THE BEAT GENERATION

A Gale Critical Companion

Barbara M. Bibel
Librarian
Oakland Public Library
Oakland, California

Dr. Toby Burrows
Principal Librarian
The Scholars' Centre
University of Western Australia Library
Nedlands, Western Australia

Ginny Chaussee
Librarian
Mountain Pointe High School
Phoenix, Arizona

Celia C. Daniel
Associate Reference Librarian
Howard University
Washington, D.C.

David M. Durant
Reference Librarian
Joyner Library
East Carolina University
Greenville, North Carolina

Nancy Guidry
Librarian
Bakersfield Community College
Bakersfield, California

Steven R. Harris
English Literature Librarian
University of Tennessee
Knoxville, Tennessee

Mary Jane Marden
Literature and General Reference Librarian
St. Petersburg Jr. College
Pinellas Park, Florida

Heather Martin
Senior Assistant Librarian
University of Alabama, Sterne Library
Birmingham, Alabama

Susan Miller
Librarian
Indiana Free Library
Indiana, Pennsylvania

Tommy Nixon
Humanities Reference Librarian
University of North Carolina at Chapel Hill, Davis Library
Chapel Hill, North Carolina

Mark Schumacher
Jackson Library
University of North Carolina at Greensboro
Greensboro, North Carolina

Gwen Scott-Miller
Assistant Director of Materials and Programming
Sno-Isle Regional Library System
Marysville, Washington

Phyllis Segor
Librarian
Braddock Holmes High School
Miami, Florida

THE BEAT GENERATION

A Gale Critical Companion

Volume 2: Authors A-H

Foreword by ***Anne Waldman***
Distinguished Professor of Poetics
The Jack Kerouac School of Disembodied Poetics, Naropa University

Lynn M. Zott, *Project Editor*

OAKTON COMMUNITY COLLEGE
DES PLAINES CAMPUS
1600 EAST GOLF ROAD
DES PLAINES, IL 60016

Detroit • New York • San Diego • San Francisco • Cleveland • New Haven, Conn. • Waterville, Maine • London • Munich

The Beat Generation, Vol. 2

Project Editor
Lynn M. Zott

Editorial
Jessica Bomarito, Tom Burns, Jenny Cromie, Elisabeth Gellert, Edna M. Hedblad, Jeffrey W. Hunter, Justin Karr, Michelle Kazensky, Jelena Krstović, Michelle Lee, Allison McClintic Marion, Ellen McGeagh, Linda Pavlovski, Thomas J. Schoenberg, Russel Whitaker

Research
Nicodemus Ford, Sarah Genik, Barbara McNeil, Tamara C. Nott, Gary Oudersluys, Tracie A. Richardson

Editorial Support Services
Mark Hefner

Permissions
Edna Hedblad, Lori Hines

Imaging and Multimedia
Lezlie Light, Kelly A. Quin, Luke Rademacher

Product Design
Pamela Galbreath, Michael Logusz

Composition and Electronic Capture
Carolyn Roney

Manufacturing
Stacy L. Melson

© 2003 by Gale. Gale is an imprint of The Gale Group, Inc., a division of Thomson Learning, Inc.

Gale and Design™ and Thomson Learning™ are trademarks used herein under license.

For more information, contact
The Gale Group, Inc.
27500 Drake Rd.
Farmington Hills, MI 48331-3535
Or you can visit our internet site at
http://www.gale.com

ALL RIGHTS RESERVED
No part of this work covered by the copyright herein may be reproduced or used in any form or by any means—graphic, electronic, or mechanical, including photocopying, recording, taping, Web distribution, or information storage retrieval systems—without the written permission of the publisher.

This publication is a creative work fully protected by all applicable copyright laws, as well as by misappropriation, trade secret, unfair competition, and other applicable laws. The authors and editors of this work have added value to the underlying factual material herein through one or more of the following: unique and original selection, coordination, expression, arrangement, and classification of the information.

For permission to use material from the product, submit your request via the Web at http://www.gale-edit.com/permissions, or you may download our Permissions Request form and submit your request by fax or mail to:

Permisssions Department
The Gale Group, Inc.
27500 Drake Rd.
Farmington Hills, MI 48331-3535
Permissions Hotline:
248-699-8006 or 800-877-4253, ext. 8006
Fax 248-699-8074 or 800-762-4058

Since this page cannot legibly accommodate all copyright notices, the acknowledgments constitute an extension of the copyright notice.

While every effort has been made to secure permission to reprint material and to ensure the reliability of the information presented in this publication, the Gale Group neither guarantees the accuracy of the data contained herein nor assumes any responsibility for errors, omissions or discrepancies. Gale accepts no payment for listing; and inclusion in the publication of any organization, agency, institution, publication, service, or individual does not imply endorsement of the editors or publisher. Errors brought to the attention of the publisher and verified to the satisfaction of the publisher will be corrected in future editions.

LIBRARY OF CONGRESS CATALOGING-IN-PUBLICATION DATA

Zott, Lynn M. (Lynn Marie), 1969-
The beat generation : a Gale critical companion / Lynn M. Zott.
p. cm. -- (Gale critical companion collection)
Includes bibliographical references and index.
ISBN 0-7876-7569-5 (hardcover set) -- ISBN 0-7876-7570-9 (v. 1) --
ISBN 0-7876-7571-7 (v. 2) -- ISBN 0-7876-7572-5 (v. 3)
1. American literature--20th century--History and criticism. 2. Beat generation. I. Title. II. Series.
PS228.B6Z68 2003
810.9'0054--dc21

2002155786

Printed in the United States of America
10 9 8 7 6 5 4 3 2

CONTENTS

VOLUME 1

VOLUME 2

VOLUME 3

FOREWORD

In a recent class I taught at the Jack Kerouac School of Disembodied Poetics entitled "Liberation Now!," students fretted over the cultural imperialism and condescension of various "moderns"—Ezra Pound, William Carlos Williams, and the mad Antonin Artaud as well as the privileged lifestyle of independently "wealthy" Gertrude Stein and H. D. who could afford a "room of one's own" in Virginia Woolf's apt phrase. There was the sense of the white male gaze toward the Balinese and Tarahumara cultures, in the case of Artaud, and of Pound's dabbling with the Noh theatre of Japan and the troubadour tradition, not to mention his problematic anti-semitism. Was "orientalism" the problem here, exoticizing the problematic "other?" I tried to give some historical context and expressed my own gratitude as a writer to the investigative nature, in particular, of Pound's passionate magpie scholarship and how he had championed James Joyce (another sexist?) and T. S. Eliot and opened the floodgates for contemporary poets back into the beauties and exquisite lineaments of the past. Reinventing Chinese poetry, just one example, for our time. William Carlos Williams's "Beautiful Thing" had also been called into question in its objectification of women.

Was there an "internalized repression" going on in Stein's own anti-semitism? Or H. D.'s aristocratic classicism? Was there a reach for the heights of Olympus? A rejection of American democratic values? My advice was: Read the work, use your heads, don't respond with knee-jerk superficial assumptions or clichéd political correctness. It's a complicated world, it's a complicated time. Be investigative, go deeper, see the subtlety of the work, understand "influence," lineage, and also the radical departure from Victorian "official"—and mostly stultifying—"verse."

But I shuddered to think of the discourse we would have around certain so-called Beat writers, known superficially for macho views presented in particular writings: the sexism of Jack Kerouac in *On The Road*; the misogyny of William S. Burroughs in *The Wild Boys*. Was it up to me to contextualize, apologize, get defensive? I had personally seen "beyond" these mindsets in the work and in my own personal experience of these writers. And I had benefited from the liberating quality of the thinking, the imagination, the radical moves of their language and grammar. Just as Marcel Proust and James Joyce and Gertrude Stein had provoked a serious probe and delight in consciousness, pursued a grammar of thinking, as it were, Burroughs and Kerouac and others were raising the ante on what was possible in language. Their writing strove to capture the passing moment, the nuances of speech, the eidolons of history and philosophy and emotion. And I was also aware of the un-mined—in some cases un-voiced—richness of the work of the women writers associated with that community and working in the 1950s—that was immensely conditioning. In those times, the struggle for female individuality, for roles not defined by the Patriarchy, was immense. To fight against the tide of post-war materialism, conformity, the anathemas of "difference" (if one was lesbian, for example, or if one was in a bi-racial relationship, or if one got pregnant out of wedlock) was a constant struggle.

I myself, although a generation younger in most cases, was also being included in the Beat canon, and I felt the resonance of these same issues in my own work which is, in some cases, staunchly feminist. But I had benefited by the previous struggle of my comrades. And there were major differences in the backgrounds and lives and aesthetics and imagination of so many of these Beat writers, compared to the Moderns and compared with one another. Comparisons are odious! It is hard to generalize a generation, a literary movement. And then there was the enormity of influence and all the art, music, and performance that was spawned out of the maelstrom. Go to the work! That is my rallying cry. There is so much there to mine, to probe, to enjoy, that will enlighten you in a spiritual sense. I think I was able, as my class's discussion took shape, to manifest the huge debt I felt to these writers who blazed the way, who turned the establishment on its head!

The Beat literary movement conjures the rhizome as a metaphor or paradigm for its incredibly rich and enduring presence in the worlds of poetry, literature, performance, politics, culture. As such, it is a social phenomenon, a movement that extended and continues to extend beyond the usual parameters of literature and art. Rhizome refers to a living tuber system, literally "an elongate stem or branch of a plant that is often thickened or tuber shaped as a result of deposits of reserves (food) and is usually horizontal and underground, producing shoots above and roots below in which persistent growth and nourishment occurs, moving horizontally rather than vertically." This rhizome pattern might also be compared to Indra's Net or the Buddhist sense of "pratitya samutpada" which translates as interconnectedness. In their book *Rhizome: Introduction* (Minuit, 1976), the critical theorists Gilles Deleuze and Félix Guattari invoke the rhizome as creative paradigm: "Form rhizomes and not roots, never plant! Don't sow, forage! Be neither a One nor a Many, but multiplicities! A rhizome doesn't begin and doesn't end, but is always in the middle, between things, interbeing, intermezzo."

It is a useful perspective in examining the multi-layered writings and the lives of a very exceptional community of writers which, in mid-20th-Century America, began to change all of our lives. It was propitious that such a conjunction of minds (and hearts) should occur and stimulate each other. That such a conjunction should root and flower in such remarkable and unique ways, having a ripple effect that moved into other realms of pop culture—fashion, film, music, theatre—and now, also, has staying power in the "academy" of officialdom; the Beat influence has been felt all over the world. It has spawned communities of writers and artists the world over. From the Jack Kerouac School of Disembodied Poetics at Naropa University in Boulder, Colorado, to the Schule für Dichtung in Vienna to the City Lights bookstore and publishing house in Florence, Italy. When Allen Ginsberg died, there were memorials in Britain, France, Italy, India, the Czech Republic, and across the United States. The writings of Beat authors are some of the most translated works in the annals of contemporary literature. The Beat movement holds and inculcates promise, fuels new generations of writers and scholarship. Beat writings demand readership, exploration, and scrutiny; their subtexts of gender, sexuality, queerness, race, and addiction beg to be deciphered. Also, importantly, the influence of jazz and negritude on Beat culture. For these writers were not operating in a vacuum: One could look at the political implications and the concern for the desecration of planet earth and notions of ecology in the work of Gary Snyder and Michael McClure. One could examine notions of spirituality (particularly the philosophy and psychology of Buddhism) and vision and the use of entheogens (Yage, mushrooms, peyote, marijuana).

Beats also felt themselves in a lineage with the antinomian William Blake, who referred to imagination as "Big Vision." Ginsberg had an audio-hallucination, imagining he heard Blake speak. This sensory experience fueled Allen's own identity as a mystic and prophet. Ginsberg taught classes in William Blake at Naropa University for years. Gregory Corso invoked the radical Percy Byshe Shelley on many occasions in his "socratic poetry raps." Eliot's "The Wasteland" was one of William Burroughs's favorite poems. Joanne Kyger has led workshops that stake out "location" and sites of activity and their literary histories, herself being the guardian of the coastal town of Bolinas for many years. Diane di Prima taught classes on light in John Keats. Keats' "negative capability" is the epigrammatic slogan of the Kerouac School and also serves as a description of the quality of mind of the Beat Generation. "Subterranean," "radical," "liberating," "subversive"; these are the adjectives that arise frequently in the discourse. One could add: "learned," "visionary," "empathetic."

This three-volume set, *The Beat Generation: A Gale Critical Companion,* covers a vibrant span of the literary movement. It gives ample space to key figures as well as others who were simpatico and shared the belletristic moments "in Eternity" and in community, and who also lived an alternative (and bohemian) lifestyle. Paul Blackburn—one example—fine poet and translator of the troubadours, affiliated with the praxis of Black Mountain, was a progenitor of the Poetry Project in New York, hosting the open and taping readings with his old Wollensack recorder. Chandler Brossard, a subterranean, almost noirish prose master. Neal Cassady, flamboyant muse and hero of Kerouac's novels, fabulous talker, although less prolific on the page. Robert Duncan and Jack Spicer, more associated with their own San Francisco Renaissance—and at times a more mystical poetics (Spicer speaks of receiving dictation from Mars)—shared a mutual "composition by field" approach with the Beats. Bill Everson, printer and former priest, as well as poet, shared an oppositional pacifism and confessionalism. Barbara Guest, historically placed as key among the New York School innovators (with Frank O'Hara, John Ashbery, Kenneth Koch, and James Schuyler), is possibly the most opaque and experimentally obtuse of the writers here and has always been considered a maverick. Other writers covered in this set's biographical entries are official progenitors of the scene and need less justification for inclusion. The topic entries (volume 1) in this collection are apt, up-to-date, expansive, and extremely useful for scholarship into the future. Entries pertaining to performing and visual arts make this collection particularly salient and useful as a full-bodied rhizomic chart of the ever-layered and expanded notion of a Beat Renaissance.

And this compendium also foregrounds the sites, the presses, and further disseminations of influence. It is a living, palpable transmission that continues because in many ways the Beat movement was a radically spiritual one and, as such, continues a utopian transforming cultural intervention that is so desperately needed now, as it was in 1950s "art." The writing of poetry and fiction for many of these writers was viewed as a "sacred practice, with sacramental approach to each other as characters," as Ginsberg wrote. There's more power in a sacred approach than in a careerist one, which is why the work and activity of these writers resonates for a new audience—vital to these times, as society needs to re-examine its materialistic, conformist, and, in the case of the U.S., its Pax Americana New World Order modus operandi.

We had an ad for the creative writing program at Naropa: "Come to a school where your teachers have been jailed for their work and beliefs!" One feels that these writers and innovators had no choice in their paths. It was a calling that exacted a life commitment, demanding full attention to art and life and its concommitant camaraderie and vow of friendship. The combination of time and place with the intersection of so many prodigious "best minds" was indeed an auspicious and powerful one that is rare in literary annals. Ginsberg spoke of the establishment response to the threat of power in this movement in his introduction to *The Beat Book* (Shambhala), which I edited in 1999:

> This "beat generation" or "sixties" tolerant worldview provoked an intoxicated right wing to go into "Denial" (as in AA terminology) of reality, and reinforced its codependency with repressive laws, incipient police state, death-penalty demagoguery, sex demagoguery, art censorship, fundamentalist monotheistic televangelist quasi-fascist wrath, racism and homophobia. This counter-reaction seems a by-product of the further gulf between the rich and poor classes, growth of a massive abused underclass, increased power and luxury for the rich who control politics and their minions in the media.

These words seem ever more relevant as I write this in the shadow of war, in the aftermath of a highly publicized fracas over a planned (ultimately scuttled) literary event at the White House. First Lady Bush wanted, ironically—perhaps this is a call for help on Laura Bush's part!—to honor radical poets Emily Dickinson, Walt Whitman, and Langston Hughes (who themselves thought and wrote subtly about the horrors and implications of war). The First Lady made the mistake (at least from the perspective of the administration) of inviting Buddhist poet and editor Sam Hamill of

Copper Canyon Press. He responded by inviting poets all over the country to send protest poems opposing a war with Iraq to the White House. The situation prompted the White House to "delay" the First Lady's event. Despite this, over 5,000 poets have responded to Hamill's invitation. These writings can be seen on the poetsforpeace website, www.poets4peace.com. Lawrence Ferlinghetti, poet laureate of San Francisco, weighed in with the timely "Speak Out," first published in the San Francisco *Chronicle* (14 February 2003). In the poem he speaks to the dangers of war, the threats that confront civil liberties. He concludes with the warning lines:

> All you lovers of Liberty . . .
> Now is the time for you to speak
> O silent majority
> Before they come for you

As I sit here pondering the future of the planet, which has suffered so much war and degradation already in the last century, and I contemplate how to best teach new "best minds" in the face of a war that threatens the stability the whole world over, I realize it behooves one to speak with passion and conviction in the spirit of the Beat Generation that tried to save America from itself. Read this historic canon as one might a sacred text, as unfettered imagination that inspires, guides, and reactivates human thought and emotion towards candor, delight, and compassion.

—Anne Waldman
Distinguished Professor of Poetics
Chair, Summer Writing Program
The Jack Kerouac School of Disembodied Poetics
Naropa University, Boulder, Colorado
and
Co-founder
Poetry is News Coalition, New York City

The Gale Critical Companion Collection

In response to a growing demand for relevant criticism and interpretation of perennial topics and important literary movements throughout history, the Gale Critical Companion Collection (GCCC) was designed to meet the research needs of upper high school and undergraduate students. Each edition of GCCC focuses on a different literary movement or topic of broad interest to students of literature, history, multicultural studies, humanities, foreign language studies, and other subject areas. Topics covered are based on feedback from a standing advisory board consisting of reference librarians and subject specialists from public, academic, and school library systems.

The GCCC is designed to complement Gale's existing Literary Criticism Series (LCS) , which includes such award-winning and distinguished titles as *Nineteenth-Century Literature Criticism* (*NCLC*), *Twentieth-Century Literary Criticism* (*TCLC*), and *Contemporary Literary Criticism* (*CLC*). Like the LCS titles, the GCCC editions provide selected reprinted essays that offer an inclusive range of critical and scholarly response to authors and topics widely studied in high school and undergraduate classes; however, the GCCC also includes primary source documents, chronologies, sidebars, supplemental photographs, and other material not included in the LCS products. The graphic and supplemental material is designed to extend the usefulness of the critical essays and provide students with historical and cultural context on a topic or author's work. GCCC titles will benefit larger institutions with ongoing subscriptions to Gale's LCS products as well as smaller libraries and school systems with less extensive reference collections. Each edition of the GCCC is created as a stand-alone set providing a wealth of information on the topic or movement. Importantly, 15% or less of the critical essays included in GCCC titles have appeared in LCS, ensuring that LCS subscribers who purchase GCCC titles will not duplicate resources in their collection.

Editions within the GCCC are either single-volume or multi-volume sets, depending on the nature and scope of the topic being covered. Topic entries and author entries are treated separately, with entries on related topics appearing first, followed by author entries in an A-Z arrangement. Each volume is approximately 500 pages in length and includes approximately 50 images and sidebar graphics. These sidebars include summaries of important historical events, newspaper clippings, brief biographies of important non-literary figures, complete poems or passages of fiction written by the author, descriptions of events in the related arts (music, visual arts, and dance), and so on.

The reprinted essays in each GCCC edition explicate the major themes and literary techniques of the authors and literary works. It is important to note that approximately 85% of the essays reprinted in GCCC editions are full-text, meaning that they are reprinted in their entirety, including footnotes and lists of abbreviations. Essays are selected based on their coverage of the seminal works and themes of an author, and based on the importance of those essays to an appreciation of the author's contribution to the movement and to literature in general. Gale's editors select those essays of most value to upper high school and undergraduate students, avoiding narrow and highly pedantic interpretations of individual works or of an author's canon.

Scope of The Beat Generation

The Beat Generation, the second set in the Gale Critical Companion Collection, consists of three volumes. Each volume includes a detailed table of contents, a foreword on the Beat Generation written by noted Beat scholar Anne Waldman, and a descriptive chronology of key events of the movement. The main body of volume 1 consists of entries on five topics relevant to the Beat Generation, including 1) The Beat Generation: An Overview; 2) The Beat "Scene": East and West; 3) Beat Generation Publishing: Periodicals, Small Presses, and Censorship; 4) Performing Arts and the Beat Generation; and 5) Visual Arts and the Beat Generation. Volumes 2 and 3 include entries on twenty-nine authors and literary figures associated with the movement, including such notables as William S. Burroughs, Gregory Corso, Lawrence Ferlinghetti, Allen Ginsberg, Jack Kerouac, and Kenneth Rexroth, as well as entries on individuals who have garnered less attention, but whose contributions to the Beat Generation are noteworthy, such as Diane di Prima, William Everson, Bob Kaufman, Ed Sanders, Gary Snyder, Lew Welch, and Philip Whalen.

Organization of The Beat Generation

A *Beat Generation* topic entry consists of the following elements:

- The **Introduction** defines the subject of the entry and provides social and historical information important to understanding the criticism.
- The list of **Representative Works** identifies writings and works by authors and figures associated with the subject. The list is divided into alphabetical sections by name; works listed under each name appear in chronological order. The genre and publication date of each work is given. Unless otherwise indicated, dramas are dated by first performance, not first publication.
- Entries generally begin with a section of **Primary Sources**, which includes essays, speeches, social history, newspaper accounts and other materials that were produced during the time of the Beat Generation.
- Reprinted **Criticism** in topic entries is arranged thematically. Topic entries commonly begin with primary sources, followed by general surveys of the subject or essays providing historical or background information, followed by essays that develop particular aspects of the topic. For example, the Publishing topic entry in volume 1 of *Beat Generation* begins with a section providing primary source material on publishing during the Beat Generation. This is followed by a section providing an overview essay on the topic, and three other sections: Beat Periodicals: "Little Magazines"; Beat Publishing: Small Presses; and Beat Battles with Censorship. Each section has a separate title heading and is identified with a page number in the table of contents. The critic's name and the date of composition or publication of the critical work are given at the beginning of each piece of criticism. Unsigned criticism is preceded by the title of the source in which it appeared. Footnotes are reprinted at the end of each essay or excerpt. In the case of excerpted criticism, only those footnotes that pertain to the excerpted texts are included.
- A complete **Bibliographical Citation** of the original essay or book precedes each piece of criticism.
- Critical essays are prefaced by brief **Annotations** explicating each piece. Unless the descriptor "excerpt" is used in the annotation, the essay is being reprinted in its entirety.
- An annotated bibliography of **Further Reading** appears at the end of each entry and suggests resources for additional study. In some cases, significant essays for which the editors could not obtain reprint rights are included here.

A *Beat Generation* author entry consists of the following elements:

- The **Author Heading** cites the name under which the author most commonly wrote, followed by birth and death dates. Also located here are any name variations under which an author wrote. If the author wrote consistently under a pseudonym, the pseudonym will be listed in the author heading and the author's actual name given in parentheses on the first line of the biographical and critical information. Uncertain birth or death dates are indicated by question marks.

- A **Portrait of the Author** is included when available.
- The **Introduction** contains background information that introduces the reader to the author that is the subject of the entry.
- The list of **Principal Works** is ordered chronologically by date of first publication and lists the most important works by the author. The genre and publication date of each work is given. Unless otherwise indicated, dramas are dated by first performance, not first publication.
- Author entries are arranged into three sections: **Primary Sources, General Commentary,** and **Title Commentary.** The Primary Sources section generally includes letters, poems, short stories, journal entries, novel excerpts, and essays written by the featured author, and sometimes commentary written about the author by the author's contemporaries. General Commentary includes overviews of the author's career and general studies; Title Commentary includes in-depth analyses of seminal works by the author. Within the Title Commentary section, the reprinted criticism is further organized by title, then by date of publication. The critic's name and the date of composition or publication of the critical work are given at the beginning of each piece of criticism. Unsigned criticism is preceded by the title of the source in which it appeared All titles by the author featured in the text are printed in boldface type. However, not all boldfaced titles are included in the author and subject indexes; only substantial discussions of works are indexed. Footnotes are reprinted at the end of each essay or excerpt. In the case of excerpted criticism, only those footnotes that pertain to the excerpted texts are included.
- A complete **Bibliographical Citation** of the original essay or book precedes each piece of criticism.
- Critical essays are prefaced by brief **Annotations** explicating each piece. Unless the descriptor "excerpt" is used in the annotation, the essay is being reprinted in its entirety.
- An annotated bibliography of **Further Reading** appears at the end of each entry and suggests resources for additional study. In some cases, significant essays for which the editors could not obtain reprint rights are included here. A list of **Other Sources from Gale** follows the further reading section and provides references to other biographical and critical sources on the author in series published by Gale.

Indexes

The **Author Index** lists all of the authors featured in the *Beat Generation* set, with references to the main author entries in volumes 2 and 3 as well as commentary on the featured author in other author entries and in the topic volume. Page references to substantial discussions of the authors appear in boldface. The Author Index also includes birth and death dates and cross references between pseudonyms and actual names, and cross references to other Gale series in which the authors have appeared. A complete list of these sources is found facing the first page of the Author Index.

The **Title Index** alphabetically lists the titles of works written by the authors featured in volumes 2 and 3 and provides page numbers or page ranges where commentary on these titles can be found. Page references to substantial discussions of the titles appear in boldface. English translations of foreign titles and variations of titles are cross-referenced to the title under which a work was originally published. Titles of novels, dramas, nonfiction books, and poetry, short story, or essay collections are printed in italics, while individual poems, short stories, and essays are printed in roman type within quotation marks.

The **Subject Index** includes the authors and titles that appear in the Author Index and the Title Index as well as the names of other authors and figures that are discussed in the set. The Subject Index also lists titles and authors of the critical essays that appear in the set, as well as hundreds of literary terms and topics covered in the criticism. The index provides page numbers or page ranges where subjects are discussed and is fully cross-referenced.

Citing The Beat Generation

When writing papers, students who quote directly from the *BG* set may use the following general format to footnote reprinted criticism. The first example pertains to material drawn from periodicals, the second to material reprinted from books.

> Podhoretz, Norman, "The Know-Nothing Bohemians," *Partisan Review* 25, no. 2 (spring 1958): 305-11, 313-16, 318; reprinted in *The Beat Generation: A Gale Critical Companion,* vol. 1, ed. Lynn M. Zott (Farmington Hills, Mich.: The Gale Group, 2003), 13-19.

Rexroth, Kenneth, "Disengagement: The Art of the Beat Generation." in *A Casebook on the Beat,* edited by Thomas Parkinson (New York: Thomas Y. Crowell Company, 1961), 179-93; reprinted in *The Beat Generation: A Gale Critical Companion,* vol. 1, ed. Lynn M. Zott (Farmington Hills, Mich.: The Gale Group, 2003), 6-13.

The Beat Generation *Advisory Board*

The members of the *Beat Generation* Advisory Board—reference librarians and subject specialists from public, academic, and school library systems—offered a variety of informed perspectives on both the presentation and content of the *Beat Generation* set. Advisory board members assessed and defined such quality issues as the relevance, currency, and usefulness of the author coverage, critical content, and topics included in our product; evaluated the layout, presentation, and general quality of our product; provided feedback on the criteria used for selecting authors and topics covered in our product; identified any gaps in our coverage of authors or topics, recommending authors or topics for inclusion; and analyzed the appropriateness of our content and presentation for various user audiences, such as high school students, undergraduates, graduate students, librarians, and educators. We wish to thank the advisors for their advice during the development of the *Beat Generation.*

Suggestions are Welcome

Readers who wish to suggest new features, topics, or authors to appear in future volumes of the Gale Critical Companion Collection, or who have other suggestions or comments are cordially invited to call, write, or fax the Project Editor:

Project Editor, Gale Critical Companion Collection
The Gale Group
27500 Drake Road
Farmington Hills, MI 48331-3535
1-800-347-4253 (GALE)
Fax: 248-699-8054

The editors wish to thank the copyright holders of the excerpted criticism included in this volume and the permissions managers of many book and magazine publishing companies for assisting us in securing reproduction rights. We are also grateful to the staffs of the Detroit Public Library, the Library of Congress, the University of Detroit Mercy Library, Wayne State University Purdy/ Kresge Library Complex, Oakland University Library, and the University of Michigan Libraries for making their resources available to us. Following is a list of the copyright holders who have granted us permission to reproduce material in this edition of *The Beat Generation*. Every effort has been made to trace copyright, but if omissions have been made, please let us know.

Copyrighted material in The Beat Generation *was reproduced from the following periodicals:*

American Book Review, v. 3, May-June 1981. Reproduced by permission.—***American Literature***, v. 65, No. 1, pp. 117-130, March 1993. Copyright, 1993, Duke University Press. All rights reserved. Used by permission of the publisher. —***American Poetry Review***, v. 23, November-December 1994. Reproduced by permission of the author—***American Studies***, v. 32, 1987; v. 29: 1, Spring 1988. Copyright © Mid America American Studies Association, 2002. Reproduced by permission from American Studies.—***American Studies***, v. 43, 1998. Reproduced by permission of the author.—***The Antioch Review***, v. 31, Fall 1971. Reproduced by permission.—***The Ark***, v. 14, 1980. Reproduced by permission.—***Arshile***, v. 5, 1996. Reproduced by permission of the author. —***Atlantic Monthly***, v. 221, March 1968. Reproduced by permission of Sterling Lord Literistic, Inc.—***Beat Scene***, Autumn, 1993. Reproduced by permission.—***The Cambridge Quarterly***, v. 22, 1993. Copyright © 1993 by the Editors. Reproduced by permission of Oxford University Press. —***Chicago Review***, v. 26, 1974. Reproduced by permission.—***College Literature***, v. 27, Winter 2000. Reproduced by permission.—***Commentary***, v. 49, January 1970. All rights reserved. Reproduced by permission.—***Concerning Poetry***, v. 2, Spring 1969; v. 20, 1987. Reproduced by permission.—***Contemporary Literature***, v. 31, n. 3, Fall 1990; v. 38, n. 2, Summer 1997; v. 42, n. 3, Fall 2001. Copyright © 1990, 1997, 2001 The Board of Regents of the University of Wisconsin System. All rights reserved. Reproduced by permission. —***The Critical Quarterly***, v. 8, Autumn 1966. Reproduced by permission of Blackwell Publishing Ltd.—***ENclitic***, v. 11, Spring 1989. Reproduced by permission of the author.—***Exquisite Corpse: A Journal of Letters and Life***, 2002. Reproduced by permission.—***Extrapolation***, v. 20, Winter 1979. Reproduced by permission.—***Film Quarterly***, v. 45, Spring 1992. Copyright © 1992 by The Regents of the University of California, www.ucpress.edu. Reproduced by permission.—***The Gazette***, September 9, 2000. Reproduced by permission of the author.—***Geographical Review***, v. 86, January 1996. Reproduced by permission of the American Geographical Society.—***Harvard Theological***, v. 84, April 1991. Reproduced by permission. —***Ironwood***, 1983. Reproduced by permission of the author.—***Journal of Modern Literature***, v. 2, 1971-72, for "Theory and Practice of Gary Snyder, by Thomas Parkinson. Reproduced by permission of Indiana University Press.—***Kenyon Review***, v. 14, Winter 1992. Reproduced by permission of the author.—***Literary Review***, v. 33, Spring 1990. Reproduced by permission of the author.—***MELUS***, v. 14, Fall-Winter 1987; v. 19, Fall 1994. Reproduced by permission.—***Midwest Quarterly***, v. 14, July 1973. Copyright © 1973 by The Midwest Quarterly, Pittsburgh State University. Reproduced by permission.—***Modern Drama***, v. 22, March 1979. Copyright © 1979 University of Toronto, Graduate Centre for Study of Drama. Reproduced by permission.—***Moody Street Irregulars***, Summer 1986. Reproduced by permission.—***The Nation***, v. 185, November 9, 1957; v. 186, March, 1958; v. 187, October 11, 1958. © 1957, 1958 The Nation magazine/The Nation Company, Inc. Reproduced by permission.—***New Orleans Review***, v. 19, Spring 1992. Copyright © 1992 by Loyola University. Reproduced by permission.—***New York Times***, August 9, 1996. Copyright © 1996 by The New York Times Company. Reproduced by permission.—***New York Times Book Review***, November 25, 1984. Copyright © 1984 by The New York Times Company. Reproduced by permission. —***New York Times Magazine***, November 16, 1952. Copyright © by Estate of John Clellon Holmes. Reproduced by permission of Sterling Lord Literistic, Inc.—***Newsweek***, November 22, 1971, Newsweek, Inc. All rights reserved. Reproduced by permission.—***North Dakota Quarterly***, Fall 1987. Copyright 1987 by The University of North Dakota. Reproduced by permission.—***Parnassus***, v. 1, 1973; v. 3, Fall-Winter 1974. Copyright © 1973, 1974 Poetry in Review Foundation, NY. Reproduced by permission of authors.—***Partisan Review***, v. 25, Summer 1958, for "The Know-Nothing Bohemians," by Norman Podhoretz. Copyright © 1958 by Norman Podhoretz; v. 25, Summer 1958, for a letter to the editor, by LeRoi Jones; v. 26, Spring 1959, for "The Other Night at Columbia: A Report from the Academy," by Diana Trilling. Copyright © 1959 by Partisan Review, renewed 1987 by Diana Trilling. Reproduced by permission of the author, publisher, and Wylie Agency respectively.—***Playboy Magazine***, v. 6, June 1959, "The Origins of the Beat Generation," by Jack Kerouac. Reproduced by permission of the publisher and Sterling Lord Literistic, Inc.—***Poetry***, v. 90, April 1957, for "Two New Books by Kenneth Rexroth," by William Carlos Williams. Copyright © 1957 by Paul H. Williams and the Estate of William Eric Williams. Reproduced by permission of New Directions Publishing Corp., agents.—***Publishers Weekly***, v. 248, May 7, 2001. Copyright 2001 by Reed Publishing USA. Reproduced from Publishers Weekly, published by the Bowker Magazine Group of Cahners Publishing Co., a division of Reed Publishing USA. Reproduced by permission.—***Religion and the Arts***, v. 2, 1998. Reproduced by permission.—***Review of Contemporary Fiction***, v. 3, Summer 1983; v. 7, Spring 1987; v. 19, Spring 1999. Copyright 1983, 1987, 1999 by John O'Brien. Reproduced by permission.—***Sagetrieb***, v. 2, Spring 1983. Copyright © 1983 by the author. Reproduced by permission of the author.—***The San Francisco Chronicle—Sunday Review Section***, April 22, 2001. Republished with permission of The San Francisco Chronicle, conveyed through Copyright Clearance Center, Inc.—***Sixties***, Spring 1962. Reproduced by permission of the Eighties Press.—***Small Press: The Magazine and Book Review of Independent Publishing***, August 1990. Reproduced by permission.—***Social Research***, v. 68, Fall 2001. Copyright 2001 by New School for Social Research. Reproduced by permission.—***Southern Humanities Review***, v. VI, Fall 1972. Reproduced by permission.—***Southern Review***, v. 21, January 1985. Reproduced by permission.—***Texas Studies in Literature and Language***, v. 44, n. 2, Summer 2002, pp. 211-28. "'The Brake of Time' Corso's Bomb as Postmodern God(dess)," by Christine Hoff Kraemer. Copyright © 2002 by the University of Texas Press. All rights reserved. Reproduced by permission.—***Third Rail***, v. 8, 1987. Reproduced by permission of Mr. Uri Hertz, Editor of Third Rail and the author.—***Times Literary Supplement***, June 3, 1983, pp. 586-7, for "Camp Follower," by James Campbell. © The Times Supplements Limited 1983; March 22, 1991, p. 21, for "The Steinberg Case," by Brian Masters. Reproduced by permission.—***TriQuarterly***, v. 43, Fall 1978. Reproduced by permission of author.—***Western American Literature***, v. 3, Fall 1968. Copyright 1968, by the Western American Literature Association. Reproduced by permission.—***Whole Earth***, v. 98, Fall 1999. Reproduced by permission. —***Women's Studies***, v. 30, 2001. © Gordon and Breach Science Publishers. Reproduced by permission.—***Woodstock Journal***, v. 7, February 2- 16, 2001; v. 7, May 11-25, 2001. Reproduced by permission.—***The Wordsworth Circle***, v. 22, Summer 1991. © 1991 Marilyn Gaull. Reproduced by permission of the editor.

Copyrighted material in The Beat Generation *was reproduced from the following books:*

Amram, David. From "This Song's For You, Jack: Collaborating With Kerouac," in ***Beat Culture: The 1950s and Beyond***. Edited by Cornelis A. Minnen, Jaap van der Bent, and Mel van Elteren. VU University Press, 1999. Copyright © 1999 by Amerika Instituut, Amsterdam. All rights reserved. Reproduced by permission.—Berger, Maurice. From "Libraries Full of Tears: The Beats and the Law," in ***Beat Culture and the New America: 1950-1965***, by Lisa Phillips et al. Whitney Museum of American Art, 1995. Copyright © 1995 by Whitney Museum of American Art. All rights reserved. Reproduced by permission.—Blaser, Robin. From "The Practice of Outside," in ***The Collected Books of Jack Spicer***, by Jack Spicer. Edited by Robin Blaser. Black Sparrow Press, 1975. Copyright © 1975 by the Estate of Jack Spicer. All rights reserved. Reproduced by permission.—Burroughs, William S. From Introductory Essay to ***Mindfield***. Thunder's Mouth Press, 1989. Copyright © 1989 by William Burroughs. Reproduced by permission of The Wylie Agency, Inc.—Burroughs, William S. From ***Naked Lunch***. Grove Press Inc., 1959. Copyright © 1959 by William S. Burroughs. All rights reserved. Reproduced by permission.—Burroughs, William S. From ***The Yage Letters***. City Lights Books 1963. Copyright © 1963, 1975 by William S. Burroughs and Allen Ginsberg. All rights reserved. Reproduced by permission. —Bush, Clive. From "'Why Do We Always Say Angel?': Herbert Huncke and Neal Cassady," in ***The Beat Generation Writers***. Edited by A. Robert Lee. Pluto Press, 1996. Copyright © 1996 by Lumiere (Cooperative) Press Ltd. and Pluto Press. All rights reserved. Reproduced by permission. —Campbell, James. From "Behind the Beat: Neurotica," and "The Muses: Huncke-Junkie and Neo-Cassady," in ***This Is the Beat Generation: New York—San Francisco—Paris***. Secker and Warburg, 1999 and the University of California Press. Copyright © 1999 by James Campbell. All rights reserved. Reproduced by permission of The Random House Group Limited and by the Regents of the University of California and the University of California Press.—Carpenter, David. From "Introduction: She That Looketh Forth as the Morning," in ***The Integral Years: Poems 1966-1994***, by William Everson. Black Sparrow Press, 2000. Copyright © 2000 by David A. Carpenter. All rights reserved. Reproduced by permission.—Carroll, Paul. From "I Lift My Voice Aloud/Make Mantra of American Language Now.../I Here Declare the End of the War!" in ***The Poem in Its Skin***. Follett Publishing Company, 1968. Copyright © 1968 by Paul Carroll. All rights reserved. Reproduced by permission.—Cassady, Carolyn. From "Afterword," in ***The First Third and Other Writings***. Edited by Lawrence Ferlinghetti and Nancy J. Peters. City Lights Books, 1981. Copyright © 1981 by City Lights Books. All rights reserved. Reproduced by permission.—Cassady, Neal. From Letter to Jack Kerouac (Kansas City, MO, March 7, 1947), in ***The First Third & Other Writings***. City Lights Books, 1971. Copyright © 1971 by City Lights Books. All rights reserved. Reproduced by permission.—Cherkovski, Neeli. From "Bob Kaufman," and "The Memory of Love: John Wieners," in ***Whitman's Wild Children: Portraits of Twelve Poets***. Steerforth Press 1999. Copyright © 1999 by Neeli Cherkovski (a.k.a. Neeli Cherry). All rights reserved. Reproduced by permission.—Christensen, Paul. From Introduction to ***Two Novels: You Didn't Even Try: Imaginary Speeches for a Brazen Head***. Zephyr Press, 1989. Copyright © 1989 by Paul Christensen. All rights reserved. Reproduced by permission.—Christian, Barbara. From "Whatever Happened to Bob Kaufman," in ***The Beats: Essays in Criticism***. Edited by Lee Bartlett. McFarland, 1981. Copyright © 1981 by Lee Bartlett. All rights reserved. Reproduced by permission.—Clark, Walter Houston. From "Historical Notes: The Harvard Incident," in ***Chemical Ecstasy: Psychedelic Drugs and Religion***. Sheed and Ward, 1969. Copyright © by Sheed and Ward, Inc. All rights reserved. Reproduced by permission. —Clay, Steven, and Rodney Phillips. From "A Little History of the Mimeograph Revolution," in ***A Secret Location on the Lower East Side: Adventures in Writing 1960-1980***. The New York Public Library and Granary Book, 1998. Copyright © 1998 by The New York Public Library, Astor, Lenox and Tilden Foundations and Granary Books. All rights reserved. Reproduced by permission. —Cohen, Ronald D. From "Singing Subversion: Folk Music and the Counterculture in the 1950s," in ***Beat Culture: The 1950s and Beyond***. Edited by Cornelis A. Minnen, Jaap van der Bent, and Mel van Elteren. VU University Press, 1999. Copyright © 1999 by Amerika Instituut, Amsterdam. All rights reserved. Reproduced by permission.—Corso, Gregory. From "Marriage," in ***The Happy Birthday of Death***. Copyright © 1960 by New Directions Publishing Corp. Reprinted by permission of New Directions Publishing Corp. —Creeley, Robert. From Introduction to ***Black Mountain Review: Volume 1, 1954***. AMS Press, 1969. Copyright © 1969 by AMS Press Inc. All rights reserved. Reproduced by permission.—Creeley, Robert. From Preface to ***Cultural Affairs in Boston: Poetry and Prose, 1956-1985***, by John Wieners. Edited by Raymond Foye. Black Sparrow Press, 1988. Copyright © 1988 by Robert Creeley. All rights reserved. Reproduced by permission.

—Davidson, Michael. From "'Spotting That Design': Incarnation and Interpretation in Gary Snyder and Philip Whalen," and From "'The City Redefined': Community and Dialogue in Jack Spicer," in ***The San Francisco Renaissance: Poetics and Community at Mid-Century***. Cambridge University Press, 1989. Copyright © 1989 by Cambridge University Press. All rights reserved. Reproduced by permission of Cambridge University Press and the author.—Dickey, James. From "Kenneth Patchen," in ***Babel to Byzantium Poets and Poetry Now***, by James Dickey. Copyright © 1968 by James Dickey. Reproduced by permission of Farrar, Straus, and Giroux, LLC.—Douglas, Ann. From "'Punching a Hole in the Big Lie': The Achievement of William S. Burroughs," in ***Word Virus: The William S. Burroughs Reader***. Edited by James Grauerholz and Ira Silverberg. Grove Press, 1998. Copyright © 1998 by Grove Press. All rights reserved. Reproduced by permission.—Duncan, Robert. From "Often I am Permitted to Return to a Meadow," in ***The Opening of the Field***. Copyright © 1960 by Robert Duncan. Reprinted by permission of New Directions Publishing Corp. —Dylan, Bob. From "Blowin in the Wind," in ***The Free Wheeling Bob Dylan***. Copyright © 1962 by Warner Bros. Inc. Copyright renewed 1990 Special Rider Music. All rights reserved. International copyright secured. Reproduced by permission. —Dylan, Bob. From "The Times They are a Changin'," in ***The Times They are A-Changin'***. Copyright © 1963 by Warner Bros. Inc. Copyright renewed 1991 Special Rider Music. All rights reserved. International copyright secured. Reproduced by permission.—Edmiston, Susan, and Linda D. Cirino. From "The East Village," in ***Literary New York***. Houghton Mifflin Company, 1976. Copyright © 1976 by Susan Edmiston and Linda D. Cirino. All rights reserved. Reproduced by permission of the authors.—Ferlinghetti, Lawrence, and Nancy J. Peters. In ***Literary San Francisco: A Pictorial from Its Beginning to the Present Day***. City Lights Books and Harper & Row, 1980. Copyright © 1980 by Lawrence Ferlinghetti and Nancy J. Peters. All rights reserved. Reproduced by permission of HarperCollins Publishers Inc., and the author.—Ferlinghetti, Lawrence, and Robert Dana. From "Lawrence Ferlinghetti," in ***Against the Grain: Interview with Maverick American Publishers***. Edited by Robert Dana. University of Iowa Press, 1986. All rights reserved. Reproduced by permission of the author.—Ferlinghetti, Lawrence. From "Horn on Howl," in ***On the Poetry of Allen Ginsberg***. Edited by Lewis Hyde. University of Michigan Press, 1984. Copyright © 1984 by University of Michigan Press. All rights reserved. Reproduced by permission of the author.—Ferlinghetti, Lawrence. From "I am Waiting," in ***A Coney Island of the Mind***. Copyright © 1958 by Lawrence Ferlinghetti. Reprinted by permission of New Directions Publishing Corp. —Ferlinghetti, Lawrence. From "Number 13: It Was a Face Which Darkness Could Kill," in ***Pictures of the Gone World***. City Lights, 1955. Copyright © 1955 by Lawrence Ferlinghetti. All rights reserved. Reproduced by permission of the author.—Foster, Edward Halsey. From "Corso," and "Hipsters, Beats, and the True Frontier," in ***Understanding the Beats***. University of South Carolina Press, 1992. Copyright © 1992 by University of South Carolina Press. All rights reserved. Reproduced by permission.—Foye, Raymond. From Introduction to ***The Herbert Huncke Reader***. Edited by Benjamin G. Schafer. William Morrow, 1997. Copyright © 1997 by the Estate of Herbert E. Hencke, Jerome Poynton, Executor. All rights reserved. Reproduced by permission.—Foye, Raymond, and John Wieners. From Introduction to ***Cultural Affairs in Boston: Poetry and Prose, 1956-1985***, by John Wieners. Black Sparrow Press, 1988. Copyright © 1988 by Raymond Foye and John Wieners. All rights reserved. Reproduced by permission.—French, Warren. From "On the Road: Work in Progress," in ***Jack Kerouac***. Twayne Publishers, 1986. Copyright © 1986 by G.K. Hall & Co. All rights reserved. Reproduced by permission.—Fuller, Robert C. From "Psychedelics and Metaphysical Illumination," in ***Stairways to Heaven: Drugs in American Religious History***. Copyright © 2000 by Westview Press. Reproduced by permission of Westview Press, a member of the Perseus Books, L.L.C.—Gelpi, Albert. From "Introduction: Everson/Antonius: Contending with the Shadow," in ***The Veritable Years: Poems 1949-1966***, by William Everson. Black Sparrow Press, 1998. Copyright © 1998 by Albert Gelpi. All rights reserved. Reproduced by permission.—George, Paul S., and Jerold M. Starr. From "Beat Politics: New Left and Hippie Beginnings in the Postwar Counterculture," in ***Cultural Politics: Radical Movements in Modern History***. Edited by Jerold M. Starr. Praeger, 1985. Copyright © 1985 by Praeger Publishers. All rights reserved. Reproduced by permission.—Ginsberg, Allen, "Early Journal Entries," found at ***http://www.allenginsberg.org***. Copyright © 2000 by the Allen Ginsberg Trust. Reprinted with permission of The Wylie Agency, Inc.—Ginsberg, Allen. From An interview in ***Jack's Book***, by Barry Gifford and Lawrence Lee. St. Martin's Press, 1978. Copyright © 1994 by Barry Gifford and Lawrence Lee. Reproduced by permission of St. Martin's Press, LLC.—Ginsberg, Allen. From Foreword to "Out of the World," ***Deliberate Prose: Selected Essays 1952-1995***. Edited by Anne Waldman. Crown Publishers, 1991. Copyright © 1999 by Allen Ginsberg Trust. All rights reserved.

Reproduced by permission of HarperCollins Publishers Inc.—Ginsberg, Allen. From Foreword to ***Selected Poems, 1958- 1984***, by John Wieners. Edited by Raymond Foye. Black Sparrow Press, 1986. Copyright © 1986 by Allen Ginsberg. All rights reserved. Reproduced by permission. —Ginsberg, Allen. From "Howl," in ***Howl and Other Poems***. Copyright © 1956 by the Allen Ginsberg Trust. Reproduced by permission of The Wylie Agency, Inc.—Ginsberg, Allen. From "On Corso's Virtues," in ***Mindfield***. Thunder's Mouth Press, 1989. Copyright © 1989 by The Allen Ginsberg Trust and © 2000 by the Allen Ginsberg Trust. Reproduced by permission of The Wylie Agency, Inc.—Ginsberg, Allen. From "Sunflower Sutra," in ***Collected Poems: 1947-1980***. Harper Collins, 1984. Copyright © 1955, 1984, 1988 by Allen Ginsberg. All rights reserved. Reproduced by permission of HarperCollins Publishers Inc. —Gold, Herbert. From "When North Beach Made an Offer, Old Bohemia Couldn't Refuse," in ***Bohemia: Where Art, Angst, Love, and Strong Coffee Meet***. Reproduced with the permission of Simon & Schuster Adult Publishing Group. Copyright © 1993 by Herbert Gold.—Hassan, Ihab. From "William Burroughs: The Subtracting Machine," in ***Rumors of Change: Essays of Five Decades***. University of Alabama Press, 1995. Copyright © 1995 by University of Alabama Press. All rights reserved. Reproduced by permission.—Hicks, Jack. From "Poetic Composting in Gary Snyder's Left Out in the Rain," in ***Critical Essays on Gary Snyder***. Edited by Patrick D. Murphy. G.K. Hall, 1991. Copyright © 1991 by Patrick D. Murphy. All rights reserved. Reproduced by permission.—Holmes, John Clellon. From "Crazy Days and Numinous Nights, 1948-1950," in ***The Beat Vision: A Primary Sourcebook***. Copyright © by Estate of John Clellon Holmes. Reproduced by permission of Sterling Lord Literistic, Inc.—Holmes, John Clellon, Letter to Jim White (On Writing a Novel: Three Letters from John Clellon Holmes), found at ***http://www.americanartists.org/Articles/Holmes/ on_writing_a_novel.htm***. Published by American Center for Artists, (1999). Copyright by Estate of John Clellon Holmes. Reprinted by permission of Sterling Lord Literistic, Inc. —Howard, Richard. From "Gregory Corso: 'Surely There'll Be Another Table...,'" in ***Alone with America: Essays on the Art of Poetry in the United States Since 1950***, Enlarged Edition. Reproduced with the permission of Scribner, an imprint of Simon & Schuster Adult Publishing Group. Original edition copyright © 1969 Richard Howard. This Enlarged Edition copyright © 1980 Richard Howard.—Huncke, Herbert. From "Elsie John," in ***Elsie John and Joey Martinez***. Pequod Press, 1979. Copyright © 1979 by Pequod Press. All rights reserved. Reproduced by permission. —Hunt, Tim. From "An Interview with John Clellon Holmes," in ***The Unspeakable Visions of the Individual, Volume 8: The Beat Journey***. A. and K. Knight, 1978. Copyright © 1978 by Arthur & Kit Knight. All rights reserved. Reproduced by permission.—In Introduction and "The Decision," in ***Howl of the Censor***. Edited by J.W. Ehrlich. Nourse Publishing, 1961. Introduction copyright © 1961 by J.W. Ehrlich. All rights reserved. Reproduced by permission.—Jarolim, Edith. From Introduction to ***The Collected Poems of Paul Blackburn***. Edited by Edith Jarolim. Copyright © 1985 by Edith Jarolim. Reproduced by permission of Persea Books, Inc. (New York).—Johnson, Joyce. From "Beat Women: A Transitional Generation," in ***Beat Culture: The 1950s and Beyond***. Edited by Cornelis A. van Minnen, Jaap van der Bent, and Mel van Elteren. VU University Press, 1999. Copyright © 1999 by VU University Press. All rights reserved. Reproduced by permission. —Johnson, Joyce. From "On Women in the Beat Generation," in ***The Rolling Stone Book of the Beats: The Beat Generation and American Culture***. Edited by Holly George-Warren. Copyright © 1999 Holly George-Warren. Reprinted by permission of Hyperion.—Johnson, Ronna C. "'An then she went': Beat Departures and Feminine Transgressions in Joyce Johnson's Come and Join the Dance," in ***Girls Who Wore Black: Women Writing the Beat Generation***. Edited by Ronna C. Johnson and Nancy Grace. Copyright © 2002 by Ronna C. Johnson. Reproduced by permission of Rutgers University Press.—Kaprow, Allan. From "The Legacy of Jackson Pollock," in ***Jackson Pollock: Interviews, Articles, and Reviews***. Edited by Pepe Karmel. Copyright © 1958, ARTnews LLC. All rights reserved. Reproduced by permission. —Kaufman, Bob. From "Jazz Chick," "O, Jazz, O," "On," and "Round about Midnight," in ***The Golden Sardine***. City Lights Books, 1967. Copyright © 1967 by City Lights Publishing Company. All rights reserved. Reproduced by permission of Coffee House Press, Minneapolis, Minnesota.—Kerouac, Jack. From "Belief & Technique for Modern Prose," in ***Portable Beat Reader***. Edited by Ann Charters. Penguin Books, 1992. Copyright by Jack Kerouac. Reproduced by permission of Sterling Lord Literistic, Inc.—Kerouac, Jack. From "Chapter 2," in ***On the Road***. Viking Penguin, 1997. Copyright © 1955, 1957 by Jack Kerouac; © renewed 1983 by Stella Kerouac, renewed © 1985 by Stella Kerouac and Jan Kerouac. Used by permission of Viking Penguin, a division of Penguin Putnam Inc.—Kerouac, Jack. From "Essentials of Spontaneous Prose," in ***Portable Beat Reader***. Edited by Ann Charters. Penguin Books, 1992. Copyright by Jack Kerouac. Reproduced by permission of Sterling Lord Literistic, Inc.—Kerouac, Jack. From "Scripture of the Golden Eternity," in ***Scripture of the Golden Eternity***. Totem Press, 1960. Copyright © 1960.by Jack Kerouac. All rights reserved. Reproduced by permission of Sterling Lord Literistic, Inc.—Kerouac, Jack. In ***The Dharma Bums***. Copyright © 1958 by Jack Kerouac, © renewed 1986 by Stella Kerouac and Jan Kerouac. Used by permission of Viking Penguin, a division of Penguin Putnam, Inc. and Sterling Lord Literistic, Inc.—Kesey, Ken. From "Flowers for Tim," foreword to ***On the Bus***, by Paul Perry. Thunder's Mouth Press, 1996. Copyright © 1964 by The Estate of Ken Kesey. All rights reserved. Reproduced by permission of Sterling Lord Literistic, Inc.—Kesey, Ken. From "The Day after Superman Died," in ***Demon Box***. Copyright © 1979 by Ken Kesey. Used by permission of Viking Penguin, a division of Penguin Putnam Inc. and Sterling Lord Literistic, Inc.—Knabb, Kenneth, "The Relevance of Rexroth: Magnanimity and Mysticism," at ***http://www.bopsecrets.org/PS/rexroth2.htm***. Published by Public Secrets, Bureau of Public Secrets, (1997). Reprinted with permission. —Knight, Brenda. Excepted from "Joan Vollmer Adams Burroughs: Calypso Stranded (1924- 1951)," "Anne Waldman: Fast Speaking Woman," "Eileen Kaufman: Keeper of the Flame (1922-)," "Joanne Kyger, Dharma Sister," "Joyce Johnson: A True Good Heart," and "ruth weiss: The Survivor (1928-)," in ***Women of the Beat Generation: The Writers, Artists and Muses at the Heart of a Revolution***. Conari Press, 1996. Copyright © 1996 by Brenda Knight. All rights reserved. Reproduced by permission of Conari Press, an imprint of Red Wheel/ Weiser. Ordering information: Red Wheel/Weiser 1-800-423-7087 Website: Conari.com. —Kowalewski, Michael. From "Jack Kerouac and the Beats in San Francisco," in ***San Francisco in Fiction: Essays in a Regional Literature***. Edited by David Fine and Paul Skenazy. University of New Mexico Press, 1995. Copyright © 1995 by University of New Mexico Press. All rights reserved. Reproduced by permission.—Kupferberg, Tuli, and Theresa Stern, An interview with Tuli Kupferberg, ***www.furious.com/perfect/tuli.html***. Published by Furious, (1997). Reprinted with permission.—Lauridsen, Inger Thorup, and Per Dalgard. From An Interview with Gary Snyder, in ***The Beat Generation and the Russian New Wave***. Ardis, 1990. Copyright © 1990 by Ardis Publishers. All rights reserved. Reproduced by permission of Overlook Press, Inc.—Leavitt, Craig. From "On the Road: Cassady, Kerouac, and Images of Late Western Masculinity," in ***Across the Great Divide: Cultures of Manhood in the American West***. Edited by Matthew Basso, Laura McCall, and Dee Garceau. Routledge, 2001. Copyright © 2001 by Routledge. All rights reserved. Reproduced by permission of Routledge, Inc., part of the Taylor & Francis Group.—Levy, Peter B. From "Beating the Censor: The 'Howl' Trial Revisited," in ***Beat Culture: The 1950s and Beyond***. Edited by Cornelis A. Minnen, Jaap van der Bent, and Mel van Elteren. VU University Press, 1999. Copyright © 1999 by Amerika Instituut, Amsterdam. All rights reserved. Reproduced by permission.—Maynard, John Arthur. From Introduction to ***Venice West: The Beat Generation in Southern California***. Copyright © 1991 by John Arthur Maynard. Reproduced by permission of Rutgers University Press. —McCarthy, Mary. From "Burroughs' Naked Lunch," in ***William S. Burroughs at the Front: Critical Reception, 1959- 1989***. Edited by Jennie Skerl and Robin Lydenberg. Southern Illinois University Press, 1991. Copyright © 1991 by Southern Illinois University Press, reprinted by permission of Harcourt, Inc.—McClure, Michael, and Eduardo Lipschutz-Villa. From "Wallace Berman and Semina," in ***Lighting the Corners: On Art, Nature, and the Visionary, Essays and Interviews***. University of New Mexico College of Arts and Sciences, 1993. Copyright © 1993 by Michael McClure. All rights reserved. Reproduced by permission.—McClure, Michael. From "A Mammal Gallery," in ***Scratching the Beat Surface***. North Point Press, 1982. Copyright © 1982 by Michael McClure. All rights reserved. Reproduced by permission of the author.—McClure, Michael. From "Bob Dylan: The Poet's Poet," and "Sixty-six Things About the California Assemblage Movement," in ***Lighting the Corners: On Art, Nature, and the Visionary, Essays and Interviews***. University of New Mexico College of Arts and Sciences, 1993. Copyright © 1993 by Michael McClure. All rights reserved. Reproduced by permission.—McClure, Michael. From "Point Lobos: Animism," in ***Hymns to St. Geryon and Other Poems***. Auerhahn Press, 1959. Copyright © 1959. by Michael McClure. All rights reserved. Reproduced by permission of the author.—Meltzer, David. From "Diane di Prima (1999)," and "Lew Welch (1969)," in ***San Francisco Beat: Talking with the Poets***. City Lights Books, 2001. Copyright © 2001 by David Meltzer. All rights reserved. Reproduced by permission.—Meltzer, David, and Jack Shoemaker. From "Lawrence Ferlinghetti I (1969)," in ***San Francisco Beat: Talking with the Poets***. Edited by David Meltzer. City Lights Books, 2001. Copyright © 2001 by David Meltzer. All rights reserved. Reproduced by permission.—Meltzer, David, and Jack Shoemaker with Michael McClure. From "Michael McClure I (1969)," in ***San Francisco Beat: Talking with the Poets***. Edited by David Meltzer. City Lights Books, 2001. Copyright © 2001 by David Meltzer. All rights reserved. Reproduced by permission.—Meltzer, David. From "Poetry and Jazz," in ***Beat Down to Your Soul: What Was the Beat Generation***. Edited by Ann Charters. Penguin, 2001. Copyright © 2001 Ann Charters. All rights reserved. Reproduced by permission.—Merrill, Thomas S. From "Ginsberg and the Beat Attitude," in ***Allen Ginsberg***. Twayne Publishers, 1988. Copyright © 1988 by G.K. Hall & Co. All rights reserved. Reproduced by permission.—Merrill, Thomas F. From "Allen Ginsberg's Reality Sandwiches," in ***The Beats: Essays in Criticism***. Edited by Lee Bartlett. McFarland, 1981. Copyright © 1981 by Lee Bartlett. All rights reserved. Reproduced by permission.—Miles, Barry. From "The Beat Generation in the Village," in ***Greenwich Village: Culture and Counterculture***. Edited by Rich Beard and Leslie Cohen Berlowitz. Copyright © 1993, by the Museum of the City of New York. Reproduced by permission of Rutgers University Press.—Miller, Henry. From "Patchen: Man of Anger and Light," in ***Kenneth Patchen: A Collection of Essays***. Edited by Richard G. Morgan. AMS Press, Inc. 1977. Copyright © 1977 by Richard G. Morgan. All rights reserved. Reproduced by permission.—Nelson, Raymond. From "Patchen: A Mystical Writer's Career," in ***Kenneth Patchen and American Mysticism***. University of North Carolina Press, 1984. Copyright © 1984 by University of North Carolina Press. All rights reserved. Reproduced by permission.—O'Grady, John P. From "Kenneth Rexroth," in ***Updating the Literary West***. Edited by the Western Literature Association. Texas Christian University Press, 1997. Copyright © 1997 by Western Literature Association. All rights reserved. Reproduced by permission.—Olson, Kirby. From "Gregory Corso: Doubting Thomist," in ***Comedy after Postmodernism: Rereading Comedy from Edward Lear to Charles Willeford***. Texas Tech University Press, 2001. Copyright © 2001 by Texas Tech University Press. All rights reserved. Reproduced by permission.—Ossman, David and Imamu Amiri Baraka (LeRoi Jones). From "LeRoi Jones: An Interview on Yugen," in ***The Sullen Art: Interviews by David Ossman with Modern Poets***. Corinth Books, 1963. Reprinted by permission of the author.—Parkinson, Thomas. From "Poets, Poems, Movements," in ***Casebook on the Beat***. Edited by Thomas Parkinson. Thomas Y. Crowell Co., 1961. UMI Research Press, University Microfilms, Inc., Ann Arbor, Michigan, 48106. Copyright © 1987 by T. Parkinson. Reproduced by permission.—Patchen, Kenneth. From "The Artist's Duty," in ***The Journal of Albion Moonlight***. Copyright © 1941 by Kenneth Patchen. Reprinted by permission of New Directions Publishing Corp.—Perloff, Marjorie. From "On the Other Side of the Field: The Collection Poems of Paul Blackburn," in ***Poetic License: Essays on Modernist and Postmodernist Lyric***. Northwestern University Press, 1990. Copyright © 1990 by Marjorie Perloff. All rights reserved. Reproduced by permission. —Perry, Paul. From "Origins," in ***On the Bus***. Edited by Michael Schwartz and Neil Ortenberg. Thunder's Mouth Press, 1990. Copyright © 1990 by Paul Perry. All rights reserved. Reproduced by permission of the author.—Phillips, Rod. From "'Let Us Throw Out the Word Man': Michael McClure's Mammalian Poetics," and "'The Journal of Urban Withdrawal': Nature and the Poetry of Lew Welch," in ***"Forest Beatniks" and "Urban Thoreaus": Gary Snyder, Jack Kerouac, Lew Welch, and Michael McClure***. Peter Lang, 2000. Copyright © 2000 by Peter Lang Publishing, Inc. All rights reserved. Reproduced by permission. —Porter, M. Gilbert. From "Kesey: The Man and the Artist," in ***The Art of Grit: Ken Kesey's Fiction***. University of Missouri Press, 1982. Copyright © 1982 by The Curators of the University of Missouri. All rights reserved. Reproduced by permission of the University of Missouri Press.—Ratner, Rochelle. From "Loba," in ***Trying to Understand What It Means to be a Feminist: Essays on Women Writers***. Contact II Publications, 1984. Copyright © 1984 by Contact II Publications. All rights reserved. Reproduced by permission of the author.—Rexroth, Kenneth. From "Disengagement: The Art of the Beat Generation," in ***A Casebook on the Beat***. Edited by Thomas Parkinson. Thomas Y. Crowell Company, 1961. Copyright © 1961 by Thomas Y. Crowell Company. All rights reserved. Reproduced by permission.—Rexroth, Kenneth. From Introduction to ***The Residual Years: Poems 1934-1948***, by William Everson. Copyright © 1968 by New Directions Publishing Corp. Reprinted by permission of New Directions Publishing Corp.—Rexroth, Kenneth. From "On Jazz and Poetry," in ***The San Francisco Poets***. Edited by David Meltzer. Ballantine, 1971. Copyright © 1971 Ballantine. All rights reserved. Reproduced by permission.—Rexroth, Kenneth. From Letter to ***The Village Voice Reader***. Doubleday, 1962. Copyright © 1962 by Doubleday. All rights reserved. Reproduced by permission. —Rexroth, Kenneth. From "Thou Shalt Not Kill," in ***Collected Shorter Poems***. Copyright © 1956 New Directions Publishing Corp. Reprinted by permission of New Directions Publishing Corp. —Ricci, Claudia, "Anne Waldman: A Profile," ***http://www.albany.edu/writers-inst/olv1n2.html***. Published by New York State Writers Institute, (Fall 1996). Reprinted with permission.—Roszak, Theodore. From "Journey to the East ... and Points Beyond: Allen Ginsberg and Alan Watts," in ***The Making of a Counter Culture: Reflections on the Technocratic Society and Its Youthful Opposition***.

The Cult of Information: The Folklore of Computers and the True Art of Thinking. University of California Press, 1995. Copyright © 1986 by Theodore Roszak, the University of California Press, publisher. Reproduced with permission.—Russo, Linda. From "To Deal with Parts and Particulars: Joanne Kyger's Early Epic Poetics," in ***Girls Who Wore Black: Women Writing the Beat Generation***. Edited by Ronna C. Johnson and Nancy Grace. Copyright © 2002 by Linda Russo. Reproduced by permission of Rutgers University Press. —Saroyan, Aram. From "Interview with Aram Saroyan," in ***Off the Wall: Interviews with Philip Whalen***. Edited by Donald Allen. Four Seasons Foundation, 1978. Copyright © 1978 by Four Seasons Foundation. All rights reserved. Reproduced by permission of Aram Saroyan.—Skau, Michael. From "'The Comedy Gone Mad': Corso's Surrealism and Humor," in ***"A Clown in a Grave": Complexities and Tensions in the Works of Gregory Corso***. Southern Illinois University Press, 1999. Copyright © 1999 by the Board of Trustees, Southern Illinois University. All rights reserved. Reproduced by permission.—Smith, Larry R. From "A Vision of Light and Art," in ***Kenneth Patchen***. Twayne Publishers, 1978. Copyright © 1978 by G.K. Hall & Co. All rights reserved. Reproduced by permission.—Smith, Richard Candida. From "Woman's Path to Maturation: Joan Brown, Joy DeFeo, and the Rat Bastards," in ***Utopia and Dissent: Art, Poetry, and Politics in California***. University of California Press, 1995. Copyright © 1995 by The Regents of the University of California. All rights reserved. Reproduced by permission.—Snyder, Gary. From "Riprap," in ***Riprap and Cold Mountain Poems***. Four Seasons Foundation, 1958, 1965. Copyright © 1958, 1965. All rights reserved. Reproduced by permission of the author.—Snyder, Gary. From "The Smokey the Bear Sutra," in ***The Fudo Trilogy***. Shaman Drum, 1973. Copyright © 1973 by Shaman Drum. All rights reserved. Reproduced by permission of the author.—Solnit, Rebecca. From "Culture and Counterculture: San Francisco's Fifties," and "Heyday," in ***Secret Exhibition: Six California Artists of the Cold War Era***. City Lights Books, 1990. Copyright © 1990 by Rebecca Solnit. All rights reserved. Reproduced by permission. —Spicer, Jack. From "A Postscript to the Berkeley Renaissance," in ***One Night Stand and Other Poems***. Grey Fox Press, 1980. Copyright © 1980 by Grey Fox Press. All rights reserved. Reproduced by permission.—Spicer, Jack. From "Sporting Life," in ***The Collected Books of Jack Spicer***. Black Sparrow Press, 1975. Copyright © 1975 by Black Sparrow Press. All rights reserved. Reproduced by permission.—Stafford, William E. From "Brother Antoninus—The World as a Metaphor," in ***The Achievement of Brother Antoninus: A Comprehensive Selection of His Poems with Critical Introduction***. Scott, Foresman and Company, 1967. Reproduced by permission of Pearson Education, Inc. —Stephenson, Gregory. From "Friendly and Flowing Savage: The Literary Legend of Neal Cassady," in ***The Daybreak Boys: Essays on the Literature of the Beat Generation***. Southern Illinois University Press, 1990. Copyright © 1990 by the Board of Trustees, Southern Illinois University. All rights reserved. Reproduced by permission.—Stephenson, Gregory. From "Gasoline," and "The Happy Birthday of Death," in ***Exiled Angel: A Study of the Work of Gregory Corso***. Hearing Eye, 1989. Copyright © 1989 by Gregory Stephenson. All rights reserved. Reproduced by permission. —Stephenson, Gregory. From "Homeward from Nowhere: Notes on the Novels of John Clellon Holmes," "The 'Spiritual Optics' of Lawrence Ferlinghetti," and "Allen Ginsberg's Howl: A Reading," in ***The Daybreak Boys: Essays on the Literature of the Beat Generation***. Southern Illinois University Press, 1990. Copyright © 1990 by the Board of Trustees, Southern Illinois University. All rights reserved. Reproduced by permission.—Sterritt, David. From Introduction to ***Mad to Be Saved: The Beats, the '50s, and Film***. Southern Illinois University Press, 1998. Copyright © 1998 by David Sterritt. All rights reserved. Reproduced by permission.—Stitch, Sidra and Brigid Doherty. From "A Biographical History," in ***Jay DeFeo: Works on Paper***. Edited by Sidra Stitch. University of California, Berkeley Art Museum, 1989, pp. 11-25. Copyright © 1989 by The Regents of the University of California. All rights reserved. Reproduced by permission.—Sukenick, Ronald. From "Bleecker Street," in ***Down and Out: Life in the Underground***. Beech Tree Books, 1987. Copyright © 1987 by Ronald Sukenick. All rights reserved. Reproduced by permission of the author.—Swartz, Omar. From ***The View from On the Road: The Rhetorical Vision of Jack Kerouac***. Southern Illinois University Press, 1999. Copyright © 1999 by the Board of Trustees, Southern Illinois University. Reproduced by permission.—Tanner, Stephen L. From "Influences and Achievement," in ***Ken Kesey***. Edited by Warren French. Twayne Publishers, 1983. Copyright © 1983 by G.K. Hall & Company. All rights reserved. Reproduced by permission.—Theado, Matt. From "Tristessa (1960), Visions of Gerard (1963), and Buddhism," in ***Understanding Jack Kerouac***. University of South Carolina Press, 2000. Copyright © 2000 by University of South Carolina Press. All rights reserved. Reproduced by permission.—Thurley, Geoffrey. From "The Development of the New Language: Michael McClure, Philip Whalen, and Gregory Corso," in ***The Beats in Criticism***. Edited by Lee Bartlett. McFarland, 1981. Copyright © by 1981 Lee Bartlett. All rights reserved. Reproduced by permission.—Tytell, John. From "Allen Ginsberg and the Messianic Tradition," and "The Black Beauty of William Burroughs," in ***Naked Angels: The Lives and Literature of the Beat Generation***. McGraw-Hill Book Company, 1976. Copyright © 1976 by John Tytell. All rights reserved. Reproduced by permission of the author.—Tytell, John. From "The Frozen Fifties," in ***Paradise Outlaws: Remembering the Beats, with Photographs by Mellon***. William Morrow and Company, Inc., 1999. Copyright © 1999 by John Tytell and Mellon. All rights reserved. Reproduced by permission of the author.—Waldman, Anne, "Angel Hair Feature," ***http://jacketmagazine.com/16/ah1-wald.html***. Published by Jacket 16, (March 2002). Reprinted with permission of the author.—Waldman, Anne. From Foreword to ***Strange Big Moon, The Japan and Indian Journals: 1960-1964***, by Joanne Kyger, published by North Atlantic Books. Copyright © 2000 by Joanne Kyger. Reproduced by permission of the publisher.—Waldman, Anne. From "Our Past," in ***Blue Mosque***. United Artists Books, 1988. Copyright © 1988 by United Artist Books. All rights reserved. Reproduced by permission of United Artists Books and author.—Waldman, Anne, "The Weight of the World is Love," ***www.naropa.edu/ginstributes8.html***. Published by Naropa Institute, (2002). Reproduced with permission of the author and Coffee House Press, Minneapolis, Minnesota.—Weinreich, Regina. From "The Sound of Despair: A Perfected Nonlinearity," in ***The Spontaneous Poetics of Jack Kerouac: A Study of the Fiction***. Southern Illinois University Press, 1987. Copyright © 1987 by The Board of Trustees, Southern Illinois University. All rights reserved. Reproduced by permission of the author.—Whitmer, Peter O. with Bruce Van Wyngarden. From "The Beat Begins," in ***Aquarius Revisited: Seven Who Created the Sixties Counterculture that Changed America***, William Burroughs, Allen Ginsberg, Ken Kesey, Timothy Leary, Norman Mailer, Tom Robbins, Hunter S. Thompson. Copyright © 1987 by Peter O. Whitmer. Reproduced by permission of Scribner, an imprint of Simon & Schuster Adult Publishing Group. —Widmer, Kingsley. From "The Beat in the Rise of the Populist Culture," in ***The Fifties: Fiction, Poetry, Drama***. Edited by Warren French. Everett/Edwards, Inc., 1970. Copyright © 1970 by Warren French, reassigned 1985 to Kingsley Widmer. All rights reserved. Reproduced by permission. —Wilentz, Elias. From Introduction to ***The Beat Scene***. Edited by Elias Wilentz. Corinth Books, 1960. Copyright © 1960 by Fred McDarrah and Elias Wilentz. All rights reserved. Reproduced by permission of the author.—Williams, Mary Elizabeth with Chuck Workman, "The Beats Go On: Filmmaker Chuck Workman on The Source, His Fawning Tribute to the Beat Generation," at ***http:www.salon.com***. Published by Salon, (June 1, 1999). Reprinted with permission.—Williams, William Carlos. From "A Counsel of Madness: A Review of The Journal of Albion Moonlight," in ***Kenneth Patchen: A Collection of Essays***. Edited by Richard G. Morgan. AMS Press, Inc., 1977. Copyright © 1977 by Richard G. Morgan. All rights reserved. Reproduced by permission. —Wisker, Alistair. From "An Anarchist among the Floorwalkers: The Poetry of Lawrence Ferlinghetti," in ***The Beat Generation Writers***. Edited by A Robert Lee. Pluto Press, 1996. Copyright © 1996 by Lumiere (Cooperative) Press Ltd. and Pluto Press. All rights reserved. Reproduced by permission.—Zurbrugg, Nicholas. From "Will Hollywood Never Learn? David Cronenberg's Naked Lunch," in ***Adaptations: From Text to Screen, Screen to Text***. Edited by Deborah Cartmell and Imelda Whelehan. Routledge, 1999. Copyright © 1999 by Nicholas Zurbrugg. Selection and editorial matter © Deborah Cartmell and Imelda Whelehan. All rights reserved. Reproduced by permission. —Zweig, Paul. From "A Music of Angels," in ***On the Poetry of Allen Ginsberg***. Edited by Lewis Hyde. University of Michigan Press, 1984. © *The Nation* magazine/The Nation Company, Inc. Reproduced by permission of *The Nation* Magazine.

Photographs and illustrations in The Beat Generation *were received from the following sources:*

Beatniks, San Francisco, California, photograph. © Bettmann/Corbis. Reproduced by permission. —Berman, Wallace. *Semina,* assemblage of various photographs. Wallace Berman Estate, Courtesy of LA Louver Gallery. Reproduced by permission. —Blackburn, Paul, photograph. © by Fred W. McDarrah. All rights reserved. Reproduced by permission.—Bremser, Ray, photograph. Original caption: "Ray Bremser, Jazz-ear sound-Poetry genius, syncopating wow-sound word walloper, original N.Y. late-1950s coffee shop bard with Kerouac & Leroi Jones, his long-ago jail songs were noted by Bob Dylan in 'The Times They are a Changin,' at kitchen table, March 15, 1987, he stayed over to read poetry and teach my 'Literary History of Beat Generation' class Brooklyn College, come down from A.A. halfway house in Utica, N.Y., rare trip to the Apple for survivor with big fine beard." Allen Ginsberg/Corbis. Reproduced by permission.—Brown, Joan. *Fur Rat,* sculpture consisting of wood, chicken wire, and raccoon fur, photograph. Berkeley Art Museum, University of California. Reproduced by permission.—Burroughs, William S. (left), and Jack Kerouac in an apartment in New York City, photograph. © Corbis. Reproduced by permission. —Burroughs, William S., sitting in front of a typewriter, at his home in Paris, France, photograph. © Bettmann/Corbis. Reproduced by permission.— Burroughs, William S. (left to right), Lucien Carr, and Allen Ginsberg, sitting together in an apartment in New York City, photograph. © Allen Ginsberg/Corbis. Reproduced by permission. —Campus of Black Mountain College in North Carolina. Courtesy of the North Carolina Offices of Archives and History, Raleigh, North Carolina. Reproduced by permission.—Cassady, Neal, San Francisco, California, 1966, photograph by Ted Streshinsky. Corbis/Ted Streshinsky. Reproduced by permission.—Chase, Hale (left to right), Jack Kerouac, Allen Ginsberg, and William Burroughs, in Morningside Heights near Columbia University campus, New York, c. 1944-1945, photograph. © Allen Ginsberg/Corbis. Reproduced by permission.—City Lights Bookstore, San Francisco, photograph. City Lights Books, Inc. Reproduced by permission.—Corso, Gregory, photograph. © Christopher Felver/Corbis. Reproduced by permission.—Cover of the Black Mountain College publicity booklet, 1936-1938, photograph. Courtesy of the North Carolina Offices of Archives and History, Raleigh, North Carolina. Reproduced by permission.—Cover of "The Black Mountain Review," photograph. Courtesy of the North Carolina Offices of Archives and History, Raleigh, North Carolina. Reproduced by permission.—Defeo, Jay. *After Image,* artwork consisting of graphite, gouache, and transparent acrylic on paper with cut and torn tracing paper, photograph. The Henil Collection, Houston. Reproduced by permission. —di Prima, Diane, photograph. © Chris Felver. Reproduced by permission.—di Prima, Diane, sitting on top of piano, reading selections from her first published book of poetry "This Kind of Bird Flies Backward," to an assembled crowd at the Gas Light Cafe in New York City, photograph. © by Fred W. McDarrah. All rights reserved. Reproduced by permission.—Donlin, Bob, Neal Cassady, Allen Ginsberg, Robert LaVinge, and Lawrence Ferlinghetti (left to right) standing outside Ferlinghetti's City Lights Bookstore, photograph. © Allen Ginsberg/Corbis. Reproduced by permission.—Duncan, Robert, photograph by Nata Piaskowski. Courtesy of New Directions. Reproduced by permission. —Dylan, Bob, photograph. AP/Wide World Photos. Reproduced by permission.—Everson, William, photograph. © Chris Felver. Reproduced by permission.—Ferlinghetti, Lawrence, photograph. AP/Wide World Photos. Reproduced by permission. —Ginsberg, Allen, reading his poem "Howl," outside the U.S. Court of Appeals in Washington, D.C., photograph. AP/Wide World Photos. Reproduced by permission.—Ginsberg, Allen, with fellow poets, original caption: "Philip Whalen, Jerry Heiserman (Hassan later as Sufi) & poet Thomas Jackerell who drove us Vancouver to San Francisco returning from poetry assemblage, we stopped to sightsee Portland where Philip had gone to Reed College with Gary Snyder & Lew Welch. End of July 1963. Vancouver," photograph. © Allen Ginsberg/Corbis. Reproduced by permission. —Ginsberg, Allen, speaking into microphone, 1969, photograph. AP/Wide World Photos. Reproduced by permission.—Guest, Barbara, photograph by Chris Felver. Reproduced by permission.—Guest, Barbara, standing and holding paper in hands while reading poetry at the Living Theatre, photograph. © by Fred W. McDarrah. All rights reserved. Reproduced by permission. —Gysin, Brion, portrait by Carl Van Vechten. The Library of Congress. Reproduced by permission. —Gysin, Brion, portrait by Carl Van Vechten. The Library of Congress. Reproduced by permission. —Holmes, John Clellon, photograph by Chris Felver. Reproduced by permission.—Huncke, Herbert, photograph by Chris Felver. Archive Photos. Reproduced by permission.—Johnson, Joyce, photograph. © Jerry Bauer. Reproduced by permission.—Kandel, Lenore, photograph. The Library of Congress.—Kaufman, Bob, reading his poems at Living Theatre, photograph. © by Fred W. McDarrah. All rights reserved. Reproduced by permission.—Kerouac, Jack, photograph. © Jerry Bauer. Reproduced by permission.—Kerouac, Jack (clockwise from top left), Allen Ginsberg, Gregory Corso, Peter Orlovsky and his brother Lafcadio on vacation in Mexico City, 1956, photograph. © Allen Ginsberg/Corbis. Reproduced by permission. —Kerouac, Jan, photograph. AP/Wide World Photos. Reproduced by permission.—Kesey, Ken, 1990, photograph. AP/Wide World Photos. Reproduced by permission.—Kyger Bolinas, JoAnne, photograph. © Chris Felver. Reproduced by permission.—Landesman, Fran, in a still from the documentary film "Gaslight Square—The Forgotten Landmark" by Bruce Marren. © 2002 Bruce Marren. Reproduced by permission.—Landesman, Jay Irving, in a still from the documentary film "Gaslight Square—The Forgotten Landmark" by Bruce Marren. © 2002 Bruce Marren. Reproduced by permission.—The Merry Pranksters' Bus, preparing it for its drive to the Acid Test Graduation, San Francisco, California, October, 1966, photograph. © Ted Streshinsky/Corbis. Reproduced by permission.—McClure, Michael, photograph. © Roger Ressmeyer/Corbis. Reproduced by permission.—Mingus, Charles (center), playing bass with other musicians during a live performance at the Five Spot Cafe in San Francisco, California, photograph. © by Fred W. McDarrah. All rights reserved. Reproduced by permission.—Mingus, Charles (center), playing bass with his ensemble, while Kenneth Patchen (right) reads poetry during a live performance at the Living Theatre, photograph. © by Fred W. McDarrah. All rights reserved. Reproduced by permission.—Monk, Thelonius, photograph by Jack Vartoogian. Reproduced by permission.—Nicholson, Jack (seated at table), and Vincent Schiavelli standing at left, in the 1975 movie version of "One Flew Over the Cuckoo's Nest," written by Ken Kesey, directed by Milos Forman, movie still. The Kobal Collection/United Artists/Fantasy Films. Reproduced by permission.—Orlovsky, Peter, photograph. AP/Wide World Photos. Reproduced by permission. —Patchen, Kenneth, photograph. Archive Photos, Inc. Reproduced by permission.—Rick Allmen's Cafe Bizarre on West Third Street in Greenwich Village, photograph. © Bettmann/Corbis. Reproduced by permission.—Rexroth, Kenneth, 1952, photograph. AP/Wide World Photos. Reproduced by permission.—St. Mark's-in-the-Bowery, an Episcopal Church built in 1799, photograph. © Lee Snider; Lee Snider/Corbis. Reproduced by permission.—Sanders, Ed, photograph by Chris Felver. Reproduced by permission of Chris Felver.—Snyder, Gary, photograph. AP/Wide World Photos. Reproduced by permission.—Solomon, Carl, photograph. © Allen Ginsberg/Corbis. Reproduced by permission.—Students sitting under a tree at Columbia University, original caption: "Outdoor Class, Outdoor Class on Columbia University Campus is shown, as class was taken outside on this warm summer day," New York, May 7, 1959, photograph. © Bettmann/Corbis. Reproduced by permission.—Village Vanguard nightclub, Greenwich Village, New York, January 1, 1967, photograph. © Bettmann/Corbis. Reproduced by permission.—Waldman, Anne, photograph. © Allen Ginsberg/Corbis. Reproduced by permission.—Waldman, Anne, reading a poem in tribute to the late Allen Ginsberg at the Wadsworth Theater in Los Angeles, California, photograph. AP/Wide World Photos. Reproduced by permission.—Washington Square in Greenwich Village and an arch, photograph. © Bettmann/Corbis. Reproduced by permission.—weiss, ruth, photograph by Daniel Nicoletta. © 2002 Daniel Nicoletta. Reproduced by permission.—Welch, Lew, photograph. © by Fred W. McDarrah. All rights reserved. Reproduced by permission. —Weller, Peter, as Bill Lee in the 1992 film "Naked Lunch," based on the book written by William Burroughs, directed by David Cronenberg, movie still. The Kobal Collection/Recorded Picture Co/First Independent. Reproduced by permission. —Whalen, Philip, 1984, photograph. © Allen Ginsberg/Corbis. Reproduced by permission. —Wieners, John, photograph. © Allen Ginsberg/Corbis. Reproduced by permission.

CHRONOLOGY OF KEY EVENTS

● = historical event

■ = literary event

1914

● William Seward Burroughs is born on 5 February in St. Louis, Missouri. He is the heir to the Burroughs Adding Machine Corporation.

1915

● Herbert Edwin Huncke is born on 9 January in Greenfield, Massachusetts.

1919

● Lawrence Ferlinghetti is born 24 March in Yonkers, New York.

1922

● Jean-Louis (Jack) Kerouac is born on 12 March in Lowell, Massachusetts.

1926

● Neal Cassady is born 18 February in Salt Lake City, Utah, as his parents travel from Iowa to California.

● Irwin Allen Ginsberg is born on 3 June in Paterson, New Jersey.

1930

● Gregory Nunzio Corso is born on 26 March in Greenwich Village, New York.

1932

● Burroughs enters Harvard University as an English major.

1939

● Huncke arrives in New York City.

● Kerouac attends preparatory school before entering Columbia University on a football scholarship.

1941

● The U.S. Naval base at Pearl Harbor, Hawaii, is attacked by Japanese forces; the event spurs America's entry into World War II.

1942

● Kerouac enlists in the merchant marines, serving on the *S.S. Dorchester.*

● Burroughs finds work in Chicago as a pest exterminator.

1943

● Burroughs arrives in New York City.

- Kerouac works on the novel "The Sea Is My Brother," which remains unfinished and unpublished.
- Ginsberg meets Lucien Carr while attending Columbia. Carr introduces Ginsberg to Kerouac and Burroughs.

1944

- Ginsberg, Kerouac, and Carr formulate and discuss "The New Vision" or "New Consciousness," a literary manifesto inspired by the work of such authors as Franz Kafka, Albert Camus, and W. H. Auden. "The New Vision" provides a framework for the Beat aesthetic.
- Carr is arrested for the murder of David Kammerer; Kerouac is detained as a material witness. Kerouac marries Edie Parker as a means of raising money for Carr's defense. Carr is convicted and serves two years in prison.
- Burroughs meets Huncke.
- Kenneth Rexroth, Philip Lamantia, William Everson, and Robert Creeley orchestrate the Berkeley Renaissance.

1945

- Ginsberg is suspended from Columbia. He moves to a communal apartment occupied by, among others, Kerouac and Joan Vollmer, who will become Burroughs's common-law wife.
- World War II ends.

1946

- Kerouac begins writing his first published novel, *The Town and the City.*
- Huncke introduces Burroughs to heroin.
- Cassady arrives in New York and begins a friendship with Ginsberg and Kerouac.
- Corso begins a three-year prison sentence for grand theft; he begins writing poetry while incarcerated.

1947

- Burroughs and Vollmer move to Texas, where their son, William Seward, Jr., is born.
- Cassady meets Carolyn Robinson, who will become his second wife.
- Kerouac travels to Denver, a trip that will inform *On the Road.*
- The House Un-American Activities Committee (HUAAC) begins congressional hearings on suspected American communists.

1948

- Burroughs moves his family to Louisiana.
- Kerouac completes *The Town and the City.* He coins the phrase "Beat Generation." In the winter, he and Cassady travel the U.S., excursions which will be recounted in *On the Road.*
- John Clellon Holmes meets Kerouac and Ginsberg in New York City.
- Ginsberg has a series of visions involving William Blake.

1949

- Ginsberg is arrested for allowing Huncke to keep stolen goods in his apartment.
- Kerouac receives a $1000 advance from Harcourt, Brace for *The Town and the City.*
- Burroughs's legal troubles force him to move his family to Mexico.
- Trumpeter Miles Davis's album *The Birth of the Cool* marks the onset of the "Cool Jazz" movement and marks a period of renewed popularity for jazz music; the medium will have a great influence on Beat writers in the next decade.

1950

- Kerouac's *The Town and the City* is published.
- Burroughs starts work on *Junkie.*
- Kerouac marries Joan Haverty.
- Ginsberg meets Corso in Greenwich Village.
- Ferlinghetti moves from New York to San Francisco.

1951

- John Clellon Holmes completes *Go,* the novel is generally credited as the first to chronicle the Beat Generation.
- Burroughs begins writing *Queer.*
- Fueled by stimulants, Kerouac composes the scroll version of *On the Road* in one long writing session; the event is an early example of the nascent technique he has dubbed "spontaneous prose."

- In Mexico, Burroughs accidentally shoots and kills Vollmer; he credits her death as his motivation to seriously pursue a writing career.
- American forces join in the Korean War.

1952

- Kerouac visits the Cassadys in San Francisco, where he composes part of *Visions of Cody.* He has an affair with Carolyn Cassady. Later in the year, Kerouac will visit Burroughs in Mexico, where he writes *Doctor Sax.*
- Holmes's *Go* is published by Scribners; he writes the seminal article "This is the Beat Generation" for the *New York Times Magazine.*

1953

- Burroughs's *Junkie: Confessions of an Unredeemed Drug Addict* is published under the pseudonym William Lee by Ace Books.
- Ferlinghetti and Peter Martin open City Lights, the first paperback bookstore in the U.S.
- Burroughs and Ginsberg have a brief affair. At its end, Burroughs moves to Tangiers, where he will live for the next five years. While in Tangiers, he begins work on *Naked Lunch.*
- Kerouac writes *Maggie Cassidy* and *The Subterraneans.*

1954

- Attracted to the tenets of the religion, Kerouac begins studying Buddhism. He begins writing *San Francisco Blues* and *Some of the Dharma,* his unpublished musings on Buddhism.
- Ginsberg moves to San Francisco to work in market research and meets Peter Orlovsky; the two will become lifelong partners.
- In California, the North Beach bohemian scene, comprised of writers such as Jack Spicer, Richard Brautigan, Bob Kaufman, and John Weiners, finds expression in cafés, bars, and jazz clubs.

1955

- Corso publishes his first poetry collection, *The Vestal Lady on Brattle and Other Poems.*
- While in San Francisco, Ginsberg completes the majority of "Howl."
- Ferlinghetti founds City Lights Press; the first book on the imprint is his own *Pictures of the Gone World*; publication of works by Kenneth Patchen, Ginsberg, Corso, and Kerouac soon follow.
- Kerouac writes *Mexico City Blues* and starts work on *Tristessa.* Excerpts from *On the Road* are published in *New World Writing* and *Paris Review.*
- Kenneth Rexroth hosts the landmark poetry reading (organized by Ginsberg) at Six Gallery in San Francisco on 7 October; performers include Ginsberg, who performs a breakthrough reading of "Howl," as well as Philip Lamantia, Gary Snyder, Michael McClure, and Philip Whalen.

1956

- Kerouac completes *Tristessa* and begins work on *Visions of Gerard* and *Desolation Angels.*
- Ginsberg reads the complete "Howl" in Berkeley, California. City Lights publishes the poem in the collection *Howl and Other Poems* with an introduction by William Carlos Williams.
- Ginsberg's mother, Naomi dies; the event has a profound effect on the poet and will influence his later work, notably the poem "Kaddish."

1957

- Kerouac meets up with Ginsberg and Orlovsky in Tangiers where they assist Burroughs in the assembly of *Naked Lunch.*
- In March, copies of *Howl and Other Poems* are confiscated and later released by U. S. Customs officials. Ferlinghetti is subsequently arrested for selling the book, which is alleged to be a work of obscenity. In October, following the famous obscenity trial, Ginsberg's work is found to be "not obscene."
- Rexroth and Ferlinghetti perform their poetry accompanied by a jazz band in a San Francisco bar.
- Kerouac's *On the Road* is published by Viking. Reviews are favorable and the book and its author gain widespread popularity.
- Ginsberg begins writing "Kaddish" in memory of his mother.

- The *Evergreen Review* publishes "San Francisco Poets" by Barney Rossett and Donald Allen; the piece is a special focus on the West Coast Beats.

1958

- Ginsberg, Orlovsky, Corso, and Burroughs move into the "Beat Hotel" in Paris.
- Corso's poem "Bomb" is published as a broadside; his collection *Gasoline* is published by City Lights.
- Grove Press publishes Kerouac's *The Subterraneans*; Viking publishes *The Dharma Bums.*
- Kerouac makes an appearance on *The Steve Allen Show.*
- An excerpt from Burroughs's *Naked Lunch* is published in the fall issue of the *Chicago Review*; the work's appearance results in controversy over censorship.
- Cassady begins a two-year prison sentence for possession of marijuana.
- Ferlinghetti's *A Coney Island of the Mind* is published by New Directions.
- Random House publishes Holmes's *The Horn.*
- LeRoi and Hettie Jones found Totem Press as well as the journal *Yugen.*

1959

- Burroughs's *The Naked Lunch* is published in Paris by Olympia Press; Grove will publish the book in the U.S. as *Naked Lunch* in 1962.
- Kerouac publishes several works this year, including *Doctor Sax, Maggie Cassidy, Mexico City Blues,* and *Excerpts from Visions of Cody.*
- Gary Snyder's *Rip Rap* is published in Japan by Origin Press.
- *Pull My Daisy* is produced; the Beat-themed film features appearances by Ginsberg, Corso, and Peter Orlovsky, and Kerouac serves as the narrator.
- Ginsberg records a version of "Howl" to be released on Fantasy Records, a major jazz label.
- Beat literature and lifestyle receives significant attention in publications such as *Time* and *Life,* as well as in the highly critical publication by Lawrence Lipton, *The Holy Barbarians.*
- 29 September debut of television series *The Many Loves of Dobie Gillis,* which features a Beatnik character, Maynard G. Krebbs.

1960

- Kerouac publishes *Tristessa, The Scripture of the Golden Eternity,* and *Lonesome Traveler.*
- Corso's *The Happy Birthday of Death* is published by New Directions.
- Totem Press publishes Snyder's *Myths and Texts.*
- *The New American Poetry* is published by Grove Press; the volume is edited by Donald Allen and presents the work of several Beat poets.
- The film adaptation of Kerouac's *The Subterraneans* is produced by Metro-Goldwyn-Mayer.
- Inspired by interaction with Brion Gysin, Burroughs begins to experiment with the "Cut-up" literary technique for *Minutes to Go* and *Exterminator.*
- Seymour Krim's landmark chronicle, *The Beats,* is published by Gold Medal.
- The 7 October debut of the television series *Route 66,* which chronicles the cross-country travels of two young men; the show grew out of plans to create a television series based upon *On the Road*; the concept was rejected by Kerouac and re-tooled as *Route 66.*

1961

- Burroughs's *The Soft Machine* is published by Olympia.
- Corso publishes his only novel, *The American Express.*
- Kerouac begins writing *Big Sur* and completes *Desolations Angels*; he publishes *Book of Dreams* and *Pull My Daisy.*
- City Lights publishes Ginsberg's *Kaddish and Other Poems: 1958-1960*; Ginsberg travels to the Near and Far East.

1962

- Burroughs's *The Ticket That Exploded* is published in Japan; *Naked Lunch* is published in the U.S.
- Kerouac's *Big Sur* is published by Grove.
- Burroughs receives international notice when Norman Mailer and others hail his work at the International Writer's Conference in Edinburgh.

1963

- Kerouac's *Visions of Gerard* is published by Farrar, Strauss.

- Correspondence between Ginsberg and Burroughs is published as *The Yage Letters* by City Lights.
- City Lights publishes Ginsberg's *Reality Sandwiches.*
- Ginsberg is awarded a Guggenheim Fellowship.

1964

- Diane di Prima founds Poets Press.
- Kerouac moves to Tampa, Florida, where he resides with his mother; he and Cassady see each other for the last time.

1965

- Following his travels in France, Kerouac begins writing *Satori in Paris*; *Desolation Angels* is published by Coward-McCann.
- Poets Press publishes *Huncke's Journal.*

1966

- Burroughs moves to London and his novel *The Soft Machine* is published by Grove.
- Kerouac and his mother move to Hyannis on Cape Cod, Massachusetts, where she suffers a stroke. Kerouac marries Stella Sampas, his third wife, and the three move back to his hometown of Lowell.
- A decision is reached in the *Naked Lunch* obscenity trial, with the Massachusetts Supreme Court ruling that while the work is "grossly offensive," it is not obscene.

1967

- Kerouac begins work on *The Valley of Duluoz.*
- *The Ticket That Exploded* is published in America by Grove.
- *Nothing More to Declare* by John Clellon Holmes is published.

1968

- Kerouac's *The Valley of Duluoz* is published by Coward-McCann.
- After a night of heavy drinking, Neal Cassady wanders into the Mexican desert and dies of exposure.
- Ginsberg organizes a protest of the Vietnam War to coincide with the Democratic National Convention in Chicago, Illinois; rioting ensues and the National Guard is called out.

1969

- Kerouac completes his final work, *Pic*; his alcoholism is chronic by this point; on 21 October, a vein in his stomach bursts, and Kerouac dies in St. Petersburg, Florida; he is later buried in Lowell.
- Ginsberg is awarded a poetry grant from the National Institute of Arts and Letters.

1970

- Burroughs's *The Last Words of Dutch Schultz* is published in London; U.S. publication in an enlarged and revised format in 1975 by Viking.

1971

- Burroughs's *The Wild Boys: A Book of the Dead* is published by Grove.

1973

- Viking publishes Burroughs's *Exterminator!.*

1974

- Burroughs returns to America and takes a teaching post at the City College of New York.
- Ginsberg's *Fall of America* wins the National Book Award, and he is inducted into the American Academy of Arts and Letters.
- The Jack Kerouac School of Disembodied Poetics, Naropa Institute, is founded by Ginsberg and Anne Waldman in Boulder, Colorado.

1978

- Ginsberg's *Mindbreaths: Poems 1972-1977* is published by City Lights.
- *As Ever: The Collected Correspondence of Allen Ginsberg & Neal Cassady* is published by Creative Arts.

1981

- Burroughs moves to Lawrence, Kansas.

1982

- The Naropa Institute holds a twenty-fifth anniversary celebration of Kerouac's *On the Road.* In attendance are, among others, Ginsberg, Burroughs, Corso, Ferlinghetti, Michael McClure, Ken Kesey, Abbie Hoffman, Anne Waldman, Timothy Leary, and Herbert Huncke.

1985

- Viking publishes *Queer* by Burroughs.

1989

- Burroughs appears as the Tom, the Junky Priest, in director Gus Van Sant's film *Drugstore Cowboy.*

1990

- Burroughs releases the album *Dead City Radio,* which features readings of unpublished material.
- Director David Cronenberg's loose film adaptation of Burroughs's *Naked Lunch* is released; Peter Weller plays Bill Lee and Judy Davis plays Joan Vollmer.
- Burroughs has triple bypass heart surgery.

1992

- Burroughs and Kurt Cobain of the rock group Nirvana collaborate on the album *The Priest They Called Him.*

1993

- Burroughs collaborates with musician Tom Waits and director Robert Wilson on the musical play and album (released under Waits's name) *The Black Rider.*

1994

- Burroughs appears in Nike television advertisements.
- "The Beat Legacy and Celebration" is held on 18-21 May; sponsored by New York University, the event is chaired by Ginsberg and Ann Charters; speakers include Carolyn Cassady, Corso, Ferlinghetti, Hettie Jones, Ed Sanders, Hunter S. Thompson, and Anne Waldman, among others.

1995

- New York University sponsors "The Writing of Jack Kerouac Conference" on 4-6 June.

1996

- Huncke dies on 8 August from congestive heart failure in NewYork City.

1997

- Ginsberg dies on 5 April from complications of liver cancer in New York City.
- Burroughs dies on 2 August following a heart attack in Lawrence, Kansas.

2001

- Corso dies on 17 January from prostate cancer in Minnesota.

PAUL BLACKBURN

(1926 - 1971)

Paul Blackburn. Copyright © Fred W. McDarrah.

American poet and translator.

A prolific poet of the 1950s and 1960s, Blackburn was active in promoting the fledgling poets of the Beat Generation. Considered one of the fathers of the New York literary scene, he was a key organizer and disseminator of the contemporary poetry of his day, arranging poetry readings that provided many young poets the opportunity to present their works. Because of his contributions to the *Black Mountain Review*—a landmark literary journal and forum for innovative and experimental verse—Blackburn is often classified as a Black Mountain poet. Critics have praised the musical quality and lyricism of Blackburn's poetry, his ability to make poetry out of everyday events, and his masterful use of complex forms. Blackburn is also known as one of the foremost translators of Provençal troubadour verse.

BIOGRAPHICAL INFORMATION

Blackburn was born on November 24, 1926, in St. Albans, Vermont. His parents, William Blackburn and Frances Frost, separated when he was three years old, leaving him and his sister in the care of their elderly maternal grandparents. At the age of fourteen, Blackburn went to live in Greenwich Village with his mother, a poet and writer of children's books. In the mid-1940s, with the encouragement of his mother, Blackburn began writing poetry. He attended New York University in 1945, left after one year to join the U.S. Army, and resumed his education in 1947. He received his B.A. at the University of Wisconsin in 1950. Blackburn met his mentor, Ezra Pound, in 1947. Pound, a major influence on Blackburn's career, was the impetus behind the publication of Blackburn's first poem. Pound also helped him make connections with the writers who would eventually form his literary circle, such as poets Robert Creeley and Charles Olson. During the early 1950s Blackburn contributed to both *Origin* and *Black Mountain Review*; his brief association with the latter is what prompted several scholars and critics to classify him as a Black Mountain poet. In 1954 Blackburn won a Fulbright Scholarship and moved to Europe with his new wife, Winifred Grey. The scholarship allowed him to pursue his study of Provençal troubadour literature, a subject that had interested him for a number of years. Creeley published Blackburn's first collection of troubadour translations, *Proensa,* in 1953, and his first book of poetry, *The Dissolving Fabric,* in 1955. Blackburn returned to New York in 1958 and assumed a pivotal role in the burgeoning poetry community of Manhattan's Lower East Side. He organized poetry readings at various locations, arranged for guest appearances by members of the Beats, the New York School, and the Black Mountain group, and welcomed and encouraged young poets just arriving in the literary community. Blackburn was also interested in politics, and was involved in a number of anti-war and pro-civil rights organizations; much of his poetry reflects his political views. Over the next decade, in addition to his poetry, Blackburn supported himself with a variety of jobs, including editing, translating, and teaching. He divorced his second wife, Sara Golden, in 1967, the same year that his first major commercial collection, *The Cities,* was published. Shortly after his divorce he returned to Europe on a Guggenheim Fellowship to work on his translations and poetry. He married his third wife, Joan Miller, in 1968. The last few years of Blackburn's life are recorded in his posthumously published book *The Journals* (1975). Blackburn died of esophageal cancer in 1971.

MAJOR WORKS

Blackburn began publishing his work in journals and reviews in the early 1950s with the encouragement and assistance of Pound and Creeley. In 1953 Creeley published *Proensa,* Blackburn's translations of Provençal troubadour poetry, and two years later *The Dissolving Fabric,* a collection of poems related to Blackburn's college and early New York years. His second collection of poetry, *The Nets* (1961), was written during his time in Spain and southern France. Unlike his first book, which includes poems concerned with the everyday events of life, his second collection contains poems based on the numerology and symbolism of the Celtic tree alphabet, which was inspired by Robert Graves's *The White Goddess.* In 1960 Blackburn produced his third volume, *Brooklyn-Manhattan Transit: A Bouquet for Flatbush,* a small collection based on the themes of city life. The volume includes "Clickety Clack," one of his most famous "subway poems," a subgenre that came to be associated with Blackburn. In 1967 Blackburn published his first major collection of poetry, *The Cities,* which spans his career from the 1950s to mid-1960s. The following year he published *In. On. Or About the Premises,* a smaller volume of his urban pieces that is also devoted to themes associated with the city. One of Blackburn's best-known works, *The Journals,* was published posthumously and chronicles the last four years of his life. It was hailed by many as the culmination of his progress as a poet.

CRITICAL RECEPTION

Blackburn's poetry has been well received by his contemporaries, but has not achieved wide recognition. Some modern scholars have been critical of Blackburn's sexually aggressive lyrics, and even his admirers have commented on the alleged sexism found in his works. Marjorie Perloff claims that modern readers may find Blackburn's reductive images of women problematic and describes his characterization of women as "irritatingly macho." Peter Baker, while disagreeing with Perloff's assessment, acknowledges that Blackburn's "persistent and aggressive sexism is a drawback to a continuing appreciation of his work." Edith Jarolim expresses approval for Blackburn's lyrical talent but dissaproval of his portrayal of women as sex objects. She notes in her introduction to *The Collected Poems of Paul Blackburn* that Blackburn's treatment of women in his poetry "may be seen not only as a product of its times, but also as the flip side of a fear of women." Many critics laud the musical quality of Blackburn's poetry and the skill with which he illuminates the interrelations between his life and his work. Other commentators praise the casual, simple language of his poems, maintaining that Blackburn paid careful attention to structure and formal elements in order to create his seemingly spontaneous verse. Robert Buckeye explains that Blackburn wrote about everyday events and observations, what he calls "out-the-window" poems, in a way that might seem careless, or even sloppy. This, according to Buckeye, was the essence of Blackburn's talent—his ability "to record the poetry inherent in the everyday without the *apparent* intervention of the voice, skill, or ego of the poet."

PRINCIPAL WORKS

Proensa [translator] (poetry) 1953; revised edition 1978

The Dissolving Fabric (poetry) 1955

Brooklyn-Manhattan Transit: A Bouquet for Flatbush (poetry) 1960

The Nets (poetry) 1961

Sing-Song (poetry) 1966

16 Sloppy Haiku and a Lyric for Robert Reardon (poetry) 1966

The Cities (poetry) 1967

The Reardon Poems (poetry) 1967

In. On. Or About the Premises (poetry) 1968

Two New Poems (poetry) 1969

Three Dreams and an Old Poem (poetry) 1970

Early Selected Y Mas: Poems 1949-1966 (poetry) 1972

Halfway Down the Coast (poetry) 1975

The Journals (poetry) 1975

The Selection of Heaven (poetry) 1980

The Collected Poems of Paul Blackburn [edited by Edith Jarolim] (poetry) 1985

GENERAL COMMENTARY

EDITH JAROLIM (ESSAY DATE 1985)

SOURCE: Jarolim, Edith. Introduction to *The Collected Poems of Paul Blackburn,* edited by Edith Jarolim, pp. xxi-xxxv. New York: Persea Books, 1985.

In the following introduction, Jarolim explores the connections between Blackburn's life and his poetry.

Was it Paul Blackburn's modesty? The prevailing winds of poetic fashion? The reasons are more complicated and less important than the fact: until now the work of one of our most talented poets has been largely unavailable. Early Blackburn volumes were slim and published in very limited editions (***The Dissolving Fabric,*** 1955; ***Brooklyn-Manhattan Transit,*** 1960; ***The Nets,*** 1961). By the time two larger, more widely distributed collections of middle-period work appeared (***The Cities,*** 1967, and ***In. On. Or About the Premises,*** 1968), the first books were out of print. ***Early Selected Y Mas*** recovered those volumes in 1972, and three years later ***Halfway Down the Coast*** and ***The Journals*** made available a substantial portion of the late poems—but by this time the collections of the middle years were no longer in print. Furthermore, over one-third of Blackburn's published poetry appeared only in magazines and anthologies, many of them ephemeral and obscure.

This collection brings together, in the order in which they were written, the original poems published during Blackburn's lifetime (November 24, 1926-September 13, 1971) and those in clear preparation for book publication at the time of his death.[1] What does this gathering and arrangement reveal? At first glance—or heft—it becomes clear that he was a prolific poet, especially considering that he died at the age of 44. But then it's common lore that he had a great facility with language, "one of the best ears in poetry," and "perfect pitch." More surprising is the cumulative evidence here of his *achieved* naturalness, of the erudition and artifice that underlie even the most casual-seeming later poems. Blackburn made only rare—and usually misleadingly informal—statements about his poetic practice, but in a 1958 letter to Gregory Corso he summed it up neatly. "It seems to bug you," he wrote, "that I set down 'real' experiences . . . but in ordered form, strictly controlled. My own life is somewhat disorderly, and when not, is on the point of becoming so, almost always. I order my life in my work."

Certainly Blackburn's life was intricately connected with poetry from very early on. Poetry took his mother, Frances Frost, from the family home in St. Albans, Vermont, when Paul was four and his younger sister, Jean, three. Frost (no relation to Robert) was selected for the Yale Series of Younger Poets in 1929; she separated from her husband William Blackburn the next year. He went to California and she went to the big city—first Burlington, then New York—to try to earn a living as a writer, leaving the children in St. Albans with her strict and elderly parents. Only rarely, and not until much later, did Blackburn write about his unhappy childhood; the bitterness of such a poem as **"My Sainted"** may be explained by the beatings he would get daily from his grandmother.

After age 14, when his mother brought him to New York City to live with her on Horatio Street, his contact with poetry was more direct and on the whole more salutary. She encouraged him to write and gave him a wide variety of poetry to read, although her own verse was fairly conventional. (Her private life was much less so. She and her lover, Paul's "Aunt" Carr, struggled to earn even enough money to keep themselves in—admittedly prodigious—supplies of scotch.)

Blackburn's formal education in poetry at New York University was interrupted the year it began: hoping to be sent overseas, he joined the Army in 1945. An armistice was declared within days of his enlistment and he was sent to Staten Island instead. After two years in the service, working mostly as a lab technician, he went back to NYU where he studied with M. L. Rosenthal and was briefly poetry editor of the school literary magazine, *The Apprentice*. It was at NYU that he began reading the poetry of Ezra Pound.

When Blackburn transferred to the University of Wisconsin in 1949, he started corresponding with Pound, occasionally hitchhiking to St. Elizabeth's to visit him. Pound was soon responsible for Blackburn's first publication in a major literary journal: he encouraged James Laughlin to print the work of the unknown poet in *New Directions* in 1951. Blackburn also attributed what became a lifelong involvement with Provençal poetry to an initial frustration over not understanding the snatches of it he came across in *The Cantos.* Pound encouraged him in this direction—or rather he didn't *dis*courage him. Pound's wife, Dorothy Shakespeare, told Blackburn he was the only one who expressed an interest in the subject that Pound didn't vigorously warn away.[2]

And it was to Pound that Blackburn owed his first—and last—affiliation with a literary school, for better and for worse. In 1949 Pound prompted the voluminous correspondence between Blackburn and "a chicken farmer in New Hampshire," Robert Creeley. Creeley in turn put Blackburn in touch with Charles Olson, Jonathan Williams, Joel Oppenheimer, and other members of the group later dubbed the "Black Mountain Poets." Creeley also introduced him, via the mails, to Cid Corman, whose historic literary magazine *Origin* was the first to publish regularly a good deal of Blackburn's work in the early 1950s.

Blackburn always opposed the division of poets into schools and did not like the role of Black Mountain poet into which he was cast by Donald Allen's anthology *The New American Poetry* (1960). He embraced all types of poetry, citing the value of "all work, if you work 'em right" to Robert Creeley in 1961, apropos another so-called poetic movement. His association with the Black Mountain group was in fact a tenuous one. He never attended Black Mountain College or taught there, and his affiliation with the *Black Mountain Review,* established in 1953 to raise money for the financially floundering experimental college, was short-lived. He was contributing editor and New York distributor of the first two issues only, and then a quarrel with editor Creeley caused him to sever his connection with the journal.

But if Blackburn disliked the label, and if the styles of the poets with whom he is generally linked are often dissimilar (for example, Blackburn uses a longer, more varied line than Creeley and is less directly allusive, more consistently musical than Olson), all these writers did share aesthetic concerns. They were, as Blackburn later put it, "all working at speech rhythms, composition by field. . . . By 1951 Olson had tied a lot of it together in that 'Projective Verse' essay. So we even had a lot of principles to keep in our heads." Blackburn, whose typing skills had been polished in the Army, took naturally to Olson's concept of the typewriter as a means of notating the oral performance of a poem, on the analogy of a musical score. More than anyone else associated with the Black Mountain aesthetic, he refined the use of punctuation, line breaks, and text alignments that characterize the practice.

During the years of his most extended contact with the *Origin/Black Mountain* writers, 1950-54, Blackburn was living in New York and working in various print shops. The first thirty-six poems in the present collection, representing—with the exception of the earlier opening poem—these four years and the preceding one at the University of Wisconsin, bear clear traces of Blackburn's literary education. His Provençal studies show up in such poem titles as **"Alba"** and **"Cantar de Noit,"** in the characters of unkind ladies who don't give signs and birds who offer sympathy, in the casting of the poet as singer and half-crazed purveyor of truth. Other literary traditions are on parade as well: we find shepherds and Greek gods, a sensitive young voyager-poet who makes a trip to the underworld—represented, à la Hart Crane, by the New York subway system—etc.

Perhaps inadvertently, Blackburn created an accurate self-portrait in his young painter of **"The Innocents Who Fall like Apples."** Like the artist's picture, some of his early work is stylized and relies overmuch on convention, but, as the poem puts it, "this dabbler speaks truth also." In **"The Innocents"** Blackburn had already begun to undercut the poetic devices on which he continued to rely. The opening lines of the poem irreverently address the prophet of their exotic Eastern setting: "Mohamet, old navigator, your flying coffin suspended between heaven and earth." And the conventions he chose early on—the trope of the unkind lady, the romantic linking of love and death—naturally held more than literary interest for him. Over the years he developed them, built a set of personal associations around them—in short, made them his own.

Other signs of the mature poet are discernible in the early pieces. An impulse toward formal control and a simultaneous drive toward relinquishing it are played out thematically in such complementary poems as **"The Search"** and **"What the Tide Gave."** The first sees the poet seeking a defining, totemic image for his art; the second uses sea imagery to project an ambivalence about loss of control (= loss of identity = death), which Blackburn continually associates with love. The recurrent "limits," "lines," and "definitions" that begin to turn up in the vocabulary of the poems are at once desirable and restrictive, as the repeated image of gull flight mixes admiration for its grace with a simultaneous antipathy for its predatory nature. The as-yet unnamed gull of **"The Birds"** and the literary "ur-gull" of **"The Lanner"** are the first of many surrogates for a poet who is a master of form and works continually to do away with it.

In the poems written around 1953-54, we especially recognize the subjects and techniques with which Blackburn became associated:

On the farm it never mattered;
behind the barn, in any grass, against
any convenient tree,
the woodshed in winter, in
a corner
if it came to that.

But in a city of eight million, one
stands on the defensive.
("**The Assistance**")

Later on Blackburn is not so coy about the scatological "it" in the first line, but riddling opening sentences or cryptic titles remain his rhetorical trademarks. So too he later perfects the wit of the final two lines of this passage—the visual pun of separating "one" from the "city of eight million"; the verbal play of "stands on the defensive" on the psychic and physical posture of the speaker; the mock-heroic tone.

But alongside the jazzy, street-wise voice of **"The Assistance"** and, to an even greater degree, **"The Continuity,"** we hear sonorous intonations of a (rather precocious) sage in such pieces as **"The Dissolving Fabric."** And in fact it is the quieter rhythms of the early imagistic lyrics—**"Friends," "The Sunlit Room,"** and **"The Quest"**—that predominate in the next group of poems, written during the three-and-a-half years Blackburn spent in Europe:

The one-half moon is over the mountain
and the star is over the sea.
The star will go down
into the sea.
The moon will also go down.
("**The Gift and the Ending**")

When, in the spring of 1954, Blackburn was awarded a Fulbright Fellowship to study Provençal language and literature, he and his new wife Winifred Grey left almost immediately for Europe. They spent several months in Majorca, Spain, until Blackburn was assigned to Toulouse in southern France. His increasing dislike of that city (see, especially, **"Sirventes"**) didn't prevent him from staying on there for another year as Fulbright "lecteur Américain." He simply escaped as often as possible, usually to nearby Spain, where he spent most of his post-Fulbright time in Europe (1956-57) as well. He grew increasingly, romantically, to admire Spain, its people and especially its language and literature. It was during this time that he bought a copy of Federico García-Lorca's *Obras Completas* and acquired his lifelong habit of translating from it.[3] And at the end of Blackburn's stay in Europe, a friend who knew of his interest in Spanish-language literature introduced him to the work of a little-known Argentinian writer living in Paris. Although he didn't manage to meet Julio Cortázar then, he eventually became his close friend, U. S. literary agent, and sometime translator.

A few of the poems in this European group recount Blackburn's diverse travels. Most of them show him already arrived, sitting and watching—

Today makes 20 days
that some ants follow the same route
across 2 of these steps
never varying from the line.
("**Canción de las Hormigas**")

or walking the streets and listening—

Que buen
números me quedan!

Mañana
luck is
always for tomorrow
or tonight, when
the lottery is drawn
("**The Lottery**")

The literary traditions of Europe naturally enter into these poems, but far less obtrusively than they did in the earlier work. Mostly Blackburn focuses on the living history of the continent, the everyday activities that continue to be performed as they have been for centuries. Poems such as **"Atardecer"** and **"The Misunderstanding"** evoke a timeless, almost mythical Europe. The sacerdotal aura they bestow on secular routines anticipates that of the series of "ritual" poems Blackburn began on his return to the States. As for the "official" rituals, the Christian festivals witnessed in **"Ramas, Divendres, Diumenga"** and **"Verbena,"** Blackburn emphasizes their sensual, celebratory character, their closeness to pagan nature-worship sources.

So he religiously counts the number of days a group of ants walk across some steps, and confers significance on configurations of people sitting "five and six" and "seven and eight" to a bench (**"Plaza Real with Palmtrees"**). But just as he mocks the rhetoric of easy solutions in his numerous "how to" titles (**"How to Get Through Reality," "How to Live with One Another Somehow"**), he often steps back in these poems from a Noah-like propensity for grouping and tallying: **"Café at Night"** is a mock-heroic account of the poet's venturing to break the dominant color-pattern of food in a local restaurant and **"Song for a Cool Departure"** finds him wondering "where to put" the "2 cypresses, 3 elms" of his poem.

If self-irony sometimes undercuts aspects of his, the poet's, vocation, the value of that vocation is never in doubt in these European poems. It is often expressed in terms of an aesthetic pragmatism Blackburn shares with the other New England-bred members of the Black Mountain group—the notion that poetry must be utilitarian, be functional, be work:[4]

> The principle, the demarcation
> of my fascination
> is use
> (**"City Museum, Split"**)

Also characteristic is his democratic notion that "poet" is just one among many potentially meaningful occupations: the balloon seller of **"Plaza Real,"** the eponymous **"The Captain"** and **"The First Mate"** are afforded equally respectful attention. What one does is ultimately less important than *how* one does it; the "easy, confident step" of the driver in **"The Busride"** of 1957 is a precursor of "the organized waddle" of the waiter Blackburn elegizes in **"The Touch"** ten years later. With the Elizabethans as much as with Ernest Hemingway, Blackburn shares the notion that style—not as surface attribute, but as "coherence" or outward manifestation of inward clarity and intactness—is all-important.

The Blackburns returned to New York in late 1957, ostensibly just to recoup finances, but things didn't work out quite according to plan. The marriage soon broke up and Blackburn had a good deal of trouble finding a job. In 1958 and early 1959 he supported himself by doing publisher's reader reports and occasional translations; for the rest of 1959 through 1962 he worked as an in-house editor for Funk & Wagnall's New International Year Book.

This was a time of turmoil, but not all of the turmoil was negative. There were new loves for Blackburn—most important, Sara Golden, whom he married in 1963—and a new literary scene. Blackburn had returned to New York at a time when the beginnings of the Beat poets' influence had awakened an interest in local poetry readings. His own interest in oral tradition made natural the active role he soon took on New York's Lower East Side. For one thing, his enthusiasm for the troubadours led to his arranging and taking part in a number of programs offering translations of medieval European poems, along with the original Provençal or middle English lyrics, to jazz accompaniment.

Readings at the Deux Megots Coffeehouse and, later, Le Metro Café provided the main outlet for Blackburn's interest in contemporary poetry. The Wednesday night guest program he hosted at Le Metro in the early 1960s was known for its quality and eclecticism, having as participant readers key members of the (so designated) Beat, New York, Deep Image, and Black Mountain poetry schools. Blackburn also helped with the poetry and drama series at the Judson Church (among other things, he played Doc Watson in Joel Oppenheimer's production there of "Billy the Kid"), and he was poetry editor of both the *Judson Review* and *The Nation* in 1962.

The poems Blackburn wrote in the five between-marriage years, 1958-63, are among his best known and most successful. The time spent in Europe had confirmed his sense of vocation; this confidence combined with a continuing youthfulness to produce work at once energetic and highly crafted. A number of these poems retain a timeless, European feeling—some, in the beginning, are still set in Europe—but Blackburn soon returned to transcribing the sights and sounds of American life. In baseball and space travel he found new rituals to observe; by the end of the period he was reporting increasingly on the rites of American politics.

And in late 1957, with **"The Yawn,"** Blackburn inaugurated the subgenre (so to speak) with which he is most often associated: the subway poem. Such pieces as **"Clickety-Clack"** show him at his most deceptively simple:

> I took
> a coney island of the mind
> to the coney
> island of the flesh
> the brighton local
> riding
> past church avenue, beverly, cortelyou, past
> avenues h & j
> king's highway, neck road, sheepshead bay,
> brighton, all the way to stillwell
> avenue
> that hotbed of assignation
> clickety-clack

We take a joy ride of the senses as we follow the poet through Brooklyn, listening to him read poetry aloud and watching him unsuccessfully attempt to engage the affections of a not-so-amused female passenger. Blackburn skillfully duplicates the lurching rhythms of the train, and anyone familiar with what is now New York City's "D" line might observe that he eliminates those stations that don't fit into his rhythmic scheme. But the poem also has a wide outside frame of reference, a broad range of literary allusion. A tribute to Lawrence Ferlinghetti, its typography and rhythms evoke the San Francisco poet's *A Coney Island of the Mind* as well as the subway's movement. **"Clickety-Clack"** also offers echoes of Edward Fitzgerald's "Rubbaiyat" ("Let's fling that old garment of repentance, baby"), lines from Yeats' "Under Ben Bulben" ("Cast a cold eye / on life, on death . . .") and less direct evocations of numerous other poems and poetic traditions.

One of the standard comic devices of **"Clickety-Clack"**—and indeed too many of Blackburn's other poems—the characterization of woman as (often prudishly unwilling) sex object, is no longer the unquestioned source of amusement it was when Blackburn wrote these pieces. For Blackburn, the type of bravado expressed through this device may be seen not only as a product of its times, but also as the flip side of a fear of women and love expressed much more powerfully, if still obliquely, in **"The Purse-Seine"**:

> the sea
> lies in its own black anonymity and we here on
> this bed
> enact the tides, the swells, your hips rising
> toward me,
> waves break over the shoals, the
> sea bird hits the mast in the dark and falls
> with a cry to the deck and flutters off . Panic
> spreads, the
> night is long, no
> one sleeps, the net
> is tight
> we are caught or not, the torn sliding down
> ponderous
> shall we make it?
> The purse closes.

Earlier in the poem Blackburn warns, "Never look a gull in the eye." He follows his own advice: the vatic tone of **"The Purse-Seine"** and, to an even greater degree, the group of poems based on the Celtic tree alphabet, as elaborated in Robert Graves' *The White Goddess* (see, for example, **"Venus, the Lark . . . ,"** **"The Vine the Willow Lurch to and Fro,"** and **"Bk. of Numbers"**), lends the distance and authority of myth to painful personal events. Nor does Blackburn's alternate lighter, colloquial voice tend to address love directly, even when the experience recounted is a positive one. Such pieces as **"Remains of an Afternoon,"** **"Ciao,"** and **"Love Song"** are inclined to "study the artifacts," as Blackburn puts it in **"Good Morning, Love!"**—to examine carefully the traces or *after*-effects of physical love.

Often cryptic, Blackburn's long, autobiographical **"The Selection of Heaven"** is nevertheless one of the exceptions to his general practice of avoiding the gull's stare. Its first sixteen sections, written in the early months of 1963, concern the deaths of Blackburn's paternal grandparents; the death of Blackburn's second marriage is the subject of the final section, appended in the summer of 1967. The years encompassed by this poem were in some ways Blackburn's most active and productive ones. He was enjoying a new degree of success as a poet: two major collections, ***The Cities*** and ***In. On. Or About the Premises,*** were slated for publication, and poems were being accepted by an unprecedented number of anthologies and journals (including, to Blackburn's bemusement, *Poetry* and *The New Yorker*). Large and interesting translation projects were offered him: the Spanish medieval epic *Poem of the Cid* for Studymasters in 1966 and Julio Cortázar's *Blow Up and Other Stories* for Pantheon in 1967. And for the first time he was getting teaching positions: he was poet-in-residence at New York's City College from 1966 to 1967 and ran poetry workshops at the Aspen Writer's Conference in the summers of 1965, 1966, and 1967.

Nor did Blackburn's activities on the New York poetry scene let up. From 1964 to 1965 he ran a show on radio station WBAI of interviews with and readings by poets. (It was terminated a few weeks before the completion of its contract because of the—even more than usually—"strong" language of one of his participating friends, LeRoi Jones.) It was Blackburn's idea to move the readings at Le Metro Café to St. Mark's Church-in-the-Bowery, and he was instrumental in establishing what officially became (and still continues as) the Poetry Project there in 1966. He was an indefatigable attender of all types of poetry readings, and he carried his large, double-reel tape recorder with him wherever he went; his tape collection, now at the University of California, San Diego, is probably the best oral history of the New York poetry scene from the late 1950s up until 1970. And through all this Blackburn continued, with increased demand for his services, to do what he had done since the early 1950s: serve as a kind of unofficial one-man reception committee for poets coming into the city. He helped them get readings, gave them advice about publication, gave them practical assistance in such matters as finding jobs and places to stay. These activities—which also included such less successful schemes as trying to get poetry placed in jukeboxes across the country—attest to Blackburn's commitment to making a reality his belief in a genuine community of poets.

The poems written during this period provide a graph of American life on the left in the 1960s. The pieces Blackburn wrote against the Vietnam War focus particularly on the way in which the government originated and maintained the war through deliberate distortions of language. There are satirical reports on sports events and the space program: **"Laurel,"** for example, probes the economic superstructures of horseracing and **"Newsclips 2,"** takes a literal look at the men inside the space suits. We get news of the music scene in the wonderful jazz variations inspired by **"Listening to Sonny Rollins at the Five-Spot,"** and of the poetry world in **"Torch Ballad for John Spicer: d. 8/17/65."**

But into these songs of active engagement with world events and with the art scene there increasingly enters a counter-strain of bitterness and despair. Images of helplessness, passivity, and death begin to proliferate. Love, friendship, the meaningfulness of the past—all eventually come into doubt. Even faith in the constructive powers of poetry, literally and metaphorically demonstrated in the impressive edifice of **"The Watchers"** in 1963, is eroded. Less than three years later Blackburn says, in one of his **"Sixteen Sloppy Haiku"** dedicated to writer Robert Reardon:

> Love is not enuf
> Friendship is not enuf
> Not even art
> is / Life is too much

A body of work which had always stressed the importance of alertness and attention now shows a strong drive toward eliminating, or at least diminishing, consciousness.

"What do you do about love?" Blackburn's friend Joel Oppenheimer asks him in "The Answer." Blackburn had already replied earlier in **"Two Songs for the Opp"**: "Stay drunk . . . / then you'll never have to know / if the girl loves you or no." The advice about this particular consciousness-reducing method is often followed in poems populated by men who sit in bars together, sometimes talking about baseball, often not talking at all. In one of the best of these pieces, based on an Andy Capp cartoon strip, Blackburn elaborates on the character's misguided effort to explain his presence at a wake:

> He t'ought it were a weddin but
> it was a funeral . So?
> what is the question . or,
> who is a friend of the groom?
> (**"Night Cappy"**)

The drive toward relinquishing consciousness is likely the impetus as well for the group of dream poems written from 1963-67. Earlier, Blackburn had incorporated dream sequences into his work—see, for example, **"Park Poem"**—but now for the first time entire poems are based on dream transcriptions. **"At the Well,"** the most successful of them, expresses the dreamer's desire to rid himself of civilization's discontents. At one point he longs to join the group of mute tribesman who come to him "at the edge of the desert" and with them

> terrify the towns, the villages
> disappear among bazaars, sell our
> camels, pierce our ears

Such atavistic impulses, ultimately rejected at the end of **"At the Well,"** resurface in the first significant group of poems to retreat into the past, both that of Blackburn's childhood (**"Concomitants," "Hesper Adest"**) and a rather romanticized version of America's past (**"The Old Days," "Ritual XIII: The Shot"**). The child's vulnerability in the first group throws light on the man's *machismo* in the second. Experimentation with "found" poetry (**"Ya Lift a Cold One"**) and purely associative verse (**"The Pain"**) are other progeny of this period of decontrol.

Not all of these mid-1960s poems are successful. Some are needlessly cryptic; others, fatalistic or simply morose. But some pieces derive a strong evocative power from their lack of clear external referents:

> KEEP no names that give us not
> our death . . .
> O swift current, O buffalo .
> (**"Baggs"**)

The desire for death, described as "that softness we rut toward," is made more palatable here by its projection unto unfamiliar, mythic terrain. Then, too, if this non-sober lurch toward the past is responsible for such darkly comic poems as **"The Assassination of President McKinley"**—which might boast, among its other attributes, being the only poem in the language to contain the phrase "schluk-schluk"—we have reason to be grateful.

Whatever the cause—the dissolution of his second marriage, the imminence of return to scenes of a retrospectively happier past, or the shipboard romance with his third wife-to-be, Joan Miller—almost immediately after embarking for Europe on a Guggenheim Fellowship in September 1967, Blackburn experienced a psychic or spiritual renewal, made incarnate in a poetic form he soon came to designate "journals." The pieces written in this form are generally longer and more discursive than his earlier work; they tend to be divided into discrete, if related, sections, and to cover a relatively wide time-range—days, or even weeks. Chronicles of everyday life—and the public, reportorial sense of Blackburn's chosen term should be kept in mind—the journals came increasingly to use a wide variety of structures, including prose, to capture its textures. Final evidence of Blackburn's continual struggle, often with himself, to extend the boundaries of what could be considered poetry's fit subject and form, the journals offer bits and pieces of his own sights and insights as examples.

The journals and other poems of this period selectively detail the final four years of Blackburn's life. After his 1967-68 year in Europe, with a brief interim return to the U.S. South for a Woodrow Wilson Fellowship reading and teaching tour of black universities, Blackburn spent two years back in New York City teaching in City College's pre-baccalaureate SEEK program, at Mannes School for Music, and at the New School for Social Research. In these years he translated Pablo Picasso's long, surrealistic poem *Hunk of Skin* (City Lights, 1968) and Julio Cortázar's *Cronopios and Famas* (Pantheon, 1969). In addition to his continued local poetry activities—to cite just one, he helped set up the reading series at Dr. Generosity's coffeehouse—he began accepting increasingly frequent invitations to give out-of-town readings. The birth of a son, Carlos, to Joan Blackburn in 1969 changed the family's census status but not their way of life. Within weeks of Carlos's birth the three took an extended cross-country trip in the Gaucelm Faidit Uzerchemobile, the VW van Blackburn bought in Europe and named after the portliest of the troubadours.

What had promised to be a relatively quiet year of teaching at the State University of New York, Cortland, turned active in a new and terrible way within months of the family's move upstate. In December 1970 Blackburn was diagnosed as having cancer of the esophagus. A series of radiation treatments proved ineffective against (and perhaps accelerated) the disease, but at least, as the poetry shows, neither they nor the cancer seriously curtailed Blackburn's routines until the very end. Journals written little more than a month before his death in Cortland on September 13, 1971 record Blackburn's still-acute observations of the events at the National Poetry Festival in Allendale, Michigan.

In typically paradoxical fashion, however, there is a retrospective cast to poems written long before Blackburn learned of his illness. In the 1967 European journals, Blackburn the seasoned traveler alludes with some irony to the poems Blackburn the neophyte poet had written some ten years earlier in Europe. The fourth section of **"The Glorious Morning"** quotes lines from the 1957 **"La Vieille Belle"** describing the same rainy reception by the same city at the same time of year: "September, O Christ, Paris. tout à fait normal." Now, however, he notes in words he would not have used in the much more romantic earlier poem, that the Place Dauphine-en-L'Isle is "all fucked up by construction." Setting the original 1956 **"Plaza Real with Palmtrees"** against his 1968 **"Second Take"** of the Spanish square, the terms of the change are clarified: the first poem is like a Greek vase, figures poised, potential but frozen, while the second is more akin to a contemporary painterly canvas, full of movement and boldly displaying the artist's brushstrokes.

By the last year of his life Blackburn was using the journals form exclusively, but before then, and particularly during the year in Europe, he was still writing what he liked wryly to distinguish as "poems." A number of these poems, later slated by him for the posthumously published ***Halfway Down the Coast,*** show an intense preoccupation with death that predates by almost three years any conscious knowledge of illness, and that differs, in its bitterness and ferocity, from the resigned fatalism of the mid-1960s poems. In spite of what must be seen here as an exacerbation of Blackburn's usual association of death and love, he seems concomitantly to have arrived at the metaphorical middle ground of the collection's title poem. At least the possibilities of reciprocity and nurturing, expressed only jokingly in the poem's final punning line—"And love? What is that many-faceted mother?"—are taken up seriously in some of the later domestic journals. **"Journal April 19: The Southern Tier,"** for example, asserts the value of setting aside destructive memories of past relationships in order to make way for new ones.

When they do come in, in the last 30 or so poems, Blackburn's reactions to his illness are much like his reactions to other bad news: wry, ironic, bitter, for the most part resigned. He also treats the subject with characteristic delicacy—not lightness, but deftness and subtlety. Apropos of waiting for death, in **"Journal 26. VI. 71 The News,"** Blackburn writes that it is "NOTHING I CAN'T STAND"—only to admit in the next line "I don't believe that, either." His penchant for the self-ironic and mock-heroic underplays the genuine strength that lies precisely in his ability to resist being heroic. These final poems attest to Blackburn's rare gift for precision without reductionism, his talent for resisting all definitive solutions save musical ones in his poetry.

The same intellectual openness and flexibility may have been responsible too for Blackburn's avoidance throughout his life of any strict adherence to a single belief system. Neither purely rationalistic nor rigorous in his spiritual views, Blackburn used transcendent or religious symbology—often out of the Catholicism of his youth, but also from Greek mythology, Celtic goddess-cults, alchemical lore, and Buddhism—to suit particular poetic purposes. His last poems continue to play with the possibilities. At one moment he employs liturgical Christian language in describing himself as

> a doomed man planting tomatoes
> backyard of a house he lives in
> belongs to somebody else . kneeling
> on the earth
> his hands move earth
> **("Journal: June 1971. 110 in the Shade")**

and in the next he dismisses the entire system, asserting acidly in **"Untitled (We cannot agree)"** that "There are no resurrections planned."

If any controlling idea can be gleaned from this collection of Blackburn's work, it might well be the one he expressed mid-career in **"Pre-Lenten Gestures"**:

> Every organic thing, o philosophers, man
> plant or animal, containing as seed the flower
> its own destruction, its own rebirth

Such a belief would account for both the fatalism of the poetry and the potentiality for significance Blackburn saw, and made others see, in the most mundane things. At its best, the work offers a feeling like Blake's "Everything is holy."

Perhaps the only change in Blackburn's eschatological views at the end is the result of the perceived loneliness and "otherness" of death. Many of the last poems wishfully project familiar, anthropocentric afterlives. In **"Journal: 26. V. 71 The News"** Blackburn asks a friend, "Will I talk to you then, fill / yr / ears with words"—only to retreat bravely in the next line, "Let / each man's words be his own." In the next-to-final sequence, heaven is humorously imagined as a kind of ideal poetry festival, with Blackburn still in charge of smoothing the proceedings. These visions of death are entirely in keeping with the final representations of his life. The last journals find Blackburn reading poetry, attending poetry readings and festivals, directing nearly all his farewells toward poet friends.

Clearly Blackburn did not so much allow his life to enter his poetry as—to an unusual degree—allow poetry to enter his life. It was not only the astounding amount of time he spent involved with poetry and poets, but also the quality of attention he consistently gave everyday occurrences. Early on, in **"The Routine,"** he transformed a bleak winter interior into a spring garden by leaving an onion to sprout in his kitchen cabinet; to the end he retained his gift for seeing ordinary things anew. In the second-to-last journal he reappraises the formerly disparaged hollyhocks of his youth: "Those delicate blooms. The awkward stems. The hairy leaves." Although his ear was also unfailing, it would be difficult to refute his perception of his impending death as, most of all, an obscuring of sight. **"Journal Nov/Dec. 1970,"** the poem in which Blackburn obliquely announces his illness, opens: "The darkness wins here." But finally it doesn't, at least not for long. Not here, in these poems.

Notes

1. Although the vagaries of publishers necessarily played some role, the 523 poems comprising this volume (out of a total of approximately 1250, including juvenilia and scribbled and abandoned drafts) are essentially those Blackburn wished to have published. If he liked a poem he would keep submitting it until it got into print, sometimes many years after he wrote it. The present volume is arranged chronologically by date of composition rather than book-by-book because there was sufficient overlap within the collections to necessitate either repeating poems or deciding from which collection a poem or several poems should be eliminated. More important, a presentation based on dates of publication would perpetuate an already distorted view of Blackburn's creative development. He began writing in the middle 1940s, but not until some twenty years later did he have regular access to publication. The title index to this volume provides a listing of the earlier collections in which the poems were printed.

2. Almost from the start there developed a symbiosis between Blackburn's poetry and his translations from the Provençal. He brought to the troubadours the rhythms and idioms of American speech; they gave him much of his knowledge of lyrical tone and poetic form. *Proensa,* a small collection of Blackburn's Provençal translations, was published by Robert Creeley's Majorca-based Divers Press in 1953. A larger anthology was accepted by Macmillan Co. in 1958, but Blackburn was never able to complete it to his

satisfaction, and Macmillan finally abandoned the project in 1961. The excellent translations of troubadour verse on which Blackburn worked for nearly twenty years were not published as a group until after his death (*Proensa,* ed. George Economou, Univ. of California, 1978).

3. Some of Blackburn's Lorca translations were published in *Origin, New Directions,* and *Evergreen Review* during these years. *Blackburn / Lorca,* a collection of these and later translations, was published posthumously (Momo's Press, 1979).

4. Look, for example, at the rhetoric of Olson's 1951 "Projective Verse" essay: "[Poetry] is a matter of, at *all* points (even, I should say, of our management of daily reality as of the daily work) get on with it . . . the whole business, keep it moving as fast as you can, citizen. And if you also set up as a poet, USE USE USE the process at all points. . . ."

ROBERT BUCKEYE (ESSAY DATE FALL 1987)

SOURCE: Buckeye, Robert. "Rock, Scissors, Paper." *North Dakota Quarterly* (fall 1987): 153-61.

In the following essay, Buckeye situates Blackburn's poetry within the cultural context of America in the 1950s and 1960s.

Blackburn published his first poems in 1950 and his last in 1971, just months before his death from cancer. It is a crucial twenty years in American history. In the wake of World War II, we had become suddenly both the world's power and its savior, assuming responsibility for the homeless, redressing wrongs everywhere, keeping bullies at bay. Or so we thought. *Pax Americana* ruled. It extended into the Cold War, Korea, Vietnam. At home, however, the rhetoric, clearly, had become hollow: the struggle for civil rights began and would not go away; rock and roll threatened family values; the beats went on the road. Then rapidly in the sixties so much came down so fast that the simple recitation of name and place and event could not begin to measure the shocks to each of us, and to the system, though each of us reserved our own roll call to count off—Tet, Chicago, Woodstock, JFK, Malcolm, King, Bobby. And then as rapidly as we had been shaken, some of us transformed, by the age, it crested: Janis, Jimi, and Morrison dead hard upon Woodstock; Kent State and its massacre of innocents; Nixon elected president. The sixties were over. The button-down collar, gray-flannel suit organization man who had walked out the door, let his hair grow, dropped acid, and believed in free love was back in the board room, though, sure, he still listened to Aretha, did drugs (safely), had a little something on the side for cold nights, and may even have kept his pigtail. "Black is beautiful" got retooled to the demands of consumerism. Hippies were no longer hip. Only feminism has thus far risen from these ashes.

In the fifties for the first time the American poet found himself looked to for influence as the cultural arm of the world's first power. Suddenly, America was no longer culturally suspect, second-rate. And for the first time the poet was likely not only to be trained in the university but also to remain there as a teacher. The cultural network, as Hugh Kenner has pointed out, had become Berkeley, Ann Arbor, Cambridge, not New York. The sixties changed all that. The poet's place in the classroom and in society, his role as cultural ambassador, his use of received forms, and the traditional expectations of audience became problematic if not impossible. The New Criticism was seen to be an establishment tool, a means of social control. Some writers struggled to recast themselves, to find out "how to use the conditions of artistic production without being defined by them."[1] And then it too was over. Poets were back in classrooms asserting classroom truths.

We may read this time in the poetry of most of its contemporaries, Lowell, say, who began in the modernist tradition of Eliot and Stevens, moved to freer, looser forms, the more directly personal (the confessional poem), political involvement (everyone had his Vietnam poem), Williams and before him, Whitman, now the presiding influences, and then the closing down: the academy triumphant, Yuppies on the horizon, *Pax Reagan* just down the road. Bourgeois society had once more made art its own.

Blackburn does not fit this description; his is no normative career of the times. During this period, his poetry is remarkably of a piece; there is some refinement of skills, a greater mastery of his materials (some of the early poems are derivative Williams and Olson); and there is some shift of emphasis from the more specifically personal of this moment (what he sees out the window) to a broader personal of the later journals (Aspen that summer, teaching at Cortland this year) as Edith Jarolim points out.[2] He did write Vietnam poems, but these merely confirm views he already held ("as if / the earth were anything else but / what it is, a hell"[3]). And he was, at the last, a poet who taught in universities, but his was never a university sensibility (or training for that matter); nor was his poetry to be influenced by teaching. From the beginning, Blackburn knew the poetry he wanted to write, and he had gone to school with those poets he could learn from—the troubadours, Pound and Williams, those associated with Black

Mountain (Olson, Creeley, Corman), some others of his contemporaries (Kelly, Spicer, Whalen). In the fifties such writing was little known and, even if it were, was not likely to be in fashion; in the sixties it was, suddenly, unexpectedly, there; by the seventies it was understood to be the nostalgia of the graybeard who seemed to have had a more interesting past than present. In the last fifteen years, the *MLA Bibliography* lists only seven citations for Blackburn, one an interview, two the same bibliography listed twice (once as a dissertation, once as a book), and two articles by poets whose poetics were, like Blackburn's, formed outside classrooms, even though they were dependent on libraries. The place of Blackburn in our poetry is a measure of cultural capital in our time.

II

In his author's note to ***The Cities,*** Blackburn comments that the "secret of this book is / three: scissors, rock, and paper."[4] "Rock," he explains later in an interview, "say, is the concrete. The center of the poem is the object in Williams' sense, a person or thing. It has as much sense as words can bring to it. That's the rock. Paper is where the form is basically an idea, even if the idea is never mentioned. And scissors, what do they remind you of? That's love poems, man. It's the legs opening and closing."[5] If Blackburn's comment is in part ironic, our understanding of how he uses these terms is complicated further by our knowledge that Rock, Scissors, Paper is a game children play, in which chance dictates actions and the rules are circular—rock smashes scissors, scissors cut paper, paper covers rock. To what extent Blackburn's gloss of a poetics is further deepened by our knowledge of the children's game is only in part the point. That the rules of the game do work for his poetry or that his poetry is, like the game, dependent upon chance and the moment must have amused Blackburn.[6] That such correspondences exist, however, are necessary to his poetics.

For Blackburn it is crucial not simply to use everyday details but, more importantly, not to ignore them. His is a poetry of the moment, of the daily and ordinary, of "the thing seen each day," Oppen had noted, "whose meaning has become the meaning and color of our lives."[7] We read our lives minute by minute. Like the gulls Blackburn comes back to time and again in his poetry, the poet feeds upon what comes his way. To suggest, however, that his poetry is like *bricolage,* action painting, jazz riffs, as accurate and illuminating as these comparisons are, is, nevertheless, too formal a description of Blackburn's method. Rock, Scissors, Paper are there to be found, not invented, and what the poet finds he records, documents. The poet does not transform them into poetry, with the tools he has at hand—voice, meter, metaphor, ornament of one kind or another. But if he refuses to make the world over in his image, he finds nevertheless that there is poetry in the world, if we but recognize it. If one aim of traditional, particularly academic, poetry is to remove the terrain of the poem from the everyday, it is Blackburn's effort to situate it once more in the world. The problem for Blackburn, Eric Mottram notes, is "how to articulate the contingent daily experience and imply that it is both just that and also exemplary of the human condition."[8] His achievement is to record the poetry inherent in the everyday without the *apparent* intervention of the voice, skill, or ego of the poet.

At various points in a concert by the Art Ensemble of Chicago, the tenor sax may play a conch or the bassist blow a police whistle. The intention is not to make these sounds of the everyday world appear to be like instrumental music, but to insist upon their objectification—these sounds *are* music, as deployed by the musicians. Grocery lists, Williams never tired repeating, may be poetry. And for Blackburn it is not sufficient merely to write of the everyday, of the moment; it is crucial that he do so exactly, as to its objectness—he does not so much write poetry as recognize that what he writes about is poetry. The risks such poetry takes are enormous: Blackburn's poetry is likely to seem careless, slapdash, the work of a moment; inconsequential, trivial; confessional in the dreariest manner.

We should understand what the implications of this poetics are. In the first place, this writing is, like much of modernism, an effort to return art to a material world and to utilize fewer established and preconceived forms. To write of what you see and hear is further a measure of perception (a test of exactitude), and is, consequently, at base a moral question; to elaborate, decorate, or ornament is to lie. This poetics forces the poet to pay attention, to understand that one moment is like another, not intrinsically more or less significant; the poet defines himself in the act of observation. Thus it insists that everything is of use and resists the categorizing demands, the calls for hierarchies of one kind or another, the strictures of institution and audience. "Two American college chicks," Blackburn writes,

> at a table of the cafe nearest calle Fernando
> ". . . highly unnecessary—" no

words I can use, everything's necessary, even
snotty American college girls.[9]

Everything is necessary: it defines the field of the poem for Blackburn, accounts in part for his achievement, explains his failure.

III

> Say something about the method of composition itself; how everything that comes to mind has at all costs to be incorporated into the work one is doing at the time.[10]
>
> —Walter Benjamin

For Blackburn it is finally not sufficient just to call attention to the significance of the ordinary, the *quidditas* of moment, even the inherently poetic in all language ("The words are always there"[11]). The materials of the poem must be deployed in such a way that the poem is the shape of its materials. If we understand the sentence, say, rather than the paragraph to be the unit of measure (of significance) for Emerson, or the life's work to be the measure for Zukofsky, we know how individual parts relate to one another, what their significance is, and how we are to approach the whole. Here, for Blackburn, it is the poetic act itself which is the defining measure. The process of writing for Blackburn, M. L. Rosenthal points out, is "a disciplining *subject* of the poem as well as its range of action."[12] In the field of the poem, the poet acts, limited by what he sees, thinks, or remembers; and by the tools he has at hand. The time of the poem is not only the act of its writing but also becomes one of the subjects of the poem if not its subject ("And I do not know what the job is / or when it will be finished"[13]). The poet—and here the analogy is more nearly exact—is like the action painter, or Thoreau in his journals.

The question becomes what elements of the poem are necessary to this poetics, and for Blackburn two are crucial. Voice, "the noise that it makes," Edward Brathwaite notes, "is part of the meaning, and if you ignore the noise (or what you would *think* of noise, I shall say) then you lose part of the meaning."[14] The development of the poem, consequently, its pace and structure, its closure, is dependent upon the rhythms of everyday speech, and its pauses and hesitations, its emphases, resolutions. This says not only that there is poetry in everyday speech, that utterance is poetry, but also that poetry is not something removed from the world, separate, in a zone we characterize as culture, art, aesthetics, and the institutions which support such formulations—classrooms, libraries, museums. "That is why," Blackburn comments, "a poem will very often seem to have no obvious structure whatsoever—in terms of what is conventionally thought as form."[15]

FROM THE AUTHOR

PREAMBLE FROM BLACKBURN'S "STATEMENT"

My poetry may not be typically American, or at least in matter, not solely so: but I think it does make *use* of certain techniques which, even when not invented by American poets, find their particular exponents there in contemporary letters, from Pound & Doctor Williams, to younger writers like Paul Carroll or Duncan or Creeley.

Blackburn, Paul. Opening paragraph to "Statement" in *The Parallel Voyages.* Tucson, Ariz.: Sun-Gemini Press, 1987.

Blackburn orders and structures the materials of the poem in a second basic way, through the contrast, correspondences, counterpoint, or reinforcement that juxtaposition establishes; it permits him to generate resonances between disparate realities or to underline their differences. In **"Affinities I,"** for example, Blackburn notices the manufacturer's name on a brass plate cork for the sink in a pension he has rented is the same as that of a troubadour poet whose work he knows well and that his landlady remembers Garcia Lorca who "always wore broad-rimmed Cordoban hats."[16] When Blackburn looks out the window, he recognizes the clouds and mountains of a Lorca poem. Here, the conjunction of two poets important to him with the room he rents underlines for Blackburn the sources of the poetic for him, the ground upon which it is nourished, which he recognizes further when he sees in the landscape outside the landscape of a Lorca poem. (Juxtaposition is also often a comic device in his work; see the frequently referred to **"The Slogan,"** in which a logo of the Consolidated Edison Electric Company—Dig We Must—carries with it a second injunction when a beautiful woman walks by ConEd workers.)

If Blackburn's insistence on ordinary speech—man talking—in his poems is democratizing, his use of juxtaposition similarly equalizes the elements of the poem: one thing, no matter how different, *is* just next to another. In addition, however, for Blackburn to place, say comment about the legendary photograph of the naked Vietnamese girl blinded and burnt by napalm next to Mussolini's son-in-law's reaction to bombs exploding and that followed by the image of a dead horse nibbling dead grass in a poem addressed to the Senate Foreign Relations Committee as he does in **"Foreign Policy Commitments Or You Get Into the Catamaran First, Old Buddy,"** cannot escape comparison. By definition juxtaposition broadens or qualifies meaning. At the same time, such juxtaposition is also inevitably for Blackburn, as I have implied, a discrete series of elements (one thing next to another) and underlines consequently the limitations of any one of its elements; no one element is sufficient, intrinsically of greater importance. For Blackburn the poem (its structure) is an accumulation of points on a grid, which do not, necessarily, form an image (the rose in the steel dust), achieve completion (the story get told), or conflate meaning (gather ye rosebuds while ye may), but which do cohere at the last in a resolution of some kind, however momentary or temporary, as a jazz performance concludes. Closure for Blackburn is merely the field of the poem as it is recorded, a taking-stock at this moment, noting.

IV

> . . . died May 17, 1958, and February 11, 1959; rebirth May 9, 1963 (future deaths and rebirths should be noted in subsequent editions).[17]

Blackburn is a poet of love and death, of longing and loneliness, loss, of completion, temporary as it sometimes, often, may be, of failure. Love is his stay against "the materialistic pig of the technological world."[18] This, and only this, counts. What the politician's sweetheart sits on is more meaningful than anything the politician can say or the poet for that matter, an answer, if anything is.[19] However good Blackburn is as a political poet (and he is good; see, for example, the aforementioned **"Foreign Policy Commitments Or You Get Into the Catamaran First, Old Buddy"**), his politics only emphasize the importance and necessity of love for him, "that choice / not so much taken / as come to."[20] You drown, he writes in "Venus," if you do not follow love, though you may drown in doing so. (Scissors, he says. It is dangerous.)

In **"The Two Kisses,"** Blackburn describes how the forehead of his dying mother to his lips is like the forehead of his dying grandfather kissed many years before. The understanding that we carry death inside us—that the cancer Blackburn carried the last years of his life is merely a metaphor for the human condition—forces us to measure life and love more profoundly if not exactly, and Blackburn's best poems of death, such as **"The Selection of Heaven," "The Two Kisses,"** some of his last journal entries, the Reardon poems, are about love as well. The extent to which love and death give each other meaning in his work is a register of his unflinching honesty in the face of things, a vision which acknowledges inherent imperfection, and loss. In a deeply philosophical sense for Blackburn, every moment counts. It is the world we live in. (We see here how his poetics may be extrapolated from his subject, that an art predicated upon love and death, its transience, its moments of transcendence, would find its expression necessarily in the moment and the everyday.) To see our experience of the daily contingent as our glory and burden, as transcendence and limitation, as dross, as poetry, is the singular achievement of Blackburn's art.

V

ANY WINDOW OR YOU GIVE IT A FRAME[21]

Blackburn writes out-the-window poems. We see in these that image central to his poetry, that of the man at the typewriter, late at night or early in the morning, remembering what has happened during the day, what he has thought or read, what he sees. What we read, however, is not just transcription (the record of the daily life) but also the intelligence of the artist at the moment of action, the field through which he moves when he sits down at his typewriter. Here in this crucial image of his writing, however, we also find the underlying irony upon which the tension of his work rests: in a poetics based on contact, the poet cannot make contact. There is always a window as it were between him and what he writes about: he can see out of it, but not break through. Whether he is on the subway or street, at the typewriter or in bed after making love (with the woman sleeping beside him), the poet looks on from the outside, often even standing outside himself. Here, Blackburn is much like the flaneur Walter Benjamin characterized Baudelaire to be: restless, uncomfortable, alienated. John Berger argues that home is not simply a place to live but also an ontological shelter, a metaphysical center, and that, in the twentieth century, romantic love "unite[es] or hop[es] to unite two displaced persons."[22] For Blackburn there is no home to go to other than love, and, except for the journals of his last years, he is preeminently a poet of homelessness, of late nights in subways or bars, sitting at his typewriter in his apartment, looking on.

VI

"'AND ROBERT FROST? NO RELATION,' HE SMILED."[23]

We live in a time when the writing of poems is a recreational activity, therapy, not much more than a cottage industry (even if more people probably write poems than ever before). Which is not to say that the poetry nor its practitioners are not serious. Just that the place of poetry in our society is diminished. Gone is the last generation of poets to believe that poetry could make a difference, that it was a measure of ourselves as a people, that it was "an active battle to stay alive—as you are able, in whatever place one be in, or care to be in, or succeed in being in."[24] Today, the poems Blackburn wrote, what they risk, and the sacrifices he made to make the life accountable and critical to the poetry are likely to seem eccentric if not incomprehensible behavior. In a letter written in 1955, Blackburn notes that "there are probably not ten people in the world interested in my work."[25] For different reasons there would not be many more today. Yet Blackburn knew absolutely that what he did is what he had chosen to do, and that it was important. In his carefully measured assessment of his life and poetry, we may read, by implication, the measure of our lives.

Notes

1. T. J. Clark, *The Absolute Bourgeois; Artists and Politics in France, 1848-1851* (Princeton: Princeton University Press, 1982) 179. Although Clark refers to nineteenth-century France, his comment, applies, I believe, to sixties America.
2. Paul Blackburn, *The Collected Poems of Paul Blackburn* [Hereafter referred to as *CP*] (New York: Persea Books, 1985). Edited, with an introduction, by Edith Jarolim.
3. Blackburn, *CP,* 47.
4. Blackburn, *The Cities* (New York: Grove Press, 1967) [12].
5. Blackburn, Interview in *Contemporary Literature,* XIII:2 (Spring 1972) 143.
6. For Blackburn the world we live in destroys desire and love; the driving force of love and desire cuts through any idea (Olson, who was an important influence for Blackburn, said we go furthest with our bodies); poetry is necessary for us to live in the world.
7. George Oppen, "The Mind's Own Place," *Kulchur,* III:10 (Summer 1963) 2.
8. Eric Mottram, "The Ear and Muscle under Music," *Six-pack,* 7/8 (Spring-Summer 1974) 188.
9. Blackburn, *CP,* 498.
10. "N [Theoretics of Knowledge; Theory of Progress]," *The Philosophical Forum,* XV:1-2 (Fall-Winter 1983-84) 1.
11. Blackburn, *CP,* 91.
12. M. L. Rosenthal, "Poets & Critics & Poets-Critics," *Poetry,* CXIV:2 (May 1969) 130.
13. Blackburn, *CP,* 96.
14. Edward Kamau Brathwaite, *History of the Voice* (London: New Beacon Books, 1984) 17.
15. Blackburn, Interview in *The Sullen Art* (New York: Corinth, 1963) edited by David Ossman, 24.
16. Blackburn, *CP,* 91.
17. Blackburn, in *A Controversy of Poets* (Garden City, New York: Anchor Books, 1965), edited by Paris Leary and Robert Kelly, 524. In his biographical note, Blackburn refers, presumably, to the end of love with his first wife, Winifred, and to his marriage to his second wife, Sara, in 1963.
18. Blackburn, "Twenty Poems," *Sulfur* 4 (1982) 65.
19. "And Art? / A Debussy tone poem, she often says, / is that an answer to anything?" Blackburn, *CP,* 233.
20. Blackburn. *CP,* 486.
21. Blackburn. *CP,* 302.
22. John Berger, *And Our Faces, My Heart, Brief as Photos* (New York: Pantheon Books, 1984) 66.
23. Blackburn, interview in *The Burlington Free Press,* ca. 1957. Article by Ann Della Chiesa. The poet Frances Frost was Blackburn's mother.
24. William Carlos Williams, "A Tentative Statement," *The Little Review,* XII:2 (May 1929) 98.
25. Blackburn, letter, 1955, September 15 [Banalbafur] to Larry Bronfman. Abernethy Collection of American Literature, Middlebury College.

MARJORIE PERLOFF (ESSAY DATE 1990)

SOURCE: Perloff, Marjorie. "On the Other Side of the Field: *The Collected Poems of Paul Blackburn.*" In *Poetic License: Essays on Modernist and Postmodernist Lyric,* pp. 251-65. Evanston, Ill.: Northwestern University Press, 1990.

In the following essay, Perloff claims that Blackburn's sexually aggressive verse seems dated in the post-feminist, post-Derridean world of the late twentieth century.

Like Frank O'Hara, with whom he must inevitably be compared, Paul Blackburn died young (he was forty-four in 1971 when he succumbed to cancer) and left behind literally hundreds of unpublished poems. Like O'Hara, Blackburn had in his lifetime published primarily chapbooks with minuscule print runs and was known, if at all, through magazine publication in such avant-garde journals as *Origin, Black Mountain Review, Trobar,*

Evergreen Review, Yugen, Big Table, and *Caterpillar.* Like O'Hara, who published in many of the same journals, he was a prominent figure on the sixties New York poetry scene, his own particular nexus being less the art-ballet-new music world of O'Hara, John Ashbery, Kenneth Koch, and their friends, than the Charles Olson-inspired "open form" poetics as practiced by poets like Robert Creeley, Cid Corman, Denise Levertov, Ed Dorn, Jonathan Williams, Gilbert Sorrentino, Robert Kelly, Jerome Rothenberg, George Economou, Rochelle Owens, David Antin, Armand Schwerner, Clayton Eshleman, and Diane Wakoski.

O'Hara's blockbuster *Collected Poems,* edited by Donald Allen and with a concise and brilliant preface by Ashbery (still, for my money, the best single essay on O'Hara's work), appeared in 1971 and immediately changed the poetic landscape. Not that every poetic scrap preserved in its meticulously edited pages was worthwhile, but that O'Hara's jaunty and deliciously absurd "action poems" (in which the words became the actors) implicitly challenged the increasingly tedious confessionalism that dominated the early sixties, thus paving the way for a poetry in which, to paraphrase Lyn Hejinian, "vocabularies" would generate ideas, rather than ideas vocabularies.

The case of Paul Blackburn is very different. A faithful practitioner of Olsonian projective verse, of open form, of what M. L. Rosenthal calls, in his foreword to Blackburn's ***Collected Poems,***[1] the "natural," his racy vernacular seems oddly out of step with the cool and mannered artifice of the late eighties. In 1969 Stephen Berg and Robert Mezey could declare, in the foreword to their popular anthology, *Naked Poetry,* "We began with the firm conviction that the strongest and most alive poetry in America had abandoned or at least broken the grip of traditional meters and had set out, once again, into 'the wilderness of unopened life.'"[2] Two decades later, young New Formalist poets like Brad Leithauser have reversed this doctrine in attacking precisely "the confinement of free verse" and declaring that "iambic pentameter—in the hands of a Richard Wilbur, anyway—thrives today in a form Chaucer would feel at home with."[3] As for "the wilderness of unopened life," this cornerstone of "naked poetry" is rejected not only by New Formalists like Leithauser but also by the poetic Left (Charles Bernstein, say, or Ron Silliman), which stands in opposition to what Joan Retallack has called, in an essay for *Parnassus,* the "theory of poetry" as "squeegee-cleaned window on transcendent Truth," as "self-effacing medium to a world fully furnished and ready for inspection."[4] Free verse, open form, projectivism, oral poetics—these are as inimical to the poetic Left as they are to the Right, given the poststructuralist emphasis, all but inescapable these days, on writing as not just a reproduction of speech but as something radically other.

In this context the "natural" and "passionate" speech-based poetry of Paul Blackburn, now enshrined in Edith Jarolim's scholarly and monumental ***Collected Poems,*** appears as something of an anomaly. Blackburn is a poet I personally feel I *should* admire. He carried on the Pound-Williams tradition, which is to my mind the central tradition of postmodernism, and was the chief disseminator of Black Mountain poetics from Olson and Creeley to the younger New York poets I cited above. Indeed, many of his closest writer-friends—for example, Gilbert Sorrentino and David Antin—have gone on to transform "open-field" poetics into complicated performance strategies, intermedia works, and new narrative genres. Blackburn's poems appeared in the most interesting little magazines and in the key anthologies, like Donald Allen's *New American Poetry* (1960). Perhaps most important, Blackburn was a superb translator, especially of Provençal poetry, as his posthumous anthology ***Proensa,*** recently edited by George Economou, testifies.[5]

Given all these admirable associations, why does the ***Collected Poems*** inspire the uneasy feeling that the whole is less than its parts? Perhaps because, unlike O'Hara, Blackburn was primarily a consolidator rather than an innovator—everyone's favorite poet and best friend precisely because he was not, after all, a very powerful rival. It is always interesting, in retrospect, to watch a so-called school or movement unravel. Imagism, Vorticism, Black Mountain, Beat poetry, the New York school, Deep Image—in hindsight, all these movements were meaningful entities only insofar as individuals have transcended them. Was H. D. primarily an "Imagiste," as Pound called her? Was John Cage, who organized the first happenings at Black Mountain College, "a Black Mountain artist"? Is John Ashbery a "New York poet"? And, conversely, does inclusion in Ron Padgett and David Shapiro's well-known *Anthology of New York Poets* (Random House, 1970) give importance to the work of, say, Joseph Ceravolo or Dick Gallup? The current controversy about the value of "language poetry," for that matter, will change its character once we stop talking about *the* language poets and look at the actual work of specific writers.

What kind of "New American Poet," then, was Paul Blackburn? Here is an early previously uncollected poem called **"A Song"**:

Of sea and the taking of breath
and to match the impress of it, the
giving of breath :
of mercy, the true quality of,
and the rhythm of certain
movements I
sing, lady

How heavy and soft
your flesh at morning
when we wake together
O lady, how heavy and soft
your eyes when I reach for you
the

line of your back
half circumscribes our summer
centers love, that
tall sweet mast to your vessel
and we enact
how underneath the pleasure piers the seas
move.

(p. 22)[6]

From the first, it seems, Blackburn was drawn to Provençal love lyric, especially as that lyric had been "made new" by Pound. The short emphatic free-verse line, the inversion of the opening stanza played off against the no-nonsense monosyllables, the line cuts in quirky places, as in "I / sing, lady"—these are Poundian signatures. But the visual layout of the poem is less Pound's than Olson's: the stanza on the right side of the page balancing the one on the left, the lines ending on function words like "the," "of," and "that" and containing a relatively high degree of abstraction, as in the playful twist on Portia's words, "of mercy, the true quality of."

At the same time, this **"Song"** is much more openly erotic, more intimate than Pound's so-called love poems (exercises really) in *Personae,* and much less conceptually dense than Olson's. The rhythm of the sea paralleling the rhythm of love: the analogy is conventional enough, but Blackburn's rendition goes beyond the convention. Thus it is oddly the "line of your back," rather than, say, the lady's eyes or breasts, that leads to arousal, calling up the poet's own "tall sweet mast to your vessel." The enactment of love "underneath the pleasure piers" is conveyed visually through the repeated *ea* diphthong—"breath" (twice), "heavy" (twice), "reach," "underneath," "pleasure," "seas"—while the final line break of "seas" / "move" mimes the push/pull of the love act itself.

Here, then, is the Blackburn signature in embryo: the first person, present-tense mode, the intimate yet nonconfessional "I" (we don't know this speaker and his mistress in the way that we know, say, the couple of Lowell's "Man and Wife"), the direct address to a more or less archetypal feminine "you," the line as breath unit, likely to break off at odd intervals and arranged in pseudostanzas that reach no point of closure, the delicate sound echoes. **"A Song"** is on all counts a "lovely" poem, a charming expression of erotic desire.

Yet it is only fair to say that the poem is also a little thin, that its words do not markedly resonate. Compare Blackburn's poem with, say, William Carlos Williams's "Love Song" ("I lie here thinking of you . . .")[7] and the difference is clear. In reading Williams, we are immediately put to work: Why, to begin with, is "love" regarded as a "Yellow, yellow, yellow" "stain" "upon the world"? Or again, if this "honey-thick stain" is that of "love," why is it described as "spoiling the colors / of the whole world"? Different readers will have different responses. Whereas in Blackburn's **"Song,"** such phrases as "the rhythm of certain movements" or "How heavy and soft / your flesh at morning / when we wake together" make no particular demands on us. Nice, we say, and go on to the next page.

It is not fair, of course, to judge Blackburn by such a relatively slight early poem. To take a more challenging example, here is a later **"Love Song,"** this one from what Edith Jarolim calls Blackburn's best period (1958-63), and chosen by the poet for inclusion in ***The Cities*** (1967) as well as by Michel Deguy and Jacques Roubaud for their Blackburn selection in *Vingt poètes américains* (Paris: Gallimard, 1980):

Upon returning home tonite
and it is a home
now
surely,
being the animal I am
when I had undressed, I
wrapped my hand around my
balls, and their now-limp appendage.
And afterward
smelled my hand.

It was you.
As your perfume is still on my undershirt
so this perfume also.

(p. 127)

This vein of Blackburn's poetry has been highly praised for its naturalness, its candor, its ability to capture a particular aspect of sexual (or rather postsexual) pleasure, its wry self-mockery. In such lyric, as Gilbert Sorrentino has remarked of Blackburn's ***Journals,*** "The 'I' . . . is as much artifice as the poem it speaks—and yet it can locate itself with such immediacy that it looks like the vehicle for common speech."[8] Certainly, the sound structure is highly wrought, the delay of the single-word lines, "now" and "surely," building up to the rhyming contentment of "animal I am," followed by the successive, halting "I"s that are, so to speak, "now-limp" like the poet's "appendage," and the delicate internal rhyme and consonance of "*And a*fterwor*d* / smelle*d* my *hand*."

Still, I would argue that this poem is more successful when read than reread, especially since its coda, "It was you. / As your perfume is still on my undershirt / so this perfume also," spells out what the preceding stanza has already told us. Indeed, poems like **"Love Song"** seem especially designed to be heard at poetry readings. Black Mountain was, of course, a movement heavily invested in an oral poetics: the poet was to be, so Olson taught, a "man on his feet talking" ("man" being by no means accidental, given the inherently chauvinist character of Olsonian poetics); the line was to image the "breath," so as to insure the speed and motion of the "energy discharge" and to allow "composition by field" to take place. Picture Blackburn, by all accounts (and judging from recordings) an extraordinary reader, getting up in front of a receptive Village audience and reciting **"Love Song,"** beating out the rhythm of the first six lines slowly so as to build up to the comic punch. Surely, given the context of the poetry reading, in which verbal subtlety and semantic complexity are inevitably less important than immediate impact, a poem like **"Love Song"** would have struck a responsive chord. More heat, we might say, than light.

But, it will be objected, wasn't Frank O'Hara's an equally casual, lighthearted, and purposely free-form poetry? And isn't it unfair to judge Blackburn by what seem to be New Critical standards of complexity and ambiguity, of double entendre, tropical discourse, and so on? Such questions raise the larger issue of what constitutes poetic language and how that language relates to the poet's culture. Consider, for example, the series of poems written in the "subgenre" that, according to Edith Jarolim, Blackburn "inaugurated" and "with which he is most often associated: the subway poem" (p. xxvii). One of the earliest of these is **"The Yawn"** (1957-58):

The black-haired girl
with the big
brown
eyes
on the Queens train coming
in to work, so
opens her mouth so beautifully
wide
in a ya-aawn, that
two stops after she has left the train
I have only to think of her and I
o-oh-aaww-him
wow!
(p. 104)

Immediacy, precision, vernacular accuracy, directness—it is these qualities that Blackburn's fellow poets evidently admired here. And sexual innuendo as well, the "mouth" opening "so beautifully / wide" to "ya-aawn" referring, of course, to that other "mouth" the thought of whose opening is enough to make the poet-observer "come" along with the Queens train. Then too, there's the witty lineation of lines 1-4, the "black-haired girl / with the big" producing the expectation that the word "breasts" will follow, only to be coyly deflated by the reference to "brown / eyes."

Twenty years and the feminist revolution later, Blackburn's "o-oh-aaww-him / wow!" seems less charming than irritatingly macho: here, and too frequently in Blackburn's poetry, woman (referred to as "girl") equals desirable body, period. It is not that the poet's response to this or that attractive woman, seen on a subway train, cannot be a fit occasion for poetry but that Blackburn's language is mimetically reductive, providing no sense of the complex and confusing contexts within which desire actually occurs.

Consider, for example, a related and, in Jarolim's words, "deceptively simple" "subway poem" called **"Clickety-Clack,"** which begins as follows:

I took
a coney island of the mind
to the coney
island of the flesh
the brighton local
riding
past church avenue, beverly, cortelyou, past
avenues h & j
king's highway, neck road, sheepshead bay,
brighton, all the way to stillwell
avenue
that hotbed of assignation
clickety-clack

I had started reading when I got on
and somewhere down past newkirk reached
number 29 and read aloud

The crowd
in the train
looked startled at first but settled down. . . .
(p. 123)

Jarolim comments, "We take a joy ride of the senses as we follow the poet through Brooklyn, listening to him read poetry aloud and watching him unsuccessfully attempt to engage the affections of a not-so-amused female passenger. Blackburn skillfully duplicates the lurching rhythms of the train, and anyone familiar with what is now New York City's 'D' line might observe that he eliminates those stations that don't fit into his rhythmic scheme" (pp. xxvii-iii). Certainly, the catalog of subway stops, with its internal rhymes ("avenue" / "cortelyou" [for Cortelue]; "h & j" / "king's highway" / "sheepshead bay" / "all the way") and girl's names ("beverly"), is a delightful tour de force, preparing us for the "stillwell" (the last stop) of the mystery girl to come.

Still, the scene of sexual arousal is less than amusing:

. . . when I reached the line : "the cock
of flesh at last cries out and has his glory
moment God"
some girl sitting opposite me with golden hair
fresh from the bottle began to stare dis-
approvingly and wiggle as tho she had ants
somewhere where it counted.

Which is enough to make the subway troubadour forget all about his reading; rather, he mentally undresses the girl, "imagining / what she had inside those toreador pants besides / her bathing suit," "pants" rhyming with the "ants" of the previous passage. Getting off at the same stop ("well / we both got off at stillwell"), he can hardly wait to make a move on her. But desire outstrips bravery: "smitten, I / hadn't noticed her 2 brothers were behind me / clickety-clack." Under the circumstances he can only retreat: "Horseman," he tells himself, alluding to Yeats with mock-heroic self-deflation, "pass by."

In anticipating this final twist, Blackburn sketches in the subway-stop landscape, with its "tattoo artists," its "franks" that are phallically "12 inches long," its "wax museum" (an obvious death image) and "soft-drink stand with its white inside"—insides being, of course, what regularly interest this observer. Still, for all its documentary realism, its edgy and nervous vernacular, **"Clickety-Clack"** is as flatly opaque as its title. It's fun, the poet seems to be saying, to pass the time on the dreary Brooklyn train reciting one's poetry and attracting the attention of "some girl . . . with golden hair / fresh from the bottle." Fun to watch "her high backside sway and swish down that / street," it being an object so much more desirable than the other objects in "the wax museum" and at the "soft-drink / stand." But for the contemporary reader, this image of a young girl as a piece of meat is surely problematic.

It is interesting to read Blackburn's "subway poems" against O'Hara's comparable "lunch poems," in which the poet-speaker (presented, like Blackburn's, in the first-person present tense) similarly makes his way around New York by subway or taxi or on foot, all the while thinking about the person (or persons) he loves. The obvious difference between Blackburn's aggressive heterosexuality and O'Hara's equally aggressive homosexuality aside, we find in these poems of the late fifties/early sixties a similar trajectory that makes their divergences all the more important.

Take "Poem (Khrushchev is coming on the right day!)," whose occasion is evidently a newspaper headline announcing the impending arrival in New York of the Soviet leader:

Khrushchev is coming on the right day!
the cool graced light
is pushed off the enormous glass piers by hard
wind
and everything is tossing, hurrying on up
this country
has everything but *politesse,* a Puerto Rican cab
driver says
and five different girls I see
look like Piedie Gimbel
with her blonde hair tossing too,
as she looked when I pushed
her little daughter on the swing on the lawn it
was also windy.[9]

At first the items rapidly presented for our contemplation here seem to be merely disparate. The poet, on his way to work in a cab in the early morning, finds it delightful that Khrushchev is about to arrive at Penn Station, but why? According to the absurd logic of O'Hara's poem, because it is a bright and windy day—"everything is tossing, hurrying on up"—and wind is the poet's own emblem for the intensity, speed, and exhilaration he wants from life. Here is the poem's climax:

New York seems blinding and my tie is blowing up the street
I wish it would blow off
though it is cold and
somewhat warms my neck
as the train bears Khrushchev on to
Pennsylvania Station
and the light seems to be eternal
and joy seems to be inexorable
I am foolish enough always to find
it in wind.

But what does Khrushchev have to do with the poet's mood? Nothing at all, except that, it being such a gorgeous September day, this must surely be the "right" day for anyone, even for such an unlikely person as Khrushchev, to come. The irony, of course, is that dour, single-minded Khrushchev, who "was probably being carped at / in Washington," couldn't care less what the weather is like since he obviously has other things on his mind. Indeed, there is no right day for Khrushchev to arrive—no *"politesse"*—which is precisely O'Hara's point, the poem comically dismissing anything that stands in the way of sheer momentary buoyancy: "where does the evil of the year go / when September takes New York / and turns it into ozone stalagmites / deposits of light."

Like Blackburn's **"Clickety-Clack,"** O'Hara's is a process poem, charting the mental antics of the poet as he moves around the city. But whereas Blackburn's organizing principle is that of straightforward narrative (i.e., I did this and then this happened and then that), O'Hara's is a genuine energy construct in that words not only point to the words that follow them in a given phrase or clause but also, so to speak, signal to a whole network of others that are metonymically related. Thus "coming" (in "Khrushchev is coming on the right day") anticipates "graced," "pushed," "tossing," "blinding," and "blowing," whereas "cool graced light" modulates into "Grace Hartigan's painting *Sweden,*" and then into "ozone stalagmites," "New York seems blinding," and "the light seems to be eternal." Further, these wind and light images dissolve the distinction between past and present even as the actual verb forms sustain it.

Blackburn's journey "to the coney / island of the flesh" on "the brighton local" catalogs place names that, as I noted above, provide documentary accuracy as well as a source for punning: for example, "cortelyou" ("courting you") or "neck road." But these puns constitute more or less local jokes, whereas O'Hara's seemingly random roll call of names is structured around the polarity that the poet takes to be the source of Manhattan's "cool graced light." Thus we are presented with North (Sweden) and South (the "Puerto Rican cab driver" who says that "this country / has everything but *politesse*"), East (Khrushchev, Ionesco) and West (Hans, Beckett), young (Piedie Gimbel's little daughter) and old (Vincent's mother), gentile (Purgatorio Merchado) and Jew (Gerhard Schwartz), poetry (François Villon) and painting (Grace Hartigan's painting *Sweden*), drama (Ionesco, Beckett) and film, in the shape of the "movie" to which "we went . . . and came out." But perhaps the most amusing polarity is that between the Soviet Russian Khrushchev and the one-time czarist Russian "blueberry blintzes" eaten with Vincent (the dancer Vincent Warren, who was O'Hara's lover at the time) the night before. The train bearing Khrushchev on his one-way journey to Pennsylvania Station is finally less "inexorable" than the "joy" of recurrence: "I go home to bed," "I get back up," "last night . . . Vincent said," "the early morning as I go to work." Indeed, Khrushchev's arrival never actually takes place: suspension, the arc of expectancy, the potential for action—these are the emotive notes that keep O'Hara's poem open, that make it impossible for closure to occur.

Black Mountain poetics, we recall, had as its cornerstone Olson's prescription in the "Projective Verse" essay to "USE, USE, USE the process at all points, in any given poem always, always one perception must must must MOVE, INSTANTER, ON ANOTHER!" What I hope the comparison between **"Clickety-Clack"** and "Khrushchev is coming on the right day!" makes clear is that, movement and speed aside, it is in the arena of "using everything," as Gertrude Stein put it, that Blackburn is deficient. In the Khrushchev poem, "USE, USE, USE the process" (an echo of Pound's Imagist credo, "Use no word that does not contribute to the presentation") means that every detail, no matter how small, turns out to be somehow relevant. But in the case of **"Clickety-Clack,"** we can pull many threads out of the web without making a hole in the rug. Does it matter that the girl has on a bathing suit rather than, say, a bra and panties, "inside those toreador pants"? That "somewhere down past newkirk" the poet "reached / number 29" of his sequence? That "sorry to say / 5 lines later the poem finished," he "started to laugh like hell?" Language is used here to provide narrative continuity, to "keep it moving," but *textually* the poem goes increasingly limp.

Which is to say, I suppose, that we are now less excited than we were in the sixties about the liberating potential of a speech-based poetics. "Of the poets working in these past three decades," declared Robert Kelly in his introduction to ***The Journals,*** "I would say Blackburn is the paradigm of the processual—the one who most allowed his life and work to intertwine, who sought and found in the happenstance of experience a mysterious beauty called music when we hear it, that is, the Form made clear."[10] *Form,* it is implied here, is something that will take care of itself, provided the poet is true to his or her experience. "What I most value in ***The Journals,***" writes Kelly, "is the further transcendence of the closed poem (that museum piece, that haunting but snake-like urn) his work had long been moving from. And what gave his achievement of the open poem its peculiar power is, in some awful and simple way, just how well he could sing."

Surely this is the classic refrain of the late sixties and early seventies, the late Romantic faith in an "idiolect in the written language" that would quite simply reproduce the poet's "idiolect in the spoken language." Was not form, after all, never more than the extension of content? And wasn't the great American poet Walt Whitman the father of open-field poetics?

Ironically, even as this doctrine was being disseminated in poetry workshops around the country, Derrida's famous seminar "Structure, Sign, and Language," held at Johns Hopkins in 1967, was published in Richard Macksey and Eugenio Donato's *The Structuralist Controversy* (1972). For "composition by field," with its faith in an aesthetic of presence, of immanence, of form as the natural extension of content, and "writing" as the direct making present of speech, Derrida substituted the notion of the decentered structure, the absence of the transcendental signified, the treatment of text as a system of differences, and the recognition that speech does not necessarily have priority over writing.

One needn't be a Derridean to see that deconstruction has forced us to question the very notion of "projective verse." For if "content" can never be abstracted from the linguistic base itself, if we take the materiality of the signifier seriously, then phonemics, morphology, and especially syntax are not just ancillary "devices" that flesh out the poet's meter-making argument, and "song" is not just something that flows "naturally," given the right poetic instincts.

Indeed, Blackburn's ***Journals,*** distinctive for their candor, their clean simplicity, their willingness to bring so much of the poet's actual life onto the page, may now strike us as barely distinguishable from reportage, whereas it is, paradoxically, his more "formal" poems that seem least dated. **"Sirventes"** of 1957-59 is a case in point. A *sirventes* is an Old Provençal genre, strophic in form, whose "main themes are personal abuse or (occasionally) praise. . . . The tone is mostly satiric, and gross vituperation is common."[11] Blackburn's *sirventes* is "made . . . against the city of Toulouse," where he spent his 1955 Fulbright lectureship year:

> Whole damn year teaching
> trifles to these trout with trousers
> tramping thru the damp
> with gout up to my gut
> taking all the guff, sweet
>   jesus crypt,
>   god of the he
> brews, she blows, it bawls, & Boses
> (by doze is stuffed)
> by the balls of the livid saviour, lead be
> back hindu eegypt-la-aad
> before I'b canned for indisciblidnary reasons.
>
> (p. 88)

Highly conventionalized as this is, the poem curiously has a more freewheeling, playful, and open-ended air than do Blackburn's subway poems or his "journals." The strophic unit becomes a kind of generative device, sound determining what comes next, as when we move from "trifles" to "trout," "trousers," and "tramping," and then, via rhyme, from "tramping" to "damp" and from "trout" to "gout." The elaborately punning lines splutter along, their sound play ("Boses," the cold victim's pronunciation for "Moses," as is "by doze" for "my nose"; "lead be / back hindu eegypt-la-aad" a wonderfully droll twist on the gospel song) culminating in the witty complexities of "indisciblidnary" which anagrammatically contains (or rather, cannot contain) the poet's *libido,* his *indiscretions,* his boredom with the *bible,* and so on. **"Sirventes"** may have no sensitive insight to convey, no larger meaning to divulge; it is simply good fun:

>   in the street I piss
>   on French politesse
> that has wracked all passion from the sound of
>   speech.
> A leech that sucks the blood is less a lesion.
>   Speech!
> this imposed imposing imported courtliness, that
> the more you hear it the more it's meaningless
>   & without feeling.
>
> (p. 89)

Like O'Hara, Blackburn claims to have little use for politesse, for bourgeois decorum, the joke here, as in the Khrushchev poem, being that the politesse rejected by the speaking voice everywhere informs the poem's language, O'Hara's "cool graced light" finding its counterpart in Blackburn's formal rhythms, for example, "A leech that sucks the blood is less a lesion. Speech!" whose alliterating and rhyming iambic hexameter nicely offsets the more imitative speech rhythms of "in the street I piss / on French politesse."

And it is the offset, of course, that matters. For the danger of projectivism was what Charles Bernstein has wittily called "the *ph*allacy of the heroic stance, grounded as it is in the anthropomorphic allegory of language as the stride of a man, with all the attendant idealization of 'speech syntax' and a voice of authority."[12] I myself would posit that Blackburn's best poems are those that sabotage, whether consciously or not, the "heroic stance" of the poet-as-man on his feet talking by heightening the system of contiguities in which the "I" operates. **"Pre-Lenten Gestures"** (1963-65) is such a poem.

The setting is a bakery where "Aunt Ella" officiates while the poet, sometimes bemused, sometimes attentive, sometimes bored, observes the shoppers, listens to the radio, thinks of friends, and tries as hard as he can not to think about a love that has ended. The poem begins:

> Thank God one tone or
> one set of decibels is
> not all there is.   The
> *Dies Irae,* the radio behind me, is
> due to the mad programmer we never know, fol-
>   lowed
> by a selection of military band music.
>   How kind.   I
> can't help thinking of
>   Ed Dorn, his line: *Why*
> *can't it be like this all the time?*
>   "as my friend said"
> the band, the binding, the
> bound from one state to the next, and
>   sometimes
>   one is not even asked.
> What may be revealed, given.
>   What?
>   that it be revealed.
>
> (p. 239)

"One set of decibels is / not all there is." In **"Pre-Lenten Gestures"** one perception immediately leads to a further perception. The radio begins by playing *Dies Irae,* thanks to "the mad programmer we never know," but quickly modulates into military band music. A line from an Ed Dorn poem cuts to another by Robert Creeley, "as my friend said." The "band" brings to mind "the binding" (of a book), and then in a mock conjugation of the verb, "the bound from one state to the next," with its memories of journeys the poet has made but also the states of mind he has passed through. "Sometimes," he comments, "one is not even asked." But we don't yet know what it is that is asked or "What may be revealed, given."

Whatever the subject of the poet's meditation, it is now displaced by the entrance of the "girl [who] comes in with her little fur hat / and wants to buy T H A T / cake that looks like a group of buns in the window. / Impulse buying." In a series of "pre-Lenten gestures" that resemble comic film stills, we see the girl in the fur hat, her young husband outside, Rudolph Valentino saying "Foolish little girl," on the radio, and so on. It is all entertaining, both for us and for the poet, but the camera soon zeros in on the "I":

> I AM BACK to an earlier question:
> someone had found it strange
> I should think of the concomitant physical cul-
>   mination of love,
> fucking, in short, as a release, some
>   times a relief from
>   the pain of loving itself.
>
> Surcease of pain. The idea
>   is medieval at least:
> "o lady, give me some relief,
> cure me of that sweet sickness
> I am subject to"
>
> (p. 241)

In the remainder of the poem, which is visually arranged on the page so as to get a maximum of intensity from the successive juxtapositions and the use of white space, the anguish of the present is seen through the prism of the troubadour love song, whether secular or addressed to the Virgin, as well as through the lens of Yeats's Crazy Jane poems, specifically "Her Anxiety" (no. 10), which begins "Earth in beauty dressed / Awaits returning spring,"[13] the subsequent four lines being reproduced in Blackburn's poem:

> All true love must die
> Alter at the best
> Into some lesser thing.
> *Prove that I lie.*
>
> (p. 243)

Blackburn must have assumed his readers would know how this particular poem continues:

> Such bodies lovers have,
> Such exacting breath,
> That they touch or sigh.
> Every touch they give,
> Love is nearer death.
> *Prove that I lie.*

Yeats's second stanza presents a chilling twist on the first. For it is one thing to say that "All true love must die" (a venerable cliché), but quite another to suggest that love itself is what moves us toward death. And it is this love-death equation that now preoccupies Blackburn's "I": "the act fore- / tells its own, what- / ever-breaking-now, its own / end . revealed (p. 243).

But the poem closes on a note of resignation, a "gesture" no longer "pre-Lenten" but of contrition, presented in a minimalist coda that is, to my mind, one of Blackburn's most moving passages:

It always is,
always was
this way, Ed.
all the time.
It is not that it does not happen.
It does,
and there is no help for it.
And
there is no end to it,
until there is.

(p. 244)

Here Blackburn picks up all the pieces: Dorn's "*Why can't it be like this all the time?*" now refers, not to pleasure, but to pain and death, and the Yeatsian refrain becomes the frightening "there is no end to it, / until there is." It is a somber conclusion to what began as a lighthearted poem about "radio days," shopping for buns in the bakery, the red Jaguar and "Robin's-egg Ford" seen through the "squeegee"-cleaned window, and the Provençal landscape ("the tower risen out of the olive grove"). At the end, the pre-Lenten "gestures" have given way to the season of repentance. And here poetry has made it happen.

Blackburn is not often as good as this. Seven-hundred pages of his poems may be more than all but a handful of former friends, disciples, or scholars of the period care to read. Again, the small-press collections of his poetry may well have been more user friendly, more intimate vehicles for Blackburn's particular sensibility, than is the heavy book under review. My own guess is that a *Selected Poems* of, say, one hundred pages would win this poet a more enthusiastic readership than the ***Collected Poems*** is likely to do. Still, we should not dismiss the importance of Jarolim's project or of Persea Books's production. For I know of no better place to learn what the sixties in American poetry were all about. Not the sixties of our most prominent poets—that would by now be familiar territory—but the sixties as represented by what is, so to speak, the decade's second string. As Blackburn puts it in "**Bluegrass**" (1966): "the work is only / what is not done."

Notes

1. *The Collected Poems of Paul Blackburn,* ed. Edith Jarolim (New York: Persea Books, 1985). All parenthetical references in the text are to this edition.
2. Stephen Berg and Robert Mezey, eds., *Naked Poetry: Recent American Poetry in Open Forms* (Indianapolis and New York: Bobbs-Merrill, 1969), p. xi.
3. Brad Leithauser, "The Confinement of Free Verse," *New Criterion* 5 (May 1987): 11.
4. Joan Retallack, "The Meta-Physik of Play: *L-A-N-G-U-A-G-E* U. S. A.," *Parnassus: Poetry in Review* 12 (Fall-Winter 1984): 218.
5. Paul Blackburn, comp. and trans., *Proensa: An Anthology of Troubadour Poetry,* ed. George Economou (New York: Paragon House, 1986).
6. Jarolim's text follows Blackburn's own lineation, spacing, and layout. Some poems are single-spaced, others double-spaced. For convenience, all poems quoted in this chapter are single-spaced.
7. *The Collected Poems of William Carlos Williams,* vol. 1: *1909-1939,* ed. A. Walton Litz and Christopher MacGowan (New York: New Directions, 1986), p. 107.
8. Gilbert Sorrentino, "Singing, Virtuoso," *Parnassus: Poetry in Review* 4 (Spring-Summer 1976); reprinted in Sorrentino, *Something Said: Essays* (Berkeley, Calif.: North Point Press, 1984), p. 109.
9. *The Collected Poems of Frank O'Hara,* ed. Donald Allen (New York: Alfred A. Knopf, 1971), p. 340.
10. Robert Kelly, "Introduction," in *The Journals of Paul Blackburn,* ed. Kelly (Santa Barbara, Calif.: Black Sparrow Press, 1975), unpaginated.
11. Alex Preminger, Frank J. Warnke, and O. B. Hardison, Jr., eds., *Princeton Encyclopedia of Poetry and Poetics,* enl. ed. (Princeton, N.J.: Princeton University Press, 1974), p. 770.
12. Charles Bernstein, "Undone Business," in *Content's Dream, Essays 1975-84* (Los Angeles: Sun & Moon Press, 1986), p. 332.
13. *The Collected Works of W. B. Yeats,* vol. 1: *The Poems,* ed. Richard J. Finneran (New York: Macmillan, 1989), p. 262.

FURTHER READING

Criticism

Apter, Ronnie. "Paul Blackburn's Homage to Ezra Pound." *Translation Review* 19 (1986): 23-6.

Discusses the influence of Pound on Blackburn's translations of troubadour poetry, claiming that this work amounts to an act of homage to Pound.

Baker, Peter. "Blackburn's Gift." *Sagetrieb* 12, no. 1 (spring 1993): 43-54.

Examines the element of time in Blackburn's poetry and attempts to establish his importance as a poet.

Buckeye, Robert. "The Principle, the Demarkation Is Use: Selected Letters of Paul Blackburn in the Abernethy Library." *Credences* 3, no. 2 (spring 1985): 53-90.

Includes a small selection of Blackburn's correspondence, noting that the letters constitute a record of the poet's life and work.

Conte, Joseph M. "Against the Calendar: Paul Blackburn's *Journals.*" *Sagetrieb* 7, no. 2 (fall 1988): 35-52.

Suggests that the series of poems that constitute The Journals *is defined not by a temporal progression but by a selection process that resists closure.*

Eshleman, Clayton. "A Mint Quality." *boundary 2* 2, no. 3 (spring 1974): 640-8.

Review of Blackburn's Early Selected Y Mas *that praises the poet's tone and precision.*

Kelly, Robert. Introduction to *Paul Blackburn: The Journals.* Los Angeles: Black Sparrow Press, 1975.

Brief discussion of The Journals *that praises the musical quality of Blackburn's poetry and his style.*

Ossman, David. Interview with Paul Blackburn. *The Sullen Art: Interviews with Modern American Poets,* pp. 22-6. New York: Corinth Books, 1963.

Brief interview with Blackburn that explores the elements of music and "common speech" in his poetry.

Sorrentino, Gilbert. "Singing, Virtuoso." *Parnassus: Poetry in Review* 4, no. 2 (spring/summer 1976): 57-67.

Review of The Journals *that contends the poems, which initially appear to be spontaneous and unstructured, in reality constitute "form perfected."*

Sturgeon, Tandy. "Doing that Medieval Thing: Paul Blackburn's Provençal Premises." *Sagetrieb* 9, nos. 1-2 (spring-fall 1990): 147-68.

Discussion of Blackburn's translations of Provençal troubadour lyrics and their relationship to his poetry.

OTHER SOURCES FROM GALE:

Additional coverage of Blackburn's life and career is contained in the following sources published by the Gale Group: *Contemporary Authors,* Vols. 81-84; *Contemporary Authors New Revision Series,* Vol. 34; *Contemporary Literary Criticism,* Vols. 9, 43; *Dictionary of Literary Biography,* Vol. 16; *Dictionary of Literary Biography Yearbook,* 1981; and *Literature Resource Center.*

CHANDLER BROSSARD

(1922 - 1993)

(Has also written under the pseudonyms Daniel Harper and Iris-Marie Brossard) American novelist, nonfiction writer, short story writer, and playwright.

Brossard's novels are often steeped in political commentary, relying on provocative themes to probe post-World War II American identity. While Brossard was a contemporary of the Beat Generation, he was never an active participant in the group, despite the fact that his 1952 novel *Who Walk in Darkness* achieved notoriety as one of the first "Beat" novels. Brossard contributed to the body of existential literature of the 1960s, and challenged mainstream American social values in the majority of his works.

BIOGRAPHICAL INFORMATION

Brossard was born July 18, 1922, in Idaho Falls, Idaho, the son of Mormon parents. His father was an alcoholic, and the family lived in poverty. Brossard was forced to leave school at age eleven to help support his family, and as a result, he was largely self-educated. At the age of eighteen he took a job at the *Washington Post,* beginning a journalism career that supported him throughout much of his life. Brossard moved to New York City in the early 1940s and served as a journalist for the *New Yorker* from 1942 to 1943; it was there that Brossard was encouraged to write fiction. Under the guidance of the magazine's editors, Brossard's work was refined to fit the *New Yorker's* style, but the author felt he was being untrue to his artistic voice in molding his work to fit their expectations. Breaking away from this environment, Brossard took a position as senior editor with *Time Magazine* in 1943 at the age of twenty-two.

In 1952 Brossard published his first novel, *Who Walk in Darkness,* a work centered on life in Greenwich Village in the 1940s. This novel has been associated with the Beat Generation largely because of its style and subject matter. Brossard, however, did not align himself with this movement and his subsequent works have little connection to Beat literature. Brossard claimed that his work tended to be anti-Romantic, while the Beat writers espoused what he considered a Romantic vision. Brossard became interested in drama in the 1960s and wrote a number of plays that were performed at the Crystal Palace in St. Louis. In 1968, after nine of his novels had been published, Brossard left journalism and took a position as an associate professor at Old Westbury College in Long Island. In 1970 he took a one-year visiting professorship at the University of Birmingham in England. While overseas, Brossard was able to find European publishers for several works that had been declined by publishers in the United States. Throughout his career, Brossard had a difficult relationship with American publishing houses, rarely working with the same publisher twice, facing frequent rejections, and receiving little support of his works once they were released. In the late 1970s Brossard moved to California, where he served as writer-in-residence at the University of California, Riverside, and San Diego State University in 1977 and 1978. Brossard died of cancer on August 28, 1993, in the Bronx, New York.

MAJOR WORKS

Brossard's first novel, *Who Walk in Darkness,* is often associated with the Beat Generation and has been variously called the first existential American novel and the first Beat novel. With its stark language, the essentially plotless novel follows the protagonist, Blake Williams, through a month in Greenwich Village in the 1940s. Williams describes in colorless, scientific language the world around him as he struggles with the absurdity of life. Only after experiencing love with a woman named Grace can Blake begin to find a sense of meaning in life. Likened to the works of Jean Paul Sartre and Albert Camus, *Who Walk in Darkness* delineates a violently absurd world and closes on a fearful, apocalyptic note at the end of the summer of 1948. While the narrator records the activities of beat/hipster characters in the Village—drinking, experimenting with drugs, engaging in a hedonistic lifestyle—he never participates in that world. Too absorbed with his own existential plight, Blake Williams merely reports on what he observes.

Brossard's next novel, *The Bold Saboteurs* (1953), is arguably his most widely read book. A violent, sexualized work, it relates the narrator's childhood experiences and their effects through a language stylized with street-slang and surrealism. The narrator, George Brown, struggles with an Oedipal hatred for his abusive father that impacts his relationships with authority figures and older men throughout his life. George experiences hallucinations that dramatize his unconscious struggles with the psychological damage caused by his alcoholic father. Using surrealistic imagery, humor, and a blending of fantasy and reality, Brossard depicts his character going through the process of complete psychological disintegration.

Though Brossard continued to write primarily novels and short stories, he also wrote a nonfiction travel book on his two-month stay in Spain during spring 1967. In *The Spanish Scene* (1968) Brossard impressionistically recreates his experiences with the Spanish people and culture. His later fiction focuses heavily on political commentary and satire. He offers a scathing account of the Vietnam War in *Raging Joys, Sublime Violations* (1981), in which famous American politicians and public figures engage in often bizarre, sometimes violent, sexual activities that affect the war in Vietnam. Brossard's works commonly examine what it means to be an American; he varies the presentation of this theme by alternating between traditional narrative, grim existentialism, and outrageous satire.

CRITICAL RECEPTION

The overall critical interest in Brossard's prose has been limited. Although examples of his earlier works are included in several anthologies of Beat literature—most notably, *Who Walk in Darkness*—scholars have found little connection between his later work and the Beat movement. Commentators have examined the political and sexual satire in Brossard's works; his *Dirty Books for Little Folks* (1978)—violent and sexually explicit versions of traditional fairy tales—generated debates surrounding the cultural truths hidden in fairy tales. Many reviewers have offered possible explanations for the lack of critical interest in Brossard's works; some argue that his inconsistent relationships with publishers are to blame, others maintain that his sharp criticism of American culture left American audiences and critics alienated. The latter argument is seemingly supported by the comparative success of Brossard's works in Europe.

PRINCIPAL WORKS

Who Walk in Darkness (novel) 1952

The Bold Saboteurs (novel) 1953

Paris Escort (novel) 1953

All Passion Spent: A Realistic Novel (novel) 1954; revised as *Episode with Erika,* 1963

The Wrong Turn [as Daniel Harper] (novel) 1954

The Double View [as Daniel Harper] (novel) 1960

The Girls in Rome (novel) 1961; revised as *We Did the Strangest Things,* 1968

Harry the Magician (play) 1961

The True Test of Friendship (play) 1962

Illya: That Man from U.N.C.L.E. [as Iris-Marie Brossard] (biography) 1966

The Insane World of Adolf Hitler (biography) 1966

Love Me, Love Me (novel) 1966

A Man for All Women (novel) 1966

In Other Beds (short stories) 1968

The Spanish Scene (nonfiction) 1968

Wake Up. We're Almost There (novel) 1971

Did Christ Make Love? (novel) 1973

Dirty Books for Little Folks (short stories) 1978

Raging Joys, Sublime Violations (novel) 1981

A Chimney Sweep Comes Clean (novel) 1984

Closing the Gap (chapbook) 1986

Postcards: Don't You Just Wish You Were Here! (short stories) 1987

As the Wolf Howls at My Door (novel) 1992

Over the Rainbow? Hardly: Collected Short Seizures (short stories) 1994

The Unknown Chandler Brossard: Collected Works 1971-1991 (prose) 2002

GENERAL COMMENTARY

WILLIAM CRAWFORD WOODS (ESSAY DATE SPRING 1987)

SOURCE: Woods, William Crawford. "The 'Passed' White Negro: Brossard and Mailer at the Roots of Hip." *Review of Contemporary Fiction* 7, no. 1 (spring 1987): 94-102.

In the following essay, Woods considers how Norman Mailer and Brossard, with their differing perspectives and professional antagonism, had varying approaches to the notion of the hipster.

Chandler Brossard and Norman Mailer share membership in the same literary generation, and there resemblances cease. But there was a time in the mid-1950s when their paths crossed. Both men had published novels that explored the phenomenon of Hip, and Mailer was about to publish an essay that would define it. Brossard, for his part, had written off the hipster altogether. So if their subjects were similar, their minds were hardly attuned. But they made some marks on each other.

Brossard recalls a visit to Mailer's Connecticut house in 1956 or '57 that was marred by the usual macho posturing and finally spoiled by Mailer's insistence that they box. "No, Norman," Brossard told him, "what you really want is for us to fall into each other's arms and cry and hug, covered with blood. . . . I don't like blood, and also it sounds kind of homosexual to me" (Manso, *Mailer,* 245). Mailer laughed the moment off, but it may have been in his mind a year or two later when he entered a mixed judgment on the competition in *Advertisements for Myself*:

> Chandler Brossard is a mean pricky guy who's been around, and he'd have been happier as a surgeon than a novelist, but he is original, and parts I read of ***The Bold Saboteurs*** were sufficiently interesting for me to put the book away—it was a little too close to some of my own notions. Brossard has that deep distaste for weakness which gives work a cold poetry. I like him as a man but I think there are too many things he does not understand.
>
> (469)

It's the perfect combination of hugs and blood.

Brossard, for his part, was to be offered a second shot many years later in that interesting mass of useful interviews Peter Manso published as a "book," *Mailer*: "In a terribly paradoxical way, there's a very usable emptiness in Norman. The fact that he assumes these various accents . . . he's got the Chandler Brossard one too, which at one point made me think: You, Norman, really are an unemployed actor looking for a big role" (327). The remark is critically intended, but, as we'll see, the play of self against role is a defining characteristic of Hip. And the brief encounters between these writers, no more than literary gossip at one level, have a role to play in introducing the subject at hand, in part because Hip is the art of encounter and such moments offer a fine display of the art: writers at war with the gloves off (one bow to Papa Hem), letting their match subside into the brittle nuance of one or another literary form.

Under all this something more serious was stirring. It looks like a wax-works now: the sharp suits and shades, the gliding walk, the pot, the bop, the language! But Hip was not made of Lucite, some passing fad to be lost in the pages of *Life.* It's still around—as a mournful humanism, an ethical nihilism, a fact in life and a possibility for fiction that is far from exhausted. Brossard and Mailer were present at the creation. Some notes on that connection follow.

. . . . .

Norman Mailer's essay "The White Negro" first saw print in *Dissent* in 1957, was embedded in the quickie anthology *The Beat Generation and the Angry Young Men* a year later, and was finally published, together with a clutch of related documents by Mailer and others, in *Advertisements for Myself* in 1959. The essay thus offers its own definition of Hip well after Chandler Brossard had introduced the figure of the hipster into his first novel in 1952, a fact Mailer himself was ready to note, though, interestingly, he saw Brossard's achievement as more lexical than literary: "Hipster came first as a word—it was used at least as long ago as 1951 or 1952, and was mentioned in the New Directions blurb on Chandler Brossard's ***Who Walk in Darkness***" (*Advertisements,* 372). But for both writers the type was less invention than discovery.

While Hip as a term and the hipster as a figure may be difficult to date precisely, they are easy enough to trace. Etymologically, the word derives from "hep," the prewar jazz musician's sobriquet for an alert and intuitive performer; historically, the man may have taken his title from Harry "the Hipster" Gibson, a postwar pianist in New York. This immediate identification with jazz, a music first mastered by blacks and long associated with drug use if not addiction, provided both Brossard and Mailer with three of the key images they needed, the one to record a social subculture, the other to craft a street-smart philosophy whose gnarled argument may be condensed to something like this sequence of ideas: out of the era of conformity enforced by the postwar American peace would emerge the American existentialist, a new man driven by private imperatives to model his prospects on the plight of the American black, whose skin had sentenced him to alienation from the wider social order. This sentence the "white Negro" reads as a declaration of freedom, in that it separates both black and hipster from a poisonous official culture best met by rebellion—sometimes creative, sometimes criminal, and often productive of the "philosophical psychopath" (Mailer 343). The hipster in fact might serve society by countering its totalitarian drift with the example of his liberation, though often at terrible cost, since that liberation could sometimes require violent action against the status quo.

Thus did "The White Negro" evolve its captivating metaphor into an intricate analysis of the unsentimental education that black experience might offer alienated members of white society. Brossard had sketched these possibilities in ***Who Walk in Darkness,*** but had failed to provide them with a convincing theoretical base; he had, however, set at the center of his circle of characters a man to whom the term "white Negro" literally applied, though twenty years would pass before many readers could know this. In the meantime, no black character would seem to hold the novel's center stage, and those who do appear are treated with no special sensitivity. Mailer himself, given his noble-savage treatment of the "Negro," was seen by some as subscribing to an inverted racism, but a close reading of the essay suggests he was less interested in offering reactionary sociology than revolutionary image: from the black bank of jazz, crusading sex, bold dope, and private language, the white man at odds with his official culture might draw the psychic funds he needed for survival. (Left unanswered in "The White Negro" is the question of the black hipster: a self-reflexive mode, or an impossibility?)

There were, to be sure, other elements in the mix: "The bohemian and the juvenile delinquent came face-to-face with the Negro, and the hipster was a fact in American life" (340). What may interest us in the sentence now is the way it names four categories that have all but vanished from the language; but in its time it proposed as fact what Mailer, more than Brossard, went on to celebrate in his fiction—most notably, perhaps, in the characters of Stephen Rojack in *An American Dream* and Gary Gilmore in *The Executioner's Song*: two murderers, one real and one imagined, but both illustrative of the homocidal and suicidal tendencies of Hip.

This deathward drift of the philosophy is something neither Mailer nor Brossard failed to see, though while the one put it in his books, the other sensed it in their author. "That was the scary thing about [Norman]," Chandler Brossard has observed. "He was willing to become a victim of ecstasy. He was capable of the ultimate act" (Manso, 328). Which capacity "The White Negro" locates as much in history as in psychopathology: in a postwar world witness to the concentration camps and the threat of nuclear war, "the only life-giving answer is to accept the terms of death" (359). This view is classic existentialism, and it licenses both Mailer's claim that the hipster is the American existentialist—a national style imposed on an international, though largely French, model—and Brossard's assertion that ***Who Walk*** is an existential novel, though hardly, as he hopes, the first such tale to come out of this country (Hawthorne's "Wakefield" and Melville's "Bartleby" come at once to mind).

Indeed there must have been times when Chandler Brossard could hardly be certain ***Who Walk in Darkness*** would ever be published at all. He has discussed its history in an unpublished essay in which he also tells something about its composition:

> For several months before starting on it, I had committed myself to the discipline of writing one imaginary episode a day . . . in doing so, I was learning the feel and control of a certain kind of chaste fiction language. . . . I felt confident about what I could do with the language and the fiction I planned to create. As a result of the almost religious preparation I wrote the book with a certain amount of ease. . . . It was about what people do to one another when their sustaining sociological context collapses, and it was done with the aesthetic sensibility/form of a documentary hallucination.
>
> (24)

The novel was turned down all over New York for a year and a half before being picked up by the French novelist and editor Raymond Queneau for Gallimard in Paris. Queneau also passed along the manuscript to James Laughlin at New Directions, which brought it out to largely incomprehending reviews in the United States only after an editorial controversy that leaves the author understandably bitter to this day. In Brossard's version of the tale, the poet Delmore Schwartz, a consultant to the publisher, objected to the book on the grounds that it included libelous portraits of two recognizable people. In the end, the author agreed to a relatively small number of changes, but one was of great importance. It occurs in the first line of the novel: "People said Henry Porter was an illegitimate" (7). The manuscript had used quite another term.

"I ended up changing a few words here and there," Brossard writes, "but the substantive change was to remove two words five times: those two words were 'passed Negro,' a characterization, as I employed it, of total inauthenticity" (25). Only the time will excuse the context. Today the very notion of a "Negro" needing or seeking to "pass" seems both offensive and deeply dated, but in the 1950s this unhappy phenomenon must have been real enough—and evocative enough for Norman Mailer to synchronistically invert the phrase in finding a title for his essay.

In any case, since authenticity is the key to all existential being, inauthenticity—whether Sartre's "bad faith" or Heidegger's "forfeiture"—effected a transformation, not corrected until a much later edition, that did substantial damage, which was to be compounded by the book's weak American reception and by the—in the author's view—devious path along which it finally gained a wider readership and a precarious place in literary history. The problem may be traced to that publisher's blurb, a gem of defensive misreading: "***Who Walk in Darkness*** is . . . one of the best books about the 'Beat Generation,' 'hipsters,' and their girls in New York's Greenwich Village." ***Who Walk***'s advertisement for itself goes on in the same coy vein, evoking an obligatory image of the "underground" while continuing to hedge its summary with a flurry of distancing quotes—all of which can hardly have pleased Brossard, who disclaims any Beat connection. Moreover, it misleads the reader, who encounters hipsters in these pages only in passing and only from the point of view of a narrator who shares the author's posture of disdain.

That attitude is one Brossard has insisted on all along. In **"The Dead Beat Generation,"** an essay published a year after "The White Negro," he was to call hipsters "the gentle jackals of the Village" (7) and to conclude that their swelling presence could best be accounted for by seeing them as "the natural products of an urban middle class that has lost its nerve" (9). And many years later he would again seek to sever all ties between himself and his presumed companions, remarking to an interviewer, "I have absolutely no affinities with the Kerouac group" (4), and citing (in the same unpublished essay) links to a different tradition altogether: "No matter what version you've heard, I was not a member of that euphoric troup of highway buskers. . . . [They] got their act together several years after a far less romantic, perhaps less huggable, and certainly less publicized group of pioneers" (2). But the historical project Brossard claims for his own elect—the creation of an existential art to illustrate the downside of life in postwar America—is identical to the one taken on by the self-professed Beat writers, and it's hard in any case to separate his early work from its shared historical field. "Despite [Brossard's] protest," one critic has reasonably noted, "his novel will continue to be discussed as a document of the early Beat movement, if not as an example of Beat writing, then for the glimpse it gives of emerging Beat consciousness" (Charters, 44).

Still, this persistent attempt to link Brossard's early work to the art of the Beat Generation, while understandable, is fundamentally flawed, as may be shown by a fuller excerpt from the same article: "Although Brossard's writing has covered a wide range of styles and concerns, he is often associated with the early Beat writers for his first novel . . . [which] drew from his own experiences living in Greenwich Village in the 1940s, and the milieu of the novel covered some of the same general terrain as sections of Kerouac's first novel *The Town and The City* (1950), and John Clellon Holmes's novel *Go* (1952). . . . The novel was essentially plotless, and Brossard deliberately used a language that was rhythmically monotonous and unliterary" (44). While factually accurate, this description misses the mark in several significant ways. Kerouac's book has much more to do with his boyhood in Massachusetts than his young manhood in New York, and while some (by no means all) of his work may have been plotless, it was never unliterary; rhythmic complexity, given its stated origins in improvised jazz, was the very essence of Kerouac's style.

The problem here is a common one: the confusion of Hip and Beat, something the mass media were repeatedly guilty of, but a distinction both Mailer and Brossard, if for very different reasons, were ordinarily careful about. Indeed, Mailer feels that a Beat (and particularly in the decayed form of "beatnik") is a *failed* hipster, a rebel with energies grown so passive that he can no longer act against society but can only vanish from it: "This is the terror of the hipster—to be beat" (352). But the terror of those who, in Brossard's fiction, choose instead to observe the hipster is something very different. The characters of ***Who Walk in Darkness***—often typified as "empty" or "spiritually incommunicado" (168)—lack the restorative energies of Hip and sometimes even question the style's legitimacy; as one remarks, "I don't know when to take this underground business as a laugh or when to take it as a real thing" (73).

The author himself is more certain. He knows it's real, and he knows where it comes from—Dostoyevsky's *Notes from the Underground,* a "formidable document," as Brossard was to put it in **"Tentative Visits to the Cemetery: Reflections on My Beat Generation."** "[It] was so . . . beguilingly characteristic of our demonic, dedicated group: to metamorphose an intellectual European horror story into our proud, embattled cry" (3). Mailer doesn't cite Dostoyevsky as a source, but the Hip life he calls for, with its repudiation of positivist thought and social controls and its insistence on the authority of individual experience, is an effort Dostoyevsky's underground man would readily endorse—just as he would, for example, second the case both Mailer and Brossard make against psychoanalysis, [The author adds in a footnote: No anachronism here. The underground man is a permanent type, not a temporal character.] whose reductive enterprise may, for the former, be supplanted by the hipster's dangerous explorations ("the associational journey into the past . . . lived out in the theater of the present" [347]). This view finds its parallel in Brossard's protagonist's own objection to the method: "I'm afraid it will make me just like everybody else" (71).

But Hip also risks making its proponents just like everybody else—hipper than thou, in a phrase of the time. Programmatic rebellion is simply another form of obedience, something Brossard's characters see a bit more clearly than Mailer's new man. There's a rigidity hiding in the drama of Mailer's thought that may be what Brossard had in mind when he observed that the more famous writer "had no central sensibility. He's a kind of intellectual hermit crab, looking for the cast-off shell of other animals to throw himself into their house" (Manso, 372). This is wrong, but not completely. It might carry more force were not Brossard much given to uncharitable judgments on other writers, one of which is of special interest when seen in the light of ***Who Walk in Darkness,*** a book which is as much literary parody as social study of Hip and anti-Hip routines.

The writer in question, surprisingly, is Ernest Hemingway—to Brossard, "a catatonic dreamer with an affected and unfortunate Castilian lisp" (**"Tentative,"** 2).

What's strange about this particular injection of venom is that one reads no more than a few pages into ***Who Walk*** before recognizing it as a second *Sun* rising, the rebirth of a generation less Beat than Lost. Not only do the truncated sentences and mannered speech forcibly remind us of their famous original, specific scenes and characters are paralleled and certain social attitudes—racist, sexist, and homophobic—mark both books as well. (Probably no more so than would be "normal" for their times; nor do I mean to impute to the authors attitudes held by occupants of their texts.) And the parallels run deeper: ***Who Walk*** has the same discursive, random feel of *The Sun Also Rises*; it is centered on sport, with boxing replacing the bullfight; it assesses the impact of jazz; it even sends its characters to the seashore for relief from the city, just as Jake Barnes and his friends head for the mountains to get Paris out of their pores. Both novels have first-person narrators more likely to observe than participate in their actions; both specify a wound to their narrator's sexuality, physical in one instance, psychic in the other. Even in small details there is specific mimicry: Brossard's dialogue on "involved" echoes Hemingway's famous comic use of "utilized." (To make matters stranger, there's a Gatsbyesque "old sport" thrown in here and there for good measure.) Just so, on the largest scale, we note a complete consonance of theme: both books propose a milieu of public and private malaise from which their protagonists can make temporary escapes only along the paths of sex, drink, drugs, and sometimes violence.

Given all this, ***Who Walk in Darkness*** might simply be written off as labored parody, Brossard gutting Papa just as the latter did Sherwood Anderson in *The Torrents of Spring*. But it's also true that many of the figures in *The Sun Also Rises* are early hipsters under other names, and one must cede Brossard a certain seriousness and even inspiration in his choice of models used in reflecting on America after the Second, as Hemingway had after the First, World War. And the author has made for his work still larger claims, that must command attention if not unqualified belief, calling it "the first existential novel to come out of America" as well as "the first anti-novel," and a book "done with the aesthetic sensibility/form of a documentary hallucination" (**"Tentative,"** 26). Such a self-assessment suggests transatlantic sources, which the author was quick to acknowledge in his *Gargoyle* interview: "I can say that I was very taken by European writing . . . and not at all interested in American writing. I never really felt American, to tell you the truth. So you might say that my sensibility developed in response to reading and identifying with European sensibilities" (4).

Brossard's intriguing view of himself as a displaced European novelist may derive as well from his odd fortune in having first found a French publisher, but his claim to the authorship of the first "anti-novel" has some basis in truth. Many of the doldrums of ***Who Walk*** are dispelled if we grant its flat style, faded story, affectless actors, and Brownian motion to be the products of the author's stated intention to produce a "documentary hallucination"—an effect Robbe-Grillet and other theorists of the *nouveau roman* would strive for only some years after Brossard had achieved it. But in the exploration of Hip the issue is less the book's spot on a literary timetable than its role as an hallucinatory document, an exercise in social forecasting in which the fifties hipster first mounts the literary stage, as there can be no doubt he does; for not only does Brossard adopt the term, he also, *pace* Mailer, introduces the man:

> "What happened to that underground man you came in with?"
>
> "He's casing the joint," Porter said. "He'll be back."
>
> "What do you mean by the underground man?" Goodwin asked.
>
> "The man who will do anything. He's a spiritual desperado."
>
> "He means Max Glazer," Porter said. "He's a smart guy. Really very hip."
>
> "I didn't say he wasn't. He is a desperado, though. Do you know what his ideal is? His ideal is to look like a street-corner hoodlum and be the finest lyric poet in America at the same time."
>
> (65)

To look like the one, to be the other: this need for a countervailing mask to play against the fundamental role is characteristically Hip, and, again, classically existential, in that authenticity is achieved not through public display but by contact with the core of one's most deeply-guarded being, which is what Mailer calls for in directing the hipster on an "uncharted journey into the rebellious imperatives of the self" (339), and what Brossard finds lacking in his less-favored characters insofar as they fail to achieve it. "I'm so tired of everything being reduced to a kick," a young woman remarks at one point (189), when the repetitious kicks have failed to produce any depth to her relationships; though other characters, dreaming of a more rebellious time, conclude the fault to be not in themselves, but in their stars, that they're not having one hell of a lot more meaningful fun:

> "Makes me feel wild, like the Twenties," said Joan.
>
> "That must have been a great time," said Harry. "I wish I had been around."
>
> "Why don't you stick in your own time?" I said. "What's wrong with now?"
>
> "Something," he said. "But I don't know exactly what it is."
>
> (22)

Brossard and Mailer both knew, exactly, and they explored well past the catch phrases—"Eisenhower," "cold war," "conformity"—so often used to sum the era up. And both directed their efforts toward finding a readership whose own rebellions they could nourish, though at the cost of an irony of which they could hardly have been unaware: by sticking to their pages the hipster they found in the street, they reproduced his simulacrum in the world again—the death of the cool, as it were, with men making motions they'd first read about in books and so forswearing the very authenticity they mimed; life imitating art, the most common of predicaments, and hardly to be urged against either author. But it does add a dimension to the debate that may have led Brossard to his "gentle jackals" dismissal, and Mailer to his insistence that man must be not only character but context—in this instance, the context of a character produced partly by a book.

For Hip and the hipster, however, the influence of art on life may matter less than that of art on art. Both figure and philosophy seem dated today, but the passions they embody have traveled on into our letters in the last forty years, and there are few contemporary novelists who don't owe at least some small debt to Norman Mailer and Chandler Brossard for the ideas mulled over here. Which takes me past, and so ties off, my discussion.

Leave it that, in the patterns traced above, we may see that Brossard and Mailer had something to give each other in their parallel developments of Hip, a sensibility at once inherited and invented by both. But what finally matters here is probably less the old easy question of "influence" than the fact that, at the same time and in something like the same way, two serious writers were working to record a new type in their fiction and define him in their critiques. Though "new" here is a little misleading, for Hip by any other name sends its tendrils back in time as well as forward. The figure of the rebel, in flight from the horrors of history, haunted by dreams of salvation or apocalypse, and answerable only to his own inner lights, is hardly a newcomer to American fiction. In that sense, hipsters crowd the pages of Hemingway, Hawthorne, Faulkner, Fitzgerald, James M. Cain, Melville, and Poe. But Hip and the hipster as Brossard and Mailer proposed them were indeed new to the American fifties, and if their titles have faded, their continuing claim to a hold on our imaginations have not.

Works Cited

Brossard, Chandler. "The Dead Beat Generation." *Dude.* July 1958: 7-9.

———. Interview. "Politics and Libidos: The Irreverent World of Chandler Brossard." *Gargoyle.* With Eric Baizer and Richard Peabody. 14 (1980): 3-8.

———. "Tentative Visits to the Cemetery: Reflections on *My* Beat Generation." Unpublished essay. No date given.

———. *Who Walk in Darkness.* New York: New Directions, 1952.

Charters, Samuel. "Chandler Brossard." *Dictionary of Literary Biography,* 1983 ed.

Mailer, Norman. *Advertisements for Myself.* New York: Putnam, 1959.

Manso, Peter. *Mailer: His Life and Times.* New York: Simon and Schuster, 1985.

STEVEN MOORE (ESSAY DATE SUMMER 1987)

SOURCE: Moore, Steven. "Chandler Brossard: An Introduction and Checklist." *Review of Contemporary Fiction* 7, no. 1 (spring 1987): 58-86.

In the following essay, Moore offers a comprehensive examination of Brossard's writing, including some of his short stories, Who Walk in Darkness, The Bold Saboteurs, *and* Wake Up. We're Almost There.

Chandler Brossard has always been an outsider, scornful of the country-club rules of literary decorum. In his 1955 review of Dan Jacobson's novel *The Trap,* Brossard concluded with the hope "that in his subsequent work he will discover himself 'outside' literature, and come upon a way of expressing himself—or conveying his vision—that is truly fictional and not literary."[1] As Brossard sees it, "literature" is the thin-blooded offspring of moribund literary conventions, tricks of the trade, writer's workshop mentality, and the homogenizing midwifery of unimaginative editors. "The fiction writer's primary responsibility," he insists in the same review, is to father "his own 'myth'" and to find a voice appropriate to this vision. Only then will the writer succeed at "extending the reader's (or listener's) vision and experience, and heightening his total sense of awareness."

Brossard's own development as a writer began "outside" literature in the early '40s with gritty short stories based on his experiences as a child (and later incorporated into ***The Bold Saboteurs***) which startled his *New Yorker* co-workers precisely because the fiction lacked any of the superficial polish or mannerisms of the "well-made" story. Efforts were made to fit his fictional talent into the *New Yorker* mold, but these failed when Brossard realized his vision and that of the magazine were worlds apart. Central to his conception of fiction was the spoken word (as opposed to "literary" locution), the vehicle of "the original source of literature, the oral storyteller."[2] Although the oral tradition was out of fashion in the mainstream fiction of the time (*The Catcher in the Rye* is the exception that proves the rule), it was the common denominator of those Brossard considered America's finest writers:

> Anderson, Twain, Stein, and Hemingway all wrote this spoken language, whether or not the particular work was written in the third person or in the first. If it was in the third, the presence of a narrator was always heavily felt throughout; there was not the feeling of a piece of fiction that had anonymously written itself. The idea was that the written language, or the literary language, was exhausted, just about dead, and there had to be a

Washington Square Park in Greenwich Village, circa 1940, as portrayed in Brossard's *Who Walks in Darkness.*

> return to the continually moving, continually developing vigor of the spoken English.

Here we have the two basic components of all of Brossard's fiction: a close attention to the vernacular and the presence of a distinctive, visionary sensibility. The result has been a unique body of work spanning forty years (and still in progress) which not only defies literary classification but challenges many of the assumptions held on what constitutes legitimate fiction. Belonging to no school or literary coterie, Brossard remains "outside" literature, a bold saboteur of entrenched conventions of any sort: literary, political, sociological, or religious.

For his first book of fiction, ***Who Walk in Darkness,***[3] Brossard stripped language of all its unnecessary literary trappings and reduced it to the flat, unemotional voice of a black-and-white documentary movie. The lean, chaste language reminded many of the book's reviewers of Hemingway (specifically of *The Sun Also Rises,* with which it has a superficial similarity), but a more illuminating parallel would be Camus's *The Stranger.* "Sartre has shown," Susan Sontag notes in her essay "On Style," "in his excellent review of *The Stranger,* how the celebrated 'white style' of Camus's novel—impersonal, expository, lucid, flat—is itself the vehicle of Meursault's image of the world (as made up of absurd, fortuitous moments)."[4] This image of the world is shared by Brossard's narrator Blake Williams (a stunted William Blake?), the passive recorder of a month in the lives of his Greenwich Village circle at the beginning of the summer of 1948. The Camus parallel is significant for other reasons: ***Who Walk in Darkness*** may or may not be (as it is sometimes called) the first Beat novel—Mandel's *Flee the Angry Strangers* and Holmes's *Go* were published the same year (1952), though I believe Brossard wrote his earliest—but it certainly appears to be American literature's first existential novel. Narrator Blake's first spoken word is "nothing," a word carrying the full weight of both Sartre's *Being and Nothingness* and Camus's *The Myth of Sisyphus.* Like Meursault, Blake describes rather than explains, and like *The Stranger,* ***Who Walk in Darkness*** is a demonstration of (rather than an argument for) the existential absurdity of life. Wanting only to perform "clean work" somewhere where "you did not have to tell lies" (177),[5] Blake documents his movement toward love and authenticity by contrasting it with his nemesis Henry Porter's flagrant inauthenticity. Blake displays none of the "self-righteousness" Delmore Schwartz ascribes to him;[6] his observations are as objective as a scientist's, taking special care to avoid subjective judgments of any sort. Only after he experiences tenderness with Grace (her name carries as much religious symbolism as godless existentialism will allow) does he venture a few speculations and metaphors (see pp. 246-47), eventually working up to such remarks as his sardonic response to a recording of Khachaturian's "Saber Dance" sung by the Andrews Sisters: "It sounded like the swan song of my decade. After that there could be nothing" (262).

Who Walk in Darkness takes place in what Jewish mystics called "the Abyss of Nothingness," as Brossard probably learned (if from nowhere else) from Milton Klonsky's 1948 essay "Greenwich Village: Decline and Fall" (and which Brossard reprinted in his excellent sociological anthology ***The Scene before You***). Klonsky took as his epigraph this quotation from Gershom Scholem:

> Rabbi Joseph ben Shalom of Barcelona maintains that in every change of form, in every transformation of reality, or every time the status of a thing is altered the Abyss of Nothingness is crossed. . . . Nothing can change without coming into contact with this region of pure absolute Being which the mystics call Nothing. . . . It is the abyss which becomes visible in the gaps of existence.[7]

Everyone in the novel is in such a state of transformation (as was Greenwich Village at the time, Klonsky shows), and the flat narrational tone and general meaninglessness of the characters' actions are meant to evoke this abyss of nothingness. Nothing in the novel is sensationalized or melodramatically exploited, though both the narrative and setting offered numerous temptations that would have overpowered a less ascetic writer. (Burroughs faced and overcame the same temptation in *Junky,* another even-toned "documentary.")

Brossard's superb control of tone also throws into high relief any dialogue contaminated by the slightest dishonesty, ambiguity, or pretension. Only Grace's dialogue approaches the purity of Blake's own, and she consequently emerges as the only other person of "good faith" (to return to Sartre). Porter, Max, and (to a lesser extent) Harry all illustrate Sartre's inauthentic men of "bad faith," and Brossard accomplishes this as much by the inauthenticity of their language as by their deeds.

This philosophic demarcation is dramatized by the Coster-Phelps boxing match at the heart of the novel. Blake and Grace favor the former: "Coster was a skillful, clean-fighting boy who knew his way around in the ring. He never bragged. He played the rules" (117). Porter favors Phelps, a brutal, dirty fighter; Max is too busy putting the make on a girl to participate, and fastidious Harry doesn't know if he's attracted to or repulsed by the fight. A boxing match may seem an inadequate objective correlative for an existential crisis, but clearly Brossard incorporated it because the boxing ring is one place where inauthenticity of any sort is quickly exposed. George's defense of "the esthetic form of a premeditated criminal act" in ***The Bold Saboteurs*** is equally valid for boxing:

> The only difference between this creative form and others is that you live this form; it is not something that exists apart from you in musical notes or words on paper. There is not the safety of distance. Form and content are inextricably one, and it is as if you yourself, for example, and not the fourteen lines, are the sonnet. The demands of this particular art form are stricter than most and the margin for error almost nonexistent. You can write a clumsy short story and get away with it but you cannot bungle a crime with very much impunity.
>
> (98)[8]

Coster's defeat at the hands of the vicious Phelps, however, seems to argue that those who fight clean and play by the rules (the rules for authenticity, that is, not the rules of social convention) are endangered most by those who have no rules, like the ubiquitous hoods in the novel (who finally mug Harry and leave him for dead) or "underground" men like Max and Porter. It is for this reason that the novel ends on a fearful, apocalyptic note as Blake and Grace realize their authenticity is no protection against the violently absurd world they live in.

That world is even more violent and absurd in Brossard's second novel, ***The Bold Saboteurs,*** where a passive narrator is replaced by an aggressively active one who goes on the rampage with a subversive language of exceptional power and energy. Again it is a spoken language, but the detached, dispassionate tone of Camus has been exchanged for the deliriously energetic tone of Céline. Like *Death on the Installment Plan,* ***The Bold Saboteurs*** relates the experiences of childhood in a style that mixes idiomatic street-slang with otherworldly surrealism, often veering into (and indeed ending with) lyrical hallucination. The result is not so much an autobiographical Bildungsroman (though it is based on Brossard's childhood in Washington, D.C.) as a terrifying exploration of psychic disintegration.

Perhaps Brossard's most widely admired book, ***The Bold Saboteurs*** has elicited a variety of responses. Like ***Who Walk in Darkness,*** it has been assigned a privileged (if inappropriate) place in Beat literature: its first chapter was reprinted in Feldman and Gutenberg's classic anthology *The Beat Generation and The Angry Young Men* (1958), and in 1971 Bruce Cook wrote that ***The Bold Saboteurs*** "had a teen-age hero who seems even today the model of a hipster."[9] Jerry H. Bryant has written some insightful pages on the book's sociological implications,[10] but perhaps Seymour Krim, one of the novel's earliest champions, has come closest to grasping the book's most significant achievement. Linking it with Ellison's *Invisible Man,* Krim points out that such "novels"

> are more truly imaginative explorations into the maze of personal being rather than novels in any traditional sense. The story they tell is primarily the psyche's story. The nightmarish sequences in both books, and many others like them, are a testimony to the devilish heat imposed on anyone with imagination who is just being today; it is the slice-of-life technique applied to the pressure-cooked head. There is invention in these books, but it is all directed to the description of, and the attempt to find, new colors, new sounds, new equivalents for the extremity to which the Self has been pushed.[11]

Narrator George Brown operates at the extremes of consciousness where sanity is occasionally flooded by the rebellious unconscious. In fact, one of the more remarkable sections of the book is a three-page letter of warning addressed to George's conscious from "Your inseparable partner, / until death do us part," his unconscious (201-04). From "the twisted smoking wreckage of my childhood" (37) George tries to maintain some semblance of sanity, but the psychic havoc inflicted upon him in childhood proves irreversible.

Brossard uses hallucination to dramatize the irruption of the unconscious into consciousness, largely the result of George's violently ambivalent feelings toward his father. Freud often used police action as an image for his theory of repression, and George's running conflict with the authorities throughout the novel is given its full psychological value in the sequence Brossard placed at the beginning of the book. Chapter one opens achronologically with George's arrest at the age of sixteen (chapter two begins when he is eight and the narrative unfolds chronologically thereafter) and reveals his ambiguous fear of and desire for punishment. Seeing a police car cruise toward him, he admits: "My body was a block of iced fear. I was afraid to let myself feel luxuriantly scared because then I knew I would disintegrate into hysteria, which is what I may have wanted to do anyway" (14). When he is finally caught, his reaction is tinged with masochistic satisfaction (16-17)—anticipating the "purifying" beating he later welcomes from his brother, when he passes out "in a coma of ecstasy and pain" (179).

The book's first surrealistic sequence follows his arrest; feeling "that the police house had always been my goal" (17), George finds in the depths of his hallucination the man responsible for his disintegrating psyche:

> Now I was in an absolutely quiet corner of the station house. Here I experienced a strange tidal sensation all around me and inside myself: it was very emotional and a little sexual. Before me was my father, very bloated and dreamy looking and dressed in what resembled a policeman's uniform. He smiled vastly at me but I did not smile back. My father reminded me of some giant fish, a whale or porpoise, that had been stranded on the beach. He was murmuring vast, oceanic nothings to a small man in a black raincoat who was pretending to write it all down in a very official-looking black notebook. . . .
>
> And almost before I knew what I was doing, I had pushed the man away and had climbed into my father's arms. Now I felt happily helpless and I was sobbing and sobbing, and my father was caressing my head.
>
> "I was hoping you would be here," I said, or felt myself say for there was still an absolute, overwhelming silence all around me.
>
> "That makes me feel very proud, son," my father replied in his vast, oceanic voice.
>
> I began to play with his police badge, but under my fingers the badge turned into an ordinary button. I was suddenly stunned by this, and I looked into my father's face for an explanation. But my father now looked old and sick and disgusting, and he stank terribly of whiskey. His uniform had become a shabby suit of clothes.
>
> "You've tricked me! You've tricked me!" I shouted. "Why? Why?"
>
> And I was hitting my father in the face, blow after blow. My father, however, did not react at all to these blows; he just stared helplessly at the floor.
>
> (20-21)

George's love-hate relationship with his father, an unredeemable drunkard, sets into play a classic Oedipal psychodrama. Hatred for his father is distributed to other authority figures and institutions, as can be expected: he avoids school, convinced they want "to emasculate whatever originality and spirit" he has (57), and his fierce blasphemy is illuminated by his brother Roland's delirious evocation of "my father who art in heaven drunk" (231).[12] Similarly, George's first mugging victim is an older man who tries to dissuade him by crying out, "I could be your father" (134) and shortly afterwards George maliciously entraps an older pederast—a delayed reaction, perhaps, to George's disgust at being forced to sleep with his father when younger (28). The drunken father appears sporadically throughout the novel, and each time George retreats into hallucination rather than bring into consciousness and resolve his hopelessly ambivalent feelings toward him. To complicate matters further, almost all of George's love affairs are with women old enough to be his mother.

George's brother Roland at first receives all the love and devotion George cannot give to his parents, but after Roland kicks the old man out of the house, he becomes the father figure (going so far as to disallow his mother remarrying), triggering similar conflicts George experiences with his father. A brother-substitute is temporarily found in a criminal wunderkind named Victor, but their idyllic relationship is short-lived. At the end of the novel George learns of his death, and his visit to pay his respects to Victor in a shabby funeral parlor is the most touching scene in the book. "Always looking for that brother, aren't you?" a policeman asks in George's final hallucination (302).

At the end of the book, lost to friends and family in "a still grey world beyond communication" (296), George finds a job caring for a final father figure, an invalid named Mr. White. Carrying him one night (after reading to him from the Book of Judges), "trying to do it so that I would not have to touch the repulsive old man too much with my arms and body, really trying to juggle him, and now with an unusual lack of muscular interest, I dropped him." (Note how the syntax delays the confession as George struggles to admit responsibility.) Panicking, he carries the half-dead body to bed and nearly strangles him. Guilt overwhelms him, and after finally proclaiming his deed like a Dostoyevskian hero, George flees from the house and, after a period of hunger and illness, lapses into the hallucination that closes the book. Traveling by boat to a Kafkaesque otherworld, George is abandoned, either struggling to break out of his hallucination—"running from pier to pier, looking for the boat which I hoped would take me back" (303)—or perhaps dying, if the archetypal boat symbolism is used in its mythic sense. Either way, it is a chilling conclusion to a remarkable study in neuroses.

But ***The Bold Saboteurs*** is obviously more than a Freudian case study. In a style as racy as the first novel's was chaste, George's picaresque adventures are always absorbing and often hilarious, and the novel undoubtedly remains Brossard's most popular for these very reasons. But the psychological conflicts dramatize a theme that Brossard would examine with increasing audacity in succeeding works, namely the conflicting claims of the Dionysian unconscious and the Apollonian intellect. At the beginning of the decade that would later produce *Eros and Civilization* and *Life against Death,* Brossard demonstrated the necessity of allowing the liberating unconscious to revitalize the grey flannel conscious, and in ***The Bold Saboteurs*** he gives a stunning dramatization of both the rewards and dangers that attend this process.

It is difficult to fathom why the one-two delivered to literature by ***Who Walk in Darkness*** and ***The Bold Saboteurs*** failed to make a greater impact. Much of the blame rests with the reading public's allegiance to the drab realism of most fiction—then as now. The hyper-realistic trompe-l'oeil narrative of ***Who Walk in Darkness*** owes more to the illogical detail of a surrealistic painting or a nightmare than to the realistic fictional conventions of the time, and the blending of fantasy and reality in ***The Bold Saboteurs*** is a technique European readers respond to more readily than Americans. Other than their obvious influence on such emerging writers as Gilbert Sorrentino and Hubert Selby in America and on various New Wave novelists and filmmakers in France, the novels attracted little critical attention.

Disappointed by this lack of response and desperately needing money, Brossard next wrote the first two of several potboilers: ***Paris Escort*** (1953) and ***The Wrong Turn*** (1954), both written under a pseudonym, to be followed in later years by ***All Passion Spent, The Girls in Rome,*** and ***A Man for All Women*** (a revision of ***Paris Escort***). These Brossard now dismisses as "threepenny dreadfuls," and although they all have occasional points of interest, they probably would not repay close study.

In the late '50s Brossard also edited the first of many paperback short-story anthologies, each carrying anywhere from one to five of his own stories, most appearing under a variety of pseudonyms. The short-story form was not a new departure for him; Brossard's earliest publications in fiction were in this form, and like Hemingway's earliest stories,[13] they dramatize epiphanic moments in a style of scrupulous meanness. The best among them conjure up the existential dread inherent in the quotidian world, offering interesting asides on the themes treated at greater length in his novels. **"Sunday Revelation,"** written while Brossard was still at the *New Yorker* but not published until 1953 (and included in his first anthology, *The First Time* [1957]), is both a grimly original portrayal of the loss of innocence, and symbolic (as he later realized) of the subtly corrupting influence of Brossard's mentor at the *New Yorker,* novelist William Maxwell. A skewed sort of voyeurism disrupts the deceptively placid surface of **"A Very Nice Place"** (1947), and the repeated image of garfish staying "stiffly together in speckled angles, unmoving"—an image Ezra Pound singled out for praise[14]—effectively characterizes the tensions between the threesome in **"Vacation for Three"** (1951). **"Jewel of the Soul"** (1951) is a harrowing story of the loss of identity, and the exquisite **"The Closing of This Door Must Be Oh, So Gentle"** (1962) is an equally effective study of a desperate attempt to maintain an identity. In a more exuberant style (anticipating his later work), **"One If for Sorrow, Two If for Joy"** (1966) reads like an Isaac Bashevis Singer story adapted by Stanley Elkin, and **"The Robber Next Door"** (1966)—which Brossard used as the closing sequence of ***Wake Up. We're Almost There***—was praised by Richard Nason as "a short story as good as any of its kind, Virginia Woolf and Katherine Mansfield not aside."[15] Plans to publish a collection of the early stories around 1953-54 fell through, but there is a good chance that these and his other short stories will be published by a small press in England soon.

Brossard's next novel was published in 1960; originally entitled "The Double Dealers," it appeared as ***The Double View*** to much better reviews than his first two received. The original title sharpens the contrast between most of the book's characters—New York pseudo-intellectuals suffering in various degrees from a kind of cultural schizophrenia—and more straightforward characters like Shanley, "no dillier with identities, no dallier with self, a single dealer of infinite simplicity" (183). The rest dilly-dally with their identities in a number of ways: Margaret, a wealthy socialite, leads a complicated double life as an organizer of foreign charities and private orgies; Phillips has ambivalent feelings toward his Jewish heritage (as his gentile name suggests); Christopher Hawkins is a black professor who wants to be white so intently that he wears a white "skin-tight suit of long woolen underwear" (111) and has such a tenuous grip on his identity that he is not even named during his early appearances; Rand has a doppelgänger relationship with his best friend Carter Barrows, sharing both Carter's wife and his nervous breakdown. Carter, the book's protagonist, is in an insane asylum throughout the novel, wondering when and where he took "the fatal fork in the road" that separated "his strange self and his not strange self" (150, 186).

The most interesting of the double dealers is Harry. Here it is worth noting that the book was written in 1953, for it anticipates in several essentials Norman Mailer's 1957 essay "The White Negro." ***The Double View***'s most ingenious character, Harry perfectly illustrates Mailer's hipster as "a philosophical psychopath, a man interested not only in the dangerous imperatives of his psychopathy but in codifying, at least for himself, the suppositions on which his inner universe is constructed."[16] An intellectual radical (who nonetheless "writes lies for an advertising agency" [28]), Harry has decided, in Mailer's words, "to set out on that uncharted journey into the rebellious imperatives of the self . . . to encourage the psychopath in oneself, to explore that domain of experience where security is boredom and therefore sickness." Harry leads a secret life as Eddie Brien, a vulgar small-time hood, doing no more than practicing what he preaches in an early chapter; asked what he means by "exploiting schizophrenia," he replies:

> "Oh that. Well, instead of destroying yourself with anxiety by repressing certain aspects of your whole self, aspects that conflict with the so-called moral self, why, it would be better to try to express them all. For example, if you have some criminal desires, become a part-time thief, or at least let the emotion have some badly needed exercise. See what I mean?"
>
> (34)

As good as his word, Harry goes from entrapping and mugging some out-of-towners to knocking over a bowling alley with his small gang, and finally to raping Margaret and burglarizing her apartment with two other masked assailants. Harry's actions are a dramatization of Mailer's notorious definition:

> Hip, which would return us to ourselves, at no matter what price in individual violence, is the affirmation of the barbarian, for it requires a primitive passion about human nature to believe that individual acts of violence are always to be preferred to the collective violence of the State; it takes literal faith in the creative possibilities of the human being to envisage acts of violence as the catharsis which prepares growth.

No growth, however, takes place; three double dealers are destroyed or debilitated during this climactic scene, and only the single dealer Shanley escapes unharmed.

The masked mass murder is a convention of Elizabethan drama, including Tourneur's *The Revenger's Tragedy,* the closing lines of which supply the epigraph to Brossard's book. In fact, the numerous parallels between these two works are instructive: like the play, the novel has a dramatic structure, eschewing prosaic transitions in favor of quick cuts to scenes of dialogue or internal monologues that read like theatrical asides. The characters in both play and novel frequently resort to disguises and live in the same climate of moral corruption. And like Tourneur, Brossard is a stern moralist, and his remarks on his novel apply equally well to *The Revenger's Tragedy*:

> I like to think of ***The Double View*** as a stringently moralistic book. It tries to show what happens when people lose sight of God; when they begin to use each other, the way we use commodities, rather than love each other; and what happens when a person does not know truly who he is and what he should do on this earth.[17]

Just as Vindice the revenger becomes tainted with evil in the very process of seeking revenge and thus must be destroyed, Harry likewise perishes, as much from a "failure of belief" (150) as from the policeman's bullet. Harry had rationalized his crimes with a variant of Ivan Karamazov's challenge: "In a society which has no meaning, Hawkins, my boy, what could be a more appropriate gesture than ours?" (178).

FROM THE AUTHOR

BROSSARD'S MULTIPLE VOICES

When I think about it, I realize that my writing life has not been happenstance in terms of my character makeup. I think I went into writing for the very simple reason that very deeply I needed a number of voices in order to survive. . . . In other words, some character deformation brought me into fiction. It is the perfect objective correlative for my problem. I was a multiple schizophrenic, if you like, but I was aching and aching to be a variety of people. I didn't come to fiction as a straight by any means, and I realize that it's essential to understanding me and my fiction and the wide variety in terms of the characters within the particular books—but it was an organic need. . . . So I was kind of lucky I fell into it; some deep urge said look for that situation in which you could be a variety of people because you'll be saved—otherwise you'll crack up.

Moore, Stephen. Interview with Chandler Brossard in the *Review of Contemporary Fiction* VII, no. 1 (spring 1987).

A more constructive attitude is taken by Carter, who struggles to learn how authenticity slipped through his fingers:

> "Failure of belief must have been the reason I'm here now, otherwise why would any one wish to leave a world, or anything else, that he believed in? Question before the accused is, how to regain Belief *and in what.* Without that there is simply no point in accused leaving present address. One is not required to have anything here except a pulse. In the place I left, outside, living without belief is even crazier than it is in here, and I know. At what point did I lose it and why? That's what must be discovered. The fatal fork in the road."
>
> (150)

On the same night Harry and his cohorts execute their burglary, Carter escapes from the asylum with his black friend (an act that looks back to *Huckleberry Finn* and forward to *One Flew Over the Cuckoo's Nest*) and plans a similar bloody revenge against his unfaithful wife and friend. But at the very moment he plans to consummate his deed, "a beatific, transcendent lucidity" illuminates him—conveyed in sexual imagery—and he lays down his knife in order to return "back down that long, long highway, to the fatal fork in it, to the town where he was born, where the wrong direction had been chosen or forced upon him. . . . He would return to the particular fragrant spawning street of his childhood and begin there to search for the person he had been" (187-88).

It's a nervy, compact book written with economy and a flair for unusual imagery, accomplishing in less than two-hundred pages what Brossard's friend William Gaddis took nearly a thousand pages to do in *The Recognitions,* namely to chart a pilgrim's progress from hell through purgatory, leaving him poised for a paradisical rediscovery of authenticity and atonement.

These religious implications are at the heart of Brossard's next novel, ***Did Christ Make Love?***[18] Here the implicit religious argument of ***The Double View*** is made explicit as Alfred Harrison, an Episcopalian priest, suffers a "passion" in both the religious and erotic sense of the word. A parish priest in East Harlem, he is driven by his smarmy wife Leslie (a latent homosexual) into the arms of a mulatto hooker named Monique. His sexual reawakening is twice compared to St. Paul's illumination on the road to Damascus (46, 73) as he discovers that fork in the road where sex and religious worship parted ways millenia ago. Harrison attempts to reunite the two, using biblical texts in sexual contexts (reversing the procedure theologians have used on sublime erotica such as the Song of Solomon and the poems of St. John of the Cross) and like Harry in ***The Double View*** he exults in the liberation of his repressed instincts. His exultation, however, is short-lived; again like ***The Double View,*** the novel ends in mass murders, from which only Leslie escapes, running off to Puerto Rico (after desecrating her husband's church) with her new lesbian lover.

Brossard underscores the radical conflicts between his characters by shifting styles as each character takes the stage. Mixing narration and interior monologue, the author clothes his characters in language that mirrors the psychosociological reality of each. In the opening chapter, for example, both Harrison's academic background and psychological conflicts are conveyed in a paratactic sentence structure that frequently fractures itself with parenthetical qualifications. (After his sexual experience, his language loosens up as much as he does.) Chapter two introduces Rojas, a streetwise young welfare worker and a parishioner of Harrison's, in a jazzy style appropriate to his playful outlook on life. (He reads, and occasionally quotes from, Huizinga's *Homo Ludens* throughout the book.) Chapter three features Leslie in a coy, saccharine style reminiscent of the Gerty MacDowell chapter in *Ulysses.* The last major character, a pimp named Dancer, has his own language of "viciously thin corrupted words" (35). The close juxtaposition of these clashing language codes heightens the various religious, sexual, and racial tensions throughout the book, giving it more the quality of a play than a novel. (It is worth noting that Brossard was heavily involved in playwrighting at the time.)[19]

Common to these diverse conversational styles is a careful and consistent use of imagery. Glimpses of Eden are caught sporadically by way of the nature and garden imagery in the sexual scenes, but animal imagery prevails in the gritty picture of an urban jungle. Rats, lizards, snakes, dogs, cockroaches, wolves, and alligators infest the novel; after a brutal rape, for example, the boys leave "much as beasts of prey will ultimately pad heavily away from the half-devoured body of a gazelle, innocent, unsuspecting, which, wandered from its herd, they have brought down" (84). In addition, a variety of figurative demons, ghosts, dwarfs, gargoyles, dragons, trolls, hunchbacks, and ghouls haunt the pages of this nightmare world. At least one critic has pronounced this Brossard's best book.[20]

Did Christ Make Love? was followed by two novels that remain unpublished; Brossard describes them as follows: "They were a shortish novel, very brutal, almost B-movie kind of novel but with a very exquisite kind of super-realism, situated in New York, about crazy people. It was called **'I Came To See You but You Were Asleep.'** That book was rejected by several people so I withdrew it, and then I did a sort of campy porn novel called **'Your Place or Mine?'** That too was rejected by a couple of people and I withdrew it."[21]

He had better luck with several non-fiction books he wrote during the same period. Two were popularized biographies written for money—***Illya*** (using his daughters' names as a pseudonym) and ***The Insane World of Adolf Hitler*** (both 1966)—but both have their own appeal. ***Illya*** is a frequently hilarious parody of pop journalism (a point no doubt lost on its gushing readers) and the Hitler book, despite its negligible, somewhat improvised text, constitutes an invaluable photographic record.

In a special category, however, is Brossard's 1968 travel book ***The Spanish Scene.*** Based on interviews and observations made during a trip in the spring of 1967, ***The Spanish Scene***'s non-fiction status may be called into question when one considers the rather extraordinary circumstances in which it was written. Brossard explains:

> ***The Spanish Scene***—non-fiction, more or less—took me two weeks. I was in an elegant sort of trance while I was doing it. I was very high, and very happy. I had spent two months in Spain collecting material for the book—just talking to people, really—and I was experiencing ecstasy during the whole time. I seemed to understand everything in Spain even though I did not speak a word of Spanish. My ESP was working divinely. A Spanish department had opened up in my brain. I could hear Cervantes talking, and Lope de Vega and Ortega. It was incredible.[22]

Consequently, it might be better to consider the book more as an imaginative recreation, an impressionistic historical fiction even, than as a straightforward travel book—reliable as it may be in that regard.

One of the book's most interesting aspects can easily go unnoticed: the subtle identity crisis the self-effacing narrator suffers and overcomes in the course of the book. Daniel Talbot, a consistently reliable reviewer of Brossard's work, noticed one facet of this crisis: "***The Spanish Scene*** is not so much a book about the Spanish scene as a gifted novelist's predicament in explaining why he is so bugged by life in his own country."[23] More accurately, it is an account of a man who has lost touch so completely with any kind of nurturing reality that he must make contact with something real before he loses touch altogether. In this regard the narrator recalls Blake Williams of ***Who Walk in Darkness,*** and the travel book has much the same kind of chaste, noncommittal style as the earlier book.

The book is made up largely of monologues by various Spaniards in which the narrator does little more than ask an occasional question; rarely does he express any kind of evaluation or value judgment. On the few occasions he does register a response, it more often than not concerns his own shortcomings: he feels "like an idiot in my innocence and non-participant role" (32) or feels "thick with stupidity and frustration" (48); occasionally he simply agrees because he can't "think of anything else to say" (60). Not surprisingly, he finds the sight of his fellow-Americans—tourists and GIs stationed in Spain—repugnant after his encounters with such vivid Spaniards.

We learn he is going through a divorce at one point (and from the dedication to his doctor can infer he almost lost his life shortly before) and learn that he is so vulnerable that a few lines from Rilke are almost enough to cause a breakdown (49). Not until the end of the book, however, do we fully realize how cathartic his encounter with Spain has been. Discovering "I knew that something in this world made sense, if you kept your eyes open to notice" (97), the Spanish scene allows him to free himself from his earlier, frustrated self: "The man with my name who had waited with premature exhaustion in the departure section of the airport in New York was still there. I was someone else" (99). Picking up a copy of *Time* and reading a misleading article on the Basques (7 April 1967, p. 31), he reacts to this compact symbol of all that is wrong with America by reestablishing contact with the real, the visible:

> I found myself concentrating on the faces of the people more, staring at particular Spanish details of stores and buildings, gestures of differentness, in order to kill the dirty-taste feeling left in me by reading the insults in the magazine; and, with microscopic urgency, I was seeing a full, curved mouth, a thick brooding eyebrow, a stone flower on a façade, and as I was thus healing myself, I began to analyze why I felt so tranquil and no longer in small angry pieces. . . . I could isolate one feeling for sure—that I felt more like myself, in those places, than I generally did in my own country. And feeling more like myself meant, quite simply, not feeling those other personalities that I had been forced to invent to deal with those countless situations and humans in New York that I, the me of myself, did not want any part of. The stage of me became so crowded with those others: a ghostly repertory company that refused to go home when the curtain came down. Those other hungry, manipulated, angry pseudo-humans were not with me here, and it was me and me alone that was responding to and becoming part of—no longer a spectator, object scene—the fold in the stone martyr's robe, the reflection of light on the shy wet street, the ache in the tolling of the bells. The singleness of myself allowed me to discover how much a part of this natural world I truly was. (101-02)

This episode, significantly, is followed by one that begins with a Spanish businessman's confession: "'I used to think I could find myself and my destiny somewhere else'" (105); he discovered that he couldn't, and the narrator soon learns likewise. The next two episodes—the last in the book—deal with the brutal, repressive side of Spain, disqualifying it as the Eden it may have appeared to be. The narrator must return to his own country, but vows not to forget those aspects of Spain that brought him back to himself: "'I won't [forget],' I said. I couldn't. To do that would be to forget myself" (112-13).[24]

This crisis of personal disintegration and integration is handled almost indirectly, so unobtrusively that it could easily be lost among the more vivid vignettes of Spanish life with which the book is largely concerned. But the theme is one that is central to Brossard's work, as is his concern with the dark, repressed side of human nature—the subject of an interesting monologue by a government official (93-96). An elegant, beguiling work, ***The Spanish Scene*** illuminates Brossard's fiction as much as it does the Iberian peninsula.

Writing of Brossard in 1959, Mailer prophesied, "It would not surprise me if he appeared with a major work in ten or fifteen years, or however long it takes for the rest of the world to become as real to him as Chandler Brossard" (*Advertisements for Myself,* 469). In 1971 that major work appeared under the strange title ***Wake Up. We're Almost There,*** a mammoth surrealistic epic (with twenty-four chapters, as in Homer's epics) with a protean repertory company of characters improvising scenes ranging in time and space from the fields of Troy to the battlefields of Vietnam, from Renaissance Italy to Hitler's Germany. Like *Finnegans Wake* (its closest literary analogue), ***Wake Up*** features a small group of archetypal characters in the dreamworld of a down-at-the-heels New Yorker called (for our purposes) Gelb. Just as George in ***The Bold Saboteurs*** blacked out into hallucinations to avoid facing his Oedipal conflict, narrator Gelb finds fantasy more hospitable than life with his shrewish wife Sylvia. Their psychotic marriage is driving him up the wall (an image he literalizes on the first page) and at the simplest level ***Wake Up*** constitutes the psychotic fantasy world he seeks refuge in. But this is only the simplest of the series of increasingly complex levels on which the book operates.

"'I feel like Everyman himself'" Gelb admits early in the book (58), and at the next level ***Wake Up*** illustrates the unconscious weltanschauung of a well-meaning but beleaguered man trying to make sense of the chaotic '60s. Given these surreal times, Brossard cut what few ties he still had with social realism in favor of a full-fledged visionary surrealism. In an essay written shortly after the publication of ***Wake Up***—an essay which illuminates Brossard's conception of his own book—he noted:

A true visionary fiction, like a myth structure, magically combines, orders, and dramatizes multiple realities. A single level of action, or plot or behavior, does not hold sway, nor does arbitrary sequential time obtain sovereignty. It is not imprisoned within one language system: it has many tongues and voices. One identity does not dominate the speaker's platform and restrict the play and range of sensibility many identities perform, and they flow in and out of one another. Thus we have a symphonic *communal* statement, in which the culture of the community and its members are resonantly and clearly the same thing, and not separated strangers and antagonists.

For an American "novel" to qualify as authentic fiction-vision, as far as I am concerned, it would have to contain an imaginative orchestration of the sensibilities and actions of Shirley Temple, Dickie Nixon, Lieutenant Calley, General Westmoreland, Blaze Starr, and Huck Finn, and include the spacious sexual folklore of *Screw* and *Suck* and the sniffy mores of *The New Yorker.* In any ten waking hours, all of these identities and genres and their behavior patterns are experienced directly and in fantasy by any intelligent, reasonably sophisticated American. Many, many more are experienced by this same person when he is "dreaming" (though that is such a simplistic and denigrating designation for that extraordinary world and its experiences). Why, then, should it be asking too much of our fiction that it represent this rich state of being, this absolutely unalterable fact?[25]

The first paragraph is an exact description of the structure of ***Wake Up***; although Gelb is the ostensible narrator, his voice repeatedly gives way to a torrent of other "tongues and voices." (Returning to the simplest level, however, he may be doing no more than "talking to myself in different voices" [464].) A plot summary would be unintelligible if not impossible and, as Brossard indicates, would be antithetical to the nature of this visionary fiction. The "symphonic *communal* statement" that emerges is a radical affirmation "of the wonders, and therefore the chaos, of the human imagination" (465), set in contrast to all forms of authoritarianism that fear and therefore try to subjugate the imagination by means of enforced conformity, reactionary/imperialistic politics, and a puritanical denial of the senses.

Written during the second half of the tumultuous '60s, ***Wake Up*** is the ultimate countercultural Happening, a psychedelic light show love-in that captures nearly every nuance of that reckless, explosive decade. Tom Wolfe once expressed dismay that novelists for the most part turned their backs on the '60s; publishers, he later discovered,

had been practically crying for novels by the new writers who must be out there somewhere, the new writers who would do the big novels of the hippie life or campus life or radical movements or the war in Vietnam or dope or sex or black militancy or encounter groups or the whole whirlpool all at once. . . . The—New Journalists—Parajournalists—had the whole crazed obscene uproarious Mammon-faced drug-soaked mau-mau lust-oozing Sixties all to themselves.[26]

Not quite; Wolfe read Brossard's *Harper's* essay on the fiction scene—he quotes from it later in the same piece (39)—but he obviously did not read ***Wake Up,*** for Brossard did indeed take on "the whole whirlpool all at once" in his book: hippies, radical movements and protest marches, black militancy, pop art, encounter groups, Vietnam, mod clothes, Zen, sitar music, protest buttons, sexual liberation, acid rock, terrorism, Kennedy assassination conspiracy theories, nothing less than "the whole crazed obscene uproarious Mammon-faced drug-soaked mau-mau lust-oozing Sixties" in a hallucinatory form that embodies the times better than any work—fiction or non-fiction—written since then. ***Wake Up*** is indisputably *the* novel of the '60s.

The '60s called into question nearly all the values and assumptions upon which western civilization rests, and, true to that spirit, ***Wake Up*** also challenges (and gleefully violates) most literary conventions of the standard novel. Brossard, of course, had been at odds with the traditional novel from the beginning; a truculent statement on the dustjacket of his very first book had warned that his next "book of fiction will not be a novel because the author feels the novel is not adequate to express certain contemporary experiences." Brossard apparently associates the conventional novel with conventional thinking, conventional beliefs, and the political status quo. Given the radical political vision propounded by ***Wake Up*** ("Sometimes I wonder if all western civilization will have to vanish—or be vanished—before mankind can begin to be truly himself in all his magnificence" [278]), Brossard obviously felt his medium must be part of the message. Consequently, the organization and sociological orientation of the book is trans-schematic, subversive, alogical, achronological, pagan, sensual, and goes to extremes that in a conventional novel would be tasteless, incomprehensible, or obscene. The very form of the book is thus calculated to unseat the reader's usual expectations and cultural assumptions (in life or fiction), never allowing the reader to settle back and be told what he or she already knows.

At the most basic level, this is accomplished by way of Brossard's unconventional imagery. The reader with conventional expectations founders at such descriptions as these (all culled from irritated, conventional reviewers):

> Her look was a Roman soldier's spear covered with cow dung.
>
> I'm beginning to feel like the arch of a fallen woman.
>
> The big trouble with people is that they look at themselves as a mouse would look in a mirror.
>
> We made it to a cobbler's shop which had not fixed a shoe for easily a lifetime.

The liberated reader, however, can take such lines two ways: to laugh and move on, or to treat them as Zen koans—alogical propositions calculated to break down and subvert imprisoning modes of thinking. One of the main characters in the book is a Zen archer named Zachary from whom the reader learns enough about Zen to take Brossard's hint that much of his imagery functions as koans and that many of his apparently unconnected episodes function as edifying tales such as those told of Zen masters. Brossard does not preface his book with a koan as Salinger does in *Nine Stories,* but the same aesthetic assumptions concerning the applicability of Zen to fiction can be seen at work in both books.

Such imagery also draws upon the rich tradition of European visionary fiction that has played so important a part in shaping Brossard's literary sensibility. The antecedents for the style of ***Wake Up*** are not to be found in American literature (with the possible exception of *Moby-Dick*) but in writers like Rabelais, Rimbaud and the French symbolists, Babel, Kafka, Celine, Genet, Bataille, and the best middle European writers. Brossard's bizarre imagery is not as disconcerting when placed alongside similar uses of synaesthesia in Malaparte's *Kaputt* ("An icy wind was blowing, the color of a dead child's face") or when aligned with Rimbaud's program for the dislocation of the senses in *A Season in Hell.* Among Brossard's American contemporaries, only Burroughs is as bold a saboteur of "literary" English.

After more than five-hundred pages of such anarchistic prose, the final episode (533-40) comes as a bit of a shock. Narrator Gelb, "scattering" as does Slothrop near the end of *Gravity's Rainbow,* is transformed into a female character for a slice of suburban life right out of the pages of the *New Yorker,* with no apparent connection with the rest of the book. The formal juxtaposition is instructive: although the story is superb by conventional standards (see Nason's remarks quoted earlier), the language is curiously flat and the characters insipidly shallow after the verbal extravaganza the reader has been through. Returning to such fiction as this is like returning to ditch water after champagne. But the more important implication concerns the shallowness of *any* non-visionary fiction that does not plumb "the rich state of being" opened up through fantasy and dreams.

Through a dazzling feat of literary sleight of hand, Brossard makes his freak-show narrative appear more "realistic" than this or any other realistic story. He stressed this point in a book review published at the time he was finishing ***Wake Up***:

> An amusing thought: The true absurdists of our time are not the avant-garde at all; they are the institutional realists. For what is more absurd than maintaining erect, dignified postures, setting up smooth-working, clean-cut structures, and saying "sensible" things, when all this "reality" is unleashing madness and surrealism? Our avant-garde absurdists in the arts are, by comparison, drones of reality. What they are acting absurd about is *real,* not at all absurd. The hatred felt by the establishment groups toward the activists-absurdists (in politics as well as in the arts) is based on the realization that these latter groups *are attempting to introduce reality into their world.*[27]

The contrast between Brossard's reality—imaginative, unfettered, soaring—and that of realistic writers could not be greater, and by the end of this phantasmagoric book, the reader should have no doubt which provides the more accurate picture of the human psyche.

Near the middle of ***Wake Up,*** a hunchback reveals his plans for "a real spicy underground film movement for emotionally deprived young. Smut for small fry. I've never understood why pornography should be reserved for grown-ups" (255).[28] Brossard's next publication was a book along these lines retitled ***Dirty Books for Little Folks,*** which he began while teaching at Old Westbury College at the end of the '60s. Privately printed in France by a friend of the author's and suitably illustrated by Max Soumagnac, ***Dirty Books*** is a hilarious collection of Rabelaisian renditions of classic fairy tales in which the Brothers Grimm hit the streets in zoot suits, selling French postcards. (Although the book has done well in Europe in both its English and French versions, it remains all but unknown here because of the lack of a distributor.) The seven stories in this book concern Jack (of beanstalk fame), a streetwise hustler; Piccolo Pete, the Pied Piper of Hamlin ("I'm to rats what James Joyce was to the contemporary novel"); Hansel and Gretel, an incestuous pair of juvenile delinquents whose most recent prank was derailing the 5:14 train from the Land of Nod ("Twenty-seven fairies killed and fourteen baby sitters injured"); Rumpelstiltskin, dressed as a Hell's Angel and expecting kinky returns for his straw-spinning scam; and three versions of Little Red Riding Hood, a sassy skirt into bestiality. Cameos are made by other fairy tale immortals engaged in very un-Disney-like pursuits: Sleeping Beauty rehearsing catatonic trances ("'I think you've just about got it, doll,' said an Old Fairy Coach with her. 'Let's take it from the top one more time.'"); Bambi in her first screen test; Snow White in a gang-shag with the seven dwarfs; and Tom Thumb and the Goose That Laid the Golden Egg getting drunk together on dago red. Everyone uses a racy street slang laced with loopy metaphors, and the result is so absurdly funny that one can easily overlook the subtle implications of these risqué tales. By letting out of the closet the sexual symbolism latent in fairy tales, Brossard not only dramatizes the tales' sexual dynamics but also draws attention to other social dynamics at work therein, such as power structures, class struggles, and economic exploitation—fairy tales as psycho-sociological case studies.

In their own way, Brossard's tales are closer in spirit and subject matter to the tales actually circulated by the peasantry before they were sanitized and immortalized by Perrault and the Brothers Grimm. The original tales contained everything "from rape and sodomy to incest and cannibalism," Robert Darnton has pointed out. "Far from veiling their message with symbols, the storytellers of eighteenth-century France portrayed a world of raw and naked brutality."[29] Brossard portrays just such a world, and in a sense ***Dirty Books*** is a daring attempt to remedy the efforts of generations of "bony, tight-lipped, self-appointed censors and translators [who have] disguised, rerouted, suppressed, and sometimes eliminated entirely certain meanings and messages, whole layers of involvement, that would have made childhood substantially richer, more interesting, less feeble-minded and smelly."[30] But it would be a mistake to overread these tales; they contain depths, to be sure, but are satisfying enough at the surface level to be admitted into the small circle of genuinely funny erotica.

In 1970 Brossard left Old Westbury for the University of Birmingham in England, where he spent a year as a visiting professor at the Centre for Contemporary Cultural Studies. There he wrote his only book with a British setting, a novella entitled ***A Chimney Sweep Comes Clean.*** (The first chapter was published in *Evergreen Review* in 1971, but the book was not published in its entirety until late 1984.) At least three narrators—none of whom, by the way, is actually a chimney sweep—come clean on a variety of British foibles and eccentricities in a comic style that mixes surreal metaphors, Beckettian dialogue, Zen koan one-liners, and philosophical cobwebs spun from puns and non-sequiturs. The result is something like cultural anthropology as written by the Marx Brothers.

Ten loosely linked episodes turn a funhouse mirror on British customs and expose the fundamental propositions underlying that culture. As a gamesome English mum explains (while carnally engaged with the narrator): "The prototypical Englishman-woman is held together by an anxiety system that prevents him from seeing or otherwise making significant contact with emotions or events that would precipitate an irrevocably intimate moment of thereness. The English exist, in a very real sense, by not existing. He is a compilation of seedy abstractions, interlocking arrangements of distancing that permit him to be, at all times, a spectator to his own pseudo-participation. He is the goodbye to his own hello." Although British culture is as ridiculous as its American counterpart, it lacks the viciousness Brossard finds inherent in much of the American experience, and as a result there is a lighter tone here than in most of Brossard's other works.

To be sure, there are some ugly facets to British life that surface here and there in the novella, and Brossard's laughter may indeed be masking the cry of Pagliacci. (In a recent letter to me, he explained: "I wrote ***Chimney*** while I was teaching at Birmingham while living in a charming, nutsy bed-sit—freezing, etc.—in West Kensington. I think I was off my rocker at the time—at the absurdness of my life, at the awfulness of the quality of life in England, at the amusing fucking lunacy of the people—I became the sensibility in the book, out of pain, out of a need to adapt or perish. Laughing while sobbing, you might say.") But the final result is a comic send-up that seems to owe more to amused outrage than to contempt.

But utter contempt is without a doubt the predominant tone of the next book Brossard wrote—the outraged and outrageous ***Raging Joys, Sublime Violations.*** Of the growing body of Vietnam fiction, this book has to be one of the most bizarre literary responses to the war and one of the most damning indictments of the American sensibility responsible for that war. ***Raging Joys*** is not a war novel in any conventional sense, but rather a series of field reports narrated by a cultural anthropologist who describes himself late in the book as "a freelance vulture circling over the compost heap that is western civilization, an insatiable deathbird waiting to plunge upon any morsel of rottenness and decay." (The telling original title for the book was "History as Language and Human Garbage.")

The narrative strategy is brilliant: in each of these episodes Brossard develops a surreal, often raunchy ambience in which official statements on the Vietnam war intrude at unexpected moments: inter-departmental softball strategy in Washington gets mixed up with military tactics in Vietnam; a discussion of Linda Lovelace doubles as a discussion of the Kennedy assassination; a guided tour of Minorca is interrupted by recitations by Vietnamese victims of American bombing missions. Severed from their original contexts, these statements join the surrealistic sideshows going on around them (often a sexual scenario, reinforcing the rape metaphor inherent in imperialism of any sort) and thus become as bizarre as any of Brossard's fantasies. In their new contexts, official statements sound like the ravings of madmen. Several other language permutations occur: the boring predictability of governmental policy announcements clash against the lively unpredictability of Brossard's language. The reader will find him/herself swinging along from vine to vine with Brossard's dazzling language only to suddenly hit a tree in the form of State Department rhetoric. The language of politics emerges as dead and deceptive as the culture it speaks for, whereas Brossard's daring metaphoric prose—free of causality and logic as well as of bourgeois ideology—asserts the primacy of the imagination.

The seventeen "field reports" that make up ***Raging Joys*** range from Tibet to Belgium, from "la belle France" to Washington, D.C., ending in a Minorca that seems to belong more to William Burroughs's Interzone than to Spain. (There is also an interview with an ex-Peace Corpsman in Nicaragua on the problems of American intervention there—a remarkable piece of prophecy on Brossard's part considering he wrote the book in 1971-73.) Also included are a number of scandalously funny interviews with political figures such as Acheson, Allen and John Foster Dulles, Lodge, Reagan, the Kennedy brothers, Nixon, Kissinger, and a letter home to mother by Hubert Humphrey. Each episode is a guerrilla attack against some ideological aspect of the American intervention in Vietnam: the attacks are quick, unexpected, rule-breaking, and retreat back into the hills of disorienting language before the reader knows quite what hit him. This is guerrilla fiction at its most trenchant.

The very form of ***Raging Joys*** represents an attack on conventional writing as yet another facet of imperialist American ideology. Just as Wagner inserted a traditional aria in *Tannhäuser* to show he could write such things if he wanted to, Brossard at one point includes a realistic description of a Nicaraguan outpost that is splendid by conventional literary standards. But this is followed by a fierce denunciation (which in itself exemplifies Brossard's unconventional style) of such conventions:

> Va bene. Traditional literary demands have been met. The illusion of physical reality has been created. Atmosphere and all that. Socio-political implications and details have been cannily supplied. The age old bourgeois writer-reader arrangement has been carried out. And to what end? Smugness and self-deception, esthetic and political status-quoism, cultural and humanistic fraud, and endless spectatorship empathy—those are the ends of such trickery and brown-nosing. You might as well be practising whaling by sticking needles into your favorite drunken blackie. Enough and begone! Vamoos! Can coupling grub worms give birth to dauntless oil rigs? Does standing on your head in a pile of cow manure produce mus of golden rich wheat for our noodles and dumplings? There you have it. In compliance with the demands of the masses, and keeping in mind at all times the affectionate, sincere, and eye-catching principles of self-determination and correct analysis, rather than self denigration and fly-by-night Lin Piao scannings, we shall continue our able bodied struggle for revolutionary change and equal, interest-free socialist brotherhood throughout the emerging Third World. We shall enthusiastically swim swollen torrents of blood even if the blood happens to be our own, to destroy the black hearted aggressor, however, clothed he may be, in sheep's wool or Brooks Bros. suits.

Each reader will have to decide how to field that one; one of the more sobering implications is that we are as much victims of our own language systems as the North Vietnamese were victims of our bombing raids. At any rate, this startling book should earn a privileged place in any future discussions of the American literary response to Vietnam.

After a four-year break from writing in the mid-'70s (the only break in a forty-five year career), Brossard began a mammoth two-headed fictional project that resolved itself into two books. The shorter is entitled ***Postcards: Don't You Just Wish You Were Here!*** and consists of eighteen folksy walking tours through a Kafkaesque Amerika of towns like Over My Dead Body, Minnesota; Cast a Cold Eye, New Jersey; and Horse of Another Color, Maine. As eerie as it is funny, ***Postcards*** extends Brossard's use of the non-sequitur to expose the general non-sequitur nature of modern America.[31] The longer work, ***Come Out with Your Hands Up!,*** begins with a "postcard"—Mum's the Word, South Carolina—but soon opens out into a vast surrealistic fiction of bewildering proportions. Like ***Wake Up,*** which it resembles in some ways, ***Come Out*** uses a central narrative consciousness through whom a torrent of voices rushes, flooding the book with the collective unconscious of our psychotic age, with special attention to countercultural movements in Europe. ***Postcards*** has recently been published in England, but ***Come Out*** awaits a publisher.

Closing the Gap is Brossard's latest, shortest, and most ethereal book. All ties with recognizable fiction are finally cut in these ten "meditations" (for lack of a better word) on such subjects as intimacy, cave explorers, handmaidens, backbiting, den mothers, and clochards. But such unlikely subjects are merely subjects for brilliant improvisations in a style that combines dazzling wit and wordplay with an edgy sense of foreboding. Here, for example, is Brossard on intimacy:

> Isn't it about time we laid down some guidelines for intimacy? Is it unreasonable to suggest that intimacy be required to account for itself? There are those among us who feel that it should have a strong sense of the past. These people argue that in no way is this interchangeable with nostalgia. They say that nostalgia is a cover-up.
>
> Intimacy has friends in high places. It would like to rule the roost, but we're not going to let it. In all too many circumstances, it has carte blanche. On more than one occasion, it has refused to pay the piper.
>
> Up in the mysterious north, a disease-resistant strain of it is developing. Frankly, this is no cause for rejoicing.
>
> We must start somewhere. Time is running out, as usual. First, victims of intimacy must be reinstated. Second, we must keep it from our children, *no matter what the price!*

Elsewhere, he rings punning changes on a particular word or phrase; confiding that "Evidence is mounting that we have been neglecting our handmaidens," Brossard pulls one rabbit after another out of his vernacular hat:

> They are walking about in hand-me-downs. They are living from hand to mouth. Making do with handouts. And it would appear that they are getting absolutely no feedback. Throwing them completely on the mercy of hearsay. They're still too proud to stoop to lip service.

And so on, concluding with mock solemnity: "Can the common man in our streets really be expected to make a wise choice between Made by Hand and Hand In Your Maidens?"

This is obviously language at play, words sporting on the page like dolphins in the sea. The principle at work here can be found in Huizinga's *Homo Ludens* (with which, as ***Did Christ Make Love?*** shows, Brossard is familiar):

> In the making of speech and language the spirit is continually "sparking" between matter and mind, as it were, playing with this wondrous nominative faculty. Behind every abstract expression there lie the boldest of metaphors, and every metaphor is a play upon words.[32]

Closing the Gap reminds us of the metaphoric origin of our most common words and phrases by putting the oldest of dogs through lively new tricks.

Encroaching upon this playfulness, however, is a faint air of dread and menace, a premonition of danger, and in fact the book closes on such a note:

> Covering one's tracks.
>
> It's never too early to begin.

Like receiving somber advice in a dream that turns to gibberish upon waking, the reader will find the otherworldly language of ***Closing the Gap*** as difficult to comprehend as a Zen koan and often as unsettling as the deadly wit of Lear's Fool. Time and again, the smile is wiped from the reader's face, the carpet pulled out from under him by an unnerving witticism. A glimpse is caught of "the abyss which becomes visible in the gaps of existence" (to quote again from Gershom Scholem). But in the end, Brossard more often than not closes these gaps with bravura feats of wordplay reminiscent of Shem the Penman:

> Maintaining our balance, but at the same time not paying all that much attention to overdraughts, keeping our nose up wind, yet always on the ready to sniff out a dead beat, planning eventually to put our best foot forward, though not so swellheaded as to overlook mounting evidence that other strategies have taken the adversary more by surprise, fingering the stone around our neck with the same illicit elegance that old Walt fingered his girlish ambiguities, we smile and prepare to face the music. We have an edge. We have discovered something: the beat of that distant drummer is a recording.

It is safe to say that the distance Brossard has traveled from ***Who Walk in Darkness*** to ***Closing the Gap*** is as great as that of any writer of our time. The variety and scope of his enormous output makes it difficult to categorize Brossard's work, although Robert Buckeye's "psychic novel" probably comes closest to the mark.[33] Suffice it to say Chandler Brossard is a unique presence on the American literary scene and deserves far greater attention than he has hitherto received. If you missed Lear's Fool doing his stand-up routine at Dachau, catch Brossard's act: he wrote the Fool's material, and works matinees to boot.

Notes

1. Chandler Brossard, "Fiction and 'Literature'" (1955), 508; the quotations that follow are from 507—see the checklist for full bibliographic details on all cited works.
2. Chandler Brossard, "Sherwood Anderson" (1951), 612; the block quotation that follows is from the same page.
3. The title is taken from part five of Eliot's "Ash Wednesday," but echoes a number of biblical texts: Pss. 82:5, 88:14-18 (the epigraph to the novel), 91:6; Eccles. 2:14; John 8:12, and 1 John 2:11. Brossard's original title was "Night Sky," but his editor James Laughlin preferred its present title.
4. Susan Sontag, *Against Interpretation and Other Essays* (New York: Delta, 1966), 16-17.
5. I quote from the 1972 unexpurgated version of *Who Walk*; all other references to Brossard's books will be to the first editions (see checklist) and will be placed parenthetically within my text.
6. Delmore Schwartz, "Fiction Chronicle: The Wrongs of Innocence and Experience," *Partisan Review* 19 (1952): 355. For Schwartz's discreditable role in the novel's publication, see Brossard's "Tentative Visits to the Cemetery" earlier in this issue.
7. *The Scene Before You,* 16. This collection also reprints Anatole Broyard's "A Portrait of the Hipster" (1948); taken together, Klonsky and Broyard's essays furnish useful background material for Brossard's novel. Coincidentally, these two were the ones Delmore Schwartz thought he recognized in the book (see n. 6) as Max Glazer (Klonsky) and Henry Porter (Broyard). Similarly, William Gaddis thought he recognized himself in Harry Lees, the Harvard dandy who drinks too much and is mugged at the end. But Brossard wrote me (18 June 1983): "I am not into, nor was I ever into, the roman à clef, or other such cleft palates, wop or otherwise."
8. See the "aesthetics" of burglary propounded in Genet's *Miracle of the Rose*; Brossard is a great admirer of Genet's work.
9. Bruce Cook, *The Beat Generation* (New York: Scribner's, 1971), 48.
10. Jerry H. Bryant, *The Open Decision: The Contemporary American Novel and Its Intellectual Background* (New York: Free Press, 1970), 219-21.
11. Seymour Krim, "'Fiction'—and Total Imaginative Writing" (1958), rpt. in his *Views of a Nearsighted Cannoneer,* rev. ed. (New York: Dutton, 1968), 224. See also Krim's letter to the editor of the *New York Times Book Review* (25 October 1953, p. 48) protesting Herbert Mitgang's incompetent review (6 September 1953, p. 12).
12. In another hallucination, George watches a crowd passing around his father's clothes and ripping them to shreds (78), reminiscent of an incident in Christ's passion: Matt. 27:35.
13. There are some close parallels: Brossard's "fictional moments" in *American Mercury* (1951) resemble the brief interchapters in Hemingway's *In Our Time,* and his story "Some Other Way" seems deliberately modelled on Hemingway's "The Sea Change." (It is perhaps only coincidental that the name of the father in the Oedipal psychodrama *The Bold Saboteurs* is Ernest.) For Brossard's opinion of Hemingway, see his essay "Everybody's Old Man" (1950).
14. Brossard and Pound corresponded in the early '50s, and occasionally the poet would evaluate Brossard's works in progress.
15. Richard Nason, "A Man For All Obsessions," *Village Voice* 17 (26 July 1973): 26.
16. Norman Mailer, *Advertisements for Myself* (New York: Putnam's, 1959), 343; the succeeding quotations are from 339 and 355. Because of the close connection in thought between Mailer and Brossard, it should come as no surprise to learn that Mailer once wrote that "parts I had read of *The Bold Saboteurs* were sufficiently interesting for me to put the book away—it was a little too close to some of my own notions" (ibid., 469). But Mailer told Brossard privately that he had not only read the whole book but "liked it enormously" (Peter Manso, *Mailer: His Life and Times* [New York: Simon and Schuster, 1985], 244).
17. From the dustjacket copy.
18. Written in 1961 and originally entitled "The Wolf Leaps" (from Villon's *Testament*: "Necessity makes men misapprehend / Hunger makes the wolf leap from the woods"), it was retitled by Bobbs-Merrill when they published it in 1973. A reference to the Viet Cong (124), however, indicates Brossard made at least a few changes in the intervening dozen years.
19. I have omitted a discussion of Brossard's half-dozen plays because, with the exception of two one-act plays reprinted in *Wake Up,* the texts remain unpublished. See Brossard's account of his brief dramatic career in *Contemporary Authors Autobiography Series,* 69—hereafter abbreviated *CAAS.*
20. Nason, 24.
21. *CAAS,* 69-70. The first book (under the title "She Cried Out to Me") is among Brossard's papers at the George Arents Library, Syracuse University; the second is in the hands of his former wife.
22. Eric Baizer and Richard Peabody, "Politics & Libidos: The Irreverent World of Chandler Brossard" [interview], *Gargoyle* 14 (1980): 7. See *CAAS,* 70.
23. Daniel Talbot, "The Way To Get at Spain," *The Nation* 206 (20 May 1968): 674. Brossard disagrees with this reading.
24. Brossard would repeat this pattern of flight and return in the 1970s. His decision to return to America, neces-

sary if he were to continue writing, is the subject of one of his best and most engaging essays, "Coming Back" (1977).

25. Chandler Brossard, "Commentary (Vituperative)" (1972), 110. This essay is required reading for students of Brossard's work.

26. Tom Wolfe, *The New Journalism* (New York: Harper & Row, 1973), 30-31.

27. Chandler Brossard, "All Fall Down: The Culture of Collapse" (1969), 16.

28. There is an earlier reference to "Smut for small fry" in Brossard's rollicking program notes for the movie *Dead of Night*: "Problems of Being the Real Me" (1960; rpt. 1974), where they figure as a series of stories to which J. Edgar Hoover is addicted.

29. Robert Darnton, *The Great Cat Massacre and Other Episodes in French Cultural History* (New York: Basic Books, 1984), 15.

30. From Brossard's unpublished fiction *Come Out with Your Hands Up!*—a work that rivals *Wake Up* in length and complexity. The quotation is from p. 322 of the typescript.

31. Roughly half of the collection appeared in the first issue of *Pacific Poetry and Fiction Review* (1978), where it is described as "from an ongoing fiction titled Somebody's Been Sleeping In My Bed"—an early title for *Come Out.*

32. Johann Huizinga, *Homo Ludens* (Boston: Beacon, 1955), 4.

33. Robert Buckeye, "The Anatomy of the Psychic Novel," *Critique* 9, no. 2 (1967): 33-45.

A Checklist of Writings by Chandler Brossard

BOOKS

Who Walk in Darkness

New York: New Directions, 1952

London: John Lehman, 1952.

New York: New American Library, 1954.

Ciel de Nuit. Trans. Janine Ribes. Paris: Gallimard, 1954.

New York: New Directions, 1962 (paperback).

New York: Lancer, 1966.

London: Sphere, 1971.

New York: Harrow, 1972 (unexpurgated version).

The Bold Saboteurs

New York: Farrar, Straus and Young, 1953.

New York: Dell, 1954.

Les Vailliants saboteurs. Trans. Jean Rosenthal. Paris: Gallimard, 1955.

New York: Lancer, 1962, 1966.

London: Sphere, 1971.

New York: Harrow, 1972.

Paris Escort by "Daniel Harper"

New York: Eton, 1953.

The Wrong Turn by "Daniel Harper"

New York: Avon, 1954.

All Passion Spent

New York: Popula, 1954.

Episode with Erika. New York: Belmont, 1963.

London: Sphere, 1971.

The Double View

New York: Dial, 1960.

Lo Scorno. Trans. Adriana Pellegrini. Milan: Longanesi, 1964.

New York: Award House, mind-'60s.

London: Sphere, 1971.

New York: Harrow, 1972.

The Girls in Rome

New York: New American Library, 1961.

London: New English Library, 1962.

Ein Amerikaner in Rom. Heyne-Bucher, 1962.

We Did the Strangest Things. New York: Belmont, 1968.

A Man For All Women (an expanded version of *Paris Escort*)

Greenwich, CT: Fawcett, 1966.

London: Sphere, 1971.

Illya: That Man from U.N.C.L.E. by "Iris-Marie Barrosard"

New York: Pocket Books, 1966.

The Insane World of Adolf Hitler

Greenwich, CT: Fawcett, 1966.

The Spanish Scene

New York: Viking, 1968.

Wake Up. We're Almost There

New York: Richard W. Baron, 1971.

New York: Harrow, 1972.

Did Christ Make Love?

Indianapolis: Bobbs-Merrill, 1973.

Dirty Books for Little Folks

La Chapelle la Reine, France: Daniel Cointe, 1978.

Contes cochons pour les petits. Trans. and published by Daniel Cointe, 1978

Raging Joys, Sublime Violations

Silver Spring, MD: Cherry Valley, 1981 (cloth and paper).

A Chimney Sweep Comes Clean

San Jose, CA: Realities Library, 1984.

Closing the Gap

Heslington, Yorskhire: Redbeck Presss, 1986.

Postcards: Don't You Just Wish You Were Here!

Heslington, Yorkshire: Redbeck Press, 1987.

BOOKS EDITED BY CHANDLER BROSSARD

The Scene Before You: A New Approach to American Culture

New York: Rinehart, 1955.

The First Time

New York: Pyramid, 1957.

London: Panther, 1962.

Desire in the Suburbs

New York: Lancer, 1962.

The Pangs of Love: Stories of the Young

Evanston, IL: Regency, 1962.

The Nymphets, ed. "Daniel Harper"

New York: Lancer, 1963.

18 Best Stories by Edgar Allen Poe, with Vincent Price

New York: Dell, 1965.

Wives and Lovers

New York: Dell, 1965.

Esposas y Amantes. Trans. Leonor Tejada. Organización Editorial Novano, S. A. 1967.

Love Me, Love Me!

Greenwich, CT: Fawcett, 1966.

Marriage Games

New York: Pyramid, 1967.

I Want More of This

New York: Dell, 1967.

In Other Beds

New York: Belmont, 1968.

STORT STORIES (EXCLUDING THOSE REPRINTED FROM—OR INCORPORATED INTO—THE NOVELS)

"A Very Nice Place." *Prairie Schooner* 21 (Winter 1947): 454-58.

"A Sense of Relief." *Tomorrow* 8 (January 1949): 43-45.

"An Early Snow." *New American Mercury* 71 (December 1950)

[Untitled "fictional moments"] *American Mercury* 72 (March 19510: 358; (April 1951): 466; 73 (August 1951): 115.

"The Way It Was in Italy." *American Mecury* 72 (April 1951): 442-44.

"Vacation for Three." American Mercury 72 (June 1951): 670-74.

"Jewel of the Soul." *New Directions in Prose & Poetry*: 13 Ed. James Laughlin. New York: New Directions, 1951, 220-31.

"Sunday Revelation." *Tales of Love and Fury.* Ed. Daniel Talbot. New York: Avon, 1951, 105-11; rpt. in The First Time.

"Mascara." In *The First Time* (pseud. Janet Ney); rpt. in *Desire in the Suburbs and In Other Beds.*

"Playground." In *Desire in the Suburbs.*

"The Closing of This Door Must Be Oh, So Gentle." *The Dial: An Annual of Fiction.* New York: Dial/Apollo Editions, 1962, 44-62; rpt. in Nelson Algren's *Own Book of Lonesome Monsters* (Lancer, 1962; Bernard Geis, 1963; Panther, 1964).

"The Peculiar Husband." *Cavalier* 15 (December 1965): 52, 77-78, 80.

"A New World for Deborah." In *Love Me, Love Me!* (pseud. Martha Backer); rpt. in *In Other Beds.*

"One If for Sorrow, Two If for Joy." In *Love Me, Love Me!*

"Some Other Way." In *Love Me, Love Me!* (pseud. Eugenie Motherlant Clark).

"What of These Pleasures?" In *Wives and Lovers* (pseud. Mimi Harper); rpt. in *Marriage Games* and *In Other Beds.*

"The Castle At Last." In *Wives and Lovers*; rpt. in Marriage Games.

"Trespassers Will Be Violated." In *Marriage Games* (pseud. Kenneth C. Parker).

"The Strange Pick-Up." In *Marriage Games* (pseud. Guy de Maupassant).

"Othello's Sister." In *In Other Beds* (pseud. Angela B. Garrison).

ESSAYS (A SELECTION)

"Plaint of a Gentile Intellectual." *Commentary* 10 (August 1950): 154-56; rpt. in *The Scene Before You.*

"Everybody's Old Man." *New American Mercury* 71 (December 1950): 698-701.

"Nize Baby, Et Op All de Prose." *New American Mercury* 72 (january 1951): 88-92.

"The Patterns of Tyranny." *American Mercury* 72 (March 1951): 354-58.

"Sherwood Anderson: A Sweet Singer, 'A Smooth Son of a Bitch.'" *American Mercury* 72 (May 1951): 611-16.

"Reefers and Glowworms." *American Mercury* 73 (August 1951): 92-95.

"Unstable Equilibrium." *American Mercury* 73 (August 1951): 111-15.

"Fictions and 'Literature.'" *Commentary* 19 (May 1955): 505, 507-08.

"A Visit with Dr. Erich Fromm." *Look* 28 (5 May 1964): 50, 52, 56.

"Whatever Became of Fiction?" *Cavalier* 16 (August 1966): 67-69.

"Dr. Edgar Friedenberg: Our Most Devastating Critic." *Look* 31 (30 May 1967): 73-75.

"The Ritual of Originality." *The Nation* 206 (29 April 1968): 575-76.

"All Fall Down: The Culture of Collapse." *Guardian,* 26 April 1969, book supplement, 15.

"Why the Death Machine Could Die Laughing." *Penthouse* 3 (April 1972): 32-34, 104, 106.

"Commenatry (Vituperative): The Ficition Scene." *Harper's* 244 (June 1972): 106-10.

"Problems of Being the Real Me." *Film Comment* 10, no. 3 (May-June 1974): 21.

"Letter from Exile." *Harper's* 253 (September 1976): 30–31.

"Coming Back." *San Francisco Review of Books,* June 1977, 19–21.

[Autobiographical essay] *Contemporary Authors Autobiography Series,* vol. 2 Ed. Adele Sarkissian. Detroit: Gale Research, 1985, 63-78.

FURTHER READING

Criticism

Beidler, Philip D. "*Raging Joys, Sublime Violations*: The Vietnam War in the Fiction of Charles Brossard." *Review of Contemporary Fiction* 7, no. 1 (spring 1987): 166-75.

Assesses Raging Joys, Sublime Violations, *particularly its characterization of the Vietnam War.*

Bowers, John. "My Chandler Brossard." *Review of Contemporary Fiction* 7, no. 1 (spring 1987): 91-3.

Includes personal recollections of Brossard, whom many considered the consummate literary hipster.

Bryant, Jerry H. "Chandler Brossard, Cynic." *Review of Contemporary Fiction* 7, no. 1 (spring 1987): 143-9.

Examines the lack of critical interest in Brossard and traces how his prose style changed over time from Who Walk in Darkness *to* Dirty Books for Little Folks.

Coyne, John. "*Dirty Books.*" *Review of Contemporary Fiction* 7, no. 1 (spring 1987): 156-60.

Examines Dirty Books for Little Folks *for its political and sexual content, its use of non-language, and the truth that resides within fairy tales.*

Friedenberg, Edgar Z. "*The Bold Saboteurs.*" *Review of Contemporary Fiction* 7, no. 1 (spring 1987): 120-5.

Examines the narrative language of The Bold Saboteurs *and considers the ultimately dislikable character Yogi and his relation to 1960s American culture.*

Holland-Skinner, Con. "Chandler Brossard—A View from England." *Review of Contemporary Fiction* 7, no. 1 (spring 1987): 103-08.

Briefly considers four of Brossard's novels and discusses how their presentation and themes have held up over time.

Keifetz, Norman. "The Labors of Yogi." *Review of Contemporary Fiction* 7, no. 1 (spring 1987): 128-31.

Provides a character sketch of Yogi in The Bold Saboteurs *that considers him to be a Herculean figure.*

Krim, Seymour. "Chandler, *WWD,* and, Inevitably, Hopefully Not Intrusively, Me." *Review of Contemporary Fiction* 7, no. 1 (spring 1987): 87-90.

Offers personal reflections on the Greenwich Village of the 1940s as presented in Who Walk in Darkness *and considers how the work has stood the test of time.*

Lykiard, Alexis. "The Bright Wonderful Surface." *Review of Contemporary Fiction* 7, no. 1 (spring 1987): 113-19.

Examines several of Brossard's novels from a European perspective, centering on his writing style and the ways he challenged western society's concept of identity in a post-World War II world.

Moore, Steven. "An Interview with Chandler Brossard." *Review of Contemporary Fiction* 7, no. 1 (spring 1987): 28-53.

Discusses Brossard's life and career, his thoughts on contemporary American literature, his improvisational approach to writing, and the reasons his work has garnered such limited critical attention.

———. Foreword to *Who Walk in Darkness,* by Chandler Brossard. New York: Herodias, 2000, 245 p.

Foreword to the 2000 edition of Who Walk in Darkness *that likens the novel to a black-and-white documentary of post-World War II American malaise. Moore also explores some of the novel's significant themes and traces its publication history.*

Ramnath, S. "Chandler Brossard: A Critical Study of *Lusty Books for Little Folks.*" *Review of Contemporary Fiction* 7, no. 1 (spring 1987): 154-5.

Examines Dirty Books for Little Folks *for its political commentary embedded within the sexual, lewd retellings of famous fairy tales.*

Solomon, Barbara Probst. "*The Spanish Scene.*" *Review of Contemporary Fiction* 7, no. 1 (spring 1987): 150-3.

Considers The Spanish Scene, *praising Brossard's clear understanding of the political climate of 1960s Spain and his ability to go beyond cultural myth to present a more realistic picture of the country and its people.*

Talbot, Daniel. "The Way to Get at Spain." *Nation* (20 May 1968): 674-5.

Review of The Spanish Scene *that argues Brossard was able to capture the real Spain by cutting below the surface of language and popular misconceptions about the country and its political culture.*

OTHER SOURCES FROM GALE:

Additional coverage of Brossard's life and career is contained in the following sources published by the Gale Group: *Contemporary Authors,* Vols. 61-64, 142; *Contemporary Authors Autobiography Series,* Vol. 2; *Contemporary Authors New Revision Series,* Vols. 8, 56; *Dictionary of Literary Biography,* Vol. 16; and *Literature Resource Center.*

WILLIAM S. BURROUGHS

(1914 - 1997)

(Full name William Seward Burroughs. Also wrote under the pseudonym William Lee) American novelist, short story writer, and essayist.

Along with Jack Kerouac and Allen Ginsberg, Burroughs was one of the founding members of the Beat Generation. His most famous work, *Naked Lunch* (1959), is a nonlinear narrative involving drug addiction, homosexuality, and outrageous social and political satire. The bizarre events of Burroughs's life and his unconventional writings are often intertwined in both the public imagination and the critical reception of his work.

BIOGRAPHICAL INFORMATION

Burroughs was born in St. Louis, Missouri, to Laura Lee Burroughs, a descendant of Robert E. Lee, and Mortimer P. Burroughs, whose family owned the Burroughs Corporation, manufacturers of adding machines. Ivy Ledbetter Lee was young Burroughs's uncle and a pioneer in the field of public relations whose clients included John D. Rockefeller and Adolph Hitler. Burroughs's uncle, and his ability to manipulate language to less-than-honorable ends, had a profound effect on his nephew's views on the controlling powers of language. Burroughs was educated at New Mexico's Los Alamos Ranch School and at Harvard University, where he earned a B.A. in English literature in 1936. He briefly studied medicine at the University of Vienna and did graduate work at Harvard and Mexico City College. Supported by an allowance from his wealthy family, Burroughs traveled to Europe after his graduation, where he married Ilse Herzfeld Klapper in 1937, apparently to help her escape from the Nazis; they were divorced in 1946. In 1943 Burroughs accompanied his friend Lucien Carr to New York City, where he met Allen Ginsberg and Jack Kerouac at Columbia University. There he became involved in the local drug scene and began financing his habit with petty thievery. Although Burroughs was homosexual, he married Kerouac's friend Joan Vollmer in 1946, and the couple moved first to Texas, where their son, Billy, was born in 1947, and then to Mexico City two years later. In 1951, Burroughs accidentally killed Vollmer while attempting to shoot a glass off the top of her head; both were drunk at the time. Burroughs left Mexico and traveled to South America, Europe, and eventually North Africa, where he met artist Brion Gysin, with whom he would later collaborate on several experimental art and literary projects. During this period Burroughs's heroin habit began to seriously impair his ability to function and was reaching a point where he could no longer afford to supply his increasing need for the drug. He enrolled in a new treatment program in London and for a time was cured of his addiction. Two years later, in 1959, Burroughs published his most famous work, *The Naked Lunch* (better known simply as *Naked Lunch*). He continued to write novels into the late 1980s and enjoyed a cult following as a counterculture figure. He served as inspiration for both the hippie and punk movements; for the science fiction subgenre known as cyberpunk; for musicians such as Laurie Anderson, who appropriated his famous saying "language is a virus"; and for filmmaker David Cronenberg, who made a film of *Naked Lunch* in 1991. Burroughs died in Lawrence, Kansas, on August 2, 1997.

MAJOR WORKS

Burroughs's first published work was the autobiographical novel *Junkie: Confessions of an Unredeemed Drug Addict* (1953), written under the name William Lee. The book's subject matter—a detailed description of drug addiction and the life of petty crime required to support a heroin habit—was so controversial that only the small paperback house Ace Books would consider publishing even an edited version; the unedited version was not published until 1977. Burroughs's most famous work, the experimental novel *Naked Lunch,* was apparently cobbled together in random order from notes Burroughs had made during his stay in Tangier. The work has no discernible point of view, and the varied events of the narrative appear to be completely unrelated to one another. *Naked Lunch* was the first of what many critics consider a tetralogy that also includes *The Soft Machine* (1961), *The Ticket That Exploded* (1962), and *Nova Express* (1964). In these works Burroughs continued to employ his unconventional narrative style and added two new composition techniques: the cut-up method and the fold-in method. The first, inspired by Burroughs's friend Brion Gysin, involves cutting texts—either original or found—into pieces and reassembling them randomly; the second involves folding sections of text in half and putting two unrelated halves next to each other to create a new arrangement of words. In the 1970s, Burroughs for the most part abandoned these techniques in the composition of his second series of novels, which included *The Wild Boys: A Book of the Dead* (1971), *Exterminator!* (1973), and *Port of Saints* (1973). A third wave of novels, sometimes referred to as a trilogy, appeared in the 1980s and included *Cities of the Red Night* (1981), *The Place of Dead Roads* (1984), and *The Western Lands* (1987).

CRITICAL RECEPTION

Burroughs's work has been variously regarded by critics as either incomprehensible and pornographic or as the inspired work of a literary genius. His unconventional narrative techniques, particularly in his early works, have inspired both positive and negative critical assessments of the effectiveness of the end result. Ihab Hassan has stated that there is a certain order and method behind even the more bizarre elements of Burroughs's style. Hassan contends that the cut-up method is used very skillfully, juxtaposing language in a way that creates unexpected meaning of significant value. John Tytell calls Burroughs "the most experimental of the Beats" and finds his novels to be characterized by "a labyrinthine density." David Lodge, however, views Burroughs as "deeply confused" and judges *Naked Lunch* to be a "very indecent book" and *Nova Express* a "very tedious book." Several critics have pointed out the frequency with which Burroughs employs metamorphosis as a metaphor and central theme in his work. Hassan characterizes the mutations of characters, both human and non-human, in Burroughs's works as a "process of disintegration." Mary McCarthy claims that such metamorphoses are used as punishments and that Burroughs himself is essentially a reformer, albeit one whose message gets lost in the depth of his pessimism and the bizarre quality of his satire. Referring to *Naked Lunch,* McCarthy concludes: "The book is alive, like a basketful of crabs, and common sense cannot get hold of it to extract a moral." Tytell shares this perception of Burroughs's fiction, referring to the author's "cruel pessimism and the absolute lack of hope." Duncan Wu, however, views Burroughs as a writer in the tradition of William Wordsworth, who was also fascinated with the process of metamorphosis. In addition, according to Wu, both Burroughs and Wordsworth believed in paradise or a promised land, and thus Burroughs's writings are "essentially moral." Perhaps most at odds with the evaluations of other critics is Wu's contention that "Burroughs has always been an optimistic writer," a trait which he claims can be traced to the writer's ability to recover from his heroin addiction. Despite the many differences among scholars, the fact remains that although Burroughs's most famous work was produced more than forty years ago, it continues to inspire heated academic discourse. Geoff Ward believes that Burroughs's significance endures because he, alone among the Beat writers, remained unregenerate and "incorruptibly deviant."

PRINCIPAL WORKS

Junkie: The Confessions of an Unredeemed Drug Addict [as William Lee] (novel) 1953; republished as *Junky* 1977

The Naked Lunch (novel) 1959

The Soft Machine (novel) 1961; revised edition 1966

The Ticket That Exploded (novel) 1962; revised edition 1967

Nova Express (novel) 1964

The Wild Boys: A Book of the Dead (novel) 1971; revised edition 1979

Exterminator! (novel) 1973

Port of Saints (novel) 1973

The Third Mind [with Brion Gysin] (essay) 1978

Cities of the Red Night (novel) 1981

The Place of Dead Roads (novel) 1984

The Adding Machine: Collected Essays (essays) 1985

Queer (novel) 1985

The Western Lands (novel) 1987

The Letters of William S. Burroughs, 1945-1959 (letters) 1993

PRIMARY SOURCES

WILLIAM S. BURROUGHS (LETTER DATE 1953)

SOURCE: Burroughs, William S. "In Search of Yage (1953)." In *The Yage Letters,* pp. 3-48. San Francisco: City Lights Books, 1963.

Following the accidental shooting death of his wife, Joan, in Mexico, Burroughs was forced to leave that country. For a time afterwards, he traveled throughout South America in search of a drug called yage. The following letter excerpts, written in 1953 and published in 1963, find Burroughs relating his travels and experiences to Allen Ginsberg.

March 3

Hotel Nueva Regis, Bogota

Dear Al:

Bogota horrible as ever. I had my papers corrected with the aid of U.S. Embassy. Figure to sue the truss off PAA for fucking up the tourist card.

I have attached myself to an expedition—in a somewhat vague capacity to be sure—consisting of Doc Schindler, two Colombian Botanists, two English Broom Rot specialists from the Cocoa Commission, and will return to the Putumayo in convoy. Will write full account of trip when I get back to this town for the third time.

April 15

Hotel Nuevo Regis, Bogota

Dear Al:

Back in Bogota. I have a crate of Yage. I have taken it and know more or less how it is prepared. By the way you may see my picture in *Exposure.* I met a reporter going in as I was going out. Queer to be sure but about as appetizing as a hamper of dirty laundry. Not even after two months in the brush, my dear. This character is shaking down the South American continent for free food and transport, and discounts on everything he buys with a "We-got-like-two-kinds-of-publicity-favorable-and-unfavorable-which-do-you-want-Jack?" Routine. What a shameless mooch. But who am I to talk?

Flashback: Retraced my journey through Cali, Popayan and Pasto to Macoa. I was interested to note that Mocoa dragged Schindler and the two Englishmen as much as it did me.

This trip I was treated like visiting royalty under the misapprehension I was a representative of the Texas Oil Company travelling incognito. (Free boat rides, free plane rides, free chow; eating in officers' mess, sleeping in the governor's house.)

The Texas Oil Company surveyed the area a few years ago, found no oil and pulled out. But everyone in the Putumayo believes the Texas Company will return. Like the second coming of Christ. The governor told me the Texas Company had taken two samples of oil 80 miles apart and it was the same oil, so there was a pool of the stuff 80 miles across under Macoa. I heard this same story in a back water area of East Texas where the oil company made a survey and found no oil and pulled out. Only in Texas the pool was 1000 miles across. The beat town psyche is joined the world over like the oil pool. You take a sample anywhere and it's the same shit. And the governor thinks they are about to build a railroad from Pasto to Macoa, and an airport. As a matter of fact the whole of Putumayo region is on the down grade. The rubber business is shot, the cocoa is eaten up with broom rot, no price on rotenone since the war, land is poor and there is no way to get produce out. The dawdling psychophrenia of small town boosters. Like I should think some day soon boys will start climbing in through the transom and tunneling under the door.

Several times when I was drunk I told some one, "Look. There is no oil here. That's why Texas pulled out. They won't ever come back. Understand?" But they couldn't believe it.

We went out to visit a German who owned a finca near Macoa. The British went looking for wild coca with an Indian guide. I asked the German about Yage.

"Sure," he said, "My Indians all use it." A half hour later I had 20 pounds of Yage vine. No trek through virgin jungle and some old white haired character saying, "I have been expecting you my son." A nice German 10 minutes from Macoa.

The German also made a date for me to take Yage with the local Brujo (at that time I had no idea how to prepare it.)

The medicine man was around 70 with a baby smooth face. There was a sly gentleness about him like an old time junkie. It was getting dark when I arrived at this dirt floor thatch shack for my Yage appointment. First thing he asked did I have a bottle. I brought a quart of aguardiente out of my knapsack and handed it to him. He took a long drink and passed the bottle to his assistant. I didn't take any as I wanted straight Yage kicks. The Brujo put the bottle beside him and squatted down by a bowl set on a tripod. Behind the bowl was a wood shrine with a picture of the Virgin, a crucifix, a wood idol, feathers and little packages tied with ribbons. The Brujo sat there a long time without moving. He took another long swig on the bottle. The women retired behind a bamboo partition and were not seen again. The Brujo began crooning over the bowl. I caught "Yage Pintar" repeated over and over. He shook a little broom over a bowl and made a swishing noise. This is to whisk away evil spirits who might slip in the Yage. He took a drink and wiped his mouth and went on crooning. You can't hurry a Brujo. Finally he uncovered the bowl and dipped about an ounce more or less of black liquid which he handed me in a dirty red plastic cup. The liquid was oily and phosphorescent. I drank it straight down. Bitter foretaste of nausea. I handed the cup back and the medicine man and the assistant took a drink.

I sat there waiting for results and almost immediately had the impulse to say, "That wasn't enough. I need more." I have noticed this inexplicable impulse on the two occasions when I got an overdose of junk. Both times before the shot took effect I said, "This wasn't enough. I need more."

Roy told me about a man who came out of jail clean and nearly died in Roy's room. "He took the shot and right away said, 'That wasn't enough' and fell on his face out cold. I dragged him out in the hall and called an ambulance. He lived."

In two minutes a wave of dizziness swept over me and the hut began swimming. It was like going under ether, or when you are very drunk and lie down and the bed spins. Blue flashes passed in front of my eyes. The hut took on an archaic far-Pacific look with Easter Island heads carved in the support posts. The assistant was outside lurking there with the obvious intent to kill me. I was hit by violent, sudden nausea and rushed for the door hitting my shoulder against the door post. I felt the shock but no pain. I could hardly walk. No coordination. My feet were like blocks of wood. I vomited violently leaning against a tree and fell down on the ground in helpless misery. I felt numb as if I was covered with layers of cotton. I kept trying to break out of this numb dizziness. I was saying over and over, "All I want is out of here." An uncontrollable mechanical silliness took possession of me. Hebrephrenic meaningless repetitions. Larval beings passed before my eyes in a blue haze, each one giving an obscene, mocking squawk (I later identified this squawking as the croaking of frogs)—I must have vomited six times. I was on all fours convulsed with spasms of nausea. I could hear retching and groaning as if I was some one else. I was lying by a rock. Hours must have passed. The medicine man was standing over me. I looked at him for a long time before I believed he was really there saying, "Do you want to come into the house?" I said, "No," and he shrugged and went back inside.

My arms and legs began to twitch uncontrollably. I reached for my nembutals with numb wooden fingers. It must have taken me ten minutes to open the bottle and pour out five capsules. Mouth was dry and I chewed the nembutals down somehow. The twitching spasms subsided slowly and I felt a little better and went into the hut. The blue flashes still in front of my eyes. Lay down and covered myself with a blanket. I had a chill like malaria. Suddenly very drowsy. Next morning I was all right except for a feeling of lassitude and a slight back-log nausea. I paid off the Brujo and walked back to town.

We all went down to Puerto Assis that day. Schindler kept complaining the Putumayo had deteriorated since he was there ten years ago. "I never made a Botanical expedition like this before," he said. "All these farms and *people*. You have to walk miles to get to the jungle."

Schindler had two assistants to carry his luggage, cut down trees and press specimens. One of them was an Indian from the Vaupes region where the method of preparing Yage is different from the Putumayo Kofan method. In Putumayo the Indians cut the vines into 8 inch pieces using about five sections to a person. The pieces of vine are crushed with a rock and boiled with a double handful of leaves from another plant—tentatively identified as ololiqui—the mixture is boiled all day with a small amount of water and reduced to about two ounces of liquid.

In the Vaupes the bark is scraped off about three feet of vine to form a large double handful of shavings. The bark is soaked in a liter of cold water for several hours, and the liquid strained off and taken over a period of an hour. No other plant is added.

I decided to try some Yage prepared Vaupes method. The Indian and I started scraping off bark with machetes (the inner bark is the most active). This is white and sappy at first but almost immediately turns red on exposure to air. The landlady's daughters watched us pointing and giggling. This is strictly against Putumayo protocol for the preparation of Yage. The Brujo of Macoa told me if a woman witnesses the preparation the Yage spoils on the spot and will poison anyone who drinks it or at least drive him insane. The old women-are-dirty-and-under-certain-circumstances-poisonous routine. I figured this was a chance to test the woman pollution myth once and for all with seven female creatures breathing down my neck, poking sticks in the mixture fingering the Yage and giggling.

The cold water infusion is a light red color. That night I drank a quart of infusion over a period of one hour. Except for blue flashes and slight nausea—though not to the point of vomiting—the effect was similar to weed. Vividness of mental imagery, aphrodisiac results, silliness and giggling. In this dosage there was no fear, no hallucinations or loss of control. I figure this dose as about one third the dose that Brujo gave me.

Next day we went on down to Puerto Espina where the governor put us up in his house. That is we slung our hammocks in empty rooms on the top floor. A coolness arose between the Colombians and the British because the Colombians refused to get up for an early start, and the British complained the Cocoa Commission was being sabotaged by a couple of "lazy spics."

Every day we plan to get an early start for the jungle. About 11 o'clock the Colombians finish breakfast (the rest of us waiting around since 8) and begin looking for an incompetent guide, preferably someone with a finca near town. About 1 we arrive at the finca and spend another hour eating lunch. Then the Colombians say, "They tell us the jungle is far. About 3 hours. We don't have time to make it today." So we start back to town, the Colombians collecting a mess of plants along the way. "So long as they can collect any old weed they don't give a ruddy fuck," one of the Englishmen said to me after an expedition to the nearest finca.

There was supposed to be plane service out of Puerto Espina. Schindler and I were ready to go back to Bogota at this point, so there we sit in Puerto Espina waiting on this plane and the agent doesn't have a radio or any way of finding out when the plane gets there if it gets there and he says, "Sure as shit boys one of these days you'll look up and see the Catalina coming in over the river flashing in the sun like a silver fish."

So I says to Doc Schindler, "We could grow old and simple-minded sitting around playing dominoes before any sonofa-bitching plane sets down here and the river getting higher every day and how to get back up it with every motor in Puerto Espina broke?"

(The citizens who own these motors spend all the time fiddling with their motors and taking the motors apart and leaving out pieces they consider non-essential so the motors never run. The boat owners do have a certain Rube Goldberg ingenuity in patching up the stricken motor for one last more spurt—but this was a question of going up the river. Going down river you will get there eventually motor or no, but coming up river you gotta have some means of propulsion.)

Sure you think it's romantic at first but wait til you sit there five days onna sore ass sleeping in Indian shacks and eating yoka and same hunka nameless meat like the smoked pancreas of a two toed sloth and all night you hear them fiddle fucking with the motor—they got it bolted to the porch—"buuuuurt spluuuu . . . ut . . . spluuuu . . . ut," and you can't sleep hearing the motor start and die all night and then it starts to rain. Tomorrow the river will be higher.

So I says to Schindler, "Doc, I'll float down to the Atlantic before I start back up that fuckin river."

And he says, "Bill, I haven't been 15 years in this sonofa-bitch country and lost all my teeth in the service without picking up a few angles. Now down yonder in Puerto Leguisomo—they got like military planes and I happen to know the commandante is Latah." (Latah is a condition occurring in South East Asia. Otherwise normal, the Latah cannot help doing whatever anyone tells him to do once his attention has been attracted by touching him or calling his name.)

So Schindler went on down to Puerto Leguisomo while I stayed in Puerto Espina waiting to hitch a ride with the Cocoa Commission. Every day I saw that plane agent and he came on with the same bullshit. He showed me a horrible looking scar on the back of his neck. "Machete," he said. No doubt some exasperated citizen who went berserk waiting on one of his planes.

The Colombians and the Cocoa Commission went up the San Miguel and I was alone in Puerto Espina eating in the Commandante's house. God awful greasy food. Rice and fried platano cakes three times a day. I began slipping the platanos in my pocket and throwing them away later. The Commandante kept telling me how much Schindler liked this food—(Schindler is an old South American hand. He can really put down the bullshit)—did I like it? I would say, "Magnificent," my voice cracking. Not enough I have to eat his greasy food. I have to say I like it.

The Commandante knew from Schindler I had written a book on "marijuana." From time to time I saw suspicion seep into his dull liverish eyes.

"Marijuana degenerates the nervous system," he said looking up from a plate of platanos.

I told him he should take Vitamin B1 and he looked at me as if I had advocated the use of a narcotic.

The Governor regarded me with cold disfavor because one of the gasoline drums belonging to the Cocoa Commission had leaked on his porch. I was expecting momentarily to be evicted from the governmental mansion.

The Cocoa Commission and the Colombians came back from the San Miguel in a condition of final estrangement. It seems the Colombians had found a finca and spent three days there lolling about in their pajamas. In the absence of Schindler I was the only buffer between the two factions and suspect by both parties of secretly belonging to the other (I had borrowed a shot gun from one of the Colombians and was riding in the Cocoa Commission boat).

We went on down the river to Puerto Leguisomo where the Commandante put us up in a gun boat anchored in the Putumayo. There were no guns on it actually. I think it was the hospital ship.

The ship was dirty and rusty. The water system did not function and the W.C. was in unspeakable condition. The Colombians run a mighty loose ship. It wouldn't surprise me to see someone shit on the deck and wipe his ass with the flag. (This derives from dream that came to me in 17th century English. "The English and French delegates did shit on the floor, and tearing the Treaty of Save-all into strips with such merriment did wipe their backsides with it, seeing which the Spanish delegate withdrew from the conference.")

Puerto Leguisomo is named for a soldier who distinguished himself in the Peruvian War in 1940. I asked one of the Colombians about it and he nodded, "Yes, Leguisomo was a soldier who did something in the war."

"What did he do?"

"Well, he did *something.*"

The place looks like it was left over from a receding flood. Rusty abandoned machinery scattered here and there. Swamps in the middle of town. Unlighted streets you sink up to your knees in.

There are five whores in town sitting out in front of blue walled cantinas. The young kids of Puerto Leguisomo cluster around the whores with the immobile concentration of tom cats. The whores sit there in the muggy night under one naked electric bulb in the blare of juke box music, waiting.

Inquiring in the environs of Puerto Leguisomo I found the use of Yage common among both Indians and whites. Most everybody grows it in his backyard.

After a week in Leguisomo I got a plane to Villavencenio, and from there back to Bogota by bus.

So here I am back in Bogota. No money waiting for me (check apparently stolen), I am reduced to the shoddy expedient of stealing my drinking alcohol from the university laboratory placed at disposal of the visiting scientist.

Extracting Yage alcoloids from the vine, a relatively simple process according to directions provided by the Institute. My experiments with extracted Yage have not been conclusive. I do not get blue flashes or any pronounced sharpening of mental imagery. Have noticed aphrodisiac effects. The extract makes me sleepy whereas the fresh vine is a stimulant and in overdose convulsive poison.

Every night I go into a cafe and order a bottle of pepsi-cola and pour in my lab alcohol. The population of Bogota lives in cafes. There are any number of these and always full. Standard dress for Bogota cafe society is a gabardine trench coat and of course suit and tie. A South American's ass may be sticking out of his pants but he will still have a tie.

Bogota is essentially a small town, everybody worrying about his clothes and looking as if he would describe his job as responsible. I was sitting in one of these white collar cafes when a boy in a filthy light gray suit, but still clinging to a frayed tie asked me if I spoke English.

I said, "Fluently," and he sat down at the table. A former employee of the Texas Company. Obviously queer, blond, German looking, European manner. We went to several cafes. He pointed people out to me saying, "He doesn't want to know me any more now that I am without work."

These people, correctly dressed and careful in manner, did in fact look away and in some cases call for the bill and leave. I don't know how the boy could have looked any less queer in a $200 suit.

One night I was sitting in a Liberal cafe when three civilian Conservative gun men came in yelling "Viva los Conservadores" hoping to provoke somebody so they could shoot him. There was a middle aged man of the type who features a loud mouth. The others sat back and let him do the yelling. The other two were youngish, ward heelers, corner boys, borderline hoodlums. Narrow shoulders, ferret faces and smooth, tight, red skin, bad teeth. It was almost too pat. The two hoodlums looked a little hang dog and ashamed of themselves like the young man in the limerick who said, "I'll admit I'm a bit of a shit."

Everybody paid and walked out leaving the loud mouthed character yelling "Viva El Partido Conservador" to an empty house.

May 5

930 Jose Leal, Lima

Dear Allen:

This finds me in Lima which is enough like Mexico City to make me homesick. Mexico is home to me and I can't go there. Got a letter from my lawyer—I am sentenced in absentia. I feel like a Roman exiled from Rome. Plan to hit Peru jungle for additional Yage material. Will spend a few weeks digging Lima.

Went through Ecuador fast as possible. What an awful place it is. Small country national inferiority complex in most advanced stage.

Ecuadorian Miscellanea: *Esmeraldas* hot and wet as a turkish bath and vultures eating a dead pig in the main drag and everywhere you look there is a Nigra scratching his balls. The inevitable Turk who buys and sells everything. He tried to cheat me on every purchase and I spent an hour arguing with this bastard. The Greek shipping agent with his dirty silk shirt and no shoes and his dirty ship that left Esmeraldas seven hours late.

On the boat I talked to a man who knows the Ecuador jungle like his own prick. It seems jungle traders periodically raid the Auca (a tribe of hostile Indians. Shell lost about twenty employees to Auca in two years) and carry off women they keep penned up for purposes of sex. Sounds interesting. Maybe I could capture an Auca boy.

I have precise instructions for Auca raiding. It's quite simple. You cover both exits of Auca house and shoot everybody you don't wanna fuck.

Arriving in Manta a shabby man in a sweater started opening my bags. I thought he was a brazen thief and gave him a shove. Turns out he was customs inspector.

The boat gave out with a broken propeller at Las Playas half way between Manta and Guayaquil. I rode ashore on a balsa raft. Arrested on the beach suspect to have floated up from Peru on the Humboldt Current with a young boy and a tooth brush (I travel light, only the essentials) so we are hauled before an old dried up fuck, the withered face of cancerous control. The kid with me don't have paper one. The cops keep saying plaintively:

"But don't you have any papers *at all?*"

I talked us both out in half an hour using the "We-got-like-two-types-publicity-favorable-and-unfavorable-which-do-you-want?" routine. I am down as writer on tourist card.

Guayaquil. Every morning a swelling cry goes up from the kids who sell Luckies in the street—"A ver Luckies," "Look here Luckies"—will they still be saying "A ver Luckies" a hundred years from now? Nightmare fear of stasis. Horror of being finally *stuck* in this place. This fear has followed me all over South America. A horrible sick feeling of final desolation.

"La Asia," a Chinese restaurant in Guayaquil, looks like 1890 whorehouse opium den. Holes eaten by termites in the floor, dirty tasselled pink lamps. A rotting teak-wood balcony.

Ecuador is really on the skids. Let Peru take over and civilize the place so a man can score for the amenities. I never yet lay a boy in Ecuador and you can't buy any form of junk.

P. S. Met a Pocho cab driver—the Pocho is type found in Mexico who dislikes Mexico and Mexicans. This cab driver told me he was Peruvian but he couldn't stand Peruvians. In Ecuador and Colombia no one will admit anything is wrong with his jerk water country. Like small town citizens in U.S. I recall an army officer in Puerto Leguisomo telling me:

"Ninety percent of the people who come to Colombia never leave."

He meant, presumably, they were overcome by the charms of the place. I belong to the ten percent who never come back.

WILLIAM S. BURROUGHS (NOVEL DATE 1959)

SOURCE: Burroughs, William S. Excerpt from *Naked Lunch*, pp.15-18. New York: Grove Press, 1984.

Originally published in 1959, Naked Lunch *is Burroughs's best known work. This short passage about a narcotics agent named "Bradley the Buyer" exemplifies Burroughs's unique narrative technique.*

"Selling is more of a habit than using," Lupita says. Nonusing pushers have a contact habit, and that's one you can't kick. Agents get it too. Take Bradley the Buyer. Best narcotics agent in the industry. Anyone would make him for junk. (Note: Make in the sense of dig or size up.) I mean he can walk up to a pusher and score direct. He is so anonymous, grey and spectral the pusher don't remember him afterwards. So he twists one after the other . . .

Well the Buyer comes to look more and more like a junky. He can't drink. He can't get it up. His teeth fall out. (Like pregnant women lose their teeth feeding the stranger, junkies lose their yellow fangs feeding the monkey.) He is all the time sucking on a candy bar. Baby Ruths he digs special. "It really disgust you to see the Buyer sucking on them candy bars so nasty," a cop says.

The Buyer takes on an ominous grey-green color. Fact is his body is making its own junk or equivalent. The Buyer has a steady connection. A Man Within you might say. Or so he thinks. "I'll just set in my room," he says. "Fuck 'em all. Squares on both sides. I am the only complete man in the industry."

But a yen comes on him like a great black wind through the bones. So the Buyer hunts up a young junky and gives him a paper to make it.

"Oh all right," the boy says. "So what you want to make?"

"I just want to rub against you and get fixed."

"Ugh . . . Well all right . . . But why cancha just get physical like a human?"

Later the boy is sitting in a Waldorf with two colleagues dunking pound cake. "Most distasteful thing I ever stand still for," he says. "Some way he make himself all soft like a blob of jelly and surround me so nasty. Then he gets well all over like with green slime. So I guess he come to some kinda awful climax . . . I come near wigging with that green stuff all over me, and he stink like a old rotten cantaloupe."

"Well it's still an easy score."

The boy signed resignedly; "Yes, I guess you can get used to anything. I've got a meet with him again tomorrow."

The Buyer's habit keeps getting heavier. He needs a recharge every half hour. Sometimes he cruises the precincts and bribes the turnkey to let him in with a cell of junkies. It gets to where no amount of contact will fix him. At this point he receives a summons from the District Supervisor:

"Bradley, your conduct has given rise to rumors—and I hope for your sake they are no more than that—so unspeakably distasteful that . . . I mean Caesar's wife . . . hrump . . . that is, the Department must be above suspicion . . . certainly above such suspicions as you have seemingly aroused. You are lowering the entire tone of the industry. We are prepared to accept your immediate resignation."

The Buyer throws himself on the ground and crawls over to the D.S. "No, Boss Man, no . . . The Department is my very lifeline."

He kisses the D.S.'s hand thrusting his fingers into his mouth (the D.S. must feel his toothless gums) complaining he has lost his teeth "inna thervith." "Please Boss Man, I'll wipe your ass, I'll wash out your dirty condoms, I'll polish your shoes with the oil on my nose . . ."

"Really, this is most distasteful! Have you no pride? I must tell you I feel a distinct revulsion. I mean there is something, well, rotten about you, and you smell like a compost heap." He put a scented handkerchief in front of his face. "I must ask you to leave this office at once."

"I'll do anything, Boss, *anything*." His ravaged green face splits in a horrible smile. "I'm still young, Boss, and I'm pretty strong when I get my blood up."

The D.S. retches into his handkerchief and points to the door with a limp hand. The Buyer stands up looking at the D.S. dreamily. His body begins to dip like a dowser's wand. He flows forward . . .

"No! No!" screams the D.S.

"Schlup . . . schlup schlup." An hour later they find the Buyer on the nod in the D.S.'s chair. The D.S. has disappeared without a trace.

The Judge: "Everything indicates that you have, in some unspeakable manner uh . . . assimilated the District Supervisor. Unfortunately there is no proof. I would recommend that you be confined or more accurately contained in some institution, but I know of no place suitable for a man of your caliber. I must reluctantly order your release."

"That one should stand in an aquarium," says the arresting officer.

The Buyer spreads terror throughout the industry. Junkies and agents disappear. Like a vampire bat he gives off a narcotic effluvium, a dank green mist that anesthizes his victims and renders them helpless in his enveloping presence. And once he has scored he holes up for several days like a gorged boa constrictor. Finally he is caught in the act of digesting the Narcotics Commissioner and destroyed with a flame thrower—the court of inquiry ruling that such means were justified in that the Buyer had lost his human citizenship and was, in consequence, a creature without species and a menace to the narcotics industry on all levels.

GENERAL COMMENTARY

IHAB HASSAN (ESSAY DATE 1963)

SOURCE: Hassan, Ihab. "William Burroughs: The Subtracting Machine." In *Rumors of Change: Essays of Five Decades,* pp. 36-52. Tuscaloosa: University of Alabama Press, 1995.

In the following essay, originally published in 1963, Hassan examines the widely disparate critical views of Burroughs's work.

To speak is to lie

—William Burroughs

I

Some works stand in judgment on the world although the world rules their judgment invalid. Their authors cannot be punished, for they have put themselves beyond any punishment the world can dispense. William Burroughs may be one of these authors. "I offer you nothing. I am not a politician," Burroughs says in his introduction to the trilogy, ***Naked Lunch, The Soft Machine,*** and ***The Ticket That Exploded.*** He offers the black and bodiless specter of human betrayal, the dreadful algebra of absolute need. He offers a deposition against the human race, a testimony of outrage in the metallic voice of a subtracting machine.

It is not surprising that his testimony is subject to extravagant praise and hysterical denunciation. In the view of some, Burroughs is the underground king of the Beat movement for which sweet Jack Kerouac is merely the publicist; in that view, ***Naked Lunch*** (1959) is the secret masterpiece through which the movement is vindicated. There is, of course, some truth in this view. Yet the "masterpiece," thanks to the dauntless publishers of the Grove Press, is now public, and the shadowy status of its author is compromised by the encomium he received at a recent Edinburgh Festival from Norman Mailer and Mary McCarthy. Others, however, remain unimpressed. In a classic snort of common sense, John Wain has said, "From a literary point of view," the novel "is the merest trash, not worth a second glance." Wain then proceeded, through seven columns of small print, to glance at the novel, comparing it with the work of Henry Miller, Louis-Ferdinand Céline, and the Marquis de Sade, to prove a different point—that Burroughs is a partisan of death.

Controversy may profit the sales of Burroughs's works; it will surely dull their terror. We begin to understand that terror when we refuse to accept it exclusively as a literary phenomenon. From Arthur Rimbaud to Samuel Beckett, a dangerous strain in modern literature has evaded Wain's "literary point of view." Vision in that strain seems incommensurate with language; experience seems incommensurate with sanity. If that peculiar literature retains any form, it is the form of outrage. In the end, outrage is an existential category, a testimony of the self concerning the world in shuddering images. True outrage is autobiography become a universal stutter.

Burroughs's life is itself an affront. Born in 1914 in St. Louis to affluent parents—related, presumably, to the Burroughses of the computing machines—he was from the beginning a solitary soul. In his autobiographical work, ***Junkie*** (1953), written under the pseudonym of William Lee, Burroughs says, "Actually, my earliest memories are colored by a fear of nightmares. I was afraid to be alone, and afraid of the dark, and afraid to go to sleep because of dreams where a supernatural horror seemed always on the point of taking shape. . . . I said: 'I will smoke opium when I grow up.'" As a boy, he was fond of hiking and fishing, but he was also a malingerer and a petty criminal, breaking into factories and houses. He was eventually sent to Harvard, from which he took a degree "without honors" in English literature. A trust fund, which provided him with $150 a month, gave him some security during the Depression. He drifted through Europe for a year and returned to the United States in 1936. On the surface, these first twenty-two years do not seem eventful. What happened to lead Burroughs since that time through the slums and prisons and hospitals of three continents, forcing him to jostle with hoodlums and pimps and pushers? In two decades, he acquired a drug habit and kicked it many times, shot his wife by accident, cultivated homosexuals, took an apomorphine cure, exiled himself from civilization only to reemerge as the unregenerate legend of the Beat movement, the mentor of Kerouac and Allen Ginsberg, and the author of ***Naked Lunch,*** which Robert Lowell describes, on the dust jacket, as "one of the most alive books written by any American for years."

The psychiatrist who diagnosed Burroughs as a paranoid schizophrenic begs the question, as indeed the question begs itself. We may outlaw madness without comprehending it, but we must still ask what monition is there in insanity and how the affront of crime is relevant. The silence of an outlaw remains demonic; the testimony of the damned gives meaning to damnation. Burroughs not only testifies, but he also indicts. Burroughs is a didactic writer who affirms his moral passion in the language of denial and derision. Like the later Jonathan Swift, like Pieter Breughel or Hieronymus Bosch, he pushes satire toward the threshold of pathology, claiming from self-hate the hate humanity harbors. Personal outrage may be made into an indictment of history.

The indictment is even larger. "In ***Naked Lunch, The Soft Machine*** and ***Nova Express***—work in progress—i am mapping an imaginary universe. A dark universe of wounded galaxies and novia [*sic*] conspiracies where obscenity is coldly used as a total weapon," Burroughs writes. And again: "The purpose of my writing is to expose and arrest Novia Criminals." Burroughs not only maps out, he also exposes. His universe is imaginary only in the sense that it is distilled from abstract terrors, dominated by Regulators and Exterminators, by Ovens and Infernal Machines. His universe is as inhuman as interstellar spaces, yet it swarms with insect people, floats on sentient ooze. The central metaphor of his universe is science fiction, which is the nightmare that our machines dream when they dream of history. The myth of technology, in Burroughs's work, is the dreadful reality of a world in which humanity makes a last effort to resist nonbeing. In *New Maps of Hell,* Kingsley Amis amiably reads into science fiction the secret aspirations of humanity. Burroughs renders through science fiction the cold apocalypse of the race. The machine always sounds the rhythm of death. The rhythm of the social mechanism is simple: first mendacity, then control, finally death:

> A POST SCRIPT OF THE REGULATOR
>
> I would like to sound a word of warning: To speak is a lie. To live is to collaborate. Any body is a coward when faced by the Nova Ovens. There are degrees of lying collaboration and cowardice. That is to say degrees of intoxication. It is precisely a question of REGULATION. The Enemy is not Man is not Woman. The Enemy exists only where no life is and moves always to push life into extreme untenable positions. You can cut the enemy off your line by the judicious use of apomorphine and silence. USE THE SANITY DRUG APOMORPHINE. Signed The Regulator Interstellar Board of Health

This is a long way from autobiography. Outrage expands to embrace the universe. Its dominant metaphor is the machine of death. Three other metaphors, equally life draining, amplify the first: sexual obscenity, junk, and money. Each has a social and political correlative.

In Burroughs's work, sex is usually violation. It is sterile, inhuman, malevolent. It is a perversion of the life instinct, an organic process turned mechanical. Sadism, masochism, and pederasty prevail; tenderness, love, and knowledge are absent. Sex is simply the obscene correlative of alienation. Despite the elaborate depiction of homosexuality in Burroughs's work, there is no attempt to understand or justify the homosexual. "A room full of fags gives me the horrors," Burroughs wrote in ***Junkie.*** "They jerk around like puppets on invisible strings, galvanized into hideous activity that is the negation of everything living and spontaneous. The live human being has moved out of these bodies long ago." Sex remains the desperate embodiment of an absence, of a lie.

Junk, however, is still a more complete embodiment of the negative. Burroughs understands that junk wins in a person's life simply by default. Junk is the aboriginal hunger of the cells, the physical correlative of nihilism. The addicts themselves are bodiless, their ghastly corpses needle cushions. They are brought back to temporary life by the kick, a state of pure and solipsistic consciousness defined mainly by its horrible absence. "Kick is momentary freedom from the claims of the aging, cautious, nagging, frightened flesh," Burroughs ruefully says. A freedom of lascivious death. Antonin Artaud saw the point, with the dark eye of poetry, in one of his letters: "I believe the opium we now have, the black juice of what we call the poppy, is the expulsion of an ancient eradicating power, which man no longer wanted, and those who were weary of the seminal fluid and of the erotic twistings of the self in the fluid of the first offense recoiled toward opium as toward a different lubricity." It is the lubricity of death again. Here is Burroughs, in a "Deposition" prefacing ***Naked Lunch,*** on the terminal addict who sits around "with a spine like a frozen hydraulic jack . . . his metabolism approaching Absolute ZERO."

Sex and junk express for Burroughs the extinction of life. So does money. "Junk is the mold and monopoly of possession," he states. "Junk is the ideal product . . . the ultimate merchandise. No sales talk necessary." Both junk and money are quantitative; both are perversions of work and leisure in a capitalist society. Money, then, is simply the counter of control, the price of need; it is the gainful term in an equation of degradation and loss. As Burroughs puts it, "The face of 'evil' is always the face of total need." The addict will do anything for junk; the pusher will do anything for money. Hence money always appears in Burroughs's work as the social correlative of exploitation.

Obviously, Burroughs's death machine operates on obscenity, junk, and money. It is the diabolic metaphor of control. Metaphor, however, is the root of language, the very principle of its life. It is natural, therefore, that Burroughs's language should reflect the quality of the metaphor that animates it. The language is desiccated, automatic. Its final aim is self-abolition. It presupposes the fact of extinction, cooling of novas and abandonment of the earth. The language of testimony testifies even against itself. This is perhaps the most original aspect of Burroughs's work.

Much of that work is rendered in a special idiom: hipster speech. Its meanings are as restricted as its vocabulary. And as Burroughs himself indicates, hipster words are polyvalent and their meanings are constantly changing. Hipster language confesses its ephemeral character; furthermore, it openly accepts the inability of words to describe felt reality. Referring to ***Naked Lunch,*** Edward Dorn astutely remarks, "This is probably the first time a book has been written in translation instead of the normally original language." Burroughs's distrust of language, however, is more radical than Dorn implies. To speak is to lie. "I will tell you: 'THE WORD.' Alien Word 'THE.' 'THE' Word of Alien Enemy imprisons 'THEE' in Time. In Body. In Shit. Prisoner, come out. The great skies are open. I Hassan i Sabbah RUB OUT THE WORD FOREVER," he screams. Scream he may, yet write he must. Burroughs is forced to devise ways of circumventing language. His commentary on Jacoubi's "The Night Before Thinking," which Jacoubi wrote under the influence of *majoun,* a form of hashish jam, is a montage; the account of Jacoubi and the experience of Burroughs with a hallucinogen, "dim-N," are spliced to reveal the "underlying unity of words and images that blossoms like bottle genie from the hallucinogens now open to all the world of The Thousand and One Nights." This technique is carried further in Burroughs's novels. The method, which owes something to the Dadaist antics of Tristan Tzara, is further developed by Brion Gysin, a painter who is a friend of Burroughs:

> Method is simple: Take a page or more or less of your own writing or from any writer living or dead. Any written or spoken words. Cut into sections with scissors or switch blade as preferred and rearrange the sections. Looking away. Now write out result. . . .
>
> Applications of cut up method are literally unlimited cut out from time limits. Old world lines keep you in old world slots. Cut your way out.

The aim is to cut oneself out of language, cut oneself from language. The aim is to escape a world made by words and perhaps to discover another. Chance denies the order we have brought ourselves to accept, an order Burroughs feels has viciously betrayed us. The death machine, Burroughs implies, can only be destroyed by destroying its logic, its logos. But what lies beyond logos? Characteristically, the answer of Burroughs, the addict saved by apomorphine, is inconclusive. "Yage may be the final fix," he says at one point. And at another: "LEARN TO MAKE IT WITHOUT ANY CHEMICAL SUPPORTS." Death is its own answer; language is the equivocation of reality. A vision equally uncontaminated by words or substance beckons him. The vision slashes in rare moments through his work. It is a broken vision.

II

Fugitive and somewhat provisional in its character, Burroughs's work does not invite systematic consideration. Its development is obvious from the contrast between his earliest book, ***Junkie,*** and a brief experimental work, a collaboration with Gysin, of later date, ***The Exterminator*** (1960). The former remains a pungent autobiographical narrative, written largely in a spare, naturalistic style. The structure is tight and conventional; the transitions are clear. The interest of the book lies mainly in its cold depiction of the sordid and implacable world of addiction.

The Exterminator, however, is a jumble of passages and motifs used elsewhere by Burroughs, a cut-up and patched job. It is randomly illustrated with Arabic script by Gysin, who also provides exhaustive permutations of such phrases as "Kick that habit man," "Rub out the words," and "Proclaim present time over." The metaphors are those of science fiction, pathology, and politics, and they are all animated by the sense of revulsion, as if an unspeakable virus were taking over the whole of life. In the background, a malevolent Control Machine moves to eliminate all "non-qualitative data." Misogyny and misanthropy blend. "Scientists suggest That Life on Earth originated and or implemented by garbage shit deposited by Space Travellers?" Burroughs queries; elsewhere he states, "Now any American will admit women are all bitches. . . . But find an Englishman to call the Queen a Bitch?" The violence and crudity of the feelings expressed are checked by bilious humor, restrained by clipped rhythms: "Hook an ape . . . When he learns to say 'Where Is The Man?' He is a sick human junky . . . With the Monkey on his back" (peculiarities of punctuation in the original).

But how authentic is the cut-up method, and how unique are its effects? "You can cut the truth out of any written or spoken words," Burroughs claims. The fact remains that in the first part of this work, which is by far the most effective, the cut-up method is used cannily and sparingly. Catchphrases acquire force because they are forced into sudden proximity with other slogans. The commentaries on Caryl Chessman and on the bombings in Madrid, on sex and on narcotics, have a common context that the author slyly provides. The shock of surprise is a contrived shock, and the method turns out, in this case, to be more cerebral than Burroughs admits. Its chief value lies not in atomizing language but rather in disclosing the connections between the separate facts of outrage in our time. In his later trilogy, however, Burroughs worked more wildly.

III

Naked Lunch (1959, 1962), the first book in Burroughs's unholy trilogy, must be acknowledged as an impressive achievement. The novel, if it can be termed such, is a sequence of dramatic or fantastic episodes without plot or developed characters. The vision is infernal, a glimpse of the abyss that Dante defined in his time by another theology. This is how Burroughs defines his inferno: "The Word is divided into units which be all in one piece and should be so taken, but the pieces can be had in any order being tied up back and forth, in and out fore and aft like an innaresting sex arrangement. This book spill off the page in all directions, kaleidoscope of vistas, medley of tunes and street noises, farts and riot yipes and the slamming steel shutters of commerce, screams of pain and pathos and screams plain pathic, copulating cats and outraged squawk of the displaced bull head, prophetic mutterings of brujo in nutmeg trances, snapping necks and screaming mandrakes, sigh of orgasm, heroin silent as dawn in thirsty cells."

The vision is infernal and also satiric in a surrealistic fashion. Burroughs can be misunderstood when he says, "There is only one thing a writer can write about: *what is in front of his senses at the moment of writing.* I am a recording instrument." The recording machine is more accurately described a few lines later: "No matter how tight Security, I am always somewhere *Outside* giving orders and *Inside* this straight jacket of jelly that gives and stretches but always reforms ahead of every movement, thought, impulse, stamped with the seal of alien inspection."

The previous statement explains why, beyond the familiar techniques of distortion and hallucination, ***Naked Lunch*** refers all its philosophic and political themes to the decayed substance of the human body. The technique is harshly reductive, a reversal of the process of Freudian sublimation, but it serves to debunk the complexities of civilization by thrusting upon us that strange reality that underlies them all: the diseased and obscene flesh. Disease and obscenity are the corporal evidence of our maladies. Most organisms are therefore presented as putrid. The virus prevails; the virus "can exhibit living qualities only in a host, by using the life of another—the renunciation of life itself, a *falling* toward inorganic, inflexible machine, towards dead matter." Hence, too, "The end result of complete cellular representation is cancer. Democracy is cancerous, and bureaus are its cancer." The collector for Friendly Finance turns out to be a toothless Egyptian eunuch, and the procedures of capital punishment are presented in terms of sadistic, homosexual fantasies under the shadow of the gallows.

Burroughs employs other techniques to convey his infernal vision in ***Naked Lunch.*** Among the more striking is metamorphosis, usually the spontaneous transformation of the human body into lower forms of life. Men turn into crabs or larva. Doctor "Fingers" Schafer, the Lobotomy Kid, witnesses with horror the change in his patient from a Complete All American Deanxietized Man to a monstrous black centipede. The Buyer, a narcotics agent, turns into a noxious blob of jelly that swallows the District Supervisor. The sudden change from realistic to surrealistic narration is terrifying enough. Metamorphosis, however, achieves more than a literary effect of terror. It destroys the objective reality of the world, the identity and separateness of things; it is the actual process of disintegration.

Disintegration is indeed the end of Burroughs's vision. Poetic hallucination and technological fantasy both proclaim, in their different ways, a dark apocalypse. We begin with a fallen world: "America is not a young land: it is old and dirty and evil before the settlers, before the Indians. The evil is there watching." We end with death or depravity. Dr. Benway, who is in charge of total demoralization, states, "Western man is externalizing himself in the form of gadgets." This is mild. From the rooftop of the Reconditioning Center we observe a howling spectacle of the world. Burroughs asks with mock horror, "Gentle reader, the ugliness of that spectacle buggers description. . . . Oh Christ what a scene is this! Can tongue or pen accommodate these scandals?" And later we observe the frightful market in the City of Interzone: "A place where the unknown past and the emergent future meet in a vibrating soundless hum. . . . Larval entities waiting for a Live One." These apocalyptic scenes, flashed on our consciousness with a hellish projector—"fade-out" is one of the author's favorite directions—fuse the poetic visions of Rimbaud and the lucid nightmares of George Orwell into a reel of grotesque malevolence.

The grotesque power of the book is egregious. There are fine scenes, like "The Black Meat," in which the poetic mood predominates; we participate silently in their awesome metaphors. And there are other discursive scenes, like "Benway" or "Islam Incorporated and the Parties of Interzone," in which the satiric content emerges from the vocabulary of pseudoscience. But the quality of Burroughs that sets him apart from both Rimbaud and Orwell is his grotesque humor. Above all, ***Naked Lunch*** is a parody of evil; it crackles with gargoyle laughter. The revolting sequence on the talking ass is one example. This is another: "American Housewife (opening a box of Lux): 'Why don't it have an electric eye the box flip open when it see me and hand itself to the Automat Handy Man he should put it inna water already. . . . The Handy Man is outa control since Thursday, he been getting physical with me and I didn't put it in his combination at all. . . . And the Garbage Disposal Unit snapping at me, and the nasty old Mixmaster keep trying to get under my dress.'"

In satire, the cold passions of Burroughs find release, and the techniques of outrage find a goal. Satire also defines the range of the author's contempt. The range is wide. It includes authority, conformity, colonialism, commerce, capital punishment, café society, patriotism, political parties; it focuses on doctors, policemen, profiteers, gourmets, hipsters, racists, academics, women, and even junkies. The central motive of Burroughs is, of course, anarchic; his paranoiac fear is of the Dream Police. Thought control, political exploitation, and social responsibility—which he usually associates with attachment to women—haunt his dreams. Ostensibly, he desperately wishes for a whole and free man. This is the positive image that lies behind all the atrocities he depicts, an image of implicit denunciation. Yet what he sees is only that "The broken image of Man moves in minute by minute and cell by cell. . . . Poverty, hatred, war, police-criminals, bureaucracy, insanity, all symptoms of the Human Virus."

The Virus, it must be concluded, has affected Burroughs more than he realizes. His denunciation of infamy slips into acquiescence to it; outrage cancels itself by a partial relish of outrage. One feels of Burroughs, as one does not of the most morbid moments of Swift, that in some secret part of him he rejoices in the humiliation of man. "Citizens who want to be utterly humiliated and degraded—so many people do, nowadays, hoping to jump the gun—offer themselves up for passive homosexual intercourse to an encampment of Sollubis," he writes. The irony of the statement is limited by the bitter relish of its larger context. In ***Naked Lunch,*** the relentless accent on perversion denotes the violation of all human relations, but it also betrays a compulsive character. The accent on addiction is equally ambiguous. There is judgment and deprecation and icy pity in Burroughs's statement, "The world network of junkies, tuned on a cord of rancid jissom . . . tying up in furnished rooms . . . shivering in the sick morning." But there is also a certain spite in his statement that "The President is a junky but can't take it direct because of his position. So he gets fixed through me." Pervert or addict, more often both, Outsiders expose the rest of the world even while they envy it. Envy breeds revenge. Outsiders seek to revenge themselves by abolishing the world. But the world remains. Burroughs rages at the world for not being a better place and rages at it again for not being more completely depraved. The revenge would be perfect if all men were junkies and women were thrown out of creation.

Naked Lunch begins with the narrator's flight from "the fuzz." We meet in stagnant, imaginary rooms the Vigilante; the Rube; Lee the Agent; A. J.; Clem and Jody, the Ergot Twins; Autopsy Ahmed; Hepatitis Hal; Hassan O'Leary, the After Birth Tycoon; the Sailor; the Exterminator; the Buyer; "Fats" Terminal; and Doc Benway. They vanish again in a green mist. In the end, the narrator pretends to take the junk cure and to climb out of that space-time that is the junkie's death. Lazarus is back. We have been Nowhere. Narrow, repetitive, diseased, this extraordinary work still deserves what Burroughs demands for it: "***Naked Lunch*** is a blueprint, How-To Book. . . . Black insect lusts open into vast other planet landscapes. . . . How to extend levels of experience by opening the door at the end of a long hall. . . . Doors that open in *Silence*. . . . ***Naked Lunch*** demands Silence from the Reader. Otherwise he is taking his own pulse."

IV

The Soft Machine (1961), the second book in the trilogy, shows certain differences from the earlier work. The collage technique of ***Naked Lunch*** yields to the more random effects of composition by a thoroughly cut-up method. All verisimilitude vanishes. Moreover, the focus on drug addiction shifts to a vague and pervasive evil that can still be identified, despite the phantasmal setting, by its perverted and excremental character. The limbo depicted by Burroughs proves to be a wasteland no less infernal than his hell. Unfortunately, it also proves to be less interesting.

The book's dust jacket claims, "Stroboscopic flicker-lights playing on the Soft Machine of the eye create hallucinations, and even epilepsy. Recurrent flickering of Cut-Up opens up the area of hallucination and makes a map for the human race to invade." These are brave words. More than ever, Burroughs seems determined to alter the human condition. The satirist invokes hallucination because it is more effective in restoring humanity to its true estate. The theory, no doubt, is attractive. Its results, however, often appear banal or inchoate; and in long stretches of the book gibberish prevails over revelation.

The work is divided into four units that carry the following titles: "Red: Transitional Period"; "Green: Thing Police Keep All Board Room Reports"; "Blue: Have You Seen Slotless City"; and "White: Poison Our Dead Sun in Our Brains." Each unit is composed of episodes with enigmatic subtitles. The routines of Burroughs in these episodes are in many ways similar to his routines in ***Naked Lunch:*** metamorphosis, parody, distortion, etc. The innovation consists in sketching a portrait or situation early in each unit and cutting and permutating its components in the sections that follow. The method, of course, heightens the phantasmagoric quality of the work, and, in some cases, it creates fresh contexts and connections that might have been missed in a sequential narrative. Furthermore, the method occasionally permits Burroughs to strip an event from the coils of sentiment or illusion that surround it, rendering it into brutal poetry. More often, however, the effect is quite different. We feel in the presence of a relentless mechanism, equally repetitive and reductive. All human activities are ground into slogans, compressed into recurrent images. Our imagination is not freed; it is rather constricted by a horrible rhythm of encounters and defeats, by a sinister and inescapable necessity. Permutation produces not variety but sameness. The whole of life seems in the grip of a subtracting machine. The machine prescribes not only the ethics of outrage but also the aesthetics of revulsion. Perhaps without realizing it fully, Burroughs seems to have devised in the Cut-Up method a means not so much of liberating humanity as of declaring its bondage. For bondage is the central theme of the cryptic episodes that comprise the book. The hand of necessity lies heavily on sex, commerce, politics; humanity is always controlled, diminished, or infected. Explorers of strange and exotic lands, like Carl the Traveller, invariably discover the same degradation that blights their own cities. And Doc Benway is forever engaged in creating cretins or automatons.

The familiar bias of Burroughs is crudely dramatized on the first page. An ugly War Between the Sexes is described. There are Lesbian Colonels and Mongolian Archers in it; what is at stake is the Baby and Semen Market. The Hate Wave disintegrates the sexual Violator in a flash of White Light. "It was a transitional Period because of the Synthetics and everybody was raising some kinda awful life form in his bidet to fight the Sex Enemy," Burroughs states. These mutant forms include black centipedes and green newt boys with purple fungoid gills. Other factions are converting to still lower forms of life: "Do not be alarmed citizens of Annexia—Report to your Nearie Pro Station for Chlorophyll Processing—We are converting to Vegetable State—Emergency measure to counter the Heavy Metal Peril! . . . 'Citizens of Gravity we are converting all out to Heavy Metal. Carbonic Plague of The Vegetable People threatens our Heavy Metal State.'" Meanwhile, the homosexual tandem, "Mr. Bradly Mr. Martin," is preparing to leave earth. As in Annexia, Death in Orgasm prevails in Minraud. "All resident doubles in rooms of Minraud grow living legs for death in orgasm of the Nova Guard." The evil, of course, is traced back to language itself. "Picture the [Nova] guard as an invisible tapeworm attached to word centers in the brain on color intensity beams. . . . The Head Guards are captives of word-fallout only live in word and image of the host," Burroughs explains. The solution? "Rub out your stupid word. Rub out separation word 'They' 'We' 'I' 'You' 'The!' Rub out word 'The' forever. . . . Go back to Silence. Keep Silence. K. S. K. S. . . . From Silence re-write the message that is you."

This is Burroughs's eternal theme, and all its permutations into sexual attitudes or color imagery add little to it. There are, of course, surrealistic descriptions of the city of man. And there are also grotesque parodies of fertility rites involving the Young Corn God. The "soft machine" of the eye can only register horror; the ear always listens to "Phantom jissom in the nettles and dry sound of scorpion"; the nose only smells "locker room smell of mouldy jockstraps." The primitive and sensuous roots of life that D. H. Lawrence joyfully celebrated are execrated by Burroughs. There is never sacrament; there is always revulsion. Everything must be cut. As always, change is regression, contact is torture, property is control, and all desire is addiction. Burroughs is an allegorist—witness his stark events, his epithets and personifications—and he has written the allegory of a moldy universe. He has chosen technological fantasy as the frame of his allegory to dramatize a vision that could be called puritanical were it not so obscene. And yet is not obscenity the other face of puritanical outrage? ***The Soft Machine*** is like a book written in a secret code. When the code is deciphered all the messages read the same: Out!

V

Burroughs's trilogy is a grotesque commedia that comes to a "happy" end in ***The Ticket That Exploded*** (1962). The new setting is sweepingly galactic. The style once again alternates between technical jargon and poetic hallucination. There is, of course, no plot, only a cut-up of scenes and images. Some of the earlier characters—Mr. Bradly, Mr. Martin, A. J., etc.—reappear. The conspiracy against creation described in the earlier books is finally resolved on a grand scale.

We begin with a dreamy dissolution of reality. A room on the roof of a ruined warehouse, "swept by the winds of time," becomes a spaceship. A "blue metal boy" and a "green boy-girl" copulate, twisting "free of human coordinates." A world of acrid ectoplasms and nitrate flakes, of flickering ghosts and mineral silences, unfolds. Newt boys appear, unite, and vanish; nerve patterns become visible in orgasm; a slow, sexual movement ebbs and flows underwater. We are apprised that a certain Bradly explodes the dungeons of the Garden of Delights, releasing all its prisoners, releasing himself from time and human flesh. Hypnotic images lace every page with memories of captive pleasures. We are bewildered, yet we feel that the theme somehow has been stated.

The mood then suddenly changes to satire. A medley of old songs and homosexual fantasies offers a savage parody of sentimental love. But not until the sections entitled "Operation Rewrite" and "The Nova Police" does Burroughs reveal his scheme. The galaxy, it seems, is ruled by a Nova Mob that perpetuates every kind of misery and addiction in man; the task of the Nova Police is to break up the Mob. The basic technique of the mob is to create and aggravate insoluble conflicts. "This is done by dumping on the same planet life forms with incompatible conditions of existence," says Inspector J. Lee of the Nova Police. The Nova criminals are a Virus; they feed on human organisms. "The point at which the criminal controller intersects a three-dimensional human agent is known as a 'coordinate point. . . .' Some move on junk lines through addicts of the earth, others move on lines of certain sexual practices and so forth—It is only when we can block the controller out of all coordinate points available to him and flush him out from host cover that we can make a definitive arrest," explains the Inspector.

Equally matter of fact and fantastic, Burroughs's scheme comes to focus in his view of love, which is the primary concern of ***The Ticket That Exploded.*** One is compelled by the strangeness of the material here to quote at length:

> The Venusian invasion was known as "Operation Other Half," that is, a parasitic invasion of the sexual area taking advantage . . . of an already existing fucked up situation. . . . The human organism is literally consisting of two halves from the beginning word and all human sex is this unsanitary arrangement whereby two entities attempt to occupy the same three-dimensional coordinate points giving rise to the sordid latrine brawls which have characterized a planet based on "The Word," that is, on separate flesh engaged in endless sexual conflict—The Venusian Boy-Girls under Johnny Yen took over The Other Half, imposing a sexual blockade on the planet—(It will be readily understandable that a program of systematic frustration was necessary in order to sell this crock of sewage as Immortality, The Garden of Delights, and LOVE).

The vocabulary of science fiction conceals a radical theory of love, indeed of life. The Mob, which is also the All Powerful Board, controls thoughts, feelings, and flesh with "iron claws of pain and pleasure from birth to death." It uses the division of the sexes, the cant of love or responsibility, the needs of the human body to sustain its control. Above all, it uses the power of Word and Image to exercise its influence. Hence the parallel redemptive functions of the Biological Courts and of the Rewrite Department; the first must refashion the body of humanity and the second must remodel language. Ideally, the aim is to make humans bodiless and language silent. Burroughs, we see, has given a terrible twist to the Biblical equation of word and flesh. His radical hope is to redeem creation by abolishing both.

It is hard to judge whether Burroughs's notion is a consummation of Western nihilism, a rediscovery of Oriental nirvana, or a viciously ironic commentary on our world. Of this we can be more certain: the Mob can call on the Old Doctor, whatever dying, fraudulent god he may be, but it can never call on him twice. It is later than the Mob thinks, only Minutes to Go, and the Nova Heat of the Police is on. Our ticket on this journey through life has exploded. Like Prospero, Burroughs makes his weird farewell. The epilogue of the book requires "Silence to say goodbye."

The Ticket That Exploded, however, is not the programmatic work that this account may suggest. Like its predecessors, it is both satiric and visionary, perhaps more so. Its logic is disrupted by random and transposed scenes or images, fantastic metamorphoses, discursive notes on scientific theory or orgone therapy, calligraphs by Gysin, travelers' diaries, bulletins in newspeak, parodies of space fiction, dream and delirium sequences, political commentaries, hipster dialogue, and such fleeting characters as Green Tony, Bradly, Sammy the Butcher, Izzy the Push, Hamburger Mary, the Fluoroscopic Kid, and Hassan i Sabbah. Its method, that is, is a constant shifting in the levels of discourse. And its aim is to diffract time, language, and flesh in a crazy kaleidoscopic vision through which filters a utopian image of man. Like an image track or reel, running intolerably silent and slow, the book blurs all the contours of the visible, the known, world, and dissolves its stationary symbols. Will a new face of reality, then, reveal itself?

VI

The question of reality in Burroughs's work is finally elusive. We know the grounds on which he rejects the world: "Take it from an Old Property, Total Fear and Hate is more of a habit than using." But we are never certain of what he affirms instead. Reality, therefore, is a negative concept where Burroughs is concerned. Despite his apocalyptic gifts, he remains a satirist more than a visionary, an ironist more than a prophet, an allegorist more than a poet. "I offer you nothing," he confesses. He offers more than he pretends, compounding the horrors of our lives with his own grotesque experience. And yet he offers less than the major writers of our century—Thomas Mann, Franz Kafka, James Joyce, and William Faulkner—have offered, not because his scope and knowledge are less than theirs, which is indubitably true, but because his love is also smaller. At times, the extent of Burroughs's love—and love is energy of the soul, the will to life—seems contained in this advice: "Flesh junkies, control junkies, heavy metal junkies—That's how you get caught, son—If you have to have it well you've had it—Just like any mark—So slide in cool and casual on the next pitch and don't get hooked on the local line: If there is one thing to write on any life form you can score for it's this: Keep your bag packed at all times and ready to travel on." Ready to travel right out of this world. The refrain is "Man, like goodbye."

In the end, too much is left out. The whole of nature is excluded. An urban writer, Burroughs has inhaled the flowers of evil growing on the pavements of every-city since the time of Baudelaire. He has tasted or inhaled little else. Like human beings, nature is corrupt. Nature is out.

Society is monstrous. Society is out. Woman is out. All the races and people crowding his books, a vestige, perhaps, of his anthropological interests, bring no virtues that civilization lacks. Mexicans, Arabs, and Chinese are out. Nothing escapes the Subtracting Machine. Again and again, Burroughs turns to the reader belligerently to ask: "Wouldn't you?" And again and again some readers want to cry, "No."

It is no accident that utopianism and nihilism have often crossed paths in history and have often shared the same human passions. To neglect that history or suppress those passions is fateful in our moment. The work of William Burroughs takes its nauseous sense of life from that moment. It gives a new meaning, however limited, to outrage. Above all, it assaults language savagely, declaring thus its opposition to the deeper assaults that human consciousness suffers.

DAVID LODGE (ESSAY DATE AUTUMN 1966)

SOURCE: Lodge, David. "Objections to William Burroughs." *Critical Quarterly* 8, no. 3 (autumn 1966): 203-12.

In the following essay, Lodge contends that Burroughs's work is unsatisfactory from both a moral and an aesthetic perspective.

I

Have we come to handle the *avant-garde* too gently? From the *Lyrical Ballads* to *Ulysses* our literary history is very much a chronicle of revolutionary works hooted and reviled by the literary establishments of their times, appreciated by a small élite of initiates, and belatedly elevated to classic status by succeeding literary establishments. Since the 1920's, however, the time lag between the publication and the public recognition of such works has got shorter and shorter, until now we are, perhaps, more in danger of mistaking than neglecting masterpieces. Part of the reason is the radical change which has overtaken academic criticism in this period: the groves of academe, that were once enclaves of conservative literary taste, are now only too eager to welcome what is new. Another, and perhaps more important reason is that through the development of the mass media and what one might call the boom in the culture market, the 'small élite of initiates' which in the past has constituted the only audience for experimental art, good and bad, is now able to bring its influence to bear very swiftly and powerfully on the larger public.

Nothing illustrates this latter process more strikingly than the way the reputation of William Burroughs has grown since Mary McCarthy praised ***The Naked Lunch*** at the Edinburgh Writers' Conference of 1962. (Miss McCarthy has since complained that her words on that occasion were distorted and exaggerated by the press; but it could be argued that writers who participate in such events, which are peculiar to our own cultural era, must expect and accept such treatment.) What is noteworthy about Burroughs' reputation is not so much the encomiums his work has received from such confreres as Miss McCarthy, Norman Mailer ('I think that William Burroughs is the only American novelist living today who may conceivably be possessed of genius') and Jack Kerouac ('Burroughs is the greatest satirical writer since Jonathan Swift'), as the way in which this body of opinion has acted on the public mind so as to secure the smooth acceptance and accommodation of such books as ***The Naked Lunch*** and ***Nova Express.*** It seems to illustrate very well what Lionel Trilling has described as the institutionalisation of the adversary culture of modernism; and like him, I do not see this process as a symptom of cultural health. ***The Naked Lunch,*** whatever else it may be, is a very indecent book, and ***Nova Express,*** whatever else it may be, is a very tedious book. These novels' pretensions to serious literary significance which, if realised, would justify the indecency and the tedium (or rather force us to redefine these qualities) need to be examined rather more rigorously than our present literary climate generally encourages. Before doing so, it may be advisable to attempt a description of these books. I say 'attempt' because they both resist any conventional summary of character and action.

II

The Naked Lunch begins with the first person narrative of a drug addict who, pursued by the New York police, travels across America with a companion to Mexico; his account of the journey is mingled with reminiscences of various characters from the drugs underworld. In the second chapter the novel parts with actuality and takes on the quality of dream. The action shifts abruptly from place to place, sometimes between mythical states called Freeland, Annexia and Interzone, which bear a parodic relationship to the actual world. There is no plot, but a general impression of intrigue and pursuit, sometimes on a cops-and-robbers level, sometimes on a political level. The narrative mode shifts from first person to third person to dramatic dialogue. Many of the scenes have a hallucinatory, surrealistic quality reminiscent of the Circe episode in *Ulysses*. The images of the book are primarily of violence, squalor and sexual perversion. There is a notorious orgiastic sequence in which orgasm is achieved by hanging and finally eating the sexual partner. We seem to be sharing the dream, or nightmare, of an addict—perhaps, as Miss McCarthy has suggested, one who is taking a cure and suffering the agonies of 'withdrawal'.

In ***Nova Express*** the dislocation of narrative and logical continuity is much more radical, for here Burroughs has used what he describes as a 'cut-up' or 'fold-in' technique—that is, a montage of fragments of his own and other people's writings, achieved, for instance by overlapping two pages of text and reading straight across. Basically the book is a science fiction fantasy based on the premise that the earth has been invaded by exterrestrial gangsters, the 'Nova Mob', whose mission is to infiltrate human institutions and encourage all forms of evil in order to accelerate this planet's progress on the path to destruction. They are pursued by the 'Nova Police', who also work invisibly through human agencies, causing, it would seem, almost as much havoc. Only such fantastic suppositions, it is implied, will account for the political lunacy and moral decay of the modern world. That the fantasy is more real than what we take to be actuality is emphasised by such conceits as that life is a 'biological movie' created and manipulated in a 'reality Studio' for the control of which the Nova factions are competing.

III

Burroughs has, principally, two claims on the attention of serious readers: as a moralist, and as an innovator. On both counts, it seems to me, he cannot be considered as more than a minor, eccentric figure. Undoubtedly he has a certain literary talent, particularly for comedy and the grotesque, but in both precept and practice he is deeply confused and ultimately unsatisfying. ***The Naked Lunch*** seems to offer an appropriate epitaph on his work: 'Confusion hath—his masterpiece'.

To begin with, there is a deep confusion, not only in Burroughs but in his admirers too, on the subject of narcotics. Much of Burroughs's notoriety derives from the fact that he is a morphine addict, who has been cured, but who still writes very much out of the experience of addiction. He tells us in the Introduction to ***The Naked Lunch*** that it is based on notes taken during the sickness and delirium of addiction. He is our modern De Quincey; and undoubtedly this accounts for his adoption by the hipster wing of the American literary scene. Herbert Gold has called ***The Naked Lunch*** 'the definitive hip book' and Burroughs tells us that the title was donated by the arch-hipster Jack Kerouac. 'I did not understand what the title meant until my recovery. The title means exactly what the words say: NAKED lunch—a frozen moment when everyone sees what is on the end of every fork'. These words clearly imply that the drugged state gives access to a special vision of truth—that the junkie, like Conrad's Kurtz, is an inverted hero of the spirit who truly sees 'the horror, the horror' that ordinary, conforming humanity refuses to face. But in other places Burroughs undercuts this argument, which alone could justify his distressingly explicit (so much more explicit than Conrad's) descriptions of the horror. In an interview published in the *Paris Review* (35, Fall 1965) he agreed that 'The visions of drugs and the visions of art don't mix'; and both novels contain a great deal of obtrusive propaganda against the use of narcotics and on behalf of the apomorphine treatment by which Burroughs himself was cured. The interviewer challenged him on this point—'You regard addiction as an illness, but also a central human fact, a drama?'—and Burroughs' reply is revealing:

> Both, absolutely. It's as simple as the way in which anyone happens to become an alcoholic . . . The idea that addiction is somehow a psychological illness is, I think, totally ridiculous. It's as psychological as malaria. It's a matter of exposure . . . There are also all forms of spiritual addiction . . . Many policemen and narcotics agents are precisely addicted to power, to exercising a certain nasty kind of power over people who are helpless. The nasty sort of power: white junk I call it—rightness . . .

It will be noted how Burroughs slides here from a literal, clinical view of addiction to a figurative or symbolic one. Both views are at odds with the assumption behind ***The Naked Lunch*** that the junkie's delirium yields truth; and they are also at odds with each other. In the first view addiction is seen as a preventable sickness, in the second it is seen as a metaphor for authoritarianism. On the one hand it is not 'psychological', on the other hand it can be 'spiritual'. In the first place the junkie is a sick man in need of society's protection, in the second place he is a victim of society.

This kind of equivocation is particularly evident in Burroughs' treatment of the police. In ***The Naked Lunch*** a certain sympathy is generated for the junkies on the run from the police, yet it is difficult to see how the exposure of the individual to drugs, which according to Burroughs is the cause of addiction, could be prevented without the police. In ***Nova Express*** the Nova Police seem to be the 'goodies' as the Nova Mob are the 'baddies', but Burroughs, in the interview already cited, says, 'They're like police anywhere . . . Once you get them in there, by God, they begin acting like any police. They're always an ambivalent agency'. In this case, how are we to read the following passage about the Nova Police:

> 'The difference between this department and the parasitic excrescence that often travels under the name 'Police' can be expressed in metabolic terms: The distinction between morphine and apomorphine . . . The Nova Police can be compared to apomorphine, a regulating instance that need not continue and has no intention of continuing after its work is done.

The confusion that surrounds these two novels of Burroughs can, I think, be partly explained by the fact that they are very different works which Burroughs is trying to present as in some sense continuous, two stages in a coherent programme. ***The Naked Lunch*** is essentially a nihilistic work and as such it must be granted a certain horrible power; but it is prefaced by an Introduction which seeks to justify it on orthodox moral grounds, and to present its hero as a brand snatched from the burning.

> Since ***The Naked Lunch*** treats this health problem [addiction], it is necessarily brutal, obscene and disgusting. Sickness has often repulsive details not for weak stomachs.
>
> Certain passages in the book that have been called pornographic were written as a tract against Capital Punishment in the manner of Jonathan Swift's *Modest Proposal*. These sections are intended to reveal capital punishment as the obscene, barbaric and disgusting anachronism that it is.

How literature can deal with evil without morally compromising itself is of course a perennial and perhaps insoluble problem, but Burroughs' defence is either naive or disingenuous. The analogy with Swift won't stand up. Whereas in *A Modest Proposal* Swift maintains a constant logical connection between his fable (the monstrous 'proposal') and his facts (the miseries of the Irish people), so that in revolting from the former we are compelled to revolt from the latter, it is doubtful whether the uninformed reader would see any connection at all between the Orgasm Death Gimmick and Capital Punishment. It may be that the disgust Mr. Burroughs feels for Capital Punishment has been transferred to the antics of his sexual perverts, but the reverse process which should occur for the reader is by no means to be relied upon. The power of Swift's piece inheres very largely in the tone of calm reasonableness with which the proposal is put forward, so that we feel obliged to supply the emotion which is missing. In ***The Naked Lunch,*** instead of this subtly controlled irony we have a kinetic narrative style which suspends rather than activates the reader's moral sense, and incites him to an imaginative collaboration in the orgy. Since I do not propose to quote from this particular scene here, I shall illustrate my point with a rather less offensive passage:

> Rock and Roll adolescent hoodlums storm the streets of all nations. They rush into the Louvre and throw acid in the Mona Lisa's face. They open zoos, insane asylums, prisons, burst water mains with air hammers, chop the floor out of passenger plane lavatories, shoot out light-houses, file elevator cables to one thin wire, turn sewers into the water supply, throw sharks and sting rays, electric eels and candiru into swimming pools . . . in nautical costumes ram the *Queen Mary* full speed into New York Harbor, play chicken with passenger planes and busses, rush into hospitals in white coats carrying saws and axes and scalpels three feet long . . .

This is vivid, inventive writing, but it is scarcely satire. There is a note of celebration here, a hilarious anarchism which relishes the mindless destruction it describes; and it extends to the most successfully drawn characters in the book, the brutal surgeon Benway and the inspired practical joker A. J. There *are* patches of effective satire in ***The Naked Lunch*** (notably a parody of conversation between some 'good old boys' of the Deep South—'These city fellers come down here and burn a nigger and don't even settle up for the gasoline'), but the tone and structure of the whole will not support the serious moral significance that is claimed for it. Indeed the account of the Nova Mob's subversive activities in ***Nova Express*** seems damagingly appropriate to ***The Naked Lunch:*** 'We need a peg to hang evil full length. By God show them how ugly the ugliest pictures in the dark room can be' . . . 'Take orgasm noises sir and cut them in with torture and accident groans and screams sir and operating-room jokes sir and flicker sex and torture film right with it sir'. Burroughs' reference to himself as an undercover agent of the Nova Police who wrote 'a so-called pornographic novel' as a bait to lure the Nova Mob into the open seems an arch evasion of responsibility.

Nova Express itself is a much more 'responsible' book, much more consistent with the avowed moral intentions of its author—and also much more boring. I find Burroughs more impressive (if no more congenial) as a nihilist than as a moralist, and the sick fantasies of the junkie more interesting than the portentous salvationism of the reclaimed addict. While it is good to know that Mr. Burroughs has been cured of addiction, his attempt to load this private experience with universal significance, equating morphine with evil and apomorphine with redemption, becomes tiresome. But what most makes for boredom in this novel is its technical experiment.

IV

First, an example, taken from a chapter vulnerably entitled 'Are These Experiments Necessary?':

> Saturday March 17th, 1962, Present Time of Knowledge—Scio is knowing and open food in The Homicide Act—Logos you got it?—Dia through noose—England spent the weekend with a bargain before release certificate is issued—Dogs must be carried reluctant to the center—It's a grand feeling—There's a lot ended—This condition is best expressed queen walks serenely down dollar process known as overwhelming—What we want is Watney's Woodbines and the Garden of Delights—And what could you have?—What would you?—State of news?—Inquire on hospitals? what?

This seems to be a 'cut-up' of English newspapers, advertisements, public notices etc. One can identify the likely contexts from which the fragments were taken. But does their juxtaposition create any significant new meaning? I think not.

The comparisons which have been canvassed by Burroughs and his admirers between his method and the methods of Eliot and Joyce (Burroughs has described *The Waste Land* as 'the first great cut-up collage', and a reviewer in the *New York Herald-Tribune* has likened ***Nova Express*** to *Finnegans Wake*) will not bear scrutiny. Compare:

> There I saw one I knew, and stopped him, crying: 'Stetson!
> 'You who were with me in the ships at Mylae!
> 'That corpse you planted last year in your garden,
> 'Has it begun to sprout? Will it bloom this year?
> 'Or has the sudden frost disturbed its bed?
> 'Oh keep the Dog far hence, that's friend to men,
> 'Or with his nails he'll dig it up again!
> 'You! hypocrite lecteur!—mon sembable,—mon frere!

> riverrun, past Eve and Adam's, from swerve of shore to bend of bay, brings us by a commodius vicus of recirculation back to Howth Castle and Environs.

What these passages have in common, and what is signally lacking in the Burroughs passage, is continuity. In the Eliot passage it is a thematic and dramatic continuity: the lines, incongruous, anachronistic and inconsequential as they are, nevertheless all relate to the idea of the 'Burial of the Dead' and communicate a very lively sense of the speaker's complex mood of surprise, impudence, admonition and complicity. In the Joyce passage it is a narrative or descriptive continuity: we hold on tight to the lightning tour of Dublin's topography, while being dimly aware that it is also a tour of human history from Adam and Eve onwards according to the cyclic theories of Vico. The more you read each passage the more you get out of it, and everything you get out of it thickens and confirms the sense of continuity and hence of meaning (for in the verbal medium meaning *is* continuity: discrete particulars are meaningless).

Burroughs has much less in common, both in precept and practice, with these modern classics, than with the art which Frank Kermode has dubbed 'neo-modernism', in a very penetrating article, 'Modernisms Again: Objects, Jokes and Art' (*Encounter,* April 1966, pp. 65-74). Extreme examples of neo-modernism are the tins of Campbell's soup which Andy Warhol signs and sells as *objets d'art,* or the piano piece 4'33" by composer John Cage, in which the performer sits before a closed piano in total silence and immobility for the prescribed time while the audience, in theory, becomes aesthetically aware of the noises around them, inside and outside the auditorium. Behind all these experiments is the principle of chance. Chance is allowed to determine the aesthetic product and the aesthetic experience; the artist confines himself to providing an aesthetic occasion within which the random particulars of our environment may be perceived with a new depth of awareness. As Kermode points out, 'Artists have always known that there was an element of luck in good work ("grace" if you like) and that they rarely knew what they meant till they'd seen what they said'; but neo-modernism trusts, or tries to trust, completely to luck. Kermode's conclusion seems to me the right one; that neo-modernism, apart from its merely humorous intent and value, is involved in a logical contradiction, for when it succeeds it does so by creating an order of the kind which it seeks to deny. 'Research into form is the true means of discovery, even when form is denied existence. So it becomes a real question whether it helps to introduce indeterminacy into the research'.

This seems very relevant to Burroughs's experiments, about which he is characteristically equivocal. The cut-up or fold-in technique is clearly designed to introduce a radical element of chance into literary composition. You run two pages of text into one another and allow chance to produce new units of sense (or nonsense). Burroughs defends such experiments (in the *Paris Review* interview) by an appeal to experience. Thus, he describes how he was struck, during a train journey to St. Louis, by the congruence of his thoughts and what he saw outside the window:

> For example, a friend of mine has a loft apartment in New York. He said, 'Every time we go out of the house and come back, if we leave the bathroom door open, there's a rat in the house'. I look out of the window, there's Able Pest Control'.

'Cut-ups,' says Burroughs, 'make explicit a psycho-sensory process that is going on all the time anyway'. Precisely: that is why they are so uninteresting. We can all produce our own coincidences—we go to art for something more. One might guess that Joyce's discovery of a Vico Road in Dublin was a lucky break for him, a coincidence like Burroughs's observation of Able Pest Control (which reappears, incidentally, in a piece of imaginative writing, ***St. Louis Return,*** published in the same issue of the *Paris Review*). But in the case of Joyce we are not aware of it *as* coincidence because it is incorporated into a verbal structure in which innumerable effects of a similar kind are created by means that are palpably not due to luck but to art. I do not mean to imply that we value works of literature solely in proportion to the conscious artifice we are able to impute to the process of composition (though this consideration always has some weight). Rather, that in the experience of successful literature we feel compelled to credit all its excitement and interest, whether this was produced by luck or not, to the creating mind behind it.

There is an essay by Paul Valéry, 'The Course in Poetics: the First Lesson' (reprinted in *The Creative Process* ed. Brewster Ghiselin, Mentor Books 1955), which deals very profoundly with the difficult problem of indeterminacy in artistic creation. Valéry admits, indeed insists, that 'every act of the mind is always somehow accompanied by a certain more or less perceptible atmosphere of indetermination'. But he goes on to point out that the finished art-work 'is the outcome of a succession of inner changes which are as disordered as you please but which must necessarily be reconciled at the moment when the hand moves to write under one unique command, whether happy or not'. As a romantic-symbolist, Valéry is prepared to grant the indeterminate a great deal of play—'the dispersion always threatening the mind contributes almost as importantly to the production of the work as concentration itself'—but the dispersion is a threat, concentration is essential. The cut-up method, by which the writer selects from random collocations of ready-made units of discourse, seems a lazy short-cut, a way of evading the difficult and demanding task of reducing to order the personally felt experience of disorder.

Fortunately Burroughs does not always practice what he preaches. Kermode remarks: 'Admirers of William Burroughs' ***Nova Express*** admit that the randomness of the composition pays off only when the text looks as if it had been composed straightforwardly, with calculated inspiration'. I would wager that the following passage *was* composed straightforwardly:

> 'The Subliminal Kid' moved in and took over bars and cafés and juke boxes of the world cities and installed radio transmitters and microphones in each bar so that the music and talk of any bar could be heard in all his bars and he had tape recorders in each bar that played and recorded at arbitrary intervals and his agents moved back and fourth with portable tape recorders and brought back street sound and talk and music and poured it into his recorder array so he set waves and eddies and tornadoes of sound down all your streets and by the river of all language—Word dust drifted streets of broken music car horns and air hammers—The Word broken pounded twisted exploded in smoke—

Here it does not seem inappropriate to invoke Eliot and Joyce. There is continuity here—narrative, logical, syntactical and thematic. The language is disordered to imitate disorder, but it is orderly enough to form a complex, unified impression. It is worth noting, too, that the meaning of the passage is a conservative and traditional one—a criticism of those forces in modern civilization that are mutilating and destroying words and The Word, and the values they embody and preserve. The passage thus contradicts Burroughs' protestations (see the *Paris Review* interview) that his experiments are designed to break down our 'superstitious reverence for the word'.

V

The function of the *avant garde* is to win new freedom, new expressive possibilities, for the arts. But these things have to be *won,* have to be fought for; and the struggle is not merely with external canons of taste, but within the artist himself. To

FROM THE AUTHOR

BREAKING NEW GROUND

In my writing I am acting as a map maker, an explorer of psychic areas . . . a cosmonaut of inner space, and I see no point in exploring areas that have already been thoroughly surveyed.

Burroughs, William S. Quoted in *William Burroughs: The Algebra of Need* by Eric Mottram. Buffalo: Intrepid Press, 1971.

bend the existing conventions without breaking them—this is the strenuous and heroic calling of the experimental artist. To break them is too easy.

I believe this principle can be extended to cover not only formal conventions, but also the social conventions that govern the content of public discourse. From the Romantics onwards the revolutionary works have commonly affronted not only their audience's aesthetic standards, but also their moral standards. *Madame Bovary* and *Ulysses,* for example, shocked and dismayed the publics of their respective periods by mentioning the unmentionable. But these works gradually won acceptance because discriminating readers appreciated that their breaches of existing decorums were not lightly or irresponsibly made, and that their authors had substituted for received disciplines and controls, disciplines and controls of their own even more austere and demanding. Much of the work of today's *avant garde,* including that of Burroughs, carries no such internal guarantee of integrity. Its freedom is stolen, not earned. The end product is hence startling and exciting on the first impression, but ultimately boring.

Finnegans Wake deliberately violates the conventions of language: it seeks to overthrow the law that we can only think and communicate lineally, one thing at a time. Most of us can manage the same trick—we can throw off a Joycean pun once in a while (I offer one free of charge to Mr. Burroughs: 'fission chips'). But to produce hundreds and thousands of such puns, as Joyce does, and to weld them all into a complex whole—this is to create not destroy convention, and is a task of staggering difficulty. Similarly, most of us can compose a good obscene joke on occasion, or produce a powerful emotive effect by the use of obscene words; but to give these things authority as public discourse we have to ensure that they will survive the passing of the initial shock—we have not merely to violate, but to recreate the public sensibility, a task requiring precise imaginative control. One can't avoid the conclusion that a lot of Burroughs' most immediately effective writing (e.g. 'A. J. the notorious Merchant of Sex, who scandalised international society when he appeared at the Duc du Ventre's ball as a walking penis covered by a huge condom emblazoned with the A. J. motto "They Shall Not Pass"') has the short-lived appeal of a witty obscenity; or, in its more grotesque and horrific forms amounts to a reckless and self-defeating squandering of the powerful emotive forces that great literature handles with jealous care and economy.

JOHN TYTELL (ESSAY DATE 1976)

SOURCE: Tytell, John. "The Black Beauty of William Burroughs." In *Naked Angels: The Lives and Literature of the Beat Generation,* pp. 111-39. New York: McGraw-Hill, 1976.

In the following essay, Tytell discusses Burroughs's use of unconventional composition techniques and satiric content, claiming that the author is commonly misunderstood by critics who consider his work either incomprehensible or obscene.

They have no conversation, properly speaking. They make use of the spoken word the same way that the guard of the train makes use of his flags or his lantern.

—Samuel Beckett *Malone Dies*

"Twilight's Last Gleamings," written by Burroughs at Harvard in 1938, but not published until 1964 in ***Nova Express,*** offers a clear illustration of his intentions as a writer. The story is a painful but hilarious parody of the sinking of the *Titanic,* except that Burroughs' vessel is allegorically named the S.S. *America.* An explosion occurs in the boiler room, but an "air-conditioned" voice advises that there is no cause for alarm. Ship's Doctor Benway, drunkenly lurching through an emergency operation, dropping cigarette ashes on his patient, sweeps his instruments and drugs into his bag and boards the first lifeboat. A politician from Clayton, Missouri (the suburb of St. Louis where Burroughs was raised), rushes into the first-class lounge and orders the musicians to play "The Star-Spangled Banner." The captain, confronted by Lady Bradshinkel, owner of the ship, seizes her wig as the deck tilts and shoots her to obtain her kimono. On his way to the lifeboats, he finds the purser ransacking money and jewels from the safe, draws a gun hidden in his brassiere, shoots him, seizes the valuables, then forces his way onto the lifeboat. The scene is hysterical pandemonium as wealthy American passengers attempt to flee. Burroughs' eye moves along the decks, burlesquing the tragedy, punctuating the mayhem with fragments of the national anthem. The parable is a premonition of the fall of America—everyone desperate for escape, but stealing, pillaging, abusing their authority at the end as they have been doing all along. Just as in Burroughs' mature works, there is no organizing narrative presence, no explaining omniscient intelligence, no judgment. The author's eye moves swiftly, cinematically, uninterested in formal transitions or artificial connections, concerned primarily with capturing the sense of chaotic flux, the terror of disaster; the exposure of false disguises is brutally candid, scathingly comedic.

Burroughs' vision is the most impersonal of all the Beat writers. As early as 1948, Burroughs announced in a letter to Allen Ginsberg a philosophy he termed "factualism:"

> All arguments, all nonsensical condemnations as to what people 'should do' are irrelevant. Ultimately there is only fact on all levels, and the more one argues, verbalizes, moralizes, the less he will see and feel of fact. Needless to say I will not write any formal statement on the subject. Talk is incompatible with factualism.

Although Burroughs has never deserted the factualist ideal, his aesthetic has evolved from the bare documentary realism of his first book, ***Junkie,*** to the structural intricacies of ***Naked Lunch*** and the complex textures of the cut-up technique. His inventive art has been infused with what Allen Ginsberg has aptly called a Yankee practicality, but its features have been difficult to decipher. Burroughs is the most experimental of the Beats, a writer who, like Henry James, is first read by other writers greedy to learn the secrets of the craft, and then later by a larger audience. "An advance in art" Harold Rosenberg has argued, "is considered to take place to the degree that art divests itself of the characteristics of art." In this sense Burroughs may be a novelist of the future, but one with a compelling message for us now.

For many readers, William Burroughs' complexity is a formidable, sometimes intimidating obstacle. His novels are composed of scenes which are often without the narrative focus provided by recognizable characters, or the scenic unity provided by a particular locale. Characters metamorphose into other characters, appear without introduction only to disappear without explanation; scenes shift sharply from New York City to South American jungles without transition. Such difficulties are compounded by the presence of alien forms that seem derived from the world of science fiction—annihilating insects, viral parasites, succubi and other demons, all merging with humans, invading their bodies and manipulating their minds, acting through their beings bizarrely, disruptively creating what Burroughs calls *nova:* the aggravation of insoluble conflicts and incompatible political situations resulting in a planetary explosion.

Burroughs continues the experimental tradition in fiction, the modernist movement of Gertrude Stein, Joyce, Gide, and others who sought to free fiction from the confining boundaries of the conventional novel. His novels court to the ultimate limits an idea expressed by William James in *A Pluralistic Universe* that can stand as a keynote for modernist fiction: "In the end nothing less than the whole of everything can be the truth of anything at all." It was the simultaneous truth of this "whole" that Burroughs, like Kerouac and Ginsberg, was dedicated to capture. As he told Ginsberg when he sent him examples of what was to become ***Naked Lunch,*** he was not trying to compose a historical novel where the events had already transpired, but writing narrative that "is happening."

Burroughs' experiments with narrative forms have profoundly developed the dimensions of fiction. Just as the cut-up extends Joyce's stream of consciousness, Burroughs' exceptional fluidity is a magnification of Henry James' principle of shifting point of view. The Jamesian tradition as developed by Conrad, Ford Madox Ford, Virginia Woolf, successfully ruptured the umbilical passivity of a reader dependent on an omniscient narrator, and placed that reader in the active center of a situation that could not be resolved by absolute judgments. The events of the story, the facts of the milieu, would swirl about the reader with all the contradictions and misunderstandings felt in any real situation. The demands on the reader's intelligence amounted to a combination of the detective's perspicacity and the psychoanalyst's intuition. Clues, vitally meaningful signs, would form the basis of interpretation. But the masters of modern fiction, from James to Faulkner, despite their intensive development of technique, were all still predominantly interested in telling a story.

Burroughs, like Poe or the French Symbolists, creates an ambiance, an atmosphere of conflicting particles whose points of contact reveal a dark and hidden interior. His medium may best be approached through analogies to the new physics. Whereas Newton's mechanical view of the cosmos, like Victorian omniscience in the novel, resulted in a morality of predictable absolutes, Burroughs' world, like Einstein's, projects a relativity of endless exfoliation. What first intrigued Einstein and led to his theory of relativity was the very unpredictability of the rate at which atoms absorb or emit electrical energy. Before the assumptions of quantum mechanics, the ultimate constituents of matter were thought to be the negatively charged electron, the positively charged proton, and the chargeless neutron. Today, instead of a determinable universe, scientists are faced with an immeasurable uncertainty. Quantum mechanics successfully destroyed the possibility of absolutes for our time, but also revealed a baffling array of highly relative bodies acting without evident controls. Take the case of the neutrino, which offers a perfect analogy for the way in which Burroughs treats many of his characters: it has no physical properties, neither mass nor electric charge nor magnetic field; it is neither attracted by gravity, nor captured or repelled by the electromagnetic fields of other particles, even as it may fly past or through those particles. The neutrino, unlimited by any apparent boundaries, deepens our understanding of dimension in space just as the positron—an electron temporarily engaged in moving backward in time—challenges our linear and chronological concepts of history. And space and time in Burroughs' work correspond to such cosmological laws.

In *Improvised Poetics,* Ginsberg suggested that Burroughs does not conceive of words as he writes, but instead sees flashing pictures. In a lecture at Tufts University, Ginsberg spoke of observing Burroughs while writing with his eyes gazing into a "middle distance." Ginsberg asked Burroughs what he was thinking about, and he answered "Hands pulling in nets from the ocean." Ginsberg explained that this was a "pictograph" of what they had seen on the shore that night.

Burroughs' speed of observation moves too quickly for sequential prose or the unit of the paragraph. The three books that complete the ***Naked Lunch*** tetralogy, ***Nova Express, The Soft Machine, The Ticket That Exploded,*** have a labyrinthine density deriving from Burroughs' use of the cut-up—a technique that juxtaposes fragments collected from random reading, snatches of conversation, newspaper items, quotations from writers like Rimbaud and T. S. Eliot, recurring motifs from Burroughs' own work, all rearranged into a mosaic with no overtly centralizing idea. Burroughs learned the cut-up from his friend Brion Gysin, a painter who tape-recorded a message that became a touchstone for Burroughs:

> I come to free the words
> The words are free to come
> I come freely to the words
> The free come to the words

Burroughs wrote Ginsberg in September of 1960 that the cut-up was a tool, a transitional bridge for passages that could not be logically connected. Often, from a page of cut-ups, he might select a line to be merged into his text. The technique was extended by a process he called the fold-in, where he would take a page of his text and someone else's, fold each down the middle, and place them side by side on the same page. The result, he felt, was analogous to the flashback in film.

Both the cut-up and the fold-in can be seen as a response to Kerouac's ideal of spontaneity. While Burroughs believes the spontaneous cannot be willed, the unpredictable can result from a dextrous use of scissors. The cut-up was to become a means through which he would objectively detach himself from romantic images, from tenderness, from personal associations and ties to his own words. It eliminated habitual reactions and conditioned reflexes, separated words from traditional referents, violated the normal syntax that influences rational behavior. It was also, curiously, a step in the direction of Eastern thought with its basis in chance and coincidence.

Burroughs' intention as a writer, beginning with ***Naked Lunch,*** has been to show how certain word combinations produce specific effects on the nervous system. By "cutting the word-lines," he believes he can find clues to the nature and function of words, as well as anticipate, suggest, or predict future events. As such, the cut-up threatens what Burroughs calls the Control Machine: any political system that through repression and social stratification ensures the power of the few and the subjection of the many, reinforcing the situation with such institutional means as police, religion, education, patriotic indoctrination through mass media.

Burroughs argues that media is now able to control events by emphasizing certain news stories, by editorializing, advertising, and selecting entertainment. "Cutting the word-lines" means severing the hypnotizing authority of newspapers, magazines, radio, and television, whose sources of power are obscured. It becomes a way of resisting the constant bombardment of images to which modern city man is subject that blunts his receptivity, dazes his senses with a permanent image haze. As a means of exploring subliminal awareness, the cut-up can establish fresh connections between images.

Burroughs has pointed to antecedents of the cut-up in the work of the Surrealist poet Tristan Tzara (who caused a riot in a theater when he pulled the lines of a poem from a hat) and T. S. Eliot. Another possible influence was a tape Burroughs heard by Jerry Newman, a friend of Kerouac's who was a record producer. The tape was called "The Drunken Newscaster," and on it a tipsy announcer confused the news with the interpolation of unrelated fragments of anecdotes. According to Ginsberg, Burroughs laughed so hard when he heard Newman in 1953 that he nearly fell out of his chair.

The form of the cut-up perfectly captures the disorder and confusion of madness, and Burroughs (like Borges, or Nabokov in *Pale Fire*) metaphysically refutes any distinctions between reality and fantasy. He writes from the viewpoint of the deranged drug addict whom he has compared to the schizophrenic. Madness becomes the expected behavior of the authorities, the political and institutional powers of the Control Machine. Their activities are a barrier, an obstacle to be overcome, and this premise motivates the swift metamorphoses of Burroughs' absurdist characters.

The result is less a world of sensibility than one of hallucinatory fear, a kind of para-awareness, for Burroughs articulates what Conrad's Kurtz would barely utter as "the horror, the horror!" The comparison is not fortuitous: Burroughs' voyage is into the miasma of Conradian darkness, though without the empathy that Marlowe's naïve journeyman's perspective affords in *Heart of Darkness*. Burroughs' landscape is a grotesque version of Conrad's exotic terrain, a spectacle of horrid insects and parasites, crabs emerging from chemical gardens, piles of rotting garbage, molds and fungi, diseased flesh and decaying carrion, weeds and rancid swamps.

T. S. Eliot, of course, first realized the value of the Conradian inferno and used it as a correlative for his own time. And Burroughs quotes from "The Love Song of J. Alfred Prufrock," from "Preludes," from "Rhapsody On A Windy Night," from "The Waste Land" itself, as he fashions a neon version of Eliot's vision of sterility with iridescence gleaming out of offal, mysterious energy sources congealing in places of death. By ***The Ticket That Exploded,*** Burroughs seems to have assimilated Eliot's desiccating, acerbically ironic view of nature in an entropic state of decomposition and rottenness. Burroughs' vision, like Eliot's, feeds on precise, clinically observed and unemotionally rendered details; these objects are presented cinematically, with all the speed of the motion-picture lens, and all transitions, even the formalities of infinitives, prepositions, and definite articles are omitted for the sake of increased tempo. It is speed that most characterizes Burroughs' prose, an accelerating quality demanding brevity of focus, appropriate surely to the surprising dislocations of the surrealistic eye as well as to Burroughs' proposition (like the Buddhist notion of *maya*) that all apparent sensory feelings, thoughts, and impressions are illusory. The rapidity of shifts of points of view and transformations of character creates an exceptional momentum that leaves the reader in the center of a maelstrom, caught in an exhilarating dance of desperation that invariably leads to death and obliteration—through the addict's needle, through the orgiastic excesses implied by Burroughs' favorite hanging metaphor, through a number of violent avenues that Burroughs has imagined with the ferocity of his contemporary, Jean Genêt.

The response to so excremental a vision may be one of simple revulsion, and it is true that many readers cannot bear much of Burroughs' incessant flagellation, sexual torture and mutilation, terrible deprivations of body and spirit all set in so fetid an environment. The initial depiction of the addict Lee (Burroughs' pseudonym in his first book, and a figure who recurs throughout his work) in ***Naked Lunch*** is typical:

> Lee lived in a permanent third-day kick, with, of course, certain uh essential intermissions to refuel the fires that burned through his yellow-pink-brown gelatinous substance and kept off the hovering flesh. In the beginning his flesh was simply soft, so soft that he was cut to the bone by dust particles, air currents and brushing overcoats while direct contact with doors and chairs seemed to occasion no discomfort. No wound healed in his soft, tentative flesh. . . . Long white tendrils of fungus curled round the naked bones. Mold odors of atrophied testicles quilted his body in a fuzzy grey fog. . . .

Lionel Abel, when reviewing ***Naked Lunch*** in *Partisan Review,* grudgingly accorded the book "only a tiny bit of literary merit," and quarreled with Norman Mailer's view (offered in *Advertisements For Myself*) of its beauty. Burroughs is so excessive in the above description of Lee's decomposition as to approach a kind of lushness, a richness and profusion that one finds in Poe's stories of hysteria, or in Baudelaire's *Les Fleurs du Mal.* Abel judged ***Naked Lunch*** from a rather heavy-handed moral perspective, and for him the novel had no aesthetic. In the way that "black comedy" describes the ironically sinister laughter of writers like Beckett, the term "black beauty" evokes the tone of joyous terror in Burroughs' work. "Beauty," Rilke has written, "is nothing but the beginning of terror that we are still just able to bear," and behind the psychology of such a remark lies an aesthetic that has eluded many of Burroughs' critics.

Consider another illustration of Burroughs' kind of beauty, this time from the "black fruit" chapter of ***The Ticket That Exploded:***

> From an enormous distance he heard the golden hunting horns of the Aeons and he was free of a body traveling in the echoing shell of sound as herds of mystic animals galloped through dripping primeval forests, pursued by the silver hunters in chariots of bone and vine—Lonely lemur calls whispered in the walls of silent obsidian temples in a land of black lagoons, the ancient rotting kingdom of Jupiter—smelling the black berry smoke drifting through huge spiderwebs in ruined courtyards under eternal moonlight—ghost hands at the paneless windows weaving memories of blood and war in stone shapes—A host of dead warriors stand as petrified statues in vast charred black plains—Silent ebony eyes turned toward a horizon of always, waiting with a patience born of a million years, for the dawn that never rises—Thousands of voices muttered the beating of his heart—gurgling sounds from soaring lungs trailing the neon ghost writing—Lykin lay gasping. . . .

Two notes are necessary for clarification: Lemurs, in Burroughs' world, are beings so spontaneous as to die when confined; black berry smoke signifies drug intoxication. The passage depends on a variety of sensuous experiences and several striking images. The bone and vine chariots, the golden hunting horns, the obsidian temples are set in the frozen splendor of a Keatsian eternal moment that recalls the picture on the Grecian urn. The dominant color of the passage, as it is throughout Burroughs' work, is black: the temples of obsidian, the lagoons, berries, charred plains, and ebony eyes function as signs of the death-in-life which forms Burroughs' typical moment. Yet, near the end of the passage, a strange sense of disembodied force, a transfer of secret energies, creates a haunting if peculiar animation. It is this sense of vitality in the very throes of death that informs Burroughs' world with its eerie, morbid beauty. Burroughs enacts a fragile balance between the most extreme instances of suffering and the kind of transported radiance that excess of pain provides in Mantegna's *Saint Sebastian,* in the Renaissance paintings of martyrdom and crucifixion, even in the more spasmodic visions of Breugel and Bosch whose entangled horrors are presented with the same calm certainty as Burroughs'.

To Poe's belief that the death of a beautiful woman was the ideal subject for poetry, Wallace Stevens has offered the modern symbolist corollary, "death is the mother of beauty." Stevens' formula is surely useful when considering how much of twentieth-century fiction and poetry emanates despair and points to death, and Burroughs, more than any other writer of his time, has sought death as an end, for and of itself. This search is characterized by a brutal self-immolation in explosions of pain. As André Breton prophesied during World War II, "Beauty will be convulsive, or not be." And Burroughs' distortions of the body and spirit create a spectacle of suffering in the Dadaist and Surrealist tradition. The apocalyptic intensity of Burroughs' blackness reminds us of the uncontainable fury of Antonin Artaud, another doomed addict, who warned that for theater to have meaning it would have to signal through the flames like some desperate victim being burned at the stake. Artaud's demand for a "theater of cruelty" offers a proper analogue for Burroughs' parabola of violence and mounting degradation, and just as Artaud's visions in the thirties presaged the inquisitorial terrors of the concentration camps, Burroughs' antennae may be tuned into strange circuits revealing the future. His compressed, obscure, and extremely visual sequences are like flashes of a barely glimpsed and terrifying extraterritorial existence. It is intriguing to remember, in this connection, that at the end of ***Junkie*** Burroughs declared that his "final fix" would be yage, a drug used by Indians at the headwaters of the Amazon that supposedly increases telepathic sensitivity.

The relationship of savage torture and sensuous pleasure is integral to Burroughs' fiction. A characteristically repeated scene describes a man being hung during an orgy; as he is homosexually ravished, his neck snaps in conjunction with orgasm. There are occasions when passion and violence have been interfused with a transcendentally regenerative power—as when Nietzsche accounts for the origins of classical tragedy in pre-Doric Dionysian rites—but such higher possibilities are not as easily derived from Burroughs' bloody dismemberments. Yet the demonic drive of scenes like the hanging sequences is rendered with a compulsion that is total and convincing as fantasy.

A typical illustration of what Burroughs sarcastically calls the "Garden of Delights" occurs as a screenplay, the section of ***Naked Lunch*** called "A.J.'s Annual Party." The film begins with Mary, a thin brunette, performing fellatio on Johnny, front and rear. She then straps on a rubber penis and assaults him. Mark enters and forces Johnny to commit similar homosexual acts, culminating on a vibrating chair as Johnny screams. Johnny is then escorted to a gallows platform covered with moldy jockstraps and hung as Mary impales herself on his erect member. In contrast, we may recall Beckett's more passive tramps who, in *Waiting For Godot,* only speculate on the possibilities of hanging. Since they barely exist, they can hardly muster the courage to be, to perform so decisive an act, and the ensuing tone is ironic. But Burroughs' figures enact a frenzy of perpetual becoming. Mary, after Johnny has been hung, cannibalistically sucks out his eyes, and bites away his nose, lips, and sexual parts. Mark then leaps on her and "they roll from one end of the room to the other, pinwheel end-over-end and leap high in the air like great hooked fish." Mark then hangs Mary during intercourse, and is transformed into Johnny. Up to this point the scene borders on pornography; it is ecstatically kinetic in its depiction of violence, giving us no explanation of its significance—only the speed of flashing sensation. The resurrected Johnny then leaps madly about the room and out into space, fulfilling the impulse of the symbolist hero to narcissistically embrace his image while plunging into an abyss:

> Masturbating end-over-end, three thousand feet down, his sperm floating beside him, he screams all the way against the shattering blue of sky, the rising sun burning over his body like gasoline, down past great oaks and persimmons, swamp cypress and mahogany, to shatter in liquid relief in a ruined square paved with limestone. Weeds and vines grow between the stones, and rusty iron bolts three feet thick penetrate the white stone, stain it shit-brown of rust.

Burroughs then rewrites his ending. First Johnny and Mary embrace sexually after being anointed with gasoline and they both burst into flames; then Johnny douches her with jungle bonesoftener and transfixes her with neon nails. It is an ever-accelerating pattern of violence and horror, the intensity increasing with each new barbaric act. The scene is finally resolved with a note of gothic lyricism sounding like a perverse parody of D. H. Lawrence:

> Damp hairs on the back of his balls dry to grass in the warm spring wind. High jungle valley, vines creep in the window. . . . A long tuber root creeps from Mary's cunt, feels for the earth. The bodies disintegrate in green explosions. The hut falls in ruins of broken stone. The boy is a limestone statue, a plant sprouting from his cock, lips parted in the half-smile of a junky on the nod.

Scenes like this one may be appalling to some sensibilities, overtly pornographic and shocking, but the lines are imbued with a phosphorescent luminosity and rendered in a spurting rhythm. In exaggerating sexual fantasy, Burroughs has gone further than predecessors like Joyce and Henry Miller. The Beats believed that absolutely anything was suitable as subject matter. The idea of taste was something they distrusted entirely, seeing it as a polite rationalization for elements of life that could not be faced artistically, the result of a legacy of Victorian prudishness that persisted far into the twentieth century. If Burroughs challenges the socially acceptable in his hanging scenes, pursuing them with reckless obsessiveness as if their horror—what he has called "terminal sewage"—was too great for a single exposure and required the cumulative impact of successive visits, his effort should be appreciated within the context of the tradition created by de Sade, Joyce, Lawrence, and Henry Miller, all writers who have tried to redeem our repressed fears and desires.

Burroughs has always treated taboo subjects with clinical candor. His use of physical abuse, of obscene detail and language is partly his correlative for a failed civilization. He introduced homosexuality and drug addiction as subjects in the fifties, but refused to exploit this material naturalistically. He writes with a devastating nightmarish flatness as if out of some hopeless vacuum—like the oracle in a bottle providing Eliot's epigraph to "The Waste Land"—of "human aggregates disintegrating in cosmic insanity, random events in a dying universe," as he observed in ***Junkie,*** his first book.

Junkie is a realistic account of Burroughs' initiation into the drug experience. The book's preface suggests how his perpetual childhood fear of nightmare, his tendency to hallucinate, and an awareness of some omnipresent impinging supernatural horror were premonitions of the underworld of drug addiction. But what is most revealing about ***Junkie,*** written when Burroughs was thirty-five and after several years on drugs, is the manner in which a realistic mode is extended almost to the surrealistic intensity of ***Naked Lunch*** and the following works. Early in the book Burroughs compares his first morphine experience

ABOUT THE AUTHOR

BURROUGHS AND JOAN VOLLMER

In 1944, Burroughs began living with Joan Vollmer in an apartment they shared with Kerouac and Edie Parker, Kerouac's first wife. Vollmer became Burroughs's common-law wife in 1946, and their son, William S. Burroughs, Jr., was born in 1947 in Texas. By the late 1940s, Burroughs's increasing passion for drugs had attracted the attention of law enforcement, and the family was forced to move to Mexico City, Mexico, to avoid his arrest. While in Mexico, the writer alternated morphine binges with periods of drug-free withdrawals; these extremes led to a significant deterioration of his physical and mental states. This decline reached its nadir in 1951, when Burroughs accidentally shot and killed Vollmer, purportedly while attempting to shoot a glass off her head William Tell-style. Burroughs was forced to leave Mexico in 1952 as a result of the shooting. He toured South America for several months, visited New York City briefly in the fall of 1953, then settled in Tangier, Morocco, for several years.

to floating without outlines, and recalls a series of pictures passing, as on the cinema screen; these qualities become essential characteristics of his later fiction. As he describes the horrors of withdrawal, Burroughs imagines New York City in ruins, with huge centipedes and scorpions (later favorite images) crawling in and out of empty bars, cafeterias, and drugstores on 42nd Street. Burroughs' critics have not observed the extent to which the key motifs of the later fiction are anticipated in ***Junkie.*** Some of these are offered with a realistic reserve and a precise attention to details—as when Burroughs explains how difficult it is for the addict to locate a vein—that makes sadism seem casual. Burroughs relates how he once supported his drug habit by stealing from helpless drunks, men susceptible to a hierarchy of scavengers who eventually will strip away all possessions as if robbing a corpse. These marauders anticipate the Liquifactionists of ***Naked Lunch*** who absorb one's protoplasmic being, and the hostile intruders of ***Nova Express*** and ***The Ticket That Exploded*** who take over human bodies.

Two typical images occur during the withdrawal process, a condition explaining many of the surreal dislocations of Burroughs' later imagery. The first image, of orgasm experienced after hanging, first appears after Burroughs has been arrested in New Orleans for possession of an unregistered pistol:

> I lay on the narrow wood bench, twisting from one side to the other. My body was raw, twitching, tumescent, the junk-frozen flesh in agonizing thaw. I turned over on my stomach and one leg slipped off the bench. I pitched forward and the rounded edge of the bench, polished smooth by the friction of cloth, slid along my crotch. There was a sudden rush of blood to the genitals at the slippery contact. Sparks exploded behind my eyes; my legs twitched—the orgasm of a hanged man when the neck snaps.

The second image, basic to Burroughs' imagination, presents a dissolving amoeboid mass. Burroughs, now in Mexico, has withdrawn from morphine, but has regressed to an alcoholic stupor:

> When I closed my eyes I saw an Oriental face, the lips and nose eaten away by disease. The disease spread, melting the face into an amoeboid mass in which the eyes floated, dull crustacean eyes. Slowly, a new face formed around the eyes. A series of faces, hieroglyphs, distorted and leading to the final place where the human road ends, where the human form can no longer contain the crustacean horror that has grown inside it.

Junkie may be considered a blueprint for all of Burroughs' work: it offers an introduction to the macabre and bizarre characters who reappear in his later fiction. There is Subway Mike who looked like "some specialized kind of underground animal that preys on animals of the surface." Or Mary, whose system could not absorb calcium so that "there was something boneless about her, like a deep sea creature. Her eyes were cold fish-eyes that looked at you through a viscous medium she carried about her. I could see those eyes in a shapeless, protoplasmic mass undulating over the dark sea floor." Or Doolie, who became for Burroughs "the focal point for a hostile intrusive force. You could feel him walk right into your psyche and look around to see if anything was there he could make use of." In his later fiction Burroughs calls this point of entry a coordinate, a place where an alien controlling agent would enter. And Doolie becomes the prototype of the carriers in the later fiction: "The envelope of personality was gone, dissolved by his junk-hungry cells. Viscera and cells, galvanized into loathsome insect-like activity." The insect image, a fusion of Gothic fantasy and science fiction, dominates all of Burroughs' work, and it is presented with remarkable force in his picture of the typical drug pusher:

> This man walks around in the places where he once exercised his obsolete and unthinkable trade. But he is unperturbed. His eyes are black with an insect's unseeing calm. He looks as if he nourished himself on honey and Levantine syrups that he sucks up through a proboscis.
>
> What is his lost trade? Definitely of a servant class and something to do with the dead, though he is not an embalmer. Perhaps he stores something in his body—a substance to prolong life—of which he is periodically milked by his masters. He is as specialized as an insect, for the performance of some inconceivably vile function.

Junkie, unlike the rest of Burroughs' work, is an ordered narrative, and the full grotesquerie of death as the ultimate reality is not felt with the force of the later fiction. Burroughs traces his involvement with addictive chemicals along a linear route from New York City to New Orleans to Mexico. While the experiences are quite painful, especially during the instances of drug deprivation, the horrors are cushioned by the narrator's journalistic presence, his retrospection, his guiding perspective through the infernal regions of drug abuse. When the same experiences are presented in the later books through the vehicle of the terminal addict, the difficulties for the reader are comparable to those confronted in Joyce's attempt to articulate the language of dreams in *Finnegans Wake* or Faulkner's use of the idiot Benjy in *The Sound and the Fury.* Drugs, Burroughs explains in his *Paris Review* interview, create a "random craving for images," and his cinematic sequences which seem to float across the page and almost evanesce respond to such a need. The reader searching for patterns, contrasts, or the thematic connections of conventional fiction must waive such expectations.

Burroughs cannot be fully appreciated by reading only ***Naked Lunch,*** for he develops crucial situations in ***The Soft Machine, Nova Express,*** and ***The Ticket That Exploded.*** The cumulative message of these novels is a warning of throttling controls on freedom and a world ruled by robot forces. Burroughs never really specifies the origins of this evil. In ***Nova Express*** and ***The Ticket That Exploded,*** the evil consists of agents planted by other galaxies to foment clashes on earth; later, the source is a virus from Venus. It is tempting to classify Burroughs as a writer of science fiction. However, because the content of science fiction is usually so difficult to believe, the writers of the genre have tended to employ conventional narrative techniques. None are as fragmentary as Burroughs, who will present a series of disconnected, unintegrated episodes without the narrative framework of plot or story.

Modern experimental novelists have struggled to reject classical notions of harmony, though some, like Joyce in *Ulysses,* have substituted cohering unities that greatly facilitate the reading of their works. In *Ulysses,* for example, the Homeric myth parallels Stephen Dedalus' flights and Bloom's more dogged pursuits, giving substance and meaning to the whole, just as the concentration on a day in Dublin provides additional focus and direction. Burroughs deliberately excludes such unifying conceptions from his books although, like Joyce, he uses stream of consciousness to enter deeply internalized states of being. In his *Paris Review* interview he claimed that he thought in "association blocks" rather than words, rejecting ordinary logic; and he asserted that the "Aristotelian construct is one of the great shackles of Western Civilization."

In what he calls an "atrophied preface" near the end of ***Naked Lunch,*** Burroughs offers several insights into his idea of the novel and the writer's role in composition. The writer can only record what exists in front of his sense; he cannot presume the imposition of plot or continuity. Burroughs implies that he has been possessed in the process of composition by alien agents. His characters are "subject to say the same thing in the same words" at different points in the narrative because their multiple disguises form the fused identity necessary to reveal the drug experience. As a result, readers can "cut into ***Naked Lunch*** at any intersection point." The book becomes a "kaleidoscope of vistas"; the world cannot be expressed directly, but requires a "mosaic of juxtaposition like articles abandoned in a hotel drawer, defined by negatives and absence. . . ." In ***The Ticket That Exploded,*** a character observes that "This is a novel presented in a series of oblique references," and the comment stands for all of Burroughs' work after ***Junkie.***

Burroughs has commented that his experiences with drugs did not induce a visionary quality as much as a sense of "moving at a high speed through space." This results in the floating metaphor first distinguished in ***Junkie,*** but becoming more pronounced as Burroughs progresses as a writer. Except for Pound's *Cantos,* no modern writer presents so rapid a series of transformations as Burroughs, and this is a feature that in Burroughs' case may be derived from film. Much as film exclusively captures the immediate presence of what is being photographed, Burroughs uses no past or future. Instead he relies on juxtaposition to create dimension and body. Since he has no real central characters, since his figures fade out of his narratives so quickly, since events change so rapidly, he violates all the ordinary features of novelistic perspective, what most readers take for "reality" in fiction—that is, a mirror of the familiar world. The result is as difficult to comprehend as Cubist painting was when it first exploded the logic of representational construction in art.

A good illustration of Burroughs' presentation occurs in ***Nova Express.*** Called "Shift Coordinate Points," it is an account of the struggle between different galactic forces for control of earth and the universe. K 9 is William Lee, the agent who detects and tracks down other hostile and threatening figures like The Subliminal Kid, Sammy The Butcher, and Izzy The Push, all of whom occupy drug addicts and work through their bodies:

> K 9 was in combat with the alien mind screen—Magnetic claws feeling for virus punch cards—pulling him into vertiginous spins—
>
> "Back—Stay out of those claws—Shift coordinate points"—By Town Hall Square long stop for the red light—A boy stood in front of the hot dog stand and blew water from his face—Pieces of grey vapor drifted back across wine gas and brown hair as hotel faded photo showed a brass bed—Unknown mornings blew rain in cobwebs—Summer evenings feel to a room with rose wallpaper—Sick dawn whisper of clock hands and brown hair—Morning blew rain on copper roofs in a slow haze of apples—Summer light on rose wallpaper—Iron mesas lit by a pink volcano—Snow slopes under the Northern shirt—Unknown street stirring sick dawn whispers of junk—Flutes of Ramadan in the distance—St. Louis lights wet cobblestones of future life—Fell through urinal and the bicycle races—On the bar wall the clock hands—My death across his face faded through the soccer scores—Smell of dust on the surplus army blankets—Stiff jeans against one wall—And Kiki went away like a cat—Some clean shirt and walked out—He is gone through unknown morning blew—"No good—No beano—Hustling myself—" Such wisdom in gusts—
>
> K 9 moved back into the combat area—Standing now in the Chinese youth sent the resistance message jolting clicking tilting through the pinball machine—Enemy plans exploded in a burst of rapid calculations—Clicking in punch cards of redirected orders—Crackling shortwave static—Bleeeeeeeeeeeeeep—Sound of thinking metal—
>
> "Calling partisans of all nations—Word falling—Photo falling—Break through in Grey Room—Pinball led streets—Free Doorways—Shift coordinate points—"

This example of what Burroughs calls an "association block" with its sense of eerie dislocation, and its events that seem so unordered by ordinary logic, realized shapes, or recognizable places, depends upon an unusually free notion of juxtaposition. When such evidently lyrical images as that of the rose wallpaper or the rain in cobwebs are yoked to an environment of electronic combat, some gap in expectation is widened, intending to diffuse and broaden the reader's focus rather than attempting to concentrate it as most fiction conventionally does. The result may be an unfamiliar music, rather like John Cage's dissonant compositions that almost impale ordinary sounds onto a musical structure.

Perhaps the most cogent analysis of Burroughs' method may be achieved by applying Charles Olson's descriptions of projective verse. Olson was fascinated by the kinetics of poetic movement since he saw the poem as an energy transfer, highly potent, very special, and, if successful, as meaningful as the most profound spiritual insights or messages. He claimed that the problem for the poet was an awareness of the process through which the energy that prompted the writing becomes the energy in which the reader participates. He believed that this interchange best occurred in as open a literary structure as possible, and Olson's key was transformation:

> ONE PERCEPTION MUST IMMEDIATELY AND DIRECTLY LEAD TO A FURTHER PERCEPTION. It means exactly what it says, is a matter of, at *all* points (even, I should say, of our management of daily reality as of the daily work) get on with it, keep moving, keep in, speed, the nerves, their speed, the perceptions, theirs, the acts, the split second acts, the whole business, keep it moving as fast as you can citizen. And if you also set up as a poet, USE USE USE the process at all points, in any given poem always, always one perception must must must MOVE, INSTANTER, ON ANOTHER!

Reacting like Pound against the nineteenth-century poets' tendency to flat statement, Olson, concerned with the artistic process of becoming, carries the tenets of Pound's Imagism to its logical extreme.

Burroughs, however, has another purpose that exists in particular accord with the Beats' desire to transform language so that it cannot be used as a conditioning agent. Since the eighteenth century, writers have appreciated the ability of the word to determine morality. In our own time, writers with such divergent political outlooks as George Orwell and Ezra Pound have agreed on how media corrupts language, reducing its efficacy by confusing the meaning of words. Orwell's fear, like McLuhan's anticipations of the end of fiction, is that language will be replaced by pictures as the chief conditioning agent, and the world of modern advertising seems to support this view. In *Tristes Tropiques,* Claude Levi Strauss asserted that writing itself has historically favored the exploitation rather than the enlightenment of mankind. From its original connections with early architectural enterprises, as a form of artificial memory and a method for organizing the present and future, writing became a source of power, ultimately a tool whose primary function was "to facilitate the enslavement of other human beings" through colonization or the internal regulations which all had to obey. In ***The Ticket That Exploded,*** Burroughs compares the present state of language to a viral infection caused by a parasitic organism. He agrees that "what we see is determined to a large extent by what we hear," and advocates a linguistic purge. In his final chapter (called "the invisible generation" and written in collaboration with Brion Gysin) he proposes a number of ways in which the conditioning influences of language can be reduced, such as playing a tape recorder backward slowly so that one can "learn to unsay what you just said . . . such exercises bring you a liberation from old association locks." Burroughs and Gysin recommend a variety of such methods: running tapes at different speeds to hear new words being formed, and splicing in body or animal sounds. Burroughs' point is that "the use of irrelevant response will be found effective in breaking obsessional association tracks," and sometimes his own anarchy of references in the cut-ups seems directed to this end.

Of course, the paradox of writing to end dependence on the word can be extended to Burroughs' centripetal rather than centrifugal conception of narrative structure. If his field is as vast as it is, if readers cannot find plot or story on which to focus, can he teach them to destroy the "control machine?" Actually, reading Burroughs, experiencing the circularity of his broadened field of reference, does serve to reshape perceptions so that the conditioning influences of the ordinary linguistic system become more apparent, and therefore less effective. But to successfully read the novels in the first place one has to want to be freed from those prejudices, and thus to have been partly liberated already.

In a sense, the unusual degree of violence in Burroughs' world—corresponding, of course, to the excesses of a spectacularly violent nation—frees the reader from normal expectations. The violence may itself be regarded as an assault on conditioning. In ***Nova Express,*** Burroughs reflects that "some ugly noxious disgusting act sharply recorded becomes now part of 'Photo falling—Word falling,'" that is, Burroughs' refrain for the breakdown of the supportive structures for our present technological civilization.

Burroughs himself provides the barest amount of thematic statement to bolster his views: indeed, if this is possible, he is a writer almost without a point of view, purely existing as a kind of supercharged literary centralizing and focusing neutrino in a world of ordinary movement. Occasionally he will comment directly, the very sparsity of such remarks giving them added weight and importance. In his *Paris Review* interview, for example, he equates the nova police he imagines in ***Nova Express*** with the forces of technology. Burroughs (like Conrad in *The Secret Agent,* Chesterton in *The Man Who Was Thursday,* or Mailer in *An American Dream*) believes that police and criminal elements share a similar mentality. The point of his equation of nova with technology is that both separate man from his naturally supportive conditions, replacing them with the antagonisms of competition and specialization.

The fear of control and pattern is endemic to Burroughs' vision. In ***Naked Lunch,*** he speculates on the future of biocontrol, a system of bioelectric signals injected into the nervous system which will telepathically regulate physical movement, mental processes, emotional reactions, and sensory impressions. The result would be robotized existence, for as he warns, "*You see control can never be a means to any practical end. . . . It can never be a means to anything but more control. . . .*" Burroughs feels that the United States is particularly the place for such an unhappy transformation, despite its myths of freedom and independence, because it has almost invented the thinking machine and as he advises near the end of ***Naked Lunch,*** "Americans have a special horror of giving up control, of letting things happen in their own way without interference. They would like to jump down into their stomachs and digest the food and shovel the shit out."

Burroughs' more overt declarations usually occur near the beginnings or ends of his novels. For instance, ***The Ticket That Exploded*** begins with the revelation of a biological weapon that reduces men to slobbering, inhuman things, and ends with an illustration of the effects of word conditioning:

> what are newspapers doing but selecting the ugliest sounds for playback by and large if its ugly its

news and if that isn't enough i quote from the editorial page of the new york daily news we can take care of china and if russia intervenes we can take care of that nation too the only good communist is a dead communist lets take care of slave driver castro next what are we waiting for let's bomb china now and let's stay armed to the teeth for centuries this ugly vulgar bray put out for mass playback you want to spread hysteria record and playback the most stupid hysterical reactions. marijuana marijuana why that's deadlier than cocaine.

Such direct imitations are infrequent in Burroughs' fiction. His indirectness is characteristically conveyed by allegory. The descriptions of the various political groups in ***Naked Lunch***'s Interzone, a complex of rooms forming one huge building like a vast beehive, exemplifies Burroughs' allegorical tendencies. The Liquifactionists believe in the "merging of everyone into One Man by a process of protoplasmic absorption." The Divisionists are similar products of conformist homogeneity: they cut off tiny bits of their flesh and nurture exact replicas of themselves in embryo jelly. Opposed to these groups are the Factualists who struggle against the use of control to "exploit or annihilate the individuality of another living creature." Motivating such fantasies is a paranoid vision of Western competitiveness, like Kerouac's more direct prediction in *Big Sur:* "like raving baboons we'll all be piled on top of each other. . . . Hundreds of millions of hungry mouths raving for more more more."

Burroughs' mode is parody. His ambition to expose the controls created by institutions, his exaggerated allegories of hospital operating rooms, of police and customs bureaucracies, result, as John Clellon Holmes has observed in *Nothing More To Declare,* in a rewriting of *1984* by W. C. Fields. The carnival mood of Burroughs' burlesque does balance the sense of violent terror in his work. The best illustration of Burroughs' grotesque humor is the figure of Dr. Benway in ***Naked Lunch,*** a man who deplores brutality only because of its inefficiency. Benway, who directs a Reconditioning Center in the Freeland Republic, is an expert on interrogation, brainwashing, and control. His macabre medicinal machinations are an ironic reflection of Burroughs' belief that there is no technological cure for spiritual disease. Burroughs' description of a typical operation stands as a primal influence on more recent absurdist fiction:

"I had a Yage hangover, me, and in no condition to take any of Browbeck's shit. First thing he comes on with I should start the incision from the back instead of the front, muttering some garbled nonsense about being sure to cut out the gall bladder it would fuck up the meat. Thought he was on the farm cleaning a chicken. I told him to go put his head back in the oven, whereupon he had the effrontery to push my hand severing the patient's femoral artery. Blood spurted up and blinded the anesthetist, who ran out through the halls screaming. Browbeck tried to knee me in the groin, and I managed to hamstring him with my scalpel. He crawled about the floor stabbing at my feet and legs. Violet, that's my baboon assistant—only woman I ever cared a damn about—really wigged. I climbed up on the table and poise myself to jump on Browbeck with both feet and stomp him when the cops rushed in.

Burroughs' comedy of hilarious excess is frequently tinged by nausea and sickness, like the menu for transcendental cuisine in ***Naked Lunch:*** "The After-Birth Suprême de Boeuf, cooked in drained crank case oil, served with a piquant sauce of rotten egg yolks and crushed bed bugs." It is a comedy that always verges on death, disease, and excrement. Surely no writer since Swift has expressed contempt and disgust in such brazenly uncomplimentary terms, and the Yahoos of *Gulliver's Travels* become the perfect model for Burroughs' view of man. Of course this sort of comic indulgence in ugliness and bestiality, in misfortune and maladjustment, is complementary to what I termed "black beauty" near the beginning of this essay. In this sense Burroughs does manage a unity of tone as he insists on a cruel pessimism, and the absolute lack of hope. Burroughs' characters will leap ferociously like Violet, Dr. Benway's baboon assistant, or will grovel like the president of Interzone who, in an annual Swiftian parody of the political process, crawls across the municipal garbage heap and in full view of the entire populace delivers the renewed lease to the British governor. The point is that human features in Burroughs' world are blurred, distorted, and eventually disappear.

The criticism that in ***Nova Express, The Soft Machine,*** and ***The Ticket That Exploded,*** Burroughs does not develop beyond the techniques of ***Naked Lunch*** is invalid: the three subsequent books form part of a larger whole, compiled partly from the same original manuscript, continuing the same vision, but always extending it. Developed after ***Naked Lunch,*** the cut-up adds a major difference in texture and atmosphere, creating its own strange profusions and impassable blocks. Sacrificing clarity and the element of narrative, it increases the chaos Burroughs wants his reader to feel. In the more recent works, ***Exterminator!*** and ***The Wild Boys,*** Burroughs uses the cut-up much more sparingly, mostly in isolated instances to create poetic bridges, integrating refrains, repeated passages that emphasize material in new perspectives. The result is generally an increase in coherence and continuity.

The two recent books represent a definite departure from the aesthetic of the objective recording instrument announced near the end of ***Naked Lunch.*** Burroughs' own political views have become more pronounced and visible, and accordingly his own sense of self is felt with greater presence in his writing now. While the ***Naked Lunch*** tetralogy has practically no identifiable persona, no single voice speaking for the author—due to the rapid metamorphoses and the obscuring miasma of junk—certain characters like Audrey in ***Exterminator!*** and ***Wild Boys*** directly reflect aspects of Burroughs' own past—his study of medicine in Vienna, for example, or his early sketch **"The Autobiography of a Wolf."** The strength of these later books is due less to experimentation than to power of vision. Both books are composed of brief sketches relating to a common anticipation of apocalypse.

In ***Exterminator!,*** the wind stops blowing in a Caribbean town called "Puerto de los Santos"; monstrous scorpion women appear in a pastoral English town; ladies are ravished on Fifth Avenue in New York City by American soldiers. Such omens of final disaster are counterpointed by quotations from songs like "The Battle Hymn of the Republic" or Burroughs' favorite, "The Star-Spangled Banner." The first sketch is a straightforward account, in the manner of ***Junkie,*** of Burroughs working as an exterminator of rats and roaches in Chicago. The following pieces reinforce this subject, except that the extinction becomes human.

In **"The Perfect Servant,"** a Pentagon official's butler is a Chinese agent who employs mind control to send a group of CIA agents into paroxysms, and releases a secret virus that will cause unborn children to speak Chinese at birth. In another sketch, a guerrilla group tries to explode a train carrying nerve gas. Another character stores electricity during shock treatment and releases it as a death ray. In **"Seeing Red,"** a brilliantly effective short parable on obscenity and politics, Lee imports a red picture through customs, the very sight of which enrages the police to the point of asphyxiation. In **"The Coming of the Purple Assed Better One,"** Burroughs mixes his observations of the 1968 Chicago Democratic convention with a fantasy on the political process, as Homer Mandrill, a demagogic baboon, runs for president on an ultraconservative platform. The book's tone is incongruously grotesque and bizarre: a Yiddish grandmother passionately protests the visit of the bedbug exterminator, moaning "like the Gestapo is murdering her nubile daughter engaged to a dentist"; the Queen of England supports herself by running a small grocery and lives in a semidetached cottage in a suburb.

The humor in ***The Wild Boys*** is more laconic and sadistic: the Green Nun assumes her Christ costume every night and visits one of the young nuns in her convent with a dildo while imagining herself in a poem by Sara Teasdale. The book begins and ends with a procession of stunted, maimed figures, and throughout there is the narrative tension of victims rising to murder their exploiters. The first piece is about Mexicans who love to humiliate Americans, and near the end of the book an old servile gardener stabs his master, a general who has just screamed that "Man is made to submit and obey." Ironically, the cult of the wild boys succeeds because they agree with their enemy, the general. Hints of their presence—a tribal affiliation of young homosexual guerrillas—appear through the early parts of the book, juxtaposed to the many signs of imminent disaster for those still in power. The time is the last decades of the twentieth century. Famine and plague have widened the gaps between rich and poor. In North Africa, where the wild boys originate, all institutional procedures have collapsed: the wealthy are protected by private mercenaries; travel is by stagecoach or mule since there is no longer much oil available. An American expeditionary force of twenty thousand soldiers is annihilated by the extraordinarily savage tactics of the wild boys who fight like animals and spread over the world. Their battle skills are in the tradition of the *lútíyeh,* the eighteenth-century bands of marauding sodomites in India who attacked rich travelers and merchant caravans, or the Pariah women of the same time and place, followers of the goddess Kali, who hunted men in packs and raped them. Like the satyrs and sirens of sodomite and Amazonian myth, the wild boys are impervious to ordinary needs. They descend from the Moslem *ghâzíyeh,* the berserkers, founded by Hassan-ben-Sabah-Momairi who appears in ***Naked Lunch*** as an obvious source of admiration for Burroughs. Hassan's followers believed in him as a messiah; they were pledged to complete obedience, and would eat hashish before battle to become indifferent to pain or death. The wild boys are a highly ritualized group whose sacraments are sex and hashish. Using eighteen-inch bowie knives, crossbows, karate, claws treated with cyanide, they develop a mixture of primitive battle tactics and sophisticated technology. Some of them use no language at all, others have developed "cries, songs, words as weapons":

> Words that cut like buzz saws. Words that vibrate the entrails to jelly. Cold strange words that fall like icy nets on the mind. Virus words that eat the brain to muttering shreds. Idiot tunes that stick in the throat round and round night and day.

Attacking with fanatical devotion, the wild boys take no prisoners, instead making hash pouches from human testicles. They renounce women and are exclusively homosexual. The tension in the book is between scenes of incredible violence and homoeroticism without love, existing almost for the sake of sensation itself. The world of ***The Wild Boys*** is as frightening as the drug-deranged environment of ***Naked Lunch,*** and it is Burroughs' best book since then.

Like the image of vultures swooping down a black funnel near the beginning of ***Naked Lunch,*** Burroughs' vision is intensely surreal. He transmits a feeling of desperate urgency, of apocalyptic disaster and warning. Tony Tanner, in *City of Words,* has interpreted this message in terms of entropy, the idea of matter returning to lower forms of organization. According to this point of view, the nightmares Burroughs concocts are recidivistic, a return to some primitive feared state. As Burroughs writes in ***Naked Lunch*** on the ritual role of untouchables in India, who "perform a priestly function in taking on themselves all human vileness," so, too, this aspect of his art is shamanistic, a warding off of evil through the public exorcism of his fiction.

But another view of Burroughs' art is possible. According to the new physics that seems to have informed Burroughs' world, as well as the possibility of telepathy induced by the drug experience, Burroughs may be introducing us to a futuristic vision of the cybernetic reality slowly replacing human perspectives in the West. Living organisms form open systems (unlike the Deist view of the world as clock, running down in time because of friction), and feed on energies and materials found in the environment. Instead of dissipating energy—which as Einstein argued cannot be destroyed—the organism builds up more complex chemicals from the chemicals nourishing it, more complex forms of energy from the energy it absorbs, and more complex forms of information—perceptions, memories, ideas—from the input of its receptors. In Burroughs' fiction, the human form is "building up" to a perceptual level that suggests a new stage of experience. Yeats, who used automatic writing and a kind of telepathy in experiments with his wife, felt that man would pass into a new unrecognizable stage in the year 2000, the time that ecologists currently claim is the approximate limit of nature's sustenance of human growth. Burroughs' books point to some new time when communication will occur through combinations of intense sensory but nonverbal experience, where we may wander through existence like neutrinos, unhampered in our flight and connecting only in silence.

Rimbaud called for the hallucination of the word. As Gertrude Stein was for the Lost Generation, Burroughs is our theoretician of language, our cabalist of the word. He has deconditioned himself with drugs, and purifying his vision, has used the cut-up as a way of objectively reproducing the process of his own consciousness. His reputation has depended on one book, ***Naked Lunch.*** Since then the critics have failed to understand his accomplishments. Marshall McLuhan was amused by reviews of Burroughs' work which regarded it as failed science fiction: "It is a little like trying to criticize the sartorial and verbal manifestations of a man who is knocking on the door to explain that flames are leaping from the roof of our house." Burroughs is the Beat archangel of apocalypse: though his content will always be obscene to those still trapped in the legacy of puritanism, his method is cleansing and purgative, however terrifying in implication.

DONALD PALUMBO (ESSAY DATE WINTER 1979)

SOURCE: Palumbo, Donald. "William Burroughs's Quartet of Science Fiction Novels as Dystopian Social Satire." *Extrapolation* 20, no. 4 (winter 1979): 321-9.

In the following essay, Palumbo suggests that Burroughs uses some of the conventions associated with science fiction to produce a scathing satire aimed at addicts of drugs, sex, or power.

In ***Naked Lunch*** and its three less well-known sequels, ***The Soft Machine, Nova Express,*** and ***The Ticket That Exploded,*** William Burroughs weaves an intricate and horrible allegory of human greed, corruption, and debasement. Like Orwell's *1984* and Huxley's *Brave New World,* Burroughs' four works, taken collectively, seize on the evils or tendencies toward a certain type of evil that the author sees as being particularly malignant in his contemporary world and project them into a dystopian future, where, magnified, they have grown monstrous and taken on an exaggerated and fantastic shape. And like these classics of dystopian fiction, Burroughs' works are more novels of ideas that cleverly utilize the trappings of science fiction than they are what most people would consider "pure and simple" science fiction.

Even to the sophisticated reader they are troublesome puzzles; they are clearly more impenetrable than most popular literature. In his review of ***The Soft Machine,*** Stephen Koch states that Burroughs' "books are without meaning just as they have no stories and are not imitations of life. They are unparaphrasable experiences . . . The reader's mind plays over their broken surfaces at liberty, discovering correspondences, making associations, experiencing images of the impossible, accepting, rejecting—creating the work himself."[1] Significantly, this is not to say that they are without meaning or story, or that they are not imitations of life. But these elements are both realized differently here than they are in more conventional fiction. Although they share the same themes, metaphorical images, characters, and stylistic approach, this quartet—Burroughs' most serious novels—becomes more bizarre and takes on more of the appearance of science fiction as the novels progressively clarify and develop the author's thought. Each volume contributes to a single plot—or rather combines with the others to suggest the elements of what little plot there is. Thus, they may each be considered sections of one large work that encompasses them all.

Burroughs experiments with a style that has its closest analog in the cinematic technique of montage, although that technique is here most radically employed. He juxtaposes one scene with another without regard to plot, character, or, in the short view, theme to promote an association of the reader's negative emotional reaction to the superficial content (sexual perversion, drug abuse, senseless violence) of certain scenes with the implied narrative content (examples of "addictions": to drugs, money, sex, power, i.e., the allegory) of others. One clear instance of this technique is Burroughs' treatment of homosexuality, a practice that, while it is repeatedly equated with excrement and death (and is likely to have a negative connotation in the minds of most readers), is also endlessly juxtaposed to various addictions, particularly heroin addiction. The theory is that if such juxtapositions recur often enough, the feeling of revulsion strategically created by the first set of images will form the reader's attitude toward the second set of examples. Burroughs' protagonist in ***Naked Lunch,*** William Lee, reveals, "So I got an exclusive why don't I make with the live word? The word cannot be expressed direct. . . . It can perhaps be indicated by mosaic of juxtaposition like articles abandoned in a hotel drawer, defined by negatives and absence."[2] And a later reincarnation of this character, Inspector J. Lee of the Nova Police, in explaining the technique used by the Nova Mob to control subject populations, notes in ***Nova Express*** that "The basic law of association and conditioning is known to college students even in America: Any object, feeling, odor, word or image in juxtaposition with any other object, feeling, odor, word, or image will be associated with it."[3] It is for this reason, as Burroughs himself warns, that "***Naked Lunch*** demands silence from the reader. Otherwise he is taking his own pulse."[4] The reader must allow the juxtaposition of images to work unobstructedly within him. It is in this way that he will be "creating the work himself." As Marshall McLuhan observes, "Burroughs is unique only in that he is attempting to reproduce in prose what we accommodate every day as a commonplace aspect of life in the electric age."[5]

Anything written in such a style must be to a large extent unparaphrasable; as William Phillips laments, "It is impossible to explain what happens"[6] in ***Nova Express,*** for instance. It is possible to make general statements describing the action of these four novels, however, for in treating these works simultaneously we are far enough removed from each to begin to distinguish outlines, much as we see that the spots and blobs of paint in an impressionistic painting form a coherent image when viewed from a sufficient distance. Surely, as many critics, such as John Ciardi, have recognized, "What Burroughs has written is a many leveled vision of horror."[7] He has constructed a science fiction-like fantasy wherein, on a literal level, it is seen that the earth and its human inhabitants have been taken over by the Nova Mob, an assortment of extraterrestrial, non-three-dimensional entities who, somewhat like metaphysical viruses, live parasitically on the reality of other organisms. These evil creatures are, we learn in ***Nova Express,*** "sucking all the flavor out of food the pleasure out of sex the color out of everything in sight—precisely creating the low pressure area that leads to Nova—so they move cross the wounded galaxies always a few light years ahead of the Nova Heat."[8] Nova is the destruction of a planet, an inevitably necessary action taken by the Nova Mob to destroy any evidence of their activity and thus to escape detection by the Nova Police and prosecution in the Biologic Courts.

In these novels exploitation of the earth has reached such proportions that the Nova Police have been alerted. They are attempting to thwart the Nova Mob without so alarming them that they will destroy the planet in trying to make what escape they can. The most direct form of nova control, control that enables the Nova Mob to carry on its parasitic activity with impunity, is thought control of the human population achieved through control of the mass communications media; and, as we are told in ***The Ticket That Exploded,*** "the basic nova technique is very simple: always create as many insoluble (human) conflicts as possible and always aggravate existing conflicts."[9] Since the middle of ***Nova Express,*** the reader has been in the midst of a science fiction-like war of images fought with cameras and tape recorders. The Nova Police and the inhabitants of earth, having discovered how to combat the techniques of the Nova Mob with similar techniques, of which these novels are themselves examples, are fighting a guerrilla war of images with the Nova Criminals, who are desperately trying to escape. The ending of ***The Ticket That Exploded*** is optimistic but inconclusive. The reader never does discover if the earth will be rid of the Nova Mob before they succeed in destroying it.

Naked Lunch is the complex of impressions and sensations experienced by William Lee, an agent of the Nova Police who has assumed the cover of a homosexual heroin addict because with such a cover he is most likely to encounter Nova Criminals, who are all addicts of one sort or another and who, therefore, prefer to operate through human addicts. (Burroughs considers homosexuality to be a form of sexual addiction.) As Inspector J. Lee of the Nova Police, Lee states in ***Nova Express*** that "The purpose of my writing is to expose and arrest Nova Criminals. In ***Naked Lunch, Soft Machine*** and ***Nova Express*** I show you who they are and what they are doing and what they will do if they are not arrested . . . With your help we can occupy the Reality Studio and retake their universe of Fear Death and Monopoly."[10] Consequently, ***Naked Lunch*** is, on one level, as Ciardi expresses it, "a monumental descent into the hell of narcotic addiction."[11] Although there is very little hint here of the fantastic plot I have outlined, the novel's individual episodes are still peculiarly non-realistic. An example is this description of Lee: "In the beginning his flesh was simply soft, so soft that he was cut to the bone by dust particles, air currents and brushing overcoats while direct contact with doors and chairs seemed to occasion no discomfort. No wound healed in his soft, tentative flesh. . . . Long white tendrils of fungus curled around the naked bones."[12] It is only toward the conclusion of the novel that we discover that Lee is some sort of an agent "clawing at a not-yet of Telepathic Bureaucracies, Time Monopolies, Control Drugs, Heavy Fluid Addicts."[13]

The "naked lunch" of the title is the reality seen by Lee, what Burroughs describes as that "frozen moment when everyone sees what is on the end of every fork."[14] From the bleak homosexual encounters and desperate scrambles to make drug connections into which the book plunges come two central ideas: the concepts of addiction, the primary motif of these novels, and "the algebra of need," which states simply that when an addict is faced with absolute need (as a junkie is for heroin or a control addict for power), he will do anything to satisfy that need. The Nova Criminals are non-human personifications of various addictions. The Uranians, addicted to Heavy Metal Fluid, are prototypes of drug addicts. Dr. Benway, Mr. Bradley Mr. Martin (a single character), and the insect people of Minraud—all control addicts—are prototypes of the human addiction to power. The green boy-girls of Venus, addicted to Venusian sexual practices, are prototypes of the human addiction to sensual pleasure. The Death Dwarf, addicted to concentrated words and images, is the prototype of the human addiction to various cultural myths and beliefs; he is perhaps the most pathetic of these depraved creatures. Burroughs explains in ***Naked Lunch*** that "Junk yields a basic formula of 'evil' virus: the face of evil is always the face of total need. A dope fiend is a man in total need of dope. Beyond a certain frequency need knows absolutely no limit or control."[15] In ***The Ticket That Exploded*** he testifies, "Fact is we were all junkies and thin after a long ride on the White Subway—flesh junkies, control junkies, heavy metal junkies."[16] And, as Ciardi notes, "Only after the first shock does one realize that what Burroughs is writing about is not only the destruction of depraved men by their drug lust, but the destruction of all men by their consuming addictions, whether the addiction be drugs or over-righteous propriety or sixteen-year-old-girls."[17]

Burroughs sees ***The Soft Machine*** as being "a sequel to ***Naked Lunch,*** a mathematical extension of the Algebra of Need beyond the Junk Virus."[18] Here the consuming addiction, displayed again in juxtaposition with scenes of drug abuse and sexual perversion, and through a number of shifting narrators, is the addiction to power over others. The central episode is the destruction of the control apparatus of an ancient Mayan theocracy by a time-traveling agent; this is a direct analog of the struggle between the Nova Police and the Nova Mob that breaks out into the open in the subsequent two novels. The time traveler uses the same technique to prepare himself for time travel as Burroughs does in writing his novels, a type of montage; he reports, "I started my trip in the morgue with old newspapers, folding in today with yesterday and typing out composites."[19] Since words tie men to time, this character is given apomorphine to break this connection. Apomorphine is the fictitious drug that cures heroin addiction in Burroughs' novels and is thus an analog of the camera-recorder gimmick through which the Nova Police combat the control techniques of the Nova Mob. (The scenario on pages 105-109 of ***Nova Express*** is another prototype of the nova situation. A prototype of the control techniques used by the Nova Mob is found in the "Dr. Benway" section of ***Naked Lunch,*** pages 21-45.)

Burroughs contends that any addiction dehumanizes its victims. The Mayan priests tend to become half-men/half-crab creatures who eventually metamorphosize into giant centipedes and exude an erogenous green slime. This type of transformation strikes Lee in his human, addict disguise. Bradley the Buyer, in fact, who reappears as Mr. Bradley Mr. Martin, Mrs. and Mrs. D., and the Ugly Spirit, has a habit of turning into a blob-like creature who is addicted to and who absorbs drug addicts. He is destroyed by flame throwers early in ***Naked Lunch,*** "the court of inquiry ruling that such means were justified in that the buyer had lost his human citizenship and was, in consequence, without species and a menace to the narcotics industry on all levels."[20] Florence Howe notes that "throughout ***Naked Lunch*** one sees man, controlled by junk and/or other men, turning into a monstrous larva-like creature or a savage beast."[21] Another example is found in ***The Soft Machine*** where one homosexual character, while being strangled with a scarf, suddenly "gasped coughing and spitting, face swollen with blood—His spine tingled—Coarse black hair suddenly sprouted all over him. Canines tore through his gums with exquisite toothache pain."[22] Instances of metamorphosis are almost innumerable in the last three novels and particularly in ***The Ticket That Exploded.***

The "soft machine," the title of the second book in the quartet, is both the "wounded galaxy," the Milky Way seen as a quasi-biological organism diseased by the virus-like Nova Mob, and the human body, riddled with parasites and addictions and programmed with the "ticket," obsolete fictions, myths, and dreams, written on the "soft typewriter" of culture and civilization. Here, in ***The Soft Machine,*** the first mention of nova activity, that of Uranian Willy—Willy the Rat, the Heavy Metal Kid, is made: "His plan called for total exposure—Wise up all the marks everywhere Show them the rigged wheel—Storm the Reality Studio and retake the Universe."[23]

Nova Express and ***The Ticket That Exploded*** most clearly reveal the plot situation and explore the Nova Mob's exploitation of media. Here addiction to language is investigated. As Koch argues, here

> The "moralist" in Burroughs addresses himself to . . . The freedom or bondage of consciousness, insofar as consciousness is a function of language. . . . Burroughs' ideology—the theme explicitly developed in ***Nova Express,*** his least impressive book so far, is based on an image of consciousness in bondage to the organism: better, of consciousness as an organism, gripped by the tropisms of need. Consciousness is addicted—it is here the drug metaphore [*sic*] enters—to what sustains it and gives it definition: in particular, it is addicted to the word, the structures of language that define meaning and thus reality itself. The linguistic formulas that fill our lives, he assumes, have hardened into independent, imprisoning realities.[24]

Thus, in ***The Soft Machine,*** the time traveler is sent to Trak News Agency, whose motto is "We don't report the news—we write it," to learn how to defeat the Mayan theocracy, which exercises its control through the manipulation of myths by first learning "how this writing the news before it happens is done."[25] And in ***The Ticket That Exploded*** it is axiomatic that "you can run a government without police if your conditioning program is tight enough but you can't run a government without bullshit."[26]

Contemporary existence is seen as a film that is rerun again and again, trapping the human soul like an insect imprisoned in amber, negating any possibility of real freedom. A character complains in ***Nova Express,*** "What you are offering me is a precarious aqualung existence in somebody else's stale movie."[27] In ***The Ticket That Exploded*** we are told that "Martin's reality film is the dreariest entertainment ever presented to a captive audience . . . Martin's film worked for a long time . . . The reality film has now become an instrument and weapon of monopoly. The full weight of the film is now directed against anyone who calls the film in question with particular attention to writers and artists."[28] The problem seems to be that "any image repeated loses charge and that loss is the lack that makes this Hell and keeps us here . . . Because ugliness is repetition to maintain precarious occupation."[29] Burroughs' last cry before the conclusion of ***The Ticket That Exploded,*** which attempts to capture the essence of "endingness," is one of revolt:

> See what I mean boys? It is time to forget. To forget time. Is it? It was it will be it is? No. It was and it will be if you stand still for it. The point where the past touches the future is right where you are sitting now on your dead time ass hatching virus negatives into present time into the picture reality of a picture planet. Get off your ass boys. Get off the point.[30]

It has been claimed that satire is "that literature which expresses feelings appropriate to what is vicious, inadequate, defective, etc."[31] Burroughs meant for his works to be the most vicious of allegorical satires, in his own words, "necessarily brutal, obscene and disgusting,"[32] as are the situations from which he drew his images and metaphors. ***The Ticket That Exploded*** begins with a character who confesses,

> I am reading a science fiction book called ***The Ticket That Exploded.*** The story is close enough to what is going on here so now and again I make myself believe that this ward room is just a scene in an old book far away and long ago . . . everything is coming apart like rotten undervest . . . but the show goes on . . . love . . . romance . . . stories that rip your heart out and eat it.[33]

Burroughs claims, in his introduction to ***Naked Lunch,*** "There is only one thing a writer can write about: what is in front of his senses at the moment of writing."[34]

On one level of interpretation Burroughs' satire is leveled at those men addicted to pleasure or power in any of the many forms that either may take—men who, obeying the dictates of "the algebra of need," will stop at nothing to fulfill their desires. They have "lost their human citizenship." They are the Nova Mob, non-human parasites feeding on the essences of others; they shamelessly lie, cheat, and manipulate to attain what has come to be equated in the reader's mind with perversion, excrement, and death. The narrator of ***The Ticket That Exploded*** explains,

> In three-dimensional terms the board is a group representing international big money who intend to take over and monopolize space . . . As word dust falls and their control machine is disconnected by partisan activity they'll be in the bread line without clothes or a dime to buy off their "dogs" their "gooks" their "errand boys" their "human animals"—liars—cowards—collaborators—traitors—liars who want time for more lies—cowards who cannot face your "human animals" with the truth—collaborators with insect people, with vegetable people—with any people anywhere who offer them a body forever—traitors to all souls everywhere sold out to shit forever.[35]

Burroughs' satire goes deeper than this, however. He attacks not only the men, but also the structure of the culture that enables their practices to continue. He attacks the fictions and the myths that imprison the men, that limit thought and action through invisible stone walls of patriotism and religion while distracting body and mind through dreams of romantic love. He demands that man free himself from these "word and image addictions." He demands that everyone heed the last words of Hassan I Sabbah (cribbed from Dostoevski's Ivan Karamozov—although here they have an even more universal meaning): "Nothing is True—Everything is Permitted."[36]

In ***Nova Express*** Burroughs wails, "Listen: their Garden of Delights is a terminal sewer—I have been at some pains to map this area of terminal sewage in the so-called pornographic sections of ***Naked Lunch*** and ***The Soft Machine.***"[37] In ***The Ticket That Exploded*** he rages,

> Better than the 'real thing?'—There is no real thing—Maya—Maya—It's all show business.
>
> . . . Love falling permutated through body halves—Static orders clicking—word falling—Time falling—Love falling—Flesh falling—Photo falling—Image falling . . .
>
> Workers paid off in a thing called "Love"—the junk man at the outskirts . . .
>
> "Look through the human body the house passes out at the door—What do you see?—It is composed of thin transparent sheets on which is written the action from birth to death—written on 'the soft typewriter' before birth—a cold deck built in" . . .
>
> The human body is transient hotel memory pictures . . .
>
> Two young bodies stuck together like dogs' teeth bared . . . Two dead stars . . . They went out a long time ago in empty back yards and ash pits . . . a rustle of darkness and wires . . . They went out and never came back a long time ago . . .
>
> "I lived your life a long time ago . . . sad shadow whistles cross a distant sky . . . adios marks this long ago address.. didn't exist you understand.. ended.. stale dreams Billy . . . worn out here . . . tried to the end . . . there is a film shut up in a bureau drawer . . . boy I was who never would be now . . . a speck of white that seemed to catch all the light left on a dying star . . . and suddenly I lost him . . . my film ends . . . I lost him long ago . . . dying there . . . light went out . . . my film ends."[38]

Notes

1. Stephen Koch, "Images of Loathing," *Nation,* 203, pp. 25-26.
2. William S. Burroughs, *Naked Lunch* (New York: Grove Press Black Cat Edition, 1966) p. 116.
3. William S. Burroughs, *Nova Express,* (New York: Grove Press Black Cat Edition, 1965) p. 78.
4. Burroughs, *Naked Lunch,* p. 225.
5. Marshall McLuhan, "Notes on Burroughs," *Nation,* 199, pp. 517-19.
6. William Phillips, "New Immoralists," *Commentary,* 39, pp. 66-69.
7. John Ciardi, "Book Burners and Sweet Sixteen," *Saturday Review,* 42, p. 22.
8. Burroughs, *Nova Express,* p. 70.
9. William S. Burroughs, *The Ticket That Exploded,* (New York: Grove Press Black Cat Edition, 1968) pp. 54-55.
10. Burroughs, *Nova Express,* p. 70.
11. Ciardi, p. 22.
12. Burroughs, *Naked Lunch,* p. 70.
13. Burroughs, *Naked Lunch,* p. 217.
14. Burroughs, *Naked Lunch,* p. xxxvii.
15. Burroughs, *Naked Lunch,* p. xxxix.
16. Burroughs, *Ticket,* p. 143.
17. Ciardi, p. 22.
18. Burroughs, *Naked Lunch,* p. xliv.
19. William S. Burroughs, *The Soft Machine,* (New York: Grove Press Black Cat Edition, 1967) p. 85.
20. Burroughs, *Naked Lunch,* p. 18.
21. Florence Howe, Letter, *The New Republic,* 141, p. 31.
22. Burroughs, *Soft Machine,* p. 60.
23. Burroughs, *Soft Machine,* p. 155.
24. Koch, pp. 25-26.
25. Burroughs, *Soft Machine,* p. 152.
26. Burroughs, *Ticket,* pp. 150-51.
27. Burroughs, *Nova Express,* p. 41.
28. Burroughs, *Ticket,* pp. 150-51.
29. Burroughs, *Ticket,* pp. 188-89.
30. Burroughs, *Ticket,* p. 196.
31. H. V. S. Ogden, "Imaginative Literature as a College Study," *College English,* XXIX, footnote, p. 9.
32. Burroughs, *Naked Lunch,* p. xliv.
33. Burroughs, *Ticket,* pp. 5-6.
34. Burroughs, *Naked Lunch,* p. 221.
35. Burroughs, *Ticket,* pp. 139-40.
36. Burroughs, *Nova Express,* p. 40.
37. Burroughs, *Nova Express,* p. 13.
38. Burroughs, *Ticket,* pp. 77, 105, 146, 159, 181, 187, 202.

DUNCAN WU (ESSAY DATE SUMMER 1991)

SOURCE: Wu, Duncan. "Wordsworth in Space." *The Wordsworth Circle* 22, no. 3 (summer 1991): 172-9.

In the following essay, Wu asserts that Burroughs is "the inheritor of the Romantic tradition that begins with Wordsworth."

"What am I trying to do in writing?" William S. Burroughs asked himself in his Tangier journal some time during the late 1950s. He's not the only one who wants to know. Ever since ***The Naked Lunch*** was published in July, 1959, Burroughs' detractors and admirers have been asking exactly the same question. John Calder's 1982 edition of ***The Naked Lunch*** helpfully includes in an Appendix what has become known as the "Ugh" correspondence, so-called after John Willett's 1963 review of several Burroughs novels in the *TLS. [Times Literary Supplement]* By then it was already clear that Burroughs' work would never be fully accepted by the literary establishment. Edith Sitwell's contribution to the "Ugh" correspondence is characteristic: "I do not wish to spend the rest of my life with my nose nailed to other people's lavatories. I prefer Chanel Number 5" (p. 264).

Well, I've been known to use the odd splash of Chanel myself, but I wouldn't invoke it as the basis of my literary judgment. It didn't help that Burroughs' publisher, Maurice Girodias, was also a pornographer. Girodias' Olympia Press edition of ***The Naked Lunch*** was published in the same series as *With Open Mouth* by Carmencita de las Lunas, *I've Got a Whip in my Suitcase* by Beauregard de Farniente, and *White Thighs* by Count Palmiro Vicarion. (But don't laugh too soon: Count Palmiro Vicarion was the pen-name of the poet Christopher Logue, better known for his recent translation of Homer's *Iliad,* and Carmencita de las Lunas was the novelist Alexander Trocchi.) It's to his credit that, alongside these lurid titles, Girodias published Samuel Beckett's *Watt,* the Beckett trilogy, Nabokov's *Lolita* and Donleavy's *The Ginger Man.* I hope in this paper to demonstrate, firstly, that Burroughs belongs firmly with the second group of writers rather than the first—and, more importantly, that he's the inheritor of the Romantic tradition that begins with Wordsworth.

Let's return to Burroughs' journal entry. By the time he was keeping this journal he had two novels behind him, ***Junky*** (published 1952) and ***Queer*** (completed the same year, though not published until 1985); he was at work on his third, then entitled ***Interzone.*** Having reached his mid-forties, he was also undergoing a period of profound self-doubt. The notoriety that came with ***The Naked Lunch*** was five or six years off, and he was still attempting to define his literary personality—hence the question, "What am I trying to do in writing?" His journal continues:

> This novel is about transitions, larval forms, emergent telepathic faculty, attempts to control and stifle new forms.
>
> I feel there is some hideous new force loose in the world like a creeping sickness, spreading, blighting. Remoter parts of the world seem better now because they are less touched by it. Control, bureaucracy, regimentation, these are merely symptoms of a deeper sickness that no political or economic program can touch. What is the sickness itself?[1]

Burroughs isn't the first writer to find himself obsessed by metamorphosis. Wordsworth once recalled being "so strongly attached to Ovid, whose Metamorphoses I read at school, that I was quite in a passion whenever I found him, in books of criticism, placed below Virgil."[2] And as I've suggested elsewhere, Wordsworth's ideas about imagination owe something to his childhood love of Ovid. On the face of it, Burroughs' terms are distinctive: "This novel is about transitions, larval forms, emergent telepathic faculty, attempts to control and stifle new forms." The determined physicality of his language looks back to post-war science fantasists such as Eric Frank Russell and Henry Kuttner.

Kuttner's *Fury* (1955), which Burroughs praises in his 1985 essay, **"Light Reading"** (***The Adding Machine,*** pp. 196-201) is obsessed with metamorphosis. It's set in a post-hollocaust world in which humans live underwater in vast airlocked cities. The hero, Sam Reed, revolts against the rulers, and leads the people out of the water onto dry land—a political metamorphosis that literally mimics the evolution of life on earth. "They don't want a change!" Reed exclaims against the rulers, "They're conservatives. The people on top are always conservatives. Any change has to be for the worse where they're concerned" (p. 94).

As with the best science-fiction, *Fury* transcends the level of mere fantasy. Its first readers were well aware that it was intended to be a political fable; in his Foreword to the 1955 edition published by the Science Fiction Book Club, Groff Conklin noted: "This story has its own important message for our time; for today, as always, the human race cannot vegetate. It either climbs upward to new levels of social complexity and achievement, or it drifts ever downward into a universal senility" (p. v). For Burroughs too, the failure to evolve has always had an immediate political significance. Though it often occurs in the expected science-fiction context, he relates it to the proliferation of "Control, bureaucracy, regimentation." In ***The Naked Lunch,*** control "can never be a means to any practical end. . . . It can never be a means to anything but more control. . . . Like junk . . ." (p. 164). Equated with drug addiction, it merely perpetuates itself like a virus, debarring humanity from the "transitions, larval forms, emergent telepathic faculty" that Burroughs favours. Control is a kind of ugly spirit within us all, waiting to exercise its malignant will. Even in his paintings, which he began working on in 1986 at the age of 72, he remains preoccupied with the need to escape control mechanisms. He describes his famous "shotgun technique" as follows: "The spray paint works particularly well, you put it in front of your surface, wood, and blast with the shotgun so you get an explosion of colour. Then if you do several, you get colours forming all these patterns. It's quite impossible to foresee what's going to happen. It's quite unpredictable . . . it's just a way of introducing a random factor, and letting the colours take over and do what they do."[3] Released from conscious manipulation, paint metamorphoses as it wishes, free of the painter's will. As Ted Morgan points out in *Literary Outlaw,* his biography of Burroughs, "The picture moved and changed, he found in them hidden faces and scenes. When he painted he felt a pleasant vertigo, a falling into the picture. So that he spent hours not only painting but looking at his paintings, and divining their hidden language."[4] The quest for a way of seeing that evades the manipulations of the conscious mind resurfaces in Robert Palmer's 1986 description of Burroughs' interpreting the mess made when two gunshots explode a can of yellow paint: "Yes" he says, "all sorts of things in this one. There, a face, a *terrified* face . . . and that could be the face of Jesus Christ . . . people rushing from place to place. There is a very definite way in which these paintings can be seen, you know. A technique of seeing. You look at them and you don't *try* to see anything, and things emerge, from Outside. They almost move, but not quite: you feel a shift in vision."[5] The "shift in vision" releases the viewer from the malignant spirits that define and prejudice our readings, and instead make him subject to magical, outside influences from beyond. There's a distinction here—and quite an important distinction—between malignant forces of control, and creative influences that "emerge, from Outside."

The importance of these influences to Burroughs cannot be overestimated. Yeats once confided to a friend that the occult was his "secret fanaticism"; Burroughs' equally fervent interest in the esoteric is unconcealed. His obsessive need to defy control is acknowledged in the Introduction to his second novel, ***Queer,*** here he related how in 1939 he first felt possessed by "something in my being that was not me, and not under my control" (pp. xx). This malign force led, he concludes, to the accident in which he killed his wife Joan while attempting to shoot an apple from the top of her head (Morgan, pp. 194-200): "I am forced to the appalling conclusion that I would never have become a writer but for Joan's death, and to a realization of the extent to which this event has motivated and formulated my writing. I live with the constant threat of possession, and a constant need to escape from possession, from Control. So the death of Joan brought me in contact with the invader, the Ugly Spirit, and maneuvered me into a lifelong struggle, in which I have had no choice except to write my way out" (pp. xxii). This view of control—a constant presence always threatening to return—is consistent with Burroughs' remarks about "waking suggestion," the method used by the priests of the ancient Mayan civilization to govern their people: "waking suggestion," he writes, "is a technique for implanting verbal or visual suggestions which take direct effect on the autonomic nervous system because the subject's attention is directed somewhere else."[6] As in his personal mythology, the malign spirit is implanted within the mind of the individual as a means of controlling physical behavior.

Control is fundamental to Burroughs' aesthetics. In 1972, he observed that "all art is really attempting . . . to produce very definite psychophysiological effects in the audience, reader, viewer, as the case may be."[7] He went on to add that "If I really knew how to write, I could write something that someone would read and it would kill them. The same way with music, or any effect you want could be produced if you were precise enough in your knowledge or technique" (p. 35.) Burroughs regards writing itself as a form of control, theoretically capable of killing people. It differs from the Ugly Spirit in that it derives from the artist, manifesting his creative power.

At first sight, these claims may sound like science-fiction. How, we may ask, can words have the power to kill? In fact, these ideas possess an odd and unnerving familiarity, for they repeat and amplify Wordsworth's comments on the same subject. Like Burroughs, Wordsworth believes that words have a destructive potential. In the third essay of his 1810 *Essays Upon Epitaphs,* he warns that

> Words are too awful an instrument for good and evil to be trifled with: they hold above all other external powers a dominion over thoughts. If words be not . . . an incarnation of the thought but only a clothing for it, then surely will they prove an ill gift; such a one as those poisoned vestments, read of in the stories of superstitious times, which had power to consume and to alienate from his right mind the victim who put them on. Language, if it do not uphold, and feed, and leave in quiet, like the power of gravitation or the air we breathe, is a counter-spirit, unremittingly and noiselessly at work to derange, to subvert, to lay waste, to vitiate, and to dissolve.
>
> (*Prose* ed. Owen and Smyser [1974], ii, 84-85).

The point is not the words are bad in themselves, but that their power to reveal is equalled by their destructive potential. In the wrong hands, they can indeed derange and subvert the mind of the attentive reader—just as Wordsworth was himself misled by the specious arguments of Godwin. Wordsworth's 1798 *Essay on Morals* goes so far as to accuse Godwin of attempting to "lay asleep the spirit of self-accusation & exclude the uneasiness of repentance" (*Prose,* i, 104). Pummelling Godwin, he observes that "The whole secret of this juggler's trick lies not in fitting words to things (which would be a noble employment) but in fitting things to words . . ." (*Prose,* i, 103). For Wordsworth, Godwin is blind to the world around him; instead, he has created a fiction, a world of words that bears little on reality. By implication, the true artist does precisely the opposite: his work is rooted in the everyday. Against the deceiving voice of Godwin, Wordsworth places those whose words embody "things"—that is, emotional and psychological truth. Like Burroughs, he believes that language has the power to alter people for good or bad. The moral power with which both writers credit the word is fundamental to an understanding of their writing for reasons that are, once again strangely familiar.

Wordsworth's concern with language looks back to David Hartley, whose *Observations on Man* he probably encountered through Coleridge in 1797-8. It was Hartley who speculated on the existence of an ideal, philosophical language, that might incarnate the thought of its user: "If we suppose mankind possessed of such a language, [Hartley writes] as that they could at pleasure denote all their conceptions adequately, *i.e.* without any deficiency, superfluity, or equivocation . . . this language might be termed a philosophical one, and would as much exceed any of the languages, as a paradisiacal state does the mixture of happiness and misery, which has been our portion ever since the fall." No white noise here; no arbitrary or random associations may interfere with the thought behind the word. Like Wordsworth and Burroughs, Hartley conceives of a language over which we have total control. Perfectly controlled articulation is, moreover, equated with the innocence that preceded the fall: "this language . . . would as much exceed any of the languages, as a paradisiacal state does the mixture of happiness and misery, which has been our portion ever since the fall." This is, in fact, the language of paradise. As Hartley observes: "the language given by God to Adam and Eve, before the fall, was of this kind."

Wordsworth too looks forward to paradise. *The Recluse,* his never-to-be-completed epic poem, into which *The Excursion* and *The Prelude* were subsumed, was intended to precipitate the millennium—Christ's thousand-year rule on earth. Wordsworth's linguistic theory was vital to his millennial project. If the poet possessed total control of his material, his reader would necessarily have to submit to the poet's message as incarnated in words. Whether the text is that of a poem or of nature itself, the reader, as Wordsworth put it in a blank verse passage composed in 1798,

> needs must feel
> The joy of that pure principle of love
> So deeply that, unsatisfied with aught
> Less pure and exquisite, he cannot choose
> But seek for objects of a kindred love
> In fellow natures, and a kindred joy.

Love of nature, and love of poetry, must lead to love of mankind. We have no choice, says Wordsworth; confronted with the "joy of that pure principle of love," we're compelled to search for it "In fellow natures." The millennium is on its way. All this depends on the poet's control over his medium. One false move and he could end up like Godwin, deranging and subverting. Throughout Wordsworth there lurks a basic distrust of words, a desire to communicate more directly with his reader:

> Oh, why hath not the mind
> Some element to stamp her image on
> In nature somewhat nearer to her own?
> (*Prel. [The Prelude],* ed. deSelincourt, v. 44-6).

In an ideal world, he'd prefer to impress his feelings upon some medium closer than paper and ink in its physical composition to that of the mind. In effect, his poetic quest is to adapt words to this purpose—to recreate out of our fallen tongue Hartley's philosophical language. There is a stage beyond even that, a wordless communication that Wordsworth regards as truly divine, attributed in the *Thirteen-Book Prelude* to "men for contemplation framed":

> Theirs is the language of the heavens, the power,
> The thought, the image, and the silent joy;
> Words are but under-agents in their souls;
> When they are grasping with their greatest
> strength
> They do not breathe among them . . .
> (XII, 270-74).

Those who speak silently in this manner, communicating at some sub-verbal level, are already living a millennial existence. Having outgrown the need to verbalize their thoughts, they have also transcended the fallen world; theirs is the language of the heavens. Paradise has been reclaimed.

By now you may, quite understandably, be wondering where Burroughs fits in. As we've seen, Burroughs shares with Wordsworth a belief in the power of language, when manipulated by a skilled artist, to change the world for good or bad; both are essentially moral in their view of literature. In a lesser writer this might be seen as little more than flaccid idealism, but in Burroughs' case it underpins a profound optimism comparable with Wordsworth's millennial aspirations.

Burroughs has always been an optimistic writer. This stems probably from his drug cure, which came in early 1956. Its importance to him is underlined by the first sentence in ***The Naked Lunch:*** "I awoke from The Sickness at the age of forty-five, calm and sane, and in reasonably good health except for a weakened liver and the look of borrowed flesh common to all who survive The Sickness." The Tangier journals stop short of giving it a name, but here Burroughs is quite explicit: "The Sickness is drug addiction and I was an addict for fifteen years" (p. 1). Release from chemical control brings about physical metamorphosis; of William Lee, Burroughs' persona in ***Queer,*** who also gives up drugs, he observes that "The withdrawing addict is subject to the emotional excesses of a child or an adolescent, regardless of his actual age. . . . Unless the reader keeps this in mind, the metamorphosis of Lee's character will appear as inexplicable or psychotic" (p. xiii). In other words, release from a control mechanism brings about physical change—invariably for the better.

This is important because, like Wordsworth, Burroughs draws throughout his writing on a detailed observation of himself. His self-analysis began early: in 1957, he wrote an account of his drug addiction that was sufficiently detailed and accurate to have appeared in an academic publication, *The British Journal of Addiction.* It continues to provide the main subject of his fictional writing. Burroughs is not alone among writers (or literary critics) for his self-obsession; it's for the vision underlying it that he's distinguished.

In November, 1955, he told Kerouac and Ginsberg that Tangier was "the prognostic pulse of the world, like a dream extending from past into the future, a frontier between dream and reality—the 'reality' of both called into question."[8] You don't need a critic to comprehend the Romantic tendency of these words. They establish Tangier as a half-way point between dream and reality, the kind of place Wordsworth describes in his "spots of time." This visionary realm was mythologised almost immediately: Tangier became Interzone in ***The Naked Lunch,*** "A place where the unknown past and the emergent future meet in a vibrating soundless hum . . . Larval entities waiting for a Live One" (p. 112). To the Romantic notion of timelessness Burroughs has added a science-fiction element, "Larval entities"—physical metamorphosis, in other words. He's quite specific about what this entails. Kim Carsons, the hero of ***The Place of Dead Roads,*** goes on "imaginary space trips," and "takes for granted that the only purpose of his life is space travel. He knows that this will involve not just a change of locale, but basic *biologic* alterations, like the switch from water to land" (p. 40). A page later Burroughs observes that "We have at hand the model of a much lighter body, in fact a body that is virtually weightless. I refer to the astral or dream body" (pp. 41-41). Both writers use the concept of metamorphosis in their millennial schemes: where Wordsworth envisages a psychological transformation by which love of nature leads to love of mankind, Burroughs foresees a corresponding mystic evolution by which the astral body replaces the physical body. Neither process may seem plausible, but both authors wish to account for something that they regard highly—transcendence. More to the point, they wish to do it in terms that are practicable. They believe that they can lead us to the promised land. Burroughs could be speaking for them both when he writes: "What you experience in dreams and out of the body trips, what you glimpse in the work of writers and painters, is the promised land of space. What Christians and Moslems talk about has actually to be done by living people if we are going to survive in space or anywhere else" (***The Adding Machine,*** p. 103).

Of what does Burroughs' promised land consist? In his recent trilogy comprising ***Cities of the Red Night*** (1981), ***The Place of Dead Roads*** (1984) and ***The Western Lands*** (1987), Burroughs draws on the mythology surrounding the radical Ismaili Shiaite Hassan-I-Sabbah, who took young men from the mountains, and showed them "paradise." Whether this was a vision induced by hashish, or a garden constructed by Hassan, and whether or not it included *houris,* remain matters for speculation.[9] Inspired by the vision, these men were planted in royal courts throughout the Mediterranean, Middle East and Europe, and at the least expected moment, sometimes years after being planted, they would murder royalty in a knife attack, reveal Hassan's power, and kill themselves. This form of terrorism was highly successful; it lasted from the eleventh to the thirteenth centuries, and was ended only by the military might of the Mongols. The story appeals to Burroughs because of Hassan's conviction that paradise exists on earth, and that it can be encountered without physical death. It is, in fact, a technique for evading death. For him, Hassan is a visionary: "What Hassan i Sabbah learned in Egypt was that *paradise actually exists and that it can be reached.* The Egyptians called it the Western Lands. This is the Garden that the Old Man *showed* his assassins. . . . *It cannot be faked any more than contact with the Imam can be faked.* This is no vague eternal heaven for the righteous. This is *an actual place* at the end of a very dangerous road."[10] In Burroughs' mythology, the apprehension of the Western Lands is the end result of metamorphosis. It is crucial to his thought that "This is *an actual place* at the end of a very dangerous road." Wordsworth's millennial paradise was also an actual place: Grasmere. In *Home at Grasmere,* Book I of *The Recluse,* he predicted an evolution that would lead to "the fairer world than this"[11]—which, he adds, can already be found in Grasmere Vale,

> A Centre, come from wheresoe'er you will,
> A Whole without dependence or defect,
> Made for itself and happy in itself,
> Perfect Contentment, Unity entire.
>
> (MS B 167-70)

This millennial vision is matched by a Wordsworthian distrust of language. In his 1985 essay, **"Ten Years and a Billion Dollars,"** Burroughs states that "My general theory since 1971 has been that the Word is literally a virus . . . it is an organism with no internal function other than to replicate itself" (***Adding Machine,*** p. 48). Words are simply another control mechanism. Instead, he seeks a distinctive language that will identify word and object: "Remember that the written word is an image; that the first writing was pictorial, and so painting and writing were at one time a single operation." In his 1974 ***Book of Breeething*** he even attempted to construct a "simplified pictorial script adapted to the typewriter [that] would constitute a workable international means of communication" (***Ah Pook is Here*** . . . [1979], p. 66). The aim behind that is, uncannily enough, to draw word and object together. Like Wordsworth, Burroughs is rejecting the abused language of philosophers in which things are fitted to words rather than words to things. He returns to the "thing" described, the referent itself, as a means of eluding the falsehood introduced by the inevitable slippage of semantics. Burroughs' "simplified pictorial script" is, in fact, only a stone's throw from Hartley's philosophical language. Nor are we so far away from Wordsworth's Note to *The Thorn,* in which we're told that words are "*things,* active and efficient, which are themselves part of the passion."

Burroughs also shares Wordsworth's veneration for those who have passed beyond the point at which language is necessary. He, too, honours the silent poet, the "man of contemplation." Just as Wordsworth's chosen people prefer to experience "The thought, the image, and the silent joy" rather than utter the language of fallen humanity, so Burroughs' rejects the prejudices and value judgments carried by words in favour of silence. As he remarks in a characteristically right-minded note to his 1973 volume, ***The Job:*** "To travel in space you must leave the old verbal garbage behind: God talk, country talk, mother talk, love talk, party talk. You must learn to exist with no religion no country no allies. You must learn to live alone in silence" (p. 21). Space travel functions throughout Burroughs' work like the Western Lands—as a metaphor for a spiritualized existence. He is not advising us to migrate to other planets, but is discussing an evolutionary progression, metamorphosis into an imaginative world. That is why he describes himself as "a cosmonaut of inner space" and declares that "The world is not my home" While working on ***The Naked Lunch,*** he is said to have told Kerouac that "I get these messages from other planets. I'm apparently some kind of agent from another planet."[12]

Burroughs' use of science-fiction terms has allowed him a means of discussing imaginative aspiration in a lively manner, and it's hardly surprising that he has conferred extraterrestrial status on Wordsworth. In **"Creative Reading,"** a short story published in 1985, Burroughs' fictional *alter ego,* Kim Carsons, has a revelation: "Wordsworth like so many artists was an *alien,* Kim decided, an *immortal* alien feeling the estrangement of human mortality. 'Old unhappy far off things and battle long ago'" (***Adding Machine,*** p. 46). Burroughs alludes to *The Solitary Reaper.* Between her first, distinctly mortal, appearance, "single in the field," and the final stanzas, the reaper has changed before our eyes. The songs of "old, unhappy, far-off things, / And battles long ago" effectively make her a time-traveller, capable of re-awakening the tragedies of both past and future—they have "been, and may be again!" They also bestow on her their own archetypal status: she "sang / As if her song could have no ending." By implication, she too has acquired an imaginative permanence, transcending the sorrows of which she sings. Her metamorphosis is echoed by that of the poet, who carries her music in his heart even when "it was heard no more." Both the poet and the reaper have glimpsed the millennial vision that underlies *The Recluse.*

When he casts Wordsworth as "an *immortal* alien feeling the estrangement of human mortality," Burroughs implicitly leagues himself alongside the poet as seeking an alternative to the bleakness of death. Like Wordsworth, he wishes to elevate the highland lass above the suffering of which she sings, and to partake of the permanence she represents. She has undergone precisely the metamorphosis that he envisages in his novels: in ***The Western Lands*** his alter ego, "William Seward Hall sets out to write his way out of death" (p. 3). The Wordsworthian consolation—so essential to *The Recluse*—in which the finality of death is, against all the odds, negated, is typical of Burroughs.

His use of Wordsworth in the construction of his Western Lands mythology stems from a genuine ideological affinity. They share the same desire to obliterate human pain and suffering—to subsume them into some transcendent experience. This is evident in Burroughs' portrayal of William Seward Hall, an aged gunfighter, in ***The Place of Dead Roads.*** Hall, we are told, "has known capture and torture, abject fear and shame, and humiliations that burn like acid":

> he has every contract on the planet out on him. The slow, grinding contract of age, and emptiness . . . the sharp vicious contract of spiteful hate . . . heavy corporate contracts . . . 'The most dangerous man in the world.'

And to what extent did he succeed? Even to envisage success on this scale is a victory. A victory from which others may envision further.

There is not a breathing of the common wind that will forget thee;

Thy friends are exaltations, agonies and love and man's inconquerable mind

(pp. 115-16).

The fugitive is a recurrent figure in Burroughs' work, and invariably represents the author. Here, he presents a fugitive pursued by the simple facts of human life—hatred and age. It's revealing in this light that as he envisages Hall's victory against death he turns to Wordsworth's sonnet *To Toussaint L'Ouverture*. Toussaint was the son of a negro slave who led a rebellion in Haiti against Napoleon's edict re-establishing slavery. He'd been imprisoned and sent to Paris by the time Wordsworth composed the sonnet in August, 1802. As a fugitive and underdog, "the most unhappy Man of Men" he has much in common with Burroughs' character, Hall: Like the solitary reaper, Toussaint has been transformed imaginatively during the course of the poem. The process begins with Wordsworth's refusal to let Toussaint die: "Yet die not," he writes—a rejection of Toussaint's certain fate. As a believer in the millennium, Wordsworth refuses death its power, dissolves Toussaint as a physical being, and incorporates him into the natural elements of "air, earth, and skies." Toussaint is further spiritualised into the "breathing of the common wind" and finally, allied with "love, and Man's unconquerable mind" comes to symbolize defiance—whether it be of political injustice, or of death. If we wish to be prosaic, we can say that Wordsworth was being unrealistic. Having read the memoirs of Madame Roland, Helen Maria Williams, and others who had done time in Paris' jails, he would have known full well what awaited Toussaint in France—and it can have been no surprise to learn that Toussaint died in captivity in April, 1803, eight months after Wordsworth's sonnet was composed.

It is symptomatic of Burroughs' romanticism that he should turn to this particular sonnet in his description of Hall. Like Toussaint, Hall is up against an enemy which, on one level at least, is invincible: death. But Burroughs shares Wordsworth's refusal to accept its finality. His use of the last four lines of the sonnet lend Hall the same permanence as Toussaint: "There's not a breathing of the common wind / That will forget thee." Hall is thus promoted to the same rank as the solitary reaper. We are no longer talking about physical reality, but have graduated onto a mystic plane—one in which political failure can be offset by a victory of the spirit. The poem goes on: "Thy friends are exultations, agonies, / And love, and Man's unconquerable mind." On a narrative level, Hall may be a doomed man, but he has come to stand, like Toussaint, as a symbol of human aspiration. "Even to envisage success on this scale is a victory," Burroughs writes, "A victory from which others may envision further." In the face of ignominy and failure, Toussaint's refusal to suffer Napoleon's occupation of Haiti gives encouragement to those inspired to defy the more ominous oppression of our mortal nature.

In their defiance of human mortality, both writers present time as a physical boundary. I have already quoted Burroughs' account of Tangier as "a dream extending from past into the future"—a phrase I find not merely evocative but highly Wordsworthian in tone. At the climax of ***The Naked Lunch,*** secret agent William Lee escapes from the clutches of two policemen, Hauser and O'Brien, by passing into another dimension: "I had been occluded from space-time," Lee reflects, "Locked out. . . . The Heat was off me from here on out" (p. 215). The pattern of escape from space-time into a mystic realm is repeated throughout Burroughs' work. In ***The Place of Dead Roads*** he enumerates some of those who have already opened the "door to another dimension" (p. 301), including survivors of the *Titanic* and *Hindenburg* disasters. They've undergone what he calls "*Drang nach Westen:* the drag to the West. When the Traveller turns west, time travel ceases to be travel and becomes instead an inexorable suction, pulling everything into a black hole. Light itself cannot escape from this compacted gravity, time so dense, reality so concentrated, that it ceases to be time and becomes a singularity, where all physical laws are no longer valid. From such license there is no escape . . . stepping westward a jump ahead of the Geiger . . ." (p. 301). Burroughs revitalises the old idea of time travel by describing it in oppressively physical terms. The "inevitable suction" of time and "compacted gravity" of light are heightened metaphors, referring us away from fantasy towards the physical realities of our own world. This is a special kind of time travel, since it is founded on a necessitarian principle: "From such license there is no escape . . . stepping westward a jump ahead of the Geiger."

The prototype for these time travellers is the author—like Wordsworth, Burroughs enjoys attributing to others what he wishes to claim for himself. He was one jump ahead of the Geiger, when as a boy during the 1930s he attended the Los Alamos Ranch School where, from 1943 to 1945, Oppenheimer built and tested the atom bomb. Ted Morgan notes that "Through his attendance at the Los Alamos Ranch School, Burroughs felt personally connected to the dropping of the Bomb" (p. 54-55). and it's no accident that Oppenheimer turns up as a character in ***The Western Lands.*** Other such incidents have since occurred. In his essay on Graham Greene, Burroughs recalls eating at a milk bar in Algiers which was bombed shortly after he left it (***Adding Machine,*** p. 187).

But Burroughs is not drawing only on his own experience. The other point of reference for "stepping westward" is Wordsworth's poem of that name, which explains the source of the phrase in a note:

> While my Fellow-traveller and I were walking by the side of Loch Ketterine, one fine evening after sun-set, in our road to a Hut where in the course of our Tour we had been hospitably entertained some weeks before, we met, in one of the loneliest parts of that solitary region, two well-dressed Women, one of whom said to us, by way of greeting, 'What you are stepping westward?'
>
> *'What you are stepping westward?'—'Yea.'*
> —'Twould be a wildish destiny,
> If we, who thus together roam
> In a strange Land, and far from home,
> Were in this place the guests of Chance:
> Yet who would stop, or fear to advance,
> Though home or shelter he had none,
> With such a Sky to lead him on?
>
> The dewy ground was dark and cold;
> Behind, all gloomy to behold;
> And stepping westward seem'd to be
> A kind of *heavenly* destiny;
> I liked the greeting; 'twas a sound
> Of something without place or bound;
> And seem'd to give me spiritual right
> To travel through that region bright.
> (*Poems in Two Volumes* . . . , ed. Curtis [1983]).

Like Burroughs' fugitives from the *Titanic* and *Hindenburg* disasters, Wordsworth flies from something that he dreads: if darkness and gloom lie at his back, the world before him is a "region bright"—a phrase that carries the same millennial promise as the Western Lands. Burroughs emphasises the irresistible force of the drag to the west, and Wordsworth finds himself equally compelled: "stepping westward seem'd to be / A kind of *heavenly* destiny." Both writers are delivered out of randomness and disorder into their predestined paths. The woman's question—"What you are stepping westward?"—evokes the transcendent state envisaged by *The Recluse,* for it is "a sound / Of something without place or bound." We have been drawn out of the physical realm into "a singularity, where all physical laws are no longer valid."

Burroughs uses "stepping westward" not merely to discuss physical survival; in fact, he's drawing on the same mythology of which the solitary reaper and Toussaint L'Ouverture are such important representatives. The drag to the west, that realm in which "physical laws are no longer valid" will lead, by implication, to the Western Lands. It's difficult not to be reminded of the strange journey described by Wordsworth's Rivers in *The Borderers:*

> When from these forms I turned to contemplate
> The opinions and the uses of the world,
> I seemed a being who had passed alone
> Beyond the visible barriers of the world
> And travelled into things to come
> (ed. R. Osborn [1982] IV, ii, 141-44).

Both writers describe extreme states in which the "visible barriers of the world" are transcended, and glimpses of the invisible world beyond vouchsafed. As Burroughs observes: "That is what writing is about: time travel."

In his Preface to *Poems* (1815), Wordsworth described imagination as "the conferring, the abstracting, and the modifying powers . . . immediately and mediately acting . . . brought into conjunction" (*Prose,* iii, 33). If Burroughs' work bears out his belief in the mind's transforming power, it is partly because he shares, unfashionably, Wordsworth's belief in the redemptive power of imaginative vision. Against the heightened realism of Mailer, the soured idylls of Cheever, the statuesque pomposity of Gore Vidal, and the sanctimonious self-indulgence of Bello, Burroughs stands out for having kept faith with a literary tradition that continues to nurture his work. His romanticism allows him to respond to death in a manner denied to most other writers. Like the poetry of Wordsworth, his novels maintain the fragile balance between ideal and reality. The millennial Grasmere of *Home at Grasmere,* Book I of *The Recluse,* may bear little resemblance to the place of Wordsworth's residence in 1800, but he believed that it could be made real. Similarly, the Western Lands represent a spiritual state that Burroughs believes can be realised. This emphasis on material reality distinguishes both Wordsworth and Burroughs from the mainstream of Utopian thought; both accept the place of suffering in human life, and, though they value the visionary faculty, that is where their ideals take root. It is no accident that one of Burroughs' favourite quotations should make this very point: "Allah is as close as the vein in your neck" (from the Koran).

Asked by Robert Palmer in 1972 whether he'd seen any sign of metamorphosis in the human population, Burroughs responded: "Well, occasionally you do see really quite extraordinary people that look like they might be mutating." Any thoughts of the future of writing? Palmer continued. "The future of writing," Burroughs replied, "is to see how close you can come to making it happen." (*Rolling Stone,* pp. 38-39).

Notes

1. William S. Burroughs, *Early Routines* (Cadmus, 1981), p. 30. The quotation is from a chapter entitled "Extracts from Lee's Journals and Letters" (Lee being Burroughs' name for himself). No date is given for these confessional utterances, though the contents suggest one of c. 1956-7).
2. Fenwick Note to *Ode to Lycoris,* quoted from *William Wordsworth: Shorter Poems, 1807-1820* ed. Carl H. Ketcham (1989), p. 544. Ovidian analogues occur even in Wordsworth's mature poetry. Michael Ragussis has argued the case for an Ovidian source to the Arab Quixote in *Prelude* Book V; see "Language and Metamorphosis in Wordsworth's Arab Dream," *MLQ,* xxxvi (1975) 148-65.
3. Barry Miles, 'William Seward Burroughs: Down at the Club', *Beat Scene* 9 (1990), pp. 18-21; p. 21.
4. Ted Morgan, *Literary Outlaw: The Life and Times of William S. Burroughs* (1990), p. 613.
5. Robert Palmer, 'A Shift in Vision: William S. Burroughs', liner notes to *Uncommon Quotes,* a recording of Burroughs reading at the Caravan of Dreams in 1986, published 1988 by Caravan of Dreams.
6. William S. Burroughs, *The Job: Topical Writings and Interviews,* with Daniel Odier (1984), p. 39.
7. Robert Palmer, "Rolling Stone Interview: William Burroughs," *Rolling Stone* (London edition) May 11, 1972, pp. 34-9.
8. William S. Burroughs, *Letters to Allen Ginsberg 1953-1957* eds. Ron Padgett and Anne Waldman (1982), pp. 123-4.
9. Burroughs insists that "There were no women at Alamout" (William S. Burroughs, *The Western Lands* [1988], p. 197), and that "Hashish was only an adjunct" (*The Place of Dead Roads,* p. 171).
10. *Place of Dead Roads,* p. 171; his italics. This passage is repeated in shortened form at *Western Lands,* p. 193.
11. *Home at Grasmere* MS. B 239, Book I of *The Recluse;* quoted from William Wordsworth, *Home at Grasmere* ed. Beth Darlington (1977).
12. William Burroughs, 'Censorship', *Transatlantic Review* No. 11 (Winter, 1962) pp. 5-10, p. 6; Bockris, p. 2; Morgan, p. 263.

GEOFF WARD (ESSAY DATE 1993)

SOURCE: Ward, Geoff. "William Burroughs: A Literary Outlaw?" *Cambridge Quarterly* 22, no. 4 (1993): 339-54.

In the following essay, Ward contends that despite the popularity of Burroughs's work and its inclusion in many university literature courses, Burroughs remains a "literary outlaw," and his work remains unacceptable to the cultural mainstream.

I

William Burroughs, along with Allen Ginsberg and other luminaries of the Beat Generation, can be seen several times weekly on Channel 4 Television, if only for a split second. Pepe Jeans, clearly anxious to replicate the image and hence the sales of the market leader, Levi's 501s, are sponsors of a monochrome 1950s-style ad in which a male model, bearing an uncanny resemblance to James Dean, alternates sulky and appealing poses for the camera as the voice-over intones the closing lines of a poem by Ginsberg from the *Howl* era: 'yes, yes, / that's what / I wanted, / I always wanted, / to return / to the body / where I was born' ('Song'). Burroughs and Ginsberg are seen fleetingly at the start of this piece of commercial nostalgia, photographed thirty years ago in Tangier. The poet looks sunned and genial; the novelist is pallid, wears his snap-brim Fedora low on the brow, and carries the faintly nervous expression of one who has just caught sight of two police officers stepping out of a car somewhere behind the photographer's shoulder. It will always be thus. Despite the increasing presence of his fourteen novels on best-seller lists and on the university syllabus, despite being *Commandeur de L'Ordre des Arts et Lettres,* and a member of the American Academy of Arts and Letters, Burroughs is, so to speak, incorruptibly deviant. Time and changing literary fashions have done nothing to dim the satire, combative experimentalism and general mayhem of ***The Naked Lunch*** (1959). Burroughs has always written, and can only be read, as a stranger. His books, therefore, dictate their own terms, where the soft-focus pantheism and culture-hopping of Ginsberg's *oeuvre* are susceptible to domestication at the point where New Age vagueness meets the market, the Beat Generation blurring with the Pepsi, and now the Pepe, Generation.

For a reader of my vintage to enact the impossible and 'return to the body where I was born' would involve travelling back in time to 1954, the year in which Ginsberg wrote 'Song'. At this time, publication of Jack Kerouac's *On the Road,* the hipster's Bible, was still three years off. In the previous year Burroughs' first book ***Junky*** had been published, to little effect.[1] These writers were peripheral. The Beats have now been largely absorbed by a mainstream that excluded them in the 50s, but whose 60s and 70s variants they helped to create. It is ironic that the work of Ginsberg, Gary Snyder and Gregory Corso should have become a cultural enclave, a womb-like space to which readers can return in safety, sure of what they will find. Like the bebop jazz of Charlie Parker and his inheritors, Beat poetry has become tuneful, has lost its edge and sense of alienation. That the middle-aged and dipsomaniac Kerouac went back to living with his mother, now appears merely the most sad and self-parodic illustration of the reincorporation of Beat attitudes by the society against which they rebelled. The vagabond romanticism, the enthusiasm for jazz, drugs and Eastern religions are now a familiar piece of the Cold War jigsaw. The cynicism, instability and foreboding that define the social climate of today have retrospectively bestowed an aura of warmth on the certitudes of the postwar period. The yearning for new frontiers now seems precisely a registration of the triumph of the suburbs; the cultural flipside of, and not a drastic alternative to, consumerist ideology.

What in the early 1950s were the self-protective reflex actions of an impoverished and marginal group have been made (by Ginsberg's biographer, and by weakly affectionate films such as *Heartbeat*) to seem like the antics of Tom Sawyer and his gang. In Joyce's *A Portrait of the Artist as a Young Man* Stephen Dedalus remarks bitterly that 'Ireland is the old sow that eats her farrow', and takes 'silence, exile and cunning' for his watchwords as a renegade maze-maker. Dodging back and forth between Mexico, New York and Tangier, evading firearms, drugs and manslaughter charges, Burroughs certainly made full use of exile and cunning. In return America has tried to eat the Beats alive, but whereas Ginsberg, Kerouac, Ferlinghetti and Corso have been swallowed whole, it will be the contention of this essay that Burroughs remains indigestible. To the many readers from Edith Sitwell to the present who have reacted negatively to Burroughs' more visceral or experimental efforts, the ugliness of his work is not in dispute. More provocatively, I will suggest that his is the pre-eminent achievement in postwar American fiction, and that Burroughs' importance, his isolation and his unacceptability are related.

Junky was, but did not have the appearance of, an auspicious beginning to Burroughs' career. It was published by the new paperback firm of Ace Books, through the good offices of an uncle of Carl Solomon, whom Ginsberg had met in mental hospital and to whom *Howl* is dedicated. The cover design, of a busty young woman in red being physically prevented from lighting a 'reefer' by a stern young male, sends out conflicting signals, as does the publisher's subtitle 'Confessions of an Unredeemed Drug Addict', with its arch and De Quinceyan overtones. Ace's editors appear to have been caught between the urge to make raffishness a selling point, and the need to add a moralising overlay at a time when any talk of drug use was inseparable in the public mind from serious criminality. Apart from the jazz world—essentially the black man's territory—there were no 'subcultures' at this stage, only the underworld. Also, at this point in American publishing history, paperbacks were a novelty, bought from neighbourhood stores and stations rather than bookshops, and the distinction between hardbound and paperbacked novels was absolute; in 1953, a clothbound novel would be unlikely to be paperbacked, even if its first run sold well. Consequently Burroughs was bypassing any possible chance of a serious literary review or recommendation by writing about junk, and by going with Ace Books. (Not that he had much choice: like all the major New York publishers whom Ginsberg approached on his friend's behalf, Doubleday rejected the typescript of ***Junky,*** noting that 'the prose is not very good. This could only work if it were written by someone like Winston Churchill', a concept that grows stranger the more one pauses over it.) To add to the confusion of intention, ***Junky*** was bound up with a True Detective yarn, *Narcotic Agent* by Maurice Helbrant, printed upside down with the back cover of ***Junky*** as its front cover. For his *nom de plume,* Burroughs took his mother's maiden name, calling himself William Lee.

I lay stress on the circumstances surrounding the presentation of the text, because what may appear to have been constraints forced on a first-time author are also features of psychology and self-presentation that Burroughs would replicate at a later stage, when he enjoyed far more control over his published output. In short, everything about the book conspires to queer the authenticity which would appear to have been its *raison d'être.* ***Junky*** is neither an autobiography nor a novel, neither a condemnation nor a defence of addiction, by one who is and is not 'William Lee'. The first person singular in Burroughs is always ghostly and evasive; no wonder that his nickname in Mexico was *el hombre invisible,* a sobriquet that provides the title of the latest biography (Barry

Miles, 1992). This crucial element of the inauthentic runs down to the roots of the prose, and is there from the opening page:

> I was born in 1914 in a solid, three-story, brick house in a large Midwest city. My parents were comfortable. My father owned and ran a lumber business. The house had a lawn in front, a back yard with a garden, a fish pond and high wooden fence all around it. I remember the lamplighter lighting the gas streetlights and the huge, black, shiny Lincoln and drives in the park on Sunday. All the props of a safe, comfortable way of life that is now gone forever. I could put down one of those nostalgic routines about the old German doctor who lived next door and the rats running around in the back yard and my pet toad that lived by the fish pond.
>
> Actually my earliest memories are colored by a fear of nightmares. I was afraid to be alone, and afraid of the dark, and afraid to go to sleep because of dreams where a supernatural horror seemed always on the point of taking shape. I was afraid some day the dream would still be there when I woke up. I recall hearing a maid talk about opium and how smoking opium brings sweet dreams, and I said: 'I will smoke opium when I grow up.'
>
> I was subject to hallucinations as a child. Once I woke up in the early morning light and saw little men playing in a block house I had made. I felt no fear, only a feeling of stillness and wonder . . .
>
> I went to a progressive school with the future solid citizens, the lawyers, doctors and businessmen of a large Midwest town. I was timid with the other children and afraid of physical violence. One aggressive little Lesbian would pull my hair whenever she saw me. I would like to shove her face in right now, but she fell off a horse and broke her neck years ago.
>
> (pp. xi-xii)

Prompted by Ace Books to write a straightforward account of his addiction to heroin and associated criminal activities, Burroughs proved incapable of either sticking to or relinquishing the prose style appropriate to his intention. The laconic monotone (indebted chiefly to Dashiell Hammett), at ease with dead metaphor and repetition, keeps sliding into romantic irony or poeticisms which, intrinsic to the style of the mature Burroughs, transgress the strict limits of the confessional genre to which the book would have had to stay loyal in order to fulfil its brief. The material about hypnagogic visions and the acutely literary invocation of opium threaten the credibility of the account. Realism is proffered, then withheld: 'I could put down one of those nostalgic routines . . .' throws the speaker's veracity in doubt. By contrast, the sudden viciousness of 'I would like to shove her face in right now' certainly carries the ring of truth, but is completely inappropriate in its violence to a genre purporting to describe in measured cliché 'a safe, comfortable way of life that is now gone forever'. (It is pure Burroughs, of course: he can safely be imagined putting a curse on the little girl's horse.) The net result is to throw absolutely everything into doubt. Ironically, the details of the narrative can generally be checked from other sources, and are correct. The point to be stressed is, that it is not the events related, but the persona that is inauthentic: yet this is exactly where the power of Burroughs' writing will ultimately lie.

Junky is a minor, twisted classic. It has gained in power as time has passed, not only because Burroughs' later achievements have washed back over it, allowing some extraordinary nuggets to shine through, but because the passage of time always denatures literary realism, bringing to light its underlying and defining rhetoricity, a process from which this deceptively complex and hybrid book can only gain. The prose is minimalist, but razor-sharp: 'There are no more junkies at 103rd and Broadway waiting for the connection. The connection has gone somewhere else. But the feel of junk is still there. It hits you at the corner, follows you along the block, then falls away like a discouraged panhandler as you walk on' (p. 30). This, on the art of obtaining a prescription under false pretences: 'You need a good bedside manner with doctors or you will get nowhere' (p. 21). Echoing another St. Louis collagist of a slightly earlier generation, Burroughs intones 'I have seen life measured out in eyedroppers of morphine solution' (p. xvi). The mock-confessional sonority must echo De Quincey, as well as Eliot. De Quincey was mordantly aware of the comic possibilities in the narratives of evangelical conversion put about by such groups as the Clapham Saints, of which his mother was a member. He borrowed from these, as he borrowed from the more baroque and latinate rhetoric of Jeremy Taylor's sermons, to forge a prose style flexible enough to burlesque pretension to transcendental insight in one passage, while implying it in the next. 'This is the doctrine of the true church on the subject of opium, of which I acknowledge myself to be the only member.' The suspicion of parody sits alongside a more impassioned and unironic romanticism. Burroughs, like De Quincey, alternates the deflationary possibilities of black humour with surges of visionary idealism, as in the curious ending to ***Junky,*** where Lee abandons New York for the wilds of Colombia.

What I have termed inauthenticity is not merely psychological, but a matter of literary choices, an authorial fealty to one tradition rather than another. William Burroughs writes, and has always written, as if the nineteenth-century novel had never happened. His early works recall the obsessional narratives of resilient criminality that Daniel Defoe produced towards the end of his life, *Colonel Jack* in particular. The later books are full of arcane lore, taxonomy, lists; a magpie, eighteenth-century interest in accumulating knowledge sits alongside an equally eighteenth-century rationality, and a Swiftian pessimism, over the ways in which knowledge is likely to be used and misused in society. ('Well as one judge said to the other, "Be just and if you can't be just be arbitrary"', ***The Naked Lunch,*** p. 79). The later books recall one of Burroughs' favourite novelists, Joseph Conrad; in both the approach is claustrophobically adjectival and heavily psychologised, as dramas of alienation and attraction work themselves through to a murderous climax in exotic and colonial settings:

> The Composite City where all human potentials are spread out in a vast silent market.
>
> Minarets, palms, mountains, jungle . . . A sluggish river jumping with vicious fish, vast weed-grown parks where boys lie in the grass, play cryptic games. Not a locked door in the City. Anyone comes into your room at any time. The Chief of Police is a Chinese who picks his teeth and listens to denunciations presented by a lunatic. Every now and then the Chinese takes the toothpick out of his mouth and looks at the end of it. Hipsters with smooth copper-colored faces lounge in doorways twisting shrunk heads on gold chains, their faces blank with an insect's unseeing calm.
>
> (***The Naked Lunch,*** pp. 109-10)

Burroughs writes as if the Oriental imagery of De Quincey's nightmares led directly into Conrad's *Heart of Darkness.* The prose in ***The Soft Machine*** or ***Port of Saints*** will be even heavier, as orchidaceously beautiful or monstrously ugly as jungle life-forms. Phrases suddenly bite. Ethical realism could never take root in a medium whose psychological and stylistic commitments are always to the alien.

II

Junky was begun prior to, and completed after, the defining event in Burroughs' life as an author. The narrator of that book has a wife, a shadowy figure, but the liaisons described are all homosexual. In the text, this ambivalence passes without analysis. In life, it was to have a tragic resolution. In 1951 Burroughs was living in Mexico City with his common-law wife, Joan Vollmer, and their child, William Junior. (His only wife in the legal sense has been Ilse Klapper, a German Jewess he met in Dubrovnik in the 30s, and married in an act of generosity so that she could escape the Nazis. He obtained a divorce in Mexico in 1945.) Though he and Joan were evidently close, there were difficulties. She was addicted to amphetamines, a dependency she passed on to the newborn baby. In 1951 Burroughs Senior was off heroin, but drinking very heavily. In keeping with the habits of a lifetime, he carried, and frequently used, a gun; in this case a.380 automatic, which had a tendency to shoot low. Accounts of what happened on the afternoon of September 6th vary, partly because the participants were all drunk. In conversation, Burroughs gave this account:

> Joan was sitting in a chair, I was sitting in another chair across the room about six feet away, there was a table, there was a sofa. The gun was in a suitcase and I took it out, and it was loaded, and I was aiming it. I said to Joan, 'I guess it's about time for our William Tell act.' She took her highball glass and balanced it on top of her head. Why I did it, I don't know, something took over. It was an utterly and completely insane thing to do. Suppose I had succeeded in shooting the glass off her head, there was a danger of glass splinters flying out and hitting the other people there. I fired one shot, aiming at the glass.
>
> (as given by Ted Morgan, in *Literary Outlaw,* p. 194)

The 'one shot' hit Joan in the temple, causing death almost immediately. The glass, still intact, rolled around on the floor.

Burroughs was arrested, but his lawyer managed to get him out on bail after thirteen days, a record. After being charged and found guilty of *imprudencia criminal* for an action that would certainly have incurred a charge of homicide in the United States, Burroughs was released on bail until sentencing one year later. In the event this judgment would be rendered somewhat technical, by virtue of the perpetrator's having physically absented himself from Mexico in the meantime; *el hombre invisible,* once again. The bribing of ballistics experts and other wheel-oiling operations had promised a relatively painless run through the courts until Burroughs' lawyer, a heroin user, shot dead a teenager who had dented his Cadillac, and fled to Brazil. When the other lawyers in the firm raised his bail payments to extraordinary levels, Burroughs became disinclined to await the verdict of the court. (A detailed and authoritative account of these events can be found in Ted Morgan's *Literary Outlaw* (1988), by far the better of the two biographies.)

In the Preface to ***Queer,*** a transitional work that precedes ***The Naked Lunch,*** Burroughs writes of the tragedy in Mexico with a degree of special pleading: 'This was in the time of Alemán, when the *mordida* was king, and a pyramid of bribes reached from the cop on the beat up to the Presidente. Mexico City was also the murder capital of the world, with the highest per-capita homicide rate' (p. 7). For thirty years, Burroughs maintained a virtual silence about the shooting. Since the publication in 1985 of the 'lost' manuscript of ***Queer,*** he has been at pains to go over and over the drama, stressing its centrality to his work:

> I am forced to the appalling conclusion that I would never have become a writer but for Joan's death, and to a realization of the extent to which this event has motivated and formulated my writing. I live with the constant threat of possession, and a constant need to escape from possession, from Control. So the death of Joan brought me in contact with the invader, the Ugly Spirit, and maneuvred me into a lifelong struggle, in which I have had no choice except to write my way out.
>
> (***Queer,*** p. 18)

Clearly, there is much that could be said against what Burroughs writes and the particular terms in which he chooses, while saying 'I have had no choice', to express it. That said, this crux on which his life foundered, and on which his writing life may or may not have depended, is so appallingly resonant as to make consideration of the writing in complete separation from the life a distortion, if not an impossibility. Any such truncated and sketchy account as I have given is bound to deal reductively with matters both too gross and too subtle for reduction. It is clear, at least, that the crisis forced a monumental self-revision, and, although ***Junky*** was mostly written before the shooting, the quantum leap from the early writing to ***The Naked Lunch*** is startling. The first page of ***The Naked Lunch*** is more or less a rewriting of an incident from the earlier book. Here, for comparison, are both passages:

> 'There's an agent outside in a white trenchcoat,' Ray told me. 'He followed me over here from Tony's and I'm afraid to go out.' . . .
>
> I drank my cup of tea, thanked him for the information, and left ahead of him. I had the stuff in a package of cigarettes and was ready to throw it in the water-filled gutter. Sure enough, there was a burly young man in a white trenchcoat standing in a doorway. When he saw me he started sauntering up the street ahead of me. Then he turned a corner, waiting for me to walk past so he could fall in behind. I turned and ran back in the opposite direction. When I reached Sixth Avenue, he was about fifty feet behind me. I vaulted the subway turnstile and shoved the cigarette package into the space at the side of a gum machine. I ran down one level and got a train up to the Square.
>
> (***Junky,*** p. 54)

> I can feel the heat closing in, feel them out there making their moves, setting up their devil doll stool pigeons, crooning over my spoon and dropper I throw away at Washington Square Station, vault a turnstile and two flights down the iron stairs, catch an uptown A train . . . Young, good looking, crew cut, Ivy League, advertising exec type fruit holds the door back for me. I am evidently his idea of a character. You know the type: comes on with bartenders and cab drivers, talking about right hooks and the Dodgers, calls the counterman in Nedick's by his first name. A real asshole. And right on time this narcotics dick in a white trench coat (imagine tailing somebody in a white trench coat—trying to pass as a fag I guess) hit the platform. I can hear the way he would say it holding my outfit in his left hand, right hand on his piece: 'I think you dropped something, fella.'
>
> But the subway is moving.
>
> 'So long flatfoot!' I yell, giving the fruit his B production. I look into the fruit's eyes, take in the white teeth, the Florida tan, the two hundred dollar sharkskin suit, the button-down Brooks Brothers shirt and carrying *The News* as a prop.
>
> (***The Naked Lunch,*** p. 12)

The prose of the first excerpt is effective, in a monochromatic way, but gains much of its force from what it excludes. The participants in its narrative of pursuit and escape are weary matchstick men, and the ultimate implication of the drama is that to be definitively located as either the police or the policed is to forfeit autonomous identity. Ducking and weaving along the perimeter of legality merely flushes out into the open conditions of Control, to use a favourite Burroughs term, that are silently operative elsewhere, and to which in the sullen conformity of the Eisenhower years there was no evident political alternative. The style is shaped by a reductive version of the terse sentences and even tone of Hammett and ultimately Hemingway: delinquent in content, it is filial in style.

The ***Naked Lunch*** version is, like the rest of the book, a virtuoso display of styles, each of which is expertly deployed, only to be gutted of authenticity in a sarcastic exposure of Control mechanisms. What is metaphorical, factual, narrated and imagined are jammed together without pointers or hierarchy, so that 'devil doll stool pigeons' and 'spoon and dropper' sound equally literal. This is a device frequently used by Surrealist poetry, but a radical departure for an American novelist. The speaker's prediction of the way the

Brion Gysin, 1916-1986.

trenchcoated agent would behave if he got the chance to make an arrest ('I think you dropped something, fella.') is presented with the same vividness as the 'real' actions of the 'advertising exec type' who watches with voyeuristic pleasure. Both are, precisely, types. The scornful tone of 'imagine tailing someone in a white trench coat' comes from seeing how the narcotics agent conforms all too neatly to the sartorial and behavioural code set out in books like ***Junky*** or *The Big Sleep*. The scorn directed at 'the type' who 'comes on with bartenders and cabdrivers' takes him in vampirically, and drains him of external reality, from the button-down shirt to the Ivy League manner, leaving nothing behind. Carrying his newspaper 'as a prop', the type is in fact a walking collage of props.

The signs that confer social authenticity are quite literally seen through by the junky, a social ghost exercising all the ghost's privileges of haunting and provocation. ***The Naked Lunch*** enacts the gleeful revenge of the inauthentic, exposing (mon semblable! mon frère!) the construction of identity and norms by society's dominant narratives. The Burroughs voice can play the game, yelling 'So long, flatfoot!' as he jumps onto the train, because that is the exact code, code of the 'B production', that his audience has been conditioned to expect. But the rules of the game have been exploded, now, by a writer who refused to play and then exiled himself. ***Naked Lunch*** is the revenge of the invisible man. He shows up the hollowness of everything except language. Writing exposes the linguistic foundations of systems of social control, and language, as Burroughs famously remarked, is a virus. The function of ***The Naked Lunch*** and, by implication, of contemporary art, is one of inoculation.

Since the end of the eighteenth century, European writing which has declared itself at odds with the ethos and mechanisms of the State, tends in consequence to have situated itself outside, operating at an intellectual distance. American radicalism has tended to face a different and more contradictory set of difficulties, caused by the very establishment of American independence in an act of dissidence. Sentimentally attached to the era of Whitman and Thoreau, Ginsberg's 1960s radicalism assumes that the modern State has deviated, or rather, fallen, from its own Edenic origins, and that what is needed is a return to the promise of the Constitution, rather than the replacement of the existing order. American radicalism is therefore susceptible to rapid incorporation by a State to whose history and myths it finally professes loyalty. On the face of it, Burroughs is much closer to the European *non serviam,* partly through the vituperation of his writing but also in his sharp sense of the distance between the language of power, and the language of literature; the second is there to deconstruct the first by methods that are essentially analytical, but which work through a style that relishes hallucinatory vividness, carnival, uproar. If there is an identifiable political position in Burroughs' work, it would be an anarchistic individualism. His extreme allergy to all systems of social containment cuts him off from Marxism as much as capitalism, and one of his most American traits is his membership of the NRA, and enthusiastic support for the right of the people to bear arms. Forever cut off from the body of middle-class beliefs and attitudes into which he was born, Burroughs conforms to only one American archetype, the outlaw; albeit, in this case, a literary one. Therefore the satirical attacks on social control in ***The Naked Lunch*** operate across the widest possible range of political scenarios, fighting paranoia with paranoia. The country 'Annexia' was actually based on Sweden, but the attacks on intrusive bureaucracy and thought-control recall Kafka and the dystopian nightmares that have been central to literature of the twentieth century:

> Every citizen of Annexia was required to apply for and carry on his person at all times a whole portfolio of documents. Citizens were subject to be stopped in the street at any time; and the Examiner, who might be in plain clothes, in various uniforms, often in a bathing suit or pyjamas, sometimes stark naked except for a badge pinned to his left nipple, after checking each paper, would stamp it. On subsequent inspection the citizen was required to show the properly entered stamps of the last inspection. The Examiner, when he stopped a large group, would only examine and stamp the cards of a few. The others were then subject to arrest because their cards were not properly stamped. Arrest meant 'provisional detention'; that is, the prisoner would be released if and when his Affidavit of Explanation, properly signed and stamped, was approved by the Assistant Arbiter of Explanations. Since this official hardly ever came to his office, and the Affidavit of Explanation had to be presented in person, the explainers spent weeks and months waiting around in unheated offices with no chairs and no toilet facilities.
>
> (p. 31)

A few hallucinatory touches notwithstanding, the style here is droll and lucid. As conditions in Annexia worsen and the events described become an intensification *ad absurdum* of state control, the imagery becomes more hectic, providing an almost poetic level of linguistic play antithetical in spirit to, but brought into life by, its objects of satire:

> Documents issued in vanishing ink faded into old pawn tickets. New documents were constantly required. The citizens rushed from one bureau to another in a frenzied attempt to meet impossible deadlines.
>
> All benches were removed from the city, all fountains turned off, all flowers and trees destroyed. Huge electric buzzers on the top of every apartment house (everyone lived in apartments) rang the quarter hour. Often the vibrations would throw people out of bed. Searchlights played over the town all night (no one was permitted to use shades, curtains, shutters or blinds.)
>
> No one ever looked at anyone else because of the strict law against importuning, with or without verbal approach, anyone for any purpose, sexual or otherwise.
>
> (pp. 31-2)

Similar but worse things were to happen in Pol Pot's Cambodia, and could do so again. Even Burroughs' most hyperbolic satire has been vindicated by events, and his writing offers a standing rebuke to contemporaries such as Saul Bellow, whose novels explore a respectable and suburban conscience and imagination protected from the realities of the twentieth century by their literary debts to the nineteenth. The naked lunch means, as Burroughs notes in the preface to the first edition to follow the famous obscenity trial, 'a frozen moment when everyone sees what is on the end of every fork' (p. 1). Both the strength and the unpleasantness of Burroughs' writing lie in its urge towards a dark carnival, a Mexican Day of the Dead which finds revelry in ruin, and takes heart from a full look at the worst.

ON THE SUBJECT OF...

BRION GYSIN

During his lifetime, Brion Gysin's creative powers were regarded as influential and visionary—both within and outside of the Beat Generation. A poet, painter, inventor, restaurateur, songwriter, and musician, Gysin's primary influence on the Beats came from his association with William S. Burroughs, to whom he introduced his "cut-up" technique. Cut-up involves cutting a work into numerous parts and rearranging them to expose new meanings and perceptions. The technique had a profound influence on Burroughs's work, providing a model for his landmark novel, *Naked Lunch.* The collaborations of Burroughs and Gysin are viewed as some of the most important literary work of the latter twentieth century. While he regarded himself as primarily a painter, Gysin' literary output is noteworthy; his works include *The Exterminator,* (1960) written with Burroughs, and *The Process* (1969), an obscure novel described as disquieting, groundbreaking, and influential.

III

Charges of inauthenticity have been laid against Burroughs' writing since his controversial innovation, the 'cut-up'. This process, discovered accidentally by the writer's friend and sometime collaborator Brion Gysin, is used extensively in the novels of the 1960s, chiefly ***The Ticket that Exploded*** and ***Nova Express.*** Cross sections of writing—including, but not necessarily, Burroughs' own—are set in juxtaposition to create new and frequently Surreal collages. The effect is to replace narrative by image-clusters. Delivered in a staccato tone, their organisation is poetic and visual:

> His style is cool like his head was sewed on a Russian version of James Dean—filtering black aphrodisiac ointment in Spanish fly that will take photo turnstile through flesh—Two faces tried to rush entirely into his face—He was in the you-me in you with all the consequences—burning outskirts of the world—Character took my hands in dash taught you from last airport typical of his decision to intersect on new kind of daring in memory of each other—
>
> 'I say nothing and nothing is now in Rome with the film—Intersected eleventh hour paper—Star failed yesterday—Screen went dead—Young face melted'—. . .
>
> Allies wait on knives—Street gangs had to be you—You won't cut word lines?
>
> (***The Ticket that Exploded,*** pp. 148-49)

This is in one sense the disintegration of writing, a refusal of authorial integrity; the words operate at intersections, 'in the you-me', 'in dash', the lines that would have linked them to a firm phenomenology of traditional author-reader relations 'cut'. Everything in a cut-up existed 'in memory', was a pre-existing text, but a 'new kind of daring' tears out the context and so destroys the memory. The new text is amnesiac and disembodied, moving by unexpected association rather than ethical or informational supervision. Two aspects of the practice deserve to be emphasised and distinguished. It is in one sense a radical assault on conventional premises of communication, as well as a filleting of novelistic tradition. Writing by these lights is driven by a pleasure rather than a reality principle, random and promiscuous coupling of phrases; Burroughs' cut-ups resemble (and indeed include, from time to time) the utopian conjunctions of Rimbaud's *Illuminations* more than they do any novel. Even so redoubtable an avant-gardist as Samuel Beckett upbraided Burroughs face-to-face for including material that was not his own, having first bestowed on Burroughs what may be the most fulsome tribute Beckett ever paid a contemporary: 'Well, he's a writer'. He is never more a writer in the pure sense than in these experiments, which tend to cut themselves off from the outer world, that satirical invective always invokes. The question therefore must be, are the cut-ups interesting in theory but as tedious in practice as some of the music of John Cage, an artist of Burroughs' generation who also made drastic commitments to chance procedure? Or do they resemble a piece of art like Marcel Duchamp's ready-mades, the urinal signed 'R. Mutt' for example, which have an interventionist validity as conceptual art but from which very little is gained by actually seeing them?

The cut-ups are not as severed from internal as from external realities, to judge by the high rate of recurrence of certain phrases, images and forms of phrase. Nor is it the case that the cut-ups destroy a certain recognisable Burroughs style:

> Calling Panama alternations—flesh empty in the trade winds—ebbing carbon dioxide as punctuation—Silver flakes closed your account—Nothing here now but dust falling from demagnetized patterns—Departed have left Mr Bradly Mr Martin—Five times good night under surges of silence—Shadow actors walk through dream—No one is there to listen—Someone walking from Rewrite to microphones trails Summer dawn sounds and old dream—
>
> (***Ticket*** p. 177)

Most of the words used appear repeatedly elsewhere in Burroughs' work, and so become encrusted with (chiefly elegiac) associations that trigger word-links to the experienced reader just as the cut-up announces that such ties have been severed. This ambivalence runs through all of Burroughs' work: the urge to erase experience and fly beyond it co-exists with the melancholy and lyrical return to memory, much as Burroughs has alternated periods of addiction and kicking the habit. Ultimately the cut-up technique exposes a form of intertextuality that was always there in writing, but which these 1960s experiments theorise and clarify. All writing is collaborative; texts overlap. To use language at all is immediately to be located in a pre-existing network of associations and codes. In one sense, Burroughs' writing is still intensely original; no one could mistake the passage quoted above for the work of another: but the cut-up technique turns on to the process of writing itself the corrosive glare that pulled apart the 'type' into his component parts. Originality, whether textual or other, is viewed as a myth of authenticity which can be seen through by the constructive but knowingly inauthentic device of the cut-up.

It still disturbs, and raises awkward questions. Equally disturbing are the short films, such as ***Towers Open Fire*** and ***The Cut Ups*** which Burroughs made in collaboration with a young British director, Antony Balch, in the early 1960s. The films applied to image as well as soundtrack the splicing and fragmentation pioneered in the novels. As with the books, there is a vein of lyricism and beauty; Balch painted the colour sequence in ***Towers*** directly onto each print of the film, by hand. Ironically, ***The Cut Ups*** had to be cut further, when staff at the Oxford Street Cinephone began to suffer disorientation after watching this short film five times a day. They also reported an unusually large number of bags, coats and other articles left behind by the audience.

IV

Those who dislike the Beats tend to belittle their achievements by labelling Burroughs, Kerouac and Ginsberg as one book writers. It is true that each had, if not a false start, then a second beginning to their writing careers in the late 1950s, through particular books that brought the constriction as well as the boost of celebrity. Kerouac drank himself into self-parody, and Ginsberg's work suffered after he took on the mantle of spokesman for the 1960s generation. Burroughs is not a one book writer, but he may be a four phase writer. The first phase produced ***Junky, Queer*** and the various bits and pieces collected belatedly in the overlapping anthologies ***Early Routines*** (1982) and ***Interzone*** (1989). (These last do not contain Burroughs' most powerful writing, though both contain the disturbing story **'The Finger'**, which explains, in graphic detail, how the author came to lose a small part of his left hand.) The second, crucial phase began in the mid-1950s, with Burroughs installed in the Hotel Muniriya in Tangier, free of addiction, using one wall of the room as a shooting gallery in moments of high excitement, and typing out the thousand pages that would form the basis of ***The Naked Lunch*** (1959), ***The Soft Machine*** (1961, 1966, 1968), ***The Ticket that Exploded*** (1962, 1967) and ***Nova Express*** (1964). The middle two books exist in different versions, but whereas the final version of ***Ticket*** is basically an expansion, the first and the last ***Soft Machine*** are radically different. Burroughs' revisions of the tetralogy established a pattern of mood and approach that would be repeated in the next two phases of his writing. A first book explores new themes in a dramatic and often satirical mode: ***The Wild Boys*** (1971) and ***Cities of the Red Night*** (1981). A second novel resembles the first thematically, but is written in a more poetic and elegiac mode: ***Port of Saints*** (1973) and ***The Place of Dead Roads*** (1983). The third volume sets up a critical distance from what is now thoroughly reworked material, in order to produce a text which is primarily didactic and theoretical: ***The Third Mind*** (1978) and ***The Western Lands*** (1987). Each phase also produces various short, satellite texts, some of which appear later in omnibus editions, of which ***Ah Pook is Here*** (1979) and ***The Burroughs File*** (1984) are probably the most important.

Despite the variation in published versions of the same text, admirers of Burroughs who attend closely to his many recordings and public readings are wont to complain, perhaps with justice, that the 'wrong' draft was published. Burroughs has always relied heavily on discussion and outside advice concerning the final organisation of his typescripts. Where early advisors such as Ginsberg were benign and constructive, the commercial pressures exerted in the fourth phase of publication in particular, have been ruinous. None of the 1980s books is as strong as ***The Wild Boys,*** let alone the tetralogy. However, Barry Miles records in his new biography that the extant version of ***Place of Dead Roads*** is the action-centred fifth draft, which was only published in preference to the more poetic sixth draft after a fight. I recall when organising a reading by Burroughs in Liverpool in 1982 that he was reading from a newly completed draft which contained material not in the published book, and which less partial observers than I concurred in thinking on a par with his best work.

This kind of bibliographical detour may alarm the first time reader, but it is in a sense induced by Burroughs, who is clearly an author for whom writing is *ab initio* an act of revision. Like Conrad, he lived with danger in the first part of his life, then wrote about it in the second; ***The Naked Lunch*** was published when he was forty-five years old. As an *hombre invisible,* he had flitted through a variety of countries and occupations, like a spirit possessing a new body briefly, before moving on. At different points before becoming a writer he majored in English Literature at Harvard, studied medicine in Vienna, semantics with Count Korzybski in Chicago; arrested on a number of occasions for firearms, drugs and other offences, he was briefly a private detective, a bartender and (the only job he claims to have enjoyed) a public exterminator; he underwent psychoanalysis; photographs show him carrying a pith helmet, in the jungle outside Macao, searching for the mysterious yage vine, said to confer telepathic powers on the user. (He found it. It didn't.)

T. S. Eliot once wrote to Herbert Read saying that someday he would like to write an essay about a man who 'wasn't anything, anywhere'. As the man who felt himself to be hollow, one who wasn't anything anywhere, Eliot was able to try on the voice of anybody, anywhere, offering in *The Waste Land* a *tour de force* of ventriloquial pastiche signalling the ruin of integrity, both from a psychological and a social perspective. Burroughs too has used poetic techniques to give life to flickering pseudocharacters whose ultimate point is to present all human communication as half-collage, half-seance, in a world that is cut up *ab initio* but striated by impalpable memory and regret. For all the stridency and repetition of his writing, he has stared down various forms of twentieth-century horror without retreating into ritual and conservatism, as Eliot did. This is an implacable and an intrepid writing, caustic and poetic by turns. Built upon personal ruin, it reminds us of the real tensions and social contradictions that the current, sentimental commercialisation of the suburban 1950s and the Pop 1960s has tried so hard to suppress.

Notes

1. *Junky* was originally printed as *Junkie.* I have used the spelling preferred by Burroughs for the first unexpurgated edition (Penguin, 1977), from which I have also quoted. Quotation from the other novels uses the first British edition in each case.

ANN DOUGLAS (ESSAY DATE 1998)

SOURCE: Douglas, Ann. "'Punching a Hole in the Big Lie': The Achievement of William S. Burroughs." In *Word Virus: The William S. Burroughs Reader,* edited by James Grauerholz and Ira Silverberg, pp. xv-xxix. New York: Grove Press, 1998.

In the following essay, Douglas provides an overview of Burroughs's life, writing career, and critical reception of his work.

"When did I stop wanting to be President?" Burroughs once asked himself, and promptly answered, "At birth certainly, and perhaps before." A public position on the up-and-up, a career of shaking hands, making speeches, and taking the rap held no appeal for one who aspired to be a "sultan of sewers," an antihero eye-deep in corruption, drugs, and stoic insolence, watching "Old Glory float lazily in the tainted breeze."

Burroughs started out in the 1940s as a founding member of the "Beat Generation," the electric revolution in art and manners that kicked off the counterculture and introduced the hipster to mainstream America, a movement for which Jack Kerouac became the mythologizer, Allen Ginsberg the prophet, and Burroughs the theorist. Taken together, their best-known works—Ginsberg's exuberant take-the-doors-off-their-hinges jeremiad *Howl* (1956); Kerouac's sad, funny, and inexpressibly tender "true story" novel *On the Road* (1957); and Burroughs' avant-garde narrative ***Naked Lunch*** (1959), a Hellzapoppin saturnalia of greed and lust—managed to challenge every taboo that respectable America had to offer.

Over the course of his long career, Burroughs steadfastly refused to honor, much less court, the literary establishment. Invited in 1983 to join the august Academy and Institute of Arts and Letters, he remarked, "Twenty years ago they were saying I belonged in jail. Now they're saying I belong in their club. I didn't listen to them then, and I don't listen to them now." Adept in carny routines and vaudevillian sleights of hand, Burroughs was a stand-up comic, a deadpan ringmaster of Swiftian satire and macabre dystopias, who claimed an outsider role so extreme as to constitute extraterrestrial status. "I'm apparently some kind of agent from another planet," he told Kerouac, "but I haven't got my orders decoded yet."

Unlike Ginsberg and Kerouac, however, Burroughs, born in 1914 to a well-to-do Wasp family in St. Louis, was part of the American elite. Indeed, as he often noted, his personal history seemed inextricably intertwined with some of the most important and ominous events of the modern era. In the 1880s, his paternal grandfather had invented the adding machine, a harbinger of the alliance of technology and corporate wealth that made possible the monstrously beefed-up defense industry of the Cold War years. Burroughs' maternal uncle, Ivy Lee, a pioneer of public relations, had helped John D. Rockefeller Jr. improve his image after the Ludlow Massacre of 1914, in which Colorado state militia shot two women and eleven children in a dispute between miners and management. In the 1930s, Lee served as Hitler's admiring publicist in the United States, an achievement that Congressman Robert LaFollette branded "a monument of shame."

Thin, physically awkward, with a narrow, impassive, even hangdog face as an adolescent, Burroughs qualified easily as the most unpopular boy in town. One concerned parent compared him to "a walking corpse." (Burroughs agreed, only wondering whose corpse it was.) Already interested in drugs, homosexuality, and con artistry, devoid of team spirit and "incurably intelligent," he was at best a problematic student, a troubling presence at several select schools, among them the Los Alamos Ranch School in New Mexico, the site J. Robert Oppenheimer commandeered in 1943 for the scientists engaged in the Manhattan Project. Los Alamos birthed the bombs that destroyed Hiroshima and Nagasaki and brought into being what Burroughs sardonically referred to as "the sick soul, sick unto death, of the atomic age," the central theme of his work.

In 1936, Burroughs graduated from Harvard, a place whose pretensions he loathed; a blank space appeared in the yearbook where his photograph should have been. He then traveled to Vienna and saw for himself what the Nazi regime his uncle had promoted was up to. For Burroughs, as for Jean Genet, one of his literary heroes, Hitler became a seminal figure; he never forgot that everything Hitler had done was legal. During the 1940s, Burroughs worked as a drug pusher and a thief, but he was guilt-free; a life of petty crime was less "compromising" than the "constant state of pretense and dissimulation" required by any job that contributed to the status quo. When gangsters write the laws, as Burroughs was sure they did, not only in the Third Reich but in most of the post-WWII West, ethics become fugitives, sanity is branded madness, and the artist's only option is total resistance. "This planet is a penal colony and nobody is allowed to leave," Burroughs wrote in ***The Place of Dead Roads*** (1984). "Kill the guards and walk."

In September 1951, in a drunken attempt at William Tell-style marksmanship, Burroughs inadvertently shot and killed his wife, Joan, while the couple was living in Mexico with their four-year-old son, Billy. Burroughs never considered himself anything but homosexual. He saw his intermittent sexual relations with Joan as a stop-gap measure when the "uncut boy stuff" he preferred was unavailable. Joan worshipped him, but he admitted to a friend that the marriage was in some sense "an impasse, not amenable to any solution." Regarding the feminine sex in general as a grotesque mistake of nature, a biological plot against male independence and self-expression, he never made a woman central to his fiction. Starring roles went instead to wickedly updated, flagrantly queer versions of the classic male hero, to tricksters, gunmen, pirates, and wild boys. Like Genet, Burroughs saw homosexuality (as opposed to effeminacy and faggotry, for which he had no tolerance) as inherently subversive of the status quo. Women were born apologists; (queer) men were rebels and outlaws. Nonetheless, Burroughs knew that rules are defined by their exceptions. He adored Joan's brilliantly unconventional mind and elusive delicacy. He never fully recovered from her death.

Cool, even icy in manner, acerbic in tone, Burroughs once remarked that all his intimate relationships had been failures—he had denied "affection . . . when needed or supplied [it] when unwanted." He had not responded to his father's sometimes abject pleas for love nor visited his mother in her last years in a nursing home. In 1981, after an impressive debut as a novelist, Billy Burroughs, who had been raised by his grandparents, died of cirrhosis, believing that his father had "signed my death warrant."

Although the cause of Joan's death was ruled "criminal imprudence" and Burroughs spent only thirteen days in jail, he held himself responsible. He had been "possessed," and, in the magical universe Burroughs believed we inhabit, to be the subject of a successful possession was the mark of carelessness, not victimhood. If you knew, as he did, that life is a contest between the invading virus of the "Ugly Spirit" and the vigilant, if existence is predicated on preternatural watchfulness, what excuse could there possibly be for falling asleep on the job? In a sea swarming with sharks, he remarked, it is strongly advisable not to look like a "disabled fish."

In the introduction to ***Queer*** (1985), he tells his readers that Joan's death "maneuvered me into a lifelong struggle in which I had no choice but to write my way out"; his art was grounded in his culpability. It mattered greatly to him that Calico, one of the beloved cats of his later years, who reminded him of Joan, had never been mistreated, had never required or suffered discipline at his hands. A matchless revisionist of received wisdom, Burroughs thought there was a very real point in closing the barn door after the horse had gone. Mistakes, he explained in ***Exterminator!*** (1973), are made to be corrected. Filled with the ironies of belatedness as it is, life is education to the last breath, and beyond.

In the same spirit, Burroughs rejected the notion that his familial and geographic proximity to the forces of darkness represented by corporate wealth, Hitler, and the Manhattan Project were "coincidence," a word he disdained. For his first novel, ***Junky*** (1953), he took his nom de plume, "William Lee," from his mother and his uncle; always uncannily alert to the subterranean implications of his friend's personae, Kerouac described ***Junky*** as the work of a "Goering-like sophisticate." Nor did Burroughs leave unexamined the class and race privileges to which he had been born. As a lifelong student of the ways in which power passes itself off as nature, he believed that nothing happens without our consent; we are always complicit in what we take to be our God-given circumstances. "To speak is to lie—to live is to collaborate."

"I don't mind people disliking me," Burroughs wrote in ***Queer.*** "The question is, what are they in a position to do about it?" In his case, the answer was "apparently nothing, at present," but he knew how and where his relative immunity was manufactured. He escaped the full rigor of the law not only in the case of Joan's death, but on various occasions when he was caught red-handed with illegal drugs, not because the wind is ever tempered to the shorn lamb, but because those who have usually get more. He always had some family funds at his disposal, and he was quite aware that he possessed, in Kerouac's word, "finish"—it was visible at all times that he did not belong to the "torturable classes."

Almost alone among the major white male writers of his generation, Burroughs viewed whiteness and wealth as in some sense criminal and certainly man-made, a con job passed off as a credential. Whites, he liked to complain, were the only ethnic group who marshaled an army before they had enemies. This hardly meant that Burroughs wanted, as both Genet and Kerouac on occasion said they did, to cease being white; he conducted no romance with negritude, an infatuation he took to be simply another form of the sentimentalism he disdained. He remained imperturbably himself in all climates, speaking no language but English despite the years he spent living in various parts of North Africa and Latin America. Strangers sometimes mistook him for a banking official, even a CIA or FBI agent, and he was never averse to trading on his patrician aura in a tight spot. "Keep your snout in the public trough" was a Burroughs maxim.

Burroughs remarked in ***Junky*** that one reason he drifted into a life of "solo adventure" and addiction was that a drug habit supplied the close-to-the-margin knowledge of emergency his comfortable background had forestalled. Yet, finally, his aim was not to undertake slumming expeditions among his social inferiors but to use his wit and his mind to write his way out of his condition. It was a task for which he was superbly equipped.

Among his contemporaries, only Thomas Pynchon and Kurt Vonnegut begin to match the wild brilliance of Burroughs' laconic extravaganzas of black humor. In one inspired moment in ***The Place of Dead Roads*** (1983), Burroughs' stand-in, William Hall, is driving on a dimly lit road at night, wondering if he'll be able to summon the "correct emotions" for the parents of the child he imagines himself running over. Suddenly a man swings into view, carrying a dead child under one arm; he slaps it down on a porch, and asks, "This yours, lady?" None of Burroughs' peers were his equal in brainpower megawattage, in sheer, remorseless intelligence. In his own phrase, he was a "guardian of the knowledge," a Wittgenstein of the narrative form. A critique of the family is implicit in Burroughs' fantasy about the dead child; even the most hallucinatory inventions of his imagination are grounded in hard, clear, powerfully analytic and authoritative thought. Dickens and Tolstoy remind us that great authors need not be intellectual geniuses, but part of the special excitement and pleasure in reading Burroughs at his best lies in the shock of encountering someone so much smarter than oneself. Burroughs' work is an intellect booster, Miracle-Gro for the mind—the reader has been handed the strongest binoculars ever made and for the first time sees the far horizon click into focus.

Burroughs claimed that after one look at this planet, any visitor from outer space would say, "I WANT TO SEE THE MANAGER!" It's a Burroughs axiom that the manager is harder to locate than the Wizard of Oz, but Burroughs holds what clues there are to his whereabouts; his work draws the "Wanted, Dead or Alive" poster, and his delineations are executions, fearless and summary. "The history of the planet," he wrote, "is a history of idiocy highlighted by a few morons who stand out as comparative geniuses." In an essay titled **"The Hundred-Year Plan,"** he compared Cold War politicians, bravely proffering patriotic stupidity, crass ignorance, and a gung-ho weapons program as qualifications for office, to prehistoric dinosaurs, whom he imagined gathering for a convention many millennia past. Faced with down-scaling or extinction, a dinosaur leader announces, "Size is the answer . . . increased size. . . . It was good enough for me. . . . (Applause) . . . We will increase . . . and we will continue to dominate the planet as we have done for three hundred million years! . . . (Wild Applause)." In this arena, Burroughs believed his elite status worked for him. Revolutionaries are always disaffected members of the ruling class; only the enemy within can lay hands on top-secret information. The insider is the best spy.

Like Hemingway, like Ginsberg and Kerouac, Burroughs aspired to "write his own life and death," to leave something like a complete record of his experiment on the planet; by his own admission, there is finally only one character in his fiction—himself. In a guarded but uncannily astute review of ***The Wild Boys*** (1971), Alfred Kazin analyzed what he took to be the solipsism of Burroughs' narrative form; Burroughs wanted "to make the fullest possible inventory and rearrangement of all the stuff natural to him . . . to put his own mind on the internal screen that is his idea of a book." Yet Burroughs was not in any usual sense a confessional or autobiographical writer.

A leader of postmodern literary fashion in the 1960s, Burroughs early discarded the Western humanistic notions of the self traditionally associated with autobiography. In a 1950 letter, he commented severely on Ginsberg's recent discovery that he was "just a human like other humans." "Human, Allen, is an adjective, and its use as a noun is in itself regrettable." Burroughs took his starting point to be the place where "the human road ends." In his fiction, identity is an affair of ventriloquism and property rights—everything is potentially up for reassignment or sale. In a compulsive gambling session described in ***Naked Lunch,*** a young man loses his youth to an old one; lawyers sell not their skills, but their luck to the hapless clients they defend. Most things in Burroughsland function as addictive substances, and the "self" can be simply the last drug the person in question has ingested. Or it may be a random object, someone else's discard, an "article abandoned in a hotel drawer."

Yet if postmodernism is, as a number of its critics have said, a disavowal of responsibility, Burroughs was no postmodernist. In his view, the elite's last shot at virtue lay in taking responsibility for the consequences of its power, and Burroughs for one—and almost the only one in the ranks of recent, major, white male American authors—was willing not only to shoulder responsibility, but to extend it. In Burroughs' magical universe, if we are everywhere complicit, we are also everywhere active. "Your surroundings are *your* surroundings," he wrote in ***The Soft Machine.*** "Every object you touch is alive with your life and your will."

When Burroughs wrote, in a famous line from ***Naked Lunch,*** that he was merely a "recording instrument," he wasn't implying, as a number of his critics and fans have thought, that he made no choices, exerted no control over what he wrote, but rather that he wanted to learn how to register not the prepackaged information he was programmed by corporate interests or artistic canons to receive, but what was actually there. In a 1965 interview with *The Paris Review,* he explained that while the direction of Samuel Beckett, a novelist he admired greatly, was inward, he was intent on going "outward." For Burroughs, the "control machine" is almost synonymous with the Western psyche. The point, as he saw it, was to get outside it, to beat it at its own game by watching and decoding the extremely partial selections it makes from the outside world and then imposes on us as "reality."

Like Marshall McLuhan, himself a fan and brilliant expositor of Burroughs' work, Burroughs saw that Western man had "externalized himself in the form of gadgets." The media extend to fabulous lengths man's nervous system, his powers to record and receive, but without content themselves, cannibalizing the world they purportedly represent and ingesting those to whom they in theory report, like drugs inserted into a bodily system, they eventually replace the organism they feed—a hostile takeover in the style of *The Invasion of the Body Snatchers.* Instead of reality, we have the "reality studio"; instead of people, "person-impersonators" and image-junkies looking for a fix, with no aim save not to be shut out of the "reality film." But Burroughs believed that a counteroffensive might still be possible, that the enemy's tactics can be pried out of their corporate context and used against him by information bandits like himself. Computers might rule the world, but the brain is the first computer; all the information people have forgotten is stored there. The problem is one of access.

In the 1960s, as he developed the "cut-up" method of his first trilogy, ***The Soft Machine*** (1961), ***The Ticket That Exploded*** (1962), and ***Nova Express*** (1964), Burroughs became fascinated by tape recorders and cameras. A how-to writer for the space age for whom science fiction was a blueprint for action, dedicated to "wising up the marks," he instructed readers in the art of deprogramming. Walk down the street, any street, recording and photographing what you hear and see. Go home, write down your observations, feelings, associations, and thoughts, then check the results against the evidence supplied by your tapes and photos. You will discover that your mind has registered only a tiny fraction of your experience; what you left unnoticed may be what you most need to find. "Truth may appear only once," Burroughs wrote in his journal in 1997; "it may not be repeatable." To walk down the street as most people perform the act is to reject the only free handout life has to offer, to trample on the prince in a rush for the toad, storming the pawnshop to exchange gold for dross. What we call "reality," according to Burroughs, is just the result of a faulty scanning pattern, a descrambling device run amok. We're all hard-wired for destruction, in desperate need of rerouting, even mutation.

How did this happen? How did Western civilization become a conspiracy against its members? In his second trilogy, ***Cities of the Red Night*** (1981), ***The Place of Dead Roads*** (1984), and ***The Western Lands*** (1987), which taken as a whole forms his greatest work, Burroughs fantasized the past which produced the present and excavated its aborted alternatives, the last, lost sites of human possibility. The first is the United States that disappeared in his boyhood, the pre- and just post-WWI years when individual identity had not yet been fixed and regulated by passports and income taxes; when there was no CIA or FBI; before bureaucracies and bombs suffocated creative consciousness and super-highways criss-crossed and codified the American landscape—"sometimes paths last longer than roads," Burroughs wrote in ***Cities of the Red Night.*** In the heyday of the gunman, of single combat, and of the fraternal alliances of frontier culture, the promises of the American Revolution were not yet synonymous with exclusionary elite self-interest. Now, however, Burroughs wrote, there are "so many actors and so little action"; little room is left for the independent cooperative social units he favored, for the dreams that he saw as the magical source of renewal for whole peoples as well as individuals.

Globally, Burroughs located a brief utopian moment a century or two earlier, a time when one's native "country" had not yet hardened into the "nation-state" and the family did not police its members in the interests of "national security"; before the discovery by Western buccaneers and entrepreneurs of what was later known as the Third World had solidified into colonial and neocolonial empire, effecting a permanent and inequitable redistribution of the world's wealth; before the industrial revolution had produced an epidemic of overdevelopment and overpopulation and capitalism had become an instrument of global standardization.

Burroughs had no sympathy for the regimented, Marxist-based Communist regimes of Eastern Europe. He saw the Cold War administrations of the U.S. and the U.S.S.R. not as enemies but as peers and rivals vying to see who could reach the goal of total control first. Yet both Burroughs and Karl Marx had an acute understanding of just how revolutionary the impact of plain common sense could be in a world contorted by crime and self-justification, and in a number of areas their interests ran along parallel lines. Unlike Ginsberg or Kerouac, Burroughs unfailingly provides an economic assessment of any culture, real or imaginary, he describes; how people make a (legal or illegal) living is always of interest to him. Like Marx, he was certain that "laissez-faire capitalism" could not be reformed from within: "A problem cannot be solved in terms of itself." He, too, saw the colonizing impulse that rewrote the world map between the sixteenth and nineteenth centuries as a tactic to "keep the underdog under," an indispensable part of capitalism's quest for new markets and fresh supplies of labor.

Burroughs never accepted the geopolitics that divided the American continent into separate southern and northern entities. Both were part of the same feeding system, though the South was the trough, the North the hog. Traveling in Colombia in search of the drug *yagé* in April 1953, Burroughs reported to Ginsberg that he was mistaken for a representative of the Texaco Oil Company and given free lodging and transportation everywhere he went. In fact, as Burroughs knew, Texaco had surveyed the area, discovered no oil, and pulled out several years before. The Colombian rubber and cocoa industries, totally dependent on American investment, were drying up as well. Colombians, however, refused to believe it; they were still expecting the infrastructure of roads, railroads, and airports that U.S. industry could be counted on to build to expedite the development, and removal, of a Third World country's material wealth. Burroughs had no more sympathy for the losers in the neocolonial con game than he did for any other "mark." "Like I should think some day soon boys will start climbing in through the transom and tunneling under the door" was his derisive comment on Colombian delusions about U.S. investment.

The literary critic Tobin Siebers, writing about post-WWII literary culture, has speculated that the postmodern disavowal of agency, almost entirely the work of First World, white, male writers and theorists, is both an expression and an evasion of racial and economic guilt. Looking at the defining phenomena of the twentieth century, its holocausts, genocides, gulags, and unimaginably lethal weapons of destruction, who would want to advertise himself as part of the group that engineered and invented them? Postmodernism allows whites to answer the question "Who's responsible?" by saying, "It looks like me, but actually there is no real 'me'"—no one, in postmodernspeak, has a firmly defined or authentic self. In the universe of total, irreversible complicity postmodernism posits, the cause-and-effect sequence of individual action and consequence, motive and deed, is severed. Where Burroughs breaks with the postmodern position is that in his fiction, though everyone is complicit, everyone is also responsible, for everyone is capable of resistance. There are no victims, just accomplices; the mark collaborates with his exploiter in his own demise.

"We make truth," Burroughs wrote in his journal shortly before his death on August 2, 1997. "Nobody else makes it. There is no truth we don't make." What governments and corporations assert as truth is nothing but "lies"; such bodies are inevitably "self-righteous. They have to be because in human terms they are wrong." For Burroughs as for the postmodernists, identity was artifice, but for him it was made that way, betrayed that way, and can be remade differently. To deny the latter possibility is the last and worst collusion because it's the only one that can be avoided. Burroughs' final trilogy is a complex, funny, impassioned attempt, with one always aware of the death sentence under which it apparently operates, to "punch a hole in the big lie," to parachute his characters behind the time lines of the enemy and make a different truth.

As he explained it in ***Cities of the Red Night,*** what Burroughs had in mind was a globalization of the Third World guerrilla tactics that defeated the U.S. in Vietnam. He prefaces the novel with an account of an actual historical personage, Captain Mission, a seventeenth-century pirate who founded an all-male, homosexual community on Madagascar, a libertarian society that outlawed slavery, the death penalty, and any interference in the beliefs and practices of its members. Although Captain Mission's relatively unarmed settlement didn't survive, Burroughs elaborates what its "New Freedoms" could have meant if it had: fortified positions throughout the Third World to mobilize resistance to "slavery and oppression" everywhere.

Despite his scorn for those lining up to welcome their destroyers, Burroughs did not traffic with the racialized thinking that—in historical fact—buttressed and excused the empire-building process, the definition of Third World people of color as inherently lazy, dishonest, incorrigibly irrational, and unable to look after their own welfare. The Western virtues of rationality and instrumentalism were largely suspect to Burroughs in any case; he shared the so-called primitive belief in an animistic universe which the skeptical West categorically rejected. In ***Cities of the Red Night,*** Burroughs is explicit that whites would be welcome in his utopia only as "workers, settlers, teachers, and technicians"—no more "white-man boss, no Pukka Sahib, no Patróns, no colonists." As he recounts the history of seven imaginary cities in the Gobi desert thousands of years ago, Burroughs explains that before the destruction of the cities by a meteor (itself a forerunner of late-twentieth-century nuclear weaponry), an explosion which produced the "Red Night" of the title, all the people of the world were black. White and even brown and red-skinned people are "mutations" caused by the meteor, as was the albino woman-warrior whose all-female army conquered one of the original cities, reducing its male inhabitants to "slaves, consorts, and courtiers."

Burroughs' cosmological myth resembles the Black Muslim fable, embraced notably by Elijah Muhammad and Malcolm X, about the creation of a white race of "devils" by an evil black scientist named Yacub intent on destroying the all-black world that has rejected him. Yet Burroughs never signed up for the fan clubs of the Third World revolutionaries so compelling to young, left-wing Americans in the 1960s; to his mind, heroes like Che Guevara were simply devices for those running the "reality film," a gambit designed to leave the "shines cooled back . . . in a nineteenth century set." Burroughs claimed to belong to only one group, the "Shakespeare squadron"; in the historical impasse in which he lived, language was his only weapon.

Language as he found it, however, was rigged to serve the enemy, an ambush disguised as an oasis—in the West, language had become the "word virus," the dead heart of the control machine. Burroughs' avant-garde experiments in montage, the cut-up, and disjunctive narrative were attempts to liberate Western consciousness from its own form of self-expression, from the language that we think we use but which, in truth, uses us. "Writers are very powerful," Burroughs tells us; they can write, and "unwrite," the script for the reality film.

Defending ***Naked Lunch*** during the obscenity trial of 1966 as an example of automatic writing, Norman Mailer noted that "one's best writing seems to bear no relation to what one is thinking about." Many post-WWII writers showed a quickened interest in the random thought that reroutes or classifies the plan of a novel or essay, but Burroughs came closest to reversing the traditional roles of design and chance. For him, conscious intent was a form of prediction, and prediction is only possible when the status quo has reason to assume it will meet no significant opposition. In his fiction, the continuity girl, the person who keeps the details of one sequence of film consistent with the next, has gone AWOL; there are no shock absorbers. Jump cuts replace narrative transitions;

straight chronological, quasi-documentary sequences are spliced with out-of-time-and-space scenes of doom-struck sodomy and drug overdoses. Lush symbolist imagery and hard-boiled, tough-guy slang, the lyric and the obscene, collide and interbreed. Burroughs' early style was founded on drug lingo and jive talk; he was fascinated by their mutability, their fugitive quality, the result of the pressure their speakers were under to dodge authority and leave no records behind. His later work elaborates and complicates this principle. No one form of language can hold center stage for long. Fast-change artistry is all; sustained domination is impossible.

The novelist Paul Bowles, a friend of Burroughs', thought the cut-up method reflected an "unsatisfied desire on the part of the mind to be anonymous," but it also came out of Burroughs' need to work undercover, at the intersections where identities and meanings multiply faster than language can calculate or record. The cut-up method was not a refusal of authorship. The writer still selects the passages, whether from his own work, a newspaper, a novel by someone else, or a sign glimpsed out a train window, which he then cuts up and juxtaposes. You always know what you're doing, according to Burroughs. Everyone sees in the dark; the trick is to maneuver yourself into the position where you can recognize what you see.

The first step is to realize that the language, even the voice that you use, are not your own, but alien implants, the result of the most effective kind of colonization, the kind that turns external design into what passes for internal motivation and makes what you are allowed to get feel like what you want. In ***The Ticket That Exploded,*** Burroughs challenged his readers to try and halt their "subvocal speech," that committee meeting inside the head that seldom makes sense and never shuts up, the static of the self, the lowest idle of the meaning-fabricating machine. Who are you talking to? Burroughs wants to know. Is it really yourself? Why has Western man "lost the option of silence"? The nonstop monologue running in our heads is proof of possession, and the only way to end it is to cut the association lines by which it lives, the logic by which we believe that "b" follows "a" not because it in fact does, but because we have been aggressively, invasively conditioned to think so. Like the Jehovah who is its front man, Western language has become prerecorded sequence, admitting of no alternatives.

"In the beginning was the word," the Bible says, but the only beginning the line really refers to, Burroughs reminds us, is the beginning of the word itself, the recorded word, literacy as the West understands it, a period that makes up only a tiny fraction of human history. Burroughs suggests that people try communicating by pictures, as the Chinese and Mayans did, even by colors and smells; words are "an around-the-world oxcart way of doing things." English as spoken shuts out the infinite variations in which meaning presents itself; the body thinks too, though the Western mind can only imperfectly translate its language. Burroughs wanted to abolish "either/or" dichotomies from our speech, change every "the" to an "a," and root out the verb "to be," which is not, as it claims, a description of existence, but a "categorical imperative of permanent condition," a way of programming people to disavow change, no matter how imperative.

Burroughs' ambitions amounted to nothing less than an attempt to uproot and transform Western concepts of personhood and language, if not personhood and language themselves, to produce a new emancipation proclamation for the twenty-first century. Inevitably, in his last novel, ***The Western Lands,*** he judged his attempt a failure, but he also noted that even to imagine success on so radical a scale was victory. By the time of his death, Burroughs was recognized as one of the major American writers of the postwar era and he had become a formative influence, even a cult figure, for several generations of the young, leaving his mark on punk rock, performance art, and independent film.

When Norman Mailer shared a podium with Burroughs at the Jack Kerouac School of Disembodied Poetics of the Naropa Institute in Boulder in 1984, he found him an impossible act to follow. The kids loved him, Mailer noted with some envy; they laughed uproariously at his every line. They knew he was "authentic." The critic Lionel Abel thought that Burroughs and his Beat colleagues had established the "metaphysical prestige" of the drug addict and the criminal; though modern skepticism destroyed the belief in transcendence, the human "need for utterness," not to be denied, had found its satisfaction in "transdescendence." In a cameo role in Gus Van Sant's *Drugstore Cowboy* (1989), a movie about young addicts in Seattle, with his dead-white poker face, dark, quasi-clinical garb, and low-pitched, deliberate, nasal intonation, Burroughs is clearly an iconic apparition from the underground, the hipster as Tiresias, the master of "the crime," as he described it in ***Naked Lunch,*** "of separate action."

Burroughs was never comfortable with the "Beat" label. In a 1969 interview with Daniel Odier, while acknowledging his close personal friendships with several of the Beat writers, he remarked that he shared neither their outlook nor their methods. Kerouac believed that the first draft was always the best one and emphasized spontaneity above all else; Burroughs counted on revision. He used the word "beat" sparingly and literally, to mean "no fire, no intensity, no life," while Kerouac and Ginsberg said it meant "high, ecstatic, saved." Unlike Ginsberg, Kerouac, or Gregory Corso, whose entire careers can be seen as part of the Beat movement, Burroughs belongs to another literary tradition as well, that of the avant-garde novelists headed by Vladimir Nabokov, Thomas Pynchon, John Hawkes, William Gaddis, John Barth, and Don DeLillo. His affinities with their direct forebears, T. S. Eliot and Ernest Hemingway in particular, are defining ones; for all his innovations, he is visibly carrying on the work of high modernist irony, as Kerouac and Ginsberg most decidedly are not, and this fact may account for the willingness of the American critical establishment to grant Burroughs a more respectful hearing than it has yet accorded his Beat peers.

Nonetheless, the affinities between Burroughs and the Beats are stronger than those he had with any other group. When he first met the much younger Ginsberg and Kerouac in 1944, he instantly took on a mentor role, handing Kerouac a copy of Oswald Spengler's *Decline of the West,* with an instruction to "EEE di fy your mind, my boy, with the grand actuality of fact." Ginsberg said that while Columbia University (where both Ginsberg and Kerouac had been students) taught them about "the American empire," Burroughs instructed them about the "end of empire." As John Tytell has pointed out, their pathway to "beatitude" sprang directly out of his "nightmare of devastation." In Tangiers in 1955, as Burroughs began the work that would become ***Naked Lunch***—a book that Kerouac named and that he and Ginsberg helped to type and revise—he wrote Kerouac that he was trying to do something similar to Kerouac's "spontaneous prose" project, whose guidelines Kerouac had written out in 1953 at Ginsberg's and Burroughs' request; Burroughs was writing "what I see and feel right now to arrive at some absolute, direct transmission of fact on all levels."

Kerouac's extended, astute, funny, and loving portraits of Burroughs as "Will Dennison" in *The Town and the Country* (1950) and "Old Will Lee" in *On the Road* not only served as advance publicity for ***Naked Lunch,*** but by Burroughs' own admission helped to elaborate the persona he adopted. In his essay "Remembering Kerouac," Burroughs said that Kerouac had known Burroughs was a writer long before he himself did. Over the course of his long life, Burroughs had other seminal, creative friendships and partnerships, most notably with the avant-garde artist Brion Gysin. Yet in some not altogether fanciful sense, Burroughs became what Kerouac and Ginsberg had first imagined and recognized him to be.

The novelist Joyce Johnson, a friend of Kerouac's, claims that the Beat Generation "has refused to die." Unlike the "Lost Generation" of the 1920s headed by F. Scott Fitzgerald and Hemingway which, within a decade, as the "Jazz Age" gave way to the Depression, was decisively repudiated by its own members, the Beat movement continues even today, a half century after its inception, sustaining its veterans and attracting new members—those for whom the respectable is synonymous with boredom and terror, if not crime, who regard the ongoing social order as suffocating, unjust, and unreal, who believe that honesty can still be reinvented in a world of lies and that the answers, if there are any, lie not in the political realm but in the quest for new forms of self-expression and creative collaboration across all traditional class, race, and ethnic boundaries, in fresh recuperative imaginings of ourselves and our country, in physical, spiritual, and metaphysical explorations of roads still left to try. "What's in store for me in the direction I don't take?" Kerouac asked.

Burroughs deconstructed the word, but he never abandoned it; it was, after all, his "fragile lifeboat," the "mainsail to reach the Western lands." Though he turned to painting as his main artistic outlet and published no novels after 1987, he continued to write, as Kerouac and Ginsberg had, up to the very day he died. If he had never been known as a Beat writer, if there had been no Beat movement, his avant-garde experiments in form, his wit, his mastery of language would ensure his inclusion in college courses on the post-WWII narrative. But it is his talismanic power to beckon and admonish his readers, to recoute their thoughts and dreams, that has made him widely read outside the academy as well as within it, and this is what he shares with his Beat companions and no one else, certainly not with the reclusive

Thomas Pynchon or the at times grotesquely overexposed Norman Mailer. Like Ginsberg and Kerouac, Burroughs is there yet elsewhere. He, too, practiced literature as magic.

The uncannily perceptive Herbert Huncke, a hustler, homosexual, addict, and writer, was the fourth seminal figure of the first Beat circle. Initially, he had been troubled by Burroughs' coldness. On one occasion, however, when Burroughs passed out drunk in his apartment, Huncke saw a different man. Awake, Burroughs was "the complete master of himself," Huncke wrote in *The Evening Sun Turns Crimson* (1980), but asleep, he seemed a "strange, otherworld" creature, "relaxed and graceful," touched with a mysterious beauty, "defenseless and vulnerable . . . lonely and as bewildered as anyone else." At that instant, Huncke said, "a certain feeling of love I bear for him to this day sprang into being." At moments, Kerouac glimpsed in Burroughs "that soft and tender curiosity, verging on maternal care, about what others think and say" that Kerouac believed indispensable to great writing. Burroughs was a Beat writer because he, too, wanted to decipher what he called the "hieroglyphic of love and suffering," and he learned about it largely from his relations with other men.

In the age that coined the word "togetherness" as a synonym for family values, the Beats, each in his own style, mounted the first open, sustained assault in American history on the masculine role as heterosexual spouse, father, and grown-up provider. In the midst of the Cold War crusade against all deviations from the masculine norm, in the era that could almost be said to have invented the idea of classified information, they openly addressed homosexuality, bisexuality, and masturbation in their work, declassifying the secrets of the male body, making sexuality as complex as individual identity, and pushing their chosen forms to new limits in the process.

Though Kerouac did not consider himself homosexual, he had intermittent sex with Ginsberg throughout the 1940s and early 1950s. Ginsberg and Burroughs had also been lovers, and their deep and steady friendship outlasted their physical affair. Shortly before his death from cancer on April 5, 1997, Ginsberg telephoned Burroughs to tell him that he knew he was dying. "I thought I would be terrified," Allen said, "but I am exhilarated!" These were his "last words to me," Burroughs noted in his journal; it was an invitation a "cosmonaut of inner space," in his favored phrase of self-description, could not fail to accept. He died four months later.

Some of Burroughs' last journal entries were about Allen and "the courage of his total sincerity." Though Kerouac's self-evasions had strained Burroughs' patience long before Kerouac's death in 1969, he always loved the passage in *On the Road* in which Kerouac spoke of feeling like "somebody else, some stranger . . . my whole life was a haunted life, the life of a ghost." Burroughs, too, knew what it was to be "a spy in somebody else's body where nobody knows who is spying on whom." In ***The Western Lands,*** Burroughs imagined a new kind of currency, underwritten not by gold or silver but by moral virtues and psychological achievements. Rarest of all are the "Coin of Last Resort," awarded those who have come back from certain defeat, and the "Contact Coin," which "attests that the bearer has contacted other beings." Finally, love between men was simply love, and love, Burroughs wrote in his journal the day before he died, is "What there is. Love."

Selected Bibliography

Abel, Lionel. "Beyond the Fringe." *Partisan Review.* 30 (1963): 109-112.

Burroughs, William S. "Final Words." *The New Yorker.* (August 18, 1997): 36-37.

Fiedler, Leslie A. "The New Mutants." *Partisan Review.* 32 (1965): 505-525.

Huncke, Herbert. *The Herbert Huncke Reader.* Ed. Benjamin G. Schafer. New York: William and Morrow Company, 1997.

Johnson, Joyce. "Reality Sandwiches." *American Book Review.* 18 August-September (1997): 13.

Kazin, Alfred. "He's Just Wild about Writing." *The New York Times Book Review.* (December 12, 1971): 4, 22.

Kerouac, Jack. *Vanity of Duluoz: An Adventurous Education, 1935-1946.* 1968; rpt., New York: Penguin Books, 1994.

Knickerbocker, Conrad. "William Burroughs: An Interview." *The Paris Review.* 35 (1965): 13-49.

McCarthy, Mary. "Burroughs' Naked Lunch." *William S. Burroughs at the Front: Critical Reception, 1959-1989.* Ed. Jennie Skerl and Robin Lydenberg. Carbondale: Southern Illinois University Press, 1991: 33-39.

McLuhan, Marshall. "Notes on Burroughs." *The Nation* (December 28, 1964): 517-519.

Morgan, Ted. *Literary Outlaw: The Life and Times of William S. Burroughs.* 1988; rpt., New York: Avon Books, 1990.

Siebers, Tobin. *Cold War Criticism and the Politics of Skepticism.* New York: Oxford, 1993.

Tanner, Tony. *City of Words: American Fiction 1950-1970.* London: Jonathan Cape, 1971.

Tytell, John. *Naked Angels: Kerouac, Ginsberg, Burroughs.* New York: Grove Weidenfeld, 1976.

Watson, Steven. *The Birth of the Beat Generation: Visionaries, Rebels, and Hipsters, 1944-1960.* New York: Pantheon, 1995.

Naked Lunch

MARY MCCARTHY (ESSAY DATE 1963)

SOURCE: McCarthy, Mary. "Burroughs's *Naked Lunch.*" In *William S. Burroughs at the Front: Critical Reception, 1959-1989,* edited by Jennie Skerl and Robin Lydenberg, pp. 33-9. Carbondale: Southern Illinois University Press, 1991.

In the following essay, originally published in 1963, McCarthy claims that Naked Lunch *represents a new type of novel based on statelessness, with the part of the exile being played by the drug addict and the homosexual.*

Last summer at the International Writers' Conference in Edinburgh, I said I thought the national novel, like the nation-state, was dying and that a new kind of novel, based on statelessness, was beginning to be written. This novel had a high, aerial point of view and a plot of perpetual motion. Two experiences, that of exile and that of jet-propelled mass tourism, provided the subject matter for a new kind of story. There is no novel, yet, that I know of, about mass tourism, but somebody will certainly write it. Of the novel based on statelessness, I gave as examples William Burroughs' ***The Naked Lunch,*** Vladimir Nabokov's *Pale Fire* and *Lolita.* Burroughs, I explained, is not literally a political exile, but the drug addicts he describes are continually on the move, and life in the United States, with its present narcotics laws, is untenable for the addict if he does not want to spend it in jail (in the same way, the confirmed homosexual is a chronic refugee, ordered to move on by the Venetian police, the Capri police, the mayor of Provincetown, the mayor of Nantucket). Had I read it at the time, I might have added Günter Grass' *The Tin Drum* to the list: here the point of view, instead of being high, is very low—that of a dwarf; the hero and narrator is a displaced person, born in the Free City of Danzig, of a Polish mother (who is not really a Pole but a member of a minority within Poland) and an uncertain father, who may be a German grocer or a Polish postal employee. In any case, I said that in thinking over the novels of the last few years, I was struck by the fact that the only ones that had not simply given me pleasure but interested me had been those of Burroughs and Nabokov. The others, even when well done (Compton-Burnett), seemed almost regional.

This statement, to judge by the British press, was a shot heard round the world. I still pick up its reverberations in Paris and read about them in the American press. I am quoted as saying that ***The Naked Lunch*** is the most important novel of the age, of the epoch, of the century. The only truthful report of what I said about Burroughs was given by Stephen Spender in *Encounter,* October 1962. But nobody seems to have paid attention to Spender any more than anyone paid attention to what I said on the spot. When I chided Malcolm Muggeridge in person with having terribly misquoted me in the *New Statesman,* he appeared to think that there was not much difference between saying that a book was one of two or three that had interested you in the last few years and saying that it was one of the "outstanding novels of the age." According to me, the age is still Proust, Joyce, Kafka, Lawrence, Faulkner, to mention only the "big names," but to others evidently the age is shrinking to the length of a publishing season, just as a literary speaker is turned into a publisher's tout. The result, of course, is a disparagement of Burroughs, because if ***The Naked Lunch*** is proclaimed as the masterpiece of the century, then it is easily found wanting. Indeed, I wonder whether the inflation of my remarks was not at bottom malicious; it is not usually those who admire Burroughs who come up to me at parties to announce: "I *read* what you said at Edinburgh." This is true, I think, of all such publicity; it is malicious in effect whatever the intention and permits the reader to dismiss works of art and public figures as "not what they are cracked up to be." A similar thing happened with *Dr. Zhivago,* a wonderful book, which attracted much hatred and venom because it was not Tolstoy. Very few critics said it was Tolstoyan, but the impression got around that they had. Actually, as I recall, the critics who mentioned Tolstoy in connection with Pasternak were those bent on destroying Pasternak's book.

As for me, I was left in an uncomfortable situation. I did not want to write to the editors of British newspapers and magazines, denying that I had said whatever incontinent thing they had quoted me as saying. This would have been ungracious to Burroughs, who was the innocent party in the affair and who must have felt more and more like the groom in a shotgun literary wedding, seeing my name yoked with his as it were indissolubly. And the monstrousness of the union, doubtless, was what kept the story hot. In the end, it became clear to me that the only way I could put an end to this embarrassment was by writing at length what I thought about ***The Naked Lunch***—something I was reluctant to do because I was busy finishing a book of my own and reluctant, also, because the whole thing had assumed the proportions of a *cause célèbre* and I felt like a witness called to the stand and obliged to tell the truth and nothing but the truth under oath. This is not a normal critical position. Of course the critic normally tries to be truthful, but he does not feel that his review is some sort of pay-off or eternal reckoning, that the eye of God or the world press is staring into his heart as he writes. Now that I have written the present review, I am glad, as always happens, to have made a clean breast of it. This is what I think about Burroughs.

"You can cut into ***The Naked Lunch*** at any intersection point," says Burroughs, suiting the action to the word, in "an atrophied preface" he appends as a tailpiece. His book, he means, is like a neighborhood movie with continuous showings that you can drop into whenever you please—you don't have to wait for the beginning of the feature picture. Or like a worm that you can chop up into sections each of which wriggles off as an independent worm. Or a nine-lived cat. Or a cancer. He is fond of the word "mosaic," especially in its scientific sense of a plant-mottling caused by a virus, and his Muse (see etymology of "mosaic") is interested in organic processes of multiplication and duplication. The literary notion of time as simultaneous, a montage, is not original with Burroughs; what is original is the scientific bent he gives it and a view of the world that combines biochemistry, anthropology, and politics. It is as though *Finnegans Wake* were cut loose from history and adapted for a Cinerama circus titled "One World." ***The Naked Lunch*** has no use for history, which is all "ancient history"—sloughed-off skin; from its planetary perspective, there are only geography and customs. Seen in terms of space, history shrivels into a mere wrinkling or furrowing of the surface as in an aerial relief-map or one of those pieced-together aerial photographs known in the trade as (again) mosaics. The oldest memory in ***The Naked Lunch*** is of jacking-off in boyhood latrines, a memory recaptured through pederasty. This must be the first space novel, the first serious piece of science fiction—the others are entertainment.

The action of ***The Naked Lunch*** takes place in the consciousness of One Man, William Lee, who is taking a drug cure. The principal characters, besides Lee, are his friend, Bill Gains (who seems momentarily to turn into a woman called Jane); various members of the Narcotic Squad, especially one Bradley the Buyer; Dr. Benway, a charlatan medico who is treating Lee; two vaudevillians, Clem and Jody; A. J., a carnival con man, the last of the Big Spenders; a sailor; an Arab called Ahmed; an archetypal Southern druggist, Doc Parker ("a man don't have no secrets from God and his druggist"); and various boys with whining voices. Among the minor characters are a number of automobiles, each with its specific complaint, like the oil-burning Ford V-8; a film executive; the Party Leader; the Vigilante; John and Mary, the sex acrobats; and a puzzled American housewife who is heard complaining because the Mixmaster keeps trying to climb up under her dress. The scene shifts about, from New York to Chicago to St. Louis to New Orleans to Mexico to Malmö, Tangier, Venice, and the human identities shift about too, for all these modern places and modern individuals (if that is the right word) have interchangeable parts. Burroughs is fond too of the word "ectoplasm," and the beings that surround Lee, particularly the inimical ones, seem ectoplasmic phantoms projected on the wide screen of his consciousness from a mass séance. But the haunting is less visual than auditory. These "characters," in the colloquial sense, are ventriloquial voices produced, as it were, against the will of the ventriloquist, who has become their dummy. Passages of dialogue and description keep recurring in different contexts with slight variations, as though they possessed ubiquity.

The best comparison for the book, with its aerial sex acts performed on a high trapeze, its con men and barkers, its arenalike form, is in fact with a circus. A circus travels but it is always the same, and this is Burroughs' sardonic image of modern life. The Barnum of the show is the mass-manipulator, who appears in a series of disguises. *Control,* as Burroughs says, underlining it, *can never be a means to anything but more control—like drugs,* and the vicious circle of addiction is reenacted, worldwide, with sideshows in the political and "social" sphere—the "social" here has vanished, except in quotation marks, like the historical, for everything has become automatized. Everyone is an addict of one kind or another, as people indeed are wont to say of themselves, complacently: "I'm a crossword puzzle addict, a hifi addict," etc. The South is addicted to lynching and nigger-hating, and the Southern folk-custom of burning a Negro recurs throughout the book as a sort of Fourth-of-July carnival with fireworks. Circuses, with their cages of wild animals, are also dangerous, like Burroughs' human circus; an accident may occur, as when the electronic brain in Dr. Benway's laboratory goes on the rampage, and the freaks escape to mingle with the controlled citizens of Freeland in a

Peter Weller in David Cronenberg's 1992 film adaptation of *Naked Lunch,* written by William Burroughs.

general riot, or in the scene where the hogs are let loose in the gourmet restaurant.

On a level usually thought to be "harmless," addiction to platitudes and commonplaces is global. To Burroughs' ear, the Bore, lurking in the hotel lobby, is literally deadly ("'You look to me like a man of intelligence.' Always ominous opening words, my boy!"). The same for Doc Parker with his captive customer in the back room of his pharmacy (". . . so long as you got a legitimate condition and an RX from a certified bona feedy M.D., I'm honored to serve you"), the professor in the classroom ("Hehe hehe he"), the attorney in court ("Hehe hehe he," likewise). The complacent sound of snickering laughter is an alarm signal, like the suave bell-tones of the psychiatrist and the emphatic drone of the Party Leader ("You see men and women. *Ordinary* men and women going about their ordinary everyday tasks. Leading their ordinary lives. That's what we need. . . .").

Cut to ordinary men and women, going about their ordinary everyday tasks. The whine of the put-upon boy hustler: "All kinda awful sex acts." "Why cancha just get physical like a human?" "So I guess he come to some kinda awful climax." "You think I am innarested to hear about your horrible old condition? I am not innarested at all." "But he comes to a climax and turns into some kinda awful crab." This aggrieved tone merges with the malingering sighs of the American housewife, opening a box of Lux: "I got the most awful cold, and my intestines is all constipated." And the clarion of the Salesman: "When the Priority numbers are called up yonder I'll be there." These average folks are addicts of the science page of the Sunday supplements; they like to talk about their diseases and about vile practices that paralyze the practitioner from the waist down or about a worm that gets into your kidney and grows to enormous size or about the "horrible" result of marijuana addiction—it makes you turn black and your legs drop off. The superstitious scientific vocabulary is diffused from the laboratory and the mental hospital into the general population. Overheard at a lynching: "Don't crowd too close, boys. His intestines is subject to explode in the fire." The same diffusion of culture takes place with modern physics. A lieutenant to his general:

"But chief, can't we get them started and they imitate each other like a chained reaction?"

The phenomenon of repetition, of course, gives rise to boredom; many readers complain that they cannot get through ***The Naked Lunch.*** And/or that they find it disgusting. It *is* disgusting and sometimes tiresome, often in the same places. The prominence of the anus, of feces, and of all sorts of "horrible" discharges, as the characters would say, from the body's orifices, becomes too much of a bad thing, like the sado-masochistic sex performances—the auto-ejaculation of a hanged man is not everybody's cantharides. A reader whose erogenous zones are more temperate than the author's begins to feel either that he is a square (a guilty sentiment he should not yield to) or that he is the captive of a joyless addict.

In defense, Swift could be cited, and indeed between Burroughs and Swift there are many points of comparison; not only the obsession with excrement and the horror of female genitalia but a disgust with politics and the whole body politic. Like Swift, Burroughs has irritable nerves and something of the crafty temperament of the inventor. There is a great deal of Laputa in the countries Burroughs calls Interzone and Freeland, and Swift's solution for the Irish problem would appeal to the American's dry logic. As Gulliver, Swift posed as an anthropologist (though the study was not known by that name then) among savage people; Burroughs parodies the anthropologist in his descriptions of the American heartland: "the Interior: a vast subdivision, antennae of television to the meaningless sky. [. . .] Illinois and Missouri, miasma of mound-building peoples, groveling worship of the Food Source, cruel and ugly festivals." The style here is more emotive than Swift's, but in his deadpan explanatory notes ("This is a rural English custom designed to eliminate aged and bedfast dependents"), there is a Swiftian laconic factuality. The "factual" appearance of the whole narrative, with its battery of notes and citations, some straight, some loaded, its extracts from a diary, like a ship's log, its pharmacopoeia, has the flavor of eighteenth-century satire. He calls himself a "Factualist" and belongs, all alone, to an Age of Reason, which he locates in the future. In him, as in Swift, there is a kind of soured utopianism.

Yet what saves ***The Naked Lunch*** is not a literary ancestor but humor. Burroughs' humor is peculiarly American, at once broad and sly. It is the humor of a comedian, a vaudeville performer playing in "One," in front of the asbestos curtain of some Keith Circuit or Pantages house long since converted to movies. The same jokes reappear, slightly refurbished, to suit the circumstances, the way a vaudeville artist used to change Yonkers to Renton when he was playing Seattle. For example, the Saniflush joke, which is always good for a laugh: somebody is cutting the cocaine/the morphine/the penicillin with Saniflush. Some of the jokes are verbal ("Stop me if you've heard this atomic secret" or Dr. Benway's "A simopath [. . .] is a citizen convinced he is an ape or other simian. It is a disorder peculiar to the army and discharge cures it"). Some are "black" parody (Dr. Benway, in his last appearance, dreamily, his voice fading out: "Cancer, my first love"). Some are whole vaudeville "numbers," as when the hoofers, Clem and Jody, are hired by the Russians to give Americans a bad name abroad: they appear in Liberia wearing black Stetsons and red galluses and talking loudly about burning niggers back home. A skit like this may rise to a frenzy, as if in a Marx Brothers or a Clayton, Jackson, and Durante act, when all the actors pitch in. *E.g.,* the very funny scene in Chez Robert, "where a huge icy gourmet broods over the greatest cuisine in the world": A. J. appears, the last of the Big Spenders, and orders a bottle of ketchup; immediate pandemonium; A. J. gives his hog-call, and the shocked gourmet diners are all devoured by famished hogs. The effect of pandemonium, all hell breaking loose, is one of Burroughs' favorites and an equivalent of the old vaudeville finale, with the acrobats, the jugglers, the magician, the hoofers, the lady-who-was-sawed-in-two, the piano-player, the comedians, all pushing into the act.

Another favorite effect, with Burroughs, is the metamorphosis. A citizen is turned into animal form, a crab or a huge centipede, or into some unspeakable monstrosity, like Bradley the Narcotics Agent who turns into an unidentifiable carnivore. These metamorphoses, of course, are punishments. The Hellzapoppin effect of orgies and riots and the metamorphosis effect, rapid or creeping, are really cancerous onslaughts—matter on the rampage multiplying itself and "building" as a revue scene "builds" to a climax. Growth and deterioration are the same thing: a human being "deteriorates" or grows into a one-man jungle. What you think of it depends on your point of view; from the junky's angle, Bradley is better as a carnivore eating the Narcotics Commissioner than he was as "fuzz"—junky slang for the police.

The Naked Lunch contains messages that unluckily for the ordinary reader are somewhat arcane. Despite his irony, Burroughs is a prescriptive writer. He means what he says to be taken and used literally, like an Rx prescription. Unsentimental and factual, he writes as though his thoughts had the quality of self-evidence. In a special sense, ***The Naked Lunch*** is coterie literature. It was not intended, surely, for the general public, but for addicts and former addicts, with the object of imparting information. Like a classical satirist, Burroughs is dead serious—a reformer. Yet, as often happened with the classical satirists, a wild hilarity and savage pessimism carry him beyond his therapeutic purpose and defeat it. The book is alive, like a basketful of crabs, and common sense cannot get hold of it to extract a moral.

On the one hand, control is evil; on the other, escape from control is mass slaughter or reduction to a state of proliferating cellular matter. The police are the enemy, but as Burroughs shrewdly observes in one passage: "A *functioning* police state needs no police." The policeman is internalized in the robotized citizen. From a libertarian point of view, nothing could be worse. This would seem to be Burroughs' position, but it is not consistent with his picture of sex. To be a libertarian in politics implies a faith in Nature and the natural, that is, in the life-principle itself, commonly identified with sex. But there is little affection for the life-principle in ***The Naked Lunch,*** and sex, while magnified—a common trait of homosexual literature—is a kind of mechanical man-trap baited with fresh meat. The sexual climax, the jet of sperm, accompanied by a whistling scream, is often a death spasm, and the "perfect" orgasm would seem to be the posthumous orgasm of the hanged man, shooting his jism into pure space.

It is true that Nature and sex are two-faced, and that growth is death-oriented. But if Nature is not seen as far more good than evil, then a need for control is posited. And, strangely, this seems to be Burroughs' position too. *The human virus can now be treated,* he says with emphasis, meaning the species itself. By scientific methods, he implies. Yet the laboratory of ***The Naked Lunch*** is a musical-comedy inferno, and Dr. Benway's assistant is a female chimpanzee. As Burroughs knows, the Men in White, when not simple con men, are the fuzz in another uniform.

The Naked Lunch, Burroughs says, is "a blueprint, a How-To Book. [. . .] How-To extend levels of experience by opening the door at the end of a long hall." Thus the act of writing resembles and substitutes for drug-taking, which in Burroughs' case must have begun as an experiment in the extension of consciousness. It does not sound as if pleasure had ever been his motive. He was testing the controls of his own mechanism to adjust the feed-in of data, noting with care the effects obtained from heroin, morphine, opium, Demerol, Yage, cannabis, and so on. These experiments, aiming at freedom, "opening a door," resulted in addiction. He kicked the imprisoning habit by what used to be known as will power, supplemented by a non-addictive drug, apomorphine, to whose efficacy he now writes testimonials. It seems clear that what was involved and continues to be involved for Burroughs is a Faustian compact: knowledge-as-power, total control of the self, which is experienced as sovereign in respect to the immediate environment and neutral in respect to others.

At present he is interested in scientology, which offers its initiates the promise of becoming "clears"—free from all hang-ups. For the novel he has invented his cut-out and fold-in techniques, which he is convinced can rationalize the manufacture of fictions by applying modern factory methods to the old "writer's craft." A text may be put together by two or three interested and moderately skilled persons equipped with scissors and the raw material of a typescript. Independence from the vile body and its "algebra of need," freedom of movement across national and psychic frontiers, efficiency of work and production, by means of short cuts, suppression of connectives, and other labor-saving devices, would be Uncle Bill Burroughs' patent for successful living. But if such a universal passkey can really be devised, what is its purpose? It cannot be enjoyment of the world, for this would only begin the addictive process all over again by creating dependency. Action, the reverse of enjoyment, has no appeal either for the author of ***The Naked Lunch.*** What Burroughs wants is out, which explains the dry, crankish amusement given him by space, interplanetary distances, where, however, he finds the old mob still at work. In fact, his reasoning, like the form of his novel, is circular. Liberation leads to new forms of subjugation. If the human virus can be treated, this can only be under conditions of asepsis: the Nova police. Yet Burroughs is unwilling, politically, to play the dread game of eugenics or euthenics, outside his private fantasy, which, since his intelligence is aware of the circularity of its utopian reasoning, invariably turns sardonic. *Quis custodet custodes ipsos?*

FURTHER READING

Biography

Whitmer, Peter O., and Bruce VanWyngarden. "There's No Place Like Home." In *Aquarius Revisited: Seven Who Created the Sixties Counterculture That Changed America: William Burroughs, Allen Ginsberg, Ken Kesey, Timothy Leary, Norman Mailer, Tom Robbins, Hunter S. Thompson,* pp. 103-30. New York: Macmillan, 1987.

An examination of the events of Burroughs's life and the role these events play in his fiction.

Criticism

Ayers, David. "The Long Last Goodbye: Control and Resistance in the Work of William Burroughs." *Journal of American Studies* 27, no. 2 (August 1993): 223-36.

Explores Burroughs's fictional treatment of control mechanisms—including addiction to drugs, sex, and power—and the ways to resist those controls.

Baldwin, Douglas C. "'Word Begets Image and Image Is Virus': Undermining Language and Film in the Works of William S. Burroughs." *College Literature* 27, no. 1 (winter 2000): 63-83.

Discusses the influence of film, television, and video on Burroughs's writing.

Friedberg, Anne. "'Cut-Ups': A Synema of the Text." In *William S. Burroughs At the Front: Critical Reception, 1959-1989,* edited by Jennie Skerl and Robin Lydenberg, pp. 169-73.

Examines Burroughs's cut-up and fold-in composition techniques in his collaborations with artist Brion Gysin.

Guzlowski, John Z. "The Family in the Fiction of William Burroughs." *Midwest Quarterly* 30, no. 1 (autumn 1988): 11-26.

Contends that Burroughs's fiction, despite its apparent concern with cosmology, is thoroughly grounded in "more mundane issues" related to the psychology of the family.

Harris, Oliver. "Can You See a Virus? The Queer Cold War of William Burroughs." *Journal of American Studies* 33, no. 2 (August 1999): 243-66.

Asserts that Burroughs was a fascinating individual whose work continues to confound critics and influence countercultures.

Hilfer, Anthony Channell. "Mariner and Wedding Guest in William Burroughs's *Naked Lunch.*" *Criticism* 22, no. 3 (1980): 252-65.

An analysis of the relationship between narrator and reader in Naked Lunch.

Hummel, William. "Original Chaos Restored: Paternal Fictions in William S. Burroughs." In *Naming the Father: Legacies, Genealogies, and Explorations of Fatherhood in Modern and Contemporary Literature,* edited by Eva Paulino Bueno, Terry Caesar, and William Hummel, pp. 288-311. Lanham, Md.: Lexington Books, 2000.

Examines the complexities of Burroughs's treatment of fatherhood in his fiction.

Lydenberg, Robin. "Sound Identity Fading Out: William Burroughs's Tape Experiments." In *Wireless Imagination: Sound, Radio, and the Avant-Garde,* edited by Douglas Kahn and Gregory Whitehead, pp. 409-37. Cambridge, Mass.: MIT Press, 1992.

Discussion of the role of voice and performance in Burroughs's writing.

Mannes-Abbott, Guy. "The Beats Go On." *New Statesman & Society* (27 October 1995): 47-8.

Reviews My Education, *suggesting that Burroughs's "carefully forged work will prove the accompaniment to [T. S.] Eliot's evocation of our century's waste lands."*

McNicholas, Joseph. "William S. Burroughs and Corporate Public Relations." *Arizona Quarterly* 57, no. 4 (winter 2001): 121-49.

Exploration of the role of Burroughs's uncle, public relations pioneer Ivy Lee, in the author's writings about the nature of language.

Murphy, Timothy S. "Intersection Points: Teaching William Burroughs's *Naked Lunch.*" *College Literature* 27, no. 1 (winter 2000): 84-102.

Discusses the difficulties of teaching Naked Lunch, *citing the work's "relentless scatology" and its unconventional narrative style.*

Skerl, Jennie. "Freedom through Fantasy in the Recent Novels of William S. Burroughs." *Review of Contemporary Fiction* 4, no. 1 (1984): 124-30.

Discussion of Burroughs's later fictional series that includes The Wild Boys, Exterminator!, Port of Saints, *and* Cities of the Red Night. *Skerl claims that these texts exhibit differences in technique and content from Burroughs's earlier, better known, works.*

Stull, William L. "The Quest and the Question: Cosmology and Myth in the Work of William S. Burroughs, 1953-1960." *Twentieth-Century Literature* 24, no. 2 (summer 1978): 225-42.

Claims that Burroughs's work is firmly grounded in the traditional mythology of the quest, despite claims by many critics and by Burroughs himself that his novels represent a rejection of such mythology.

Vickers, Scott. "Summer Reading." *Bloomsbury Review* (May-June 1994): 7.

Details the insights on Burroughs's life and writings provided by The Letters of William S. Burroughs *and* William Burroughs: El Hombre Invisible.

White, Edmund. "This Is Not a Mammal: A Visit with William Burroughs." In *The Burning Library,* edited by David Bergman, pp. 107-14. New York: Alfred A. Knopf, 1994.

Recounts a visit to Burroughs's residence shortly after reading Cities of the Red Night, *commenting on its themes and relation to other works.*

Wood, Brent. "William S. Burroughs and the Language of Cyberpunk." *Science-Fiction Studies* 23 (March 1996): 11-26.

Explores the connections between Burroughs's work and cyberpunk fiction and theory of the 1980s and 1990s.

OTHER SOURCES FROM GALE:

Additional coverage of Burroughs's life and career is contained in the following sources published by the Gale Group: *Authors in the News,* Vol. 2; *American Writers Supplement,* Vol. 3; *Beacham's Encyclopedia of Popular Fiction: Biography & Resources,* Vol. 1; *Contemporary Authors,* Vols. 9-12R; *Contemporary Authors New Revision Series,* Vols. 20, 52, 104; *Contemporary Literary Criticism,* Vols. 1, 2, 5, 15,

22, 42, 75, 109; *Contemporary Novelists,* Ed. 7; *Contemporary Popular Writers; Dictionary of Literary Biography,* Vols. 2, 8, 16, 152, 237; *Dictionary of Literary Biography Yearbook,* 1981, 1997; *DISCovering Authors; DISCovering Authors 3.0; DISCovering Authors: British Edition; DISCovering Authors: Canadian Edition; DISCovering Authors Modules: Multicultural, Novelists,* and *Popular Writers; Literature Resource Center; Major 20th-Century Writers,* Eds. 1, 2; *Reference Guide to American Literature,* Ed. 4; *St. James Guide to Horror, Ghost & Gothic Writers; St. James Guide to Science Fiction Writers,* Ed. 4; *Twentieth Century Literary Criticism,* Vol. 121; and *World Literature Criticism.*

NEAL CASSADY

(1926 - 1968)

American poet, autobiographer, and letter writer.

Cassady is widely considered the muse of the Beat Generation. Though Cassady did write poetry, extensive letters of literary quality, and the start of an autobiography, his reputation rests on his inclusion in the writings of other Beat authors. Jack Kerouac's novels almost always featured a main character based on his friend Cassady; and though many readers thought Dean Moriarty of *On the Road* was Kerouac himself, his bohemian hero was Cassady, down to the smallest details. Cassady is also the hero "N.C." of Allen Ginsberg's classic poem "Howl" and figures in other poems among Ginsberg's early works. His inclusion in these famous Beat writings resulted in Cassady's subsequent notoreity as a cult literary figure. Cassady's enormous appetite for life and immense energy fascinated his friends as well as the readers of Beat literature.

BIOGRAPHICAL INFORMATION

Cassady was born in Salt Lake City on February 8, 1926. Cassady's parents had a troubled marriage, in large part due to his father's severe alcoholism and illegal moneymaking schemes, and they divorced when Cassady was six years old. Left in the care of his father, Cassady moved to the slums of Denver and lived in flophouses among the skid row derelicts. During the summers he traveled with his father, who educated him in hitchhiking and conning passersby for spare change. When he visited his mother he was tormented by his unusually cruel stepbrothers. He had his first sexual experience at the age of nine, and before he turned twenty-one he had served fifteen months in reformatories, stolen some five hundred cars, and worked as a male hustler. Despite his troubled youth, Cassady developed a deep interest in philosophy and literature. At the age of fifteen he met Justin Brierly, a lawyer and high school counselor who attempted to help Cassady further his education. Cassady's connection with Brierly eventually led him to Kerouac and Ginsberg. In 1946 Cassady married fifteen-year-old LuAnne Henderson and headed to New York in a stolen car, where Kerouac was waiting to meet the storied wild man. Kerouac and Cassady became friends almost instantly, and Cassady was soon introduced to Ginsberg. Cassady and Ginsberg maintained an intense sexual relationship until Cassady returned to Denver in 1947. In transit to Denver, Cassady met up with two young women whom he attempted to seduce, one successfully, and wrote to Kerouac about it in a letter later known as "The Great Sex Letter." The document is considered one of Cassady's most important writings and had a powerful influence on the jazz-like style of Kerouac. In Denver, Cassady met Carolyn Robinson, who would later become his second wife. Cassady continued to write Kerouac and Ginsberg while he tried to straighten out his disastrous romantic life. Finding Carolyn pregnant, he annulled his marriage to LuAnne, and married Carolyn in April 1948. During this time he began working for the Southern Pacific Railroad as a brakeman, which he did well and enjoyed. He was laid off within a year, however, and was unable to maintain his family responsibilities. Over the next two years he went back and forth between LuAnne and Carolyn, moved between Denver, San Francisco, and New York, and began writing his autobiography, which he never finished. In New York he started a relationship with Diana Hansen, who would become his third wife. Though his divorce was never finalized, Cassady married Hansen in 1950, using money he stole from Kerouac, and then immediately returned to San Francisco, the railroad, and Carolyn. This same year Cassady wrote the 23,000-word letter known as "The Joan Anderson Letter" to Kerouac. Considered to be Cassady's greatest work, it was a major influence on Kerouac's *On the Road,* inspiring him to write his novel as Cassady had written his letter—using only materials from his own life. In 1958, evading the troubles of his relationships and possibly threats on his life due to his debts, Cassady got himself arrested for possession of marijuana in order to protect himself in jail, and was incarcerated for two years at San Quentin. His letters to Carolyn, which were collected in *Grace Beats Karma: Letters from Prison, 1958-1960* in 1993, document his intense remorse. Upon his release in 1960, he again tried to live up to his family responsibilities, but failed. He became addicted to Benzedrine after he met novelist Ken Kesey and joined his gang of followers known as the Merry Pranksters, a group that attempted to free themselves from all social structures and revered Cassady as a the father of their generation. Carolyn divorced Cassady in 1963, and he spent the next five years with Kesey and the Pranksters. In 1968 Cassady left for Mexico, ostensibly to work on an avant-garde film. He was depressed when he left, feeling that he had in fact become a shiftless derelict like his father. After mixing alcohol and the drug Nembutal—known to be fatal—Cassady wandered nude along the railroad tracks and was discovered dead the next morning.

MAJOR WORKS

Although Cassady's literary output consists only of letters to his friends and an unfinished autobiography, he was a major influence on the Beat movement. The novels of Kerouac and the poetry of Ginsberg are deeply indebted to Cassady. Both Kerouac and Ginsberg made extensive use of Cassady as muse, caricature, and correspondent, and his letters, which Kerouac hailed as masterworks of American literature, served to fuel Kerouac's writing. It has been argued that the two authors' dependence on Cassady may have actually drained him of any sustained output of his own, and that Kerouac's insistence on making Cassady into a literary outlaw may have prevented him from living a more stable lifestyle. Cassady's letters, which stand as his primary literary achievements, are collected in *As Ever: The Collected Correspondence of Allen Ginsberg and Neal Cassady* (1977) and *Grace Beats Karma.* Two of his most famous letters, both written to Kerouac, are "The Great Sex Letter" and "The Joan Anderson Letter." Kerouac felt that these letters demonstrated Cassady's superior literary genius; they also spurred Kerouac to begin writing directly from his own life, as in such novels as *On the Road.* A fragment of "The Joan Anderson Letter" was published in the magazine *Notes from the Underground* in 1964. Despite the obvious interest in them, an edition of the letters between Kerouac and Cassady remains forthcoming. Cassady was unable to finish his autobiography *The First Third and Other Writings;* the depression that ensued after his imprisonment and the chaos of his personal life after taking up with Kesey left him unable and unwilling to write, even at the urgings of Ginsberg and Lawrence Ferlinghetti of the Beat publishing house City Lights Books. Although a substandard copy of the unfinished autobiography appeared in 1971, a corrected and more complete version, which includes the "Prologue," was finally published by City Lights in 1981. Unlike his letters, in which Cassady used long strings of alliteration, partial stream-of-consciousness form, and a jazz and be-bop style, his autobiography is written in a more conventional tone. Both his letters and his autobiography reveal a man often in desperate straits; his autobiography, which trails off when Cassady was only nine years old, concludes with Cassady in the midst of narrating yet another grisly episode of parental neglect and abuse.

CRITICAL RECEPTION

Cassady's friends—Kerouac, Ginsberg, Ferlinghetti, among others—considered Cassady brilliant as a writer and thinker, even long after he had disappointed them as a friend. After the publication of *On the Road, Howl,* and several other works in which Cassady was fictionalized as a major character, fans of the published Beat authors longed to learn more about the larger-than-life hero. Critical interest in Cassady generally stopped at this point: Cassady's biographers and students of the Beat Generation have more often written about Cassady's fictionalized legend than about Cassady's own writings. However, the publication of Cassady's letters has helped critics to better understand his literary influence on the Beat movement. Albert Huerta examines the effect of Cassady's alliterative writing style on Kerouac's writing, and states that "Neal's letters to Jack were that overflow of the energy found in jazz and which Kerouac subsequently grasped, harnessed and articulated in his celebrated novel of 1957." Craig Leavitt suggests that Cassady's openness, in both his life and his writing, drew out self-revelations from his peers, allowing them to create a masculine culture in which intimate connections were celebrated. In larger terms, Gregory Stephenson traces in the literary history of Cassady a movement from the Beat hedonism of the 1950s to the more spiritually oriented (if still more hedonistic) counterculture of the early 1960s. In Cassady's own writings, Carolyn Cassady and several scholars note the influence of two of his early favorites, Arthur Schopenhauer and Marcel Proust. Although many scholars consider Cassady's works to be a major influence on the Beat style, critics have noted that Cassady never took himself seriously as a literary figure. Huerta contends that rather than his writings, "Cassady might well have wished to be remembered for his human vitality."

PRINCIPAL WORKS

The First Third and Other Writings [edited by Lawrence Ferlinghetti and Nancy J. Peters] (unfinished autobiography, poetry, and fragments) 1971; revised edition, 1981

As Ever: The Collected Correspondence of Allen Ginsberg and Neal Cassady (letters) 1977

Grace Beats Karma: Letters from Prison, 1958-1960 (letters) 1993

PRIMARY SOURCES

NEAL CASSADY (LETTER DATE 7 MARCH 1947)

SOURCE: Cassady, Neal. Letter to Jack Kerouac. Kansas City, Mo., 7 March 1947. *The First Third and Other Writings*, edited by Lawrence Ferlinghetti and Nancy J. Peters, pp. 124-6. San Francisco: City Lights Books, 1971.

Dubbed "The Great Sex Letter," this correspondence—written in 1947 and published in 1971—from Cassady to Kerouac relates the former's success in seducing a woman he met during a bus trip.

Dear Jack:

I am sitting in a bar on Market St. I'm drunk, well, not quite, but I soon will be. I am here for 2 reasons; I must wait 5 hours for the bus to Denver & lastly but, most importantly, I'm here (drinking) because, of course, because of a woman & *what a woman!* To be chronological about it:

I was sitting on the bus when it took on more passengers at Indianapolis, Indiana—a perfectly proportioned beautiful, intellectual, passionate, personification of Venus De Milo asked me if the seat beside me was taken!!! I gulped, (I'm drunk) gargled & stammered NO! (Paradox of expression, after all, how can one stammer No!!?) She sat—I sweated—She started to speak, I knew it would be generalities, so to tempt her I remained silent.

She (her name Patricia) got on the bus at 8 PM (Dark!) I didn't speak until 10 PM—in the intervening 2 hours I not only of course, determined to make her, but, how to *DO IT.* I naturally can't quote the conversation verbally, however, I shall attempt to give you the gist of it from 10 PM to 2 AM.

Without the slightest preliminaries of objective remarks (what's your name? where are you going? etc.) I plunged into a completely knowing, completely subjective, personal & so to speak "penetrating her core" way of speech; to be shorter (since I'm getting unable to write) by 2 AM I had her swearing eternal love, complete subjectivity to me & immediate satisfaction. I, anticipating even more pleasure, wouldn't allow her to blow me on the bus, instead we played, as they say, with each other.

Knowing her supremely perfect being was completely mine (when I'm more coherent, I'll tell you her complete history & psychological reason for loving me) I could conceive of no obstacle to my satisfaction, well "the best laid plans of mice & men go astray" and my nemesis was her sister, the bitch.

Pat had told me her reason for going to St. Louis was to see her sister; she had wired her to meet her at the depot. So, to get rid of the sister, we peeked around the depot when we arrived at St. Louis at 4 AM to see if she (her sister) was present. If not, Pat would claim her suitcase, change clothes in the rest room & she and I proceed to a hotel room for a night (years?) of perfect bliss. The sister was not in sight, so She (not the capital) claimed her bag & retired to the toilet to change——long dash——

This next paragraph must, of necessity, be written completely objectively—

ON THE SUBJECT OF...

WHEN CAROLYN MET NEAL

The advance publicity on this man had already made him unique, but I was not prepared for his appearance—not so much the physical aspects—which were all pretty average—it was his suit. Though not the authentic "zoot," it had the same aura, and I'd never been closer to one than the movie screen. It gave him a Runyonesque flavor, a dangerous glamor heightened by the white T-shirt and bare muscular neck.

Neal walked across the room to the phonograph and turned to me, a statue by the door.

Cassady, Carolyn. Excerpt from Chapter 1 of *Off the Road: My Years with Cassady, Kerouac, and Ginsberg,* pp. 1-3. New York: Morrow, 1990.

Edith (her sister) & Patricia (my love) walked out of the pisshouse hand in hand (I shan't describe my emotions). It seems Edith (bah) arrived at the bus depot early & while waiting for Patricia, feeling sleepy, retired to the head to sleep on a sofa. That's why Pat & I didn't see her. My desperate efforts to free Pat from Edith failed, even Pat's terror & slave-like feeling toward her rebelled enough to state she must see "someone" & would meet Edith later, *all* failed. Edith was wise; she saw what was happening between Pat & I.

Well, to summarize: Pat & I stood in the depot (in plain sight of the sister) & pushing up to one another, vowed to never love again & then I took the bus to Kansas City & Pat went home, meekly, with her dominating sister. Alas, alas——

In complete (try & share my feeling) dejection, I sat, as the bus progressed toward Kansas City. At Columbia, Mo. a young (19) completely passive (my meat) *virgin* got on & shared my seat . . . In my dejection over losing Pat, the perfect, I decided to sit on the bus (behind the driver) in broad daylight & seduce her, from 10:30 AM to 2:30 PM I talked. When I was done, she (confused, her entire life upset, metaphysically amazed at me, passionate in her immaturity) called her folks in Kansas City, & went with me to a park (it was just getting dark) & I banged her; I screwed as never before; all my pent up emotion finding release in this young virgin (& she was) who is, by the way, a *school teacher!* Imagine, she's had 2 years of Mo. St. Teacher's College & now teaches Jr. High School. (I'm beyond thinking straightly).

I'm going to stop writing. Oh, yes, to free myself for a moment from my emotions, you must read 'Dead Souls' parts of it (in which Gogol shows his insight) are quite like you.

I'll elaborate further later (probably?) but at the moment I'm drunk and happy (after all, I'm free of Patricia already, due to the young virgin. I have no name for her. At the happy note of Les Young's 'jumping at Mesners' (which I'm hearing) I close till later.

To my Brother

Carry On!

N. L. Cassady

GENERAL COMMENTARY

ALBERT HUERTA (ESSAY DATE SUMMER 1983)

SOURCE: Huerta, Albert. "The Inner Quest of Space: Twenty-Five Years Later." *Review of Contemporary Fiction* 3, no. 2 (summer 1983): 41-5.

In the following essay, Huerta focuses on Cassady's prison letters as examples of how Cassady pushed the boundaries of time and space in his writing. Huerta's reading of Cassady's prose is part of his effort to distinguish Cassady as author from the Cassady of Kerouac myth.

1982 marked the 25th anniversary of two important launchings: Jack Kerouac's *On the Road* and *Sputnik,* the first satellite in space. Since 1957, both have arched different paths with distinctive ends. Kerouac's book inaugurated the quest for inner space through Jesus' teaching and Buddha's *dharma*—truth seeker—via *satori*—that spontaneous illumination similar to the dynamics found in the beat and rhythm of jazz. *Sputnik* initiated the conquest of outer space through the development of technology and computer science. Both creations involved astrophysics and quantums—light and speed—but established unique realms. Kerouac's concern was for a metaphysics of the heart that would enable him to touch tenderly all that was intensely human. *Sputnik* opened the frontiers of a new age of space to instant telecommunications and mass media.

Kerouac's legacy was celebrated and appraised at Boulder, Colorado, with a ten-day marathon

(July 23-August 1, 1982) of lectures, panel discussions, poetry readings, concerts, and the reminiscences of those who remembered the great rememberer himself, who translated the musical qualities of jazz into ". . . deep form, poetic form—the way the consciousness really digs everything that happens."[1] The second event has yet to be commemorated. But until *Sputnik*'s effects are appraised and celebrated, we may wonder what its legacy will be. Has it brought us closer to the edge of an impersonal and cataclysmic *Nineteen Eighty-four*? We may sense with trepidation an Orwellian nightmare spinning the Earth into digital oblivion. As laser and spy satellites circle the earth at incredible speeds, and inflated military budgets project more sophisticated satellites with the potential to rain upon the human race the blinding megatons of demonic fury, we may embarrassingly discover a space odyssey in contradiction to the heart's desire to touch tenderly the inner forces of nature.

Although the Kerouac Conference was a deeply human event, it also cautioned scholars to demythologize Kerouac's and Cassady's overly romanticized images—Jack as the glorified author of *On the Road,* and Neal as his fun-loving travelling companion (or sputnik) and the fictionalized Dean Moriarty—whom many fans had distorted to the degree of ignoring the merits of their joint literary contribution. This concern to abandon further mythologizing and media exploitation surfaced at various stages of the Conference proceedings, and was reinforced by the sad and bitter recollection of their early deaths. Kerouac (1922-1969) died at forty-seven from alcoholism in St. Petersburg, Florida. Cassady (1926-1968) was found dead at forty-two along the railroad tracks leading from San Miguel de Allende, Mexico. And even though the Conference did not overlook the complexities of Kerouac's and Cassady's backgrounds—conditioned as they were by religious dogmatism in the '40s and '50s and the inner desire for self-actualization and possessed by the inherent turmoils of Dionysian-like personalities[2]—as important biographical factors which may have structured such personal tragedy, the participants at Boulder, nonetheless, affirmed the real need for a deeper study of the relationship of their literary personae. For whatever might be argued or written about the psychological and mythological characteristics of these two fascinating men, it is the sense of the pure consciousness of language found in Kerouac's novels which has invited so many to read him seriously. Moreover, it is precisely this element of spontaneous prose, charged and shared by Cassady's electrifying Whitman-like energy, that confirms beyond any doubt Kerouac's place in contemporary American literature.

Neal Cassady—"I Sing the Body Electric"

If we are to understand and deepen our appreciation of the harmonics of spontaneous prose which rhythmically and freely conduct us across the vast spaces of human consciousness, we are obligated to reflect upon the inspirational force that motivated Kerouac to write his final version of *On the Road.* From various unpublished Kerouac letters to his Denver friend Ed White, we know of the author's obsession with Neal Cassady's electrifying energy that never seemed to short out. John Tytell assesses well the reasons for Kerouac's attraction to Cassady: "Kerouac was inspired by the directness and emotional honesty he found in letters he received from Neal Cassady, letters whose racy colloquialism and syntactical ellipses affected his own style. . . ."[3]

Unfortunately, Neal lost or destroyed a good portion of Jack's letters. However, many of Neal's letters to Jack are preserved in the library of the University of Texas at Austin, while others are in the hands of private collectors. A few letters appear at the end of the 1981 revised edition of Cassady's partial autobiography, ***The First Third.***[4] Also since the mid-seventies, scholars have had access to the collected letters of Allen Ginsberg and Neal Cassady.[5] These letters are important and have motivated scholars in recent years to examine more closely the Kerouac-Cassady relationship. Surprisingly, Cassady's partial autobiography is written in a direct, expository, biographical style, lacking the momentum and elliptical qualities of spontaneous prose—that *floor-boarded* acceleration of a fast car, whose sudden abbreviated breaks along dangerous turns simulate the curves and high-energy quantum leaps found in physics—and which Kerouac attributed to Cassady's longer letters.

Neal's Prison Letters: 1958-60

To my knowledge, the fifty-six prison letters dated between May 1, 1958 and May 19, 1960, which Neal wrote to his wife and three children while serving time in the California Correctional System (primarily at San Quentin) for possession of marijuana, constitute the only extant corpus of unpublished material.[6] In 1981, Prentice-Hall commissioned William Plummer to write Cassady's biography. However, Plummer was more inclined to sensationalize the sociological dimensions of Cassady's life at this time of imprisonment, rather than analyze or evaluate the letters for their literary merits.[7] When commenting upon this conflictive period, Plummer emphasizes the domestic effects of Neal's incarceration upon his wife and children.

Albeit these letters have been made available to every Kerouac-Cassady biographer, few have considered them very seriously. These letters span an important interlude in Cassady's life, and are undoubtedly valuable source material concerning a series of extremely significant issues: Cassady's view of prison life, the judicial system and the law; his efforts to transform this time into a monasticlike existence leading to personal conversion, and a return to Catholicism through the spiritual direction of a Jesuit priest; and the energetic writing style that is reminiscent of Kerouac's spontaneous prose.

Jazz Consciousness—Prose Alliteration

Jazz was the voice of Kerouac's and Cassady's generation.[8] Without this cultural matrix Kerouac and Cassady would have lived very different lives. They would have produced a different kind of literature. The jazz era of the '40s offered them the necessary inspiration that was essential to the discovery and actualization of the self in terms of a renovated vision of America. Jazz was also the motivation for their creative energies. For Kerouac it was Cassady who best embodied the transposition of jazz sounds into the harmonics of spontaneous living. Neal was the medium by which the beat and rhythm of jazz seemed to have found their integrated human plasticity.

Moreover, it was also Neal's alliterative writing style that affected Kerouac's own writing. Neal's letters to Jack were that overflow of the energy found in jazz and which Kerouac subsequently grasped, harnessed and articulated in his celebrated novel of 1957. Because of the instrumental relationship of jazz sounds to alliterative prose, Cassady's letter-writing assumes a primary place in our appreciation and interpretation of Kerouac's work. Therefore, an understanding of Neal's prison letters is a major step in illuminating this jazz-alliterative experience leading to spontaneous prose. And although these letters were written after the publication of *On the Road,* they are worth examining for stylistic clues that may elucidate further the foundation of Kerouac's writing.

Inner Time and Space: Connotative Meaning

Prison regulations structure Cassady's letters in a unique way. Since Neal was confined to a different dimension—prison time and prison space—he was necessarily forced to compress his ideas and feelings into tightly woven patterns of writing. Also, the careful censorship of all prison mail required some original response to evade this affront upon his privacy. It can be said, so it seems to me, that the effects of these external restraints and controls to monitor Cassady's writing impelled him to turn deeply inward to the open regions of the mind and of the imagination. In that inner-space that was truly free, Neal discovered the rich arsenal of words, phrases and sentences which he had gleaned from his readings of the masters, particularly Proust. However, his limited situation impeded complete disclosure of his thoughts and feelings. Because of this predicament, Neal economized on language, often choosing to write elliptically and symbolically, while always communicating a sense of spontaneity.

Consequently, in these letters Neal detonates this linguistic reserve of the mind into the conscious explosion of words, words that connote his feelings and moods far better than their denotative definitions and their usual syntactical ordering to the parts of speech. The denouement of this communicative process is an intense word collage of color, candor and literary conceit. He will address Carolyn in a traditional manner, but then he will suddenly break off into an effervescent rhapsody of alliteration—words, words, words—to confide his real affective state. Words, however, in search of sounds to articulate and synthesize the core of his thoughts and feelings.

In two handwritten letters from San Quentin, dated October 31 and November 22, 1958, Cassady effusively postulates his love for Carolyn:

> Dearest daft dove deliberately doubling deft devotion despite despair dripping dumbly down delicate imdecolletage deserving diametrically different disectional dressing—drenched daily in deepest dedication to you, Lady . . .

The letter of November 22, 1958, is more intense and includes a reference to the *dharma*—truth seeker. However, the reader will notice that Neal gently remonstrates with Carolyn over her doubts and anxieties. Neal encourages Carolyn to treat these feelings as temptations, and to trust "Dependence" on the "Divine":

> Dearest Devoted Deeply Disturbed Darling Distaff Driver Distributing Delightful Dream Dividends Despite Dear Dispaired Doing Doubtless Disbeliev-

ing Directly Discerned Dharma De[ten]tion Denouncing Detestable Doubt Declaiming Defense Demanded Diligent Divine Dependence Diametrically Deriding Diabolic Disquietude Dastardly Disregarding Dross Destiny Doubly Distasteful Duty Dipped Delineation Determinally Devolving Dull Disinclination Detaching Degrilled Decades Dreaded Delay Daily Diverting Disolute Debilitation Duel Decreasing Distantly Deporting Decent Desires Dallying Disportment with you Dear Dismembered, Carolyn, Wife . . .

In one of his most moving letters, Neal reiterates to Carolyn his sincere desire to symbolically purge himself of his bad karma during the Christian penitential season of Lent. Unlike the two previous letters where "d's" predominate to emphasize the complete emotional content of "Dearest," in this handwritten letter of February 3, 1959, Neal castigates himself severely through a volcanic irruption of "b," "p" and "k" sounds. The alliteration of these three consonants function as a kind of self-flagellation, which strikes the reader's psyche as a whiplashing of the soul. Neal's Jansenistic self-guilt is intensified by this catharsis of "boiling" and "putrid" sounds. The reader will notice that the absence of cadence and the emphasis of discordant, gutteral "k" sounds communicates a cacophonous state of soul, which in Neal's terms makes it "a Correctional Crucifixtion":

. . . I choose, this Tuesday, the day of the week dedicated to Pureness esp., exercise those few precious remnants left of penial personality, shattered will, choose Purity, 1st last and forever since, as you know, as is exemplified by the very obviously, among the usual pyramid of others to be attack[ed] each as they arise, can best be tackled while repugnancy, built bigger by bile boiling a baneful brother belaboring this belly made daily more nauseated turning over unavoidable even droppings on the pitiful psychotic plans puked paranoidly forth in painfully putrid perennially prutrescing, panegyric praising Peon Power, repeatedly reaps sickening samples of karma kappers kollected in this krazy klink kollering Kaught Korruption to, [and] until, which for me I'm sure is now, reach a personal point of saturation from whence, saluting strictest sobriety forever hence, one may fortudiously hold at bay, and furthermore, with His Help, even enjoy enduring the oblation of overcoming, that vice St. Augustine claimed kept more from Heaven than any other, namely, what else?, Impurity.

Two other typewritten letters, July 15, 1959 and February 8, 1960, are a description of what Neal imagines Carolyn's feelings to be as the wife of a felon, while at the same time depriving her of freedom. Again, we experience Neal's frustration as articulated through the alliteration of "f" sounds—fricatives that fracture any real sense of freedom for Neal and Carolyn. The July 15 letter reads in part:

. . . I had to advise you to spend that buck for final freedom from being a felon's mate, with all the lonely fear, fixations, frustrations, failures, frictions, fallow fields, faltering fervors, feeble fun farces, fat faults, fermenting ferocities, fiendish fidelities, flab fortitudes, fragile fortunes, fractured fancies, familiar feminine famines, frantic freaks, frugal frigid frivolities, funeral futile fussy furtive futurities, etc., that being married to one . . .

In the letter of February 8, 1960, Neal admits:

I vaguely realize that picking on you is but a form of expressing my own self-hatred for being a phooney (you see, even my phoney is phony!), and that though "Must forgive self first, then others," find myself more & more freezing into a vampire who on you is fastening filthy feet to feebly feed find few festering fumes from freedom's fickle flickering flames: FORGIVE?

The pitiful conclusion communicates his guilt and need for forgiveness.

Neal's alliterative outpouring is not merely expressive of these depressed and guilt-ridden emotional and spiritual states. He is also buoyant, lively and playful. In a typewritten letter of August 20, 1959, he teases with the sounds and the meanings of words, while admitting his innate penchant for alliteration. He compliments Carolyn:

. . . you are beautiful, benevolent, buoyant, blooming and a blushing blonde bouquet of blessings beyond belief . . .

He then describes the role of their friend, the prison teacher of comparative religion, Gavin Arthur, grandson of United States President Chester Arthur. As we can see, the poor man is duty bound to these prisoners who are his heirs:

. . . poor harassed harbinger harnessed to hazard on harvesting hard highwaymen's hallow homage to His Holy Honor however hopelessly hidebounded heinous His hesitant Heirs hectoring hybrid heterodoxes hinder Him.

Neal subsequently praises his son Johnny for the success at summer camp. In the process he acknowledges to being an alliterator:

Can't count the cheers coursing thru my cranium cause Johnny carried the Camp campaign with such flying colors, can comment without committing compound crassness, 'cept crap coming out these asine alliterations, that Cassady's got the manliest Mama's boy ever made in 'Merica, many many thanks to Mama . . .

I have examined closely a few examples of Cassady's alliterative style as found in the prison letters, 1958-60. There can be no doubt that these samples reveal the vital and zestful forces of a unique nature, one seething freely over the edge of human consciousness, in order to touch spontaneously and more effectively the bodies and souls of those whom he loved. And as the reader has seen, these various patterns of alliterative prose—flashes from within—also convey the drama of an imprisoned spirit desiring to break through the darkness of his circumstances. But in spite of these barriers, Cassady breaks the chains of his bondage by communicating through these sound and word games. In a way, they mitigate the pain of his imprisonment.

Earlier I stated that it was the experience of jazz which motivated this highly kinetic generation with Whitman-like energy. The synesthetic alliterative sounds that we hear in these letters are analogous to the intense activity of a jazz musician while improvising. A jazz player will first pick up on a sound or a beat. He will then kick this sound around for a while, transform it, and finally surrender this new improvisation to another musician, who in turn will syncopate the beat and rhythms already articulated by the other voices. In this way the musical composition acquires a new richness that is essentially free and spontaneous. Cassady does the same with the phonetics of language, creating jazzily new composite wholes out of the emphasis of one word, such as "dearest," "felon," "beautiful," and "harassed." To each word he brings forth the consciousness of syncopated and improvised rhythms—flatted and blue-like notes.

So, what did Neal give to Jack? And what was it that Jack was trying to do in *On the Road*? Jazz, man, jazz! It was all about the inner freedom of the jazziest duo on earth, Jack Kerouac and his orbiting sputnik Neal Cassady. It was this inner quest for freedom that was celebrated twenty-five years later in Boulder, Colorado.

Postscript: The Cassady Legend

But even with this modest academic effort to appreciate Cassady's literary contribution at a more intellectual level, his Whitmanesque legend and paradoxical nature may long continue to dominate the minds of Kerouac's readers. For as in Whitman's "A Song for Occupations," Cassady might well have wished to be remembered for his human vitality, rather than paper and types: "I pass so poorly with paper and types . . . I must pass with the / contact of bodies and souls."

Notes

1. Jack Kerouac to John Clellon Holmes. See John Clellon Holmes, *Nothing More to Declare* (New York: E.P. Dutton, 1967), p. 78.
2. For an understanding of the Dionysian in Kerouac, see Lee Bartlett's study which recapitulates and expands further William Everson's and Albert Gelpi's discussion of this theme. "The Dionysian Vision of Jack Kerouac," in *The Beats: Essays in Criticism,* ed. Lee Bartlett (Jefferson, NC & London: McFarland, 1981), pp. 115-26.
3. John Tytell, *Naked Angels: The Lives and Literature of the Beat Generation* (New York: McGraw-Hill, 1976), p. 145.
4. The first edition of Cassady's *The First Third* was published in 1971. Unfortunately, it was edited from an incomplete manuscript. The 1981 edition includes the complete manuscript. See Neal Cassady, *The First Third,* 2nd printing (San Francisco: City Lights Books, 1981).
5. Barry Gifford, ed., *As Ever: The Collected Correspondence of Allen Ginsberg and Neal Cassady* (Berkeley, CA: Creative Arts, 1976).
6. The corpus of Neal Cassady's Prison Letters to his wife and children consists of fifty-six items: eighteen letters in 1958; twenty-five letters and one postcard in 1959; and twelve letters in 1960. An envelope dated July 11, 1958 from Vacaville, California confirms the absence of one letter. As of June 1982, these letters were placed on permanent loan with the Gleeson Library of the University of San Francisco, where they are housed for the work of future scholars. The author expresses his indebtedness to Carolyn Cassady for making Neal's prison letters available, and is grateful for her generosity in reading the manuscript.
7. William Plummer, *Holy Goof: A Biography of Neal Cassady* (New Jersey: Prentice-Hall, 1981).
8. Ralph J. Gleason, "Jazz was the Voice of Kerouac's Generation," in *This World, San Francisco Chronicle,* September 1, 1957, p. 16. For further confirmation of jazz as the voice of this generation, see *Jam Session: An Anthology of Jazz,* Ralph J. Gleason, ed. (New York: G.P. Putnam's Sons, 1958), and John Clellon Holmes, *The Horn* (New York: Random House, 1958).

GREGORY STEPHENSON (ESSAY DATE 1990)

SOURCE: Stephenson, Gregory. "Friendly and Flowing Savage: The Literary Legend of Neal Cassady." In *The Daybreak Boys: Essays on the Literature of the Beat Generation,* pp. 154-71. Carbondale: Southern Illinois University Press, 1990.

In the following essay, Stephenson traces the multiple appearances of Cassady as a literary character in the works of Kerouac, Allen Ginsberg's poetry, John Clellon Holmes's Go, *and Tom Wolfe's* The Electric Kool-Aid Acid Test. *Stephenson emphasizes the common depictions of Cassady as a mystic or Holy Fool.*

The friendly and flowing savage, who is he?
Is he waiting for civilization, or past it and
mastering it?

Wherever he goes men and women accept and
desire him,
They desire he should like them, touch them,
speak to them, stay with them.
Behavior lawless as snow-flakes, words simple as
grass, uncom'd head, laughter and naiveté.
Walt Whitman "Song of Myself"

Neal Cassady (1926-1968) achieved within his lifetime the status of a modern folk hero, a contemporary legend. Both during and after his life, that legend has found expression in a number of written works, on film, and in popular song. In the following I am concerned specifically with Neal Cassady's literary legend; that is, with the manner in which he is depicted as a character in literary works. Cassady's own autobiographical writing, his published correspondence, the recordings and transcriptions of his monologues, and the works of memoir and biography that treat his life are inapposite to my purpose, which is to assess the particular values, the myth, and the mystery which he represented for the various authors who were inspired to write about him.

The earliest work in which a character based on Neal Cassady appears is John Clellon Holmes' novel *Go,* first published in 1952. The character, called Hart Kennedy, is a secondary figure in the book. He enters the story suddenly about a third of the way through the novel, appears intermittently for about a hundred pages, and then hastens away again. As in many of the subsequent works in which he appears, the Cassady figure is profoundly ambiguous, manifesting both positive and negative aspects, inspiring admiration and disapproval on the part of the other characters in the works, on the part of the author, and on the part of the reader.

The physical description of Hart Kennedy emphasizes the negative, manipulative-opportunistic aspects of his character: "small, wiry Hart, who moved with itchy calculation and whose reddish hair and broken nose gave him an expression of shrewd, masculine ugliness" (114). He is further described as having eyes that are "continually sizing everything up" (117). And Hart's actions in the story bear out the suggestions of his physiognomy. He exploits every situation, every friend, and every acquaintance in the service of his amoral hedonism. He is dishonest, irresponsible, inconstant, callous and on one occasion, shows himself capable of violence. Such is the confusion and destructiveness of his life that his wife, Dinah, remarks that "you can't stick close to him if anything matters to you" (149).

FROM THE AUTHOR

CASSADY ON THE VALUE OF ART

Art is good when it springs from necessity. This kind of origin is the guarantee of its value; there is no other.

Cassady, Neal. Quoted in *Memory Babe: A Critical Biography of Jack Kerouac* by Gerald Nicosia, chapter 5, section 5. New York: Grove, 1983.

And yet, together with his negative and destructive qualities, Hart represents an intensity and an excitement, a responsiveness to life that provokes awe and imitation among many of the novel's characters. He is a catalyst—initiating, inciting action, urging others on to pleasure and abandon. His ebullience and exuberance are infectious. He communicates an awareness of existence as possibility, as promise, and as wonder that denies the self-limiting cautions and conventions by which most people live their lives.

In the context of the story Hart embodies a type of response to what Holmes sees as the spiritual predicament of postwar man. Hart's response is extreme, primitive, almost atavistic; indeed, he is likened to "an euphoric savage who erupts into a magic rite at the moment of his seizure" (139). He is a prophet of the libido, of the instincts and appetites. His desperate hedonism is not, however, an end in itself but rather the means to an end: the transcendence of personal consciousness and time. His message, incoherent and inarticulately expressed, is of the perfection and essential unity of all experience:

> Hell, you can't explain it; all this intellectual terminology drags me now. It isn't that really . . . it's nothing you can explain that way. It's just getting your kicks and digging *everything* that happens. Like everything was perfect. Because it really is, you know? . . . It's just that *everything's* really true, on its own level. See? . . . Everything's really true. I mean the same as everything else.
> (144-45)

Paul Hobbes, the main character of the novel, finds Hart's conduct to be frequently dubious and blameworthy and his ideas specious. Hobbes is capable at best of only a grudging acceptance of Hart and his wife, whom he regards as "amoral, giggling nihilists" (166). The other two central figures of *Go,* Gene Pasternak and David Stofsky, revere Hart, though Stofsky finds cause to remonstrate with him for his callousness. Finally, there is no attempt in the novel to reconcile or resolve the creative and destructive aspects of Hart Kennedy, but by virtue of his duality and ambiguity, he becomes something of a mythic figure in the story, something elemental, a force more than a man—ultimately an enigma.

Probably the best-known and certainly the most extensive of the portrayals of Neal Cassady in literature is his appearance as the character Dean Moriarty in Jack Kerouac's novel *On the Road.* Moriarty is, aside from the narrator, the central figure of the story. His character is fuller, more nuanced, and significantly more sympathetic than that of Hart Kennedy in *Go,* though the essential ambiguity of the character is at least equally profound.

The relationship between the narrator of *On the Road,* Sal Paradise, and Dean Moriarty is that of neophyte to adept. As the novel opens, Sal, though still a young man, has reached the end of himself. He has ended his marriage, suffered a serious illness, is weary and has the feeling that everything is dead. At this critical point of his life he meets Dean Moriarty and with that meeting his life begins to change direction. For Sal, Dean represents a psychological and spiritual reorientation, a new pattern of conduct, and a new system of values, including spontaneity, sensuality, energy, intuition, and instinct. In contrast to Sal's eastern, urban-intellectual friends who are "in the negative, nightmare position of putting down society and giving their tired bookish or political or psychoanalytical reasons" (11), Dean, "a sideburned hero of the snowy West," affirms and celebrates life (6). Dean retains an eager receptivity to experience that Sal associates with childhood innocence; and from the beginning of their friendship, Sal believes of Dean what he later states in his defense: "He's got the secret that we're all busting to find" (161).

Dean brings Sal into contact with his own lost self, guides him in reestablishing the primacy of his instincts and intuition, instructs him in nonrational modes of knowing. He aids him in disencumbering himself of systems of thought in order to perceive and to experience directly and without preconceptions: "Everything since the Greeks has been predicated wrong. You can't make it with geometry and geometrical systems of thinking. It's all *this*!" (99). Dean initiates Sal into the religion of "IT," which is the transcendence of personal, rational consciousness and the attainment of a synchronization with the infinite.

Dean also attempts to instill in Sal his own sense of energetic receptivity to events, his joyous passivity to life. Dean advises a total acceptance of oneself and of the world without resistance or despair, an attention and a response to circumstances that amount to a cosmic optimism. Throughout the story Dean assures Sal of the inevitable rightness of things as they are and as they will be: "I am positive beyond doubt that everything will be taken care of for us" (100). "Everything takes care of itself. I could close my eyes and this old car would take care of itself" (132). And again later: "I *know* that everything will be all right" (153). "We know what IT is and we know TIME and we know that everything is really FINE" (172). The key concepts of his code are affirmation and ecstatic resignation, expressed in his refrain of "Yes!"

But together with his irresistible charm, his irrepressible energies, and his hip mysticism, there are other features of Dean's character that make him an ambiguous figure in the book. There is, from the beginning, an element of the con artist in him, as Sal recognizes, something of the self-seeking trickster, the amoral hipster looking for kicks, the young man on the make. His treatment of people often parallels his treatment of cars: using them, breaking them under the strains of his demands, and then abandoning them. Dean is alternately innocent and demonic, tender and destructive, and Sal responds to him with admiration and with fear. Sal identifies Dean both with his "long-lost brother" (10) and with the Shrouded Traveler of his recurrent nightmare. He sees him both as "a new kind of American saint" (34) and as "the Angel of Terror" (193). Sal's ambivalence is manifested most clearly during the climactic Mexican adventure when, while euphoric with marijuana, he sees Dean as God, and then later after his illness and his abandonment by Dean, he states: "I realized what a rat he was . . ." (249).

Dean is neither altogether angelic nor altogether demonic. He is energy, both positive and negative. He can be benevolent, libidinous, sage, or baleful. Always he operates beyond the boundaries of rational consciousness. In the manner of a mystic, he can communicate directly with such other surrational persons as the idiot girl with her visions, the ecstatic spastic in the Denver bar, the wild, sweating bop musicians, and the fellahin of Mexico whose spoken language he does not know. Dean is as protean, as powerful, and as unknowable as the human subconscious mind with which he may be identified—as a votary, a prophet, and as an embodiment of its energies and mysteries.

Dean may be seen as a parallel to the shadow figure of Jungian psychology. The shadow is the personification of the latent unconscious traits, the hidden and repressed aspects of the personality, both favorable and unfavorable, destructive and creative. "The shadow usually contains values that are needed by consciousness but that exist in a form that makes it difficult to integrate them into one's life . . . sometimes everything that is unknown to the ego is mixed up with the shadow, including even the most valuable and highest forces."[1] In the novel, Dean serves as Sal's shadow, and in a larger context, the Cassady figure may be seen to represent the shadow of postwar American society.

In addition, Dean represents an earlier American spirit (the American Adam, the American innocent) that has been stifled by what Huck Finn termed "sivilization," the insipid, insidious systematizing of life. Parallels between Huck Finn and Nigger Jim, and Sal Paradise and Dean Moriarty, between the river and the road, are numerous. The trailblazer, the pioneer, and the cowboy are also very much part of his makeup. Sal describes him as "a young Gene Autry—trim, thin-hipped, blue-eyed" (6) and as "a wild yea-saying overburst of American joy," "an ode from the Plains," "a western kinsman of the sun" (11). The irony and tragedy of his situation is that there are no geographical frontiers left for him in industrial, suburban America. The remarks of the poet Gary Snyder speaking about Neal Cassady are particularly relevant to this point.

> My vision of Cassady is of the 1890s cowboys, the type of person who works the high plains of the 1880s and 1890s . . . he is the Denver grandchild of the 1880s cowboys with no range left to work on. Cassady's type is that frontier type, reduced to pool halls and driving back and forth across the country. . . . Cassady was the energy of the archetypal west, the energy of the frontier, still coming down. Cassady is the cowboy crashing.[2]

Dean may also be considered in light of what W. H. Auden has termed "the American child-hero" who is "a Noble Savage, an anarchist, and, even when he reflects, predominantly concerned with movement and action. He may do almost anything except sit still. His heroic virtue . . . lies in his freedom from conventional ways of thinking and acting: *all* social habits, from manners to creeds, are regarded as false and hypocritical or both. All emperors are really naked."[3] This characterization is entirely applicable to Dean Moriarty; indeed, it would seem to be a description specifically of him. In this manner, the Cassady figure represents something archetypally American, something closely connected with American literature, American history, and with deep-seated patterns of the American psyche.

More than being a resurgence of the American revolutionary and frontier spirits, Moriarty also represents for Kerouac a fulfillment and a culmination of American identity and an evolutionary step. He is "something new, long prophesied, long a-coming" (34). Kerouac sees him as a precursor, a potentially redemptive, visionary figure: "the HOLY GOOF" (160) whose spiritual condition is "BEAT—the root, the soul of Beatific" (161).

There are also significant affinities between the character of Dean Moriarty and Norman Mailer's idea of the hipster expressed in his essay *The White Negro.* Mailer characterizes the hipster as "a philosophical psychopath" (Alan Harrington classified Neal Cassady as a psychopath in his *Playboy* article "The Coming of the Psychopath.") for whom "movement is always to be preferred to inaction" and whose quest is for "the apocalyptic orgasm." The fundamental decision of the hipster's nature, according to Mailer, is to seek "to open the limits of the possible for oneself." The metaphysic of the hipster is a belief in "God who is It, who is energy, life, sex, force, . . . the paradise of limitless energy and perception just beyond the next wave of the next orgasm." For Mailer, the hipster represents "the first wave of a second revolution in this century, moving . . . toward being and the secrets of human energy." Parallels with the character, conduct, and ideas of Dean Moriary are unmistakable. Indeed, so similar are Kerouac's Moriarty and Mailer's hipster that the essay makes (unintentionally) one of the most perceptive criticisms ever written of *On the Road.*[4]

Kerouac was, however, dissatisfied with his rendering of Neal Cassady as Dean Moriarty, and a year after writing *On the Road,* he began another book in an attempt to more closely and completely delineate the man in whom he saw such heroic qualities. *Visions of Cody* is an ambitious and original novel that essays a total portrait of a human mind and soul from within and without. The author approaches Cody Pomeray (the novel's pseudonym for Neal Cassady) through a careful depiction of the places and scenes of his life, through a detailed account of Cody's boyhood and young manhood, through transcriptions of recorded conversations between himself and Cassady, and through abstract language and stream-of-consciousness imagery that attempts to communicate the very rhythms and sounds of Cody's soul.

Despite its beauty of expression and truth of observation, *Visions of Cody* fails to contribute substantially to the characterization of Cassady already achieved in *On the Road.* The endeavor testifies though to the complexity and significance that Kerouac sensed in Cassady and the intensity of his desire to record an accurate and comprehensive image of him.

Neal Cassady also appears (usually under the pseudonym of Cody Pomeray) in a number of Kerouac's subsequent works, components of *The Duluoz Legend,* though never again as a main character. Throughout Kerouac's writing he remains a somewhat ambiguous figure. In *Book of Dreams* (1961) he is a fearful presence—sullen, silent, cold. In the screenplay and film *Pull My Daisy* (1961) he appears as Milo, an essentially anarchic-poetic spirit trying to fulfill the demands of a working, family man. Cody makes a brief, minor appearance in *The Dharma Bums* and a more substantial one in *Desolation Angels* where he is still revered by the narrator as "a *believing* man" (*Desolation,* 138). Only in *Big Sur* is he a real presence again, his energy and his optimism undiminished—"a grand and ideal man" (55). But he has become something of a tragic figure to Kerouac, "a martyr of the American night," an ex-convict, reduced to grueling physical labor and later jobless (57). The narrator recognizes that Cody has failed to fulfill his enormous promise as a man. Watching him chop wood furiously but ineffectively, the narrator views the activity metaphorically—"vast but senseless strength, a picture of poor Cody's life" (84). Ultimately though, whatever his ambivalence and reservations about his hero, Cody remains for Kerouac an angel, "so much like St. Michael" (100), still emitting an angelic, golden aura, "that strange apocalyptic burst of gold" that seems to derive from "the golden top of heaven" (101). The spiritual energy of Cody's psyche far exceeds his occasional and minor failings as a man.

For the poet Allen Ginsberg, Neal Cassady represented a man in whom spiritual and sexual energies were harmonious and complementary—"the ultimate psycho-spiritual sexo-cock jewel fulfillment."[5] As such Cassady was an ideal to be celebrated, and after his death, elegized.

An important early Ginsberg poem in which Neal Cassady appears, as "N.C." and "Neal," is "The Green Automobile" from the collection *Reality Sandwiches: 1953-60.* The green automobile of the poem is the vehicle of the imagination, of poetic vision. Ginsberg acknowledges Cassady as "the greater driver" of that vehicle. Together in the green automobile, the poem affirms, they will ascend "the highest mount," driving up "the cloudy highway," and will attain a state of vision, experiencing time-in-eternity, discerning the eternal in the temporal. Ginsberg sees "N.C." as a "sexual angel" and a "native saint." He declares, "Neal, we'll be real heroes now / in a war between our cocks and time."[6]

A close parallel exists between the sort of homoerotic comradeship and visionary partnership that Ginsberg eulogizes in "The Green Automobile" and that celebrated by Whitman in his *Calamus* poems (1860) and prophesied in *Democratic Vistas* (1871): a redemptive, adhesive, democratic brotherhood, a "virile fraternity" of "manly love."[7] For Whitman such relationships would in time manifest themselves in America, counterbalancing the nation's materialistic tendencies, and would be of a character "fond and loving, pure and sweet, strong and lifelong, carried to degrees hitherto unknown—not only giving tone to individual character, and making it unprecedentedly emotional, muscular, heroic and refined, but having the deepest relations to general politics."[8] Ginsberg also sees his relation to "N.C." in such terms, heralding an era of "princely gentleness" and "supernatural illumination" ("Green Automobile," *Sandwiches,* 14).

Neal Cassady is one of the dedicatees of Ginsberg's volume *Howl and Other Poems* and in the title poem figures prominently in the catalog of outcast and persecuted spiritual questers. As "N.C." he is named "secret hero of these poems" and celebrated as "cocksman and Adonis of Denver," a sensualist whose ultimate purpose in "ecstatic and insatiate" copulation is to achieve spiritual enlightenment (12). The poem "Wild Orphan," in the same collection, would also seem to be drawn from the life of Neal Cassady. The poem depicts an orphaned boy, lonely, growing up among "dead souls", but who "imagines cars / and rides them in his dreams" (42). He is a boy of rare spiritual power which will eventually find expression in "a cock, a cross, / an excellence of love" (43). As in "The Green Automobile," both poems of the *Howl* volume emphasize Cassady's role as "sexual angel," an embodiment of great sexual and spiritual energy without tension, division, or contradiction.

A theme similar to that of "Howl" informs Ginsberg's poem "The Names," collected in ***As Ever, The Collected Correspondence of Allen***

Ginsberg and Neal Cassady, which laments the deaths of American "saints," martyred by a materialistic-militaristic-rationalistic society. Cassady is named as one such martyr, condemned to a living death in the frustration, suppression, and gradual dissipation of his natural energies and joy. Again, the heroic proportions of Cassady as the "Angel" of desire and of "cock kindnesses," the "Lamb" of suffering, "patience & pain," are celebrated and are contrasted to the repressive and insensitive nature of the society in which he is abused and persecuted (211-12).

Cassady is elegized in a group of poems in *The Fall of America* in which Ginsberg assesses the personal significance and defines the larger metaphysical and social contexts of Neal Cassady's life and death. Cassady is seen in these poems as a hero of human consciousness and spirit whose thoughts and acts opposed maya (illusion, ignorance) and its manifestations: "If anyone had strength to hear the invisible / and drive thru Maya Wall / you *had* it."[9] The poems contrast the ephemerality of the maya manifestations, such as tyranny, violence, fear, and acquisitiveness, to the eternality of acts of tenderness, of passion, and of compassion, such as were performed by Cassady. In this respect Cassady's life was that of a teacher, a liberator. Ginsberg consoles himself for his sense of grief and loss with the discovery of a new dimension of personal relationship to Cassady: after the sometimes confused affections of "flesh forms," there is the endless, pure, and direct discourse of "spirit to spirit" ("Elegy for Neal Cassady," 77).

Interestingly, the work in which Neal Cassady is most unequivocally depicted as a mythic figure, a living legend, is neither fiction nor poetry, but Tom Wolfe's nonfictional *The Electric Kool-Aid Acid Test.* Wolfe's book is an account of the adventures of Ken Kesey and the Merry Pranksters in which Cassady is a central figure. Wolfe emphasizes in the book the religious nature of the group's experience, the parallels that may be drawn to the historical process of the foundation of new religions around the *Kairos,* or supreme experience, and its prophet. In Wolfe's account Kesey is clearly the prophet, but Cassady is both his precursor and his closest disciple.

At the outset Cassady is valued by the group only as "the holy primitive . . . the *natural,*" admired for his *On the Road* reputation but not (except by Kesey) esteemed intellectually.[10] Later, however, all reservations concerning him are forgotten, when as the driver of the Prankster bus, he exhibits exemplary resourcefulness and dependability and manifests his intuitive astuteness and spiritual understanding. As Kesey explains to the others, "Cassady doesn't have to think anymore" (160).

As a member of the "mystical brotherhood" of the Merry Pranksters, Cassady continues and consummates his role as the "HOLY GOOF" in *On the Road.* He distinguishes himself as a spiritual clown, a mystical acrobat, "a monologuist . . . spinning off memories, metaphors, literary, Oriental, hip allusions" (16-17), a mystagogue, a living parable, and a man in continual and rapid pursuit of "the westernmost edge of experience" (362).

Cassady's name in the Prankster group is "Speed Limit," in recognition not only of his driving skills but of his ability to approach the infinite present, the eternal now. As Wolfe explains there is "a sensory lag" built-in to the human mind: "the lag between the time your senses receive something and you are able to react. One thirtieth of a second is the time it takes, if you are not the most alert person alive, and most people are a lot slower than that. Now Cassady is right up against the 1/30th of a second barrier. He is going as fast as a human can go . . ." (145). The Pranksters equate the "sensory lag" with the concept of samsara or maya of Eastern religions and the "Now" with satori or enlightenment: "It was as if Cassady, at the wheel, was in a state of satori, as totally into this very moment, Now, as a being can get . . ." (102).

This conception of time and being (a recurrent topic of Dean Moriarty in *On the Road* in his pursuit of IT) corresponds in many respects with Bergson's idea of "pure duration."[11] The self, according to Bergson, could, by means of a union of intellect and intuition achieve a state of consciousness in which its own inner essence and its identity with the cosmos, become fused in a single experience of perpetual becoming. A more direct parallel exists between Cassady's endeavor and that myth that the critic Leslie Fiedler finds central to American culture: "the hope of breaking through all limits and restraints, of reaching a place of total freedom. . . ."[12] For Cassady such a place is not geographical but a state of being. The manifest on the Prankster's bus, of which Cassady is driver, reads: "Further" and that is Cassady's spiritual destination: beyond the limitations of the body, beyond the restraints of the mind, and into the total freedom of pure being (69).

Cassady's role as catalyst is now extended to that of a cultural catalyst, his energies inspiring and helping to define the shape and direction of postwar American culture: "Here was Cassady between . . . [Kerouac and Kesey] . . . once the mercury for Kerouac and the Beat Generation and now the mercury for Kesey and the whole—what?—something wilder and weirder out on the road" (103).

Present at all the epiphanous moments of the Prankster experience—the cross-country bus trip, the Acid tests, exile in Mexico—Cassady helps bring the adventure to its termination by officiating at the Acid Graduation Ceremony. His death, occurring soon thereafter, concludes Wolfe's account of the Pranksters and lends a note of finality, and perhaps also of futility, to their endeavor.

A character based on Neal Cassady but considerably fictionalized, not drawn from life as in the previous works considered here, appears in Robert Stone's story "Porque No Tiene, Porque Le Falta." The character, named Willie Wings, is identifiable as a Cassady figure by his prodigious amphetamine use, his being "a very good driver," his pet parrot, his inspired monologues, and a number of other personal characteristics and attitudes.[13] But he is also endowed with attributes and traits that are entirely fictional, such as his possession of a pistol and his occasional aggressiveness and hostility.

Willie Wings, a middle-aged speed freak and ex-dealer, is an ambiguous character, though ultimately he may be seen as the moral center of the story. His friend Fencer considers him "an avatar" (203), while the main character of the story, Fletch, neither likes nor respects him, believing that "his mind is running off its reel" (203). For his part, Willie Wings does not like or respect Fletch either; he is contemptuous of Fletch as a "literary" type and accuses him of living "unawares," not living "the conscious life" (206). Wings considers Fletch "dead" in perception, "like a dead nerve in a tooth" (207).

The issues of the story are courage and imagination, known here in combination as "corazon." In the beginning Fletch lacks "corazon" utterly. He is paranoid and a heavy drinker whose chief wish is for stasis, constancy, and safety. Like the cockroach in the song "La Cucaracha," to which the title of the story refers, Fletch "doesn't want to travel on," so to speak, because he lacks the metaphorical marijuana of the imagination; that is, creative courage. In contrast to Fletch, Fencer and Willie Wings approach life with daring and fantasy, experiencing the world as a mystery, events as symbols to be read. Their lives are correspondingly enriched with hazard and adventure, dangers faced, and perils overcome. In the course of the story Fletch learns (or regains) the sort of "corazon" necessary to endure and prevail in life and thereby wins the respect of Willie Wings who pronounces, "I had you wrong, brother. You really are a poet" (226).

Willie Wings, as his name implies, maintains such a degree of grace and fluidity of thought and action that it may be likened to a flight through life, almost a transcendence of the conditions of living. Imagination (true poetry for him, not "literary" poetry) is the key to both physical and psychic survival for Willie Wings. He expresses his code or philosophy through the parable-anecdote that he relates (for Fletch's edification) concerning the man alone in the hotel room whose masturbation becomes an act of imagination and spiritual affirmation, an act of poetry. For Willie Wings boredom and inertia are far more dangerous than uncertainty and insecurity and surviving intact (with joy, humor, fantasy, style) far more important than merely surviving.

Neal Cassady also serves as the basis for Ray Hicks, the hero of Robert Stone's novel *Dog Soldiers*. Hicks is an idealized Cassady figure, fictionalized to a much greater extent than any previous character based on Cassady—a Cassady as he might have been. Nevertheless, Ray Hicks is clearly recognizable (as the author intends) as having cardinal aspects of his character and personal history inspired by those of Neal Cassady. He is a quintessential Cassady figure—perhaps in some measure a truer, deeper portrait than those drawn from life.

Hicks, like Dean Moriarty, has significant affinities with Mailer's "philosophical psychopath." (He is introduced in the novel reading a volume of Nietzsche, and a few pages later we learn that his closest friend considers him a psychopath.) He is, at once, a man of strict physical and mental discipline and yet impulsive, erratic; a man of scrupulous personal honor and honesty involved in immoral and illegal activities. Hicks thinks of himself as "a kind of samurai," "a serious man" who has chosen out of all the numberless illusions of the world "the worthiest illusion."[14]

Obvious parallels exist between the relation of Hicks to his former Zen Master, Dieter Bechstein, and that of Neal Cassady to Ken Kesey, as described in *The Electric Kool-Aid Acid Test*. Kesey's place at La Honda with its painted trees, outdoor mobiles, speakers and lights, is the model for Dieter's similarly equipped mountaintop *rosha* at El Incarnacion del Verbo, "the last crumbling fortress of the spirit" (274). The Merry Pranksters are fictionalized as and elevated to the brotherhood of "Those Who Are" (212).

As in the case of previous Cassady figures, Hicks is possessed of both physical and spiritual energy. Dieter says admiringly of him, "He was your natural man of Zen. . . . He was incredible. He acted everything out. There was absolutely no difference between thought and action for him. . . . It was exactly the same. An enormous self-respect. Whatever he believed in he had to embody absolutely" (271). Ultimately, Hicks assumes the role of a sacrificial figure, becoming "the pain carrier," the bearer of the suffering of the world (330). His death alone, walking on a desert railroad track (as Neal Cassady died), bearing his "weight" or burden, is his final sacrificial act, a fusion of his physical and spiritual disciplines.

Using the same man as inspiration, Robert Stone creates two disparate characters: Wilie Wings and Ray Hicks. At the deepest level, however, they have in common their personal integrity and their advanced but imperfect spiritual development. In their different ways both men embrace "the worthiest illusion" (poetry for Wings, human love for Hicks) and actively oppose the agencies of negativity (the Sinister Pancho Pillow and such devils as Antheil and Danskin). And both Wings and Hicks share a fluidity of psyche, a quality of attunement with and attention to the total environment, the inner and the outer, the visible and the invisible worlds. They manifest a singular ability to maneuver in the moment, to respond quickly and correctly to the flow of events, to flow with the events. They have recognized the unpredictability of life, its lack of constants and fixities, and they have mastered the flux, knowing, though, that their mastery is only temporary, knowing that it must end, that defeat is ultimate and inevitable. In this recognition and in their response to the terms of life, Wings and Hicks share a code, a style which is, again, very similar to that of "Hip" as defined by Mailer. Both men act out of "a dialectical . . . dynamic conception of existence" in which the alternatives are "to stay cool or to flip," to control or to be defeated. Finally, only the particular strategies of Wings and Hicks differ. Their views of existence and the essential nature of their response to it are the same.

Neal Cassady is incarnated as "Sir Speed" Houlihan in two works by Ken Kesey: the play *Over the Border* and the short story "The Day after Superman Died." In the former he is a central figure, and in the latter he is the subject and the pivot of action and meaning, although he is present only in the memories and the minds of the other characters.

Over the Border is Ken Kesey's poeticized version of the experiences of himself and the Merry Pranksters, here called Devlin Deboree and the Animal Friends. The essential situations, events, and characters are clearly recognizable from Tom Wolfe's account but are here altered, embroidered, recombined. The title refers to the group's flight to and exile in Mexico and also to their state of consciousness, over the border of rational, ego consciousness and in the terra incognita of the personal subconscious and the collective unconscious. The title also suggests the ultimate goal of the group, a sort of neo-Nietzschean transcendence of the human condition, and may also be read as suggesting the nature of their failure, crossing over the border of common sense and human mercy into megalomania.

Houlihan is a key figure among the Animal Friends. His relation to Devlin Deboree is very similar to that of Lear's Fool to Lear. His earthy, antic metaphysics are the ballast of the group. His humor and sensuality represent a sense of proportion that counterbalances Deboree's insidious messianism. Houlihan's personal characteristics are very much those of some earlier Cassady figures: catalytic, kinetic, irrepressible in his energy, eloquent and humorous in his endless free-association monologues, resourceful, imperturbable in the face of adversity. His presence dispels stasis and immobility and inspires humor and courage. As Dieter said of Hicks, Houlihan embodies implicitly what he believes to the extent that he is a living parable. And in the manner of many of his fictional predecessors, he flows with events, maintaining a Taoist balance, participating simultaneously at the physical and metaphysical levels of existence.

Flight is the central motif of the play, in both of the principal meanings of the word: as escape and as movement through the air. The Animal Friends escape from the forces of law and authority (restraint and limitation) in the United States and in Mexico, and they rescue their comrades from imprisonment in Mexico. Their aim of transcendence is both an escape from the confinement of rational, ego consciousness and a soaring flight in the limitlessness of the Infinite Mind. Houlihan personifies the group experience of flight in both of these senses. He is imprisoned in Mexico but escapes from the prison into the sky (by means of a helicopter). And the group's ultimate failure in their quest for transcendence, their "aerodynamic error," as the play's narrative voice characterizes it, is epitomized by Houlihan's kite, which soars for a time but then, through a miscalculation, an overextension, plummets into the sea.[15] "Houlihan forlornly reeling the drowned carcass of the kite up the cliff, calling over his shoulder through a hole in the electronic noise: 'The sharks got 'im mates.'—holding aloft the bedraggled skeleton: 'I went out too far . . .'" (*Garage,* 157).

The question of whether or to what extent the Cassady figure is psychopathic arises again in *Over the Border* with reference to Alan Harrington's article—"some *Playboy* hack calling your buddy a psychopath" (*Garage,* 65). Kesey addresses the issue by allowing the deceased spirit of Houlihan to speak in his own defense. "Joyce was blind in one eye. Would you let James Joyce go down for posterity with Here Lies a One-Eyed Man as his only epitaph? Nothing about his style, his genius, his innovative influence?" (*Garage,* 65). Obviously, Kesey views this as a trivial matter, a minor imperfection at worst, and utterly irrelevant to the real significance of Houlihan's life. Through his Devlin Deboree persona, the author promises to consider this larger issue, the meaning of Houlihan's life, at some future date.

Kesey fulfills his promise to treat the significance of Houlihan's life in his story "The Day after Superman Died." The title refers to the death of Houlihan, and the narrative focuses on the consequences of his death for Devlin Deboree and by extension, for the world at large. The movement of the story is from denial to affirmation, from despair to renewal of faith. The central motif is the eye, or sight—obscured vision versus clear vision.

The story opens with images of death, conflict, weariness, sorrow, tension. It is a "blighted afternoon" of harsh, raw light and "eye-smiting smoke."[16] A day on which there seem to be "no satisfactory answers" to questions, doubts, and accusations, both external and internal (150). The imagery and the mood culminate in the revelation of Houlihan's death. For Deboree this knowledge is the final, ominous sign that "the movement," or "the revolution" in which he believes, is losing.

Far worse for Deboree is the apparent nonsense of Houlihan's final words: "Sixty-four thousand nine hundred and twenty-eight." Deboree is, in his despair, "begging for some banner to carry on with, some comforter of last-minute truth quilted by Old Holy Goof Houlihan, a wrap against the chilly moss to come." But Houlihan, "the Fastestmanalive," has left only "a psycho's cipher" (168). Deboree cannot avert the conclusion that Houlihan's senseless death invalidates all that had gone before: "That it had *all* been a trick, that he had never known purpose" (189).

The turning point of the narrative occurs when Deboree learns the circumstances of Houlihan's death, the context in which his last words were spoken. Drunk and doped, Houlihan had accepted a challenge to count the railroad ties between two Mexican villages; he died in the attempt. His last words were a record of the extent of his endeavor. For Deboree this knowledge constitutes "the banner" for which he had hoped: "Houlihan wasn't merely making noise: he was *counting.* He didn't lose it. We didn't lose it. We were all counting" (192). Such sudden renewal of hope and purpose precipitates a sort of satori or illumination in the stricken psyche of Deboree. He experiences a profound sense of acceptance, the joyous passivity and receptivity, the cosmic optimism that was Houlihan's message in life and his legacy in death.

In the context of Kesey's story, Houlihan is identified with "the movement," "the revolution," relating more to the Taoist term of the Great Awakening of the consciousness or the spirit rather than to the political sense of the terms. In the movement Houlihan is "Hero, High Priest of the Highway, . . . Hoper Springing Eternally" (176). Despite his failures and shortcomings, his life is seen as an example for others pursuing similar spiritual goals: "that faith that saw him through his lapses had become a faith for everybody that knew him, a mighty bridge to see them across their own chasms" (189).

The larger implications of the story seem to be that Houlihan is a key figure in an American (and international) cultural-philosophical-spiritual movement, that the movement is an important step in human evolution, and that this step represents, in turn, an important phase in cosmic evolution. In this manner, Kerouac's prophecy of Cassady as "a new kind of American saint," possessor of "the secret that we're all busting to find," would seem to have been fulfilled, a quarter of a century later, in Kesey's canonization of Houlihan.

The Cassady figure, as represented in the works of fiction, the poems and plays in which he appears, is protean, disparate. A common denominator of his various incarnations, however, would seem to be his psychic (consciousness and spirit) energy, which is manifested in one or another of its aspects in every appearance.

There is a clear development of the figure in terms of this psychic energy in the course of the works in which he is depicted. His movement is, to borrow Kerouac's image, from Beat to beatific. Hart Kennedy is obviously primarily a hedonist, but he is struggling toward an essentially mystical insight concerning time, consciousness, and reality. Dean Moriarty, though no less of a sensualist, is more pronouncedly mystical in orientation. He is a young man beginning to form his experiences and his perceptions into a new coherence. Ginsberg's "N.C." is a man who has resolved his contradictions, who has attained a degree of mastery in directing the poetic imagination—unequivocally a spiritual hero. Robert Stone's figures have achieved personal discipline and formulated codes by which they live. They are able to direct their thoughts and actions in accordance with what they perceive as the flow of existence. Tom Wolfe's "Speed Limit" Cassady and Ken Kesey's Houlihan represent the final unfolding of the character: the Holy Fool, the cosmic jester, master of the flow within and without, teacher of courage and faith.

What the Cassady figure represents in American literature and culture is a populist mysticism: the reemergence of a heterodox, syncretic, religious impulse that has previously found expression in such figures as Whitman and Henry Miller. The Cassady figure is an embodiment of transcendental primitivism—the American response to the cultural-spiritual crisis of Western civilization to which such movements as dadaism, surrealism, and existentialism have been the European response. His alliance with the renewing forces of the unconscious, his cultivation of surrational intelligence, his leverage through passivity, and his ability to determine the flow of events and to move with it closely resemble elements of various oriental, spiritual disciplines. In this sense the Cassady figure represents a marriage of West and East, helping to accomplish the spiritual circumnavigation of the globe prophesied by Whitman in his "Passage to India," evolving toward a new synthesis, a new paradigm. Whitman's admonition of "O farther, farther, farther sail" has become the manifest on the magic bus driven by the Fastestmanalive: "Furthur." The modes of locomotion (physical and metaphysical) may have altered greatly in the century between Whitman and Cassady, but the destination remains the same.

Notes

1. Franz [M. L. von. "The Process of Individuation." In *Man and His Symbols*, edited by Carl G. Jung, 157–245. New York: Dell, 1968.], 183.
2. Ann Charters, *Kerouac, A Biography* (San Francisco: Straight Arrow Books, 1973), 286-87.
3. W. H. Auden, "Today's Wonder-World Needs Alice," in *Aspects of Alice*, ed. Robert Phillips (London: Victor Gollancz, 1972), 8.
4. Norman Mailer, *The White Negro* (reprint, San Francisco: City Lights Books, 1957).
5. Allen Ginsberg, "The Art of Poetry VII," *The Paris Review* 10 (Spring 1966): 36.
6. Allen Ginsberg, *Reality Sandwiches: 1953-60* (San Francisco: City Lights Books, 1963), 11-16. Further parenthetical references are to this edition; when necessary for clarity page references are preceded by *Sandwiches.*
7. Walt Whitman, *Complete Poetry and Selected Prose and Letters* (London: Nonesuch, 1971), 110.
8. Whitman, 710.
9. Allen Ginsberg, "Elegy for Neal Cassady," in *The Fall of America* (San Francisco: City Lights Books, 1972), 75. Further parenthetical references are to this edition; when necessary for clarity page references are preceded by *Fall.*
10. Tom Wolfe, *The Electric Kool-Aid Acid Test* (New York: Farrar, Straus & Giroux, 1968), 63. Further parenthetical references are to this edition; when necessary for clarity page references are preceded by *Electric.*
11. Henri Bergson, *Creative Evolution,* trans. Arthur Mitchell (New York: Modern Library, 1944), 218.
12. Leslie Fiedler, *Love and Death in the American Novel* (London: Palladin, 1970), 135.
13. Robert Stone, "Porque No Tiene, Porque La Falta," *New American Review* 6 (April 1969): 203. Further parenthetical references are to this edition; when necessary for clarity page references are preceded by "Porque."
14. Robert Stone, *Dog Soldiers* (Boston: Houghton Mifflin, 1974), 168. Further parenthetical references are to this edition; when necessary for clarity page references are preceded by *Dog.*
15. Ken Kesey, *Over the Border,* in *Kesey's Garage Sale* (New York: Viking, 1973), 151. Further parenthetical references are to this edition; when necessary for clarity page references are preceded by *Garage.*
16. Ken Kesey, "The Day after Superman Died," *Spit in the Ocean* 6 (1981), 147. Further parenthetical references are to this edition; when necessary for clarity page references are preceded by "Day."

TITLE COMMENTARY

The First Third and Other Writings

CAROLYN CASSADY (ESSAY DATE 1981)

SOURCE: Cassady, Carolyn. "After-word." In *The First Third and Other Writings,* edited by Lawrence Ferlinghetti and Nancy J. Peters, pp. 139-41. San Francisco: City Lights Books, 1981.

In the following essay, Cassady provides some background on the text of her husband's biography, The First Third and Other Writings, *and notes the influence of Marcel Proust on his writing.*

In 1979 when Ken Kesey and Ken Babbs decided to devote an issue of their magazine, *Spit In The Ocean* to Neal Cassady, Babbs solicited contributions from the memories of Neal's former friends and acquaintances. One of these, Ed McClanahan consulted his files and there discovered a long-forgotten sheaf of typewritten pages yellowed with age and heavily endowed with penciled corrections and additions. Babbs passed these pages on to me, and I recognized them as a carbon copy of the published manuscript of Neal's ***The First Third,*** this new find being a later and last draft Neal had done.

Ed says he got the manuscript from Gordon Lish, and Gordon says he got it from Neal along with some letters. He sold the letters, but neither man can remember the whys of the manuscript. My guess is that Neal gave it to Gordon to read and comment on, and when Gordon moved to New York he gave it to Ed to return to Neal. This must have occurred in the mid-60s when Neal wasn't easy to pin down, so the manuscript was filed and forgotten.

Buried in my own files was a mysterious page of Neal's writing in progress and its carbon copy numbered page 118. The manuscript Babbs gave me ended on page 117. My orphaned page had found its mother. Subsequently, in comparing this manuscript with the published version, I found vast differences.

Neal had worked on the book in erratic spurts of intensity over a six-year period between 1948-1954, during which time he was also reading the works of authors he admired. The then-current passion was Marcel Proust's *Remembrance of Things Past.*

The last concentrated efforts to rewrite were made in 1954 while Neal was immobile from a railroad accident and we were living in San Jose. After our move to Los Gatos in the fall of 1954 he managed only half-hearted attempts in response to urgings by Allen Ginsberg and Lawrence Ferlinghetti to polish and finalize for publication as much as he'd already written of his autobiography. We worked together on it from the beginning, but I made as few suggestions as possible to guarantee the book would reflect his thinking and his style exclusively, for better or for worse.

The influence of Proust was clearly apparent to me as I worked to decipher and incorporate Neal's revisions in the latest draft. The prose of the Prologue, on the other hand, written much earlier, is far simpler and more direct. The complexity of the later prose, however, is still true as a mirror of Neal's personal style as well as Proust's. He enjoyed the challenge of finding words or expressions that described his observations, feelings and impressions in as minute detail as possible. He reveled in the game of continuing a sentence as long as he could before resorting to a period. (Rather like his favorite feat of driving a car as far as possible before applying the brakes.) He knew he was neither trained nor equipped to think of writing in terms of literary merit, but he also knew what he wanted to convey, and in order to discipline himself to do it at all he invented games for motivation. I find his writing more enjoyable if read in the same spirit.

Personally, I am grateful Neal played with his written words to the extent he did. We may find some of it uphill reading but from both his letters and his various drafts of this manuscript, we are fortunate to have a legacy of a far more intimate understanding and communication with the man himself.

CRAIG LEAVITT (ESSAY DATE 2001)

SOURCE: Leavitt, Craig. "On the Road: Cassady, Kerouac, and Images of Late Western Masculinity." In *Across the Great Divide: Cultures of Manhood in the American West,* edited by Matthew Basso, Laura McCall, and Dee Garceau, pp. 211-30. New York: Routledge, 2001.

In the following essay, Leavitt discusses the multiple literary characterizations of Cassady as well as his self-portrayal in The First Third, *observing that Cassady appeared to embody the contradictions of Western masculinity in decline.*

I walked back in with crazy Dean; he was telling me about the inscriptions carved on toilet walls in the East and in the West.

"They're entirely different; in the East they make cracks and corny jokes and obvious references, scatological bits of data and drawings; in the West they just write their names, Red O'Hara, Blufftown Montana, came by here, date, real solemn . . . the reason being the enormous loneliness that differs just a shade and cut hair as you move across the Mississippi."

—Jack Kerouac, *On the Road*[1]

In 1947, when a young writer from Massachusetts named Jack Kerouac set off on a journey to parts west, the United States stood at a crossroads. The Euro-American civilization of the Atlantic had just exerted itself in world war; with renewed strength it would soon sweep across the American continent in a wave of economic growth that would everywhere replicate the tamed and subdued East. Interstate freeways sliced across the Great Plains and through the vast spaces of the West, bringing with them the homogenized culture of American capital and conformity. Franchised hamburger stands replaced rickety roadhouses. Large-scale commercial farming and ranching transformed the independent man of the West into an anachronism, a caricature safe for mass consumption in Hollywood movies. Television beamed the official, sanitized American culture into every home. Sprawling suburban tract housing arose from coast to coast, obliterating any sense of place. The virility of the mythical western man would be neutered, shrunken to fit into the emerging plastic, prefab postwar world—a world too small and too civilized to contain his vast, violent energies.

The Old West had essentially disappeared long ago, but its magnetic power continued to draw men like Kerouac, who sought to find some of its mythic flavor and energy. "I'd been poring over maps of the United States in Patterson for months, even reading books about the pioneers and savoring names like Platte and Cimarron," he wrote.[2] He wanted to rediscover something about his country, and about himself, by going west. It was a philosophical quest of sorts: "Somewhere along the line I knew there'd be girls, visions, everything; somewhere along the line the pearl would be handed to me."[3]

The man who handed it to him was Neal Cassady. When Kerouac met his friend and guide, the latter was a footloose youth from Denver, a sometime rancher who had recently been released from a Colorado reformatory and had drifted eastward. Cassady's youth, beauty, keen intellect, and especially his boundless energy inspired much of Kerouac's true-to-life fiction, and thereby the Beat movement.[4] He represented an authenticity Kerouac found lacking in his intellectual New York circles, where he saw his friends "in the negative, nightmare position of putting down society and giving their tired bookish or political or psychoanalytical reasons," but Cassady "just raced in society, eager for bread and love."[5] Philip J. Deloria notes, "Because those seeking authenticity have already defined their own state as inauthentic, they easily locate authenticity in the figure of an Other . . . the quest for such an authentic Other is a characteristically modern phenomenon."[6] For the urban, eastern, introverted Kerouac, Cassady became this more authentic Other and an idealized image of an alternate Self. The Easterner's literary efforts, including the posthumously published *Visions of Cody* (1972) and especially the highly influential 1957 best-seller *On the Road,* would turn Cassady into a new icon of masculine western freedom and sexual power, an archetype for the Beat and hippie movements, one of the last authentic cultural heroes to emerge from the Wild West.

"With the coming of Dean Moriarty began the part of my life you could call my life on the road," wrote Kerouac, using the character name he had given to the portrait of his friend, Cassady. "Dean is the perfect guy for the road because he was actually born on the road, when his parents were passing through Salt Lake City in 1926, in a jalopy, on their way to Los Angeles."[7] Cassady was indeed fated for a restless and roaming life. Some of his childhood was spent with his mother in the slums of Depression-era Denver. For much of the rest he tagged along with his alcoholic father, a classic western hobo, on his seasonal ramblings in search of warm weather and drink. Watching his father and his companions, young Neal studied a distinct culture of manhood.

In ***The First Third,*** a partial autobiography published posthumously in 1971, Cassady himself wrote about learning the empty, ritualized language common to a certain brand of uncultured western man:

Their conversation had many general statements about Truth and Life, which contained the collective intelligence of all America's bums. They were drunkards whose minds, weakened by liquor and an obsequious manner of existence, seemed continually preoccupied with bringing up short observations of obvious trash, said in such a way as to be instantly recognizable to the listener, who had heard it all before, and whose own prime concern was to nod at everything said, then continue the conversation with a remark of his own, equally transparent and loaded with generalities. The simplicity of this pattern was marvelous, and there was no limit to what they could agree on in this fashion, to say nothing of the abstract ends that could be reached.[8]

This hobo's dialectic reveals the origins of Cassady's own virtuoso verbal style, which Kerouac marveled at and portrayed with great care. But unlike the vagrants and their anti-intellectual western forefathers, young Neal did not scorn book learning. He craved it, managing to give himself a fair education as he survived on the streets of Denver with the father who could not care for either of them properly. "In the West he'd spent a third of his time in the poolhall," Kerouac wrote, "a third in jail, and a third in the public library."[9] Cassady asked Kerouac to teach him to write, but Kerouac would later insist that Cassady's rambling letters inspired his own free-flowing prose style. One of these, written to a mutual friend from reform school before Cassady and the Massachusetts writer crossed paths, charmed Kerouac with its intellectual ambition. "I was tremendously interested in the letters because they so naively and sweetly asked Chad to teach him all about Nietzsche and all the wonderfully intellectual things."[10] Biographer William Plummer notes that young Cassady's favorite writers included "Schopenhauer and Proust: the philosopher who portrayed man as a creature of will and desire rather than intellect; the novelist who fabricated a world of sensation and pure consciousness, who measured time not by the clock but on the pulse."[11] Cassady's energies turned back from the closed frontier to the project of entering the great body of world knowledge, albeit in his own highly informal way. But as Kerouac would show, Cassady was most at home not in a library, but behind the wheel of a fast car.

As machine-driven industrialized civilization strengthened its grasp on the American West, the old symbols of virility and power changed. One of Kerouac's contemporaries, author Edward Abbey, portrayed the decline of the horse, once an all-important extension of the cowboy's physical presence, in the opening pages of his 1956 novel *The Brave Cowboy.* When his anachronistic hero tries to ride into town on a mare named Whisky, man and beast find their way blocked by a bustling highway built for trucks and automobiles. Whisky "recoiled at the touch of pavement"; the barriers to horsemanship presented by the burgeoning postwar highway system were such that "though he rode for years he would find no end to it; the track of asphalt and concrete was as continuous and endless as a circle or the walls of a cell."[12]

Like the horse, the six-shooter no longer reigned supreme as phallic projector of western masculine power; the automobile took its place as well. It was no longer necessary for the Euro-American to battle Native Americans to dominate the wide-open spaces of the West. That deathly work had been done, and now the postwar white male could "reconquer" the West for himself with the car. A fast and powerful automobile became the ultimate symbol of manhood in postwar America, especially in the West, where the machine gives man power and dominance over the once daunting geographical expanses. Wolfgang Zuckermann notes that the "sexual symbolism equating the automobile with masculinity is well-known," and is often exploited by car advertisers who play upon the fragile self-images of young men who feel constant pressure to reaffirm their masculinity.[13]

"I stole my first automobile in 1940," Cassady wrote, "by '47 when swearing off such soul-thrilling pleasures to celebrate advent into manhood, I had had illegally in my possession about 500 cars—whether just for the moment and to be taken back to its owner before he returned (I.E. on Parking lots) or whether taken for the purpose of so altering its appearance as to keep it for several weeks but mostly only for joyriding."[14] As a Denver teenager, Cassady regularly stole a car in the afternoon, went by East High School as classes were letting out to pick up girls, and, if he was "lucky," drove one up to the mountains for a sexual encounter before returning girl and car to the city limits in the evening. In *On the Road,* in one of the several cross-country trips, an older Cassady leaves his friends to wait while he uses a borrowed Cadillac to pick up a waitress for a quick score:

> From where I stood in the door I saw a faint flash of the Cadillac crossing Cleveland Place with Dean, T-shirted and joyous, fluttering his hands and talking to the girl and hunching over the wheel to go as she sat sadly and proudly beside him. They went to a parking lot in broad daylight, parked near the brick wall at the back (a lot Dean had worked in once), and there, he claims, he made it with her, in nothing flat. . . . Thirty minutes and Dean roared back, deposited the girl at her hotel, with kisses, farewells, promises, and zoomed right up to the travel bureau to pick up the crew.[15]

Auto and libido were synonymous throughout Cassady's life, and the natural symbolism of car as cock was irresistible to the novelist Kerouac. He portrayed Dean Moriarty as "the greatest driver in the world," a force of nature who terrified good citizens with his frightening speed and recklessness behind the wheel.

> Dean came up on lines of cars like the Angel of Terror. He almost rammed them along as he looked for an opening. He teased their bumpers,

> he eased and pushed and craned around to see the curve, then the huge car leaped to his touch and passed, and always by a hair we made it back to our side as other lines filed by in the opposite direction and I shuddered. I couldn't take it any more. . . . All that old road of the past reeling dizzily as if the cup of life had been overturned and everything had gone mad.[16]

In *On the Road,* the automobile takes on a metaphysical quality, projecting its occupants beyond ordinary time and space into a realm of mythic freedom and power. "Ah, man, what a dreamboat," Moriarty says as he and Kerouac's self-styled narrator, Sal Paradise, hurtle through the Nebraska night at 110 mph in a borrowed car.

> "Think if you and I had a car like this what we could do. Do you know there's a road that goes down Mexico and all the way to Panama?—and maybe all the way to the bottom of South America where the Indians are seven feet tall and eat cocaine on the mountainside? Yes! You and I, Sal, we'd dig the whole world with a car like this because, man, the road must eventually lead to the whole world. Ain't nowhere else it can go—right?"[17]

Cassady would have not only the world, but all its women. Observable throughout Kerouac's literary reckoning with the West is an implicit recognition of a culture with much looser sexual mores than the relatively staid and civilized Massachusetts of his youth. Cassady embodies this freer sexuality. Kerouac takes pains to show the titanic virility of his hero asserting itself in early adolescence, writing that "ever since thirteen Cody [another pseudonym for Cassady] was able to handle any woman and in fact had pushed his drunken father off Cherry Lucy Halloween night 1939 and taken over so much that they fist fought like rivals and Cody ran away with the five dollar stake."[18] Cassady himself wrote of his sexual initiation at age nine. Young Neal accompanied his father to the home of a drinking buddy, "a feeble-minded German drunkard," who lived with his wife and no less than twelve children in an old barn in southwest Denver. "Here, made freer by watching the numerous brothers unselfconsciously smoke, cuss and fight together on outlaw forays through sparse neighborhood between creekbed and field, I soon followed the leader in screwing all the sisters small enough to hold down—and those bold enough to lead."[19] This scene of debauchery, incest, and rape, while only a sample of the bizarre environs of Cassady's childhood, sheds much light on the sexual ethics, or lack thereof, of the mature man. Under the eyes of his own inebriated father, who should have represented authority and discipline in the boy's life but who in fact knew nothing of such things himself, Neal learned about sex in an orgy in which the line between pleasure and force was blurred, and any female was a potential sex object. Plummer comments, "It was no wonder that in full maturity, Cassady was never able to fully credit the idea of rape."[20]

Early in *On the Road,* Dean steals a young Denver beauty named Camille from a friend and keeps her ensconced in a hotel room while he pursues his all-night kicks with male buddies and other women. Camille tries to establish when he will return to her:

> "Well, all right, Dean, but please be sure and be back at three."
>
> "Just as I said, darling, and remember not three but three-fourteen. Are we straight in the deepest and most wonderful depths of our souls, dear darling?" And he went over and kissed her several times. On the wall was a nude drawing of Dean, enormous dangle and all, done by Camille. I was amazed.[21]

In fiction and in reality, Cassady's life was an impossible tangle of connections to different women. He sometimes had two wives at once, and much of the travel portrayed in *On the Road* involves racing back and forth between them. Each woman served a temporary purpose in his ongoing quest for "more"; all were ultimately expendable. But despite—or perhaps because of—its amoral quality, the ecstatic, open-ended sexuality of Moriarty and *On the Road* appealed to readers and foreshadowed the coming rejection of traditional sexual mores by many young American women and men in the 1960's.

Cassady, however, was not all speed and phallic projection and dominance. His was a deeply wounded and nuanced sexuality. Unlike the cowboy tough-guy, Cassady represented a masculinity that was interested in self-knowledge. Reading and jazz helped develop his sensitivity to the human condition. His aggressive sexuality aside, Cassady loathed violence. During the months spent in a Denver tenement with his mother and her family, Cassady's older half-brother Jimmy bullied him and his feeble, alcoholic father mercilessly and forced Neal to fight other boys in the neighborhood. Jimmy and his friends also enjoyed drowning or thrashing stray cats to death, horrifying the young Neal. The negative example of Jimmy's brutality influenced Neal's sensibilities greatly. As a child, "Neal was always the youngest and smallest in a volatile world of desperate men and men-children," and he soon learned that "competition with others was unavailing: it only brought on potentially violent situations."[22] This stance is at wide variance with the traditional western attitude, in which manly skills and manhood itself had to be frequently tested and proved, often through violent means.

Another dramatic change from the older western model of masculinity was Cassady's propensity for enthusiastic self-expression. Western heroes of the past were not known for being extraordinarily articulate; seldom did the lone gunman ride into town, belly up to the bar, and pour out his soul to his peers. In Jack Warner Shaefer's *Shane,* a novel that represents "a kind of archetype, exhibiting with remarkable purity all the basic components of the classical Western,"[23] the hero for whom the story is named enters the community as a total stranger—"he has no family, no friends, and no ties."[24] At the conclusion of the tale, after Shane has vanquished the villain and saved the community, he disappears again into the wilderness without having revealed much of his own story; he remains a mystery to the community he has rescued.

The Cassady image of western masculinity takes the opposite tack: in the Beat milieu it is manly to tell all. Cassady enters the community, represented by Kerouac and his New York circle of friends, and ignites the Beat movement by awing the easterners with his endless tales of life in the West. He tells about the adventures and deprivations of childhood on the street, about his highly unconventional sex life, about the pain and isolation of his lonely condition. In so doing, he helped other men come out of themselves as well. As the last road trip of *On the Road* begins, Dean Moriarty, Sal Paradise, and their friend Stan Shephard hurtle south from Denver toward Mexico. Kerouac shows the power Cassady had to help other men bring their inner lives into the open:

> We all decided to tell our stories, but one by one, and Stan was first. "We've got a long way to go," preambled Dean, "and so you must take every indulgence and deal with every single detail you can bring to mind—and still it won't all be told. Easy, easy," he cautioned Stan, who began telling his story, "you've got to relax too." Stan swung into his life story as we shot across the dark. He started with his experiences in France but to round-out ever-growing difficulties he came back and started at the beginning with his boyhood in Denver . . . Stan was nervous and feverish. He wanted to tell Dean everything. Dean was now arbiter, old man, judge, listener, approver, nodder. "Yes, yes, go on please."[25]

The far-ranging self-disclosure of Cassady's confessions to Kerouac, the basis of both *On the Road* and *Visions of Cody,* mark a watershed for the western male: a celebration of his ability to reveal self and soul to another man.

Cassady was also bisexual, in dramatic counterpoint to the rigidly heterosexual traditional cowboy masculine ideal. ***The First Third*** records several homosexual assaults on Neal as a child. The beginning of his friendship with Allen Ginsberg, gay poet and giant of Beat literature, was marked by a sexual affair that continued on and off for months. "My soul melted, secrecy departed, I became / Thenceforth open to his nature as a flower in the shining sun,"[26] gushed Ginsberg in a poem about the first night of the affair. Cassady's heart was not in it; like so much else in the drifter's life, sex with another man was an experiment. Ginsberg, however, was smitten with the handsome young Cassady, and even persuaded him to kneel by a Texas roadside and take improvised vows of eternal spiritual union. Later Ginsberg acknowledged, "By hindsight I realize he was obviously just being nice to me, humoring me."[27]

In *On the Road,* Cassady tries to use his flexible sexuality for strategic gain with a man who has offered the travelers a ride. The more conventional, eastern Kerouac distances himself with homophobic language:

> In the hotel room, Dean tried everything in the book to get money from the fag. It was insane. The fag began by saying he was very glad we had come along because he liked young men like us, and would we believe it, but he really didn't like girls and had recently concluded an affair with a man in Frisco in which he had taken the male role and the man the female role. Dean plied him with businesslike questions and nodded eagerly. The fag said he would like nothing better than to know what Dean thought about all this. Warning him first that he had once been a hustler in his youth, Dean asked him how much money he had. The fag became extremely sullen and I think suspicious of Dean's final motives, turned over no money, and made vague promises for Denver. . . . Dean threw up his hands and gave up. . . . "Offer them what they want and they of course immediately become panic-stricken." But he had sufficiently conquered the owner of the Plymouth to take over the wheel without remonstrance, and now we really traveled.[28]

Cassady's openness to the full range of human experience was one of the qualities Kerouac admired most in him. In a short essay entitled "America's New Trinity of Love: Dean, Brando, Presley," Kerouac discusses the expanded emotional capabilities of a new kind of ideal man: "Up to now the American Hero has always been on the defensive: he killed Indians and villains and beat up his rivals and surled. He has been good-looking but never compassionate except at odd moments and only in stock situations. Now the new American hero . . . is the image of compassion in itself. It is as though Christ and Buddha were about to come again with masculine love for the woman at last."[29] The new ideal clearly extends to and is indeed embodied by Keroauc's new western hero.

Once dismissed by the intellectual establishment, Kerouac is now the subject of growing posthumous popularity and respect. In 1998, the *Atlantic Monthly* proclaimed his "full ascension to academic respectability."[30] *On the Road* is indisputably the major foundation of his reputation. So why did a rambling narrative about the travels of a college dropout from Massachusetts and his promiscuous, fast-talking friend from Colorado become an important cultural document? Its impact on American culture in the late 1950s and the 1960s was considerable. "Especially for young males, *On the Road* was something far more than an apology for hipsterism," writes Plummer. "They felt in their marrow what was classically American in Kerouac's book. . . . Like so many American tales, *On the Road* is about escape, about lighting out for the perpetually receding territory ahead."[31] The "escape" many young people wanted to make in the 1950s and 60s was from what they saw as a restrictive and repressive middle-class American culture. Conformity was king and personal expression was frowned upon. Plummer writes, "As Dean Moriarty, [Cassady] was hugely attractive to countless alienated and emotionally hamstrung young men and women."[32] To understand why Cassady became an icon of western masculinity with a national profile, it is helpful to consider certain components of American masculinity and their development over the years.

American masculinity reached another of its perpetual crisis points in the years after World War II.[33] The sweeping triumph of technological capitalism made the strong back of the American worker irrelevant. For upper-and middle-class white men, the rise of corporate office culture created a vast divide between fathers and sons. When a boy grew up working with his father in the fields of the family farm or at an old-style trade such as blacksmithing or shoemaking, the day-to-day physical closeness and the transmission of expertise from father to son usually created deep sympathy and love. Even the factory labor that engaged so many American men in the twentieth century was relatively rich in fraternal camaraderie and filial sensibility. But what happened when a father worked away from his children in the stereotypical suburban corporate commuter arrangement that took hold in the postwar years and beyond?

> When a father, absent during the day, returns home at six, his children receive only his temperament, not his teaching. If the father is working for a corporation, what is there to teach? He is reluctant to tell his son what is really going on. The fragmentation of decision-making in corporate life, the massive effort that produces the corporate willingness to destroy the environment for the sake of profit, the prudence, even cowardice, that one learns in bureaucracy—who wants to teach that?[34]

Even more distance was created in the 1960s between young men and the society of their fathers by the Vietnam War. American militarism after World War II increasingly served an unjust, oligarchic capitalism, yet perversely dressed itself in the rhetoric of an idealized democracy that did not really exist in the segregated and unequal United States. The military masculine model was tarnished for a whole generation, and the unfulfilled democratic ideal unmasked. "The older men in the military establishment and government did betray the younger men in Vietnam, lying about the nature of war, remaining in safe places themselves, after having asked the young men to be warriors and then in effect sending them out to be ordinary murderers."[35]

Just as Cassady was coming of age, the emergence of new musical forms into the mainstream of American life further contributed to the distance between old and young. Jazz, rhythm and blues, and later rock and roll became available to whites on a mass scale due to radio and phonograph technology, and they excited middle-class white youth with their passion and sexual energy, qualities not welcomed by the "polite" Anglo-American establishment.

Changes in the culture of work, and disagreement over the meaning of American democracy and how its interests were best served, coupled with the growing influence of provocative African-American music, served to alienate young, white, middle- to upper-class men from the ideas of masculinity held by their fathers. Many sought a new cultural paradigm that would allow them to make sense of the world and their place in it, a way of being male that would permit more freedom from conformity and would allow for greater expression of masculine passions. The result was the "existential hero."[36]

Anthony Rotundo, author of *American Manhood,* notes a change in the male relation to self in the twentieth century. "Middle-class Americans of the 1800's often viewed the inner movings of the self with Calvinistic suspicion," he writes.[37] Self-expression was considered dangerous. Masculine passion, originating in the self rather than in society, was to be carefully controlled. The self was to be manipulated to other ends, generally economic in nature and derived from the salient "Protestant work ethic." But Rotundo perceives a change. "Where nineteenth-century views had regarded the self and its passions suspiciously as objects of manipulation (self-control, self-denial), twentieth-century opinion exalted them as the source of identity and personal worth (self-expression, self-enjoyment)."[38]

But, paradoxically, most American men in the 1950s lacked true outlets for their passions. Consumerism, mainstream society's major means of creating and measuring identity, was utterly unsatisfying for many. Social roles grew more constrained just as the pressure on masculine identity grew stronger. Rotundo argues that in this tumultuous period, the existential hero represents a new "strategy for establishing a relationship between male passion and modern life." In a formulation that summarizes the Beat mystique as rendered by Kerouac, he asserts that "this ideal grows out of a belief that there is, in fact, no proper place for true masculine impulse within modern society. The hero who lives by this belief is suspicious of authority, wary of women, and disgusted by corrupt civilization. If he would be true to the purity of his male passions and principles, he must—and can only—live at the margins of society."[39]

Rotundo cites such popular figures as Humphrey Bogart, Ernest Hemingway, and John Wayne as existential icons in this mold. He also points to the American cult of the entrepreneur, the economic renegade who powers advances in capitalism by taking risks in speculative ventures without the collective safety of the corporation. Rotundo, however, steers clear of examining the real existential movement in America: the counterculture. His profile of the existential hero is more accurately personified by rebellious postwar personalities like James Dean, Bob Dylan, and Jack Kerouac, though none fits the type better than Neal Cassady. Under the pressures of a shallow and materialistic culture, middle- and upper-class American men looked to the ostracized poor and minority cultures for models, for modes of living that would allow a man to live passionately, true to himself in a larger culture that seemed anything but genuine. The African-American blues singer was one such model; the attitude affected by every rocker from Elvis Presley on owes much to the existential pose of the traveling blues singer who lives on the margins of society. Kerouac jolted American literature in much the same way Presley did music, by bringing the new existential hero to the fore. Cassady represents a white, Western version of this passionate, alienated masculine persona. As portrayed by Kerouac in *On the Road,* Cassady was a breath of fresh air to readers who admired his uninhibited sexuality, sly philosophical humor, and most of all his total commitment to personal freedom. He was one of the first western icons of the American counterculture, and would later, after parting ways with Kerouac, preside over the flowering of a uniquely western counterculture that endures to this day.

One of the most striking connections between Kerouac's vision and that of the traditional western writer is his use of what scholar Max Westbrook would call "sacrality."

> Certainly a substantial number of Western writers believe that Western experience . . . is the nation's best chance of healing the wounds caused by the Puritans when they made us feel ashamed of our bodies, afraid of the voice that comes from our dark and inner selves, apologetic for our worldly ambitions. Western writers have thus faced anew the ancient and sometimes American hope—the effort to discover the unity of body, soul, and land.[40]

Westbrook gives this acceptance of the spiritual quality inherent in the material world, in the flesh and its desires, the name *sacrality:* an "other way of thinking—a belief in the possibility of knowing through the unity of thought and things."[41] Within such a paradigm, virile masculinity can be celebrated without Puritanical hesitation or guilt. Sacrality is perhaps the major theme of *On the Road* and Dean Moriarty one of its staunchest champions in American literature. Puritanical shame was unknown to him; the record of his exploits in Keroauc's books served as an important volley in the counterculture's assault on the barrier between soul and body in American culture. "To him, sex was the one and only holy and important thing in life," Kerouac wrote, "although he had to sweat and curse to make a living and so on."[42] Kerouac and Cassady believed that through sex, as well as through travel, meeting and "digging" different people of all kinds, through sheer intensity of experience, they could reach the truth about themselves and the world. "'Everything is fine,'" Moriarty proclaims from behind the wheel, "'God exists, we know time. Everything since the Greeks has been predicated wrong. You can't make it with geometry and geometrical systems of thinking. It's all this!' He wrapped his finger in his fist; the car hugged the line straight and true."[43] And yet the acceptance of the holiness of life did not solve the problem of living. For all their philosophical acumen, the heroes of *On the Road* found no lasting satisfaction, no resolution to their yearnings, no place where they were content to hang their hats for long. Instead, they wandered on.

For Cassady, the desperation and isolation of his troubled life redoubled his masculine sexual need. Camille Paglia could have been referring to Cassady when she wrote, "Male sexuality is inherently manic-depressive. Men are in a constant state of sexual anxiety, living on the pins and needles of their hormones. In sex and in life they are driven *beyond*—beyond the self, beyond the body. . . . But to be beyond is to be exiled from the center of life. Men know they are sexual exiles. They wander the earth seeking satisfaction, craving and despising, never content."[44] The male heterosexual mania to reenter the woman, to regain the center, has shaped and indeed dominated the lives of many men. Kerouac writes of hearing his friend make love to his wife in the next room: "I could hear Dean, blissful and blabbering and frantically rocking. Only a guy who's spent five years in jail can go to such maniacal helpless extremes; beseeching at the portals of the soft source, mad with a completely physical realization of the origins of life-bliss; blindly seeking to return the way he came."[45]

Neal Cassady, "exiled from the center of life" with no family, no fixed home, and little stake in the world of money-making and consumerism, had nowhere to go but "beyond." Like the mythic cowboy, he was outside of society, outside of the law. The protagonists of *On the Road* circle endlessly, looking for but never quite finding the center of America, the world, themselves. This sense of lonely wandering and isolation from community is one of the many links between Kerouac's book and the tradition of Western books and films, from which the American culture derives its image of western masculinity. As Will Wright explains, the primary theme of the Western is the relationship between an independent heroic figure and the society he defends—an often difficult and ambiguous relationship. Wright shows that early Westerns, using what he calls the "Classical" plot, generally featured a lone hero with special talents (usually for violence) entering a community to which he is a stranger, defeating a villain or other evil that threatens this community, then becoming an accepted citizen of the grateful town, often sealing this new status by marrying a woman from the rescued population. But as time went on, Wright notes, more and more Westerns presented heroes who rejected membership in the communities they had delivered from evil. Some heroes seemed unwilling to give up their special independent (existential) status, or simply deemed the community in question unworthy. This change reflects the growing existential suspicion of society and its values in the post-World War II decades.

In such an era, Neal Cassady made a natural hero for a generation of disaffected youth. His special talent was not for gun-fighting but for passionate living: lovemaking, drug-taking, spontaneous action without regard to social norms. While often these are highly debatable behaviors, they were in fact the core values of the '60s generation's counterculture. Alienated by the materialism and rigidity of the dominant culture, many took to the Beat vision described by Kerouac and personified by his wandering hero.

This juxtaposition between "hip" and "square" resonates in the Beat worldview and reflects the Beats' perception of a large gap between virile, independent Western settlers and their "softer" eastern contemporaries. "Luxury," wrote Mody C. Boatright of the eastern way of life resisted by protagonists of the earliest, genre-setting cowboy fiction, "had . . . created an effete society, governed not by natural human relationships but by convention, which tended to deprive men of their masculinity and women of their natural social role."[46] There was nothing effete about Neal Cassady. Kerouac waxed eloquent when writing about just how far on the outside of all convention, social respectability, and protection the young Cassady really was:

> Have you ever seen anyone like Cody Pomeray?—say on a street corner in Chicago, or better, Fargo, any mighty cold town, a young guy with a bony face that looks like it's been pressed against iron bars to get that dogged rocky look of suffering, perseverance . . . poor pitiful kid actually just out of reform school with no money, no mother, and if you saw him dead on the sidewalk with a cop standing over him you'd walk on in a hurry, in silence. Oh life, who is that? There are some young men you look at who seem completely safe, maybe just because of a Scandinavian ski sweater, angelic, saved; on a Cody Pomeray it immediately becomes a dirty stolen sweater worn in wild sweats. . . . It is a face that's so suspicious, so energetically upward-looking like people in passport police lineup photos, so rigidly itself, looking like it's about to do anything unspeakably enthusiastic, in fact so much the opposite of the rosy

> Coke-drinking boy in the Scandinavian ski sweater ad, that in front of a brick wall where it says *Post No Bills* and it's too dirty for a rosy boy ad you can imagine Cody standing there in the raw gray flesh manacled between sheriffs and Assistant D.A.'s and you wouldn't have to ask yourself who is the culprit and who is the law.[47]

Cassady did indeed have trouble with the law. His poverty, orphanhood, and Beat cultural orientation made him a target for the police throughout his life. As a teen, he spent much time answering to the authorities due to his predilection for stealing cars. In 1958, just after the success of *On the Road* had given him some modicum of fame, he was arrested and served more than two years in prison for giving two joints of marijuana to undercover policemen who picked him up in their car, offering him a ride to his job on the railroad. Friends suspected the authorities had singled him out because of his counterculture notoriety. Ginsberg and other prominent writers attended Cassady's legal proceedings and agitated for his release, painting him as a martyr of antidrug and anti-Beat hysteria. Marijuana, something of a totem for the existential counterculture, signified the user's rejection of corrupt material society and commitment to a new idea of personal freedom, the all-important western value.

Cassady's letters to his wife Carolyn, compiled in ***Grace Beats Karma: Letters from Prison 1958-1960,*** show a man struggling to maintain his masculinity and self-respect despite the humiliation of prison life. He became heavily involved in a Catholic prayer practice and excelled in courses in comparative religion while behind bars. Nonetheless, jailing a man of Cassady's independence and boundless energy took its toll. Being deprived of the ability to care for his wife and children (for after all his wandering and adventure, he had settled down and tried to content himself with family life for several years as he worked on the railroad in California) was particularly painful. He wrote to his wife that upon release, "I want to work myself to death, seriously, a kind of legitimate suicide."[48] But after Cassady's release from jail in 1960, the marriage soured. Carolyn had refused to put up the house for Neal's bail money, fearing he would take to the road and leave his family in the lurch. In addition, she made plans to travel overseas at the expense of a male friend whom she hinted would make a good father and provider for the children. Cassady's resentment over this perceived betrayal smoldered. He lost a good job on the railroad due to his long incarceration. Now in his mid-thirties, Neal faced the extinction of work, home, and family; things he craved deeply but which were ultimately incompatible with his freewheeling nature.

Cassady's relationships with women had always been passionate, unstable, even dangerous. The tremendous need Neal felt for women had a dark underside. Though he was much more likely to abandon a woman than to physically harm her, the latter was not out of the question. Kerouac reports: "Marylou [LuAnne, Neal's first wife] was black and blue from a fight with Dean about something; his face was scratched."[49] A fair "fight" between the teenage LuAnne and her muscular husband was impossible. Second wife Carolyn also reported moments of brutality: "He was a raging animal; this could only be lust, not love. . . . The only way he was not able to do it was when I was offering or willing. It had to be rape. Until finally I only submitted because I was afraid of him. At last, then, I said, 'I can't stand it anymore, kill me or whatever,' and much to my surprise he was very nice about it, he seemed to understand."[50] The links between young Neal's bizarre sexual initiation in the German drunkard's barn, his adult desire to dominate women, and his proclivity for flight from commitment are hard to miss.

"It was equally his motif, as it was his father's," writes Plummer about twenty-two-year old Neal learning of Carolyn's first pregnancy in 1948, "to dismantle 'families,' to flee and disappoint his loved ones at precisely the moment he felt the pressure of their expectation. Now, confronted with fatherhood and weighed down by assorted failures, he could not shake the feeling of 'ennuied hysteria.'"[51] His work hours cut due to a slowdown in railroad traffic, unable or unwilling to cope with the pressure, Cassady took the family savings, bought a '49 Hudson Hornet, picked up first wife LuAnne, and raced cross-country to find Kerouac for one of the rounds of traveling recorded in *On the Road.* Beat writer and friend William Burroughs was harsh in his assessment: "Wife and child may starve, friends exist only to exploit for gas money. Neal must move."[52] True to Rotundo's profile of the existential male hero, Cassady was more committed to the fulfillment of his fickle passions than he ever could be to a particular woman. Kerouac wrote uncritically about his friend's cavalier attitude toward women; he intimated that the moral fallout and emotional debris created by Neal's wild twists and turns were a fair price to pay for the freedom thus gained.

But not even in the decidedly masculine world of *On the Road* could a man avoid the wrath of women scorned forever. One scene places Dean on the hot seat in front of a group of women led by Galatea Dunkel, a tarot-card reader whose husband, Ed, has been lost to her for months due to Dean-inspired wanderings. Dean's thumb has grown infected from an injury sustained in a fight with Camille [Carolyn], who has just kicked him out the house, and he paces in a nervous sweat as his crimes against women and humanity in general are enumerated:

> It wasn't anything but a sewing circle, and the center of it was the culprit, Dean—responsible, perhaps, for everything that was wrong. . . . "I think Camille was very, very wise leaving you, Dean," said Galatea. "For years now you haven't had any sense of responsibility for anyone. You've done so many awful things I don't know what to say to you." . . . They all sat around looking at Dean with lowered and hating eyes, and he stood on the carpet in the middle of them and giggled—he just giggled. He made a little dance. His bandage was getting dirtier all the time; it began to flop and unroll. . . . "You have absolutely no regard for anybody but yourself and your damn kicks. All you think about is what's hanging between your legs and how much money or fun you can get out of people and then you just throw them aside . . ." Then a complete silence fell over everybody; where once Dean would have talked his way out, he now fell silent himself, but standing in front of everybody, ragged and broken and idiotic, right under the lightbulbs, his bony mad face covered with sweat and throbbing veins, saying, "Yes, yes, yes," as though tremendous revelations were pouring into him all the time now, and I am convinced they were.[53]

Kerouac's invocation of mysticism to defend Cassady's irresponsible behavior is at best only partially satisfying. The existential strategy comes with enormous costs; it represents a reaction to society, but not a new model upon which societies can be built. The generation inspired by *On the Road* would learn this the hard way as their movement collapsed under the weight of drugs and sexual chaos in the late '60s. Kerouac probably understood this well, but favored the freedom of the individual at whatever cost.

The Massachusetts author was transformed by his travels with the charismatic Westerner. By the end of *On the Road,* the narrator has absorbed the lonely wandering persona of his drifting friend, if not all of his monstrous energy. A deep feeling for the great wide-open spaces west of the Mississippi emanates from his flowing prose. He offers his own melancholy cowboy song as he rolls across the darkened plains on a midnight bus to Denver:

> Home in Missoula,
> Home in Truckee,
> Home in Opelousas,
> Ain't no home for me.
> Home in old Medora,
> Home in Wounded Knee,
> Home in Oglalla,
> Home I'll never be.[54]

The success of the book did little to give Kerouac peace. In the '60s, he grew increasingly reclusive; he was living with his mother, drinking heavily, reading Buddhism, and writing, but with greatly diminished energy. Cassady's achievements as a writer were slim; he lacked the focus and discipline to get much done at the typewriter. Kerouac would come to see this as a virtue. In one of his last and best books, *Big Sur* (1962), the eastern observer praised Cassady's commitment to worldly action over literary abstraction: "I can see from glancing at him that becoming a writer holds no interest for him because life is holy for him there's no need to do anything but live it, writing's just an afterthought or a scratch anyway at the surface."[55] Kerouac's writings about Cassady, among other things, represent the detached eastern intellect romanticizing the vigorous Western masculine principle. Though Kerouac eventually got off the road, Cassady could not stay off it for long. He knew no other way.

Independently of his friend Jack, Cassady became a leading figure in a uniquely western branch of the emerging American counterculture. On October 13, 1955, the San Francisco Poetry Renaissance began with a much-heralded poetry reading at the Six Gallery in the city by the bay. Beat poets from the East Coast symbolically linked arms that night with a circle of talented San Francisco writers, including Gary Snyder and Lawrence Ferlinghetti, effectively expanding the province of Beat literature from a small New York cabal to a national movement. Easterner Ginsberg organized the Six Gallery event and used it to introduce his best-remembered poem, "Howl." After *On the Road,* "Howl" is the most famous document of the Beat movement and, like Kerouac's book, took Neal Cassady as its major inspiration and archetype: "N.C., secret hero of these poems, cocksman and Adonis of Denver."[56] Cassady attended the reading in his railroad brakeman's uniform and is reported to have enjoyed himself immensely.

After his turn-of-the-decade jailing and final break with Carolyn, Neal was on the road again. Another hip young novelist, Ken Kesey, took Cassady under his wing. Cassady became part of Kesey's "Merry Pranksters," a communal cult based in northern California and bound by psychedelic drugs and a determination to unmask the empty social role-playing "games" Kesey felt dominated the American culture. The main weapon in Kesey's quixotic campaign to free America from itself was LSD. Mid-'60s "acid test" parties brought together literary figures with groups as disparate as pacifist rockers The Grateful Dead and aggressive motorcycle gang the Hell's Angels in a free-form atmosphere in which the now stereotypically Californian[57] values of freedom, individuality and free love were the common denominator. Neal's celebrity was used as a draw to lure the curious into the bacchanalias of drugs and amplified guitar music; his monologues entranced roomfuls of people at a time. Grateful Dead lyricist John Barlow describes the advanced state of Neal's verbal abilities: "He would carry on five different conversations at once and still devote one conversational channel to discourse with absent persons and another to such sound effects as disintegrating ring gears or exploding crania. To log into one of these conversations, despite their multiplicity, was like trying to take a sip from a firehose."[58] "Cassady's raps," as they were known, were rhapsodic monologues in which the Denver hobos' empty, self-concealing drone-chatter about "Truth and Life," as described in ***The First Third,*** exploded into a singular art form of deeply felt and exhaustively articulated self-expression. For all their psychedelic wit, the Cassady raps retained the flavor of the dusty West. Novelist Robert Stone called Neal's epic musings "Forties stuff . . . old-time jail and musician and street patter." "American-Denver talk," Plummer surmises, "what Kerouac liked to think of as Okie drawl, but with free-lancing Proustian detail."[59]

Cassady's stint with Kesey sealed his image as a titanic, larger-than-life icon of western masculinity. At the age of forty, his physique was rock-hard; his favored pastime flipping a small sledgehammer endlessly to maintain and display his chiseled torso in the California sun. The sexual conquests continued unabated. The burgeoning West-coast hippie scene and Neal's unique celebrity ensured a steady stream of willing women. "Neal would take his women through a whole lifetime of relationships in about an hour," reported Grateful Dead bandleader Jerry Garcia. "He would keep them up for about a week and they'd all become sort of blank from the intensity of the relationship."[60]

Best of all for Cassady, he was given the driver's seat on "Furthur," a converted 1939 International Harvester school bus that Kesey bought to drive the Merry Pranksters around the country for a series of acid-inspired publicity stunts. The bus' very name, deliberate misspelling notwithstanding, indicates a continuation of the *On the Road* motif of motor vehicle as instrument for conquest of both physical and psychic terrain. The bus journeys as well as the California acid parties were recorded by Tom Wolfe in *The Electric Kool-Aid Acid Test* (1968). Though several notches below Kerouac's road book as literature, the popular success of the latter tome did repeat and fix the image of Cassady as existential helmsman of the highway. The road trip has since become an enshrined institution of American youth, a favored rite of passage for thousands of young men and women who travel the roads each summer, often simply for the sake of movement itself.

But not even Cassady could keep moving forever. The years of nonstop drugs, sex, wandering, and kicks took their toll. Friends reported a growing sense of blankness, a loss of the once inexhaustible sense of fun. In a last desperate visit to Carolyn in 1967, Neal confessed he was losing his ability to perform, to play the role of existential acid-cowboy that friends and strangers alike expected from him. Everyone "expected him to be Superman, and he couldn't."[61] The titanic masculine image, first created by Kerouac's earnest observations of a Colorado kid being himself, had grown so heavy and burdensome that the man who inspired it could no longer carry its considerable weight. "Kerouassady," he jokingly called himself; by then he was an amalgam of himself and a mythic hero invented by another man. In February 1968, Neal died from an overdose of alcohol and pills while walking a long stretch of railroad near a town called Celaya in Mexico, traditional retreat of Western heroes.

Notes

1. Jack Kerouac, *On the Road* (New York: Viking, 1957), 267.
2. Ibid., 12.
3. Ibid., 11.
4. John Holmes defined the Beat generation as "A cultural revolution . . . made by a post-World War II generation of disaffiliated young people coming of age into a Cold War world without spiritual values they could honor." Introduction to Anne Charters, ed., *The Portable Beat Reader* (New York: Viking Penguin, 1992), xx. Beat Literature was characterized by its rebellious attitude toward the social order, its embrace of sexuality, drugs, and spirituality, and by its focus on the unique visions and experiences of the individual.
5. Kerouac, *On the Road,* 10.
6. Philip J. Deloria, *Playing Indian* (New Haven: Yale University Press, 1998), 101.

7. Kerouac, *On the Road,* 3.
8. Neal Cassady, *The First Third* (San Francisco: City Lights, 1971), 48.
9. Keouac, *On the Road,* 7.
10. Ibid., 4.
11. William Plummer, *The Holy Goof: A Biography of Neal Cassady* (New York: Paragon House, 1981), 24.
12. Edward Abbey, *The Brave Cowboy* (New York: Dodd, Mead, 1956), 26.
13. Wolfgang Zuckermann, *End of the Road: The World Car Crisis and How We Can Solve It* (Post Mills, Vt.: Chelsea Green Publishers, 1992), 59-60.
14. Cassady, 170. All text from Beat writers is here reproduced as it stands in the original works; misspellings, unorthodox grammar and punctuation, and invented words are not uncommon.
15. Kerouac, *On the Road,* 225.
16. Ibid., 233-34.
17. Ibid., 230.
18. Jack Kerouac, *Visions of Cody,* (New York: McGraw-Hill, 1972), 56.
19. Cassady, 133.
20. Plummer, 21.
21. Kerouac, *On the Road,* 44.
22. Plummer, 21.
23. Will Wright, *Sixguns and Society: A Structural Study of the Western* (Berkley and Los Angeles: University of California Press, 1975), 33.
24. Ibid., 20.
25. Kerouac, *On the Road,* 269.
26. Allen Ginsberg, "Many Loves," in *Selected Poems, 1947-1995* (New York: HarperCollins, 1995), 65.
27. Barry Miles, *Ginsberg* (New York: Simon and Schuster, 1989), 90.
28. Kerouac, *On the Road,* 209.
29. Various Artists, *Kerouac: Kicks Joy Darkness* (compact disc; Ryko 10329; 1997).
30. Douglass Brinkley, "In the Kerouac Archive," *Atlantic Monthly,* (November 1998), 49.
31. Plummer, 55.
32. Plummer, 9-10.
33. For more about changing masculine roles in America, see Elizabeth H. Pleck and Joseph H. Pleck, *The American Man* (Englewood Cliffs, N.J.: Prentice-Hall, 1980); Jane C. Hood, ed., *Men, Work, and Family* (Newbury Park, Calif.: Sage Publications, 1993); Edward Klein and Don Erikson, eds., *About Men: Reflections on the Male Experience* (New York: Poseidon Press, 1987); Perry Garfinkel, *In a Man's World: Father, Son, Brother, Friend, and Other Roles Men Play* (New York: NAL Books, 1985); and Harvey Deutschendorf, *Of Work and Men* (Minneapolis: Fairview Press, 1996).
34. Robert Bly, *Iron John: A Book about Men* (Reading, Mass.: Addison-Wesley, 1990), 96-97.
35. Ibid., 95.
36. For more about changing social attitudes in the post-World War II decades, see John Patrick Diggins, *The Proud Decades: America in War and Peace 1941-1960* (New York: W. W. Norton, 1988); Irwin Unger and Debby Unger, *America in the 1960s* (St. James, N.Y.: Brandywine Press, 1988); and David Reisman with Nathan Glazer and Reuel Denney, *The Lonely Crowd* (New Haven: Yale University Press, 1961). For more about the Beat reaction to their contemporary social and historical context, see Edward Halsey Foster, *Understanding the Beats* (Columbia: University of South Carolina Press 1992).
37. Anthony Rotundo, *American Manhood: Transformations in Masculinity from the Revolution to the Modern Era* (New York: Basic Books, 1993), 280.
38. Rotundo, 6.
39. Ibid., 286.
40. Max Westbrook, "The Western Esthetic," in *Critical Essays on the Western American Novel,* ed. William T. Pilkington (Boston: C. K. Hall, 1980), 73.
41. Ibid., 78.
42. Kerouac, *On the Road,* 4.
43. Ibid., 120.
44. Camille Paglia, *Sexual Personae* (New York: Vintage Books, 1990), 19.
45. Kerouac, *On the Road,* 132.
46. Mody C. Boatright, "The Beginnings of Cowboy Fiction," in Pilkington, ed., *Critical Essays on the Western American Novel,* 42.
47. Kerouac, *Visions of Cody,* 48.
48. Neal Cassady, *Grace Beats Karma: Letters from Prison 1958-1960* (New York: Blast Books, 1993), 158.
49. Kerouac, *On the Road,* 133.
50. Plummer, 82.
51. Ibid., 49.
52. Ibid., 64.
53. Kerouac, *On the Road,* 193-95.
54. Ibid., 255.
55. Jack Kerouac, *Big Sur* (New York: Farrar, Straus and Cudahy, 1962), 141.
56. Allen Ginsberg, "Howl," in Ann Charters, ed., *Reader,* 65.
57. For more about Beats in California, see John Arthur Maynard, *Venice West: The Beat Generation in Southern California* (New Brunswick, N. J.: Rutgers University Press, 1991).
58. John Barlow, "Cassady's Tale," *http://www.charm.net/~brooklyn/Topics/BarlowOnNeal.html.*
59. Plummer, 129.
60. Ibid., 142.
61. Ibid., 155.

FURTHER READING

Biographies

Campbell, James. *This Is the Beat Generation: New York-San Francisco-Paris.* London: Secker and Warburg, 1999, 320 p.

Collects anecdotes about the lives of Beat writers, including several chapters devoted to Cassady.

Cassady, Carolyn. *Off the Road: My Years with Cassady, Kerouac, and Ginsberg.* New York: Morrow, 1990, 436 p.

Cassady was Neal Cassady's wife. In this memoir she discusses her life with Cassady and with the rest of the Beats.

Plummer, William. *The Holy Goof: A Biography of Neal Cassady.* Englewood Cliffs, N.J.: Prentice-Hall, 1981, 162 p.

Standard biography of Cassady that emphasizes Cassady's role as the "muse of the Beat Generation."

Watson, Steven. *The Birth of the Beat Generation.* New York: Pantheon Books, 1995, 387 p.

Biography of the Beat writers, in which Cassady is often at the center of sexual and literary relationships.

Criticism

Harris, Oliver. "Old War Correspondents: Ginsberg, Kerouac, Cassady, and the Political Economy of Beat Letters." *Twentieth-Century Literature* 46, no. 2 (summer 2000): 171-92.

Discusses the central importance of Cassady's letters to the development of Kerouac's writing.

OTHER SOURCES FROM GALE:

Additional coverage of Cassady's life and career is contained in the following sources published by the Gale Group: *Contemporary Authors,* Vol. 141; *Dictionary of Literary Biography,* Vols. 16, 237; and *Literature Resource Center.*

GREGORY CORSO

(1930 - 2001)

(Born Nunzio Gregory Corso) American poet, novelist, and playwright.

Critics cite Corso, in conjunction with Allen Ginsberg, William S. Burroughs, and Jack Kerouac, as an essential founding member of the Beat Generation. Corso's poetry reiterates the basic tenet of the movement: rejection of the established social order in favor of experimentation. Although Corso was not a prolific writer, his poetry has increasingly been heralded by critics and the public, particularly his poetry collections *The Happy Birthday of Death* (1960) and *Long Live Man* (1962). Building on personal experiences garnered as a result of his turbulent background and lack of formal education, Corso explores the meaning of life and death, employing a subtle humor and an element of fantasy. Through interviews with the popular press, Corso became a representative of the Beat movement to the American public, creating an avant-garde, anti-establishment, rebel persona. In addition to his poetry, Corso wrote a novel and numerous plays.

BIOGRAPHICAL INFORMATION

Corso was born March 26, 1930, in New York City, to two young Italian immigrants, Fortunato Samuel and Michelina (Colonni) Corso. His mother returned to Italy, abandoning her family before Corso was a year old. He spent his early years in orphanages and foster homes, as well as a brief period in the observation ward of the Bellevue Mental Hospital. Corso received very little formal education during his childhood. When he was a young teenager, he was arrested for theft and housed in the infamous New York City Jail as a material witness for several months. There he learned the power of using imagination and fantasy to counteract the grueling, harsh aspects of reality, a theme that would play a paramount role in his poetry. At the age of sixteen, Corso was arrested again for theft and sentenced to three years in Clinton Prison. During his incarceration, Corso discovered literature, spending his time reading poets such as Percy Bysshe Shelley and studying an antiquated dictionary. Internalizing Shelley's message about the moral duty of poetry, Corso began to write his own verses. Upon his release, Corso was directionless, having been institutionalized for most of his life. A fortuitous meeting with Allen Ginsberg in a Greenwich Village bar in 1950 inspired Corso to pursue a life of writing. Ginsberg introduced Corso to Columbia professor Mark Van Doren who read Corso's poetry, commented on it, and encouraged the poet to keep writing. In the early 1950s, after spending a year as a seaman on a Norwegian freighter, Corso settled near Harvard University, where he spent two years pursuing his self-education, reading and writing in the library and befriending students. In 1955, a group of Harvard students offered to finance the self-publication of Corso's first volume of poetry, *The Vestal Lady on Brattle and Other Poems*. Through his ongoing friendship with Ginsberg, Corso was introduced to other members of the Beat Generation, among them Jack Kerouac and William S. Burroughs. After his first book of poetry failed to attract critical attention, Corso traveled, spending much of his time in Europe and relying on Ginsberg to help ensure the publication of his writings. Ginsberg arranged for the publication of Corso's second collection, *Gasoline* (1958). By this time, the Beats were garnering public and critical attention. Through interviews and public appearances, Corso gained recognition as an innovative poet, the quirky clown of the Beat movement. In 1960, Corso published *The Happy Birthday of Death,* a collection that contains many of his best-known poems, including the title poem and "Bomb." Two years later, Corso published *Long Live Man.* In 1963 Corso married Sally November and accepted a teaching position at the State University of New York in Buffalo. During this time he began experimenting with heroin, a decision that Corso and his friends later agreed destroyed his poetry career and prevented him from fully developing his talent. Corso and November divorced, and he lost his teaching position in 1965 for refusing to sign a statement denying that he was a member of the Communist party. Corso married Belle Carpenter in 1968; his second marriage also ended in divorce. Corso's next major publication, *Elegiac Feelings American* (1970), was a tribute to Kerouac, who died in 1969. Plans for a mid-1970s collection of poems ceased when the manuscript was stolen, and Corso's next collection of verse, *Herald of the Autochthonic Spirit,* was published in 1981. This volume signalled Corso's return to poetry, revealing a writer lamenting the wasted years of heroin addiction and describing a struggle to recommit himself to poetry. *Mindfield* (1989), Corso's final book of published verse, serves as a collected works but also introduces several new poems. Corso continued writing and teaching throughout his life, often at the Naropa Institute in Boulder, a center operated by several other Beat poets. He traveled frequently in Europe, financed chiefly through the benevolence of patrons. His publishing became increasingly sporadic as the social mood of the country changed and the popularity of the Beat movement waned. Corso died January 17, 2001, in Minnesota, of cancer.

MAJOR WORKS

Corso's first volume of poetry, *The Vestal Lady on Brattle and Other Poems,* earned him scant critical attention. However, with the publication of his next volume—*Gasoline*—he established his voice, identifying the issues that would continue to interest him throughout his career. The volume brought Corso greater critical acclaim, partially as a result of the rising public interest in the Beats. Corso's poetry is marked by a playfulness, sly wit, and sense of humor. In such poems as "Hair" and "Marriage," he infuses humor along with poignant observations about society and humankind. Throughout his career, Corso focused on the meaning of life and death in his verse, topics that play an increasingly important role in his later poetry. In addition, his poetry examines such issues as the conflict between the need for assimilation in society and the desire for individuality, the difficulties of making choices, and the conflicted nature of man. In his verse, he advocates experimentation and exploration, portraying characters on the fringe of society and incorporating anti-establishment messages in his verse. Many of his poems, such as "Bomb" and "Police," portray his views on contemporary matters of the time. While most of his poetry, particularly his earliest verse, is based on personal experience, Corso uses events from his past as a springboard for discussion of broader themes. The mood in his early poems varies greatly. Even short works fluctuate between the serious and the blackly comedic, simultaneously depicting both intense and carefree attitudes, the outrageous and the fantastic. In such later volumes as *Elegiac Feelings American, Herald of the Autochthonic Spirit,* and *Mindfield,* Corso is increasingly critical of American society and exhibits an evermore somber mood.

The Happy Birthday of Death exhibited similar feelings, employing surrealistic imagery and absurdist humor. Corso also strengthens his commitment to poetry as a social act with the poems in this collection, exploring topics including marriage, power, and mortality. These poems employ a questioning tone, humor, and satire. Nonsensical word pairings in "Food," for example, provide humourous touches as the poet moves from consuming "sugared meats" and "orangestuffed duck" to "Fried chairs, poached mattresses, [and] stewed farms." *Long Live Man* reflects Corso's optimistic views that are layered beneath the violence and ridicule presented on the surface in his poetry. While poems like "Death Comes at Puberty" and "Suburbia Mad Song" detail the suffocation of spirit Corso sees in American life, other poems assert the potential of that spirit. The opening poem, "Man," acknowledges mankind's selfishness but also imagines a world filled with beauty and wisdom. *Elegiac Feelings American* similarly portrays danger and oppression alongside infinite possibility. The title poem, an elegy, describes Kerouac as the spirit of America. According to the poem, Kerouac observed and wrote of the failings of America, but his spirit became poisoned by his alcoholism, paralleling the self-poisoning of American society and the American landscape. However, the poem concludes on an optimistic note, embracing Kerouac's vision with an image of possible redemption.

When Corso released *Herald of the Autochthonic Spirit,* critical attention for the Beats had largely faded, and the work was not widely read. Nonetheless, the collection contains significant poems from Corso's oeuvre, especially "Columbia U Poesy Reading—1975," an allegorical rendering of Corso's guilt over abandoning his muse and his decision to begin again and expiate past failings. The book also shows Corso coping with age and coming to terms with his career as a poet in such poems as "I Gave Away . . ." and "The Whole Mess . . . Almost." *Herald of the Autochthonic Spirit* demonstrates many of Corso's hallmarks as a poet: ironic and compassionate humor, a facility with various poetic forms, and a strong belief in the power of poetry as a force for social awareness and change.

CRITICAL RECEPTION

Throughout Corso's career, critics have consistently praised his writing as quirky yet thought-provoking. In particular, reviewers have noted a number of important traits: his sense of humor; his insight into human frailty; his view of social issues; and his advocacy of a reexamination of social values. Additionally, many scholars have characterized his voice as refreshingly accessible, informal, and honest. Kirby Olson has declared that, "Corso's work might best be described . . . thanks to its often comic character, [as] the most unjustly neglected poetry in American literature." Commentators have argued that Corso's unaffected worldview lends power and resonance to his works. Critics have also maintained that Corso's writing is best when he speaks in his own voice about common, personal events, asserting that when he adopts a more formal and imitative writing style, he loses the strength and appeal of his natural, emphatic tone. Corso's intensely individual references and nonsensical phrasing have been a source of derision for several critics who have felt that the larger meaning in his works is frequently lost in the midst of whimsical allusions and wording. Other reviewers have observed that the quality of Corso's work varies greatly, not only within single volumes of poetry but even within individual poems, ranging broadly across the emotional and ideological scale. Shelley and other Romantic poets, as well as Surrealists André Breton and Arthur Rimbaud strongly influenced Corso's work; many reviewers have noted this influence, as well as the contrast between Corso's satirical, biting, violent imagery and his sense of optimism and affinity for themes of renewal. For example, commenting on Corso's optimism and passion, Gregory Stephenson has remarked that, "Corso shares with Shelley a zeal for liberty and . . . passionate faith in humankind." Stephenson asserts this point despite his analyses of *Gasoline,* in which he noted the presence of "the motif of predatory devouring and destruction of innocence and beauty . . . familiar from Corso's first collection." Overall many critics have agreed that despite being overlooked as one of the most important writers in the Beat movement, Corso's poetry is deserving of more critical attention.

PRINCIPAL WORKS

In This Hung-Up Age (play) 1955

The Vestal Lady on Brattle and Other Poems (poetry) 1955

Gasoline (poetry) 1958

The Happy Birthday of Death (poetry) 1960

The American Express (novel) 1961

The Minicab War: The Gotla War-Interview with Minicab Driver and Cabbie (poetry) 1961

Long Live Man (poetry) 1962

Selected Poems (poetry) 1962

The Mutation of the Spirit (poetry) 1964

The Geometric Poem (poetry) 1966

10 Times a Poem (poetry) 1967

Elegiac Feelings American (poetry) 1970

Ankh (poetry) 1971

Gregory Corso (poetry) 1971

The Night Last Night Was at Its Nightest (poetry) 1972

Earth Egg (poetry) 1974

Way Out: A Poem in Discord (poetry) 1974

Gregory Corso: Writings from 'Unmuzzled Ox' (poetry) 1981

Herald of the Autochthonic Spirit (poetry) 1981

Mindfield: New and Selected Poems (poetry) 1989

PRIMARY SOURCES

GREGORY CORSO (POEM DATE 1960)

Corso, Gregory. "Marriage." In *The Happy Birthday of Death*, pp. 29-32. New York: New Directions, 1960.

In the following poem, "Marriage," Corso employs humor and satire to comment on the institution of marriage. This poem, along with "Bomb," is one of Corso's best-known works.

Should I get married? Should I be good?
Astound the girl next door with my velvet suit and faustus hood?
Don't take her to movies but to cemeteries
tell all about werewolf bathtubs and forked clarinets
then desire her and kiss her and all the preliminaries
and she going just so far and I understanding why
not getting angry saying You must feel! It's beautiful to feel!
Instead take her in my arms lean against an old crooked tombstone
and woo her the entire night the constellations in the sky—

When she introduces me to her parents
back straightened, hair finally combed, strangled by a tie,
should I sit with my knees together on their 3rd degree sofa
and not ask Where's the bathroom?
How else to feel other than I am,
often thinking Flash Gordon soap—
O how terrible it must be for a young man
seated before a family and the family thinking
We never saw him before! He wants our Mary Lou!
After tea and homemade cookies they ask
What do you do for a
living?

Should I tell them? Would they like me then?
Say All right get married, we're losing a daughter
but we're gaining a son—
And should I then ask Where's the bathroom?

O God, and the wedding! All her family and her friends
and only a handful of mine all scroungy and bearded
just wait to get at the drinks and food—
And the priest! he looking at me as if I masturbated
asking me Do you take this woman for your lawful wedded wife?
And I trembling what to say say Pie Glue!

I kiss the bride all those corny men slapping me on the back
She's all yours, boy! Ha-ha-ha!
And in their eyes you could see some obscene honeymoon going
on—

Then all that absurd rice and clanky cans and shoes
Niagara Falls! Hordes of us! Husbands! Wives! Flowers!
Chocolates!

All streaming into cozy hotels
All going to do the same thing tonight
The indifferent clerk he knowing what was going to happen
The lobby zombies they knowing what
The whistling elevator man he knowing
Everybody knowing! I'd almost be inclined not to do anything!
Stay up all night! Stare that hotel clerk in the eye!
Screaming: I deny honeymoon! I deny honeymoon!
running rampant into those almost climactic suites
yelling Radio belly! Cat shovel!
O I'd live in Niagara forever! in a dark cave beneath the Falls
I'd sit there the Mad Honeymooner
devising ways to break marriages, a scourge of bigamy
a saint of divorce—

But I should get married I should be good
How nice it'd be to come home to her
and sit by the fireplace and she in the kitchen
aproned young and lovely wanting my baby
and so happy about me she burns the roast beef
and comes crying to me and I get up from my big papa chair
saying Christmas teeth! Radiant brains! Apple deaf!
God what a husband I'd make! Yes, I should get married!
So much to do! Like sneaking into Mr Jones' house late at night
and cover his golf clubs with 1920 Norwegian books
Like hanging a picture of Rimbaud on the lawnmower
like pasting Tannu Tuva postage stamps all over the picket fence
like when Mrs Kindhead comes to collect for the Community Chest
grab her and tell her There are unfavorable omens in the sky!

And when the mayor comes to get my vote tell him
When are you going to stop people killing whales!
And when the milkman comes leave him a note in the bottle
Penguin dust, bring me penguin dust, I want penguin dust—

Yes if I should get married and it's Connecticut and snow
and she gives birth to a child and I am sleepless, worn,
up for nights, head bowed against a quiet window, the past behind
me,

finding myself in the most common of situations a trembling man
knowledged with responsibility not twig-smear nor Roman coin
soup—

O what would that be like!
Surely I'd give it for a nipple a rubber Tacitus
For a rattle a bag of broken Bach records
Tack Della Francesca all over its crib
Sew the Greek alphabet on its bib
And build for its playpen a roofless Parthenon

No, I doubt I'd be that kind of father
Not rural not snow no quiet window
but hot smelly tight New York City
seven flights up, roaches and rats in the walls
a fat Reichian wife screeching over potatoes Get a job!
And five nose running brats in love with Batman
And the neighbors all toothless and dry haired
like those hag masses of the 18th century
all wanting to come in and watch TV
The landlord wants his rent
Grocery store Blue Cross Gas & Electric Knights of Columbus
impossible to lie back and dream Telephone snow, ghost parking—
No! I should not get married! I should never get married!
But—imagine if I were married to a beautiful sophisticated woman
tall and pale wearing an elegant black dress and long black gloves
holding a cigarette holder in one hand and a highball in the other

and we lived high up in a penthouse with a huge window
from which we could see all of New York and even farther on
clearer days

No, can't imagine myself married to that pleasant prison dream—

O but what about love? I forget love
not that I am incapable of love
It's just that I see love as odd as wearing shoes—
I never wanted to marry a girl who was like my mother
And Ingrid Bergman was always impossible
And there's maybe a girl now but she's already married
And I don't like men and—
But there's got to be somebody!
Because what if I'm 60 years old and not married,
all alone in a furnished room with pee stains on my underwear
and everybody else is married! All the universe married but me!

Ah, yet well I know that were a woman possible as I am possible
then marriage would be possible—
Like SHE in her lonely alien gaud waiting her Egyptian lover
so i wait—bereft of 2,000 years and the bath of life.

WILLIAM S. BURROUGHS (ESSAY DATE 1989)

SOURCE: William S. Burroughs. "Introductory Notes." In *Mindfield*, pp. xvii-xix. New York: Thunder's Mouth Press, 1989.

In the following essay, Burroughs focuses on personal recollections of Corso, including Corso's sense of himself as a poet.

Someone asked Samuel Beckett what he thought of William Burroughs, and he reportedly replied, somewhat grudgingly: "Well, he's a writer." I have always cherished the compliment.

And I can say, ungrudgingly: Gregory Corso is a poet. He has the rare calling of a pure lyric gift. And he has never doubted his calling.

I first met Gregory in Allen Ginsberg's apartment on East 7th Street in New York, in 1953. At this time I had just returned from an expedition in search of *yagé* in South America. My only published work was *Junky.* Allen told me about this gifted young poet who was to arrive momentarily and fix breakfast for us. Gregory arrived and burned the toast. When I upbraided him with unnecessary asperity, he said, in effect, that after all, he was a *poet.*

After that I saw Gregory from time to time at Allen's, and in the San Remo Bar. There was a special quality about him, a radiant, childlike charm. I did not at that time appreciate the quality of his poetry. Recognition came much later, in Paris, when Brion Gysin, Sinclair Beiles, Gregory, and your reporter were working on *Minutes to Go.* Brion was knocked out by Gregory's poems, and quite suddenly I saw and heard and realized: Gregory *is* a poet.

Little incidents come to mind. We ordered wild boar in a French restaurant around the corner from rue Git-le-Coeur, where we all stayed. When the wild boar arrived, Gregory took one sniff and refused to taste it. I chided him overbearingly for being provincial, and took a mouthful myself—and came near to spitting it right out on the plate, with the words of Samuel Johnson when he spat out some over-hot food: "A fool would have swallowed that." It had a horrible, rank musky taste. But I did gag down one mouthful for the experience.

As I said, Gregory has never doubted his calling. Years ago, when he called W. H. Auden on the phone, Auden said:

"Who is *this?*"

"Gregory."

"Gregory *who?*"

"Gregory *the poet!*"

Auden, in his prime, donnish valiance, would have none of it. I think he felt that it was vaguely indecent—"Girls from one to ten / Beware of Englishmen."—or at least in questionable taste, to call oneself a *poet.*

"What have I done? / A lamb mess drawing flies."

The English knee-jerk liberal, who threw a shoe when Gregory read "**Bomb**," will never understand poetry or poets, for poetic reality has nothing to do with political or social reality.

And Gregory has another rare gift: he has a voice. When you think of Gregory, you will hear his voice. This is not always an endearing gift but it becomes Gregory, because the voice is good. Gregory's voice echoes through a precarious future. It will be heard so long as there is anyone there to listen.

There are those who say that Gregory has grave flaws of character. Poetry is made from flaws. A flawless poet is fit only to be a poet-laureate, officially dead and inperfectly embalmed. The stink of death leaks out: "Rarely, if once, will Nature give / The power to be a Laureate and live."—(with apologies to E. A. Robinson)

I think that Gregory would survive even the laurel crown, for the smell of *life* would leak out.

I stroll through Gregory's poems, stopping here and there: ah, yes, I remember you, and you, and you . . . We all stop in different places, but there are stopping places for anyone who knows what poetry is:

Fierce, with mustaches of gold
Guns rusting in arthritic hands
Don't shoot the warthog!
Pasting posters of mercy
On the stark posts of despair
A young child doomed by his sombrero
The cactus outlives you
Dirty Eyes aims a knife at me
I pump him full of soft watches
A favorite doll
Buried in the attic, it dies forever
Here, touch my electric hand
Laughter dies long after jest
The joker smiles no joke
He had no foes, he made them all into *friends*
Some friends want to be everybody's friends
Some friends always want to do you favors
Some always want to get *near* you
Those who haven't any friends and want them
    are creepy
Those who have friends and don't want them
    are doomed
Those who haven't any friends and don't want
    them are
        grand
Does one need a friend in heaven?
The mean cat in a little dark corner
Trembles the entire room
And so I gave the Gods away
And thought is all I know of Death . . .

Gregory is a gambler. He suffers reverses, like every man who takes chances. But his vitality and resilience always shine through, with a light that is more than human: the immortal light of his Muse.

Gregory is indeed one of the Daddies.

ALLEN GINSBERG (ESSAY DATE 1989)

SOURCE: Ginsberg, Allen. "On Corso's Virtues." In *Mindfield,* pp. xiii-xv. New York: Thunder's Mouth Press, 1989.

In the following essay, the foreword to Mindfield, *Ginsberg praises Corso's precision and wit, as well as his knack for capturing the essence of ideas.*

Gregory Corso's an aphoristic poet, and a poet of ideas. What modern poets write with such terse clarity that their verses stick in the mind without effort? Certainly Yeats, Pound, Williams, Eliot, Kerouac, Creeley, Dylan & Corso have that quality.

Corso's handling of ideas is unique, as in various one-word-title-poems ("**Power**", "**Bomb**", "**Marriage**", "**Army**", "**Police**", "**Hair**", "**Death**", "**Clown**" and later "**Friend**"). He distills the essence of archetypal concepts, recycling them with humor to make them new, examining, contrasting and alchemizing common vernacular notions into mindblowing (deconstructive or de-conditioning) insights. In this mode, his late 1950's poems (like Kerouac's 1951-52 scriptures on "Joan [Crawford] Rawshanks in the Fog" & "Neal and The Three Stooges") manifest a precursor Pop artistry, the realized notice of quotidian artifacts.

Poetic philosophe, Corso's uncanny insight mixes wisdom & logopoeia. "I'd a humor save me from amateur philosophy," he writes: "Fish is animalized water"—"knowing my words to be the acquainted prophecy of all men / and my unwords no less an acquaintanceship"—"Nothing sits on nothing in a nothing of many nothings a nothing king"—"I found God a gigantic fly paper"—"Standing on a street corner waiting for no one is Power"—"A star / is as far / as the eye / can see / and / as near / as my eye / is to me"—"And how can I trust them / who pollute the sky / with heavens / the below with hells."

As poetic craftsman, Corso is impeccable. His revision process, which he calls "tailoring," generally elision and condensation, yields gist-phrasing, extraordinary mind-jump humor. Clown sounds of circus, abstracted from plethora are reduced to perfect expression, "Tang-a-lang boom. Fife feef! Toot!" Quick sketch, sharp mind scissors.

As engineer of ideas, certain concepts recur retailored for nuance, such as "I shall never know my death," (i.e. dead he won't know it) and "You can't step in the same river once."

His late work, **"The Whole Mess . . . Almost"** is a masterpiece of Experience, the grand poetic abstractions Truth, Love, God, Faith Hope Charity, Beauty, money, Death, & Humor are animated in a single poem with brilliant & intimate familiarity.

As poetic wordslinger he has command of idiomatic simplicity, to wit: "A hat is power," "fried shoes" or:

O Bomb I love you
I want to kiss your clank eat your boom
You are a paean an acme of scream
a lyric hat of Mister Thunder

as well as exuberant invention as "an astrologer dabbling in dragon prose":

. . . Bomb
from your belly outflock vulturic salutations
Battle forth your spangled hyena finger stumps
along the brink of Paradise

Corso also excels as political philosophe; his many years as classic artist wanderer dwelling in European hotels, castles, & streets gives him perspective on North America. His crucial position in world cultural revolution mid-XX century as originator of the "Beat Generation" literary movement, along with Kerouac, Burroughs, Orlovsky and others, grants him an experience inside history few bards or politicians have known. Readers of the poem cluster **"Elegiac Feelings American"** will appreciate Corso's generational insight into Empire sickness. Earlier poems like **"Power,"** **"Bomb"**, **"Army"**, & many brief expatriate lyrics prove Corso to be Shelley's natural prophet among "unacknowledged legislators of the world."

Corso is a poet's Poet, his verse pure velvet, close to John Keats for our time, exquisitely delicate in manners of the Muse. He has been and always will be a popular poet, awakener of youth, puzzlement & pleasure for sophisticated elder bibliophiles, "Immortal" as immortal is, Captain Poetry exampling revolution of Spirit, his "poetry the opposite of hypocrisy," a loner, laughably unlaurelled by native prizes, divine Poet Maudit, rascal poet Villonesque and Rimbaudian whose wild fame's extended for decades around the world from France to China, World poet.

ED SANDERS (ESSAY DATE 2-16 FEBRUARY 2001)

SOURCE: Sanders, Ed. "Gregory Corso: 1930-2001." *Woodstock Journal* 7, no. 3 (2-16 February 2001).

In the following essay, Sanders eulogizes Corso.

"We brought about change without a drop of blood!" I once heard Gregory Corso exclaim at a reading at Columbia University in 1975. He was speaking of course of the Beat Generation, a generation that had great force beginning in the late 1950s, and especially in the early '60s when racist sheriffs in the South were known to snarl at Civil Rights demonstrators as "Beatnik race-mixers."

Gregory's best poems reached out way beyond the Beats, and touched the hearts of poetry readers around the world. You can read "Marriage," "Bomb" and his elegy for Jack Kerouac, "Elegiac Feelings American," to get started.

As *Journal* readers know we ran a series of tributes to Gregory Corso last fall, during his illness, from such writers as Robert Creeley, Raymond Foye, Joanne Kyger, Diane Di Prima, Michael McClure, Gary Snyder, Lawrence Ferlinghetti, Bob Rosenthal, Patti Smith, Oliver Ray, Rosebud Pettet and others.

And so, it was with sadness of course, that we took the 6:30 am Trailways to NYC on January 24 for Gregory's funeral at the beautiful Our Lady of

Pompei church on Carmine Street, where he was baptized 70 years ago. The service had dignity, about as much dignity as you can achieve, given the ashes-to-ashes, dust-to-dust quality of tearful memory that suffuse such events.

I last spoke with Gregory late last year, when he called from his daughter, Sheri Langerman's house in Minnesota, where he had moved from his long-time pad in the West Village. He had just about completed a final book, which was a miracle, given how close he had been to death last summer. Sheri, a professional nurse, adjusted his medicine regimen back then, and began to oversee his care. From then on, he seemed to perk up. He was watching a Jean Cocteau movie and quite eloquent when I visited last fall before he moved to Minnesota. In short, the efforts of Sheri and some of his close friends gave him an extra few months during which he was able to finish a book, as his soul-mate Allen Ginsberg also had done during his final weeks.

There were hundreds on hand at Our Lady of Pompei. I bet the church hadn't seen such a full crowd in quite a while. Our Lady of Pompei has a European quality. You would think you were in one a little church off the Piazza Campo Dei Fiori in Rome.

Patti Smith was in great vocal form as she sang a hymn to the accompaniment of the great pipe organ. Later she sang another song, backed by Oliver Ray on guitar. David Amram, who spoke with eloquence and played a very beautiful flute tune based Charley Parkeresque on the chord changes for "Amazing Grace." Long time Corso caretaker Roger Richard also spoke, and afterwards there was a gathering at a loft on the Lower East Side which was packed with several generations of Gregory's friends and admirers, some of whom had flown in from California.

I was intrigued to learn that Gregory's ashes will be interred in Rome in the very same cemetery in which Percy Bysshe Shelley's ashes are buried! Wow.

Buried with Shelley

Shelley and two others were in a small schooner called the "Don Juan" on the way to the beautiful seaside town of Livorno, on Italy's west coast, in the late, hot afternoon of July 8, 1822 when a sudden storm overwhelmed the boat and Shelley the two others drowned. In Shelley's pocket was a book of John Keats' verse.

When Shelley's body washed ashore several weeks later, Edward John Trelawney burned it, in ancient Greek fashion, on the beach at Via Reggio, after which Shelley's ashes were brought to the then new Protestant cemetery in Rome.

And now, Gregory Corso is coming to join the author of "Ode to the West Wind."

I wanted to find out the specifics so I spoke with attorney Robert Yarra, who lives in Fresno, California, and is a long time friend of Beat literature, and Gregory in particular. Mr. Yarra's speciality is immigration law, and it was he who was responsible for setting in motion the requests and permissions required to get Gregory into the Roman cemetery.

"George Scrivani and I had thought about that. George asked Gregory if it was something he'd want and he seemed very positive about that. He wanted Rome or Venice." Robert Yarra has friends with connections, as they say, in Rome, so he called a woman named Hannalorie, a friend of his, and asked if it would be possible to bury Gregory at the Protestant Cemetery. "She then spoke to the director," Yarra told me, "and he said no, it was very difficult. And then I said can you still try again, and so she did, and she was finally able to persuade them to bury him there."

When did this occur? I asked. Yarra replied, "This about six months ago, and Gregory knew of the results." Hannalorie is a long time friend of Robert Yarra, and lives in Rome. "She met Gregory about two years ago, and they got along very well. She's a very forceful lady, and usually gets what she wants."

Sheri Langerman, Gregory's daughter, will bring the ashes to Rome in May. It's going to cost about $5,000 to bury him there. "We're going to try to bury him near Shelley, if possible," said Yarra.

What a marvelous tale!

LAWRENCE FERLINGHETTI (ESSAY DATE 11-25 MAY 2001)

Ferlinghetti, Lawrence. "Untamed Poet Crosses River." *Woodstock Journal* 7, no. 10 (11-25 May 2001).

In the following essay, Ferlinghetti offers an unsentimental yet favorable portrayal of Corso.

Most obituaries are total eulogies, uncontaminated by any unkind cuts at the beloved or other straight talk. Don't "dis" the dead, etc. Well, that's OK for some dead folk, but not for Gregory Nunzio Corso who crossed the big river this past January 17th.

The announcement of a memorial service for him in lower Manhattan proclaimed he was

"America's greatest lyric poet," although he certainly wasn't as lyrical as Whitman or Edna St. Vincent Millay, or even the early e. e. cummings.

But that kind of judgment is always subjective and personal, isn't it? Corso was lyrical all right, but in a highly original, cutting sort of way.

On the back of Corso's early City Lights book, ***Gasoline,*** Jack Kerouac said, "Gregory was a tough young kid from the Lower East Side who rose like an angel over the rooftops and sang Italian songs as sweet as Caruso and Sinatra, but in words. 'Sweet Milanese hills' brood in his Renaissance soul, evening is coming on the hills. Amazing and beautiful Gregory Corso, the one and only Gregory the Herald." Very poetic—but "sweet" is one thing Corso wasn't every day. ("Bittersweet" would be closer.) And it wasn't Milanese hills in his soul. He was no refined northern Italian, but a Calabrese, born in 1930 in Greenwich Village of parents from the very depths of the Mezzogiorno. And Gregorio was mezzogiorno through and through, handsomely dark, heavy-browed, often brooding, like that savage landscape on the unshod boot of southernmost Italy, swept with burning sun and storms. And he had its dark lyric spirit that could burst forth untutored and raw in great raves of poetry.

And he was always in your face, often not singing sweetly, but challenging you in some wild way, daring you or putting you on, shaking you up or at least mocking your ordinary way of looking at things. How many times did I hear him interrupt some solemn voice on stage with a loud shout from the back of the hall, comic or obscene, the outsider challenging the whole scene? But he was no mere egocentric wiseacre. He was a tragicomic poet with a crazy sense of humor, as in poems such as his much-quoted **"Marriage"** with its parody of T. S. Eliot's "Love Song of J. Alfred Prufrock."

And a trait of his that has never been noted is that he had a great graphic talent and could have been a great painter, if he hadn't been so heavily into poetry, drugs, booze, and women. Some of his classic paintings and drawings were exhibited early in the 1990s at New York University's Beat Art show.

Graphically, he was the equal of any of the New York School painters who hung out with the poets at the old Cedar tavern in Greenwich Village in the 1950s and 60s. When he drew with pentel or brush he had a classic line that was instantly recognizable as his own, much in the way Picasso's line was distinctively his and no one else's.

Ed Sanders' *Woodstock Journal* published a beautiful obit, including a note from poet Robert Creeley that said Corso "had been ill for much of the past year but had recovered from time to time, saying that he'd got to the classic river but lacked the coin for Charon to carry him over. So he just dipped his toe in the water." Some of Corso's most powerful poems focussed on death, as was the case with so many other great poets. (The second and last reading that Dylan Thomas gave in San Francisco in the 1950s was totally centered on death, with poems by many others as well as himself.) Corso's mad mouthfuls challenged death as he challenged everything else. Read his dire comic eulogy to it in **"Bomb"** to get the full blast.

But even in death, this gadfly wordslinger is triumphing on his own terms. He wanted to be buried in Venice or Rome, and in the latter he might well have been happy under the paving stones of the Campo dei Fiori, in the center of which is a statue of Giordano Bruno, the heretic burned unrepentant by the Church in 1600, whom Corso no doubt saw as a brother. But the British Romantic, Percy Bysshe Shelley, was Corso's most loved poet, and Shelley is in the Protestant cemetery in the working-class Testaccio district of Rome. That's where Gregory's going, thanks to the initiative of his friends, including attorney Robert Yarra, George Scrivani, and a powerful lady in Rome named Hannalorie.

So, farewell, devilish angel poet, hail and farewell!

GENERAL COMMENTARY

RICHARD HOWARD (ESSAY DATE 1969)

SOURCE: Howard, Richard. "Gregory Corso: 'Surely There'll Be Another Table . . .'" In *Alone with America: Essays on the Art of Poetry in the United States Since 1950,* pp. 57-64. New York: Atheneum, 1969.

In the following essay, Howard offers an early estimation of Corso's poetic output, concluding that while much of his verse may be overwrought or self-absorbed, many of Corso's poems reflect great breadth of vision and humor. Howard concludes with an analysis of Corso's poem "Marriage."

No poet likes to be clumsy. But I decided to heck with it, so long as it allows me to speak the truth. If the poet's mind is shapely then his poem will come out shapely." The poet's mind! Surely the last place one would expect to find shapeliness in the case of a poet who has announced, with characteristic, with indeed programmatic glee, "thought is all I know of death." But it is the mind under critical circumstances that Corso intends, the mind in its stretch toward transcendence, when he speaks of his poems as celebrating "an entranced moment in which the mind accelerates"—the speed and the magic are everything here, and the mind itself, "a subterranean lashed to a pinnacle," merely a machine to be driven wild:

> O for that madness again
> Where illusion spoke Truth's divine dialect!

Gregory Corso's decision,[1] then, to rely upon himself as both medium and message—"I discard my lyre of Orphic futility"—rather than upon an imposition of shapeliness within the conventions of written communication, may be due to his higher loyalty to the art, or to his lack of insight as an artist. In either case, the risk of that decision is our own as we consider, or perhaps a better action would be to *consent to* four volumes of poems (though almost never of *verse* in any acceptation of the word collected from the traditional disposition of language ordered in some regular accord with its metrical possibilities) published between 1955, when the poet was 25 and had "learned, through Allen Ginsberg, how to handle myself in an uninstitutional society, as I was very much the institutional being . . . ," and 1962, when Corso already promised, though he has as yet failed to produce, a fifth collection with the rueful but viable title (for a man whom Jack Kerouac once called Gregory the Herald): "There Is Yet Time to Run Back Through Life and Expiate All That's Been Sadly Done."

A childhood of destitution and loss, an adolescence of vagrancy and imprisonment account for Corso's image of himself as an "institutional being," a youth with the imagination of confinement seeking to effect a supreme escape ("where all beyond is true Byzantium") yet repeatedly baffled by his disastrous circumstances, as he translated them in his first book, ***The Vestal Lady on Brattle,*** where the poet's *daemon,* "my vision-agent," is flouted by the surrogate of conformity, "the deserter":

> I don't know the better things that people know
> All I know is the deserter condemned me to
> black—
> He said: Gregory, here's two boxes of night
> one tube of moon
> And twenty capsules of starlight, go an' have a
> ball—
> He left and the creep took
> all my Gerry Mulligan records with him.

And though on the evidence of the enormous publicity Corso has provoked ("They've reached the moon and I've reached Greece," he proclaims, the two exploits evidently making an equivalent impact upon the news agencies of the world and even beyond), the "handling" Corso congratulates himself upon must seem more a matter of applause than of restraint, of back- rather than wrist-slapping, still there is no question that the orphanages of Manhattan, the cells of Clinton Prison, and the crew quarters of a Norwegian freighter brought the frightened kid—

> Candy-colors fade
> long pants lead us elsewhere
> and a child's hands are getting hair

—to a poetry of this world: "time a long long dog having chased its orbited tail comes to grab my hand and leads me into conditional life," however freakishly delivered. Corso moralizes his situation in the note to Donald Allen's anthology of *The New American Poetry,* announcing with the sententiousness also typical of his associates Ginsberg and Kerouac that "sometimes hell is a good place—if it proves that because it exists so must heaven. And what was heaven? Poetry." To avoid the institutional, to transcend the System, then, is to deny the systematic. What is wanted is what Bacon called "a knowledge broken," arrived at by broken flesh, broken mind, broken speech—*parataxis* rather than method, exaggeration and grotesquerie rather than generality, excess rather than economy. The onset and origin of such knowledge is, to the poet, a natural mystery—"it comes," he says of his poetry, "a dark arriviste, from a dark river within"—and its presence at the moment of composition, or rather of transcription, for this poetry is a dictation from the Unknown, or as one of his symbolic titles has it, **"Notes After Blacking Out,"** is a bewilderment, even an abnegation:

> I renounce the present
> like a king blessing an epic . . .
>
> and I, as though tipping a pitcher of milk,
> pour secrecy upon the dying page;

as for the future, the predictable continuation of such knowledge as poetry affords ("a poet is a spy . . . mankind's spy"), only the example of organic life, preferably in its least accessible forms ("impossible for me to betray even the simplest tree"), supplies the hope of an answer there. It is the kind of power which comes from below the intellect that reminds the poet of his own pulverized responsibilities, his own dashed hopes:

And so it's spring again so what
The leaves are leaves again no tree forgot.

Hence a poetry of fragments, of scatterings, even of droppings (one of Corso's regrets about "losing the horror of that 12-year-old Gregory" is the impoverishment of what was once a highly gratifying *Analerotik*); regenerative, seminal, fertilizing, but without sequence or lineal order. This is what Allen Ginsberg means, I think, when he says, in his introduction to Corso's second book ***Gasoline*** (1958), that "he wants a surface hilarious with ellipses" and underlines the organic analogy: "Corso's got the angelic power of making autonomous poems, like god making brooks."[2] Any process which spreads the self around after the fashion of nature is welcomed as constructive, even the mortal one, for in Corso's Commandments, "poetry is seeking the answer, joy is in knowing there is an answer, and death is knowing the answer." Hence in the very properly titled third collection ***The Happy Birthday of Death*** (1960), one comes across the kind of necrophiliac nursery-rhyme whose tonality, a Gongoristic conjugation of the cute and the heroic, only this poet could get away with, though where he takes it *to* is less apparent than the claustration, the bondage, even, of life itself that he is abducting his consciousness *from*:

Let's all die
Let's practice a little
Let's play dead for a couple of hours
Let's everybody weave elegant everlasting cerements
build fantastic tombs
carve lifelong coffins
and devise great ways to die let's!

What we confront in all these insistent fooleries, each of which has the wonderful quality of assigning itself a new genre even as it hilariously judges itself—

I lean forward on a desk of science
an astrologer dabbling in dragon prose

—Corso will begin, and we think: that's it! dragon prose, and *dabbling* in it, that's just what he does, and then the poet continues with his high or highty-tighty mode which flings us into an ideal uncertainty:

knowing my words to be the acquainted
prophecy of all men

—what we must endure in Corso's work is a poetry which insists that its own process, its own fragmentary ritual—

No meaning to life can be found in this holy language
nor beyond the lyrical fabricator's inescapable theme
be found the loathed find—there is nothing to find

—is *all that there is:* no meaning hinted, no symbolism proposed, no subjectivity revealed. For Gregory Corso the escape from inhibition is, merely, exhibition. In fact he does not write poems, he writes only poetry, and his refusal to select, to emphasize, to reject ("any door locked against a man is a sad business") is part of his general revulsion from the dialectic of our culture, in which the notion of weeds is automatically created by the notion of a garden, or as Corso's death-hymn **"Bomb"** puts it: "to die by cobra is not to die by bad pork." For Corso, like Freud, sees our civilization as one in which not only sexuality is repressed, but any form of transcendence; in the famous closing lines of **"This Was My Meal"** the bafflement of the orphaned corybant is celebrated, even as it is mourned, in overwhelming images of defeat:

I turned to father
and he ate my birthday
I drank my milk and saw trees outrun themselves
valleys outdo themselves
and no mountain stood a chance of not walking

Dessert came in the spindly hands of stepmother
I wanted to drop fire-engines from my mouth!
But in ran the moonlight and grabbed the prunes.

The great thing, for Corso, is *not to choose,* not to settle for the possible, but to take everything, to invent the new nourishment as well as to feed on the old. "Time takes me by the hand / born March 26, 1930 I am led 100 mph over the vast market of choice / what to choose? what to choose?" And with appropriate appetite and an inventiveness that is really hysterical, Corso answers in his last book, ***Long Live Man*** (1962):

Surely there'll be another table . . .
Wisconsin provisions
Insufficient when I have absolute dairy visions:
Corduroy eggs, owl cheese, pipe butter
Firing squad milk;
The farmer will never love me
Nor I, he . . .

The impulse to inventory as a form of invention is evident in all of Corso's shrinkings from choice, from singleness, from being "stuck here"; he offers an enormous list of alternative names for his third book of poems, what he calls "saleable titles," my favorites among which are

Fried Shoes
Remarkable
Cars are love
The Wet Sea
The Rumpled Backyard
Caesarean operation . . .

That last is another of his approximations to genre—all of Corso's poems are hasty productions, untimely ripped and never quite free of the shreds and shrieks of selfhood; in fact, he rejoices in a certain fakery, the suggestion that out of the anthology of Being he has never quite chosen, never really made his commitment to anything more than infinite potentiality: "Ah, this surfeit of charlatanry will never leave my organic pyx thank god . . ." He would not be "caught in a single fate," yet Gregory Corso's *poems* are thereby caught, for they cannot be complete or at least completed so long as their author must declare "all life is a rotary club," in the sense of a blunt instrument revolving endlessly, as well as a good-humored civic organization: "I still question if all life is a rotary club and if it's death to resign." And there are moments, beautiful ones, in Corso's production when the poet acknowledges the terrible waste in it all, the debauchery of talent and titanic hopes in his own method, or abnegation of method. Once "death has distributed its categorical blue," once

My body's quilt hath split
and the porter sweeps
what was once my meat,

then the poems as he has dripped and dribbled and spattered them upon existence will have to create Gregory, and no longer Gregory them. Doubt, self-doubt is not a sentiment we expect to find very emphatically registered in Corso's *oeuvre,* but once "the horns are still and marriage drops its quiet shoe," there comes an occasion when the poet confronts what he has not so much made as failed to make of himself; it is a supreme occasion in the revels, and a moment of unsurpassable pathos:

Am I the person I did not want to be?
That talks-to-himself person?
That neighbors-make-fun-of person?
Am I he who, on museum steps, sleeps on his
side?
Do I wear the cloth of a man who has failed?
Am I the loony man?
In the great serenade of things
am I the most cancelled passage?

I think that if we were to seek one hostage to fortune out of Corso's work, one poem that is not merely a collage of high spirits, the "imitation of power" as Corso calls himself in a poem dedicated to Ginsberg, it is to be found smack in the middle of his output, which rises in a long slope to the crowning achievement **"Marriage"** in the third book, and then diminishes down to mutterings and defensiveness, as in the late **"Paranoia in Crete"**:

Just sit here, knees up, amid amphora & aloe
reading lusty potsherd, gobbling figs, needing no
one—
mine the true labyrinth, it is my soul, Theseus,
try a ball of string in that . . .

The shape, then, is that of a fronton (Corso has been categorical about his architectural affinities in defining his charge: "I must *create* the room of my truth's desire; and then, and only then, may I enter and dwell in peace and joy"), as the poet corroborates in this beautiful, Cocteau-haunted distich:

The caryatid I am is Truth
Lo! my pediment of Lie

A glance, then, at this central poem in the pediment, a triumph of 112 lines, necessarily about the impossibility of choosing: "Should I get married? Should I be good?" The poet runs through a number of possible girls and what he would do to them, samples their favors and families:

O how terrible it must be for a young man
seated before a family and the family thinking
We never saw him before! He wants our Mary
Lou!

Agonizing over the horrors of the wedding ("And I trembling what to say say Pie Glue!"), Gregory finds himself protesting over the singleness of wedlock, Corso as some kind of wizard of promiscuity at Niagara Falls:

Everybody knowing! I'd be almost inclined not
to do anything!
Stay up all night! Stare that hotel clerk in the
eye!
Screaming: I deny honeymoon! I deny
honeymoon!
running rampant into those almost climactic
suites
yelling Radio belly! Cat shovel!
O I'd live in Niagara forever! in a dark cave
beneath the Falls
I'd sit there the Mad Honeymooner
devising ways to break marriages, a scourge of
bigamy
a saint of divorce . . .

Yet the prospect of withholding himself from the common fate is just as painful for Corso as the doom of conformity, and the whole of his poetic career is summed up in the terrors of the poem's final strophes:

Because what if I'm 60 years old and not married
all alone in a furnished room with pee stains on
my underwear
and everybody else is married! All the universe
married but me!

And "**Marriage**" closes with the apocalyptic consolation of an ultimate energy milked from the universe as the poet milks his own from himself—it is the final mythological comfort of choosing nothing but experience, or Everything:

Ah, yet well I know that were a woman possible
as I am possible
then marriage would be possible—
Like SHE in her lonely alien gaud waiting her
Egyptian lover
So I wait—bereft of 2,000 years and the bath of
life.

. . . . .

I suspect that one reason for Corso's silence the last five years is his outrage upon discovering the irreversibility of somatic processes. If he refuses to choose a poetry that is more than "an assembly of great eye sounds," then his body will choose for him, as the later poems testify:

My beautiful hair is dead . . .
How to stand thunderous on an English cliff
a hectic Heathcliff?
O my lovely stained-glass hair is
dry dark invisible
not there!
Wigmaker! help me!
I want a wig of winter's vast network!
Samson bear with me! Just a moustache . . .

The capacity to project himself alive and kicking and screaming into every and any possibility is being leached out of Gregory by living, or by *having lived*: "I am 32 years old and finally I look my age, if not more." The last poem in ***Long Live Man*** finally faces the possibility—and follows it with silence—that the very act of making, the poetic act, is a moral gesture because it involves choosing, the preference of one thing (life) over another (death):

I love poetry because it makes me love
and presents me life.
And of all the fires that die in me,
there's one burns like the sun;
it might not make day my personal life. . . .
but it does tell me my soul has a shadow.

It is easy to dismiss the truncated, violent work of Gregory Corso ("I cried," he says at the end, "for that which was no longer sovereign in me, stinking of dead dreams"), and indeed I have quoted in this essay all that I care to recall of his entire output, making my own anthology from the welter of alternatives. So much is a dither of self-promotion, illiteracy and native *strain* that to "care" in the common phrase as Corso himself cares for these productions—

Must I dry my inspiration in this sad concept?
Delineate my entire stratagem?
Must I settle into phantomness
and not say I understand things better than
God?

—is to entertain one's prepossessions as a malady and a doom. But in all its vulgarities and distractions and boastings, there lie, disparate, yearning for union and the release of choosing, the elements of a giant art.

Notes

1. Which he supports by this engaging contention, with its significant admission of fallibility: "I never felt badly about losing my early works because I felt myself to be inexhaustible—like I had a great big supply of this stuff called poetry. The only care I took, and maybe not even that so well, was not to lose the poet. As long as I had the poet I would have the poems." The little concessive clause here suggests that the poet himself is aware of the desperately marginal nature of his enterprise, its swelling omens of failure even in its apocalyptic finding: "Athene requests my unbecoming."
2. The second part of this remark of Ginsberg's is distressing: to speak of "autonomous" poems is either a tautology or it is nonsense; but the comparison with (lower-case) god making brooks strikes a good note, and in its context in the introduction the description has the kind of generous rightness Ginsberg's comments characteristically achieve.

EDWARD HALSEY FOSTER (ESSAY DATE 1992)

SOURCE: Foster, Edward Halsey. "Corso." In *Understanding the Beats,* pp. 128-49. Columbia: University of South Carolina Press, 1992.

In the following essay, Foster argues that Corso's poetry is deeply personal, citing poems from throughout his career and providing supporting biographical details from his past, especially from his difficult youth. Foster emphasizes the dark and violent images from Corso's poetry, though he notes that in his later verse Corso could be reflective and at times optimistic.

The poet and poetry are inseparable. You got to dig the poet. Otherwise the poetry sucks.
—Gregory Corso, in an interview with Robert King and John Little collected in *The Beat Vision,* ed. Arthur and Kit Knight

Allen Ginsberg met Gregory Corso in 1950. Corso had recently been released from Clinton Prison, where for three years he had served a sentence for robbery and according to a note in Corso's second volume, ***Gasoline,*** had read his way through "books of illumination."[1]

Corso knew more about life on the street than the other Beats did. Burroughs, Kerouac, and Gins-

ON THE SUBJECT OF...

LAWRENCE LIPTON

Poet, novelist, and critic Lawrence Lipton is best known for *The Holy Barbarians* (1959), a sociological analysis of the Beats. The book chronicles Beat writers such as Ginsberg and Kerouac, examining their ways of life, attitudes, cultural achievements, and roles in society. The book also features biographical sketches of some well-known Beat Generation personalities. In addition, Lipton transcribed conversations he had taped, including one between Ginsberg and Corso as they discussed their trip down the coast from San Francisco. But Lipton's book went beyond discussing well-known Beats, offering a snapshot of the bohemian lifestyle that pervaded Venice, California, where Lipton made his home. His other publications include *Rainbow at Midnight* (1955) and *Bruno in Venice West & Other Poems* (1976).

berg were from middle- or lower-middle-class homes, but he had seen intimately the world of derelicts and thieves that the others watched from cafeteria windows on Times Square. They had read Spengler and Nietzsche and knew from such friends as Huncke and Garver what the underside of American life was like, but Corso spent most of his childhood and adolescence in foster homes and prisons. He was, like Cassady, a survivor, and as Kerouac described him in the character of Raphael Urso in *Desolation Angels,* he also had "a great mellifluous mind, deep, with amazing images"(*DA,* 249).

The other Beats learned the hipster's code of values, but these were Corso's by necessity. Abandoned by his mother and then turned over to foster parents by his father, he learned firsthand the hipster's streetwise sense that no one, no institution, is really disinterested and that finally the only reliable place to turn is oneself.

Corso's poetry, as a result, is deeply personal—so much so as to be at times hermetic and obscure. It takes more from Poe than Whitman, and at least at the beginning was influenced by André Breton and surrealism. Poe and Breton's focus on dreams and the subconscious led Corso to a poetry similar to what Kerouac and Ginsberg found in expressionism. Corso has written spontaneous works, notably **"Elegiac Feelings American,"** but generally his poetry, like Poe's, is the product of careful revision and craft. Poe, as he wrote in a poem entitled **"After Reading 'In the Cleaning,'"** is for him the "only American poet."[2] "I don't think I could let things go without a change," he told an interviewer, adding elsewhere that "revision is where you really find out how skillful you are. You have to be like a magician."[3] Nonetheless, Corso's poems are never merely imitative; they are "spontaneous, literally," he has said, but in a statement that might be understood as an extension or refinement of Kerouac's technique, he also pointed out that "spontaneous poetry is also spontaneous change when you're working on it." Corso's poetry "insists that its own process, its own fragmentary ritual," in Richard Howard's words, ". . . is *all that there is.*"[4]

Corso, who was born in New York in 1930, never went beyond the sixth grade, but he developed a private visionary and imaginative world which may have helped to cultivate the facility for startling images which marks much of his poetry.[5] When Corso was eleven, he lived with his father again, but the next year he was living on the streets and broke into a restaurant to get food. As he was leaving, he was arrested and sent to the Tombs, the New York City prison, where "they abused me terribly, and I was indeed like an angel then because when they stole my food and beat me up and threw pee in my cell, I, the next day would come out and tell them my beautiful dream about a floating girl who landed before a deep pit and just stared."[6]

When he was thirteen, he ran away from home. Looking for a place to sleep, he broke into a building and was arrested and sent back to the Tombs for four months. The next two or three years were spent largely in homes for boys. He was then arrested for his part in a robbery using walkie-talkies to warn when the police were coming. The judge, Corso recalled in an interview, decided that he "was a menace to society because [he] had put crime on a scientific basis" and sentenced him to Clinton Prison for three years.[7]

Before his arrest, Corso had written his first poem, **"Sea Chanty,"** in which the speaker says that his mother was eaten by the sea when she did not heed his warning not to hate "the sea, / my sea especially." He found on the shore an unusual kind of food, which the sea told him he could eat. When he asked what it was, he was told that it was his mother's feet. As one might guess, Corso had already been reading surrealist poetry, particularly André Breton's, and it would have a major effect on his work, although he insisted it was "just another toy to play with."[8]

In prison, Corso read his books given to him, he commented, by "angels . . . , from all the cells surrounding me" (***G*** [***Gasoline***], 4). He read a 1905 dictionary and "for three lucky years . . . just got that whole book in me, all the obsolete and archaic words." He read the English romantics, Stendhal, Dostoevsky, and Hugo, but "the one who really turned me on," he said, "was Shelley, not too much his poetry, but his life." Gregory Stephenson, who is responsible for the only extended study of Corso's work to date, has pointed out that "Corso shares with Shelley a zeal for liberty and . . . passionate faith in humankind." Stylistically, however, he learned more from the Surrealists, Randall Jarrell, and, somewhat later, Kerouac. "I don't owe respect to nobody," Corso said in an interview, "'cause all I learned I learned on my ownsome. Although I did learn from humankind, it was myself and humankind; ergo I have added to it."[9]

In 1954 Corso lived near Harvard, "met lots of wild young brilliant people who were talking about Hegel and Kierkegaard," and was published in the *Harvard Advocate*.[10] His first book, ***The Vestal Lady on Brattle and Other Poems,*** was published in Cambridge in 1955 with funds raised by Radcliffe and Harvard students. He sent a copy to Randall Jarrell, who responded warmly and invited him to visit.

Jarrell was the poetry consultant at the Library of Congress. He had studied with John Crowe Ransom, had written for *Partisan Review* and the *Kenyon Review,* and was associated with Delmore Schwartz, Robert Lowell, and John Berryman. His work was representative of that which in a few years would be stigmatized as "academic," but his poetic interests as a critic were not narrow or elitist, and he served Corso much as Williams served Ginsberg. Jarrell's work showed Corso how to write poems in terms of specifics rather than general ideas or emotions. Asked by an interviewer where he had learned about poetry, Corso named Jarrell, who "made me see things around me—fat ladies at the supermarket. Look at that, he says. What? you say, because you don't see anything great about them. But then suddenly you do! He illuminated me this way, got me to see."[11]

Jarrell may have shown Corso far more. Much of Jarrell's poetry is concerned with innocence and youth in a world of war and death. In these poems, young men who wish no one harm are trapped in situations where survival means being decisive and cruel. In ***The Vestal Lady on Brattle,*** as Gregory Stephenson says, Corso "wants us to look at our society and our lives with the eye of a child." The subject matter is often terrifying, but it is seen with a child's clear vision and innocence. The title poem concerns an aged woman who each morning creates a child, drowns him, and then "drinks" his body. In **"12 Ash St. Place,"** an old man drips colors from his hands. The poet stops to talk to him and is friendly, but the old man drips "a purple color on [his] hand" and it burns.[12]

The poems in ***The Vestal Lady on Brattle*** return repeatedly to thoughts and images of death. **"Greenwich Village Suicide"** concerns a woman and whose face is covered with a copy of the *Daily News* (***VL,*** 5). The speaker in **"In the Morgue"** is dead and watches two gangsters laid out near him. Several of the poems, like **"Sea Chanty,"** suggest hatred or fear of mothers. In **"Dialogues from Children's Observation Ward,"** a mother visits her child but doesn't say hello to him. According to **"In My Beautiful . . . And Things,"** the speaker will share his "beautiful things" with a woman if she is "not like a mother or a bitch" (***VL,*** 16).

The principal motif of the poems in ***The Vestal Lady on Brattle,*** according to Stephenson, "is that of a predatory devouring or destruction of innocence and beauty."[13] But if the world in this book is largely ugly and cruel, the poet has his work and, as he adds in **"Cambridge, First Impressions,"** his dreams. There are no visions out on Cambridge's "Revolutionary Road," but he can leave that and turn, alone,

> . . . to books to cans of beer to past loves.
> And from these gather enough dream
> to sneak out the back door.
>
> (***VL,*** 35)

Although the subjects and images in the poems are frequently macabre and frightening, their tone is not. Poetry, commented Corso in a statement quoted at the beginning of ***Gasoline,*** "comes . . . from a dark river within" (***G,*** 4), but an innocent tone transforms it into poems that on the surface are playful and clever. The images are often more startling than terrifying. The poet shows himself and his readers extraordinary things but will not be defeated by nightmares and is always "[sneaking] out the back door." In this sense, the poems, are redemptive; they do not deny the dark river but they deflect it from destructive ends. "The creative artist," as Stephenson writes, "is the embodiment of heroic resistance to the ravening, repressive forces of death and negativity."[14]

In the introduction to Corso's second book, ***Gasoline*** (1958), Ginsberg said that Corso "wants a surface hilarious with ellipses, jumps of the strangest phrasing picked off the streets of his mind like 'mad children of soda caps'" (***G***, 7).[15] The language in ***Gasoline*** is in fact kinetic and delightful, although the poems propose a world one would never want to enter. There is a nightmare just on the other side of the words, and it is the words alone which keep it from breaking through. If one is distracted from the intricate phrasing, one is alone and helpless in that "dark river." **"In the Fleeting Hand of Time"** for example, evokes a childhood abandoned to "all too real Mafia streets," where desperation ends with the desire to be thrown "beneath your humanity of cars" and with the poet abandoning his "lyre of Orphic futility." The suicide, who has "betrayed" poetry and life returns to the paradise from which he originally came, but once there, he is simply led back "into conditional life" (***G***, 15).

Perhaps the best-known poem in the book is **"Birthplace Revisited,"** in which the poet decides to return to the apartment where he was born, but on his way up the stairs sees "Dirty Ears" with a knife and "[pumps] him full of lost watches" (***G***, 31). There are many other startling images and bizarre juxtapositions here. In **"This Was My Meal,"** a child says that his father "ate my birthday," that the cow brains at dinner look like snow (***G***, 43). In **"But I Do Not Need Kindness,"** the poet talks about a "little old lady," who "rode a spiked car over my head" (***G***, 33-34). Paris, in the poem of that name, is the city of "deathical Notre Dame." It is "Aprilcity," where Baudelaire, Artaud, and other poets now have "worms in hair" (***G***, 48). In **"Vision of Rotterdam,"** that city, repeatedly bombed during the war, "is dying again," but a plan to rebuild it is trapped "amid a madness of coughing bicycles" (***G***, 17). In San Francisco, according to **"Ode to Coit Tower,"** there are "black-jacketed saints . . . Zen potsmokers / Athenians and cocksmen," but

> . . . not one
> pure Shelleyean dream of let's say hay-
> like universe
> golden heap on a wall of fire
> sprinting toward the gauzy eradication of
> Swindleresque Ink.
>
> (*G*, 13)

Transcendence in Corso's poetry is found through language and surreal vision. The "pure Shelleyean dream" is a great blaze that could destroy the Swindler writer (such as a counterfeit Shelley like Swinburne?), but it exists only in the poem, transforming dark emotion and nightmare into astonishment. In **"2 Weird Happenings in Haarlem,"** windmills are "spied . . . eating tulips" (***G***, 18), and in **"Three,"** Death spends the day at the movies "when a child dies" (***G***, 39).

Although Shelley is the poet with whom Corso is conventionally associated, he is closer, especially in the early books, to Rimbaud. As Stephenson points out: "Words for [Corso] possess a magical, incantatory power. . . . Like that of Rimbaud, Corso's poetic enterprise is the *alchemy of the word,* the verbal transmutation of the world. His expressive, explosive, explorative utilization of language is at once destructive and constructive, subverting traditional modes of thought and conventional notions of reality, as it exalts desire, freedom and vision."[16]

"I could very precisely see a mosque instead of a factory," Rimbaud said in "Second Delirium: The Alchemy of the Word", "a drum corps of angels, horse carts on the highways of the sky, a drawing room at the bottom of the lake; monsters and mysteries."[17] Similarly in Corso, windmills eat tulips, and the poet sees himself as "the last gangster."

Poe, Corso's "only American poet," is the greater influence, however. In the introduction to ***Gasoline,*** Ginsberg wrote that Corso wrote "pure abstract poetry, the inside sound of language alone" (***G***, 7). The modern interest in "pure poetry" can be traced to Poe's essay "The Poetic Principle," in which he argued that a poem's objective was aesthetic rather than moral or intellectual. Corso, at least in his early poems, has no interest in judging or analyzing whatever rises from the "dark river." He wants simply the image or observation that is astonishing in itself, such as the American cows on exhibit in the Mexican zoo (***G***, 24).

Some of the poems in ***The Happy Birthday of Death*** (1960) contain surreal imagery like that in ***The Vestal Lady on Brattle*** and ***Gasoline.*** The speaker in **"Death,"** for example, remembers that before he was born, "owls appeared and trains departed."[18] In **"Transformation & Escape,"** God is "a gigantic fly paper," and St. Michael is a sticky material that the poet pastes onto his head (***HBD***, 19). But the better poems in ***The Happy Birthday of Death*** tend to be more discursive and less imagistic. Corso said that when he first began writing, he thought of poetry as "a concise form, built like a brick acropolis" but decided, after writing the poems in ***Gasoline,*** that "if I could just go with the rhythm I have within me, my own sound, that that would work, and it worked."[19] The result can be seen here in poems like **"Hair," "Marriage," "Power,"** and **"Army."**

Of these, **"Marriage"** is the best known. Corso and Ginsberg gave readings together many times in the late 1950s, and Corso often read **"Marriage"** as a comic piece to balance the anger in "Howl." The poem begins in the tone of a serious young man contemplating marriage, and the structure is correspondingly formal. The opening line, which hints at iambic pentameter ("Should I get married? Should I be good?"), rhymes with the second. The third and fifth, and the sixth and ninth lines also rhyme, but at that point, the poem abandons any pretense of formality and simultaneously begins to portray weddings and marriage as formal obligations and traps. The poet imagines the priest at the wedding "asking me Do you take this woman for your lawful wedded wife? / And I trembling what to say say Pie Glue!" (***HBD,*** 29). Instead of taking "the girl next door" to the movies, the poet would take her "to cemeteries / tell all about werewolf bathtubs and forked clarinets" (***HBD,*** 29). At Niagara Falls, he would scream, "I deny honeymoon!" at the hotel clerk and run into the honeymoon suite "yelling Radio belly! Cat shovel!" And back home, he would "[hang] a picture of Rimbaud on the lawnmower" (***HBD,*** 30). Nonetheless, although he "can't imagine [himself] married to that pleasant prison dream," he knows that without a wife, he could end "all alone in my furnished room with pee stains on my underwear" (***HBD,*** 32).

The same week that Corso wrote **"Marriage,"** he wrote **"Bomb,"** his other well known poem from the 1950s. **"Bomb,"** which is printed in the shape of a nuclear explosion, is an attempt, in Corso's words, to bring "all the energy of all the lyric that I could name" together so as "to know" what the bomb is: "if I start with hating it, with the hate of it, I get no farther than a piece of polemic, a political poem."[20] The bomb, according to the poem, is the "Budget of history" and the "Brake of time." It is inevitable and apparently, like death, morally neutral. When the bomb finally explodes, "Penguins [will be] plunged against the Sphinx," and "St. Sophia [will be] peeling over Sudan." The bomb is the new apocalypse, greater than God: "thy BOOM His tomb." The bomb is declared to be the new master, and the poem ends:

> Know that the earth will madonna the
> Bomb
> that in the hearts of men to come more bombs
> will be born
> magisterial bombs wrapped in ermine all
> beautiful
> and they'll sit plunk on earth's grumpy
> empires
> fierce with moustaches of gold.
> (***HBD,*** between 32 and 33)

Corso's early poems involve distinct, sharp moments of illumination, but **"Marriage"** and **"Bomb"** and many other works in ***The Happy Birthday of Death*** are constructions in which subconscious revelation is replaced by politics and social observation. The imagery can be no less startling—as when Corso tells the bomb,

> I want to put a lollipop
> in thy furcal mouth
> A wig of Goldilocks on thy baldy bean
> and have you skip with me Hansel and Gretel
> along the Hollywood screen.
> (***HBD,*** between 32 and 33)

Because of their political concerns, the poems are generally less hermetic, their observations and ideas more accessible and less ambiguous, yet their emotional power can be as appalling as the dark rivers that run beneath the surface in ***The Vestal Lady on Brattle*** and ***Gasoline.*** As Corso says in **"Notes After Blacking Out,"** "Truth's author itself is nothingness." In a poem, one searches for "the answer," but "Death is knowing the answer" (***HBD,*** 11). According to **"1959,"** the final poem in ***The Happy Birthday of Death,*** "No meaning to life can be found in this holy language" (***HBD,*** 90).

Elsewhere, however, Corso's view was less desperate. In the late 1950s, Corso collaborated with Burroughs, Brion Gysin, and Sinclair Beiles in a collection of cut-ups called *Minutes to Go* (1960). When the book was ready for publication, Corso added a note saying that his own poetry "was from the soul and not from the dictionary," and if by doing cut-ups he had seemingly destroyed his own work, it was "poetry I care not for, and so should be cut-up." Burroughs saw words as a form of oppression and wanted cut-ups to dispel their power, but Corso insisted that "you can't destroy language" and that Burroughs would merely "add to it."[21] Corso never published any more cut-ups and had reservations about publishing those in *Minutes to Go.*

Corso's novel ***The American Express*** (1961) includes a character named Mr. D, "tall and spectral," who, says another, would "unspeak the word and so have done with the human *and* universal predicament."[22] Mr. D. is based on Burroughs during the period of the cut-ups, but the character is not developed, which is unfortunate since Corso lived at that time in the same building as Burroughs, knew him well, and was one of few who could provide an objective description of him as he moved from his early work to his more radical fictions published in the 1960s. The book, which is Corso's only novel, "was written in one month, and it's the one I hate because I really did a fast job on that. It's written so awkwardly."[23] There are comic passages, but the book is not as a whole effective. It was published in Paris in 1961 but has never been published in the United States.

Conceivably Burroughs's destructive intentions in his cut-ups led Corso to reconsider the dark undercurrents in his own work. The poems in his next collection, ***Long Live Man,*** are, in any case, very different from what he had written before. ***The Happy Birthday of Death*** ends with **"1959,"** but **"Man,"** the first poem in ***Long Live Man*** (1962), claims in Whitmanesque lines

> That man can *think* soul is a great strange
>   wonderful thing—
> In the beginning was the word; man has
>   spoken—
> The Jews, the Greeks; chaos groping behind;
> Exalted dignity sings. . . .
>   (***LLM*** [***Long Live Man***], 9-10)

"I love poetry," Corso says in **"Writ on the Eve of My 32nd Birthday,"** "because it makes me love / and presents me life," though it also "does tell me my soul has a shadow" (***LLM,*** 93). The "dark river" is still there, and **"Death,"** he says in **"Writ on the Steps of Puerto Rican Harlem,"** "remains the same" (***LLM,*** 77). The difference is in the way things are seen. If nothing in ***Long Live Man*** is as strong as the best of the earlier work, the poems can be joyful, celebrating life in ways the others had rarely done.

There were five major books between 1955 and 1962, but between 1962 and ***Mindfield,*** his collection of "new and selected poems" published in 1989, there were only two. In 1967 Corso said that he had "spent four years thinking, trying to get right back to the source of things. I had this scary feeling that all I know about is writing and poetry, and so I made up my mind to learn." He had gone to Europe, lived in Crete and Greece, and had "read the oldest books—*Gilgamesh,* the Bible, the *Book of the Dead,* all the Greek literature—just trying to put it together for myself."[24]

In Paris he spent six months studying hieroglyphs, and this led to his next major effort, ***The Geometric Poem*** (1966), not published in the United States until 1970, when it was included in ***Elegiac Feelings American.*** The poem is important in understanding the transcendental sensibility that runs through Corso's work. According to Stephenson, "'**The Geometric Poem**' represents the fullest expression of Corso's fundamental themes of vision and the emancipation of the spirit. In the myths and history of ancient Egypt the poet discovers a metaphor for the visionary society, and he is inspired to prophesy the coming of a 'perfect Egypt' in which poetic truth and imagination finally triumph over objective reality."[25]

Egyptian civilization survived for four thousand years, longer than any other in history. It was in part a gnostic culture, dependent less on reason than on revelation. As Stephenson points out, "The ancient Egyptians recognized no distinction between the divine realm and the world, all was unity. . . . It is this essential mythos . . . that Corso wishes to revivify. . . ."[26] Geometric forms had mystical as well as logical properties—the line, which seems to have neither beginning nor end, the circle, which is "the highest + purest geometrical form."[27] But nothing in Corso is ever finally triumphant except the dark river, and the poem ends with "3 Prophetic Versions of An Egyptian Downfall." Even this "perfect" civilization is ultimately dissolved.

"Mutation of the Spirit," which was written on heroin in two days in 1964, is in some ways a counterpart to **"The Geometric Poem." "Mutation"** is in effect a series of gnostic revelations or hermetic texts. Some passages are private illuminations:

> I speak what is demanded of one such as I
> TRUTH ABOVE ALL the demand
> I am a wreck of truth Damn such demand
> I cried I would rather my value be true
> than truth be my value.
>   (***EFA*** [***Elegiac Feelings American***], 23)

Others evoke a private, surreal imagery:

> Chicken cries Sacramental sobs from the chapel
>   A window
>   closes
> Loneliness grandeur and blue lambs whorled
>   eyes rinsed
>   light

Swimming deer And now the long hike back to
the city.

(*EFA*, 18)

In addition to **"Mutation of the Spirit"** and **"The Geometric Poem,"** ***Elegiac Feelings American*** brings together Corso's poetry from the 1960s together with several earlier works (**"Spontaneous Requiem for the American Indian"** [1958], **"Pot"** [1957], **"The Poor Bustard"** [1956], and others) which had not been previously collected in his books.

The hipster's political vision of America as a regimented and repressive society is especially obvious in these poems, but they are also marked by Corso's surreal humor. "I'm afraid to return to America," Corso says in **"The American Way"**:

I am telling you the American way is a hideous
monster
eating Christ making Him into Oreos and
Dr. Pepper
the sacrament of its foul mouth.

(*EFA*, 70)

"The American Way" absorbs even those who resist it. The Beats "acquire for themselves their own habits" but

become as distinct and regimented and lost
as the main flow
because the Way has many outlets
like a snake of many tentacles—.

(*EFA*, 74)

The only answer is "a new consciousness" (*EFA*, 74). The poem was finished in 1961, and **"Mutation of the Spirit"** and **"The Geometric Poem"** seem to have been Corso's attempts to reach that "new consciousness." His elegy for Kerouac, the book's title poem, suggests that it was Kerouac who had found the alternative and, together with his friends, had become "the very roots themselves" (*EFA*, 4): "We came to announce the human spirit in the name of beauty and truth," Corso says, and the proof of Kerouac's success is "the children of flowers" (*EFA*, 5, 12).

"Columbia U Poesy Reading—1975," collected in Corso's 1981 book, ***Herald of the Autochthonic Spirit***, is a meditation on the Beats' influence and achievement. On the one hand, the Beats had the kind of rewards offered by the very culture they resisted: "the New York Times paid [Ginsberg] 400 dollars for a poem he wrote about being mugged for 60 dollars."[28] But the poem declares that Corso, Kerouac, Burroughs, and Ginsberg were "Revolutionaries of the Spirit," who had managed to "boot the ivory apple-cart of tyrannical values / into illusory oblivion / without spilling a drop of blood" (*HAS* [*Herald of the Autochthonic Spirit*], 2). But Corso then talks about his own involvement with drugs, particularly heroin, as a treason to poetry. At the end he hears the Muse "moan: 'O Gregorio, Gregorio / you'll fail me I know,'" but his spirit replies, "Not so" (*HAS*, 5). **"Columbia U Poesy Reading—1975"** is Corso's rededication to poetry.

When the poem was written, Corso was planning a new book to be titled "Who Am I—Who I Am." His only copy of the manuscript was stolen, however, and there were no further books until ***Herald of the Autochthonic Spirit*** was published in 1981. By then, of course, he could no longer be a young Rimbaud. He had, as he wrote in **"Feelings on Getting Older,"** "entered prison the youngest and left the youngest / of Ginsberg Kerouac Burroughs . . . the youngest," but now he had "vintage eyes" (*HAS*, 52-53). The poems in ***Herald of the Autochthonic Spirit*** include reflections on youth (such as **"What the Child Sees," "Youthful Religious Experiences,"** and **"When a Boy . . ."**) and meditations on aging (such as **"The Mirror Within," "Getting to the Poem," "How Not to Die"**). Among the latter, the best may be **"The Whole Mess . . . Almost,"** in which the poet tells how he threw out of his window "Truth, squealing like a fink," God, Love, Beauty, and other things which had once been important to him. Having second thoughts about Beauty, however, he ran outside in time to catch her before she hit the ground. Then he threw out Death, so that all he had left, beside Beauty, was Humor, to which he could only say, "Out the window with the window!" (*HAS*, 48-49). The dark river, at least here, was gone.

Mindfield: New & Selected Poems (1989) is largely a selection of poems from Corso's earlier books, but it also includes a section of previously unpublished poems including several written since ***Herald of the Autochthonic Spirit*** (1981). **"Poet Talking to Himself in the Mirror"** asserts again his essential role as a poet. He says he doesn't have an agent as Ginsberg and Ferlinghetti do, and he wonders if he should get one and make money but then concludes, "No way, Gregory, stay / close to the poem!!!"[29]

"Field Report," the long, rambling poem which follows **"Poet Talking to Himself in the Mirror"** and with which the volume ends, is a series of reflections and meditations in which Corso reaffirms the importance of poetry and his own position as a poet. The poem is largely discursive and very different from his early hermetic work, but there are still effective metaphors. "Old age," Corso says near the end of the poem,

> . . . comes
> like a stranger cat in the night
> purring its head against your head
> quiet old age . . .
> (*M* [*Mindfield: New & Selected Poems*], 267)

"Field Report" continues Corso's general direction since the 1960s away from the extraordinary surreal imagery for which he was first known. Nonetheless, like his earliest work, it is personal, lyrical, and deeply serious. As he insisted many years earlier, "I, as a poet, am the poetry I write." "After all," he told an interviewer, "I know what I am putting down there and why I am putting it down."[30]

And that is the way Corso's work should be read and understood. The poetics behind the poems are antithetical to any critical position which would discuss the work as separate from its creator. The poems are not confessions, but they are profoundly personal, the expression of the poet's preoccupations and sensibility. In the preface to his *Collected Poems* Ginsberg said that he arranged the volume "in straight chronological order to compose an autobiography" (*CP,* xix), and in effect that is also what Corso did in ***Mindfield.***

By its very nature, Corso's poetry denies the validity of formal critical evaluation. The reader or listener is left simply to recognize whether a correspondence exists between his or her experience and the poet's. Richard Howard found the poems plagued with "vulgarities and distractions and boastings" yet manifesting at the same time "the elements of a giant art."[31] Corso, however, would never edit out those "vulgarities and distractions and boastings," for that would suggest that there was an ideal the poet should achieve, while in fact what matters is the record of what the poet already is. To read Corso's poems is to encounter the complexity of the poet himself. "The poet and his poetry," he said, "are inseparable."[32]

Notes

1. Gregory Corso, *Gasoline/The Vestal Lady on Brattle* (San Francisco: City Lights, 1958) 4. Subsequent references are given parenthetically in the text.
2. Gregory Corso, *Long Live Man* (New York: New Directions, 1962) 89. Subsequent references are given parenthetically in the text.
3. Michael Andre, "An Interview with Gregory Corso," *Unmuzzled Ox* 22 (Winter 1981): 157; quoted in Neeli Cherkovski, *Revolutionary of the Spirit:* Gregory Corso," *Whitman's Wild Children* (Venice and San Francisco: Lapis, 1988) 191.
4. Andre, "Gregory Corso," 157; Robert King and John Little, "I'm Poor Simple Human Bones: Gregory Corso," *The Beat Vision,* ed. Arthur and Kit Knight (New York: Paragon, 1987) 172; Richard Howard, "Gregory Corso," *Alone in America: Essays on the Art of Poetry in the United States Since 1950* (New York: Antheneum, 1980) 79.
5. See Gregory Corso, "When I Was Five I Saw a Dying Indian," *Evergreen Review* 48 (August 1967) 29-30, 83-87 for his account of his childhood visionary experiences.
6. Gregory Corso, Biographical Note, *The New American Poetry,* ed. Donald Allen (New York: Grove, 1960) 430.
7. Gavin Selerie, ed., *Riverside Interviews 3: Gregory Corso* (1982) 23.
8. Quoted in Cherkovski, "*Revolutionary of the Spirit,*" 181.
9. Andre, "Gregory Corso," 127; King and Little, "Poor Simple Human Bones," 154; Gregory Stephenson, "'The Arcadian Map': Notes on the Poetry of Gregory Corso," *The Daybreak Boys: Essays on the Literature of the Beat Generation* (Carbondale and Edwardsville: Southern Illinois University Press, 1990) 76; Selerie, ed., *Riverside Interviews,* 41.
10. Corso, Biographical Note, *The New American Poetry,* ed. Allen, 430.
11. Quoted in Bruce Cook, *The Beat Generation* (New York: Scribners, 1971) 144.
12. Gregory Stephenson, *Exiled Angel: A Study of the Work of Gregory Corso* (London: Hearing Eye, 1989) 14; Gregory Corso, *The Vestal Lady on Brattle* (Cambridge, MA: Brukenfeld, 1955) 1, 25. Subsequent references to *The Vestal Lady* are given parenthetically in the text.
13. Stephenson, *Exiled,* 11.
14. Stephenson, *Exiled,* 13.
15. Conceivably Corso acquired his sense of ellipses from Ginsberg, but he could also have derived it from Surrealism.
16. Stephenson, *Exiled,* 30.
17. Arthur Rimbaud, *Complete Works,* trans. Paul Schmidt (New York: Harper and Row, 1975) 205.
18. Gregory Corso, *The Happy Birthday of Death* (New York: New Directions, 1960) 38. Subsequent references are given parenthetically in the text.
19. Andre, "Gregory Corso," 125.
20. Andre, "Gregory Corso," 132.
21. Sinclair Beiles, William Burroughs, Gregory Corso, and Brion Gysin, *Minutes to Go* (Paris: Two Cities, 1960) 63; Andre, "Gregory Corso," 132.
22. Gregory Corso, *The American Express* (Paris: Olympia, 1961) 17, 141.
23. Andre, "Gregory Corso," 128.
24. Cook, *The Beat Generation,* 147.
25. Stephenson, *Exiled,* 65.
26. Stephenson, *Exiled,* 65.

27. Gregory Corso, *Elegiac Feelings American* (New York: New Directions, 1970) 50. Subsequent references are given parenthetically in the text.

28. Gregory Corso, *Herald of the Autochthonic Spirit* (New York: New Directions, 1981) 1. Subsequent references are given parenthetically in the text.

29. Gregory Corso, *Mindfield: New & Selected Poems* (New York: Thunder's Mouth, 1989) 237. Subsequently referred to parenthetically in the text.

30. Gregory Corso, "Some of My Beginning . . . and What I Feel Right Now," *Poets on Poetry,* ed. Howard Nemerov (New York: Basic, 1966) 72; Andre, "Gregory Corso," 140.

31. Howard, "Gregory Corso," 83.

32. Andre, "Gregory Corso," 140.

MICHAEL SKAU (ESSAY DATE 1999)

SOURCE: Skau, Michael. "'The Comedy Gone Mad': Corso's Surrealism and Humor." In *"A Clown in a Grave": Complexities and Tensions in the Works of Gregory Corso,* pp. 88-99. Carbondale: Southern Illinois University Press, 1999.

In the following essay, Skau links the humorous and surrealist strains of Corso's poetry, suggesting that both are an effective way of confronting the tragic or horrific aspects of life. Though Skau acknowledges the conclusions of earlier scholars that Corso's humor often consists simply of shallow wordplay or childish sport, he concludes that the poet's comic approach reflects his ultimately optimistic views.

He was born with a gift of laughter
and a sense that the world was mad.
—Rafael Sabatini, *Scaramouche*

One of the most critically overlooked aspects of the literature of the Beat Generation writers has been their use of humor. The Beats were outspoken in their objections to what they saw as the stagnant literature prevalent at the mid-twentieth-century mark, characterizing it as academic, as literature to be studied rather than enjoyed. In contrast, the Beat writers steered toward a populist response, attempting to provide serious literature that was also entertaining. Amusing word play and comic situations are significant elements in even their most compelling works, for, as Corso has pointed out, "Man is great and mad, he was born mad and wonder of wonders the sanity of evolution knoweth not what to do" (qtd. in Gaiser 271). Corso is among the most consistent and proficient of the Beat writers in the comedic mode. His poetic voice is often puckish, as he gives conventions ironic twists, situates images in alien environments, and spins language through unfamiliar contortions. The result is an uncomfortable system of conflicts and warps that disturb the conventions of language, imagery, and perceived reality. Corso's most effective strategies involve his peculiar strain of surrealism, with its unsettling combination of humor and threat.

More than many of the other Beat poets, Corso employs surrealist departures from rational patterns. Asked by an interviewer, "Did you read Philip Lamantia? Because you've got some images which really get into surrealism," Corso replied, "Yeah, yeah, him early, and Andre Breton" (Interview with R. King 24).[1] Bill Beyle has also noted the surrealist elements in Corso's work, but demurred in that Corso's technique "is less 'spontaneous' in the manner of Kerouac or Breton than 'rapid'" (73). Breton himself, however, postulates that "I resolved to obtain from myself . . . a monologue spoken as *rapidly* as possible without any intervention on the part of the critical faculties, a monologue consequently unencumbered by the slightest inhibition and which was, as closely as possible, akin to *spoken thought*" (22-23; first emphasis added). In fact, Beyle's complaint calls to mind a humorous section from Kerouac's *The Subterraneans* in which Leo Percepied (based on Kerouac himself) confronts Yuri Gligoric (modeled on Corso) about the latter's poetic phrase "seldom nocturne": Leo complains, "I would say rather it was great if you'd written it suddenly on the spur of the moment"; Yuri protests that "it sounds like it's been planned but it wasn't, it was bang! just like you say, spontaneous vision"; and Leo concedes that "his saying 'seldom nocturne' came to him spontaneously made me suddenly respect it more" (114). In a similar vein, "Gregory said he once asked Jack if spontaneity forbade him from revising anything he wrote. According to Gregory, Jack replied, 'Well, if I want to change a word spontaneously, I do it'" (Jones 8). Both incidents wryly suggest that the quality of product is less important than the process, even though the process may not be readily identifiable in the product. On the other hand, one might also note that Corso describes his **"Writ on the Eve of My 32nd Birthday"** as *"a slow thoughtful spontaneous poem"* ([***Long Live Man,*** abbreviated] ***LL*** 92). Nevertheless, whether "spontaneous" or "rapid," terms that Corso apparently does not find equivalent, Corso's approach affords significant parallels to the works of the surrealists. Radical juxtapositions of sheer unlikelihood abound, particularly in the early volumes: "Radio belly," "Apple deaf," "Penguin dust," "Telephone snow" (**"Marriage,"** [***Happy Birthday of Death,*** abbreviated] ***HB*** 30-31); "Corduroy eggs, owl cheese, pipe butter, / Firing squad milk"

("**Food,**" *HB* 33); "Fried chairs, poached mattresses, stewed farms" ("**Food,**" *HB* 35). These images all depend upon totally unconventional or nonrational objective derangement that Corso, in the original sense of the word, appropriates. Coming as they do in lists, series, and catalogs, some are bound to be more effective than others. The reader's response is likely to be very subjective: while "Corduroy eggs" may conjure a sense of comically textural innovation, "pipe butter" may seem to be merely arcane juxtaposition.

At other times, more dramatic in his imagery, Corso energizes fantastic activity: "May 1940 stevedores lead forth a platoon of leukemia" ("**Vision of Rotterdam,**"[***Gasoline/Vestal Lady,*** abbreviated] ***G/V*** 16); "Four windmills, acquaintanceships, / were spied one morning eating tulips" ("**2 Weird Happenings,**" ***G/V*** 18); "all the trees in the vicinity went insane" (***American Express*** 186). Frequently these patterns occur in settings of violence, where Corso's wrenched situations reflect the dislocation of emotions. Thus, in the passages just cited, the first two examples occur in poems portraying the scars of the wartime era and evoke the apocalyptic terror faced by the populace, and the third example conveys the effects of war's violence on Nature. In fact, Corso often employs the surrealist image as a harshly disruptive force: he can imagine the possibility that "planets kick dust in my eyes" ("**Clown,**" ***HB*** 57), a frighteningly paranoiac vision with cosmic dimensions. He can also elaborate a conceit into disturbingly farcical but pregnant proportions:

> Together they ate a rose
> and together they dried their tongues
> upon the ashes and remaining bits of fur
>
> They loved and loved
> until their eyes fell within them
> and their faces fell away.
>
> ("**The Crime,**" ***G/V*** 76)

The threat of love to individual identity becomes alarmingly clear. The type of malevolent, surrealistic violence that Lautréamont developed in *Maldoror* fascinates Corso and repeatedly controls the dramatic action of his poems. In a temporal vendetta, he exacts revenge for a distressed childhood: "Dirty Ears / aims a knife at me . . . / I pump him full of lost watches" ("**Birthplace,**" ***G/V*** 31). In addition, he repeatedly employs a Rimbaudian symbolic violence against personifications:

> I ran to Kindness, broke into Her chamber,
> and profaned!
> with an unnamable knife I gave Her a thousand
> wounds,
> and inflicted them with filth.[2]
>
> ("**But I Do Not,**" ***G/V*** 34)

In "**Transformation & Escape,**" the narrator assaults Saint Peter in heaven after having dismembered himself. At an extreme, Corso can envision himself as a mad, transhistoric assassin:

> By the throat I smote the Age of the Reptile!
> So too the Age of the Mammal!
> So too O very much so the Ancestry of Man!
> Man descended from a walking ape!
> I awake the lazy greasy Neanderthal and spit in
> his big sad stupid eye!
> I pummel my Colt .38 into the iron skin of the
> Palaeolithic muralist!
>
> ("**Lines Written,**" [***Elegiac Feelings American,*** abbreviated] ***EF*** 28)

Antonin Artaud has ventured to explain the success of violence in art: "A violent and concentrated action is a kind of lyricism: it summons up supernatural images, a bloodstream of images, a bleeding spurt of images in the poet's head and in the spectator's as well" (82). The perverse thrill in violence leads Corso repeatedly to derive his materials from the world of the gangster, that ambiguous American hero, borrowing his language and employing him as an ominous symbol. Nonetheless, in his poetry he refrains from exploiting the sensationalism of violence: unlike Burroughs, Corso does not inflict on the reader the graphics of mutilated bodies, but instead portrays the actions as schoolboy bullying (which, of course, can have disturbing psychological effects), reduces the effects by blunting the casualties, or turns the recipients into generalizations. Corso's violence is that of the rebellious spirit, and its victims are distanced into abstractions. Thus, "**The Whole Mess . . . Almost**" catalogs the speaker's defenestration of Truth, Love, Faith, Hope, Charity, Beauty, and Death. Again, the surrealist manifestoes provide an explanatory model: Breton suggests that surrealism made

> for itself a tenet of total revolt, complete insubordination, of sabotage according to rule, and . . . expects nothing save from violence. The simplest Surrealist act consists of dashing down into the street, pistol in hand, and firing blindly, as fast as you can pull the trigger, into the crowd.
>
> (125)

In Corso's poetry, only the weapon has changed:

> Last night I drove a car
> not knowing how to drive
> not owning a car
> I drove and knocked down

people I loved
. . . went 120 through one town.
I stopped at Hedgeville
and slept in the back seat
. . . excited about my new life.[3]

("**Last Night I Drove,**" *G/V* 46)

Breton stops short of depicting specific violence and detailing the writhing pain and bloody gore, just as Corso's mayhem merely "knocked down" his victims. This is poetic violence, that of the page rather than that of the streets.

Devoid of gory details, Corso's surrealism is primarily of the humorous stamp. Seldom does a brutal image appear unrelieved by comedy, for

I've new delight—and eternally toward delight
I've a possession to assume
to bestow.

("**Greece,**" *LL* 27)

Corso's attitude toward humor is constantly ambivalent because of his perception that he is a clown straitjacketed by the inhumane brutality of the world:

I know laughter! I know lots of laughter!
Yet all I do is walk up and down hands behind back
dreaming dungeons spikes and squeaking racks.

("**Clown,**" *HB* 53)

Although he warns, "I can commemorate black laughter, too," he would that his situation were otherwise: "o there's that in me wishes each laugh / would knit an eternity of hilarity" ("**Clown,**" *HB* 54, 56). As a realist, however, he admits with frustration that human conditions obviate the possibility that such an ideal could be imminently realized. Thus, his approach is similar to the laughter that convulses into a choking fit, "a charred humor and spidered smile" ("**Written While Watching the Yankees,**" *HB* 47). Torn between the roles of jester and of indicter, a position most frequently occupied by the Juvenalian satirist, Corso's poetry usually lacks the bite associated with this satire, the complexity of which he shows himself aware: "A bee's both honey and sting" ("**Logos,**" *LL* 79). However, without the satirist's sting, his normal tone mingles humor and sadness. He has a gentle openness that undermines violence; for example, when he encounters British fog for the first time, he conjures up a stereotypical Jack the Ripper in search of one of his victims, but with a comic deflation:

So out into it I go
and ho the detective's hollow walk
Mary Dare? Art thou Mary Dare?
And banged straight into a tree
and said: Excuse me.[4]

("**Nature's,**" *LL* 49)

His good heart even compels him to entertain the position of devil's advocate: thus, he can turn atomic warfare into a delightful spectacle in "**Bomb,**" write a poem celebrating "**Power**" that Ferlinghetti would refuse to publish because he saw it as "fascistic,"[5] decline to embrace the liberal position of so many of his compatriots in endorsing Fidel Castro's revolution in "**Upon My Refusal to Herald Cuba,**" and even compose a poem whose title seems to challenge the conventional excoriation of racists—"**In Honor of Those the Negroes Are Revolting Against.**" In fact, he often seems to adopt a contrary stance simply as a way of asserting his own independence, as though merely denying affiliation with contemporary avant-garde positions is a way of carving out an identity. The complexities of life impress him with both wonder and concern. He sees himself as what he calls "The Double Axe," "Ulcerated by clown turned phantom, / Dragging behind bright colors, profound melancholy" (*LL* 71), as in his "Harlequin death-trap" ("**Paris,**" *G/V* 48) or in the funereal circus where "[f]ifty shrouded clowns pile out / from a tiny tomb," for the clown's "red nose / is antideath" ("**Clown,**" *HB* 61, 59). His humor becomes a pointed jest, a weapon, or, as he has repeatedly called it, a "butcher," for "[a]nything destroyed has got to be with humor" (Interview with M. Andre 132).[6] Corso then is the clown of the apocalypse: "That hand-grenade humor dropped down the hatch / Of an armoured suit my proposed bit come doomsday Power!" ("**Power,**" *HB* 80). He performs as a court clown, armed with a seltzer bottle of stagnant water, for his is an embittered jestership, leading Gordon Ball to suggest that Corso "may be our strongest poet who can say 'Nay!' in laughter." In "**Clown,**" he compares himself to a jester, but a wise one who is completely aware both of his place in the social structure and of human vulnerability and mortality: "My joy could never wedge free / from sorrow's old crack" (*HB* 58). Nevertheless, he realizes the value of the clown's role in alleviating, if only momentarily, the havoc and the horror of the world. Corso sees this approach as characteristic of the Beat poets:

> The new American poet is not serious, he laughs at everything, the situation is hilarious, he laughs, his poetry is pained, one senses the pain, the poet especially senses his pain, sensing it, he laughs, what more can he do.
>
> ("**Literary**" 193)

Thus, he explains in "**Bomb**" that "I am able to laugh at all things / all that I know and do not know thus to conceal my pain" (*HB*),[7] echoing

Lord Byron's sentiment: "And if I laugh at any mortal thing, / 'Tis that I may not weep" (*Don Juan*, 346). Humor becomes not merely a means of coping, but also a tactic for emotional survival, for, as his character Simon states in ***The American Express,*** "clowns know how to bring joy" (175). One of the most celebrated modern clowns, Emmett Kelly, has offered an explanation of the process involved:

> By laughing at me, they [the audiences] really laugh at themselves, and realizing that they have done this gives them a sort of spiritual second wind for going back into the battle.
>
> (126)

Thus, humor offers no tangible succor—only a fresh perspective that renews the spirit.

Corso's humanistic concerns ordinarily prevent him from indulging in meaningless frivolity, a common weakness of writers for whom humor is a frequent tool. He is careful to establish his serious intentions, despite the comedic hues of his poems: "I hoped and prayed and sought a meaning / It wasn't all frolic poesy"; on the other hand, the same poem goes on to show that the humorous elements are personally salutary: "I'd a humor save me from amateur philosophy" (**"Writ on the Steps,"** ***LL*** 77). However, occasionally Corso's use of surrealism and humor does appear to be mere diversion, an imagistic counterpart of what the Beats called "goofing"—playful, if pointless, verbal recreation. Thus, in **"Poets Hitchhiking on the Highway,"** he portrays a contest of surrealistic wits:

> Of course I tried to tell him
> but he cranked his head
> without an excuse.
> I told him the sky chases
> the sun
> And he smiled and said:
> 'What's the use.'
> I was feeling like a demon
> again
> So I said: 'But the ocean chases
> the fish.'
> This time he laughed
> and said: 'Suppose the
> strawberry were
> pushed into a mountain.'
> After that I knew the
> war was on—
> So we fought:
> He said: 'The apple-cart like a
> broomstick-angel
> snaps & splinters
> old dutch shoes.'
> I said: 'Lightning will strike the old oak
> and free the fumes!'
> He said: 'Mad street with no name.'
> I said: 'Bald killer! Bald killer! Bald killer!'
> He said, getting real mad,
> 'Firestoves! Gas! Couch!'
> I said, only smiling,
> 'I know God would turn back his head
> if I sat quietly and thought.'
> We ended by melting away,
> hating the air!
>
> (***HB*** 28)

The careless lack of variety in the repeated credit tags for the direct quotations, together with the purposeless imagistic stunting, can lead the reader to echo the speaker's companion: "What's the use?" Furthermore, Corso's dialectics suggests a complexity that can be disturbing: despite the companion's smile and laugh and the narrator's own eventual smile, the contest develops violent components independent of the actual discursive exchange. The narrator feels demonic and realizes that he is fighting in a war; his opponent gets "real mad," and the rivalry results in a displaced abstract hatred. What begins as a potential remedy for bored frustration turns into creative battle, with both combatants vying for imagistic one-upmanship in a nonrational exchange for which the surreal code seems to be mutually accepted. The status of the antagonists as poets is of little consequence: their behavior resembles children in a surreal game of king of the mountain. The struggle for dominance is as pointless as the final discontent with earthly—as opposed to verbal—existence, because the surrealistic currency has no established system of priorities, turning the contest into mutual cheating. The interchange itself is filled with threatening images and language: "chases," "pushed," "snaps," "splinters," "strike," "mad," and "killer." Dueling with words is no less aggressive than dueling with s(words), and the contest manages to climb only short rungs above the childish taunts that "your mother wears army boots" or "so is your old lady." In addition, Corso's humor sometimes gives the appearance of unintegrated jokes: "I predict Jeanne Dixon will die" (**"Field Report,"** [***Mindfield,*** abbreviated] ***M*** 260).[8] "Describe freedom / I'm not at liberty" (**"Verse,"** [***Herald of the Autochthonic Spirit,*** abbreviated] ***HA*** 25) seems to have the same throwaway quality, but, preceded as it is by the lines "I always believed freedom to be / a matter of individuality," this passage evokes the sociological dimensions of the tensions between individual freedom (no restraint) and political liberty (no unwarranted restraint); however, Corso does little to explore the conflict inherent here.

At other times, he can play games with language conventions: thus, toying with the cliché "fair and square" and the slang that equates a square with a member of the conventional or established world, he claims that a horse "won the race fair and hip" (**"At"**); similarly, reversing another cliché and playing with the physically bloated image of Kerouac late in his life, Corso indicates that his friend "poofed into fat air" (**"Columbia U,"** ***HA*** 1). In addition, catalogs of surreal juxtapositions, as occur in, for example, **"Food,"** smack of childish self-indulgence rather than creative disorder. One is reminded of W. H. Auden's advice to Frank O'Hara in a 1955 letter: "I think you . . . must watch what is always the great danger with any 'surrealistic' style, namely of confusing authentic non-logical relations which arouse wonder with accidental ones which arouse mere surprise and in the end fatigue" (qtd. in Perloff 62). The edge is a narrow one, and length is obviously a factor contributing to the level of exhaustion. Thus, the overstuffed **"Food"** turns into a belabored catalog resembling an out-of-control response to a writer's workshop exercise; the occasionally witty and surprising images are not enough to rescue the poem from its self-indulgent courses.

On the other hand, **"Bomb,"** from the same volume, switches its focus and perspective before the point of tedium is reached: imagining the explosion as a "Zeusian pandemonium," Corso creates a futuristic and time-levelling Olympic scene with transhistoric figures competing in a baseball game: "the spitball of Buddha / Christ striking out / Luther stealing third." However, rather than offering the reader Joseph Smith being walked, Mohammed getting picked off first base, the pope committing an error, and a bench full of evangelical pinch-hitters, Corso moves on erratically, refusing to go into melodramatic extra innings. The triplet of baseball lines, however, illustrates one of Corso's favorite surreal techniques: he establishes a dislocation by conflating temporal periods and then populates that new setting with similarly displaced figures. Thus, in the poem **"At the Big A,"** he imagines the Freak Stakes, a race at Aqueduct track in which the entries include Centaur, Nightmare, Winged Horse, Unicorn, Sea Horse, the Lone Ranger's Silver, and Hippo (River Horse)—and the race is won by Corso's longtime favorite "horse," heroin, "the only horse that wasn't running." Although the poem could hardly be classified among Corso's major works (it remains as of this moment uncollected in any of his volumes), it does effectively illustrate his control of the catalog technique: he keeps the field limited, declining to include Alexander the Great's Bucephalus, Robert E. Lee's Traveller, Black Beauty, Flicka, Hopalong Cassidy's Topper, Roy Rogers's Trigger, Gene Autry's Champion, *de combat,* and *d'oeuvre,* among numerous other possibilities. What he has done then is to employ poetic economy, including only as many examples as are necessary to provide variety and to provoke wonder, without indulging in the exhaustive and exhausting comprehensiveness that sometimes mars his explorations of narrowed topics, too much like the exasperating, monomaniacal enthusiasm of children.

Much of Corso's humor depends upon a childlike sense of wonder and incongruity, and as Breton asserts, "The mind which plunges into Surrealism relives with glowing excitement the best part of its childhood" (39), when transgression against adult standards and restrictions is less inexcusable. Perhaps for Corso, whose orphaned childhood was less than idyllic, surrealism offers an opportunity not only to experience that period again, but also to create a new childhood. Corso was the youngest of the prominent Beat writers, and his reckless behavior and literary eclecticism sometimes resemble the precocious teenager's exasperating testing of his family's love, with the Beats serving as a family substitute. In Corso's poetry, childhood, children, zoos, and animals offer recurrent subjects as he uses innocence of vision as both topic and technique to portray "the best part" and the worst part in disturbing surrealistic detail:

> I turned to my father
> and he ate my birthday
> I drank my milk and saw trees outrun
> themselves
> valleys outdo themselves
> and no mountain stood a chance of not walking
>
> Dessert came in the spindly hands of stepmother
> I wanted to drop fire-engines from my mouth!
> But in ran the moonlight and grabbed the
> prunes.[9]
>
> (**"This Was,"** ***G/V*** 43)

Here the child's dismal experience is rescued from the spoiled birthday and from the unpleasant climax of prunes by a pilfering manifestation of Nature. Even the loveless, oppressive conditions cannot stifle the imaginative exuberance of youthful humor. The childlike perspective also results in occasional moments of "off-color" humor, particularly in the taboo areas of sexuality and excretion.[10] Thus, in **"Open the Gate,"** his narrator, warned not to curse, "let out a big dirty word" (57); in **"Marriage"** he envisions a honeymoon night on which everyone, including hotel clerks, elevator operators, and bellboys, knows "what was going to happen" (***HB*** 30), where the reader becomes complicit in imagining the wedding night copulation that is never specified; the death-wish of "**Seaspin**" is relieved by the narrator's "sea-ghost" as he pauses to "[f]eel the mermaid up" (***HB*** 13), an adolescent male vision of sexuality that, when imposed on an imaginary figure, takes on the irrepressible satyriasis of Harpo Marx; he can imagine himself in unmarried old age, "all alone in a furnished room with pee stains on my underwear" ("**Marriage,**" ***HB*** 32); in a small Greek village, Corso's narrator and fellow drinkers in a tavern without a toilet go out in back and "all did wondrously pee" ("**Some Greek Writings,**" ***LL*** 69). Liberated from social conventions by death, projected old age, and provincial setting, he can indulge, as in dreams, childish licentiousness and unpunished violation of adult expectations.

At other times, the childlike naiveté offers a wide-eyed perception of reality, while humanity provides its own absurdity:

> The Berlin Zoo
> has two pay entrances.
> One for the West
> and one for the East.
> But after the tickets are bought
> they both join at the gate
> and stream toward the monkeys.
>
> ("**Berlin Zoo,**" ***M*** 215)

Visitors converge to watch simian antics that are hardly less ludicrous than the human behavior that splits a city and country in two or that arbitrarily separates people into geographical divisions and political factions. Similarly, a found poem creates unlikely neighbors in a "**Direction Sign in London Zoo**":

> Giant Panda
> Lions
> Humming Birds
> Ladies.
>
> ([***Selected Poems***, abbreviated] ***SP*** 51)

No reasonable person could suspect that the zoo includes women on exhibit, but the humorist's eye catches an absurdity conjuring such a comical possibility (nor is the observation sexist; the poem would work equally well if the last line were "Gentlemen").

At his best, Corso's wit and precise sense of timing function to provide materials that satisfy the classical criteria of *utile et dulce*. Focusing on his poetic role, he characterizes himself as

> devoted to Mercurio
> the greatest messenger of them all
> in Greece they know him as Hermes
> in India as Ganesha
> in Egypt as Toth
> in Israel as Moses
> in Scandia as Loki
> in the Northern reaches as the Bellosurian arrow
> in America as CBS.[11]
>
> ("**Field Report,**" ***M*** 244)

Thus, he humorously caps the catalog with a telling observation on the loss of mythic mystery and of wonder in modern times.

In "**The Whole Mess . . . Almost,**" Corso provides a model for his approach. The speaker throws out the window Truth, God, Love, and a series of other "things most important in life." Finally, he finds himself facing the last occupant of the room—Humor: "All I could do with Humor was to say: / 'Out the window with the window!'" (***HA*** 48-49). The jesting twist reveals Corso's belief that human beings, even when deprived of most of life's values and verities, still have a significant alternative to which to turn. The poem portrays and embodies this message, providing both illumination and delight. It also illustrates Corso's poetic technique. Once asked, "Why write poetry rather than prose?" he answered, "There's nothing more to say, man, now you've gotta play" and went on to explain "his preference . . . for the play theory of art" (Scully 245). The combination of the words *play* and *theory* offers clues to the strategy that he uses in his writings—and to the problems that he recognizes in his approach. He even seems to realize that some of his early work may be vulnerable to charges of comedic posturing and that maturity (a quality seldom applied to Corso by his critics) has taught him the need to make his humor pointed:

> I don't act silly any more.
> And because of it I have to hear from so-called friends:
> "You've changed. You used to be so crazy so great."
> They are not comfortable with me when I'm serious.
> Let them go to the Radio City Music Hall.
>
> ("**Writ on the Eve,**" ***LL*** 92)

Clearly, Corso believes that his humor has outgrown mere entertainment and must have a point to satisfy his poetic goals.

In a world that often seems disintegrating and destructive, Corso employs humor and surrealism in his works as ways of reducing or relieving the tensions of an oppressive age: "'It takes humor to get you through this life,' he [Corso] stated with a knowing smile" (Dossey). In such conditions, these techniques encounter the danger of becoming tainted by the very disorders they might alleviate: "The comedy gone mad! / Poor clown, the weather of sorrow" (**"Clown,"** ***HB*** 60). Corso, however, indicates that humor can serve to enhance the treatment of sociopolitical problems: "And if one must by one's need see civic social how much grander it'd be if one worked that see into a wild mad illuminating humour" (Letter to Editor, *Cambridge*). Whether challenging conventional positions (liberal or conservative), discarding accepted ideals and values, or even rejecting the gods, Corso is game for the action—a three-card monte dealer in life, a hustler with such élan that even his victims are entertained. Corso's ultimate effect is the enhancement of the values of life. He celebrates his own poetic power in terms of comedic potential: "Alive with a joy a sparkle a laugh / That drops my woe and all woe to the floor / Like a shot spy" (**"Power,"** ***HB*** 80). Breton has pointed out that true Surrealism is not an end, but a means—its aim is "*the creation of a collective myth*" through the medium of art (232). For Corso, both the myth and the medium must be allowed to frolic in their natural, humorous dimensions.

Notes

1. Lamantia (b. 1927) is an American surrealist poet.

2. The first lines of this passage parallel an early line from Rimbaud's "A Season in Hell": "One evening I pulled Beauty down on my knees. I found her embittered and I cursed her" (173). Corso used Rimbaud poems for several of his cut-ups in the *Minutes to Go* collection and refers to him in "Marriage," among other poems. Stephenson and Foster have both called attention to the influence of Rimbaud on Corso.

3. Another version of this poem appears as "Hedgeville," *Elegiac* 81. Corso discusses the multiple appearance of the poem in his interview with Andre. . . .

4. The Mary Dare line also occurs in "Of One Month's Reading of English Newspapers." The coincidence is likewise revealing of Corso's sensitivity. "Of One Month's Reading" appeared in the American avant-garde periodical *Evergreen Review* in the January/February 1962 issue; "Nature's Gentleman" first appeared in the British collection of Corso's work *Selected Poems,* published in November 1962. The *Evergreen Review* publication includes a contributor's note in which Corso asserts that he intended no offense to the English: "I love the English and really mean no meanness." With a different title, the British publication, of course, contains less possibility of offense and even turns the joke around on the narrator.

5. See also a Ferlinghetti postcard to Corso postmarked 27 September 1958 and a Ferlinghetti letter to Corso dated 5 March 1963, both held in a collection housed in the Humanities Research Center at the University of Texas at Austin. Corso responds to Ferlinghetti's objections in an undated (1957?) letter and in letters from September 1958 and October 1958 held in the Bancroft Library at the University of California at Berkeley.

6. Corso also refers to humor as a butcher earlier in the same interview on p. 124; in his interview with King on p. 6; in "Columbia U Poesy Reading—1975," *HA* 2; and in "Who I Am" 28 [in Skau, Michael. *"A Clown in a Grave": Complexities and Tensions in the Works of Gregory Corso*].

7. In a letter to *Cambridge Opinion,* Corso explains, "politics and betterment of earthly conditions is death to poetry, unless these newspaper subjects be treated with light, love and laughter, like Allen's Howl and my Bomb."

8. Jeane (not Corso's Jeanne) Dixon (1918-97) was an American prophet, psychic, and astrologer; among her many accurate predictions were the assassinations of Mahatma Gandhi and John F. Kennedy, the suicide of Marilyn Monroe, and the death in a plane crash of United Nations Secretary General Dag Hammarskjöld.

9. In the original City Lights Pocket Poets Series publication of *Gasoline,* the word *Dessert* was spelled as *Desert.*

10. On the other hand, the adolescently homophobic "White Swallow faggot bar" of "Hi" (*WW* 8) is revised as the "White Swallow bar" in a later collection (*M* 228).

11. Mercurio, Italian form of Mercury, the Roman renaming of Hermes dating from the fifth century, was the messenger of the gods. Hermes, son of Zeus, was the Greek messenger of the gods and divine herald. Ganesha, the elephant-headed Hindu god, is "the lord of beginnings" and "is assigned the role of scribe for Vyasa's dictation of the *Mahabharata* in the eighth-century interpolation to this text" (Brown 1, 3). Thoth (Corso spells his name correctly in "Columbia U Poesy Reading—1975," among other references), the ibis-headed Egyptian moon god, was the messenger and scribe of the gods. Moses, the Hebrew prophet from the Old Testament of the Bible, is a messenger in transmitting God's laws, including the Ten Commandments, to the Israelites. In Norse mythology, Loki's role as messenger is less clear, but Thor sent him to negotiate with Thrym for the return of Thor's hammer; Loki also shares with Mercury and Hermes the role of mischief-maker or trickster. CBS is the acronym for the Columbia Broadcasting System, one of America's major television networks.

Works Cited

Beyle, Bill. "Gregory Corso: Introductory Shot." *Unmuzzled Ox* 2.1-2 (1973): n. pag. Rpt. in *Unmuzzled Ox* 6.2 (#22) (Winter 1981): 73-78.

Dossey, Steve. "Gregory Corso: Another View." *Moody Street Irregulars: A Jack Kerouac Newsletter* 12 (Fall 1982): 6.

Gaiser, Carolyn. "Gregory Corso: A Poet the Beat Way." *A Casebook on the Beat.* Ed. Thomas Parkinson. New York: Crowell, 1961. 266-75.

Jones, James T. Letter to Editor [14 June 1995]. *Blue Beat Jacket* 7 (1995): 6-12.

Scully, James. "The Audience Swam for Their Lives." *Nation* 9 Mar. 1964: 244-47.

Stephenson, Gregory. "'The Arcadian Map': Notes on the Poetry of Gregory Corso." *Writers Outside the Margin: An Anthology.* Ed. Jeffrey H. Weinberg. Sudbury: Water

Row, 1986. 21-36A. Rpt. in *The Daybreak Boys: Essays on the Literature of the Beat Generation.* By Gregory Stephenson. Carbondale: Southern Illinois UP, 1990. 74-89.

———. *Exiled Angel: A Study of the Work of Gregory Corso.* Toronto: Hearing Eye, 1989.

Abbreviations

EF Elegiac Feelings American

G Gasoline

G/V Gasoline/Vestal Lady

HA Herald of the Autochthonic Spirit

HB Happy Birthday of Death

LL Long Live Man

M Mindfield

MF Mind Field

SP Selected Poems

VL Vestal Lady

WW Wings, Wands, Windows

KIRBY OLSON (ESSAY DATE 2001)

SOURCE: Olson, Kirby. "Gregory Corso: Doubting Thomist." In *Comedy after Postmodernism: Rereading Comedy from Edward Lear to Charles Willeford*, pp. 45-73. Lubbock: Texas Tech University Press, 2001.

In the following essay, Olson considers Corso's humor in the context of modernist and postmodernist philosophy. Olson maintains that Corso introduces questions into his poetry about ethics and subjectivity that resonate with the concerns of Friedrich Nietzsche and Jacques Derrida.

Gregory Corso is often thought of as a comic sidekick to the more serious Beat poet Allen Ginsberg. As the leader of the Beat movement, Ginsberg received serious critical attention, and it is no longer doubtful whether he will be included in the mainstream canon. Corso's zany work places him as a lightweight Beatnik, remembered outside the movement for his poem **"Marriage"** and inside the movement largely as a problematic character for whom the other Beats felt the burden of responsibility.[1] Corso's work has been consistently misread, even by his own close friends, who do not see the seriousness of his themes. Corso's humor questions the conceptual boundaries of what it means to be animal, human, or divine, and he rearranges these categories, creating incongruous creatures that are half-animal and half-divine and showing both the divine and the animal within the human. The reasons he does this are seemingly obvious, yet they have never been noted by any of Corso's perceptive critics. Corso grew up Catholic in an era in which that church was the under the domination of St. Thomas Aquinas and his idea of the great chain of being. Thomism was declared official church theology by Pope Leo XIII in 1879 and continues to have this status today. Aquinas had a monistic conception of the universe, in which God was one great being, possessor of all liberty, and from there, there was a declension in the powers of each category of creature from the angels, to man, to animals, to plants, to minerals. Something of this system can be seen briefly in G. K. Chesterton's description of Aquinas's interest in angels. "It was a part of that strong interest in things subordinate and semi-independent, which runs through his whole system; a hierarchy of higher and lower powers. He [St. Thomas] was interested in the problem of the Angel, as he was interested in the problem of the Man, because it was a problem; and especially because it was a problem of an intermediate creature. I do not pretend to deal here with this mysterious quality, as he conceives it to exist in that inscrutable intellectual being, who is less than God but more than Man" (Chesterton [1943] 1956, 132).

Throughout his poems, Corso takes on the difficulty of being ethically human within nature, a theme that is touched upon frequently by postmodern philosophers. But Corso seems to outstrip even them in terms of his ontological transgressions and his understanding of their ramifications thanks to his initial orientation within the Thomist system, which outlines these categories and their various faculties quite clearly, if rarely as succinctly as Chesterton. In this chapter, we will investigate the way Corso works against and within this system by focusing on his investigation of the ontological categories of animal, human, and divine and what category is permitted to eat the others.

The basic question, as Corso puts it, is, "Can we be ethical when we must eat other creatures in order to live?" If other creatures have the right to coexist with us and to be considered as subjects, and since we must eat other creatures in order to survive, is there a possibility of ethics and morality in our world? The obvious answer is no. Corso's work for several decades was to see if he could find a loophole in this pessimistic theodicy, or theological explanation of evil. Corso could find no such loophole and often lapsed as a result into an almost Gnostic nihilism, in which grace was anywhere but here on this planet. The result of Corso's investigation is that he has been ignored because his ecological suspicions do not accord with the contemporary optimism regarding the food chain as it is perceived by various pragmatic poets of the nature school.

At a midpoint in Gregory Corso's career, he began to write poems in which animals appear without humans. Completely overlooked by any of Corso's commentators thus far, yet retained by Corso in his ***Selected Poems*** (Corso 1989), the short poem **"Active Night,"** from the collection ***Long Live Man*** (Corso 1962), contains many secrets to Corso's vision:

"ACTIVE NIGHT"

A tarsier bewrays the end of an epical rain
Burying beetles ponderously lug a dead rat
A moth, just a few seconds old, tumbles down
fern
Bats are drinking flowers
The lonely tapir walks the river bottom
And up comes a manatee with a sea-anemone on
its nose.

(*Long Live Man*, 1962, 72)

In this poem, set in the Malaysian rain forest, a variety of animals return to their feeding after a long, pensive wait. A tarsier's appearance "bewrays," or prophesies, the end of the rain. The action and diction turns to New York street talk with "lugs a dead rat," as the end of the "epical" rain is reached. This ecosystem functions much like a utopian nightlife scene—every individual going about the business of pleasure—hence its title. Since groups mean the death of the individual to Corso, the two groups presented here, burying beetles and bats, are explicitly or implicitly linked to death. The burying beetles, like pallbearers, lug a dead rat to a softer place, where they will then bury it and live off the fly larvae that will develop inside its underground carcass. The bats, with images of vampires flitting through our cultural image bank, in this instance drink from flowers, a sexy image in which the bats, simply by following their natural instincts, end up all doing the same sweet thing together. Corso's initial hypothesis seems to be that if everyone just minds their own business by following their own nature, then everyone can be content within nature. But the last few lines debate this conclusion. A tapir, a smaller animal related to the rhinoceros, is walking along the river bottom feeling lonely, when he sees a manatee surface—with a sea anemone on its nose. The sea anemone, which eats small sea creatures, has apparently mistaken the manatee's nose for something to eat, and the manatee surfaces in this humorous close, an ending akin to a mousetrap on a clown's nose in a tiny circus. The tapir, we may assume, now relishes his loneliness, as his nose at least is not being chewed by someone else, so perhaps, the poem seems to say, it is better to be lonely. Corso, in a sense, denies the very possibility of community between species in the poem. Although the poem has a circus feeling, there is a bitterness at the heart of the poem, in that creatures are forced to perceive each other with suspicion.

In the above poem, Corso appears to be questioning the anarchism of the San Francisco Beat movement. For decades before the arrival of the Beat writers in San Francisco, Kenneth Rexroth and others had prepared the ground for philosophical anarchism through offering extensive lecture series. G. K. Chesterton, already at the beginning of the twentieth century, was able to write about the libertarian Herbert Spencer that "his books became sacred books for a rising generation of rather bewildered rebels, who thought we might perhaps get out of the mess if everybody did as he liked" (*The Victorian Age in Literature* [1911] 1966, 106).

Corso does not follow the libertarian program on the right, or the ecological program on the left. He interrogates them, rather, in the poem **"Active Night."** Long before this poem was written, Corso had already written against an optimistic Gaia concept of nature in his poem, **"A Pastoral Fetish,"** which appeared in his first collection of poems, ***Vestal Lady on Brattle.*** This book was the only one to have at least one poem in it written before Corso had met the other members of the so-called Beat generation (he met Ginsberg in 1950, and **"Sea Chanty"** had been written in 1945) and thus shows that his antiecological suspicions were not conceived against the other Beats, but were part of his original vision of nature and society. Poems such as **"Sea Chanty," "Song,"** and especially **"Pastoral Fetish"** are the most obvious examples of this tendency in Corso's early verses, but nearly all of the early poems touch on this same theme. As Gregory Stephenson writes in his book on Corso, "The central motif of the poems in this collection is that of a predatory devouring or destruction of innocence and beauty. This theme is first treated in the title poem of the collection where an aged woman devours a child; a vampiric, cannibalistic act that is apparently part of her daily regimen. In **'You Came Last Season,'** a lover consumes his beloved, while the poem **'Coney Island'** presents a comedian-crab and a fungi-man whose common and consuming interest is eating the feet of the bathers on the beach. The sea itself is seen as a cruel devourer in **'Sea Chanty'** in which the narrator's mother is first eaten by the sea and is then unknowingly eaten by the narrator himself. In **'Song,'** it is the 'pig's daughter' who is to be betrayed, killed, and eaten by her husband. Other predators in these poems include the mouse-eating mandrill in **'Vision Epizootic'**; the 'drooling Desirer' with his 'long greasy coat, and the bloodstained fingernails' who stalks his human prey in **'The Early Morning'** . . . and the perverse, flower-murdering Old MacDonald in **'A Pastoral Fetish'**" (1989, 11-12).

> Old Mac Donald wears clod-hoppers
> in his walk through fields of lilac and dandelion
> A storm-trooper, like a Klee twittering machine,
> he stomps:
> Crunch one lilac here; crunch another dandelion
> there,
> here, there, everywhere (he's got no mercy at all)
> crunch crunch here and a crunch crunch there
> crunch everywhere
>
> There comes a time when he's got to stop
> take off his shoes; go to bed . . .
> ah, that's when Old MacDonald's in his glory.
> Green blood and mud-caked leather he digs the
> most.
> He makes it a habit to sleep his nose by his toes
> so that all night long he could snore in the
> sticky smell
> of murdered lilac and dandelion.
> It's the old bastard's greatest kick
> (***Mindfield,*** Corso 1989, 13)

Comparing the nursery rhyme figure of Old Mac Donald to a Klee storm-trooper and calling him an old bastard subverts the innocence of the children's genre and gives the poem an adult realism, while also calling art into question through the juxtaposition of the work of Paul Klee and Nazis, as well as through the mixing children's rhymes with psycho-killers' actions. In a sense Corso is stomping on the innocence of childish rhymes and showing the bitter truth of life in a food chain, in which flowers can be murdered and nobody can say anything about it because even today plants do not have subjectivity and they are unlikely to get it before a court of law even if animals are well on their way. The fun of destroying nature is something that almost everyone has felt—stomping on beauty, pulling the wings off insects, and shooting guns at birds. It is something wired into people, who are after all predators, with teeth, hard nails, and stomachs they are forced to fill. The poem is not simply a comic work intended for laughs, however. It calls into question ontological categories of human, plant, and animal and asks us to ask again which should have rights.

The long philosophical tradition from Plato to the Church fathers through Martin Heidegger denies animals the power of rationality and speech in order to rationalize our dominance over them. Critic John Lewellyn writes of Heidegger that "his problem here is very much Kant's problem: how to understand the classical definition of man as a rational animal without implying that Dasein and the animal are species of a shared genus. The same problem surfaces in [Emmanuel] Levinas' remark 'We understand the animal, the face of an animal, in accordance with Dasein.' Levinas, Heidegger and Kant are all preoccupied, like the Stoics, with the problem of safeguarding the dignity of man" (1991, 83). Corso's perspective is mostly Catholic, but his poetic investigations stem from Darwinism, which has had an impact on virtually every domain of humanist philosophy. Humanism assumed that man does not have continuity with the animals. DNA testing has conclusively proved Darwin correct: the paternity of the human species is linked to animals. We not only are animals, but we eat them, too, which makes us cannibals.

Corso's humor consists largely of continually unmasking the foundational truth that we live in a food chain and must eat other creatures in order to live. The food chain, though never named as such, emerges in his earliest poetry from such poems as **"Song," "A Pastoral Fetish,"** and **"The Sausages,"** from ***Vestal Lady on Brattle*** (1955), inscribing the unassimilable and disturbing content of the food chain within the absurd feel-good rhymes of childhood. Within the self-cannibalizing convoy of subjects known as a "food chain," Corso relentlessly questions the possibility of a logical ethics, and the most he can achieve is an absurdist aesthetics. In the later poem **"This Was My Meal,"** from the collection ***Gasoline*** (1958), Corso writes:

> In the peas in the upside down letters of MONK
> And beside it, in the Eyestares of Wine
> I saw Olive & Blackhair
> I decided sunset to dine
>
> I cut through the cowbrain and saw Christmas
> & my birthday run hand in hand through the
> snow
> I cut deeper
> and Christmas bled to the edge of the plate
>
> I turned to my father
> and he ate my birthday
> I drank my milk and saw trees outrun
> themselves
> valleys outdo themselves
> and no mountain stood a chance of not walk-
> ing

Dessert came in the spindly hands of stepmother
I wanted to drop fire-engines from my mouth!
But in ran the moonlight and grabbed the
prunes.

(***Mindfield,*** 1989, 39)

In the upside down letters of MONK, the poem begins. If we turn MONK upside down we get the word KNOW. What is it that monks would know if their world were righted? It is that we eat. When the narrator cuts through the cowbrain he sees Christmas—not only a critique of Christianity, but of the traditional foods we eat at Christmas. Everything is busy eating in the poem, pleased with the taste of other things, and there is real fear as the father eats the child's birthday. Trees take off running, mountains run to escape the general mayhem, and, finally, even something as insubstantial and traditionally poetic as "moonlight" runs in and grabs the prunes.

Corso does not simply accept the ethical face of humanity. He would never accept the project of Heidegger and Levinas of "safeguarding the dignity of man" (Lewellyn 1991, 83). Cannibalizing other beings, something that we must do by our very nature in that there is nothing we can eat that did not first have a life of its own, seemingly undoes any morality we might claim to possess as soon as we grant spiritual being to other creatures. Morality is, Corso avers, merely a series of conventions or masks. Eating is a public secret that we must repress in order to continue the fiction of living in an ethical world.

In his novel ***American Express,*** Corso presents a scene in which a seal-trainer's seal is stolen from him at a party and cooked. The seal meat is then passed around. Very quickly, the seal disappears. The seal-trainer remains in the room, and after the orgy of consumption is accomplished, he is accused of having partaken:

"You ate it all!" Vatic accused Sgarlotto.

"Would I eat but a morsel? I could not. I too am hungry, but ate nothing. A sacrifice of the stronger need—disposed in ethics—the animal was my pet, sir"

(1961, 128).

A few pages later Corso pushes the cannibalistic theme even further. A statue of Christ is smashed, cut into small pieces, and cooked in oil. "'Carroll,' I said, 'have you ever thought of frying bits of Christ?' I had chopped off an entire foot and he watched it fry with horror in his eyes" (1961, 139).

Corso's character Mr. Plow argues that, "Man can live without food. There are ways. But these ways are held back. There are certain forces, the restaurant industry in particular, that put all their effort into keeping these ways out of man's consciousness. Farmers, cattlemen, the entire scheme of eating would crumple were the ways exposed" (***American Express,*** 1961, 133). These lines are some of the few that Corso marshals against the general slaughter of everything by everything, a wall to wall bloodbath of eating and carnage that is spread from one end of Corso's art to the other, over a period of more than forty years, from the first poem, **"Sea Chanty,"** written at the age of fifteen (Stephenson 1989, 11), to the drawing of knights slaughtering each other at the end of Corso's ***Selected Poems*** on page 265, with the title **"Life is a Battlefield."** This is Corso's unrelenting theme, which is mitigated, as Stephenson writes, by "love, humor, compassion . . . and the imagination" (1989, 19). But which is predominant in Corso's vision—the slaughter or the love? It seems to me that slaughter wins, just as it does in life, eventually, even if Corso does hold out the hope of an afterlife and with it a sense of a spirit that can rise above the food chain and act beyond the nature that is granted to animals.

In **"A Dreamed Realization,"** from ***The Happy Birthday of Death,*** Corso writes that "Back there in God creatures sat like stone / . . .— no light in their various eyes." "It was Life jabbed a spoon in their mouths. / Crow jackal hyena vulture worm woke to necessity" (1960, 49). The price of life, which is death, is also distressingly recounted in **"Food,"** in the same collection. Even if in this short section Corso abstains from eating, this abstention can only be momentary, an ethical pose permitted by a full stomach. Corso writes, "The farmer will never love me / Nor I, he. / I'd rather go hungry / Than assist his chicken slaughter, / Attend his State Fair, / Or screw his famous daughter" (1960, 33-34). In the second section, the narrator goes wild, indicating that the first half of the poem was Lent, which was only meant to play up the second half, which is Carnival.

Goose legs stream from my eyes!
I plunge my hands into apegrease!
The plate avalanches!
Baked lions, broiled camels, roasted fennecs,
Fried chairs! Poached mattresses! Stewed farms!

(***The Happy Birthday of Death,*** 1960, 35)

Corso writes often of zoos in poems such as **"Berlin Zoo," "Puma in Chapultepec Zoo,"** and **"A Difference of Zoos"** because they accentuate the captivity of animals, but Corso always implies that the metaphor is easily reversible, to show the captivity of the animal-like instincts in man. Because they help to erase the humanist line that reserves a special place for humanity, Corso shows a special affinity for those creatures that lie somewhere between man and animal, in that zone that Gilles Deleuze and Félix Guattari call in *Thousand Plateaus* "Becoming-Intense, Becoming-Animal."

"A DIFFERENCE OF ZOOS"

I went to the Hotel Broog;
And it was there I imagined myself singing Ave
    Maria
  to a bunch of hoary igneous Brownies.

. . . . .

I sang Ave Maria
  for the Heap, for Groot,
  for the Mugwump, for Thoth,
  the Centaur, Pan;
I summoned them all to my room in the Broog,
the werewolf, the vampire, Frankenstein,
every monster imaginable
And sang and sang Ave Maria—
The room got to be unbearable!
I went to the zoo
and oh thank God the simple elephant.
(***Long Live Man,*** 1962, 62)

In the final line, Corso thanks God for the comparatively simple elephant. Corso's Italian-Catholic upbringing upheld the dignity of man but, at least in the lives of certain saints such as St. Francis, also upheld the dignity of animals. This is a major source of lyric tension in Corso's work, as it contrasts so painfully with the actual nature of the world, in which one eats creatures in order to live. In the poem **"Saint Francis,"** Corso writes:

I praise you your love,
Your benediction of animals and men . . .

. . . . .

I see you with eagle,
Penguin, vulture, seagull;
Nor be it a bird
But an elephant, a herd!
All on your goodly compassionate shoulders.
(***Long Live Man,*** 1962, 36)

If we are all fragile beings placed in an immanent world, rather than immortal beings in a transcendent one, questions of morality arise with the problem of mortality. If we must treat this world with respect, since there is no possibility of an afterlife, we are yet simultaneously prevented from doing so by having to eat our neighbors: the animals and vegetables. In the poem above, St. Francis does very well with birds on his shoulders, but then Corso piles on the heavier facts of the food chain: not just one elephant, but a whole herd, and one can imagine the saint being crushed into a blood pancake.

The way out of this horrible realization that "life is a battlefield," recently, has been to grant animals subjectivity and to argue for vegetarianism. Soon, there will probably be laws passed against eating meat, just as there are laws against eating people, if this alarming trend continues. It all began innocently enough. For two millennia male European philosophers held that women possessed limited moral understanding.

Aristotle wrote in *Politics,* "For the slave has no deliberative faculty at all; the woman has, but it is without authority . . . The courage of a man is shown in commanding, of a woman in obeying" (1260a), and he cites Sophocles to the effect that "Silence is a woman's glory" (1260a). In the *Summa Theologica,* St. Thomas argues along with Aristotle that women have "a defect in the active power," perhaps coming from some "external influence, such as that of a south wind, which is moist," which preclude them from the clearer, drier reasoning necessary for moral judgment (Aquinas 1945, 880). Today such chauvinistic thinking is considered more and more antiquated, as Western democracies have accepted for at least fifty years the right of women to vote, to be educated, and to hold increasingly complex professional positions, including the presidency. Now to grant men souls, and not women, is ridiculous. But must we then grant all of nature a soul?

A paradoxical double movement is taking place in ecofeminist discourse, the contemporary French philosopher Luc Ferry says, in which women are held to be more "natural" than men, thus undermining women's right to rationality and humanity: consigning women to the precise roles that Aristotle laid out for them twenty-five hundred years ago—irrational, emotional beings whose irrationalism consigns them to certain positions outside the logos.

Luc Ferry is a contemporary Enlightenment thinker concerned with the destruction of human subjectivity among postmodernist philosophers and argues for rights among the human genus that he would deny to animal species. He argues that "To assert that women are more 'natural' than men is to deny their freedom, thus their full and whole place within humanity" (1995, 126). Without full human subjectivity, women will have the same status as animals, which Ferry argues must not be accorded the same privileges as humanity. Rights and the idea of women's subjectivity were launched by the early feminist movement, properly, Ferry believes, only to be challenged unwittingly by more recent ecofeminists who would place women back among the animals.

Should animals have the same rights as people? Ferry sees this as preposterous. The animal rights movement is now trying to extend the notion of subjectivity and rights to other mammals, and even trees, which, Ferry thinks, makes the entire idea of rights ridiculous. Which way is it going to be? Is humanity going to extend rights to animals, thus granting everything subjectivity, or will people be stripped of rationalism as well, and stripped of rights? To grant everything the right to vote would be fun, but would it mean anything to grant a worm the right to vote and hold office?

Without the ontological category of subjectivity, of a precious autonomy outside the food chain, there can be no vote granted. A worm would have to speak, as would a tree, in order to take its place in the legislature. Humanity, and nowhere more so than in the Thomist tradition, has always found reason to be that which sets it apart from the animals. To again quote Chesterton from his intellectual biography of St. Thomas, "To be brief, in all humility, I do not believe that God meant Man to exercise only that peculiar, uplifted and abstracted sort of intellect which you are so fortunate to possess: but I believe that there is a middle field of facts, which are given by the senses to be the subject of the reason; and that in that field the reason has a right to rule, as the representative of God in Man. It is true that all this is lower than the angels; but it is higher than the animals, and all the actual material objects Man finds around him" ([1943] 1956, 22). The decisions we make over rights for each category of creature, the contemporary philosopher Luc Ferry asserts, are not whimsical philosophical debate but will affect the legal realm and the way every category of life is treated in the future. What counts as food, and what is exempt from being eaten? What will be treated as object, and what will be treated as subject?

Christopher D. Stone's landmark article, "Should Trees Have Standing? Towards Legal Rights for Natural Objects," appeared in 1972 in the *Southern California Law Review* and was later reprinted as an influential short book (cited in Ferry 1995, xvi). Although the notion of radical democracy for all beings continues to spread, Corso is working in the other direction, a direction of many postmodern scholars, in arguing that humankind does not possess rationality and in fact is merely animal. Corso has gone further than any of the postmodern philosophers in asserting the animality of people and thus seems to implicitly accept cannibalism, as he does from his earliest poetry on forward, but there is in this acceptance the kind of moral teasing that Corso is always carrying out, a teasing that awakens uncomfortable questions of ontology. Corso sometimes seems to argue that if animals do not have subjectivity, then neither does man. Meanwhile, animal rights activists assert that "all animals are born equal and have equal rights to exist" (quoted in Luc Ferry 1995, 3).

The philosopher Luc Ferry sees this spreading of ontological subjectivity as a continuation of the French Revolution of 1789 (1995, 3), a spreading of a radical democracy that he thinks must be curtailed, if it is not to end in nonsense. "Law is always for men, and it is for men that trees or whales can become objects of a form of respect tied to legislation—not the reverse . . . the most common response among [ecological] fundamentalists is that it is the 'biosphere' as a whole, because it gives life to all beings, or at the very least allows them to sustain their existence. But the biosphere gives life both to the AIDS virus and to the baby seal, to the plague and to cholera, to the forest and to the river. Can one seriously claim that HIV is a subject of law, equal to man?" (1995, 139-140)

Ferry asserts that humanity has greater freedom than animals, and this makes us separate and special, above the general slaughter. Animal cultures, he says, persist over thousands of years without any change. Human cultures are constantly changing, constantly evolving, and thus we have a freedom that distinguishes us from animals. "For unlike an animal, which is subject to the natural code of instinct particular to its species more than to its individuality, human beings have the possibility of emancipating themselves, even of revolting against their own nature. It is by so doing, that is, by breaking away from the order of things, that one gives proof of an authentic humanity and simultaneously accesses the realm of ethics and culture" (1995, 115).

Is Ferry's argument more than simple conservativism, a hope to keep things as they are? If nobody has rights, then the world is a free-for-all in which murder is as legitimate as negotiation. If everything has rights, then to step on a flower inadvertently would mean that one could be charged with murder. Is there a balance that we could strike between these two extremes?

Ferry wants us to see that human beings have the gift of being able to think over a certain period of time, outside of instinct, outside of natural needs, which allows us to create a culture, a legal realm, thanks to the length of our memories (a pigeon, by comparison, has a memory of approximately twelve seconds).[2] This and speech allow us to think and communicate important moral concepts that other animals cannot access.

It is Gregory Corso's cynical laughter over this so-called separation of man and animals that led him to write, during the first hours after President John F. Kennedy's assassination, a poem in praise of the animalistic aspects of man. Corso, in the first part of this poem, sees murder as legitimate, as a part of a long tradition going back to Rome, back through the animal species, back to the very beginning of life. Corso does not see anything "emancipating" in man that is essentially worth preserving. He sees no ethics because there is no such thing as an "authentic humanity," and he sees no culture. The radiant moments of mankind are dimmed by its blacker moments, which are part of our legacy in a natural world. This does not mean he is happy about it: it is devastating to him, even if it is also funny:

> Come you illiterate creepy dumbbells harken the cry of
> the true Assassin
> I damn! I hail!
> I summon the Blessed Lord of the Ice Cold Nanook
> Country and eat raw seal meat with Him!
> I curse the earth in Space and in Time!
> I pee upon the evolution of the Rocks!
> I weep upon the first living things!
> Bang my fists on the unknown age of the world!
> I vomit up Natural Selection and the change of the
> Species!
> I laugh like a sick dinosaur o'er
> the invasion of the dry lands by Life!
> I smirk at the butterfly like a pimply-faced stumble-bum!
> By the wings I yank by the wings the wings the lovely
> wings
> By the throat I smote the Age of the Reptile!
> So too the Age of the Mammal!
> So too O very much so the Ancestry of Man!
> Man descended from a walking ape!
> I awake the lazy greasy Neanderthal and spit in his big sad
> stupid eye!
> I pummel my Colt .38 into the iron skin of the Paleolithic
> muralist!
> I look contemptuously down upon the screwed-up
> Neolithic creep!
> (from **"Lines Written Nov. 22, 23, 1963—in Discord,"** ***Mindfield,*** 1989, 141)

Corso sees the good in man, the democratic, freedom-loving part, as being hopelessly eclipsed by a demonic animalistic agency that has made its way into every living thing. "I have made goats of every King every Pope every puny club-footed Elect" (***Mindfield,*** 1989, 141). Corso sees even God himself as being merely an animal or as having animal faculties in the poem **"God is a Masturbator"** (***Elegiac Feelings American,*** 1970, 112). There is nothing that is not immanent and nothing that is not damned, fatally flawed, and utterly animalistic to the core, Corso implies, yet at the end of the poem Corso contradicts this perception and writes:

> When the captain dies
> The ship doesn't sink
> (***Elegiac Feelings American,*** 1970, 30)

Corso is not willing to accept the human dignity of the face; yet he has been unwilling to dispense with all spiritual traditions and regard man as a vicious and unredeemable animal, as the end of the above poem shows. Cultural institutions outlast single individuals and provide a kind of stability to humanity, a stability that animals attain through their unchanging qualities.

Whereas Levinas, Heidegger, and Kant are preoccupied with "safeguarding the dignity of man" (Lewellyn 1991, 83), Corso increasingly questions the face of this civilized, alienated man and posits a lurking rapist who rapes and murders innocent schoolgirls, yet he is never comfortable simply condemning humankind. "The kind man behind the kind man / Is the kind of man who could and can" (***Elegiac Feelings American,*** 1970, 77), Corso writes about British sexual psycho-killers. As Corso distances himself from his early Catholicism,[3] his writing grows darker, he turns to heroin and drink, and his output diminishes at the same time that he begins to explore Gnostic and other heresies and to develop a Manichean world view. St. Thomas's entire theology was built on defeating the Manichean heresies by proclaiming that all of creation was divine and that Satan, who had been created by God, was the originator of evil. Corso gradually fell away from this world view and began to see evil as an aspect of the world that could never be gotten rid of. The central problem for him lay in eating. If we eat other creatures, then this entire world has to be evil.

From 1958 to 1962, Corso produced three ebullient volumes. Corso says in his interview in *The Beat Vision* that he began to take drugs at the age of thirty-three, which would have been in 1963 (Knight and Knight 1987, 179). Did Corso begin to take drugs in response to the Kennedy assassination, which threw him into discord, or was his moral disarray already in effect when the assassin(s) destroyed the first Catholic president? After this year, there have been only two complete volumes, and these later poems (when they are successful, such as **"On One Month's Reading of English Newspapers"** on rape quoted just above) are even more bitter because the qualifying aspect of humor is often muted or even extinguished.

Corso cannot find a transcendent truth, but he cannot find the actual world to his taste either, as long as there remains the "drudgery and insult of food" (***American Express,*** 1961, 104). Unlike the more popular American ecopoets such as the Luddite Wendell Berry or Zen naturalist Gary Snyder, who are busy finding delicious truths that we can live with and then pointing the way, Corso finds despicable truths that he cannot live with and reveals his fruitless attempts at ethical reconciliation.

Corso is treated with concern by Gary Snyder in an interview in the collection *The Beat Vision,* where Snyder suggests a confrontation with Corso because Corso does not share the consensus vision that the Beats, Snyder says, were coming toward in the seventies. "It's very interesting that we find ourselves so much on the same ground again, after having explored divergent paths; and find ourselves united on this position of powerful environmental concern, critique of the future of the industrial state, and an essentially shared poetics, and only half-stated but in the background very powerfully there, a basic agreement on some Buddhist type psychological views of human nature and human possibilities" (*The Beat Vision,* Knight and Knight 1987, 3-4).

Corso does not fit into any of this—denying religion, denying a critique of anything—he writes down what he sees, and is not a social reformer at all. "In some ways I'm a good Maoist," Snyder says (Knight and Knight 1987, 15), echoing the Maoist program of a cultural revolution that was popular at the time (1974). Corso is not with the program at all, and Snyder considers him to be a problem. "I haven't really tried to deal with where Gregory's at; but he's had a lot of self-created hard times . . . But we're all responsible collectively in some sense for Gregory, so what I would like to do is all of us (Lawrence, myself, and Allen and so forth) sit down and have a collective meeting with Gregory. That's what I'm going to suggest, too. I've learned how to do that where I live. Collective meetings of mutual and personal self-criticism" (Knight and Knight 1987, 24-25). Snyder's Maoist-inspired program of "mutual and personal self-criticism" would indicate that unless Corso was willing to get with the program, he would be excommunicated, or worse. Snyder actually suggests violence to one of the interviewers who is having a hard time understanding one of his friends who has adopted an Eastern viewpoint. "I'd kick the fuck out of him, that's all," Snyder says (Knight and Knight 1987, 27). And then he says, blandly, "Say, 'Make sense, you son of a bitch.' That's what I do with people" (Knight and Knight 1987, 27). Such truculence, even when presented in a jocular manner, overrides the delicate problem of understanding Corso on his own terms, rather than forcing him to make sense on Snyder's terms.

Corso's thinking undoes the Buddhist ecologist's insistence that nature make sense. But does the food chain make sense? Can it be understood? Should Corso be stomped for this? Can Corso be forced to make sense on Snyder's Buddhist ecological grounds, in which Snyder wants to write about nature without including any of nature's terror, its nightmarish aspect in which creatures die without dignity in the maws of others? In which predators race through the jungles killing things for nutrition? If Snyder were asked (by a group of writers sympathetic to Corso) to make more sense on Corso's terms, he might find it difficult to speak as well.

Corso shares a similar problem with postmodern philosophers and Gary Snyder. He questions the special place accorded man in Western philosophy's arrogant relationship to the natural world, but Corso came from a world of gangs, prisons, and hard beatings as he grew up in the Italian-American section of New York City. He does not have the kind of privileged background Gary Snyder, Allen Ginsberg, or most other members of the cultural elite took for granted in their childhood, and thus they can perhaps more easily idealize the world. Jacques Derrida, the well-to-do French postmodernist, in his interview "Eating Well," says, "one must begin to identify with the other, who is to be assimilated, interiorized, understood ideally . . . The sublime refinement involved in this respect for the other is also a way of 'Eating well,' in the sense of good eating but also doing well to eat" (1991, 115). This project of "respect for the other" whom we must eat has been left out of Western civilization since Plato said that animals were outside of the realm of Being, unworthy of respect because they could not speak. Derrida asserts that we ought to at least have respect for the animals we devour and say as much, as if that would somehow matter to them. Corso distrusts all speech and points out "Everything that is said is said by man—I say it is stupid, disgusting, to listen!" (***American Express,*** 1961, 43).

In an interview with Jean-Luc Nancy, Jacques Derrida, too, questions the artificial boundary between man and animal. He extends subjectivity as far as the vegetable realm, but my question is whether this matters, since we are still eating them. Should a vegetable say, "Thanks for the rights, Jacques," as it is being spread over his steak tartar in thin slices to make a tasty accompaniment?

> "J.-L. N.: When you decide not to limit a potential "subjectivity" to man, why do you then limit yourself simply to the animal?
>
> J. D.: Nothing should be excluded . . . The difference between 'animal' and 'vegetal' also remains problematic"
>
> (Nancy 1988, 106).

Corso sometimes looks half-heartedly to the American Indian for a philosophical answer to the dilemma, but only for laughs. The American Indians considered humans to be members of the same family as animals, making no crucial distinction between man and animal, even though they ate their brothers willingly. Does it matter if we treat animals and vegetables as brothers and sisters as long as we are still eating them, or does that just augment the horror? Can we return to that early table the Pilgrims were offered by the Indians and not have any moral compunctions? Gregory Corso describes the collision of cultures in the Massachusetts Bay colony in his **"Spontaneous Requiem for the American Indian"**: "Pilgrim blunderbuss, buckles, high hat, Dutch, English, pat- / ent leather shoes, Bible, pray . . . o but feast, turkey, corn, pumpkin, sweet confused happy hosty guests, Iroquois, Mohawk, Oneida, Onondaga, Thanksgiving!" (***Elegiac Feelings American,*** 1970, 16). Can we make friends with the beings that we eat? After all, their brothers and sisters (termites, worms, etc.) in turn will eat us when we die. Corso opened this question and was aware of its difficulty some years before the major postmodern thinkers began dodging the question. In contrast to the easy righteousness of the ecological movement, which shares the apparently common American Indian belief that animals willingly gave up their lives to be food for humans, it is obvious that humans are the narrators in this picture.

How it is that ecological fundamentalists and their Native American counterparts can eat things they consider to be human, or at least on the same level as themselves, is a puzzle. Animals are not saints. They eat whatever they can, without apparent attacks of conscience. Meanwhile, they try to protect their own skins. No human would willingly feed an animal with his or her own body, so it seems rather arrogant to assume that an animal would want to feed us. Berry bushes have spikes all over them to protect their fruit, so apparently even they do not willingly give up their fruit.

Corso depicts man as a member of an obscene and comical animal world and presents another aspect of Indians in **"Spontaneous Requiem for the American Indian."** At the end of the poem an Indian on a motorcycle screams into New York to sit at Horn & Hardart's with Western women, and Corso writes "O, he's an angel there / though sinister sinister in shape of Steel Discipline smoking / a cigarette in a fishy corner in the night" (***Mindfield,*** 1989, 139). Corso does not buy the idea of Indians as angels of perfect ecological insight. After all, they too slaughtered the buffalo, as well as each other, before whites came, and when they came, they burned the white settlers, scalped them, and torched their houses. "Dust, hordes, tribes, death, death, blonde girls to die, gowns / of ladies to burn, men of redcoats and bluecoats to / die, boys to drum and fife and curse and cry and die, / horses . . . to die, babies . . . to die," (1989, 139) in the miserable "battlefield of life" (1989, 265). Corso, always questioning categories, does not buy the saintliness of Indians, but insists in his poetry on showing their sinister side. They were beaten by superior technology, and Corso is sometimes sentimental about it, but more often simply realistic, just as Indian tribes before whites came slaughtered one another, and held each other as slaves and were not exactly sorry about it. The following conversation took place in the interview with Michael André:

> [*André*]: *One of the questions I was going to ask you was about your elegy for the Indians. You were interested in the same thing, that say, Gary Snyder and Allen [Ginsberg] are interested in.*
>
> [Corso]: Yes.
>
> [*André*]: *But you handle it in a completely different way. You just elegize them and describe them today, rather than attempt to revivify their whole value system.*
>
> [Corso]: Yes. Now there you go. I wrote that Indian thing very early, in 1958. That was not done when the Indians started, you know—the opening up with the Blacks and civil rights. The feeling was the loss and I still feel that today. Of course they didn't build the nation, but the land that they did have and the life they did have is gone. There are

> the hippies and the new Indians, but it will never be the same, it's changed. I look upon it as a stain . . . There is nothing I could do for the Indians before they went, although there are nine million Indians today, they say, the same as there was when the white man first came to this country.
>
> [*André*]: *Really?*
>
> [Corso]: Less buffalo, of course, but the same number of Indians. The genocide wasn't exactly genocide. It was the genocide of taking their land. (André 1981, 129-130)

At least one place in the interview Corso dismisses the Indian way of life as something as worthy of study as Mediterranean culture:

> [*André*]: *In many ways there is as much left to study in the American Indian civilization as in Greek civilization.*
>
> [Corso]: Oh, not in architecture, anyway, except the pueblo. I would think the Indians had a better way of life, but. . . . The Greeks could have had technology. The Renaissance picked up on that, through the Byzantine; Giotto learned the two dimensional Christ from the Byzantine. (André 1981, 154)

Corso's dismissal of Indians on account of their having no architecture does not take into account that many Native Americans were nomads and had no settled domiciles or lived in small settlements, not in large cities. This does not make sense, yet to look to American Indians for answers to the problems of a settled society, which does live in cities, especially when those answers are now proposed by anthropologists and nature poets who work in universities within a Western tradition, also does not make sense. Can answers come from other paradigms without destroying the paradigm of Western culture? The Western world was superior to the Indian world in at least one area—martial ability. Just as the Iroquois Indians were superior to the Delaware and used that advantage to make the Delaware warriors lay down their arms and take the names of women (Parkman [1908] 1944, 10-17), so the Western Europeans destroyed Native American cultures and made them lay down their weapons.

Now the West is about to be conquered by Native American ontology, since many have complained that Western ontology is inadequate. The Western viewpoint saw the world as composed of things, with humans alone having a soul, whereas the Indians lived in an immanent world where everything, even trees and animals and tools, had subjectivity, and thus could not be used without some sense of respect. But how does one eat something respectfully? If someone were to eat me, I would not care if they did it respectfully. What would it matter? If a mosquito were to say a short prayer while taking blood out of my foot, it would just make me more irritated. Thanks to the ecology movement, Western civilization is going back to this notion that everything is imbued with a spirit. But for what good reason?

We invite each other out to dinner, celebrate good times over food, and go happily to the grocery store, but we are rarely conscious that we are eating other beings. Would it be a better thing if we were to realize it? We can recognize and empathize with animals' sufferings, and we can even find some signs of sentience in plants, but our lives are based on their exploitation. As the animal rights movement declares that all living beings are created equal, Corso's poetry will be increasingly relevant to describing and understanding the ethical dilemma that we face.

The spiritual diaspora accepted in the Western tradition beginning in Plato and continuing with the Gnostic theologians, in which man is trapped here in an alien body and on an alien planet, was an initial answer to the question of evil. They concluded there is evil on this earth because this is *not paradise*. Paradise was in heaven. Early theologians sought to remove the animal aspects of man in order to recreate heaven on earth and prepare us to go to heaven. Gregory Corso's comic poetry, by bringing the violent animal nature of man back into the center of the *polis,* opens up an ontological conduit that goes both ways. It challenges the dignity of man. Not only does "humanity" flow into animals, but "animality" flows into humanity.

Corso's Western orientation seems at first to be irreligious. He appears to only accept facts, the factual nature of the world, and sees the world as a machine, engineered for comfort. He appears to have much in common with postmodernist Gilles Deleuze, who writes, "What is required is humor, as opposed to the Socratic irony or to the technique of the ascent" (*The Logic of Sense,* 1990, 135). "Deeper than any other ground is the surface and the skin . . . The tragic and the ironic give way to a new value, that of humor. For if irony is the co-extensiveness of being with the individual, or of the I with representation, humor is the co-extensiveness of sense with nonsense" (Deleuze 1990, 141). Deleuze concludes, "The values of humor are distinguished from those of [Socratic] irony: humor is the art of surfaces and the complex relations between the two surfaces" (1990, 248). Corso's humorous writing is ahead of its time in America because it takes up the Ni-

ABOUT THE AUTHOR

PATTI SMITH ON CORSO'S PASSING

He has left us two legacies: a body of work that will endure for its beauty, discipline, and influential energy, and his human qualities. He was part Pete Rose, part Percy Bysshe Shelley. He could be explosively rebellious, belligerent, and testing, yet in turn, boyishly pure, humble, and compassionate. He was always willing to say he was sorry, share his knowledge, and was open to learn.

Smith, Patti. "Gregory Corso: 1930-2001." *Village Voice* (24-30 January 2001): 75ff.

etzschean problem of a world without transcendent values, but he does not just stop there and accept it.

Without some standard that stands outside the whole system, there is no objective way to judge good and evil and thus no reason to feel guilt, which Nietzsche saw as a leftover of the priestly mentality. From a purely animalistic viewpoint, ethics makes no sense. To inform a tiger that he should not have destroyed a deer would be wasted effort. Nietzsche thought the same should go for humans. Nietzsche writes against morality throughout his work as a tool of the priestly caste who "concentrated their effort on arousing moral and religious responses, and the moral norm was vicariously invoked where by rights a powerful aesthetic magic should have transported the listeners" (*The Birth of Tragedy,* 1956, 134-135).

Nietzsche laughs explicitly at the "vegetarian absurdity," which had already swept Europe in his day, as a ramification of the growing guilt over the subjectivity of formerly objectified animals (1956, 267). The face of man, in Levinas's and Heidegger's sense, is for Corso merely a mask whose sole function is to hide his animal nature from himself. In his deconstruction of human subjectivity, Corso closely parallels recent trends in French postmodern thought, but he goes further. What is needed is a reevaluation of Corso's poetry within the light of his anticipation and taking of these developments in French postmodernism to their furthest extreme. Aside from a few in-group appreciations from the likes of fellow Beats Ginsberg, Kerouac, and Burroughs,[4] Corso's writing has received scant critical attention, much of which has been negative, and almost all of it has misunderstood or skimmed over Corso's intentions.

Until recently, Corso has not fit into any of the reigning critical paradigms. His impiety has gotten him rejected from serious consideration. Yet at least a decade before Derrida and Deleuze, Corso interrogated all the transcendent economies of being and found the exits blocked. The important puzzle of the ethics of eating has yet to be satisfactorily addressed by either the ecological movement or postmodern philosophy. If we are neighbors and not ontologically superior to the creatures we eat, the idea of ethics goes out the window when we are eating, and we must eat every day or die. Corso's paradoxical poetry deals with this notion in a manner more profound and more vivid than anything yet written by Deleuze or Derrida. Corso knocked out the absurdity of an eternal God, universal judgment, and impartial ethics years before postmodernism, but what are we left with? Mere cannibalism, without justification!

For Corso it has meant that all of his early hopes for an ethical aesthetic reaction to the natural world were broken; his hopes as a utopian philosopher were dashed at the same time he was reborn as a no longer ebullient poet, but a tougher and a more realistic poet just the same. Corso's thinking led him to poetry, which is where he remained. Friedrich Nietzsche, the godfather of postmodernism, shows that art takes over where logic and science can go no further. Nietzsche writes, "Every noble and gifted man has, before reaching the mid-point of his career, come up against some part of the [scientific] periphery that defied his understanding, quite apart from the fact that we have no way of knowing how the area of the circle is ever to be fully charted. When the inquirer, having pushed to the circumference, realizes how logic in that place curls about itself and bites its own tail, he is struck with a new kind of perception, which requires, to make it tolerable, the remedy of art" (*Birth of Tragedy,* 1956, 95).

In the aporia between the need for eating and respect for the other "logic curls about itself and bites its own tail." It is right here that Corso's art is centered. In the heart of immanence lies Corso's crowning curse: if humanity is animal and has no transcendent soul, is ethics, then, just for laughs? Surprisingly, Corso would say no. Because animals do not have imagination they thus cannot change things, and they do not have agency in Luc Ferry's sense, but humans do, and this gives us the imperative to act ethically. Corso's final response is somewhat similar to Nietzsche's. Nietzsche transformed himself into a deity—Dionysus. Corso transformed himself into yet another deity, a poet, which in many places he links to the deification that the Romantics accorded to the poet. In order to be personally transcendent and to thus stand apart from the general battleground of life, Nietzsche and Corso both opted for the pose of a magical being. In one of Corso's final poems in his ***Selected Poems*** he writes:

"FIRE REPORT—NO ALARM"

And that I did not adhere
  to any man's God
neither a comprehensible
  Absolute
nor the inexplicable
  unseen breath
    of Omnipotent power
—that I did indeed feel
    the awesome lack
that in Heirophantic
    ardour
      is awesomely contained
and not fall to
  my knees
    in abject piety
or even for a failing
  moment
give in
  to the warmth
  and secure
of God-embracement
—that I did not adhere
  to arcane trinities
or bow to lettered
  ambiguity
so that my soul
  be stencilled
  in wanton faith
—that I stood
  amongst the brethren
and aided the old
  and poor
as well the young
all for whom I
    did open the door
like an act of Jesus
Such be my metaphor
who with autochthonal
    spirit
stands before the
    universe alone
God-free
    father of my children
and upon my finger
    the ring of poetry—
(***Mindfield,*** 1989, 234-235)

This would indicate that Corso was not willing to dispense with beauty, love, and chivalry simply because the soul is not necessarily transcendent. For this reason, Corso was not simply triumphant concerning the white destruction of Indian cultures and considered it to be a stain upon the American conscience. He was contrasting Native American culture with classical Greek culture when he dismissed the former, not with contemporary American culture, for which Corso shared the general Beat dislike. Corso's implicit argument is that classical civilization held superiority over both Native American and European society in America. Corso saw that, in the variable scale of things, the Indians might have had some things to offer, but apparently he never studied them the way that Gary Snyder and others in the Beat movement have done, because he thought the greater beauty was in classical culture.

Corso's lineage goes back to the Romantic poets. He was given a copy of Percy Shelley's verses while in prison, and it was one of the most important "books of illumination" that the "angels of Clinton Prison" handed to him in his "17th year" (dedication page to ***Gasoline***). Corso's role of the poet was probably defined by Shelley in such poems as "Hymn to Intellectual Beauty," in which Shelley claimed to have pledged allegiance to this spirit.

I vowed that I would dedicate my powers
  To thee and thine—have I not kept the vow?
. . . . .
  Thus let thy power, which like the truth
  Of nature on my passive youth
Descended, to my onward life supply
  Its calm, to one who worships thee
  And every form containing thee,
Who, SPIRIT fair, thy spells did bind
To fear himself, and love all human kind.
(cited in Perkins 1967, 971)

Corso's vocation as a poet was probably formulated in lines such as those, in which Shelley saw the poet as someone who had dedicated himself to the spirit of intellectual beauty, to receiving this message from a Platonic world above and beyond this one and relaying this truth to others in an attempt to spread justice and loveliness in contemporary human affairs. Shelley wrote in the preface to "Prometheus Unbound" that morality was a part of poetry. "We owe the great writers of the golden age of our literature to that fervid awakening of the public mind which shook to dust the oldest and most oppressive form of the Christian religion. We owe Milton to the progress and development of the same spirit: the sacred Milton was, let it ever be remembered, a republican, and a bold inquirer into morals and religion. The great writers of our own age are, we have reason to suppose, the companions and forerunners of some unimagined change in our social condition or the opinions that cement it. The cloud of mind is discharging its collected lightning, and the equilibrium between institutions and opinions is now restoring, or is about to be restored" (cited in Perkins 1967, 982). Corso probably took seriously this calling in his youth, this calling to be the one to listen to the divine and translate it into human terms, yet he often parodied it as well. Shelley, who was an atheist, had discovered in poetry some last vestige of the divine. To this extent, ontological hierarchies are reconstructed in that the poet has a "higher calling" than other humans. In the poem "**Sunrise**," Corso writes a rather irreverent version of this mission.

> I sat on the toilet of an old forgotten god
> and divined a message thereon
> I bring it to you
>   in cupped hands
>
> (***Herald***, 1981, 6)

Corso's intentional parody of the messenger-spirit motif comes just after his fresh minting of the image of an eternal relay and recalls Mikhail Bakhtin's work on the comic literature of the Middle Ages. "Here, as in Rome, the tendency was towards a laughing double for every serious form. We recall the role of medieval clowns, those professional creators of the 'second level,' who with the doubling effect of their laughter insured the wholeness of the serio-laughing word. We recall all the different kinds of comic intermedia and entr'actes that played a role in the 'fourth drama' of Greece and in the cheerful exodium of Rome" (*Dialogic Imagination,* 1981, 79).

Corso's implicit argument, which wavers but often comes back quite strong, is that we can still have faith in ourselves and in our imaginations. It is our imagination that created God. Therefore, we can act with the magnanimity of God. St. Thomas had accorded to all of nature the role of being an aspect of God's creation. In Umberto Eco's *The Aesthetics of St. Thomas,* Eco writes, "For the medievals, the fact that goodness was a transcendental meant that there could be nothing evil in being—not, that is, in the metaphysical sense. In the same way, defining beauty as a transcendental implied the elimination of the seeming deformities and dissonances in the universe. Such an enterprise involved a kind of ardor and an aesthetic optimism which, on its own theoretical level, reflected the sentiments of St. Francis' *Cantico della creature*" ([1956] 1988, 22). Similarly, Eco writes of a group of Franciscans, "The authors of the Summa Fratris Alexandri were like their contemporaries in wanting to show that even monsters were beautiful, in that they are beings, because every being is beautiful and God creates nothing that is not beautiful" ([1956] 1988, 44). Corso is a long way from seeing everything as beautiful in his later work, which is probably one reason why there is so little of it. Nevertheless, in Corso's later God-free logic, he seems to come to a new position. If we can imagine a decent thing, then we can do it. Against nature and nature's darkest inclinations, Corso posits the classical humanist spirit of humor and imagination and love. As he turns toward a world of divine powers, his humor is somewhat eclipsed, and a very serious and different kind of poet steps forth, but Corso just as often "gooses" this more serious poet. Corso's poetry is based on an exploded Thomism, which retains some of the Catholics' incredible optimism about the universe, while God, angels, men, and animals fly through his poems with dizzying interchangeability. Corso's comedy, such as it is, is very close to tragedy and leads him toward an extremely powerful and often moving lyricism. He is perhaps the greatest surviving poet of a tradition that began with St. Francis's canticles, St. Thomas's philosophy, and Dante's epic poetry. Corso's work might best be described as that of a doubting Thomist: his doubts and his Thomism being intertwined in a stunning vision that is perhaps, thanks to its often comic character, the most unjustly neglected poetry in American literature.

Notes

1. During a gathering of the Beats in Grand Forks, South Dakota in 1974, Corso is described by Allen Ginsberg rather disparagingly as "the last Beatnik" (Knight and Knight 1987, 7), and Gary Snyder describes Corso as a "casualty" (Knight and Knight 1987, 23), along with Lew Welch and Jack Kerouac, as if Corso, too, had died, even though he was there at the conference! Corso is still living twenty-five years after this comment by Snyder, but Snyder's remark shows that Corso's life and poetics were quite different from that of other members of the Beats. Snyder says of the Beats, "We weren't high school dropouts. We were graduate school drop-outs—all of us" (Knight and Knight 1987, 9). Again this would exclude Corso, who audited some undergraduate classes at Harvard, but never even attended high school. He spent much of his teenage years in prisons and homes for wayward youth. He left school after the sixth grade.

2. According to D. F. Kendrick, noted animal memory researcher, Middle Tennessee State University, <http://www.mtsu.edu/~pyskip/ltlec13.htm>.

3. Corso does still offer optimistic lyric efforts into the 1970s and 1980s, but the poems seem to depend on human magic rather than on a vision of nature as being wonderful all by itself. See "Sunrise" (*Mindfield,*

1989, 166), in which Corso depicts the poet as Hermes, or "Alchemy" (*Mindfield,* 1989, 202), in which Corso sees nature herself as an alchemist, uniting a Franciscan view of nature with his later more magic-oriented vision:

ALCHEMY

A bluebird alights upon a yellow chair
—Spring is here

4. A summary of some of the more important Corso criticism is offered in Gregory Stephenson's *Exiled Angel: A Study of the Work of Gregory Corso* (Stephenson 1989, 97). A more extensive bibliography is available in Michael Skau's *Clown in a Grave: The Poetry of Gregory Corso* (Carbondale: Southern Illinois University Press, 1999).

Bibliography

André, Michael. "An Interview with Gregory Corso." *Unmuzzled Ox* 22 (Winter 1981): 123-158.

Aquinas, Thomas. *The Basic Writing of St. Thomas Aquinas,* edited by Anton C. Pergis. Vol. 1. New York: English Dominican Press, 1945.

Chesterton, G. K. *St. Thomas Aquinas.* 1943. Reprint, London: Hodder and Stoughton, 1956 (page citations are to reprint edition).

———. *The Victorian Age in Literature.* 1911. Reprint. London: Oxford University Press, 1966.

Corso, Gregory. *American Express.* Paris: Olympia Press, 1961.

———. *Elegiac Feelings American.* New York: New Directions, 1970.

———. *Gasoline.* San Francisco: City Lights, 1958.

———. *The Happy Birthday of Death.* New York: New Directions, 1960.

———. *Herald of the Autochthonic Spirit.* New York: New Directions, 1981.

———. *Long Live Man.* New York: New Directions, 1962.

———. *Mindfield: Selected Poems.* New York: Thunder's Mouth Press, 1989.

———. *The Vestal Lady on Brattle.* Cambridge: Richard Brukenfeld, 1955.

Deleuze, Gilles. *The Logic of Sense.* Translated by Mark Lester. New York: Columbia University Press, 1990.

Eco, Umberto. *The Aesthetics of Thomas Aquinas.* Translated by Hugh Bredin. 1956. Reprint, Cambridge: Harvard University Press, 1988.

Ferry, Luc. *The New Ecological Order.* Translated by Carol Volk. Chicago: University of Chicago Press, 1995.

Knight, Arthur, and Kit Knight. *The Beat Vision.* New York: Paragon House, 1987.

Lewellyn, John. *The Middle Voice of Ecological Conscience.* London: MacMillan Academic, 1991.

Nancy, Jean-Luc. *L'Expérience de la Liberté.* Paris: Galilée, 1988.

Nietzsche, Friedrich. *The Birth of Tragedy and the Genealogy of Morals.* Translated by Francis Golffing. New York: Doubleday, 1956.

Parkman, Francis. *The Conspiracy of Pontiac,* Vol. 1. 1908. Reprint, London: Dent, 1944.

Perkins, David. *English Romantic Writers.* New York: Harcourt Brace Jovanovich, 1967.

Stephenson, Gregory. *Exiled Angel: A Study of the Work of Gregory Corso.* London: Hearing Eye, 1989.

TITLE COMMENTARY

Gasoline

GREGORY STEPHENSON (ESSAY DATE 1989)

SOURCE: Stephenson, Gregory. "*Gasoline.*" In *Exiled Angel: A Study of the Work of Gregory Corso,* pp. 21-30. London: Hearing Eye, 1989.

In the following essay, Stephenson examines Gasoline *noting two important traits: Corso's love of words and sounds; and his debt to several Romantic poets such as William Wordsworth, Samuel Taylor Coleridge, and Percy Bysshe Shelley.*

Gasoline

Gasoline, published in 1958, is the book that established Gregory Corso's literary reputation both in the United States and internationally. It is a seminal work of what has been called "the new American poetry", interjecting a spirit of wild, improvisatory freedom of creation and unbridled vision into the literature of the postwar period. We recognize in the poems of this collection the same vitality and inventiveness, the same zany humour and euphoria of metaphor that animated the poet's first volume, together with a greater fluency and deftness, a surer sense of shape and focus. A small book, 32 poems on 37 pages, ***Gasoline*** lives up to its title: it is a volatile and combustive collection.

The opening poem of the volume, **"Ode to Coit Tower"**, announces the nature and the terms of the conflict that informs and encompasses the other poems in the book, namely the conflict between imagination and the material world, between vision and the real. In Corso's ode, humankind's aspiration toward beauty and vision is emblemized by Coit Tower, while all that confines, represses, restrains and oppresses that aspiration is emblemized by the island prison of Alcatraz.

In a sequence of images the tower is associated with "illuminations" and "visions", with children, with poetry and with sexuality, that is to say with the creative, the visionary, the innocent and ecstatic. The prison, by contrast, is seen to be the visible sign of the "petrific bondage" in which the sense and the spirit are held, and is further seen as a symbol of the destructive agencies of the world that seek to vanquish and subdue all dream and song, all manifestations of the visionary.

From the summit of the tower, the poet experiences a vision of Mercy herself crucified against the wind above the prison, "weeping . . . for humanity's vast door to open that all men be free that both hinge and lock die".

The poet mourns not only the imprisoned state of humanity in the world but his own loss of vision and his consequent affliction by "reality's worm". He grieves for the loss of his imaginative faculties, for "that which was no longer sovereign in me", and longs to regain the "dreams that once jumped joyous bright from my heart", together with "that madness again that infinitive solitude where illusion spoke Truth's divine dialect".

In place of the mythic splendours, the grandeurs, the joy and the intense response to natural beauty that characterized the poet's youthful perception and imagination, he now experiences a vision of Death and can hear only "a dark anthem" of foreboding and fear.

There are, however, two sources of solace for the poet. The first of these consists of the "heroes" and "saints" of vision who continue to uphold and to affirm dream, delight, energy and imagination in the face of the tyranny of materialism. The second solace is the knowledge that the physical world is written in "Swindleresque ink", that is disappearing ink. Material reality, the phenomenal world, are, then, ephemeral; they are illusions which will ultimately fade and vanish to reveal the true and eternal reality that they now obscure.

Corso's ode reverses the meaning of *the imaginary,* for the imagination is seen to be a mode of perceiving the Eternal, while what we consider to be reality, the world of the senses, is seen to be imaginary, a mere semblance with no substantial existence. The poem also proposes the essential premise of the poet's art: the universal struggle of the forces of spirit and matter, truth and falsehood, in which conflict poetry is a weapon in the arsenal of vision. The battle is waged at all levels, in the macrocosm of the world, and in the microcosm of each psyche, including, of course, that of the poet himself. This is Corso's grand theme, the essential context and argument of virtually all of his poems.

Both in structure and in theme, **"Ode to Coit Tower"** has affinities with certain poems of the English Romantics, including William Wordsworth's "Ode: Intimations of Immortality from Recollections of Early Childhood", Samuel Taylor Coleridge's "Dejection: An Ode", and Percy Bysshe Shelley's "Ode to the West Wind", (the latter of which Corso's poem alludes to in its concluding section). Certain parallels to the thought of William Blake may also be discerned in the poem. These likenesses and correspondences do not, in my estimation, diminish the achievement of Corso's ode, but rather serve to enrich and illuminate his poem, establishing also a kinship and a continuity of concern with the poet-seers of the past.

Stylistically, the ode is, perhaps, Corso's most uncharacteristic poem, blending echoes of Whitman and Ginsberg, and of Wordsworth and Shelley, with the poet's own wild imagery, his quirky syntax and diction. The long lines in which the poem is cast seem too dense, too heavy, working against Corso's quick, brilliant bursts of words, and overweighing the cursive character of his phrasing. Each stylistic component of the poem remains a disparate element, never really attaining coherence, equilibrium, integrity or significant interrelation with the other component elements. Yet, despite these technical flaws, the poem remains a forceful and cogent statement of the poet's vision, and serves effectively as an overture to the collection.

The motif of confinement, introduced in **"Ode to Coit Tower"**, recurs in separate poems throughout the volume, (e.g. **"The Last Warmth of Arnold"**) and provides the central image for **"Puma in Chapultepec Zoo"**. The poem begins with a description of the caged puma, emphasizing its grace and beauty, and contrasting the narrow closeness of the animal's present confinement with the expansiveness of its former freedom in the mountains. The predicament of the puma brings to the poet's mind the recollection of a distant friend:

> I think of Ulanova
> locked in some small furnished room
> in New York, on East 17th Street
> in the Puerto Rican section.

Despite the specificity of the poet's association, I think that by extension both the situation of the caged puma and of Ulanova, "locked in some small furnished room", may be read as metaphors of the human predicament: the spirit caged in the material world, vision locked in the senses, beauty and grace held prisoner in a fallen world.

Similarly, the poem "**Amnesia in Memphis**" presents an unnamed speaker who may be seen to represent all humankind. The narrator of the poem lives in a twilight state between life and death, perhaps a posthumous existence in his own dead body. He cannot recall his identity but only vague images of his former life as he lies "half-embalmed" and helpless. His loss of life and identity seems to have coincided with a general failure of magical, divine and prophetic powers at this period, apparently the end of ancient Egyptian civilization. The final prophecy foretells calamity, collapse and dissolution:

> The papyrus readers have seen the Falcon's head
> Fall unto the Jackal's plate.

This prophecy would seem to relate to our own time, the post-mythic era, when that which was noble, celestial and airborne (the Falcon) has been overthrown and devoured by that which is ignoble, earthbound and base, (the Jackal). And, in a manner much like the state of the narrator of the poem, we are all of us only half-alive and unaware of who we are, oblivious to our divine potential. The poem reinforces the volume's theme of mankind's state of "petrific bondage", and prefigures Corso's later interest in Egyptian mythology.

Further images of the confinement of the human spirit in the material universe are presented in "**To a Downfallen Rose**" and in "**Sun**". In the first poem, the downfallen rose is an emblem of the plight of the spirit, which once existed in an Edenic state and is now caught in "the vast fixedness" of matter, and which is subject to "the hateful law" of the phenomenal world, to time, decay and physical death. Trapped and helpless, the rose screams in anguish, distress and despair. In the second of the two poems, the sun is celebrated for its life-giving qualities, for its divine character as "helion, apollo, rha, sol", and it is seen to be not a material entity, not a giant ball of fiery gases, but, instead, an aperture. In the poet's mythopoeic vision the sun represents an opening to the realm of true life and light, a passage to the dominion of beauty and vision:

> O constant hole where all beyond is true Byzantium.

A celestial realm of light and vision is portrayed in the poem "**In the Fleeting Hand of Time**", which contrasts the state of non-material or astral being with life in the world. Corso invokes an intense, dreamlike atmosphere charged with supernatural beauty and solemn splendour to represent the celestial world, in contrast to which the physical world is depicted as stark, bleak and drab.

The poem records the poet's experience of a state of pre-existence (including the memory of a former incarnation) and his birth again on earth. From the radiant beauty and grandeur of the astral plane he descends to the raw, drear material world in which he feels acutely alien. Gradually, in the world's taint and stain he loses every remnant of grace and glory, and longs for death. Through death, he re-ascends and regains a "room of paradisical light", finding renewal and truer life.

"**In the Fleeting Hand of Time**" bears, of course, a glancing resemblance to Wordsworth's famous "Ode: Intimations of Immortality from Recollections of Early Childhood" in its poetic treatment of the notion of pre-existence. The resemblance goes no further, though, than that of a shared idea, and Corso's poem is in no way imitative or derivative. The poem represents an important expression of Corso's personal cosmography and mythology, the essential metaphysic of his work, and it is characteristically (and appropriately) personal, visual, image-rich, proposing not a systematic theology but an inspired poetic vision.

In the poems of ***Gasoline*** we encounter again the motif of predatory devouring and destruction of innocence and beauty, already familiar from Corso's first collection. This motif is clearly and powerfully expressed in "**Don't Shoot the Warthog**", where a child, personifying Beauty, is abused and devoured in a cannibal frenzy. It is appropriate that the child is first seen "swinging an ocean on a stick", for this type of exercise of the impossible, the fabulous, is entirely in keeping with the poet's essential surrealist aesthetic. Similarly, it is fitting that when the other children in the poem hear the name of Beauty they respond by leaping with joy and running to see, while it is the adults who are the persecutors of and the predators upon Beauty.

Parallel sorts of unjust, undeserved injury and harm are inflicted upon innocents in "**The Last Warmth of Arnold**" and in "**The Mad Yak**". In the former poem, the eponymous hero, Arnold, is a sensitive, shy, gentle boy whose interests include religion, literature, music and his pet pigeon. He is in love with a classmate, Eleanor, but his love is unreturned. He is a fearful child who hides under the porch and seeks out warm places in the cold world. Arnold is an alien, "from somewhere else / where it was warm"; an idealistic child in a sordid, hopeless environment of bookies and chicken pluckers, bums and sad old ladies who sit all day in the park. Arnold is rejected by the world (as is the cause to which he gives his allegiance, the Wilkie campaign). He is unfairly assaulted, after which he starves and dies, another innocent martyr in a cruel, ugly, uncaring world.

Another pitiful victim of human cruelty is the yak whose interior monologue comprises the poem, "**The Mad Yak**". Here, Corso effects a reversal of the conventional connotations of the terms "human" and "animal", contrasting the patient, compassionate yak to the callous and greedy human beings who exploit and slaughter the yaks. The humans are quite insensitive to both the beauty and the suffering of the animals, viewing them only in terms of products, such as scarves, caps, buttons and shoelaces. The yak, on the other hand, feels sorrow and compassion for its fellow creatures, and a deep sense of relatedness to them. It mourns the loss of its brothers and sisters, and feels pity for its uncle: "Poor uncle, . . . / How sad he is, how tired!" In short, the yak exhibits all the best qualities that we normally associate with human beings, while the humans of the poem (including the monk!) are base and "animalistic".

"**The Mad Yak**" bears several themes. It is an expression of the poet's compassion for all sentient beings, and of his sense of man's ideal relation to nature and of the essential unity of all life. At the same time, the poem may be read as a criticism of man's disposition to sacrifice natural beauty and freedom (including his own) to mundane, practical ends. The poem also reinforces the theme of the world's brutal persecution of the innocent, its destruction of beauty.

The ultimate embodiment of the persecuted, innocent victims of mankind's vicious malice is the figure of Christ in the poem, "**Ecce Homo**". Contemplating a painting of the crucified Christ by Theodoricus, the poet expresses his sense of grief and horror at the tortures inflicted upon this most gentle of all men, the very incarnation of divinity. Such is the fierce, fell quality of the cruelty that motivated the act that the poet concludes that the worst wounds "went thru the man to God". As the title of the poem suggests, the figure of Christ is capable of being understood in two senses: it can be seen to represent the most ignoble and vile of all of man's acts, the torture and murder of the Prince of Peace; and, it can be seen as the symbolic embodiment of all of mankind's highest and noblest aspirations. Significantly, it is the artist, Theodoricus, and the poet who ally themselves with the sufferer, and thus with all victims, and who accuse and reprimand the perpetrators, and thus by extension all tyrants and bullies together with their supporters.

The conspiracy against joy and beauty by the forces of repressive cruelty and death is further instanced and elaborated in the poems, "**Vision of Rotterdam**" and "**Paris**". In both poems the cities are metaphors for civilization in the best sense of the word, that is the cultivation of the mind and spirit. The armies that have attacked and occupied the cities during the past represent all that is barbarous, brutal and retrograde in man. Both poems celebrate the indominatable, irrepressible character of joy and beauty, in that the two cities have survived bombing and occupation, they have prevailed over their conquerors.

In "**Vision of Rotterdam**", the poet envisions a bombardment of mercy and miracles, of gentleness and kindness that will rout the invisible occupying armies of anti-life, deliver the populace and regenerate the city. "**Paris**" asserts that the forces of uncreation and unlife have their collaborators among us, their fifth column of "informers and concierges" who aid and abet them and who attempt to enforce their dictates. But, at the same time, there are those who heroically oppose the occupying forces: "Spirits of angels crouching in doorways / . . . beautiful Baudelaire, Artaud, Rimbaud, Appolinaire", and others.

Neither the occupation of the world by the combined forces of lifelessness, lovelessness, joylessness, banality, blandness and stasis, nor the domination of true life by matter, are stable, permanent conditions, Corso asserts. The victors are constantly at risk, ever vulnerable to harassment, ambush and sabotage by the resistance movement, the angelic underground of poets, artists, lovers, saints, clowns and children.

The poems "**Botticelli's *Spring***", "**Uccello**", and "**This Was My Meal**", treat the theme of the transforming power of the imagination. In the first of these it is the magical property of art to affect the external world that is manifested when Botticelli causes spring to appear in the physical world by the act of painting it on canvas. In the second poem, the poet praises the power of art to transfigure the disorder and even the violence and cruelty of life and to impose upon them, or discover in them, harmony, unity and beauty. The third poem celebrates the imagination in its purest and most potent form, as it is exercised by children. An ordinary, and indeed rather unappetizing meal of peas, cow's brain and milk, with a prune dessert, occasions in the fantasy of a child an extraordinary adventure in which wonders and marvels abound. In each of the poems the imagination triumphs over the material world, evidence that it is a powerful instrument of human redemption.

As in Corso's first collection, images of violence and death, especially the death of children, are frequent in the poems of ***Gasoline***. In addition to the persecuted victims already discussed, there are the "young child—doomed by his sombrero" who is glimpsed in **"Mexican Impressions"**, and the dead month-old infant in **"Italian Extravaganza"**. There are the deaths of the streetsinger, the gardener and child in **"Three"**, and the murder of Kindness in **"But I Do Not Need Kindness"**. Further images of violence occur in **"D. Scarlatti"**, **"Birthplace Revisited"**, and **"The Last Gangster"**.

Closely related to the violence-and-death motif in Corso's poetry are the recurring images of alienation and loss. The windmill "alone, alien, helpless" among cacti in a windless land (in **"Mexican Impressions"**) is one such figure, the doll abandoned in the attic in **"Doll Poem"** is such another, together with the narrators of **"On the Walls of a Dull Furnished Room"** and **"I Miss My Dear Cats"**. These two clusters of images combine to create a sense of the barreness and terror of human existence.

The effect of such imagery is offset, however, by the poet's impish humour and by the energy and excitement and the magical lyricism of his poems. ***Gasoline*** presents a myth or metaphysic of a fallen world, a debased state of existence from which man can be delivered by means of the imagination and the faculty of vision. Thus, despite their preoccupation with suffering, persecution, alienation and death, these poems affirm man's potential victory over the external world.

Among the strategies enacted by Corso's poems to serve this end is their cultivation of a mythic, animistic sensibility, and their corresponding emancipation of language through a dissolution of syntactical restrictions and denotative lexical meanings.

In the poems of ***Gasoline*** Corso ascribes consciousness to windmills, flowers, dolls, trees, valleys, mountains and moonlight. He personifies Time, Mercy, Kindness, Beauty, Truth and Death. He alludes to Egyptian, Greek and Aztec mythologies, and invents his own myths. By means of such actions and processes, such feats of the imagination, the poet endeavours to lift the malediction of habit and limitation, to restore life to the inanimate and the abstract. He gives names and forms to the mysterious powers latent in the life of the world, returning them to their sacred status. He joins together again that which has been separated, aiding in the re-establishment of primordial unity.

In the poem, **"No Word"**, Corso declares his independence from the conventional uses and banal ends of language:

> It is better man a word elongate
> and eat up what another spake
>
> . . . . .
>
> It is better man give up his diction
> become mouthless
> it is better
> than another man, myself
> heed his restriction

Corso "elongates" and "eats up" words by means of copulative coinages such as "redsmash", "joyprints", "hungersulk", "eyehand", "rosefamed", "sunbone", and "wheatweather"; and by metamorphic fusions such as "eucharistic feet", "ventriloquial telegram", "brides of wheat", "windless monkage", "spider thirst" and "dome heirloomed". He forms adjectives such as "swindleresque", "visionic", "vegetic" and "deathical"; and alters temporal, logical and syntactic relations among the components of his sentences to create ellipsis, associative connections, condensation, shifts of context, displacements, juxtapositions, or for rhythmic effect: "Sun misery sun ire sun sick sun dead sun rot sun relic!"

For Corso language is an instrument of exploration and revelation. Words for him possess a magical, incantatory power. He is intoxicated with words, fascinated by their sounds and meanings, their strange conjunctions and disjunctions. Like that of Rimbaud, Corso's poetic enterprise is the *alchemy of the word,* the verbal transmutation of the world. His expressive, explosive, explorative utilization of language is at once destructive and constructive, subverting traditional modes of thought and conventional notions of reality, as it exalts desire, freedom and vision.

Gasoline is an urgent, audacious yet graceful collection that confirms an uncommon and an important poetic talent.

The Happy Birthday of Death

GREGORY STEPHENSON (ESSAY DATE 1989)

SOURCE: Stephenson, Gregory. *"The Happy Birthday of Death."* In *Exiled Angel: A Study of the Work of Gregory Corso,* pp. 31-43. London: Hearing Eye, 1989.

In the following essay, Stephenson focuses on The Happy Birthday of Death, *observing the use of surrealism and a growing trend toward satire in Corso's poetry.*

The Happy Birthday of Death

Corso resolutely sustains his assault upon the real in his third volume of poems, ***The Happy Birthday of Death*** (1960), unleashing an arsenal of antic, vatic babble and bombast against all the various agencies that debase the human spirit and impair true life. In a series of longer poems, each centered upon a single concept, Corso denounces and ridicules the faults and failings that obstruct the development of mankind; while in the shorter lyrics of the collection he presents epiphanic glints and glimpses, praises the heroes and martyrs of visionary consciousness, and affirms the sovereign power of life.

The longer, reflective poems of the volume, **"Hair"**, **"Marriage"**, **"Bomb"**, **"Food"**, **"Death"**, **"Clown"**, **"Power"**, **"Army"** and **"Police"**, eschew formal organization, reasoned argument and explicit formulation in favour of anarchic humour and intensity of emotional conviction. The poems are less meditations or discourses upon their themes than they are imaginative explorations, proceeding by associative leaps and oblique correspondences, by expansions and fusions and transformations. These extended single-theme poetic statements are developed by means of a succession of images rather than a rational sequence of propositions; they unfold with the wild logic of a dream, and might be named anti-odes.

The principal and most central in this series of free-wheeling and reflective poems is **"Power"**, which may be read as an enunciation of Corso's poetics and of his conception of the role of the poet and of poetry in the world. The poem turns upon the contradictory duality inherent in the word *power,* which means both the possession of control, authority or influence over others, and the ability to act or to produce an effect. (Erich Fromm has distinguished these two qualities of the word power as "domination" and "potency", and has recognized their mutually exclusive nature.) The first meaning of the term involves the exercise of external, physical power, while the second sense of the word is expressive of an inner, impalpable power. Thus, the word reflects the irreconcilable dual nature of the world as material or as spiritual reality. Accordingly, we may say that the kind of power that each of us seeks to possess in life reflects our view concerning which level of existence, the physical or the metaphysical, is primary.

The poem opens with the declaration that "We are the imitation of Power", which I understand both in a Platonic sense, that we are each of us counterfeits of an essential and transcendent idea of Man; and in the sense explained above, that we each choose to seek either mundane or transcendental power. The Platonic, or more accurately, the neo-Platonic or Plotinian theme is developed further by the statement that "The senses are insufficient", and by the second stanza in which this idea is amplified:

> Since I observe memory and dream
> And not the images of the moment
> I am become more vivid
> And need not open the eye to see

This belief that there is a greater reality than that which is present to our senses and that true knowledge is apprehended by reminiscence or through inspired vision is clearly neo-Platonic. Corso's assertions here also recall William Blake's famous statement in his commentary on his painting, *The Last Judgement,* where he distinguishes between "Spiritual Perception" and the "Corporeal or Vegetative Eye". In these opening sections of the poem Corso is establishing what reality is and how it may be perceived, and what true power is and how it may be attained.

In the next stanza the poet alludes to three heroes of popular culture: Ted Williams, baseball player, and the comic-book heroes Captain Marvel and Buck Rogers. These figures represent to Corso embodiments of man's heroic impulse, his aspiration to oppose the forces of evil and to exceed the limits of the physical world. They have each attained mastery, achieved potency, and they are invoked by the poet as exemplary heroes of Power.

In common cause with these heroes the poet declares his own heroic endeavour: "I contradict the real with the unreal". This brief statement expresses in essence the guiding principle of all of

Corso's work: his rejection of the tyranny of the real and his assertion of freedom from limitation, from causality, from "impossibility". Poetry for Corso is a mode of rebuking, rebutting and refuting the phenomenological universe and of imposing inner desire on the external world. The poet is, in Corso's view, a prophet of the Ideal, the Transcendental; he is a plenipotentiary of the Eternal, an "ambassador of Power".

Corso unequivocally condemns all forms of dictatorial and destructive power, and aligns himself with the forces of Life in their struggle against the forces of Death:

> I *Ave* no particular Power but that of Life
> Nor yet condemn fully any form of Power
> but that of Death
> The inauguration of Death is an absurd Power
> Life is the supreme Power

Significantly, the poet is composing his poem as he sits in a playground, for he has succeeded in retaining something of the Power of Innocence, the Power of childhood vision, the spirit of play and fun, and the faculty of imagination. In contrast, he reflects on his childhood friends, "the feeble boys of my youth", now grown to adulthood and toiling factories, powerless prisoners in the graceless realm of industrial might and monetary empires, sad thralls to profane Power.

It is the poet's task to liberate these prisoners and to redeem the ravaged world, the "Awful blank acreage once made pastoral by myths". Against the violence, indifference, fraud, denial and despair of the fallen world, the poet possesses two weapons: vision and humour. By means of vision he may remythicize the drear, bleak wasteland, restoring it again to a fertile, pastoral Arcadia; and by means of laughter he can defy the forces of Death-in-Life and battle against the institutionalized repression of the human spirit.

In the closing stanzas of the poem Corso extols the weapon of wit, "That hand-grenade of humour dropped down the hatch / Of an armoured suit . . .", and proclaims that "The child of Power is laughter!" He embraces laughter as "My Power!" and concludes with an affirmation of the redemptive, revitalizing potentialities of humour:

> . . . a laugh
> That drops my woe and all woe to the floor
> Like a shot spy.

The theme of humour is taken up again in the poem, **"Clown"**. Here, the poet contrasts the vital position occupied by the jester or court fool in Medieval society with the current low estate of the clown in this "laughless age". Corso characterizes the present era as a spiritual winter but prophesies a vernal renewal to be ushered in by the clown, the "good mad pest of joy" whose "red nose / is antideath".

Certain of the more significant attributes of our frozen age, our human winter, are treated by the poet in **"Bomb"**, **"Death"**, **"Army"**, and **"Police"**. The titles speak for themselves, and taken as a group the poems serve to communicate a vision of an infernal era dominated by destructiveness, negation, violence and oppression. Enthroned in human consciousness like a baleful and obscene deity sits "Horned Reality its snout ringed with tokens of fear / pummeling child's jubilee, man's desire". (**"Police"**) But arrayed against this evil, usurping demon, against its armies, its police and all their deadly weaponry, stand the ragged clowns and holy fools of the world: "Their happy light is forged phalanx, charge!" (**"Clown"**) The struggle rages on all fronts.

Humour figures as a central technical element in the poems, **"Hair"**, **"Food"** and **"Marriage"**, all of which are comic monologues satirizing various social attitudes and forms of behaviour. The narrators of these poems are in some cases very clearly not the poet himself but a persona employed by him for dramatic purposes, while at other times (as in **"Marriage"**) the question of identity is more problematic.

"Hair" is a lament by an unnamed narrator-persona who alternately rages and weeps at the loss of his hair through baldness. So dismayed is he at the prospect of a hairless head that he calls it "a blunder only God could allow", and reproves the Deity for having been so "careless" in permitting such a calamity to be visited upon him. Dejectedly, he considers the courses that remain for a bald man: a change of image or identity (to an intellectual or to a wrestler), the purchase of a wig, the cultivation of facial hair as a compensation. The narrator concludes by cursing hair and rejecting it as inconvenient, unsanitary and expensive to maintain, but it is obvious that his sudden aversion to hair is motivated solely by frustration and envy.

The comic effect of the poem derives, of course, from the exaggerated emotion and the hyperbole provoked by an essentially trivial event. Corso's theme here is that of human vanity, the blinding conceit that engenders blasphemy, anger, abjectness, despair and envy. The poet also reveals how frail a thing is human identity or personality for most people, for it is dependent upon external appearance rather than upon inner qualities of character. In this manner, false values and self-deception are shown as serving to perpetuate the illusion of the real.

"Food" follows the development of another persona-narrator from fastidious ascetic to glutton. In the beginning the narrator scorns and refuses ordinary food in favour of visions of impossible, ethereal delicacies, rejecting the "murdered meat" and "chicken slaughter" of the farmer, and denouncing hunger itself as the "petty agent of death". He perceives the very act of eating as absurd and unaesthetic, and starves himself rather than accept "so dreadful a nourishment" as the farmer or the restaurateur have to offer.

In the second part of the poem, however, the narrator has become as voracious and insatiable as he once was abstemious. He consumes indiscriminately a gargantuan banquet of "Sugared meats! Badger tongues! Chinese lineaments! . . . orang-estuffed duck . . . apegrease . . . Baked lions, broiled camels, roasted fennecs, Fried chairs, poached mattresses, stewed farms!" Although living only to eat, he is aware that ultimately he is but fattening himself as a feast for "the inevitable wolf" of death.

As I read it, **"Food"** dramatizes and derides the extremes of denial and indulgence in relation to physical appetite. The two positions are seen as being equally absurd and untenable. The gourmand is merely an inverted ascetic and vice-versa. (These twin tendencies are later embodied by Corso in the characters of Angus Plow and Scratch Vatic in his novel, ***The American Express.***) Both denial and indulgence serve to confirm appetite rather than transcending it, and both represent what are essentially life-denying attitudes, dogmatic, deviational obsessions that narrow and distort consciousness and thus impede expanded vision.

The superbly humourous **"Marriage"** satirizes the rituals and conventions of courtship, sexuality and marriage, contrasting the individualistic, imaginative, poetic spirit of the poem's narrator with the norms and expectations of society. The poem also pokes fun at the bizarre impulses of the narrator and at his inability to cope with practical matters or the responsibilities of a job and children. The poem points out that what is all too frequently obscured or lost among all the social usages, customs and practices connected with marriage is its very reason and motive: love. The mystery, the miracle of love must not be reduced to mediocrity, must not become domesticated or trivialized. The poem concludes with a celebration of pure, passionate love as exemplified by Ayesha, the beautiful, terrible sorceress of H. Rider Haggard's *She,* reminding us that true marriage can only be founded upon the recognition of love as a primal force, subversive, illimitable, partaking of the character of the divine. True marriage is not a social contract but a covenant of flesh and spirit both within and between lovers.

The shorter lyrics of the collection treat a variety of themes most of which are centered around the struggle between vision and the real, between life and death. As I have previously noted, this struggle is not merely observed and recorded by the poet but enacted ceaselessly in his spirit. Accordingly, the mood of the individual poems varies from one to the other as ardent affirmation gives way to anguish and even to black despair, out of which, in turn, new aspiration is born.

Transformation of the self and of the external world continues to be a central theme in the poems of this collection. In **"Seaspin"**, metamorphosis of the self is imaged as a drowning and a descent into the depths of the ocean where the solid body becomes fluid and graceful as the mind merges with the vast power and the abounding beauty of the sea. The sea-change undergone by the narrator of the poem is a sensuous dissolution, an attaining of ultimate freedom and fulfilment. With limpid lyricism the poem expresses the deep universal desire for such transcendence, and implicitly contrasts the aquatic world so rich with mystery and beauty, a metaphor for the realm of the imagination, with dry land, the familiar world of dullness and suffering which we inhabit.

The aperture between the realms of the actual and the visionary that may sometimes be chanced upon or may be sought and discovered, or at other times formed or forced, yields fleeting views of the unknown and the marvellous. Such glimpses are recorded by Corso in the poems **"Under Peyote"**, **"Early Morning Writings"** and **"No Doubt What He Saw"**. In the first of these a breach is effected by means of a vision-inducing drug under the influence of which new relationships among unrelated elements are revealed. The inanimate becomes animated, the intangible is made palpable, the disparate is unified, all in a manner inexplicable to reason, beyond categories of coherence or order, that is to say in accordance with desire and in complete freedom.

"Early Morning Writings" is a sequence of ten short haiku-like poems presenting observations of and reflections on occurrences taking place between dawn and noon on a single morning. Each short poem in the sequence may be seen as an aperture, a passage communicating with the realm of vision. Encountering the ellipsis which Corso employs as a central device in these poems the reader's mind is compelled to bridge the gap between the two juxtaposed images and thus for a brief instant traverses the passage, glimpsing the super-real, the marvellous.

> Two men look into each others eyes
> —one shoe is missing
>
> The mother's talk
> The child's ear
> —the plans of a kingdom burn

By creating poetic equations in this manner the poet indicates the mysterious links and kinships that secretly connect widely dissimilar entities, qualities and events, revealing the latent enchantment and the essential unity of the world.

The joining together of the unlike is also the theme of **"No Doubt What He Saw"**, which, in evidence of the natural occurrence of this phenomenon, provides a childhood memory. The poet recalls that once as a child he observed a horse with a daisy dangling from the side of its mouth, and remembers how he was struck by the strange conjunction of the large and powerful beast with the tiny, delicate flower. He speculated that the occurrence might herald a permanent union of the two kingdoms of living things, the daisy eventually becoming "ancestral to the makeup" of the horse. The poet's young companion of the time was incapable of perceiving or comprehending this sort of imaginative vision and "doubted it all". Later, however, the poet convinced his doubting friend by showing him "a pastoral metamorphosis": a bull and a daisy joined to form "a Daisytaur".

In its charming fashion the poem attests to the poet's belief that the primordial union of the world, of all life and being, shattered by some unimaginable cataclysm, is ever seeking to restore itself to its original state, the disparate parts striving to come together again. Seemingly strange attractions and affinities, incongruous unions of unlike things are therefore in full accordance with the deepest natural law, and nature's great enterprise is abetted by the redintegrative power of the poet's art.

Further instances of the transforming power of the imagination are presented in **"Medieval Anatomy"** and **"Looking at the Map of the World"**; but in other poems Corso expresses the dark aspect of the visionary experience: the acute sense of loss, the feeling of exile and forfeiture when vision fails, the frustration and despair attendant upon finding oneself trapped again in the raw, drear, unyielding material world.

In **"How Happy I Used To Be"** the poet again laments the diminution of the visionary faculty of his childhood (a theme treated previously in **"Ode to Coit Tower"**). Obviously, though, his imaginative power has not failed completely. Though it may be lessened in intensity, he yet retains a sufficient degree of vision to enable him to perceive as a poet. He remains keenly aware, however, that such power is constantly under the threat of destruction by material and social pressures, and that it is, by its very nature, fickle and fugitive.

In **"On Pont Neuf"** Corso cries out in anguish at the sense of death-in-life and at the bleakness of the world in the aftermath of the visionary experience.

> I leave paradise behind me
> My paradise squandered fully
> What dies dies in beauty
> What dies in beauty dies in me—

The extreme difficulty of summoning and sustaining vision is made painfully explicit in **"1959"** where vision is characterized as a "dreadful privilege" that compels one to seek "to inherit what is necessary to forfeit", and that in its inevitable recession leaves life drab, oppressive and meaningless. The hopes begotten of vision are succeeded by despondency; "confident births" lead only to "lucid deaths". The poet mourns that, in the absence of vision, "there is no mystery" only "Cold history", no myth but merely a "Multitudinous deathplot!"

Despite such occasional moods of dejection and disconsolation, the poet continues to resist and endeavour and contend, striving against the agencies of negation, cultivating his sources of strength and inspiration. The spirit of abiding vitality, of renewal and vision is frequently imaged by Corso as a young girl or a young woman. Like Dante's Beatrice, Nerval's Aurélia, Coleridge's Abyssinian maid, or Breton's Nadja, the child-woman in Corso's poetry emblemizes the miraculous redemptive principle latent in the world.

This figure, innocent sorceress, elusive muse and mythic apparition, assumes various guises in Corso's poems. In **"The Sacré Coeur Café"** she is envisioned by the poet as Cosette, the heroine of Victor Hugo's *Les Misérables*. Sitting in a café the poet awaits her appearance, "little Cosette—the size of eternity". He dreams of following her, serving her, sacrificing himself for her, but then awakens again to the "plastic tables" of the café and to the ordinary calamities and banalities of everyday life. She is glimpsed again in the form of a lovely "childgirl" in the poem **"Written in Nostalgia for Paris"**, and pursued by the poet through the bloody and violent streets of Paris during the Algerian war. She is awaited reverently in a park in **"Spring's Melodious Herald"**, where the poet expresses his hope that her "primordial beauty" will overthrow "winter's vast network". Embodiment of hope and of regeneration, Corso's child-woman is a radiant enigma appearing unexpectedly and fleetingly, anticipated incessantly.

The motifs of confinement and persecution, already familiar from Corso's first two collections, continue to be developed by the poet in ***The Happy Birthday of Death.*** In **"For K. R. Who Killed Himself in Charles Street Jail"**, Corso elegizes a friend and fellow-poet who represents for him the type of the visionary quester destroyed both by the inner torments inevitably engendered by the spiritual quest, and by the abuse and persecution inflicted upon him by an uncomprehending materialist society. The death of such a person is at one level a victory for cruelty, for confusion, for the demonic forces of darkness, yet Corso celebrates the "illuminated rose of pain" that grew within the spirit of the man, nourished by his sufferings, as the truer triumph. By nurturing light in the darkness of the world, K. R. achieves, after death, communion with the Light: "By light follow, O child of dark, by light embrace!"

A new and more hopeful variant of the persecution and confinement motif is introduced in this collection, that is the theme of escape. In the poem **"Transformation & Escape"** Corso depicts a flight from heaven which he reveals to be "syrupy . . . and oppressively sweet", and which is in reality a vicious totalitarian state, an inferno rather than a paradise! In the end, after an eternity of confinement at hard labour, the poet escapes the celestial chain-gang and falls from heaven, free. As I read it, the poem records in symbolic terms Corso's rejection of institutionalized religion, which under the appearance of mercy and benevolence has so often shown itself to be inhumanly cruel and oppressive. Like Blake, Corso champions the archetypal rebel over the divine tyrant. The cloying, saccharine sweetness of counterfeit piety, the poem tells us, is not to be confused with the true ambrosia of love.

Another symbolic escape is described in the poem **"1953"**, in which a mass prison-break is accomplished by means of magic and imagination. Marching "Chagall-like" past the entranced warden, past turnkey, trusty, stoolie and guards, leaping the high confining walls and regaining their freedom, the aged prisoners make for a sanctuary where they are awaited by "gentle children". The poem may be read as an allegory of human spiritual liberation.

Confinement of another sort and escape of a different variety are presented in **"Paranoia in Crete"**. The poem is a monologue spoken by an unnamed narrator who may be identified by means of allusions in the text as the legendary King Minos, son of Zeus and Europa, and ruler of Crete. In Corso's version of the myth the semi-divine king is living in exile within his own kingdom from whose throne he has been deposed. (The poem is unclear as to why this has occurred, perhaps it is a further punishment for Minos' defiance of Poseidon.) The king lives alone in a cave, subsisting on a diet of figs, and engaged in plastering up the crevices of his crude rock chamber in order to perfect his isolation from his enemies.

I think the poem can be read as a metaphor both for the situation of the creative artist in the world and for the human situation. Minos' defiance of the established powers and of his persecutors recalls the creed of "non serviam" espoused by James Joyce's artist-hero, Stephen Daedalus, while the king's response to his oppressors recalls Daedalus' threefold strategy of "silence, exile and cunning". Corso's King Minos has refused to serve a tyrannical god, has accepted the consequences for his act and has chosen to cultivate solitude and thus to reign in the one kingdom that cannot be usurped, that of the spirit. In proud defiance of his foes, Minos declares:

> Mine the true labyrinth, it is my soul, Theseus;
> try a ball of string in *that*!

Certainly, too, the condition of a semi-divine king driven into exile, living in a cave rather than in his rightful palace, subject to the persecution of his enemies and striving to maintain an interior resistance may be seen as a dramatic analogue to the state of the exiled and dispossessed human spirit. In this sense Minos is the epitome of all men.

In a similar reversal of the conventional roles of hero and villain in classical mythology, in the poem **"Mortal Infliction"** Corso condemns Ulysses for having blinded Polyphemus. Again, the poet defends the natural, immortal inhabitant against the mortal interloper, the devious trespasser.

Corso also mythicizes contemporary heroes, as in **"Dream of a Baseball Star"**. In this instance Ted Williams serves as representative of the artist and of all mankind, his batting prowess as a symbol of the struggle waged by the spirit against the limitations of the physical world. The poem makes original, engaging and effective use of sports as a metaphor for metaphysics.

Baseball as a trope for the cosmic struggle provides a point-of-departure for the poet in **"Written While Watching the Yankees Play Detroit"**, in which Corso prophesies the final victory of the spirit, its liberation from the confinement of "creation". The poem affirms the ultimate deliverance, elevation, glorification and transfiguration of the human spirit: "the spheres will be known", "the spheres are ours", we shall dwell in "solar palaces", ride upon light, transcend our petty humaness. In the realm of "creation" we are like Plato's prisoners chained in their cave, knowing only"A sort of shadow, a warped cluster, a sad foliage", while our true destiny is "Beyond the banks of life and death", beyond the world, among the spheres. Images of enclosure, such as "banks" and "houses" are opposed and succeeded in the poem by images of egress, apertures of door and window. Fire serves as the image of apocalyptic transformation, of the consummation of the material world. The image of the "spring fig" with which the poem concludes serves as an appropriate symbol of paradisical renewal and rebirth.

Corso's metaphysics is of his own eclectic, syncretic, eccentric variety; he is, as I have previously emphasized, a poet of visions and not an expounder of doctrines, dogma or systems. Indeed, he is disposed to be deeply suspicious of all that presents itself as being absolute, definite, fixed or final. There are, of course, coherent and consistent ideas implicit in his work but he chooses not to formalize or codify them, knowing that "the letter killeth but the spirit giveth life". The poet expresses this fundamental attitude, one possessing certain affinities with Keats' "negative capability", in the poem **"Notes After Blacking Out"**:

> All is answerable I need not know the answer
> Poetry is seeking the answer
> Joy is in knowing there is an answer
> Death is knowing the answer

The Happy Birthday of Death is a search for answers, a mythopoeic inquiry into life, into the heart of man, into the world and the cosmos. Undermining, discrediting, rebuking and rebutting all that is inimical to freedom and to growth, Corso urges us to pursue our "pilgrimage toward that splendor" that is heralded by beauty, vision, liberty, desire and delight.

CHRISTINE HOFF KRAEMER (ESSAY DATE SUMMER 2002)

SOURCE: Kraemer, Christine Hoff. "The Brake of Time: Corso's Bomb as Postmodern God(dess)." *Texas Studies in Literature and Language* 44, no. 2 (summer 2002): 211-28.

In the following essay, Kraemer asserts that despite the dark and chaotic images within "Bomb," Corso maintains a sense of humor in the poem.

Since its initial publication in 1958, Gregory Corso's surreal and ambiguous ode to the destructive power of the bomb has consistently aroused extreme reactions in its readers. In a 1959 *Time* magazine one reviewer scathingly quoted from **"Bomb"**'s enthusiastic final lines as a prime example of "Beat blather" that, in his eyes, was "certainly not literature" but was excellent for recitations in the bathtub ("Bang," 80). Corso's presentation of the poem to a poetry group at New College in England was met with frank hostility, ending with Corso and Allen Ginsberg being heckled and bombarded with the shoes of the offended members of the Campaign for Nuclear Disarmament (Moraes, 67). In contrast to this negative reception, Ginsberg defended the poem in extravagant aesthetic terms, arguing that "it just reduces the bomb to insignificance because the poem is greater than the bomb" (Horovitz, 67). Even Ginsberg's reaction, however, fails to acknowledge that the poem is more than just a powerful, provocative, and often amusing piece of poetry. Corso's style is wild and impressionistic, but **"Bomb"** nevertheless articulates sophisticated social and religious questions that continue to plague us even after the fear of total nuclear holocaust has been eased somewhat by the end of the Cold War. Though **"Bomb"** overflows with surreal juxtapositions and farcical absurdity, the humor is not an end in itself but rather a tool to destabilize the reader's ingrained assumptions about nuclear apocalypse. Only after the reader has been disarmed by Corso's often hilarious treatment of a matter that is still deadly serious does the poet slip in the powerful, underlying central image—the bomb as a bringer of ultimate chaos, the brake of time itself, a postmodern god for a world that at Hiroshima suddenly realized its potential for self-annihilation.

Yet Corso does not leave the reader to morbidly ruminate over these dark images. Instead, the poet recovers his sense of humor, courting the bomb with a passionate love letter and finally launching into a wild celebration of destruction, reminiscent of a small boy's delight with a home chemistry set:

> BOOM BOOM BOOM BOOM BOOM
> BOOM ye skies and BOOM ye suns
> BOOM BOOM ye moons ye stars BOOM [. . .]
> Yes Yes into our midst a bomb will fall
> (lines 165-67, 176)

Corso's journey into darkness is a direct prerequisite for this final ascent into a new and surprising light. The bomb is a reality; death is a reality, and for Corso, the only reasonable reaction is to embrace, celebrate, and laugh with the resulting chaos. Though **"Bomb"** contains a whisper of social criticism, it offers no impetus to fight to change the system. Corso himself, in fact, denied that the poem had any political message at all. As he explained in a rambling interview with Michael Andre and Robert King, his reaction to the anti-nuclear protests of the 1950s focused more on death itself than on the fear of nuclear holocaust: "People were worrying about dying by the Bomb in the Fifties. So I said, what about falling off the roof, what about heart attack . . . old age I picked as being the heaviest—'old age, old age'" (Skau, "On Bomb"). Though Corso always distanced himself from the Buddhist beliefs of fellow Beats Ginsberg and Kerouac, **"Bomb"**'s embrace of death has Eastern influences of which Corso himself may have been unconscious. In the face of postmodern fragmentation, Corso's position is one that is extremely compatible with both Hindu and Buddhist traditions—a sense of resignation, coupled with a casting aside of order as a source of meaning in favor of increasingly ubiquitous chaos.

Critics of Stanley Kubrick's notorious satire *Dr. Strangelove: or, How I Learned to Stop Worrying and Love the Bomb* have suggested that the effectiveness of the film's humor is directly related to the taboo nature of its subject matter. In 1964 the Cuban missile crisis was just a few years in the past; the film *Failsafe,* which *Dr. Strangelove* consciously parodied, had freshened fears that a nuclear power might unintentionally trigger World War III. As a result, the film's mockery of the government, the military, and the bomb itself were deeply shocking—and, therefore, joltingly, hysterically funny. Corso's intent seems to be much the same in his humorous presentation of the bomb. In an era during which all discussions of nuclear war were tainted with anti-Communist rhetoric and a brutal us-versus-them competitiveness, Corso needed a way to temporarily remove these connotations and create a clear zone within which his readers could contemplate the bomb from a slightly less ethnocentric point of view. Ironically, though Corso literally "dresses up" the bomb, the net result is revelatory, demonstrating our collectively imagined bomb to be much more than a political tool in the international power struggle.

The primary device that Corso uses to decontextualize the bomb is juxtaposition. Fragmentation abounds as incomplete phrases and concepts butt up against each other, and puns, wordplay, and nonsensical images reminiscent of the visual art of Dalí or Magritte plunge the reader into a chaotic world of dreams and half-glimpsed impressions. The result is characteristically postmodern, as Corso draws heavily from both pop and classical culture, shoving the sundry elements together with a deliberate disregard for consistency or order. The poem's larger structure is equally loose; **"Bomb"** lacks clear transitions, skipping almost randomly from topic to topic. More often, however, Corso creates bizarre contrasts within a single line, throwing together elements that do not and could not meet in the real world.

> Turtles exploding over Istanbul
> The jaguar's flying foot
> soon to sink in arctic snow
> Penguins plunged against the Sphinx
> The top of the Empire State
> arrowed in a broccoli field in Sicily
> (30-35)

Corso gives the reader only one clue to interpreting this mishmash of images: the association of disparate objects is always presented in conjunction with the exploding bomb. Even the poem's appearance reinforces the primacy of the moment of explosion: the piece is shaped like a rising mushroom cloud. Though the effect is lost in later printings, the original pamphlet edition of **"Bomb"** published by City Lights particularly emphasizes the poem's sense of instability and intruding chaos—the text itself, apparently printed on a relatively primitive press, marches unsteadily across the page with individual letters slightly askew. Clearly, the poet's bomb represents something more complex than mere fiery destruction. Unlike a real nuclear bomb, Corso's does not merely obliterate; instead, it breaks connections, producing chaos and forcing incompatible elements together. In a world dominated by the bomb, contradictions are the order of the day, and sly paradoxes reign: pieces of human monuments (perhaps monuments *to* humans?) are mixed with fragments of the animal world, the normally conquering Christ strikes out at baseball, astrologers lean on "desk[s] of science," and (more didactically) children play in parks while men die in electric chairs.

In the first section of the poem (contained in the head of the mushroom cloud), Corso takes on death itself with equally cheerful impiety. His verse has the singsong quality of a child's recitation, the lurid images rendered cartoonish by Corso's puns and childlike neologisms.

> O there are deaths like witches of Arc Scarey
> deaths like Boris
> Karloff
> No-feeling deaths like birth-death sadless deaths
> like old pain
> Bowery
> Abandoned deaths like Capital Punishment
> stately deaths like
> senators
> And unthinkable deaths like Harpo Marx girls
> on Vogue
> covers my own
> (16-19)

Corso emphasizes death's unreality in these lines, helping the reader to temporarily distance herself from it as well. Death can be "scarey," in the way that a child quails at an old black-and-white monster movie; lonely, like the state-sponsored executions that the public never sees; dignified, as one might imagine a government official's to be; or unthinkable, in the way that we do not contemplate the deaths of icons of our society: beloved clowns like Harpo Marx, who was still alive at the time of Corso's writing ("Harpo"), or beautiful Vogue models whose reified youth seems timeless. Though the short, sudden "my own" at the end of this section adds a trace of seriousness, most of the passage examines death from the point of view of an external observer, using simple categories that a child might understand. Even the gravity of Jeanne d'Arc's terrible death is undermined by the poet's word choice—though he elevates her specific death by making it symbolic of an entire class (the unjust deaths of martyrs?), his use of the word "witches" rather than "saints," "martyrs," or even "Joans" irreverently diminishes the famous young mystic by labeling her as her executioners did. These techniques distance the reader from the grotesque, concrete details that characterize death in the real world. By examining the experience of death so broadly, Corso has achieved much the same effect that an artist might by portraying death as a black-cloaked Grim Reaper—death is sanitized and simplified, encouraging the reader to contemplate associated ideas and images rather than the full horror of its reality. Even here, however, Corso hints at the direction the poem will take later: these superficial descriptions of death provide no context for contemplating the nature of one's own mortality. Corso's inability to characterize his death with a glib adjective indicates an uneasy awareness of his own death's ineffability.

This distancing passage leads directly into a description of New York being destroyed by a nuclear bomb. Corso's description stops with the participants' last conscious moments as they huddle in the shelter of a subway.

> a city New York City streaming starkeyed subway
> shelter
> Scores and scores A fumble of humanity High
> heels bend
> Hats whelming away Youth forgetting their
> combs
> Ladies not knowing what to do with their
> shopping bags
> Unperturbed gum machines [. . .]
> The smiling Schenley poster will still smile
> (22-25, 28)

Corso plays here with a *memento mori* theme, which appears in the literary canon with some frequency starting in the Middle Ages. Works such as Thomas Nash's "A Litany in Times of Plague" show the ephemerality and vanity of human endeavor in the face of certain mortality. Just as the plague served as the mechanism for apocalypse and a symbol of looming death for medieval writers, so the bomb has been for post-World War II writers.[1] Thus, Corso's emphasis in this scene is on the sad absurdity of humanity in the face of "Bombdeath"—people fumbling about fearfully, still worrying about their personal possessions even in their last moments, their surroundings (gum machines, advertisements, etc.—all symbols of human culture) unchanged, prosaic, and trivial. Corso notes, "I do not know how horrible Bombdeath is I can only imagine / Yet no other death I know has so laughable a preview" (20-21). The humor here has a bit of an edge. The poet's laughter is both condescending and sad, mocking the confusion of the humans unable to grasp the enormity of their fate. Yet as in Nash's "Litany," Corso's mention of his own death implicitly includes him in the foolish crowd, so befuddled by the confusion that they fail to even recognize their plight. Given the distancing passage above, as well as the fact that Corso steers us away from identifying with any individual in the huddling crowd, the overall effect of this passage is ironic. From the poet's point of view, the doomed humans are both pitiable and laughably absurd, their death's suddenness robbing it of significance and dignity.

From this ambiguous point in the passage, Corso moves through the series of outrageous juxtapositions quoted above ("Penguins plunged against the Sphinx," etc.) and then dives unapologetically into pure whimsy. Though the humor of the previous sections might easily be described as black, Corso's mad baseball game is unabashedly playful. Once again, the poet obliquely implies that the incompatible elements that make up the baseball game have come together as a result of the bomb: "O Athletic Death Sportive Bomb," he says, and describes "Electrons Protons Neutrons" (perhaps the only things that remain after the explosion?) marching to enter the "final amphitheatre" (38, 41, 45). Though the exact origins of the game are unclear, its positioning within the poem after the lines describing the destruction of New York suggests that it may be a kind of chaotic heaven or afterlife, thrown together by the antics of the "sportive" bomb. In Corso's game lyres and tubas play together in the same band, Hermes races Olympic star Jesse Owens, and concession stands serve a strange combination of ancient Greek and American cuisine, while major religious figures—including Christ and Buddha—compete on the field.[2]

Despite the poet's pronounced tendency to indulge in mad fantasies like the above, "**Bomb**" is not entirely devoid of social commentary. Later in the poem, the reader has a sudden, surprisingly personal glimpse of the poet as he moves back into the first person.

> That I am unable to hate what isnecessary
> to love
> That I can't exist in the world that
> consents
> a child in a park a man dying in an
> electric-chair
> That I am able to laugh at all
> things
> all that I know and do not know thus to
> conceal my pain
> That I say I am a poet and therefore love all man
> [. . .]
>
> (109-14)

The flippancy with which the poet treats the destruction of New York is not the product of a jaded or uncompassionate soul. These short but complex lines encapsulate Corso's conundrum: as a poet, he feels a duty to love humanity and to celebrate the world as it is; but the world contains both beauty and horror in equal amounts, making it "necessary to love" the horror as well as the beauty. Corso's response to this paradox is simple: he laughs, thus removing himself from the paradox and placing himself above it, where the absurdity of the human condition is clear.

This particular section of "**Bomb**," in which Corso struggles with the horror he perceives in the world, resonates well with Ginsberg's slightly earlier "Howl." Like a slide machine flicking through images too quickly for the watcher to absorb or really comprehend them, the first section of "Howl" is highly fragmented, each line a separate clause in a sentence that stretches over many pages of text. Each of these clauses contains a different image of the pain, desperation, or oppression of what Ginsberg calls "the best minds of my generation," a group of nonconformists in search of spiritual enlightenment and meaning. Unfortunately, Ginsberg implies, the structure of society is such that the spiritually minded are systematically put down, injured, or eradicated. They flounder in a disconnected mess of pop culture, unable even to determine what is it they are looking for: whether "jazz or sex or soup," "Plotinus Poe St. John of the Cross telepathy [or] bop kabbalah." Ultimately, writes Ginsberg, they are "destroyed by madness [. . .] dragging themselves through the negro streets at dawn looking for an angry fix" (Ginsberg, 9-26). These same problems—alienation, apathy, cruelty—are sore spots for Corso as well, though his reaction in "**Bomb**" is more melancholy and less defiant than Ginsberg's.

This existential angst, however, was hardly unique to the Beats. The despair resulting from the inability to find meaning either in the surrounding world or in the self is discussed most famously by Kierkegaard in his *The Sickness Unto Death* as well as immortalized in Beckett's *Waiting for Godot* and Camus's *The Stranger.* The subjects of Ginsberg's "Howl" react to this seemingly inescapable reality by engaging in self-destructive behavior: ravaging their bodies with fasting and drugs, committing crimes, attempting suicide, and finally adding to the chaos around them with random acts—throwing potato salad at lecturers or writing obscene poetry on walls. It is these latter acts that may provide one explanation for Corso's morbidly exuberant joy in the explosion of nuclear bombs. In Beckett's *Waiting for Godot* Didi and Gogo suffer miserably unless they play, laugh, and avoid contemplating the futility of their situation. Similarly, we can easily imagine Ginsberg's Beats eking out a little relief from their acts of "poetic terrorism": seriously rebelling against the Enlightenment-derived worship of rationality that they saw as enslaving but also rejoicing in the liberating pleasure of absurdity and relishing the shocked, uncomprehending reactions of the squares. Corso's exploding bombs provide the same relief of breaking out of the system—this time by breaking the oppressive and contradictory system itself.

To say that "**Bomb**" is merely Corso's irreverent way of coping with a paradoxical and oppressive world, however, ignores the poem's religious elements. Although Corso rejected the Roman Catholic upbringing of his childhood, his work as a whole demonstrates a continuing dialogue with various conceptions of God, of which that presented in "**Bomb**" is only one. Though the bulk of this imagery appears about halfway through the poem, Corso has not left us entirely unprepared. The poet places heavily loaded language even in the most ridiculous and lighthearted section of the poem, the baseball game: "the visiting team of Present / the home team of Past" (50-51). These lines suggest that the bomb has united the past and the present, recalling the opening lines, "Budger of history Brake of time" (1). Cast in these terms, the bomb is not merely a weapon; it takes on godlike powers, enabling it to interfere with the progression of time itself. Corso reinforces these characterizations with a pastiche of religious imagery, playfulness, and suggestions of cosmic power, setting up a tension in the image of the bomb that will not be articulated fully until later in the poem.

> Toy of universe Grandest of all snatched-sky I
>   cannot hate you
> Do I hate the mischievous thunderbolt the
>   jawbone of an ass
> The bumpy club of One Million B.C. the mace
>   the flail the axe
>
> [. . .]
>
> And hath not St. Michael a burning
>   sword
>   St. George a
>   lance David a sling
> Bomb you are as cruel as man makes you
>
> (2-4, 6-7)

This passage is full of apparent contradictions. The bomb is presented as tremendously powerful, compared to a thunderbolt, and called "Grandest of all snatched-sky"—an ambiguous image evoking, perhaps, a stormy horizon or the mushroom cloud itself. Its destructive power, however, is presented as potentially neutral. Corso evokes beloved religious figures, symbols of all that is good and righteous, and notes that they too have the power to kill and destroy. The bomb, however, is only "as cruel as man makes [it]," notes the poet, observing that our tendency to anthropomorphize objects leads us to perceive the bomb as cruel when it is merely fulfilling its function. Despite these images of power, Corso also strikes a discordant note by calling the bomb the universe's toy. This paradox, in which Corso assigns the bomb both childlike and godlike attributes, is a recurring trope of "**Bomb.**"

Corso's celebration of chaos and apocalypse resonates strongly with the Eastern philosophy that his associates Ginsberg and Kerouac favored, in which destruction is seen as necessary and natural—death being, in fact, a prerequisite to new life. Corso finds a fiery beauty in the bomb as well as carnage and horror:

> You are due and behold you are due
> and the heavens are with you
> hosannah incalescent glorious liaison
> BOMB O havoc antiphony molten cleft
> BOOM
> Bomb mark infinity a sudden furnace
> spread thy multitudinous encompassed Sweep
> set forth awful agenda
> Carrion stars charnel planets carcass elements
> Corpse the universe tee-hee-finger-in-the-mouth
> hop
>   over its long long dead Nor
> From thy nimbled matted spastic eye
> exhaust deluges of celestial ghouls
> From thy appellational womb
> spew birth-gusts of great worms
> Rip open your belly Bomb
> from your belly outflock vulturic salutations
> Battle forth your spangled hyena finger stumps
> along the brink of Paradise
>
> (76-93)

The destruction imagined here is cosmic in scope. Corso was hardly the first to assign the bomb godlike qualities, however. Robert Oppenheimer's famous response to the first Los Alamos nuclear test was to recall Krishna's words from the Bhagavad-Gita: "I am become Death, shatterer of worlds."[3] Interestingly, however, Corso's language describes a female bomb. "[Y]ou are due" suggests pregnancy and labor, and a few lines later the bomb does indeed give birth to cosmic destruction from its "appellational womb." Corso's choice of the word "appellational" is oddly appropriate to the Hindu destroyer/mother goddess Kali. His phrasing suggests a simultaneous act of naming and bringing into creation, much as the Judeo-Christian god is portrayed as bringing the world into creation through the Logos, or Word. Similarly, Kali wears fifty human skulls representing the letters of the Sanskrit alphabet, "the manifest state of sound from which all creation evolved" (Harding, 43). Some mystics also interpret her protruding tongue as the expression of sound by which the universe is created (55). Even the time-related language quoted above ("Brake of time," etc.) has a potential connection to imagery associated with the Hindu goddess. The word "Kali" comes from the Sanskrit word "kala," or time, and Kali herself is considered to have "the power of time which devours all" (41). This conception resonates well with Corso's image of the bomb as something that can both stop time and force past and present together as though they were one and the same.

The organic quality of the words Corso uses to describe the bomb's destruction is also strongly reminiscent of Hindu legends of Kali, who is often pictured as wearing the dismembered limbs of her victims. Though Corso's intent seems to be to portray the bomb's destructive power as godlike, he does not primarily focus on the bomb's most seemingly awesome destructive power, the intense initial explosion that instantaneously vaporizes everything within a wide radius. Instead, Corso lingers on the disturbingly organic aftermath, suggesting images of mangled and rotting flesh: "carrion," "charnel," "carcass," "corpse." This imagery resonates with the myth of Kali's creation by the other gods as told in the Chandi,[4] in which she is given form in order to defeat a marauding army of demons. Elizabeth U. Harding retells this myth in the introduction to her book, *Kali: The Black Goddess of Dakshineswar*:

> Dust clouds gathered the stench of singed skin and rotting flesh to the blood-red horizon. The demons had been killed, and their blood flowed, accumulating here and there in small pools around carcasses of elephants and horses. Only some headless torsos of demons who refused to give up life still fought the Devi. The battle shrieks had died and the only cries now were those of jackals and hyenas. There was nothing left to kill, but the blood-intoxicated Mother in the form of Kali continued the carnage—smashing and slashing dead demons all over again.
>
> (xxii)

This apocalyptic scene very much echoes the carnal quality of Corso's word choices. Significantly, however, the poet does not portray the bomb destroying buildings and men, or even devils and demons. Corso's bomb makes a corpse of the universe itself, slaying the stars and planets, marking infinity (all of creation) with fiery annihilation. Clearly, the apocalyptic imagery that Corso employs encompasses much more than nuclear holocaust—this apocalypse is cosmic in nature, worthy of a god, as Corso clearly acknowledges with his biblical use of "thy" and "thou."

Unsurprisingly, this is not the only work in which Corso experiments with images influenced by Eastern religion. The title of his poem **"God? She's Black"** potentially has religious as well as political significance (Corso, Ferlinghetti, and Ginsberg, 25). Given the religious atmosphere in America in the early 1960s, the suggestion that God might be not only female but also African American would have been construed as aggressively offensive toward the mainstream Christian establishment, a fact that Corso would certainly have relished.[5] Secondly, the title recalls Kali's traditionally black skin. In explanation of Kali's blackness, one Tantric scripture comments, "Just as all colors disappear in black so all names and forms disappear in Kali."[6] As an aspect of Devi, the Great Mother, Kali represents both time itself and the limitless Void from which creation came (comparable, say some scholars of comparative mythology, to the "formless void" of Genesis 1:2). Kali, who is always pictured as nude aside from her bloody adornments, is also said to be clad in infinite space in order to symbolize her lack of boundaries (Harding, 52).

Though it is unclear whether Corso was aware of this imagery when he wrote about the infinite goddess of physics and space that appears in **"God? She's Black,"** his deity serves very well as an interpretation of Kali through a scientific Westerner's eyes. In it God(dess) is literally portrayed as the physical laws of nature by the first lines of five parallel stanzas: "Gases & liquids Her nature"; "Solids & solutions Her procedure"; "Formulae & equations Her law"; "Metals & alloys Her chore"; "Sound & Light Her Store." Like the Hindu Mother goddess, this God(dess) is all-encompassing, giving birth to "stars like eggs" from an "All Central Womb"; like Kali, she is described in terms of space and void, as in the phrase "Her All Void Hand." Corso uses the word "All" to describe the God(dess) a total of five times in six stanzas—clear indication of her omnipresence and limitlessness.

Given these commonalities between Hindu myth and the imagery Corso uses in **"Bomb,"** it is likely that Corso was at least indirectly influenced by Eastern myth in creating the poem's apocalyptic vision. This may also help explain why Corso's struggle with chaos and contradiction in the world around him ends with his total embrace of apocalypse at the end of the poem. If the reader interprets the poem with the similarities between Kali and the bomb in mind, then the bomb's role as a catalyst for the cycle of death and rebirth that is central to Eastern thought becomes clear. The connection between the nuclear bomb of Hiroshima and that of the poem, in fact, may be purely symbolic. The bomb's association with juxtaposition and postmodern fragmentation suggests that instead Corso's bomb serves to pull down systems of meaning and identity—causing, in other words, the symbolic death of those identities. In true rebellion against his Roman Catholic upbringing, primary among those systems of meaning that the bomb blows apart is the Judeo-Christian notion of God.

> Bomb O final Pied Piper
> both sun and firefly behind your shock waltz
> God abandoned mock-nude
> beneath His thin false-talc'd apocalypse [. . .]
> His Kingdom an eternity of crude wax
> Clogged clarions untrumpet him
> Sealed angels unsing Him
> A thunderless God A dead God
> O Bomb Thy BOOM His tomb
> (94-97, 101-5)

It is obvious from Corso's choice of details that this "dead God" is the Judeo-Christian Jehovah. In the New Testament the place where God dwells is often referred to as "the Kingdom of Heaven," which the poet pictures as a lifeless shell. Further, the trumpets and angels that are the traditional trappings of God's messengers are now engaged in his destruction. Corso's use of the phrase "Sealed angels" is likely an allusion to Revelation, in which seven seals are broken before God's wrath—Judgement Day—is unleashed on the world. God, however, is dead, a casualty of the bomb's archetypal, technological might, and his promised apocalypse has been rendered thin, false, and impotent. Instead, it is the bomb that will entice humanity to its end (note the word "final"), much as the Pied Piper of the folktale led first the rats and then the children out of Hamelin.

By echoing Nietzsche's notorious and often misunderstood statement that "God is dead," the poet also seems to agree with the philosopher that the traditional, anthropomorphic, lawgiving Western god has become inadequate for the spiritual needs of the late twentieth century. In an age of technology, it is the bomb, the "final Pied Piper," that is capable of calling humanity to death and beyond, not the biblical God of Judgement Day. God has been rendered "thunderless" by modern thought, unable to smite wrongdoers with a Jovian thunderbolt or even, given the very real and equivalent power of the bomb, to make anyone believe that godlike power actually requires a God. Corso's line "Thy BOOM His tomb" suggests that the bomb has, in a sense, stolen God's thunder; it is the might of the bomb that people fear and hold in awe, not the Judeo-Christian God's power. Clearly, Corso's poem is more than a love song to a bomb. By personifying cosmic destruction in the form of a technological reality, Corso has demonstrated the force with which technology is now changing the archetypes that populate our psychic landscape. If it is primarily the bomb that evokes fear and awe in people while God no longer does, then in some sense, technology has usurped a place in our psyches previously held only by religion.

Comparative religion scholar Ira Chernus discusses exactly this point in his 1986 book *Dr. Strangegod.* Arguing that the image of the nuclear bomb encompasses many of the elements of major religions' godfigures—infinite power, the notion of inevitability or fate, the day of apocalypse/judgement—Chernus suggests that one of the most significant experiences of the numinous for modern man is contemplating, in person or on film, the destructive power of the bomb. "[R]eligious symbols are paradoxical," Chernus writes in his introduction:

> They tell us that when we reach life's depths and extremities, order and disorder—the rational and the irrational, life and death—meet in the unifying embrace of a limitless power. Hence they tell us that to gain order and life we must accept, and perhaps experience intensely, disorder and death.
> (8-9)

This seems to be exactly the process that the poet experiences—and, ideally, helps the reader to experience—in the course of the poem. The poet begins in a state of confusion and uncertainty, telling the bomb "I cannot hate you" but failing to directly address its reality. Instead, he retreats behind humor and absurdity, sanitizing his portrayal of New York being destroyed and launching into the frankly silly description of the eclectic baseball game. His explanation for this behavior comes much later in the poem: "I am able to laugh at all things [. . .] thus to conceal my pain" (112-13). The poet is clearly cognizant of the world's contradictory nature and of the kinds of suffering that human beings can inflict. In particular, the poem contains a total of three references to capital punishment, an issue that in the poet's eyes seems to represent man's basic injustice to man.[7] From this point of tension and discomfort, the poet descends to contemplate chaos and destruction in its full, cosmic, primal majesty ("hosannah incalescent glorious liaison / BOMB O havoc antiphony molten cleft BOOM" [78-79]), and then to consider directly, for the first time, his ambivalent feelings about the world he perceives ("That I am unable to hate what is necessary to love" [109]). The result is a revelation that the reader is only privy to if she shares it. Having contemplated his own inability to make the world around him fit a coherent pattern, Corso chooses to embrace and accept it, moving into an affectionate love song to the bomb and finally into a mad paean to destruction. Though previously the poet seems to have sought order, that is, a world in which horror and beauty cannot coexist, at the close of the poem he has chosen the overwhelming reality of chaos as a viable substitute. Hindu theologians have been known to note that it is the very certainty of the death/rebirth cycle that makes it so comforting; similarly, in "**Bomb**," chaos is a constant that can be molded into a source of stability.

In seemingly direct contrast to this vision of the bomb as a godlike destroyer/creator, however, is the representation of the bomb as playful, childlike, and occasionally innocent that follows. The bomb is described as "impish" and "sportive"; Corso exhorts it to foxlike play with "Leap Bomb Bound Bomb frolic zig and zag" (72), praising its "binging bag" and "jubilee feet" (73, 74). The energy and cheerfulness of this language is unmistakable. "Binging bag" is onomatopoetic, perhaps suggesting the celebratory explosion of firecrackers; "jubilee" and "frolic" suggest energetic, joyful, dancelike motion, as does the phrase "Satyr Bomb," which evokes the destructive but oddly spiritual ecstasy of a springtime Dionysian revel. Even in the most dramatic exposition of the bomb's annihilative power, Corso includes the phrase "tee-hee-finger-in-the-mouth hop" (84), a disturbing image that suggests a bouncing child, apparently innocently delighted at the carnage. The bomb is still unmistakably female, however. In one of the poem's most surreal and hilarious passages, Corso dotes on the bomb, writing affectionately:

> Poor little Bomb that'll never be
> an Eskimo song I love thee
> I want to put a lollipop
> in thy furcal mouth
> A wig of Goldilocks on thy baldy bean
> and have you skip with me Hansel and Gretel
> along the Hollywoodian scene
>
> (133-39)

The pity and sympathy that Corso feels for the bomb are even stronger here than in the opening section. Here, he visualizes it as childlike, a being that could be comforted with candy and drawn into a friendly brother-sister frolic. Disturbingly, however, the bomb is now literally a bomb—a blunt metal object with a "baldy bean" and "bunky seat." The image of the bomb's blank face, topped with a friendly golden wig, presents a disquietingly subversive contrast between innocence and destruction.

This image may well be the key to understanding "**Bomb**," both in terms of Corso's initial conflict and his final resolution. The bewigged bomb both symbolizes the conflict between beauty and horror that so frustrates Corso and is shockingly, hysterically absurd—an emblem of Corso's initial inability to reconcile the opposites he perceives. Yet the indulgent attitude Corso takes toward the bomb suggests that the poet has emerged from his contemplation with an appreciation for the dual nature of reality, particularly as symbolized by the joyful disorder of postmodern pastiche. Harding notes that in India on certain feast days, three-, four-, and five-year-old girls are consecrated and worshipped as incarnations of Kali. Corso also seems to share the intuitive notion that in this paradoxical world, the destroyer and the child are two sides of the same coin, each an equally good face to put on the bomb's chaotic complexity. Perhaps this is an example of the numinous union of opposites that Chernus describes.

Corso's vision of the bomb as a small child may also serve to put himself into a direct, personal relationship with his subject. According to Harding, the worship of Kali in human beings and in images also helps the worshippers develop a personal relationship with their goddess. To contemplate Kali as the Void is often to depersonalize the relationship, as the worshipper assumes an insignificant position in relation to the godhead. Instead, many worshippers will characterize Kali as a mother or occasionally as a sister or daughter in order to focus their adoration and contemplation. Appropriately, this part of the poem makes frequent use of the first person, and Corso imagines himself performing physical actions toward the bomb, something that does not occur elsewhere in the poem. Though the bomb has played various feminine roles (as a dark mother, and then as a daughter or perhaps sister to Corso, as suggested by "Hansel and Gretel"), it is only at the close of the poem that Corso chooses to approach it in the intimate role of a lover.

> O Bomb in which all lovely things
> moral and physical anxiously participate
> O fairyflake plucked from the
> grandest universe tree
> O piece of heaven which gives
> both mountain and anthill a sun
> I am standing before your fantastic lily door

I bring you Midgardian roses Arcadian musk
Reputed cosmetics from the girls of heaven
Welcome me fear not thy opened door
(140-49)

The tone of this section is strangely ambiguous. The bomb's godlike attributes are pronounced: it is the fruit or the offspring of the "grandest universe tree," the might of its explosion serving as a second sun for "both mountain and anthill." Nevertheless, Corso imagines himself as an almost archetypal suitor on the doorstep of his love, bringing gifts from Edenic, mythic lands (roses from the Norse Midgard, musk from the Greek Arcadia, "reputed" (reputable?) cosmetics from an unspecified heavenly realm) to coax out his shy beloved. Corso's imagery is not unlike the writings of some mystics in their search for divine revelation. Gershom Scholem notes that the *Zohar,* the primary text of medieval Jewish mysticism, conceptualizes the Torah as a coy woman shut up in a palace who must be properly courted before she reveals her secrets, and even characterizes the mystic as a hopeful suitor who "haunts the gate of her house" (55). Here the text suggests that the poet is courting the true meaning of apocalypse—the divine revelation in which opposites meet.

The ecstasy of the climactic lines suggests that the poet's desire to see his beloved is fulfilled. All is thrown into chaos by the bomb's jubilant explosions, and Corso rejoices wildly in the barrage:

Bomb I love you
I want to kiss your clank eat your boom
You are a paean an acme of scream [. . .]
BOOM BOOM BOOM BOOM BOOM
BOOM ye skies and BOOM ye suns
BOOM BOOM ye moons ye stars BOOM
nights ye BOOM ye days ye BOOM
[. . .]
ya BANG ye BONG ye BING
the tail the fin the wing
Yes Yes into our midst a bomb will fall
Flowers will leap in joy their roots
aching
Fields will kneel proud beneath the halleluyahs
of the wind
(160-62, 165-68, 174-76)

Robert Lifton may have described it best when he called apocalypse "the orgiastic excitement of wild forces set loose" (165)—Corso imagines nature itself vibrating ecstatically at the moment of destruction, responding joyously to the resulting chaos. Just as the universe, in many traditions, rejoices in its creation, Corso imagines the earth celebrating its death with equal fervor. No whimpers for Corso; his world ends with a bang.

Corso's final lines make it clear that his vision is not one of literal nuclear holocaust. His bomb is much more metaphysical, symbolic of psychological and spiritual forces, not mere physical destruction.

Yet not enough to say a bomb will fall
or even contend celestial fire goes out
Know that the earth will madonna the
Bomb
that in the hearts of men to come more bombs
will be born
magisterial bombs wrapped in ermine all
beautiful
and they'll sit plunk on earth's grumpy
empires
fierce with mustaches of gold
(181-87)

This passage holds Corso's final thoughts on the bomb, and in fact cryptically summarizes the poem's main idea. It is not enough, says the poet, for us to know that chaos (both literal and symbolic death) is assured, to argue that even the sun ("celestial fire") will eventually burn out. The poet urges the reader to realize that life itself gives rise to this chaotic force. Birth, implies Corso, ensures that there will inevitably be death; order yields to chaos, and in the end, even the mightiest empires will bow before its equalizing might. This very Eastern conclusion summarizes one of that tradition's most troublesome truths: life is a continual struggle with irreconcilable contradictions, of which birth and death are but one inseparable pair.

Throughout the poem, Corso equates the bomb with various incarnations of the godhead, speaking of it in religious terms and assigning it cosmic powers of creation and destruction. The poet's suggestion that the technological bomb might serve as a partial replacement for God, however, carries serious metaphysical consequences. In a post-World War II world, the destructive power of the bomb is as awe-inspiringly real and terrifying as the might of a wrathful Jehovah must have seemed in a more superstitious age. Though the bomb might not have the universe-obliterating power that Corso imagines for it, nevertheless the United States alone contains enough nuclear weaponry to render Western civilization a smoking ruin, and possibly to so contaminate the rest of ecosphere as to render the earth deadly to humans for centuries to come. As China moves to expand its nuclear capabilities and reports of Russia's malfunctioning defense systems filter in, an accidental or deliberately triggered nuclear holocaust still represents a compelling reinterpretation of biblical Armageddon.

Significantly, however, the bomb is a creation of human beings, brought into existence by the collective will and effort of many individuals and the tacit support and approval of millions more. To say that the bomb serves as a god-figure suggests not only that human beings have the ability to create their own gods, but also that God (in this context, the arbiter of the fate of humanity) may be in fact an extension or a kind of emergent consciousness of a people's will. Never before, however, have human beings created a god-figure that they consciously understand is under their control. With the advent of the bomb, we have been confronted with our collective ability to self-determine—with the realization, in other words, that we have the power to choose whether or not to continue to exist, and not just on an individual level. Frighteningly, however, the individual gains no power from this knowledge. The collective will of the human race may still choose self-destruction, with individuals no more capable of effectively dissenting or escaping than a single cell of a human body could rebel against the whole. "**Bomb**" responds to this by reminding us that our lack of control is, after all, inevitable and noting that "the earth will madonna the Bomb" (183)—in other words, that creation will give birth to its own end. Taken out of its metaphysical context and made tangible by examining our group tendency to stockpile the weapons of our own physical destruction, this sentiment becomes material for a deep spiritual crisis that "**Bomb**" only begins to explore.

Though Corso does not attempt to examine the full implications of a God-bomb in his poem, he approaches the confused and chaotic world he describes with a sense of resignation, softened only by his ability to laugh. Corso's final embrace and celebration of a symbolic nuclear apocalypse suggest a belief that chaos is inevitable and inescapable; our options do not include changing the system, but only finding ways to live meaningfully within it. For Corso, this lies in embracing, celebrating, and laughing with that chaos, as he does himself with fragmented verse and surreal humor. This acceptance, however, is not arrived at easily. To fully wrestle with our participation in the cycle of life and death requires that we determine our own role—and our own responsibility—in how and whether we will continue to live.

Notes

1. This comparison is made most compellingly by Ingmar Bergman's masterpiece film *The Seventh Seal* (1957), which was released the year before "Bomb" was first published. The film is set in a plague-stricken medieval Europe and uses the Black Death to metaphorically address contemporary concerns about the bomb.
2. The selection of mainly ancient Greek elements to represent the past may not be precisely planned—Skau notes that some of the lines for "Bomb" were taken from an earlier manuscript entitled "In a Grecian Garden" (Skau, *Clown* 157).
3. From the Bhagavad-Gita, 11.32 (Jungk, 201).
4. A sacred book of the Shakta Tantras (Harding, xxiii).
5. Skau writes of Corso, "Like the Native American figure of Coyote, the Trickster, he has served as a disruptive force—self-centered, as unpredictable as a summer storm, unsettling the comfortable patterns of convention, and provoking those in contact with him to reassess their values, often much against their will" (Skau, *Clown* 1-2).
6. From the Mahanirvana Tantra (Harding, 47).
7. The poet writes, "I can't exist in a world that consents / a child in a park / a man dying in an electric chair" (110-11). The implication is that the poet cannot bear to live in a world that allows for such a contrast to exist. As a result, the repeated image of the electric chair serves as the poet's shorthand for the unbearable coexistence of joy and pain that he observes.

Works Cited

"Bang bong bing." *Time*, 7 Sept. 1959: 80.

Chernus, Ira. *Dr. Strangegod: On the Symbolic Meaning of Nuclear Weapons.* Columbia: University of South Carolina Press, 1986.

Corso, Gregory. *Bomb.* San Francisco: City Lights Books, 1958.

———. *The Happy Birthday of Death.* New York: New Directions Publishing, 1960.

Corso, Gregory, Lawrence Ferlinghetti, and Allen Ginsberg. *Penguin Modern Poets 5.* Harmondsworth, Middlesex, U.K.: Penguin Books, 1963.

Ginsberg, Allen. *Howl and Other Poems.* San Francisco: City Lights Books, 1956.

Harding, Elizabeth U. *Kali: The Black Goddess of Dakshineswar.* York Beach, Me.: Nicolas-Hays, 1993.

"Harpo Marx." *The Internet Movie Database.* 6 Mar. 2000 <http://us.imdb.com/Name?Marx,+Harpo>.

Horovitz, Michael. "On the Beat with Gregory Corso." In *The Riverside Interviews 3: Gregory Corso,* edited by Gavin Selerie. London: Binnacle, 1982.

Jungk, Robert. *Brighter Than a Thousand Suns.* New York: Harcourt, Brace, 1958.

Lifton, Robert Jay. "The Image of the 'End of the World.'" In *Visions of Apocalypse: End or Rebirth?,* edited by Saul Friedländer, Gerald Horton, Leo Marx, and Eugene Skolnikoff. New York: Holmes & Meier Publishers, 1985.

Moraes, Dom. "Somewhere Else with Allen and Gregory." *Horizon* 11.1 (Winter 1969): 67.

Nash, Thomas. "A Litany in Times of Plague." *A Small Anthology of Poems.* 01 May 26 <http://www.wmich.edu/english/tchg/lit/pms/nash.litany.html>.

Scholem, Gershom. *On the Kabbalah and Its Symbolism.* New York: Schocken Books, 1965.

Skau, Michael. *"A Clown in a Grave": Complexities and Tensions in the Works of Gregory Corso.* Carbondale: Southern Illinois University Press, 1999.

———. "On Bomb." *Gregory Corso.* 25 Sept. 2000 <http://www.english.uiuc.edu/maps/poets/a_f/corso/bomb.html>.

FURTHER READING

Bibliography

Wilson, Robert A. *A Bibliography of Works by Gregory Corso.* New York: Phoenix Book Shop, 1966.

Details Corso's periodical publications, recordings, and drawings in addition to book and broadside collections of poetry.

Biography

Cherkovski, Neeli. "Revolutionary of the Spirit." In *Whitman's Wild Children,* pp. 229-51. South Royalton, Vt.: Steerforth Press, 1999.

Focuses on personal remembrances of Corso and his early life, including explication of some of his poetry.

Honan, William H. "Gregory Corso, a Candid-Voiced Beat Poet, Dies at 70." *New York Times, www.nytimes.com/* (19 January 2001).

Highlights turning points in Corso's life that helped develop his poetry, including his relationship with poet Allen Ginsberg.

King, Robert. "Gregory Corso." In *unspeakable visions of the individual: The Beat Diary,* edited by Arthur Winfield Knight and Kit Knight, pp. 4-24. California, Pa.: 1977.

Interview with Corso covering his thoughts about poetry, other Beat writing, and friends such as Jack Kerouac and Allen Ginsberg.

Silberman, Steve. "Poet Was Ever a Subversive Spirit: Gregory Corso Despised Pretension." *San Francisco Chronicle,* (19 January 2001).

Appreciates Corso for his individualism and his ties to poetic tradition, reflecting on Corso's lifelong irreverence.

Criticism

Ball, Gordon. "Corso's Triumphant Surrender: *Herald of the Autochthonic Spirit.*" *American Book Review* 4, no. 6 (1982): 84.

Review of Herald of the Autochthonic Spirit *noting the strengths of Corso's earlier work and asserting a growth in his poetic vision.*

Challis, Chris. "The Fabulous Wordslinger." In *Quest for Kerouac,* pp. 183-94. New York: Faber and Faber, 1984.

Places Corso's career in the context of the Beat movement, praising his sense of form and compassion.

Gaiser, Carolyn. "Gregory Corso: A Poet, the Beat Way." In *A Casebook on the Beat,* edited by Thomas Parkinson, pp. 266-75. New York: Thomas Y. Crowell Company: 1961.

Distinguishes Corso from other Beats by noting his interest in form, his irreverent sense of humor, his youth, and his troubled background.

Kraemer, Christine Hoff. "The Brake of Time: Corso's Bomb as Postmodern God(dess)." *Texas Studies in Language and Literature* 44, no. 2 (summer 2002): 211-29.

Argues that the postmodern composition of Corso's poem "Bomb" places the idea of nuclear threat in a new and more organic context.

Seigel, Catharine. "Corso, Kinnell, and the Bomb." *University of Dayton Review* (1987): 95-103.

Compares Corso's poem "Bomb" to the work of Galway Kinnell, a poet noted for politically engaged verse, and discusses "Bomb" as a response to nuclear threat.

Stephenson, Gregory. "'The Arcadian Map': Notes on the Poetry of Gregory Corso." In *The Daybreak Boys: Essays on the Literature of the Beat Generation,* pp. 74-89. Carbondale: Southern Illinois University Press, 1990.

Identifies the central themes that constitute Corso's poetic vision, such as the struggle of light against darkness, and includes an abridged version of several sections of Stephenson's 1989 study of Corso and his poetry.

Thurley, Geoffrey. "The Development of the New Language: Wieners, Jones, McClure, Whalen, Corso." In *The American Moment: American Poetry in the Mid-Century,* pp. 187-209. London: Edward Arnold, 1977.

Declares that Corso's best poetry demonstrates the full potential of the Beat movement and counters the deadening spirit of academic poetry.

OTHER SOURCES FROM GALE:

Additional coverage of Corso's life and career is contained in the following sources published by the Gale Group: *American Writers Supplement* 12; *Contemporary Authors,* Vols. 5-8R; *Contemporary Authors New Revision Series,* Vols. 41, 76; *Contemporary Literary Criticism,* Vols. 1, 11; *Contemporary Poets; Dictionary of Literary Biography,* Vols. 5, 16, 237; *DISCovering Authors 3.0; Literature Resource Center; Major 20th-Century Writers; Poetry Criticism,* Vol. 33; and *World Poets.*

DIANE DI PRIMA

(1934 -)

American poet, essayist, playwright, screenwriter, translator, and editor.

In the male-dominated Beat Generation, di Prima stands out as a prominent female voice. In addition to her many works of poetry and prose, she was influential as an editor involved with *Yugen* and *Kulchur,* two magazines that featured Beat authors, and with *The Floating Bear,* a newsletter she coedited with LeRoi Jones.

BIOGRAPHICAL INFORMATION

Di Prima was born in Brooklyn, New York, on August 6, 1934, the eldest of three children born to Francis and Emma di Prima. She was raised in a middle-class Italian-American household, and both of her parents had graduated from college. Di Prima graduated from Hunter College High School, an elite public college preparatory program in New York City, and later attended Swarthmore College for two years. She left Swarthmore in 1953 to pursue a more unconventional lifestyle in Greenwich Village, joining a counterculture that opposed middle-class values and encouraged sexual freedom and the use of drugs. Her first collection of poetry, *This Kind of Bird Flies Backward* was published in 1958, and was followed by a collection of poetry and prose titled *Dinners and Nightmares* in 1961. Di Prima coedited *The Floating Bear,* a monthly poetry journal, with Jones between 1961 and 1969. *The Floating Bear* provided a forum for young writers in the New York area and included contributions by many of the well-known Beats, including Jack Kerouac, Philip Whalen, William Burroughs, and others. Although Jones and di Prima often disagreed about the journal's contents, their diverse interests and opinions resulted in a varied selection of work published in the journal. The journal published writings that dealt with controversial subject matter, and Jones and di Prima were eventually arrested on the grounds that they had used the mail to distribute obscene materials. Demanding a grand jury hearing, Jones defended himself and di Prima by reading "obscene" portions of classics such as James Joyce's *Ulysses*; the jury failed to return an indictment. In 1965, di Prima moved to Monroe, New York, and the following year to Millbrook, New York, where she joined Timothy Leary's experimental community. In 1968, di Prima went to San Francisco. She is the mother of five children and has been married and divorced twice.

MAJOR WORKS

Earthsong: Poems 1957-1959 (1968) is a collection comprised of di Prima's early work from the 1950s on the theme of love. The poems explore her love for her partners and her children and are explicit in their portrayals of sexual love, evidencing di Prima's exploration of unconventional poetic form and expression. The poetry and prose collection *Dinners and Nightmares* is dedicated to di Prima's "pads and the people who shared them with me." The first section, "dinners," is a sequence of prose narratives based on mealtime events, while the "nightmares" section contains a series of poems. The 1963 poetry collection *The New Handbook of Heaven* contains poems in which di Prima's treats the theme of death, often in poems about missing or deceased friends and relatives. In 1969 di Prima's *Memoirs of a Beatnik* was published. In this autobiographical account (thinly disguised as fiction), di Prima relates her life from the time she was a seventeen-year-old college dropout to the time she recognizes herself as being part of the Beat Generation. *Memoirs* generated controversy, largely due to di Prima's explicit delineation of her encounters with a variety of lovers, both male and female; the "characters" are easily recognizable as di Prima's friends. She provides glimpses into Greenwich Village bohemian life of the 1950s, describing gay bars, popular dances like the Fish, modeling for photopornographers and for painter Raphael Soyer, sleeping in hallways and Washington Square Park, and an excursion to an upstate New York hootenanny, with time out for a visit to Ezra Pound at St. Elizabeth's Hospital in Washington. Di Prima also discusses the "rule of Cool," a code of behavior that meant a controlled aloofness and studied ambiguities, especially with respect to personal emotions. Di Prima's most comprehensive and complicated work is her book-length poem *Loba, Parts I-VIII* (1978), in which she endeavors to express the full range of feelings and being of the "she-wolf," or woman. Di Prima's memoir, *Recollections of My Life as a Woman: The New York Years* (2001), provides an account of her participation in the artistic renaissance that occurred in New York and on the West Coast during the 1960s. She also describes events of her early years, including memories of an abusive father and mother, her attendance at a high school for the gifted, and details of her life experiences during the 1950s and 1960s.

CRITICAL RECEPTION

Critics regard di Prima's works as honest, accessible, reflections on her life as part of the Beat Generation, as a woman, and as an artist. Di Prima has been lauded for the universality of her subject matter; readers easily identify and empathize with her narrators and the experiences they share, and find this experience quite moving and personally illuminating. Blossom S. Kirschenbaum notes that extended family is oten a focus of di Prima's poetry. In an analysis of *Loba,* Rochelle Ratner describes this work as illustrative of di Prima's full absorption in writing about the female experience. As Ratner states: "In a strange way, di Prima seems to be speaking for all those women who make poems out of their anger, and for those women who still hold their pain silently within them." In di Prima's continuing exploration of the female experience, her memoirs *Reflections of My Life as a Woman,* provide readers with a view of her life—a conflicting world of family obligations and pressure from friends who felt that writing poetry required freedom. In his review of *Reflections,* Jeff Zaleski comments: "She tells her story well, skillfully interweaving events with lyrical commentary on her inner life."

PRINCIPAL WORKS

This Kind of Bird Flies Backward (poetry) 1958

Dinners and Nightmares (poetry and prose) 1961; revised edition, 1974

The New Handbook of Heaven (poetry) 1963

Poet's Vaudeville (poetry) 1964

Haiku (poetry) 1966

Earthsong: Poems 1957-1959 (poetry) 1968

Hotel Albert: Poems (poetry) 1968

L.A. Odyssey (poetry) 1969

Memoirs of a Beatnik (memoirs) 1969

The Book of Hours (poetry) 1970

Kerhonkson Journal: 1966 (poetry) 1971

Revolutionary Letters (poetry) 1971

XV Dedications: Poems (poetry) 1971

Loba: Part I (poetry) 1973

Brass Furnace Going Out: Song After an Abortion (poetry) 1975

Selected Poems, 1956-1975 (poetry) 1975

Loba: Part II (poetry) 1977

Loba: Parts I-VIII (poetry) 1978

Pieces of a Song (poetry) 1990

Recollections of My Life as a Woman: The New York Years (memoirs) 2001

GENERAL COMMENTARY

BLOSSOM S. KIRSCHENBAUM (ESSAY DATE FALL-WINTER 1987)

SOURCE: Kirschenbaum, Blossom S. "Diane di Prima: Extending *La Famiglia.*" *MELUS* 14, nos. 3-4 (fall-winter 1987): 53-67.

In the following essay, Kirschenbaum focuses on the manner in which di Prima handles the various aspects of family life in her poetry.

In her scandalous little book ***Memoirs of a Beatnik*** (1969), Diane di Prima tells how one afternoon someone handed her a copy of Allen Ginsberg's *Howl and Other Poems* (1956); she kept thinking the phrase "breaking ground," and she felt she was about to meet her brothers.[1] In fact, a year later she did meet Allen Ginsberg and Jack Kerouac. Another year later Lawrence Ferlinghetti, introducing her book ***This Kind of Bird Flies Backward*** (1958), wrote: "Here's a sound not heard before. The voice is gritty. The eye turns. The heart is in it." Di Prima was meeting brothers—members of the Beat confraternity. Reacting to postwar consumerism, conformity and boredom, they were in spiritual crisis. They reacted with wild expenditures of energy: fast cars, wild parties, jazz, sex, drugs and kicks. This is the confraternity of John Clellon Holmes' novel *Go* (1952), generally credited as the first and most vivid literary account of early Beat life. Characters can be recognized as Ginsberg and Kerouac, with portraits too of Herbert Huncke, Neal Cassady, and William S. Burroughs. Kerouac's *On the Road* came out in 1957. The media promptly promoted the movement. By 1958, when Ferlinghetti's *A Coney Island of the Mind* appeared, *Esquire* also published "The Philosophy of the Beat Generation." In 1959, when Burroughs' *The Naked Lunch* was issued, so was di Prima's ***13 Nightmares.*** Mainstream and counterculture seemed in competition to perpetrate the outrageous and the perverse—and in competition to define basic values. As a difficult daughter flouting parental standards, di Prima affirmed familial relationships; in both work and personal life she was seeking out a family of affinity.

"Family" has multiple meanings and, as *The New York Times* has reported (September 2, 1988), family law is even now the battleground of social revolution. Biologically, the term is genetic and implies descent from a common ancestry. It also includes relationships recognized by law, such as marriage and adoption. Sometimes it refers to members of a household who function together as a family. The dispersed extended family of "blood" relatives and in-laws may include attached and honorary members. Most broadly, and especially in a religious spirit, one may speak of the Family of Humanity within the parenthood of God. "Family" can take on a pejorative sense also, as in reference to criminal "families." As a result of changes in family structure, childbearing, and personal relationships, the concept of family is now being challenged. According to the *Times*, "new reproductive technology, the crumbling of stereotypes about women's roles and a new assertiveness on the part of fathers converged" to force reexamination of the government's role in defining, sustaining, and even destroying a family. Professor Martha Minow of Harvard Law School is cited as noting "that the law sometimes looks at families as a unit, entitled to protection against government interference, while at other times it elevates the individual rights of some family members over others." Unwed fathers now seek recognition for families that in a legal sense never existed and even press claims against women wishing to abort a pregnancy. Conventions are changing—sometimes because individuals have been unsocialized, delinquent, or just blundering; sometimes because different groups have upheld different standards; and sometimes because the good-hearted have refused to accept what they perceived as cruel, oppressive, or unnatural regulation by a society that is corrupt. Hence family quarrels may in essence be quarrels over the definition of "family."

As a poet concerned with the meaning of words, and as a woman of childbearing capability, di Prima participated deliberately in changing the meaning of the term "family." At the time when she came of age, the counterculture was asserting, and demanding recognition of, relationships not previously sanctioned. Some associations termed familial were voluntary rather than legal, in protest against the legal apparatus of the time; some were associations for which no legal provision existed. Certainly the privileged status of conventional, heterosexual, ostensibly monogamous marriage was being challenged, and the status of the nuclear family too, as no worthier than other forms of love and other domestic arrangements. Alternatives competed with officially endorsed patterns.

Neither marriage nor women had a privileged status among the Beats. Joyce Johnson (novelist and sometime lover of Kerouac, and also high-schoolmate of di Prima) referred to women, in the title of her prizewinning memoir, as *Minor Characters* (1983). Women were relegated to supporting roles, caretakers or spoilsports, for the Beats preferred each other's male company and as men they had greater confidence in their own artistic roles. Di Prima's resentment of the assumption that a man's creativity is more important emerges in her poem **"The Quarrel,"** from ***Dinners and Nightmares*** (1961), in which a man named Mark draws while the "chick," brooding that she too has work of her own to do, resenting his arrogance and innocence, goes to the kitchen to wash dishes; "Hey hon," he calls after her, "It says here Picasso produces fourteen hours a day." A woman had to be tough and cunning to break through stereotyped roles without being unsexed.

Di Prima could have assumed the role of "queen bee;" instead, she paid tribute to other women poets. She has poems to sister-spirits like Audre Lorde, another classmate at Hunter High, who was midwife to her second child Dominique (Minnie), fathered by LeRoi Jones (now Imamu Amiri Baraka). Di Prima also wrote the introduction to Lorde's *The First Cities* (1968) and published Lorde's group of seven poems *Between Our Selves* through Eidolon Editions at Point Reyes in 1976. Some talented women were not brazen enough for what the times required. Hettie Green, for instance, whose Jewish family sat *shiva* for her when she married LeRoi Jones, found courage to stand in the freezing wind near Cooper Union and hand out leaflets advertising her husband's reading—but she would never read her own work and only years later asserted that it was any good. (*Minor Characters,* 212-218). Gradually women have gained recognition as poets by publishing and reading, inclusion in anthologies, critical studies devoted to their works. Di Prima honors some of them. In ***Loba, Parts I-VIII*** of 1978, di Prima's list "**Some of the People This Poem Is For**" includes poets Lenore Kandel, Audre Lorde, Anne Waldman, Alta, Muriel Rukeyser, H. D., Jane Bowles, Laura Riding, and Adrienne Rich.[2] Nevertheless, as Helen Barolini remarked of di Prima, in introducing poems included in the anthology *The Dream Book,* "She is the most important woman poet of the counterculture which grew out of the 1960's" (366).

This poet who had to find siblings, and who would later celebrate her Italian heritage, was born in New York in summer of 1934, to parents who were lawyers. Early poems expressed an abstract, idealized kind of love. One dated "May 29, 1951" in three parts invokes "Brother of mine, when they first spoke of you I knew you for all things Beethoven meant." It continues "Friend, and I could not help you for you never turned to flesh." The last part beseeches, "Love I will call you now I call you true"—and it concludes most intimately and with the most diffusion, "for you are rain by now and wind and all the nights of my life black and young and yes my lad I love you first and truest." These lines sing conviction, openness, aspiration; they echo Edna St. Vincent Millay. In other poems from the same book (***This Kind of Bird Flies Backward,*** 1958), the speaker has leapt ahead to a hip bravado:

> So here I am the coolest in New York
> what dont swing I dont push.
>
> In some Elysian field
> by a big tree
> I chew my pride
> like cud.

It is a contained posture, but defiant. Difficult daughters breaking rules of family, church, and state seem disloyal to their affronted and aggrieved elders, when often they are quarreling fiercely over the terms of relationships they value most.

"Nineteen-year-old girls did not leave home except for dormitories or marriage," Joyce Johnson has remarked about the 1950s. "If you wished to live free, you could not also expect to live well" (*Minor Characters,* 63). Though she had planned to become a theoretical physicist, di Prima stayed at Swarthmore only one year. Her 1961 book ***Dinners and Nightmares*** is dedicated "To my three pads & the people who shared them with me. . . ." It details the grungy, improvised, uneven Beat life. The first entry in the section "What I Ate Where" describes "menstrual pudding," potatoes in tomato sauce pretending to be stew, eaten in a room with taupe walls during four grey November days (9-11). Immediately following in the text is a courtship dinner, martinis, shrimp and wild rice in a cream sauce, he half-Cherokee and handsome, she radiant and not yet aware she is pregnant; they talk of classical Chinese and of Cape Cod in winter, all in anticipation of sex by firelight. Sensual delights make hard times endurable, even when hard times include rats in the kitchen. Recollected meals of "nothing but Oreos" (15) and of Kraft cheese spreads on Pepperidge Farm bread are interspersed with February 1954's "anything that came in small enough jars. [W]e lived off what we could steal from the a & p" (19). Hot Plate Cooking alternates with holiday feasts.

One can imagine parental distress. It is explicit in a scene with an Old Family Friend (21):

> it was chinese food but so expensive you didn't know it was chinese . . . then the Old Framily Fiend [sic] and I had an argument, which I will not mention by name, . . . anyway it was the kind that ends with you are killing your parents, what right have you got to breathe out just because you breathed in, and there are already too many babies in ny.

The angry narrator later vomits and cries—then cleans up and goes with her friend to Rumpelmayer's, too brightly lit for weeping, to warm herself there with onion soup. The generations are at war. Yet in ***Dinners and Nightmares*** di Prima confides, "once in a while I like it to go back to brooklyn and see those houses, not more than four stories with lawns out front, even in winter that's nice, the houses are set back and there's light and air" (36). By then, she already has a baby with her, and the baby's father is not her husband.

Di Prima has been twice married: to Alan S. Marlowe, an actor-model-director (1962-69), and to Grant Fisher (1972-75). Marital commitment is obviously not forever, for her, nor does it replace vocation; it only parallels work and childrearing. Her affair with LeRoi Jones included coediting *Floating Bear* for two years (she went on editing it afterwards); her ***The New Handbook of Heaven*** (1963) is for him. Poems flaunt defiance of family even while enlarging the circle of quasi-family, which comes to include other poets, those who share the pads, those with whom one eats—one's true "com-panions,"—and those with whom one maintains enduring relationships. The tradition of family persists.

Holding to tradition while seeming to flout it is also evident in *Various Fables from Various Places* (1960), which she edited. Here fables from Legends of Florence and some by da Vinci are listed along with fables from thirteen other cultures world-wide—including Africa, India and Tibet. Di Prima is universalizing the context of gems from her own heritage as they are to be passed along to the next generation. Her Afterword expresses an eclectic and relativist stance:

> The shape of a fable seems to be something like this: there is a situation given or postulated from which something is bound to come. Something comes from it; that is, in most cases somebody gets his deserts—just or unjust. A comment is made thereon, either explicit . . . or implied in the action itself. And that's, in most cases, that. The distinguishing thing about the shape of a fable, in contrast to most folk literature, is its brevity and sharp focus.
>
> (183)

The thrust is for a longer history than that of the United States, for transcending national boundaries, and for tuning in to lasting stories that preserve experience of the whole human race.

Brevity and sharp focus characterize many of di Prima's own poems. **"Love Poem #11"** consists of four short lines; **"Nightmare 5"** has just one single line, "Get your cut throat off my knife." **"More or Less Love Poem #10"** is cast synoptically:

> you are not quite
> the air i breathe
> thank god.
>
> so go.

She chose another succinct form for a volume of haiku which was issued in 1966. However aphoristic, though, di Prima was no formal innovator. She used "hip" diction and laconic lines to practice stances and thereby evolve a mythos.

Consciously di Prima was both ancestor and descendant, and several poems celebrate her lineage. ***Revolutionary Letters*** (1971), dedicated to Bob Dylan, opens with **"April Fool Birthday Poem for Grandpa"**:

> thank you
> for honestly weeping in time to
> innumberable heartbreaking
> italian operas for
> pulling my hair when I
> pulled the leaves off the trees so I'd
> know how it feels, we are
> involved in it now, revolution, up to our
> knees and the tide is rising, . . .

She recalls the Bronx park in spring dusk where she learned anarchism, hearing her grandfather "thunder Dante, and Giordano Bruno," and she wants him to know

> we do it for you, and your ilk, for Carlo Tresca,
> for Sacco and Vanzetti, without knowing
> it, or thinking about it, as we do it for Aubrey
> Beardsley

—she is working out her own definition and membership for "family." She names more names before concluding

> we do it for
> the stars over the Bronx
> that they may look on earth
> and not be ashamed.

Even as she distances her parents, she carries forward an understanding of her grandfather's legacy.

She refuses to "know her place" so long as that place is assigned rather than chosen. In ***Revolutionary Letters*** (#49) she therefore makes little distinction between revolutionary and criminal, for according to di Prima "All prisoners are political prisoners," and that includes pot-smokers, holdup men, forgers, whores, and pimps; murderers too. The ***Letters*** advise:

> get up, put on your shoes, get
> started, someone will finish.
>
> (#2)
>
> store water; make a point of filling your bathtub
> at the first news of trouble: . . .
>
> (#3)
>
> take vitamin B along with amphetamines, try
> powdered guarana root, available
> at herb drugstores, it is an up
> used by Peruvian mountainfolk, tastes
> like mocha (bitter) can be put in tea
>
> (#5)
>
> are you prepared
> to hide someone in your home indefinitely
> say, two to six weeks, you going out
> for food, etc., so he never
> hits the street, to keep your friends away

coolly, so they ask no questions, to nurse
him, or her, as necessary, . . .

(#14)

Self-dramatizing? not in context of the 1968 Democratic convention in Chicago, not in context of Kent State, not if we connect newspaper headlines with our private lives, as di Prima insists on doing. In her poems di Prima addresses not only her intimates, with whose names she is thereby acquainting her readers, but also public figures: Huey Newton, Kwame Nkrumah. Her inveighing against "ecology / totally fucked up" (#37) and announcing that she "dropped acid in Tompkins Square Park with my / brothers & sisters" (#39) may not seem like effective resistance; but it is a kind of bearing witness, a refusal of complicity with the Establishment. And di Prima is redefining family: "brothers & sisters" are political allies. While her "we" (as in "we buy the arms and the armed men, we have placed them / on all the thrones of South America") accepts complicity as an American—this is no finger-pointing to "you" or "they,"—she thereby assumes the obligation to know and resist. It is the commitment of feminists who work to integrate their own lives with historical processes.

Is this really poetry? For the past two decades, the flow of poetry by women demonstrates "a need to reveal rather than to conceal, to use a language bare not only of adornment but of obliqueness," as Suzanne Juhasz has put it (*Naked and Fiery Forms, Modern American Poetry by Women, A New Tradition,* 178-179). The first freedom is the freedom to say everything. Like Alta (founder of Shameless Hussy Press) and others, di Prima writes not for eternity, but for now—and like Alta, Judy Grahn, and Susan Griffin, she avoids publication by the very establishment against which she is in revolt. These women prefer to operate their own presses.

Even in revolt, though, or especially in revolt, di Prima claims precedents in her own cultural past. In **"Minnesota Morning Ode,"** (from ***Selected Poems, 1956-76,*** 1977, 294-295), she calls Giordano Bruno "brother, waiting in prison / eight years to be burned, to find the sun at last / on the Campo de Fiori . . ." and identifies with him:

yes, you are right—what's a millennium
or two to us, brother? The gods can wait

for she is determined to build where she is, or to build

. . . at Attica
& Wounded Knee
on the Campo de Fiori, at the Vatican:
the strong bright light of flesh which is the link
the laughter, which transmutes.

From her personal past she commemorates **"Backyard"** (320) and apostrophizes Brooklyn, remembering

where fences crumbled under the weight of
rambling roses
and naked plaster women bent eternally white
over birdbaths
the icicles on the chains of the swings tore my
fingers
& the creaking tomato plants tore my heart as
they wrapped their
roots around fish heads rotting beneath
them
& the phonograph too creaked Caruso come
down from the skies; Tito
Gobbi in gondola; Gigli ridiculous in
soldier uniform; Lanza frenetic

—and she regrets the inattention and claustrophobia of the people among whom she lived.

"To My Father," confrontational in tone, implores and urges rhetorical questions, but goes beyond rebellion. Incompatibility is accepted, in this poem, and that acceptance is the basis for acceptance of the self and of continuity:

In my dreams you stand among roses.
You are still the fine gardener you were.
You worry about mother.
You are still the fierce wind, the intolerable force
that almost broke me.
Who forced my young body into awkward and
proper clothes
Who spoke of his standing in the community.
And men's touch is still a little absurd to me
because you trembled when you touched me.
What external law were you expounding?
How can I take your name like prayer?
My youngest son has your eyes.

With respect and hurt love di Prima pays tribute to what she must reject.

Inspired by her grandfather, defying her father, finding brothers and sisters and lovers, di Prima goes on to share specifically female experiences. She is frank, even blatant, about subjects that in her own girlhood were kept private to the point of secrecy. Menstruation, for instance, is a subject that has only lately entered both poetry and prose. Joyce Johnson has recalled her mother's instruction in the shames of "down below," and Toni Morrison in *The Bluest Eye* has a girl character's mispronunciation of "ministration" highlight religious implications of blood and life. The popular culture has come so far that tampons are now advertised on television instead of being asked for in hushed tones from the pharmacist.

Yet some readers, perhaps those who still refer to "the curse" or to "being unwell," can no doubt be shocked by

"I GET MY PERIOD, SEPTEMBER 1964"

How can I forgive you this blood?
Which was not to flow again, but to cling joy-
ously to my womb
To grow, and become a son?

(*Selected Poems,* 136)

In **"Brass Furnace Going Out: Song after an Abortion"** di Prima writes:

I want you in a bottle to send to your father
with a long bitter note. I want him to know
I'll not forgive you, or him for not being born
for drying up, quitting
at the first harsh treatment
as if the whole thing were a rent party
& somebody stepped on your feet

In her poem **"Marriage"**—quite different from Gregory Corso's marvelous parody of Eliot—di Prima speaks as a wife, calmly accepting difference as "a thing of value, a bone of contention." **"Prayer to the Mothers"** appeals to the ancient who

attend on
births, dance on our dead, croon, fuck, embrace
our weariness, you lurk here still, mutter
in caves, warn, warn & weave . . .

These are her guardians against

the metal men who walk
on all our substance, crushing flesh
to swamp

(*Selected Poems,* 249)

"Song of Black Nana" begins "An unloved woman is a gnarled, misshapen thing / whatever her form."

Collected Poems, dedicated to di Prima's children, includes several addressed to and about them: **"Jeanne Poems"** (29—for her eldest), **"Letter to Jeanne"** (268), **"To Tara"** (her fourth, 255), **"Tara"** (198). The book functions, though, to redefine the family—commemorating dear ones living and gone, letting the children know who are their people, and with whom they have a history of reciprocal allegiance.

In the most recent work discussed here, ***Loba I-VIII,*** the poet, who considers herself Buddhist, in her **"Ave"** addresses the goddess:

you lie with the unicorn
you lie with the cobra
you lie in the dry grass
you lie with the yeti
you flick long cocks of satyrs with your tongue

—this is the "gypsy mother" by turns fierce and cowering, killing and birthing. **"Loba in Childbed"** (42-44) is a poem of screaming, but also of the mantra and the mandala—of focusing one's private archetypal magic. It is followed by **"The Loba Sings to Her Cub"**: "O my mole, sudden & perfect / golden gopher tunneling / to light, . . ." The image is wild, brave, wise:

The horned lady
stands on lions.
She is winged &
flanked by owls.

In this book the poet identifies with **"Lilith. Huntress. Guinevere."** As in the earlier **"Poem to a Statue of Shiva in the Garments of Kali"** (***Selected Poems,*** 157), the goddess is definitely not virgin mother, nor nurturer merely, but female power in all manifestations, evil as well as good.

This fierceness is not reconciled with contemplative Buddhism; but it accords with what Gary Snyder wrote about the Beats in "Note on the Religious Tendencies" (quoted by Bruce Cook, *The Beat Generation,* 155-156). Three things go on, he said: Vision and illumination-seeking; Love, respect for life, abandon, Whitman, pacifism, anarchism, etc.; and Discipline, aesthetics, and tradition. He summarizes: "real commitment to the stewpot of the world and real insight into the vision-lands of the unconscious." Buddhism, in contradistinction to Catholicism, has no Messiah, no afterlife, no limiting hagiology, and no history of corruption or exhaustion in the West. The androgynous image of the Buddha, gender-neutral, offers escape from stereotyped sex-attributes and -roles, suggesting rather the complete individual harmonious with Jungian psychology. In any case, di Prima's corpus of poetry has never promised a coherent rational philosophical system. Its guiding postulate seems rather what is given in the poem **"Bob Creeley, Reading"** (from ***Selected Poems,*** 304):

"everything is permitted
nothing
is free" . . .

In whatever way a reader evaluates the Beat and subsequent counter-culture, whether as Norman Podhoretz's "Know-Nothing Bohemians" or as Lawrence Lipton's "Holy Barbarians," unquestionably it was very American and globally exported. Abroad too some saw the Beats as adolescent rebels, juvenile delinquents, and sensation-seekers (and would have seen Scott Fitzgerald and Ernest Hemingway that way too), while others recognized the Beats' refusal to be insulated, propagandized, and bribed, their insistence on authentic experience. After all, not everyone found "squares" simply respectable; others saw them as complacent, stodgy, sterile, and spiritually dead. It was a time of polarization between "palefaces" and "redskins," a time of the battle of the anthologies. Culture was being politicized, or increasingly recognized as political.

Both here and abroad, culture-heroes once considered criminal moved on to careers of respectability and honor. Genet, after a career of theft, blackmail, and prostitution, became a poet/playwright and culture hero of Paris; di Prima was responsible for translating a pirated bilingual edition of his *The Man Condemned to Death/Le condamńe a mort.* So too William S. Burroughs, whose *Junkie* was first published pseudonymously, now lectures at universities, and has been honored by the American Academy of Arts and Letters, and is welcomed by socially prominent hostesses. Allen Ginsberg too is respectable; by 1978 he got the literature medal of the National Arts Club, awarded a decade earlier to Louis Auchincloss; his *Collected Poems 1947-1980* were published under terms of a six-figure contract and scored a critical success; he has taught at Brooklyn College and he read at the December 1986 national convention of the Modern Language Association.

The anti-academicism of the Beats has come full circle—not the first such turnaround. As earlier fugitives from academe followed Charles Olson to Black Mountain College in North Carolina, this generation frequents the Naropa Institute in Boulder, Colorado. Di Prima teaches there and also at New College of California and the San Francisco Institute of Magical and Healing Arts. She travels to other campuses to give workshops.

While becoming respectable and institutional, the counterculture has changed the dominant culture's mores. In the time since nice girls did not leave home except for dormitories or marriage, women have evolved "a pattern more like men's—sowing wild oats, then marriage, then maybe some affairs. Women have taken charge of their sex lives," as Barbara Ehrenreich, author and social historian, put it when interviewed by Steven Findlay for *USA Today,* October 28, 1986, 11A. She traces the first real mass expression of female sexuality not to the Beat movement but rather to Beatlemania, which was both commercial culture and counter-culture—it was innovative music, a new sound. Ehrenreich optimistically sees the sexual revolution as supporting monogamy, since women are now more capable of invigorating a sex life with one other person. Women's independence, she says, is no threat to the family because "Women's sexual revolution is more oriented towards staying and working it out." Some men feel threatened; and for women "Self-confidence is not easy at the minimum wage." It was di Prima's stance, though, to live as though the revolution had already been accomplished—to separate sex from marriage and marriage from childrearing, and to improvise a quasi-familial supportive network. Once, such behavior was a disgrace. By now, the radical writers of the 1960s have come to be recognized as citizens, taxpayers and recipients of awards.

It is not the intent of this paper to measure di Prima's poetic achievement. I have not seen her plays, though six have been produced in New York, and I have not seen her most recent publications. They are hard to come by, issued in limited editions of 100 to 2,000 copies, sometimes printed by hand like ***The Book of Hours,*** or even including hand-written poems, as do twelve of the 112 copies of ***Haiku*** (1967); such work is only later picked up for wider distribution. It can be fairly said, though, that her innovation is not metrical or formal. Her diction resembles that of other Beat poets in inclusion of argot from jazz musicians, narcotics users, prostitutes—those who gamble with life, live marginally, evade the law or claim allegiance to a higher law, and connive to gratify socially disapproved desires. Di Prima's stance has been imitated, however: tough, cool, revolutionary; "honest, terse, hurt in a way that counts," as Seymour Krim said as long ago as 1960, when he printed ***13 Nightmares*** in his anthology *The Beats.* Through their own public-relations skills and through cooptation by the media, the Beats have succeeded fabulously. The gap is now closed.

How, then, has di Prima extended *la famiglia*? She is very Italian in the mode described by Luigi Barzini, distinguished Milan-born American-educated journalist. The thesis of his book *The Italians,* written in English for Americans, is that Italy's "lively, brave, energetic" people were slow to unify and lost foreign wars because of excessive individualism—yet "The Italians," he wrote, "seem happy" (57). He infers, "the pleasure of Italy comes from living in a world made by man, for man, on man's measurements." It is this individualism and human scale, recollected from her New York childhood and ancestral images, that di Prima upholds—though she insists that the world be made also by woman, for woman, on woman's measurements.

Further, according to Barzini, "The strength of the [Italian] family is not only . . . the bulwark against disorder, but, at the same time, one of its principal causes. It has actively fomented chaos in many ways especially by rendering useless the development of strong political institutions" (191). He continues:

> Italians' family loyalty is their true patriotism. In the outside world, amidst the chaos and the disorder of society, they often feel compelled to employ the wiles of underground fighters in enemy-occupied territory.

Such views were updated in an article in *Time* (August 17, 1981) in the epigraph to which Barzini is quoted, along with businessman Domenic Barili, who remarks, "We say—and it is only partly a joke—that provided there is no government, we are safe." Further along in "Land of Miracles—And *Malgrado,*" Italo Calvino is quoted:

> The real Italian miracle is that the society holds together economically and morally while its public life disintegrates. Italians know that they can count only on their own individual strength, that it is useless to expect anything from an authority whose institutions do not function.
>
> (9)

Clientelismo, the *economia sommersa,* and the conviction of *il piccolo è bello* that supports cottage industry and family factories in efficient decentralization: these are techniques for survival. In a comparable spirit, loyalty to reconstituted family and the wiles of an underground fighter are notably exemplified in di Prima's ***Revolutionary Letters*** and in her oeuvre generally.

Barzini alleged in his book (202) that though nominally male-chauvinist, Italy was really a "cryptomatriarchy"—that is his term. In his not uncontroversial formulation, traditionally self-sacrificing womanhood was honored, from the phrase *Mamma mia!* through invocations of the Madonna. By rejecting self-sacrifice, and by sexualizing (even bestializing) the female goddess, di Prima has veered away from traditional Italian values and content. Yet in Italy too values have changed. Migration, legalized divorce, emancipation of the young, social acceptance of "illegitimate" couples, and the growing number of nuclear rather than extended families do alter inherited patterns. Perhaps this "cryptomatriarchy" emerges in di Prima, relocated.

Confirming this cooptation and transmutation of inherited patterns, Todd Gitlin (*The Sixties; Years of Hope, Days of Rage,* 1987) has recently commented:

> The beats were adept at turning established values against the society that enshrined them. Was this the era of worship, when families were supposed to "pray together" in order to "stay together"? The beats preached love, too, and spoke their own home-style Buddhist language of the spirit. Were the suburbs clannish about "togetherness"? The beats celebrated epiphanies of companionship in the form of their own selective and exclusive human buddyhood—a fragile community, for the buddies were always having lovers' quarrels.

As descriptions of Establishment and Counterculture merge, the main effect seems to be a blurring of standards. With respectability discredited and outrageousness acclaimed, the dialectic may have to be resolved through new attention to the concept of human decency.

La famiglia, then, is extended both biologically and socially—and metaphorically too. The sense of tribal life appears in di Prima's work as not only Italian. Traditionally, as Barzini and many others have noted, the Chinese and the Jews also went in for extended family; but di Prima lengthens the cultural list to include also Africans and Native Americans. She has a strong sense of artists as confraternity and sorority. Relatives, friends, and lovers conjoin as family here; the published list of those for whom she is writing includes someone with her mother's maiden name as well as the different surnames of her children. In directly challenging the concept of legitimacy, in revising the index of *who really counts,* and in using non-Anglo verse forms (free verse, haiku, Indian chants, blues), di Prima has been rewriting history and, by implication, genealogy. She widens the concept of common ancestry and common progeny. Instead of contracting defensively or expanding self-aggrandizingly, the family is considered in concentric circles until it becomes the Human Family.

Since the Second World War, Americans and Europeans alike have lost a sense of cultural preeminence. The Atlantic can no longer be regarded as the only ocean to lap the shores of Civilization, for the whole of what we call the Third World is insisting on decolonization and cultural recognition. Decolonization is a central motif for di Prima. She defines her own usable past to include the Italian heritage that does not however limit her. She insists on her own concepts of history, country, and self. Confidence in that self sustains her openness to the world of other selves. This is her legacy to her children and grandchildren—and to her readers.

Notes

1. Bruce Cook quotes this passage in *The Beat Generation*, 66.

2. Di Prima names also predecessors Djuna Barnes and Anais Nin, and singers Joan Baez, Janis Joplin, and Bessie Smith, among others. In their lives and their works, di Prima's sister-spirits testify abundantly to their motives, obstacles, embroilments, and provisional successes in defying middle-class values. Lenore Kandel, for instance, born in New York and raised in Los Angeles, went to live in Haight-Ashbury; she had modeled, folksung, bellydanced, and waitressed, before *The Love Book* was in 1966 seized by police and subjected to an obscenity trial. Audre Lorde in *Zami: A New Spelling of My Name* (Trumansburg, N.Y.: The Crossing P, 1982) explicitly affirms values and motives for her generation of women that set these sister-spirits at odds with the dominant culture.

Works Cited

Barolini, Helen (ed.). *The Dream Book.* New York: Schocken, 1985.

Barzini, Luigi. *The Italians.* New York: Atheneum, 1964.

Burroughs, William S., Jr. ("William Lee.") *Junkie.* New York: Ace, 1953. Reissued as *Junky,* with preface by Allen Ginsberg. New York, Penguin, 1977.

———. *The Naked Lunch.* Paris: Olympia Press, 1959; New York: Grove, 1972.

Cook, Bruce. *The Beat Generation.* New York: Scribner's, 1971.

Davidson, Spencer (reported by Barry Kolb and Wilton Wynn in Rome). "Land of Miracles—and *Malgrado,*" *Time,* August 17, 1981, 8-15.

di Prima, Diane. *This Kind of Bird Flies Backward.* New York: Totem Press, 1958.

———. *Various Fables from Various Places.* New York: Putnam, 1960.

———. *Dinners and Nightmares.* New York: Corinth, 1961.

———. *The New Handbook of Heaven.* San Francisco: Auerhahn Press, 1963.

———. *Haiku.* Topanga, California: Love Press, 1966.

———. *Memoirs of a Beatnik.* Paris: Olympia Press, 1969.

———. *The Book of Hours.* New York: Brownstone Press, 1970.

———. *Revolutionary Letters.* San Francisco: City Lights, 1971.

———. *Brass Furnace Going Out: Song After an Abortion.* Syracuse, New York: Pulpartforms Unlimited, 1975.

———. *Selected Poems, 1956-76.* Plainfield, Vermont: North Atlantic, 1977.

———. *Loba, Parts I-VIII.* Berkeley, California: Wingbow Press, 1978.

di Prima, Diane (tr.). *The Man Condemned to Death. Le condamñe a mort.* New York: The Poets Press, ca. 1960.

Ehrenreich, Barbara, interviewed by Steven Findlay in *USA Today,* October 28, 1986, 11A.

Ferlinghetti, Lawrence. *A Coney Island of the Mind.* New York: New Directions, 1958.

Ginsberg, Allen. *Howl and Other Poems.* San Francisco: City Lights, 1956.

Gitlin, Todd. *The Sixties; Years of Hope, Days of Rage.* New York: Bantam, 1987.

Greenhouse, Linda. "Family Law: Battleground in Social Revolution," *The New York Times,* Friday, September 2, 1988, B-6:3-6.

Holmes, John Clellon. *Go.* 1952. Mamaroneck, New York: P. P. Appel, 1977.

Johnson, Joyce. *Minor Characters.* Boston: Houghton Mifflin, 1983.

Juhasz, Suzanne. *Naked and Fiery Forms; Modern American Poetry by Women, A New Tradition.* New York: Harper & Row, 1976.

Kerouac, Jack. *On the Road.* New York: Viking, 1957.

Krim, Seymour. *The Beats.* Greenwich, Connecticut: Fawcett, 1960.

Lipton, Lawrence. *The Holy Barbarians.* New York: Julian Messner, 1959.

Lorde, Audre. *The First Cities.* New York: The Poets, 1968.

———. *Between Our Selves.* Point Reyes, California: Eidolon Editions, 1976.

———. *Zami: A New Spelling of My Name.* Trumansburg, New York: The Crossing Press, 1982.

Morrison, Toni. *The Bluest Eye.* 1970. New York: Washington Square Press, 1972.

Podhoretz, Norman. "The Know-Nothing Bohemians," *Partisan Review,* 25 (Spring 1958): 305-318.

DIANE DI PRIMA AND PETER WARSHALL (INTERVIEW DATE FALL 1999)

SOURCE: di Prima, Diane, and Peter Warshall. "The Tapestry of Possibility: Diane di Prima Speaks of Poetry, Rapture and Invoking Co-responding Magic." *Whole Earth* 98 (fall 1999): 20-2.

In the following interview, di Prima discusses her career and body of work.

[*Warshall*]: *Classic metaphor is presented as X is Y. "My love is a red rose." "My life is a journey."*

[di Prima]: Well, I think metaphor is exactly the opposite. All of those definitions make things less than they are. When you talk about metaphor, it's understanding that every single thing is multidimensional, and that behind each jade plant, there are a million layers. There's Chinese poetry, there's jade itself, there's the way it flowers and tumbles. The way everything falls. Sort of floats downhill in it.

What I'm talking about is some apprehension of correspondences that makes everything richer, constantly richer. There's more than meets the eyes, as we like to say. There's more than actually meets the brain and the thinking part of the brain, too. So that in a good poem, you don't even know why you're taken. Why you're "rapt away"—like the rapture Jehovah's Witnesses are waiting for—into a much larger comprehension of how things speak to us, how things fit together, how there are all these levels beyond the material and yet with their roots right in the material.

When I was young, by reading alchemical texts I began to understand that everything meant more than I thought; that people used to think in a multilayered way. There was no simpleminded way to read, say, a text from the 1500s. You had to be able to let every thing and every statement in it go to places or depths that were more than its surface. For me, there's a feeling in them, of them resounding.

Having realized that all these people thought in a way that was so much more than one thing at a time, I was trying to listen to music that way, to look at a painting that way. I kept trying to open to these other possibilities, and that was kind of going to school, in a way, to the past. Now, I'm sure sometimes it happens other ways, like a sudden revelation, like when Jacob Boehme saw the light on the piece of pewter and the world opened up. I wouldn't know how everyone comes to multiple layers, but I think that coming to it completely changes you. Changes your life and changes your relation with the world as well as with other people. There are no equations in it; there's no "this equals that."

Against the studying of Western magical system that we in the West, the Gentiles, based on Cabala, Agrippa, and so on, you get that sense of depth too. You can talk about Jupiter, or you could pick up this sapphire and put it on the shrine, or you can move toward the color blue. There's an interlocking of relations between all these different things. They are not intellectual. They become living. So that the color of something, or its basic energy, or something it exudes, or the number of its petals if it's a flower, all speak to you.

So if I think of metaphors like "life is a journey" as reducing metaphor to equation, all that stuff wants to make a very clear line between one thing and another and another, and is not willing to also see that things have these energies and live off of them forever—the actual force that anything has, moving off of it into your heart, into your eye, into your soul, whatever. I don't even know if there are souls, but into your soul anyway. That energy is what corresponds, "co-responds"; and when it co-responds and you co-respond to it in writing, you move toward something that seems like metaphor.

There is a woman author who said that metaphor is a physical pictograph of a spiritual condition.

That's another one of those equations. It's sort of like saying that the only thing we're writing about is our own spiritual states. I'm not sure that's true. Sometimes I'm really actually writing about the rock wall in the canyon. Maybe the rock wall in the Wind River Canyon isn't a metaphor for my spiritual state but it is just so beautiful and so moving and pours out such an energy that I need to write it. Or be a voice for it, just be a voice for it.

It may be that some metaphors are correlations for spiritual states, but there may be many, many metaphors, or whatever those things are, those images that arise that don't necessarily relate to the human. I think it's kind of a species-centric statement. When you're a poet, you spend a long time writing the 'I' poem, and whether you hide the 'I' or, because you're being a language poet and don't use "I," it's still an 'I' poem for a long long time. And then when you reach the point where that's not so interesting, maybe you spend a long time, who knows—I'm not sure—writing poems that include your human family and the human landscape.

I'm not certain that there aren't entities that want voice. Robert Duncan used to talk about presences of a poem that arrived in the room and were just presences, having to be spoken. Sometimes the dead want voice. Sometimes the dead who have had a good voice want still more voice. "Shut up, Dante!" That kind of thing.

I'm not really sure exactly where metaphor begins, in the sense that you're starting with this world—which is where we all have to start all the time—and, starting with this world, you come up against the natural object. Where does it turn into a metaphor? Where is the mind. Where is the swift apprehension of relations in the mind? That bird leaving no trace in the sky is correspondence to one's thought. Thought leaves no trace.

For instance, in writing ***Loba*** [Diane's book-length poem], there wasn't any "Oh, I think I'll pick the wolf as a metaphor for a woman. . . . "No. Wrong. First there was a dream that contained a world that I did not associate with a poem for over a year after I started the poem. The poem began as words in my head. Sometimes I get these broadcasts; and when I get them, I have to write them down or else they keep repeating like a broken record. And they won't go on to the next lines, but they won't stop.

So in the process of these first few broadcasts, around the third or fourth, it showed up that there was a wolf. At the beginning of Part I, there was no wolf. But, by the end of Part I, the wolf was like Shiva. She's dancing and bringing down the city around her ("she treads the salty earth, she does not raise breath cloud heavenward / her breath itself is carnage"). I really didn't know anything about where the thing was going or what it was. I still don't. At that point, I was conscious that it was a wolf; I wasn't conscious it was related to the dream. I had no idea for another year or two. I had almost forgotten the dream. But the door was opened for more of the poem.

Then the conscious part: that there was a wolf and some women—women and wolves here. I had the days to write; three days a week in the morning when a baby-sitter came. I would begin with collaging. I was making all these collages of wild animals, or animals and women, or women in improbable wild scenery. Eventually the poems would start. And would just go. So it was like making an invocation. Mostly, it was visual imagery. You suddenly find two things are adjacent to each other and you say, Oh that's what I want, or that somehow is satisfying.

I love that moment where the wolf, Loba, looks down and you can see her fur over her socks and—

She's dancing in the bar, yeah. We have that always. Somebody's going to look and notice the fur. Last year at the Sonoma Mountain Zen practice, I actually experienced the true sense of my core feralness. And everything spoke to me constantly, every butterfly on the path when I would walk and do mantra and so on.

It plugged into me with Loba, twenty-eight years earlier. So now when people say "What is ***Loba*** about?" I'm able to say it's about the feralness of the core of women, of the feminine in everything. In everyone. If you want an "about"—I didn't have an "about" for twenty-eight years.

Man in the Street

How do all these variants of imagery move people?

Imagery is a tool. The closer you come to those primal images that are in us all, the more you do move people. I think we'd like to use the term "collective unconscious." But, it's too reductive, too squishy.

There's also the so-called "man in the street"—anyone, not consciously aware of metaphors or imagery, who responds to it, responds to correspondence. We all know it on some level.

I remember when politics was raging in the late sixties and early seventies, and I was writing all those revolutionary letters and reading them on the street and putting them in 200 of those guerilla-type newspapers around the country, through that Liberation News Service. I would go back East, where people are more inclined to be programmatic, to do poetry readings and things, and people would say to me, "What is your plan for the people of San Francisco?" or "the people of northern California," or "the people of the West," or whatever size they wanted to make it. As if because I wrote those poems, I had a clear-cut program in mind. And of course I didn't.

The Tapestry of Possibility

I chose poetry because I first read almost all the philosophers that were in the Carroll Street branch of the Brooklyn Public Library—and then I stumbled upon Keats. I realized how stupid it is to try to be consistent in a program or in a system of philosophy or of anything, when, through poetry, you hold all these different possibilities without having to resolve them.

There's a tapestry of possibility that we all live with, sort of a theater backdrop. There's a level of human life that's the outer scrim, the transparent fabric that creates special effects of light and atmosphere. And if you light the scrim up, this tapestry is infinite—or if not infinite, huge—possibility. You can write that scrim, which is transparent—it's like the material world is transparent—and look through it to the full tapestry of possibility. That vastness . . . if you plug into some part of that, what comes alive and seeks you—"rapts" you away—grabs you as the artist. I wasn't looking for it. I think I would say I wasn't looking for it when that particular vast thing which now kind of informs all my work came to me.

If you plug into that place, people respond. You can do it for ill or for good. It's like one of those forces, like electricity. It's just there. Most people don't even talk about that tapestry, that cycle of birth, life, and death, and the blood at the beginning and at the end of it. The mess at the beginning and at the end of it, and how beautiful that is.

Diane di Prima's Brooklyn-born street wisdom never dismisses anything, be it the pattern of the stars, the destinies of children (she has five), dark timbers, fragile ankles, or the meandering of the mind. Acumen and heart. She teaches privately and studies Buddhism and Western magick. She's known as an outstanding poet of the Beat period, constructs great collages, and has published thirty-two books, including the eight part ***Loba.***

DIANE DI PRIMA, MARINA LAZZARA, AND DAVID MELTZER (INTERVIEW DATE 1999)

SOURCE: di Prima, Diane, and David Meltzer. "Diane di Prima (1999)." In *San Francisco Beat: Talking with the Poets,* pp. 1-21. San Francisco: City Lights Books, 2001.

In the following interview, conducted in 1999, di Prima discusses her early life and her writing. Her opinions on the label "Beat Generation" are also covered, along with her feelings about children and marriage.

July 21, 1999: Marina, Jim, and I meet up at the BART station close to Diane's apartment in San Francisco. Her partner, Sheppard Powell, opens the door for us, and we walk up to the second floor into a book-filled living room. The usual awkwardness about where to plug in the tape recorder and set up the microphone. Diane asks if we want tea or coffee, and once everyone is settled, the interview commences.—DM

[Meltzer]: *Your grandfather introduced you to Dante. Was that your earliest encounter with poetry?*

[di Prima]: Yeah, I was about four or so. He took out this old paperback . . . one of those European ones . . . and told me that this book had traveled around the world. I thought, oh, that's why it looks so beat up. I pictured housewives in the Bronx reaching from one window to another like they would pass food and, instead, passing the same book all the way around the world.

[Meltzer]: *Around the clotheslines.*

Around the clotheslines, right. Dante on the clothesline! Yeah, that was the first poetry. We also listened to a lot of opera together. He was forbidden opera because it was bad for his heart. He had heart trouble and he'd get so worked up about the opera.

[Meltzer]: *You say you'd made a lifetime commitment to poetry at the age of fourteen. What happened to lead up to that?*

In order to stay sane, I found the public library, or my father actually showed me how to walk to the library. Girls weren't allowed out much. I was allowed to go to the library. And I read my way. . . . I found that if you were caught in the adult section, they told you that you couldn't be there. But if you got the books to the counter, they checked them out for you. Everything was a double message. So I was reading my way through philosophy. I had written answers to Plato in all the margins of the Jowett translation, when I was eleven, twelve, thirteen. I fell in love with Schopenhauer. I was sure Schopenhauer would have been happier if I would have been with him. Meanwhile, I was also reading novels. [*laughter*]

[Lazzara]: *Was that your first crush?*

One of my very first crushes, yes. I had a pretty big thing for Spinoza, too. Anyway, somewhere in that reading there was a Somerset Maugham novel—maybe it was *The Razor's Edge*—where he quotes Keats: "Beauty is truth, truth beauty." So I went looking with my little library skills for this person named Keats, and I found the

FROM THE AUTHOR

DI PRIMA ON POSTMODERNISM AND PHILOSOPHY

Western thought always keeps stopping on the brink. It never really makes that extra step. It could really do with an infusion of Buddhist logic. At least 4 fold logic and then what's beyond that. It seems that although it's dressed up in new language, nothing really new has happened in philosophy in the 20th century. Well, maybe not since Wittgenstein. It seems like the same old thing. You know, sometimes when people ask me for poems now, I'll send out poems that have been lying around for years, I don't always have new poems lying around everywhere, and these things that I wrote as cut-up stuff, cutting up each others dreams in workshops and such. I'll send these out. Everyone seems to be taking them very seriously and publishing them. They think I'm working off of some language theory when actually these are just things I did for fun.

Matheny, Joseph. "Interview with Diane di Prima." *Incunabula* (website) <www.incunabula.org> (22 September 1992).

poetry section. Whereupon I began to read nothing but poetry. I couldn't understand why anybody would bother with philosophy because clearly any point you had to reach consistently couldn't be completely right. Any logic couldn't be completely right, and poetry could hold all the contradictions.

So then a lot of poetry . . . the people who were my people at that point were Romantics, Shelley and Keats mostly. And reading all of Keats's letters, which I was doing when I was age thirteen or fourteen. And finally one day it hit me that this wasn't just out there, it wasn't just heroes, other people, it was me. I could do this. I could do this. I cried a lot when I realized that. I was very sad because with it came the understanding that I was going to have to give up a lot of things regular people have. I wasn't going to be able to snuggle into regular human life. I don't know how I knew all that, but I did. And that's when I made my commitment to poetry. I was sitting in my backyard, and it hit me. Like that. If that's the case, then I better start writing every day. So I bought a new notebook, and every day I wrote something. By then I was in high school.

[*Meltzer*]: *In high school was there encouragement for this?*

Yes. I was in Hunter High School, which in those days was for women only. And you got in by exam, so there were the brightest women from all kinds of backgrounds. And in my age group, in my class, there were about eight of us who wanted to write. By the time we were sophomores or thereabouts, we would get together in the morning and go to one of the home rooms a little early and read what we'd written the day before. A few of the teachers were very encouraging—very interesting women teachers dedicated to teaching women.

I graduated in '51. One summer I went to summer school because people had these crazy notions back then that it's better to do everything faster. . . . I skipped a grade in grammar school, which made life miserable in grammar school—all the kids hated me. At summer school, there was an off-the-wall teacher, a crazy man in a beret named Anton Serota who I let read one of my poems, and he had me read it out loud to the class, and he was very encouraging. And also very helpful about the way you write when you're young, with so many abstractions. "This part works because I can make pictures in my mind; this part doesn't work." It was just one summer, but it was a really helpful and close friendship. Those things happen. Then I went to Swarthmore College and got the opposite of encouragement.

I wanted to major in Greek and Latin. I'd gotten a city prize for Latin translation. I was in the top two percentile in math and physics. There was a lot of propaganda that the U.S. needed scientists. So their little claws were out there: come and be a scientist. I majored in physics at Swarthmore. However, they weren't equipped. They were teaching nineteenth-century physics; nobody was teaching relativity. So it was very boring and didn't work, and I dropped out of school when I was a little more than eighteen.

[*Meltzer*]: *What were your feelings as a young person growing up in the Second World War and then in the aftermath of the war with the unveiling of the atomic bomb and the Holocaust. How did that affect you—or did it?*

While we were growing up, there was no war news in the house. Before the war started, half of my family went back to Italy. My father's father's brother and his half of the family went back, but my paternal grandfather stayed. We all went down to the boat, and half of them sailed off. We never traced that part of the family again. Rudi, my oldest son, recently tried. There was this feeling of enormous Greek tragedy going on. And it would be an understatement to say that my mother and father were very controlling. We never saw a paper, we never heard the news, we never read a comic, and we never went to the movies except for about four Disney films until I was in high school. As far as the war went, it was blocked out except for the nuns having us pray for all the children—on both sides—at school.

I write about a lot of this in ***Recollections of My Life as a Woman.*** I remember the day the war was over and everyone was waiting with their boxes of confetti to throw them out the window, and all that . . . there was a feeling of horror for me in that. My neighborhood was very primitive, and everybody had something like doll's heads on sticks with slanted eyes painted on them. They were running up and down the street like that. In my neighborhood, they burned politicians in effigy from lampposts when they lost elections.

The bomb fell on my eleventh birthday. August 6. And that was a moment that I talk about in the book. My father came home. We were waiting for him for the birthday party, and he threw down the paper and said, "Well, we lost." He said, "Whatever we do now, we've lost." I remember that. Consciousness flooded in with the dropping of that bomb. Consciousness of the war. But then it was only two weeks more and the war was over. But I don't remember the slow unveiling, as you put it, of the information about the concentration camps.

[Meltzer]: *We used to go to newsreels a lot. Everyone in the neighborhood was also a newspaper junkie. We'd sit on the stoops talking politics.*

Yeah, I remember the stoops. . . . But, no, the discourse didn't happen around the kids. It's nuts. I was eleven, and two years later I'm in high school and there's a whole world of God-knows-what kind of conflicts going on that you had not heard a word about. I'm sure they talked about the war in Italian, but I was only interested in whatever intrigue might affect me and my brothers in terms of who was mad at who, and what was going to make another blow-up happen in the family. So the war was a metaphor for the other war.

[Meltzer]: *So you leave Swarthmore at eighteen? How did this come down in terms of your relationship to your family?*

It was very traumatic for them.

[Meltzer]: *Did you go back home?*

Yeah, I was home for the Christmas holidays when I decided that I wasn't going to go back to school. I had a group of friends at Swarthmore, and everybody I was close to was dropping out. It was just too straight and precious and protected—class-conscious and definitely not my class, not my kind of place. Two of my friends, women who were lovers, asked me to join them in renting an apartment in New York. I said yes. It turned out that one of their mothers threatened them both with the police because between the ages of eighteen and twenty-one your parents could bust you for being homosexual . . . your parents could call the police. You had no rights then. One of them decided to do what her mother wanted and went on to some school in Connecticut, so it was left to me to get an apartment alone. Really no regrets. I mean there was nothing happening for me at Swarthmore.

[Meltzer]: *What was it to be alone for the first time?*

It was great. I wasn't terribly alone, because of lovers and friends, but having your own say over your own place was heaven. I got a place on Fifth Street between Avenue B and Avenue C. In those days women weren't doing that. It was 1953. Forty-five dollars a month. A nice-size room and a little room, a kitchen, and bathroom. I was the only woman living alone in that block that I know of. People thought I was a whore.

[Meltzer]: *When did you seek out a literary community?*

Well, there was already the people from Hunter and a couple of friends from Swarthmore. I used to go hang out in the first coffee shop that opened that for us—the Rienzi. I used to hang out there some, and I hung out in Washington Square Park. I wasn't so much looking for poets or writers as looking for artists of any sort. Writers talk too much. I liked creativity that was more intuitive, so I hung with painters. Took dance classes. Did that for a while. Actually, ever since my parents first let me out of the house. Not having been able to play actively as a kid made my first dance classes a matter of reclaiming the body. I became friends with dancers and painters and met people from the Arts Students League and Ballet Theater and the New Dance Group, and took classes all over the place. At the New School of Social Research. I took some classes at Brooklyn College at night and some at Hunter and some at Columbia.

[Meltzer]: *What kind of classes were you taking?*

I was still very interested in math. I loved math. Pure math. I took integral calculus in Brooklyn and theory of equations at Columbia. And took Greek at Hunter, classical Greek, and just whatever I wanted, rather than going for a degree. At the New School it was really more like theater because they typecast their professors. The Russian literature professor was a guy with a shock of gray hair and he "suffered" a lot in the classroom. The existentialist professor had a very thin profile and blond hair and a French accent, and he'd show us his profile. But it was fun. For me, it was learning about other literatures and all that. Everywhere I went I met people—and people talked to each other in those days. I have a daughter who moved to New York recently, and it seems like people don't know how to meet each other anymore. Back then you would sit on a park bench, and someone would sit down next to you, and you started a conversation. And then you went somewhere and drank coffee and continued. It wasn't necessarily about picking people up. It was more like: who are you and what's going on?

[Meltzer]: *How'd you make a living?*

The first year I worked downtown on Wall Street doing an office job. I didn't need to work that much, but I was helping one of my gay women friends with some of my money. The next thing was a part-time job at Columbia at the electronics lab. I got security clearance! That gave me access to free classes at Columbia. And then one day I was in Washington Square, and the painter Nicolai Cikovsky came up to me, one of the Eastern Europeans who migrated just before the war, and asked me if I would model for him. I said sure. His studio was right off the park there, and other painters came to visit. Those guys passed their models from hand to hand. That led to years and years of just modeling for painters for a living. (There's one of Raphael Soyer's paintings over there on the wall.) We were making $3.50 an hour in 1953. . . . That would be like $50 an hour now. All under the table, all in cash. We worked two-hour shifts. I wound up working twenty hours a month. The rest of my time was for writing and studying and filling in holes in my education. I went to movies at the Museum of Modern Art almost every day.

[Meltzer]: *Did you ever go to the Thalia?*

Went to the Thalia a ton. I used to bring my lunch and see the same movie over and over, and if I didn't want to see the second feature, I'd go sit in the lobby and read during that one.

[Meltzer]: *You hadn't been allowed to go to movies as a kid and started going to movies at eighteen. Do you remember what that opened up?*

It's hard to express it, but a whole sense of manipulation of light and time, like the heart of magic, the heart of art. The first film I saw—besides Walt Disney and one Shirley Temple film—the first film I consciously saw was Cocteau's *Blood of the Poet* when I was fifteen in a little theater on Irving Place, when I was going to summer school. From then on, it was all the Cocteau movies. . . . The Museum of Modern Art would show series. They'd show everything that Von Stroheim ever directed, for instance. You got a total education without anybody blathering at you, lecturing. Everything by Carl Dreyer. All the movies Garbo was ever in. One thing after the other. You got a pass. It was $3 a year if you were an art student. And Raphael Soyer always signed that I was an art student. You could go to the museum every day for a year. I was busy trying to fill in the holes in my information as an artist.

[Meltzer]: *Can you describe your writings at that time?*

Some of the stuff that's in ***Dinners and Nightmares*** was written around then. I was very interested in making it as sparse as possible—I was influenced by Hemingway, among others. Also by the Matisse line drawings that came out in a Dover paperback around that time. I noticed that there was not only dimensionality but color . . . a hint of color to the eye from those black-and-white line drawings. I wanted to know how much information you could give with how few words, just like the lines in a Matisse drawing. And so I would cut and cut and cut. The first book has some of that stuff—***This Kind of Bird Flies Backwards***—and the "More or Less Love Poems" that are in ***Dinners and Nightmares.*** I was reading a lot. When I left Swarthmore I charged a lot of books the day I was leaving. One was *The Cantos.*

[Meltzer]: *To the library?*

No, I charged them in the bookstore at Swarthmore and paid the bill off about thirty years later. I got Auden and cummings and those people you would expect. But I got *The Cantos* and *Personae,* too.

[Meltzer]: *Was Pound informing at that point?*

The most. I read and did what he tells you to do in *ABC of Reading.* I was doing a little Homeric Greek. I had some wonderful books of the troubadours with glossaries in the back and that kind of stuff. I didn't really meet the poets or start meeting the literary community until '56. So there's three years that were more dancers and painters and Actors Studio people. My friend Bret Rohmer was a painter. Bret had been a child actor. He was friends with all those Actors Studio guys—Bill Gunn, Marty Landau—so they would come over. Allen Ginsberg came through town in '56, early '57, maybe.

[Meltzer]: *What was the impact of Allen?*

Well, I had been writing all this slang from '53 on. I loved the street language. My friends who I lived with and other serious artists were saying, no, you can't do that. Nobody's going understand it in ten years. People were pretty down on me in my group. We were all nineteen years old. There was an argument about whether or not you could use the vernacular. But my friend Joan O'Malley said no. At one point, somebody got upset. We had a whole wall collaged full of photos of the artists and actors we loved. We all started tearing down all the photographs, yelling that we weren't worthy of these people if we had these terrible ideas about art. So in a way it was like oil on troubled waters to see *Howl* published. It legitimized things that were already happening in my work.

Within a year after Allen came through, people started looking me up. People started showing up at my house, and that would be anywhere from people of my age like LeRoi Jones to Edward Dahlberg and Kenneth Rexroth. Dahlberg and Rexroth acted like lecherous old guys. In the world I was in, all of that seemed quite natural. I didn't wonder what piece of the woodwork they had come out from or why they had looked me up.

[Meltzer]: *Besides being lecherous, did you learn anything from Rexroth?*

I love Rexroth. I love Rexroth. He was valiant and wonderful and helped me many times, especially in terms of my political writing or information that I had or thought I had or wanted to find out about in history. He sat in on a workshop once of mine that was called History as Paranoia. Everything I said, he would answer from the back of the room, "And furthermore, did you know that . . ." and he'd add six more things. He was quite wonderful. It's just that I don't think guys of that generation had ever encountered a girl who was writing but wasn't particularly on the make. I slept around a lot, but I wasn't on the make when I met a guy who was a writer. So it took them a little while to adjust. They did good. [*laughter*]

[Meltzer]: *OK. Let's see . . . what about the Beat movement?*

Yeah, what is that thing rumored to be the Beat movement?

[Meltzer]: *Help me. I'm having a crisis here. You're known as an important writer of the Beat movement. Do you want to tell me what it is or was?*

I and people I knew were disgusted with the whole thing of a label, and the label came late, and the label brought all those little girls from Jersey with their eyeliner and their black tights, and you had to take care of them because they were going to bed with the wrong people, and they were going to get hurt. Do you remember those girls from Jersey?

[Meltzer]: *I remember the girls who came to North Beach from the suburbs.*

Same thing. When did you move out here?

[Meltzer]: *Let me see . . . maybe '60, '61.*

Those girls were showing up by about '57 or '58.

I have no idea about the Beat movement. To this day, I find it very difficult, as I'm sure you do, or anyone does, that people assume that whatever we were doing then we are doing now. What I'm doing now is what I'm doing now, and if you want to read ***Loba*** as a Beat poem, more power to you, but it doesn't make sense to read it that way.

[Meltzer]: *To what do you attribute this great renewed fascination by primarily young males toward what they imagine was the Beat? It seems to be almost exclusively a male fantasy.*

This is such a repressive age we're in right now. It's really disgusting right now. So the idea of a time when it was OK to blah, blah, blah.

[Meltzer]: *For guys.*

For guys. Not just for guys. It was OK for me. Look at how awful it is right now for everybody. I mean, it is fucking difficult. Drugs have been given a bad name. Traveling freely on the road would be a form of insanity. Money is so tight, nobody works twenty hours a month and studies their art. You know Edward Dorn's phrase, "crazy with permission," from *Gran Appacheria?* There was some kind of wild permission that we took. It certainly hadn't been handed to us. McCarthy didn't hand it to us, nor did our parents. But the biological facts of life weren't against it. We weren't going to die if we slept around. Which you might now.

Robert Duncan used to say all the time that when something is leaving the planet it enters the realm of the imagination. When Dante wrote about the Church, the Church was failing—and so it *could* enter the realm of the imagination. Maybe that's part of it now. Real life, as we lived it, is fading, so there's this terrific Beat fantasy.

[Lazzara]: *Spoken word poetry might be inspired by the Beats, don't you think?*

Not to me. My experience of the whole thing was not an experience of the public arena much. I would read if people asked, and friends were doing it, at some of those places along the Lower East Side, but the heart of it for me was making my first book and editing *The Floating Bear.* It was always the word on paper and getting it out, much more than it was performance per se. Performance was the theater. We had the theater. . . .

[Meltzer]: *The New York Poet's Theatre? Could you tell us a little bit about how that originated and what it did?*

Yeah, at that point I was married to a guy who was a performer, Alan Marlowe.

[Meltzer]: *That's a great actor's name.*

Yeah, but his name was Meyorwitz, but he didn't even find that out until later. We did one-act plays by poets, with sets by painters. People who weren't directors directed—choreographers and dancers or whatever. George Herms did the set for McClure's *The Blossom,* or *Billy the Kid.* Alex Katz did a set for a James Schuyler play. Peter Agostini sculpted the hanged man for *Three Travelers Watch Sunrise* by Wallace Stevens. We had some beautiful, beautiful things. It ran for about a four-month season each year over a period of four or five years.

[Meltzer]: *Where was the theater located?*

Different places, different years. We would rent different spaces. The plays would run on the weekends, and during the week there'd be contemporary music night, a dance night, an experimental film night, something else. Different people would run those. And then on Sunday afternoons, before the evening play, we would have poetry readings right in the set of the play. We did a whole series where we invited poets to come and read their favorite poems by others. Red Grooms made a set for Kenneth Koch. It was exciting and beautiful. *That* was the performance thing. By the time the coffee shop thing got big, it was it was a little too raucous for me. There's a part of me that prefers being able to read poetry in a more subtle and quiet way. I never was really into the "performance" part of all that, although I read with musicians a few times. I worked with the Chicago Art Ensemble at the University of Chicago, for example.

[Meltzer]: *When did you have your first child?*

In '57.

[Meltzer]: *Were there difficulties?*

Yeah, there were a lot of difficulties. I had decided I wanted a kid, right? I decided I didn't want to live with a man. My family experience of growing up made me think that living with men wasn't a nice idea. I had lots of lovers, and I asked people if they wanted to father a kid, and everybody thought I was insane, and finally I didn't ask—I just got pregnant and had Jeanne. That part was not a problem. The problem was, for example, I didn't dare let people at the hospital know that I wasn't married, because they were looking hard for white babies to put up for adoption. They had babies of every other color under the sun, but if you were a single parent with a white child the pressure put on you to give up that baby before you left the hospital was enormous. So I made up a husband for the birth certificate. A lot of problems like that.

Of course, my family, my poor family, was completely freaked out already about this. It wasn't hard for me in the sense of daily life because I just worked at home. I had bought a mimeograph machine, and I made a home business. I did the scripts for the off-off Broadway theaters. I would do them at the house, and people would come and pick them up. That was fine. I tried getting not welfare but child care so that Jeanne could be somewhere when I did this work, and the only way you were allowed Social Service child care was to be on welfare, and if you were on welfare, you had to turn in the name of a father. None of which was of any interest to me. So Jeanne just stayed home and played. I worked at the Phoenix Bookstore when she was two, and she'd come in the stroller and play in the back. I did that for about two years.

[Meltzer]: *You had more children and sometimes had more than one to deal with.*

Having one, you take her everywhere, do everything together. She used to sleep backstage when I was at the Living Theater, when I worked there with Jimmy Waring. Having two meant you had to arrange things. But it was so difficult anyway between me and Roi after I had Dominique. I left for the West Coast with Alan Marlowe, who was breaking up his affair with Fred Herko. Alan had money coming in from TV residuals. For some reason, and I'm not sure what his reason was, he wanted to marry me. I knew that he was a man I'd never fall in love with, so he seemed like a good person to marry. I had two kids with him, Alex and Tara, over six years. But most of the time, we weren't even sexually involved. It was an open marriage, and he was mostly with guys. We ran the theater and we ran the press. I really wasn't alone with more than one child that much. Although the men weren't much use in terms of taking care of the house or taking care of kids or making money. Once the residuals stopped, Alan had no idea what else to do. He could raise money for the theater for a season, but he had no idea about day-to-day things like rent.

[Meltzer]: *I'm interested in* The Floating Bear *project—it had a lasting impact in the strange history of poet-produced bulletins. It came out in mimeograph form and was an incredible repository of poetry and poetry news, reflecting a coast-to-coast poetic network. I wonder if we could talk about the whole process of co-editing with LeRoi Jones, Amiri Baraka. How were the editorial meetings?*

Roi and I had gotten together as lovers about a year before we got together as editors. A. B. Spellman and I were going to do a magazine called *The Horse at the Window.* We had this whole stack of interesting manuscripts, and A. B., the first time he had to reject something, decided he couldn't be an editor because he couldn't reject anybody. So we had this whole stack of manuscripts, which I think he then gave to Roi, and then Roi approached me about the idea of a newsletter. At first, it was an every-two-week thing. Later, it got to be once a month, and very much later it got very big and came out only a few times a year. But when Roi and I did it the first year or so it was every two weeks.

We started out with the addresses in our two phone books. One hundred seventeen people got the first issue. It was always free. It always broke even. People would send contributions and things. Painters gave us money. Painters had lots of money in those days. In terms of the editorial meetings, there were a lot of ways that Roi and I saw eye to eye about literary stuff, and a lot of ways we didn't at all. There was a lot of hard-edge macho stuff that he loved a lot more than I, like early Dorn, and there was a kind of mystical work, like Robert Duncan's stuff and other work, that I liked more than he. But we just put both in. That gave the *Bear* its odd flavor. It was an amalgam of the two kinds of taste. We basically trusted each other's point of view or taste. I did the typing, everybody did the proofreading, and we would have collating parties. Roi did most of the correspondence and staying in touch with the writers.

After I married Alan, Roi resigned. For personal reasons, he said. I kept going with the *Bear* 'til '69. I had some guest editors. John Wieners edited one issue.

[Meltzer]: *You say in '65 you went up to Millbrook, Timothy Leary's psychedelic community. Could you describe what that was like?*

I visited it in '65; I lived there in '67. It was wonderful, amazingly wonderful. Tim had this idea that he wanted to gather a lot of very creative people in one place and give them all the acid they could possibly take and make sure they had no worries or responsibilities and see what happened.

I and my kids and Alan Marlowe had kind of a house. It was the upper floor of this place that was built like a Swiss chalet. The lower floor was a bowling alley, and the upper floor was meant to be a huge billiard room, and that's where we lived.

Tim's plan was that we were not supposed to want for anything, we weren't supposed to worry about anything. If there was anything we needed . . . I mean, if I had the vague idea or mentioned to someone that I might like to try watercolor painting, an elaborate watercolor paint set would show up on my desk by the next day. It was very unnerving, because I was used to struggling. Very hard to get used to not struggling. The place was set up with the basic rule, which I broke all the time, that you were supposed to trip once every five days. Nobody was supposed to go more than five days without tripping. Now this gets very boring after a while.

[Meltzer]: *And exhausting.*

And exhausting. So I would take my LSD and say thank you very much and stash it. It wasn't hard to act as if you were tripping. Nobody knew the difference. That was the main rule, but since everybody was tripping every five days, nothing ever was the same in the community two days in a row. We'd figure out how we were doing the meals. We'd figure it out again different the next day. I did the cooking there for the first month or two. Which was nice because I couldn't give up on taking care of business. Tim's group on the top floor ate meat and wanted lots of alcohol. Then an ashram moved in while I was there, and they wanted lots of milk and white bread and sugar, and then there were the macrobiotics. Jean McCreedy's children were crying because there was no Campbell's soup for them. You learned a lot. You also had incredible space.

There was a place called the Meditation House. I'm sure people have written about this. It was a one-room house, with windows all around. The sun came up on one side of the room and went down on the other side. We took turns being "the spiritual watch" for the place. You were there, doing solitary tripping for twenty-four hours, and the guard was changed in the evenings. We all came and meditated with the person who had been tripping, and then the next person moved in and took her post as watcher. Usually you were on watch for twenty-four hours, but once I did it for three or five days just before I left Millbrook. It was like indigenous American religion just beginning to grow. The nights as the trip came on . . . it was incredibly lovely and very deep. With the support of the whole place, unspoken around you, with ten square miles of property between you and whatever was trying to stop this whole thing from happening. There was a leather-bound blank book in the Meditation House. Everybody either left a drawing or a message or something from each trip. I wrote "Rant from a Cool Place" while I was there tripping. Later, I published it in ***Revolutionary Letters.***

[Meltzer]: *I'm interested in your long-term involvement with the hermetic and, then later, with Buddhism.*

There was an involvement with the hermetic at Hunter. This often happens with adolescents, both girls and boys, if you let it. I and my writer friends, including Audre Lorde, would work with things like ESP and trance and trying to have séances. And then Buddhism. I read a lot of Eastern stuff from around 1960. Zimmer, *Philosophies of India.* I met Shunryu Suzuki Roshi in '62 when I was out on this coast with Alan Marlowe. Suzuki Roshi married us.

[Meltzer]: *I remember.*

I don't remember who was there. There were only twelve or so of us. Marilyn Rose was there, Kirby Doyle was there, you were there, Dee Dee Doyle was there. And a whole lot of Suzuki's wife's friends. Because it's so auspicious to have the place full for a wedding, they invited all these Japanese ladies.

I started sitting then. When I met Suzuki it felt like the first time in my life I had met somebody I could really trust. That was an interesting thing for a Brooklyn girl. And so I took home a cushion, got some basic instruction, and wrote Dick Baker once or twice a year to say this is what's happening. He would tell Roshi, and sometimes I'd get a message back. Whenever I was on the road and I was here, I would hitch to the Zen center and sit in the morning with them. Zen practice began in '62. I had been playing with stuff before that. I had been playing with *The Six Yogas of Naropa* from Garma C. C. Chang's book and stuff like that.

New Year's Eve '63 was when I took my first acid. What happened to me on that first acid trip was that a whole lot of stuff I'd been reading about became clear as day. About time and about emptiness—I could just see it. So that put things in a different light, as it were. Probably this is where the mysticism starts to come back into the poetry in a much more clear way. Although in '59 there was a peyote trip, and that's when the poems broke open to long lines like those in ***The New Handbook of Heaven.*** That book started after the peyote trip in '59 in my apartment on the Lower East Side. Jimmy also helped as a teacher of mine—James Waring. He said to follow precisely wherever the poem went—"the graph of the moving mind" (that's Philip Whalen's phrase), rather than this thing that I was doing earlier of cut, cut, cut, and make it sparse. I think I was doing that to learn certain techniques. This wasn't about technique now, it was about really following and being obedient to consciousness, as Robert Duncan liked to put it. That started in 1959.

[Meltzer]: *You've been involved with Buddhism as well studying the Western hermetic tradition for twenty-five, thirty years.*

Oh, easily. Easily. If you don't count the séances. It's about thirty-three years of Western studies. I would say around '66 I started really studying the Tarot.

[Meltzer]: *Because of your earlier background in physics and math, did the alchemical material make more immediate sense?*

Could be. And my anarchist grandfather used to run a pharmacy, even though he didn't a have a license—his son-in-law had the license. I remember hanging out with all those glass bottles of herbs and powders and scales. Grinding things for him. I started to work with the cards when I lived in New Mexico in '66. I'd just hang out with a card—I was using the Waite deck then—and fall asleep nearly every afternoon. And I'd have a dream about that card. It seemed very simple. It wasn't like I was trying. Within the next few years I got hold of the tool of the Tree of Life, as it's used in Western magic, then everything fell into place. That was '71.

[Meltzer]: *Do you mean a combination of the various symbolic systems?*

The using of the Tree as a way to synchronize the systems.

[Meltzer]: *And is that compatible with Buddhism?*

You know, in Vajrayana Buddhism there are two truths. There's absolute truth and relative truth. Absolute truth is emptiness, but it's luminous, creative, constantly moving and changing. But it's empty. Or we call it mind. Big Mind. It's the same thing. Relative truth is *kundzop,* which means costume. It's all the costumes of the empty, and they're seen as inseparable from the absolute. Throughout the world there are techniques of working with and sometimes, yes, even manipulating relative truth, as in Western magic. I have a Buddhist shrine room and also a Western magical shrine, which is a landing place (and launching pad) for all the elemental forces. But it's not a place where I meditate, in the Buddhist sense.

I had this same question for Suzuki Roshi one of the last times I saw him. I said exasperatedly, "I'm a poet. I want images, and here Zen is supposed to be empty!" He said, "Two sides of the same coin." He was telling me the same thing that I learned again in Vajrayana. He said: "You have image, you write. But when you do zazen it should be like going to sleep in your mother's arms."

[Meltzer]: *When did you first meet Robert Duncan?*

I met him at Michael McClure's in 1961. Michael invited Robert to meet me. Invited him over for breakfast. Robert was clearly not very interested in meeting me. And at one point, I was barely awake, I went over to the window and started brushing my hair, which was very, very long and very, very red. All of a sudden Robert looked up and said: "You have the most beautiful hair I've ever seen! Will you come to lunch?"

[Meltzer]: *Could you tell me what you learned from him as a mentor?*

It sounds odd, but I think Robert was probably one of the closest, most intimate lovers I ever had, even though we never had a physical relationship. I learned a lot of different kinds of things from him. One of the things I learned—in a way no teacher of Buddhism ever showed me—was how precious my life was. How precious the whole ambience of the time. A real sense of appreciating every minute. He used to come and do Christmas with us and eat hash brownies and talk. All Christmas morning. He would come up and stay with us in Marshall on Tomales Bay, and there was something about that—more than all the exchanges which were about hermeticism and one thing or another. Something about this ineffable quality of the time and the energy that was there—I can't describe it. He trapped me into a whole field of study. Remember that first year of the New College poetics program that we did? I was supposed to be chairwoman that year and tell everybody what they should teach—not that anybody ever managed to tell anybody what to do in that program. I said: "Robert, I think you should do a course that covers nonorthodox threads of thought in the West, maybe from the caves to the present. Give us some sense of continuity, how it all relates to one another, Gnosticism and the heresies and this and that." He said, "I think you're supposed to teach that, dear." I said, "Robert, I don't know anything about it." He said, "Well, that's why we teach, isn't it?" Of course, after I taught it for two years, everybody was on my neck. "You have to stop teaching that."

[Meltzer]: *What was the New College of California poetics program all about in those days?*

It was whatever Robert thought it was. He felt that it was time to make a model, as he probably said a million times to all of us, of what a curriculum in poetics—as opposed to one in writing poetry—would be and what it would constitute. Not that he thought we had to do it forever or push it through and make it happen, but that we had to make a *model* that would exist for future times. I think that was what mainly it was about. I took that as my permission when I and some friends, Sheppard Powell and Janet Carter and Carl Grundberg, started San Francisco Institute of Magical Healing Arts. Again it was Robert's idea of making a model of what would it be to teach Western hermeticism.

[Meltzer]: *How does it feel to write an autobiography?*

You know, I started that book because I wanted to write something for my daughters, especially about the stupid things I did because of myths I bought into about being a woman. But it just changed and grew. It feels like . . . deep diving. You don't know that you remember the thing you remember until you're writing it down, and then later you don't remember that you remembered it. It's been very helpful. Part of it is about what women do that they don't really have to, because they think they should. Part of it is an exploration of my Italian American roots, and a lot of it is the dance of being an artist with all these guys, and the problems of having kids on your own in the 1950s. It stops in '65 when I'm thirty-one years old.

[Meltzer]: *Is there a second volume?*

If I get around to it. I'm sixty-five, and at first I thought there's definitely going to be a volume two, but I don't know if I feel like doing that again. I'm not sure I'd do it with a big publisher. I hate working with New York. It's unpleasant. It's all about money and stardom, and the legal department wants a list of everybody in the book and little marks next to their names, are they alive or dead? I told them let's wait a while till everybody's dead, so then you don't have to have this list. But writing the book itself was great. It's an imagination of an autobiography.

[Meltzer]: *We didn't talk about the sixties. . . .*

There were two reasons to move out here: to study with Suzuki Roshi and to work with the Diggers. I came out in '67 with John Braden, who was a lover of Alan Marlowe's, to perform. We did poetry readings and music. He was a song person. And we stayed with Lenore Kandel. She was right in the thick of it. Lenore was wonderful as the woman on the scene, the matriarch, and she made it so clear that I was welcome; otherwise, it could have been very different.

Moving out to California was very much talked about during that trip. Peter Berg said, "You did the ground work, now come and enjoy the fruits." Fruits, I don't know about. I enjoyed something, but it was pretty chaotic. Yet I had always wanted to live out here ever since I first saw it. There was no place else I wanted to live.

We found a house on Oak Street. It was fourteen rooms at $300 a month, with an in-law apartment, a big yard, two-car garage. On Oak between Cole and Schrader. Built in 1914 or 1915. John Braden flew back out and found the house. We rented it immediately. And then we got all these people. A whole slew of grown-ups, some of them crazy, some with children. I had a VW van with rifles and electric typewriters. People decided that's what I needed, so at my going-away party they gave me rifles and electric typewriters. Alan Van Newkirk drove them all out, together with some of my kids.

Our new VW van was used by the Diggers for food pickup and delivery. Our house did two vegetable runs and a fish run every week, and delivered to twenty or twenty-five communes. That was our gig. I wrote lots of ***Revolutionary Letters,*** and they were going out through Liberation News Service to all the underground newspapers in the country. It was nice because I always had the feeling that I could believe this stuff but there was no way I could ever actually *do* anything, because it was McCarthy time and the FBI was chasing some of my friends because they were here without papers. Everything was like that in the '50s. Suddenly to be able to be out in public and do anything, delivering food, having be-ins—it just took a weight off your heart about having kept your mouth shut too long. So it was great. It was really great.

[*Meltzer*]: *How long did that last?*

We got out here in June of '68, and by the fall of '69 the FBI was at the door every day. People from the White Panthers were staying with me; they were wanted, of course. The Black Panthers were in and out of the house. . . . We really didn't know what the FBI was after, but there was somebody knocking on the door just about every day. So we went up to Black Bear Ranch. Elsa and Richard Marley invited us up. I forwarded all my mail to a dead-end post office box where nothing was traceable. Keith Lempe picked it up and readdressed the mail to "Lucy Fur" and sent it on in a plain envelope. We came back a year and a half later. The FBI was still coming to that house, which by then had passed through other hands and a series of other communes. They were still looking for us at that house.

[*Meltzer*]: *What do you think led to all that?*

Well, I think partly we were set up. We were naive as hell. We're still (as a generation) naive as hell or we wouldn't have let KPFA get into such a bad situation. That's been going on for years. We are heads-in-the-sand people. There were too many people with no survival skills at all who came to San Francisco and needed too much for the small number of people who had real vision and really wanted to do something. I think any time that anything interesting happens, heroin is dumped into the scene. Besides our being naive and besides the dope and besides the too many kids who didn't know how to take care of themselves, none of us knew how to deal with our own egos. There was a big revolutionary ego game. With those same egos and a sense of humor, maybe we could have made something work.

[*Meltzer*]: *Well, if you had a sense of humor you wouldn't have those big egos.*

I remember Ginsberg saying to Leslie Fiedler about Vietnam, "I, Allen Ginsberg—single-handed—will stop it!" It was that "single-handed," you know. We were crazy like that, but it was a good kind of crazy. And, of course, the women-and-men thing was impossible.

[*Meltzer*]: *Do you want to discuss that further?*

No, I think we've talked about it. It will be volume two of my book!

[*Meltzer*]: *Isn't it interesting that in all these radical social movements from the turn of the century, the early twentieth century, the sixties, sex politics falls into that same kind of male-privilege model?*

Still doing it right now, this minute. Many of the young artists, couples that I could name, they think they're being fair and equal, and yet the girl's still doing all the money work and housework as well as trying to do her art, and the guy goes up to the attic and just does his art. Still.

You need centuries of change. In the sixties it was a kind of mythologizing: the women had the babies and the men went out hunting. They got very mad at me at Black Bear because I moved up there with not one but two men. And the men chopped wood and carried water. They said those are women's jobs, you're not supposed to be doing that. They got Grant Fisher very upset because he wanted male approval so badly. I said if you don't do some work, you're leaving. So he was doubly upset. Poor guy! The other thing is we didn't and we don't know any history. We don't know what worked and didn't work.

[Meltzer]: *What works, then? What can a poet do to reach the world?*

It's important to self-publish and make your work available. Form small collectives. Start small. You have to remember, you don't have to think of going national. Each small city and its surrounding area is the size of a country from a long time ago. Handle it that way. If you can get books from here to L.A., that's good. Part of what we're hypnotized by from the media is that we have to hit millions of people at once. Back then 117 people got the first *Floating Bear.* And I sold 1,000 copies of my first book out of the stroller wheeling Jeanne around New York. They all went in less than a year. Two years later somebody came to me from one of the federal prisons and told me that twelve carbon copies of that first book had been typed in prison and passed around. Which to me was a bigger honor than any Pulitzer Prize.

TITLE COMMENTARY

Loba

ROCHELLE RATNER (ESSAY DATE 1984)

SOURCE: Ratner, Rochelle. "*Loba.*" In *Trying to Understand What It Means to be a Feminist: Essays on Women Writers,* pp. 15-7. New York: Contact II Publications, 1984.

In the following essay, Ratner examines di Prima's book-length poem Loba.

Loba—she-wolf, wolf-woman, woman as wolf, Goddess. [Di Prima's ***Loba***] is one of the most important books of poetry that has been written in the past decade, and the finest book by a woman since H. D.'s *Trilogy* (1944-46). The poem has been a long time in the making, and is still listed as "in progress": "The author reserves the right to juggle, rearrange, cut, osterize, re-cycle parts of the poem in future editions. As the Loba wishes, as the Goddess dictates" [author's note].

As you might have guessed from the above quote, this is not so much a poem *about* the Goddess as much as an interaction *with* the Goddess. Di Prima makes no attempt to describe her experience in a watered-down fashion so that all her readers will understand. She enters the poem at the precise moment of interaction, and vividly captures it. Thus many poems become fragments, mysterious moments—but any reader who cares enough can be easily caught up in their not-quite-rational intensity.

These are "persona" in its finest sense. At the end of the first invocatory poem, "**Ave,**" she says: "I am you / and I must become you / I have been you / and I must become you / I am always you / I must become you." Who is she? The entire first section presents image-filled notes on who and what she might be:

See the young, black, naked woman riding
a dead white man. Her hair
greasy, she whips him & he flies
thru the smoky air. Her hand
is in her mouth, she is eating
flesh, it stinks, snakes wind
around her ankles. Her hand
touches the (wet) earth. Her hand
shakes a rattle, she laughs, her fangs
flash white & red, they are set
with rubies.

Once the poem is begun, absorbed into the poet's flesh, DiPrima is able to step in and out of the persona. It's not that she's rejecting it, but transcending it. Thus the Loba becomes every woman: "she strides in blue jeans to the corner / bar; she dances / w/the old women, the men / light up, they order wine, / sawdust is flying under her feet / her sneakers, thudding soft / her wispy hair falls sometimes / into her face." For fleeting moments she becomes: a white crow, mistress owl, a black cat, the wind you never leave behind, etc. And once the Loba establishes herself as Goddess, another field is open to explore in relation to other Goddess figures: Loba as Eve, Helen, Persephone, Iseult, Heloise, Guinevere, Mary. In a fascinating interlude she speaks in praise of Lilith. This is DiPrima's totem animal, leading and guiding her:

she-who-was-to-have-devoured me
stood, strong patient
                    recognizably
goddess.
          Protectress
great mystic beast of European forest.
green warrior woman, towering.
                    kind watchdog I cd
leave the children with.
                    Mother & sister.
                    Myself.

This is not just any Goddess, but one who has come through torture. In a very strange way, DiPrima seems to be speaking for all those women who make poems out of their anger, and for those women who still hold their pain silently within them. In Part VI, **"The Seven Joys of the Virgin,"** she turns **"The Annunciation"** into a scene of rape. **"Nativity"** (like **"Loba in Childbed,"** 100 pages earlier in the book) is a powerful poem of today's woman in her humiliating scene of hospital birth: "They fettered me / w/leather straps, on delivery table. I cd not / cry out. Forced gas mask over mouth, / slave. I cd not / turn head. Did they fetter me / w/breath of a fish? these poison airs? I cd not / turn head, move hand, or leg / thus forced. They tore the child from me. Whose?"

Several essays could be written about the various philosophies at work here. Lesser poets than DiPrima would have written essays instead of poems. I can think of no other poet who has made so many personal statements vital to our times. There is the political statement (art, not rhetoric) which DiPrima used so perfectly before in her ***Revolutionary Letters,*** the zen-like, meditative, quiet acceptance seen previously in her ***Kerhonkson Journal*** poems, alchemical images, Catholicism, and a mystical, kabbalistic sense new to DiPrima's work, just to name five obvious philosophies at work here. Something about reading these poems makes you want to dig deeper into the philosophical literature itself. And at the same time, she doesn't boast about her knowledge. She doesn't make you feel as if you don't know enough as a reader to keep up with her, in the way that Ezra Pound or Charles Olson often do. It's all so clear and simple that you get the sense it's been a part of her lifestyle for so long that it's comfortable and natural to her.

The poems have such a graphic preciseness—you ask yourself how anything this explicit could be anything but real. Like in William Blake's best visionary pieces, you get the feeling that DiPrima sees, feels, even smells the Loba. "I am always you / I must become you." If at the beginning the reader doubted the sincerity of this quest, at the end you realize that, not only was she sincere, but she succeeded.

Pieces of a Song: Selected Poems

DAVID BAKER (ESSAY DATE WINTER 1992)

SOURCE: Baker, David. "Probable Reason, Possible Joy." *Kenyon Review* 14, no. 1 (winter 1992): 146-57.

In the following excerpt, Baker reviews di Prima's Pieces of a Song: Selected Poems *and comments on her poetic style.*

California must be a big place indeed: di Prima lives up the coast from Coulette's Los Angeles, in San Francisco where (as the biography printed in ***Pieces of a Song*** states) she is "writing and teaching at San Francisco Institute of Magical and Healing Arts. Continuing to study and practice Tibetan Buddhism, as well as magic, alchemy, and healing." . . . Diane di Prima is a wild, woolly, sometimes unaccountably daffy inheritor of Romantic zest. Her career in poetry has its most fundamental recent grounding in the aesthetics of the Modernist experimentalism of Pound and H. D., and follows through to the Beats and the Black Mountain group; like Gary Snyder, she turns these influences toward a more mystical, natural Romanticism. Where Neoclassicism most values the elements of wit and reason, Romanticism is readier to contain the irrational impulses of magic, mystery, and sensation. Diane di Prima beckons them with a smile. Her poems are loose, open-ended, informal (tonally as well as technically), sounding at times like tribal chants, at times like nonce improvisations, and elsewhere like prayers. She's as likely to be exasperating as inspiring, but I admit to finding her brash energy and her willingness to find wonder and joy in the world refreshing.

The second section of her poem **"Deer Leap,"** from a sequence entitled ***Loba,*** speaks clearly of her desire to maintain a direct connection to the mysteries of the natural world. Having observed her "little Brother" holding still for a moment while he drinks at a brook, she continues:

> Wonder is light
> at wood's edge, falling
> reflecting green, wonder
> is open space where the forest
> closes itself, and nothing
> protects or shelters.
> Outside the forest, no law
> shelters the beast of the wood.
> No law outside   where wonder
> sings limpid, glances
> sideways. Let us go then
> love, where light
> twinkles in the gap
> between the Law
> and ourselves.
>
> (192)

Where Eliot's Prufrock issued a like-sounding invitation, asking his would-be lover to journey through the maze of city streets and museums, through his own paralyed subconscious, di Prima's poem moves toward an act of imaginative freeing, toward wonder, toward the primitive laws of nature, and toward union with the wild things in the woods, far more reminiscent of Kinnell or Dickey than of Eliot. Her most lovely and lyrical writing typically concerns such desires—to touch the heart of mystery and possibility, to become more naturally uninhibited, to reach a place where nature will "let us be what we are." So the poem concludes "mid leap," precisely at the point of the self's giving-over to natural fate, when the speaker has transformed from singular to plural. This is an act of unification, but also of necessary acceptance that the aboriginal woods contain both beauty and annihilation:

let us be what we are,   mid leap
let us fall or rise
on the breath the Will
                    yields to.

there are eyes
under all the leaves,   there are
lynxes, yes
        & the whisper
of passing shadows, but wonder
is there where boundary
breaks against itself
                    & the Law
shivers & bursts like diamonds
                    in the heart

(194)

I am sometimes, however, less convinced or less fully engaged by di Prima's more social and secular poems. Here, among exclusively human goings-on, her tendency is toward the flakier side of Beat Romanticism with its hip phonetics and often facile, surprisingly inflexible politics. Her **"Short Note on the Sparseness of the Language"** is a little narrative about two lovers' decaying relationship:

wow man I said
when you tipped my chin and fed
on headlong spit my tongue's libation fluid

and wow I said when we hit the mattressrags
and wow was the dawn: we boiled the coffee-
    grounds
in an unkempt pot

wow man I said the day you put me down
(only the tone was different)
wow man oh wow   I took my comb
and my two books and cut and that was that

(19)

The poem tries to attain the terseness of a Creeley poem, but I find the brief, nonchalant language merely tiresome, more pathetic than cool, more inexpressive than meaningfully "sparse." It is bereft of any real figurative resonance; it suggests no special import in its sketchy details. Even more disappointing, the poem is a feeble literary paradigm, if indeed its purpose is to provide us with an acting-out of its arch, literary title. If its desire is to represent irony or to dramatize a certain Imagist aesthetic, its result is closer to mere sarcasm or flat happenstance. Perhaps it is true that the poem's limitation stems partly from the immaturities of a young writer. It falls early in the present collection, which does seem to be arranged in rough chronology. But the editors have not assisted such understanding; they have neither dated the poems nor designated in which of di Prima's many individual collections they may have appeared first.

My complaint about **"Short Note on the Sparseness of the Language"** is not to say that di Prima cannot write about politics or culture. **"The Practice of Magical Evocation"** (20), despite its rather Loopy title, is a significant statement of feminist poetics and selfhood; and di Prima is sometimes convincing in her many poems written in sympathy with Native American culture, ritual, and perception. It is characteristic of a Romantic sensibility to turn for guidance toward primitive, archetypal, and tribal practices. Di Prima's fascination here—in her many prayers, chants, and spells—perhaps better signifies her active criticism of the more conventionally modern or urbane ways of living.

The real secret to di Prima's best work, however, lies in her occasional ability to integrate all of her otherwise separate impulses. In what is surely her most fully realized achievement, the long sequence ***Loba,*** she pushes her poetry past the charming or easy—perhaps the most damaging temptations of a Beat aesthetic-and past the exclusively natural. The she-wolf provides di Prima with a fierce, elemental female hero: a rapidly moving perspective able to maneuver from ecology and politics to erotics and religion, a perspective alternately predatory and nurturing. The ambition of the sequence is to contain as much as possible, including elements of Buddhism, Christianity, and Romantic naturalism, and to employ a wide-ranging rhetorical variety—narrative tales, lyric chants, visionary prayers, hallucinations. Here, loping through antique mythology ("I chant / a voice like angels from the heart / of virgin gold, / plaint of the unicorn caught in the boundless circle" 178) as well as through recent cultural history ("who walked across America behind gaunt violent yogis / &. died o-d'ing in methadone jail / scarfing the evidence" 184), di Prima finds her most memorable voice and her most significant visionary stance, wholly if ideally American in its equality:

that she is black, that she is white
that you always know who she is

when she appears
that she strides on battlements, that she sifts
like stones in the sea. . . .

that there is anything about her
which cannot be said
that she relishes tombstones, falls
down marble stairs
that she is ground only, that she is not ground
that you can remember the first time you met
that she is always with you
that she can be seen without grace

that there is anything to say of her
which is not truth

(176)

These lines from **"Some Lies about the Loba"** strain to contain the multitudes that Whitman envisioned. . . . Di Prima's challenge—the point of her successes and failures alike—is to contain, accept, and still be able to discern.

Recollections of My Life as a Woman: The New York Years

JAMES SULLIVAN (REVIEW DATE 22 APRIL 2001)

SOURCE: Sullivan, James. Review of *Recollections of My Life as a Woman: The New York Years,* by Diane di Prima. *San Francisco Chronicle,* Sunday Review Section (22 April 2001): 5.

In the following review, Sullivan assesses Recollections of My Life as a Woman. *Sullivan praises passages in which di Prima focuses on the dilemma of being both a poet and a single mom—and faults other portions of the book, which he deems less interesting.*

When she was an adolescent, the poet Diane di Prima recalls, she liked to say she was going to be a pirate when she grew up. Her mother had different plans: She insisted her daughter take typing lessons.

"I can't say how she imagined a typing pirate, but anyway there I was, and here I am," writes di Prima, so often described as the leading woman writer of the Beat Generation.

The image is apt for di Prima's new memoir, ***Recollections of My Life as a Woman: The New York Years,*** which recounts her years as a poet, theater impresario, small-press publisher and hip mama in Manhattan through the mid-1960s. Now a longtime San Francisco resident, in her younger years the author navigated uncharted waters even in an arts scene that prided itself on the new. Di Prima, mother of five, had three children before she left New York for good, and her "open-minded" friends weren't always supportive of her experimental mix of progressive and traditional lifestyles. The poet Robert Creeley, for one, has recounted a popular myth that di Prima refutes here. Spending an evening with Jack Kerouac, Allen Ginsberg and Philip Whalen, di Prima announced she had to get home to the babysitter. "Di Prima," Kerouac teased, "unless you forget about the baby-sitter, you're never going to be a writer." In Creeley's version, she gave in, staying for an orgy with her fellow writers. Di Prima thinks her colleague might have mixed up the incident with the orgy she wrote about in her Beat-exploitation book, ***Memoirs of a Beatnik*** (1969).

If she had in fact stayed, ignoring her familial obligations, "there would be no poems," the author stresses. Such a lack of discipline would have made the "Chinese puzzle" of being both a poet and a single mom impossible.

When di Prima's memoir sticks to her thoughts on that particular conundrum, it sings. Occasionally, especially near the end of the book, she resorts to a more orderly account of the period, her days with her family, the theater and her own Poets Press. Then the voice wears a bit thin.

Still, as a series of snapshots of the artistic renaissance that invaded Manhattan and the West Coast in the early-to-mid '60s, these "Recollections" are full of light and wonder. Explaining the mulish stoicism of the women of her Italian-immigrant family, di Prima writes how they were deadened by the endless chores: "Never to take a walk with an empty head. Lest something come upon you from the skies."

She learned early to let the skies open as they would. Of her adventures—the affairs, the unpremeditated moves, the peyote and LSD, middle-class repudiations all—di Prima makes no apologies. "It was not that I held my life so cheap, but held experience, the savoring of life so dear."

Those experiences make for rich reading. The memory of an early apartment, she writes, where friends came and went at will, still burns: "The good smell of wood fire. Smell of oil paint . . . The smells of sweat from dance clothes thrown in a heap, smells of the catbox, the stew."

Di Prima's circle of friends extended well beyond the Beats, from the poets Frank O'Hara, Michael McClure and LeRoi Jones (famously, a lover) to filmmaker Jonas Mekas, free-jazz pianist Cecil Taylor, Andy Warhol's Factory proteges and many others.

But this is not a tell-all. She declines to name, for instance, the "prominent poet and translator," a neighbor who disapproved of her bohemian lifestyle and, she learned years later, helped kill a prestigious publishing deal for di Prima's ***Selected Poems.***

For the author, dealing with the blustery male ego, even in a creative world that accepted the gay lifestyle long before the rest of America could acknowledge it, was inevitable.

"My choice: to overlook their one-upmanship, their eternal need to be right," she writes. "Or I took it in stride as not important. A minor part of their Act."

Sometimes she did things the old-fashioned way; at others, she could be downright anarchic. Always she followed her instincts.

"I could be wrong about some things," writes di Prima in her Author's Note. "Most everybody is."

Guileless as her memoir is, the disclaimer seems unnecessary.

JEFF ZALESKI (REVIEW DATE 7 MAY 2001)

SOURCE: Zaleski, Jeff. Review of *Recollections of My Life as a Woman: The New York Years,* by Diane di Prima. *Publishers Weekly* 248, no. 19 (7 May 2001): 240.

In the following review of Recollections of My Life as a Woman, *Zaleski contends that the memoirs recount the atmosphere of the 1950s and 1960s Beat scene and details of di Prima's own life with "honesty and wit."*

Di Prima, perhaps the best known and certainly among the most talented of the beat generation poets, captures [in ***Recollections of My Life as a Woman***] the heady atmosphere of New York's avant-garde community in the 1950s and 1960s, while rendering her own life with intimacy and grace. Born in Brooklyn in the mid-1930s, she remembers her Italian immigrant grandmother with great affection. But she describes frightening incidents from her earliest childhood: her father, a sullen, brooding, man, once beat her until her nose bled; her relationship with her mother was equally abusive. In elementary school, di Prima was bullied relentlessly; it was not until she entered Hunter High School for gifted students that she found a circle of friends; there, reading the great poets, she resolved to become a poet herself. Leaving Swarthmore College after what she perceived as unproductive years, di Prima returned to New York City, and embarked on an independent life as a writer. She describes her bohemian lifestyle—love affairs with men and women, experiments with drugs—with honesty and wit. Friend to many of the best known figures of the beat world, including Allen Ginsberg, Audre Lorde and LeRoi Jones, di Prima found fulfillment in her work as an editor and poet, and as a single mother. She tells her story well, skillfully interweaving events with lyrical commentary on her inner life.

FURTHER READING

Biography

Knight, Brenda. "Diane di Prima: Poet Priestess." *Women of the Beat Generation: The Writers, Artists, and Muses at the Heart of a Revolution,* p. 123-40. Berkeley, Calif.: Conari Press, 1996.

Presents a short biography of di Prima that touches on her relationships with Allen Ginsberg, Jack Kerouac, and LeRoi Jones and provides examples of her poetry.

Criticism

Gargan, William. Review of *Loba,* by Diane di Prima. *Library Journal* 123, no. 13 (1 August 1998): 94.

Review of di Prima's book-length poem Loba.

Johnson, Ronna C., and Maria Damon. "Recapturing the Skipped Beats." *Chronicle of Higher Education* 46, no. 6 (1 October 1999): B4ff.

Discusses Beat writers and their ethnicity; includes discussion on di Prima.

Peabody, Richard. *A Different Beat: Writing by Women of the Beat Generation.* London and New York: Serpent's Tail Press, 1997, 235 p.

An anthology of poetry and autobiographical text by female Beat writers, including di Prima.

OTHER SOURCES FROM GALE:

Additional coverage of di Prima's life and career is contained in the following sources published by the Gale Group: *Contemporary Authors,* Vols. 17-20R; *Contemporary Authors New Revision Series,* Vol. 13; *Contemporary Poets,* Ed. 7; *Contemporary Women Poets; Dictionary of Literary Biography,* Vols. 5, 16; *Literature Resource Center,* and *World Poets.*

ROBERT DUNCAN

(1919 - 1988)

(Born Edward Howard Duncan; has also written under the pseudonyms Robert Edward Duncan and Robert Edward Symmes) American poet, playwright, and essayist.

An important member of the San Francisco Bay poetry community, Duncan also is often identified as a Black Mountain poet. His writing is highly intertextual, referring to large numbers of other literary texts and even to other art forms, such as painting, music, and dance. Stylistically, Duncan's work is characterized by mixtures of poetry and prose, unconventional syntax and punctuation, odd line breaks, and verse that begins with lower case letters or semicolons. Duncan is associated with the Beat Generation writers through their admiration for his confessional tone, his questioning of social as well as literary norms, and through Lawrence Ferlinghetti's publication of his *Selected Poems* (1959).

BIOGRAPHICAL INFORMATION

Duncan was born January 7, 1919, in Oakland, California, to Edward Howard, a day laborer, and Marguerite Wesley Duncan, who succumbed to the 1919 flu epidemic shortly after her son's birth. He was adopted a year later by architect Edwin Symmes and his wife, Minnehaha, followers of theosophy; the fables and myths he learned as a child from family members became a major influence on his later work. Duncan was reared as Robert Edward Symmes, and although he published originally under that name, he changed his surname back to Duncan at the age of twenty-one. In 1936 he enrolled in the University of California at Berkeley, but left after two years, traveling to New York to become part of the literary circle that included Anaïs Nin and Henry Miller. Duncan was drafted by the U. S. Army in 1941, but received a psychiatric discharge shortly afterwards. In 1943 he was briefly married to Marjorie McKee. Two years later Duncan returned to the San Francisco Bay area, where he became a prominent member of the local literary community led by Kenneth Rexroth. He attended Berkeley again from 1948 to 1950, studying medieval and Renaissance civilization. In 1950 Duncan met painter Jess Collins and the following year the two began a lifelong domestic partnership, a relationship that had a stabilizing effect on Duncan's personal life and a strong influence on his poetry as well. Although he occasionally appeared with some of the most famous of the Beat poets, he maintained a deliberate distance from the movement itself. Duncan also was associated with the Black Mountain group, having taught at North Carolina's Black Mountain College for a short time in 1956. He was active throughout his life in Bay Area poetry and politics, publishing numerous collections of verse and providing encouragement to younger poets. Throughout his career, Duncan received many literary awards and grants, including a Guggenheim Fellowship in 1963, National Endowment for the Arts grants in 1966 and 1967, the National Poetry Award in 1985, and the American Book Award that same year. Duncan died of a heart attack in San Francisco in 1988.

MAJOR WORKS

Duncan began publishing his poems at Berkeley, but did not become well known until 1944 when his controversial essay "The Homosexual in Society" appeared in *Politics* magazine. Collections of his early poems were published during the 1960s in three volumes: *The Years as Catches: First Poems (1939-1946)* (1966); *The First Decade: Selected Poems 1940-1950* (1968); and *Derivations: Selected Poems 1950-1956* (1968). Many of the concerns he expressed in his later, more notable poetry appear first in these early works. One of his most famous collections, *The Opening of the Field* (1960), consists of some of the pieces he composed at Black Mountain College. Reflecting poet Charles Olson's call for open form in poetry, these works have prompted some critics to suggest that Duncan took the notion of open poetry further than his mentor by completely rejecting boundaries of any kind. The poems of the 1968 collection *Bending the Bow* are largely political, dealing with Duncan's opposition to the Vietnam War and nuclear arms, as well as his devotion to environmental causes. Also in 1968, Duncan published a collection of essays *The Truth and Life of Myth,* explaining his theory of poetry and its relationship to myth and mysticism. Duncan announced in 1968 that he would not publish another major collection for fifteen years, hoping to work on the process of writing poetry without the pressures of publication deadlines. The resulting collections are *Ground Work: Before the War* (1984), which won the National Poetry Award in 1985, and *Ground Work II: In the Dark* (1987). In 1993 a collection of poetry spanning Duncan's entire career was published under the title *Selected Poems.*

CRITICAL RECEPTION

Reviewers have qualified Duncan's verse as postmodern due to its self-referential qualities and its intertextual allusions and references to the works of other poets, musicians, and artists. Dennis Cooley has claimed that "even a partial list of writers and subjects from which he [Duncan] has often drawn is staggering," listing the numerous literary figures from Dante to H. D. that Duncan quotes or cites as influential in his work. Michael Davidson has asserted that "many of Duncan's finest poems are 'readings' of other texts, his own poem serving as meditation and transformation." Such individual works as "A Poem Beginning with a Line by Pindar" (1960), or such collections as *Dante* (1974) or *Poems from the Margins of Thom Gunn's "Moly"* (1972) are examples of Duncan's work that treat the texts of others "not as privileged signs of cultural order . . . nor as allusions but as generative elements in the composing process." A. K. Weatherhead has noted Duncan's attempt in much of his poetry, "to take over the prerogatives of painting and to exist in spatial terms." Most critics have agreed that although Duncan intended his poetry to be read aloud, much of his verse must also be seen in print to be appreciated since it contains figures and pictographs that cannot be spoken. Norman M. Finkelstein has positioned Duncan's work at a point between Romanticism and Modernism, claiming that it "is frequently uneven, for he is at the mercy of Modernist fragmentation as well as the excesses of hermetic, visionary Romanticism." Dennis Cooley has maintained that Duncan's views on order and chaos inform his work to a large degree. "According to Duncan's view of the universe," Cooley reports, "the poet's job is not to impose order but to discover it." Duncan often blends poetry and prose resulting in an unconventional composition method that can be disturbing to readers. Cooley has further contended that this is a deliberate strategy intending to jar the reader out of traditional ways of thinking. Thomas Parkinson has summed up the views of many of Duncan's critics, claiming that his work, "taken as a whole, has a grandeur to it that is complemented by the scope and intelligence of his theoretical and practical work on the life of a poet."

PRINCIPAL WORKS

Heavenly City Earthly City (poetry) 1947

Poems 1948-49 (poetry) 1949

Medieval Scenes (poetry) 1950; revised edition 1978

Caesar's Gate Poems 1949-1950 (poetry) 1955; revised edition 1972

**Faust Foutu: An Entertainment by Robert Duncan in Four Parts* (play) 1959

Selected Poems (poetry) 1959

The Opening of the Field (poetry) 1960

Roots and Branches (poetry) 1964

The Sweetness and Greatness of Dante's Divine Comedy (poetry) 1965

A Book of Resemblances Poems: 1950-1953 (poetry) 1966

The Years as Catches: First Poems (1939-1946) (poetry) 1966

Bending the Bow (poetry) 1968

Derivations: Selected Poems 1950-1956 (poetry) 1968

The First Decade: Selected Poems 1940-1950 (poetry) 1968

The Truth and Life of Myth (essays) 1968

Poems from the Margins of Thom Gunn's "Moly" (poetry) 1972

Dante (poetry) 1974

Ground Work: Before the War (poetry) 1984

Ground Work II: In the Dark (poetry) 1987

Selected Poems (poetry) 1993

* This play was first produced in 1955 in San Francisco, California, as *Faust Foutu: Act One of Four Acts, A Comic Mask, 1952-1954* and later in New York in 1959 through 1960.

PRIMARY SOURCES

ROBERT DUNCAN (POEM DATE 1960)

SOURCE: Duncan, Robert. "Often I am Permitted to Return to a Meadow." In *The Opening of the Field,* p. 7. New York: Grove Press, 1960.

In the following poem from the 1960 collection The Opening of the Field, *Duncan writes in a nearly linear progression in contrast to much of his subsequent poetry.*

as if it were a scene made-up by the mind,
that is not mine, but is a made place,
that is mine, it is so near to the heart,
an eternal pasture folded in all thought
so that there is a hall therein
that is a made place, created by light
wherefrom the shadows that are forms fall.
Wherefrom fall all architectures I am
I say are likenesses of the First Beloved
whose flowers are flames lit to the Lady.

She it is Queen Under the Hill
whose hosts are a disturbance of words within
words
that is a field folded.
It is only a dream of the grass blowing
east against the source of the sun
in an hour before the sun's going down
whose secret we see in a children's game
of ring a round of roses told.
Often I am permitted to return to a meadow
as if it were a given property of the mind
that certain bounds hold against chaos,
that is a place of first permission,
everlasting omen of what is.

GENERAL COMMENTARY

NORMAN M. FINKELSTEIN (ESSAY DATE SPRING 1983)

SOURCE: Finkelstein, Norman M. "Robert Duncan, Poet of the Law." *Sagetrieb* 2, no. 1 (spring 1983): 75-88.

In the following essay, Finkelstein presents Duncan as a poet of self-conscious lyrics that assert moral and rhetorical authority, displaying the responsibility of the poet towards the political events of his time.

Robert Duncan is a poet of lawfulness; not only is his best work lawful in the most rigorous historical and philosophical terms, but the notion of the Law is deliberately made the subject of the poetry itself. By lawfulness is meant the measure, in a work of art, of appropriate response to historical exigencies, the recognition, which is itself freedom, of what must be done in the realm of necessity.[1] What *must* the poet say, given his personal and social history? If he is sufficiently self-conscious, his work will be imbued with the necessity of utterance, and in this necessity he will discover lawful artistic freedom. Art attains to greatness insofar as it is lawful, and lawfulness, of necessity, permeates the totality of the work, its craft or form as well as its subject matter. As Duncan himself says, "lawful action to me is total responsibility to what is present."[2] Because Duncan recognizes the necessity of the poet to work under Law, a very rare perception among poets today, his opus has become a high point in contemporary poetic self-consciousness, and has taken its place alongside the work of his most important Romantic and Modernist precursors.

As the first real synthesis of Romantic and Modernist modes, Duncan's work is frequently uneven, for he is at the mercy of Modernist fragmentation as well as the excesses of hermetic, visionary Romanticism. But despite the problems imposed by past poetic modes, he still maintains that "The morphology of forms, in evolving, does not destroy their historicity but reveals that each event has its origin in the origin of all events."[3] Thus the poem becomes the vessel of Poetry and of culture as an on-going historical event. Totally process-oriented, Duncan's efforts impel us to read his entire opus, particularly his three major books to date, as a single open form, in which mythic themes rise and fall in conjunction with the most contemporary events. Continuing in the synchronic techniques of Pound and Olson, Duncan can shift rapidly from a mythic hymn of praise to a blistering condemnation of the Vietnam War, incorporating interior psychological events and exterior political occurrences into the single woven texture of the poem. As he says in his most coherent testament, ***The Truth & Life of Myth*** (1968):

> my purpose here has been to give some idea of how little a matter of "free" association and how much a matter of an enduring design in which the actual living consciousness arises, how much a matter of actual times and actual objects the living reality of the myth is for the poet. Just these times, just these objects, just these persons come to mind—at once things-in-themselves and things in ourselves.
>
> (*TL,* [*The Truth & Life of Myth,*] p. 21)

As is implied here, the source of this highly synthetic conception of poetic composition is the vision of a mythic, spiritual presence embodying itself in the immediate, material world. Duncan's most explicit statement of the process by which he comes to write appears in ***The Sweetness & Greatness of Dante's Divine Comedy*** (1965):

> With Dante I take the literal, the actual, as the primary ground. We ourselves are literal, actual beings. This is the hardest ground for us to know, for we are *of* it—not outside, observing, but inside, experiencing. It is, finally, I believe, the only ground for us to know; for it is Creation, it is the Divine Presentation, it is the language of experience whose words are immediate to our senses; from which our own creative life takes fire, *within which* our own creative life takes fire. This creative life is a drive towards the reality of Creation, producing an inner world, an emotional and intellectual fiction, in answer to our awareness of the creative reality of the whole.
>
> (*SG,* [*The Sweetness & Greatness of Dante's Divine Comedy,*] pp. 4-5)

To one versed in *either* Modernism or Romanticism, such a statement may seem positively eerie: as if Blake were speaking through Williams, or vice versa. But for Duncan, the foster-child of members of "an Hermetic Brotherhood, similar to and contemporaneous with the Order of the Golden Dawn" (***TL,*** p. 9), the immediate world is a means by which the spiritual world may be understood, and to write of one is to write of the other. This leads to Duncan's rediscovery of the myth of the world as book, a spiritual text that the poet seeks to embody in his verse. As Charles Altieri observes:

> Natural forces pass by, and as they pass they are given form in textual passages. Textual passages then free us to pass from one realm of being to another, from outer to inner nature and from literal natural orders to the spiritual and transcendental orders of the letter.[4]

This new freedom, genuine as it may be, also has its drawbacks, which arise from its very origins. Searching for the mythic in the actual may obscure the causes of material events, and even Duncan's most impassioned political poetry never touches the heart of historical and social contradictions as, say, George Oppen's does. Instead, his poetry more often engages itself with the "pretentious fictions" of which he himself speaks, leading at times to a kind of phantasmagoric silliness in which flights of fancy supplant more urgent poetic desires. Duncan is aware of this tendency, however; as he says of the combination of heroic and commonplace myths in his work:

> But it is in the Romantic vein—to which I see my own work as clearly belonging—that the two worlds, the lordly and the humble, that seemed to scholars irreconcilably at odds, mythological vision and folklorish phantasy, are wedded in a phantasmagoria—as Goethe called his Helen episode—the spiritual romance . . . where chastity and lewdness, love and lust, the philosopher king and the monstrous clown dance together in all their human reality.
>
> (*TL,* p. 38)

Still he is open to criticism for this attitude, particularly when placed in comparison to his great Romantic precursors, Blake, Coleridge and Shelley, whom he otherwise resembles. The High Romantics were almost never self-indulgent in their fictions in the way that Duncan can be; their mythopoeic works have an urgency derived from the dialectic of inner freedom and outer circumstance that Duncan is too apt to abandon. Again, Duncan is conscious of this pitfall:

> This is the great temptation of all true poets to be so enraptured by the beauty of the language in love of which they have been called to their life work, so taken in by the loveliness of words or by

> the wonder of images and persons that the art projects, that they lose the intent of the whole, the workings of the poem towards the fullness in meaning of its form.
>
> (*SG*, pp. 11-12)

But this is perhaps the inevitable outcome of the translation of the Romantic sensibility into the contemporary open form.

For beyond the ideological mystifications that a mythic poetry perforce creates for itself lies the even greater problem of form. In the act of creation, Duncan claims, "self-consciousness is not lost in a void but in the transcendent consciousness of the dance."[5] Here too, a sense of mythic reality may impinge on the poet's drive towards the discovery of poetic causation, which is felt in the poem as a sureness of rhythm and a coherence of syntax that is too often missing in Duncan's verse. Self-consciousness enters the cosmic dance too readily, and the result is a diffusion of energy, the same fragmentation that plagues Olson and Pound. Arguably, Duncan's best work *arises out of* field poetics, but actually manifests itself as beautifully controlled lyric outbursts, poems in which the *logos* and the *melos* move together in a very traditional way. Perhaps this is to say that the Romantic lyric is the better vehicle for creative ideation than the post-Modern open form. But that would be reductive, for Duncan's finest poems are the furthest extensions of his synthetic methodology, in which the urgency of visionary utterance leaves both mythic and immediate events behind, creating what can only be described as eternally original imaginative ground, "that is a made place, created by light / wherefrom the shadows that are forms fall" (***OF*, [*The Opening of the Field*,]** p. 7). It is from this place that Duncan is capable of speaking with the voice of universal Law, invoking the Utopian desire that becomes the object of his verse as well as its inspiration. Thus he is able to declare "That Freedom and the Law are identical / and are the nature of Man—Paradise" (***BB*, [*Bending the Bow*,]** p. 74).

The process through which Duncan matures into a poet of lawfulness is a long one, carrying him up to the well-known turning point in his career, ***The Opening of the Field*** (1960). As we have seen, Duncan's understanding of the Law is directly related to his synthesizing poetic, in which the Modernist faith in direct, objective experience is aligned with Romantic interiority, the transcendental world that is both an outgrowth of and a reaction to immediate circumstance. Duncan's early work involves a dialectical movement between Modernist and Romantic modes of discourse, a kind of Yeatsian vacillation that eventually takes the poet to the philosophical juncture of interiority and exteriority. As he declares in **"I Am A Most Fleshly Man"**:

> Come unto me, questioning dark spirit.
> You dwell upon the threshold of my mind.
> This yearning is a vast eternity
> that waste about us questioning lies,
> and we, in the limbo of disem bodied love,
> stare upon the bodies we deny.
>
> (***YC*, [*The Years as Catches*,]** p. 81)

Such lines, fraught with sensuality yet broodingly abstract, may be attributed to a poetic consciousness that maintains outer experience whole while still remaking it in the interior "limbo of disembodied love." When the poet realizes that such a stance frees him from both the constraints of the immediate and the isolation of the transcendental, he recognizes the lawful freedom granted his historical position.

Duncan is now free to move between interior and exterior realms, a poetic capability that he realizes for the first time in **"The Song of the Borderguard."** In this poem, which is metonymic of the transformation that Duncan's poetry undergoes before ***The Opening of the Field***, words themselves are self-consciously depicted as "a barbarian host at the borderline of sense," and poetry is a lion always ready to pounce on the unsuspecting borderguard/poet. The relationship between the "Poet on Guard" and the lion is strangely ambivalent:

> The man shedding his belief
> knows that the lion is not asleep,
> does not dream, is never asleep,
> is a wide-awake poem
> waiting like a lover for the disrobing of the
>   guard;
> the beautiful boundaries of the empire
> naked, rapt round in the smell of a lion.
>
> (***FD*, [*The First Decade: Selected Poems 1940-1950*,]** p. 135)

Duncan here depicts the process by which he releases himself, hesitantly, from his former preconceptions. On the border between interior and exterior worlds, he is still afraid of the full visionary implications of his role, and he guards himself. But the guards are "enamord" and half-wish for the lion of the poem, which comes as much as a lover as a destroyer to the threshold, this "borderline of sense." The form of the poem opens outward to this experience even as the lion, the jungle beast, comes out from within the interior self. The border opens, and the poet with his guitar, singing "believe, believe, believe," awaits the coming of inspiration.

He has not long to wait. Duncan's absorption with primal acts of language, acts which "take place" in a poetic terrain that is invoked by the poet's utterance but also maintains an independent metaphysical existence, leads him to ***The Opening of the Field.*** This volume, with its prophetic title, fluid open forms and magnificent lyricism, marks the beginning of Duncan's mature work, that continues with no interruption through ***Roots and Branches*** (1964) and ***Bending the Bow*** (1968). ***The Structure of Rime*** and ***Passages,*** the two series poems that wind their ways through these volumes and beyond, argue for the unification of Duncan's poetic efforts in ways unprecedented in his earlier work. Themes reappear continually in these books, providing a sense of unity that works against the boundaries of discrete poems. Adhering strictly to chronological order, Duncan allows his individual lyrics to punctuate the flow of the open forms. The result is a genuine tapestry, or more precisely, a world/book that serves as a vessel for the continual inclusion of myth, current events and enduring cultural and literary antecedents. This is Duncan's unique version of field poetics, in which the poem, as Michael Davidson notes, "does not imitate but enacts natural and cosmic orders: it does not seek to 'contain' meaning but to discover immanent meanings."[6]

The lawfulness of this stance becomes apparent in the first poem of ***The Opening of the Field,*** the seminal post-Modern lyric **"Often I Am Permitted To Return To A Meadow."** Here, the idea of composition by field literally becomes the dominant metaphor for the discovery of creative freedom within the bounds of necessity:

> as if it were a scene made-up by the mind,
> that is not mine, but is a made place,
>
> that is mine, it is so near to the heart,
> an eternal pasture folded in all thought
> so that there is a hall therein
>
> that is a made place, created by light
> wherefrom the shadows that are forms fall.

The meadow is of the poet, but is Other than the poet as well, and in such ambiguity resides the linguistic tension needed for the poem to resolve itself as completed utterance. Turning continually on the dichotomy of inner and outer worlds, the syntax rushes breathlessly forward, shaping the poem into the image of Duncan's ideal Form, which exists simultaneously in the mind, in the poem, in the exterior world and in a transcendental spiritual reality. The poem, the made place, is the manifestation of the creative will, Duncan's muse, "the Lady," "the First Beloved," who is also the Kabbalistic *Shekinah,* coexisting with God at the Creation. She inspires the poem even as she brings the poet his dream of children in a ring dancing in the wind-blown field, "the place of first permission," the scene of initiation into visionary experience. It is here that the poet is *permitted* to go each time inspiration comes to him, and it is this notion of freedom found in necessity that secures the poem's lawfulness.

As we learn in **"The Law I Love Is Major Mover,"** Duncan's permission comes from universal Law itself. The poet insists that form discovers itself under the guidance of such Law, which permeates natural existence, human activity and the higher spiritual orders. Political systems at their best are reflections of this Law as is human love and the poets' worship of their Muse:

> No nation stands unstirred
> in whose courts. *I, John, testify:*
> *I saw.* But he who judges must
>   know mercy
> as a man knows a woman
>   in marriage,
> for She is fair, whom we, masters, serve.
>
> The Which, says John Adams,
>   "requires the continual exercise of virtue
>   "beyond the reach
>   "of human infirmity, even in its best
>   estate."
>
> (*OF,* p. 10)

From such intuitions, Duncan generalizes that "Responsibility is to keep / the ability to respond." Such a post-Modern literary axiom (compare Olson's "ONE PERCEPTION MUST IMMEDIATELY AND DIRECTLY LEAD TO A FURTHER PERCEPTION") in this instance takes on great significance, for it is clearly meant to be not only an aesthetic rule, but genuine testimony to the workings of universal will. The universe responds to itself through a continual act of creation, as creativity perpetuates itself from form to form:

> The scale of five, eight, or twelve tones
>   performs a judgment
> previous to music. The music restores
>   health to the land.
>
> (*OF,* p. 10)

The evolving forms of music are directly related to the "health of the land," in both the natural and political senses of the term. In all cases of creativity, the same Law holds true.

As in music the lawful determination of the scale creates a system of composition, so too in poetry does syntax determine the formal integrity of the work:

Look! the Angel that made a man of Jacob
made Israel in His embrace
was the Law, was Syntax
Him I love is major mover.

(*OF*, p. 11)

Jacob wrestling the angel, one of Duncan's most important mythic references, signifies the poet's struggle to uncover the hidden laws of form that lie unrealized in the raw material of experience. The dormancy of mere existence would keep the poem from coming into being, but in the wrestling with syntax, even as Jacob wrestled, the laws of language are revealed. Thus, in **"The Structure of Rime I,"** immediately following **"The Law I Love,"** we are told that

Jacob wrestled with Sleep—you who fall into
Nothingness and dread sleep.
He wrestled with Sleep like a man reading a strong
sentence.

(*OF*, p. 12)

Duncan himself later glosses these lines:

It has seemed to me that I wrestle with the syntax of the world of my experience to bring forward into the Day the twisted syntax of my human language that will be changed in that contact even with what I dread there. And recently I have come to think of Poetry more and more as a wrestling with Form to liberate Form. The figure of Jacob returns again and again to my thought.

(*TL*, pp. 15-16)

As Duncan implies throughout ***The Structure of Rime,*** all of Creation operates under the "sentence" of lawful syntax. Such being the case, questions of human morality bear re-examination in the light of a higher spiritual reality. Such a re-examination takes place in **"This Place Rumord To Have Been Sodom,"** one of the most fully-sustained and syntactically complete poems in ***The Opening of the Field.*** In the repetition and variation of this lyric, the lust that we think of as the reason for Sodom's destruction is gradually revealed to be an aspect of divine love. Sodom becomes a scene of Blakean contrariety in which spirit and flesh are merged in the desire of consciousness to perpetuate itself:

This was once
a city among men, a gathering together of spirit.
It was measured by the Lord and found wanting.

It was measured by the Lord and found wanting,
destroyed by the angels that inhabit longing.
Surely this is Great Sodom where such cries
as if men were birds flying up from the swamp
ring in our ears, where such fears that were once
desires walk . . .

(*OF*, p. 22)

But because "the faithful hold this place green," the vitality of Sodom survives, and its mythic destruction gives way to its mythic renewal, a new dispensation in which men come to understand the dialectical contradictions through which universal Law works its ends:

Only these new friends gather joyous here,
where the world like Great Sodom lies under
fear.

The world like Great Sodom lies under Love
and knows not the hand of the Lord that moves.

Human interpretations of mythic events are contingent upon the degree of man's understanding of the Law, which in the poem creates a series of linguistic variations that cause us to reinterpret the story of Sodom, to see its destruction and renewal as an act of love. What endures in the poem is syntax itself, the structure of language which, stirred by desire, renews itself like the fallen city.

For Duncan, then, desire assumes form in language to renew itself continually, following syntactic laws. As Duncan's verse progresses, it becomes, to a certain extent, polarized by this notion, and may be regarded as either a celebration of the Law or a defense of it in the face of political and cosmic disorder. More and more frequently, Duncan resorts to purely open forms to express this polarization, for within such poems both the Utopian urge towards an alchemical marriage of spirit and flesh, and the entropic forces of materialism, greed and political tyranny may be contained. The lyrical affirmation of ***The Opening of the Field*** becomes increasingly more difficult to achieve throughout the Sixties, as immediate political realities impose themselves more and more forcefully upon any merely ideal or mythic totality. Duncan's increasing awareness of the United States' international policy of imperialism and the national ferment it causes leads him to reassert his vision of unity, while at the same time he begins to attack unlawful political and economic policies and the men who coordinate them. ***Roots and Branches,*** containing poems from 1959 to 1963, is a predominantly celebratory volume, and as such is a strong contrast to the strenuous political verse of ***Bending the Bow,*** the volume of poems from 1964 to 1967. The former volume is weaker; its open forms, despite their many moments of beauty, seem desultory in the light of ***Passages,*** the more recent series of political poems that begins in ***Bending the Bow.***

Nevertheless, ***Roots and Branches*** is Duncan's most extensive and personal exploration of his Romantic sources, a volume that pleases more for what it attempts within a certain stance than for what it accomplishes. The title poem, for example, is a Shelleyan fragment that honors the natural world as the bearer of inner spiritual knowledge:

> How you perfect my spirit!
> almost restore
> an imaginary tree of the living in all its doctrines
> by fluttering about,
> intent and easy as you are, the profusion of you!
> awakening transports of an inner view of things.
> (***RB***, [***Roots and Branches,***] p. 3)

Equally authoritative in its visionary tone is section five of the series poem "**Apprehensions,**" a sublime hymn to the sun as the symbolic home of human life and knowledge:

> It is the earth turning
> that lifts our shores from the dark
> into the cold light of morning,
> eastward turning,
> and that returns us from the sun's burning
> into passages of twilight and doubt,
> dim reveries and gawdy effects.
> The sun is the everlasting center of what we
> know,
> a steady radiance.
> (***RB***, pp. 39-40)

These are only two of the volume's many outbursts of Romantic identification which, in reinforcing Duncan's commitment to what he "apprehends" to be a universal "directive" for creative endeavor, brings together the various "orders" of the natural, the personal, the social and the spiritual in a unified linguistic design:

> the orders of the sentence in reading;
> the orders of what is seen in passing. There was
> the swarming earth;
> the orders of commanding images;
> the orders of passionate fictions and themes of
> the poet in writing;
> the orders of the dead and the unborn that
> swarm in the floods of a man embracing his
> companion;
> the orders of the Lord of Love.
> (***RB***, pp. 42-43)

The result is an overriding Law of poetry:

> *L'idée poétique,* the idea of a poetry that rises from the movement, from the outswirling curves and imaginary figures round this ship, this fate, this sure thing,
>
> *est l'hypothèse d'une être vaste, immense, compliqué, mais eurythmique.*
> (***RB***, p. 78)

By the time Duncan is challenged by the political events of the middle Sixties and moved to incorporate them into his mythopoeic structure, he is so immersed in his sense of lawfulness that the confrontation produces some of his finest work. ***Bending the Bow*** is the political testament of a man who would as soon eschew politics for "pretentious fictions," but who nonetheless deeply senses that his *poetic* responsibility lies in the meeting of this political challenge. The Introduction to the book presents Duncan's dilemma clearly, in a way that bridges the gap, as does the poetry, between exterior event and interior response. The poet's description of his participation in an anti-war demonstration reminds one of the Peterloo Massacre that inspired some of Shelley's greatest work:

> I had step forward to speak, when the men were ordered to march upon us and force us to retract our stand, and we, under our own orders, moved each to sit or lie upon the ground, to hold the ground of our testimony stubbornly, the individual volition of a non-violent action. It was like the presence of the poet's intent in the hearts of the people of a poem, we meant to fulfill our humanity. But we were, in turn, members of a company of men, moving forward, violently, to overcome in themselves the little company of others kneeling and striving to speak to them, a refusal of all common speech that strove to maintain itself before us.
> (***BB***, p. iii)

Duncan here applies his sense of literary dialectics to political realities: he simultaneously places himself among the demonstrators and among the soldiers in an effort to understand the motivations of men who would otherwise appear to him as two-dimensional stick figures of violence and hate. He insists on discovering essential truths about complex political actions; for him, such acts are congruent with his renewed interior stance, in which events in the real world simultaneously resound in the life of the imagination as part of a process of dialectical self-realization he can only call *It*:

> The gnostics and magicians claim to know or would know Its real nature, which they believe to be miswritten or cryptically written in the text of the actual world. But Williams is right in his *no ideas but in things;* for It has only the actual universe in which to realize Itself. We ourselves in our actuality, its thingness, are facts, factors, in which It makes Itself real. Having only these actual words, these actual imaginations that come to us as we work.
> (***BB***, p. vii)

"Actual imaginations": this seemingly paradoxical phrase summarizes Duncan's notion of poetic composition from the beginning, and is now expanded to lay as much stress on the first term as on the second. Thus Williams takes his place next to the gnostics, an unavoidable master when the poet aspires to a high degree of objectivity in what has become a political as well as a poetic enterprise.

It is for this reason that "**Passages,**" the open series that begins in ***Bending the Bow,*** joining the continuing ***Structure of Rime,*** has a greater resemblance to such works as *The Cantos, Paterson* or *Maximus* than any of Duncan's previous poetry. Duncan's subject matter demands the moment-by-moment dictation and interweaving of cultural and political fragments that open form provides, though the tapestry-like texture of ***Passages*** is actually much more of a piece than Duncan's earlier and shorter open forms. Duncan describes his technique in "**At The Loom,**" Passages 2:

> my mind a shuttle among
> set strings of the music
> lets a weft of dream grow in the day time,
> an increment of associations,
> luminous soft threads,
> the thrown glamour, crossing and recrossing,
> the twisted sinews underlying the work.
>
> (***BB,*** p. 11)

The difference between this poetry and the veiled psychological symbolism of ***The Structure of Rime*** is clear: whereas the former sensuously enacts and informs its subject matter, capturing it in the pervasive rhythm of the open form, the latter describes the workings of the mind in contact with the subject matter, presenting in flowing prose a pictorial representation of that meeting. "**Structure of Rime XXIV,**" the best of that sequence in ***Bending the Bow,*** *pictures* its Utopian city, though it rises out of music:

> In the joy of the new work he raises horns of sublime sound into the heat surrounding the sheets of crystalline water to make walls in the music.
>
> And in every repeat majestic sequences of avenues branch into halls where lovers and workers, fathers, mothers and children gather, in a life, a life-work, the grand opus of humanity, the old alchemists' dream.
>
> (***BB,*** p. 36)

On the other hand, "**Where It Appears,**" Passages 4, relies on musical rhythm (and breath stops indicated on the field of the page) to convey its message:

> I'd cut the warp
> to weave that web
>
> in the air
>
> and here
>
> let image perish in image . . .
>
> (***BB,*** p. 15)

And when the two series meet, in a poem that is simultaneously Passages 20 and Structure of Rime XXVI, the prose paragraphs and symbolic figures with which the piece begins open outward into free verse in a brief but powerful evocation of political and spiritual union:

> Where the tents of the Great Assembly stand,
> I used to make up my
> tents, my treasuries,
> my powers within powers
>
> (***BB,*** p. 69)

The kind of union herein described is the goal towards which the verse in ***Passages*** strives, though the poet acknowledges that such a goal can never be reached, but must remain as a Utopian ideal to constantly re-inspire the composition of the poem.

Despite the fact that Duncan's poetry remains one of struggle, of the ceaseless *becoming* of open form, in recent years he has attained a level of mastery that allows for powerfully definitive statement and magnificently formal rhetoric. As implied by the very title of the volume containing "**Passages 31-35,**" ***Tribunals,*** Duncan has become so much the poet of the Law that he may stand as the judge of the nation. This was already clear in ***Bending the Bow,*** when, drawing upon such precursor poems as the Hell and Usura Cantos, as well as *The Inferno,* Duncan inveighed against

> the great dragon himself so confronted
> whose scales are men officized—ossified—
> conscience
> no longer alive in them,
> the inner law silenced . . .
>
> (***BB,*** p. 70)

Tribunals supplies the mystical underpinnings of this stance, the spiritual authorization of Duncan's hermetic masters, who represent the lawful tradition of philosophical studies. At its most extreme such verse can sound less like Blake or the Neo-Platonists than like pop fantasy: "but the Golden Ones meet in the Solar Councils / and their alphabet is hidden in the evolution of chemical codes" (*T,* [***Tribunals***] p. 23). Nevertheless, Duncan's voice rings out clearly when he enjoins us to

> come into these orders as they have come-
> , stand
> as ever, where they are acknowledged,
> against the works of unworthy men, unfeeling
> judgments & cruel deeds.
>
> (*T,* p. 29)

As the poet of Law, Duncan has moved from his initial point of recognition, in which his unique historical situation granted him renewed

FROM THE AUTHOR

FROM DUNCAN'S POEM "THIS PLACE RUMOR'D TO HAVE BEEN SODOM"

The world like Great Sodom lies under
Love and knows not the hand of the
Lord that moves.

Duncan, Robert. From "This Place Rumor'd to Have Been Sodom." In *The Opening of the Field.* New York: Grove, 1960.

compositional capabilities, to a point of action, from which he may speak with a moral and rhetorical authority that marks him as a true heir of Romanticism. Duncan has vowed that his next major collection will not appear until 1983, at which time we may judge to what extent his sense of lawfulness has contributed to his fully mature work. But whether or not Duncan's philosophical insights will benefit from a totalizing sense of poetic form, we may be sure that the Utopian desire for universal Law will continue to speak through him, as it has done throughout his exemplary career.

Notes

1. Despite the fact that I approach the notion of lawfulness from a somewhat different philosophical tradition than does Duncan himself, my conception of the principle remains consistent with that of the poet. My own definition of lawfulness is derived from a line of thought that culminates in Hegel and Marx, as for example in the "Law of the Heart" section of the *Phenomenology of Mind* and the "Trinitarian Formula" of *Capital,* Volume III. Duncan's more eclectic training, which includes Neo-Platonism, Kabbalism, Gnosticism and such contemporary philosophy as that of Whitehead, still leads him to an understanding of universal Law that is remarkably rigorous in its poetic application.

2. *Towards A New American Poetics: Essays & Interviews,* ed. Ekbert Faas (Santa Barbara: Black Sparrow Press, 1978), p. 64.

3. *The Truth & Life of Myth* (1968; rpt. Freemont, Michigan: Sumac Press, 1972), p. 51. Cited in the text as *TL.* Other Duncan works abbreviated in the text are: *The Sweetness & Greatness of Dante's Divine Comedy* (San Francisco: Open Space, 1965), *SG; The First Decade: Selected Poems 1940-1950* (London: Fulcrum Press, 1968), *FD; The Years As Catches* (Berkeley, Oyez, 1966), *YC; The Opening of the Field* (New York: New Directions, 1960), *OF; Roots and Branches* (New York: New Directions, 1964), *RB; Bending the Bow* (New York: New Directions, 1968), *BB; Tribunals* (Los Angeles: Black Sparrow Press, 1970), *T.*

4. "The Book of the World: Robert Duncan's Poetics of Presence," *Sun & Moon* 1 (1976), 72.

5. "Towards an Open Universe," in *The Poetics of The New American Poetry,* ed. Donald M. Allen & Warren Tallman (New York: Grove Press, 1973), pp. 219-220.

6. "A Book of First Things: *The Opening Of The Field,"* in *Robert Duncan: Scales of the Marvelous,* ed. Robert J. Bertholf & Ian W. Reid (New York: New Directions, 1979), p. 59.

MICHAEL DAVIDSON (ESSAY DATE 1983)

SOURCE: Davidson, Michael. "Cave of Resemblances, Caves of Rimes: Tradition and Repetition in Robert Duncan." *Ironwood* (1983): 33-45.

In the following essay, Davidson explains Duncan's theories of repetition and the generative role of traditional texts in the composition of his own poetry.

In attempting to characterize the tone of Bay Area poetry during the 1940's, Kenneth Rexroth used the term "elegiac" to refer to its brooding, somewhat nostalgic quality.[1] The elegiac mood was a response to the War's devastation, to be sure, but it was also a reaction to the literary climate of the time. The heroic innovations of the Modernists had been reified into more palatable substitutes by a new generation and as Delmore Schwartz observed, ". . . what was once a battlefield (had) become a peaceful public park on a pleasant summer Sunday afternoon."[2] Presiding over the expanding New Critical hegemony in literary periodicals and university classrooms was the example of Eliot, both as poet and as cultural critic. His literary essays could be (and were) read as directives for a new sensibility, one in which thought and action, art and culture, individual talent and tradition could, after an interregnum of two centuries, be once again reconciled. The latter pair provided, of course, an aesthetic that extended far beyond Eliot's 1919 essay, "Tradition and the Individual Talent," and perhaps a good deal beyond his original concerns. Any rapprochement between tradition and innovation could be had only at the expense of personality. The introduction of the "really new" work of art to the canon was seen to alter the "existing monuments," not by any contingent relationships to the author's biography or historical moment but by art's universal appeal. In order to write and write well, one had to keep "the whole of the literature of Europe from Homer" in one's bones at the same time one fought to "extinguish" the private ego—an intimidating task for any young poet.

For those young poets who gathered around Rexroth in the 1940's, the critical problem was not Eliot's version of tradition—an organic totality in which the values among the canon are altered by the non-canonical—but, rather, the prescriptive application of certain aspects of Eliot's criticism in order to delimit "a" tradition, presumably one circumscribed by western, Judaeo-Christian culture. Certainly the methodological imperative behind an aesthetics of "impersonality" was anathema to the kind of testamentary and expressive poetry being written not only in San Francisco but in other avant-garde circles during the late 1940's. Robert Duncan, looking back to this period from the vantage of the later 1950's, remembered "powers of love"

> and of poetry,
> the Berkeley we believed
> grove of Arcady—
>
> that there might be
> potencies in common things,
> "princely manipulations of the real"[3]

calendar	1936-37 begins	1936-37 ends	1937-38 begins	1937-38 ends
Fall Semester	sept. 7	dec. 19	sept. 9	dec. 18
winter vacation	dec. 19	jan. 25	dec. 18	jan. 24
Spring Semester	jan. 25	june 5	jan. 24	june 4
spring vacation	march 27	april 5	march 26	april 4

Black Mountain College publicity booklet, 1936-38.

The cult of romance in which he, Jack Spicer and Robin Blaser participated during the "Berkeley Renaissance" is the most obvious contrast to the New Critical version of Eliot's tradition with its strong valorization of the seventeenth-century metaphysical poets, its anti-romantic stance, its neo-Kantian aesthetics. It is not that Duncan and his peers substituted the romantic tradition for some neo-classical fashion of the times—a replacement of one canon with another—but that he so radically transformed the notion of tradition altogether. This transformation was made possible partly through the terms of romanticism itself, but only by means of a rather idiosyncratic and expansive definition.

For Robert Duncan, the romantic tradition represents more than a historical period or canonic body of texts. It represents an ancient quest for knowledge about the nature of life forms—knowledge which, for a variety of reasons, cannot be summoned or articulated according to the usual channels. In cultural terms, this quest is most vital when informed by a diversity of sources. The Hellenistic period is the most obvious example of such diffusion and interpenetration, and Duncan often refers to theological and philosophical writings from this era as exempla of a fruitful admixture of eastern and western, classical and modern, pagan and Christian influences. In literary terms, this quest is reflected through those works in which a mythopoeic strain is dominant. Mythopoeia occurs in two forms, "the lordly and humble, . . . mythological vision and folklorish phantasy."[4] Thus, the quest romance is as much a dimension of *The Odyssey* as it is of "The Owl and the Pussycat" or "Wynken, Blynken and Nod." For Duncan, romanticism involves "powers of love" that are primordial, locked in the forms of biological and psychological life. Because of their potency, these ideas cannot appear except in veiled or occult forms. What Duncan calls "permission" refers to the poet's ability to participate in these "potencies in common things" and release them, beyond all reference to literature, to a swirling, changing universe.

This participatory stance toward the "lordly and humble" aspects of tradition has little to do with what we characteristically designate as "originality," the creation of new or unique artistic artifacts. In a paradox central to his poetics, Duncan often speaks of his originality in terms of an ability to resuscitate origins. In an unpublished preface to ***The Opening of the Field,*** he defines his own relationship of originality or individual talent to tradition:

> In this sense, in that I am concerned with forms and not with conventions, with an art and not with a literature, I may be a modernist. But I do not care particularly about the brand-newness of a form, I am not a futurist, I work toward immediacy; and I do not aim at originality. The meanings in language are not original, any more than the sounds; they accrue from all the generations of human use from the mists of the *schwa* and first objects to the many vowels and common universe of things of today; they are radical, sending roots back along our own roots. I am a traditionalist, a seeker after origins, not an original.[5]

The poet's individual talent may be expressed not in his originality—his transformation of the tradition as Eliot had defined it—but in his ability to respond to the demands of immediacy. Implicit in this idea is the notion of repetition, or what Duncan prefers to call "rime," by which original moments, events, ideas are interrelated in a dense weave. The structure of rime or repetition is the dynamic rendering of original moments that, in order to be such moments, can only be responded to, not invented out of whole cloth. To put it in other terms, the structure of rime refers to the poem's ability to resonate with the world without either destroying or representing it. Where "tradition," to the hegemonous New Critical aesthetic, implied artisanal mastery within a specifically literary history, for Duncan and others of his generation it meant cooperation with and response to the open field of creative life.

Duncan's radical "traditionalism" marks him as one of the most paradoxical of contemporary poets. He resolutely refuses to accept the designation "Modernist" or (more vehemently) "Post-Modernist." As he says in an interview, ". . . I'm not a Modernist . . . I read Modernism as Romanticism; and I finally begin to feel myself pretty much a 19th century mind."[6] This idiosyncratic stance produces a series of seeming contradictions: he is a poet of "open" forms who continues to write, as well, in classical modes like the sonnet and the ballad; he is a firm believer in verbal immediacy and testimony who, nevertheless, uses a heightened rhetoric more appropriate to the Victorian age; he is an avowedly romantic poet who has written masques in the Augustan manner worthy of Swift or Dryden; he is a political poet who, while attacking American imperialism in Southeast Asia, is still capable of celebrating war. The list of artists whom he is ambitious to "emulate, imitate, reconstrue, approximate, duplicate" would confuse even the most subtle genealogist of literary influence. It includes

> Ezra Pound, Gertrude Stein, Joyce, Virginia Woolf, Dorothy Richardson, Wallace Stevens, D. H. Lawrence, Edith Sitwell, Cocteau, Mallarmé, Marlowe, St. John of the Cross, Yeats, Jonathan Swift, Jack Spicer, Céline, Charles Henri Ford, Rilke, Lorca, Kafka, Arp, Max Ernst, St.-John Perse, Prévert, Laura Riding, Apollinaire, Brecht, Shakespeare, Ibsen, Strindberg, Joyce Cary, Mary Butts, Freud, Dali, Spenser, Stravinsky, William Carlos Williams and John Gay.
>
> Higglety-pigglety: Euripides and Gilbert. The Strawhat Reviewers, Goethe (of the *Autobiography*—I have never read *Faust*) and H. D.[7]

Such paradoxes are very much a part of Duncan's aesthetic, ". . . a poetics not of paradigms and models but of individual variations and survivals. . . ."[8] He cares little for "good and bad works" but of "seminal and germinal works cast abroad in the seas of the world."[9] What offends some critics is Duncan's refusal to stay put, to obey some paradigmatic version of what the poet must be. A poet of this order seems irresponsible, unable to synthesize a strong literary ethos or heritage into his own work. But responsibility, as Duncan points out, means "the ability to respond,"[10] the ability to read the fluctuating pattern of reality as a meaningful text and to read all texts as versions of the "Grand Collage" of man's representations.

Perhaps the most important negatively critical assessment of Duncan's view of tradition came not from a conservative critic but from his peer and mentor, Charles Olson. In "Against Wisdom as Such," Olson admonishes Duncan for what he takes to be a sectarian fetish of wisdom, extricable from its sources and processes. Wisdom, Olson feels, "like style, is the man." It is not

> extricable in any sort of a statement of itself; even though—and here is the catch—there be "wisdom," that it must be sought, and that "truths" can be come on (they are so overwhelming and so simple there does exist the temptation to see them as "universal"). But they are, in no wise, or at the gravest loss, verbally separated. They stay the man. As his skin is. As his life. And to be parted with only as that is.[11]

Reading between the lines of Olson's cryptic prose we may see a Coleridgean faith in the organic synthesis of ideas and form. Duncan is accused of trafficking in knowledge for its own sake without reference to its immediate applicability to the individual's life and projects. Wisdom, for the creator of Maximus, is the product of the self-reliant individual, wresting time out of a continuum in order to create rhythm rather than witness its effects.

Duncan's response to Olson exhibits a Freudian bias in favor of surfaces: wisdom regarded as story rather than as symbol:

> In a sense (Olson) is so keen upon the *virtu* of reality that he rejects my "wisdom" not as it might seem at first glance because "wisdom" is a vice; but because my wisdom is not real wisdom. He suspects, and rightly, that I indulge myself in pretentious fictions. I, however, at this point take enuf delight in the available glamor that I do not stop to trouble the cheapness of such stuff. I like rigor and even clarity as a quality of a work—that is, as I like muddle and floaty vagaries. It is the intensity of conception that moves me.[12]

The argument between the two men (an enormously generative one, as Don Byrd points out[13]) is an argument over two notions of tradition: one as the archaeological (and archetypal) structure of certain dynamic ideas realized throughout history by a few capable imaginations, the other as the open-ended series of variations on a corrupt and corruptible text. Olson's theory of tradition is recuperative; Duncan's is interpretative. For Olson, a writer like Melville transforms not only literature but physical space as well; he exists as a nodal point in the nineteenth-century imagination, along with Keats, Rimbaud, the geometers, Bolyai and Lobatschewsky, and the mathematician Riemann, within which constellation an entirely new conception of space was developed.[14] For Duncan, on the other hand, Dante and Shakespeare represent spirit guides in the poet's attempt to reanimate a core myth of creation. But as Michael Bernstein says, this treatment of past masters involves a reciprocal recognition on the part of both master and ephebe:

> But if . . . a poet's "permission" to enter into his poethood depends upon a reciprocal selection—his being "called" by a certain constellation of "masters" requires, of course, that he himself also be ready to heed just those voices, be ready, that is, to constitute himself as their successor—then one of the surest indices of a potentially new voice is the enrichment/subversion he can bring to the established heritage of his own mentors, his capacity significantly to add to the horizon of "pretexts" already marked out as canonic by the prior selection of his teachers.[15]

As verification of Bernstein's remarks, one has only to look into Duncan's encyclopedic meditation on the Modernists, ***The H. D. Book,*** in which the poet's own personal history is fused with a reading of certain modern masters so that, ultimately, the distance between private and literary life is broken down. The poet H. D. is the subject of the book, but not simply as an "influence" on Duncan's own work. Rather she projects and anticipates Duncan's life and art. By reading through her works (and the works of her generation), Duncan is permitted to re-enter the world of his own personal identity in which fictions, stories, poems and tales were formative influences. In fact, a substantial portion of the early chapters of ***The H. D. Book*** are devoted to the very earliest hearings of certain poems (H. D.'s "Heat," Basho's frog-pond-plash poem, Joyce's "I Hear an Army Charging Upon the Land") and to the circumstances of their encounters. He wants to record the luminous aura surrounding his own inaugural entry into story so that he may suggest how this moment "rhymes" with his later vocation as a poet. The great reading of Modernism (and ultimately of tradition in general) becomes a reading of origins as well.

For Duncan, the task of reading is never passive. It implies a readiness to receive and grapple with a story larger than himself, beyond the immediate event of reading. Jacob's wrestling with the angel is as much an allegory of reading as it is of Christian salvation, and Duncan often makes use of the story in exactly this double sense. Instead of hermeneutically recovering the text in an act that leaves it essentially unchanged, the poet actively translates its terms into a new text:

> Our work is to arouse in a contemporary consciousness reverberations of old myth, to prepare the ground so that when we return to read we will see our modern texts charged with a plot that had already begun before the first signs and signatures we have found worked upon the walls of Altamira or Pech-Merle.[16]

This charged, participatory act of reading has its origins in another kind of tradition: the hermetic, theosophical tradition inherited from his adopted parents and from his grandmother, the latter of whom had been an elder in an hermetic brotherhood.[17] For his parents,

> . . . the truth of things was esoteric (locked inside) or occult (masked by) the apparent, and one needed a "lost" key in order to piece out the cryptogram of who wrote Shakespeare or who created the universe and what his real message was.[18]

In his childhood environment every event was significant as an element in a larger, cosmological scheme. Although Duncan never practiced within any theosophical religion, he easily translated its terms into Freud's dreamwork, which proposes a similar sort of interpretation. Within both theosophical and Freudian hermeneutics, story is not simply a diversion or fiction but an "everlasting omen of what is." The dream becomes a model for how that omen is received as a cryptic condensation and displacement of a "sentence":

> I ask the unyielding Sentence that shows Itself
> forth
> in the language as I make it,
> Speak! For I name myself your
> master, who come to serve.
> Writing is first a search in
> obedience.[19]

These "sentences" from the first of his **"Structure of Rime"** series reflect the basic double-bind in Duncan's version of romanticism. The poet must become both subject and object of his creation, open to a language he does not invent and yet, by the agency of this language, a maker. The Sentence is both an imperative (an "unyielding Sentence") and a grammatical construct just as the dream text is both *beyond* yet *of* the dreamer:

> It is in the dream itself that we seem entirely creatures, without imagination, as if moved by a plot or myth told by a story-teller who is not ourselves. Wandering and wondering in a foreign land or struggling in the meshes of a nightmare, we cannot escape the compelling terms of the dream unless we wake, anymore than we can escape the terms of our living reality unless we die.[20]

The consequences of this collapsing of subject and object is a poetry deeply self-conscious of its textual nature without, at the same time, reducing itself to an endless series of footnotes on its own operations. Many of Duncan's finest poems are "readings" of other texts, his own poem serving as meditation and transformation. ***Medieval Scenes*** (1947) originated around a series of epigraphs that led directly into the individual poems; **"A Poem Beginning With A Line By Pindar"** reads the story of Eros and Psyche into a line by the Greek poet; ***Passages*** begins with two texts from the Emperor Julian's "Hymn to the Mother of the Gods," and includes many other texts within its separate poems; ***A Seventeenth-Century Suite*** consists of variations on poems by Raleigh, Southwell, Herbert and others; ***Dante Etudes,*** similarly, involves poetic reflections on passages from Dante's prose; and poems often begin in the margins or blank pages of the poet's own books (***Poems From the Margins of Thom Gunn's* "Moly"**, ***The Five Songs***). The point is that texts appear within Duncan's poems not as privileged signs of cultural order (as they often do in Pound and Eliot) nor as allusions but as generative elements in the composing process.

Duncan's mythopoeic hermeneutics derives, as I have said, from his family's theosophy as well as from Freudian dream-analysis and romanticism. All of these traditions propose a search for "first things," but for Duncan this search is not some sort of constitutive recollection of innocence. Returning to a "place of first permission" is to see it for the first time since, to adapt Williams, ". . . the spaces it opens are new places / inhabited by hordes / heretofore unrealized. . . ." That is, the poetic descent into origins occurs in time, the present thus contributing to and changing how those early stories and traumas are re-experienced. A naive reading of Duncan's poetic statements on the subject of origins might see him yearning toward some totalized scheme of correspondences whereby time, in a Proustian or Joycean epiphany, is at last stilled or transcended. As Joseph Frank has observed, Modernist texts like *A la Recherche du Temps Perdu, Ulysses* or *The Waste Land* rely for their unity on epiphanic moments that transcend temporal flux, allowing for a spatialized time that the text recovers.[21] Duncan's moments of "permission" are not recuperative; although they serve to link him to the past, they do so only to more fully engage the present. On the one hand he desires a kind of Emersonian participation in the world; on the other, he recognizes that the temporal apprehension of the world structures how that involvement might occur:

> Working in words I am an escapist; as if I could step out of my clothes and move naked as the wind in a world of words. But I want every part of the actual world involved in my escape. I bring the laws that bound me into an aerial structure in which they are unbound as outlines of a prison unfolding.[22]

Duncan's structure of repetition is similar to that described by Kierkegaard in his essay, "Repetition." Here, Kierkegaard makes a distinction between "recollection," the attempt at reconstituting that which has been, and "repetition," the adumbration of what has been in a new formation. Recollection, he says, is what the Greeks called knowledge: the realization of eternal forms. Repetition continually generates life out of that which was once partially glimpsed, but never fully realized. "The dialectic of repetition is easy," Kierkegaard says, "for that which is repeated has been—otherwise it could not be repeated—but the very fact that it has been makes the repetition into something new."[23] For Duncan, poetry is the structure of repetition in exactly these terms: a return to "roots of first feeling" and yet a projection forward based on terms discovered in that return.

> The morphology of forms, in evolving, does not destroy their historicity but reveals that each event has its origin in the origin of all events; yes, but in turn, we are but the more aware that the first version is revised in our very turning to it, seeing it with new eyes.[24]

A useful place to explore Duncan's ideas on repetition as well as his inheritance from the romantic tradition is his open-ended series, ***The Structure of Rime.*** Originally conceived as imitations (readings) of Rimbaud's prose poems in *Illuminations*, ***Structure of Rime*** has become the poet's ongoing study of the role of rhyme, measure and correspondence. These categories are experienced, by the poet, as "persons of the poem," dramatic voices that speak from various aspects of language: from the vocalic resources of the voice to syntax and, ultimately, to the informing matrix of myth and story.

> I started a series without end called ***Structures of Rime*** in which the poem could talk to me, a poetic seance, and, invoked so, persons of the poem appeared as I wrote to speak. I had only to keep the music of the invocation going and to take down what actually came to me happening in the course of the poem.[25]

"Persons of the poem" are not fictive, in the sense of dramatic personae, nor is their apprehension, to extend our Kierkegaardian terms, "recalled." They are encountered as "rhymes" with the creative order of life and are translated into the poet's creative order. The various mythic and daemonic figures who appear (Black King Glélé, The Woman Who Resembles the Sentence, The Master of Rime, The Beloved, etc.) appear in various guises throughout the series, but their participation in a basic configuration of powers and dominions remains. They are elemental forces in a cosmic drama, played out upon the stage of language.[26]

Like Duncan's other open-ended series, ***Passages, The Structure of Rime*** is an ongoing project that appears throughout the poet's *oeuvre*, occasionally intersecting with other sequences (as in "**Apprehensions**" and ***The Five Songs***) and at least once with ***Passages***.[27]) More recently, Duncan has dropped ordination (as he has with ***Passages***), presumably to eliminate any notion of sequence or chronology.

Presiding over the series is "The Master of Rime" who acts as a daemonic muse on the order of Nietzsche's Zarathustra or Blake's Orc:

> The master of Rime, time after time, came down the arranged ladders of vision or ascended the smoke and flame towers of the opposite of vision, into or out of the language of daily life, husband to one word, wife to the other, breath that leaps forward upon the edge of dying.[28]

The Master of Rime represents poetry's ability to penetrate into the larger text of the world by creating "an absolute scale of resemblance and disresemblance." He enters through the "language of daily life," a language unheard until engaged by the poem. Within the poem, rhymes and resonances occur that the poet, aided by the visionary faculty of the Rime Master, is able to translate. The individual "Structure of Rime," as the passage above should illustrate, does not replicate this daily language, but provides a rhetorical mise en scène in which the process of visionary translation occurs. Rimbaud and Blake are not far behind the Master of Rime for their own entry into Duncan's language.

As the theory and practice of rime, it is perhaps all the more appropriate that the series is, for the most part, written not in lined verse but in prose. ***The Structure of Rime*** is not an *ars poetica* on the order of Pope's "Essay on Criticism" or Shapiro's "Essay on Rime," versified discussions of poetics. It is, instead, a dramatization of poetics, acted out by Duncan's heightened rhetoric and convoluted syntax:

> You too are a flame then and my soul quicken-
> ing in your gaze a draft upward carrying the
> flame of you. From this bed of a language in
> compression, life now is fuel, anthracite
> from whose hardness the years spring. In
> flame
>
> beings strive in the Sun's chemistry
> as we strive in our meat to realize images of
> manhood immanent we have not reacht,
> but leave, as if they fell from us, bright fell
> and fane momentary attendants . . .[29]

Duncan is here describing the power of the Beloved, but the force of syntactic subordination, suspension and combination works to destroy linguistic boundaries. To adapt the imagery of the passage, the language has taken fire from a "language in compression." The passage enacts what it describes; qualifying phrases and subordinate clauses suspend the syntactic term while predicates are further and further separated from their subjects. The fullest use of acoustic values (assonance, alliteration, rhyme and near-rhyme) are exploited to give the passage the same sense of excitement and wonder inspired by the gaze of the lover. Language does not simply describe the erotic; words, by their sensual interplay, are eroticized.

If the Master of this ordering and disordering of language is Master of Rime, the Muse of the series is the "woman who resembles the sentence." At one level, she represents Duncan's own mother, lost at the time of his birth and thus the lost link to his own biological past:

> She has a place in memory that moves language. Her voice comes across the waters from a shore I don't know to a shore I know, and is translated into words belonging to the poem . . .[30]

On another level, she is syntax itself, the scale of resemblances and disresemblances upon which the poet plays his individual variations. Biological life (genetic coding) and creative life (linguistic coding) are thus fused under one common law:

> *Have heart,* the text reads,
> *you that were heartless.*
> *Suffering joy or despair*
> *you will suffer the sentence*
> *a law of words moving*
> *seeking their right period.*
>
> I saw a snake-like beauty in the living changes of syntax.
>
> *Wake up,* she cried
> *Jacob wrestled with Sleep—you who fall into Nothingness*
> *and dread sleep.*
> *He wrestled with Sleep like a man reading a strong sentence.*[31]

What appears to be going on in the interchange between the "I" and the "woman who resembles the sentence" is a re-telling of the fall of man. The poet seeks to return to that "place in memory" before which language had become plural, a prelapsarian state in which words and things are not separate, in which discourse and poetry are one and the same. But he may only return via the language as he has inherited it, the original speech having been lost through an obsession with a "snake-like beauty in the living changes of syntax." His punishment, if indeed this is how we must characterize it, is to "suffer the sentence" of that first mother of language, to struggle, like Jacob, with the Angel of syntax. Thus, as the end of this opening Structure of Rime indicates, the poet will remain an adept in the service of language, creating "sentence after sentence" in her image:

> In the feet that measure the dance of my pages I hear cosmic intoxications of the man I will be.[32]

We have heard versions of this allegory of creative life throughout romantic literature (notably in Blake, Emerson, Shelley, Whitman, Stevens), and in one sense, ***The Structure of Rime*** is a homage to that tradition, without naming it as such.[33] What differentiates Duncan's version of the Adamic mythos from that of Emerson or Stevens, for example, is his dramatic rendering of voice and presence. His method is often dialogical, voices entering into the poem to cajole, warn, debate and invoke, while being responded to by the poet himself:

> The actual world speaks to me, and when it comes to that pitch, the words I speak with but imitate the way the mountain speaks. I create in *return.* In the structures of rime, not "I" but words themselves speak to you.[34]

In order to create "in return," Duncan must empty out what Olson called the "lyrical interference of the ego" and allow the complexities of image and syntax free reign. Here, for example, he invokes the Muse who commands:

> *Return your intelligence into the threshold of the real from the chamberd brain to the seeing fingers of the eye that feels, to the equilibrations of the inner ear to dwell in the light and dark of the rainbow from which color streams towards the music sound imitates; in the heavy and light in which desire arrives, burrow deep if you would reach that Grand Burial of the Mind where it may rest.*[35]

The complex image presented here is of a body extended into the world it senses so that there is, finally, no boundary of Mind and no objective world. The accumulation of phrases and their seeming lack of closure accomplish on a linguistic level the very dissolution described. This and others of the series thus become a reading of the romantic tradition through the agency that it bequeaths to poets.

Structure of Rime, as a continuing poetic series, is informed by a doctrine of linguistic and mythological correspondences. The history of our language, from our entry into it at childhood to its most complicated manifestations in poetry, is also the history of fictions by which we mutually cohere. To differentiate phonemes or recognize similar sounds is to become engaged with the realm of story—and of tradition—at its most basic level. As a conceptual field, ***Structure of Rime*** is informed by a cellular model in which all parts contribute to the whole and yet whose boundaries are continually evolving. Darwin's picture of evolution is, for Duncan, a visionary proposition of our heritage that claims, for man, relationships with the species beyond the historical moment. At the same time, it is in the immediacy of the moment, in its specific and time-bound nature, that our sense of commonality is discovered: "We must begin where we are. Our own configuration entering and belonging to a configuration being born of what 'we' means."[36] And the real "we," as Duncan points out, is "the company of the living."

In attempting to differentiate Duncan's theory of tradition from that of Eliot and his New Critical followers, I have perhaps glossed over what might be seen as a shared organicism. Duncan would probably not argue with Eliot's sense that innovation affects the past as much as it affects the present, nor that the poet must work with the "historical sense" in his bones. What works like ***Structure of Rime*** and ***Passages*** illustrate, however, is the breadth and range of materials thus incorporated into the dynamics of literary change. And at the same time, these highly speculative, processual works involve immediacy and passional statement where Eliot would encourage discretion.[37] In making this contrast I have availed myself of a model of repetition, derived from contemporary hermeneutics, that introduces into Duncan's doctrine of rime and correspondence what I hope is a more dialectical movement. Thus the phrase from which my title derives, "Cave of Resemblances, Cave of Rimes," should not only evoke the cave of Plato but that of Freud as well.

Notes

1. See Duncan's letter to Rexroth printed in Robert Duncan and Jack Spicer, *An Ode and Arcadia* (Berkeley, CA: Ark Press, 1974) n.p.
2. Delmore Schwartz, "The Present State of Poetry," in *Selected Essays of Delmore Schwartz,* ed. Donald A. Dike and David H. Zucker (Chicago, 1970), p. 44.
3. Robert Duncan, *The Opening of the Field* (N.Y.: Grove Press, 1960), p. 14.
4. Robert Duncan, *The Truth and Life of Myth: An Essay in Essential Autobiography* (Fremont, Mich.: The Sumac Press, 1968), p. 38.
5. Robert Duncan, "Notebook A," in the papers of Robert Duncan at the Bancroft Library, University of California, Berkeley, p. 99.
6. "Interview with Robert Duncan," in *Towards a New American Poetics: Essays and Interviews,* ed. Ekbert Faas (Santa Barbara, CA: Black Sparrow Press, 1978), p. 82.
7. Robert Duncan, "Pages from a Notebook," in *The New American Poetry,* ed. Donald M. Allen (N.Y.: Grove Press, 1960), p. 407.
8. Robert Duncan, "Notes on Grossinger's *Solar Journal: Oecological Sections* (Santa Barbara, CA: Black Sparrow Press, n.d.), n.p.
9. "Notes on Grossinger's *Solar Journal,*" n.p.
10. *The Opening of the Field,* p. 10.
11. Charles Olson, "Against Wisdom as Such," in *Human Universe and Other Essays,* ed. Donald Allen (N.Y.: Grove Press, 1967), p. 68.
12. Robert Duncan, "From a Notebook," in *The Poetics of the New American Poetry,* ed. Donald Allen and Warren Tallman (N.Y.: Grove Press, 1973), p. 185.
13. Don Byrd provides an excellent account of Olson's and Duncan's relationship in his essay, "The Question of Wisdom as Such," in *Robert Duncan: Scales of the Marvelous,* ed. Robert J. Bertholf and Ian W. Reid (N.Y.: New Directions, 1979), pp. 38-55.
14. See Olson's essay, "Equal, That Is, to the Real Itself" in *Human Universe and Other essays,* pp. 117-122.
15. Michael A. Bernstein, "Bringing It All Back Home: Derivations and Quotations in Robert Duncan and the Poundian Tradition," *Sagetrieb* I:2 (Fall, 1982), p. 184.
16. Robert Duncan, "Two Chapters from *H. D.", Tri-Quarterly* (Spring, 1968), p. 67.
17. See Duncan's discussion of the occult tradition in part I, chapter 5 of the *H. D. Book,* printed as "Occult Matters," (*Stony Brook,* 1/2), pp. 4-19.
18. *The Truth and Life of Myth,* p. 8.
19. *The Opening of the Field,* p. 12.
20. "Occult Matters," p. 18.
21. Joseph Frank, "Spatial Form In Modern Literature," in *The Widening Gyre* (Bloomington, Indiana: Indiana U.P. 1963) pp. 3-62.
22. Robert Duncan, *Bending the Bow* (N.Y.: New Directions, 1968), p. v.
23. Søren Kierkegaard, *Repetition,* ed. and trans. Howard V. Hong and Edna Hong (Princeton, N.J., Princeton U.P., 1983), p. 149.
24. *The Truth and Life of Myth,* p. 51.
25. Robert Duncan, "Man's Fulfillment in Order and Strife," *Caterpillar* 8/9, p. 239.
26. Duncan discusses the role of "persons of the poem" in *Structure of Rime* in an interview with Kevin Power, "A Conversation with Robert Duncan," *Revista Canaria de Estudios Ingleses* 4 (April, 1982), pp. 100-103.
27. Robert Duncan, "Apprehensions," in *Roots and Branches* (N.Y.: Scribners, 1964), pp. 30-42; "Structure of Rime *Of the Five Songs"* in *The Five Songs* (La Jolla, CA, The Friends of the UCSD Library, 1981); "Passages 20 (Structure of Rime XXVI)" in *Bending the Bow,* p. 68.
28. *The Opening of the Field,* p. 17.
29. *Bending the Bow,* 37.
30. *The Opening of the Field,* p. 12.
31. *The Opening of the Field,* p. 12.
32. *The Opening of the Field,* p. 12.
33. Duncan provides an extensive discussion of the romantic roots of *Structure of Rime* in *Maps* 6, pp. 42-52.
34. "Man's Fulfillment in Order and Strife," p. 238.
35. Robert Duncan, "The Shadow of the Muse," in *Ground Work* Vol. I (privately published), p. 38.
36. *Bending the Bow,* p. ii.

37. Duncan has, on numerous occasions, pointed out the discrepancies between Eliot's theory and practice when it comes to personal confession. I am speaking less about Eliot's actual practice in the poems than I am of the canonization of his theory of "impersonality" by a later generation of critics.

TITLE COMMENTARY

Ground Work

THOMAS PARKINSON (REVIEW DATE JANUARY 1985)

SOURCE: Parkinson, Thomas. "Robert Duncan's *Ground Work.*" *Southern Review* 21, no. 1 (January 1985): 52-62.

In the following review, Parkinson discusses Duncan's concept of originality and its importance in the development of Duncan's poetry.

Robert Duncan's ***Ground Work*** is his first extensive book from a national publisher since his ***Bending the Bow*** of 1968. Segments of the book have appeared from small presses ranging from San Francisco to New York to France and Australia. His work has been the subject of a critical book by several hands, and the essays in *Robert Duncan, Scales of the Marvelous* include extensive comments on some poems included in ***Ground Work.*** Duncan is fortunate in his critics, especially Jayne Walker, Michael Davidson, Thom Gunn, Ian Reid, and Sean Golden. The essays testify to the fact that Duncan's poetic work, taken as a whole, has a grandeur to it that is complemented by the scope and intelligence of his theoretical and practical work on the life of the poet. By "life" I mean here the continuing vigor and spirit of the work, and Duncan is a working poet, a maker, and as his admired predecessors are, part of a process that is at once natural, historical, and spiritual. Hence language and life become identified while remaining autonomous, so that they do not exclude or substitute for each other. The most extended and revealing appearances of his critical and theoretical work remain scattered in the numerous publications of sections of his ***H. D. Book,*** which reminds me more of Coleridge's *Biographia Literaria* than any other nineteenth- or twentieth-century work.

I do not compare Duncan and Coleridge accidentally or in order to grant Duncan high prestige. From all accounts, Coleridge's conversation was rather like Duncan's, and his extended prose shows, as does Duncan's, a remarkable appetite for being and for all forms of knowledge that can be subsumed in the poetic. The primary difference between the two resides in Duncan's playfulness, with language, and consequently with experience, that varies from the often magisterial seriousness of Coleridge. Duncan continuously experiments without conclusion, so that if a conclusion is drawn, that becomes in turn the occasion for fresh development. Nothing is "finished," both in the sense of intellectual and historical development and in the sense of the work of art, so that Duncan follows Whistler in that respect as he follows so many other American artists. Finish and accomplishment are not the ends of art, though they occasionally occur in the work. Keeping the imagination of possibilities matters more than any finality.

Duncan embodies many other qualities of the American poetic tradition, based in turn on the American political and philosophical traditions. Merely to pun on William James, his concern with the varieties of religious experience is validated by his pluralistic humanism and his espousal of radical empiricism rather than vicious intellectualism. As Dewey took James for a master Duncan in turn accepted both James and especially the Dewey of *Art as Experience* as part of his pantheon. Jefferson and Adams became mentors and he shared the anti-Hamiltonism of his immediate poetic masters Pound and Williams. And his beloved Whitman was always present as releaser of possibilities.

I stress the immediate American intellectual and poetic backgrounds because they rest quietly below the exotic, the Egyptian and Hermetic, the Caballistic, the Renaissance rhetorical poetics, the Dantesque, the Homeric, the French surrealist, in short, the Grand Collage which is at once the universe and the great continuous work of the world's artists. Duncan talks of himself as an imitative and derivative artist, but this seems to me his way of describing himself without pretension, even with ironic self-depreciation, as a traditional rather than conventional artist. He derives from the past, initiates and innovates for the future, and maintains a coven of contemporaries. The artistic community knows no break.

Continuity and tradition do not mean repetition. Originality for a poet like Duncan means getting at origins, finding the ground from which the images of the work arise and to which they return. Whether he is working from Dante's prose, Renaissance meditative poems, or Thom Gunn's *Moly* sequence, he works *from* them and *to* what they leave open or unexamined, so that the implications of Southwell's "The Burning Babe" extend to napalmed children in Vietnam, martyrdom enriched by and commenting upon martyrdom. I use the term "enriched" in a quantitative sense and with some ambiguity: the children are at once magnified and granted a wider human extension into a permanent horror that only love can counter and endure. As images they are enriched; as children they cannot be healed or saved.

The construction that Duncan forms around the Southwell instigation takes first the consuming greed of jealousy from his own experience and then contains the consuming impersonal military violence. The personal failing can through the image of the babe reach an alchemical balance. Southwell's vision is a trial to the soul, a difficulty, a judgment, that, revealing the unconsumable detritus of the person that is the bitter core, can bring a purging fire to the heart:

Robert Southwell, "The Burning Babe"

As I in hoarie Winters night
Stoode shivering in the snow,
Surpris'd I was with sodaine heate,
Which made my hart to glow;

And lifting up a fearefull eye,
To view what fire was neare,
A pretty Babe all burning bright
Did in the ayre appeare;

Who scorched with excessive heate,
Such floods of teares did shed,
As though his floods should quench his flames,
Which with his teares were fed;

Alas (quoth he) but newly borne,
In fierie heates I frie,
Yet none approach to warme their harts
Or feele my fire, but I;

My faultlesse breast the furnace is,
The fuell wounding thornes:
Love is the fire, and sighs the smoake,
The ashes, shames and scornes;

The fewell Justic layeth on,
And Mercie blowes the coales,
The mettall in this furnace wrought,
Are mens defiled soules:

For which, as now on fire I am
To worke them to their good,
So will I melt into a bath,
To wash them in my blood.

With this he vanisht out of sight,
And swiftly shrunk away,
And straight I called unto minde,
That it was Christmasse day.

[St Peter's Complaint with other Poems, April 1595—following his martyrdom in the Roman Catholic cause by edict of Queen Elizabeth on February 21st, 1595, at Tyburn, after three years imprisonment with rack and torture]

"From Robert Southwell's 'The Burning Babe'"

The vision of a burning babe I see
doubled in my sight. The one
alight in that fire of passion that tries the soul
is such a Child as Southwell saw his Christ to be:

This is not a baby on fire but a babe of fire,
flesh burning with its own flame, not toward
death
but alive with flame, suffering its *self*

ON THE SUBJECT OF...

MICHAEL RUMAKER

Primarily a short story writer, Rumaker is counted among a group of writers who deliberately call attention to the artifice of their writing, and employ a conspicuous style in an effort to delve into both conscious and unconscious meanings. Rumaker's early stories are naturalistic in their details, juxtaposing considerable dialogue with passages of vivid description, though the narrator is often unidentified and speaks in the third person. Though many of these stories are based on Rumaker's experiences, critics have maintained that the author's technique imparts a detached quality. The stories considered among Rumaker's best—"Gringos," "The Pipe," and "The Desert"—depict elemental figures in raw natural settings. *The Butterfly* (1962), Rumaker's first novel, concerns a man just released from a mental institution who is trying to reestablish his life. The book is based on a similar breakdown Rumaker suffered in 1958; notebooks kept during his hospitalization inform the novel. In *Robert Duncan in San Francisco* (1996), Rumaker recalls his early years as a writer and his associations with the artists of Black Mountain College, the Beats of San Francisco, and the gay artists of the 1960s.

the heat of the heart the rose was hearth of;
so there was a rose, there was a flame,
consubstantial with the heart,

long burning me through and through,
long time ago I knew and came
to a knowledge of the bitter core of me,
the clinker soul, the stubborn residue
that needed the fire and refused to burn.

Envy of the living was its name, black jealousy
of what I loved it was, and
the pain was not living, it was ashes of the
wood;
the burning was not living, it was
without Truth's heat,
a cold of utter Winter that refused the Sun,
an adversary in the body against its youth.

In this I am self possesst of such a hoarie
Winter's night
as Southwell stood in shivering—
a shivering runs me through and through.

O Infant Joy that in Desire burns bright!
Bright Promise that I might in Him burn free!
His faultless breast the furnace,
my inner refusal the thorny fuel!

All the doors of Life's wounds I have long closed
in me
break open from His body and pour forth
therefrom fire that is His blood
relentlessly

*"Who scorcht with excessive heat, such
floods of tears did shed"*

—it is no more than an image in Poetry—as
though

*"his floods should quench his flames,
which with his tears were bred"* until

tears breeding flames, flames breeding tears,
I am undone from what I am, and in
Imagination's alchemy
the watery Moon and fiery Sun are wed.

The burning Babe, the Rose,
the Wedding of the Moon and Sun,
wherever in the World I read
such Mysteries come to haunt the Mind,
the Language of What Is and I

are one.

Duncan's imagination transforms the energy derived from Southwell into terms at once personal and international, so that the cosmic powers of "The Burning Babe" metamorphose into a Christ that sees suffering without purgation, the main horror spiritually and socially of the modern experience:

"A pretty Babe"—that burning Babe
the poet Southwell saw—
a scorching, a crying, that made his cold heart
glow,
a fuel of passion in which
the thought of wounds delites the soul.
He's Art's epiphany of Art new born,
a Christ of Poetry, the burning spirit's show;
He leaves no shadow, where he dances in the air,
of misery below.

Another Christ, if he be, as we are,
Man, cries out in utter misery;
and every Holy Martyr must have cried
forsaken in some moment
that from Christ's "Why hast Thou forsaken
me?"
has enterd our Eternity
or else is not true to itself. But now

I am looking upon burnd faces
that have known catastrophe incommensurate
with meaning, beyond hate or loss or
Christian martyrdom, unredeemd. My heart
caves into a space it seems
to have long feard.

I cannot imagine, gazing upon photographs
of these young girls, the mind
transcending what's been done to them

From the broild flesh of these heretics,
by napalm monstrously baptised
in a new name, every delicate and
sensitive curve of lip and eyelid
blasted away, surviving . . .
eyes? Can this horror be calld their
fate? Our fate grows a mirroring face
in the accusation beyond accusation
of such eyes,
a kind of hurt that drives into the root
of understanding, their very lives
burnd into us we live by.

Victor and victim know not what they do
—the deed exceeding what we would *know;*
the knowledge in the sight of those eyes
goes deep into the heart's fatalities.
And in our nation's store of crimes long
unacknowledged, unrepented,
the sum of abject suffering, of dumb incalculable
injury increases
the sore of conscience we long avoid.

What can I feel of it? All hurt
rushes in to illustrate that glare
and fails. What can I feel of what was done?
All hatred cringes from the sight of it
and would contract into self-loathing
to ease the knowledge of what no man
can compensate. I think I could bear it.

I cannot think I could bear it.

Even in the other sections of the Renaissance Suite, Duncan does not follow the same procedure; the works evade categories. Moving from Southwell and Jonson and Herbert to Dante creates another set of possibilities, as do the marginalia to Gunn's *Moly* suite [***Poems from the Margins of Thom Gunn's*** **"Moly"**] and the designedly disparate and inconclusive series of ***Passages*** and the **"Structure of Rime."** The book sounds a bravura chord, exhibiting a range of tones and voices, in a mode that Duncan mocked with playful seriousness in the first of the ***Letters*** of 1956 (published 1958):

Lists of imaginary sounds I mean sound signs I mean things designed in themselves I mean boundary marks I mean a bounding memorizations I mean a memorial rising I mean a con glomerations without rising

1. a dead camel
2. a nude tree
3. a hot mouth (smoking)
4. an old saw (rusty edge)
5. a copy of the original
6. an animal face
7. a broken streetcar
8. a fake seegar
9. papers
10. a holey shawl
11. the addition of the un planned for interruption: a flavor stinking coffee (how to brew another cup in that Marianne Moore-E. P.-Williams-H. D.-Stein-Zukofsky-Stevens-Perse-surrealist-dada-staind pot)
12. a table set for breakfast

Duncan deliberately situates himself at the center of American and European modernism, vintage 1924 or 1925 (the date wavers), including all his American coven and his contemporaries, especially those first encountered through the pages of *Origin* magazine and known immediately at Black Mountain College, most notably Olson and Creeley.

"Post-modern"—the term comes to mind almost automatically, which should serve as warning: Duncan does not ease into categories. He admired and emulated Pound and Williams, but he loved the nineteenth century, and although Eliot is not mentioned in this 1956 list, he too was one of Duncan's honored ancestors, as was John Milton, and Duncan's love of Whitman is much more unequivocal and passionately informed than that of Pound or Williams. Whitman was much too oratorical and operatic for Williams, and for Duncan the high rhetoric and the overarching arias of Whitman were both invitations and satisfactions. Where Eliot and Pound qualified their enthusiasms, narrowing their openings to poetry and reality in the process, Duncan proposed reckless devouring appetites. He would not follow Eliot, Pound, Moore, and Stevens in "the contraction and even the retraction of sympathies" that he saw growing from their "sense of what respectable educated opinion is, the tolerance and intolerance of schoolmasters of English Literature and Philosophy the world over." So he saw them, however briefly, in ***The Truth and Life of Myth,*** his essay in essential autobiography of 1968. His exclusion of H. D. from the list of the squeamish is, in the context, clearly intentional, for she does not speak or think as modernist but as embodying and instigating what Duncan himself seeks, participation in primal creation that is artistic and religious; he is not making a religion of art or an art of religion but finding in the reality of experience and signs, especially linguistic signs, the reality at once in and of the universe that is many.

The universe that is many—that may seem a semantic solecism. What I am attempting to express is that for Duncan's poetry a belief underlies that artistic enterprise, a belief in an unfinished, unknowable but penetrable mystery that can be realized and momentarily stabilized through art. The way to exploration runs through multiple myths through which in turn the soul and the world undergo transformation and realization. This is a frame of being in which, as in the work (and universe) of Freud, there are no mistakes, even the slightest apparent error being a revelation and transformation.

The aesthetic that accompanies inevitably Duncan's sense of the ground and the work troubles commentary. In the preface to his **"Dante Études,"** he says of the moment of writing, and of reading Dante,

> What we took to be a stream of consciousness, we take now to be a light streaming in a new crystal the mind ever addresses. Dante again enters my thought here—even as I disgress—and I feed upon prime.

There are no digressions possible to this universe in which nothing is casual and there are no accidents. Later in the **"Études"** (Book Two) the poem is interrupted by the parenthetical statement:

> (thank you, Jack Clarke, for sending me the Latin)

meaning the original form of Dante's *De Monarchia*. By definition what seems at first glance to be part of the stream of consciousness becomes a fusion of writing the poem and reading Dante, "a light streaming in a new crystal the mind ever addresses." Jack Clarke's place is justified as are those of Pound, Olson or Shelley, being necessary to both ground and work. The poet's mythopoeic faculty makes him part of the work.

Allusions in the modernist poetic bear the risk of attaining the onerous status of poetic diction in the eighteenth century which Gray celebrated in his letter to Mason because of its total separation from the language of prose. Duncan in his omnivorous way takes all proper names and all language of poetic tradition and everyday life as part of an unending vocabulary of potential forms. Duncan extends the possibilities of the modernist poetic to a field without bounds.

I deliberately invoked the "field" and with it Duncan's carefully unified and structured book ***The Opening of the Field*** because ***Ground Work*** presents a differing set. With ***Roots and Branches*** and ***The Bending of the Bow, The Opening of the Field*** paid obeisance to the modernist concept of the book, Yeats's *The Tower,* Eliot's *Four Quartets,* Stevens's *Harmonium,* Williams's *Spring and All*—the list is indefinitely extendable, but all these works can be subsumed under the notion of the intended and integrated. ***Ground Work*** does not so insistently stick or hang together. ***Ground Work*** fulfills the resolve made by Duncan in 1972 when Sand Dollar printed the new edition with preface of ***Caesar's Gate***:

> I do not intend to issue another collection of my work since ***Bending the Bow*** until 1983 at which time fifteen years will have passed.

The inclusive book ***Ground Work*** collects collections and composes an aggregate or conglomerate. There is reason also to doubt that this is a collection of fifteen years of poetry, Duncan being naturally prolific and most of the poems centering around the period from 1969 through 1974.

Ground Work indicates several directions. First, there is the quality of the book itself, its vigor and range, and the one element in it that the book's aesthetic forbids comment on, that is, the unevenness of the poems and their discontinuity. Second, there are the implications of that very problem for the tradition that Duncan embraces and continues, the tradition that he (very properly) sees in Whitman and the line from Pound, Williams, and H. D. through Zukofsky and the Objectivists to Olson and Creeley and their associates. Basil Bunting's defense of the *Cantoa* concedes what critics consider their unevenness and then asserts their value in his expressed contempt for negative reactions: "Fools! These are the Alps." The problem with the aesthetic involved in the tradition that Duncan carries onward resides in distinguishing Alps from molehills, or as Williams wrote to Pound in momentary annoyance with college students concerned with poetry, he wished they would be interested in poems. The autonomous poem can become a conventional notion justified only in pedagogical situations, but for Williams it remained a valid concept, so that even an Alp should be a mountain. His practice does not always suit the idea of autonomy from poem to poem, and his later and most influential writing holds to dramatic and narrative strains rather than the isolated or isolatable lyric. ***Ground Work*** pushes the notion of the serial poem beyond that incorporated in Duncan's preceding books, and it raises major poetic questions. Duncan is a grand poet, large in aspirations, omnivorous in appetite for experience, greatly learned and ideologically complex. His poetry can, accordingly, hardly be called modest.

Ground Work is a trial work, for Duncan a movement away from and beyond his preceding books. It would have been easy for him to avoid this shift and troubling of the image of his work, but the risk was to go on and become the imitator of Duncan. Instead he chose a breaking point. The book also places the tradition that is Duncan's on trial. The recent study of *The Modern Poetic Sequence* by Rosenthal and Gall is uneasy with that tradition and manages to leave Duncan out of consideration. Without him the tradition is not only incomplete (it will always be incomplete) but will appear almost blandly secular, for Whitman, Pound, and Williams are Enlightenment figures and Duncan is a heterodox mystic in the heroic mold of Blake, as the variations on Southwell suggest. With H. D. he could admire Freud because he saw that the childhood of the individual was the childhood of the race, and form his mythopoeic imagination on that order.

Ground Work, then, has symbolic or sympotatic stature in the development not only of Duncan's poetry but of the American imagination. The poems range widely in mode of reference while maintaining unity of tone. Readers coming to Duncan for the first time or after earlier but not full readings will find the following poems good inductions, and to my mind among the best work now being done in the art: **"Achilles' Song," "A Song from the Structures of Rime Ringing As the Poet Paul Celan Sings," "Bring It Up from the Dark,"** all the ***Poems from the Margins of Thom Gunn's*** **"Moly"**, readings in the **"Seventeenth Century Suite"** and the **"Dante Études,"** especially **"Book Three,"** and the concluding poems beginning with **"The Missionaries."**

In addition to the poems, the prefatory ***Some Notes on Notation*** grows from the fact that this text has been prepared by Duncan himself as typist and photographically reproduced, so that the notation of this book is as accurate to the poet's imagination as can be. Duncan is a genuinely expert typist and for years made his major income by typing scholarly manuscripts or what work came to his hands. The prosodic problems posed by Duncan's poetry parallel those growing from the work of Whitman, Pound, and Williams, and Duncan indicates his mode of settling a way of noting the dance of language. The day may come when poetry returns through sophisticated electronics to its original vocal being; then the written or printed poem will be, in all senses of the term, a score. Notation of verse outside the syllabic and accentual modes has been puzzling and unsatisfactory, and the modes of verse that seem, at least superficially, measurable are hardly satisfactory, partly because of the often irrelevant application of the concept of the prosodic foot as unit.

Duncan's notes on notation are eminently sensible, and although they reflect his specific practice, they grow, as does the practice, from careful and reasoned participation in the imaginative modes of modern verse. These notes seem to me essential movements toward a rationale of verse that will bring into proper emphasis the basically kinesthetic nature of all poetry, its weights, measures, and silences. Poetry grows from the body and its being in the universe and returns through language to the body in its finest articulations. ***Ground Work*** accomplishes this grand intent, showing forth in the poems means of being and in the brief theoretical (and practical) notes on notation suggesting linear and syntactical rationales. Only greed would ask for more.

FURTHER READING

Biographies

Faas, Ekbert. *Young Robert Duncan: Portrait of the Poet as Homosexual in Society.* Santa Barbara: Black Sparrow Press, 1983, 361 p.

A combination of literary history and biography that traces the development of "the new American poetics" along with Duncan's personal development.

Jarnot, Lisa. "Robert Duncan: The Ambassador from Venus." *Chicago Review* 45, no. 2 (1999): 24-47.

Discussion of Duncan's birth and adoptive families and their influence on his poetry.

Criticism

Bernstein, Michael André. "Robert Duncan: Talent and the Individual Tradition." *Sagetrieb* 4, nos. 2-3 (fall-winter 1985): 177-90.

Examines Duncan's work as both a continuation of and a challenge to the tradition of American poetry begun by Ezra Pound, H. D., and William Carlos Williams.

Bertholf, Robert J. "Robert Duncan: Blake's Contemporary Voice." In *William Blake and the Moderns,* edited by Robert J. Bertholf and Annette S. Levitt, pp. 92-110. Albany: State University of New York Press, 1982.

Explores the influence of Blake on Duncan and their "spiritual affinities." Also compares their poetic treatment of Jesus Christ, Eros, memory, war, innocence, freedom, and the self.

Brien, Dolores Elise. "Robert Duncan: A Poet in the Whitman-Emerson Tradition." *Centennial Review* 19, no. 4 (fall 1975): 308-16.

Analyzes the importance of Walt Whitman and Ralph Waldo Emerson on Duncan's poetry as manifested in such themes as love, self, God, the body, the creative process, and the role of poetry in society.

Cooley, Dennis. "The Poetics of Robert Duncan." *boundary 2* 8, no. 2 (winter 1980): 45-73.

Discusses the aesthetic principles and concepts of order and chaos that guided Duncan's composition process and informed his poetry.

Guy-Bray, Stephen. "Song and Sonnet: Robert Duncan and the Earl of Surrey." *ANQ: A Quarterly Journal of Short Articles, Notes, and Reviews* 12, no. 4 (fall 1999): 39-42.

Examines the influence of the Earl of Surrey's "Alas, so all thinges nowe doe holde their peace" on Duncan's 1968 poem "Song."

Johnson, Mark Andrew. *Robert Duncan.* Boston: Twayne, 1988, 155 p.

Introduction to Duncan's life and career, with chapters on his poetics and several of his major collections of poetry.

Kamenetz, Rodger. "Realms of Being: An Interview with Robert Duncan." *Southern Review* 21, no. 1 (winter 1985): 4-25.

Discussion of Duncan's views on the influence of Jewish mystical texts and tradition on Letters *and* The Opening of the Field *as well as comments on language, law, his parents' religion, and the relationship between his art and life.*

Materer, Timothy. "Robert Duncan and the Mercurial Self." *Sagetrieb* 9, nos. 1-2 (spring-fall 1990): 7-24.

Discussion of Duncan's use of alchemy and the occult in his work.

Meachen, Clive. "Robert Duncan: 'To Complete His Mind.'" In *Modern American Poetry,* edited by R. W. (Herbie) Butterfield, pp. 204-17. Totowa, N.J.: Barnes & Noble Books, 1984.

Discusses the open and inclusive nature of Duncan's poetry as well as his treatment of apocalypse, God, and rebirth.

Michelson, Peter. "A Materialist Critique of Robert Duncan's Grand Collage." *boundary 2* 8, no. 2 (winter 1980): 21-43.

Asserts that Karl Marx, from a historical perspective, and Duncan, from a mythopoeic perspective, share a similar aim of improving people's lives.

Mossin, Andrew. "In the Shadow of Nerval: Robert Duncan, Robin Blaser, and the Poetics of (Mis)Translation." *Contemporary Literature* 38, no. 4 (winter 1997): 673-704.

Analyzes the differences between Duncan's and Blaser's translations of Gerard de Nerval's "Les Chimeres."

Nelson, Carey. "Between Openness and Loss: Form and Dissolution in Robert Duncan's Aesthetic." In *Our Last First Poets: Vision and History in Contemporary American Poetry,* pp. 97-144. Urbana: University of Illinois Press, 1981.

Examines Duncan's theory of open form as well as several of his themes, including loss, sexuality, religion, history, language, and war.

Nelson, Rudolph L. "Edge of the Transcendent: The Poetry of Levertov and Duncan." *Southwest Review* 54, no. 2 (spring 1969): 188-202.

Explores the similarities and differences between Duncan and Denise Levertov who are often classified together because of their affiliation with the poetic theories of Charles Olson.

Rosenthal, M. L. "The 'Projectivist' Movement: Robert Duncan." In *The New Poets: American and British Poetry Since World War II,* pp. 174-84. New York: Oxford University Press, 1967.

Comments on The Opening of the Field *and* Roots and Branches *and extols Duncan as the most naturally gifted of the Black Mountain poets.*

Wallace-Whitaker, Virginia. "Robert Duncan and the Creative Process: Writing Reading." *Sagetrieb* 8, nos. 1-2 (spring-fall 1989): 247-54.

A discussion of Duncan's approach to the writing process, based on the poet's participation in a study of the creative personality held at the Institute of Personality Assessment and Research at the University of California-Berkeley in the 1950s.

Weatherhead, A. K. "Robert Duncan and the Lyric." *Contemporary Literature* 16, no. 2 (spring 1975): 163-74.

Discusses Duncan's attempts to abandon temporal progression in his poetry and his wish to express himself in the spatial terms normally associated with painting.

Wheaton, Bruce. "Bound to be Present: Memory and Imagined Space in the Work of Robert Duncan." In *The Green American Tradition,* edited by H. Daniel Peck, pp. 228-44. Baton Rouge: Lousiana State University Press, 1989.

Assesses the role of memory in Duncan's poetry.

OTHER SOURCES FROM GALE:

Additional coverage of Duncan's life and career is contained in the following sources published by the Gale Group: *Contemporary Authors,* Vols. 9-12R; *Contemporary Authors New Revision Series,* Vols. 28, 62; *Contemporary Literary Criticism,* Vols. 1, 2, 4, 7, 15, 41, 55; *Dictionary of Literary Biography,* Vols. 5, 16, 193; *DISCovering Authors Modules: Poets; Literature Resource Center; Major 20th-Century Writers,* Eds. 1, 2; *Poetry Criticism,* Vol. 2; *Poetry for Students,* Vol. 13; *Reference Guide to American Literature,* Ed. 4; and *World Poets.*

WILLIAM EVERSON

(1912 - 1994)

(Full name William Oliver Everson; also known as Brother Antoninus) American poet.

Called the "Beat Friar" by his fellow poets, Everson used religious themes in his poetry, and this set his work apart from that of the rest of the Beats, even though he shared the movement's search for enlightenment and understanding. Deep religious feelings and the inner conflict that arose from his choice to live as a celibate monk infuse his poetry with a unique, often shocking tension that captured the imagination of his fellow San Francisco artists.

BIOGRAPHICAL INFORMATION

Born September 10, 1912, in Sacramento, California, to Norwegian immigrant Louis Waldemar Everson and German-Irish farm girl Francelia Maria Herber, Everson was the second of three children. His mother was reared as a Catholic but she reared her children as Christian Scientists. Like his father, Everson declared himself agnostic as an adolescent, thus beginning his life-long journey to define for himself his spirituality and religion. In 1931, and again in 1934 and 1935, Everson attended Fresno State College, spending 1932 and 1933 as a cannery worker and laborer for the Civilian Conservation Corps. During his second term in college, Everson discovered the work of poet Robinson Jeffers. Jeffers's influence was profound and lifelong, and in large part the inspiration for Everson's decision to become a poet.

Deciding to focus on writing and commune with nature, Everson dropped out of college and married Edwa Poulson, his high school sweetheart. During this time he published poetry in journals and magazines and issued several collections of work including *These Are the Ravens* (1935) and *The Masculine Dead: Poems 1938-1940* (1942). However, with World War II, Everson's plans were altered. Unwilling to participate in a war, Everson declared himself a conscientious objector and was placed in the forestry service at Camp Angel in Waldport, Oregon, where he spent more than three years. This was an important time for the young poet, as it brought him into contact with other pacifists and anarchists. There he cofounded an experimental literary press and continued to write poetry.

Having divorced his wife, when he was released from work camp in 1946 Everson moved to San Francisco and came under the influence of poet Kenneth Rexroth. Their relationship was to begin as one of mentor-disciple, but became strained as their philosophies diverged. Their friendship remained throughout their lives—despite professional differences—and Rexroth was in large part the reason for Everson's honored place in what would come to be known as the San Francisco Renaissance. In San Francisco, Everson met and married writer and artist Mary Fabilli, whose struggle to embrace her Catholicism led Everson to convert to the Catholic faith. Rules of the church at the time prevented the couple from remaining married and becoming baptized, so with great difficulty, the couple chose faith over marriage and went their separate ways, each entering the service of the church. After his baptism in 1949, Everson spent the next several months working as a layman, and in 1951 became a lay-brother without vows in the Dominican order, thereafter known as Brother Antoninus. During his seven years of monastic withdrawal he produced a significant outpouring of poetry, became a master hand-press printer, and worked on fine printed volumes of religious works.

In 1957 Brother Antoninus emerged from his monastic life and moved to San Francisco. In 1967 he met a young woman named Susanna Rickson who came to him for spiritual counseling. The two fell in love, and after a reading from his work *Tendril in the Mesh* (1973), he removed his Dominican robe and announced that he was marrying Susanna. He left his order and the newlyweds took up residence in Marin County. In 1971 he was invited to become poet in residence at Kresge College of the University of California at Santa Cruz, where he lectured on poetry and gave classes on the art of fine-press printing. He and his students revived the Lime Kiln Press and produced a number of widely acclaimed fine-press editions of contemporary works. Throughout the 1970s and 1980s, he published poetry under the name of Everson, and raised a son, Jude, with Susanna. By 1993 Everson was suffering from Parkinson's disease and was hospitalized. Everson continued to work on the definitive collection of his poetry from the final period of his life with the help of Albert Gelpi until his death on June 2, 1994.

MAJOR WORKS

Everson's work fits into three distinct periods of the author's life: pre-Catholic, Catholic, and secular. The poetry from the first period is collected in *The Residual Years: Poems 1934-1948* (1968). These works are concerned with nature themes stemming from Everson's early years as a farmer and as a forest worker during World War II. In his introduction to the collection, Rexroth challenged contemporary poetry readers to turn to Everson if they were interested in seeing what modern poetry could and should be. The next period in the poet's work comprises *The Veritable Years: Poems 1949-1966* (1977). Containing work produced as Brother Antoninus, this collection includes poems selected by the author concerning his conversion and early religious life and the turmoil that erotic desire can cause in a man of God. Much of the Brother Antoninus poetry replaces the male notion of God and Catholicism with more feminine representations. His poetry is also erotic and mystical, often intermingling sexual desire with attainment of spiritual enlightenment. The final period of Everson's work is collected in *The Integral Years: Poems 1967-1994* (2000). This collection, which Everson was working on at the time of his death in 1994, contains themes surrounding his motivation to leave the Dominican order and the psychological ramifications of this decision. The tone of the work from this final period is more contented and harmonious, suggesting that Everson had found peace and meaning in his life.

CRITICAL RECEPTION

The unique experience of Everson's agnostic background, his conversion to Catholicism, his life as a Dominican monk, his eventual exit from monastic life, and the perspective his latter years afforded have all been subject to critical examination. Everson's inner struggle as he moved toward a life of spirituality and then resigned from religious duty is of particular interest to those studying modern Christian literature. Scholarly commentary has also focused on Everson's role as the Beat Friar, his influence within the San Francisco Renaissance, his connection to the Beat movement, and his interaction with other artists. Lee Bartlett, leading expert on Everson's works, considers the significant influence of Jungian analytic psychology on this later work, while other critics have traced the importance of Robinson Jeffers on Everson's poetic development. Albert Gelpi, who worked closely with Everson on *The Integral Years* and who helped complete it after Everson's death, has analyzed the erotic mysticism of Everson's work and his feminization of traditionally masculine concepts in religion. Many critics maintain that Everson is often gratuitous in his frank confessionals about his sexual desire and the constraints of his religious vocation, and others fault him as didactic in his consideration of spirituality.

PRINCIPAL WORKS

These Are The Ravens (poetry) 1935

San Joaquin (poetry) 1939

The Masculine Dead: Poems 1938-1940 (poetry) 1942

X War Elegies (poetry) 1943; revised and enlarged as *War Elegies* 1944

The Residual Years: Poems 1940-1941 (poetry) 1944

Waldport Poems (poetry) 1944; enlarged as *The Residual Years: Poems 1934-1946* 1948; enlarged as *The Residual Years: Poems 1934-1948* 1968

Poems: MCMXLII (poetry) 1945

A Privacy of Speech: Ten Poems in Sequence (poetry) 1949

Triptych for the Living (poetry) 1951

An Age Insurgent [as Brother Antoninus] (poetry) 1959

The Crooked Lines of God: Poems 1949-1954 [as Brother Antoninus] (poetry) 1959

There Will Be Harvest [as Brother Antoninus] (poetry) 1960

The Year's Declension [as Brother Antoninus] (poetry) 1960

The Hazards of Holiness: Poems 1957-1960 [as Brother Antoninus] (poetry) 1962

The Poet is Dead: A Memorial for Robinson Jeffers [as Brother Antoninus] (poetry) 1964

The Blowing of the Seed (poetry) 1966

Single Source: The Early Poems of 1934-1940 (poetry) 1966

The Achievement of Brother Antoninus; A Comprehensive Selection of His Poems with a Critical Introduction (poetry) 1967

In the Fictive Wish (poetry) 1967

The Rose of Solitude (poetry) 1967

A Canticle to the Waterbirds [as Brother Antoninus] (poetry) 1968

Robinson Jeffers: Fragments of an Older Fury [as Brother Antoninus] (poetry) 1968

The Springing of the Blade (poetry) 1968

The City Does Not Die [as Brother Antoninus] (poetry) 1969

The Last Crusade [as Brother Antoninus] (poetry) 1969

Who Is She That Looketh Forth as the Morning [as Brother Antoninus] (poetry) 1972

Black Hills (poetry) 1973

Tendril in the Mesh (poetry) 1973

Man-Fate: The Swan Song of Brother Antoninus (poetry) 1974

Archetype West: The Pacific Coast as a Literary Region (criticism) 1976

River-Root: A Syzygy for the Bicentennial of These States (poetry) 1976

The Mate-Flight of Eagles (poetry) 1977

Blame It on the Jet Stream (poetry) 1978

Rattlesnake August (poetry) 1978

The Veritable Years, 1949-1966 (poetry) 1978

Earth Poetry: Selected Essays and Interviews of William Everson, 1950-1977 (essays and interviews) 1980

The Masks of Drought (poetry) 1980

William Everson, on Writing the Waterbirds and Other Presentations: Collected Forewords and Afterwords, 1935-1981 (essays) 1981

The Excesses of God: Robinson Jeffers as a Religious Figure (criticism) 1988

The Engendering Flood: Book One of Dust Shall Be the Serpent's Food (poetry) 1990

Naked Heart: Talking on Poetry, Mysticism, and the Erotic (essays and lectures) 1992

The Blood of the Poet: Selected Poems (poetry) 1994

Prodigious Thrust (poetry) 1996

The Integral Years: Poems 1966-1994 (poetry) 2000

GENERAL COMMENTARY

WILLIAM E. STAFFORD (ESSAY DATE 1967)

SOURCE: Stafford, William E. "Brother Antoninus—The World as a Metaphor." In *The Achievement of Brother Antoninus: A Comprehensive Selection of His Poems with a Critical Introduction,* pp. 1-18. Glenview, Ill.: Scott, Foresman and Company, 1967.

In the following essay, Stafford assesses Brother Antoninus's work as confronting the reader with a tone of bleakness and insistent emotional involvement, a delight in shocking the reader, and an often overly didactic style.

Racked out in the spread of poetry to follow is one of the most notable, extreme, jagged figures of modern American poetry—the intense, religious, wholly committed *persona* of Brother Antoninus, and his earlier self, the aggressively secular anarchist rebel William Everson. Between these two selves, or aspects of one self, there hums a line of poems held closely along a sustained documentary sequence, portraying, overall, the slow turning of a character under duress:

> I speak from a cold heart.
> I cry out of a cold climate.
> I shake the head of a cold-encrusted man.
> I blow a blue breath.
> I come from a cold place.
> I cry out for another future.
>
> —**"The Blowing of the Seed"**

The progression of the sequence is from the young man influenced by his farm background in the California valley:

> You cannot shake it, the feeling of mountains, deep in the haze and over the cities,
> The mass, the piled strength and tumultuous thunder of the peaks.
> They are beyond us forever, in fog or storm or the flood of the sun, quiet and sure,
> Back of this valley like an ancient dream in a man's mind,
> That he cannot forget, nor hardly remember,
> But it sleeps at the roots of his sight.
>
> —**"Walls"**

Through early love and its recollection:

> The bruise is not there,
> Nor the bullying boy,
> Nor the girl who gave him the bitter gift,
> Under the haws in the hollow dark and the windless air;
> But the rue remains,
> The rue remains in the delicate echo of what was done;
> And he who labors above the lines,
> Leans to an ache as old almost
> As the howl that shook him in his own birth,
> And the heavy blow that beat him to breath
> When the womb had widened.
>
> —**"The Answer"**

Into the clash with the warring state:

> And I vow not to wantonly ever take life . . .
> And seek to atone in my own soul
> What was poured from my past.
>
> —**"The Vow"**

Coming to adult love:

> Under my hand your heart hits like a bird,
> Hushed in the palms, a muffled flutter,
> And all the instinct of its flight
> Shut in its wings.
>
> —**"The Blowing of the Seed"**

And into announced faith:

> The light woke in the windows.
> One by one the saints existed,
> The swords of their martyrdom healed in their hands.
> The linnet opened his voice;
> He blistered his throat in the seethe of that rapture.
> The suddenness split my skull.
>
> —**"A Frost Lay White on California"**

Pressures in the long development spring from the distinguishing issues of our time—World War II, the moral crises incident to war and the uprootings that go with it, the political turmoil felt by a whole alienated group, and the emotional revulsions of a conscientious and sensitive human being subjected to such pressures. And the solution or resolution, or asserted prospect, hacked out in the poems is most abrupt, emphatic, and extreme. Finally, the unifying element is an announced faith, a religious commitment maintained forcefully in the struggle and sweep of modern challenges.

Those who have found this poetry realize its distinction. but it is not for everyone. For some, it is too disturbing. For all, however, it is phenomenal, a reference point of the modern sensibility.

The poetry of Brother Antoninus confronts the reader with two main hazards, the first an immediate and obvious quality, and the second a more pervasive demand. The immediate quality is that of bleakness and insistent emotional involvement, lying at an extreme from prettiness, and even from recent, more generously updated conceptions of poetry's content. Modern poetry is no valentine, but Brother Antoninus has done more than leave off the lace:

> .. the great elk, caught midway between two scissoring logs,

Arched belly-up and died, the snapped spine
Half torn out of his peeled back, his hind legs
Jerking that gasped convulsion, the kick of
spasmed life,
Paunch plowed open, purple entrails
Disgorged from the basketwork ribs
Erupting out, splashed sideways, wrapping him,
Gouted in blood, flecked with the brittle sliver of
bone.

—**"In All These Acts"**

This passage is from a late, religious poem, and in the development of Brother Antoninus' work it seems that the more intense his religious commitment becomes, the more violent the content of his poetry. But even the earliest work has this quality, as a glance at the sequence cited earlier will show: ". . . howl that shook him . . . heavy blow." Even the linnet's song "blistered his throat."

This bleak aspect of the work impressed critics from the first. Kenneth Rexroth, in an article which helped to launch "the beat generation" into public notice ("San Francisco Letter," in the second issue of *Evergreen Review*), calls William Everson "probably the most profoundly moving and durable poet of the San Francisco Renaissance," and continues: "His work has a gnarled, even tortured honesty, a rugged unliterary diction, a relentless probing and searching, which are not just engaging, but almost overwhelming." And Rexroth goes on to say, "Anything less like the verse of the fashionable literary quarterlies would be hard to imagine." The implication is meant to be honorific: "rugged unliterary diction," not like "the verse of the fashionable quarterlies." But that implication, though understandable, is quite misleading. Rugged as the poems are, they are lavishly literary.

Consider the organization of sound in the following passages. The striking words and pictures may pose as unliterary but are in fact elaborate with repeated sounds and varied, rhymed, slurred progressions:

They came out of the sun with their guns geared,
Saw the soft and easy shape of that island
Laid on the sea,
An unwakening woman,
Its deep hollows and its flowing folds
Veiled in the garland of its morning mists.

—**"The Raid"**

"No pride!" cried God, "kick me I come back!
Spit on me I eat your spittle!
I crawl on my belly!"

—**"A Frost Lay White on California"**

It is clear that the immediate quality of bleakness and shock looms here, but everything is tuned and heightened and artful, even relentlessly artful. Consider the syllables and their sounds, no matter where they come in the lines, no matter how casually they seem to fall—the sun-gun-geared of the first line, the saw-soft, easy-shape of the second line. Think of the hovering erotic implication of the scene in **"The Raid."** How could you find in any "fashionable quarterly" any verse with more density of repetition than pride-cried-God-kick-come-back? The reader may trust his sense of something special in the language of these poems; they are both rugged *and* literary. The immediate quality of feeling, the shock, derives from something other than just rough words, and in order to identify the cause of the obvious bleakness and shock, we must cast back to the first statement made about the self, the *persona,* which is created out of contrasts.

One kind of poetry—and the poetry of Brother Antoninus is a distinguished example of it—flourishes because it expresses many impulses which practical, politic life coerces most of us to avoid. That is, many of our everyday actions and sayings we adjust to calculations about effects on others; we are purposeful and instrumental with language. But there is another way to live, a way to stay honest without staying silent; and the poetry of Brother Antoninus demonstrates this other way—it is a shock and a delight to break free into the heart's unmanaged impulses. All literature lives in one way or another with this freedom, but the Everson-Antoninus poetry lives openly—even flagrantly—by continual recourse to shock.

Brother Antoninus has committed his whole life to conduct and communication which maintain independence, a stance of accepting what the immediate being can find, and a readiness to reject anything else; he is a passionate romantic. As a radical in politics, as a conscientious objector in war, as a recklessly individual spokesman in his religion, Everson-Antoninus exemplifies to an extreme degree a quality which marks current literature—the exhilaration of rebellion. A reader must accept a certain view if he is to read such a writer sympathetically; he must relish how the literature stiff-arms the genteel, how the author delights in presenting abruptly topics often avoided. Brother Antoninus requires this kind of acceptance immediately and repeatedly.

The shock method is evident in the following passages, chosen from early and late work. Note that the passages do not necessarily prove anything unusual, nor do they have to consist of inherently shocking materials; but each one deliberately confronts the reader with a certain almost electric realization that the writer has shoved against commonly slurred-over or conventionalized human expectations. After an introductory poem, the selection in this text begins with the line: "These verses are lies." Immediately the writer has begun his attack on the reader's expectations. The following demonstrate the prevalence of this *challenge* as a way of writing; the author subjects his reader to a world that hurts:

When they rode that hawk-hearted Murietta
down in the western hills
They cut the head loose to prove the
bounty. . . .

—**"Lines for the Last of a Gold Town"**

He is a god who smiles blindly,
And hears nothing, and squats faun-mouthed on
the wheeling world. . . .

—**"Circumstance"**

Churchill: the sound of your voice from the
eastern air. . . .
Who listen beyond the hammering tongue
For the eloquent fallacy wound at its root
Are not to be wooed. . . .

—**"The Unkillable Knowledge"**

These are typical passages. They demonstrate the punishing quality in the poems: the reader is to suffer while he receives something that promises an eventual, bitter, satisfying reward.

Bleak, rugged passages, though extreme in the work of Brother Antoninus, and hence an immediate hazard to some readers, do not constitute so much of a barrier as does his other main distinction, the more pervasive quality mentioned earlier. That quality is, bluntly put, didacticism. Brother Antoninus takes a conspicuously unfashionable stand on the issues of belief, assertion, and authority in literature. The results of his stand pervade his poems, which consequently baffle or estrange some readers.

We are accustomed today to accept for the duration of a literary experience all kinds of moral reversals, anti-universes, and ordinarily outrageous assumptions. We ride with the work, accepting the author's most emphatic statements temporarily, without yielding ourselves in any vital way to his assumed authority. We accept his tone as part of the literary experience, but we know that the writer cannot through personal authority coerce our belief. He can only provide us with experiences which we can value for their shimmer and excitement. The fine arts cannot impose; they have to appeal.

However, a generation ago, or longer, an author was a sage, sometimes almost a prophet, a model of some kind. Brother Antoninus is in that tradition, and his poems take on a prophetic, oracular tone. What he presents, he presents as an insight, a truth, not merely as an exercise of the imagination. In his work his voice is direct; he does not turn aside to flirt with fancies and baffling temporary allegiances; there is no Emperor of Ice Cream in his poetry, no Raven saying "Nevermore" to enhance a temporary feeling chosen for literary exercise. Brother Antoninus sets up to be a thinker and guide, a statesman of letters. His stance is that of responsibility. "These verses are lies," yes; but only because they come from a limited intelligence and will, not because the writer is setting out to create passing sensations for the reader.

So the reader of Everson-Antoninus finds himself presented with metaphors intended as truth. The world that is asserted must be linked in its largest events and in its details with a belief that is asserted triumphantly, but then subjected to the terrors and horrors and weaknesses of our existence, and then asserted again. It is the vicissitudes of this faith, surviving in the modern world and in the particulars of the author's life, that have become more and more central in the work of Brother Antoninus.

Even his earlier work is tied to the soul's program of development: his poetry inducted him into his religion, and his religion shapes his poetry. The reader who is unwilling to accept that pattern, who is reluctant to suspend his disbelief in the significance of the particulars of the author's life as the author sees them, will be continually under a strain in reading the poetry; for it asks the reader's participation and makes the author's discoveries into the central rewards of the later poems:

And I crawl.
I will get there.
Like a clubbed snake
I hitch toward freedom.
Out of this skin, this slough,
Across these illusions,
Upon this blood.

—**"The Face I Know"**

In addition to the evidence in poem after poem that Brother Antoninus is using literature deliberately for purposes other than just the literary, the author himself, outside his poems, declares his objectives. He says in a letter about his work, "I strive for spiritual perfection and make the striving the subject and the themes of my poetry." The Foreword to his 1962 collection, ***The Hazards of Holiness,*** elaborates:

> This is not to say that I despise craftsmanship, but only that the struggle with language is the struggle to make myself comprehensible to myself, to orient my inner and outer being. . . .
>
> Thus I can truthfully say that I have no interest in the conquest of language, as understood by those who seek to achieve a hypostatized aesthetic object. The victories I seek, those of "appeasement and absolution, and something very near to annihilation," are one and all victories over myself, the unremitting attempt to exorcize the demon.

Important as the author's attitude is, and pervasive as its effect is, in the work of Brother Antoninus, the disclaimer of literary ambition need not greatly change the reader's approach. For Brother Antoninus—whatever his explicit intention—is manifestly and even almost helplessly poetic. He maintains creative momentum partly because he continues to be surprised at his own religiousness; he continues to make the kind of visionary statement a discoverer makes. The world says straight to him what it is supposed to say, and for the reader it is the intensity, rather than the validity, of the statements that counts. Almost to the pitch of a Saint Francis, Brother Antoninus encounters the intricate sermons of God acted out by the creatures around us:

> Curlews, stilts and scissortails, beachcomber
> gulls,
> Wave-haunters, shore-keepers, rockhead-holders,
> all cape-top vigilantes,
> Now give God praise.
> Send up the articulation of your throats
> And say His name.
>
> —**"A Canticle to the Water Birds"**

The rugged shock effect of his writing and the pervasive didactic or moral tone are, then, the most distinctive qualities in the poetry of Brother Antoninus; but two further characteristics—both having to do with the distinctive content of the poetry and both related to the struggle of the self which runs through all the work—may distance for many readers the poems in this text. One characteristic is the extreme alienation modern war has forced on him, and the other is the decidedly personal focus of many of his poems relating to the breakup of a marriage.

In the content of his poetry, and in his life, Brother Antoninus demonstrates forcefully how intense, abrupt, and devastating to the soul modern war is. His distinction in this regard is somewhat blurred by a common supposition that war literature must come from participants, like Wilfred Owen, or Siegfried Sassoon, or Ernest Hemingway; but the young William Everson was even more of a casualty; he did not have even the relative immunity to war which is necessary for reluctant involvement; he did not survive the vision of mass destruction, and was a soul casualty. In common with Robinson Jeffers, who greatly influenced his topics and his style, William Everson saw modern war, from its first flare upon the imagination, as demanding that participants abdicate their humanness; he found himself a spokesman for a kind of being from whom modern warriors cannot be fashioned.

It is difficult to overstate the alienation this writer works from: he gives ordinary readers a view of the place of the absolutist, of the principled rebel. This is not to say that his stance is one of moral superiority; but he has taken the much-contemplated step of saying no to the state, and has been imprisoned for it. That passionate individuality referred to earlier resulted in long-suffering rebellion, in circumstances which continue to test individual values. It is unlikely that many readers even today can participate emotionally, without some qualms, in such a poem as **"The Unkillable Knowledge"** or, as expressed more simply, in this passage from **"The Vow"**:

> I flinch in the guilt of what I am,
> Seeing the poised heap of this time
> Break like a wave.
> And I vow not to wantonly ever take life;
> Not in pleasure or sport,
> Nor in hate . . .
> And seek to atone in my own soul
> What was poured from my past. . . .

This pronounced alienation from the "national purpose" when the main group of citizens were mobilized for war has marked one section of our society, and the work of Brother Antoninus is in regard to pacifism probably the most representative of all that the "beat" poets of the San Francisco group have produced. After World War II the Bay Area in California became a center for many who had been uprooted and had come to know the attractions of the place. Brother Antoninus—then William Everson—had been a prisoner in isolated Civilian Public Service camps during the war years, and he had seen many of his friends taken away to prison. The society around him was alien enough to bring about in-group solidarity among the students, conscientious objectors, and political radicals who began to identify themselves and each other during the postwar years. That background of disaffection with a warring society is worth mention in order to point out that the literary renaissance in San Francisco, as well as later campus and political events of the Bay Area, stems partly from the kind of position exemplified by this poet.

The other markedly distinctive content in what follows comes mostly in the poems about the breaking up of a marriage. One whole section, **"The Blowing of the Seed,"** provides a very ambitious working out of the complex relation between man and woman. They are mutually attracted; they can save each other by the welcome they give to each other's needs. But even that relation carries an implied danger, for all such relations are unstable balances—precarious and disturbing.

Earlier, the poet's **"Chronicle of Division"** (printed in part here) documents an estrangement between a man and a woman, and something more than a particular estrangement—the poem becomes a religious, psychological drama of attraction and repulsion, complicated by separation enforced by war. So intense are the feelings back of **"Chronicle of Division"** that some natural image can best serve as a quick indicator; it is convenient to glance at a poem like **"Lava Bed"** to see how the intensity of vision can reveal itself through the choice of scene and a bitter selecting of components to be held up to view:

> Fisted, bitten by blizzards,
> Flattened by wind and chewed by all weather
> The lava bed lay.
> Deer fashioned trails there but no man, ever;
> And the fugitive cougars whelped in that lair.
> Deep in its waste the buzzards went down to
> some innominate kill.
> The sun fell in it,
> And took the whole west down as it died.
> Dense as the sea,
> Entrenched in its years of unyielding rebuff,
> It held to its own.
> We looked in against anger,
> Beholding that which our cunning had never
> subdued,
> Our power indented,
> And only our eyes had traversed.

In this poem a part of the world wonderfully suited for the poet's most fundamental vision is simply held up and described; in appearance, the world is delivering its own meaning by existing in materials and patterns which speak dramatically of struggle, hardness, enduring rebellion. The world is a hard bed, fisted, bitten, flattened, chewed; mankind finds itself confronting that kind of Garden of Eden in the poems of Brother Antonius. Even when what the world offers has appeal, the greater that appeal, the more poignant its brief existence; and even a poem about childhood allows a quick, strangely erotic glimpse, and then loss:

> And what lumps in the throat is the music's
> magic,
> Its exquisite trill,
> At the October fairs,
> Where the painted horses
> Bridled in gold,
> Leap up, leap up in that lifeless lope,
> With the little girls
> Who shriek with joy
> And shake out their ribboned hair . . .
> And the dream will go. . . .
> —**"The Springing of the Blade"**

This bleak view of love, and the forceful stand against war, along with the rugged bluntness of the poems and their uncompromising moral stance—all of these characteristics become pyramided and intensified as Brother Antoninus forces his poems to take upon themselves a big, coherent program—he uses the writing of poetry as a way to master emergencies in his own experience; he *writes his way through* crises and undertakes to wrestle down the ills of our time by means of what he encounters in his development as a poet. All of the poet's encounters are made valid and valued parts of the soul's venture through the world. In recognition of that large purpose, the poems in this text are selected and ordered to help the reader see three main steps in the content of the writer's career. Moreover, it is content that Brother Antoninus talks about when he considers his own work. But before settling for a quick, clear pattern of content, we should emphasize that this poet's technique, his characteristic procedure in writing, also deserves attention.

The "rugged diction" and the shock tactics discussed earlier are like the "personality" of this writer; but his *character* remains for deeper discovery. Note that in the largest, decisive maneuvers of his poems he exercises continuous firm control. He provides constant assurance for the reader, who is guided unswervingly, even as the poem gives the appearance of casual progression. The study of a poem like **"The Raid"** will demonstrate this constant, assertive control:

> They came out of the sun undetected,
> Who had lain in the thin ships
> All night long on the cold ocean,
> Watched Vega down, the Wain hover,
> Drank in the weakening dawn their brew,
> And sent the lumbering death-laden birds
> Level along the decks.
>
> They came out of the sun with their guns geared,
> Saw the soft and easy shape of that island

Laid on the sea,
An unwakening woman,
Its deep hollows and its flowing folds
Veiled in the garlands of its morning mists.
Each of them held in his aching eyes the erotic
image,
And then tipped down,
In the target's trance,
In the ageless instant of the long ascent,
And saw sweet chaos blossom below,
And felt in that flower the years release.

The perfect achievement.
They went back toward the sun crazy with joy,
Like wild birds weaving,
Drunkenly stunting;
Passed out over the edge of that injured island,
Sought rendezvous on the open sea
Where the ships would be waiting.

None were there.
Neither smoke nor smudge;
Neither spar nor splice nor rolling raft.
Only the wide waiting waste,
That each of them saw with intenser sight
Than he ever had spared it,
Who circled that spot,
The spent gauge caught in its final flutter,
And straggled down on their wavering wings
From the vast sky,
From the endless spaces,
Down at last for the low hover,
And the short quick quench of the sea.

Consider the recurrences in sound and structure, the funnel-shaped action, and the turn signals in this poem:

They came out of the *sun un*detected,
*Who h*ad la*in in* the th*in* ships

. . . . .

They came out of the sun with their *guns geared*. . . .

The action is in a clear, explicit pattern: they came out . . . they came out . . . and then tipped down . . . they went back . . . at last. . . . The reader knows from the first that the poem is sweeping along toward a definite, summarizable conclusion. Further, the world of this poem is again the typical Antoninus miracle of metaphorical rightness, with war, moral judgment, the erotic images of nature, and final retribution for presumptuous man.

Brother Antoninus' poems are not wandering and exploratory; they drive forward with an assured pattern looming throughout. Consider an early example, **"On the Anniversary of the Versailles Peace, 1936."** This example typifies the poems; it links to social and political issues; it looks rambling and baggy on the page; it is sustained by the pattern of the natural background, the scene; it subjects the reader to shocks of sensation:

Low is the light;
No red in the sky but a yellow stain;
And that killed snake the sierra all angles and
humps on the filled east. . . .

Alliteration recurs throughout this poem; the design is a pattern almost as steady as in Old English verse, with balanced alliterative assertions. And the world spreads itself before the human actors as a delphic lesson:

There is no warring nor fury nor flame, but the
hush and the balance;
And one watching can nearly accept with hope
that gospel of love which was Christ's.
But the truce fails; the light spreads, hurling
west,
And the sun bursts roaring from the rough hills,
Trampling up the sky, and is free.

Even the alternation between long and short lines adds to the reader's sense of a controlled speaker in these poems. For a time in his development Brother Antoninus shortened his lines, to maximize the kind of come-to-the end-and . . . drop-over effect continually available to the poet, but for the most part he varied the lengths of the lines and thus attained an extreme effect with abruptly bobbed utterances:

I call to mind that violent man who waded the
North.
He imagined a slight,
Killed for it;
Made outlaw, lay in the echoing wastes;
Fled to far cities;
Knew dangerous about him the subtle strands of
communication
Ticking his doom.

—**"The Outlaw"**

Many of his later poems fill the page from left to right, unloading with detailed care the full reasoning of the writer; but the intermittent short lines continue to mark the style; and often that bobbed line of the early poems turns up again as the ritual intonation of later religious poems:

Now give God praise.
Send up the articulation of your throats,
And say His name.

—**"A Canticle to the Water Birds"**

These stylistic distinctions will sustain a reader: the language promises sure advancement through the structure, and the pressured swerve of the lines carries on the assurance.

A further enhancement—so frequent as to become by anticipation a part of the reader's appetite—is intensity as communicated by strains and displacements in the language. For instance, often scenes or actions become illuminated for the reader by a word or phrase which indicates immediate technical involvement on the part of the speaker, a flashing out with terms used by adepts—a crane waits to "gig" fish; or a small bird, "the swart junket," "skits" in the thicket; a river "cuts" its way to the sea. Events come into the consciousness with immediacy, signaled in and accommodated by a writer who feels his closeness to the action.

Sometimes this effect of closeness derives from forcing the language to accept adjustments which appear to be necessary because of emergencies in stating something felt too distinctly for communication in ordinary language: a noun may be forced to become a verb, for instance. At times this procedure is like a mannerism, though it always creates an intensity:

All gone, all broken,
Smashed and smithereened. . . .
Speak from the bloodied past, the failured
venture.

—**"The Blowing of the Seed"**

The effect of this custom-made wording is to induce in the reader a realization of tension. The poems are never allowed to become inert, are never standard formulations. The effort of the self to attain its place, its soul's rescue, is reflected in the effort of the poems to attain the resolution intimated by their apparent strain. In effect, the poems act out, even in the details of their wording, the whole effort intimated from the first of this discussion, the progression of Everson to Antoninus, the evolution of the *persona* animating the successive poems.

Strangely, it is this very feeling of effort that has led some critics to assume that the fox is not cunning. Whether cunning is the right word or not, an examination of Brother Antoninus' work will certainly show that he treats the language with that same confidence and control which distinguishes the work of the most elaborately "literary" writer.

One other distinction in the style of this poet deserves recording here: he has carried all of his force and individuality into public readings; and again he qualifies as an important representative of the San Francisco group of poets in that he has helped to establish poetry reading in its current popularity, through many readings locally and in a number of trips across the country. His appearances are striking. He is tall, and though he appears to understate his posture, he is still tall. In the long robe of the Dominican, he dramatizes his stance. He adjusts to different audiences, apparently finding his manner as he goes along, but the effect is always that his poems appear to come from a need to communicate directly; in the reading as in the writing, a personal message dominates. His voice is piercing, a reed instrument. And he intones and invokes as he moves about the stage. He has confidence in his poems, and he is capable of putting the audience under a strain as they have to wait for him to begin. He challenges and taunts. He jolts and teases the audience. As he writes for purposes larger than the literary, so he reads with apparent intention of using poems for changing the lives of his hearers.

Directly using poems for the sake of his hearers, as part of his life applied to the immediate situation, is typical of the career of Brother Antoninus: he has carried from farm to camp to home to monastery the accumulation of his work and even the means to print it. As he himself was a printer and as his friends were often engaged in writing and publishing, and as they often considered their work to be independent, outside the mainstream, his bibliography has become very much tangled. His writing and publishing make an elaborate puzzle, with partial printings of certain large works, and with consequent gaps in the material he considers continuous. The selection presented herewith weaves as best it can with a range of work from the earliest to the latest in book publication; and the sequence draws into itself material not yet in book form. The acknowledgments page will enable a reader to trace some of the main strands of the bibliographical puzzle, but because the line of his development lends itself to certain simplified clarifications, it has been thought best to group the poems into the three imposed sections indicated in the Contents, and to offer a somewhat elaborated explanation here.

Each section marks a stage in chronology identified by a phrase which to a fair degree indicates a stage in the poet's development. In the later 1930's and into the 1940's, while the writer was farm worker, student, and then prisoner in a camp for conscientious objectors, he was writing what he has classed as poems of "the natural imagination," that is, poems which rely for their value on sense impressions as guides for the self. He was at this time much influenced by Robinson Jeffers. Though always alerted to overtones in natural experience, William Everson, before his change of religion and name, was not identified with any church. In fact, some of his poems from the conscientious-objector camps accurately depict a certain distance he maintained from the professedly religious objectors; in particular, the sequence called **"Chronicle of Division"** reveals that distance and some traces of rebellion against the program accepted by "conformers" in the camps:

> The newcomer marvels,
> Beholding about him wherever he enters,
> The direct head,
> The declarative face,
> That wears its look like an open hand.
> . . . . .
> Till time taught him less,
> Revealing the brittle bias
> The unseen error that makes human the
> saint. . . .

His official listing in the directory of the camps identifies him as a "farmer, poet, printer," and his religion is listed, "none."

Overlapping the first period and extending into the 1950's, was a period here labeled that of "metaphysical search." This term merely serves to identify poems which appear to move from confusion and discouragement and social indictment toward some achieved sense of direction. This division is probably the most schematic and least valid, chronologically, of the three divisions offered here for the convenience of the reader. The difficulty of achieving helpful groupings is apparent from the date appended to **"The Vow,"** which ends this section. That date is 1940, but no later poem more appropriately takes up into itself the scene, the sense of direction, and the religious overtone later to become predominant:

> Delicate and soft,
> The grass flows on the curling palms of my
> hands.
> The gophers under the ground
> Fashion their nests in the cool soil.
> I lift up my eyes,
> And they find the bearing that swings the sky,
> And I turn toward home,
> Who have gathered such strength as is mine.

The last section, representing the current stage in this poet's development, contains the Roman Catholic religious poems. They celebrate, beyond the detailed suffering, a security—a continuing struggle but in some respects a resolution of the author's long struggle to achieve a coherent self. The poems hammer a direct, religious view, and they even approximate ritual patterns at times; but they do not mark a complete change from the tone and technique of the earlier work: the writer has brought his metaphors, and his general sense of the world as a metaphor, into the frame for repeated assertion of his Roman Catholic faith. He has found it possible to view himself as one of the "crooked lines" with which God writes straight.

KENNETH REXROTH (ESSAY DATE 1968)

SOURCE: Rexroth, Kenneth. Introduction to *The Residual Years: Poems 1934-1948,* by William Everson, pp. xv-xvii. New York: New Directions, 1968.

In the following essay, Rexroth introduces Everson's collection of poetry written between 1934 and 1948, and celebrates the originality and the importance of the work.

It's long ago now, another epoch in the life of mankind, before the Second War, that I got a pamphlet of poems from a press in a small California town—***These Are the Ravens***—and then a handsome book from the Ward Ritchie Press in Los Angeles—***San Joaquin.*** They weren't much like the poems being written in those days, either in *New Masses, Partisan Review* or *The Southern Review.* They were native poems, autochthonous in a way the fashionable poems of the day could not manage. Being an autochthon of course is something you don't manage, you are. It was not just the subjects, the daily experience of a young man raising grapes in the Great Valley of California, or the rhythms, which were of the same organic pulse you find in Isaiah, or Blake's prophecies, or Whitman, or Lawrence, or Sandburg at this best, or Wallace Gould, or Robinson Jeffers. This, it seemed to me, was a young fellow out to make himself unknown and forgotten in literary circles. The age has turned round, and the momentary reputations of that day are gone, and William Everson, now Brother Antoninus, is very far from being unknown and forgotten.

I say this, not in a spirit of literary controversy, but to try to bring home to a time that accepts his idiom and his sensibility, how unusual these poems were thirty years ago. Everson has won through, and in a very real sense this whole book—a new edition of his early poems—is a record of that struggle. It is a journal of a single-handed war for a different definition of poetic integrity. There is nothing abstract or impersonal about these poems. They are not clockwork aesthetic objects, wound up to go off and upset the reader. T. S. Eliot and Paul Valéry told the young of the last generation that that's what poems were, and the young dutifully tried their best to make such infernal machines, never noticing that their masters never wrote that way at all. Everson paid no attention. He cultivated and irrigated and tied up the vines and went home in the sunset and ate dinner and made love and wrote about how he felt doing it and about the turning of the year, the intimate rites of passage, and the rites of the season of a man and a woman. He used the first person singular pronoun often, because that, as far as he could see, was the central figure in the cast of the only existential drama he knew. And what is wrong with that? Nothing at all, the critics of the last generation to the contrary notwithstanding. It wasn't an alarm clock that meditated in the marine cemetery or suffered in the wasteland of London.

Everson has been accused of self-dramatization. Justly. All of his poetry, that under the name of Brother Antoninus, too, is concerned with the drama of his own self, rising and falling along the sine curve of life, from comedy to tragedy and back again, never quite going under, never quite escaping for good into transcendence. This is a man who sees his shadow projected on the sky, like Whymper after the melodramatic achievement and the tragedy on the Matterhorn. Everything is larger than life with a terrible beauty and pain. Life isn't like that to some people and to them these poems will seem too strong a wine. But of course life is like that. Night alone, storm over the cabin, the sleepless watcher whipsawed by past and future—life is like that, of course, just as a walk on the beach is like "Out of the Cradle Endlessly Rocking," or playing on the floor while mother played the piano is like Lawrence's "Piano." Hadn't you ever noticed?

Something terribly important and infinitely mysterious is happening. It is necessary to hold steady like Odysseus steering past the sirens, to that rudder called the integrity of the self or the ship will smash up in the trivial and the commonplace. This is what Everson's poetry is about—but then, sometimes less obviously, so is most other poetry worth its salt.

I don't think there is any question but that William Everson is one of the three or four most important poets of the now-notorious San Francisco school. Most of the people wished on the community by the press are in fact from New York and elsewhere. The thing that distinguishes Robert Duncan, Philip Lamantia, William Everson and their associates is that they are all religious poets. Their subjects are the varied guises of the trials of the soul and the achievement of illumination. Everson's poems are mystical poems, records of the struggle towards peace and illumination on the stairs of natural mysticism. Peace comes only in communion with nature or momentarily with a woman, and far off, the light is at the end of a tunnel. So this is an incomplete autobiography—as whose isn't?

How deeply personal these poems are, and how convincingly you touch the living man through them. I have read them for years. Brother Antoninus is one of my oldest and best friends and the godfather of my daughters. As I turn over the pages, some of them thirty years old, I feel again, as always, a comradeship strong as blood. Evil men may have degraded those words, but they are still true and apposite for the real thing. Blood brotherhood.

ALBERT GELPI (ESSAY DATE 1978)

SOURCE: Gelpi, Albert. "Introduction, Everson/Antoninus: Contending with the Shadow." In *The Veritable Years: Poems 1949-1966* by William Everson, pp. xix-xxxiii. Santa Rosa, Calif.: Black Sparrow Press, 1998.

In the following essay, originally published in 1978, Gelpi examines twentieth-century Christian poetry, and traces Everson's work through his conversion and monastic period to his exit from monastic life and the years that followed.

In a review almost a decade ago [1968], I hailed ***The Rose of Solitude*** as the most significant volume of religious poetry since Robert Lowell's *Lord Weary's Castle* twenty years before, and argued that Brother Antoninus' poetry was more profoundly Christian than Lowell's because it was more Incarnational, whereas Lowell's lapse from Catholicism stemmed from his difficulty in accepting the awesome, violent paradoxes of the central Christian mystery. Lowell ended up caught in the ambiguities of agnosticism, revising and adding to his random *Notebook* in the same, confined fourteen-line conventions. And now, with Antoninus' early, pre-Catholic poetry, written as William Everson, available still in the collection ***The Residual Years,*** and with this new and complete collection of poems spanning his Dominican years, I would venture the judgment that if T.S. Eliot is the most important religious poet in English in the first half of the twentieth century, Everson/Antoninus is the most important religious poet of the second half of the century.

The extreme contrasts between those two poets point to a symptomatic tension in the religious commitment. The differences are less doctrinal than temperamental: Eliot the conservative classicist submitting the weaknesses of the individual to the reasonable authority of tradition and institutional structures in order to absolve him from the exigencies of personality; and Everson, the romantic individualist, trusting reason less than the undertow of passion and instinct to write out a life-long poem, as Whitman did a century ago, of the struggles with himself to realize himself.

Many would argue that authentic religious experience must be distinguished from mere intellectual commitment to an ecclesiastical structure, and that the great religious poetry of the first half of the century came not from Eliot but from such figures as Ezra Pound, D.H. Lawrence, Robinson Jeffers. Such a statement is not fair to Eliot, since the philosophical meditations of *Four Quartets* do derive from genuine religious experiences. However, the distinctions between modes of religious sensibility postulated bluntly above is fundamental and revealing.

For what links the other three poets and Everson together, for all their admitted differences, is precisely what Eliot shrank back from as from the devil: a sourcing of self in the Dionysian unconscious rather than Apollonian consciousness; a faith in the forces—pre-rational, irrational, supra-rational, what you will—instinctive in nature and emergent in the human psyche. Their poetry functions in good part to articulate the eruption into consciousness of the unconscious energies, which are for them the source and secret of life. Pound recovered such primal experiences in the Greek myths and the mysteries of the occult; Lawrence, like Whitman, in the divine carnality of the sexual drive; Jeffers, in the pantheism which sees in the sea and rocks and creatures of the shore "the brute beauty of God" beyond the predatory violences of the egoistic mind and will. And in the poetry of each, such psychological and spiritual explorations led to open form and free verse, as the poem discovered its definition.

By contrast, the explicitly Christian poets of the twentieth century have, by and large, tended to stress the constraining limits of a radically flawed creation through which the refractions of the Spirit penetrate at best tenuously and elusively, and they have generally insisted on working within the limitations of formal conventions as a way of testing and fixing "hints and guesses," as Eliot described our experience of the Incarnation. The means and the meaning, the norms and the measure have therefore been ruminative, guarded, Apollonian in the main. The elaborated patterning of the *Quartets* conveys not just the timeless moments which have transformed Eliot's life, but also the abiding disillusionment with temporal existence which qualifies and survives the moments of transcendence. Marianne Moore's intricately artful syllabics are a discipline to verify and regulate the allegorist's reading of natural experience in moral and religious terms. The virtuosity of Richard Wilbur's carefully maintained poise and symmetry epitomizes his conviction that the Incarnation calls us to attend to "things of this world" for "their difficult balance" of body and spirit. The religious pieces which conclude Allen Tate's long spiritual travail are written in Dante's *terza rima* in aspiration towards a faith that seems all but beyond his grasp. In Robert Lowell's Catholic poems, alternately stretched and clenched on their metrical and metaphorical designs till they threaten to wrench themselves apart, the Spirit moves to save human nature in death, which saves it from natural corruption; for him, the advent of the Incarnation spells Apocalypse. John Berryman enacted his religious anxiety through the knotted syntax and studied cadences of Anne Bradstreet and of Henry (protagonist of Berryman's *The Dream Songs);* and even after the poet's late return to the Church, his poems vacillate between prayers for patience and impatient anticipation of breaking free of the human tragedy.

It is the very history of religious—especially Christian—poetry in the twentieth century, with its fixation on human fallibility and its consequent insistence on necessarily prescribed forms, that makes Everson's poetry seem radical, original, transformative. Most of the Dionysians in recent poetry—Allen Ginsberg, Jack Kerouac, Lawrence Ferlinghetti, like Hart Crane in the twenties—have used alcohol or drugs for release into vision, but Ralph Waldo Emerson, who opened the way for Whitman and all the later Dionysian poet-prophets, was the first to condemn such "*quasi*-mechanical substitutes for the true nectar," which would end in "dissipation and deterioration." The distinctiveness of Everson's achievement springs, rather, from the Dionysian character of his Christianity. This has evolved in two complementary phases: from the beginning, his surrendering to primal experience until at last it yielded him the Christian mystery; and his surrendering, then, to the Christian mystery so unreservedly that it enflamed and illuminated, below and above structured rational consciousness, that dark area, at once the center and circumference of psyche, where passion and spirit reveal themselves as personhood incarnate.

. . . . .

How did this transpire through more than sixty years of living and forty of poetry? William Everson's life has been punctuated again and again by interruptions, abrupt changes and seeming reversals. What has been the continuity? Born in 1912 in Sacramento, growing up in California's San Joaquin Valley, his grandfather the founder of an evangelical sect in Norway, his stern father an agnostic, his doting mother a Christian Scientist, Everson was a dreamy, withdrawn young man, but in 1934 he discovered the master whose work made him a poet: Robinson Jeffers. Jeffers represented an "intellectual awakening and the first religious conversion, all in one." "When Jeffers showed me God in the cosmos, it took and I became a pantheist," and "that pantheism was based on a kind of religious sexuality," a sense of the universal life-force compelling all things in the sexual rhythm. Reading Lawrence a few years later confirmed for him the sacredness, even divinity, of natural life, but stylistically his lines adapted the expansive free-verse of Jeffers to his own verbal movement and timbre. Everson married Edwa Poulson in 1938 and began cultivating his own vineyard in the Valley. **"August"** is characteristic of much of the early poetry in its identification with the female earth so deep that masculine intellect relinquishes sovereignty and the poet yields virginal to the God of Nature:

> Smoke-color; haze thinly over the hills, low
> hanging;
> But the sky steel, the sky shiny as steel, and the
> sun shouting.
> The vineyard: in August the green-deep and
> heat-loving vines
> Without motion grow heavy with grapes.
> And he in the shining, on the turned earth,
> loose-lying,
> The muscles clean and the limbs golden, turns to
> the sun the lips and the eyes;
> As the virgin yields, impersonally passionate,
> From the bone core and the aching flesh, the
> offering.
>
> He has found the power and come to the glory.
> He has turned clean-hearted to the last God, the
> symbolic sun.
> With earth on his hands, bearing shoulder and
> arm the light's touch, he has come.
> And having seen, the mind loosens, the nerve
> lengthens,
> All the haunting abstractions slip free and are
> gone;
> And the peace is enormous.

That peaceful harmony was shattered by the Second World War. Everson's pantheism made him a pacifist; death and destruction in nature were part of the ecological cycle, but in the human order turned violational because egoistic and malevolent. The figure of the bloody warrior from his Nordic ancestry stalks the poetry of the late 30's as the Shadow-inversion of the feminine pacifist-pantheist. But when the holocaust broke, Everson retreated to nature and spent the years 1943-1946 as a forester in an Oregon camp for conscientious objectors. **"The Raid"** describes war as rape, and **"The Hare"** acknowledges the Shadow in himself with the awareness, "fathered of guilt," that we are all killers. Still, fascinated as he was and remained with assertive masculinity (Jeffers was similarly ambivalent), he chose the C.O. camp in the name of his feminine susceptibilities.

But only at great cost. **"Chronicle of Division"** recounts the personal crisis in the global disorder: the breakup of his marriage and the dissolution of his previous life. In 1946 he came to San Francisco to join the pacifist-anarchist group around Kenneth Rexroth who as writers were opposing the established academic poets and critics in the cause of open form and spontaneity. There he met and married the poet-artist Mary Fabilli. The sequences ***The Blowing of the Seed*** and ***The Springing of the Blade*** hymn their union and move the nature mysticism of the earlier poetry more explicitly into the area of human sexuality. But she was a lapsed Catholic undergoing a rebirth of faith, and through her ordeal Everson found his own life unexpectedly altered and clarified:

> It was my time with Mary Fabilli that broke both my Jeffersian pantheism and my Lawrencian erotic mysticism. She personalized this, her whole touch was to personalize, to humanize. . . . Also the intuition to which her course led me is that my mystical needs, my religious needs, which had not really been met in my pantheism, could only find their solution in the more permeable human context, and in a ritual and a rite, and in a mythos that was established in a historical continuity.

At Midnight Mass, Christmas 1948, Everson was overwhelmed, psychologically, almost physically, by the divine presence in the tabernacle, and that mystical encounter led directly to his baptism the next year. However, by a grotesque twist of irony, the previous marriages of both partners and the prevailing Church procedures at the time made it impossible for them to remain husband and wife. ***The Falling of the Grain*** deals with the wrenching ironies and the overriding commitment which underlay their decision to separate. Two years later he entered the Dominicans as a lay brother and served for almost nineteen years, during which time the poems written as Brother Antoninus made him a figure in the San Francisco Renaissance and the Beat Generation and a charismatic presence at readings on campuses around the country.

In fact, Everson's conversion and Antoninus' monasticism did not so much "break" his pantheism and erotic mysticism, as break them into a new set of circumstances and a new psychological and spiritual dimension. Now his life was centered on the Incarnation. Not an isolated historical event, but a daily miracle: the ongoing infusion of Creator into creation, supremely expressed in Jesus, the God-Man. The individual hangs on that cross, where all the contradictions of the human condition take on new consequence. The natural and the supernatural, soul and body, sexuality and spirituality—the Incarnation means that those seeming polarities, often vehemently at cross purposes, are meshed at the point of tension.

From the human point of view the Incarnation canceled out Original Sin, so that God could redeem man from the sinfulness which was part of his freedom. Everson had seen the killer in himself; like Eliot, he knew that the fallible will needed to be curbed by ethical restraints and external norms lest creative freedom become oppression or anarchy; and his penitential bent sought the stricter discipline of monasticism. But from God's perspective the Incarnation is the completion of the creative act. On the one hand, God could be seen as driven to descend into flesh to save soul from body: the vision of Lowell and Eliot. But on the other hand, God could be seen as having saved man in his human condition: not Spirit charging into flesh but Spirit embodied; not sinful flesh but transfigured body. The implications of this mystery were tremendous and dangerous, and Everson was driven to search them out. For when God became man, did He not submerge Himself in the sexual element? In fact, was not sexuality the manifestation of that submersion? Had He not chosen from eternity to move in and through the sexual polarity, so that our sexual natures disclose their divine impulsion? Then in the heart-beat, pulse-throb, sex-urge, the Incarnation unfolds the contingencies of time and space, and subsumes them. Now Antoninus found himself confronting these paradoxes in exactly the situation which would test them most severely: separated from the wife who was the saint of his conversion, bound by his own election to a vow of celibacy.

Consequently the poetry of Brother Antoninus is almost obsessively concerned with the Feminine—that is, not only women, but his own sexuality and the feminine component in his psyche which mediates his passional, instinctual and poetic life. Decades before he had read Jung's psychology his poetry was recording his own often conflicting encounter with the major archetypes: in the psyche of a man, the Shadow, who represents his dark, repressed, even violent aspects; the Anima, the woman within, who is his soul and leads him into engagement with his erotic and spiritual potentialities; and, most dimly, the Self, that achieved and transcendent personhood realized through the resolution of polarities, who reveals himself as the God within and of whom, Jung says, Jesus is the symbol and reality. Everson's poetry through the war had enacted an initial rejection of the Shadow; now the Anima became the primary archetypal focus in the struggle toward transcendence.

In the Fictive Wish, written in 1946 before meeting Mary Fabilli, is a marvelous evocation of what Everson was already recognizing as "the woman within":

> Wader,
> Watcher by wave,
> Woman of water,
> Of speech unknown,
> Of nothing spoken.
>
> But waits.
>
> And he has,
> And has him,
> And are completed.
>
> So she.

But what was the monk to make of her? Often she came to him as the dark temptress, allied with his own lustful Shadow and luring him on to what must now be sexual sin. Many of the poems in ***The Crooked Lines of God,*** written soon after converting and becoming a Dominican, excoriate the flesh, and the poems in the first half of ***The Hazards of Holiness*** churn in the frustration not just of lust but of his passionate nature. They recount, Everson has said, his own "dark night." **"A Savagery of Love"** makes Mary Magdalene, the patroness of the Dominicans, the image of the purified Anima, redeemed from whoredom into "a consummate chasteness," her passion focused on the Passion of the Incarnated God.

Now, in that divine identification the Anima could express her passionate nature. In **"The Encounter"** and several other remarkable poems towards the end of ***Crooked Lines*** Antoninus becomes the woman before God, his/her whole being called into activity by His totally mastering love. **"Annul in Me My Manhood"** opens with the prayer:

> Annul in me my manhood, Lord, and make
> Me woman-sexed and weak,

If by that total transformation
I might know Thee more.
What is the worth of my own sex
That the bold possessive instinct
Should but shoulder Thee aside?

"A Canticle to the Christ in the Holy Eucharist" translates the meditation into graphic imagery: the doe seized by the buck's wounding love on the slopes of Tamalpais, the woman-shaped mountain north of San Francisco:

In my heart you were might. And thy word was the running of rain
That rinses October. And the sweetwater spring in the rock. And the brook in the crevice.
Thy word in my heart was the start of the buck that is sourced in the doe.
Thy word was the milk that will be in her dugs, the stir of new life in them.
You gazed. I stood barren for days, lay fallow for nights.
Thy look was the movement of life, the milk in the young breasts of mothers.

However, by 1954 the stresses of the monastic life had dried up the inspiration, and it could resume again in 1957 only after a profound, shattering "breakthrough into the unconscious" the previous year, made possible by Antoninus' association with the Dominican Jungian Victor White, and by saturating himself in archetypal psychology. The result was a long narrative poem called ***River-Root,*** which is the most sustained orgasmic celebration in English, perhaps in all literature. Amongst the Antoninus poems collected into ***The Veritable Years, River-Root*** can be seen as a watershed: the turning away from the often austere asceticism of the years just after conversion back down again to primal nature, now transfigured in the mystery of the Incarnation. The narrative objectivity of the poem permitted Antoninus, while still under the vow of chastity, to render the intercourse between the husband and wife with a candor that, far from detracting from its sacramentality, climaxes in a vision of the Trinity. God's entry into flesh locates the sexual mystery, its source and activity and end, in the very Godhead.

River-Root, then, represented at once a recovery and synthesis and turning point. It opened the way back to poetry—and to the world. In ***The Hazards of Holiness*** the ascetic Antoninus struggled with and against the drift that had already begun to carry him, unaware, back to Everson. The last section of that divided volume expresses the full range of his experience of the feminine archetype: from the sexual force leading men to their death in the title poem (whether demonically, like Salome and the Baptist, or heroically, like Judith and Holofernes) to the Virgin mother and spiritual Wisdom of **"A Canticle to the Great Mother of God."**

Two crucial poems here state the paradox in personal terms. **"The Song the Body Dreamed in the Spirit's Mad Behest"** extends the erotic imagery of bride and bridegroom from ***The Canticle of Canticles*** to depict the plunge of God into corporeal existence in blunt sexual expression possible only after Freud and Jung in this century and possible for Antoninus only through access to the unconscious:

He is the Spirit but I am the Flesh.
Out of my body must He be reborn,
Soul from the sundered soul,
Creation's gout in the world's bourn.

Mounted between the thermals of my thighs
Hawklike He hovers surging at the sun,
And feathers me a frenzy ringed around
That deep drunk tongue.

And the counterthrust of the Incarnation lifts our straining sexuality until we too are reborn, borne at last to Godhead:

Proving what instinct sobs of total quest
When shapeless thunder stretches into life,
And the Spirit, bleeding, rears to overreach
The buttocks' strife.

. . . . .

Born and reborn we will be groped, be clenched
On ecstasies that shudder toward crude birth,
When His great Godhead peels its stripping strength
In my red earth.

"God Germed in Raw Granite" spells out the same reciprocating movement: God descending into the curves and folds of the female landscape; thence the "woman within" awakening the man erotically to the call of Spirit; and finally the synthesis of masculine and feminine twinned into a trinity by and with God:

I am dazed.
Is this she? Woman within!
Can this be? Do we, His images, float
Time-spun on that vaster drag
His timelessness evokes?
In the blind heart's core, when we
Well-wedded merge, by Him
Twained into one and solved there,
Are these still three? Are three
So oned, in the full-forthing
(Heart's reft, the spirit's great
Unreckonable grope, and God's
Devouring splendor in the stroke) are we—
This all, this utterness, this terrible
Total truth—indubitably He?

Could "she" remain merely the "woman within," the Anima arousing the monk to rapturous response to God? For if he is to find God not in some disembodied heaven but in the crucible of the heart, must he not run the risks, trusting in Him Whom the unconscious aches to disclose, and the passions burn to attain? **"In Savage Wastes,"** the concluding poem of ***Hazards,*** makes the decision to reenter the world; the way out of agonized self-absorption, like the way out of pantheism, was "the more permeable human context."

The Rose of Solitude tells of an encounter which moved him to his most exalted realization of the Feminine. The highest recognition that I can give the book, the final validation of poetry which refuses to distinguish between art and life, is the fact that it will leave the reader, too, shaken and transformed. The plot is not remarkable: Antoninus falls in love with a Mexican-American woman, breaks his vow of chastity with her, is led by her to repentance and confession; in the end they part. The remarkable quality stems from the character of the Rose herself. The sequence gradually reveals her and extols her as the apotheosis of the Feminine. Beyond the divisions which split body from soul, beyond the mental abstractions which man invents to cope ineffectually with those divisions, beyond his pity and self-pity, his hesitations, and recriminations, she emerges—all presence and act, all physical and spiritual beauty in one—spontaneous yet resting in herself, drawing him not by her will but by her being what she is.

The sequence is so densely and intricately woven that it is difficult to excerpt passages, but **"The Canticle of the Rose," "The Rose of Solitude"** and **"The Raging of the Rose"** are prodigious feats of rhetoric, the poet pitching language to the extremes of articulation (the prolonged compounding of multisyllabic philosophical concepts in the **"Canticle"**; the wild incantation and imagery of **"Solitude"**; the synthesizing of the two modes in **"Raging"**) in order to express the inexpressible fact that, in her, sexual sin becomes *felix culpa* and the Incarnation is accomplished. Accomplished in her, and, through his realization of her, in himself: **"The Raging of the Rose"** concludes with an affirmation of Selfhood sourced in the **"I Am Who Am"** of Genesis:

Rose!
Reality unfolded!

On the four wings of the Cross,
In the ecstasy of crucifixion,
In the blood of being,
In the single burn of beauty

BE!

So that
In you,
The consummate
Vision of Other:

In you
I AM!

But the relationship ends in separation: the monk returning to his cell, releasing her to her own life and to another relationship. The end of the book is muted—necessarily so, since the Rose has had to be experienced, for all her glory, as forbidden, alien finally to his chosen existence.

. . . . .

Thus, after all the years as Brother Antoninus, he still had not recovered, except in exalted moments, that unquestioned oneness which he had felt with nature in the mid-thirties. During the War his refusal of the Shadow-role of warrior had cast him, reciprocally, in a Shadow-relationship with the patriarchal institutions which said that he should fight. In middle age his commitment to the monastic ideal had made him, by contrast, ambivalent about "the woman within," though she was the source of his religious experience as well as his Muse.

It could be no simple duality. Everson had experienced Christianity "as a Dionysian phenomenon" at the time of his conversion and in subsequent moments of mystical transcendence; and, as he later recalled it, "this same movement took me into the monastery—to exclude everything from the ecstatic Dionysian core" in the life of Brother Antoninus. Dionysus symbolizes the Anima-dominated man, whose creative energy comes from his feminine affinities. In the myth Dionysus' opponent is Pentheus, the repressive law-giver, the chaste soldier-king. Dionysus is Pentheus' Shadow, but is it not true that Pentheus is Dionysus' Shadow as well, driving him to furious reprisals? What, then, of Everson and Antoninus? The situation is different because Antoninus is not Pentheus any more than Everson is simply Dionysus. If Everson and Antoninus are Shadows to each other, they are needed so within the single personality. Between them, even if we can distinguish twin aspects of the living person, lies no fight to the death, as with Pentheus and Dionysus, but a grappling toward accommodation, begun long before Everson became Antoninus. **"The Sides of a Mind"** in the late thirties is only one testimonial to how generic the struggle has been.

Thus, as psychic entity, the formative "Antoninus" had embodied a reflective, scrupulous, perfectionist dimension of character which got voiced in the earlier work mostly in his concern for revision and crafted statement. Later the monastically realized "Antoninus" brought to the work an emotional, spiritual clarity and an intellectual subtlety that made for the most powerfully achieved poems. Hence "Antoninus," whether craftsman or monk, was no extraneous imposition but constituted an inherent reality. As Everson's becoming Antoninus represented an extension and integration of identity, not a denial, so his departure from the monastery would not affect the alchemy of his character.

Still, the tension persisted. He could be a Dionysian Christian, but could he remain a Dionysian monk? In the late sixties he moved toward taking final vows, even while sounding more emphatically the erotic basis of spirituality. ***Who Is She That Looketh Forth as the Morning*** redresses the previous image of Mary as Wisdom in **"A Canticle to the Great Mother of God"** by retrieving for her, at the moment of conception by the Spirit, the erotic and chthonic powers of a goddess like Venus. ***Tendril in the Mesh,*** Antoninus' last poem as a monk, strives to assimilate and terminate another love-relationship with a woman by subsuming its graphic sexual details in an "Epilogue" which experiences Incarnation not as sanctified humanity but as animistic totem:

> Dark God of Eros, Christ of the buried brood,
> Stone-channeled beast of ecstasy and fire,
> The angelic wisdom in the serpentine desire,
> Fang hidden in the flesh's velvet hood
> Riddling with delight its visionary good.

After the first public reading of this poem in December, 1969, Brother Antoninus stripped off his religious habit and announced to his shocked audience that he was leaving the Dominican Order. Shortly thereafter he married, first outside the Church and later in the Church, Susanna Rickson, to whom ***Tendril*** is dedicated. They live near Santa Cruz, where Everson teaches at the University of California.

. . . . .

The precipitate departure indicated how much like a thunderclap it came, even to himself; and the poems of ***Man-Fate*** (1974) are the words of a man caught in a psychic crossfire: Antoninus become Everson again. During the years as Brother Antoninus, nature had remained a strong religious presence for him. The elegy for Jeffers, ***The Poet Is Dead,*** works almost completely through images of the California coast, and poems like **"The South Coast," "A Canticle to the Waterbirds,"** and **"In All These Acts"** project pantheism into Christian mystery. Now Everson withdrew again to nature to validate his break with Antoninus, but with a consciousness heightened and complicated by all that Antoninus had come to realize and value, and by the monastery life that Everson found it excruciating to leave behind. In the opacities of the elemental matrix, he would be healed or torn apart.

That venture into the primeval is enacted in a sequence of dreams and archetypal fantasies which comprise the climax of ***Man-Fate.*** In **"The Narrows of Birth,"** on Christmas night, twenty-one years after his conversion experience, he dreams of joining the clan gathered around the Great Mother of Nature. He bows before Her for absolution, but instead sees her followers begin the castration of a young man, whose body is "slumped in its unmistakably erotic swoon." The dreamer finds the Great Mother betraying him to join in the castration. The dream in **"Black Hills"** shows Everson fighting his way back in psychic as well as historical time to recover the Indians in all their splendid strength, and to seek the blessing of his dark, dead Father, whom he loves and whom civilization taught him to dread and kill. All but overwhelmed in the furious rush of the braves, he cannot wring a word of recognition from the Chief. In the aftermath of the dream he rises briefly to conscious acquiescence in the natural round, which the red men honored and the white men violated: "All Indian at last, / I lift up my arms and pray"; but even that moment is broken off anti-climactically.

The nightmares tell what Antoninus already knew: that one cannot give over to the Shadow; abandonment to the powers of darkness without a guide will end in dissolution, chaos, death. For the man, the Anima can be such a mediator. She is grounded in the Shadow-area so strongly that at times she seems merely its vassal and instrument: the Feminine as temptation or threat. But in coping with the Shadow the man also engages *her.* And if trusted and loved, she can free him from enslavement to the Shadow, mediating the unconscious and the passions, drawing them from blind automation into activity and actualization in masculine consciousness, and thus opening the way gradually to Selfhood: the apocalypse of the polarized personality into androgynous, undivided identity. The Self is the psychological equivalent of the Beatific Vision, glimpsed in our supreme moments, but mostly striven for through the polar rhythms of living. For in Selfhood the individual attains not just what is uniquely himself, but thereby attains participation in the Godhead in which we shall all find ourselves at last.

Under the onslaught of the Shadow in ***Man-Fate*** Everson's response is instinctive and right: he turns to touch his wife. She is the objective verification of the Anima: a somnolent but locating presence, waiting for his return from lonely contention with the Shadow. For after the powerful consolidation of the Anima in ***The Rose*** and the subsequent poems, now no longer alien and suspect but tallied in his marriage, she lies ready to wake again from drowsy abeyance to spring him into the next thrust towards Selfhood. The last words of the book are:

> I have made a long run.
> I have swum dark waters.
>
> I have followed you through hanging traps.
> I have risked it all.
>
> O cut my thongs!
>
> At the fork of your flesh
> Our two trails come together.
>
> At your body's bench
> I take meat.

Expressed in the archetypal terms of the human psyche, the Incarnation is God entering into, permeating and operating through the Feminine, just as the Annunciation proclaims. The concluding image above, physical yet suggestive of the sacramental act, constitutes, more immediately and elementally than with the Rose, the personalizing of the regenerative, redemptive mystery in the witness of the wife to the power of the Anima. Mother and wife and priestess in one, she administers him nourishment needed now for the way ahead.

ALBERT GELPI (ESSAY DATE 1998)

SOURCE: Gelpi, Albert. "'I Am Your Woman': The Erotic Mysticism of William Everson." *Religion and the Arts* 2, no. 2 (1998): 149-81.

In the following excerpt, Gelpi explores the religious themes and erotic mysticism in the works of William Everson, including River Root *and* The Hazards of Holiness *among others, with particular attention to the poet's interest in the feminine and its role in religion and spirituality.*

1

In a lightning-flash of discernment, William Everson knew himself as poet in the fall of 1934. He had contributed stilted verse in meter and rhyme to the high-school yearbook of his hometown Selma in California's Central Valley and to the literary magazine of Fresno State, where he was briefly a student. But his first poems in his own voice poured out from this sudden conversion, and from the outset his voice set him apart from the prevailing modes of his contemporaries. In the thirties he was neither a writer of political or proletarian protest nor a late-Modernist, language-oriented Objectivist like Louis Zukofsky or George Oppen. The Objectivists were eastern, urban, and sophisticated in ways that he had no wish to emulate, and even the circumstances of his single brief and ironic excursion into proletarian poetry expressed his contempt for that of the thirties poet as the fashionable construction of the eastern literary establishment.

Everson suspected that the rejection slips he was receiving from major reviews and monthlies reflected editorial bias against unpolitical poetry like his. In 1939, after another pink slip came, this time from *Poetry* magazine, he perpetrated a hoax to test out his hunch. He concocted "a facetious, hurried scrap with a social message" entitled **"The Sign"** and sent it to *Poetry* under the name "William Herber" (his mother's maiden name) with a biographical note in which he described himself as an itinerant "fruit bum" penning poetry in between labors in the fields (Bartlett 25-26). **"The Sign"** was snapped up and published with a breathless note from the editor, and Everson called the bluff with heavy scorn after a second faked poem of class struggle was quickly accepted by the magazine. **"The Sign"**'s final lines mimic the solidarity between the field-hand and the urban hoboes which was a shibboleth of the bourgeois left:

> And he in the field, hoeing,
> Heard the near train,
> And watching the cars saw who huddled in the
>   cold light,
> And their hands lifted, a sign,
> A symbol between them,
> The one sign caught between earth and sky,
> Like the meeting touch of their palms.
>
> (***The Residual Years*** 302)

The lines were written as pastiche, but it is easy to see how the harmonics of rhythm, pacing, and sound structure—which would become hallmarks of Everson's verse—might have moved the editors of *Poetry* to take the poem at face value. One of the several delicious ironies of this anecdote is that unlike most of the literary left writers and artists Everson was in fact a working class poet, and another irony is that even after the exposure of the hoax the editor of *Poetry*, secure in his presuppositions, replied that he would be interested in other "Herber" poems but not in any more "Everson" poems. Everson was marginal to the leftist literary establishment, partly because he was a Westerner, reared in rural California, but also because he was temperamentally a craggy and shaggy anomaly. His paternal grandfather had been a shoemaker in Norway who founded an evangelical sect called the Iversonians; his immigrant father was an itinerant newspaper printer who doubled as bandmaster, finally settling in Selma, California in the agricultural San Joaquin Valley; his mother was the daughter of German and Irish immigrants in rural Minnesota. Like "William Herber," Everson was largely self-educated, having been an indifferent student in the local high school and briefly at nearby Fresno State University; and like "Herber" he was in fact writing his pastoral poems after laboring in the fields of the muscat vineyard he worked with his wife Edwa.

What made Everson unlike "Herber" is that his pastoral poems were personal, not collectivist, and mystical, not political. Whitman was a revered forebear for many thirties writers, and of his generation Everson was the Whitmanian poet of earth and sexuality; but he was not the Whitmanian man of the people. He would have felt cramped and uncomfortable on the Brooklyn Ferry. At the same time, Everson's rooting of self in the mysticism of his local ground places him in the autochthonous tradition of American writers from Emerson and Whitman and Thoreau to Frost and Williams and Jeffers. In point of fact the epiphany that set his vocation in 1934—the words "epiphany" and "vocation" are not too strong—came when he chanced on a volume of Robinson Jeffers' poems while browsing in the library stacks at Fresno State. What he read on those pages precipitated his first conversion and made him at once a pantheist and a poet. Much later in his life he would write ***The Excesses of God,*** an exposition of Jeffers as a religious poet. Responding to Jeffers' evocation of the divine but brute beauty of his Carmel coastline, Everson touched mystery and transcendence in the vast distances, tumultuous skies, and rich fields of his own San Joaquin Valley. In the very year after his discovery of Jeffers, and of himself through Jeffers, ***These Are the Ravens,*** his first little paper-bound sheaf appeared (published partly at his own expense, as Whitman had done with the first editions of *Leaves of Grass*), and ***San Joaquin*** followed in 1939.

The poems began to show Everson's absorption of D. H. Lawrence as well as Jeffers as he intensified and humanized the erotic element in Jeffers' pantheism through the sexual mysticism of Lawrence's poetry. In the poem **"August"** the powerful evocation of the landscape reaches a climax at the end of the first verse paragraph as the virginal man in the fields yields to the power of the pantheistic sun.

> Smoke-color; haze thinly over the hills, low
> hanging;
> But the sky steel, the sky shiny as steel, and the
> sun shouting.
> The vineyard: in August the green-deep and
> heat-loving vines
> Without motion grow heavy with grapes.
> And he in the shining, on the turned earth,
> loose-lying,
> The muscles clean and the limbs golden, turns to
> the sun the lips
> and the eyes;
> As the virgin yields, impersonally passionate,
> From the bone core and the aching flesh, the
> offering.
>
> He has found the power and come to the glory.
> He has turned clean-hearted to the last God, the
> symbolic sun.
> With earth on his hands, bearing shoulder and
> arm the light's touch,
> he has come.
> And having seen, the mind loosens, the nerve
> lengthens,
> All the haunting abstractions slip free and are
> gone;
> And the peace is enormous.
>
> (***The Residual Years*** 25)

The man-virgin "comes" in the insemination of the sunlight and the elision from "has come" to "having seen" in the turn of the lines lifts orgasm into visionary transcendence. This early poem, like **"The Sign,"** places its protagonist in the fields, but the speaker is not "Herber" but Everson alone and communing with the cosmos. **"August"** stands as an adumbration of the erotic mysticism at the heart of all Everson's poetry.

These lines also show how quickly Everson absorbed and personalized the inspiration of Jeffers and Lawrence and made the long free verse line his own. The rich and dense syllabic texture and the strong stresses are at once extended and integrated by techniques that would characterize Everson's work henceforth: alliteration reminiscent of his Scandinavian and Germanic heritage (in the first lines alone, "haze," "hills," "hanging," "heat," "heavy"; "smoke" leading to all the sibilants of the second line; "green," "grow," "grapes"; the "v"s in "vineyard," "loving," "vines," "heavy"); assonance (again in the first lines only, "smoke," "over," "low," "motion," "grow"; "steel" twice, "green-deep," "heat"; "shouting," "without"); verbal repetitions ("vine," "clean," "come"); verbal modulations ("sky steel," "sky shiny as steel"; "shiny," "shouting," "shining"; "heat," "heart"; "turned," "turns," "turned"; "loose," "loosens"; "loosens," "lengthens"; "limbs," "lips," "slip"; "virgin," "nerve"); parataxis ("he has found," "he has turned," "he has come"); the accumulation of the coordinating conjunction "and" and of active participles ("hanging," "shouting," "loving," "shining," "lying," "bearing," "having seen," "haunting") concluding in a short, emphatic declaration: "And the peace is enormous."

But the enormous peace of this pantheistic vision was overshadowed and broken by the other prophecy Everson found in Jeffers: the impending threat of another world-wide war worse than the first, against which Jeffers was already sounding the alarm in the early thirties. With Jeffers he came to see war and deadly combat latent in the violence of the human ego, ready to erupt at the imminent flash-point. Jeffers adopted the embittered voice of "Cassandra" to rail in vain against World War II. In Everson the drumrolls and clamor of approaching battle sound dark warnings in early poems like **"Attila"** and **"On the Anniversary of the Versailles Peace,"** and when war broke, his deepening pacifism led him to the only public political stance he ever took in his life: the individual dissent of the conscientious objector. He spent much of the war in a number of work-camps in the coastal forests of Oregon, writing anti-war poems out of his own sense of alienation from his nation and printing them by hand from The Untide Press.

"The Raid" is an anti-war poem that encompasses and dooms both sides. The first part of the poem describes the air-strike by Japanese bombers on Pearl Harbor in terms of a brutal rape, but the second half follows the flyers, stunting in triumph, to their own emasculating death in the mother-sea when the home carriers are not at the designated point of rendezvous for return landing. Here is the last section:

> Only the wide waiting waste,
> That each of them saw with intenser sight
> Than he ever had spared it,
> Who circled that spot,
> The spent gauge caught in its final flutter,
> And straggled down on their wavering wings
> From the vast sky,
> From the endless spaces,
> Down at last for the low hover,
> And the short quick quench of the sea.
>
> (*The Residual Years* 120-21)

However, commenting on **"The Raid"** some years later, Everson saw in it not just an anti-war statement but also an unconscious enactment of his own imaginative impulse in which he projected on to the fated flyers the drive to immerse himself in the maternal matrix. In Everson's imaginative life as a poet, in his psychological and spiritual life as a man, the feminine plays the crucial role as the point of engagement and contest, of mediation and integration and transcendence. This drama of engagement and integration with the "other" in the man's psyche links the feminine with nature and with God and makes the feminine the mediatrix of the man's sexuality and spirituality. Inevitably, Everson's psychological engagement with the feminine was played out through his complicated relations with the women who played pivotal roles as muse and agent in a life characterized by dramatic turns: the doting mother whose love for her son made his father resentful and jealous, and the women who stand at every major crossroads.

The sequence **"Chronicle of Division"** finds Everson at the end of the war facing not just the ruins of a conflict he had opposed but the ruins of his marriage, because Edwa had forsaken him for an old friend while he was doing time in the CO work-camp. The chronicling of devastation and fracture within and without leads up to the powerful fifth section, entitled **"Sea,"** whose refrain of three slow-paced but insistent lines propels him again and again to immerse in the matrix:

> The film.
> The long stooping ledges.
> The drop.
>
> (*The Residual Years* 182, 184, 190)

"In the Fictive Wish" can be read as a sequel to **"Chronicle of Division"** because it marks his psychic re-emergence from the deeps through the agency of his water-woman. Here is a segment of imagined apparition and consummation:

> Wader,
> Watcher by wave,
> Woman of water;
> Of speech unknown,
> Of nothing spoken.
>
> But waits.
>
> And he has,
> And has him,
> And are completed.
>
> So she.
>
> (*The Residual Years* 215)

Lines canceled from the published text of **"In the Fictive Wish"** show that years before his immersion in C. G. Jung's writings Everson had intuited the androgynous nature of the self and the dynamics of individuation at the heart of Jungian psychology:

Does the truth tear?
That the self is whole,
Is undivided?
The man and the woman
Androgynous,
Wound in the haft
Of the body's bond?
Is it hence so hollow,
Now, that the inner is all,
Substantive pattern
By which all judgment
Marks its measure?
Self one with the self,
Woman within
Rich in reward?

(***The Residual Years*** 351)

In retrospect these prescient verses can be seen to prefigure much of the drama of all his subsequent poetry. Everson's intuitions are cast as questions because the affirmative answers implied by the questions are so awesome. The divisions within the embodied psyche are experienced in gendered terms—for the man his relation to the "woman within"—and the resolution of those divisions into an "androgynous" and "whole" self lies in the very mystery of the psyche's incarnation in the gendered body. The "substantive pattern" of the individual's "inner" identity is "[w]ound in the haft / Of the body's bond." The difficulty in achieving resolution is contained in the word "wound," which as a past participle modifying the "androgynous" union of masculine and feminine in the individual suggests the intimate "bond" uniting body and psyche but as a noun reminds us of the painful breach that must be healed by that union. Similarly, "half," in "the haft of the body's bond," echoes the more familiar word "half" but in itself can mean either "fixed abode, established ground" or "handle, especially of a cutting or piercing instrument" that can leave an open wound. The only factor left out of the volatile "pattern" adumbrated in these lines is the one that in a few years turned out to be the key determinant: the agency of God in this complex drama.

2

Everson had begun service as a conscientious objector in January, 1943, and was not discharged until July, 1946. Instead of returning to the San Joaquin Valley—his life there seemed over—Everson was drawn to the seacoast, specifically to the San Francisco Bay area, in part because of Robert Duncan's and Kenneth Rexroth's presence there. He had been in correspondence with them, and the intersection of Berkeley poets constellated around Duncan and the anarchist group constellated around Rexroth made for the San Francisco Renaissance, in which Everson found himself a brooding presence. When he met the poet-artist Mary Fabilli there in 1946, he felt instantly that he had found the woman he had been searching for. Their intense relationship led to marriage in June, 1948, but their married life was to last only a year—not through estrangement but, paradoxically, through their extraordinary symbiosis.

Mary was a born Catholic in the toils of rediscovering her faith. Everson was drawn into an inner quest of his own in part out of empathy with her and more deeply out of dissatisfaction with "my Jeffersian pantheism and my Lawrentian erotic mysticism" as an explanation of the mystery at the heart not only of nature but the individual self (Bartlett 112). By the time Jeffers was giving his pantheistic philosophy the name of "Inhumanism," Everson was restlessly seeking a more personalist basis of belief. The autobiographical prose narrative ***Prodigious Thrust,*** published only posthumously in 1996, is a soaring and delving account of his conversion; to the end of his days he said he intended it be an homage to Mary Fabilli as the mediatrix of his conversion. His search for a personal God brought him to read about the Church, and in the fall of 1948 he read Augustine's *Confessions* and identified with the saint's agonized quest so vehemently that in ***Prodigious Thrust*** he called it "my own book" (78). He began to accompany Mary to church, and at Midnight Mass, Christmas 1948, in the cathedral in San Francisco, as he gazed at the newborn Jesus to the crib to the side of the altar, he had an intimation of God not just as personal but incarnate. There, he would write, he experienced "for the first time that synthesis of sense and spirit I had so needed and never found. I was drawn across, and in the smell of the fir saw it for the first time, not merely as an existent thing, but as a created thing, witness of the Word, the divine Logos, who made all earth, and me, a soul in his own image, out of very love" (***Prodigious Thrust*** 94).

God was not just the divinity of nature but of human nature: not the faceless and self-subsistent "brute beauty" of the landscape, as Jeffers said, but the personal Creator transcendent yet immanent in creation, the Trinity of Persons incarnate in the multitude of human persons. "That was the night I entered into the family and fellowship of Christ" (95); the conversion of 1948 subsumed the conversion of 1934 and redefined the terms of his life. He would reflect later: "For me there was the earth, the Church, and the woman. The earth spoke to me of God, the Church spoke to me of worship, and the woman spoke to me of love" (***Prodigious Thrust*** 159).

Everson began catechetical instruction and was baptized on July 23, 1949, at St. Augustine's Church and with Augustine as his baptismal name. However, Mary's return to the Church and his reception into the Church did not mark the confirmation of their marriage but—in an ironic twist that tested their love and their faith—its severance, a severance they would have themselves to choose. In fact, they had separated a month before the baptism because, by the ecclesial marriage laws as interpreted and implemented at the time, Mary's previous marriage in the Church invalidated their civil ceremony at the same time that it precluded their making a sacramental union. The decision before them was to live in sin or to sacrifice the marriage which had seemed the culmination of their earlier and broken lives. The Portuguese proverb "God writes straight with crooked lines" was a paradox that Everson pondered for the rest of his life, and with remarkable courage the couple resolved to discover how God writes straight with their crooked and now divergent lives. The poetic sequence **"The Falling of the Grain,"** incorporated into the prose narrative of ***Prodigious Thrust,*** traces out the abjection and exaltation of Everson's acquiescence in the separation, a decision to which Mary, his mediatrix, was also fully committed. It stands, in his words, as a "testament to her, some final acknowledgment, in the glory of the thing that had befallen us" (***Prodigious Thrust*** 181). They would be white-haired and elderly before they would meet again, thirty-five years after their separation and only a few years before his death in 1994.

Everson threw himself into his spiritual and devotional life with an intensity remarkable even in a fervent convert. For companionship and solace he sought refuge in a Catholic Worker House in Oakland. Without warning one morning at Mass he had the most powerful mystical experience of his life. He described what happened in a notebook a couple of years later:

> I was seized with a feeling so intense as to exceed anything I had previously experienced. It was a feeling of extreme anguish and joy, of transcendent spirituality and of a great, thrilling physical character. I knelt in the pew, twisted to one side, the rosary wound in my hands, the tears streaming down my face.
>
> (Bartlett 120)

ON THE SUBJECT OF...

MARY FABILLI

Though Mary Fabilli is often linked with the Beat Generation, she never considered herself a part of the movement. Her association with the Beats came from her marriage to William Everson and through the inspiration her work gave to such poets as Robert Duncan. Fabilli's verse is informed and inspired by her Roman Catholicism and her Italian heritage. As she stated in a *Contemporary Authors Autobiography Series* essay: "All I'm trying to do is explain how I became a poet through the various experiences of my life. They are not the same as purely Wasp experiences, though I was affected by some of those too." Fabilli's publications include *The Old Ones* (1966) and *Aurora Bligh and Early Poems, 1935-1949* (1968).

Everson found himself again the yielding virgin, but this time not as "impersonally passionate" pantheist before the "symbolic sun" (as in the earlier **"August"**) but now as a Christian dazed and exalted before God radiating out of the eucharistic tabernacle:

> an intense invisible ray, a dark ray, like a ray of light seen in the mind only. I saw nothing with my eyes but I felt it powerfully in my soul. I knew instantly that the ray came from our Divine Lord, and further I knew that this ray was with the character of the Sacred Heart. It was utter concentration, the quintessence of love. It was as if all aspects of human love I had ever known, both spiritual and physical, were suddenly brought forward a thousandfold and thrust against my heart. It was as if His very lips, as if His Mouth wonderfully sweet, were pressed to my heart.
>
> (Bartlett 120)

The force of the possession slammed him to the floor of the church, at once aroused and yielding body and soul, the old oppositions between "spiritual and physical" seemingly superseded in the totality of surrender and realization.

A Freudian analyst would want to see his response as the displacement or sublimation of the erotic desire he had thwarted, but Everson intuited it as a deeper experience of the erotic, where sexuality and spiritually are understood not as the duality that afflict human nature but as coefficients of the grounding essence of human nature. Body and soul, sexuality and spirituality met and were joined at the cross-point of the Incarnation, the central and defining Christian mystery. What's more, the Incarnation did not just proclaim God's singular insertion into history in the person of Jesus—extraordinary as such an event is; but in addition the historical Jesus announced and signified for all time the Spirit's ongoing immanence in all material, bodily, and so sexual life. What were the implications and consequences of that even more awesome fact?

3

Everson began to ponder what the dark light that seized him body and soul intimated of the incarnational mystery in poems like **"The Encounter"** and **"Annul in Me My Manhood."** The apparent tension between sexuality and spirituality he knew for himself, and he could only start with that age-old dualism. His own experience as a man confirmed the association—newly explicated by Freudian and Jungian analysis—of controlling intellect and mastering will with aggressive masculine phallicism. When God became flesh, the Spirit entered the arena of gendered experience. How does the one Spirit operate in bodies gendered male or female? What does Jesus, the male victim of a masculinist culture, tells us about gender dualisms? How, from the human perspective, does the gendered individual experience the infusion of Spirit? "Male" and "female" are binaries that describe designations of physical and biological gender, as distinguished from "masculine" and "feminine," which are meant to differentiate psychological dispositions and attitudes. Doesn't the Incarnation, in fusing the divine and the human, fuse the human and the divine? And in so doing, doesn't the Incarnation locate personal identity within but beyond the binary of body and spirit and so within but beyond the double binaries, the external differentiation between male and female, and the psychological differentiation between masculine and feminine?

We know that we live within the stress and even violence of those binaries. Can we, suffering within them, reach beyond them? How do we realize the latent fact of the Incarnation in ourselves? The binaries turn inside out and back again, the paradoxes resolve only to dissolve again; but the still center of these whirling refractions is the Incarnation. When divinity and humanity were joined in the person of Jesus, their cross-point was a crucifixion. But in faith Everson believed that the crucifixion moved the conflict between eros and thanatos beyond the pessimism of Freud and Bataille. In Christ's Passion the agon ended not in death but in resurrection. The full historical unfolding of the Incarnation in Jesus' life moved from Bethlehem to Calvary to the open tomb, and the further unfolding of the Incarnation in each of our lives meant that the agon ended not in the annihilation of the self, as Freud and Bataille thought, but in the revelation of a new self more deeply grounded, more fully realized, more completely embodied and inspirited. The Incarnation offers not the end of belief but the beginning of the process of comprehending what belief in God's presence in us means. Somehow, in ways that we can only begin to understand, the violence of that meeting effectuated the resolution and transcendence of the dislocation between the human and the divine. From 1949 on Everson's poetry records his determination to enter the violence of that dislocation in the hope of reaching their Incarnational resolution.

"Annul in Me My Manhood" cites the great woman mystic Theresa of Avila observing that "The soul is feminine to God." That is to say, each person, male and female, must open and surrender himself and herself to the infusion of Spirit, the "impregnation" of "[f]ertile influxing Grace." The words of St. Theresa in the epigraph to the poem declare that the more instinctive "femininity" of women made it easier for them to accept that infusion. Theresa, anima as saint and mystic, guides Everson into modes of relation and response opposite to the aggressive assertiveness of the gendered and acculturated male in a patriarchal society. With her as mediatrix, therefore, he beseeches God to break his masculine possessiveness and prays for psychological and spiritual cross-gendering:

MAKE ME THEN
Girl-hearted, virgin-souled, woman-docile,
maiden-meek;
Cancel in me the rude compulsive tide
That like an angry river surges through,
Flouts off Thy soft lip-touches, froth-blinds
The soul-gaze from its very delight,
Outbawls the rare celestial melody.
Restless I churn. The use of sex is union,
Union alone. Here it but cleaves,
Makes man the futile ape of God, all ape

And no bride, usurps the energizing role, inverts;
And in that wrenched inversion caught
Draws off the needer from his never-ending
need, diverts
The seeker from the Sought.

(*The Veritable Years* 122-123)

In order to seek a more "feminine" disposition to God and in order to find a community in which he could have support in that search, Everson entered the monastic life with its vows of poverty, chastity, and obedience as a member of the Dominican Order. In June, 1951, at St. Albert's Priory in Oakland, he was received as a donatus, a lay brother without final vows, and was given the monastic name Brother Antoninus. In his first years as a religious, Antoninus was rigorous in his piety and devotions, but he found the emotional springs that fed his poetry drying up. In the first rapture of conversion he had written powerful religious poems, some, like **"Triptych for the Living,"** based on Gospel episodes, some, like **"A Screed of the Flesh,"** the convert's Jansenist castigation of the flesh as weak and sinful. The most famous, **"A Canticle to the Waterbirds"** (which became the signature poem opening virtually all of his many platform readings) celebrates the capacity of creatures like the birds on the California shoreline, supposedly "our lessers in the great hegemony of Being" to teach us "what a creature is / And what creation owes" because those birds are so "utterly seized in His supremacy" that they can act out their nature under His will without the alienating willfulness of the human ego and thus can "be His verification, / Outside the mulled incertitude of our forensic choices" (***The Veritable Years,*** 84-5).

But in the first years after Everson assumed the monastic discipline as Antoninus, he found his poetic output dwindling and worried that it would stop entirely. In compensation he threw himself into an ambitious project as a printer that would keep him at his hand-press for long hours day after day. He would design and print, page by single page, a limited edition of a new Latin translation of the Psalms. The task was so enormous, especially for a single printer, that he could not complete it, but the *Psalter,* even in its unfinished state, was immediately recognized as a monument in the history of hand-press books of the period. His writing during these early Dominican years concentrated on pouring out his emotions into the composition of ***Prodigious Thrust*** as an homage to Mary Fabilli and a celebration of the faith commitment that brought him to renounce life with her.

The stresses of Antoninus' spiritual and emotional life played a role in keeping him from the *Psalter,* and, not surprisingly perhaps, the sublimation of his libido into the writing of ***Prodigious Thrust*** was proving insufficient. His devotional rigor became a matter of remark and even some concern among his fellow Dominicans, but at the same time the fact that monasticism seemed to be sealing him off from the feminine and erotic matrix of his emotional life disturbed and frightened him. New poems dwindled to but one or two a year, and this constriction was an ominous sign for him not just as a poet but as a monk. Could he nurture his spirituality while denying his eroticism? Should he deny his erotic nature for the sake of his spiritual life? Could it be that the erotic was the source and ground of the spiritual? If so, could his eroticism function and flourish within the monastic vow of chastity? Could a monk be a lover?

The breakthrough that ended several years of aching sterility and self-questioning came in part through the guidance of Father Victor White, the British Dominican and Jungian who spent a year at St. Albert's and whose book *God and the Unconscious* (1952) sought to synthesize archetypal psychology with Christian theology. During White's residence in 1955 as visiting lecturer, he became for Antoninus a much-loved friend, a spiritual counselor, an intellectual mentor. At last, in July, 1956—Antoninus noted that it was on the seventh anniversary of Antoninus' baptism—release began with a dream in which he found himself confronting and confronted by a "superior" woman whose presence he later associated with his mother and also with his wives Edwa and Mary. He instantly recognized the momentous power and significance of the dream and for months thereafter furiously explored its implications in his journal. This exhausting and terrifying immersion in the unconscious was mediated through Everson's readings in Jung's psychology at the direction of White. Moreover, the purgative ordeal opened the way for the first new poem to erupt out of the renewed access to the "woman within"—Jung's "anima."

River-Root, the long fictional narrative in verse that emerged, marked a turning point in Everson's career. I have called it "the most sustained orgasmic celebration in English, perhaps in all literature" (***The Veritable Years,*** afterrword, 361). He later called it "a karmic fusion of Augustine, Whitman and Lawrence" (***On Writing the Waterbirds*** 96). Later, too, he could see that, besides the renewal of his own poetic and spiritual life, his poetic effort to sacralize and sacramentalize sexuality came at a crucial historical moment in postwar poetry and served as a counter to Allen Ginsberg's frenzied and mad promiscuity in *Howl.* His sense of the challenge of *Howl* is inscribed in the famous "San Francisco Scene" issue of *The Evergreen Review* (edited by Rexroth and published in the fall of 1957) where a segment of Ginsberg's sensational and apocalyptic poem appeared alongside several poems by Antoninus from the early fifties.

Also in contrast to *Howl, **River-Root*** is archetypally heterosexual, emphatically theological, and explicitly Christian. The narrative plot of ***River-Root*** imagines a long night of love-making between a married Catholic couple, so that the thirty-page description is contained and sanctified within sacramental marriage. ***River-Root*** is a go-for-broke poem that had to risk violating all the habituated intellectual and emotional constraints; Antoninus saw its justification and valorization in its very extremity. The effort to sacralize sex after the shocking excavations of Freud and Jung and the anatomical explicitness of Lawrence and Henry Miller and Ginsberg required that his long, strongly rhythmed, richly alliterative lines not only had to infuse the erotic plot with theological and mystical aura but also had to be as graphic and carnal in sexual detail as those secular forebears had been in their writings in order that the physical and the spiritual could match each other in intensity and in that shared, infused intensity cross and dissolve the dualistic boundaries imposed by rational differentiation.

At its measured and cumulative climax the "incarnational join" of the husband and wife at once fuses the two of them, body and soul, into one and yields a vision of the pair yoked in God as a tri-unity and thence yields a vision of the Trinity itself. The astonishing, shocking passage propels the genital into the sublime and the sublime into the genital:

> FOR THE PHALLOS IS HOLY
> And holy is the womb: the holy phallos
> In the sacred womb. And they melt.
> And flowing they merge, the incarnational join
> Oned with the Christ. The oneness of each
> Ones them with God.
>
> FOR THIS IS THE PROTOTYPAL
> Act of creation. Where the phallos
> Kisses the womb-nerve listening
> The Father is. And as the phallos flows
> So is uttered the Son. And as Father and Son
> Meld together, merging in love,
> So here Spirit flows, between taut phallos and
> tremulous womb,
> The male nerve and the female,
> Spirit moves and is one.
>
> (***The Veritable Years*** 141)

Mystics and spiritual writers have, of course, consistently resorted to erotic language and sexual imagery as the sublime human experience of finding one's self in surrender in order to articulate something of the overpowering and yielding encounter with the Beatific Vision, but even in that context these lines are shockingly, breathtakingly explicit. When theological commentators have spoken of the erotic language of the mystic, they have tended to treat the sexual act as an analogue to the ecstasy of the divine encounter. But by treating the sexual element as mere metaphor or figure of speech, albeit the nearest natural analogue, they keep the categories of grace and nature safely and ontologically distinct. By contrast, Antoninus' poetry seeks to apprehend the implications of the Incarnation by pursuing beyond figuration the essential eroticism of the mystical and the essential mysticism of the erotic. The language of the poetry seeks to be symbolic rather than metaphorical, typological rather than tropological; and the poems—almost always tormented, frequently dizzying, often sublime—stand as the record of stress pitched at and intimating transcendence.

Without claiming the insight of the great mystics, Everson/Antoninus sought the imaginative terms, beyond Whitman and Lawrence and Jeffers, beyond Freud and Jung, for a Christian understanding of erotic mysticism. He felt that as a twentieth century Christian he had to explore both the mystical dimension of the erotic, which Whitman and Jeffers had posited, and the erotic dimension of mysticism, to which St. John of the Cross and St. Theresa had given voice. The problem lay in the conflicted Christian attitude towards sexuality. Church teachings acknowledged the sanctity of sex within the permitted limits of sacramental marriage, but the dionysian power of the sexual drive so threatened the apollonian control of the will that Church felt compelled to emphasize the sinfulness of unrestrained concupiscence and the need for rational control. Antoninus knew the power of the dionysian; yet, as a Catholic and monk, he never advocated illicit sex or free love, as Lawrence and Ginsberg did, and always acknowledged the reality of sexual sin and the need for rational control. Nonetheless, his own experience and temperament drew him as a Catholic and monk and poet to recover what had been lost or glossed over in Church teaching: "the essential mystical purity of sex," "the presence in the sexual act of a high illuminate insight, entirely natural but nonetheless sublime, establishing a kind of unspeakable totality, that compels one to acknowledge in it a profound dispositive factor" (***Prodigious Thrust*** 242, 251).

The phrasing here is punctuated with the multi-syllabic latinate vocabulary of scholastic philosophy, but his meaning is clear. The sublime is where the erotic and the mystical meet in ascent and descent. Antoninus would not equate in any crude or reductive way John or Teresa's experience of God with that of the couple in ***River-Root,*** but he would see them as different and related modes of the sublime encounter. For "[i]s it not in the actuality of the sexual embrace that the material principle is incorporated in this union [with the divine], that the unifying force achieves incarnation, that the 'immaterial super-existence' [a phrase borrowed from Jacques Maritain] attains concreteness?" (256)

4

Antoninus did not know Georges Bataille's book *Erotisme,* first published in the 1950s during Antoninus' first years in the monastery but not translated into English till much later. Bataille was roughly Maritain's contemporary as a French philosopher, but secular and agnostic where Maritain was Catholic and scholastic. Nevertheless, Antoninus would have responded to Bataille's fixation on the erotic as he did to Maritain's scholasticism. For in his lapsed Catholicism Bataille's grasp of the erotic not finally as a biological drive but as the human drive towards mystical union resonates with Everson's obsessive theme. The difference lies in Bataille's agnosticism, which left human aspiration thwarted by hopeless dualism: the reality of desire and the impossibility of consummation. In *Erotisme* Bataille describes erotic desire as the limited human individual's drive to break open from his or her physical and psychological isolation into knowledge of and union with an other, and so in its highest or deepest reaches as the limited human individual's compulsion to break out of those bounds into knowledge of and union with the absolute Other. Eros and thanatos are the Janus-face of our human liminality. So isolate are the self and the other that our doomed efforts to bridge that existential gap result in violence to the self and the other. Final release from pain inflicted and endured comes only in death and as death; at that fatal cross-point speech fails and tortured desire falls silent at the void. The religious and mystical impulse in erotic desire propels us to the liminal extremes of what the human can endure as it verges on what lies beyond: for Bataille, probably nothingness.

But for a believing Christian like Antoninus, we are drawn not towards the void but towards the triune God, Father-Son-Spirit, and the Word uttered incarnate in creation empowers our speech even in those incomplete and liminal encounters. By crossing into the human, into the arena of erotic desire, God empowers us to utter in our mortal and bodily imperfection the indwelling of the Spirit. Language falters, as Bataille said, but does not fail utterly. Philosophical and theological language have a necessary conceptual function but move into the disembodied abstraction of rational discourse. The task of the poet, especially the poet of erotic mysticism, is to push the sensuality of language—its vivid and kinetic images, its rich and dense syllabic resonance, its strong and propulsive rhythms—to such extremes that verbal texture and resonance register the indwelling of Spirit, embodied and manifest in the erotics of poetic form.

Needless to say, the dangers run very high not just poetically but psychologically. Will the psyche collapse, will the poem fail under such extreme stress? The mystics served a strong warning to Antoninus. The Incarnation declares the union of the divine and the human at the highest and deepest levels, but in the ambiguous tension of our quotidian, in-between state the staggering disparity between the human and the divine makes even approaches to union, even the imaginative intimations of union risky, and the terms of such resolution violent. God cannot enter humanity without violence, and humans cannot encounter God without violence. Flannery O'Connor cited the following verse from the eleventh chapter of Matthew's Gospel and made the last clause the title of her second novel: "From the days of John the Baptist until now, the Kingdom of Heaven suffereth violence, and the violent bear it away." The mystery of the Incarnation is inseparable from the mystery of human desire and from its corollary and consequence, the mystery of human suffering, for both of which—the desire and the suffering—the Incarnation is also the resolution. Because of the dislocations and imperfections of the human, God's descent into flesh would require crucifixion, His and ours. Desire perverted to self-love has to nail Him to the Cross; desire seeking completion and transcendence has to mount the Cross and die into resurrection.

It was the burden and vocation of the poems of Antoninus' monastic years to explore the erotic mysticism that the Incarnation announces as the essential mystery of the human. Poem after poem presents the desire for crucifixion and the crucifixion of desire. Antoninus' readings in psychology gave his sense of the Cross a complex and dialectical meaning: its "intense phallic character," its feminine character as the fruitful tree of life, and the "union" of those oppositions in a *hieros gamos,* or holy marriage: "the prodigious thrust transfixed by the prone line of the horizontal, male and female interlocked, pinned together by the attraction each has for the other, Christ's Passion purifying the base generative symbol of the race" (***Prodigious Thrust*** 243, 255). **"In All These Acts"** plays out one drama of crucifixion in material creation in very much the dialectical terms suggested above.

The three verse paragraphs of **"In All These Acts,"** set off and paced by spaces, moves in a triadic development (thesis-antithesis-synthesis). The first paragraph presents a grisly but riveting account of the death by disembowelment of a buck elk caught in an avalanche along the Pacific coast; the second, the pantheistic assimilation of the mutilated and castrated elk, swept downstream to the tidal sea, back into the uninterrupted cycles of natural process. The poem would have ended here, if it had been written by Jeffers or by Everson before 1949. (**"Chronicle of Division"** ends with a long section, the only titled one, called **"Sea."**) But here the agony of the first scene and the healing of the second yield a further understanding of the action in the third paragraph:

In all these acts
Christ crouches and seethes, pitched forward
On the crucifying stroke, juvescent, that will
spring Him
Out of the germ, out of the belly of the dying
buck,
Out of the father-phallus and the torn-up root.
These are the modes of his forth-showing,
His serene agonization.
(***The Veritable Years*** 201)

The progression of paragraphs traces out the pattern: the castrating erotics of death; the maternal renewal; the immanent divinity that is the source and motive power and end of the mortal round.

The combination of "juvescence" and "spring" deliberately recalls Eliot's image in "Gerontion": "In the juvescence of the year / Came Christ the tiger"; "The tiger springs in the new year. Us he devours." But "crouches" and "seethes" gloss the fastidious eroticism of Eliot's phrasing with the brutality of Jeffers. At the same time, just as deliberately the language of the passage gives Jeffersian brutality Christian resonance through verbal echoes from Antoninus' reading of Gerard Manley Hopkins: from Hopkins' "Pied Beauty," "He fathers-forth whose beauty is past change"; from "No Words, There is None," "Pitched past pith of grief"; from "As Kingfishers Catch Fire," "For Christ plays in ten thousand places, / Lovely in limbs, and lovely in eyes not his." Antoninus' poem pushes the kinetic energy of Hopkins' "The world is charged with the grandeur of God" ("God's Grandeur") to the outbreak and subsumption of violence in the crucifixion of the buck, "caught midway between two scissoring logs."

It is of course the poet's consciousness that grasps the correlation between the buck's excruciation and the crucified Christ, for the consequences of the Incarnation are more fully realized in and by the human: in Hopkins' phrase, "I am at once what Christ is, since he was what I am" ("That Nature Is a Heraclitean Fire"). But the language of an Antoninus poem like **"The Cross Tore a Hole"** is more bluntly and violently sexual than anything in Hopkins, and is more shocking than **"In All These Acts"** because here Christ Himself replaces the buck as the focus of the erotic crucifixion. At one point in the poem, for example, "the seed sack of Christ's body" hung on the phallic Tree erupts at death into an orgiastic drench of love into the earth's womb, and so, says the poet, into "my womb":

My soul,
God's womb, is seeded
Of God's own.
My womb,
God's own, is sown
Of God's seed.
My soul,
Wombed of God's wonder,
Is seeded, sown.
(***The Veritable Years*** 115-116)

The three gnomic sentences, each beginning with "My" and a noun subject ("soul," "womb," "soul") completed by a present tense, passive verb ("is seeded," "is sown," "is seeded, sown") and a prepositional phrase ("of God's own," "of God's seed," "of God's wonder") turn the paradox round and round and inside out till the oppositions fall away: the soul enwombed and the womb ensouled; "In Thee, God, / I am Thou," Spirit enfleshed and me inspirited.

For the Catholic, communion is the daily sacramental sign and enactment of the double aspect of that "incarnational join." **"A Canticle to the Christ in the Holy Eucharist"** invokes another Theresa as anima-saint-muse: this time St.

Thérèse of Lisieux, the late nineteenth century Carmelite nun sustained in her brief life and early death by contemplation of the Incarnation doubly manifest in the Infant Jesus, innocent and vulnerable, and in the Sacred Heart, crowned with thorns and bleeding from the lance's pierce. The poem's meditation on reception of Christ incarnate, body and blood, in the eucharistic bread and wine is elaborated through the baroque conceit of a doe's impregnation by a buck on the wooded slopes of Tamalpais, the mountain that bulks above the Bay area in the shape of a supine woman. The conceit first presents Christ as "the buck that stamps in the thicket" and the poet-communicant as the "fallow doe in the deep madrone" waiting to be taken by the rampant buck.

But, as in all sacrificial mysteries, the pressures focussed at such extremes of psychic and spiritual experience turn opposites into each other in a reversal that Jung gave the cumbersome name "enantiadromia." The poem turns on the inversion of roles played by the "I" and the "you," Christ in the Eucharist. At first Christ is the rampant buck planting his quickening paternal seed, and the speaker is the maternal doe quickened to new life and full breasts. The buck's drenching stroke wounds the doe, but her sexual wound bleeds into birthing the new born and the milk to feed him. But almost immediately the relationship between "I" and "you" starts shifting: from I-doe and you-buck to you-doe and I-fawn. In human terms Christ the bridegroom-father becomes Christ the nursing mother: not one or the other but androgynously both; and that doubling makes the speaker both pregnant bride to the Christ-sire and suckling son to the Christ-mother. The wounder and the wounded become the "wound-made-one"—source and vessel, from which and into which the rush of water/wine/blood/semen/milk flow. "For each in that wound is each, and quick is quick, and we gaze": "The double gaze and the double name in the sign of the quenchless wound" (***The Veritable Years*** 120).

Two representative stanzas from the middle of the poem elaborate these inversions and convergences:

In my heart you were might. And Thy word was
the running of rain
That rinses October. And the sweetwater spring
in the rock. And the brook in the crevice.
Thy word in my heart was the start of the buck
that is sourced in the doe.
Thy word was the milk that will be in her dugs,
the stir of new life in them.
You gazed. I stood barren for days, lay fallow for
nights.
Thy look was the movement of life, the milk in
the young breasts of mothers.

My mouth was the babe's. You had stamped like
the buck in the manzanita.
My heart was dry as the dugs of the doe in the
fall of the year on Tamalpais.
I sucked thy wound as the fawn sucks milk from
the crowning breast of its mother.
The flow of thy voice in my shrunken heart was
the cling of wild honey,
The honey that bled from the broken comb in
the cleft of Tamalpais.

(***The Veritable Years*** 119)

The language here, as always in Everson's work, is intricately rhetorical, but the rhetoric is integral to the performative action of the poem. The proliferation of nouns trailing prepositional phrase and modifying clauses over-lay each other in a palimpsest of transparencies. The long, insistently anapestic lines press forward, spinning out and gathering in the shifting details into full consonance.

From start to finish Everson/Antoninus' poetic agon—and it has to be read as a man's agon played out in the archetypes of patriarchal history—transpired under the sign of woman. The exploration of erotic mysticism—his persistent and defining theme—took on fuller range during the Antoninus years because the celibate and contemplative character of his Dominican life intensified the terms of the paradox, and thereby elevated and deepened both their theological and erotic register. In the poems erotic mysticism manifests itself in two complementary aspects or impulses that open into and revert into each other, interpenetrating like the double helix or the cones in a gyre. In his mystical aspiration the male learns from St. Theresa that "'The soul is feminine to God,' / And hangs on impregnation" (***The Veritable Years*** 122). He has to summon his anima as mediatrix, and through his identification with "her" he strives to experience himself as woman before the omnipotent and transcendent Deity. Like Mary at the Annunciation, like St. Theresa in ecstasy, he becomes the fleshed vessel for the Spirit's insemination.

5

The most extreme poetic statement of this aspect of erotic mysticism is **"The Song the Body Dreamed in the Spirit's Mad Behest,"** written in the late fifties. [. . .]

Citing Hart Crane's use of this stanza in "The River"and "The Dance" sections of *The Bridge,*

Everson has commented that he felt impelled to compose this particular poem in sapphics instead of the more unfettered free verse line, because the very wildness and ferocity of the imagery and emotions needed the restraining counter-pressure of meter and rhyme and end-stopped stanzas. In effect, the final line of the end-stopped stanza, tightening from five to two beats and completing the rhyme with the second line, provides a periodic check on the powerful forward drive of this divine seduction. By Everson's own testimony poems like **"The Song the Body Dreamed"** and ***River-Root*** seek to press his imaginative meditation on the erotics of Incarnation to the limits because on the one hand he was writing for a secular culture saturated with an explicit and secular sexuality that needed to be sacramentalized and because on the other hand he required extreme statement to resist the fearful repression of sexuality in the ascetic strain within Church tradition. And here again the celibate life of the monastery exerted maximum pressure on his exploration of the Incarnational implications of erotic mysticism.

"A Frost Lay White on California," another poem in ***The Hazards of Holiness,*** renders an opposite but complementary aspect of erotic mysticism with similar bluntness and even crudity: not here, as in **"The Song the Body Dreamed,"** the "feminine" human's submission to God, but—in some ways more startlightly—God's "feminine" submitting to the human. For humans—again whether men or women—encounter God not in the realm of Spirit but in the flesh and blood of the body, not in "His" transcendence but in "Her" immanence. Donald Gelpi's *The Divine Mother* traces out the theological tradition that has from earliest Christian history imagined the Spirit as the feminine aspect of the Trinity. And in her recent study *Jesus as Mother,* the historian Carolyn Bynum examines a strain of Christian spirituality which puts the writings of contemplatives like Dame Julian of Norwich into a rich tradition of religious thinking and devotional practice quite at odds with masculinist norms and categories.

The Incarnation means that Jesus, the God-man, was born of woman and the Spirit. As a result Mary was elevated to a unique position in the Catholic tradition: one that has celebrated her as the mediatrix of all graces and the mother of the universal Church. It is true for the most part that Marian devotion has been assimilated and even institutionalized into the structures and pronouncements of the historical Church in ways that serve the purposes of the patriarchs. However, another manifestation of the Incarnation has received less institutional reflection and emphasis. Jesus' humanity not only connected him materially to His mother and thence to all of us, but defined itself in a life and set of teachings that institutional patriarchal power perceived as threateningly "feminine," so that in the end the priests delivered Him to the Roman procurator for crucifixion. Moreover, the reach of the Incarnation into history extends the Sign of the Cross generation after generation, person by person, as the Spirit incessantly assumes the material condition of mortal creation, enters again and again the contradictions of gendered life that each time and for each man and woman meet and are joined at Cross-point.

One of the consequences of the Incarnational mystery, therefore, is that in the gendered psychology of our acculturation God in material form is perceived and experienced as mother and woman. However, that manifestation inevitably came to bear the negative valence of patriarchal culture. Specifically, in the Jewish culture in which Jesus lived and died, and in the larger Middle Eastern and Greek culture in which His teachings were formalized into Church, patriarchal values were further re-enforced and given a kind of sacral authority by the gnostic asceticism of groups and cults, both within Judaism and in the Gentile cultures of the region. In its various forms—Augustine's early manicheism is the best known—gnosticism conceives of existence in a radical dualism which sets divine and human, good and evil, spirit and matter, soul and body into irreconcilable opposition and reduces mortal existence to entrapment of soul in a physically and spiritually corrupt and corrupting body from which soul must be released and freed at death into the realm of Spirit. And because gender was experienced as constituting a primary human differentiation, these binaries became genderized and those gender associations became fixed oppositional valences: light and spirit associated with the masculine and so with men; dark and materiality associated with the feminine and so with women.

Christian Incarnationalism demolishes and supersedes such radical dualisms, but the human and historical circumstances of the cultures in which the Church took form and direction resulted in the infusion and adoption of gnostic assumptions, from Augustine and other early theologians and Church Fathers, that actually contravene the implications of the essential Christian revelation. As a result, the ascetic tradition of the Church tended to set spirituality against sexuality, and one culminating expression of that gnostic asceticism was the monastic discipline under which Antoninus was living. It is no accident that he chose Augustine as his baptismal name. The *Confessions* spoke forcefully to Everson in 1948 and continued to speak forcefully to Antoninus; the poems are wracked by a gnostic tension between spirit and flesh. But the power of the poems lies in the resistance to that gnostic opposition in the effort—admittedly often tortured and conflicted—to break the possessive control of the alienated ego and lay himself open to being possessed by the erotic mysticism of the Incarnation.

"A Frost Lay White on California" breaks the gnostic taboo more shockingly even than **"The Song the Body Dreamed"** by revealing the God-Lover as woman. The epigraph to the poem is a verse from Deuteronomy voicing the patriarchal proscription of sexuality as carnal and unclean, and so female and animal: "Thou shalt not offer the hire of a strumpet, nor the price of a dog, in the house of the Lord thy God, whatsoever it be that thou hast vowed: because both these are an abomination to the Lord thy God." The narrative begins with Antoninus, anguished and alone in the bitter-cold, night-bound chapel at St. Albert's Priory, "My two arms crossed on my chest." The poem then goes on to imagine God entering the temple, despite all that he has vowed, precisely as a dog and strumpet, to seduce the monk's clenched heart.

God's blunt declaration "I am your image" inverts the Genesis notion of the creature made in the Creator's image, and then "He" persists in interrupting the monk's silent resistance with series of italicized outbursts of questions and exclamations that cumulatively explicate God's human "image" in the forbidden terms:

> "Do you know what I am?
> I am your woman.
> That is my mouth you feel on your heart,
> Breathing there, warming it.
> I am more, I am your dog.
> That is my moan you hear in your blood,
> The ache of the dog for the master.
> I am your dog-woman.
> I grieve a man down,
> Moan till he melts."
>
> (***The Veritable Years*** 182-183)

Again a little later:

> "You are of flesh," cried God, "that is your light!
> The shimmering sensitivity of the nerve.
> Not I!
> No brain to think with!
> No nerve to think through!
> I am dog in that I follow,
> Woman in that I love.
> Seek me!
>
> . . . . .
>
> Flee that Luciferian
> Light of the brain,
> Pride of your life!
> Down! Down! Behind! Below!
> Quick! I am gone!
> I, woman, moan against the bars,
> I, dog, bay against the dawn."
>
> (***The Veritable Years*** 183)

The inversions—I-you, God-man, man-woman, dog-woman, God-dog, God-woman—build to convergence: *"be what I am / Which is—yourself! / The you who am I!"*; *"I, the God-dog! / I am all woman!"* Omnipotence has, appallingly, willed dependence on the human will, the velleities of human consciousness, but that divine abasement is the condition for soliciting—wooing, winning,—human consent.

"I am your woman": God's cry has made him, for that moment of realization at least, a different man. The poem that begins with crucified paralysis ends with the dawn wind and rain, "woman-wind . . . trying for rain," blowing "out of the terrifying helplessness of God" to thaw the frost outside the chapel and melt the monk's heart within the stone walls. Wind and rain also come as potential agents of transformation at the end of "What the Thunder Said," the climactic and concluding turning-point of *The Waste Land,* and though Eliot's and Everson's poems are psychologically and spiritually very different, there are telling correlations, Eliot's terms are, of course, less explicitly eroticized and gendered than Everson's, and the Thunder speaks with the transcendent omnipotence of Yahweh. But the terms of His Sanskrit message, thundered with masculine omnipotence, actually prophesies release from human impotence in a more "feminine" attitude: break the will of the emprisoning ego, surrender control, If the women in Eliot's early poems represents the sinful, sexual body, the Lady in *Ash Wednesday* represents the soul "feminine to God"; she mediates the Incarnation, the mystery described in "The Dry Salvages" as "[t]he hint half guessed, the gift half understood." Eliot's enormous stature as a poet and specifically the Puritan/Calvinist cast of this Christian witness served to impel Antoninus to plumb the Incarnation more deeply than Eliot's gnostic distrust of the body allowed.

The juxtaposition of **"The Song the Body Dreamed"** and **"A Frost Lay White on Califor-**

nia" is enlightening, therefore, because the two poems voice complementary aspects of Everson's erotic mysticism by gendering the dual reality of the Creator as at once transcendent to Creation and immanent in it. In one dimension of the human experience of God, men and women receiving the infusion of His empowerment call out to Him: "I am your woman." At the same time, however, God incarnate is dependent on the contingencies of human choice and calls out to men and women "I am your woman" for their consent to Her indwelling. In the gendered terms of human existence God knows us—and we know God—as inseminating spirit and inspirited flesh.

In these and other poems on erotic mysticism the poet has not penetrated the Incarnational mystery sufficiently to reach beyond the old gendered binaries. The mystics may have gone farther, but perhaps in our fallen human condition no one can leave these divisions behind. Yet with the mystics Everson felt that both flesh and spirit hunger for

> something beyond the blood of the beast, some finer, more favored marriage than body and spirit had yet known, but might aspire to—not sexless, not soulless, but a mastery of the two, a fulfillment at a rare level, which loosed them from their urgency, and made them govern toward a more stable norm.
>
> (***Prodigious Thrust*** 125)

As a poet Antoninus felt called to "aspire to" that "more favored marriage" of body and spirit by using his imagination to disrupt the old categories, turn them inside-out and upside-down—though the presence of the word "mastery" betrays the difficulty of shedding the assumptions culturally encoded in body and spirit.

6

Not surprisingly the extraordinary strain that accompanied the poems of erotic mysticism after ***River-Root*** spiraled down into what Antoninus has described as his contention with the shadow, his "dark night of the soul," and those tensions are recorded in ***The Hazards of Holiness*** (1962). Speaking of himself in the third person in an "Afterward" to ***River-Root,*** he noted that while in the development of Christian spirituality monasticism arose from the "attempt to curb the power of sexuality over the emergent spiritual energies," still "Brother Antoninus' dark night was directly due to the repression of Eros which monasticism necessarily entails" (***On Writing the Waterbirds*** 88-9).

Again this time, as with Mary Fabilli, clarification came when the image of woman as muse and mediatrix found agency in an actual woman. Brother Antoninus met Rose Moreno Tannlund, a Mexican-American woman in whom sexuality and spirituality (as with Mary) were not crossed but fused into a passionate identity. He would later reflect:

> In ***The Hazards of Holiness*** I went step by step through my encounters with the shadow. Part of my assault on the psyche was an attempt to depotentiate the shadow, get it in the open where I could deal with it. This worked, but at the same time made me very vulnerable to the anima, when she came in the form of a woman.
>
> (Bartlett 179)

By the time ***The Hazards of Holiness*** appeared with the permission of his religious superiors, he was in the midst of the book-length "love-poem sequence" that was published as ***The Rose of Solitude*** (1967), in many ways his most sustained poetic achievement and the culmination of the Antoninus years. The love of Antoninus and Rose never reached physical consummation but was sufficient in their minds to constitute an infraction of his vows. Yet in the convoluted workings of grace that very lapse becomes the Augustinian *felix culpa*—a fall redemptive in its consequences. The circumstances of their love require that they choose separation over the mysticism of married love that he had imagined in ***River-Root,*** and again, as with Mary, the example and inspiration of the woman's passionate and unwavering adhesion to God's will returns the monk to his vows.

The autobiographical narrative is told in clusters of interlocking lyrics written in short, staccato, syllabically compacted lines, but two extraordinary apostrophes to the Rose—**"Canticle to the Rose"** and **"The Rose of Solitude"**—stand as the pivot on which the drama turns. Here are two strophes towards the end of the ten-page **"Canticle to the Rose,"** written in expansive lines rhetorically elaborated all along their length:

> And if I call you great, and if I call you holy, and if I say that even your sins enforce the sheer reality of what you are,
> Know that I speak because in you I gaze on Him, by you I see Him breathe, and in your flesh I clasp Him to my breast.
> So saying, let me confess the preeminent masterhood that is creation's term,
> And in your presence salute the transcendent Presence out of which you came.
> Born of the Father, like Venus from the sea, you bear the beatific Ocean's witness of divine abyss,

To pierce, in time, to the divine abyss from
which you briefly dawned.

. . . . .

Pride of the presence, bride of the translucent
Night, daughter of dawn and the resurgent
Day,
Bestow on me once more your smile of essence,
conferring in your grace my own reality,
Endowing as your perfect otherness my shape of
man, that freed from my sickliness of soul,
I might, in Christ, achieve all that as a man I
must. And of such grace
Let me once more clasp in my arms the meaning
of your fiery spirit, and burn upon my heart
your perfect signature.

Where the terse, compacted lines of the short narrative lyrics relive the passion of their fall, here the rhetoric of the "**Canticle**" circles higher and higher, stretches further and further, mingling the language of theology and passion into a sublimation of their love into love of the incarnate God. To those who objected, as some male readers and many feminist readers did, that he was talking not to Rose Tannlund but to himself, was using her to celebrate himself, he replied with unshakable conviction that he had known Rose as he had known Mary, and that he come to know God and himself in her very real presence, for which the poem was but a "signature." Different as "**The Rose of Solitude**" and the virginal Lady of *Ash Wednesday* are, they share in the archetypal power of the Marian mediatrix of grace; unlike the Lady, however, Rose was its embodiment as well as its apotheosis.

Mary led him to the monastery and Rose returned him to it. But Antoninus' meeting with Susanna Rickson, a woman just eighteen, thirty-five years his junior, brought him, to the breakpoint that ushered in the last phase of his life and poetry. In the fall of 1965, he agreed with great reluctance to see Susanna for counseling at a friend's insistence. The love that developed between them precipitated a long crisis over his vocation. ***Tendril in the Mesh*** mythologizes the lovers as Pluto and Persephone and seeks to sacralize their love by an invocation of the "dark God of Eros." After years of praying and self-examination, Antoninus read the poem publicly for the first time in December, 1969, at the University of California, Davis, and then told the stunned audience that he was leaving the Dominican Order to marry Susanna.

Deep in a canyon off the Santa Cruz coast, they settled in a cabin beside Big Creek in a glade he called Kingfisher Flat. Everson once more after almost two decades as Brother Antoninus, he adopted leather jackets and a bear-tooth necklace as the sign of his return to nature. ***Man-Fate*** is his transitional volume (1974). However, Everson regarded this return to nature not as a reversion to an earlier pantheism but rather as an immediate engagement with the mystery of the Incarnation alive in the round of material life and in the torque of human love. The poems of ***The Masks of Drought*** (1980) and its coda ***Renegade Christmas*** (1984) make the topography of Kingfisher Flat, gripped by the deadly drought that dried up California in 1976-77, into the symbolic landscape of a psyche desiccated by the onset of old age and impotence.

There is no explicit theologizing now, but the language is so charged with psychological and theological implications that the giant redwoods and the densely thicketed hillsides, the creek flowing seaward from the falls upstream, the birds and animals and fish of the canyon present a microcosm of Everson's climacteric. As before, release comes in the end with the female flux: "Woman and water in the blood-flow" (***The Masks of Drought*** 16). Rains soak the land and swell the creek; and the poet's emotional paralysis dissolves in twinned epiphanies of ascent and descent: the awakening of "God-awe" through "The High Embrace" of the giant redwoods paired (like Baucis and Philemon in ancient myth) beside the Everson's cabin, and the erotic renewal of husband and wife in the baptism of "Stone Face Falls" under "the cry of the kingfisher" (***The Masks of Drought*** 84, 89). Everson echoes Gerard Manley Hopkins' and T. S. Eliot's and Robert Lowell's invocation of the kingfisher as the Christ-presence, but he gives the image his own valence; for Everson the kingfisher's "cry" combines a summons and an expression of pain, an annunciation and a crucifixion in what we heard him describe (in the poem "**In All These Acts**") as the "serene agonization" of incarnational renewal.

Everson's last years were increasingly overshadowed by the irreversible effects of Parkinson's disease. As Susanna found the circumstances of their life in the isolated canyon increasingly difficult, Everson faced another separation. He and Susanna went their separate ways in September, 1992, on his eightieth birthday. The Dominicans had welcomed him back to St. Albert's in the early nineties for a celebratory reading. He died at Kingfisher Flat in June, 1994, and after a wake and a funeral Mass in the chapel at St. Albert's, at which Mary, Rose, and Susanna were present, he was buried in the Dominican cemetery in nearby Benicia.

7

It had been a long, crooked way from the muscat vineyard outside Selma to Kingfisher Flat, and Everson had years before resolved to call his collected poems, organized into three volumes (Everson-Antoninus-Everson) ***The Crooked Lines of God.*** As the central Christian mystery, the Incarnation posits the union of divinity and humanity from all eternity, a union to be realized again and again, personally and collectively, through time. Thereby the Incarnation posits the redemption of men and women in their humanity, body and soul, one by one and together, as they suffer out through time their integration and transfiguration.

Earlier I described the complementary aspects of Everson's erotic mysticism as spirals in a double helix or interlocking cones in a gyre: he experienced God in transcendence as "He" and God in immanence as "She." Moreover, his dionysian Catholicism stands in stark contrast to the religious imagination of T. S. Eliot and Robert Lowell—both, like him, converts: Eliot an Anglo-Catholic from about the age of forty, Lowell a Roman Catholic during his twenties. The Calvinist, gnostic temperament of both Eliot and Lowell, which sought relief in Catholicism, continued to keep them embroiled in the contention between nature and grace, body and soul, hidden God and sinful humans. The Christian poetry of both came to its finest and final expression in books, *Four Quartets* and *Lord Weary's Castle,* that found the redemptive power of the Incarnation in the apocalypse of World War II. Eliot's deep-seated conviction of human fallibility, which has made a bloody mess of history, allowed him to glimpse the Incarnation only as "the hint half guessed, the gift half understood," and he could only stoically await release from the corruption of flesh into a dimension where at last he could grasp the fire and the rose as one. Lowell strained to sustain his will to believe but could imagine the Incarnation only in terms of the annihilation rather than the redemption of humanity. So "Colloquy in Black Rock," written near the end of the war, has Christ walking on the fouled waters of creation rather than plunging into baptismal immersion, and the final lines depict Him divebombing His violent people and blasting them to bits. Not long after "Colloquy" Lowell left the Church to continue his colloquy with his unappeased soul in elegiac jeremiads of secular damnation.

The Augustinian strain in Everson's Catholicism made him, not unlike Eliot and Lowell, feel the wrench of gnostic dualisms. After his own conversion Everson had observed: "There is a persistent, under-occurring attitude of Christian piety, in this country rooted in the psychological remains of continental Jansenism, yoked to the native puritanism, which suspects sexual delight itself as being sinful . . ." (***Prodigious Thrust*** 221). But the distinctive fact of his religious life and his poetry is that he strove to push past those dualisms in the name of the Incarnation. Where Eliot's Christianity is ascetic, conservative, and apollonian—"masculine," if you will—Everson/Antoninus' strives to become radically "feminine," incarnational, and dionysian. It risks itself to the implications of the Incarnation in ways that Eliot could not countenance and Lowell failed to achieve. Everson/Antoninus' poetry is psychologically, emotionally, and theologically bolder and more liberating than theirs: at once more disturbing and more consoling, more violent and more healing. And for that reason he is the most important Christian poet writing in English in the second half of this century.

The lines that conclude **"The South Coast,"** a poem from ***The Crooked Lines of God*** (1959), his first volume as Antoninus and his first use of that title, can serve as epigraph—and now epitaph—for his large and impressive body of work:

> God makes. On earth, in us, most instantly,
> On the very now,
> His own means conceives.
> How many strengths break out unchoked
> Where He, Whom all declares,
> Delights to make be!
>
> (***The Veritable Years*** 121)

The Spirit's delight in insemination and gestation, the flesh's declaration of Spirit: again, the double helix of Everson's erotic mysticism. And the lovely pun on "clarus / light" in "declares, / Delights" underscores the linkage between language and vision that is the matrix of Everson's poetry.

Works Cited

Bataille, Georges. *Erotisme; Death and Sexuality.* 1957 (in French). Trans. Mary Dalwood. San Francisco CA: City Lights Books, 1986.

Bartlett, Lee. *William Everson: The Life of Brother Antoninus.* New York: New Directions, 1988.

Bynum, Carolyn Walker. *Jesus as Mother: Studies in the Spirituality of the High Middle Ages.* Berkeley CA: University of California Press, 1982.

Eliot, T. S. *Four Quartets.* New York: Harcourt, Brace, 1943.

Everson, William. *The Blood of the Poet: Selected Poems of William Everson.* Ed. Albert Gelpi. Seattle WA: Broken Moon Press, 1993. A single comprehensive volume of Everson's poetry that includes almost all of the poems discussed here.

———. *The Hazards of Holiness.* Garden City NY: Doubleday, 1962.

———. *The Masks of Drought.* Santa Barbara CA: Black Sparrow Press, 1980.

———. *On Writing the Waterbirds and Other Presentations.* Ed. Lee Bartlett. Metuchen, NJ: Scarecrow Press, 1983.

———. *Prodigious Thrust.* Santa Rosa CA: Black Sparrow Press, 1996.

———. *The Residual Years: Poems 1934-1948.* Santa Rosa CA: Black Sparrow press, 1997.

———. *The Veritable Years 1949-1966.* Santa Barbara CA: Black Sparrow Press, 1978.

Gelpi, Donald L., S. J. *The Divine Mother: A Trinitarian Theology of the Holy Spirit.* Lanham MD: University Press of America, 1984.

Lowell, Robert. *Lord Weary's Castle.* New York: Harcourt, Brace, 1946.

DAVID CARPENTER (ESSAY DATE 2000)

SOURCE: Carpenter, David. "Introduction: *She That Looketh Forth as the Morning.*" In *The Integral Years: Poems 1966-1994,* by William Everson, pp. xxiii-xxvii. Santa Rosa, Calif.: Black Sparrow Press, 2000.

In the following essay, Carpenter considers Everson's growth as a poet and his development of synthesis in his work, and examines the poet's celebration of the power of the feminine.

She is the Mother of Life, Mistress of Death,
Before her feet the tiger coughs and dies,
And the bony elephant gives up the boast
Of those vast passions that once filmed his eyes.
(Brother Antoninus, ***Veritable Years,*** 98 ed., 323)

What you hold in your hands, excepting the critical and textual apparatus, is the last volume of ***The Crooked Lines of God: A Life Trilogy*** as William Everson envisioned it, as he envisioned and shaped his life's work, as he envisioned and retrospectively shaped the poetic portrait of his life. Everson desired—and needed—to behold an identifiable pattern to his existence, this especially important in his last decade or so, and thus he embraced the concept of the monomyth, the three archetypal stages of the hero's quest. Everson has explained how he envisioned the pattern of his life, retrospectively delineated and arrived at, a pattern given shape to reactively, and thus we have the trilogy, as he came to see it: ***The Residual Years, The Veritable Years*** and ***The Integral Years.***

Some readers will find the poet's retrospective and aesthetically tidy demarcating of his life and poetry handy, convenient; and why not, for the three stages of the monomyth are identifiable in the trilogy as envisioned by Everson. They do seem to be valid when held up against the broad strokes, the most salient movements of the poet's life as he has arranged them in his numerous volumes of poetry. A problem exists for the reader who desires to study Everson's psychological and artistic development, however, insofar as Everson frequently arranged the poems of a given collection according to his over-arching vision of the collection, not according to the dates of composition. ***The Masks of Drought,*** for example, opens with **"Storm-Surge"** (composed 24 December 1971), the earliest of the poems in the volume, but two poems later is **"Runoff"** (composed 1 March 1976), the poem directly following this is **"Blackbird Sundown"** (composed 2 August 1972), and so on. While the two sections of **"Moongate"** were composed last (4 August 1979 and 8 August 1979, respectively), the poem is presented as the thirteenth of nineteen poems in the volume, with the last poem in the volume—**"Spikehorn"**—composed 1 October 1977.

While Everson tells us in his "Preface" to this volume that he conceived of his life "as evolving under the dynamic nuclear formula, thesis-antithesis-synthesis, with my work following suit," he further admits he discovered the pattern retrospectively: "it emerged from the actual working-out of my life, and was born, after the fact, in the consciousness of inspired revelation." Noting that, prior to the publication of ***The Masks of Drought,*** "several readers [had] expressed concern that no synthesis was apparent" in his poetry (i.e., the vitally important third part of the dialectical triad was missing from his poetry and thus, presumably, from his life), Everson then tells us that with the publication of ***The Masks of Drought*** "these misgivings were more or less put to rest. With this book readers spoke of the quality of resolution, the vibration of wholeness, and even went so far as to proclaim it my best book and a true synthesis. I can't express the import of elation and relief these expressions occasioned for me."

Given Everson's lifelong struggles with the internal and external manifestations of his psyche's shadow-side and feminine principle; given the increasing debilitations he was suffering from Parkinson's Disease—as well as the tensions in his life his sexual impotence was causing him—before, during, and after he composed the poems of ***The Masks of Drought***; given his lifelong pursuit to realize wholeness of Self, to realize the complete integration of the masculine with the feminine sides of his psyche, the complete integration of the spirit with the flesh; and given that he had determined the last volume of his life's trilogy would be the poetic expression and artistic embodiment of such integration, thus titled ***The Integral Years,*** it is no surprise he says in the "Preface" that "it devolves on ***Masks*** to assume the brunt of apotheosis."

Everson knew well that integration, synthesis, wholeness, apotheosis resulted from progressive movement toward the goal, and the arrangement of poems in a given volume could communicate progression—thematically, artistically, sexually, psychologically, spiritually. Indeed, arranged in the right order, according to the over-arching vision, the entire volume could convey a progression toward synthesis or apotheosis that the individual poems, read in the order of composition (especially important when studying Everson's psychological development), may not convey. Thus in **"Moongate,"** the poem composed last of those in ***Masks,*** the poet envisions himself pursuing the "fox" of his vocation tirelessly, experiences once again his first wife falling away from him as he continues his pursuit, the first marriage subordinated to that pursuit, and yet an unknown feminine figure takes her place but follows him who follows the fox; she doesn't see what it is the poet pursues, but she follows nevertheless. Importantly, the poet stands between the male fox and the feminine principle, and it is a stretch to suggest such a tableau represents a "true synthesis." Indeed, Everson was mindful of how dearly his pursuit of vocation had cost him on the domestic front.

However one chooses to approach Everson's poetry, what becomes hugely apparent as one reads the trilogy is this: there has never been and is not now any poet, in any language, who has celebrated the power of the feminine as much, as complexly or as unabashedly, as William Everson. The celebration, furthermore, transcends time and personalities, as readers who are not limited by the restrictive thinking of so-called "political correctness" will come to see. The poetic celebration is not without tension or struggle, of course; one sensed struggle was inevitable early on in the poet's career when, in **"In the Fictive Wish,"** Everson expressed his intensely determined desire to find "the woman within" himself in a "woman without." Indeed, he was on the lookout for her after betrayal had ended his first marriage, but he found more in Mary Fabilli than a woman willing to be malleably fashioned into the objective correlative of his "woman within"; he found through her a redefinition of his feminine side, as well as a formal religion.

No one who has studied carefully Everson's fascination with, attachment to, and love of the feminine should see irony in the fact that the poet was led by a woman into the monastic life of Brother Antoninus and then propelled out for the love of another woman. Even as Antoninus, the poet's celebration of the feminine principle continued; in fact, the celebration became most extreme, most tortured and most internalized, as we see in **"Annul in Me My Manhood,"** wherein he pleads with God to make him "woman-sexed" if that is what it would take for God to enter his being and fill the emptiness he was suffering, and if "by that total transformation / I might know Thee more" ([***The Veritable Years,*** hereafter:] ***VY*** 113). No, it was not ironic when Everson / Antoninus realized vows of celibacy weren't right for him, fell in love with Rose Tannlund and then with Susanna Rickson, the latter to become his third wife.

What does seem sadly ironic is that one of Everson's final poems should be **"Danse Macabre,"** wherein he recounts a recent dream in which he sees himself as he was in his "Waldport years," but then he—as he is forty years later—is confronted by the feminine principle of the dream: she's "hooded" but her face, he sees when she lifts it before him, is "a gaping skull, / Not bones dry from the tomb. / Rather, bluish white, glistening, tatters of flesh / Still clinging her jaws—butcher's bones / Housewives lug home for dog-gnaw" (171).

One must wonder if Everson knew Sherwood Anderson's "Death in the Woods," a story about just such a housewife, just such a type, whose sole purpose was to feed animal life. Even after her death in the woods, in the snow, her breasts exposed after her dogs rip her upper garments off her, she feeds animal life when a group of men and two boys gather around her frozen body, turn her over and stare at her breasts. In her bag had been just such "butcher's bones," which she carried home for her dogs.

In any case, after his life-long poetic celebration of the feminine, it seems as I said sadly ironic that Everson's unconscious would present him with the butchered face of the woman within: "She will not be put off," he tells us. Her unavoidable presence—regardless of what face she confronted him with over the years, what face he projected onto her—Antoninus discovered, as Everson had before the monastic years. Her power in his life would not be put off; she demanded his attention, demanded he celebrate her in his striving toward the knowledge and realization of the integral years he came to envision as comprising the last volume of his trilogy. Regardless of what face he envisioned the feminine essence with, he tells us in "**Danse Macabre**" that "I pull her to me" (172). Although the poems he wrote over a period of six decades exemplify time and again the truth of that utterance, this particular poem closes with Everson's apparent acknowledgment of and deference to an important fact: i.e., from the unsettling dream that presented him with the animatic but butchered face of the woman within, he tells us:

I jerk awake.
I am clasping the recumbent body of my wife.
She is fast asleep, faced from me,
And I press against her.

Sensing arousal
She stirs her hips, languidly, still deeply asleep,
Too lost in the wonder of her own myth
To waken to mine.

(172)

The acknowledged fact, of course, is that the woman without has a life, a personal myth and quest independent of his, independent of his previously announced intention to conjoin—or, through projection, to fuse psychologically—the woman within and the woman without. No, Susanna's identity remained undeniably her own. She lay "faced from me," Everson notes, the prevalent face of the poem thus left belonging to the woman within.

FURTHER READING

Biographies

Bartlett, Lee. *William Everson: The Life of Brother Antoninus.* New York: New Directions, 1988, 272 p.

Full-length biography considering the life and works of William Everson.

Brophy, Robert. "William Everson." In *Updating the Literary West,* pp. 337-45. Fort Worth, Texas: Texas Christian University Press, 1997.

Biographical sketch of Everson with a selected bibliography.

Criticism

Bartlett, Lee. "Creating the Autochthon: Kenneth Rexroth, William Everson, and *The Residual Years.*" *Sagetrieb* 2, no. 3 (winter 1983): 57-69.

Examines the relationship between Rexroth and Everson as it progressed from a mentor-disciple relationship through philosophical, literary differences to eventual resolution and the affirmation of a close personal friendship.

———. "Everson's 'Prologue.'" *Explicator* 41, no. 3 (spring 1983): 59-60.

Brief reading of Brother Antoninus's poem "Prologue" as influenced by Jungian psychology.

———. "From Waldport to San Francisco: Art and Politics Make Peace." *Literary Review* 32, no. 1 (fall 1988): 9-15.

Examines Everson's time as a conscientious objector in a work camp during World War II and the literary tradition that grew out of his and others' pacifist-anarchist philosophies.

———. "The Place of Poetry in the West: A Conversation with William Everson and Nathaniel Tarn." In *The Sun is but a Morning Star,* pp. 175-203. Albuquerque: University of New Mexico Press, 1989.

Bartlett interviews William Everson and Nathaniel Tarn on the reality of American poetic language and the three consider a number of American poets and works.

Carpenter, Frederic I. "'Post Mortem': 'The Poet is Dead.'" *Western American Literature* 12, no. 1 (spring 1977): 3-10.

Considers the relationship between Robinson Jeffers's poem "Post Mortem" and Everson's elegy to Jeffers, "The Poet is Dead."

Cherkovski, Neeli. "Singing the First Song: William Everson." In *Whitman's Wild Children: Portraits of Twelve Poets,* pp. 209-24. South Royalton, Vermont: Steerforth Press, 1988.

Sketch of Everson and his poetic style examining his nature and religious poetry.

Duncan, Robert. Introduction to *Single Source: The Early Poems of William Everson (1934-1940),* pp. ix-xii. Berkeley, California: Oyez, 1966.

Introduces a collection of Everson's early work as demonstrating a conversion of spirit to the poetic philosophy of Robinson Jeffers followed by a conversion of faith to Catholicism, all the while growing in spiritual depth.

Kherdian, David. "Brother Antoninus." In *Six Poets of the San Francisco Renaissance,* pp. 133-51. Fresno, Calif.: The Giligia Press, 1967.

Sketch of Brother Antoninus and an interview with the poet considering the Catholic Church, its relationship to his poetry, and its role as a muse to modern poets.

Marusiak, Joe. "Where We Might Meet Each Other: An Appreciation of Galway Kinnell and William Everson." *Literary Review* 24, no. 3 (spring 1981): 355-70.

Considers the poetry of Kinnell and Everson for its depiction of faith, the future, and the individual's struggle with difficult choices, and examines their poetic craftsmanship.

Meltzer, David. "William Everson (Brother Antoninus) (1969)." In *San Francisco Beat: Talking with the Poets,* pp. 22-60. San Francisco: City Lights Books, 2001.

An interview with David Meltzer, Jack Shoemaker, Tina Meltzer, and William Everson discussing the poet's life work and his decision to leave the Dominican monastery.

Peich, Michael. "William Everson: Fine Painter." *Printing History* 18, no. 2 (1981): 36-48.

Examines Everson's significant achievements in fine book making and printing and his role in defining contemporary American fine printing.

Williamson, Alan. "Of Sexual Metaphysics." *Parnassus: Poetry in Review* 8, no. 1 (fall/winter 1979): 184-91.

Reviews Everson's The Veritable Years *as an uneven collection of poetry centrally concerned with the conflict between sexual desire and the demands of monastic spirituality.*

OTHER SOURCES FROM GALE:

Additional coverage of Everson's life and career is contained in the following sources published by the Gale Group: *Contemporary Authors,* Vols. 9-12R; *Contemporary Authors New Revision Series,* Vol. 20; *Contemporary Literary Criticism,* Vols. 1, 5, 14; *Dictionary of Literary Biography,* Vols. 5, 16, 212; *Literature Resource Center*; and *Major 20th-Century Writers,* Ed. 1.

LAWRENCE FERLINGHETTI

(1919 -)

(Born Lawrence Ferling Monsanto) American poet, novelist, and playwright.

To fully appreciate the impact of Ferlinghetti on the American literary scene in general and on the Beat Generation in particular, it is necessary to look beyond his notable contributions as a writer, especially his poetry collection *A Coney Island of the Mind* (1958). As co-owner of City Lights, a renowned bookstore and publishing house located in San Francisco, Ferlinghetti played a significant role in promulgating the Beat school of writing. During the late 1950s and 1960s, he was a major force in encouraging and publicizing works that ran counter to both the literary and political establishment in the United States, publishing and distributing titles by such writers as Allen Ginsberg, Jack Kerouac, Frank O'Hara, Philip Lamantia, and Gregory Corso. Ferlinghetti's arrest in 1957 on obscenity charges and his subsequent prosecution helped bring widespread attention to the Beat movement.

BIOGRAPHICAL INFORMATION

Ferlinghetti was born in Yonkers, New York. After receiving a B.A. in journalism from the University of North Carolina in 1941, he served in the United States Naval Reserve during World War II and was a lieutenant commander during the Normandy invasion. When the war ended, he worked for *Time* magazine and then went on to attain advanced academic degrees: an M.A. from Columbia University in 1948 and a doctorate from the Sorbonne in Paris in 1949. Ferlinghetti eventually moved to San Francisco, where he taught French from 1951 to 1953. In 1952, along with Peter Martin, he founded City Lights Bookstore, the first all-paperback book shop in the United States. In 1955 City Lights began publishing the Pocket Poets Series, the inaugural title of which was Ferlinghetti's poetry collection *Pictures of the Gone World*. The fourth volume of the series, Ginsberg's *Howl and Other Poems* (1956), led to Ferlinghetti's arrest on charges of publishing obscene material. As a result of the publicity brought on by the ensuing trial, which was unsuccessful in convicting the publisher, Ginsberg and Ferlinghetti became internationally known literary figures. *Howl* had a first printing of fifteen hundred copies, but by the end of the trial, ten thousand copies were in print. The publicity surrounding City Lights inspired an explosion of other small presses that specialized in publishing books by controversial writers.

In addition to his notoriety as a publisher during this time, Ferlinghetti also became a public figure through his performance poetry. Along with Kenneth Rexroth, he began a series of poetry readings accompanied by jazz music in a San Francisco nightclub called The Cellar. Both Rexroth and Ferlinghetti felt that jazz, at the time considered to be "outsider music," was an appropriate complement to their poetry and a viable way of attracting a new audience for contemporary poetry. Ferlinghetti repeatedly stated that much of his poetry was designed to be heard rather than read on a printed page. Public engagement with his audience, as well as open confrontation with social and political issues, has characterized Ferlinghetti's literary career. Despite his largely radical political stance, Ferlinghetti contends that the function of the poet is to provide a dissenting voice that is independent of affiliations with either liberal or conservative organizations.

MAJOR WORKS

Ferlinghetti's first published work, *Pictures of the Gone World,* is largely composed of poems of lyric observation. While "gone" was a slang term during the Beat era similar in meaning to such later expressions as "groovy" or "far out," as applied to the poems in this collection it also denotes the sense of something that is past. His second collection and best-known work, *A Coney Island of the Mind,* is more representative of his subsequent poetic style: satirical, linguistically inventive, and structurally innovative. In 1960 Ferlinghetti published his first novel, *Her.* The form of this work is an interior monologue of the main character, Andy Raffine, who views himself as troubled and fragmented as the result of becoming an orphan at an early age. He nonetheless retains a sense of himself as being happy and whole prior to his being orphaned and seeks to recapture this state by engaging in an idealized romantic and sexual relationship, a quest that ultimately ends in failure. The poems of *Starting from San Francisco* (1961) expand on Ferlinghetti's violation of conventional poetic form and, like his earlier collection *A Coney Island of the Mind,* attempt to convey the experience of an oral reading through the use of broken, fragmentary lines that emulate the rhythms of speech. As a playwright, Ferlinghetti has published two principal collections of short, experimental dramas: *Unfair Arguments with Existence* (1963) and *Routines* (1964). Often described as surreal, the plays in these collections feature settings and situations that are symbolic rather than representational. In his later poetry collections—including *Landscapes of Living and Dying* (1979) and *Wild Dreams of a New Beginning* (1988), Ferlinghetti continued to demonstrate his faith in the poetic imagination as a means for challenging the rigid ideas and behavioral codes of conventional society.

CRITICAL RECEPTION

Critical response to Ferlinghetti's work often focuses on the formal structure of his poems. James A. Butler uses the term "projective verse" to describe the poems of Ferlinghetti, for whom, Butler states, "the syllable, not the foot or meter, is the building block of poetry. The syllables thus do not combine into a foot, but into a line. . . . Meter and rhythm are therefore unimportant in the line length; the line is determined by those places in which the poet takes, and wants the reader to take, a breath." Thematically, commentators observe that humanity in Ferlinghetti's work, is portrayed as fundamentally ununified and limited in its perception of its own possibilities. As Gregory Stephenson has written, "Ferlinghetti's art evolves out of his desire to communicate this vision and to advocate the cause of unity against disunity, love against power." While some critics have dismissed Ferlinghetti's poetry as formally undisciplined and sentimental in the social and political ideals he champions, others praise what they perceive as his honest intentions and vibrant sensibility. The pieces in the retrospective collection *Endless Life: Selected Poems* (1981) reflect the abiding concern throughout Ferlinghetti's career with not only political issues, but also with the nature of beauty and the poetic imagination. In his later collection, *Wild Dreams of a New Beginning,* Ferlinghetti clearly demonstrates what Diane Wakoski has described as "an immense belief in the power and life of imagination. Belief that it can transform the world, even change it."

PRINCIPAL WORKS

Pictures of the Gone World (poetry) 1955; enlarged edition, 1995

A Coney Island of the Mind (poetry) 1958; enlarged edition, 1968

Her (novel) 1960

One Thousand Fearful Words for Fidel Castro (poetry) 1961

Starting from San Francisco (poetry) 1961; enlarged edition, 1967

Unfair Arguments with Existence (plays) 1963

PRIMARY SOURCES

LAWRENCE FERLINGHETTI (POEM DATE 1955)

SOURCE: Ferlinghetti, Lawrence. "Number 13." In *Pictures of the Gone World.* San Francisco: City Lights Books, 1955.

The following poem is taken from Ferlinghetti's first collection of poetry.

"NUMBER 13"

It was a face which darkness could kill
in an instant
a face as easily hurt
by laughter or light
'We think differently at night'
she told me once
lying back languidly
And she would quote Cocteau
'I feel there is an angel in me' she'd say
'whom I am constantly shocking'
Then she would smile and look away
light a cigarette for me
sigh and rise
and stretch
her sweet anatomy
let fall a stocking

FROM THE AUTHOR

FERLINGHETTI ON CITY LIGHTS'S AUTHOR ROSTER

It would have been nice had we provided a nice warm stable and we were feeding them regularly—the care and feeding of poets. The care and feeding of authors is what publishers do. We didn't really have a stable. One at a time, poets would stagger in the door, drunk or sober, high or stoned. They were looking for a stable, but we didn't have one. In fact, we weren't very stable ourselves. We were a two-bit, one-room bookstore with no money. That's how it was.

Troiano, Jeff. Interview with Lawrence Ferlinghetti in the *San Francisco Reader* (online and print periodical) <www.sanfranciscoreader.com> (October 2002).

LAWRENCE FERLINGHETTI (POEM DATE 1958)

SOURCE: Ferlinghetti, Lawrence. "I Am Waiting." In *A Coney Island of the Mind,* pp. 49-53. Norfolk, Conn.: New Directions, 1958.

This poem, taken from Ferlinghetti's landmark collection A Coney Island of the Mind, *examines the state of the world, decrying its madness and proclaiming its wonders.*

"I AM WAITING"

I am waiting for my case to come up
and I am waiting
for a rebirth of wonder
and I am waiting for someone
to really discover America
and wail
and I am waiting
for the discovery
of a new symbolic western frontier
and I am waiting
for the American Eagle
to really spread its wings
and straighten up and fly right
and I am waiting
for the Age of Anxiety
to drop dead
and I am waiting
for the war to be fought
which will make the world safe

for anarchy
and I am waiting
for the final withering away
of all governments
and I am perpetually awaiting
a rebirth of wonder

I am waiting for the Second Coming
and I am waiting
for a religious revival
to sweep thru the state of Arizona
and I am waiting
for the Grapes of Wrath to be stored
and I am waiting
for them to prove
that God is really American
and I am seriously waiting
for Billy Graham and Elvis Presley
to exchange roles seriously
and I am waiting
to see God on television
piped onto church altars
if only they can find
the right channel
to tune in on
and I am waiting
for the Last Supper to be served again
with a strange new appetizer
and I am perpetually awaiting
a rebirth of wonder

I am waiting for my number to be called
and I am waiting
for the living end
and I am waiting
for dad to come home
his pockets full
of irradiated silver dollars
and I am waiting
for the atomic tests to end
and I am waiting happily
for things to get much worse
before they improve
and I am waiting
for the Salvation Army to take over
and I am waiting
for the human crowd
to wander off a cliff somewhere
clutching its atomic umbrella
and I am waiting
for Ike to act
and I am waiting
for the meek to be blessed
and inherit the earth
without taxes
and I am waiting
for forests and animals
to reclaim the earth as theirs
and I am waiting
for a way to be devised
to destroy all nationalisms
without killing anybody
and I am waiting
for linnets and planets to fall like rain
and I am waiting for lovers and weepers
to lie down together again
in a new rebirth of wonder

I am waiting for the Great Divide to be crossed
and I am anxiously waiting
for the secret of eternal life to be discovered
by an obscure general practitioner
and save me forever from certain death
and I am waiting
for life to begin
and I am waiting
for the storms of life,
to be over
and I am waiting
to set sail for happiness
and I am waiting
for a reconstructed Mayflower
to reach America
with its picture story and tv rights
sold in advance to the natives
and I am waiting
for the lost music to sound again
in the Lost Continent
in a new rebirth of wonder

I am waiting for the day
that maketh all things clear
and I am waiting
for Ole Man River
to just stop rolling along
past the country club
and I am waiting
for the deepest South
to just stop Reconstructing itself
in its own image
and I am waiting
for a sweet desegregated chariot
to swing low
and carry me back to Ole Virginie
and I am waiting
for Ole Virginie to discover
just why Darkies are born
and I am waiting
for God to lookout
from Lookout Mountain
and see the Ode to the Confederate Dead
as a real farce
and I am awaiting retribution
for what America did
to Tom Sawyer
and I am perpetually awaiting
a rebirth of wonder

I am waiting for Tom Swift to grow up
and I am waiting
for the American Boy
to take off Beauty's clothes
and get on top of her
and I am waiting
for Alice in Wonderland
to retransmit to me
her total dream of innocence
and I am waiting
for Childe Roland to come
to the final darkest tower
and I am waiting
for Aphrodite
to grow live arms
at a final disarmament conference

in a new rebirth of wonder

I am waiting
to get some intimations
of immortality
by recollecting my early childhood
and I am waiting
for the green mornings to come again
youth's dumb green fields come back again
and I am waiting
for some strains of unpremeditated art
to shake my typewriter
and I am waiting to write
the great indelible poem
and I am waiting
for the last long careless rapture
and I am perpetually waiting
for the fleeing lovers on the Grecian Urn
to catch each other up at last
and embrace
and I am awaiting
perpetually and forever
a renaissance of wonder

GENERAL COMMENTARY

LAWRENCE FERLINGHETTI, DAVID MELTZER, AND JACK SHOEMAKER (INTERVIEW DATE 1971)

SOURCE: Ferlinghetti, Lawrence, David Meltzer, and Jack Shoemaker. "Lawrence Ferlinghetti I (1969)." In *San Francisco Beat: Talking with the Poets,* edited by David Meltzer, pp. 68-95. San Francisco: City Lights Books, 2001.

In the following interview, which was originally published in 1971, Ferlinghetti discusses his career as a writer and publisher, the Beat movement, and American political and literary trends of the 1960s.

Spring 1969: Jack Shoemaker and I drove to Ferlinghetti's San Francisco house in the Potrero Hill district, a warmly worn and comfortable home filled with art and books. We sat in the living room for a while, chatting, sipping wine, and then Lawrence took us upstairs to the attic garret where he had his office. Its windows looked out over the city. He was forthcoming but also playful; sometimes I thought he was putting us on, a sly trickster with ice-blue eyes. As the interview proceeded, the sun began a spectacular descent behind the city skyline. Afterward, we went downstairs where Kirby, his wife, had made supper for us, which we ate with much wine and wonderful conversation and laughter.—DM

1

[Ferlinghetti]: I have nothing to say. I haven't got my crystal spectacles on.

[Meltzer]: *You just published a book* **[Tyrannus Nix?]**

I don't have anything to say in relation to all these other poets. I don't feel myself to be part of any scene now. I never went in for the regional point of view. I don't know anything about anything! That's the way I feel. I am living in Big Sur a lot of the time, and I really don't have much to do with what is going on now.

[Meltzer]: *Is this a transitional period for you?*

Definitely. When isn't it? In the summer I'm a nudist anarchist; in the winter I'm a Buddhist socialist.

[Meltzer]: *Your new book of poems . . . can we consider that to be a statement of your concern?*

It is the old political bullshit. Politics is a drag, but every once in a while you get dragged into it and have to sound off. But it is not my idea of an ideal kind of poetry.

[Shoemaker]: *It is not your constant concern . . . ?*

No. I keep getting dragged into that bag, and I get classified as a political poet. I had another book that came out this year called ***The Secret Meaning of Things,*** which is generally not political at all.

[Shoemaker]: *You have written a poem now about every president since Eisenhower. . . .*

That is just what Snyder said.

[Shoemaker]: *It seems you have an overwhelming historical concern. . . .*

No, I haven't. I wrote a poem about Eisenhower, and I wrote this one about Nixon. It seems to me there were very few presidents in between. I wrote about Fidel Castro in between. The last president of the U.S.A. was really Fidel Castro. He ran things from down there in Cuba even when Kennedy was president. Castro was acting, and the U.S.A. was forced to react according to its already well-established guidelines for Christian behavior and, therefore, had to react strictly according to the American way of life, which he threatened. Castro may still be president. Nixon is sort of a bush-league stand-in.

The Cuban Revolution was the Spanish Civil War of my generation. The thing that turned on the writers in the thirties was the Spanish Civil War. It would be interesting to pin down some of the other poets you have interviewed as to what their actual position is on Castro. I find a good many of the poets around are quite rightist, if not reactionary, and most of them are politically illiterate. Great Kerouac is not around anymore, so we won't go into him. But there's a Hemingway parallel there.

I recently received a list of award winners from the National Foundation of the Arts. Many poets and little presses in the country have received grants from them. This is government money in the form of grants from either the National Foundation of the Arts and Sciences or the Coordinating Council of Little Magazines and Small Presses.

Jean-Jacques Lebel and I had a running argument over the last six weeks while he was staying here. He considers himself a revolutionary, and he proposed that a young poet he met in Berkeley get a $1,000 grant from this foundation. There was a scout in town, Gus Blaisdell, from the University of New Mexico. He was looking for people to recommend for government grants. Jean-Jacques Lebel suggested Blaisdell recommend the young Berkeley poet. It happened that Blaisdell didn't dig this fellow's poetry. That wasn't my point.

My point was that it surprised me that someone who considered himself a full-blown revolutionary would be the first to accept government money. Even though I dig that using establishment money for anti-establishment ends *is* subversive—part of the cultural "rip-off." The Kayak Press in San Francisco, for instance, took $10,000 two years in a row. One of the editor's justifications was that he would sponsor a prize for the best poem on Che Guevara. The *prize* for the best poem on Che Guevara was $400, I believe. I have heard that the Kayak editor, George Hitchcock, was a radical in the thirties, and it seems to me that this is sort of what happened to the whole old liberal movement in this country. The labor unions were bought off. They loaded the ships for Vietnam. From my point of view, which I admit is disputable, poets and little presses are also being bought off. Any one of them that took the money would say, "No, that's not true. We are free to do anything we want with the money." But it's logical that if you're a real bad boy the first year, you won't get the grant renewed. And then, too—someone in another country—a radical in France or Germany—reads about your taking this money and they don't see the rationalization and the various gradations of your reasoning. All they see is the fact that you took the U.S. government money. . . . I guess mine is the "pure" purist position—though I hardly consider myself "pure"—

[*Shoemaker*]: *Perhaps what happens today is that most poets of David's generation and the younger poets of my generation don't take the whole thing that seriously. And free money is. . . .*

Jean-Jacques's argument was that it depends on what you use the money for. If you take the money to live on, that is one thing. But if you take it to instigate a plot to blow something up or to throw sand in the wheels of the machine, then it is justified. He said this kid in Berkeley is interested in using money to buy materials to hatch a big plot. . . . The kid doesn't have time to work because he is working full time on the revolution. This government money will save him from having to get a job, and he can work full time on blowing up the system. I have a note in ***Tyrannus Nix*** that I would like to get on the record, page 82. It is a note about a line called "The poets and their sad likenesses":

> Many American poets do in fact help the Government in sanctioning a *status quo* which is supported by and supports War as a legal form of murder: witness the number of avant-garde poets and Little Presses who have in recent years accepted U.S. grants directly from the National Foundation on the Arts or from its conduit, the Coordinating Council of Literary Magazines, making it clear that the avant-garde in the arts is not *necessarily* to be associated with the political Left. Cf. Marcuse's "repressive tolerance," i.e., the policy of tolerance and/or sponsorship as a self-protection against violence; or as Susan Sontag recently put it, "divesting unsettling or subversive ideas by ingesting them."

The state, whether capitalist or Communist, has an enormous capacity to ingest its most dissident elements.

[*Meltzer*]: *In what sense does a poet help revolution, if at all . . . and what is the revolution?*

It depends on which revolution you are talking about. I mean, the first thing a poet has to do is to live that type of life which doesn't compromise himself. It seems to me that taking government grants and living on them is compromising himself before he even starts writing.

[*Shoemaker*]: *I heard an answer to it while I was involved with the Unicorn Press and they were disputing the matter of taking government money. George Hitchcock presented a very realistic position for taking the money and using it in an almost anarchistic way. He stated that he wanted to be left alone and that this money would help insulate him against the system. He then brought up the point of hypocrisy in consumption. We live in America now and consume American goods and do, in fact, work and do our business in American cities. We are supporting the system in almost every way and to refuse free money seems almost silly. I mean, we are all buying goods that indirectly help support the war.*

You can't breathe, you can't live in a country, walk down its streets, use a car, and certainly not operate a business or buy anything in a store without having to cooperate against your will. The point is what you have a choice to do and what you don't have a choice to do. You are on the whole very quiet. They are certainly not engaging in any shock treatment. Neither for legalizing psychedelics or preventing ecocatastrophe or preventing world war.

[Meltzer]: *There have been probably more benefit poetry readings this last year than there have ever been. One a week almost. All concerns: ecological concerns, against the war, draft benefits, People's Park . . . it seems like it has been easy to amass large groups of poets to read for nearly any benefit and cause. . . .*

Who is reading books of poetry these days? The rock generation certainly isn't . . . say under the age of twenty-five. What books are they reading! If you went to the Fillmore and took a poll on how many people have read even Ginsberg, you would probably get about five percent. They just aren't reading books, it seems. The whole revolution of the sixties was psychedelic and visual and oral: the poster trip and the rock trip . . . the book wasn't it. Maybe now it is *Zap Comics*. The amount of *Zap Comics* we sell at the bookstore is enormous. The average dude who comes in and buys tickets to the Fillmore buys *Zap Comics*. They articulate his "community" for him. They articulate his "counterculture"—and City Lights Bookstore just got busted for selling *Zap*—we haven't been "ingested" yet.

[Shoemaker]: *What would he buy ten years ago if he came in?*

Literature . . . Ginsberg. . . .

[Shoemaker]: *I am under twenty-five, I dig rock music, but I and a circle of friends that is relatively large have always been reading, hanging around bookstores. . . .*

I was thinking of a group younger than you. Maybe it is splitting hairs about how young. . . .

[Shoemaker]: *I think a great deal of the movement is concerned with books. . . .*

Reading books isn't the greatest thing in the world, maybe. We overdid it in my generation. Maybe it's not so all-important to be literate. This new book of mine that New Directions put out, ***Tyrannus Nix,*** they printed a lot of copies, but what is it going to change? It is not going to change anything, it seems to me. A good rock concert may change people's consciousness faster. That was the argument before Altamont, anyway.

[Shoemaker]: *Let's trace one book. What about Howl? (Those early City Lights books meant a lot to people in my high school.) Let's bring it down to the nitty-gritty. . . . Is Howl selling more than it did five or ten years ago?*

Well, yes. It is selling more than it sold ten years ago and more than it sold five years ago, but this year the books on the list that sold most were the books by Brautigan. Brautigan's books outsold Ginsberg's, which is quite a surprise. Brautigan got identified with the hippie generation, though he was around long before hippies. He was around in the Beat days and the Beat nights—

There were a few new young poets in the Haight-Ashbury, but none of them ever got well known. It's as if you had to have a guitar to make it. Ginsberg, McClure, Snyder, these were all holdovers, bridge figures from the fifties. Not many others made that bridge. . . . And how did these poets from the fifties bridge the gap? Some used some kind of musical instrument to back up their voices. Like Ginsberg using finger cymbals and then the harmonium . . . and Michael McClure using the autoharp, and I use an autoharp. These were all attempts to bridge this gap. The single unaccompanied voice couldn't stand up to a rock group. I mean, it's murder to come on stage after a good rock group as a single unaccompanied voice. I did this down in Santa Barbara. They had a benefit last spring for Resist, part of Robert Bly's antiwar tour, and Rexroth was master of ceremonies. . . . I didn't get on until 1:00 a.m. I was part of an enormously long variety show program, and I had to follow Mad River. That was really murder. I did one long poem with a taped raga backing up my voice ("**Assassination Raga**").

I have been doing more with the autoharp lately. In fact, I have chanted some with Daniel Moore's Floating Lotus Magic Opera. Daniel's trip is a very definite part of revolution today. He pulls a lot of separate things together.

[Shoemaker]: *He is writing only for that now. He doesn't write any more poetry.*

The libretto is his poetry. I mean it is very much like the poetry he published in *Dawn Visions*. Daniel Moore is really a musical and dramatic genius. Like you have been through the Living Theater, and you have been through Artaud, and here comes Daniel Moore out of all of that with a ceremonial ritual drama. Daniel's solution to the single voice. He started out with the single voice and then got the whole do have the choice of deciding whether or not you are ingested by the state voluntarily and thus becoming a functioning part of it—nourishing it symbiotically, so to speak. The carrot and the stick—*Waiting for Godot* still—Pozzo with Lucky the artist on a string. The next time Nixon runs for office, for instance, he can say he sponsored or supported you. So vote for him, baby. Let's not spoil the spoils system.

From another point of view: say you are running a press . . . I was never offered a grant personally, because I didn't apply for one. But I had some correspondence with Carolyn Kizer about people to recommend for these grants. I wasn't cooperating with her at all. I didn't wish to cooperate as the director of a press. It is doubly bad for a press to take government money. It is almost like a newspaper taking it.

[*Shoemaker*]: *What about independent grants like the Guggenheim and the Ford Foundation?*

The radical would say that these large foundations are just as big murderers as the government is. Are they? I figure it is important to lead the kind of life where you don't have to take grants from any organization. You have to make it on your own without any help. At any point you can tell them to go fuck themselves. And not only can but do tell them. The real problem is to decide who's "them." . . . Well, you can say or print anything you want, according to the government foundations. The director of the program is obviously sincere in saying that there are no strings attached to the money. Grants are renewable the second year. Suppose during the first year you publish something that is really offensive politically or offensive to the sensibilities of those in Washington who hold the purse strings. If you say "Fuck you, Agnew," will you get your grant renewed the second year? Maybe yes.

Here is a part of Carolyn Kizer's reply to me:

> I see no reason why the government shouldn't subsidize attacks on itself. After all, this endowment gave $10,000 to Grace Paley whose activities in various Viet Nam and Peace movements are well known, and another $10,000 to Robert Duncan, who is not exactly friendly to our foreign policy. Why should you be? And what does that have to do with creative art? No, the attack will come, and is coming, from Congress. One congressman has just sent for all the books written by people to whom we have given grants thus far. And it will continue when our anthologies from the best writings from literary magazines appear, because every literary magazine in the country has been asked to take part in this program. I am sorry that you don't wish to accept any aid from an organization that bears the Great Seal on its letterhead. I myself don't feel that this is the same as refusing an invitation to the White House. Neither does Lowell, for that matter, with whom I am in frequent consultation. . . .

Obviously, the government and congressmen scrutinize the presses who are given money, as she says they are doing in this letter.

Here she says,

> Perhaps a similar plan would be feasible for independent small presses. Perhaps I should point out to you that some care and judgment involving considerations not wholly aesthetic will be imperative, particularly in the early stages of such a program. Work chosen for partial Federal subsidy will be subject to the closest scrutiny by persons anxious to attack the Federal Arts Program. Part of the responsibility for this program lies in the development of receptive audiences for the best works of art produced by society—irrespective of how they may offend taboos of specific groups. My own feeling is that shock treatment isn't suitable under such circumstances, but rather a slow and laborious process of increasing exposure to art in all its forms—not the least of which is books beautifully composed and beautifully produced.

Shock treatment isn't in order . . . but rather a slow easy careful development. That's it exactly—from a revolutionary viewpoint today, it *is* time when shock treatment is necessary! It sounds like the Old South when they say, "We can't have any fast changes . . . things have to develop slowly . . . you can't rush the desegregation . . ." and so forth. The blacks were fed up with that and started blowing things up. White radicals feel it is definitely time for shock treatment these days. And it seems to me that most of the poets, especially in San Francisco, Tibetan opera backing up his voice. One of the few poets who can make it on his own voice is Ginsberg.

After the blast of the rock scene—in '65 and '66—the San Francisco poets have been singularly silent. There have been a lot of poetry readings, but—for instance—the big reading we had at Norse Auditorium a couple of years ago . . . you know, an awful lot of awful poetry went down that night. Along with some great stuff.

2

There is a lot of talk about ecology, and yet they will have 5,000 people at Big Sur Hot Springs completely fouling up the landscape to attend an ecology seminar. Not to mention Altamont. There is really going to be an enormous ecological catastrophe, or ecocatastrophe, within the next ten years, unless something really drastic is done. Capitalism is an outrageously *extravagant* form of existence which is leading to an enormous ecological debacle, unless it is completely changed.

Theodore Roszak, in *The Making of a Counter-Culture,* makes a point that the young radicals are picking on capitalism when they could just as well pick on technocracy in a Communist country. It seems obvious to me that capitalism has got to go. The world ecologically cannot afford capitalism anymore. It's absolutely absurd. An unplanned economy, a laissez-faire economy, or a semi-laissez-faire economy, any kind of incentive capitalism, private incentive capitalism, these are luxuries the Earth cannot stand anymore. The resources won't stand it. The pollution of the atmosphere won't stand it.

There has to be absolute population control on a worldwide basis. Not euthanasia, not compulsory killing of old people. . . . We will have to have worldwide contraception beginning at age twelve. People are going to have to have permission to have children. This is going to be an absolute necessity. We are going to have to do away with these medieval nationalistic forms of government and have a form of central planning. The whole world has got to be run by a huge supranational nonpolitical central planning agency.

It's got to be a form of humanitarian socialism: not authoritarian but a nontotalitarian socialism. I'd like to think it could be a kind of Buddhist socialism. A planned socialist economy is the only way we can avoid the absolute devastation of Earth . . . the absolute pollution of Earth. It has got to happen. I mean, it is really coming up to the way it is laid out in *2001: A Space Odyssey,* where all directions are coming from a central control somewhere. It's a very pessimistic point of view, but some sort of totalitarian supranational state seems unavoidable. I think it is practically impossible to avoid this. This is the last thing anyone wants, but it seems inevitable—whether by cataclysmic war, which will end things up, with one strong central force in control, or by just plain ecocatastrophe. Capitalism just lays waste to too many resources. And the population jump that is going on now. . . . "One half of the people that ever lived are still alive." Think that one over.

I had a poem called **"After the Cries of the Birds Have Stopped"**—it saw the world of the future where all that was left were roving bands of mystics . . . like those that we call mutants today, would be the only ones left. Roving bands of long-haired mystics . . . the whole materialistic ideal of Western man in his business suit would go down the tube—

A lot of people think that practically any Oriental religion has more to say and has more answers today than Christianity does . . . especially for the youth in this country. It's not that they give an optimistic view of the world or of the future, it's just that they are more realistic. Who can imagine going to a Christian church these days? There are a few exceptions, like the things that have been going on at some far-out churches which are engaging the young on their own terms . . . like the Glide Memorial or the Free Church in Berkeley . . . that's where the Ho Chi Minh funeral parade ended up, at the Free Church in Berkeley. . . .

[*Shoemaker*]: *It is interesting that both of those churches you mentioned are in an Episcopalian framework. The church that most of us looked to a few years ago was the Unitarian one.*

The new Unitarian center in San Francisco . . . the architecture inside is like a Japanese building or a building somewhere in the Far East. It is a beautiful center, and when Baba Ram Das (Richard Alpert) came back from India, that is where he spoke. He and other Jewish Buddhists, "Hindu Cantors," or rabbinic saddhus—

3

I am surprised to find that quite a few poets in San Francisco keep guns. I heard that Gary Snyder, Lew Welch, and James Koller held target practice now and then. I wrote Snyder about it and said I felt it was a sellout of his own values to keep guns. He wrote back and said, well, he grew up in the Northwest where things were different from where I grew up in New York City. In the great Northwest, people had guns like household utensils, and it was just an ordinary object that everyone had for survival purposes. He stated his position, which I recognize, but it still didn't alter the basic argument, as far as I was concerned. If you keep guns, then ultimately they are going to be used for the function they were built for. As long as there are guns, they will speak, telescopically. It looks like I'm stuck with the purist position again.

I met a wandering Japanese mystic here in the summer, Nanao Sasaki. He is a friend of Gary's. He is the one that founded that ashram on Suwanose Island. In fact, he is the one that told me about Gary's having the gun. After I wrote this letter to Gary, Nanao said to me: "I'm going to add a P.S.: We do not *have* to survive."

I think there are an awful lot of misguided poets in the West, in S.F. . . . I am not thinking of Gary Snyder now . . . there are plenty of other poets that believe in violence. From this you could explore violence on the left or violence among radicals who consider themselves on the left. I think this is one reason that *Ramparts* magazine finds itself on the rocks. *Ramparts* is a good example of the radical left which supported black power right down the line. . . . Eldridge Cleaver is one of its editors, which is good, because Eldridge Cleaver has about twice as much brains as all the other black radicals that I know. What I meant was, the radical left turns out to have been supporting large elements of the radical right. The most violent elements in the Black Panthers or in the black power movement are not strictly to be identified with Eldridge Cleaver. Naturally, I think Cleaver is great because he seems at least to realize the blacks don't have a monopoly on revolution these days—

"Right on" has become the motto of black power, shouted by many white radicals who never gave support to the word "right" before—there are all kinds of rightist elements at work in radical circles these days, white and black. For instance, when you say if someone doesn't agree with you, you are going to use force on him, we are going to beat him up, we are going to pull out guns if you don't agree with us—that's also fascist. The assumption of adopting the ideas of Che Guevara, or the principles of guerrilla warfare, as something workable in this country, is absurd, because this is a completely different setup with an entrenched government so powerful it couldn't possibly be overturned by any band of guerrillas or revolutionaries blowing up power plants. Guerrilla theory is based on the assumption that in the early stages of insurrection the mass of the citizenry is going to rise up and support the guerrillas—and this just won't happen in the U.S.A., where the middle class is so well fed. Not until there is another Great Depression could it happen.

I took the plane from here to L.A. on the Friday afternoon commuter special. You are up there at 35,000 feet, sitting next to these executives. The one next to me had a plastic button that said, such and such a name, General Manager, Fairchild. These men ride along up there at 35,000 feet, and they really are the Roman emperors of the world. They have got this enormous technocracy which they control: the military-industrial complex. It's not just a myth. They are actually ruling the whole Earth, and it is so powerful that there is no possibility of this kind of entrenched establishment being overturned by any band of revolutionaries.

As, for instance, even in France it was possible for a student revolution to actually make the government fall, for the whole government to topple, and a new form of government to take its place.

[*Meltzer*]: *There are those who would say that the student revolution, or the student-based anti-Vietnam movement, fought for in this country during the last five years, caused Johnson to resign.*

I think that's true. People are always saying: what good does it do to march in peace parades? The snowballing peace movement, centered in peace parades in those days, actually did cause Johnson to decide not to run again. I mean, it seems obvious.

[*Shoemaker*]: *Well, that would seem to be an effective ploy against the military-industrial complex.*

But that's as far as it can go. It can't overthrow the government itself and, as I said the other day, the only way it can happen in this country is if there is a great economic Depression again, like in the thirties. I think that will happen. Eventually there is going to be another great boom and bust, and then we will have economic conditions where it will be possible to have a real overthrow of the government. That Great Depression might very well arrive before this is printed—

Nationalism is a medieval form of government. The whole argument during the American Civil War was that the states wouldn't give up any of their states' rights until the federal government could work. Now nations still refuse to give up any sovereignty, or states' rights, in the UN. They refuse to give up their vetoes. And the U.S.A. is the first to refuse to give any of its states' rights. You will have a civil war on a world level so long as these countries won't give up their stupid nationalistic forms. It will be an absolute catastrophe unless they do.

Maybe everyone is getting hysterical on the subject of ecology these days. But it seems to me that things are moving very fast. Every day in the papers there is another ecological disaster. Today there was a story about "strange foreign birds" landing here and there. Or, the day before, there was a "strange epidemic that killed all the fish in the Berkeley estuary."

[Meltzer]: *These things have been going on for a long time. The results via the media seem to be more interesting to the public than the process itself.*

Someone said that the danger is people may well become bored with the word "ecology" before they really comprehend what it means. If we are fortunate, there will be a political revolution in this country which will allow a new ecological control of the world (which is a very doubtful possibility). Suppose you did arrive at a point where a planned economy was instituted. Then you could get down to what would happen to the individual. Is he going to be a mystic, or what is he going to do? Then the individual is free again to write poetry.

[Shoemaker]: *Would you try to institute a government more concerned with distribution of goods, more concerned with planning, with making sure that somebody is not building too many tract homes . . . ?*

Right. That is why there needs to be an overall central planning.

[Shoemaker]: *Sure, and that kind of central planning is for distribution of goods. . . .*

Of course, this is what the socialist countries are trying to do. This is what it was all about.

[Meltzer]: *You start off working theoretically with equal distribution of goods and, all of a sudden, like in a matter of years, it winds up the same thing: somebody, a small nucleus of power, essentially more concerned with power than anything else. What is this peculiar continuity that takes place in revolution? Man reaches the point of overthrowing a so-called tyrannical government and, in turn, winds up propagating the same thing.*

Man is by nature predatory. It's too bad we can't all be just "predators of sweetness and light."

4

[Meltzer]: *One of the general questions we like to ask is, when do you recall your first responses to poetry, your first connection with it . . . ?*

Up to now, if I had some biographical question to answer, I would always make something up.

Who's Who sent a questionnaire form, and for several years I wrote "Fuck you!" on the *Who's Who* questionnaire and sent it back to them. But they are very persistent people and they keep writing and they keep saying, "If you don't answer this, we will publish something about you which may not be correct—so you may as well correct this"—so you get involved correcting a column of type that they have written about you that they have scrounged from other sources. I make up a lot of things.

Was I probably born in 1919 or 1920 in either Paris or New York? Some days it's hard to tell. I really don't see the reason for giving a straight answer. For one thing, I enjoy putting on *Who's Who*. I have done this with a lot of different interviewers, since it is valid for a poet who considers himself a semi-surrealist poet.

If you are going to write in one manner and someone comes to you with some straight questions—why should you give them a straight answer?

For instance, there was a very serious French professor from the Sorbonne who did a long serious book on American poets, and he interviewed me on tape. He asked me what my thesis was at the Sorbonne—what my doctor's thesis was there. I told him that it was the history of the pissoir in French literature. The interview was in French. And he wrote it all down, and it came out in the book that my doctoral thesis at the Sorbonne was called *The History of the Pissoir in French Literature*. He is really pissed now. He found out. They'll have to change the index cards in the Sorbonne where the damn thing is filed. Maybe the place will be burnt down in the next revolution. That would help.

The way I happened to get into surrealism just now is that I've been talking to Philip Lamantia, who has just come back into town. It's really kind of exciting. He has a place in North Beach, a block from City Lights. He is working with Steve Schwartz, who has started a surrealist magazine, *Anti-Narcissus*. Then there is Nanos Valaoritis, who is an exiled Greek poet-professor at State College. He is more or less identified with French surrealism. He edited a magazine in Greece which was a surrealist magazine. I am going to publish a book of their surrealist texts, I think. The whole thing comes together after all these years. We talk and think about some word better than surrealism. At a time when daily reality far exceeds "literary" surrealism, there really isn't any better term. I mean, maybe there is, but no one has thought of it yet. Superrealism? Hyperrealism? Unrealism?

Philip and I have had some funny surrealistic experiences since he has returned here. We wrote a poem about one, one day. I wrote a surrealist poem about the surrealist enigma of Ho Chi Minh's funeral and how a girl we met in North

Beach, whom we called Nadja, opened the door of her womb to Philip Lamantia and inside was a light bulb. Turn her on—

Anyway, I have been telling Philip that I don't see why he doesn't consider me a surrealist, too. He says I am just writing fake surrealist poems. Well, he didn't say "fake surrealist poems," but I had the feeling he thought I was doctoring up my spontaneous visions and putting "thought" in it—making it no longer a pure surrealistic product. In fact, I *was* doctoring them up. Hyping them up, might be more accurate.

[Meltzer]: *It would be interesting to know your early sources, your early teachers. . . .*

The surrealist poets were some of my earliest sources. Especially poets like Apollinaire, who was not really a surrealist. He was more or less the con man of the movement, but I think I learned more from him than others.

[Shoemaker]: *You chose to go to France to school?*

My mother was French. I was in France with her when I was a kid. . . . That's not true. [*laughter*] . . . Strike that. I was in France with one of my relatives, one of my French relatives . . . you can never tell whether these statements are true or not . . . I was kidnapped by . . . now this is absolutely true [*laughter*] . . . I was kidnapped by a man, a French cousin of my mother's, who took me to France in swaddling clothes and didn't bring me back to the U.S.A. until I was about six or seven years old.

So later I had some memory of speaking French, and it wasn't too hard to get back to it. It was a natural thing to go back to.

I went to Columbia and got an MA, but the idea of getting a Ph.D. at Columbia was so forbidding . . . the whole discipline and regime you had to go through to get an American Ph.D. . . . yet I wanted to use the GI Bill as much as I could. . . . So I went to Paris on it.

The whole thing about a doctorate at the University of Paris was that you were a free man. You just had to report to the director of your thesis like once every half-year. You could spend decades working on your thesis—some eternal students did just that—one on Rimbaud—they didn't care whether you ever came back. I remember going to the *soutenance*—the public defense of your thesis. It's like the orals they have in this country, but it is in one of those big renaissance lecture halls they have at the Sorbonne and is open to the public. You have a jury of professors up on the stage. You sit with your back to the audience, and the professors are up there in their robes, and they work your thesis over and ask you questions about it, in classical French, and you're supposed to reply in classical French. I guess that was one of the things French students revolted against about two years ago. I must say I made some classic mistakes. I defended translation mistakes by saying that a translation is like a woman—when she is faithful she is not beautiful—when she is beautiful she isn't faithful—

I was free, and this was ideal for someone who wanted to find time and bread to be a writer. To get my monthly GI check, all I had to do was sign a book once a month at the Sorbonne. I got five full years out of the GI Bill that way. And never went to class.

[Shoemaker]: *What was your thesis eventually on?*

[Meltzer]: *The pissoir?*

What thesis? [*laughter*] This is absurd. In fact . . . it was on modern poetry: the *city* in modern poetry, in French and English poetry. In English there are things like Hart Crane's *Bridge* and Eliot's *The Waste Land.* All this fits into city poetry. Things like Francis Thompson's [*sic*] *City of Dreadful Night.* And in French, long poems like Verhaeren's *Tentacular City*—

[Meltzer]: *When was this?*

It could have been after the Second World War, centuries ago.

I didn't know any literary people at all when I was living in France in those days, and I didn't know any Americans who were there writing. Rexroth later told me: "Now I remember I met you in Paris, and you knew so-and-so and so-and-so . . . I'm sure I knew you. . . ." But I didn't know any of the people he says I met. Or it was another me. The first I heard of Rexroth was when I read his introduction to the *Selected Poems of D. H. Lawrence*—he really turned me on to Lawrence. I was living with a French family over in the workers' part of town, near Père Lachaise cemetery, on Place Voltaire. I lived with the family of an old Communist. An old man who looked like Beethoven and who was a music professor, a classical music teacher. I went to the Sorbonne once a month to sign this book, and otherwise I didn't have anything to do with any literary scene.

I got a place of my own in Montparnasse which cost me about $26 a year. It was a cellar with two rooms and a little tiny air-shaft kitchen with a sink hollowed out of solid stone, which must have been there since the Middle Ages, and a front room that had a French window on a courtyard. That was the only window in the two rooms. The middle room had no windows at all. It was very damp in there. And it was dark. There was only light from this front window.

I got the place by sneaking in one night. It was absolutely impossible to find any apartments in Paris. Even today you have to buy the key, and it costs an enormous amount.

I met a plumber in a bar, and he was tubercular, and his wife and children were tubercular. He had three children, and they were all living in this dank two-room apartment, and it was very damp, and the kids were coughing, and they were all sick—and he owed everyone in the neighborhood. We agreed that I would pay up all his debts in the neighborhood so he could leave, and he would move me in at night, and when the concierge came the next day, I would tell her that I was a friend of his and that he was away in the country. So the whole thing cost me $100 to pay off all his debts. It went on like that for three years. I had this place and kept telling the concierge that he was coming back. Maybe me and the concierge and the plumber were the original models for *Waiting for Godot.* Of course, the plumber never came back, and I finally sold the place the same way. Moved out in the middle of the night. That was the place where I wrote ***Her.*** It wasn't a novel, it wasn't supposed to be a novel. It was a surrealist notebook that I kept, a "black book." It is a book which New Directions calls a novel. They have to call it something. But it never got any reviews in this country. It came out in 1958 or 1959, right after ***Coney Island of the Mind,*** although I had written the first version of it in 1949 or '50. This book has never gotten any reviews in this country. I got some in France when it came out in French, because it fits into the French tradition of the novel. Like you can fit it in the Robbe-Grillet and Breton's *Nadja.*

Nadja was one of the books I stole from them. I also stole from Djuna Barnes's *Nightwood.* It's full of all kinds of stuff I stole from *Nightwood*—which I always thought was one of the great American expatriate novels. Really great prose. I once told Djuna Barnes that I thought her prose was man's prose, and she said that was the greatest compliment I could have paid her.

The speeches of Dr. Matthew O'Connor are absolutely great prose. They find him in bed dressed as a woman, and he talks of the Night. Watchman, what of the Night. He lays it out. . . .

In this country there is no tradition for a novel like ***Her.*** The critics don't know what to do with it; they don't have anywhere to place it. It doesn't fit in anywhere. The closest thing I can think of is the work of Anaïs Nin—Virginia Woolf underwater—though what she is saying and what she is preoccupied with is completely different. In fact, she wrote a book about the novel—*The Novel of the Future*—in which she listed ***Her.*** That is the only reference I have ever seen to ***Her*** in this country. . . .

Why is it that there has never been anyone really following *Finnegans Wake* in this country? What happened after that was a complete disintegration of the language and a dissociation of imagery which went into "cut-ups." This is the same surrealist dislocation of imagery which Bill Burroughs arrived at through the physical cutting up of texts. The French and Italian surrealists did cut-ups and collages many years before. Of course, what was new in Burroughs was what he did with it. In him, you have an artifical dislocation of imagery, which is one direction writing could go after *Finnegans Wake.* Joyce had done that as far as one could possibly do it, with his enormous brain, and his superlinguistic genius. The cut-up technique produces the same dissociation of imagery, the same dislocation of imagery, only it is arrived at by mechanical means. In Burroughs's case it didn't come out of the Joycean vision at all . . . it came out of the junkie vision. It was too hard on his own body to keep up the junkie vision. To arrive at a different type of reality dislocation, he cut up the words by cutting up the paper, which was easier on his own head and body. He put down drugs and picked up a pair of scissors. Anyone who can pick up a frying pan—

[Meltzer]: *Is that what you could call native American surrealism: a strange, violent reaction to media, cutting it up and throwing it up . . . a sort of fragmenting?*

Yes. McLuhan said it all, I guess. And we end up with no Joyceans.

[Meltzer]: *I don't think so. What about Jack Hirschman?*

Like in his book *Jah?*

[Meltzer]: *Sure. That's like the American* Finnegans Wake.

Hirschman doesn't have the utter brilliance of language and articulation of Joyce. Yet Hirschman has his own. . . .

[Meltzer]: *I think it is there and will be known.*

Henry Miller never did any experimentation with language in this sense.

[Meltzer]: *But don't you think that those early books of Miller could act as a valuable contribution to native American surrealism?*

Air-Conditioned Nightmare. . . .

[Meltzer]: *Yes, and the* Tropics *and* Black Spring. *He was able to combine the lesson of Europe with the great Buffalo Bill American simplicity. Mickey Mouse faces 300 years of culture. . . .*

You know, Miller was attracted to Kerouac, at one point. He discovered Kerouac quite late, evidently. I remember when *Dharma Bums* came out. Jack was out here, and he was going to go to Big Sur to stay in my cabin. That is when he wrote a book called *Big Sur.* His editors must have named it, because it had nothing to do with Big Sur. He never really got into the Sur at all, never got south of Bixby Canyon. Miller was turned on to the *Dharma Bums.* They were talking to each other on the phone. Jack was here in City Lights and Miller was in Big Sur. They were going to meet for dinner at Ephraim Donner's house in Carmel Highlands. Miller went to Donner's, and Jack was drinking in town here. The afternoon kept getting later and later. Kerouac kept saying, "We'll get there, we'll leave soon. . . ." It got later and later, and Jack kept telling them on the phone, "We're leaving now. We'll be there in three hours . . . two-and-a-half hours, we'll make it in two . . . Cassady will drive me . . . we'll be there in no time. See you at seven." At seven Kerouac is still in town drinking. Eight o'clock. Nine o'clock . . . Miller is sitting, waiting. Kerouac never got there. And I don't think they ever did meet. That was the end of it.

Dharma Bums had all the elements that would appeal to Miller. The on-the-road trip, the air-conditioned nightmare, the mountaintops, and that freedom . . . the whole idea of dharma bums.

I haven't seen Kerouac in a long time . . . but I imagine that Jack is probably sitting in front of his TV set, wearing a baseball cap, with a bottle of Skid Row tokay, watching the ball game on TV in central Florida. Something seemed to die in him early in the 1950s—the Hemingway parallel again. Killing himself. Yet, by age forty-seven, he's written more and better than the Great Hunter. . . .

5

The French intellectual is something that I put down lately. The whole French civilization has led to their having become very effete. Even many of the ones involved in the May revolution last year. The difference between the young radical out here on the West Coast and the French intellectual is enormous. The American can do things himself with his hands . . . he is into the whole survival thing. There's no such thing as the *Whole Earth Catalog* in France. Of course, there are utopian communes there, but you have no such thing as groups that are doing everything themselves, making everything themselves, like leather, clothes, books, tools, and so on. . . .

The intellectual in Europe is like the intellectual in South America, Latin America. He doesn't wash dishes, for instance. Still a woman's place to do all that crap. The intellectual in Latin America (this isn't so in France) may talk very revolutionary ideas, but he is usually very well dressed in a white shirt, necktie, and even cuff links. When Ginsberg and I went to South America in 1959, this surprised me. We met poets and writers and intellectuals and professors from all the South American countries at this conference in Concepción. Including a lot of Communists. And practically everyone was meticulously dressed. They didn't have drip-dry shirts in those days, either. In other words, there was a housekeeper, a *criada* back home, ironing those shirts and doing the laundry. No one questioned this, in public at least. . . .

The second big difference I found was there were no mystic trips going on in France. Naturally, there are older mystics, and there have always been writers. René Daumal—for instance, *Mount Analogue*—but in the young kids, the revolutionary-age groups, there's little mysticism . . . nothing like the Hare Krishna Society or Zen or Gurdjieff. The kids who are turned on to Gurdjieff in America, however, don't realize the European background for the movement. Claude Pelieu is a French poet and translator living in the States, and he enlightened me on the history of Gurdjieff in Europe. I don't know whether this is all true, but it seems that Gurdjieff was a White Russian refugee from the Revolution. He left Russia in 1917 or so, and made quite a few counter-revolutionary statements at that time. Then he traveled to the Near East and had some contact with the Sufis. It's in his book, *Conversations with Remarkable Men.* During the Second World War, according to Pelieu, Gurdjieff was living in the suburbs of Paris and received Hitler and several of Hitler's main henchmen. In London and Paris Gurdjieff's followers were rich dilettantes. Rich old ladies and members of the upper leisure class.

They have a big hang-up on money in the Gurdjieff groups. You have to pay quite a lot of bread to attend, in some groups at least. Over here, the kids don't realize the possibly neofascist tendencies. Of course, Gurdjieff shouldn't be held responsible for what various followers have done with his ideas in America.

I mentioned before the neofascist tendencies among radicals. And it is in things like Scientology, which is very full of neofascist ideas. I would class them all together as a sort of psychic authoritarianism.

[Shoemaker]: *A friend of mine did a study at UBC. His doctoral thesis was on the fascist approach of youth today and how it is like the German youth of the late twenties and early thirties. Then the kids about my age were going to the woods and reading Hermann Hesse. They were carrying backpacks and hitchhiking all over the country. Women were hitchhiking publicly, singly. My friend firmly believed that the movement today is turning toward a kind of neofascism, toward a kind of psychic or intellectual fascism. Very strange. You can probably document it. Especially in Berkeley now. If you are not a member of the team, you are an enemy. The only escape is to claim that you are a visionary incompetent. That's the only way I make it. I go and say that I am not going to march on your line, and I am not a black power advocate, etc., etc., because I have something working in my mind that makes it impossible for me to participate in your physical revolution. They all allow me, but they won't allow another person who is just a good middle-class liberal, just simpatico. Very strange. But they will allow visionary incompetents. In fact, they encourage them. They figure these people to be as harmless as any.*

6

I came to S.F. in December of 1950. Rexroth was the center of the scene. Robert Duncan was here. There was also a scene around Duncan. Rexroth used to have Friday night open houses for all the poets who would go sit at his feet. I was very timid when I was living in France, and I would never dream of looking up a "literary figure." When Allen goes to France, he looks up everybody. He looked up Michaux or Céline. . . . I would never think of going out and meeting these people on my own.

When I came to S.F. I heard about Rexroth. I heard about him through Holly Bye, who was a friend of Kenneth Patchen's. Holly Bye was married to a printer named David Ruff, and they had a printing press. I met Patchen through Holly Bye.

The Patchens were living in North Beach. Patchen moved from the East Coast in about 1955, I think. I was living in an attic in Pacific Heights. I met Holly because she had gone to Swarthmore with Kirby, my wife. They were at Swarthmore together, and so she was the only person we knew here . . . the first person who had anything to do with any literary scene, and I think they took me over to Rexroth's house for the first time in about 1953. I was completely tongue-tied. I mean, he was a great man. I wasn't about to say anything! I went back for years before I even opened my mouth. I mean, even when he moved over to Scott Street, I was still the same way. I never said anything over there. I was too bashful to speak up. It was only in the late 1950s that I felt I could carry on a discussion with him.

[Meltzer]: *Was Kenneth Patchen sick when you first met him?*

He walked with a cane even then, but he was able to get around. He walked and shopped around North Beach. Shopping bag and cane. The Patchens lived on Green Street in North Beach, and he would come to the bookstore a lot. Except once. After we started publishing books, around 1955, it was Patchen's idea to have an autograph party for his book (*Poems of Humor and Protest*). We announced it and a crowd came, but he never showed up. That was the first and last time I ever gave an autograph party! His wife, Miriam, called up and said Patchen was feeling too bad to come.

Then his back got worse and worse. They moved to Palo Alto to be near the hospital, and they are still down there. It is in a sort of cul-de-sac off the freeway. And he just can't get out. He's just too sick. Painkillers all the time. It's a fucking tragedy. One of the great original American voices. And Stanford University has—so far as I know—never even recognized his presence. They should at least give him an honorary title of poet in residence. Even if they can't find a cent for him. It's disgraceful. Well, he doesn't need Stanford! I talked to him on the phone this week, for the first time in about a year. He said he had been a prisoner of his room for ten years. He sounds awful on the phone, obviously in pain. . . .

[Meltzer]: *Does the future look any brighter for him?*

No. He's had so many operations on his back. The Patchens once sued the doctors for malpractice, which was a very bad thing to do, because the case was thrown out of court, and the real result was that no doctor would take his case. He would come up here and sit in the lobby of the hospital, and no doctor would touch him. He's been wanting to move away from this area, to go somewhere where he isn't blackballed by the medical profession.

The Patchens have investigated Florida and places like Tucson, where the climate is good, but he said on the phone last week: "There's one thing I can't tolerate still, and that is intolerance."

[*Meltzer*]: *When did you first start publishing City Lights books?*

We started the bookstore in June of 1953. There was Pete Martin, who was an instructor in sociology at State College, and he was also a film buff. Pete Martin put out a magazine which was sociologically oriented toward film. It was called *City Lights,* an early pop-culture publication. It had people like Pauline Kael writing in it, and Mickey Martin and the Farbers.

I don't know where I saw the magazine *City Lights.* There was a total of five or six issues and, for some reason, I sent them some of my translations of Jacques Prévert. I discovered North Beach around this time, about 1952. The Black Cat was the first place I ever went to and then the Iron Pot. I met Pete Martin around then. He said, "Oh, you sent me those Prévert translations!" He used them, and I think that was the first thing I ever got published.

The bookstore was started to pay the rent for the magazine at the same location, 261 Columbus. That little second floor was the magazine office. I didn't have anything to do with the magazine, but I started the bookstore downstairs with Pete Martin. The idea was that we would open it up a few hours a day. Pete Martin was full of great ideas. He now runs a bookstore in New York, called the New Yorker Bookstore. I've never been in it, but I'm sure it's one of the most original around, knowing Pete—

In those days there were no pocket bookstores in the country. There weren't any pocket books except Penguins and the cheap ones you found in drugstores. And there was no place to buy them except in places like drugstores. It's pretty hard to imagine no paperback bookstores, but this was in 1953. So Pete Martin's idea was to have this place that had nothing but the best pocket books and to have all the political magazines, from left to right, which you couldn't get anywhere else. As soon as we opened the place, we couldn't get the door closed. Right from the beginning it was open until midnight, seven days a week, since 1953.

Pete Martin had so many ideas that he'd take off on something else before he finished the first thing. He split for New York after our first year. Got married or divorced, and the bookstore just continued. We started publishing in 1955. Just poetry. . . .

[*Shoemaker*]: *The books were typically modeled after French books . . . ?*

The little ones, the Pocket Poets series. The first ones we put out had a pasted-on label. I got this idea from Patchen's early edition of *An Astonished Eye Looks Out of the Air,* which had a pasted-on label window around the middle of it, with the title on it. The first one was done by hand. David Ruff and Holly Bye and Kirby and myself and Mimi Orr pasted on covers and gathered it by hand, like any other little press. The first printing was 1,000 copies. . . . [The first publication of the Pocket Poets series was ***Pictures of the Gone World*** by Ferlinghetti.]

Howl was the fourth book. The second was Rexroth's *Thirty Spanish Poems of Love and Exile,* and Patchen's *Poems of Humor and Protest* was the third book. And then came *Howl.* Now we are printing 20,000 at a crack on Ginsberg's books, on the reprints of all his books—*Planet News, Reality Sandwiches, Kaddish, Howl* . . . it's a lot of books of poetry. About once a year these books have to be reprinted. The first edition of *Howl* was only 1,500 copies.

We have over fifty books in print now. We were distributing a lot of other little presses up to this year, like Dave Haselwood, Four Seasons, Don Allen, Coyote, to fill out our list. It was an interesting thing to do. One bookstore where other bookstores could order all these little press books. We put them all together in one catalog and sent it across the country to libraries and book dealers. But it got to be too big, too much work. This year I decided I'd just have to slough off the little presses and just do our own books. . . . We were hung up in the city doing the dirty work on getting the books around the country, while half of the small-press editors were out in their communes turned on. I was also put off by the little presses taking government money. Most of them were taking grants from the National Foundation of the Arts, and I disagreed with doing that, and I didn't want to be caught up in cooperating in this.

I don't take any bread out of it now. I live on my royalties from New Directions. I used to work at the store like forty hours a week. Shig is the one that has always put in thousands of hours a week. The store couldn't have existed without him. He is the one that has really held it together all these years.

I haven't worked regularly at the bookstore in five or six years. In the fifties I worked there regularly, and that is what I lived on. I used to draw about $300 a month, at the most.

The bookstore really is unintentionally a nonprofit operation. Like in that old joke. For years the bookstore supported the publishing; now the publishing is better off than the bookstore. The bookstore keeps going, but there are more and more books, and there never is any cash left over after the fucking government gets paid! There are a lot of people living off it, though. We have six or eight people working. It's a good way to live, an interesting way to live—to say the least!

I have always believed in paying authors good royalties . . . as much as the New York publishers pay for paperback books. In fact, Allen Ginsberg gets more, because of the volume of his books. He gets more than paperback publishers normally pay. I don't know whether you would want to know how much royalties he got last year, but he got about $10,000 from City Lights. Which is a lot for a little press. The bottom dog on our list is Edward Dahlberg's *Bottom Dogs,* so far as copies sold each year go.

[*Meltzer*]: *I guess you will be going on a reading tour now. . . .*

Yes, I will be. It would be ideal when I go on a college reading tour to have something to back up my voice with. This is not to say that the voice can't make it on its own. It can make it on its own in a traditional reading, in a room with a lot of graduate students sitting there, the traditional type of poetry reading with a lot of polite murmuring and polite applause . . . but when you get into a mass scene where you have an enormous audience, not only do you have to have poems that have a good deal of "public surface" and might be considered performance poems, but it takes a very exceptional voice to make it with an enormous audience. Allen Ginsberg is one of the few that make it. He can be on the same program with a rock group because he has such a marvelously full voice. He could read the phone book and make it sound like a great poem.

For a person with a normal voice, like myself, it's great if you can use something like an autoharp. I can use an autoharp at home, but it is kind of cumbersome to carry around the country. . . . I can use it at home and turn on and get high chanting. But to do this at a big public reading . . . the idea is to come up with what you might call an American mantra.

One thing about the autoharp is that it is an indigenous American instrument. It's not like using the sitar or tamboura. And if you are using a guitar, you have to have a certain level of professional competence—unless you play it upside down in some cuckoo fashion and beat on it with a chopstick or play it with your teeth or something. Otherwise, I wouldn't get up on the stage with my guitar.

You can't take just any old poem and strum to it in the background. I am not talking about that. Nothing was worse than most of the poetry and jazz in the fifties. Most of it was awful. The poet ended up sounding like he was hawking fish from a street corner. All the musicians wanted to do was blow. Like, "Man, go ahead and read your poems, but we gotta blow."

Krishnamurti was here last winter and he was at a party. I asked him what he thought of chanting Hare Krishna, and he said, "Might as well chant Coca-Cola or Ave Maria." Kirby walked up and asked him for his autograph. And he refused. She really admired him. She had just finished reading one of his books and was very sincere about it. It was a faculty party after he'd given a lot of lectures in Berkeley. Mostly faculty people—everyone standing around in those cocktail dresses, suits; and he sort of away in a far end by himself. Kirby walks up with this book and pen and asks him to sign it. He would not sign it. He said: "Too much vanity." She felt really put down. It seemed to me that it is much more vain to refuse an autograph than to sign one.

I had a strange "conversation" with him, because he seemed very ill at ease at this party, like he didn't know whom to talk to. He didn't want to talk to all these people who looked like they were made of glass or plastic. He sort of looked like that, and I was the only guy in the room with a beard. This was before McClure and a whole contingent arrived. Anyway, Krishnamurti was standing around the punch bowl, but I couldn't get close enough to him to hear his voice. We were always about five feet apart. I would move up a little to hear his voice more clearly, and he moved back, as if he were afraid, as if I were going to break his bones or something. He was a very fragile-looking man. The conversation went something like this—he said: "I don't eat meat." I said: "Big deal! Neither do a lot of my friends." He said, "But I have never *tasted* it." I said: "OK, you win." That was about the sum total of my exchange with Krishnamurti. Brilliant.

Speaking of influence . . . Blaise Cendrars's *On the Trans-Siberian* was written maybe sixty years ago. Well, I read it and took the train in 1967. I took the Trans-Siberian from Moscow across Siberia—seven days and six nights—on the basis of having read this poem. I got pneumonia and was in a seamen's hospital near Vladivlostok in a town called Nakhodka, a workers' city. I damn near died! I could have died out there, and no one would have known for months and months. It was on the Sea of Japan, and there were no communications whatsoever with the outside world. None with Japan, and the only communication was back to Moscow. I don't know how we got started on that, except . . . except the power of the poem. I mean, that shows what literature can do in the way of changing the world. (I damn near died, thanks to Blaise Cendrars.)

MICHAEL SKAU (ESSAY DATE MARCH 1979)

SOURCE: Skau, Michael. "Toward a Third Stream Theatre: Lawrence Ferlinghetti's Plays." *Modern Drama* 22, no. 1 (March 1979): 29-38.

In the following essay, Skau examines Ferlinghetti's plays in Unfair Arguments with Existence *and* Routines.

One of the early practitioners of the "new theatre" was Lawrence Ferlinghetti, whose two volumes, ***Unfair Arguments with Existence*** and ***Routines,*** explore the dimensions and strategies of dramatic innovation. The influence of Bertolt Brecht, Jean Genet, Antonin Artaud, Samuel Beckett, and Eugéne Ionesco can be easily detected in many of his productions as he experiments with the forms and structures of drama. Ferlinghetti uses the expressive power of noise and silence, the disintegration of language, the integrity of production autonomy, and the involvement of the audience to disturb the conventional ambiance of the theatre, replacing the traditional with what he calls "Third Stream Theatre." Eschewing the professionalism and virtuosity of his acknowledged influences, Ferlinghetti provides effective and significant contributions to experimental theatre.

In 1966, Robert Brustein called for a "Third Theatre," offering "artistic license" as an alternative to serious dramas and those with commercial appeal.[1] Two years earlier, Ferlinghetti had defined his own dramatic form as "a 'third stream' between oldstyle dramas & spontaneous Action or improvisation, between Well Made Plays (with their coherent pictures of coherent worlds which now turn out to be the falsest) and those free-form Happenings made of primitive perceptual chaos."[2] Ferlinghetti's plays in ***Unfair Arguments with Existence*** lean more toward the "oldstyle dramas" and his ***Routines*** more toward the fledgling Happenings, but in both cases the author takes considerable liberties with the model forms. Ferlinghetti characterizes his "routines" as "nexuses of ordinary dramatics, nubs of normal plays" (***R*** [***Routines***], 1-2), and at first glance many of these do seem to have been printed in the seed stage. They are essentially situations, episodes, notions, and momentary insights, whose distortion and lack of development give them the quality of political cartoons. Most of the plays in ***Routines*** disdain dialogue, relying instead on elemental auditory or visual effects. Non-verbal cries and screams and surrealistic images, like a woman's head carried on a stick or a naked woman whose body is painted to resemble a bearded lady, dominate these plays.[3] Low humor, farce, and slapstick are also employed to enhance the alogical pattern. In ***The Alligation,*** Shooky enacts the theme of frustration which characterizes all of the plays: he raises himself to look out the window, then "*falls to floor, half raises self to window again, falls again, moves to another window, raises self slowly, falls back, half raises self again, falls back, half raises self again, falls back*" (***UA*** [***Unfair Arguments with Existence***], 22). Because the possibility of effective oral communication is no more feasible than Shooky's attempt at purposeful action, dialogue is shunned in the plays. In the longest play in ***Routines, Servants of the People,*** four loudspeakers are mounted on podiums before an audience composed of actors and the general public, and these loudspeakers dominate the play, providing as much meaningful interchange as the separate channels of a radio. The play focuses on the breakdown of communication, beginning with an introductory mingling of various voices in the audience, yielding a fragmented and colliding effect, much like the cut-up and fold-in techniques employed by William S. Burroughs (in fact, the play provides an epigraph from Burroughs). When the loudspeakers take over, their language is "*garbled,*" filled with empty political babbling and chauvinistic jargon. A woman in the audience is attacked by a perversion of communication, the logical fallacy known as the complex question: she is asked by a loudspeaker, "Have you ever been a member of the Communist Party, when did you join the Communist Party, and when did you finally irrevocably disassociate yourself from the Communist Party?" (***R,*** 47). As the loudspeakers continue, a "graduate student" rises to confront the mindless politics, but he is shouted down by the audience, and the loudspeakers once again gain control. However, the dissenter evidently has had an effect, because the audience gradually becomes a *"hum of confused voices."* The loudspeakers merge into a meaningless babble, and finally the controlling fascist forces reveal themselves, drowning out everything with their roars, whistles, and sirens. Typically, inarticulate and nonhuman sounds dominate the plays. In ***His Head,*** a man's reminiscences about his early love experiences are bombarded by incomprehensible responses: *"a headless wailing in the distance,"* a boy's lispings and cries, a recording of a woman singing until the *"phono goes slower & slower & the singing becomes a croak. It stops with a final long groan"* (***R,*** 15). ***The Jig Is Up*** substitutes for human speech screaming, roaring, wailing, and the voice of a truck—its horn, its motor starting, idling, gunned, and roaring off. ***Ha-Ha*** employs a "Laughing Record," fox-trots, explosions, martial music, jazz, and a large monkey who marks his several appearances by saying "Ha-Ha." ***An Evening at the Carnival*** concludes with a battle between *mariachi* music and the *Internationale.* The total effect of these sounds resembles the *Bruitisme,* or "noise music," proposed by the Italian futurist Russolo. At an extreme, the noises can even be brutally humanized: at the end of ***Three Thousand Red Ants,*** *"The alarm begins to ring. First it whispers, then it shouts"* (***UA,*** 18).

Several of the plays are more dependent on language, but nevertheless subvert this element. In ***Motherlode,*** the miner's monologues are filled with half-finished phrases and truncated idiomatic expressions. Characters in this play seem completely unaware of one another's vocal expressions, and ironically the miner wears a hearing-aid; at the end of the second scene, the miner and "the Schmuck" deliver their monologues simultaneously, further underlining the frustration of communication. Ferlinghetti continually employs verbal sabotage to highlight the communication impasse. Puns are a frequent tool for him. The development of ***Sleeper*** seems to depend largely on the fact that etymologically "jazz" and "jism" stem from the same root. When one recognizes that ***The Jig Is Up*** centers on the conflict of races in America, the puns in the title become obvious. In ***Our Little Trip,*** a man who was completely wrapped in a bandage exclaims, "Oh we are wounded, wound, unwound!" (***R,*** 8). In ***His Head,*** a boy lisps in the ear of a blindfolded man, who replies, "Oh, I see, I see" (***R,*** 13). In ***Bearded Lady*** **"Dies,"** an artist who exhibits paintings allegedly painted anonymously is dubbed "Anonymous Bosch." ***The Customs Collector in Baggy Pants*** is a collection of ribald jokes and double-entendres, as corny and clichéd as the jokes on vulgar cocktail napkins. In each play, the integrity of language is undermined as words slip and slide around in their meanings, usage, and connotations. Even language about language is sabotaged: the miner in ***Motherlode,*** whose pack mule loaded with books and an upright typewriter suggests that he is a symbol of the writer, says, "The Greeks had a—" and never finishes the phrase (***UA,*** 60). When language is used in these plays, it is groping or disintegrating, in either case a precarious tool for communication.

Since the role of language is reduced in the plays, the dramatic structure has to be refashioned into a more efficient vehicle. In his introductory notes to ***Unfair Arguments with Existence,*** Ferlinghetti modestly calls his dramas "rough drafts of plays for a new theatre, or for one that barely exists" (***UA,*** vii). The description seems much more appropriate to the scene-like quality of ***Routines,*** but Ferlinghetti is probably referring to the rough-hewn aspects of many of his plays. As author, he deliberately blurs the outlines of his productions. Characterization is reduced to a minimum, without a concern for personality or character traits. The personae of Ferlinghetti's plays are masks, empty shells of human beings. The playwright recognizes the dangers inherent in plays with such thin character development: "With the strangest problem still how to get real depth of emotion into such visually exciting & seemingly superficial scenes" (***R,*** 3). His rationale seems to stem from a belief that conventional characterization is invalid because identity itself is superficial. Thus, in ***Three Thousand Red Ants,*** Fat comments, "Make up our identities as we go along, on demand, as needed. Improvised names and faces! Improvised characters!" (***UA,*** 5). As a result, Ferlinghetti's characters are generic, seldom having names, usually referred to in blandly descriptive or occupational terms: Question Man, Blindfolded Man, Watch Salesman, American Diplomat, Graduate Student, etc. In ***Three Thousand Red Ants,*** the names of the characters, "Fat" and "Moth," are simply truncated forms of the generally descriptive terms, "Father" and "Mother." The villainess of ***The Alligation*** is named "Ladybird," but it is instructive to recall Ferlinghetti's disclaimer regarding the use of Eisenhower in his poem **"Tentative Description of a Dinner to Promote the Impeachment of Presi-**

dent Eisenhower": "Well, I hope all these people see that the poem is not aimed at Mister Eisenhower personally but at The President. He is a Real Nice Man. Just like Dad. Trueblue. Just not too bright in his President's uniform. It's just like the real nice man inside the cop's costume—you may hate the uniform for the power of the state it represents, but the man inside is not *it*. He's just a deluded walking symbol of it."[4] Ferlinghetti's plays attack not personalities, but the abuse of social roles, and the representatives of those social roles become the personae of his plays.

Ferlinghetti also steadfastly refuses to dictate the elements of production for the plays. By ignoring realism or authenticity, his dramas gain an autonomy which leaves them open-ended. Thus, in ***An Evening at the Carnival,*** during a battle between *mariachi* music and the *Internationale,* Ferlinghetti concludes: "This goes on indefinitely. Perhaps the native music will sound again & Fidelista rise again. No one knows how it will end" (***R,*** 33). Similarly, Ferlinghetti explains: "***The Alligation*** can be taken literally in several ways, depending upon the identity of Shooky. He may also be 'represented' as a Man in a Union Suit; his skin may change color; his suit may be striped. Directors should follow their Sisyphitic Noses."[5] In ***Swinger,*** Ferlinghetti comments about the major character: "Perhaps she was not naked when she entered but has disrobed in the dance" (***R,*** 16). An introductory note to ***The Victims of Amnesia*** states: "The female parts may or may not all be played by the same person" (***UA,*** 38). Finally, ***BORE*** presents an impassioned and eloquent manifesto for a revolutionary theatre (resembling in its principles the guerilla theatre of the Yippies) designed to point out and eventually correct the deficiencies of modern society, and the dramatic example which Ferlinghetti appends is tentative and sketchy, protecting the possibility of spontaneity.[6] The performances, thus, have a looseness which allows them to incorporate fresh materials and to adapt themselves to current events. The structure resembles the technique of minstrel poets who altered their materials to affect specific audiences in particular locales. Ferlinghetti pursued this tradition in his **"Oral Messages"** in ***A Coney Island of the Mind,*** where the printed form of the poems is not followed word for word in the poet's recording of them.[7] He used the same device in his poem **"One Thousand Fearful Words for Fidel Castro"**: "The poem has less than its thousand words. Ferlinghetti left space for a different ending in the chance that there could be a change in the political climate."[8] Likewise, recent editions of ***Tyrannus Nix?*** offer a coverleaf for the paperbound volume, appending verses entitled **"Watergate Rap 1969-1973,"** absorbing the scandal which surfaced after the original publication of the book. The result is a freedom from restriction and discipline. The poems and plays become plastic and can be refashioned for the occasion. In ***The Victims of Amnesia,*** Ferlinghetti speaks directly to the thematic effects of this freedom, when the night clerk exclaims: "I've had enough of this big con game, hear? Get somebody else to ferret things out, get somebody else to get the facts for the Register. I won't put up with it any longer, and I don't have to, either, hear? Make up your own vital statistics! Your own little reasons and rationalizations and aliases and alibis for living!" (***UA,*** 54). Ferlinghetti envisions his plays as "groping toward some tentative mystique" (***UA,*** vii), rather than imposing a vapid or unrealistic panacea. Thus, the autonomy of the dramatic productions ideally provides liberation for the audience as they pursue their own healthy and purposeful lives.

One of the most influential principles espoused by Antonin Artaud in *The Theater and its Double* involves the interaction between performers and audience: "It is in order to attack the spectator's sensibility on all sides that we advocate a revolving spectacle which, instead of making the stage and auditorium two closed worlds, without possible communication, spreads its visual and sonorous outbursts over the entire mass of the spectators."[9] Ferlinghetti uses a number of different techniques to break down the conventional barrier between the stage and the audience. In ***Servants of the People,*** the spectators merge with the performers until "it is impossible to tell the real actors from the rest of the audience" (***R,*** 36). In ***Our Little Trip,*** "The general public, the audience, or all those who come to 'bear witness' to this moment of life are given blankets as they arrive & asked to lie down under them." Clearly, Ferlinghetti's purpose is to destroy the ordinary comfort of the audience at a theatrical performance: he comments, "Naturally they stir restlessly" (***R,*** 5). In ***The Center for Death,*** the audience involvement occurs in the middle of the play, as "*From time to time the Watch Salesman steps down into the audience & hauls someone into the procession, or tries to, crying 'Time! Time!'*" (***R,*** 24). At times, the performances can become a confrontation between the stage and the audience as though they were antagonists. Thus, in ***The Victims of Amnesia,*** the night clerk swings a rifle around "*until it is aimed at front row of audience*"

(*UA,* 44), and later *"shakes fist at feet passing at windows, then at audience"* (*UA,* 53). Again, the point is to disturb the comfortable ambiance of the audience as spectators. The plays demand that the audience become accomplices in the performance, either by demanding their participation or by antagonizing them into reaction. At times, Ferlinghetti even tries to alter the theatrical setting and to specify the type of audience. His notes for ***Servants of the People,*** for example, suggest: "A stage is not needed. Any place people assemble will do. But the more distinguished the location the better. A large respectable audience is to be preferred to one made up of poets, artists and their ilk" (***R,*** 36). In addition, Ferlinghetti uses symbols designed to jar the audience out of comfortable, conventional patterns. In ***The Victims of Amnesia,*** a woman gives birth to a series of light bulbs, and Ferlinghetti notes, "Every attempt must be made to convince the spectators of the literal reality of what is happening, since it does happen & is real" (*UA,* 45). In ***Motherlode,*** the terrain is designed to resemble a human leg. In ***The Nose of Sisyphus,*** the title character attempts to push a globe up a playground slide with his nose. Michael Kirby has commented on the use of this type of symbol: "Although they may, like everything else, be interpreted, they are intended to stir the observer on an unconscious, alogical level. These unconscious symbols compare with rational symbols only in their aura of 'importance': we are aware of a significance and a 'meaning,' but our minds cannot discover it through the usual channels. Logical associations and unambiguous details that would help to establish a rational context are not available. There is no relevant framework of reason to which impressions may be referred."[10] The surrealistic images, thus, force an engagement on the part of the audience on levels which are not ordinarily involved. Ferlinghetti also has emphasized the value of non-rational communication: he celebrates "Transition from all this so-necessary dramatic anarchism to pure Poetic Action not necessarily logical or rational but with, at best, that kind of inexpressible inchoate meaning that springs from wild surmises of the imagination" (***R,*** 2). Freed from theatrical conventions, the playwright pursues imaginative truth, rather than the limited statements of reason.

Examination of a single Ferlinghetti play reveals more specifically the function of his techniques in the dramatic medium. In ***Three Thousand Red Ants,*** several concurrent themes are evident which also characterize many of the other plays and routines: man's virtually voyeuristic approach to the world outside his immediate sphere; woman's role in the resultant state of inaction; and the tyranny of the verbal medium contributing to the same disabling result. The play's bizarre setting is provided as *"a great big bed almost anyplace by the sea"* (*UA,* 3). When one of the characters wants to get up and leave, a door frame is lowered beside the bed. Later, a window frame is lowered to permit them to look out to sea. The play opens with a man named "Fat" awakening, and with him awakens language: "Mmm—*(silence)* Mmm—*(silence)* M—*(silence)* M—*(silence)* Mo—Mo—*(silence)* Moth—*(Sits up.)* Moth? *(Shakes her.)* Moth? *(Lies back.)* Moth! *(Silence)* Moth—er? *(Silence. Closes eyes, whispers.)* Moth! *(silence)* M—Mother?" (*UA,* 3). Fat is represented as an absentminded, bumbling, but humane man, more interested in cerebration than copulation. While reading in bed, he becomes fascinated by an ant which has somehow made its way onto his book. The parable of the ant becomes transparently obvious: Fat watches the ant as it crosses the words "man means," after which it falls off the edge, which reminds Fat of three thousand Red Chinese soldiers who fell through a cracked ice block and drowned. Fat's concern is somewhat qualified by the fact that he has only read about this disaster in the newspapers, which necessarily removes him from it as a reality: "those three thousand men in the paper who just got drowned" (*UA,* 7). The dialogue of the play serves to emphasize his distance from the tragedy: his wife asks, "Drowned in the where?" and Fat answers, "In the paper—Three thousand troops in Red China that just got drowned in the floods" (*UA,* 7). Nevertheless, Fat's sympathy seems genuine and sincere, and appears to be connected with his desire to get out of bed. However, his wife, "Moth," laughs off his social concern. She is frightened of ants and uninterested in the death of the three thousand soldiers. The ant and the soldiers are all the same to her: "So—a retired department store credit manager dreams about three thousand red ants in China!" (*UA,* 10). Moth is interested only in sex. She reads pornographic books, delights in bawdy jokes and sexual innuendo, recalls a recent sexual dream, and continuously attempts to seduce Fat into engaging in sexual intercourse with her. Fat, however, resists and becomes entranced by a reefed ship he sees through his window: through his binoculars he enthusiastically follows the attempts of the passengers to save themselves. A rescue plane flies overhead and its shadow crosses the bed, upsetting Moth, who finally kicks away the window and gibes at Fat. Political symbolism seems intended here: the plane is red, white, and blue; as it rushes to offer assistance to the endangered passengers, its black shadow invades the privacy of Fat and Moth in their bedroom. More importantly, however, both characters are limited in their perception of the plane: Fat sees it only as potential deliverance, while Moth sees only its frightening shadow.

Both Fat and Moth are substantially removed from the world outside their "bed." Moth is obsessed with recalling her past with Fat—"all those years." Fat is concerned with the present, but distanced from it: he can perceive it only through the newspapers and his binoculars. He is prevented from becoming involved with events, unable or unwilling to influence even the fate of the ant. Fat's inability to act is partially attributed to the debilitating, castrating influence of Moth: he confronts her, asking, "Why you always want to keep us shut in? Always close the window when I open it! Always close the doors! Why, why, why always shut the world out!" (***UA,*** 16-17). Their relationship is imaged by a passage Fat reads aloud from a book: "Like the ant queen, she carries the seed of her long-dead Prince Consort around for years" (***UA,*** 9). Later, Moth calls Fat "Prince Consort" and repeats the passage from the book. The accusation regarding women here also informs a number of Ferlinghetti's other presentations. In ***The Alligation,*** Ladybird refuses to grant Shooky his freedom, preferring to keep him in benevolent captivity. In ***Swinger,*** a woman attempts to capture a bull fiddle pendulum, a typical Ferlinghetti phallic symbol. She finally embraces it passionately, but only after she has managed to stop its swinging.

However, a more serious danger in ***Three Thousand Red Ants*** and in many of Ferlinghetti's other plays is the deterioration of the verbal process. Verbal disintegration threatens the relationship between the characters. Fat gets irritated when Moth calls him "Baby," while Moth is perturbed when Fat makes the sound "erk." At one point, Fat and Moth indulge aloud in reveries, each oblivious to the monologue of the other, lost in their own individual obsessions, speaking in tangents. The situation demonstrates the veracity of the statement made by the Graduate Student in ***Servants of the People***: "There is no dialogue. We have no basis for conducting one. And this is the true sadness of our position" (***R,*** 47). In ***Three Thousand Red Ants,*** speech patterns are continually interrupted and truncated, like the very names of the characters. Puns, language distortions, and verbal associations constantly sidetrack the characters from the active pursuit of their ideas. Verbal dislocation and subversion keep the two characters from the achievement of any purpose, whether sexual or social. The very audience itself is condemned along with the characters. When the window frame is lowered between the bed and the audience, Fat, ostensibly watching those endangered by the reefed ship, shouts encouragement. Moth tries to calm him down, and her words obviously are intended to apply to both the ship's passengers and the audience: "They can't hear you, way out there" (***UA,*** 15). By the end, an egg cup which Fat has broken, a dream he has had of eating an egg on the ice, the broken ice in Red China, a crack in the lens of the binoculars, and a crack he sees in the sky, all merge to image the fragmented psychological state: Fat is, as Moth calls him, a "Humpty Dumpty."

Like many of Ferlinghetti's other plays, ***Three Thousand Red Ants*** ends at a bleak impasse. Anticipating charges of pessimism, Ferlinghetti has pointed to "the symbolism of light in several plots" (***UA,*** vii). Following the helpful intervention by the rescue plane, the sun appears and sheds radiance. However, the dilemma of the protagonists remains unresolved and the brightening of the atmosphere seems contrived, at odds with the rest of the play. A more revealing illustration of Ferlinghetti's stance is offered by the conclusion of ***Our Little Trip.*** In this play, the Question Man badgers a couple: "Will or will not the individual endure, the free ego, the individual identity, will it always somehow manage to reassert itself in spite of all, no matter what it has to go through, no matter what it is subjected to, in spite of all—" (***R,*** 10-11). The focus then shifts to the couple: *"The two figures press against each other, fall to the ground and lie together, seeming to caress each other with a low moaning"* (***R,*** 11). This scene seems to offer Ferlinghetti's standard optimism in the power of the sensual experience—except that the two figures are completely wrapped in bandages. Their embrace has the chilling quality of the featureless kissing figures in Magritte's *Les Amants.* The optimism of the play is muffled, restrained: the proper instinct is there, but it is stifled by the conditions of existence. The tone of Ferlinghetti's plays is one of only wishful or tentative optimism, a condition he sees as integrally interwoven with the theatre itself: "Thus, feeling around on the frontiers of theatre, we may yet possibly discover some 'seeking action' in life itself" (*UA*, ix). The possibility of this discovery inspired much of the dramatic experimentation of the 1960's and led many of the playwrights to neglect stage polish and sophistication and to focus instead on visionary ideals of regeneration. For Ferlinghetti, dramatic experimentation has a moral purpose: the liberation of the theatre and freedom from dramatic conventions can offer the liberation of the individual identity and the free ego, and the "new theatre" can thus contribute to the evolution of the new man.

Notes

1. Robert Brustein, *The Third Theatre* (New York, 1969), pp. 3, 8.
2. Lawrence Ferlinghetti, *Routines* (New York, 1964), p. 2. Subsequent citations from this edition will be indicated by the letter "R" followed by the page numbers in the text. Citations from Lawrence Ferlinghetti, *Unfair Arguments with Existence* (New York, 1963) will be indicated by the letters "UA" followed by the page numbers in the text.
3. The bearded lady image seems surely to have been inspired by the painting *Le Viol* by the surrealist René Magritte.
4. Liner notes to the record album *Tentative Description of a Dinner to Promote the Impeachment of President Eisenhower and Other Poems,* Fantasy, 7004. The poem appears in Ferlinghetti's *Starting from San Francisco* (New York, 1967), pp. 41-44.
5. (UA, vii). The last phrase is an allusion to Ferlinghetti's own play *The Nose of Sisyphus,* which together with a play entitled *The Soldiers of No Country* was originally included in *Unfair Arguments with Existence.* Both plays were suppressed by the author in later editions. *The Nose of Sisyphus* now appears as the last play in *Routines.*
6. A Yippie manifesto is offered by Free [pseud. Abbie Hoffman], *Revolution for the Hell of It* (New York, 1968), p. 27: "The key to the puzzle lies in theater. We are theater in the streets: total and committed. We aim to involve people and use (unlike other movements locked in ideology) any weapon (prop) we can find. The aim is not to earn the respect, admiration, and love of everybody—it's to get people to do, to participate, whether positively or negatively. All is relevant, only 'the play's the thing.'"
7. *Poetry Readings in "The Cellar"*, Fantasy, 7002.
8. Samuel Charters, *Some Poems/Poets: Studies in American Underground Poetry Since 1945* (Berkeley, 1971), p. 83. The Castro poem appears in Ferlinghetti's *Starting from San Francisco,* pp. 48-52.
9. Antonin Artaud, *The Theater and its Double,* trans. Mary Caroline Richards (New York, 1958), p. 86.
10. Michael Kirby, *Happenings: An Illustrated Anthology* (New York, 1965), p. 20.

MICHAEL SKAU (ESSAY DATE 1987)

SOURCE: Skau, Michael. "The Poet as Poem: Ferlinghetti's Songs of Myself." *Concerning Poetry* 20 (1987): 57-71.

In the following essay, Skau illuminates Ferlinghetti's use of the first-person voice in his poetry.

> Such reflections lead me to the conclusion that criticism, abjuring, it is true, its dearest prerogatives but aiming, on the whole, at a goal less futile than the automatic adjustment of ideas should confine itself to scholarly incursions upon the very realm supposedly barred to it, and which, separate from the work, is a realm where the author's personality, victimized by the petty events of daily life, expresses itself quite freely and often in so distinctive a manner.
>
> (Breton 13)

Among the radical changes of technique and perspective in the art of the twentieth century, one that is frequently overlooked is the sociological fact that the situation of the artist has been altered by the proliferation of the mass media. Artists have become public to such an extent that their roles and reputations may easily become their major concerns—and their primary themes. The use of the first person in poetry traditionally becomes a device for universalization: an experience or sensation is employed to speak to or reveal a generalized point, embodying Lautréamont's tenet that "Whoever considers the life of a man finds therein the history of the species" (340). However, in much of the poetry of the Beat Generation writers, the personal and subjective elements become distressingly autistic: everyday trivia and personal experiences are described, as is frequently the case in Lawrence Ferlinghetti's poems, to portray and congratulate the writer himself. A chief subject of Ferlinghetti's poetry is often Ferlinghetti himself. The subjective element in the poems seems calculated to reveal the poet to the reader rather than to illuminate the reader. The success of his subjective poems is compromised when Ferlinghetti focuses self-consciously on his role as poet or on nugatory occasions and indulges in mock self-deprecation, but more frequently the genuine wit and comfortable presence of his speakers transform personal observations into significant images of the human condition.

Since World War II, the artist has become as important as—if not at times more important than—the work of art. The artist's personality and image are the most important creations. Thus, as A. Alvarez has charged, Dylan Thomas "was under

ON THE SUBJECT OF...

RAY BREMSER

Though his published output does not match that of Ginsberg, Kerouac, and other Beats, and though succeeding generations are not as influenced by his life and work, Ray Bremser is often considered the prototype for what it means to be "Beat." A troubled figure who committed a series of armed robberies and other minor crimes in the 1950s and 1960s, Bremser spent a good deal of time in jail. His publishing career began when he submitted poems to LeRoi Jones's journal *Yugen* at the behest of Ginsberg and Gregory Corso. Introduced to the New York Beats by Jones, Bremser became a social fixture on the scene and a frequent drinking buddy of Kerouac's.

Bremser's first collection of poetry, *Poems of Madness*, was published in 1965 and contains several pieces written while he was imprisoned. His second volume, *Angel* (1967), solidified his reputation as a jazz poet. Subsequent publications reinforced this label, and Bremser became known for animated readings of his work.

constant pressure from the literary Public Relations Officers to continue at all costs less with his poetry than with his act as the blindly inspired poet" (23). In addition, Salvador Dali promoted his reputation for bizarre behavior and outrageousness, as when he appeared on late night television talk shows or modeled capes in *Esquire* ("Swashbuckling" 106-09). His face, with an exquisitely sculptured moustache, is probably more readily recognizable than all but one or two of his paintings. He has created a commercially successful persona, characterized by eccentricity. Andy Warhol exploited the same propensity—and also satirized it: "'Why is *The Chelsea Girls* art?' [Warhol] inquired, referring to one of his movies. 'Well, first of all, it was made by an artist, and, second, that would come out as art'" (Quoted by Rosenberg 98), unconsciously echoing Robert Frost's "Poetry is the kind of things poets write." In addition, in 1966 Warhol advertised in a newspaper that he would sign his name to anything brought to him including dollar bills, thus converting these mundane objects into "Art" (Rosenberg 105). Likewise, he has loaned his name, as producer, to movies (*Trash*) and to rock music groups (The Velvet Underground). Warhol's use of a look-alike for personal appearances parodied this personality cult ingeniously. The more unconventional his behavior, the more public attention he would receive. After initial success the artist no longer need produce quality work (or even any work at all), so long as he remains in full view of the public eye.

This situation arises partially because the arts themselves have begun to closely approach the popular media. As the "popular" arts and the "serious" arts become virtually indistinguishable and interchangeable, the serious artists find themselves in the eminently seduceable roles of popular artists and become common property. As a result, their subsequent work, whether in the verbal, plastic, or performing arts, threatens to conform to the role in which they have been cast. The seemingly inevitable result is a diminution or sullying of the quality of their output through repetition and replication, if only to satisfy their constituency—or, at any rate, to avoid the alienation of that constituency. A viable and frequently occurring alternative is for the artists to offer themselves as substitutes for their works of art. Sometimes they, complicitly or inadvertently, find themselves performers within the world of popular art: Truman Capote, Norman Mailer, Jerzy Kosinski, and John Irving have all had bit acting parts in major films; Ferlinghetti appeared reading a poem in the film *The Last Waltz;* Allen Ginsberg toured with Bob Dylan's Rolling Thunder Review, and he has performed onstage with and recorded with the rock group The Clash on their *Combat Rock* album; Jack Kerouac is featured as a character in Tom Robbins's novel *Even Cowgirls Get the Blues,* and Ferlinghetti is a character in Richard Brautigan's novel *The Tokyo-Montana Express.* Popularity and public attention pose severe threats to artists. The quality of their production and the response of established critics to this work become inconsequential—as long as the response is extreme. Thus, a UPI release about the Surrounded Islands project of the artist Christo reveals that "project spokesmen say that reaction—any kind of reaction—is part of the point of the art work" (8 May 1983). In such a case, the very arbiters of artistic taste may await or attempt to anticipate the public verdict. Values grow eclectic until it is not rare to hear someone express enthusiasm for Beethoven *and* the Beatles, Goya *and* Christo,

Shakespeare *and* Vonnegut. The critic finds himself forced either to capitulate or to despair.

The Beat Generation writers have certainly perpetuated this problem, with their primarily subjective criteria. Their supporters have been bulwarks and proselytizers of the "I don't know what's good, but I know what I like" approach to the arts. This attitude, though thoroughly democratic, minimizes the validity of the trained eye of critical evaluation. It preaches that art is not to be understood but to be appreciated as experience. The ultimate criterion is intensity of vision; the truth or falseness of that vision matters less. To a limited degree, this intuitive approach has provided a valuable re-invigoration of the arts, but it has also left them terribly vulnerable to abuse.

Ferlinghetti is one of the most conspicuous practitioners of a new type of poetry designed as an intentional rebuke to what the Beats considered the sterility of academic poetry, what Ferlinghetti has characterized as

> the barren, polished poetry and well-mannered verse which had dominated many of the major poetry publications during the past decade or so, not to mention some of the "fashionable incoherence" which has passed for poetry in many of the smaller, *avant-garde* magazines and little presses.
>
> ("**Horn**" 134)

The new poetry demands that the reader engage it, interact with it, rather than study it (similarly, Bob Dylan once refused to allow his song lyrics to be anthologized in their entirety as poems because he did not want to be studied in the universities). Together with the development of a fresh poetics, a new type of subject matter arrives which is intensely personal and which often focuses sharply and clearly on the poet's sensibilities, what Leslie Fielder calls "the reemergence of the 'I' at the center of the poem" (233). However, this poetry is not confessional in the conventional sense. The poet details his everyday actions and reactions so that the poems become a record of his existence.

Ferlinghetti's range here is worth detailing: his subjective poems might well be seen as occasional, but the occasions inspiring them are often nugatory, as though the poet were attempting to illustrate another of Lautréamont's suggestions, that the unusual is to be found in the banal, as he tries "to write out the true poem of my life" ("**Genesis**" 445). His poem "Truth is not the secret of a few" seems to have resulted from a minor confrontation with either a librarian or an attendant at a museum. The trivial nature of the

Ray Bremser, 1934-.

complaint is reinforced by the conclusion of the poem, where the poet resorts to off-color humor:

> walking around in museums always makes me
> want to
> 'sit down'
> I always feel so
> constipated
> in those
> high altitudes.
>
> (***Pictures*** [***Pictures of the Gone World***] #9)

Similarly, in "**Bickford's Buddha**" (***Secret*** [***The Secret Meaning of Things***] 11-19), he recounts being evicted from Harvard Library by guards because he has no student identification card. He takes this eviction personally rather than considering its obviously general application. In a puerile and devastating diatribe, ***The Illustrated Wilfred Funk,*** Ferlinghetti employs a barrage of adolescent and scatalogical bile to condemn the character Funk, presumably redeeming such juvenilia by sudden self-condemnations of identification with Funk. This form of self-castigation also occurs in other poems as the poet mockingly and self-consciously deprecates himself and his artistic creations. Thus, he recalls a night during which a group of writers

> reading their worst verse
> (somewhat resembling this).
>
> ("**Overheard Conversations,**" ***Who*** [***Who Are We Now?***] 30)

ON THE SUBJECT OF...

BONNIE BREMSER

Born Bonnie Frazer on July 23, 1939, Bremser's involvement with the Beat Generation is widely considered to have commenced with her marriage to jazz poet Ray Bremser in 1959. Discussion of her life and her book *Troia: Mexican Memoirs* (1969) is frequently linked with her husband, whose significance in her career was evident when London Magazine Editions reissued *Troia* in 1971 as *For Love Of Ray.*

In his **"Populist Manifesto,"** he provides an indictment of the directions of contemporary poetry and charges himself also: "All you "Poets of the Cities" / hung in museums, including myself" (***Who*** 62).[1] In **"The Third World,"** Ferlinghetti calls attention to

> old funnyface
> myself
> the bargain tragedian.
> (***Open*** [***Open Eye, Open Heart***] 81-82)

Such self-criticism might at first glance seem to suggest that the poet's self-pitying disappointment at his supposed lack of physical beauty manifested itself in an outlook of cheap cynicism—until one recognizes how cleverly the poet has managed to link images of the conventional masks of comedy and tragedy.

Artistically damaging, however, are instances when the persona feels his poetic stature threatened. Ferlinghetti, who has described himself as "a poet against my will" (**"Genesis"** 445), incorporates his consciousness of and concern with his poetic role and reputation into the poems themselves. In "Bickford's Buddha" the poet visits the Harvard Co-op and hears a girl ask for "books by Ferlinghetti"; with the rather forced humor of colloquial spelling and grammar, he adds parenthetically, "They dint have none" (***Secret*** 11). Later, he passes the Grolier Bookshop, where photographs hang of the poets who have passed there. Because his own picture is not among them, he whines,

> Where am I
> walking by
> not announcing meself
> Phooey I'm a poet too.
> (***Secret*** 13)

Here again non-standard grammar attempts to mask the wounded pride of the speaker. In **"Mock Confessional"** he self-consciously says, "Anyway I hear people are wondering about me / and I've written this to clear the air" (***Open*** 6). In ***Back Roads to Far Places,*** he imagines himself aging:

> I'll be a strange wild
> wandering old man
> thought by some
> to be a sage.

On such occasions, self-aggrandizement can result in the embarrassment of poetic posturing. In **"Autobiography"** he gushes in celebration of his own creativity:

> I am a hill
> where poets run.
> . . . . .
> I am a hill of poetry.
> . . . . .
> For I am a still
> of poetry.
> I am a bank of song.
> (***Coney*** [***A Coney Island of the Mind***] 65; ellipses supplied)

Sometimes a single evaluative adjective accounts for the disconcerting impression of the poet's self-applause. In **"Holiday Inn Blues,"** the narrator sits in a bar "making up fantastic fictional histories" (***Landscapes*** [***Landscapes of Living and Dying***] 18) of two of the customers. After a series of sexual-religious puns in **"Mock Confessional,"** the speaker describes his jokes as "bright cocktail chatter" (***Open*** 7). **"The Love Nut"** (***Landscapes*** 16-17) depends entirely upon inverted self-congratulation: the narrator examines himself in a mirror and in mock castigation derides himself for his healthy, humane values. **"Director of Alienation"** (***Who*** 6-9), also opening with the speaker's sight of himself in a mirror, employs the very same tactic.

Closely connected with this self-concern are examples of the poet bewailing the demands made of him precisely because he is an artist. The result, of course, is obliquely self-congratulatory: the poet compliments himself by regretting the implications of his talent.[2] Thus, when Ferlinghetti states,

> Some days I'm afflicted
> with Observation Fever
> omnivorous perception of phenomena
> not just visual,
> (**"Bickford's Buddha,"** ***Secret*** 11)

the pose is that of the artist saying, "Look at me, a poet, looking at things," and the poetic middleman is not easily dismissed, for he becomes the essence of the poem. Ferlinghetti returns to the observer role often, feeling he is

really afflicted
with this observation biz
It never stops
on & on & on.
(**"Bickford's Buddha,"** ***Secret*** 12)

In a perceptive essay, Sally M. Gall examines a related tendency in contemporary poetry, "which frequently reduces to 'me talking to you about me—my thoughts, my feelings, my experiences,'" and in which she discovers a "preoccupation with the trivialities of day-to-day existence" and a "Stevensian 'Watch Me Thinking' air" (491). The stance is one which Ferlinghetti repeatedly adopts. As Wordsworth does in his preface to *Lyrical Ballads,* Ferlinghetti emphasizes the poet's ability to see more clearly than the ordinary man, and, to be sure, observation of the details of the world is artistically crucial. However, the difference between the description of this quality and the self-pluming of a man who claims to possess it is disturbing. Arrogance and effrontery do not contribute to the creation of a persona with whom the reader can feel comfortable. Camping out in the wilderness in **"Reading Apollinaire by the Rogue River,"** Ferlinghetti's narrative voice exclaims, "And I see the Rogue for real / as the Indians saw him" (***Northwest*** [***Northwest Ecolog***] 24). One is reminded of D. H. Lawrence's *Studies in Classic American Literature* with its criticism of Whitman for this type of encompassing presumption (166 ff.).

Ferlinghetti celebrates his own perception as the mystical third eye vision, his "blue blue eyes / which see as one eye / in the middle of the head" (**"True Confessional,"** ***Open*** 5). He smugly disparages a fellow passenger on a boattrain for what he assumes must be insensitivity:

That fellow on the boattrain who insisted
on playing blackjack
had teeth that stuck out
like lighthouses on a rocky coast
but
he had no eyes to see
the dusk flash past
horses in orchards
noiselessly running
bunches of birds
thrown up
and the butterflies of yesterday
that flittered on
my mind.
(***Pictures*** #20)

The effect is one of aesthetic snobbery, and the preening self-inflation is grating.

In several poems Ferlinghetti clearly adopts a voice intended to express a point of view antithetical to his own. In **"One Thousand Fearful Words for Fidel Castro,"** he employs what Samuel Charters calls the "rhetorical technique . . . of the pretended fool" (78) in order to reveal the shallowness and hypocrisy of an ultranationalistic American unsympathetic to Castro. The criticisms are hyperbolic and parodistic, until the conclusion, where the poet finally offers an endorsement of Castro's overthrow of Cuban oppression: "I give you my sprig of laurel" (***Starting*** [***Starting from San Francisco***] 52). The complexity of the problem of voice increases when one recognizes the allusions in the last stanza of the poem to Whitman's celebrations of Lincoln and the concluding line as a variant of "I give you my sprig of lilac," from "When Lilacs Last in the Dooryard Bloom'd" (234). Similarly, **"Highway Patrol"** becomes an exercise in impersonation, speaking through the persona of a bigoted, vulgar, and violent "red-neck" California patrolman; the poem concludes with a phrase identifying both the source of the persona's value and the source of Ferlinghetti's stereotyped portrait: "Just like in the movies" (***Who*** 38). In **"The Pied Piper of Iron Mountain,"** the speaker is a businessman from "the suburbs of Pittsburgh," with "steely" eyes and "iron progeny," who leads the children of the future into "the black mouth of Iron Mountain," away from what "once was a garden called Earth" (***Landscapes*** 11).

Many of Ferlinghetti's poems are verbal photographs, and the presence of a subjective quality, even if it serves only in the capacity of a commenting observer, prevents these poems from becoming flat still lifes and injects an experiential dimension. Often this dimension is necessary to maintain a realistic referent in the midst of surreal poetic fantasy. Thus, **"Overpopulation"** projects a futuristic society which is tempered by the narrator's hesitation, aroused by the hole in the newspaper he is reading: "I must have misunderstood something / in this story" (***Starting*** 28), he suggests, anticipating and disarming the reader's own skepticism. Many of Ferlighetti's poems, including **"Yes"** (***Pictures*** #7), **"The pennycandystore beyond the El"** (***Coney*** 35), **"Starting from San Francisco"** (***Starting*** 5-8), and **"Overpopulation"** (***Starting*** 28-32), face the reader with impressionistic and/or surrealistic materials, and the first-person presence provides a solidity and integrity which allow the poems to partake of natural human fantasy rather than to remain formal poetic constructs.

Ferlinghetti's subjective poems are most successful when the speaker is employed as a self-effacing, comfortable presence generating wit and warmth. The poet's preoccupation with his creative role can even be presented capably in these circumstances:

> Yet I have slept with beauty
> in my own weird way
> and I have made a hungry scene or two
> with beauty in my bed
> and so spilled out another poem or two
> and so spilled out another poem or two
> upon the Bosch-like
> world.
> (**"I have not lain with beauty all my life,"** *Coney* 24)

Here the modest choice of the word "spilled" lends the assertion the grace of humility and affords an escape from the charge of artistic egotism. **"Autobiography"** offers a generalized portrait tempered with ironic humor, beginning with a sad and disappointed American childhood:

> I looked homeward
> and saw no angel.
> I got caught stealing pencils
> from the Five and Ten Cent Store
> the same month I made Eagle Scout.
> (*Coney* 60)

The narrator goes on to describe the unfair and debilitating social conditions of modern America, which he assures the reader that he has witnessed, in an echo of Whitman's passage from "Song of Myself," "I am the man, I suffer'd, I was there" (51):

> I have seen them.
> I am the man.
> I was there.
> I suffered
> somewhat.
> (*Coney* 64)

The effect of the word "somewhat," its surprise heightened by the line break, provides a wry deflation of what could have been pomposity or sentimentality. An entry in ***Northwest Ecolog*** (14) employs a similar technique:

> A fifteen year old boy drowned here yesterday / swept way by the undercurrent / his boots on / sucked into a deep hole / We found a striped T-shirt and a pair of canvas shoes upon a beach downriver / Looked more like girls' shoes but might have been boys' if he were slightly androgynous / We turned them over to the county sheriff / who came zooming downriver / in a tin boat / with his emblem emblazoned on the bow / We didn't mention androgyny.

The control here is so tight and tough-minded that it threatens to err on the side of callousness.

Subjective poems set in specific dramatic situations require a focus on details which enables them to avoid the weaknesses of posturing and self-indulgence. Ferlinghetti's **"Great American Waterfront Poem"** (***Who*** 34-36) and **"In a Time of Revolution, For Instance"** (***Open*** 10-12) are particularly effective examples. In the former poem, the narrator finds himself in a situation increasingly familiar in America in the last half of the twentieth century: he is awaiting a phone call about his divorce decree. He finds himself on the "waterfront of existence," on the edge of land's stability, facing the treacherous freedom of the ocean. Furthermore, the narrator's personal feelings are mixed: he sees himself in a "divorce from civilization," in a classic struggle of Eros and Civilization, echoing the forces drawn by Marcuse, but he also fears that his gesture is futile, that "there isn't any longer any Away."[3] The poem is filled with personal tension, apprehension, and anxiety; it concludes realistically with a refusal to supply a facile resolution: "The tide is at the ebb The phone rings." The poem's success stems largely from its sympathetic portrait of an idealistic, vulnerable narrator, a man with more questions than answers, who sees, in convincing fashion, the helplessness of his own situation as applicable to the general human condition in an age when one cannot even expect Matthew Arnold's romantic fidelity after the Sea of Faith has begun to ebb. **"In a Time of Revolution, For Instance"** paints with telling perception the ambivalent response of a "have-not" confronted with the world of upper-class style. The mixed feelings of attraction and repulsion assert themselves immediately:

> I don't know how or why I
> thought they must be
> fucked-up except
> they were very beautiful.
> (***Open*** 10)

The detailed attention of the narrator to the appearance, manners, and behavior of the three "beautiful" people reveals the narrator's begrudging fascination. He recognizes the vast social and economic chasm that separates them from himself, and the epiphanic moment discloses his dissatisfaction with his own status, symbolized by his fishplate lunch:

> my fish finally arrived looking
> not quite unfrozen and
> quite plastic.
> (12)

Nevertheless, he admits, "I decided to eat it anyway," as he realizes that the good life, as attractive and elegant as it appears, is regrettably beyond his grasp. He resigns himself to the bleakness of his own world but allows himself the luxury of pipe dreams.

The success of these poems resides in the naturalness of the first-person voice, articulate in its depiction and development of specific situations, registering a middle range of life's common disappointments. The poems point no finger at specific villains: all are victims or potential victims. More importantly, the best of the subjective poems owe their mastery to the particular focus of perception, concentrating on the objects of observation rather than on the speaker's act of observation, thus revealing the narrator's character indirectly. In the introduction to his translation of Jacques Prevert's poems, Ferlinghetti applauds the French poet:

> Still there are many so-called poets around these days who have need of such a seeing-eye dog in the street. Prevert remains a great 'see-er' if not a great seer. He writes as one talks while walking, and 'la poesie est dans la demarche.' His ubiquitous eye enumerates the ordinary world with a 'movement transfigurateur.'
>
> (5)

The same praise can be offered to Ferlinghetti in his subjective poems—as long as that ubiquitous eye is not turned in upon itself. The "I" of the best of these poems provides a comfortable companion on those walks, a Virgil-like guide pointing to the familiar and the unfamiliar and discovering something to be marvelled at in everything perceived.

Notes

1. The allusion apparently involves Ferlinghetti's inclusion in a Dallas-organized 1974-75 exhibition entitled "Poets of the Cities New York and San Francisco 1950-1965."

2. Jack Kerouac indulges in similar affectation: in *On the Road,* Dean presses Sal about his writing, and Sal replies,

   > Hell, man, I know very well you didn't come to me only
   > to want to become a writer, and after all what do I
   > really know about it except that you've got to stick to it
   > with the energy of a benny addict.
   >
   > (7)

3. Ferlinghetti's assertion appears to echo Rupert Birkin's pronouncement that "There *is* no away" in D. H. Lawrence's *Women in Love* (238). Many of Ferlinghetti's poems reflect his interest in the themes and symbols of Lawrence, most obviously, of course, in "The Man Who Rode Away" (*Open* 34-36), which is specifically dedicated to Lawrence.

References

Alvarez, A. "Introduction: The New Poetry *or* Beyond the Gentility Principle." *The New Poetry.* Ed. A. Alvarez. London: Penguin, 1966. 21-32.

Breton, André. *Nadja.* Trans. Richard Howard. New York: Grove, 1960.

Charters, Samuel. *Some Poems/Poets: Studies in American Underground Poetry Since 1945.* Berkeley: Oyez, 1971.

Ferlinghetti, Lawrence. *Back Roads to Far Places.* New York: New Directions, 1971. N. pag.

———. *A Coney Island of the Mind.* New York: New Directions, 1958.

———. "Genesis of *After the Cries of the Birds.*" In *The Poetics of the New American Poetry.* Ed. Donald Allen and Warren Tallman. New York: Grove, 1973. 445-49.

———. "Horn on 'Howl.'" In *The Evergreen Review Reader.* Ed. Barney Rossett. New York: Castle, 1968. 134-38.

———. *The Illustrated Wilfred Funk.* San Francisco: City Lights, 1971. N. pag.

———. *Landscapes of Living & Dying.* New York: New Directions, 1979.

———. *Northwest Ecolog.* San Francisco: City Lights, 1978.

———. *Open Eye, Open Heart.* New York: New Directions, 1973.

———. *Pictures of the Gone World.* San Francisco: City Lights, 1955.

———. *The Secret Meaning of Things.* New York: New Directions, 1968.

———. *Starting from San Francisco.* New York: New Directions, 1967.

———. Translator's Note." *Selections from Paroles.* By Jacques Prévert. Trans. Lawrence Ferlinghetti. San Francisco: City Lights, 1966. 3-6.

———. *Who Are We Now?* New York: New Directions, 1976.

Fiedler, Leslie. *Waiting for the End.* New York: Stein and Day, 1964.

Gall, Sally M. "Domestic Monologues: The Problem of Voice in Contemporary American Poetry." *The Massachusetts Review* 23.3 (Autumn 1982): 489-503.

Kerouac, Jack. *On the Road.* New York: Signet, 1957.

Lautreamont, [Comte de] [Isidore Ducasse]. *Maldoror (Les Chants de Maldoror); Poesies.* Trans. Guy Wernham. New York: New Directions, 1965.

Lawrence, D. H. *Studies in Classic American Literature.* New York: Viking, 1964.

———. *Women in Love.* New York: Viking, 1960.

Poets of the Cities New York and San Francisco 1950-1965. [Dallas]: Dutton, 1974.

Rosenberg, Harold. *Art on the Edge: Creators and Situations.* New York: Macmillan, 1975.

"The Swashbuckling Cut of a Cape." *Esquire* 76.1 (July 1971): 106-09.

Whitman, Walt. *Complete Poetry and Selected Prose.* Ed. James E. Miller. Boston: Houghton, 1959.

JOHN O'KANE (ESSAY DATE SPRING 1989)

SOURCE: O'Kane, John. "Lawrence Ferlinghetti: Anarchism and the Poetry Revolution." *ENclitic* 11, no. 2 (spring 1989): 47-58.

In the following essay, O'Kane focuses on the political aspects of Ferlinghetti's works, viewing him as a "populist" poet.

Rage, rage against the dying of the light.
—Dylan Thomas

A stroll up Columbus Avenue from the looming international-style skyscrapers dwarfing the nearest BART station from City Lights Books, is not what it used to be. North Beach 1989 is a haphazard mix of trendy franchises, carnivalism catering to the always steady influx of tourists, porno paradises, and pastiched literary cafes mixed in with some of the genuine article. But it's also one of the West's celebrated Bohemias (or at least was), a site from where experiments in culture and politics have emanated, where inklings of change were first registered and nurtured to challenge the enveloping haze of these carnival utopias franchised to the American imagination. The frenzied din of challenge and experiment has rarely subsided since North Beach became part of our psyche, back in the 50s as home of the Beats and Bop.

But the mood has certainly changed a lot since the howling, angry poet-artists christened counter-culture and prepared the post-war generations for a send-off into the very different angriness of the 60s and beyond. City Lights Books, the fulcrum for the originary outbursts, is now, for many, more like a nostalgic dot on the officially-routed tourist circuit offering a little culture for the upwardly-mobile, or part of some new kind of Baedeker guide for the consumer to consult on the way to one of the better restaurants on the fringe of Little Italy.

Literary nostalgia has been institutionalized in the gridding of the streets. New street names cordon off the sectors of most importance in homage to Kenneth Rexroth, Jack Kerouac and other flashes of bohemian inspiration that will never die out in North Beach. As if these street names might help prevent the total fade into porno-paradise oblivion, remind everyone not to forget that something else existed on these slopes of Coit sometime back then, when art-making born of hunger and passion for resistance had a certain renaissance. Many, especially the fathers of SF who cooperated in this project, want to remember all that, but probably many more want to forget it. I quizzed a straw sample of the '89 resident in some of North Beach's yupscale environments about what the renaming meant to them and found that few knew of the writers being honored. Everybody's heard of Jack Kerouac, but few could offer much more than casual recollection. At Vesuvios, just across Jack Kerouac alley from City Lights Books, there was only a dim awareness of this monument (and a few—and residents of the immediate neighborhood at that—had never heard of Lawrence Ferlinghetti!). A *flaneur* at the fringe of this great city today will take a more predictable stroll than he would have in any of the stretches of time from the late 50s into the early 70s when wonderment was being born in spurts of unpredictability. Even Walter Benjamin might be taken back at the forgetful and regurgitated panorama of wonderless wanderlust, layers of more than a decade of revisionism.

It's really Lawrence Ferlinghetti's empire that sits among the arcades of croissanteria and talk-to-a-nude-woman carnival attractions. As co-founder of City Lights Books in 1951 (starting it with Peter Dean Martin, each putting up $500, to bankroll the publishing of vital literary works, already begun by Martin with *City Lights Review,* a short-lived publication lasting one more year), he's witnessed bursts of wonderment—too few in number—contained from the pressure to revise and take away that marks a conservative time. A time that has too few instances of the creative passion in resistance against god, country, and corporation (what often underwrites, he believes, the best art). One witnessing too many instances of academic imperialism (professors of poetry living off the poets, as he says). He's published the writers for over three decades that try to live up to visions of angriness and counter-revision, pass along into the 90s and beyond the raging obsession with pure freedom, the continual fascination with the "rebirth of wonder."

Is it possible this legacy can be forgotten amid the din of cultural and North Beach noise? Ferlinghetti says the establishment has a stake in squelching the rage pent-up since the early days of McCarthy, when his anarchist civil-libertarianism crystalized in poetry. Settling in San Francisco in the late 40s, after studying at the Sorbonne and Columbia on the GI Bill, he came under the influence of Kenneth Rexroth, like so many similarly-disposed youth in the early stages of the Cold War 50s. Rexroth's weekly gatherings dispensed the kernel of anarchist thinking, and this grooved Ferlinghetti's poetry and public philosophy for many years to come. He was active in the resistance to McCarthyism (San Francisco was a hotbed of anti-McCarthyism), which was steeped in anarchism (Lewis Hill, the founder of KPFA, symbolized the confluence of civil libertarianism and anarchist thought in the station's focus). His sympathies have extended toward almost every glimmer of utopian resistance, rebirths of wonder promising to offer escape from the dogmas of all systems (East, West or otherwise). Sympathy for Castro's revolution took him to Cuba in the early 60s to witness the energy of change in motion, before it too preferred rigid collectivism over individual wonderment (giving us **"One Thousand Fearful Words For Fidel Castro,"** January, 1961). Similar sympathies took him to France in the early months of '68, and to Mexico City in the fall of the same year in support of the student-fueled protests, just prior to the Olympics, against Government repression and censorship (**"Concerning the Suppression of *El Corno Emplumado*,"** in ***The Mexican Night***). Sojourns to Central America have preoccupied him to this day, especially Nicaragua where resistance struggles have had all the ingredients for a rebirth of wonder.

Ferlinghetti believes the response to his recent book, ***Love in the Days of Rage*** (Dutton, 1988), proves the point. There's little sympathy today for the raging legacy of anarchist resistance. Aside from the feature review offered by *In These Times* early in the year, there have only been a few scattered reviews-in-brief, and mostly in the fringe and alternative presses. The mainstream press has assigned it to the margins. Which makes sense in a way, Ferlinghetti admits, since the whole purpose of the book was to revive the energy which only ever exists on the margin. Especially in the late 80s, the years when post-revolutionary-rollback has been in place for nearly two decades. Anarchist thinking has fallen into disrepute among both poets and political theorists, always promising to be very bad for the GNP.

The book is very different than prior poetic ruminations on the "Coney Islands of the Mind" spewed forth endlessly by the jerky arbitration of industrial society. It is a book of prose, a novella with strong bursts of essay, that looks at "May '68" through the experiences of lovers caught up in the web of events set in motion by the student protests in March that sent the nation on a paralytic course until mid-June. Ferlinghetti was in Paris for most of this three month period, a place that nurtured his early literary and intellectual experiments before finding North Beach (also having French parental roots).

Why would Ferlinghetti write such a book in the late 80s? Why would he write a prosey novella that seems so unlike anything he's written to date (even very different from his 1960 novel, ***Her,*** a kind of surrealist parody of confessions in notebook form we have from Dostoyevsky, Rilke, Sartre and other existentialist writers)? Ferlinghetti says that this time in history was a very important one for him, and he believes as well that it was a time socially and politically unique in the West. For years, from the early ***Pictures of the Gone World*** all the way through the fairly recent Parisian poetic reflections (***Over All the Obscene Boundaries***), he has jabbed away at the repressions of industrial society with an uncommon aesthetic agility, aphorism after aphorism of usefully-fueled anger that so many have identified with. His phrases have resonated well beyond their life in poems. They are weighted with the valency of correct insight into living in the post-atomic era. In Ferlinghetti's most brilliantly crafted poetic indictments we have enough, a more than sufficient rap on the mindless excrescences of industrial life that speaks volumes.

How could any language or type of writing better render the emotional and social catharses? Is this the ruse of the aging seer who wants to make sure he saw, and was seen? A nostalgic looking back to a time romanticized by so many artists and intellectuals as the golden age beyond parochial pettifoggery, a time rife with the free-form imaginings of an anarchist philosophy? A new manifesto—manifestos are always written to be overunderstood—to innaugurate the 90s, a breeding ground for the possible revival of an anarcho-utopianism gushing forth from the dissemblage of Reaganite spite? Poets after all are read but not always *heard.* There's something about poetry that defies a true seriousness. What does poetry, conceived in moments of isolated inspiration, have to do with the revolution? We read the precious phrasings as we chase down an errand at the nearest mini-mall, end the day in arrested reflection after Arsenio Hall and just before slumber, or while seeking out the distractions of the latest trend in entertainment.

Practiced Populism

But Ferlinghetti is an admitted populist who believes poetry should be consumed in a different way. This means poetry communicating more than obsequious solipsism. It means poetry as an emotionally-charged public event cementing personal will into social bond. He has always wanted to make an impact with his readings, and performance, an emphasis on the Happening, has always been a big part of his public posture (manifestoed movements breaking free from private art have usually embraced some form of living theater of total expression). Concoctions of experimental theater and stand-up satire, echoes of Brecht-Artaud anti-theater, gave us ***Routines*** and ***Unfair Arguments with Existence.*** Many of his early poems in the 50s were conceived specifically for jazz accompaniment (melding with Bop culture). They were meant to be spontaneously spoken "oral messages" rather than poems written exclusively for the printed page, he admits (like "**Junkman's Obbligato**" and "**Autobiography**"). Doses of drama, music, poetry, and political rhetoric (we also have ***Tyrannus Nix?***) make up his magical populist Happenings.

Ferlinghetti admits that his poems—especially the early ones—are replete with plays on other lines. Playful citation marks the strong urge to overturn a master while paying respectful homage, to be accepted with his likes while outmaneuvering him. His free-form phrasings are too anarchic, and populist, to be clever academic exercises in quotation. His resistance and inversion of his forebears too satirical and ideologically motivated to be classed as harmless boudoir musings. His very diction and syntax marks popular distance from so much of our so-called canon.

Though housebroken on the likes of T.S. Eliot, Ezra Pound, W. B. Yeats, Walt Whitman, and Dylan Thomas, Ferlinghetti's populism couldn't be further from what these poets were all about (Whitman excepted). The inner-directed, reflective obscurantists of the poetic word had no place in his Cold War holocaust-crazed 50s, as if the colossal destruction of the war years just ended had made private, interior reflection an endangered species. His early offerings are riddled with lines from these fathers of the craft, but the gist of his jottings then and now is to open up to what he calls the "commonsensual public surface." In "**Junkman's Obbligato,**" he takes Eliot and Yeats to task for masturbating of high culture. There's no room for these condescending priests of mental experience: Eliot's stuffy rejection of lumpen pop everyday gleaning transcendent moments elusive to most of the throng; Yeats' romanticized spirit in one bucolic spread after another.

This speaker mocks all masters. He wants to live a life pealed back to penury and simple, direct material contact. No special christening here, he wishes to empty his pockets and disappear, missing all appointments and assigning all possessions to oblivion. The permutation of Prufrock's paralysis becomes, "let us arise and go now to where dogs do it." No Maud Gonne people's this junkyard of experiment: "Know whores thirdhand after everyone else is finished." The imminent end of civilization in a swift reach of "Wasteland" metaphor becomes a Chaplinesque playground:

Hurry up please it's time,
The end is coming.
Flash floods
Disasters in the sun
Dogs unleashed
Sister in the street
her brassiere backwards.
Let us arise and go now
into the interior dark night
of the soul's still bowery
and find ourselves anew
where subways stall and wait
under the River.

Prufrock's social pretensions and mental masturbation become a chance to point outward toward the public surface, and to call for the coexistence of egalitarianism and anarchy:

Let's cut out let's go
into the real interior of the country
where hockshops reign
mere unblind anarchy upon us . . .
Let us go then you and I
leaving our neckties behind on
lampposts
Take up the full beard
of walking anarchy
looking like Walt Whitman
a homemade bomb in the pocket.
I wish to descend in the social scale.
High society is low society.
I am a social climber
climbing downward
And the descent is difficult.

Yeats' Innisfree and woods of Arcady are mocked as escapist babble. Innisfree becomes "Manisfree," a switch to man's freedom over living the "true blue simple life of wisdom and wonderment." (Not really this anyway, since the speaker's imagination just conjures "poppies out of cowpods," and thinks "angels out of turds"). Ferlinghetti's Manisfree is "way up behind the broken words and woods of Arcady."

But he's hardly a simplistically popular populist of mass marketing. In the mid-70s, in the throes of what he calls the "revisionist decade," he took the care to put together ***the populist***

manifestos, poems and prose in defensive eulogy to a culture with hardly a trace of revolutionary consciousness (then seven or so years after the events of May '68). These statements come at the moment when utopian-anarchists of all stripes were seething in apocalyptic apologies. The economy began its slide, the first nuclear alert since the Cuban missile crisis negotiated the audacities of the oil embargo, and Watergate-inspired blows to the public conscience failed to bring about renewal, only an apathy lying somewhere between defensiveness and inactivity. The manifesto is always a defensive response, something has to be made manifest that is only latently evident. Breton was trying to reverse an imagined cultural slippage into a permanent state of anal rationality, create new markets for the spontaneous type. Ferlinghetti was trying to reverse and revise the rapidly occurring revisions.

The world was quickly becoming avidly academic and theoretically obsessed, poets and other writers carving out their slot in one sort of protective closet or another. Even the howling Allen Ginsberg had fallen into the trap of guru-seer, fondling metaphysicals in the private purview of mountainous retreat, only tangentially fulfilling the raging code of Beat ("No more chanting Hare Krishna while Rome Burns," in **"First Manifesto"**). He was seeing the "best minds of our generation destroyed by boredom at poetry readings," and called for a renewed mentality that could rejoice "over the end of industrial civilization, which is bad for earth & Man." Asking where Whitman's "wild children" have been hiding out, he bids poets to descend to the streets once more, to utter words that are the "common carrier for the transportation of the public to higher places." He lambasts the poets who write poetry about poetry, the masters of the "sawmill haiku," the "freaked-out cut-up poets," the "closet agitpropagators," the "Bolinas bucolics," and "hairy professors of poesie" who together are more interested in protecting their bohemias of private concern ("Who among you still speaks of revolution, . . . unscrews the locks from the doors in this revisionist decade?").

Ferlinghetti does, and with the force of a William Blake crying in a cultural wilderness, where industrial blights have forged mental manacles of myopia. The real enemies are the "objective gorillas & guerillas of the world," those who have colonized so much of what reality is passed off as in our age, the acquisitive rationalizers who've created nothing more than the "permanent alienation of the subjective." America has witnessed a mythical "two hundred years of freedom" only to invent, unwittingly, a state of exile for nearly every truly creative being right in country. The "subjective must take back the world" from the subverters, and make expatriation a life-style of the past. The alienated generations of creative life have lived out their expatriate visions for too long in spiteful retreat from the "short-haired hyenas who still rule everything." (Bohemian myths of vitalist exclusion from Hemingway, Lowry, Lawrence, and Miller all the way through Dylan, Cassady, and Ginsberg festering an alienated subjectivity from no contact with, and no productive direction of, the objective world, he suggests). He asks, "How many Punk Rockers waving swastikas" might it take to show us the fate of creative subjectivity in the land of the object?

He offers a non-alienated idiom of resistance against a host of symptoms. Poetic culture, taking on the bad things the objective enemy passes on, is dominated by "prose" in the typography of poetry: modern poetry is prose, the "poetic and the prosaic intellect masquerading in each other's clothes." Most of this "poetry" now is prose because it has no "passion musick." Like modern sculpture it loves the concrete, like minimal art it minimizes emotion in favor "of understated irony and implied intensity." Too separate from music, mimicking the speech of man "begun to approach the absolute staccato of machines and the hard rock and punk rock of electronic existence," it's all become a turning-inward mental masturbation in search for the discovery of the unknown within the self (poets "recording the personal'graphs of consciousness'"). Freud and Jung have replaced Marx as intellectual deities in a prose-introspection movement of the mind that, however much it is saying, sounds few "deep refrains and leitmotifs of our still mysterious existence." Too many of "our best brains simply not equal to the mass confusion of our colliding cultures nor to the confusion in how to tell poetry from prose."

He objects to writing that somehow dramatizes the alienation of the subjective from the objective in a kind of decadent mentalism (citing Ezra Pound's notion that "only in times of decadence does poetry separate itself from music"—and by implication, the emotions, erotic forces of completion). It chronicles plenty about our "soulless civilization," what it has done to "our free men to our Eros man and Eros woman the anarchist in each of us who is the poet in each of us." But what happened to the truly raging poetic idiom of challenge? This wild voice still wails in each of us every day, an "insurgent voice lost among machines and insane nationalisms still longing to break out." The objectivists colonize the insurgently wild with machines and rationally and arbitrarily imposed borders and boundaries that prevents the truly anarchist sensibility to flower.

Spring Anarchy

That's why the events of May were so attractive to Ferlinghetti. They promised a breakup of boundaries between nations, classes, political groups, and genders to celebrate the collective spirit of anarchy, the true expression of freedom at a time when individuality might find a space in collective harmony. Ferlinghetti knows this didn't last long, but has been fascinated by those brief weeks of erotic play.

He is well read in anarchist philosophy, and based the book on his interpretations of its practical usefulness. ***Love*** [***Love in the Days of Rage***] is dedicated to Fernando Pessoa, "whose anarchist Banker prefigured mine." Pessoa's novella from the 20s, *The Anarchist Banker,* is a parable about the paradoxes of anarchism expressed through the debates between two men (sort of a *My Dinner With Andre* with a little more punch). Ferlinghetti's treatment keeps the paradoxes, and touches up the ideas with a love relationship between a man and a woman that nearly puts it in the camp of Godard (a close cousin when it comes to the political-erotics of late 60s French culture). Ferlinghetti insists that anarchism is the only true philosophy to have in these times, the only check against dogmatism, the hold possessions have upon our psyche, the dictates of uniform living. He has been perpetually awaiting a "rebirth of wonder" since he wrote **"I am Waiting"** in the 50s: ". . . and I am waiting for the war to be fought which will make the world safe for anarchy and I am waiting for the final withering away of all governments and I am perpetually awaiting a rebirth of wonder." He was still waiting in 1968, and in 1988 when he penned the scenario in ***Love.***

Anti-totalitarian anarcho-utopianism buoyed the consciousness of so many of Ferlinghetti's generation, many who lived under authoritarian regimes in Europe and elsewhere, if not right here on main street USA. The extremes of total unfreedom, and the desire for absolute expression, breed one another. The intensity of anarchist thinking has always grown during times of greatest practical threat to the extinction of the individual (Bakunin's Russia for example). He grew up before and during WWII, and Fascism and Soviet Stalinism were the evils of the day that had to be met with an experimental voice of resistance. Where his European heros either leapt head first into philosophies of Being and Nothingness, codes of mental rebellion of one sort or another salvaging—or at least trying to salvage—individual selves in obscure imaginaries (varieties of Existentialism, for example), or hit the trenches with final force, Ferlinghetti became a popular sage, a translator of ideas important for us in the 20th century into an idiom specifically American.

Because what was happening right here on main street hasn't been the same as what has happened across the Atlantic. The Cold War Fascism of the 50s energizes the early poems, but all that was hardly the same as holocaust-Germany or Russia. Ferlinghetti batters away at "soft Fascisms" peculiar to America, amorphous glows of repression gathering momentum now for better than four decades, the era of post-World War II baby-boom America when a certain dark force of pessimism has weighed down on fake euphorias and promises of all kinds we associate with "progress." The contradictions of freedom dominate all of his writing. He asks, how can one exist in a *seeming* absence of overt checks on freedom of expression, a situation of political pluralism and freedom of speech and unlimited progress and all those things we live with everyday but can't quite *feel* what they mean, and have the sense of being unfree? This sensibility of living in America in this "progressive" era of post-industrial efficiency and frenetic wealth-acquisition, is what Ferlinghetti tries to capture. It's hard to really accept the cliche, bantered around by a lot of writers and intellectuals from Mumford to Mailer, that Americans live a species of Totalitarianism. Ferlinghetti has tested what this abstraction might mean for us now. This is only one reason why he has had such a large following. He performs an emotional and intellectual celebration of what freedom—and its absence—can possibly mean for the post-atomic citizen.

Attracted to Europe, especially France, spending a lot of time in Paris over the years, he's therefore a certain kind of American critic. The *real* revolutions happened there, here they become media events. Paris of Spring '68 was injected with some heavyweights offering the designer ideas that might have led to substantial change. During the same time we had the Columbia uprising, real in its way but only a middle-class (not to suggest May wasn't) playacting of the spectre of revolution, only a "strawberry statement" to the pose of rebellion (not to diminish the productive anti-war responses). Europe, the lore has it, is where the ideas come from that are experimented with in meaningful contexts for change. But what happens when they're imported to America, and then exported back after lengthy incubation? Do we get something like the inversion of De Tocqueville's fiction about America, Wenders' romanticized abstractions? Ferlinghetti has been criticized as an outsider foisting his notions on a cultural climate alien to the American imagination. He admits that the French are not very sympathetic to outsiders attempting to tamper with the events of May, but also that an outsider's view may actually have the benefit of sorting out the confusion, of coming closer to getting it right.

If so what did he get right? This summing-up novella is a sexy affair with a lot of anarchist additives, tamperings with the thought, revisions of the dogma, that leaves an attractive residue of the spirit and contradictions of what May '68 was all about (or at least what we think it was all about), its erotic logic.

Eros or Civilization

Anarchists from Bakunin onward have suspected permanence. They look at philosophies, political parties, governments, and groupings generally, with distrust. Collective formations will inevitably usurp individual freedom. They are total libertarians, always ready to break out of socially and mentally forged manacles that slot people into tracks of formulaic living. Erotics has to play a big part in truly libertarian revolts since control of sexual and fantasy life can be used to sustain the tyrannical collective. Carnal control can complete the rebellion, harness full freedom into a utopian social design. Blake and Whitman more than whisper their concerns and identities into Ferlinghetti's lines (in ***Love*** and elsewhere).

This "revolution" did lack what many others had. It wasn't 1789, 1848, or 1871 in Paris (one of those nostalgic reference points for the engaged imagination), but at heart a "libertarian revolt of the young, a youth revolt against boring society in general, a global revolt against what they saw as the false values of their elders with their entrenched hierarchies and hereditary authorities backed up by the state and the whole apparatus of control. . . ." This one of Ferlinghetti's rhetorical inserts to announce the differences. It was about the "imagination" ("power to the imagination" parlayed as a typical slogan), which was to reign in the place of "dismal bureaucracy." It wasn't even marxist in the nominal sense, the communists were against the actions of the anarchist, visonary students (the split between the unions, conventional marxists, intellectuals and others spelling the demise of the original unity a few weeks into the fray). The graffiti covering many of the buildings and public spaces at the time tells the story. Ferlinghetti gives a sampling: "The more I make love, the more I want revolution. The more I make revolution, the more I want to make love;" "Under the paving stones is the beach;" among others.

May '68 wasn't really about the shouting and struggling on the paved streets of Paris and elsewhere (though that was an important arena), but about some undefinable straining toward freedom erotically charged, and not so obvious from conventional political slogan. This was an anarchist impulse, and the logical result would be the destruction of all authority and structure, a bursting through the paved streets to a world where sensuous languor is always attached to the forces of insistent revolution. Or at least should be. Freedom has a lot more to do with self-realization and erotic expression. The State keeps people in bondage through enforcing codes of denial and limitation, and no matter how much levelling and subsidy are engineered to grease the machinery of public input, something will always be lacking.

This novella is supercharged with this unstateable absence. The "rebirth of wonder" in that aperture of utopian promise opening to view for a few short months in the Spring (the days of rage), is playacted in a love relationship. Annie is an American exile painter mired in the Sorbonne bohemia; Julian is a man of means, a banker, who also acquired some political capital in the anarchist resistance in Portugal against Salazar. The coupling ingeniously draws attention to the contradictory atmosphere May was. It destroys the illusion that choices, allegiances, and beliefs were clear-cut, that actions were somehow predictable according to one's station in life (they are unlikely bedfellows). It shows the extent to which individuals were compromised by dependence on some piece of the system, the establishment that controls everything. She's an aesthete bound to a code, and institution, that privileges imaginative reflection and shuns activism. He's a major part of the money business that controls everything, making the practical application of his political beliefs an all-or-nothing proposition (silent compromise or total destruction). The events of May, always in the background of their relationship, are always forcing them to go further, to get more involved or embrace a more complex slice of daily existence. They do finally get involved, but only according to their own imaginative, final-solution script, remaining aloof from the day-to-day engaging grit (again, like so many really were then). They are not political, but kind of eroticized by the whole affair gathering momentum day-by-day. To such an extent that it's not always easy to tell where the forces of social eruption and personal attraction either part company or fuse together. Annie says once that Julian reminded her of "a lot of people already."

Ferlinghetti presents a paradox for us to ponder, and the heros never escape its grip. Julian's anarchism remains a hyper-rational irrationalism that languishes in the anti-social, private action (never fusing with energies unleashed by the events and participated in by other well-meaning actors). Annie's aesthetic take on the events becomes a hyper-irrational rationalism that finally finds her fused with an erotics of nature in the mind, and left to *imagine* her love for Julian more than anything else. There's bound to be a certain defeatist spite in evidence, a fall into failed visions, since De Gaulle did assert power over the crippled country in June of '68, leaving aspiring revolutionaries to await a little longer for that "rebirth of wonder" fueled by the imagination. That isn't to say that since by book's end the characters—in particular Annie—are still not sure how the infinite possibilities of utopian thinking and desire for perfection can be put together with mere living, means they've failed. Incomplete realizations were ingrained in the anarchist visions governing the gist of the "new left" protest, dominated as it was by sentiments of the "poetry revolution." Species of "final answer" and urges toward perfection get intertwined on occasion, and defensive apocalyptic reactions can be (and were) the result. Julian after all devises a plan to destroy the system and capture its resources.

That isn't to say that Ferlinghetti believes anarchism, and imaginative expression, are doomed (these are his very favorites put into a new fiction). It's the symptoms of this time that are important, its unique contradictions; frustration at the seemingly unresolvable (hence "days of rage"). Julian actually becomes a terrorist who tires of babbling anarchist principles in the abstract. He recognizes that his thinking is incomplete, perhaps contradictory, that it is a question of moving to another phase, but he has to make a move. Desperation from an exemplar of a dying culture? "His name had a warmth and elegance about it that she liked, the decadent elegance of characters in pre-World War One novels like Brifault's *Europa,* that seemed to sum up a dying culture and that Annie had come across in George Whitman's bookstore down in the Rue de la Bucherie." He has a moral vision, and a history of sympathetic political resistance as a youth in Portugal against Salazar, but Annie suspects him as all talk, a wealthy banker, in the system, who has more than a few aristocratic connections with the dying culture he so despises. His political vision, kindled by the events of May, has revived his anarchism. And he seems truly sincere about becoming engaged in attempts to overthrow the tottering empire. Annie's challenges force him to take things a step further, to commit himself to an action which will vindicate him. Capitalizing on the government's instability, and his position as a banker, he will claim the large sum of money made available because of the bank's contingency plan. It is transfering its cash reserves to an undisclosed location outside the fray to await the turn of events. With the aid of Annie, armed with plastic explosives, they will move away from abstraction to concrete engagement. Annie travels separately by train to meet Julian at some pastoral retreat (in the neighborhood of his childhood), pondering all the while what it all means and what it is that obsesses her about him.

This almost seems too simple, a facile indictment of everything he—and she—supposedly represent, Ferlinghetti's way of showing the extent to which they both live a fiction. What will this do to enhance the vision of anarcho-utopia? Julian speaks and acts the anarchist paradox exactly. He feels it's important to remain separate until the revolutionary consciousness moves to a higher level because all social structures become tyrannical fictions. The only hope is to await the moment, in isolation, when action might not destroy liberty in the process, when perhaps groups can service disparate individuals. The final coup can only be accomplished through collective action, at one of these propitious moments. Until that time, Julian believes, "Work for the same ends, but work separately! Yes, that was it, that was it exactly. Working separately we'd all be separately free."

Julian never acts with anyone. Living a brief moment of idealized political theory shows the powers of reason turning back on themselves. Reason should produce healthy social-democratic compromise, but this would be just another example of collective tyranny. But utopias are hopeful dreams constructed with desire and the obsession with perfection, far cries from the rudiments of social theory. Annie's erotic take on the

May '68 scene appears to be Ferlinghetti's way of building on these limitations and failings, of moving to some other way of understanding this rebirth of wonder.

She's in constant fear of her life becoming rational (a realistic obsession in late 60s parlance: reason and anti-reason did battle in the face of the always receding permanent solution). We understand her to be typical in this respect, one among many who had attached the powers of the imagination to slithers of idealized politics, wary of the overly-intellectualized response but never shirking the pose of "intellectual" (at one point Annie and Julian saunter into a cafe to find Simone de Beauvoir and Jean-Paul Sartre intellectualizing at a table, and they reflect on how little they knew about their ideas, and how little interest in them existed among the throng of youth participating in the event). Her dreams are riddled with the bogey of reason. Priapic gods advise her against mixing love with reason (being like oil and water). Sartre appears to her once looking like "old man reason" himself. Eros will always overwhelm reason's stultifying dictates. The most important influence in her life came from a teacher she fell in love with. He showed her the artist as "the bearer of Eros, the bearer of the life force itself. . . . Eros versus civilization." The two will blindly battle one another to the end.

She paints everything she sees, having a painter's fantasy about Paris, imagining herself in the role of cafe artist at various periods of history (Impressionist, Cubist, Abstract-Expressionist, Gothic, Baroque, Surrealist etc.) framing its real essence, its aesthetic, historical and political meaning. She wants to have "nothing but a painter's dream forever and ever," taking freedoms (just like Julian) with the appearance of the outside world. They both put it in fluid perspective to meet each contingency. "Everything he was saying made perfect sense. Everything he was saying made no sense at all. He could use words, she was thinking, the way she could use paint, to say anything, to make up any perspective, to construct every kind of illusion, to construct any kind of pleasing picture, true or false."

With the outside world uncertain, the sexualized imagination too much for reason's civilized bondings in a social body, the poetry revolution—a recurring notion since the 50s for Ferlinghetti—initiates maneuvers for the emergence of some new kind of social contract, possibilities for that "rebirth of wonder." Ferlinghetti has an extended passage where they come in contact with the off-beat vanguardists of this revolution, the Poetry Police. These are a ragged band of wailing revolutionaries, a version of the YIPPIES in America who fought the war machine with doses of metaphysics (trying to bring down the military by levitating the Pentagon on the October '67 march). These police want to save the world from itself, make it safe for "beauty and love." They shout "profound wiggy formulas for eternal mad salvation." They are ready "to capture all libraries, newspapers, printing presses, and automats, and force their proprietors at pens point to print nothing henceforth but headlines of pure poetry and menus of pure love, every day's papers to be filled with nothing henceforth but pure poetry stories giving the latest positions and poses and appearances and manifestations and demonstrations of pure beauty made out of the whole cloth of naked reality itself . . ." The raging of The Haight and North Beach put to Left Bank music.

Has Ferlinghetti defined the consciousness of the poetry revolution through Annie? She finally sees Julian as a "phantom, an idea, an image in her head, or in her heart, whatever *that* was." She's a long way from a revolution. As she speeds along in the train to safety, temporarily at least, in rural France, the future looks so unfathomable that she can see better by screening out the reality of the actual landscape, "making up her own movie on the screen of her closed eyes." She becomes engaged erotically, and questions her capacity to fathom the truths and falsities of the personal and political worlds: ". . . that light hot upon her now, the Midi sun hot upon her, through the train window, and she felt aroused now in that hot sexual light that had aroused so many painters, creating their so hot paintings, their landscapes of light and desire. . . ."

Love itself may only be another thought, she wonders, the demon which the politicians and priests and marriage itself all destroy. Life on earth may be the persistent squelching of dream and vision, an endless accommodation to the way things are in all their ugly and tawdry trappings, a life of reason and compromise and, at best, social democratic common denominators. She envisions a pastoral escape, longing for physical life, lying with animals, taking in the "sexual soil hot in the sun." She imagines herself in a "gold field at the end of time, where all beings breathed as one," and seabirds cry "their unthinking threnodies."

Is this adolescent nirvana-seeking for the catchy oneness of the universe? A hip debunk of some of the testy talk of the day? Is civilization hopeless in no matter what form thought places it? Can there be no mind in anarchism? Are utopias momentary hallucinations that can never be held onto for any duration, erotic and poetic forays into seemingly civilized jungles of misdirection and chaos that expose over and over again what Freud and Marcuse found, that permanent and stable social forms are an illusion? Is civilization a fiction of guaranteed repressions which can only stifle forces of eros, the things that really matter for the evolution of man and society?

Rationally-inspired solutions were not a big part of the new, anarchist politics of the May scene (nor of the visionary new left resistance generally). And as a result, dramas played into a paradox. Visions of wonderment and alternatives to change the way things were cascaded off one another so rapidly that few could stop the drift into indecision and helplessness, what always invites the ideologists into the utopian vacuum with their measuring tools. Reason of some kind has always had to better, if only for a short time, the anarchist impulse. A lot of vision with only a modicum of design keeps dogma off on the periphery, shadowed by spontaneity, but invites nostalgia at what could have been, since nothing ever gets changed. Anarchist tropes *can* feed the dictatorship, give it reasons for existing. But Ferlinghetti knows this. We can read off his design from the parade of questions provoked by an attentive reading the book deserves.

He has something more in mind. What would a "poetry revolution" look like if we came across one in progress? Visionary art and poetry exists because something is awry in the social fabric. A perfectly crafted utopian system would render poets useless, or rather assign them different duties by merging their talents into socially-reproductive behavior. In anything shy of this perfection, art and politics will only just meddle in each others affairs, one threatening the existence of the other (vision afraid of brakes on experiment, ideas afraid of teeming unpredictability). Can the privately-generated sublime ever catalyze social and political progress? Castro brought poets and artists into his regime for the first few years, contributing to some measure of flowering freedom (as Ferlinghetti admits), and cultural life in the five or so years after the 1917 Russian Revolution was a major outpouring of the century. But the vengeful aftermath of these unleashings threatened to exterminate the sublime for several years to come, and with catastrophic results. When the erotic visions of the poet have no productive outlet, the result is "Piblokto madness," a disease Ferlinghetti refers to in ***Her,*** the 1960 novel, and elsewhere. Victims of Piblokto exhibit uncontrollable frenzies, and constant trade-offs between rational and irrational behavior, pondering solitude and agitated sociopathy.

Many are patiently awaiting the arrival of a true poetry revolution. Ferlinghetti's mission as a populist poet is to keep railing against the blights that prevent a rebirth of wonder, raging against "the dying of the light." He will keep alive the possibility of finding that delicate equipoise between art and politics.

GREGORY STEPHENSON (ESSAY DATE 1990)

SOURCE: Stephenson, Gregory. "The 'Spiritual Optics' of Lawrence Ferlinghetti." In *The Daybreak Boys: Essays on the Literature of the Beat Generation,* pp. 139-53. Carbondale: Southern Illinois University Press, 1990.

In the following essay, Stephenson analyzes the mythic concerns that he views as underlying Ferlinghetti's works.

The Sun's Light when he unfolds it
Depends on the Organ that beholds it.
"What is Man?" William Blake

The Eye of man a little narrow orb,
clos'd up & dark,
scarcely beholding the great light,
conversing with the Void.
Milton William Blake

I remember clearly that what impressed me and attracted me in the poetry of Lawrence Ferlinghetti, when I first read it as an adolescent twenty-five years ago, was its quality of mystery. By mystery I do not mean obscurity or hermeticism nor do I mean mystification, but rather, that magical, mythic, secret, and visionary power at the heart of the work of certain poets, that property that causes a poem to resonate so deeply in the mind of the reader. I continue to respond to that mystery in Ferlinghetti's work whenever I read or reread it, and for that reason I want to consider his writing with close attention, not to explain the mystery but to approach it, to honor it.

My procedure is simply to follow what I see as the inner continuity of concerns in Ferlinghetti's writing, the correlations of thought and of emotion and of image within and among the works and to trace elements of the whole design as I perceive them.

As I read it, the work of Lawrence Ferlinghetti proposes what I call (borrowing the phrase from the title of an essay by Thomas Carlyle) a "Spiritual Optics," that is, a way of being and seeing, a mode

(Left to Right) Bob Donlin, Neal Cassady, Allen Ginsberg, Robert LaVinge, and Lawrence Ferlinghetti outside of Ferlinghetti's City Lights Bookstore.

of identity and vision. Ferlinghetti's writing embodies a myth or metaphysic which conceives an original unity of being from which human consciousness, individual and generic, has fallen. The fallen state is one of division and conflict where the mind struggles toward reconciliation and reunification with original being. The impulse toward reunification involves a twofold, interrelated process in each human psyche: the integration of the fragmented, fallen consciousness into a unity; and the reconciliation of subject and object, of ego and nonego, in the communion of creative perception.

The development and definition of this "spiritual optics" is the central problem of Ferlinghetti's poetry, prose, and dramatic work. In the following I want to examine this double theme and to consider its evolution in his writing, with particular attention to his prose narrative ***Her,*** which represents a grammar of the premises and concerns of his work.

Her is an interior monologue narrated by Andy Raffine, an American painter living in Paris. In the opening paragraphs of the story, Raffine characterizes his psychic situation in terms of "a transaction with myself" and "a battle with the image."[1] These two elements of his problem are mutually reflexive. The first, the "transaction," is a quest for identity, a search for the whole or completed self, which he images as a sexual union. And the second element, the "battle," is a quest for vision, for a true perception of existence, a perception beyond habit and preconception, beyond subjectivity and objectivity. The state of being and seeing in which he hopes to unite the masculine and feminine aspects of the self, unite subject and object in vision, he calls "the fourth person singular" (90).

Raffine has a sense of an original, true, whole identity experienced in childhood and shattered when he was orphaned at an early age. He views himself as fallen and fragmented, continually seeking to refine and refind himself. He also sees his situation as a microcosm of the human condition, that we are "all of us, all splintered parts of the same whole" (40). In Raffine's view everyone, whether consciously or unconsciously, is engaged in a quest "searching for something all had lost," a condition of original human unity that is now "a lost community . . . a far country" from which we are exiled (76).

Accordingly, the world in which we live, the fallen world, is divided into the forces of redemption and liberation that would restore humankind to unity and the forces of repression and oppression that, perhaps unknowingly, enforce alienation and divisiveness. Poetry, music, visual art, eroticism, affection, ecstasy, compassion, beauty, communication, and love represent the reintegrative principles. Egotism, power, authority, dogma—as embodied by the military, the police, the clergy, the customs authorities, and others and as reflected in "regulations and protocols and codes and restrictions and taboos and constitutions and traffic regulations and accepted maxims and venerated proverbs"—represent the principles of conflict, impediment, and disunity (58).

Raffine is, potentially, a redemptive, regenerative figure who could, through his life and art, help to bring about "the true Liberation" ending "the prolonged Occupation of the world" (46). He could articulate the "final, irreducible secret" in paint, catalyze "the long overdue millenium of art and life" (88). Raffine is represented as a sort of Fisher King figure and is associated with fish imagery throughout the text ("the fishy king none other than myself, my name a brand of canned salt fish" [27]). He is sexually wounded, pursuing a female Grail in the figure of "Her."

Raffine's sexual wound is not physical but mental. It consists of his view of women as either virginal-maternal or as insatiable devourers. This fixation prevents him from consumating a sexual union. Repeatedly, at crucial moments of erotic encounter he fails, held back in fear by his illusions, abstractions, preconceptions, never learning to use "the one true key of love that could unlock all the doors" (104).

Similarly, Raffine fails continually in his art; his "orgasm" in paint is checked by an inevitable return to habit and cliché. He is unable to "break away into the free air of underivative creation" (111) and is frustrated in his attempts to "enact the new" (112).

Both Raffine's sexual and artistic failures are extentions of his essential failure to achieve identity and vision, a failure which ultimately results in his death.

Raffine's quest for identity and vision closely parallels the process of individuation as described by Carl Jung involving encounters with shadow and anima.

According to Jungian psychology, the shadow is a projection or personification of "the hidden, repressed and unfavorable (or nefarious) aspects of the personality."[2] The shadow is not altogether negative though; it also possesses creative qualities and virtues, "values that are needed by consciousness,"[3] including "even the most valuable and highest forces."[4]

Raffine's shadow in ***Her*** is Lubin, waiter at the Café Mabillon. Lubin is an ambiguous figure, whose face is "two masks, a mask of comedy superimposed on one of tragedy" (16), whose jaw "was meant to cup a violin, or to clench a bone" (65). Ferlinghetti compares him both to "a great bird of prey" (18) and to "a great shy dog" (64). Lubin is at once vulgar and wise, ragged and elegant, blasphemous and reverent. (There is a close resemblance, deliberate on the part of the author, between Lubin and Dr. Matthew O'Connor of Djuna Barnes' novel *Nightwood.*)

A drunkard and a debauchee, Lubin serves as confessor and counselor to the naive and idealistic Raffine. The identification between the two figures exists in both a paternal relationship (Lubin describes himself to Raffine as "your wandered father" [66].) and a twin relationship (doppelgänger, alter egos, opposite and complementary). To Lubin, Raffine is "my own past" (66), while he sees himself as "the billous tag-end of your future" (67) and in memory as "an earlier Andy Raffine" (68). Lubin's most important function is to disabuse Raffine of his notions concerning the virginity of "Her" and to serve as a mediator between Raffine and "Her." Lubin foresees disaster for Raffine, but his counsels and warnings to him are unheeded.

The second stage of the individuation process, according to Jungian psychology, "is characterized by the encounter with the *soul image,* . . . the complementary contrasexual part of the psyche"—for the male, the anima. The anima may manifest itself in a variety of forms including "a sweet young maiden, a goddess, a witch, an angel, a demon, a beggar woman, a whore, a devoted companion, an Amazon, etc."[5] Andy Raffine's anima takes the form of most of the named figures above, constantly metamorphosing. Like the shadow, the anima has two aspects, benevolent and malefic. In its sublime aspect the anima is often "fused with the figure of the Virgin," while in its infernal aspect it often presents itself in the figure of the femme fatale or a witch.[6]

Raffine's search for his anima is rooted in his childhood experience of the death of his mother, thus his insistence on purity and virginity. Another recurring virginal figure of Raffine's anima is "a little girl with a hoop in a dirdnl dress" (11), whose piece of white string that is "as purely white as innocence itself" becomes defiled by mud (17). These two images are inhibitory, obstructive, and finally destructive for him. During the most critical sexual encounter of the book, his failure is attributable to his fixation with such virginal purity, for he involuntarily recalls "that first face" and notices a soiled piece of white string on the floor beside the bed (118). The ultimate symbol of the manifestation of the maternalvirginal aspect of Raffine's anima is the statue of the Virgin on the cathedral Notre Dame, between whose breasts he climbs before falling, figuratively "tangled up and trussed" in string, to his death (156).

The baleful aspect of Raffine's anima is the concept of woman as the emasculator, the insatiable whore, the devourer. Raffine views women in terms of female archetypes such as the Sirens, exhausting helpless men "in perpetual orgasm" (55); the Mona Lisa, "that eternal dame having just eaten her husband, note the famous enigmatic smile of containment if not contentment" (88); Salome, "she wants more than my head she wants my body on a spit" (102); the Queen Bee, "no sooner is the union completed than my abdomen opens and my organ detaches itself" (109); and the ominous old crone flowerseller who reappears throughout the book, with her mad, raucous laugh, reminiscent of the "layer-out" figure of Robert Graves' Triple Goddess.

Raffine fails to integrate and reconcile the positive and negative qualities of his anima, fails to balance or direct the energy. In consequence, both aspects are destructive to him and result ultimately in his death. His failure is most apparent during the central romantic-erotic encounter of the story which takes place in Rome.

Raffine travels to Rome in a desperate endeavor to flee his "half-life" and to seek to achieve genuine identity and perception (84). He attempts to "see without the old associational turning eye that turns all it sees into its own" (93). Two brief unconsumated erotic encounters (one with a prostitute, the other with an Italian peasant girl) convince him of the necessity of liberating his psyche from his abstractions and preconceptions concerning women. He characterizes the restrictive grip of these habits of mind as a bird perched inside his head: "the crazy sad bird I carried in my head as the idea of woman . . . the parrot of love who kept repeating all the phrases and phases of it" (107). His quest culminates in an involvement with an American girl in a hotel in Rome. Raffine vows to himself that he will avoid all the old patterns and associations and "this time begin with the real and stick to it" (113). And, for a time, he succeeds: "Instead of a hazy image out of somebody else's painting or out of my own, I saw the girl in sharp outline, a clear incisive line . . ." (113-14). But as they are about to make love, Raffine realizes that they remain "anomymous bodies" to each other, each imposing a pattern upon or evoking an image from the other (118). Raffine cannot escape the imprint of his early experiences, the memory of his mother, his fixation with purity. They do not make love, do not comfort, warm, or awaken each other, do not save each other. Raffine recognizes that he remains on the "carrousel" of inauthentic identity and perception, revolving continually through the same experiences, never able to grab the brass ring of true selfhood and vision (119).

Still blindly and desperately seeking a union with the feminine to complete his "transaction" with himself, Raffine returns to Paris. There he ascends the cathedral Notre Dame by means of a scaffolding, embraces the statue of the Virgin, and falls to his death. Raffine's final, fatal fall is, like Finnegan's, a reenactment of the Fall of Man—"a falling away through a failure of contact through a failure of life" (147). The events of the story have taken place during the Lenten season, during Passion Week, and Raffine dies on Good Friday, a parody Christ, "a friday fish to hang upon the old hook" (149), an unhealed, unredeeming Fisher King who has lost his "battle with the image" (7).

The final images of the narrative may, however, indicate a *felix culpa,* or fortunate fall, a redemption in death for Andy Raffine: "God grips the genitals to catch illusionary me . . . he plays the deepsea catch he reels me in O god" (157). There is an echo here of a phrase of Lubin's: "The hand that grips the genitals, love plays the deepsea catch . . ." (68), which is later recalled and expanded by Raffine, "Love plays the deepsea catch, it's love will reel it in . . ." (139). Raffine is identified with fish both by means of his name, "a brand of canned salt fish," and by means of recurring fish imagery: "fished up . . . Fishface . . . swimming . . . fisheyed" (66-69) and again, "my sardine can alack . . . a fart of a fish . . . my sardine boat . . . your fishy fellow" (86). Thus, Raffine becomes "the deepsea catch" that is "played" throughout the book to be reeled in by God or by love in the end. Ferlinghetti employes a pun (a frequent device in ***Her***), perhaps a double pun, involving the use of the word *reel.* Aside from its surface contextual meaning of being drawn in as a fish on a line, it may also refer to the image of "the unwinding reel" of cinematic film that Raffine uses as a metaphor for his life and his identity, a film projected frame by frame and then recoiled (10). In the meeting of the two metaphors, fish and film, there may be another meaning created, a sound pun, a homophone. Raffine is not only reeled in (like a fish or a film) but, perhaps also, *realed* in as well; that is to say, reeled into the real. In this case, Raffine's final exclamation, "O god," may be understood not as a cry of despair but as an affirmation. He may, in death, have achieved the fourth person singular.

Her is a complex, resonant work whose themes are developed through recurring images and associations. There are paired opposites such as blindness/sight, key/lock, obesity/Lent, climbing/falling, virginity/licentiousness, sleeping/waking; and there are associative pairs or clusters such as shadow/haze/dusk/fog (suggestive of ordinary perception, that is, cliché, habit) and gramophone/film reel/carrousel (suggestive of the endlessly repetitive nature of ordinary perception and experience). In addition there are multivalent images such as string, fish, bird, film reel, door, statue, flowers, mirror, window, flushing toilets. Puns and literary allusions are frequent in the text.

Her represents the myth or metaphysic of Ferlinghetti's writing, the cosmography of his poetic imagination. His view of existence has much in common with that of the English romantic poets, particularly William Blake, but it is nonetheless distinctively and uniquely that of the author himself. According to Ferlinghetti's myth, human beings are fallen (from unity to disunity, from true perception to false and limited perception) and are, as a consequence of their fall, self-divided. Their inner divisions are reflected in the world they create that is divided between power and love. Authentic (or visionary) perception and authentic being (which in combination, constitute what I have named a "spiritual optics") are the means by which unified human identity may be regained and a return to the prelapsarian world accomplished. Ferlinghetti's art evolves out of his desire to communicate this vision and to uphold and advocate the cause of unity against disunity, love against power. Thus, the theme of vision and the absence of vision is, in its various aspects and applications, central to virtually all of Ferlinghetti's writing.

Lawrence Ferlinghetti's dramatic pieces, collected in ***Unfair Arguments with Existence*** and ***Routines,*** are extentions and expansions of the central myth articulated in ***Her.*** There is a particularly close relationship between ***Her*** and the play ***The Soldiers of No Country*** where the characters of Denny, Toledano, and Erma parallel those of Andy Raffine, Lubin, and "Her." The situation of the characters in a cave recalls certain of the images of ***Her*** and may ultimately derive from Plato's allegory in which the cave represents limited perception, the world of reflected reality, shadows. The cave is described in the stage directions as "womb-like," that is, a cave out of which we must be born.[7] Denny's complaint is similar to that of Andy Raffine: "Nobody's listening, we're just talking to ourselves. . . . They don't even see you . . . seeing only themselves or someone else, not you but another . . ." (***Unfair*** [***Arguments with Existence***], 9-10). Images of mirror, bird, white string, virginity, the Virgin, darkness and light, loss, a lost country without "evil or hate . . . only a blind urge to love" (***Unfair,*** 19) also unite the play with ***Her. The Soldiers of No Country*** seems more optimistic than ***Her,*** however, ending with Erma emerging from the darkness of the cave into the light and with a powerful image of birth.

The images of cracked binoculars, blindness, and the unwillingness to see in the plays ***3,000 Red Ants*** and ***Alligation*** evoke the eye and sight motifs of ***Her.*** In ***The Victims of Amnesia*** the conflict occurs between a Night Clerk, a benighted authoritarian who likes to play at being a conductor or a soldier, and Marie Mazda, associated with miracle, mystery, and light. ***Motherlode*** portrays another "sounding of the same eternal situation" wherein "prospecting for love, we dig flesh . . ." (***Unfair,*** vii-ix). The piece represents again the human quest for the lost and mythic "mainland" or "the land of lovers" (***Unfair,*** 91), the prelapsarian world from which we are exiled. The quest motif occurs again in ***The Customs Collector in Baggy Pants*** in which the object of the search is the lost "diamond of hope," associated also with erotic or generative powers, the power to love, "twin gems . . . King of Diamonds," which are also lost and must be recovered (***Unfair,*** 109). The figure of the customs collector and the flushing toilets of this piece recall identical images in ***Her.*** (There is, of course, a pun involved in the word *customs* in this context. The Custom's Agents represent the inner forces of custom and habituation that allow no contraband impressions or perceptions to pass.) Further images from ***Her,*** climbing and falling, are central to the final play of the volume, ***The Nose of Sisyphus.*** The opposition between vision and blindness, freedom and repression, spirit and animality, is configured in this instance as the conflict between Sisyphus, a heroic, redemptive figure, and Big Baboon, a menacing embodiment of all that is base and retrograde in humankind.

The shorter dramatic pieces of ***Routines*** reflect and explore particular aspects of existence as repetition, as habit, and as pattern. In his preface to the plays, Ferlinghetti declares that "life itself . . . [is] a blackout routine . . . [we are] lost in the vibration of a wreckage (of some other cosmos we fell out of)."[8] This metaphysical premise, already established in ***Her*** and developed in ***Unfair Arguments with Existence,*** provides a sense of the unity and continuity of the various "routines" as attempts to locate and describe the ground of our experience, with the ultimate intention of aiding us in transcending our condition.

The "question of identity" is the problem treated in ***Our Little Trip*** (***Routines,*** 9). Whether identity may be said to exist at all, whether it is attainable, and whether it is important are the issues raised by the Question Man, a dispassionate, reductive, intellectual relative of Big Baboon. The Question Man views human existence in terms of mechanics, physical properties, mental capacities, and operations, without metaphysics, without mystery, without meaning. The male-female relationship is again presented as being intimately involved with the process of identity. The central image of the piece is that of a man and a woman whose faces are wrapped in a single long bandage which attaches them to each other. We first see them "dressed conventionally," straining away from each other (***Routines,*** 6). Later, after an interval, they return to the stage naked except for the bandage around their faces and "now strain toward each other," finally rewinding themselves completely, pressing against each other and caressing (***Routines,*** 9). Their actions suggest a resolution to the question of identity, a casting aside of conventions, of defenses, a return to the true and original state of the soul, an integration of the masculine and feminine principles.

Male and female relationships are also the subject of ***His Head*** and ***Swinger,*** but these pieces seem only to describe conflicts without suggesting resolutions. They are, together with the other philosophical and political routines of the collection, provocations to the reader or to the audience, problems, questions to make us "think of life" and to precipitate "revolutionary solutions or evolutionary solutions" (***Routines,*** 23). As Ferlinghetti reminds us, "Routines never end; they have to be broken" (***Routines,*** 50).

Ferlinghetti's first volume of poems, ***Pictures of the Gone World,*** records epiphanies and vignettes of vision and satirizes and exposes elements of the conspiracy against joy and vision. In these poems, lovers, children, artists, and poets oppose librarians, cultural ambassadors, museum directors, priests, patrolmen—those who can neither love nor see because they have "been running / on the same old rails too long";[9] those who have "no eyes to see" the beauty of the world

ON THE SUBJECT OF...

CHARLES UPTON

Charles Upton is best known for his poetry collection *Panic Grass,* published by City Lights in 1968. The long poem is often described as a synthesis of *Howl* and *On the Road.* It is an apocalyptic vision provoked by a journey across a seemingly doomed America; the vision of a highly impressionable, somewhat inexperienced nineteen year old saddled with an uncompromising spirituality. The collection was followed by *Time Raid* (1969), a collection of more positive, lighthearted poems. In subsequent years, Upton traveled across America in a manner reminiscent of the Beat poets who preceded him, continuing to write about a variety of subjects. He also edited the anthology *Because You Talk* (1976).

because they are preoccupied with trivialities and superficialities (No. 20); the predatory and acquisitive; those who have no identity outside of "their hats and their jobs" (No. 26); those who have

> fatally assumed
> that some direct connection
> does exist between
> language and reality
> word and world.
> (No. 27)

The poems are also united with ***Her*** and to the plays by common imagery, including statues, mirrors, doors, virgin, and string.

A Coney Island of the Mind continues and expands the theme of vision with a unifying image of the eye. "The poet's eye obscenely seeing" discerns reality from illusion, the mysterious from the meretricious, the eternal from the temporal.[10] "The poet's eye" may be developed through response to literature or to visual art (Goya, Bosch, Chagall, Kafka help us to see) or may be retained from childhood "when every living thing / cast its shadow in eternity" (No. 19, 34). As in ***Her,*** humankind is engaged, consciously or unconsciously, in regaining "the lost shores" where there are "green birds singing / from the other side of silence" (No. 21, 36). Human beings are "all hunting love and half the hungry time not even knowing just what is really eating them"; they are "always on their hungry travels after the same hot grail" (No. 29, 44-45). In the paradise we seek there will be no clothes, no altars, no hierarchy or authority, but only "fountains of imagination" (No. 13, 28). And though we are confounded as to how to gain admittance to the castle of the "**Mystery of Existence**" where "it is heavenly weather" and "souls dance undressed / together," the poet assures us that "on the far side" there is "a wide wide vent . . . where even elephants / waltz thru" (No. 16, 31). We continually overlook the epiphanous possibilities of the obvious, the miraculous qualities of the commonplace.

In his "**Oral Messages**" section of ***A Coney Island of the Mind*** Ferlinghetti declares again and clarifies his opposition to tyranny, boredom, exploitation, nationalism, and war and reaffirms his faith in "a rebirth of wonder" and a "total dream of Innocence" ("**I Am Waiting**," 49-52). If we would return to "the true blue simple life / of wisdom and wonderment," we would reach the "Isle of Manisfree," the just and joyous society ("**Junkman's Obbligato**," 54-59). In "**Autobiography**" and "**Dog**" Ferlinghetti urges us to attention and observation of the world, to see what is around us with the innocent eye of the dog, to see directly, unintimidated, without abstractions or preconceptions, but instead "touching and tasting and testing everything" ("**Dog**," 68). And in "**Christ Climbed Down**," Christ is associated with "the poet's eye," potential in every human being, the ability to reject the superficial, to discern the essential. In a commercial, consumer society, artificial and hypocritical with a vacuum of values, Christ must seek rebirth, a Second Coming in the soul of every human: "In the darkest night / of everybody's anonymous soul / He awaits . . ." (70).

The image of a dormant, potential, redemptive force waiting in the world, waiting to be awakened in each separate psyche and in the collective human psyche, becomes the central motif of "**The Great Chinese Dragon**," which is one of the key poems of ***Starting from San Francisco.*** The dragon of the poem represents to the poet "the force and mystery of life," the true sight that "sees the spiritual everywhere translucent in the material world."[11] The dragon is guarded and restrained by the police, the agents of the conspiracy against joy and vision, who recognize and fear its apocalyptic power. The poem concludes with the image of the dragon buried in a cellar, awaiting "the final coming and the final sowing of his oats and teeth" (64). The dragon may be seen as the visionary imaginative potential within each human mind, restrained by the rational faculties and the collective regenerative qualities of humanity, repressed by the forces of authority, egotism, and materialism. (Appropriately, the ultimate etymological root of the word *dragon* is the Greek verb *derkesthai,* which means "to see.") Also closely related to the premises of ***Her*** are the concepts of the poem "**Hidden Door**" which rejects the "pathetic fallacy / of the evidence of the senses / as to the nature of reality" and explores the mystery of "our buried life," the attempt to rediscover the "lost shore of light," to find again the "mislaid visionary self" (31-35). A number of images from ***Her*** and from the plays recur in the poem, including the blind man with tin cup, key, door, climbing and falling, palimpsest, vulva, and mirror. The poem "**He**" describes a poet-prophet who is "the mad eye of the fourth person singular," who has achieved "unbuttoned vision" (36-41).

The Secret Meaning of Things is, as the title indicates, a further enquiry into visionary consciousness, an attempt to achieve and to convey a mode of observation that "leaves behind all phenomenal distinction," enabling the eye to perceive essences, inscapes, the mystery and the eternalness of temporal phenomena.[12] The volume is notable for two poems in particular, "**After the Cries of Birds**" and "**Moscow in the Wilderness, Segovia in the Snow**," which can be seen as companion pieces. In the first of the two poems, Ferlinghetti prophesies "a new visionary society . . . a new pastoral era" in America, the reconciliation of occidental and Oriental culture and thought, the American frontier translated into a metaphysical frontier, the new manifest destiny in "the wish to pursue what lies beyond the mind / . . . to move beyond the senses" (32-39). In the second of the poems, another prophecy, the Russian spirit, in the image of an ancient armadillo "asleep for centuries / in the cellar of the Kremlin," at last awakens to music, to ecstasy, and to vision (47-48). Considered together the two poems represent a prophecy, as described in Revelation, of "a new heaven and a new earth" achieved through the medium of the awakened eye.

The title to the volume ***Open Eye, Open Heart*** is again significant to the pervasive theme of vision. The phrase is taken from the poem "**True Confessional**" in which it refers to a way of seeing with the eye of "the inside self."[13] Images of light, "shining . . . bright . . . skeins of light . . . luminous," oppose those of darkness, "cobwebs of

Night . . . shadow"; the "inside self" is contrasted to the "outside with its bag of skin" (4-5). In such poems as **"Sueño Real," "The Real Magic Opera Begins,"** and **"Stone Reality Meditation"** the nature of reality is the central issue. These poems reflect an increased awareness of the ephemerality, the transitory nature, of material form with its "fugitive configurations" (21) that occur in "the eternal dream-time" (16).

The artist or poet, as in **"An Elegy on the Death of Kenneth Patchen,"** is still seen as a redemptive figure who struggles against "the agents of Death" (38) and who opposes the "various villainies of church and state" (45). Ferlinghetti again depicts art as the medium of awareness and of visionary consciousness. He mentions, in this connection, references to music by Telemann, sculpture by Giacometti, paintings by Ben Shahn, and the writings of Lorca, Whitman, Blake, and Lawrence. The absence of vision is recorded in the poem **"London, Rainy Day"** where "life's eternal situations / stutter on . . . Nothing moves in the leaded air," and the transcending, transforming power of the inner eye is inactive: "The blue rider does not appear" (46).

The "Her" figure, anima, muse of vision, psychic complement, appears again in ***Open Eye, Open Heart,*** glimpsed, lovely and elegant, in a restaurant or encountered in a Ramada Inn in Kansas, with her "far-eyed look" (13). The "Eternal Woman" remains a disturbing presence for Ferlinghetti, at once magnetically attractive and yet dreadful in her demand for absolute abnegation (29). **"Tantric Ballad"** treats the theme of man and woman as "counterparts," who in sexual union form a lotus flower, a perfected form (125).

The external and internal relationship between the masculine and the feminine and its relation to identity and vision is again a dominant theme in the poems of ***Who Are We Now?*** Man and woman relationships are the subject of several poems in the volume, including **"People Getting Divorced," "Short Story on a Painting of Gustav Klimt," "At the Bodega,"** and **"The Heavy."** In **"The Jack of Hearts,"** Ferlinghetti's paean to the prophet-visionary who can redeem "the time of the ostrich," who can awaken and enliven "the silent ones with frozen faces," the hero with open eye and open heart has found

> the sun-stone
> of himself
> the woman-man
> the whole man.[14]

And in **"I Am You,"** the poet praises and prophesies what Plato called the Spherical Man, the original and final human:

> Man half woman
>
> Woman half man
>
> And the two intertwined
>
> in each of us androgynous
> . . . . .
>
> in the end as in beginning.
> (19-20)

Further prophecies of ultimate harmony, ultimate unity, ultimate victory, occur in the poems **"A Vast Confusion"** and **"Olbers' Paradox."** In the first of these Ferlinghetti describes "a vast confusion in the universe" in which "all life's voices lost in night" and then envisions

> Chaos
> unscrambled
> back to the first
> harmonies
>
> And the first light.
> (44)

"Olbers' Paradox" is a metaphoric appropriation of the theory of an early astronomer Heinrich Olbers that "there *must* be a place / where all is light" and that the light from that place will one day reach the Earth (45). For Ferlinghetti the theory represents the final victory of light over darkness, the Great Awakening, the apocalypse of the fourth person singular:

> And then in that symbolic
> so poetic place
> which will be ours
> we'll be our own true shadows
> and our own illumination.
> (45)

In this manner the problems of identity and vision which were posited in ***Her*** are resolved in prophecy.

And in the concluding poems of the volume, **"Eight People on a Golf Course and One Bird of Freedom Flying Over"** and **"Populist Manifesto,"** Ferlinghetti reaffirms his belief in the inevitable and final triumph of the indestructible, resurrective phoenix of life, truth, and vision over the conspiracy of politics, industry, religion, the military, the media, bankers, and the police and reiterates his faith in poetry as a primary instrument of enlightenment: "Poetry the common carrier / for the transportation of the public / to higher places" (**"Populist Manifesto,"** 64).

The theme of "spiritual optics" that is articulated in the work of Lawrence Ferlinghetti is coherent and consistent but not static. Rather, it lends dynamism and invention to his writing, varying focus, tone, and response, permitting dramatic expansions and reductions of experience, fitting the poems to each other and to the plays and to ***Her*** in such a manner that they reinforce one another's meanings. The theme develops in the course of the work—from the diagnostic, essentially pessimistic ***Her,*** with its abortive poetry revolution and failed quester-hero, through the cautious hope in the plays and the early poems, with their continuing struggle from blindness to vision, from darkness to light, from power to love, from quotidian life toward "a renaissance of wonder" (**"I Am Waiting,"** ***Coney,*** 53), to the prophecies of the later poems which foresee a Great Awakening, the union of the masculine and the feminine principles, the reconciliation of Occident and Orient and of opposing ideologies, and which herald the emergence of a visionary society, "a new pastoral era," and the final victory of light over darkness.

Notes

1. Lawrence Ferlinghetti, *Her* (New York: New Directions, 1960), 9, 10. Further parenthetical references are to this edition; when necessary for clarity page references are preceded by *Her.*
2. Joseph L. Henderson, "Ancient Myths and Modern Man," in *Man and His Symbols,* ed. Carl G. Jung (New York: Dell, 1968), 110.
3. M. L. von Franz, "The Process of Individuation," in *Man and His Symbols,* 178.
4. Franz, 183.
5. Jolande Jacobi, *The Psychology of C. G. Jung,* rev. ed. (New Haven: Yale University Press, 1962), 111-12.
6. Franz, 196.
7. Lawrence Ferlinghetti, *Unfair Arguments with Existence* (New York: New Directions, 1963), 3. Further parenthetical references are to this edition; when necessary for clarity page references are preceded by *Unfair.*
8. Lawrence Ferlinghetti, *Routines* (New York: New Directions, 1964), 1. Further parenthetical references are to this edition; when necessary for clarity page references are preceded by *Routines.*
9. Lawrence Ferlinghetti, No. 2, in *Pictures of the Gone World* (San Francisco: City Lights Books, 1955). Further parenthetical references to this unpaginated edition are cited in text by poem number and when necessary for clarity followed by *Pictures.*
10. Lawrence Ferlinghetti, No. 3, in *A Coney Island of the Mind* (New York: New Directions, 1958), 13. Further parenthetical references are to this edition; when necessary for clarity page references are preceded by *Coney.*
11. Lawrence Ferlinghetti, *Starting from San Francisco* (New York: New Directions, 1961), 61-62. Further parenthetical references are to this edition; when necessary for clarity page references are preceded by *Starting.*
12. Lawrence Ferlinghetti, *The Secret Meaning of Things* (New York: New Directions, 1968), 18. Further parenthetical references are to this edition; when necessary for clarity page references are preceded by *Secret.*
13. Lawrence Ferlinghetti, *Open Eye, Open Heart* (New York: New Directions, 1973), 5. Further parenthetical references are to this edition; when necessary for clarity page references are preceded by *Open.*
14. Lawrence Ferlinghetti, *Who Are We Now?* (New York: New Directions, 1976), 4-5. Further parenthetical references are to this edition; when necessary for clarity page references are preceded by *Who.*

ALISTAIR WISKER (ESSAY 1996)

SOURCE: Wisker, Alistair. "An Anarchist among the Floorwalkers: The Poetry of Lawrence Ferlinghetti." In *The Beat Generation Writers,* edited by A. Robert Lee, pp. 74-94. London: Pluto Press, 1996.

In the following essay, Wisker provides an overview of Ferlinghetti's career as an author and publisher.

Who's this bum
crept in from the streets
blinking in the neon
an anarchist among the floorwalkers
    Lawrence Ferlinghetti: ***Director of Alienation***

I first encountered the Beats, Lawrence Ferlinghetti prime among them, in the 1960s. Two volumes served in particular: the Penguin *Modern Poets 5* and ***Pictures Of The Gone World*** published by City Lights in the Pocket Poets Series. The view quickly, and rightly, spread that here was a poetry whose voice was direct, questioning, warning, cajoling, enjoining, irreverent and in touch with the thoughts, feelings and paraphernalia of the contemporary generation.

Ferlinghetti's **'In Goya's Greatest Scenes'** held a special force:

In Goya's greatest scenes we seem to see
                                        the people of
   the world
    exactly as the moment when
       they first attained the title of
                                        'suffering
   humanity'[1]

The poem opens with these lines and then sets off to explore the characteristics of suffering humanity caught by the 'imagination of disaster': 'they are so bloody real / it is as if they really still existed'. At that point the poem shifts directly to the contemporary world in which we find the same people, albeit in a changed landscape of false windmills, 50-lane freeways and billboards, a concrete continent which has:

> more maimed citizens
> in painted cars
> and they have strange licence plates
> and engines
> that devour America

Here we have a voice of perception, engaged and angry at what it perceives. It is a committed voice, anxious about the way things seem to be going, determined to share that perception and to speak out purposefully.

This populist view of poetry was one Ferlinghetti has clearly shared with other San Francisco poets, among them Robert Duncan, Philip Whalen, Michael McClure and Gary Snyder. One meets it again in early lines from the following early (and untitled) poem:

> Constantly risking absurdity
> and death
> whenever he performs
> above the heads
> of his audience[2]

The poet-acrobat, 'a little charleychaplin man', climbs onto a high wire which he has made and reaches towards a still higher perch where 'Beauty stands and waits'. As she starts her death-defying leap it is uncertain whether or not the poet-acrobat will catch her fair, eternal form. The poet is seen as a chancer, a perceiver, an instructor, and a performer, 'the super realist / who must perforce perceive / taut truth'. All the tricks he can muster are played, by the poet, in order to perceive and communicate this 'taut truth'. At his best Ferlinghetti is a great communicator and his fascination is, very often, with oral communication—the impact of the human voice sometimes together with musical accompaniment. He has spoken of 'street poetry':

> Getting poetry back into the street where it once was, out of the classroom, out of the speech department, and—in fact—off the printed page. The printed word has made poetry so silent.[3]

Ferlinghetti's second book, ***A Coney Island Of The Mind,*** published in 1958, contains seven poems grouped together under the title **'Oral Messages'**. These are fluid, deliberately incomplete pieces in which the speaker announces:

> I am waiting for my case to come up
> and I am waiting
> for a rebirth of wonder
> and I am waiting for someone
> to really discover America[4]

One of the themes to which Ferlinghetti often returns is to be found in the idea that there is a real America still to be discovered and, as we shall see . . . , this becomes the subject of a later poem—**'After the Cries of The Birds'**—in which San Francisco sets off to become the real America. The seven **'Oral Messages'**—**'I Am Waiting'**, **'Junkman's Obbligato'**, **'Autobiography'**, **'Dog'**, **'Christ Climbed Down'**, **'The Long Street'** and **'Meet Miss Subways'**—have in common a fluidity, an atmosphere of the rebirth of wonder, and a sense of discovery. Ferlinghetti identifies the poems as 'conceived specifically for jazz accompaniment and as such [they] should be considered as spontaneously spoken "oral messages" rather than as poems written for the printed page'.[5] These poems were performed as experiments and Ferlinghetti described them as still in a state of change. They were originally available on a recording which he made with Kenneth Rexroth and the Cellar Jazz Quintet of San Francisco. **'Dog'** has been reprinted many times over the years but it is perhaps **'Autobiography'**[6] which most clearly represents the character of the set of poems. The refrain has to do with 'leading a quiet life / in Mike's place every day'. The poem is a thematic exploration of this 'quiet life' in which the speaker watches the champs of the Dante Billiard Parlor, gets caught stealing pencils from the Five and Ten Cent Store, lands in Normandy, goes on watching the world walk by, reads the Classified columns, sees Walden Pond drained to make an amusement park and is only temporarily a tie salesman whilst waiting for a top job. Here we have the same kind of apparently wandering narrative, the same kind of casual, committed, faithfully recorded, fictionalised, romantic listing of the sights and scenes of everyday life, its thoughts, dreams and disasters that gets into the lyrics of Bob Dylan and, later, of Bruce Springsteen. It is a world in which the old certainties, the old reverences and the going sense of meaning are all under scrutiny, if not lost already; a world in which the speaker, who both is and isn't Lawrence Ferlinghetti, has 'read somewhere / the Meaning of Existence' yet has 'forgotten / just exactly where'.[7]

Another 'take' on Ferlinghetti lies in a poem like **'Summer in Brooklyn'** which begins:

> Fortune
> has its cookies to give out
> which is a good thing
> since it's been a long time since
> that summer in Brooklyn
> when they closed off the street
> one hot day
> and the

FIREMEN
turned on their
hoses
and all the kids ran out[8]

As the poem proceeds, the kids reduce in number from a couple of dozen to six 'running around in our / barefeet and birthday / suits'. Finally the firemen stop their hoses and go back into their firehouse to continue their card game. The speaker in the poem is left with Molly who, embarrassed, looks at him and runs in herself: 'because I guess really we were the only ones there'.

'Summer in Brooklyn', like so many of Ferlinghetti's poems, has the infectious warmth of local humanity, and the intellectual honesty, which he found in the work of William Carlos Williams, and which he believes is the central characteristic of the Rutherford poet's continuing influence. This serves to remind the reader that he has been influenced by and has influenced a particular vein of American poetry. Ferlinghetti's early review of Williams' *Autobiography* identifies Williams as representing the other side of the coin in American literature:

> On one side, Europe and the expatriate writers, Henry James, Ezra Pound, T.S. Eliot; on the other side, America and Whitman and all those with their roots in American soil.[9]

Ferlinghetti makes it clear that he identifies Williams with the Whitman camp and quotes his now well-known view that the publication of *The Waste Land* in 1922 was 'the great catastrophe in our letters'. The San Francisco poet is also at pains to make it clear that this isn't a case of literary isolationism:

> This is not to say Dr. Williams never left home. He spent more than one year in Europe and knew many of the Americans there, especially in the 1920's, and was well up on all their movements. Yet he was for the most part an unhappy expatriate. By his own description, he is happiest when hard at his medical practice, letting the poetry germinate while he works, finding the resolution of medicine and poetry in the final, limitless search for poetic essence in the life he is able, because of his profession, intimately to touch.[10]

Ferlinghetti's poetry, too, germinates while he works and travels, and has its essence in the life he is able intimately to touch. Despite the blasphemy, the tendentious naïvety and the surrealism, there is a tough reasonableness about Ferlinghetti's views and works which reveals an intellectual grasp of the evolution of literature, especially American. He is aware that choice is as important as chance and this is especially apparent when he comes to compare Williams with his friend, Ezra Pound:

> Their ends are disparate: Williams in the same, snug harbour of Rutherford; Pound alienated from his country in St. Elizabeth's Hospital, Washington, D.C.[11]

Ferlinghetti's review of Williams was written during 1951, his first year as a resident of San Francisco. This was obviously a formative period in his life and his regular visits to 250 Scott Street, where Kenneth Rexroth had his spacious six-room, book-filled apartment, undoubtedly played a part. By all accounts Ferlinghetti was quiet at this time: 'Rexroth was the great master, and I was just a kid', he is quoted as saying.[12] The same accounts make it clear that the great master was ready to fill any silence being seldom short of a word; the point of the gatherings at his apartment seemed to Michael McClure to be 'to exercise his own genius':

> We would listen, and we'd ask him questions. Kenneth was like Godwin was to early nineteenth-century England—an anarchist, teacher, political figure, *literateur.* He was a very brilliant man and put many of us on our feet with a stance we could grow with.[13]

There is no doubt that Kenneth Rexroth helped Ferlinghetti to grow, as did Robert Duncan, whom he met at Rexroth's soirées. Meanwhile Ferlinghetti was pursuing his literary career in other directions. He had persuaded the book review editor of the *San Francisco Chronicle* to let him try some unpaid reviews. In July 1952, the then Lawrence Ferling began a series of poetry reviews, the piece on Carlos Williams being published in October of that year.

The circumstances of Ferlinghetti's life perhaps make him particularly sensitive to the influence of both choice and chance, which he has seen at work in his comparison of Pound and Williams. A parenthesis at the opening of a recent biography emphasises that both his parents had gone before he was two, he was abandoned at six, then as a teenager he was sent away by his caretakers after leading his gang into petty crime. It is argued that he subsequently raised himself out of these circumstances, not just to salvage an ordinary life with a decent job, wife, kids, car and the rest, but:

> to other circumstances as extreme as those beginnings: to become Lawrence Ferlinghetti, publisher, poet, novelist, painter, spokesman of his time.[14]

I don't want to proceed with a 'life' in this way, nor have I the space to do so. I do, however, want to sketch in just a few episodes because I believe that this helps to focus an author's work—even if the reader has been born in an age which celebrates, in the famous phrase, the death of the author. Ferlinghetti was born in Yonkers, New York, in March 1919. He gained a first degree from the University of North Carolina and an MA from Columbia University. He saw active service in the Second World War and late in 1943 he assumed command of his first ship. Ferlinghetti remembers the approach of D-Day with both clarity and drama:

> The night before the invasion started we were in Plymouth, and the side lanes leading up to the harbor were choked with transport—weapons, wagons, lorries jammed with troops—American, French, British, all lined up silent. And there was a blackout, so you'd go along these roads just packed with troops and all kinds of equipment and everything was in the dark. It was like the night before Agincourt—small campfires and men huddled around them and everything very silent, like the description in *Henry V.*[15]

After his Navy service Ferlinghetti, as he put it, emptied wastebaskets at *Time* for a while, before living in Paris between 1947 and 1951. There he added to his qualifications a Doctorat de l'Université from the Sorbonne. His dissertation was on 'The City as Symbol in Modern Poetry: In Search of a Metropolitan Tradition'. It involved studies of a number of authors including Eliot, Walt Whitman, Hart Crane, Mayakovsky, Lorca, Francis Thompson, André Breton and Djuna Barnes. The method was, as Ferlinghetti describes it, to go through the works of the selected writers and summarise what they had to say about the city, identifying which works in particular embodied it. His life and art are clearly associated with cities and with San Francisco in particular, and this association, this fascination, is there throughout Ferlinghetti's work. The poem and essays in *Literature and the American Urban Experience* are the papers of a conference on literature and the urban experience held at Rutgers, the State University of New Jersey, in 1980. Out front, as it were, is Ferlinghetti's **'Modern Poetry is Prose (But it is Saying Plenty)'**, which was composed for presentation at the poetry forum during the conference. The poem takes the shape of a history of modern poetry as seen through Ferlinghetti's eyes—naming and thus celebrating Whitman, Emerson, Sandburg, Vachel Lindsay, Wallace Stevens, Langston Hughes, Blake, Allen Ginsberg, D.H. Lawrence, Kerouac, and others:

> poetic strummers and wailers
> in the streets of the world
> making poetry of the urgent insurgent Now[16]

The poem, as it continues, speaks of poets turning inwards to record their personal graphs of consciousness—Robert Creeley and Charles Olson are there, as are Whitman and Ginsberg, who had taken poetry almost singlehandedly in new directions. The process of renewing poetry is to be traced in the San Francisco poets, of course, the New York poets, the objectivists, the projectivists and the constructivists. The still wild voice 'inside of us' is present in the 1980s of the poem (and don't we need it in the 1990s):

> a still insurgent voice
> lost among machines and insane nationalisms
> still longing to break out
> still longing for the distant nightingale
> that stops and begins again[17]

On 25 August 1944, the day Paris was liberated, Ferlinghetti and a junior officer took an abandoned jeep to the city. The vehicle broke down and the two officers stopped at a café in Saint Brieuc in Brittany for wine. Ferlinghetti noticed that a paper tablecloth had something scrawled on it, which inspection revealed to be a poem bearing the signature of Jacques Prévert. This incident began one of Ferlinghetti's fascinations. Prévert had become popular in the 1930s for his straight-talking, irreverent and often satirical view of French life and its figures of authority—a view which suited Ferlinghetti well. He took the tablecloth with him and very soon began on his translations of *Paroles* which were issued by City Lights, his own imprint, late in the 1950s and by Penguin Books in Britain in the mid-1960s. As Ferlinghetti puts it:

> What Prévert means to us is naturally quite a different thing from what he has meant to the French. Many of the poems in *Paroles* grew out of the Second World War and the Occupation in France . . . Prévert spoke particularly to the French youth immediately after the war, especially to those who grew up during the Occupation and felt totally estranged from Church and State. Since then we have had our own kind of resistance movement in our writers of dissent—dissent from the official world of the upper middle class ideal and the White Collar delusion and various other systemized tribal insanities.[18]

Of course, Ferlinghetti himself is part of the 'resistance movement' which he describes—and speaking to the same postwar generation worldwide. As he began writing, Ferlinghetti was undoubtedly influenced by Eliot, Thomas Wolfe,

Kenneth Rexroth and others, but in his early work the tone and some of the subject matter of Prévert is most apparent. This can be clearly identified in Ferlinghetti's own translation of 'Pater Noster' which begins:

> Our Father who art in heaven
> Stay there
> And we'll stay here on earth
> Which is sometimes so pretty
> With its mysteries of New York
> And its mysteries of Paris[19]

The poem develops into a catalogue of the world's mysteries, which are as attractive, paradoxical and curious as any that heaven can offer. It is reminiscent in its comic-irreverent tone and treatment of hallowed material of the fifth section of ***A Coney Island Of The Mind*** which begins:

> Sometime during eternity
> some guys show
> up
> and one of them
> who shows up real late
> is a kind of
> carpenter
> from some square-type place
> like Galilee
> and he starts wailing
> and claiming he is hep
> to who made heaven
> and earth
> and that the cat
> who really laid it on us
> is his Dad[20]

Ferlinghetti's poem is more complex, more mischievous and more dramatic than the Prévert, both in its structure and its meaning. Much of the impact is visual, the lines disturbing and breaking expectations and patterns, just as the meaning is interrogating the projected tone, complacency, and implicit righteousness of Christian belief. As Ferlinghetti has said, Prévert is at his best when he 'simply shows you something and lets you draw your own conclusions'.[21] When he goes beyond this 'showing', we are sometimes, as in **'Human Effort'**, treated to triteness. The importance of Prévert, according to Ferlinghetti, is that at his best he is:

> one of those who hold on to your sleeve and say:
> 'Don't go for it . . . keep out of it.'[22]

The influence of Prévert is helping the American poet to shape what is essentially a poetry of dissent.

Ferlinghetti returned to the United States and, after an unsuccessful stay in New York, which he said was just too tough and avaricious for him, he went to San Francisco early in 1951. The city which was to become his home and a central factor in his inspiration 'had a Mediterranean feeling about it. I felt it was a little like Dublin when Joyce was there. You could walk down Sackville Street and see everyone of any importance on one walk.'[23] Early in 1953, Ferlinghetti and his wife, Kirby, moved into an apartment in a hillside house with a view of the Bay. Here the poet began the poems which were to form the centre of ***Pictures Of The Gone World.*** These poems make reference to Brancusi, Picasso, Dada and Sarolla and the Spanish Impressionists amongst the painters and art movements, and Dante, Yeats and Rimbaud amongst the writers. But the collection is most remarkable for the painterly treatment of Ferlinghetti's immediate subject matter. Characteristic of this is his first completely San Francisco poem, as he described the piece which opens the collection:

> Away above a harborful
> of caulkless houses
> among the charley noble chimneypots
> of a rooftop
> rigged with clotheslines
> a woman pastes up sails
> upon the wind
> hanging out her morning sheets[24]

Ferlinghetti believes that style is a feeling for the weight and arrangement of words on a page. In **'Away above a harborful'**, it is clear that he is using the page as a canvas, as he develops his style in which the page is analogous to the open form of the abstract expressionist painters. Meanwhile he was also sending off his Prévert translations and it was through this activity that he came across Peter Martin's *City Lights* which has been named after a Charlie Chaplin film:

> The hero of the film . . . was the perennial outsider—dispossessed, alienated, victimized by the immense mechanism of the modern world. It was a figure with whom Ferlinghetti instinctively sympathized. Though he didn't see himself as a victim like Charlie, he clearly felt himself one of the 'common men,' threatened by the massed forces of the bureaucratic, materialist, conformist world.[25]

Pete Martin and Ferlinghetti met and, in June 1953, they opened the immediately successful City Lights Pocket Book Shop. The following year Martin sold his share in the store to Ferlinghetti and went back to his native New York to open a bookstore in Manhattan. Straightaway Ferlinghetti set about realising one of his plans, which was to base a publishing venture in the bookstore. He got together the 27 poems which became ***Pictures***

Of The Gone World—number one in the pocketbook series, published by City Lights Press on 10 August 1955. City Lights very soon became one of the major imprints in the history of American literature, and Ferlinghetti began to publish William Carlos Williams, Allen Ginsberg, Kenneth Patchen, Kenneth Rexroth, Denise Levertov, Gregory Corso, Neal Cassady, Jack Kerouac and many others—most of the writers needed for a course in the new American literature, postwar, have appeared from City Lights. The press was one of the major catalysts for the arrival and output of the Beat generation. Around 1955, poetry went public in San Francisco, based on the bringing together of the East Coast Beat writers—Ginsberg, Kerouac and Corso—with the West Coast writers—Rexroth, Ferlinghetti himself, Snyder, McClure, Whalen, Lamantia and others. One of the most inspiring outcomes of this meeting was a reading which Ginsberg organised at the Six Gallery in San Francisco, to which he invited McClure, Snyder, Whalen and Lamantia—with Rexroth as master of ceremonies. The Six Poets at the Six Gallery reading was given in October 1955. It was on this occasion that Ginsberg gave the first reading of his long poem *Howl,* which launched his career as a poet at the same time as it celebrated the inauguration of the San Francisco poetry renaissance; the event brought a new awareness to the audience of the large group of talented poets in the city; it also brought to the poets themselves a new sense of belonging to a community. What was emerging was something more than the 'New York poets' or the 'San Francisco poets'. The sum of the parts was a literary movement that was to become a national and international phenomenon.

This phenomenon turned out to be enigmatic, simultaneously a celebration and a condemnation of the postwar world, a rich compound of nihilistic, committed, romantic, modernist and existentialist impulses. Getting Ferlinghetti, Ginsberg, Kerouac, Corso, Burroughs and Cassady grouped together under an umbrella labelled 'Beat' has always been difficult; there is always a stray philosophy, an infectious idea, a broken ideal, an individuality and a commitment which has defied any such attempt. The label 'Beat' has often been used but seldom defined; indeed, one of its characteristics is that it is an embattled position which is resistant to definition. The contradictory, dialectical, tendentious character of the Beat generation has been its critical downfall; it has often seemed confused because there has been an obsession with the lifestyle rather than the works of the generation. The characteristic preoccupations of the Beats have to do with art, and particularly abstract expressionism, popular music, particularly some forms of jazz, drugs, sex, community and communal living, travel, anarchistic politics, religious experimentation, a fascination with criminality, being on the offensive against society whilst at the same time acknowledging alternative kinds of society.[26] These characteristics, which are not intended to be exhaustive, are exhibited in different measure and different combinations by the different writers who were fashioning their particular literary aesthetics in the culturally repressive America of the Cold War era. They sought to oppose its philistine and repressive mores by exploring and exploiting the extreme potential of the individual self. Not surprisingly, these characteristics become the subject of the art produced, and hence the focus on lifestyle in the contemporary critical response. It is not surprising, either, that the Beats professed close allegiances with some of the great figures of the romantic movement, and particularly with the Romantic ideology expressed by Blake, Shelley, Whitman and Lawrence. However great the debt to European Romantic ideology and indigenous American Transcendentalism, it is without doubt mediated by post-Romantic thought:

> It is hardly possible to read a classic Beat text without being aware of the way in which its Romanticism is continued, qualified and interrogated by the Modernism of Stein, Pound, Eliot, Williams (who wrote the introduction to *Howl*), Faulkner, Hart Crane, Thomas Wolfe and Henry Miller (who wrote the preface to *The Subterraneans*); the Surrealism of Apollinaire, Prévert (whose *Paroles* Ferlinghetti has excellently Englished), Eluard, Reverdy and Lorca; and the Existentialism of Hemingway, Céline, Artaud (whose *In Order to have finished with the judgement of God* Ginsberg has proclaimed a major influence on his early works), Sartre and Camus (whose *The Myth of Sisyphus* has been a touchstone for Ferlinghetti).[27]

It is precisely as a result of the containment, qualifications and interrogation of specific characteristics of Romanticism by specific characteristics of Modernism that the energy, tensions, and volatility of the best Beat writing arises. Ferlinghetti is in no way a disengaged writer; in fact, a powerful sense of commitment is evidenced in a great deal of his writing. He was incensed, whilst writing about his '**Tentative Description of a Dinner Given to Promote the Impeachment of President Eisenhower**', by those he described as Beat natives who said he could not be both Beat and committed at the same time:

> all the tall droopy corn about the Beat Generation and its being 'existentialist' is as phoney as a four-dollar piece of lettuce. Jean-Paul Sartre . . . would give the horse laugh to the idea of Disengagement and the Art of The Beat Generation. Me too. And that Abominable Snowman of modern poetry, Allen Ginsberg, would probably say the same. Only the dead are disengaged. And the wiggy nihilism of the Beat hipster, if carried to its natural conclusion, actually means the death of the creative artist himself. While the 'noncommitment' of the artists is itself a suicidal and deluded variation of this same nihilism.[28]

Ferlinghetti's sense of commitment became very clear after the Six Poets at the Six Gallery reading when he sent a telegram to Ginsberg offering to bring out *Howl* as a City Lights publication. He used the words which Emerson had used in writing to Whitman about his *Leaves of Grass*—'I greet you at the beginning of a great career'. He added, 'When do I get the manuscript?' Ferlinghetti and Ginsberg worked together, supplementing *Howl* with some other poems, including 'A Supermarket in California', which wonderfully realises a dream encounter with Walt Whitman. Ferlinghetti sent the manuscript to William Carlos Williams, who wrote an introduction to the volume describing Ginsberg as a poet who 'sees through and all around the horrors he partakes of in the very intimate details of his poem. He avoids nothing, but experiences it to the hilt.'[29] In September 1956, City Lights took delivery of the first fifteen hundred copies, but it was when the second printing arrived the following March that the trouble started.

On 25 March 1957, the Collector of Customs, Chester MacPhee, ordered the second printing to be seized. This was reported in the *San Francisco Chronicle*:

> collector of Customs Chester MacPhee continued his campaign yesterday to keep what he considers obscene literature away from the children of the Bay Area. He confiscated 520 copies of a paperbound volume of poetry entitled *Howl and Other Poems* . . . "The words and the sense of the writing is obscene," MacPhee declared. "You wouldn't want your children to come across it."[30]

Ferlinghetti was prepared for this. He demonstrated a real grasp of literary, social and political affairs over the following months. On 3 April, the American Civil Liberties Union (to which he had submitted the manuscript of *Howl* before it went to the printers) informed MacPhee that it would contest the legality of the seizure. The first printing had been done by Villiers in Great Britain, chosen by Ferlinghetti because they were both experienced and reasonable. Now he announced an entirely new edition to be printed within the United States, and thus removed from the jurisdiction of the customs. This photo-offset edition was for sale at the City Lights bookstore, while the customs held on to the few copies from Britain.

The ensuing events did much to bring together and advertise the work of the Beats. Both the customs and the police, albeit unintentionally, did much to aid this development:

> I recommended a medal be made for Collector MacPhee, since his action was already rendering the book famous. But the police were soon to take over this advertising account and do a much better job—10,00 copies of *Howl* were in print by the time they finished with it.[31]

On 19 May 1957, the book editor of the *San Francisco Chronicle,* William Hogan, gave his Sunday column over to an article by Ferlinghetti who viewed *Howl* as without doubt the most significant long poem to be published since the Second World War, and perhaps since Eliot's *Four Quartets.* As Ferlinghetti himself says, many added 'Alas' to this:

> Fair enough, considering the barren, polished poetry and well-mannered verse which has dominated many of the major poetry publications during the past decade or so, not to mention some of the 'fashionable incoherence' which has passed for poetry in many of the smaller, avant-garde magazines and little presses. *Howl* commits many poetic sins; but it was time.[32]

The unswerving commitment which Ferlinghetti revealed throughout the trial of *Howl* is characteristic. He challenged critics to identify another single long poem which was as resonant of its time and place and generation. The central part of his *Chronicle* article emphasises his own concerns and his response to Ginsberg:

> It is not the poet but what he observes which is revealed as obscene. The great obscene wastes of *Howl* are the sad wastes of the mechanized world, lost among atom bombs and insane nationalisms. Ginsberg chooses to walk on the wild side of this world, along with Nelson Algren, Henry Miller, Kenneth Rexroth, not to mention some great American dead, mostly in the tradition of philosophical anarchism.[33]

As Ferlinghetti suggest, Ginsberg's best personal defence of *Howl* appears in another poem of his, 'America', where he asks:

> What sphinx of cement and aluminium bashed
> open their skulls
> and ate up their brains and imagination?
> Moloch! Solitude! Filth! Ugliness! Ashcans and
> unobtainable

dollars! Children screaming under the stairways!
Boys sobbing in armies! Old men weeping in the parks![34]

There is no doubt that Ferlinghetti identifies with this view, and with the idea that by exhibiting the obscene wastes of the mechanised world a process of improvement may be begun. He turns Collector MacPhee's words back on himself in describing what Ginsberg exposes as:

> A world, in short, you wouldn't want your children to come across . . . Thus was Goya obscene in depicting the Disasters of War, thus Whitman an exhibitionist, exhibiting man in his own strange skin.[35]

As it turned out, collector MacPhee was only the first skirmish in a war. The customs released the books it was holding at the end of May. Then ('They were terrible nice, really', said Kirby Ferlinghetti) the police arrived and the fun really started. Captain William Hanrahan of the Juvenile Department took MacPhee's accusation about the likely corruption of children seriously. Ferlinghetti described the Juvenile Department as 'well named, in this case'. Two officers turned up at City Lights while Ferlinghetti was out and Kirby met these well-groomed college students:

> I would have sworn they were just out of Yale. They said it was all in the line of duty, ma'am, and I guess I got a little emotional about the whole thing and told them there were a lot more obscene things in books you can buy every day at any bookshop.[36]

Kirby noticed that the officers were a little embarrassed about the whole thing. Shortly afterwards, Ferlinghetti was being fingerprinted in San Francisco's Hall of Justice. He describes this as 'a dandy way for the city officially to recognize the flowering of poetry in San Francisco'. One newspaper reported all this as: 'The Cops Don't Allow No Renaissance Here'.[37] Both Ferlinghetti and Shigeyoshi Murao, who was tending the cash register when one of the police officers purchased a copy of *Howl* from City Lights, were charged with publishing and selling obscene literature.

The trial in San Francisco was widely publicised, bringing a great deal of attention to both Ferlinghetti and Ginsberg and selling thousands of copies of the book. The Beats and the San Francisco poets, represented respectively by Ginsberg and Ferlinghetti, joined forces and the literary cluster of the Beat generation was ready for orbit. Ferlinghetti's own account of the trial emphasises some of the great voices in support of *Howl*—Henry Rago, editor of *Poetry (Chicago)*, Robert Duncan and Ruth Witt-Diamant for the San Francisco (State College) Poetry Center, James Laughlin from *New Directions*, Kenneth Patchen, Barney Rossett and Donald Allen (editors of the *Evergreen Review* in which *Howl* was reprinted during the trial), Mark Schorer, Leo Lowenthal, and Kenneth Rexroth who spoke for many others in concluding that the simplest term for describing Ginsberg's books is 'prophetic'. He argued that *Howl*, Ferlinghetti's ***Pictures Of The Gone World***, and other key works of the Beat generation by Kerouac, Cassady, Snyder, Corso and others are based in a tradition of prophetic writing:

> There are the prophets of the bible, which it [*Howl*] greatly resembles in purpose and in language and in subject matter. The theme is the denunciation of evil and a pointing out of the way out, so to speak.[38]

There is no space here to explore the debate which was raised by the trial, a debate which was just as extreme and paralleled by the trial of D.H. Lawrence's *Lady Chatterley's Lover* in London in the autumn of 1960. Both acquittals led to vastly increased sales, and both were based on the evidence given by many of the critical and creative geniuses of the day. In many ways the aura which became attached to the question of the worth of *Howl*, as of *Lady Chatterley's Lover*, has to do with the significant context of such cultural moments, not in terms of a disputation with the great tradition, but in terms of their insertion into the domain of popular literature.[39] Ferlinghetti was justifiably pleased with the outcome of all this. He emerged as a master of confrontation based on commitment, and the *Chronicle* reported the happy, curious scene in which 'the Judge's decision was hailed with applause and cheers from a packed audience that offered the most fantastic collection of beards, turtle-necked shirts and Italian hair-dos ever to grace the grimy precincts of the hall of Justice'.[40] The Judge's decision was subsequently seen as a landmark in law, and Ferlinghetti believes that, since Judge Horn was re-elected to office, the People were in agreement that it was the police who had committed an obscene action. The scene was rather like the one depicted in Ferlinghetti's novel, ***Her***, in which the Poetry Revolution is growing in Paris:

> The Poetry Revolution was growing, the Poetry Revolution was shaking, transforming existence and civilization as it rolled down around the corner of the Boule Miche and down the Boulevard Saint-Germain toward Odéon where Danton watched over a Metro entrance and pocket-watches hung from trees each with a different time swinging in the breeze but all of them

> indicating it was later than you think, while crowds of black berets and herds of sandals came floating and staggering out of the Café Mabillon and the Pergola to join the much-belated Poetry Revolution, while three thousand nine hundred and forty-two alumni of the Académie Duncan came streaming out of the Rue de Seine combing their hair with Grecian lyres.[41]

Over the years Ferlinghetti has published a number of plays, travel journals, translations, and two novels—***Her*** and ***Love in the Days of Rage.*** Perhaps the best known of these is the novel ***Her,*** which he had begun in Paris, much influenced by *Nightwood* by Djuna Barnes, a copy of which had been given to him by two friends—Mary Louise Barrett and Mary Birmingham—who were living in the same street in Paris as the women in *Nightwood.* ***Her*** was published by New Directions in 1960. The passage quoted above is characteristic of the style which Ferlinghetti adopted, which echoes the tripartite structure and interior monologue of Djuna Barnes. The novel was given a mixed critical reception but it sold very well—100,000 copies had been sold by 1988 when the novel was in its thirteenth printing. Despite the range of his writing, it is in his poetry that Ferlinghetti's reason for writing exists and he describes himself as a poet against his will, with no alternative in life—'I was only interested in writing . . . too selfish to spend much time on other people.'[42] He has travelled widely giving readings, and made a number of recordings of his poetry. One of the ageless radicals and a true bard, his poetry creates its own style and shape on the page. It is sometimes whimsical, sometimes unsettling, always committed to an honest rendering of his basic motivation to be an agent provocateur and, as he puts it, subversive, anarchistic and prophetic. His third book of poetry, ***Starting From San Francisco,*** emphasised these points in a number of poems which are in effect broadsides, alive to geography and politics, to the sadness of a world seemingly shrunk and bereft of its dreams. The sadness is caught in the figure, the portrait of the brakeman who haunts the final lines of the title poem:

> this world shrunk
> to one lone brakeman's face
> stuck out of darkness—
> long white forehead
> like bleached skull of cow—
> huge black sad eyes—
> high-peaked cloth cap, grey-striped—
> swings his railroad lantern high, close up,
> as our window whizzes by—
> his figure splashed upon it,
> slanted, muezzin-like,
> very grave, very tall,
> strange skeleton—[43]

Having presented this haunting portrait, the poem asks, 'Who stole America?' The question reminds me of one of the shorts fired off by another American poet who is fully conscious of the centrality of both political and human geography—Ed Dorn. In **'What Will Be Historically Durable'**, our ear is bent by the opening statement that 'About Nixon there was / Something grandiose' and then bent again, towards perception, by the concluding statement that 'Nothing illustrates this / More than / When he stole the post office.'[44] It is the corruption that it itself engenders that steals America. In 1860 Walt Whitman had written 'Starting from Paumanok . . . I strike up for a New World' and, a hundred years later, Ferlinghetti starts up from San Francisco and explores parts, of America, South America, Europe, and the 'obscene boundaries' created by the Cold War.

At this time, his first two volumes, ***Pictures Of The Gone World*** and ***A Coney Island Of The Mind,*** were being read in many languages around the world—in England, France, Italy, Germany, Finland, Sweden, Denmark, Czechoslovakia, Japan, Canada, Mexico, Cuba, Argentina, Peru, Chile, Puerto Rico, and the former USSR. Barry Silesky, in the most recent exploration of Ferlinghetti's life and work, makes it clear just how long is the shadow that his poetry has cast in our times:

> Unparalleled in popularity, it has been read by more people, in more countries, than that of any living American poet. Countless numbers who may have read no other contemporary poetry—and maybe no poetry at all besides what was forced on them at school—have read Ferlinghetti.[45]

Apart from his writing, since the late 1940s Ferlinghetti has been a serious and obsessive painter and, in spring 1990, the University of California mounted a large retrospective exhibition of his work.

It is not surprising, therefore, that painting and responses to paintings are often his subject matter. There is a visual quality to much of Ferlinghetti's work and this is clear in a number of the poems . . .—**'In Goya's Greatest Scenes'** for instance, or **'Away above a harborful'**. The painterliness and the response to individual paintings is present right from the start of the poetry. Section eight of ***Pictures Of The Gone World***[46] begins with the lines: 'Sarolla's women in their picture hats / stretched upon his canvas beaches / beguiled the Spanish / Impressionists', and section twenty-four opens with a characteristically challenging declaration: 'Picasso's acrobats epitomize the world'. Other poems in direct response to individual paintings include **'Short Story on a Painting of Gustav Klimt'**, **'Monet's Lilies Shuddering'**, **'Returning to Paris with Pissarro'**, **'Seeing a Woman as in a Painting by Berthe Morisot'**, and the spirited, sharp and witty evocation of Chagall's 'The Equestrienne' in **'Don't Let That Horse'**:

> Don't let that horse
> eat that violin
> cried Chagall's mother
> But he
> kept right on
> painting
> And became famous[47]

The tone of voice in Ferlinghetti's poetry varies from the humorous, as in **'Don't Let That Horse'**, to the angry, as in a tirade like **'One Thousand Fearful Words for Fidel Castro'**, or the mischievous and blasphemous, as in section five of ***A Coney Island Of The Mind.*** What characterises his work is his openness and honesty of response, guided by a relentless and unstinting creativity and inventiveness. If you believe, as Ferlinghetti does, that art and poetry in particular presuppose the independence of the artist, then it is likely that such necessary independence will involve dissidence of one kind or another. The first thing that the poet has to do is to live that type of life which doesn't compromise. When Ferlinghetti got hold of his FBI file through the Freedom of Information Act, he found a note written on it by J. Edgar Hoover which said, 'Ferlinghetti is a beatnik rabble-rouser who also may be a mental case'. The poet commented, 'In my opinion you couldn't ask for a better calling card than that.'[48] Ferlinghetti believes that taking government grants and living on them is to compromise even before you start writing. It is a purist view and there is no doubt that it has become an embattled position in recent years, but it is one which he has held from the beginning, and which he expressed with special effect during the 1960s. Ferlinghetti quoted Herbert Marcuse and the notion of repressive tolerance—the policy of tolerance as self-protection against subversion or violence. Susan Sontag brilliantly described this as the process of defusing unsettling or subversive ideas by assimilating them. As Ferlinghetti puts it in ***Tyrannus Nix***:

> Many American poets do in fact help the government in sanctioning a status quo which is supported by and supports WAR as a legal form of murder . . . The State, whether Capitalist or Communist, has an enormous capacity to ingest its most dissident elements.[49]

Ferlinghetti's poetry derives from the way in which his honesty and creativity mix with his responses to actuality, be it life in San Francisco, social inequality or oppression, politics or travel. In July 1966, Ferlinghetti, who was much travelled in the external world, took an internal journey by taking LSD for the first time. There might well be a relationship between this event and his long poem **'After The Cries Of The Birds'**; it is plain enough that the poem is a response to both interior and external voyages and discoveries. It was published in December 1966 in both *The Village Voice* and the *San Francisco Oracle,* which perhaps indicates both Ferlinghetti's grasp of literary affairs and the simultaneous 'overground' and 'underground' status of the poetry. When it was published in book form by Dave Haselwood Books in 1967, Ferlinghetti had added 'Genesis of **"After the Cries of the Birds"**', which was written for presentation at the Berlin Literarisches Colloquium and read on a programme with Andrei Voznesenski. In his essay Ferlinghetti offers an exploration of the genesis of the poem and a homage to San Francisco, of which he says that its physical characteristics and its location, perched as it is high on the northern tip of its low peninsula, contribute to the city not feeling like the rest of America:

> Its political face may look the same. The same Fuzz are present in its City Hall and in its Hall of Justice built in the most advanced style of Mussolini Modern. Servants of the People armed with real guns (in the best tradition of the Wild West) still roam the streets. But its students in Black Friday City Hall riots against Congressional Committees on UnAmerican Activities, and its Berkeley Student Movement, and its Free Speech Movement, and its Sexual Freedom Movement, and its free bookstores, and its peace marches, and its Poets Peace Fasts, and its Buddhist temples and its Zen Centres and its Chinatown and its Japan-town and its psychedelic communities and its Poets Outside still telling America to go fuck itself with its atom bomb . . . all these panic ephemera creating some illusion of what San Francisco might possibly become apart from the rest of America, what San Francisco might someday become as it finally becomes detached or detaches its Self from what America still wants to be, from what the dominant material mechanical militarist Mammon money America will always still want to be.[50]

This view of San Francisco carries over into **'After The Cries Of The Birds'**. The poem has a refrain which marks off episodes based on the lines with which it opens:

Hurrying thru eternity
after the cries of the birds has
stopped
I see the "future of the world"
in a new visionary
society
now only dimly
recognizable
in folk-rock
ballrooms
free-form dancers in ecstatic clothing
their hearts their gurus[51]

It is a visionary work in which the form represents the speaking voice on the page. As it continues we share a vision of the city with the speaker hurrying through eternity 'to a new pastoral era'. For a moment, we are in the Berkeley Rose Garden 'looking West at sunset to the Golden Gate / adrift in its Japanese landscape' and, a moment later, the island of the city has floated free—'never really a part of America'. By the end of the poem, San Francisco has become the capital city of an envisioned new New World guided by Ferlinghetti, 'anarchist among the floorwalkers'. His city becomes the model of an improved future, demonstrating that Ferlinghetti is a poet, ultimately, of place—in a distinctly and distinguished American tradition. A poet of place in such a thoroughgoing manner that he reaches us all, his San Francisco becoming a San Francisco of all our minds. His version of life and art in the second half of the twentieth century is one which we may or may not share, but which we cannot ignore.

Notes

1. Lawrence Ferlinghetti, *Endless Life: Selected Poems* (New York: New Directions, 1981) p.27. Previous publication includes *Penguin Modern Poets 5: Gregory Corso, Lawrence Ferlinghetti, Allen Ginsberg* (Harmondsworth: Penguin Books, 1963).
2. Ferlinghetti, *Selected Poems,* p.43.
3. Ferlinghetti, quoted in *American Poetry of the Twentieth Century* (London: Longman, 1990), p.292.
4. Ferlinghetti, *Selected Poems,* p.59.
5. Ferlinghetti, quoted in Barry Silesky, *Ferlinghetti: the Artist in His Time* (New York: Warner Books, 1991) p.91.
6. Ferlinghetti, *Selected Poems,* 47-55.
7. Ibid., p.55.
8. Ferlinghetti, 'Summer in Brooklyn', in *Children's Poetry* (San Francisco: Kingfisher Books, 1985) p.80.
9. Ferlinghetti's review of Williams' *Autobiography* reproduced in Charles Doyle (ed.), *William Carlos Williams: The Critical Heritage* (London: Routledge and Kegan Paul, 1980) p.248.
10. Ibid.
11. Ibid.
12. Silesky, *Ferlinghetti,* p.47.
13. Ibid.
14. Ibid., p.1.
15. Ibid., p.20.
16. Ferlinghetti, in *Literature and the American Urban Experience* (Manchester: Manchester University Press, 1981) p.5.
17. Ibid., p.9.
18. *Prévert: Selections from Paroles,* trans. by Ferlinghetti (Harmondsworth: Penguin Books, 1965) p.9.
19. Ibid., p.19.
20. Ferlinghetti, *Selected Poems,* p.31.
21. *Prévert,* p.9.
22. Ibid.
23. Silesky, *Ferlinghetti,* pp.43-4.
24. Ferlinghetti, *Selected Poems,* p.3.
25. Silesky, *Ferlinghetti,* p.55.
26. This brief list of characteristic preoccupations is developed in an extremely helpful essay by John Osbourne and Peter Easy, 'Wanted: A Good "Beat" Critic' in *Over Here,* Autumn 1984, pp.16-17.
27. Ibid., p.19.
28. Ferlinghetti, in *The New American Poetry* edited by Donald M. Allen (New York: Grove Press, Inc., 1960) pp.412-13.
29. Silesky, p.67.
30. Ferlinghetti, in the *Penguin Book of the Beats* (Harmondsworth: Penguin Books, 1992) pp.254-5.
31. Ibid., p.255.
32. Ibid.
33. Ibid., p.255-6.
34. Ibid., p.256.
35. Ibid.
36. Silesky, p.70.
37. Ann Charters, op. cit., p.256.
38. Ibid., p.260.
39. This point is developed in Stuart Laing, 'Authenticating Romantic Fiction—Lady Chatterley's Daughter' from *It's My Party: Reading Twentieth Century Women's Writing,* Gina Wisker (ed.) (London: Pluto Press, 1994).
40. Ferlinghetti, in *The Penguin Book of the Beats,* pp.262-3.
41. Ferlinghetti, *Her* (London: MacGibbon & Kee, 1966) p.45.
42. Ferlinghetti, quoted in Silesky, p.50.
43. Ferlinghetti, *Starting From San Francisco* (New York: New Direction, 1967) p.8.

44. Ed Dorn, 'What Will Be Historically Durable', in *Hello, La Jolla* (Berkeley: Wingbow Press, 1978) p.19.

45. Silesky, p.254.

46. Ferlinghetti, *Selected Poems,* p.7.

47. Ferlinghetti, *A Coney Island Of The Mind* (New York: New Directions, 1958) p.29.

48. Ferlinghetti, *When I Look at Pictures* (San Francisco: Peregrine Smith Books, 1990), quoted on back cover.

49. Ferlinghetti, quoted in Silesky, p.197.

50. Ferlinghetti, 'Genesis Of' in *After The Cries Of The Birds* (San Francisco: Dave Haselwood Books, 1967) unpaginated.

51. Ibid.

TITLE COMMENTARY

A Coney Island of the Mind

M. L. ROSENTHAL (REVIEW DATE 11 OCTOBER 1958)

SOURCE: Rosenthal, M. L. "The Naked and the Clad." *Nation* 187, no. 11 (11 October 1958): 214-15.

In the following review, Rosenthal considers the themes and techniques of A Coney Island of the Mind.

Lawrence Ferlinghetti is certainly one of [the] advocates of universal nakedness . . . , but he differs from most of the others in his high-flying joyousness of spirit and in his stylistic sophistication. He knows he is not the first man to take a peek at Darien and he has learned some useful things, and gladly, from various European and American experimenters. The religion of sex-and-anarchy, like other religions and creeds, starts off with certain simplicities but does not require its communicants to reiterate them monotonously and mechanically. Ferlinghetti can preach a little tiresomely; he proves he can in the seven **"Oral Messages"** [in ***A Coney Island of the Mind***], written "specifically for jazz accompaniment," in which he tries to rival the worst of Ginsberg, Corso, et al. He doesn't quite succeed, for he is too bright and literate and many of his wisecracks and sideswipes are worth hearing, but finally he does become dull. The "great audiences" Whitman called for are not the improvised audiences of night clubs who must have their poetry ranting and obvious if they are to "get" anything at all.

Apart from the **"Oral Messages"** however, and from a few other preachy pieces, Ferlinghetti is a deft, rapid-placed, whirling performer. He has a wonderful eye for meaning in the commonplace, as in the lovely, sensual snapshot of a woman hanging clothes on a San Francisco rooftop, or in the memory of a New York candy store where

> Jellybeans glowed in the semi-gloom
> of that september afternoon
> A cat upon the counter moved among
> the licorice sticks
> and tootsie rolls
> and Oh Boy Gum

He has a fine imaginative eye, too, as the bawdy description of a contest with "the widder Fogliani" painting mustaches on the statues in the Borghese gardens shows. Even better—far better, because here he conquers his almost indomitable over-whimsicality—is the contrasting picture of laborers putting up a statue of Saint Francis ("no birds sang" despite the presence of a priest, reporters, and many onlookers) while unnoticed in the crowd, there passes to and fro

> a very tall and very purely naked
> young virgin
> with very long and very straight
> straw hair
> and wearing only a very small
> bird's nest
> in a very existential place. . . .

These quotations will indicate Ferlinghetti's obvious debt to the stanzaic and rhythmic technique of William Carlos Williams and the other "modernist" masters, and his equally obvious independence of idiom. I have mentioned his whimsy and his tendentiousness—I think they are related to his failure as yet to find a really adequate form for the intellectual and idiomatic range of which he gives such encouraging glimpses. There are poems in this volume (for instance, **"The wounded wilderness"** **"Morris Graves"** and **"In Paris in a loud dark winter"**) which demand something more than the light music into which Ferlinghetti's characteristic line virtually forces him. The nakedness-symbolism is another kind of strait jacket. "Take it off!"—or even *"Vive la différence!"*—is a fine old war-cry. But Ferlinghetti is far too gifted to let himself be mesmerized by it, or by his somewhat too-easy mastery of one kind of metrical pyrotechnics.

FURTHER READING

Bibliography

Morgan, Bill. *Lawrence Ferlinghetti: A Comprehensive Bibliography to 1980.* New York: Garland, 1982, 397 p.

Extensive primary and secondary bibliography.

Biography

Cherkovski, Neeli. *Ferlinghetti: A Biography.* New York: Doubleday, 1979, 254 p.

Biography based on the author's extensive interviews with Ferlinghetti.

Dana, Robert. "An Interview with Lawrence Ferlinghetti." *Midwest Quarterly* 24, no. 4 (summer 1983): 413-40.

Ferlinghetti discusses his poetry, publishing ventures, and City Lights Bookstore.

Silesky, Barry. *Ferlinghetti: The Artist in His Time.* New York: Warner Books, 1990, 294 p.

Chronicle of Ferlinghetti's life and writings in the context of the Beat literary scene; contains fourteen pages of photographs.

Smith, Larry. *Lawrence Ferlinghetti: Poet-at-Large.* Carbondale: Southern Illinois University Press, 232 p.

Critical biography.

Criticism

Charters, Samuel. "Lawrence Ferlinghetti." In *Some Poems/Poets: Studies in American Underground Poetry Since 1945,* pp. 77-83. Berkeley, Calif.: Oyez, 1971.

Analysis of "One Thousand Fearful Words for Fidel Castro."

Ianni, L. A. "Lawrence Ferlinghetti's Fourth Person Singular and the Theory of Relativity." *Wisconsin Studies in Contemporary Literature* 8, no. 1 (winter 1967): 392-406.

Contends that Ferlinghetti's works convey "in general a view of life based on the philosophical implications of the theory of relativity."

Ogar, Richard, editor. *The Poet's Eye: A Tribute to Lawrence Ferlinghetti.* Berkeley, Calif.: The Friends of the Bancroft Library, University of California, 1997, 127 p.

Collection of poems, memoirs, and commentaries devoted to various aspects of Ferlinghetti's life and works; includes a checklist of the Pocket Poet Series.

Oppenheimer, Joel. "Weathered Well." *New York Times Book Review* 86, no. 44 (1 November 1981): 40-1.

Evaluation of Endless Life: Selected Poems *that includes a general appreciation of Ferlinghetti as "the herald of a new age in poetry."*

Schwartz, Stephen. "Escapees in Paradise: Literary Life in San Francisco." *New Criterion* 4, no. 4 (December 1985): 1-5.

Discusses several Beat poets, including Ferlinghetti. Schwartz dismisses Ferlinghetti as a poet who "always preferred clowning to writing."

Skau, Michael. *"Constantly Risking Absurdity": Essays on the Writings of Lawrence Ferlinghetti.* Troy, N.Y.: Whitson Publishing Company, 1989, 103 p.

Introductory study of Ferlinghetti's works.

Trimbur, John. Review of *Endless Life: Selected Poems by Lawerence Ferlinghetti,* by Lawerence Ferlinghetti. *Western Humanities Review* 17, no. 1 (May 1982): 79-80.

Examines the close relationship between Ferlinghetti's poetry and politics. Trimbur praises Ferlinghetti as "a force in American poetry" whose works are "strong and clear and deeply felt."

OTHER SOURCES FROM GALE:

Additional coverage of Ferlinghetti's life and career is contained in the following sources published by the Gale Group: *Concise Dictionary of American Literary Biography, 1941-1968; Contemporary American Dramatists; Contemporary Authors,* Vols. 5-8R; *Contemporary Authors New Revision Series,* Vols. 3, 41, 73; *Contemporary Literary Criticism,* Vols. 2, 6, 10, 27, 111; *Contemporary Poets,* Ed. 7; *Dictionary of Literary Biography,* Vols. 5, 16; *DISCovering Authors Modules: Poets; DISCovering Authors 3.0; Literature Resource Center; Major 20th-Century Writers,* Eds. 1, 2; *Poetry Criticism,* Vol. 1; *Reference Guide to American Literature,* Ed. 4; and *World Poets.*

ALLEN GINSBERG

(1926 - 1997)

American poet, playwright, and nonfiction writer.

Ginsberg came to prominence as a major figure of the Beat Generation, and his poem "Howl" (1956) is one of the most famous literary works of the movement. Much of Ginsberg's poetry challenges the conventions and mores of American society, engaging in graphic explorations of previously controversial topics such as homosexuality and mental illness. Ginsberg often employed shocking imagery and profanity to communicate his ideas and experiences. Despite his unconventional literary style, he counted writers and thinkers of the literary "establishment," including William Carlos Williams, William Blake, and Walt Whitman, among those who had the most profound impact on his work. Commentators have noted such influences, remarking on Ginsberg's unique ability to employ traditional forms and ideas to advance innovative concepts, both in his writings and in his political and social activities.

BIOGRAPHICAL INFORMATION

Born in Newark, New Jersey, in 1926, Ginsberg suffered an emotionally troubled childhood that is reflected in many of his poems. His mother, Naomi, suffered from various mental illnesses and was periodically institutionalized during Ginsberg's adolescence. She was an active member of the Communist Party and other associations of the radical left. Contributing to Ginsberg's confusion and isolation during these years was his increasing awareness of his homosexuality, which he concealed from both his peers and his parents until he was in his twenties. First introduced to poetry by his father, a high school teacher and poet, Ginsberg's interest deepened through his association with William Carlos Williams, who became a mentor to the young poet. Lionel Trilling and Mark Van Doren, who had Ginsberg in their classes at Columbia University, further shaped his literary influences. More important to Ginsberg's future as a poet were the social interactions he pursued in college. It was while attending Columbia that Ginsberg significantly established friendships with writers Jack Kerouac, William S. Burroughs, and Neal Cassady. This group, along with several West Coast writers that included Kenneth Rexroth and Lawrence Ferlinghetti, among others, would form the core of the Beat movement. In 1956 Ginsberg's first major work, *Howl and Other Poems,* achieved notoriety when it became the subject of an obscenity trial. Prosecutors in the case unsuccessfully attempted to convict Ferlinghetti, whose imprint, City Lights Books, published the work.

Through both his writings and his personal life, Ginsberg served as an inspiration to those who sought alternatives to convention. In the 1960s he generated national media attention for his political activism. He helped organize protests against the Vietnam War and advocated "flower power," a strategy in which antiwar demonstrators would promote positive values like peace and love to dramatize their opposition to the death and destruction caused by the war. Ginsberg also became actively engaged in Eastern philosophy, meditation, and yoga during the 1960s, helping to popularize Zen Buddhist ideology in America. In the spring of 1997, already suffering from diabetes and chronic hepatitis, Ginsberg was diagnosed with liver cancer. After learning of this illness, Ginsberg produced twelve brief poems. The next day he suffered a stroke and lapsed into a coma. He died two days later, on April 5, 1997, in New York City.

MAJOR WORKS

The 1956 publication of *Howl and Other Poems* brought Ginsberg both fame and notoriety and proved to be the defining work of his career. "Howl" is a long-line poem in the tradition of Walt Whitman's *Leaves of Grass* (1855). The poem is a cry (or "Howl") of rage and despair against what Ginsberg viewed as the destructive and corrupt aspects of American society. "Howl" established Ginsberg as a leading voice of the Beat movement. His public reading of the poem to a spellbound audience at the Six Gallery in San Francisco in 1955 is considered to be one of the landmark events in the history of Beat literature. A lyrical lamentation on the moral and social ills of post-World War II America, the poem is dedicated to Carl Solomon, whom Ginsberg met while undergoing eight months of therapy at the Columbia Psychiatric Institute in 1948. Solomon challenged Ginsberg's academic theories about poetry and strengthened his understanding of contemporary poetry's potential for expressing political resistance. In 1957 "Howl" became the subject of an obscenity trial. Because of its graphic sexual language, the San Francisco Police Department declared the book obscene and arrested Lawrence Ferlinghetti, the owner of City Lights bookstore, which published the volume. The ensuing trial attracted national attention as such prominent literary figures as Walter Van Tilberg Clark and Mark Schorer spoke in defense of "Howl." Ferlinghetti was later acquitted of distributing obscene material and soon afterward published an article in which he stated: "It is not the poet but what he observes which is revealed as obscene. The great obscene wastes of 'Howl' are the sad wastes of the mechanized world, lost among atom bombs and insane nationalisms."

In 1961 Ginsberg followed *Howl and Other Poems* with *Kaddish and Other Poems, 1958-1960.* Written upon the death of Ginsberg's mother, "Kaddish," is a poem similar in style and form to "Howl." It is based on the traditional Hebrew prayer for the dead (commonly referred to as the "Mourner's Kaddish") and poignantly expresses the anger, love, and confusion Ginsberg felt toward his mother while at the same time rendering the social and historical milieu which informed his mother's troubled life. *Reality Sandwiches: 1953-1960* (1963) reflects Ginsberg's travels through Africa, Europe, and North and South America during the late 1950s. Ginsberg's experiences with the anti-war movement informs much of his work during the 1960s and early 1970s, including *Planet News* (1968), a collection of poems often described as literary collages. *Planet News* attacks the Vietnam War, ecological dangers, racism, and the disproportionate allotment of wealth in America. Several pieces in this collection also reveal Ginsberg's personal concern with aging and his anguish over the recent deaths of Cassady and Kerouac. *The Gates of Wrath: Rhymed Poems, 1948-1952* (1973) collects some examples of Ginsberg's earliest verse. These poems and an early letter to William Carlos Williams were misplaced for many years until singer-songwriter Bob Dylan discovered them in 1968 among his personal papers. Providing an account of Ginsberg's life up to 1952, the poems are written with traditional rhyme and metric schemes.

The Fall of America: Poems of These States, 1965-1971 (1972), Ginsberg's next major work, is a cross-country journey that observes the physical and spiritual erosion of the United States. The central piece of the collection, "Poem of These States," is a verse sequence intended, according to Ginsberg, to convey the experience of a lone consciousness travelling through the United States during the Vietnam War. Dedicated to Walt Whitman and his 1871 book *Democratic Vistas, The Fall of America* won the National Book Award for poetry in 1974. *Mind Breaths: Poems, 1972-1977* (1978) marks a change of direction in Ginsberg's verse. In an interview, Ginsberg described his previous work as politically obsessed, ephemeral, angry, and not concerned enough with issues of his personal life. The poems in *Mind Breaths* are more tranquil, inducing the sense of spiritual meditation and calm suggested in the book's title. Also included is the poem "Don't Grow Old," which commentators described as Ginsberg's personal "Kaddish" for his father. Ginsberg returned to political and social issues in *Plutonian Ode* (1982), in which he addresses the dangers of nuclear warfare. The volumes *Collected Poems: 1947-1980* (1984) and *White Shroud: Poems, 1980-1985* (1986) marked Ginsberg's overdue ascension to the respected ranks of mainstream American letters.

CRITICAL RECEPTION

Commentators have been sharply divided in their opinions of Ginsberg's work. While a vocal minority have virtually dismissed it as willfully obscene and obtuse, others acknowledge Ginsberg's contributions to experimental poetry and hail his unique forms of expression. Whatever their opinion of his work, most critics agree that Ginsberg played a pivotal role in the Beat movement and that much of his writing reflects the values associated with the Beats. Many commentators, including Paul Zweig and Darryl Pinckney, remark on the similarities between Ginsberg and Whitman, particularly in the use of long, free verse lines but also in the use of homosexual imagery. Much of the commentary on Ginsberg's poetry analyzes the spiritual and philosophical aspects of his work. Some critics, such as John Tytell, maintain that the poet's spirituality comes from both his Jewish background, as evidenced in "Kaddish," and from Eastern philosophies, as evidenced in such works as "Planet News." Critics such as Paul Carroll cite the similarity of Ginsberg's poetry to a mantra, in its author's attempts to change the world through repetitive, chant-like language, while Thomas Merrill and others emphasize Ginsberg's affinity with Existentialism and other twentieth-century philosophical movements. A great deal of critical commentary focuses on the biographical details of Ginsberg's life as they relate to his poetry; critics interpret his poetry using details of specific events and experiences in his personal life, in particular Ginsberg's family life, his mother's illness, his sexual orientation, his interest in mind-expanding drugs, political activism, and spiritual pilgrimages.

PRINCIPAL WORKS

Howl and Other Poems (poetry) 1956; also published as *Howl: Original Draft Facsimile, Transcript & Variant Versions,* 1986

Siesta in Xbalba and Return to the States (poetry) 1956

Empty Mirror: Early Poems (poetry) 1961

Kaddish and Other Poems, 1958-1960 (poetry) 1961

The Change (poetry) 1963

Reality Sandwiches: 1953-1960 (poetry) 1963

The Yage Letters [with William Burroughs] (letters) 1963

Kral Majales (poetry) 1965

Wichita Vortex Sutra (poetry) 1966

TV Baby Poems (poetry) 1967

Airplane Dreams: Compositions from Journals (poetry) 1968

Ankor Wat (poetry) 1968

The Heart Is a Clock (poetry) 1968

Message II (poetry) 1968

Planet News (poetry) 1968

Scrap Leaves, Tasty Scribbles (poetry) 1968

Wales—A Visitation, July 29, 1967 (poetry) 1968

For the Soul of the Planet Is Wakening . . . (poetry) 1970

Indian Journals: March 1962-May 1963; Notebooks, Diary, Blank Pages, Writings (journals) 1970

The Moments Return: A Poem (poetry) 1970

Notes After an Evening with William Carlos Williams (nonfiction) 1970

Ginsberg's Improvised Poetics (poetry) 1971

Bixby Canyon Ocean Path Word Breeze (poetry) 1972

Iron Horse (poetry) 1972

Kaddish (play) 1972

New Year Blues (poetry) 1972

Open Head (poetry) 1972

The Fall of America: Poems of These States, 1965-1971 (poetry) 1972

The Gates of Wrath: Rhymed Poems, 1948-1952 (poetry) 1973

The Visions of the Great Rememberer (letters) 1974

Allen Verbatim: Lectures of Poetry, Politics, and Consciousness (lectures) 1975

First Blues: Rags, Ballads, and Harmonium Songs, 1971-1974 (poetry) 1975

Sad Dust Glories: Poems During Work Summer in Woods, 1974 (poetry) 1975

Journals: Early Fifties, Early Sixties (journals) 1977

Careless Love: Two Rhymes (poetry) 1978

Mind Breaths: Poems, 1972-1977 (poetry) 1978

Mostly Sitting Haiku (poetry) 1978; revised and expanded edition, 1979

Poems All Over the Place: Mostly Seventies (poetry) 1978

Plutonian Ode (poetry) 1982

Collected Poems: 1947-1980 (poetry) 1984

White Shroud: Poems, 1980-1985 (poetry) 1986

The Hydrogen Jukebox (play) 1990

Snapshot Poetics (poetry) 1993

Cosmopolitan Greetings: Poems, 1986-1992 (poetry) 1995

Selected Poems, 1947-1995 (poetry) 1996

PRIMARY SOURCES

ALLEN GINSBERG (JOURNAL DATE 1937-1941)

SOURCE: Ginsberg, Allen. "Early Journal Entries." The Allen Ginsberg Trust (website) <www.allenginsberg.org> (2002).

These early journal entries, dating from June, 1937 to May, 1941, offer Ginsberg's musings on a variety of topics, including his home life and his thoughts on art and literature.

Excerpts from Early Journals

Monday. June 21, 1937. I heard the story of *Monsieur Beaucaire* by Booth Tarkington over the radio, it was about time. I haven't received the key yet, and my mother is worse today. I found the book *Speaking of Operations* by Cobb[1] and I expect to read it soon.

Tuesday. June 22, 1937. Haven't received the key and I stayed home from school to mind my mother. I got a haircut and two pairs of shoes and heard the Louis-Braddock fight over the radio. [Joe] Louis won and is now champion of the world.

Wednesday. June 23, 1937. My brother graduated from high school today and we had a party. The party broke up about 12 o'clock at night. We had an excellent time and my brother (for once) kissed my aunts good-by. I stayed home from school to take care of my mother.

Thursday. June 24, 1937. I stayed home from school again, only today I went to high school and saw my father teach.[2] My mother locked herself in the bathroom early in the morning and my father had to break the glass to get in.[3] She also went back to the sanitarium.

Friday. June 25, 1937. I saw a newsreel of the Louis-Braddock fight. [I] also [saw] *Dangerous number* and another picture in the movies. I developed a sty below my eye.

Wednesday. Sept. 7, 1937. Dear Diary, I went to the shore beginning of summer and did not write anything as you were not along. Worst summer ever had—poison ivy—impetigo—bad weather—cold. Saw many pictures there including *The Life of Emile Zola,*[4] *Firefly,*[5] and *Saratoga* with Jean Harlow.

Thursday Sept. 8, 1937. Started school again, my teacher is Mrs. Bisset (Biscut)—she isn't good or bad. The day was uneventful. [Written by someone else is the following] P.S.—She was bad. Dear dairy [sic]—. Miss Biscut wood [sic] give anyone indigestion.

Thursday. Dec. 23, 1937. Coming home from movies (allegedly) shouting '4 blows'.

Friday. Dec. 31, 1937. Celebrated New Year by seeing 2 movies in succession. [on May 22, 1941 Allen wrote: "should have put down which."]

1938

Saturday. Jan. 22, 1938. "Life is but an empty Dream." I had a couple of vocabulary tests and I rated [as high as] high school graduates. My brother still has his 'bigness' complex.

Sunday. Jan. 23, 1938. Came back from Newark today. My mother is still in Greystone.[6] I saw *Hollywood Hotel* and *Sgt. Murphy* [with Ronald Reagan]. I just had another quarrel with my brother.

Wednesday. Feb. 2, 1938. Saw *Rosalie* with Nelson Eddy and Eleanor Powell. Am listening to Ben Bernie[7], who said the ground hog came out, took a look at [Walter] Winchell[8] and ducked in again. When Winchell opened his mouth Sam Goldwin[9] got the idea for *Hurricane.*

Friday. Feb 25, 1938. Came to Newark.[10]

Saturday. Feb 26, 1938. I saw *Hurricane* with Jon Hall and *All American Sweetheart.* The actor in the leading man's role [Scott Colton] was exceedingly good.

Sunday. Feb. 27, 1938. Had a puppet show: "A Quiet Evening with the Jones Family." Am in Newark.

Monday. Feb. 28, 1938. Went to school. Miss Biscuit still "cracked or crackered . . ." P.S. (this my better half's writing). [Allen's father, Louis, wrote the phrase within the quotation mark].

In case you don't know, I moved.[11] So did my brother. "And father and the rest of the furniture." [Louis wrote the phrase within the quotation marks]. got some new furniture. [My brother's] bigness still going strong.

Tuesday. March 1, 1938. Nothing new today. Naomi is still in the sanitarium but will be out in about 1 month.

Saturday. March 5, 1938. Saw [Walt Disney's] *Snow white and the Seven Dwarfs*[12]—exceedingly good. I sat through the picture 3 times.

* * *

Monday. March 14, 1938. What fools these Nazis be. In later years I expect to use this book for history. The world is now in a turmoil. A party headed by Hitler (Germany) and Mooselini [sic] (Italian) and some daffy emperor of China are killing all the Jews in their countries (a little exaggeration there). It really is a tough situation (I haven't mentioned this subject before in my diary.)

[Allen saved newspapers and reported the main stories in his diary.]

Sept. 9, 1937—Italy, Reich reject bid to parley [with Russians about piracy].

Sept. 10, 1937—[English & French] draft plan to annihilate [submarine] pirates.

Sept. 11, 1937—Soviet balks British plans it's war on pirates—piracy conference reaches agreement—patrol of Mediterranean [to keep neutral shipping safe].

Sept. 17, 1937—Britain and France defy Italy [over piracy patrol].

Feb. 3, 1938—Reich war rift with Nazis widens.

Feb. 5, 1938—Hitler takes Army control ousts 15 generals shifts 25 puts Goering in command.

Feb. 16, 1938—Austria capitulates to Germany. Pro-Nazis get the key posts in Cabinet. Berlin outlines policy for Austria, gloom pervades Vienna.

Feb. 21, 1938—England speeds [peace] pact with Italy [Germany and France]. Many Jews predicting what will happen in Austria flee in panic. [Anthony] Eden resigns in crisis over Hitler's speech. Hitler defies world next move is Czechoslovakia. Hitler wants [African] colonies back [which are now British colonies]. War invited by Eden policy says [Neville] Chamberlain.

Feb. 22, 1938—House of Commons backs Chamberlain policy [to restore friendship with Mussolini].

March 11, 1938—Was Hitler's first important move. [Kurt] Schuschnigg [Austria's chancellor] is going to have plebiscite, either free Austria or German lands.

March 12, 1938—[Schuschnigg resigns] Hitler takes army into Austria and conquers it so that it will not have a plebiscite because he knows that the majority is against him.

March 14, 1938—Austria absorbed into German Reich. Hitler commander of united armies, plebiscite on April 10 Chamberlain shocked - and there you have it. Seeing Schuschnigg was going to have a plebiscite Hitler marches his troops into Austria because he knows that he will loose. All the countries see his open hand Schuschnigg made him show his real self.

March 15, 1938—Nazi Deputy warns Czech chamber.

March 17-20, 1938—Lithuania-Poland have a [border] controversy it nearly led to war. Poland won without bloodshed.

March 24, 1938—Britain will go to *war* to defend its World War treaties. But denies help to Czechs. There sure is a hot time in the old world today.

March 28, 1938—A civil war in Spain, with bombing on a grand high in one day (last week) 1,200 were killed in Barcelona [Loyalist stronghold city]. It's bad the war is about over and those damn Rebel fascists are winning. Mussolini is sending soldiers by the thousand (and that is a confirmed fact admitted by certain Italian sources) and is ready to go to war if France (or any other country) helps the loyalists. A nice kettle of fish. But there is also war in china (Chinese against the invaders which is Japan) the war has been going on people killed and it still is an undeclared war. Thank heavens the Chinese are winning. It was even at first, then the Japanese gained so many victories that Japan thought (and other countries) that it would be a cinch for her to win. Then or rather now the Chinese have cornered the Japanese in a triangle in the midst of Chinese territory (not so fast or wonderfully though.) Something is likely to break in Europe the tension is no so great but the dictators' next move may start another European (or most likely world) war.

April 10, 1938—Germany Austria approve of Hitler's grab of Austria (99%). Mussolini and England signed a treaty that may avert war for the present. The Sudeten Germans in Czechoslovakia (Nazis) are demanding a separate tract of land for themselves.

May 22, 1938—The world is all agog, nothing much happened since I spoke to you last. Today, oh, am I having fun. Oh boy, my brother thinks I saw *Girl of the Golden West* (he-he). I am leading him around the bush by telling [him] the stories and happenings of that and another picture. I really didn't see either of them. I got [the] information from a friend.

Briefly there's a war in China; Brazil had a fascist uprising (the government won thank heavens). Mexico is on the verge of a Civil War, there's a war in Spain, but most important of all [is] Czechoslovakia. There is a party in Czechoslovakia called the 'Sudeten Germans' Headed by a man called Konrad Henlein. The Sudeten Germans are Nazis consisting of [only] 3 million out of 14 ¾ million people in Czechoslovakia. They are demanding autonomy for themselves and a lot of other outrageous demands [even though] they are a small minority. The Sudetens are backed by Hitler. If he grabs [Czechoslovakia] it will be by an excuse of saving her from internal troubles. He hesitates to take her because she is armed and will fight back and France is on her side. If France fights [Germany] Great Britain will too and also Russia; if Hitler fights he will be backed up with Italy.

I haven't told you much about myself. I am [the] smallest boy in class. Hobbies—stamps, coins, minerals, chemistry and most of all (at present) movies. They afford me great pleasure and they are about the only relief from boredom which seems to hang around me like a shadow. So don't be surprised at the movies I've seen in succession. On March 14, 1938, Clarence Darrow[13] died at 80.

[Again Allen has listed the main newstories here]

Aug. 4-8, 1938—Held a little border dispute with Russia and Japan.

Aug. 8, 1938—Japan army concedes Soviet victory at border.

Aug. 29, 1938—British envoy to Berlin called home for talks in move to keep peace.

Sept. 4, 1938—Hitler army of 50,000 on Rhine.

Sept. 6, 1938—Hitler defies blockade. (War is coming I'm pretty sure). France pours reserves into frontier defenses. Blames German arming.

Sept. 9, 1938—War crisis at explosion point.

Sept. 10, 1938—Britain will fight Nazis told Roumania agrees to let Russian trespass through it to defend Czechoslovakia.

Sept. 11, 1938—Nazis demand annexation of Sudeten.

1941

May 1941. Began writing to (I suppose) satisfy my egotism. My writing has improved (slightly). A lot happened since I first entered notes in [this] book and stopped. Biggest things were graduation from public school, classical course and extracurricular activities in high [school]: L. D. S. (Literary and Debating Society), dramatic Club, S.G.A. (Student Government Association) Board of Publications. I was a good writer so I got $2 a week position beginning Sept. 1941 as Central [High School] columnist for *Paterson Evening News*.[14] Will be layout editor of the *Tatler*[15] (school paper) next term. I'm running for Treasurership of S. G. A. against Robert Hanson and Saul Liss. Haven't *too* good a chance. Am counting on my father's name and a lot of people who know me but not vice versa. Don't mind my succession of different thoughts. I have a lot to say. As I said, I am writing to satisfy my egotism. If some future historian or biographer wants to know what the genius thought & did in his tender years, here it is. I'll be a genius of some kind or other, probably in literature. I really believe it. (Not naively, as whoever reads this is thinking). I have a fair degree of confidence in myself. Either I'm a genius, I'm egocentric, or I'm slightly schizophrenic. Probably the first two.

I'm president of [the Literary and Debating Society]. As for international affairs, I have a collection of newspaper headlines. I made a collection with my brother, who by the way is a senior at college and has recovered from his attack of '17'.[16] The [headline] collection dates from somewhere in 1937 or '38 to '40. I became lazy. By the way, I'm an atheist and a combination of Jeffersonian Democrat-Socialist Communist. I don't agree with communist foreign policy and dictatorship. Also to satisfy my egotism (and for the benefit of future historians) I'm outlining and giving my opinion on every book I read, hereafter. I'm a lover of classical music and like some swing [such as:] *Playmates, Alexander the Swoose* [recorded by Johny Messner], and *Three Little Fishies*.

Started to compose my own piano concerto. Succeeded in getting introduction & main theme, about 25 bars, and didn't have patience to finish. What I have is excellent. I like Tchaikovsky,

Beethoven, Chopin, Schubert—long list. I prefer rhapsodies, overtures, piano concertos & a few suites & dances, [just] about everything. My latest fad is Tchaikovsky especially piano concerto #1 and [his] 4th, 5th & 6th symphonies. Wagner to.

Mommy came home about a year ago. Is still a little—. She came home to find Lou $3,000 in debt. Is very fat, lost her girlish laughter & figure. I don't blame her for her condition. For bout 4 months, there were violent quarrels. Lou should have known better. As for the $3,000—Je ne sais pas.

Heywood Broun[17] died and a columnist by the name of Samuel Grafton[18] has almost taken his place. Grafton's style is humorous, witty, satirical, cynical, not [as] sentimental as Broun. Grafton is more cold, political, full of facts. I admire him very much. Typical of his humor and fine phraseology is, "I get my knowledge thru osmosis." His columns are both entertaining and educational. Roosevelt elected for 3rd term, awhile ago.

I saw a great deal of movies including: *Make Way for Tomorrow, Pygmalion, Grapes of Wrath, Of Mice & Men, Great Dictator,* and other Charlie Chaplain films, *Fantasia, Dark Victory, The Letter, The Old Maid* (Bette Davis), *Wuthering Heights, Mr. Deeds Goes to Town, You Can't Take It with You,* Laurel & Hardy pix, Ed Cantor's pix, Jack Benny's pix, Bob Hope & B. Crosby's pix, *Snow White & the 7 Dwarfs,* Sabu's pix (*Aladdin?*), *Three Comrades* (with Robert Taylor, Margaret Sullivan), *It Happened One Night, All Quiet on the Western Front;* [the editors have corrected those errors].

I weigh 95 lb., by the way, and am comparatively fragile. I'm coming thru a stage of puberty and new horizons are opening up, though I can remember the baser emotions since I was about seven. In a modified way, of course. I'm capable of almost anything. Well, if I'm equipped to do things why not? I suppose I'm a coward, because I haven't exercised my beautiful theories. By the way, the lock on this [diary] is broken because I lost the key a few years ago.

I am no longer bored by life in general (as mentioned in a previous year) because of my extra-curricular activities. I haven't the time to be bored.

Notes

1. *Speaking of Operations* (Garden City, NY: Doran, 1915) by Irvin S. Cobb was a humorous account of visiting the doctor and hospital. After experiencing an operation Mr. Cobb understood why people like to talk about them. As a subject of conversation among the initiated an operation has no equal; and if it is a good subject to talk about why is it not a good subject to write about.
2. Louis Ginsberg (1896-1975) was an English teacher at Eastside High School as well as an accomplished poet.
3. Suicide attempt
4. Emile Zola [Paul Muni]
5. Jeanette MacDonald
6. Sanitorium, Morristown, NJ [Might Be Photo]
7. Ben Bernie: Popular radio celebrity on WABC, New York 9:30pm
8. Walter Winchell: Radio News commentator
9. Sam Goodwin: Motion Picture producer
10. When mom was ill Allen was staying with father's brothers and sisters, Rose Gaidemak, father's oldest sister, Clara Meltzer next oldest, Honey Litzky. Claire Gaidemak. Came weekends to Newark.
11. 288 Graham Ave. Date of move, from where, why?
12. Snow white—maybe inaugurated Radio City
13. Clarence Darrow—American criminal lawyer and social reformer.
14. INCLUDE EXAMPLE OF PATERSON EVENING NEWS COLUMN [beginning Sept 1941]
15. Tatler [AG is layout editor beginning Sept. 1941]
16. AG note what is "attaack of '17'? Merely "Of being 17."
17. Heywood Broun: 1888-1939 Newpaper Columnist, commentator.
18. Samuel Grafton (radio comentator?)

ALLEN GINSBERG (POEM DATE 1955)

SOURCE: Ginsberg, Allen. "Sunflower Sutra." In *Collected Poems: 1947-1980,* pp. 138-9. New York: HarperCollins, 1984.

Written in 1955, "Sunflower Sutra" was inspired by Ginsberg's reading of the William Blake poem, "Ah! Sunflower."

"SUNFLOWER SUTRA"

I walked on the banks of the tincan banana dock
and sat down under the huge shade of a
Southern Pacific locomotive to look at the
sunset over the box house hills and cry.
Jack Kerouac sat beside me on a busted rusty
iron pole, companion, we thought the same
thoughts of the soul, bleak and blue and
sad-eyed, surrounded by the gnarled steel
roots of trees of machinery.
The oily water on the river mirrored the red sky,
sun sank on top of final Frisco peaks, no
fish in that stream, no hermit in those
mounts, just ourselves rheumy-eyed and
hung-over like old bums on the riverbank,
tired and wily.

Look at the Sunflower, he said, there was a dead gray shadow against the sky, big as a man, sitting dry on top of a pile of ancient sawdust—
—I rushed up enchanted—it was my first sunflower, memories of Blake—my visions—Harlem
and Hells of the Eastern rivers, bridges clanking Joes Greasy Sandwiches, dead baby carriages, black treadless tires forgotten and unretreaded, the poem of the riverbank, condoms & pots, steel knives, nothing stainless, only the dank muck and the razor-sharp artifacts passing into the past—
and the gray Sunflower poised against the sunset, crackly bleak and dusty with the smut and smog and smoke of olden locomotives in its eye—
corolla of bleary spikes pushed down and broken like a battered crown, seeds fallen out of its face, soon-to-be-toothless mouth of sunny air, sunrays obliterated on its hairy head like a dried wire spiderweb,
leaves stuck out like arms out of the stem, gestures from the sawdust root, broke pieces of plaster fallen out of the black twigs, a dead fly in its ear,
Unholy battered old thing you were, my sunflower O my soul, I loved you then!
The grime was no man's grime but death and human locomotives,
all that dress of dust, that veil of darkened railroad skin, that smog of cheek, that eyelid of black mis'ry, that sooty hand or phallus or protuberance of artificial worse-than-dirt—industrial—modern—all that civilization spotting your crazy golden crown—
and those blear thoughts of death and dusty loveless eyes and ends and withered roots below, in the home-pile of sand and sawdust, rubber dollar bills, skin of machinery, the guts and innards of the weeping coughing car, the empty lonely tincans with their rusty tongues alack, what more could I name, the smoked ashes of some cock cigar, the cunts of wheelbarrows and the milky breasts of cars, wornout asses out of chairs & sphincters of dynamos—all these
entangled in your mummied roots—and you there standing before me in the sunset, all your glory in your form!
A perfect beauty of a sunflower! a perfect excellent lovely sunflower existence! a sweet natural eye to the new hip moon, woke up alive and excited grasping in the sunset shadow sunrise golden monthly breeze!
How many flies buzzed round you innocent of your grime, while you cursed the heavens of the railroad and your flower soul?
Poor dead flower? when did you forget you were a flower? when did you look at your skin and decide you were an impotent dirty old locomotive? the ghost of a locomotive? the specter and shade of a once powerful mad American locomotive?
You were never no locomotive, Sunflower, you were a sunflower!
And you Locomotive, you are a locomotive, forget me not!
So I grabbed up the skeleton thick sunflower and stuck it at my side like a scepter,
and deliver my sermon to my soul, and Jack's soul too, and anyone who'll listen,
We're not our skin of grime, we're not our dread bleak dusty imageless locomotive, we're all golden sunflowers inside, blessed by our own seed & hairy naked accomplishment-bodies growing into mad black formal sunflowers in the sunset, spied on by our eyes under the shadow of the mad locomotive riverbank sunset Frisco hilly tincan evening sitdown vision.

Berkeley, 1955

ALLEN GINSBERG (POEM DATE 1956)

SOURCE: Ginsberg, Allen. "Howl." In *Howl and Other Poems*, pp. 9-26. San Francisco: City Lights Books, 1996.

Originally published in 1956, "Howl" is considered the definitive work by Ginsberg, the poem that brought him both fame and notoriety. Emotionally complex and graphic, the work was considered obscene by some—resulting in the obscenity charges against and ensuing trial of Lawrence Ferlinghetti for his role as publisher of the poem—and praised as a work of genius by others.

For Carl Solomon

I

I saw the best minds of my generation destroyed by madness, starving hysterical naked,
dragging themselves through the negro streets at dawn looking for an angry fix,
angelheaded hipsters burning for the ancient heavenly connection to the starry dynamo in the machinery of night,
who poverty and tatters and hollow-eyed and high sat up smoking in the supernatural darkness of cold-water flats floating across the tops of cities contemplating jazz,
who bared their brains to Heaven under the El and saw Mohammedan angels staggering on tenement roofs illuminated,
who passed through universities with radiant cool eyes hallucinating Arkansas and Blake-light tragedy among the scholars of war,
who were expelled from the academies for crazy & publishing obscene odes on the windows of the skull,
who cowered in unshaven rooms in underwear, burning their money in wastebaskets and listening to the Terror through the wall,
who got busted in their pubic beards returning through Laredo with a belt of marijuana for New York,
who ate fire in paint hotels or drank turpentine in Paradise Alley, death, or purgatoried their torsos night after night

with dreams, with drugs, with waking nightmares, alcohol and cock and endless balls,

incomparable blind; streets of shuddering cloud and lightning in the mind leaping toward poles of Canada & Paterson, illuminating all the motionless world of Time between,

Peyote solidities of halls, backyard green tree cemetery dawns, wine drunkenness over the rooftops, storefront boroughs of teahead joyride neon blinking traffic light, sun and moon and tree vibrations in the roaring winter dusks of Brooklyn, ashcan rantings and kind king light of mind,

who chained themselves to subways for the endless ride from Battery to holy Bronx on benzedrine until the noise of wheels and children brought them down shuddering mouth-wracked and battered bleak of brain all drained of brilliance in the drear light of Zoo,

who sank all night in submarine light of Bickford's floated out and sat through the stale beer afternoon in desolate Fugazzi's, listening to the crack of doom on the hydrogen jukebox,

who talked continuously seventy hours from park to pad to bar to Bellevue to museum to the Brooklyn Bridge,

lost battalion of platonic conversationalists jumping down the stoops off fire escapes off windowsills off Empire State out of the moon,

yacketayakking screaming vomiting whispering facts and memories and anecdotes and eyeball kicks and shocks of hospitals and jails and wars,

whole intellects disgorged in total recall for seven days and nights with brilliant eyes, meat for the Synagogue cast on the pavement,

who vanished into nowhere Zen New Jersey leaving a trail of ambiguous picture postcards of Atlantic City Hall,

suffering Eastern sweats and Tangerian bone-grindings and migraines of China under junk-withdrawal in Newark's bleak furnished room,

who wandered around and around at midnight in the railroad yard wondering where to go, and went, leaving no broken hearts,

who lit cigarettes in boxcars boxcars boxcars racketing through snow toward lonesome farms in grandfather night,

who studied Plotinus Poe St. John of the Cross telepathy and bop kabbalah because the cosmos instinctively vibrated at their feet in Kansas,

who loned it through the streets of Idaho seeking visionary indian angels who were visionary indian angels,

who thought they were only mad when Baltimore gleamed in supernatural ecstasy,

who jumped in limousines with the Chinaman of Oklahoma on the impulse of winter midnight streetlight smalltown rain,

who lounged hungry and lonesome through Houston seeking jazz or sex or soup, and followed the brilliant Spaniard to converse about America and Eternity, a hopeless task, and so took ship to Africa,

who disappeared into the volcanoes of Mexico leaving behind nothing but the shadow of dungarees and the lava and ash of poetry scattered in fire place Chicago,

who reappeared on the West Coast investigating the F.B.I. in beards and shorts with big pacifist eyes sexy in their dark skin passing out incomprehensible leaflets,

who burned cigarette holes in their arms protesting the narcotic tobacco haze of Capitalism,

who distributed Supercommunist pamphlets in Union Square weeping and undressing while the sirens of Los Alamos wailed them down, and wailed down Wall, and the Staten Island ferry also wailed,

who broke down crying in white gymnasiums naked and trembling before the machinery of other skeletons,

who bit detectives in the neck and shrieked with delight in policecars for committing no crime but their own wild cooking pederasty and intoxication,

who howled on their knees in the subway and were dragged off the roof waving genitals and manuscripts,

who let themselves be fucked in the ass by saintly motorcyclists, and screamed with joy,

who blew and were blown by those human seraphim, the sailors, caresses of Atlantic and Caribbean love,

who balled in the morning in the evenings in rose gardens and the grass of public parks and cemeteries scattering their semen freely to whomever come who may,

who hiccuped endlessly trying to giggle but wound up with a sob behind a partition in a Turkish Bath when the blond & naked angel came to pierce them with a sword,

who lost their loveboys to the three old shrews of fate the one eyed shrew of the heterosexual dollar the one eyed shrew that winks out of the womb and the one eyed shrew that does nothing but sit on her ass and snip the intellectual golden threads of the craftsman's loom,

who copulated ecstatic and insatiate with a bottle of beer a sweetheart a package of cigarettes a candle and fell off the bed, and continued along the floor and down the hall and ended fainting on the wall with a vision of ultimate cunt and come eluding the last gyzym of consciousness,

who sweetened the snatches of a million girls trembling in the sunset, and were red eyed in the morning but prepared to sweeten the snatch of the sunrise, flashing buttocks under barns and naked in the lake,

who went out whoring through Colorado in myriad stolen night-cars, N.C., secret hero of these poems, cocksman and Adonis of Denver—joy to the memory of his innumerable lays of girls in empty lots & diner backyards, moviehouses' rickety rows, on mountaintops in caves or with gaunt waitresses in familiar roadside lonely petticoat upliftings & especially secret gas-station solipsisms of johns, & hometown alleys too,

who faded out in vast sordid movies, were shifted in dreams, woke on a sudden Manhattan, and picked themselves up out of basements hung over with heartless Tokay and horrors of Third Avenue iron dreams & stumbled to unemployment offices,

who walked all night with their shoes full of blood on the snowbank docks waiting for a door in the East River to open to a room full of steamheat and opium,

who created great suicidal dramas on the apartment cliff-banks of the Hudson under the wartime blue floodlight of the moon & their heads shall be crowned with laurel in oblivion,

who ate the lamb stew of the imagination or digested the crab at the muddy bottom of the rivers of Bowery,

who wept at the romance of the streets with their pushcarts full of onions and bad music,

who sat in boxes breathing in the darkness under the bridge, and rose up to build harpsichords in their lofts,

who coughed on the sixth floor of Harlem crowned with flame under the tubercular sky surrounded by orange crates of theology,

who scribbled all night rocking and rolling over lofty incantations which in the yellow morning were stanzas of gibberish,

who cooked rotten animals lung heart feet tail borsht & tortillas dreaming of the pure vegetable kingdom,

who plunged themselves under meat trucks looking for an egg,

who threw their watches off the roof to cast their ballot for Eternity outside of Time, & alarm clocks fell on their heads every day for the next decade,

who cut their wrists three times successively unsuccessfully, gave up and were forced to open antique stores where they thought they were growing old and cried,

who were burned alive in their innocent flannel suits on Madison Avenue amid blasts of leaden verse & the tanked-up clatter of the iron regiments of fashion & the nitroglycerine shrieks of the fairies of advertising & the mustard gas of sinister intelligent editors, or were run down by the drunken taxicabs of Absolute Reality,

who jumped off the Brooklyn Bridge this actually happened and walked away unknown and forgotten into the ghostly daze of Chinatown soup alley ways & firetrucks, not even one free beer,

who sang out of their windows in despair, fell out of the subway window, jumped in the filthy Passaic, leaped on negroes, cried all over the street, danced on broken wineglasses barefoot smashed phonograph records of nostalgic European 1930s German jazz finished the whiskey and threw up groaning into the bloody toilet, moans in their ears and the blast of colossal steam whistles,

who barreled down the highways of the past journeying to each other's hotrod-Golgotha jail-solitude watch or Birmingham jazz incarnation,

who drove crosscountry seventytwo hours to find out if I had a vision or you had a vision or he had a vision to find out Eternity,

who journeyed to Denver, who died in Denver, who came back to Denver & waited in vain, who watched over Denver & brooded & loned in Denver and finally went away to find out the Time, & now Denver is lonesome for her heroes,

who fell on their knees in hopeless cathedrals praying for each other's salvation and light and breasts, until the soul illuminated its hair for a second,

who crashed through their minds in jail waiting for impossible criminals with golden heads and the charm of reality in their hearts who sang sweet blues to Alcatraz,

who retired to Mexico to cultivate a habit, or Rocky Mount to tender Buddha or Tangiers to boys or Southern Pacific to the black locomotive or Harvard to Narcissus to Woodlawn to the daisychain or grave,

who demanded sanity trials accusing the radio of hypnotism & were left with their insanity & their hands & a hung jury,

who threw potato salad at CCNY lecturers on Dadaism and subsequently presented themselves on the granite steps of the madhouse with shaven heads and harlequin speech of suicide, demanding instantaneous lobotomy,

and who were given instead the concrete void of insulin Metrazol electricity hydrotherapy psychotherapy occupational therapy pingpong & amnesia,

who in humorless protest overturned only one symbolic pingpong table, resting briefly in catatonia,

returning years later truly bald except for a wig of blood, and tears and fingers, to the visible madman doom of the wards of the madtowns of the East,

Pilgrim State's Rockland's and Greystone's foetid halls, bickering with the echoes of the soul, rocking and rolling in the midnight solitude-bench dolmen-realms of love, dream of life a nightmare, bodies turned to stone as heavy as the moon,

with mother finally ******, and the last fantastic book flung out of the tenement window, and the last door closed at 4. A.M. and the last telephone slammed at the wall in reply and the last furnished room emptied down to the last piece of mental furniture, a yel-

low paper rose twisted on a wire hanger in the closet, and even that imaginary, nothing but a hopeful little bit of hallucination—
ah, Carl, while you are not safe I am not safe, and now you're really in the total animal soup of time—
and who therefore ran through the icy streets obsessed with a sudden flash of the alchemy of the use of the ellipse the catalog the meter & the vibrating plane,
who dreamt and made incarnate gaps in Time & Space through images juxtaposed, and trapped the archangel of the soul between 2 visual images and joined the elemental verbs and set the noun and dash of consciousness together jumping with sensation of Pater Omnipotens Aeterna Deus
to recreate the syntax and measure of poor human prose and stand before you speechless and intelligent and shaking with shame, rejected yet confessing out the soul to conform to the rhythm of thought in his naked and endless head,
the madman bum and angel beat in Time, unknown, yet putting down here what might be left to say in time come after death,
and rose reincarnate in the ghostly clothes of jazz in the goldhorn shadow of the band and blew the suffering of America's naked mind for love into an eli eli lamma lamma sabacthani saxophone cry that shivered the cities down to the last radio
with the absolute heart of the poem of life butchered out of their own bodies good to eat a thousand years.

II

What sphinx of cement and aluminum bashed open their skulls and ate up their brains and imagination?
Moloch! Solitude! Filth! Ugliness! Ashcans and unobtainable dollars! Children screaming under the stairways! Boys sobbing in armies! Old men weeping in the parks!
Moloch! Moloch! Nightmare of Moloch! Moloch the loveless! Mental Moloch! Moloch the heavy judger of men!
Moloch the incomprehensible prison! Moloch the crossbone soulless jailhouse and Congress of sorrows! Moloch whose buildings are judgment! Moloch the vast stone of war! Moloch the stunned governments!
Moloch whose mind is pure machinery! Moloch whose blood is running money! Moloch whose fingers are ten armies! Moloch whose breast is a cannibal dynamo! Moloch whose ear is a smoking tomb!
Moloch whose eyes are a thousand blind windows! Moloch whose skyscrapers stand in the long streets like endless Jehovahs! Moloch whose factories dream and croak in the fog! Moloch whose smokestacks and antennae crown the cities!
Moloch whose love is endless oil and stone! Moloch whose soul is electricity and banks! Moloch whose poverty is the specter of genius! Moloch whose fate is a cloud of sexless hydrogen! Moloch whose name is the Mind!
Moloch in whom I sit lonely! Moloch in whom I dream Angels! Crazy in Moloch! Cocksucker in Moloch! Lacklove and manless in Moloch!
Moloch who entered my soul early! Moloch in whom I am a consciousness without a body! Moloch who frightened me out of my natural ecstasy! Moloch whom I abandon! Wake up in Moloch! Light streaming out of the sky!
Moloch! Moloch! Robot apartments! invisible suburbs! skeleton treasuries! blind capitals! demonic industries! spectral nations! invincible mad houses! granite cocks! monstrous bombs!
They broke their backs lifting Moloch to Heaven! Pavements, trees, radios, tons! lifting the city to Heaven which exists and is everywhere about us!
Visions! omens! hallucinations! miracles! ecstasies! gone down the American river!
Dreams! adorations! illuminations! religions! the whole boatload of sensitive bullshit!
Breakthroughs! over the river! flips and crucifixions! gone down the flood! Highs! Epiphanies! Despairs! Ten years' animal screams and suicides! Minds! New loves! Mad generation! down on the rocks of Time!
Real holy laughter in the river! They saw it all! the wild eyes! the holy yells! They bade farewell! They jumped off the roof! to solitude! waving! carrying flowers! Down to the river! into the street!

III

Carl Solomon! I'm with you in Rockland
where you're madder than I am
I'm with you in Rockland
where you must feel very strange
I'm with you in Rockland
where you imitate the shade of my mother
I'm with you in Rockland
where you've murdered your twelve secretaries
I'm with you in Rockland
where you laugh at this invisible humor
I'm with you in Rockland
where we are great writers on the same dreadful typewriter
I'm with you in Rockland
where your condition has become serious and is reported on the radio
I'm with you in Rockland
where the faculties of the skull no longer admit the worms of the senses
I'm with you in Rockland
where you drink the tea of the breasts of the spinsters of Utica
I'm with you in Rockland
where you pun on the bodies of your nurses the harpies of the Bronx
I'm with you in Rockland

where you scream in a straightjacket that
you're losing the game of the actual
pingpong of the abyss
I'm with you in Rockland
where you bang on the catatonic piano
the soul is innocent and immortal
it should never die ungodly in
an armed madhouse
I'm with you in Rockland
where fifty more shocks will never return
your soul to its body again from its
pilgrimage to a cross in the void
I'm with you in Rockland
where you accuse your doctors of insanity
and plot the Hebrew socialist revolution
against the fascist national Golgotha
I'm with you in Rockland
where you will split the heavens of
Long Island and resurrect your living
human Jesus from the superhuman tomb
I'm with you in Rockland
where there are twenty-five-thousand mad
comrades all together singing the final
stanzas of the Internationale
I'm with you in Rockland
where we hug and kiss the United States
under our bedsheets the United States
that coughs all night and won't let us
sleep
I'm with you in Rockland
where we wake up electrified out of the
coma by our own souls' airplanes roaring
over the roof they've come to drop
angelic bombs the hospital illuminates
itself imaginary walls collapse O skinny
legions run outside O starry spangled
shock of mercy the eternal war is here
O victory forget your underwear
we're free
I'm with you in Rockland
in my dreams you walk dripping
from a sea-journey on the highway
across America in tears to the door
of my cottage in the Western night

San Francisco 1955-56

ANNE WALDMAN (ESSAY DATE 15 APRIL 1997)

SOURCE: Waldman, Anne. "The Weight of the World is Love."*Naropa University* (website) <www.naropa.edu/ginstributes8.html> (15 April 1997).

Written in 1997 following Allen Ginsberg's death, this tribute from Waldman appears on the Naropa University website.

"You'd better come over", Allen says voice steady on the other end of the pay phone. It's a mild Good Friday (March 28) afternoon in New York. I've been escorting my 16 year-old son Ambrose who's known Allen all his life and his cousin, Reed, 9 years, around town. Both live wires. We'd ended up at a showing of "When We Were Kings" not far from Union Square. It's a little after 4pm. I've been calling to see him for the past two days. I'm trembling, something's up, Allen's been seriously ill. Not recovering as quickly as he's wont to from various familiar ailments.

I'd seen him just the week before, he'd prepared lunch for me & artist George Schneeman in his new loft—a generous array of fresh cooked spinach, soup, salad, cheeses - but he couldn't sit up for long had to lie down. He'd been planning a trip to Milan. He was commenting on my new long tome, *IOVIS II,* how impressed he was who else was doing a poem like that? (*ever encouraging, empowering, oh Allen!*) George had a collaboration with Allen in mind. Another artist—George Condo—had arrived. Allen was sweet, attentive, happy we were all spending time together, that he was finally getting the two artist-George together. I had cancelled his planned trip to Naropa's Kerouac School Summer Writing Program painful as that was—*no Allen at Naropa after 23 years?—* wanting to spare him one more duty, one more obligation! He seemed to be fighting his exhaustion, lying on the sofa now, thin, sallow, wrapped in a blanket, but ever manifesting the gracious host, putting us at our ease, plans were going forward, he was curious about everything, emanating tremendous tenderness & warmth, but decidedly fragile. And just several weeks before I'd been over, taking younger poet Lisa Jarnot along to meet Allen, while we visited painter Larry Rivers, in the same loft building, for a glass of white wine. We gossiped about Frank O'Hara, other mutual poet-luminaries they both had in common and there had been, I noticed, a palpable ebb in his demeanor. And then everyone asking that week: "How's Allen?"

"Over" means to Beth Israel Hospital, 16th Street & First Avenue. A slow tense ride in what's called the "Sabbat" elevator. We enter Allen's spacious room, sweet & sour scent of flowers. His steady-as-a-rock loyal assistants Bob Rosenthal and Peter Hale sit by his bedside, sombre, visibly shaken. The children are restless. Ambrose seems nervous, standing by the window. Bob & Peter leave us alone and I hover over my dear old friend *-mentor, comrade-poet, co-founder of Kerouac School, spiritual husband, fellow Buddhist, fellow activity-demon, how many journeys, how many intimate conversations, our karma entwined for over 30 years?*—all those aspects racing & cramming into my head—facing what terrible truth?

"I'm dying", he says simply, "liver cancer. I just learned." We both burst into tears and stare hard into each others' eyes. *What lifetimes of attachment, of some indescribable desire in me in him to be on the same wave-length sustained this conjunct?* I suddenly feel the truth of "rahula"—the link, the chain, the weight that human desire & attachment brings, in a way I haven't experienced before. It's substantively different—although no less powerful than—the connection one feels with parents, child, lover. Allen belongs to the world, to others who have their own deep & profound links to him as much as he belongs to me. What I am feeling I realize is his very particular & inspired love affair with the phenomenal world, his bodhisattva's compassion that connects us all with that mystery. His obsessive attention to detail, William Blake's "minute particulars", his tireless activity on behalf of others & how that's so rare & *how can we do without it?*

> *Well, while I'm here I'll*
> *do the work—*
> *and what's the work?*
> *To ease the pain of living.*
> *Everything else, drunken*
> *dumbshow.*
>
> *("Memory Gardens")*

But there's ordinary Allen, too. The guy flossing his teeth & cooking chicken soup at the Varsity Townhouse apartment in Boulder, summer after summer. *Are we allowed to miss him too?*

"We've done some great work together", he says, to cheer us both. More crying. "The doctor's say several months, but I think less—maybe one". "You have time to put your house in order!" I added bravely. And "you've had a great life, so rich, so full!" He: "It's been a great ride!" "Thank you Allen, thank you for all your kindness, generosity, thank you, thank you. I don't want you to suffer!" He: "No pain, they're saying no pain." Then we reminisce some about Naropa, the old days. Then where the school is going from here, how inspired we should be by the students, the Dalai Lama's forthcoming visit, all the magazines, publications, arts centers & events that have been spawned by graduates, the fund-raising for minorities, the activities of the Schule fur Dichtung in Austria, the "new independents" coming out of our program, poets who think for themselves, not beholden to any school—Beat, New York, Language Poetry etc.! Poets who write with passion, conviction! "Thank god', he says with a sigh of relief. He wants to know things are OK with my home scene, his beloved musician Steven Taylor, our Naropa poetics core faculty, *that everyone's taken care of.* "Well, it's always a struggle". I say. He wants me to get David Erdman, the Blake scholar, to teach his Blake class this summer. "I'll try." We talk about Peter Orlovsky, Gregory Corso who he's not told yet, he's just gotten news today, *there's a little more time.* "You can't tell anybody", he scolds, "I want to tell them myself." *It'll be hard.* I promise I won't, bursting inside. He: "My stepmother is going to outlive me!". "I'll stay Allen, wash your feet, wait on you! Just tell me to stay! I want more of your transmission!" "No, no, you're fine". Later Ambrose is included, and we're talking about the movie we've just seen. Allen likes Mohammed Ali—his Vietnam protest, his poetic quips—we'd both met him backstage at a Bob Dylan concert. He's curious about what Norman Mailer says in the film. He queries Ambrose about museums he's been to, "Go to the Frick, I always like the quiet elegant, intimacy of the Frick." He talks about Columbia University we'd visited the day before, "It's a good program everybody's gotta do with classics, Homer, Plato, humanities." "Ambrose, you're looking sexy these days!"

We need to trim the flowers we brought, some fumbling with a pocketknife, the nurse enters with food, there's delivery of fruit and candy "for guests" from an admirer. I take the boys downstairs, trying to catch my breath, then head back up, the slow elevator to the 9th floor. Entering again, Allen's sitting calmly pen in hand fine-tuning the manuscript for his next book *Fame & Death.* He wants me to hear the title poem. "I had this big embarrassing fantasy, wasn't going to write it down, thought of something Trungpa'd said, trusting in the original embarrassing mind, did." He reads, pausing to get strength, or laugh at funny lines. It's a grand confession, a modified version of the funeral we'll get to 10 days later. I laugh at a line, the one woman in the poem speaking how the dead poet couldn't remember her name but she loved him anyway. I remind him in the old days he used to call me Diane (for Diane diPrima). *Is this it? Has it come to this? Are we really saying goodbye in eternity?*

Presumably there's more time, *yes, act like there's more time,* and I'm making plans to come back in several weeks. I can help out at his office. "I'll do anything", I say.

We speak by telephone he sounds weak. I'm in contact with the office daily and Peter Hale tells me the day Allen gets home from the hospital, the following Wednesday, he won't lie down. He's in good spirits. He's up and about for *five* hours. And calling everyone. And the press release an-

Peter Orlovsky, 1933-.

nouncing his terminal illness goes out. Two days later, April 4th, Paranirvana of Trungpa Rinpoche, Allen's in coma from stroke, I'm prostrating and sitting with the Vidyadaa's black coral-like brain relic at Dorje-Dzong in Boulder, waiting for flight, several hours away, to New York which will carry me to Allen's bedside. His corpse is still warm. *Can he still hear us? The monks chanting?* His face is extraordinarily handsome in repose. Did someone say he resembles Dostoyevsky in death? More of his lines ring in the brain like mantra:

The weight of the world

is love.
Under the burden
of solitude,
under the burden
of dissatisfaction
the weight,
the weight we carry
is love.

. . . . .

yes, yes

that's what
I wanted.
I always wanted,
I always wanted
to return
to my body
where I was born.

("Song")

GENERAL COMMENTARY

MORRIS DICKSTEIN (ESSAY DATE JANUARY 1970)

SOURCE: Dickstein, Morris. "Allen Ginsberg and the 60's." *Commentary* 49, no. 1 (January 1970): 64.

In the following essay, Dickstein reviews a poetry reading by Ginsberg in the late 1960s.

A generation is fashion: but there is more to history than costume and jargon. The people of an era must either carry the burden of change assigned to their time or die under its weight in the wilderness.

—Harold Rosenberg
Death in the Wilderness

It was almost two years ago, in the shabby auditorium of Columbia's Earl Hall, with its high crumbling plaster dome, that I last heard Allen Ginsberg read his poems. He and John Hollander were back where they had both gone to school twenty years earlier, doing a benefit for a campus literary magazine. It was an intriguing combination. I knew from Hollander's fine poem "Helicon" that they had been friends then, in a strange, intense, and perhaps mistrusting way. I also knew how archetypically their lives had since diverged. There was almost a cultural parable here: could any two closely contemporary poets have come to public notice more differently? For Hollander there had been *Partisan Review,* a Yale Younger Poets award (carrying Auden's sponsorship, for a very Audenesque book), and a successful academic career. For Ginsberg there had been San Francisco and the notoriety of ***Howl,*** cheap exploitation in *Time* and olympian put-down in *Partisan Review* (by Hollander among others).

Times had changed however. Instead of canzoni, sestinas (!), madrigals, songs, and sonnets, Hollander had published an impressive sequence of autobiographical poems, some almost as free and personal as anything Ginsberg had written. And Ginsberg, as far as I knew, might not have written any poems for years. None of his books contained anything from after 1960. Perhaps alone among the Beat poets he had survived, magnificently—that much was clear. But as I had followed his gentle, newly-bearded eminence from week to week in the pages of the *Village Voice* he seemed to have become entirely a public figure, the guru to a new generation. It was not as a poet, it seemed, that he lent his magnetic spiritual presence to so many of the most obscene and solemn moments of the 1960's, from New York to Berkeley and London to Prague; he was the elder statesman, the wise and worldly Lord of the Revels, a live link with the germinal protest culture of the 50's.

So it was the performer, the public Ginsberg, that many came to see, see even more than hear, that night in Earl Hall. Nor was anyone disappointed, not by either poet. The surprise was how close Hollander came to stealing the show. For all his change of style he remained the complete university poet in the best sense: witty, literate, brilliant, breathlessly enthusiastic yet ironical. The crowd had not come for *him* perhaps but they were his nonetheless; he knew their stops, he could sound them from top to bottom. When sustained applause finally demanded an encore he asked for Ginsberg's permission to read "Helicon." It was a touching gesture, and the poem itself was wildly received. Those in the audience, who had seen the two embrace when they first met on the stage, who perhaps did not know that Hollander had once dismissed ***Howl*** as a "dreadful little volume" exhibiting an "utter lack of decorum of any kind," understood intuitively that "Helicon" was a peace offering, a love poem and more—a propitiation of part of himself and his generation.

Ginsberg, who followed, seemed by comparison insensitive to his listeners or determined to throw them off balance. He began by chanting rather than reading, and as the *Hare Krishnas* went on, longer than anyone imagined they could, it seemed possible that he had sloughed off language entirely. There was Allen Ginsberg, ecstatic and uncool, apparently oblivious to us, doing his spiritual push-ups in public. It was troubling, and needless to say it worked its effect; gradually, grudgingly, we gave up that air of facetiousness and sophistication endemic to every college audience. Ginsberg was there not to please us but to convert us.

But the greater surprise, for me at least, was yet to come: poems, many of them, some better than anything he'd previously written. A number were funny, closer to the comic self-ironies of Hollander than to the transports we had just witnessed or the prophetic intensities of ***Howl*** and ***Kaddish.*** Had I forgotten, or never noticed, the Ginsberg of **"To Aunt Rose"** and **"America"** and **"The Lion for Real,"** bittersweet parables at once madcap and sentimental? Well, here was **"This form of Life needs Sex,"** in which the man who had shocked television interviewers by introducing Peter Orlovsky as his spouse explored his new interest in women and procreation.

ON THE SUBJECT OF...

PETER ORLOVSKY

Orlovsky has worked variously as a poet, singer, songwriter, ambulance attendant, mental hospital attendant, farmer's helper, dishwasher, and secretary (to Ginsberg). He has authored three poetry collections, cowritten a book of love poems and letters with Ginsberg, and contributed to numerous other publications. Despite his varied and colorful resume, Orlovsky is best known as Ginsberg's life-long friend and lover. Closely associated with Ginsberg's life and work beginning in 1955, when the two met in San Francisco, Orlovsky nevertheless projects a personality of his own, captured in a handful of what are considered often humorous outbursts of wildly personal lyrics.

There was more, poems too various to be classified, and when ***Planet News: 1961-1967*** was published a year ago they were there on the page, they hadn't evaporated. Ginsberg had survived as a poet too, as a poet above all.

JOHN TYTELL (ESSAY DATE 1976)

SOURCE: Tytell, John. "Allen Ginsberg and the Messianic Tradition." In *Naked Angels: The Lives and Literature of the Beat Generation*, pp. 212-57. New York: McGraw-Hill Book Company, 1976.

In the following essay, Tytell provides an overview of Ginsberg's work.

The *only* way out that they generally now prescribe, generally in India at the moment, is through bhakti yoga, which is Faith-Hope-Adoration-Worship, or like probably the equivalent of the Christian Sacred Heart, which I find a very lovely doctrine—that is to say, pure delight, the only way you can be saved is to sing. In other words, the only way to drag up, from the depths of this depression, to drag up your soul to its proper bliss, and understanding, is to give yourself, completely, to your heart's desire. The image will be determined by the heart's compass, by the compass of what the heart moves toward and desires. And then you get on your knees or on your lap or on your head and you sing and chant prayers and mantras, till you reach a state of ecstasy and understanding, and the bliss overflows out of your body. They say intellect, like Saint

Thomas Aquinas, will never do it, because it's just like getting all hung up on whether I could remember what happened before I was born—I mean you could get lost there very easily, and it has no relevance *anyway,* to the existent flower. Blake says something similar, like Energy, and Excess . . . leads to the palace of wisdom. The Hindu bhakti is like excess of devotion; you just, you know, give yourself all out to devotion.

—Allen Ginsberg
Paris Review interview

"I would call that man poet," Henry Miller once wrote, "who is capable of profoundly altering the world": **"Howl"** and **"Kaddish"** are two examples of a body of poetry that has had a tremendous impact on the values of a generation. Ginsberg has focused his vision on the forces depleting the life spirit of the West. While his inspiration has been apocalyptic, he offers us compelling alternatives to the general disaster he sees.

Allen Ginsberg comes to his readings with an implicit faith in the holiness of personal impulse. There is no holding back, no repression because of time or circumstance, no polite restraint or euphemism. "Go fuck yourself with your atom bomb," he exclaims in a poem called "**America**"—a line that has excited many audiences while making countless critics cringe. And Ginsberg is feared in America just as Whitman was feared: to believe in democracy is the first step toward making it possible, and such seriousness is dangerous. It has been difficult for some to understand the quality of this seriousness because of the necessity Ginsberg feels to become part of the absurdity he perceives. This was his message when, for example, during his testimony at the Chicago Seven trial he stated that the radicals' purpose had been to transmit joyous feelings of delight despite the horror of the 1968 Democratic political convention and Mayor Daley's army. For Ginsberg, integrating the absurd into the imagination is a process that violates the artist's sense of his own superiority, and leaves him more vulnerable to the wisdom of everyday experience.

Ginsberg's poetry is an expression of the simultaneity of what he has termed an "undifferentiated consciousness." In *Axel's Castle,* Edmund Wilson observed that the energy of poetry had been appropriated by novelists after World War I as writers like Joyce and Virginia Woolf fashioned a prose style of such imagistic intensity and linguistic density as to end all distinctions in English between prose and poetry. These writers, Joyce in particular, created an inner perspective that perceived like the unspeaking mind, that encountered reality through the full play of the senses rather than through the intellect as in omniscient fictions. This unconscious, or at least unarticulated flow that surrounds our being, that constitutes most of what we call sensibility, even as we are but dimly aware of its potential in our daily lives, is the source Ginsberg draws on for his poems.

His original intention as a poet was to achieve an emotional breakthrough of individual, subjective feeling and values as a way of overcoming the Kafkian intimidation of the fifties. Relying on natural speech and spontaneous transcription, Ginsberg sought a nonliterary poetry based on the facts of daily existence. Jazz, abstract painting, Zen and haiku, writers like William Carlos Williams and Kerouac, Apollinaire and Artaud, Lorca and Neruda, were to influence his development of a new measure that corresponded more closely to the body's breath than to the artifice of iambics. The result for Ginsberg, as it had been for Gertrude Stein earlier in the century, was composition as creation, that is, the act of writing itself leading to a pursuit of the unknown rather than to a recovery of the already revealed. As with Burroughs and Kerouac, form would not be predetermined, but would follow the sequence of perception in the course of the writing, even if the route became as irrational, intuitive, and discontinuous as the shape of the mind itself. Syntax, therefore, would not accord with the imposed logic of grammar, but would correspond to the essentially nonsequential flow of the mind. As the mind does not perceive in the orderly arrangement of expository prose, it becomes almost a pretentious fiction to write a poem or a story as if it did.

In an unpublished piece called **"A Few Notes On Method,"** Ginsberg argued that since Imagism, the movement initiated by Pound before World War I, there had been no "crystalization of real grief" in poetry, nor had poets attempted to explore "superhuman" or eternal verities. Imagism, while perfecting the poetic medium, removed from the poem a whole world of subject matter and the kind of "concretion of personal experience" that interested Ginsberg. Influenced by Burroughs' theory of factualism, Ginsberg proposed a juxtaposition of his imaginative interpretation of actual data within a narrative system that eliminated rational connectives. Ginsberg called this "ellipsis," a way of presenting images as they flashed through the mind. It was the equivalent of removing the voice of the omniscient narrator in Burroughs' work, for example. In a letter to Kerouac, Ginsberg described a dream he had about

Joan Adams Burroughs which was the occasion of a theory of how the sublime could be invoked and excited in his poems by creating several "image points in time separated by a wide gap showing the distance between them, the jump, or interval, or ellipsis of consciousness actually attaining an inner secret time shock, a sort of mystical eclipse of time." Ginsberg compared his method to Cezanne's theory of *petites sensations* of experience, which his teacher, the art historian Meyer Shapiro, had explained as an attempt to delineate through color, perspective, and brushstroke every detail in the flux of experience, sensation, and time. Ginsberg studied the Cezanne paintings in the Museum of Modern Art while on marijuana, and realized how the painter manipulated space by the alternation of hot and cold colors so that the result was a kind of "space pun," as he told Kerouac, of coexisting planes that would separate mysteriously as the light source was indeterminate and shifting. Ginsberg compared this principle of "spacetimejump" to the telescoping of time in Eliot. Ellipsis applied to both narrative and syntax—the sacrifice of what Ginsberg called "syntactical sawdust," articles, prepositions, and connectives that impeded the flow and did not actually occur in the mind. The result was a richer texture and greater density of language. The prose base of Ginsberg's unusually long line (the length Whitman used to explode all metrical confinements, and which was later sustained in American poetry only by Vachel Lindsay and Robinson Jeffers) is deliberately distorted by condensation or dislocation, a form of compression of basically imagistic notations into surrealistic or cubistic phrasing like the "hydrogen jukeboxes" of **"Howl."** The key is a rhythmic shift or acceleration like the staccato abruptness of the primitively naïve grammar of **"America"**—a kind of mock American Indian dialect used ironically—which distinguishes between the flow of a mind's perceptions and less intuitively sponsored flights.

In both his rhythm and his use of the long line, Ginsberg has acknowledged Kerouac's influence, and the following passage from *Visions of Cody,* rearranged as poetry, may indicate what Ginsberg learned:

> I've pressed up girls in Ashville saloons, danced with them
> in roadhouses where mad heroes stomp one another to death
> in tragic driveways by the moon:
> I've laid whores on the strip of grass runs along a cornfield
> outside Durham, North Carolina, and applied bay rum
> in the highway lights;
> I've thrown empty whiskeybottles clear over the trees in
> Maryland copses on soft nights when Roosevelt was President;
> I've knocked down fifths in trans-state trucks as the Wyo. road
> unreeled;
> I've jammed home shots of whiskey on Sixth Avenue, in Frisco,
> in the Londons of the prime, in Florida, in L.A.
> I've made soup my chaser in forty-seven states;
> I've passed off the back of cabooses, Mexican buses and
> bows of ships in midwinter tempests (piss to you);
> I've laid women in coalpiles, in the snow, on fences, in beds
> and up against suburban garage walls from Massachusetts
> to the tip of San Joaquin.
> Cody me no Codys about America,
> I've drunk with his brother in a thousand bars,
> I've had hangovers with old sewing machine whores that were
> twice his mother twelve years ago when his heart was dewy.
> I learned how to smoke cigars in madhouses;
> and hopped boxcars in
> New Orleans;
> I've driven on Sunday afternoon across the lemon fields with
> Indians and their sisters;
> and I sat at the inauguration of.
> Tennessee me no Tennessees, Memphis; aim me no Montanas, Three
> Forks;
> I'll still sock me a North Atlantic Territory in the free.
> That's how I feel.
> I've heard guitars tinkling sadly across hillbilly hollows
> in the mist of the Great Smokies of night long ago. . . .

The passage suggests a momentum that Ginsberg was to reproduce and extend in **"Howl"** several years later, a force that depended on the personal, the confessional, the excessive and volatile, and a rhythm that accumulates power through repetition. Kerouac sought new speech rhythms, the patterns of blacks, rednecks, westerners, hearing in them a return to the nonliterary origins of an oral tradition. He also wanted to capture the rapid, excited current of American speech, and this, too, influenced Ginsberg. Actually, each writer benefited from the other's freedom, from mutual departures from conventional approaches to literature—as when Kerouac, in a letter, advised Ginsberg to change the phrase "startle the fox" to "star the fox," or when Kerouac sat Ginsberg at his typewriter and urged him to type whatever came into his mind and accept it as a poem. It took Ginsberg several years to assimilate such lessons, and the first realization of Kerouac's mode of composition occurred with **"Howl."** In August of 1955, Ginsberg wrote Kerouac to acknowledge his debt:

> The pages I sent you of **"Howl"** (right title) are the first pages put down, as is. I recopied them and sent you the 100% original draft. There is no preexistent version. I typed it up as I went along, that's why it's so messy. What I have here is all copies cleaned & extended. What you have *is* what you want.
>
> I realize how right you are, that was the first time I sat down to *blow,* it came out in *your method,* sounding like you, an imitation practically. How far advanced you are on this. I don't know what I'm doing with poetry. I need years years of isolation and constant everyday writing to attain your volume of freedom & knowledge of the form. . . .

Ginsberg was not always able to sustain the intensity necessary for Kerouac's spontaneity, and later admitted to Kerouac that even **"Kaddish"** needed revision to avoid "wearisome repetition & draggy self-pity fatigue vagueness." Still, the essential discovery that he could release secrets of memory, free of rational restrictions since consciousness itself was without limitations, was learned from Kerouac who had derived his new rhythms from hearing jazz musicians in places like Minton's in Harlem during the war. But Ginsberg was an adept student: in *Desolation Angels,* while describing a historic visit to William Carlos Williams (then seventy-two), Kerouac compared Ginsberg to Dizzy Gillespie on trumpet because each "comes on in *waves* of thought, not in phrases." The comparison seems all the more prescient in the light of Ginsberg's recent attempts to allow blues to influence his work. The long line offered Ginsberg the necessary dimension to recreate the process of thought which occurs in visual images as well as words, taking the course of endlessly digressive associations and ramifications and confusions for there is no logic to thought (except when arbitrarily applied). As Ginsberg put it in a letter to John Hollander: "I want to get a wild page, as wild and as clear (really clear) as the mind—no forcing the thoughts into straightjacket—sort of a search for the rhythm of the thoughts & their natural occurences & spacings & notational paradigms."

This search for a form to articulate what Kerouac called "the unspeakable visions of the individual" represented a fundamentally new direction for poetry, although Pound began forging that way in *The Cantos,* and other poets like Charles Olson, Robert Creeley, and John Ashbery were on a similar journey. Ginsberg's critics, however, have failed to see the nature and intention of this voyage within. Unfortunately, most academicians are more comfortable with what might be called the confined—as opposed to the open—poem, and so Ginsberg's critics tend to admire the early work in ***Empty Mirror*** because they can cope with experiences that have recognizable formal contours like the sonnet, the dramatic monologue, or the brief lyric. But Ginsberg will not focus on a situation in the manner of Wallace Stevens or Robert Lowell, poets who will employ such familiar rhetorical devices as ironic contrast to locate a centering point. Instead, he directs his considerable energies to the hundreds of points constituting the perimeter of the experience, and then plunges beyond expansively, illogically, tumultuously encouraging digression just as the mind in the natural flow of its bewilderment does. Ginsberg argued in ***Indian Journals*** that "We don't think in the dialectical rigid pattern of quatrain or synthetic pattern of sonnet: we think in blocks of sensations & images." As Emerson advised in "The Poet," "It is not metres, but a metre-making argument that makes a poem—a thought so passionate and alive that like the spirit of a plant or an animal it has an architecture of its own, and adorns nature with a new thing."

Thomas Merrill, who wrote a book on Ginsberg for the Twayne American writers series, believes that Ginsberg's poetry is merely a means to an end, a way of delivering apocalyptic prophecy or encouraging religious awakening. Merrill subscribes to Allen Watts' denigrating idea that Ginsberg's poetry is primarily therapy, rather than art. A similar argument might be applied to Wordsworth, to Matthew Arnold's "Dover Beach," to Eliot's "The Waste Land," which was, after all, written in a Swiss sanitarium while Eliot was recovering from a nervous breakdown. Of course, this list might be extended infinitely, but the point is that Watts' distinction between art and therapy is false and misleading. Watts and Merrill seem to suspect Ginsberg all the more, however, because he seeks some integration, some useful resolution of madness, so they claim he is more concerned with healing himself than offering himself (as Edmund Wilson suggested in "The Wound and the Bow") as a totemistic scapegoat for our general illness. Theodore Roszak, in *The Making of a Counter Culture,* offers a similarly uncharitable view of Ginsberg's poetry, finding it "a subsidiary way of publicizing the new consciousness." Roszak gratuitously and foolishly suggests that Ginsberg need only appear at his readings without bothering to read the poetry at all, but simply demonstrating his person to achieve the desired effect. Merrill is forever accusing Ginsberg of "exploiting" this or that device, and finds it difficult to "digest" Ginsberg's excesses. Merrill's strangest proposal is that **"Howl"** is not an original departure, that its accomplishments were somehow anticipated by the short lines and imagistic notations of ***Empty Mirror.*** Roszak, also, prefers ***Empty Mirror*** to Ginsberg's later poetry, and so did John Hollander in his angry review of **"Howl."** The real problem for Ginsberg's critics has been that they have been unable to respond to a living example of Romanticism (besides the fact that they find his sexual references obscene and distasteful), and so they have tried to deny him his point of departure.

The reviews of ***Howl*** document Ginsberg's position in American letters through the sixties. John Hollander, poet and professor, writing in a spirit of evident distrust for what he felt was a modish façade of avant-garde posturing, deplored in *Partisan Review* the "utter lack of decorum of any kind in his dreadful little volume." James Dickey, in *Sewanee Review,* established Ginsberg as the very citadel of modern Babel, and found the poem full of meaningless utterances. Dickey, at least, had the grace to allow that Ginsberg was capable of "a confused but believable passion for values." Even Michael Rumaker, reviewing ***Howl*** for the *Black Mountain Review,* certainly a friendly organ, had few words of praise. Rumaker perversely read Ginsberg according to the expectations of New Criticism (exactly what Ginsberg was reacting against!) and found only imprecision everywhere. For Rumaker, the title poem especially was corrupted by "sentimentality, bathos, Buddha and hollow talk of eternity." The poem was uncontained, its language cumbersome and hysterical, but its most unforgivable quality was that it tried to use art to induce spiritual values.

Ginsberg's critics have been completely unresponsive to the oral tradition in poetry, and even seem to hold his marvelous abilities as a reader against him—which they never did in the case of Dylan Thomas. The fact that the eye simply cannot contain the poem on a page, the expansive scope and surreal leaps of Ginsberg's poetry have all contributed to preventing the critics from inventing the necessary categories through which to view his work.

Ginsberg has provided numerous clues to his own method in several interviews, and in a diary he kept while traveling in India from March 1962 to May 1963. In ***Indian Journals*** he includes some revealing notes for a lecture delivered to a Marxist literary conference in Benares that comment on his prosody. His reason for the change from the terse line of ***Empty Mirror,*** influenced mainly by William Carlos Williams, to the longer line of the subsequent work was an increased depth of perception on a nonverbal and conceptual level. Motivating the change as well was Kerouac's ideal of spontaneity, and the impact of his own visionary experiences. The models for the change were jazz ecstasy, mantra chanting, drug experiences, and Zen meditation. The resulting notation of simultaneous perception was an attempt to "capture the whole mind of the Poet," the process of thought occuring without any censoring factors. Ginsberg's means were the swift "jump of perception from one thing to another," like Olson's composition by field theory, which in Ginsberg's hands was to lead to a surrealistic violation of the old narrative order.

It seems clear that Ginsberg, like Blake, is seeking to purge language of stultifying formalisms. In the pure simplicity of rhythm and diction in *Songs of Innocence,* Blake reacted to the intricate rhetorical and metrical complexity of eighteenth-century verse. He needed a new language because he was to deny the emphasis of his day on the verifiable, the familiar and general, and to devote himself to the numinous mysteries anticipating the Romantic movement, and to the very real social concerns of poems like "London." It was Samuel Johnson who praised the "grandeur of generality," and who sonorously asserted that "nothing can please many and please long, but just representations of general nature." To this smugly congealing view Blake might well have retorted—"To generalize is to be an Idiot. To particularize alone is the Distinction of Merit." Instead of the generality of the commonplace, the regular and expectable (all reflected in the eighteenth-century insistence on heroic couplet as perfect form), Blake studied hermetic medieval manuscripts, and read Thomas Taylor's translations of the Gnostic texts (which Coleridge and Shelley later read, and which Bronson Alcott brought to Emerson). Blake, also, began the romantic reaction against reason and deductions resulting from observations of the senses. Such deductions, as Yeats was later to argue in *Ideas of Good and Evil,* only bind men to mortality as the senses become the exclusive means of perceiving the world; reliance on the senses, Yeats added, would also divide men from each other by revealing their clashing interests. Blake preferred relying on the imagination, Yeats asserted, because it bound men together by "opening the secret doors of all hearts."

Ginsberg's most significant relationship to Blake has been ideological—a sympathy with social concerns, a desire to transform consciousness, to use poetry as an instrument of power or as sacramental invocation. Ginsberg also shares Blake's attitude to the child in man: "Better murder an infant in its cradle than nurse unwanted desires," Blake wrote, and behind the extravagance of the remark is the idea that maturity implies the abandonment of natural spontaneity. Since Freud, we have been taught that the condition of the child is suspect and fallen. But Blake believed that man had lost the intuitive harmonies inherent in childhood. So if for modern Freudians infantile childishness is a term of condemnation, for Blake the child's delight in his surroundings, his curious whimsy, were exactly the attributes that prepared for mature judgment.

In technique, Ginsberg has maintained his link to Blake in various ways: through his musical settings of Blake's *Songs of Innocence and Experience,* and the imitations in ***Gates of Wrath,*** a collection of very early and uneven work. In "**September On Jessore Road,**" the last poem in ***The Fall of America,*** Ginsberg employs Blake's early metrical devices with great exactness. An even more pervasive influence is felt in poems like "**The Lion For Real**" or "**Sunflower Sutra.**"

The latter poem is an elegy of glorious optimism for a dead sunflower, a refutation of its "corolla of bleary spikes pushed down and broken like a battered crown" among the "gnarled steel roots of machinery" on a railroad dock overlooking the San Francisco Bay. Blake's sunflower, too, represented mutability, the transcience of the living and the inevitability of death. But Ginsberg, in a letter to Kerouac, described the sunflower he saw as the flower of industry, tough-spiked and ugly, "the flower of the world, worn, brittle, dry yellow—miracle of gravel life spring (ing to) the bud." Experimenting with rhythmic buildup without relying on a repetitive base (like the use of the pronoun *who* in "**Howl**") to sustain its powerfully increasing tempo, Ginsberg offers us a paean to the life-force within the heart of the wasteland, the sordid details of junk, treadless tires, used condoms, and abandoned tin cans and industrial grime, enveloping the desiccated sunflower in which Ginsberg chooses to believe, vigorously asserting his belief by seizing the skeleton stalk and holding it at his side like a scepter:

> —We're not our skin of grime, we're not our dread bleak dusty imageless locomotive, we're all beautiful golden sunflowers inside, we're blessed by our own seed & golden hairy naked accomplishment-bodies growing into mad black formal sunflowers in the sunset, spied on by our eyes under the shadow of the mad locomotive riverbank sunset Frisco hilly tincan evening sitdown vision.

The verse paragraph ending "**Sunflower Sutra**" recalls Walt Whitman, another seminal influence on Ginsberg, and a key figure in the visionary tradition. Malcolm Cowley has observed Whitman's close resemblance in *Leaves of Grass* to works which he could not have or probably did not read like the *Bhagavad-Gita* or *The Upanishads*. Cowley claimed that Whitman's sources were internal, the larger consciousness in which he participated being occasioned by a mystical experience that Dr. Richard Maurice Bucke—one of Whitman's disciples and author of a book called *Cosmic Consciousness*—dates around 1853-54. Whitman's experience, like Ginsberg's with Blake, resulted in an ecstatic sense of ineffable joy, a knowledge of the unity of the universe, of the bonds existing between men and all living things. In Whitman's poetry, these feelings emerged as an unprecedented celebration of his fellow men, an effusive outpouring of pity, affectionate sympathy, and love so genuinely sincere that it could only be called sentimental by cynics.

"In me the caresser of life wherever moving," Whitman wrote in "Song of Myself"; "to me all the converging objects of the universe perpetually flow." The close connection between Whitman and Ginsberg may be measured by Whitman's expectation of the poet, as he characterized it in the preface to *Leaves of Grass*—a document which along with Emerson's essay "The Poet" constitutes the first signs of a native American poetic, standing among the most significant utterances on the poetic process in any era. As the poet sees the farthest, Whitman argues, "he has the most faith. His thoughts are the hymns of the praise of things." In the following statement, Whitman could almost be predicting Ginsberg's future appearance:

> This is what you shall do: Love the earth and sun and animals, despise riches, give alms to every one that asks, stand up for the stupid and crazy, devote your income and labor to others, hate tyrants, argue not concerning God, have patience and indulgence toward the people, take off your hat to nothing known or unknown or to any man

or number of men, go freely with powerful uneducated persons and with the mothers of families, read these leaves in the open air every season of every year of your life, re-examine all you have been told at school or church or in any book, dismiss whatever insults your own soul, and your very flesh shall be a great poem and have the richest fluency not only in its words but in the silent lines of its lips and face and between the lashes of your eyes and in every motion and joint of your body.

Whitman goes on to address himself to what Bucke called cosmic consciousness: "From the eyesight proceeds another eyesight and from the hearing proceeds another hearing and from the voice proceeds another voice eternally curious of the harmony of things with man." Whitman declared that this inspiration of the inner eye would lead to a new order of poets who would replace religion. This new poet, now "priest of man," would "not deign to defend immortality or God or the perfection of things or liberty or the exquisite beauty and reality of the soul. They shall arise in America and be responded to from the remainder of the earth."

A number of American writers have struggled with Whitman's example. William Carlos Williams recognized him as the poet who "broke through the deadness of copied forms which keep shouting above everything that wants to get said today drowning out one man with the accumulated weight of a thousand tyrannies of the past, the very tyrannies we are seeking to diminish. The structure of the old is active, it says no! to everything in propaganda and poetry that wants to say yes. Whitman broke through that. That was very basic and good." But this Emersonian view of the writer was not shared by many modern American authors. Henry James later regretted his criticism of Whitman's Civil War book, *Drumtaps,* and atoned by reciting Whitman's poetry to friends visiting him at Lamb House in Rye. Pound wrote several attacks on Whitman, the most notorious of which appeared in an essay on Villon where he complained of "the horrible air of rectitude with which Whitman rejoices in being Whitman," and claimed that Whitman pretended to be "conferring a philanthropic benefit on the race by recording his own self-complacency." Pound's rage was at something he sought to release in himself, without quite knowing how. In "A Pact" he offered amends:

I am old enough now to make friends.
It was you that broke the new wood,
Now is a time for carving.
We have one sap and one root—
Let there be commerce between us.

Whitman smashed the containing forms of nineteenth-century metrical structure in the manner that Blake began to in the *Prophetic Books.* Whitman composed, properly speaking, with no logical structure, creating, as Cowley suggested, the equivalent of an oneiric, waking dream. The wavelike flow of his music was like a rhapsodic tone poem, as he released prolonged bursts of inspiration. His expansive amplitude became a kind of euphoria, a way in which, as Waldo Frank once put it in *Our America,* "We go forth all to seek America. And in the seeking we create her." This, in particular, is Allen Ginsberg's point of departure as a poet.

Ginsberg has acknowledged the formative influence for him of Whitman's concept of "adhesiveness," his feeling of kinship with all classes and kinds of people. "Who need be afraid of the merge?" Whitman proclaimed in "Song of Myself" as he lists the thief, the venereally diseased prostitute, the slave, the workingman, and the businessman in his egalitarian audience. This must have been one of the generous qualities of heart that appealed to Emerson, and which caused his famous praise of *Leaves of Grass,* for the sage of Concord himself had announced in "The American Scholar" essay that "I embrace the common. I explore and sit at the feet of the familiar, the low." It was inevitable that once such sentiments were to be taken seriously by our poets, a new and broader concept of what constituted the poetic vernacular would develop. To be sure, the idiom of the common man was the language that Wordsworth intended to recreate, but never really managed. "Language is fossil poetry," Emerson jubilantly offered in one of his disassociated exclamations in "The Poet," but no nineteenth-century ear was tuned to such a key. Even Whitman's language was often too rotund and inflated, not quite as pretty as Tennyson's or Swinburne's, but also not fully in touch with the rhythms of the ordinary ear. And Whitman, in his later years in Camden, New Jersey, became less and less receptive to the familial harmonies of familiar tongues and the louder vitalities of street speech. It was another New Jersey poet, William Carlos Williams, who discovered how to hear, as Ginsberg once put it, with "raw ears."

Blake, Whitman, and Williams are the figures who have most inspired Ginsberg, but an equally significant, if less finitely measurable, source has been Surrealist poetry and painting. Blake permitted entry into the prophetic tradition; Whitman offered the infusion of democratic optimism; Williams inspired a new diction; but Surrealism suggested the state of mind that proved liberating enough for Ginsberg to see the political realities of his day with passionate clarity.

In a poem called **"At Apollinaire's Grave,"** Ginsberg was to voice his appreciation for the insights learned from the French Surrealist poets:

> I've eaten the blue carrots you sent out of the
> grave and Van Gogh's ear and maniac
> peyote of Artaud
> And will walk down the streets of New York in
> the black cloak of French poetry
> Improvising our conversation in Paris at Père
> Lachaise
> and the future poem that takes its inspiration
> from the light bleeding into your grave

Surrealism was very much a part of the *Zeitgeist* surrounding Ginsberg in his youth. During the war, a number of the key Surrealist painters had settled in America, and by 1942 Ernst, Masson, and Tanguy were living in New York City, as well as André Breton, one of the theoreticians of the movement. Breton's belief that subconscious irrationality could provide the basis for a positive social program separated the Surrealists from the Dadaists, their more nihilistic forebears. Breton's manifestoes contain arguments that anticipate the inner flow of experience Ginsberg was to express so powerfully in his poetry. Breton sought a "monologue spoken as rapidly as possible without any interruption on the part of the cerebral faculties, a monologue consequently unencumbered by the slightest inhibition and which was as closely as possible akin to spoken thought." This "psychic automatism" proposed to express the mind's actual functioning in the absence of controls like reason, or any superimposed moral or aesthetic concern. If Ginsberg was to remain in touch with Blake's tradition of magic prophecy, he would have to find ways to release that vision without unnecessarily tampering, interfering, or distorting, and the Surrealist bias against revision that Kerouac maintained prevented the danger of any fatal loss of impetus.

The Surrealists in France had distinguished between literature as a craft or talent exercised within certain traditional and prescriptive formal limitations and poetry as a mode of visionary discovery. To induce revelation, they pursued their dreams, finding in them a route to the unconscious, and a way of capturing the uncensored maturity of Rimbaud's child-man. Like Blake's idealization of the child, the Surrealists sought a model for wonder, spontaneity, and destructiveness—which, by the way, they interpreted as the end of adult self-control and obedience to conditioning. So Breton began attending with fascination to phrases running through his mind as he fell asleep, just as Williams in *Kora In Hell* was to improvise disconnected passages composed just prior to sleep. Related to such experiments was the Surrealists' interest in Charcot's *Studies In Hysteria* and Robert Desnos' self-induced trances. As Alfred Jarry urged, true hallucination is the sustained waking dream, and this becomes the premise of much of Ginsberg's poetry as he applies the phantasmagoria of dream to everyday reality. As Breton formulated it in his *Second Manifesto*:

> Surrealism aims quite simply at the total recovery of our psychic force by a means which is nothing other than the dizzying descent into ourselves, the systematic illumination of hidden places and the progressive darkening of other places, the perpetual excursion into the midst of forbidden territory. . . .

It is quite clear that this consciousness was present in Ginsberg's earliest poems. In **"Psalm I,"** the second poem in ***Empty Mirror,*** Ginsberg refers to his poems as the product of a "vision haunted mind," and writes of "majestic flaws of mind which have left my brain open to hallucination." In the initial poem of the volume, the marvelously understated "I feel as if I were at a dead end," Ginsberg describes a state of psychic and moral impotence whose metaphor is the head severed from the body. This impotence expresses itself as a terrible inability to act in the face of a paralyzing absurdity which stalks through the poems; hallucination, visionary messages from the unconscious, serve to fuse head and body, to reconnect intellect and feeling. A number of the best poems in the collection are called dreams, like the Kafkian **"A Meaningless Institution"** where Ginsberg invents an enormous ward filled with "hundreds of weeping / decaying men and women." Everyone in the poem is impassive; everything in it is static; there is no interrelationship anywhere—and in the end the observer wanders futilely "down empty corridors / in search of a toilet." The view of the world implied by such a poem is dismal, a miasma of quiescent disappointment and stagnant despair, a pervasive mood in the book appearing with special poignance in **"Sunset," "A Ghost May Come," "A Desolation," "The Blue Angel,"** and **"Walking Home At Night."** These poems reflect terrible entrapment in mechanical situations revealing men devoid of humanity, like those "cowering in unshaven rooms in underwear" in **"Howl."** Occasionally, the depression is alleviated by childish rage, as in one of the best poems in ***Empty Mirror,* "In Society"**:

I walked into the cocktail party
room and found three or four queers
talking together in queertalk.
I tried to be friendly but heard
myself talking to one in hiptalk.
"I'm glad to see you," he said, and
looked away. "Hmn," I mused. The room
was small and had a double-decker
bed in it, and cooking apparatus:
icebox, cabinet, toasters, stove;
the hosts seemed to live with room
enough for only cooking and sleeping.
My remark on this score was understood but not appreciated. I was
offered refreshments, which I accepted.
I ate a sandwich of pure meat; an
enormous sandwich of human flesh,
I noticed, while I was chewing on it,
it also included a dirty asshole.
More company came, including a
fluffy female who looked like
a princess. She glared at me and
said immediately: "I don't like you,"
turned her head away, and refused
to be introduced. I said, "What!"
in outrage. "Why you shit-faced fool!"
This got everybody's attention.
"Why you narcissistic bitch! How
can you decide when you don't even
know me," I continued in a violent
and messianic voice, inspired at
last, dominating the whole room.

The periodic ending of the poem is a Kafkian delusion, like Joseph K criticizing court practices in *The Trial* only to learn later that he had been haranguing his judges instead of visitors to the court. The aggressively explosive tirade of "Why you shit-faced fool!" is the culmination of a series of four utterly absurdist enclosures like the room without room to live, all beautifully emphasized by the short, abruptly declarative lines. Behind the subject of the poem is Ginsberg's discomfort with his own homosexuality, and its most compelling image is the sandwich of human flesh containing the dirty asshole. Like the talking asshole in Burroughs' *Naked Lunch,* Ginsberg's image provides an apt illustration of what Lautreamont thought of as systematic bewildering—the beauty of the "fortuitous meeting of a sewing machine and an umbrella on an operating table." The image of the dirty asshole returns the reader to the uneasiness with the homosexual condition that the poem dramatizes, starting with the shift from queertalk to hiptalk. Calling the fluffy female "shit-faced" creates a continuity of image, just as the emphasis on the hosts' kitchen and cooking apparatus prepares the reader for the dirty asshole. While the continuity from eating food to defecating on those about you does unify the poem, it is by no means an apparent motif, and the categories of kitchen, asshole, and "shit-faced fool" exist like realities on different planes. The asshole image can be taken as an example of what Breton called incandescent flashes linking those different elements of reality together with a vital metaphor, even though those elements seem so far removed that reason alone could never connect them. The impact of the poem, the depth of the anxiety betrayed by its central image, defies a realistic mode. The poem, culminating as it does with a view of messianic anger "dominating the whole room," shares the qualities of self-revelation and honest exposure associated with Robert Lowell's *Life Studies.* As Ginsberg has written in a poem **"On Burroughs' Work"**:

A naked lunch is natural to us,
we eat reality sandwiches.
But allegories are so much lettuce.
Don't hide the madness.

A similar strength occurs in a number of the poems in ***Empty Mirror***—little wonder that Ginsberg's critics like the volume—especially in **"A Crazy Spiritual,"** another one of the dream poems that anticipates the bizarrely driving absurdity and fulminating ironies of the songs on Bob Dylan's *Bringing It All Back Home* album ("Maggie's Farm" and "Bob Dylan's 115th Dream" in particular).

The poems in ***Empty Mirror*** employ short lines predominantly, stripping "yakking down to modern bones" Ginsberg wrote to Cassady, and at one point Ginsberg expresses metaphorical dissatisfaction with Yeatsian terseness:

I attempted to concentrate
the total sun's rays in
each poem as through a glass,
but such magnification
did not set the page afire.

He begins to move in the direction of his long-line experiments in **"Hymn,"** a series of five verse paragraphs (animated by such antiprose and surreal formulations as "clock of meat"), or "Paterson," a poem no one seems to have noticed even though it anticipates the rhythmic power of the later poetry as well as the thematic rejection of American materialism. Rather than live in rooms "papered with visions of money," rather than cut his hair, dress properly, bathe, and work steadily for the "dead prick of commonplace obsession," the hero of "Paterson," a Beat code figure, would choose madness:

. . . gone down the dark road to
Mexico, heroin dripping in my veins,
eyes and ears full of marijuana,

eating the god Peyote on the floor of a mudhut
on the border
or laying in a hotel room over the body of some
suffering man or woman;

The hero prefers to "jar" his "body down the road" of dissipation rather than conform to the conventions of the everyday, and he lists a series of ecstatic excesses, culminating in a screaming dance of praise to an eternity that annihilates reality as in a Dionysian frenzy he impales himself in nature, "leaving my flesh and bones hanging on the trees." "Paterson" is a psychological fulcrum for Ginsberg's early poetry, charging the sense of heavy doldrum and ennui, the sentimentality of his earliest Columbia College verse, with a quality of scatological hysteria he may have learned from Céline. Actually, in a review of Céline's *Death On The Installment Plan* that Ginsberg wrote in his last year at Columbia, he recognized the persona he was later to assume in "Paterson":

> The mad author has taken the weird mask of an aggressive character, self-sufficient, skeptical, sentimental, self-disgusted, self-protecting, all because he is convinced of the dangerousness of modern life, and has passed it [the mask] off as a natural, "just" development of mind.

"Paterson" is a poem of excess, an early sign of Ginsberg's surrealism. Breton noted that surrealism acts on the mind very much like drugs, creating a need for the mysterious effects and special pleasures of an artificial paradise, but at the same time pushing men to frightful revolts as that paradise seems unattainable. Like opium-induced images, surrealistic images seem to occur spontaneously, or despotically as Baudelaire once claimed, ringing with unpremeditated juxtaposition. Apollinaire, in *Le poète assassiné,* glorified physical disequilibrium as divine, and Rimbaud, earlier, had called for a violent derangement of the senses.

Ginsberg has heeded this imperative, risking his sensibility to widen the area of his consciousness with drugs. As Coleridge claimed to have composed "Kubla Khan" during an opium reverie, Ginsberg has admitted to writing a number of poems while using marijuana or the stronger hallucinogens like peyote, LSD-25, mescaline, and ayahuasca (yage, the drug for which Burroughs traveled to South America to find the "final fix"). The experiences described in these poems, often titled by the name of the drug employed, are very similar to the effects in Burroughs' fiction: déjà vu, death hysteria, extreme paranoia, disembodied awareness of a decomposing body, demonic mind-monsters, loss of identity as in **"The Reply"** where the "universe turns inside out to devour me," and only occasionally a sense of ecstatic, spiraling energy. The greatest concentration of drug poems is in ***Kaddish,*** but they are clearly the weakest part of the volume. Oddly enough, Ginsberg is unable to suggest a convincing state of transport in these poems, and they seem grounded compared to a natural high like the one Emerson described in his first essay, "Nature":

> Standing on the bare ground—my head bathed by the blithe air and uplifted into infinite space—all mean egotism vanishes. I become a transparent eyeball; I am nothing; I see all; the currents of the Universal Being circulate through me; I am part or parcel of God.

Ironically, in the ***Kaddish*** drug poems, just where a reader might expect a sacrifice of intellect and a total involvement with the senses, the intrusion of the poet's questioning mind misdirects the tensions. Ginsberg seems almost aware of this, as when in **"Aether"** he mentions "the threat to magic by writing while high." **"Aether,"** the last poem in ***Reality Sandwiches,*** comes closest to fulfilling Ginsberg's ideal of the poem as notation of undifferentiated consciousness (drugs theoretically assisting in such an effort by deemphasizing mind), a quality felt in the poem's movement toward new line arrangements and visual impact.

Over the years, Ginsberg has defended the legalization of marijuana and spoken of his experiences with hallucinogens without proselytizing for them. He regards these drugs as the American and South American Indians have traditionally used them, as potent medicines with ritual significance. When he advocates their use, it is less for pleasure than for the sake of increased consciousness—the necessity of transcending normative behavior, "getting out of one's head" so as to view ordinary realities from an entirely different perspective. On June 14, 1966, Ginsberg testified before a special Senate subcommittee on his own drug experiences. He stated that drugs had helped him overcome stereotypes of habit by releasing inner and latent resources of feeling for other human beings, especially women, and for nature, that had been stymied and almost conditioned out of existence by the mechanization of modern culture with its emphasis on muting the senses, reducing language and thought to uniform patterns, slogans without character, monopolizing attention with packaged news and stale imagery that failed to satisfy his own need for communication. The psychedelics in particular, Ginsberg advised, had helped end the atmosphere of fear and repression induced by Cold War politics, causing a breakthrough to common sympathy:

> Now so many people have experienced some new sense of openness, and lessening of prejudice and hostility to new experience through LSD, that I think we may expect the new generation to push for an environment less rigid, mechanical, less dominated by cold-war habits. A new kind of light has rayed through our society—despite all the anxiety it has caused—maybe these hearings are a manifestation of that slightly changed awareness. I would not have thought it possible to speak like this a year ago. That we are more open to hear each other is the new consciousness itself.

Although for some hallucinogens telescope madness, they can prove—for those able to handle the situation, Ginsberg warns—therapeutically restoring. Ginsberg himself has not always been able to contain his drug experiences, and on his trip to India in 1962 he reached an apex with morphine injections and opium that produced a recurrence of the death-terror he felt in 1948 when he tried to deliberately induce the spirit of Blake. Generally, Ginsberg has used drugs as an aid to releasing blocked aspects of his consciousness which are expressed in his poetry, like the Moloch vision in "**Howl**" which was induced by peyote, or "**Kaddish**," written while using amphetamines.

"**Kaddish**" is an elegy to the suffering madness of Ginsberg's mother, Naomi. It testifies to Ginsberg's capacity for involvement with another human in torment, for the acceptance of another's weirdness. While successfully capturing the historical ambiance of the thirties—socialist idealism, communist factionalism, martyrdom, and the reflexive paranoia of fascism—the poem is most memorable as a torrential and cathartic release of Ginsberg's complex relationship to his mad mother, at times compassionately tender, full of sweet regrets and losses, at times full of the frustration, rage, and anger that poor Naomi, locked into her tormented self, provoked. The racing, breathless pace of the poem reflects its manner of composition—the stimulation of morphine mixed with meta-amphetamine (then new to Ginsberg, and a conflicting combination as well since morphine slows time while amphetamine speeds it up) as Ginsberg sat at his desk from six in the morning and wrote until ten the following night, leaving the poem only for coffee, the bathroom, and several doses of Dexedrine. While the poem was written in a very brief period of time, Ginsberg had been thinking and writing about the subject for years—as early as 1957, in a letter from France, he told his father that he was working on a requiem for Naomi. Ginsberg's intention was to purge his consciousness of his "whole secret family-self tale—my own one-and-only eternal child-youth memories which no one else could know," as he claimed in "**How Kaddish Happened.**"

The narrative, part purgation, part reconciliation and acceptance, relates a story that contains more sheer feeling than any poem of its time: Naomi was a Russian Jewess raised on the Lower East Side, who became a teacher of retarded children ("morons with dreamy lips"). After marrying Louis Ginsberg, poet and teacher, she became involved in socialist and communist circles:

> with the YPSL's hitch-hiking through Pennsylvania, in black baggy gym skirts pants, photograph of 4 girls holding each other round the waste, and laughing eye, too coy, virginal solitude of 1920

Such details are interwoven with the story of how Allen, at the age of twelve, elected to accompany his mother on a six-hour trip from Paterson to the Greyhound bus depot on Times Square to a rest home in Lakewood, New Jersey, while she was in the process of a nervous breakdown. The lyrical poignance of the memories of Naomi's past, her physical beauty, her mandolin, the left-wing summer camps and songs of revolution are juxtaposed with the sordid presence of her horrible suspicions—that her mother-in-law is trying to poison her, that Roosevelt himself has wired her room to spy on her. Naomi's anguished hysteria—demanding blood transfusions, demanding assistance from strangers on the street, demanding release from asylums—combined with the reach of Ginsberg's grief (assuming a less strident, more mournful tone in accord with the Hebrew prayer for the dead from which he quotes), allows the poem an almost unbearable threshold of pain. Naomi's intensity is like Medea's, a quality that made Ginsberg's adaptation of his poem for the stage unforgettable as theater.

The poem suggests a vast range of feelings by constantly proposing such shocking contrasts as the fifteen-year-old Allen lying in bed with his mother just after she has returned from a three-year stay in a New Jersey mental institution, proffering and imploring love, and a few lines later:

> One night, sudden attack—her noise in the bathroom—
> like croaking up her soul—convulsions and red vomit coming
> out of her mouth—diarrhea water exploding from her behind—
> on all fours in front of the toilet—urine running between
> her legs—left retching on the tile floor smeared with her black

feces—unfainted—
At forty, varicosed, nude, fat, doomed, hiding outside the
apartment door near the elevator calling Police, yelling for her
girl-friend Rose to help—

The contrasts proliferate throughout the poem with details like Naomi's insulin, Metrasol, electric-shock, lobotomy treatments, and her insistence, when living with her sister Eleanor in the Bronx after separating from Louis that, "I will think nothing but beautiful thoughts." And after the joy of her struggles to regain a semblance of sanity, working for a doctor, taking painting lessons, relating to Allen a dream of feeding God a Jewish meal, the final vision of Naomi utterly broken, again in the sanitarium:

Too thin, shrunk on her bones—age come to Naomi—
now broken, into white hair—loose dress on her skeleton—
face sunk, old! withered—cheek of crone—
One hand stiff—heavyness of forties & menopause
reduced by one heart stroke, lame now—wrinkles—a scar on
her head, the lobotomy—ruin, the hand dipping downwards to
death—

The language of the poem comes closer to prose syntax than most of Ginsberg's work, but the lines often become fragmentary and discontinuous, suggesting that certain perceptions are too intolerable to be fully developed. Ginsberg has commented on his own unease in wrestling with form through such long notations, but the result is another new direction for poetry. "Make it new," Pound said; "Invention," Williams declared—and **"Kaddish"** is a major formal departure from our expectation of what poetry should look like on the page, just as thematically the elegy departs from tradition by refusing eulogy, developing a heroic resistance by revealing Naomi's negative qualities. The moods of the poem vary widely from imprecation and curse to sympathy and physical desire (at one point, Naomi makes sexual advances to her son while dancing before a mirror), and ultimately, at the end of the poem, a ghostly disassociation as Naomi fails to recognize Allen on his last visit to her. And even that mood changes as he receives her letter of prophetic instruction just before hearing of her death: "The key is in the window, the key is in the sunlight in the window—I have the key—Get married Allen, don't take drugs—the key is in the sunlight in the window." The letter, which Ginsberg rewrote himself, revives the spirit of millenarian optimism that Naomi epitomizes throughout the poem, a pathetically disoriented yet actively striving figure.

The four final sections, each very short, relieve and disperse some of the intensities developed in the narrative, as if the momentum could not be suddenly released, but needed to be gently assuaged. The "caw caw caw" section, for example, soothes like a resolving fugue with its two parts, one representing the realistic bleakness of materialism and pain, the second a source of mystical aspiration, both harmonized by the last line with its collocation of "Lord" and "caw." Even these last sections, however, contain signs of the poem's tremendously successful excessiveness, especially a litany which brutally and without explanations lists the horrible shocks of Naomi's life.

Judging from their correspondence, the poem had a complex affect on Louis Ginsberg. While he found it on the whole "heart-wrenching" and "magnificent," he was disturbed by the implicit sexuality of the poem, finding his son's references to homosexuality, incestuous yearnings, and the allusion to Louis' affair with another woman embarrassing. He felt his son was reaching for a sensationalism that was irrelevant to the poem's literary merit, and he specifically requested the deletion of the "long black beard around the vagina" as vulgarly obscene. It was a classic illustration of generational difference. In the margin of his father's letter, Allen wrote a large NO! in red, and then answered in a separate letter:

> The line about the "beard around the vagina" is probably a sort of very common experience and image that children have who see their parents naked and it is an archtypal experience and nothing to be ashamed of—it looks from the outside, objectively, probably much less shocking than it appears to you. I think it's a universal experience which almost everyone has had though not many poets have referred to it.

The original draft of the poem, as Ginsberg told Kerouac, was changed significantly. Lawrence Ferlinghetti advised the elimination of several repetitions, urging Ginsberg to seek greater density and concentration while clarifying his narrative sequence. Ginsberg responded to these suggestions rather than to his father's more personal requests.

The overall effect of the final version of **"Kaddish"** is unlike that of any other modern poem, even **"Howl."** The reader is left in a state of utter exhaustion, the feeling one often has after a particularly harrowing dream. The aesthetic paradox of **"Kaddish"** is that despite all its terror and the shockingly relentless and obsessive manner in which Ginsberg pursues his mother's haunted memory, the result is a poetry of the sublime, the rare kind of exalted rejoicing in being that occurs in the poetry of Christopher Smart, in Richard Crashaw's description of his love for God, or Francis Thompson's "The Hound of Heaven."

The crucial question for any poet capable of creating poems like **"Howl"** or **"Kaddish"** is whether that imaginative energy can be sustained. There are those who have wondered whether Ginsberg is the agent or the vessel of his poetic inspiration, whether he is the author of his poems or whether, like Burroughs, he may be the telepathic register of some otherly source. In this connection, it is useful to remember that the poets we most admire in any age manage to leave us with only a few major poems: indeed, it would be difficult to measure the greatness of the best of Dryden, Pope, Wordsworth, Coleridge, Browning, or Tennyson without the light of their total efforts. ***Empty Mirror, Howl,*** and ***Kaddish*** are all exceptional volumes, but the beginning, not the high point, of a continuing productivity, a steady stream of poems that achieve different kinds of power and insight.

The collection after ***Kaddish*** was ***Reality Sandwiches,*** and except for **"Siesta in Xbalba"** (written in 1954, one year before **"Howl,"** and Ginsberg's first major formal innovation) and **"Love Poem on Theme By Whitman,"** it was definitely less effective than any previous book, and as such caused suspicions that Ginsberg's talents had been depleted by his other activities. A poem like **"Sather Gate Illumination"** stands for the weaknesses of the book. The poem is about self-worth as a function of love, "broken minds in beautiful bodies unable to receive love because not knowing the self as lovely." Although like **"Sunflower Sutra"** the subject is as central to Ginsberg's poetry as to Whitman's, the poem lacks imaginative tensions, and its relaxation is reflected in lines that approach prose without the surreal jumps and syntactical excitements animating Ginsberg's usual flow. Near the beginning of the poem, as Ginsberg walks through the Berkeley campus, a crippled French teacher is explaining some grammatical point to her class:

> Regarder is to look—
> the whole French language looks on the trees on
> the campus.

There is a certain intrusive and staged obviousness about using French, the traditional language of love, and a teacher who stresses the act of looking in a poem that observes instances of failed love. Making that teacher a cripple and a woman who later saunters through the poem's center "with loping fuck gestures of her hips askew" creates a rhetoric of construction that is just too apparent in a poem that encourages love of body despite external defects. The result is obviousness rather than directness, the single dimension of allegorical lettuce. The poem becomes too dogmatic in its very structure, too insistent on a generous theme that needed more deftness, delicacy, and freedom than Ginsberg could manage at the moment.

These very qualities are all present in **"Love Poem on Theme By Whitman,"** a poem that improvises on lines in one of Whitman's more mysterious poems, "The Sleepers."

> I'll go into the bedroom silently and lie down
> between the bridegroom and the bride,
> those bodies fallen from heaven stretched out
> waiting naked and restless,
> arms resting over their eyes in the darkness,
> bury my face in their shoulders and breasts,
> breathing their skin
> and stroke and kiss neck and mouth and make
> back be open and known,
> legs raised up crook'd to receive, cock in the
> darkness driven tormented and attacking
> roused up from hole to itching head,
> bodies locked shuddering naked, hot lips and
> buttocks screwed into each other
> and eyes, eyes glinting and charming, widening
> into looks and abandon,
> and moans of movement, voices, hands in air,
> hands between thighs,
> hands in moisture on softened hips, throbbing
> contraction of bellies
> till the white come flow in the swirling sheets,
> and the bride cry for forgiveness, and the groom
> be covered with tears of passion and
> compassion,
> and I rise up from the bed replenished with last
> intimate gestures and kisses of farewell—
> all before the mind wakes, behind shades and
> closed doors in a darkened house
> where the inhabitants roam unsatisfied in the
> night,
> nude ghosts seeking each other out in the
> silence.

Early in "Song of Myself" Whitman imagines God as a loving bedfellow, the "noble bridegroom" of religious love poetry whose nocturnal visit causes the poet to "scream at my eyes" in the plenitude of received energy. Several times in "Song of Myself" Whitman alludes to the bride and her groom; once he turns the groom out of bed to "tighten" with the bride all night. Among those whom Whitman visits in "The Sleepers" is a calmly reclining married couple, each with a palm on the other's hip. In an image embodying Emerson's concept of the "oversoul," Whitman dreams "all the dreams of the other dreamers" and becomes the other dreamers. Ginsberg begins at this point of intense identification (a contemporary "caresser of life"), breathing into his lovers, actually Neal and Carolyn Cassady, the divinely creative power of sexual energy that is expressed as a rhythmic whirlwind of physical passion and ecstatic release, a paean of one long and continuous line that so brilliantly renews the excitement and beauty that Whitman conveys, and whose rhythms simulate as well the overtures, passion, and climax of actual intercourse. While the poem's fierce rotation is about the body's axis, there is none of Iago's "beast with two backs" view of bestial lust in love; we are left uplifted by the poem, perhaps because of the skillful manner in which Ginsberg mixes tender images like "moans of movement" and "moisture on softened lips" with his lovers' contracting, pounding bodies.

Ginsberg has commented on the tradition he sought to continue in **"Love Poem on Theme By Whitman"** in, of all places, his testimony before Judge Hoffman at the Chicago Seven trial. Ginsberg, along with Burroughs and Jean Genêt, had attended the Democratic presidential convention in Chicago in the summer of 1968. As journalists, they were allowed entry to the convention area where they witnessed the excessively rigorous security precautions and controls, even extended to the delegates themselves, which created a suffocating and regimented atmosphere hardly conducive to political process. Ginsberg spent most of his time outside the convention hall in support of the vociferous and militant group of young dissenters who were protesting the fiasco inside. Terror and latent violence suffused the air as the threats of tear gas and more aggressive police measures were realized in vicious attacks. Ginsberg exerted an enormously calming presence, chanting mantras to relieve tensions, meditating and counseling in the midst of the turmoil and uncertainty. At the trial, however, prosecutor Foran hounded him for his views on sex with all the vulgar zeal of lawyer Carson grilling Oscar Wilde on *The Picture of Dorian Gray.* Ginsberg's reply to Foran's rude query on the religious significance of the poem is a definition of what Whitman meant by "adhesiveness," as well as an explanation of his own frequently candid use of sexuality:

> Whitman said that unless there were an infusion of feeling, of tenderness, of fearlessness, of spirituality, of natural sexuality, of natural delight in each other's bodies, into the hardened materialistic, cynical, life denying, clearly competitive, afraid, scared, armored bodies, there would be no chance for spiritual democracy to take root in America—and he defined that tenderness between the citizens as, in his words, an "Adhesiveness," a natural tenderness, flowing between all citizens, not only men and women but also a tenderness between men and men as part of our democratic heritage, part of the Adhesiveness which would make the democracy function: that men could work together not as competitive beasts but as tender lovers and fellows. So he projected from his own desire and from his own unconscious a sexual urge which he felt was normal to the unconscious of most people, though forbidden for the most part.

In an earlier poem, **"A Supermarket In California,"** addressed to Whitman "lonely old courage-teacher," Ginsberg wondered whether they could ever "stroll dreaming of the lost America of love?" In ***Planet News*** this question is reiterated with a graphic insistence, as at the end of **"Journal Night Thoughts"**:

> I come in the ass of my beloved, I lay back
> with my cock in the air to be kissed—
> I prostrate my sphincter with my eyes in
> the pillow, my legs are thrown up
> over your shoulder,
> I feel your buttocks with my hand
> a cock throbs I lay still my
> mouth in my ass—
> I kiss the hidden mouth, I have a third eye
> I paint the pupils on my palm, and an
> eyelash that winks—

Ginsberg has been progressing steadily in the tradition of Henry Miller toward a description of particulars that once would have been regarded as obscene or scatological ("How big is the prick of the President?" he humorously queries in **"Wichita Vortex Sutra"**), but which Ginsberg sees as natural speech. Whitman had proclaimed that copulation was no more rank than death, that both had aspects of holiness, and in "Song of Myself" there are several descriptions of mystical ecstasy that are rendered with the metaphor of masturbation (recalling Ginsberg's Blake visitation). Whitman's "prurient provokers" and "red marauders," as well as his *Calamus* poems, suggested a potential for American letters (which few except Henry Miller have had the courage or the folly to fulfill) that leads to poems like **"This form of Life needs Sex"** in ***Planet News.*** Sexuality, both as release and as a trigger for latent psychic energies and realizations, in short as a vehicle for awareness and liberated consciousness, has been an object of repression for a long time in America and Ginsberg has taken many public risks to widen those particular perceptual gates.

In **"Please Master"** (which appears in ***The Fall Of America*** as a part of a series of elegies to Neal Cassady), Ginsberg writes one of his most memorable poems, perhaps the finest attempt by an American poet to describe physical love between two men. The refrain of the title suggests Ginsberg's obeisance, his desire to accept both the rough and gentle pleasures of anal sex. Though the poem is exceptionality graphic, it never loses its undertones of warmth:

Please master can I lick your groin curled with
blond soft fur
Please master can I touch my tongue to your
rosy asshole

The poem's movement is from the initial disrobing, to courtly preliminaries, to easing entry and more lunging, ravishing penetration. Despite its violence, it sustains its tone of tender supplication, fusing the phallicism with receptivity of love. **"Please Master"** is characteristic of the Beats' frankness, their lack of shame or guilt, their openness to new subject matter.

As far as obscenity is concerned, there is an interesting and revealing difference between Burroughs and Ginsberg that is analogous to the pessimism of the Dadaists and Breton's belief that Surrealism could lead to a general revolutionary awakening. While both Burroughs and Ginsberg deny ordinary guilt and shame, Burroughs employs sex viciously to create the consciousness of suffering; Ginsberg is always endearing, "charming" is the word he used before Judge Hoffman, always in accord with Blake's "naked human form divine" and Whitman's "I keep as delicate around the bowels as around the head and heart." The Beats, as Michael McClure argues in *Meat Science Essays,* intended to free the word *fuck* from its chains: "The obscenity barrier is raised by censorship and fear. It is built by a fear of the natural and the idea that nature is obscene." Ginsberg has always reveled in the divinity of his own sexuality, his homosexuality, adoring his own physical propensities and urging the life of the body on his readers.

Planet News, Ginsberg's poems of the sixties, marked a sharp resurgence of power, containing at least six splendid poems: **"Television was a Baby Crawling Toward that Deathchamber," "The Change," "Kral Majales," "Who Be Kind To," "Wichita Vortex Sutra,"** and **"Wales Visitation."** In ***Planet News,*** the demands of the self so insistently pronounced in the earlier poetry are modulated to harmonize with the larger concerns of the earth, and the poet's role in dramatizing those concerns. The first and last poems in the collection, both on the dangers inherent in the American military system, form an envelope for inner unities. No one seems to have noticed the way in which so many of the poems lead into each other and relate organically (as earlier ***Kaddish*** consisted of a number of elegies). In ***Planet News*** these interconnections—**"Lost in Calcutta"** pointing directly to **"The Change"**—are part of a grand network of the poet's awareness of the planet as he travels through India, Japan, California, New York, Havana, Warsaw, Prague, and London. Ginsberg is essentially a city man writing about city life with a gregarious impulse to engage and contend with cosmopolitan energy centers.

What is most impressive about ***Planet News*** is Ginsberg's sense of himself and his place in the general order of things. He acknowledges an obligatory role as the prophetic witness of American imperialism—kind of a Rudyard Kipling in reverse—in **"Television was a Baby Crawling Toward that Deathchamber,"** a lengthy and innovative poem about technological control over consciousness that is reminiscent of Burroughs:

Screech out over the radio that Standard Oil is a
bunch of spying Businessmen intent on
building one Standard Oil in the whole
universe like an egotistical cancer
and yell on Television to England to watch out
for United Fruits they got Central America
by the balls
nobody but them can talk San Salvador, they run
big Guatemala puppet armies, gas Dictators,
they're the Crown of Thorns
upon the Consciousness of poor Christ-indian
Central America and the Pharisees are US
Congress & Publicans is the American
People

The poem, dense with associations that create a labored, staccato rhythm, builds to a point approaching hysteria as Ginsberg denounces the "Six billionaires that control America" and focuses on historic Paterson which he imagines (as Burroughs once saw Times Square crawling with centipedes) as devoid of human life. Ginsberg feels all the more impelled to address "all these lacklove / suffering the Hate" who have been conditioned by the forces of those six unnamed controllers:

all day I walk in the wilderness over white
carpets of City, we are redeeming ourself, I
am born,
the Messiah woke in the Universe, I announce
the New Nation, in every mind, take power
over the dead creation,

"Television was a Baby . . ." is a continuous cadenza, practically one long obsessive sentence of locomotive propulsion. Its spurting, trumpeting, ranting tone of indictment might be too much to bear were it not for Ginsberg's characteristic humor, his sense of the bizarrely comic absurdity of things, carrying "subversive salami" in his ragged briefcase as he put it in ***Reality Sandwiches.***

The sense of speaking directly to a "new nation" (the notion of a constituency emerging from the radical activities of the sixties) with a messianic message of salvation is continued in **"Kral Majales,"** a poem about the enthusiastic reception of Ginsberg by Prague students under the hostile surveillance of the Czechoslovakian police and secret agents who followed Ginsberg everywhere. The poem is a denial of the conspiratorial military-police closure on consciousness—communist and capitalist—and a joyous recognition of the Dionysian "King of May" spirit which, as Plato warned, has always been the great catalyst for change:

And I am the King of May, that I may be
expelled from my Kingdom with honor, as
of old,
To shew the difference between Caesar's
kingdom and the Kingdom of the May of
Man—

The poem depends on a sense of Blakean antithesis, the heavy industry and heavy heart of communism and the "shutdowns" of national statism in Cuba, America, or Czechoslovakia, dominating the first half of the poem, then with a sudden violence, an utter lack of any transition, changing into an ebullient and soaring celebration of the May Day festivities—ironically appropriated by world communism, but actually, as Ginsberg implies, belonging to the "new nation" of freed spirits who accept the hegemony of man over state.

In **"Wichita Vortex Sutra,"** a ritual declaration of the end of the Vietnam War, part of a longer project called "These States," Ginsberg offers a view and a prayer for that "new nation":

No more fear of tenderness, much delight in
weeping, ecstasy
in singing, laughter rises that confounds
staring Idiot mayors
and stony politicians eyeing
Thy breast,
O Man of America, be born!

This is a potential that Ginsberg first commemorated in ***Kaddish***'s **"Ignu,"** an "angel in comical form" that attends to life with passionate intensity, with the social concerns of Blake and Whitman, with the abandon of Rimbaud, and the native American surrealistic antics and anarchistic tactics exemplified by the Marx Brothers (as in Kerouac's poem, "To Harpo Marx" where Harpo steals the silverware at a party and sprays the guests with insect repellent). For Ginsberg, as for Kerouac, fools, idiots, hobos, and social pariahs like the retarded Iddyboy in *Doctor Sax* serve to extend our general notion of what it means to be human, and often represent potentials of almost saintly purity because they are uncontaminated by the social games and lures that so easily corrupt the rest of us.

In **"Who Be Kind To,"** as in **"The Change,"** Ginsberg suggests that it is now time to turn from Rimbaud's hedonistic and socially irresponsible escape into adventurous sensations to face the problems of this world, the looming dangers of planetary biocide. **"The Change: Kyoto-Tokyo Express"** describes Ginsberg's own evolution from a destructively obsessive refusal to deal with the social realities of the West (by traveling in India and taking drugs) to a desire to "open the portals to what Is." The poem virtually declares that the despair of the time of **"Howl"** is no longer justified as an end, that it was only the beginning of consciousness but not a program:

Come, sweet lonely Spirit, back
to your bodies, come great God
back to your only image, come
to your many eyes & breasts,
come thru thought and
motion up all your
arms the great gesture of
Peace & acceptance Abhya
Mudra Mudra of fearlessness
Mudra of Elephant calmed &
war-fear ended forever!

"The Change" also signals a return for Ginsberg to the tensions of a tightly involuted line, still dependent on surreal dislocations of image, and rhythmic power of voice, but for the moment more compactly self-contained than even the ***Empty Mirror*** poems. As in **"Journal Night Thoughts"** or **"Wichita Vortex Sutra,"** Ginsberg reveals an encouraging curiosity about new modes of presentation and formal arrangement.

"Who Be Kind To" is both an advisory and a benediction to the radical spirit in our time, urging the discoveries of **"The Change"** on a wider audience while wishing for its preservation and continuity: "Be kind to yourself, because the bliss of your own / kindness will flood the police tomorrow." Ginsberg exhorts:

For this is the joy to be born, the kindness
received through strange eyeglasses on

a bus through Kensington,
the finger touch of the Londoner on your thumb,
that borrows light from your cigarette,
the morning smile at Newcastle Central station, when longhair Tom blond husband greets the bearded stranger of telephones—

The poems ends with another vision of the "new man" that reappears throughout ***Planet News***:

That a new kind of man has come to his bliss
to end the cold war he has borne
against his own kind flesh
since the days of the snake.

Planet News is imbued with the vatic sense of the seer one finds in the best of romantic poetry, and the authenticity one feels after speaking with someone who has undertaken a long hazardous journey and returned with informing insights. Perhaps the most beautiful poem in the volume, certainly in the Wordsworthian spirit of communion with nature and the transport this can impart, is **"Wales Visitation,"** a poem written while taking LSD that successfully captures the sense of energy flow animating all living things that the drug seems to enhance. The poem flows musically with what Pound called the tone leading of vowels, and succeeds particularly in eliminating all sense of self. Instead of a human center, it lavishly records the flux of phenomena:

Out, out on the hillside, into the ocean sound, into delicate gusts of wet air,
Fall on the ground, O great Wetness, O Mother, No harm on your body!
Stare close, no imperfection in the grass,
each flower Buddha-eye, repeating the story, the myriad formed soul
Kneel before the foxglove raising green buds, mauve bells drooped
doubled down the stem with trembling antennae,
& look in the eyes of the branded lambs that stare breathing stockstill under dripping hawthorn—
I lay down mixing my beard with the wet hair of the mountainside
smelling the brown vagina-moist ground, harmless
tasting the violet thistle-hair, sweetness—
One being so balanced, so vast, that its softest breath
moves every floweret on the stillness on the valley floor,
trembles lamb-hair hung gossamer rain-beaded in the grass,
lifts trees on their roots, birds in the great draught
hiding their strength in the rain, bearing same weight

In Ginsberg's most recent work, ***The Fall of America,*** long series of poems on the spiritual condition of "these States" during the sixties, the idea of the "fall" develops out of **"Howl."** In a notebook dating back to 1957, Ginsberg wrote:

Therefore I prophecy the Fall of America
Bitter, bitter tongue to tell

The Fall of America shows Ginsberg moving closer to Kerouac's conception of the writer as memoirist: much of the book is drawn from journal transcriptions, or composed directly on the tape recorder as Ginsberg traveled about the country by car, plane, and train. The book records a cumulative pain, the anguish of Vietnam all the more wrenching because of the lies of "progress" as the nation Ginsberg observes suffers its most intense self-confrontation since the decade of abolitionist fury before the Civil War. More than ***Howl*** or ***Kaddish,*** this is Ginsberg's most despairing and least affirming book, haunted as it is by a constant sense of doom. Instead of the ecstatic resources of drugs or mysticism, the only relief Ginsberg projects—like Burroughs in *The Wild Boys*—is an apocalypse of self-destruction. Perhaps this new irredeemable despair is responsible for the purgatorial tone of the collection. In ***Planet News,*** travel, movement in space and time, was treated adventurously, euphorically, expectantly. But in ***The Fall of America,*** the motion is burdened, deliberate, weighted with sorrow and seriousness, unalleviated by new impressions or expectations, restricted somehow to the boundaries of a country in its saddest hour.

The basis of ***The Fall of America*** is an Emersonian correspondence: the violence of Vietnam is reflected in an inner violence, the destruction of foreign war is complemented by the devastation of our own natural environment. Ginsberg sees the external misadventure and the internal blindness of what we have done to our own land as organically related—like the Buddhist notion of karma that promises that any present action will affect future incarnations, or the biblical maxim on sowing and reaping. Ironically, the poem is dedicated to Whitman and prefaced by the selection from *Democratic Vistas* on adhesiveness, the sense of male comradeship that Whitman supposed would spiritually leaven American materialism. But Ginsberg's own tone is uninspired by Whitman's cheer. With brutal relentlessness, in poem after poem, Ginsberg's eye fixes on the pocks of industrial spoilage scarring the face of the land.

In ***The Fall of America,*** the Moloch of "**Howl**" has finally consumed our youthful hope, transforming any Jeffersonian aspirations of a society whose real strength was rooted in the back country to an infernal view of belching smoke-stacks, Poe's red death pervading the acrid atmosphere. Ginsberg, in his half-century on the planet, has been a Tiresian witness to this harrowing change:

I was born there in Newark
Public Service sign of the 'Twenties
visible miles away through smoke
grey night over electric fields
My aunts and uncles died in hospitals,
are buried in graves surrounded by Railroad Tracks,
tombed near Winking 3 Ring Ballantine Ale's home
where Western Electric has a Cosmic plant,
Pitt-Consoles breathes forth fumes
acrid above Flying Service tanks
Where superhighway rises over Monsanto
metal structures moonlit
Pulaski Skyway hanging airy black
in heaven my childhood
neighbored with gigantic harbor stacks,
steam everywhere
Blue Star buses skimming skyroads
beside th' antennae mazes
brilliant by Canalside—

Everywhere, the horror is the city's filth spilling over into the countryside, festering contamination and scourge, the land blighted, wasted and prone to plague like Thebes before the exorcism of Oedipus:

Living like beasts,
befouling our own nests,
Smoke & Steam, broken glass & beer cans,
Auto exhaust—
Civilization shit littering the streets,
Fine black mist over apartments
watercourses running with oil
fish fellows dead—

Ginsberg extends the scope of the disaster with a pop mosaic of complicity, a collage of simultaneous data, actual sensory details and historical referents, mixing news of Vietnam atrocities and establishment apologies—like Ambassador Lodge's infamous Christmas Eve assertion that the United States was morally justified in its actions—with the new American landscape of hamburger advertisements, motels, automobile junkpiles:

Car graveyard fills eyes
iron glitters, chrome fenders
rust—
White crosses, Vietnam War Dead
churchbells ring
Cars, kids, hamburger stand
open, barn-smile
white eye, door mouth.

The technique is primarily juxtaposition—the smell of burning oil and an advertisement for mouthwash—and no overt comment is needed because of the graphic quality of the depiction. In "**Friday The Thirteenth,**" the natural correspondence becomes more explicit:

Earth pollution identical with Mind pollution,
consciousness Pollution identical with filthy sky,
dirty-thoughted Usury simultaneous with metal dust in water courses
murder of great & little fish same as self besmirchment
short hair thought control
mace-repression of gnostic street boys identical with DDT
extinction of Bald Eagle—
Mother's milk poisoned as fathers' thoughts, all greed-stained over the automobile-body designing table—

Ginsberg's bias is humanistic and international. The awful power of American industry with its iron landscape of "Triple towers smoke-stacking steaming," of open-hearth furnaces and the smells of creosote and butane replacing alfalfa and wheat, seems to Ginsberg to be designed to burden the rest of the world, to kill peasants in South America or Asia. In a sense Ginsberg has turned a full circle, returning to the damned terrain of Eliot's wasteland, but now without the remotest flicker of hope. The agonized cry in "**Northwest Passage**" of "Wallula Polluted! Wallula Polluted! Wallula Polluted!" recalls the mounting wail of despair which Eliot expresses in "The Fire Sermon":

Weialala leia
Wallala leialala

The vision of a new nation, and a resurgence of life-forces that Ginsberg envisaged in ***Planet News*** has been blurred by fire and smoke, but is not yet extinguished despite the politics of repression. Ginsberg vaunts his fury with a Blakean sense of purpose, lashing his own resolve to "haunt these States" in "**A Vow**":

Common Sense, Common law, common tenderness
& common tranquillity
our means in America to control the money munching
war machine, bright lit industry

everywhere digesting forests & excreting soft
pyramids
of newsprint. . . .

With the ferocity and anger of Ezra Pound, Ginsberg threatens in "**War Profit Litany**" to list the names of the companies who have profited through the war in Vietnam, their corporate directors and major stockholders, the banks and investment houses that support them. In "**Returning North of Vortex,**" Ginsberg startlingly (in 1967) appeals for an American military defeat in Vietnam, prophesying that we will lose our will. Ginsberg's passion reaches an apex here, a point of crisis which diminishes, or changes course, with a group of elegies to Neal Cassady.

The vision then shifts from the city to his own farm in the country. Living without electricity, surrounded by animals rather than the carrion of stripped cars in the city, this more pastoral dimension functions ironically in the book, as a backdrop by which to measure the ruination of the land. There are very few lyrical moments in the book (as in "**Easter Sunday**") which are not used to contrast some discordantly jarring industrial rapacity. The finest poem in the volume is a vision of this unsettled pastoral, "**Ecologue,**" a long account of winter preparations on the farm that is impinged upon by the consciousness of Vietnam, of the incipient fascism Ginsberg feels in his country, of "millions of bodies in pain." The poem pivots on omens of disaster, and uses the picture of the farm as a microcosm of the larger breakdown of civilization.

Ginsberg himself becomes one of the correspondences in ***The Fall of America***: his automobile accident near the end of 1968, and a fall on the ice several years later, are a synecdoche of the general collapse he sees about him. In his earlier work, no matter how dispiriting or anguished the degree of torment, the voice was always powerful enough to sustain the reader, to suggest that existence depends on resistance and active effort, on the definition of a direction whose goal might be pleasure or personal salvation, but whose purpose would be to free the individual from the Circe of materialism. In ***The Fall of America,*** however, Ginsberg seems temporarily disoriented, despite the power of his invective:

Now I don't know who I am—
I wake up in the morning surrounded
by meat and wires,
pile drivers crashing thru the bedroom floor,
War images rayed thru Television apartments,
Machine chaos on Earth,
Too many bodies, mouths bleeding on every
Continent,

In "**Death On All Fronts,**" a poem revealing the dominating influence of Burroughs' vision in ***The Fall of America,*** Ginsberg admits to being unable to find order or even solace in his own work. In "**Friday The Thirteenth**" he wonders about the efficacy of poetry, its ability to raise consciousness in the presence of the implacable destructiveness in the world. These are very real questions for a poet who has aspired to millennial prophecy, and who has exerted himself so energetically in realizing a particular vision of the world. Part of Ginsberg's gift as a poet has been his faith in vision that has been characteristically American because of its bouyance, its ability to return with hope despite disaster. Like the American transcendentalists, that vision has been the fruit of wonder and a voyaging imagination. To discover the new, one needs to have faith in old tools. In ***The Fall of America,*** that faith seems to have been profoundly shaken. Perhaps, too, this is why Ginsberg has temporarily shifted from bhakti yoga—delight in song—to long periods of meditation, up to ten hours a day for weeks on end.

Allen Ginsberg's poetry is a record of surprising conversions—from the tersely unfulfilled anguish of ***Empty Mirror,*** the rage of "**Howl,**" the mourning dirge of "**Kaddish,**" the bare brutalities of ***Reality Sandwiches,*** the celebratory incandescence of ***Planet News,*** the apocalyptic terrors of ***The Fall of America.*** The poems exist not only as a formidably substantial body of work, but as a demonstration that poetry need not be disembodied, removed from a natural base in chant and song. Rhythm, Ginsberg has shown his own generation, is less a matter of seeing the poem on the page than hearing it sounded. As with Indian mantras or traditional religious meditation, the effect is to slow the consciousness flow, to change ordinary conditioning so that new perceptions can occur. The words repeated aloud assume a new transporting density, become a kind of magical incantatory vehicle for body and nonconceptual sensation as well as mind. The poems are made to be sung; the singer uses them to see what is there and what possibilities lie beyond. Ginsberg's most recent readings show that he is headed in a folk and blues direction enriched by the discipline of lengthy meditation and Eastern mantra. "Allen Ginsberg's naked dance" Gary Snyder called it years ago in a letter from Japan: it has been the bardic dance of our day, shocking the word from the security of the printed page and spinning it into our very midst.

THOMAS F. MERRILL (ESSAY DATE 1988)

SOURCE: Merrill, Thomas F. "Ginsberg and the Beat Attitude." In *Allen Ginsberg*, pp. 1-14. Boston: Twayne Publishers, 1988.

In the following essay, Merrill examines Ginsberg's poetry and the underlying ideology of the Beat movement.

Allen Ginsberg's collection of early poems ***The Empty Mirror*** begins with a poetic statement of the profoundest fatigue and hopelessness; but the mood is religious:

> I feel as if I am at a dead
> end and so I am finished.
> All spiritual facts I realize
> are true but I never escape
> the feeling of being closed in
> and the sordidness of self,
> the futility of all that I
> have seen and done and said.
> Maybe if I continued things
> would please me more but now
> I have no hope and I am tired.
> (***Collected Poems: 1947-1980,*** 71)

The poem expresses not exultation, not the certitude of a life that has found comfort in the evidence of things unseen, but the mood of a spirit that has long been besieged by doubts and has experienced a face-to-face encounter with the enervating specter of despair. "I am tired," the poet says, and in this weariness we hear the echo of the existentialist complaints so familiar to us in the modern age. Kierkegaard might have diagnosed the malady as the "sickness unto death"; Jack Kerouac gave it a hipster christening: "beat."

Like existentialism, the definitive boundaries of "beat" have been blurred both by the variety of attitudes that they enclose and by the notoriety that the popular press has brought to the term. The world is all too familiar with the "beatnik," but it is less so with the philosophy behind the beard and sandals. To be beat in the fifties was to feel the bored fatigue of the soldier required to perform endless, meaningless tasks that have no purpose. Society imposed authority from without, but beatniks obeyed an authority from within. Viewed as a social phenomenon, they appeared "fed up" and recalcitrant—grumbling malcontents and irresponsible hedonists. Inwardly the case was quite different. There the beatniks regarded themselves as pioneers, explorers of interior reality; in this respect, they resembled traditional religious mystics. Paul Portugés, in fact, explores what he calls Ginsberg's "visionary poetics" in the context of Christian mysticism, although he cautions that "one distinctive feature of Ginsberg's visions (and Blake's to some extent) is that they are directed toward the poetry and the poetics and *not* toward an ultimate, divine saviour."[1] The beats' much sensationalized use of drugs and hallucinogens only illustrates that their quest for inward reality had taken advantage of the resources of modern science. They could easily see themselves as jet-age Saint Johns of the Cross.[2]

The incessant search for reality within (through drugs, meditation, and intense feeling) was a quest for authenticity that reason, it was felt, deadened. It called for reconnaissance at the extremes of human experience, as far beyond the limits of reason as possible, thus placing uncommon stress upon subjective moods. Truth, for the beats as for Kierkegaard, was "an appropriation process of the most passionate inwardness." Unlike the rationalist they would not attempt to overcome their fears, guilt, dread, and cares; rather, they exploited these feelings in order to reach new levels of truth about themselves. Moods, they passionately believed, were indices to reality.

Obviously, such a commitment to internal truth not only permits but demands the uninhibited confessions that tend to make conventional readers squirm. Many beat writers, especially Ginsberg, flaunt their most intimate acts and feelings—masturbation, sodomy, drug addiction, erotic dreams—in aggressively explicit street language. To the social conservative, it is shameless exhibitionism. To the beats, such expression is the denial of shame itself, a manifesto that nothing human or personal can be degrading. If this attitude seems uncivil, even childish, consider Blake's assurance that "the fool who persists in his folly will become wise."[3]

John P. Sisk says that the beats were "locked in a dialectic" with society;[4] that is, they assumed the role of a nonbelligerent opposition, meeting the rigid rationalism of society with deliberate irrationality. It was nonbelligerent because the Beat Generation had no interest in resistance, in crusade, in movements, or in any activity, for that matter, that remotely resembled fighting. The beats were indifferent enemies of society but enemies nonetheless; because they were appalled by the ugliness of its materialism and goals and the emptiness of its values. They were indifferent because they had come to believe that they could not change society—change could only come from within. So beatniks chose not to fight. In the battle for social, spiritual, and aesthetic progress, they were conscientious objectors. They played it "cool"; they sought to "make the scene" as best they could.

Disaffiliation and Death

The words that were most often used to describe this posture were *disaffiliation* and *disengagement.* These are uneasy words to a nation of joiners where the number of organizations one belongs to can determine success as much as intellectual or occupational achievement. As Paul O'Neil rather bluntly puts it, the beats felt that "the only way man can call his soul his own is by becoming an outcast."[5] True, they were outcasts from society but intensely bound by friendships. The loose bonding of the social contract was superseded by the "responsible resoluteness of an inter-personal fidelity."[6]

Because they felt modern society had mangled the concepts of *self* and *neighbor* into grotesque hypocrisies that reduce "civilized" living to an immense lie, the beats disaffiliated for the purpose of making "interpersonal fidelity" possible. Ginsberg documents his own awakening to this "lie." In the Columbia university bookstore one day, it suddenly came to him that everyone there was concealing an unconscious torment from one another: "they all looked like horrible grotesque masks, grotesque because *hiding* the knowledge from each other."[7]

The vision of people "*hiding* the knowledge from one another" testifies to the beat conviction that people are more real (and presumably better) than society allows them to be and also that collective society has an awesome control over people that transcends their individual wills. The truth about humanity—the truth that society obdurately censors—is shouted by Ginsberg in his **"Footnote to Howl"**: "Everything is holy! everybody's holy! everywhere is holy! everyday is in eternity! Everyman's an angel!" (***CP* [*Collected Poems: 1947-1980,*]**, 134).

Religion

The beat writers generally shared a freestyle religiosity. Jack Kerouac, for instance, was concerned to emphasize his beat religious calling: "No, I want to speak *for* things, for the crucifix I speak out, for the Star of Israel I speak out, for the divinest man who ever lived who was a German (Bach) I speak out, for sweet Mohammed I speak out, for Buddha I speak out, for Lao-tse and Chuang-tse I speak out,"[8] but Gary Snyder maps its religious contours best: "[I find] three things going on: 1. *Vision and illumination-seeking.* This is most easily done by systematic experimentation with narcotics. . . . 2. *Love, respect for life, abandon, Whitman, pacifism, anarchism, etc.* . . . partly responsible for the mystique of 'angels,' the glorification of skid-row and hitchhiking, and a kind of mindless enthusiasm. . . . 3. *Discipline, aesthetics, and tradition* . . . its practitioners settle on one traditional religion, try to absorb the feel of its art and history, and carry out whatever ascesis is required."[9] The Church was "square," but religious sensitivity was "hip." On the occasions when the beat writers did use Judeo-Christian concepts, they exploited them with a fanatical application that knew no compromise. "Everyman is Holy, Every day is in eternity! Everyman's an angel!" (***CP,*** 134) bellowed Ginsberg over the blare of a saxophone. The offense of all this to organized religion was basically its lack of discipline, decorum, and its general disregard for traditional ethical teachings. Theologically, there was not so much disparity as one would expect.

Beats were prone to religious illumination. Kerouac reports, "I went one afternoon to the church of my childhood . . . and suddenly with tears in my eyes had a vision of what I must have really meant with 'Beat' . . . the vision of the word Beat as being to mean beatific."[10] But Allen Ginsberg's famous vision in a subleased apartment in Spanish Harlem of William Blake is an even more sensational example. So arresting was this experience for the poet that his spiritual-aesthetic existence orbited around it for the next fifteen years of his life.[11] "I wasn't even reading, my eye was idling over the page of *The Sunflower,*" Ginsberg explains, "and it suddenly appeared . . . and suddenly I realized that the poem was talking about *me*. . . . Now, I began understanding it, . . . and suddenly, simultaneously with understanding it, heard a very deep earthen grave voice in the room, which I immediately assumed, I didn't think twice, was Blake's voice. . . . But the peculiar quality of the voice was something unforgettable because it was like God had a human voice, with all the infinite tenderness and anciency and mortal gravity of a living Creator speaking to his son."[12]

The essential religious matrix of the beats, however, was in the Orient. Because of its conception of the holiness of personal impulse (which often was interpreted as sanction for doing whatever came naturally), Zen Buddhism was particularly attractive. Every impulse of the soul, the psyche, and the heart was one of holiness. Everything was holy if understood as such, a point Ginsberg hammered home through repetition in his **"Footnote to Howl"**:

> Holy! Holy! Holy! Holy! Holy! Holy! Holy! Holy!
> Holy! Holy! Holy! Holy! Holy! Holy! Holy!
> The world is holy! The soul is holy! The skin
> is holy! The nose is holy! . . .
> (*CP*,134)

Whatever the source—Judaism, Whitman, Buddhism, Saint John of the Cross—here is radical sacred egalitarianism, a statement that nothing is profane and that therefore no human act is not of God. As blanket a denial of evil as is possible, it represents a genuine fusion of Western and Eastern theological attitudes. The Judeo-Christian dualism of good versus evil is obliterated by a oriental relativism that neatly does away with the consequences of the spiritual pride that has bloodied the pages of Western ecclesiastical history.

The alternative to ethical dualism is a sense of the natural balance of things: an appreciation not of good versus evil but of good and evil. In the *Hsin-hsin Ming* or "Treatise on Faith in the Mind," a poem attributed to Seng-ts'an, a sixth-century Zen master, can be found the following words:

> If you want to get the plain truth
> Be not concerned with right and wrong
> The conflict between right and wrong
> Is the sickness of the mind.[13]

The view represented by this fragment, that the conflict between right and wrong is an unnecessary and harmful concern, had enormous appeal for beat writers. The basic corruption of the "square world," as they saw it, was its compulsion to be right. This compulsion had done great harm in Western cultural history, because it had insisted upon a perspective of ethical dualism in which good had always been set in taut opposition to bad with the result that people had suffered the burdens of shame and guilt, which seemed to them the most significant by-products of Western cultural psychology. And, shame and guilt were considered overwhelming obstacles to a view of life that celebrated the holy integrity of humanity and the world.

Buddhism

According to Zen, evil is not considered the natural enemy of good but its inevitable companion. They are sides of the same coin, and the proper stance of a reasonable person toward them is not to pursue one and resist the other but to accept the claims of both. A person consists of both good and bad attributes; to deny, therefore, part of oneself through an arbitrary moral code is to deny one's claim to the name *human being*. The argument is really between what might be called a "natural humanity" and an "artificial ideal." The ideal is artificial because it runs counter to natural inclination, and produces a contradiction in the personality that usually reveals itself in guilt or psychoneurosis. Zen serves to eliminate artificiality and to sweep away the psycho-ethical tensions that have marked the course of most Western philosophies. Life is restored to a natural harmony with the world; the staggering moral burdens of duty, honor, and "proper" conduct are seen as foreign accretions to the pure effortless simplicity of human existence. "In Buddhism," says T'ang master Lin-chi, "there is no place for using effort. Just be ordinary and nothing special. Eat your food, move your bowels, pass water, and when you're tired go and lie down. The ignorant will laugh at me, but the wise will understand."[14]

Such wise and ordinary effortlessness informs Ginsberg's technique of spontaneous writing (sometimes called "First thought, best thought")[15]: "The whole point of spontaneous improvisation in song is that you have to accept whatever thought presents itself to your rhyme—on the wing, so to speak. . . . You let your tongue go loose! . . . You can't change your mind—your mind is its own. And there's nothing heroic about that acceptance. . . . That's the whole point—it's ordinary mind!"[16]

Like Keats's "Negative Capability," which eschews all "irritable reaching after fact and reason," the spontaneous, "ordinary mind" (often with the assistance of drugs) relinquishes rational aloofness and reintegrates with the body and the world. "In 'Wales Visitation,'" Ginsberg reports, "I guess what I had come to was a realization that me making noise as poetry was no different from the wind making noise in the branches. It was just as natural. It was a *very important point*."[17]

Whereas so much of traditional philosophy and theology stresses the disparity between humans and the natural world, Zen Buddhism offers the comfort of reintegration with nature. Material and spiritual boundaries are permitted to overlap; the conscious and the unconscious merge; an armistice is declared between ego and nature; and the satori experience—the awakening of an individual to a knowledge of his or her "inseparability" with the universe—is not a remote hope half-hidden in the shadows of eschatology but a very real, very immanent possibility.

Zen appealed to the beat personality in two other practical ways. First, it did not repress sexual feelings or activities. Sex was seen as a healthy, natural human instinct and was treated with respect and understanding. Second, its view of the inseparability of the universe precluded the stringent moralizing that characterizes Western religions. To be right was to follow one's natural bent; to be wrong was to resist instinct and to allow an artificial standard from outside the personality to govern one's life.

Zen submerges the ego into the "oneness" of the universe so that believers at no time consider themselves "something special" but rather as things among other things. The Zen follower, Alan Watts explains, views the ego as "his *persona* or social role, a somewhat arbitrary selection of experience with which he has been taught to identify himself. (Why, for example, do we say 'I think' but not 'I am beating my heart'?) Having seen this, he continues to play his social role without being taken in by it. He does not precipitately adopt a new role or play the role of having no role at all. He plays it cool."[18]

Beat Zen exaggerates two aspects of "pure" Zen: the holiness of the personal impulses and the idea of the Zen-lunatic or holy maniac. The sanctity of the spontaneous impulse justifies the principle of "spontaneous writing" as well as the characteristic confessional quality of beat literature. Art does not discriminate; every thought and feeling is sacred and thus appropriate for aesthetic registration.

The second aspect of beat Zen, the idea of the holy lunatic, is closely allied with the holiness of personal impulse. Such persons are revered because they deliberately confound the rational (artificial) tendencies of their disposition and therefore come closer to pure natural existence. Lunacy, in other words, is cultivated as a part of a long discipline of disaffiliation from rational and material thought patterns. One deliberately deranges the senses that organize those patterns. Since LSD and narcotics are biochemical aids to this process of deliberate derangement, their popularity among the beats is understandable.

Though Ginsberg unmistakably arose from a beat matrix, both profiting and suffering from the media attention that was virtually guaranteed, we should be alert to how he has over the years outgrown many of its exaggerations and developed many of its positive orientations into a consistent and integrated life. Most markedly, he has mellowed with age, transcending (through Buddhist meditation) the chip-on-the-shoulder social protest stance that characterized his work in the sixties, acknowledging, perhaps, Confucius's counsel that it is better to be "human hearted than righteous."[19] When asked in 1976 how his meditation study changed his outlook on world politics, Ginsberg replied: "It has changed it somewhat from a negative fix on the 'fall of America' . . . into an appreciation of the fatal karmic flaws in myself and the nation. Also with an attempt to make use of those flaws or work with them—be aware of them—without animosity or guilt; and find some basis for reconstruction of a humanly useful society, based mainly on a less attached, less apocalyptic view."[20] Reviewing his life's work in 1984 for his ***Collected Poems,*** Ginsberg assessed his sixties poetry as "politically obsessed, ephemeral, too much anger, not enough family, not enough of my personal loves."[21]

Allen Ginsberg Himself

"**Collected Poems,**" writes Ginsberg (in the "Author's Preface" to this 1984 compilation of his work) "may be read as a lifelong poem including history, wherein things are symbols of themselves." As with no other poet, Ginsberg's poems are his most comprehensive and intimate biography. Little is left out. Still some chronological and conceptual ordering of his life may help to complement and perhaps "de-symbolize" some of the less than obvious events.

During his high school years in Paterson, Ginsberg remembers thinking of himself "as a creep, a mystical creep. I had a good time, was lonesome; but I first read Whitman there."[22] A Jewish homosexual, raised in a household strangely presided over by a politically obsessed mother on the ragged fringes of sanity and an utterly straight conventional father (himself a poet and high school teacher), Ginsberg inevitably felt himself the lonely outsider, a stance he assumed throughout his life and rendered symbolically in his poems through the figure of "the shrouded stranger."[23] He was seventeen years old when he entered Columbia as a prelaw student, following, as he tells us in ***Kaddish,*** his "high school mind hero, a jewish boy who became a doctor later" (***CP,*** 214). Although he originally studied economics, joined the debating team, became editor of the *Columbia Review* and president of the Philolexian Society, he was most impressed with Lionel Trilling's great books seminar, which he took as a freshman. One of his classmates, Lucien Carr, encouraged him to write poetry, and he received further encouragement from Mark Van Doren.

Two years later Ginsberg's friendship with Carr, who was involved in a fatal stabbing, was a contributing factor in Ginsberg's expulsion from the university. The actual charge was partly that Ginsberg wrote an obscenity on his dorm window,[24] but his main offense was being allegedly discovered in bed with Jack Kerouac, by Dean McKnight.

He moved to an off-campus apartment later shared by Kerouac and William Burroughs who, Ginsberg later claimed, "educated me more than Columbia, really."[25] Burroughs, thirteen years older than Ginsberg and later the author of the notorious satire *Naked Lunch*, was yet another mysterious "outsider" of the "shrouded stranger" mold who introduced Ginsberg to the subterranean Times Square world of drugs, gay bars, and crime. Kerouac, too, served as Ginsberg's tutor during this period, and the trio's apartment became a kind of beat salon, attracting a circle of friends including John Clellon Holmes, Lucien Carr, and eventually the mythical superhero and literary muse of the beat imagination, Neal Cassady.

Cassady, a product of Denver reform schools, was a "shrouded stranger" with flair, a supersensual, charismatic talker (immortalized as Dean Moriarty in Kerouac's *On the Road*), with whom Ginsberg immediately fell in love. They became sexual partners, but Ginsberg's passion was not equally reciprocated and the affair ended bitterly.[26] Even so, Cassady lived as a kind of mythic love-hero, even beyond his death in 1968, in Ginsberg's work and heart. The poem **"Many Loves"** (*CP,* 156-58) intimately documents the love affair, as does **"The Green Automobile"** (*CP,* 83-87) and the seventeen **"Elegies for Neal Cassady"** (*CP,* 487-508).[27]

Ginsberg returned to Columbia as an English major in the fall of 1946 after working at a variety of odd jobs and taking a four-month training course at the Merchant Marine Academy. After graduation from the academy he embarked on a seven-month voyage along the Atlantic and Gulf coasts, which probably gave him his first taste of adult nonacademic life.

Cassady had moved back to Denver, and in the spring of 1947 he wrote to Ginsberg of his compulsive need for him. As Harold Beaver puts it, Cassady "had a giant inferiority complex and was constantly afraid of letting Ginsberg slip as if (in his own words) he 'were a woman about to lose her man.'"[28] Ginsberg went to Denver only to find that Cassady had little time nor feeling for him. Ginsberg shipped out again on a freighter, the *John Blair,* to Africa via Marseilles for two months, making it impossible for him to register for fall classes at Columbia.

Throughout Ginsberg's stormy years at Columbia, the staid and traditional Lionel Trilling and Mark Van Doren respected and championed his unruly but brilliant promise, even though their young protégé was pursuing his own quite different interests in the literary underground. Diana Trilling described her husband's student as "middling tall, slight, dark, sallow; his dress suggested shabby gentility, poor brown tweed gone threadbare and yellow," but her maternal insight fixed on the pathos of his personal background: "His mother was in a mental institution, and she had been there, off and on, for a long time. This was the central and utterly persuasive fact of the young man's life. . . . Here was a boy on whom an outrageous unfairness had been perpetrated: his mother had fled from him into madness and now whoever crossed his path became somehow responsible, caught in the impossibility of rectifying what she had done."[29] The long moving elegy to his mother, ***Kaddish,*** substantiates her insight. A similar corroboration may be found in Ginsberg's observation: "I cut myself off from all women because I was afraid I'd discover my mother in them, or that I'd have the same problems with them that I had with her."[30]

After graduating in 1948, Ginsberg held a number of odd jobs: dishwasher at Bickford's Cafeteria, book reviewer for *Newsweek,* market research consultant, and reporter for a labor newspaper in Newark, a position he used as a pretext for meeting and interviewing the poet William Carlos Williams, who had a long and abiding prosodic influence on Ginsberg's work. Williams patiently read and criticized Ginsberg's early poems (particularly those collected in ***The Gates of Wrath*** and ***Empty Mirror***), provided an introduction to ***Howl,*** and even included two of Ginsberg's personal letters in the fourth book of his epic ***Paterson.***

In June of 1948, when his affair with Cassady (who had written of his marriage in April) had clearly ended, and when his mother's mental illness was growing worse, Ginsberg experienced the now legendary Blake vision that oriented the spiritual and vocational direction of his life for the next fifteen years. That same year, his friend Herbert Huncke (another criminally oriented "shrouded stranger" who had just been released from prison)[31] stored some stolen goods in Ginsberg's apartment. When, at Ginsberg's insistence, they removed the goods in a stolen car, they were arrested by the police. In lieu of prison, Ginsberg was sent to the New York State Psychiatric Institute for eight months where he met Carl Solomon, the dedicatee of ***Howl.***

Solomon, the "lunatic saint" of ***Howl,*** introduced Ginsberg to the French surrealists and reinforced his sensitivity to the uses of literature as a political force. An outsider and antirationalist, Solomon was no doubt directly responsible for much of the rebellious rage against the system that erupted in ***Howl.***

Ginsberg was released in the summer of 1949 and returned home to Paterson for several months. He visited Williams whose admiration and encouragement increased. Many of the poems in ***The Gates of Wrath*** and ***Empty Mirror*** reveal his fidelity to Williams's imagist and objectivist poetics.

After drifting back to Manhattan and supporting himself at various dead-end jobs, he journeyed to Mexico by way of Cuba in December of 1953 and, while exploring Mayan ruins, lived for six months as a guest on the *finca* of Karena Shields, an archaeologist and former actress who once played Jane in the Tarzan movies. It was here that he wrote the moving meditation **"Siesta in Xbalba"** (*CP,* 97).

Moving on to the San Francisco Bay area, he endured an uncomfortable reunion with Neal Cassady, who by this time had settled into a life of marriage and children; Ginsberg was once again reduced to amorous despair. He found employment in San Francisco as a marketing researcher and moved into an apartment with a girl friend. He quickly entered into San Francisco's literary scene and became acquainted with Kenneth Rexroth, Gary Snyder, Robert Duncan, Lawrence Ferlinghetti, and eventually Peter Orlovsky, who was to become his lifelong lover, friend, and spouse.[32] The most notable literary event of Ginsberg's San Francisco period was his now famous reading of the yet unpublished ***Howl*** at Six Gallery on 13 October 1955. The performance was electrifying and launched Ginsberg as a major poetic voice of the San Francisco Renaissance.

There was somewhat of a falling our between Ginsberg and the older San Francisco writers after this reading. Grudges and hurt feelings developed that troubled Ginsberg enough for him to ship out on a freighter for the Arctic and eventually return to New York. During the next few years he embarked on a series of travels: Tangier (to visit Burroughs), Spain, Italy, Vienna, Munich, Paris (where he wrote part four of ***Kaddish***).

Naomi Ginsberg died at the Pilgrim State Mental Hospital on Long Island in 1956 and Allen completed his elegy to her, ***Kaddish,*** in 1959. In February 1960 he left for a writers' conference in Chile, which developed into six months of travel through Bolivia and the Peruvian Amazon in search of the hallucinogenic drug *yage,* a quest documented in the correspondence with William Burroughs published as ***The Yage Letters.***[33] During this period he also experimented with several hallucinogens with Timothy Leary.[34]

By 1961 Ginsberg had become an internationally recognized poet and he once more traveled to France, Morocco, Greece, Israel, India, Vietnam, and Japan. In the Orient his commitment to Buddhist beliefs galvanized, an event documented in ***Indian Journals: March 1962-May 1963*** and in **"The Change: *Kyoto-Tokyo Express*"** (*CP,* 324). This was a decisive point in Ginsberg's spiritual development, for it marked his abandonment of the gods, devils, and angels that had haunted his visions since the Harlem Blake experience fifteen years before. It is important to acknowledge Ginsberg's spiritual shift here from a theistic Judeo-Christian to a nontheistic Buddhist base. Lewis Hyde reports Ginsberg's later reflection on this change: "at the time I believed in some sort of God and thus Angels, and religiousness—at present as Buddhist I see an awakened emptiness *(sûnyatâ)* as the crucial term. No God, no Self, not even Whitman's universal Self"[35] In 1972 Ginsberg made a formal commitment to the Buddhist faith.

Ginsberg suffered international political notoriety in 1965 when he was crowned *Kral Majales* (King of May) by the students of Prague and was subsequently expelled from Czechoslovakia by the authorities, who were alarmed and offended by his uninhibited behavior and political comments. Back in the United States he remained politically visible during the Democratic National Convention in Chicago in 1968. "Few people realized what a locked-up police state Chicago was," he recounted, "just like Prague."[36] But in Chicago, he was able to practice his Buddhist chanting techniques with practical success: "As a matter of fact, [the chanting] did stop a lot of violence; it really calmed several scenes where police didn't have remote-control orders to attack."[37]

In ***Planet News*** (1968) and ***The Fall of America*** (1972), written in a frenetic travelogue style, Ginsberg poetically crisscrosses the continent making taped descriptions on the run, which to Helen Vendler, at least, represent "the largest attempt since Whitman to encompass the enormous geographical and political reality of the United States."[38]

During the seventies and eighties, Ginsberg's media exposure has fallen off sharply. The times mellowed and, despite Ginsberg's demurral, he seems to have mellowed too. During summers, he receives instruction in meditation from his teacher Chögyam Trungpa and teaches himself at the Naropa Institute and the Jack Kerouac School of Disembodied Poetics, which he cofounded, in Boulder, Colorado.

Today, Ginsberg lives in modest style in his $260-a-month tenement apartment on the lower East Side of Manhattan. Although he lives penuriously (he owns no car, no television, buys his suits at the Salvation Army), he says he spends "$32,000 a year on secretaries, photocopying, printing photos, for travel, and for expenses for musicians who appear with him."[39] Peter Orlovsky, still his close friend, has moved out to live with Denise Mercedes and raise children.

"People ask me if I've gone respectable," he told an interviewer recently. "It's just the difference between reality and commercial imagery. These days it's a different stereotype. Before, I was disreputable; now I'm a yuppie. The stereotype used to be the rebel, the buffoon. Now it's the older man gone mellow, losing his inspiration."[40]

Much of his time and energy goes to fulfilling a $160,000 contract with Harper and Row for six volumes of his journals, letters, literary essays, lectures, and poems to be published within six years as a sequel to the 837-page ***Collected Poems: 1947-1980.***

"Assembling the ***Collected Poems*** gave me the chance to see the whole spectrum of what I've been through," Ginsberg says. "I'm astounded and amazed at the thought." What did that whole spectrum teach? "My intention," he reports, "was to make a picture of my mind, mistakes and all. Of course, I learned I'm an idiot, a complete idiot who wasn't as prophetic as I thought I was. The crazy, angry philippic sometimes got in the way of clear perception." Poetically, he sounds today as though he has come full circle to a Buddhist version of the Williams-like poetics with which he began: "[I] . . . turned away from a theistic mind, using abstractions like 'the Infinite,' and toward a non-theistic, Buddhist concentration on seeing what's there, paying attention to the thing itself." Politically, he feels he made errors of judgment in his youth: "I thought the North Vietnamese would be a lot better than they've turned out to be and I shouldn't have been marching against the shah of Iran because the mullahs have turned out to be a lot worse."[41]

Notes

1. Paul Portugés, *The Visionary Poetics of Allen Ginsberg* (Santa Barbara, Calif.: Ross-Erikson, 1978), xiv.
2. Note this stanza from *Howl*:

    who studied Plotinus Poe St. John of the
      Cross telepathy and bop kaballa
    because the cosmos instinctively vibrated at
      their feet in Kansas. . . .
    (*CP*, 127)

3. Quoted in Alan W. Watts, *Beat Zen, Square Zen, and Zen* (San Francisco: City Lights Books, 1959), 22.
4. John P. Sisk, "Beatniks and Tradition." *Commonweal.* 17 April 1959, 76.
5. Paul O'Neil, "The Only Rebellion Around," *Life,* 30 November 1959, 115.
6. Carl Michalson, "What Is Existentialism?" in *Christianity and the Existentialists,* ed. Carl Michalson (New York: Scribners, 1956), 13.
7. Thomas Clark, "The Art of Poetry VIII," *Paris Review* 37 (Spring 1966): 42-43.
8. Jack Kerouac, "The Origins of the Beat Generation," *Playboy,* June 1959, 32.
9. Gary Snyder, "Note on the Religious Tendencies," *Liberation,* June 1959, 11.
10. Kerouac, "Origins of the Beat Generation," 42.
11. See Portugés, *Visionary Poetics,* for a full treatment of this experience, in addition to Ginsberg's own account excerpt ahead.
12. Clark, "Art of Poetry VIII," 36-37. "Psalm IV" (*CP,* 238) is Ginsberg's poetic rendering of his "secret vision" of Blake.
13. Quoted in Alan W. Watts, *The Way of Zen* (New York: Mentor, 1959), 116.
14. Watts, *Beat Zen,* 3.
15. "'First thought, best thought.' Spontaneous insight—the sequence of thought-forms passing naturally through ordinary mind—was always motif and method of these compositions" ("Author's Preface, Reader's Manual," *CP,* xx).
16. Portugés, *Visionary Poetics,* 161-62.
17. Ibid. 122.
18. Watts, *Beat Zen,* 9.
19. Watts, *Way of Zen,* 40.
20. Peter Chowka, Interview with Ginsberg, *New Age Journal,* April 1976; reprinted in *Poetry of Ginsberg,* ed. Hyde, 320.
21. Quoted by Francis X. Clines, "Allen Ginsberg: Intimations of Mortality," *New York Times Magazine,* 11 November 1984, 92.
22. Quoted in Richard Kostelanetz, "Ginsberg Makes the World Scene," *New York Times,* 11 July 1965, sec. 4, 27.

23. Paul Christensen reports that "the outcast version of himself came to him in a dream . . . a monster of instinctual desire who has been rejected by society" ("Allen Ginsberg," *Dictionary of Literary Biography,* Vol. 16 [Detroit: Gale Research Co., 1983], 217).

24. According to Tytell, "When a chambermaid reported that 'Fuck the Jews' and 'Nicholas Murray Butler has no balls' had been inscribed on the dirty film of Ginsberg's window, Dean of Students McKnight was outraged and wanted Ginsberg expelled" (*Naked Angels,* 85).

25. Kostelanetz, "Ginsberg," 28.

26. According to Harold Beaver's characterization, "Ginsberg was the big city shepherd to this intellectual sucker from Denver. Cassady was the moronic adolescent to the Faustian father, apprentice to professional poet, Goy to Jew, Dedalus to Bloom" (Review of *Mind Breaths, TLS,* 7 July 1978, 754).

27. In the notes to *CP,* Ginsberg specifies that four poems ("A Further Proposal," "A Lover's Garden," "Love Letter," and "Dakar Doldrums") were "dedicated to Neal Cassady in the first years of our friendship, [and] were set among 'Earlier Poems: 1947,' appended to *Gates of Wrath,* a book of rhymed verse" (*CP,* 749-56).

28. Beaver, 754.

29. Diana Trilling, "The Other Night at Columbia," *Partisan Review* (Spring, 1959); reprinted in *Poetry of Ginsberg,* ed. Hyde, 58.

30. Paul Carroll, "*Playboy* Interview," *Playboy,* April 1969, 86.

31. "Friend and early contact for Kerouac, Burroughs and the author [Ginsberg] in explorations circa 1945 around Times Square, where he hung out at center of the hustling world in early stages of his opiate addictions. . . . Huncke introduced Burroughs and others to the slang, information and ritual of the emergent 'hip' or 'beat' subculture" (Ginsberg's note [*CP,* 758]).

32. Ginsberg identified Peter Orlovsky as his "wife" in the biographical fact sheet he was invited to submit to *Who's Who.*

33. See *The Yage Letters* [with William Burroughs] (San Francisco: City Lights Books, 1963).

34. See Timothy Leary's account of Ginsberg's experience "under the mushroom" in "In the Beginning, Leary Turned on Ginsberg and Saw That It Was Good," in *Poetry of Ginsberg,* ed. Hyde, 231-39.

35. Hyde, ed. *Poetry of Ginsberg,* 6.

36. Carroll, "*Playboy* Interview," 236.

37. Ibid., 237.

38. Helen Vendler, "A Lifelong Poem Including History," *New Yorker,* 13 January 1986, 83.

39. Les Berton, "Allen Ginsberg: No Longer Howling in the Wilderness," *Wall Street Journal,* 11 March 1986, 28.

40. Quoted in David Remnick, "The World & Allen Ginsberg," *Washington Post,* 17 March 1985, K4.

41. All quotations ibid.

TITLE COMMENTARY

"Howl"

GREGORY STEPHENSON (ESSAY DATE 1990)

Stephenson, Gregory. "Allen Ginsberg's 'Howl': A Reading." In *The Daybreak Boys: Essays on the Literature of the Beat Generation,* pp. 50-8. Southern Illinois University Press, 1990.

In the following excerpt, Stephenson argues that Ginsberg's focus in "Howl" is transcendence in contemporary life.

In the quarter century since its publication by City Lights Books, Allen Ginsberg's poem **"Howl"** has been reviled and admired but has received little serious critical attention. Reviewers and critics have generally emphasized the social or political aspects of the poem, its breakthrough use of obscenity and its allusions to homosexuality, or its long-line, free-verse, open form. For these reasons **"Howl"** is already being relegated to the status of a literary artifact. I want to consider **"Howl"** as essentially a record of psychic process and to indicate its relationship to spiritual and literary traditions and to archetypal patterns.

The concept of transcendence with the inherent problems of how to achieve it and where it leaves us afterward is central to romantic literature. This complex has its antecedents in Orphism, Pythagoreanism, Platonism, heterodox Judaism, Gnosticism, and the mystical tradition. **"Howl"** expresses a contemporary confrontation with the concept of transcendence and examines the personal and social consequences of trying to achieve and return from the state of transcendence.

Transcendence and its attendant problems may be summarized in this way: the poet, for a visionary instant, transcends the realm of the actual into the realm of the ideal, and then, unable to sustain the vision, returns to the realm of the actual. Afterwards the poet feels exiled from the eternal, the numinous, the superconscious. The material world, the realm of the actual, seems empty and desolate. (Poe, in *The Fall of the House of Usher,* describes this sensation as "the bitter lapse into everyday life, the hideous dropping off of the veil.") The poet (like Keats' knight at arms) starves for heavenly manna. This theme of transcendence is treated in the work of Coleridge, Wordsworth, Keats, Shelley, Nerval, Rimbaud, and many other poets and writers. **"Howl"** describes and resolves the problems, using as a unifying image the archetype of the night-sea journey.

Carl Solomon, 1928-.

The night-sea journey (or night-sea crossing) is perhaps the earliest of the sun myths. "The ancient dwellers by the sea-shore believed that at nightfall, when the sun disappeared into the sea, it was swallowed by a monster. In the morning the monster disgorged its prey in the eastern sky." Carl Jung discusses the myth in his *Contributions to Analytical Psychology* and Maud Bodkin applies it to "The Rime of the Ancient Mariner" in her book *Archetypal Patterns in Poetry.* The essential situation, in one form or another, may be found in a number of myths, legends, and folktales, and in literature.

For Jung and Bodkin the night-sea journey is a descent into the underworld, a necessary part of the path of the hero. It is "a plunge into the unconscious . . . darkness and watery depths. . . . The journey's end is expressive of resurrection and the overcoming of death." The swallowing of Jonah by a great fish in the Old Testament, the *Aeneid* of Virgil, and the *Inferno* of Dante are records of night-sea journeys.

The movement of **"Howl"** (including **"Footnote to Howl"**) is from protest, pain, outrage, attack, and lamentation to acceptance, affirmation, love and vision—from alienation to communion. The poet descends into an underworld of darkness, suffering, and isolation and then ascends into spiritual knowledge, blessedness, achieved vision, and a sense of union with the human community and with God. The poem is unified with and the movement carried forward by recurring images of falling and rising, destruction and regeneration, starvation and nourishment, sleeping and waking, darkness and illumination, blindness and sight, death and resurrection.

In the first section of **"Howl,"** Ginsberg describes the desperation, the suffering, and the persecution of a group of outcasts, including himself, who are seeking transcendent reality. They are "starving" and "looking for an angry fix" in a metaphorical more than a literal sense. Both metaphors suggest the intensity of the quest, the driving need. (William S. Burroughs uses the phrase "final fix" as the object of his quest at the end of his novel *Junkie.*) The metaphor of narcotics is extended by their search for "the ancient heavenly connection." (Connection suggests not only a visionary experience in this context—a link to or a union with the divine—but also refers to the slang term for a source of narcotics in the 1940s and the 1950s.) These seekers are impoverished, alienated, arrested, and driven to suicide both by the hostility of the society in which they pursue their quest and by the desperate nature of the quest itself, by its inherent terrors and dangers.

Ginsberg's "angelheaded" seekers follow a sort of Rimbaudian "derangement of the senses" to arrive at spiritual clarity; they pursue a Blakean "path of excess to the Palace of Wisdom." They "purgatory" themselves in the manner of medieval flagellants with profligate and dissolute living (alcohol, sexual excess, peyote, marijuana, benzedrine). And through these means they achieve occasional epiphanous glimpses: angels on tenement roofs, "lightning in the mind," illuminations, brilliant insights, vibrations of the cosmos, gleanings of "supernatural ecstasy," visions, hallucinations; they are "crowned with flame," tantalized when "the soul illuminated its hair for a second," "crash through their minds," receive "sudden flashes," and make incarnate "gaps in Time & Space"; they trap "the Archangel of the soul" and experience the consciousness of "Pater Omnipotens Aeterna Deus." For such sensualized spirituality and for their frenzied pursuit of ultimate reality, they are outcast, driven mad, suicided (as Artaud says) by society, driven into exile, despised, incarcerated, institutionalized.

Ginsberg has phrased the issue in the first section of the poem as "the difficulties that nuts and poets and visionaries and seekers have. . . . The social disgrace—disgrace—attached to certain states of soul. The confrontation with a society . . . which is going in a different direction . . . knowing how to feel human and holy and not like a madman in a world which is rigid and materialistic and all caught up in the immediate necessities. . . ." The anguish of the visionary in exile from ultimate reality and desperately seeking reunion with it is intensified by a society which refuses to recognize the validity of the visionary experience and maintains a monopoly on reality, imposing and enforcing a single, materialist-rationalist view.

A number of the incidents in the first section are autobiographical, alluding to the poet's own experiences, such as his travels, his expulsion from Columbia University, his visions of Blake, his studies of mystical writers and Cézanne's paintings, his time in jail and in the asylum. Some of the more obscure personal allusions, such as "the brilliant Spaniard" in Houston, may be clarified by reading Ginsberg's Journals. Other references are to his friends and acquaintances—Herbert Huncke, William S. Burroughs, Neal Cassady, William Cannastra, and others. (Certain characters, incidents, and places in **"Howl"** are also treated in Jack Kerouac's *The Town and the City,* John Clellon Holmes' *Go,* and William S. Burroughs' *Junkie.*) Ginsberg presents not only the personal tragedies and persecutions of his generation of seekers but alludes back to an earlier generation with embedded references to Vachel Lindsay "who ate fire in paint hotels" and Hart Crane "who blew and were blown by those human seraphim, the sailors." And for the poet, the prototype of the persecuted and martyred visionary is his own mother, Naomi Ginsberg, who is twice mentioned in the poem and whose spirit provides much of the impetus for the poem. "'**Howl**' is really about my mother, in her last year at Pilgrim State Hospital—acceptance of her later inscribed in Kaddish detail."

The personal nature of the references in **"Howl"** do not make it a poem á clef or a private communication. Nor is the poem reduced or obscured by its personal allusions. To the contrary, as images the persons, places, and events alluded to have great suggestive power. They possess a mythic, poetic clarity. We need know nothing of Ginsberg's experiences at Columbia University to understand the poetic sense of the lines who passed through universities with radiant cool eyes hallucinating Arkansas and Blake-light tragedy among the scholars of war,

> who were expelled from the academies for crazy
> & publishing obscene odes on the windows
> of the skull.

ON THE SUBJECT OF...

CARL SOLOMON

Carl Solomon met Allen Ginsberg at the Columbia Psychiatric Institute in 1949, when both were patients there. The meeting proved fortuitous to both. Ginsberg spurred Solomon to creativity, and the latter has often said that he would not have pursued a writing career had he not met the poet. For Ginsberg, Solomon's political, Dada, and surrealist experimentation provided new avenues of intellectual adventure to explore, and he was fascinated with Solomon's life and character, which he portrayed in *Howl.* The legend is that Solomon related elements of his life (many apocryphal) to Ginsberg who in turn transcribed the autobiographical musings and later incorporated them into his masterwork. The landmark poem made Solomon a literary icon, and he spent the rest of his life alternately attracted to the role he played and repelled by it. Solomon is often described as the secret heart of the Beat Generation, far more influential than his modest publications would suggest, though his 1966 volume *Mishaps Perhaps* is cited by some as a key Beat text.

And we do not have to know that the line "who walked all night with their shoes full of blood. . . ." refers to Herbert Huncke before we are moved to pity and terror by the picture. For Ginsberg, as for Whitman, the personal communicates the universal. The images are ultimately autonomous and multivalent engaging our poetic understanding by their very intensity and mystery.

Ginsberg was not alone in lamenting the destruction of a generation of frenzied, Dostoyevskian questers. In an early article on the Beats, Jack Kerouac mourned "characters of a special spirituality . . . solitary Bartlebies staring out the dead wall window of our civilization. The subterranean heroes who'd finally turned from the 'freedom' machine of the West and were taking drugs, digging bop, having flashes of insight, experiencing the 'derangement of the senses,' talking strange, being poor and glad, prophesying a new style for American culture . . . [but who] . . .

after 1950 vanished into jails and madhouses or were shamed into silent conformity." Ken Kesey, in his novel *One Flew over the Cuckoo's Nest,* also treats the issue of the imposition of a false, shallow, materialist-rationalist reality on the human spirit and the consequent persecution and oppression of those who cannot or will not accept the official reality.

Several lines near the end of the first section (from "who demanded sanity trials" to "animal soup of time—") describe the exploits and sufferings of the dedicatee of the poem, Carl Solomon, the martyr in whom Ginsberg symbolizes his generation of oppressed celestial pilgrims. Ginsberg's statement of spiritual solidarity with Solomon—"ah Carl, while you are not safe I am not safe"—presages the climactic third section of the poem. This compassionate identification with a fellow quester-victim is very similar to the Bodhisattva vow in Buddhism and anticipates the poet's later interest in Buddhist thought.

After a statement on the technique and intention of the poem, the section ends with strong images of ascent and rebirth and with a suggestion that the martyrs are redemptive, sacrificial figures whose sufferings can refine the present and the future.

The second section of the poem continues and expands the image of pagan sacrifice with which the first section concludes. To what merciless, cold, blind idol were the "angelheaded" of section one given in sacrifice?, Ginsberg asks. And he answers, "Moloch!" Moloch (or Molech), god of abominations, to whom children were sacrificed ("passed through the fire to Molech"), the evil deity against whom the Bible warns repeatedly, is the ruling principle of our age. To him all violence, unkindness, alienation, guilt, ignorance, greed, repression, and exploitation are attributable. The poet sees his face and body in buildings, factories, and weapons—as Fritz Lang saw his devouring maw in the furnace of *Metropolis.*

Ginsberg presents a comprehensive nightmare image of contemporary society, an inventory of terrors and afflictions that is as penetrating as Blake's "London." And like Blake in "London," Ginsberg places the source of human woe within human consciousness and perception. Moloch is a condition of the mind, a state of the soul: "Mental Moloch!"; "Moloch whose name is the Mind!" We are born, according to Ginsberg, in a state of "natural ecstasy," but Moloch enters the soul early. (See Blake's "Infant Sorrow.") We can regain that celestial, ecstatic vision of life ("Heaven which exists and is everywhere about us!") by emerging from the belly of Moloch, the monster that has devoured us, who "ate up . . . [our] brains and imagination." We can "wake up in Moloch!"

The remainder of the second section returns to a lament for the visionaries of section one. American society is seen as having consistently ignored, suppressed, and destroyed any manifestation of the miraculous, the ecstatic, the sacred, and the epiphanous.

In the pivotal section two of **"Howl,"** Ginsberg names Moloch as the cause of the destruction of visionary consciousness and describes the manifestations of this antispirit, this malevolent god. Ginsberg also indicates that the Blakean "mind forg'd manacles" of Moloch can be broken and that beatific vision can be regained. In this section the poet has also made clear that transcendence is not merely of concern to poets and mystics but to every member of the social body. Ginsberg has shown the effects of a society without vision. Commercialism, militarism, sexual repression, technocracy, soulless industrialization, inhuman life, and the death of the spirit are the consequences of Mental Moloch.

The third section of the poem reaffirms and develops the sympathetic, affectionate identification of Ginsberg with the man who for him epitomizes the rebellious visionary victim. The section is a celebration of the courage and endurance of Carl Solomon, a final paean to the martyrs of the spirit, and an affirmation of human love.

The piteous and brave cry of Solomon from the Rockland Mental Hospital is the essence of the poem's statement; his is the howl of anguished and desperate conviction. "The soul is innocent and immortal it should never die ungodly in an armed madhouse." The image of the "armed madhouse" is both macrocosmic and microcosmic. Each human soul inhabits the defensive, fearful "armed madhouse" of the ego personality, the social self, and the American nation has also become "an armed madhouse." (Kesey also uses the madhouse as metaphor in his novel *One Flew over the Cuckoo's Nest.*) The psychic armor that confines and isolates the individual ego selves and the nuclear armaments of the nation are mutually reflective; they mirror and create each other. At both levels, the individual and the national, the innocent and the immortal soul is starved, suffocated, murdered.

The imagery of crucifixion ("cross in the void," "fascist national Golgotha") reemphasizes

Ginsberg's view of the visionary as sacrificial redeemer. Such images culminate in the poet's hope that Solomon "will split the heavens . . . and resurrect your living human Jesus from the superhuman tomb." I understand this to mean that Solomon will discover the internal messiah, liberate himself from Mental Moloch ("whose ear is a smoking tomb"), and attain spiritual rebirth.

The final images of "**Howl**" are confident and expansive, a projected apocalypse of Moloch, the Great Awakening "out of the coma" of life-in-death. Confinement, repression, alienation, and the dark night of the soul are ended. The "imaginary walls collapse" (walls of egotism, competition, materialism—all the woes and weaknesses engendered by Mental Moloch), and the human spirit emerges in victory, virtue, mercy, and freedom. The "sea-journey" of Solomon and of the human spirit is completed.

"**Footnote to Howl**," originally a section of "**Howl**" excised by Ginsberg on the advice of Kenneth Rexroth, extends the poet's vision of Blake's phrase "the Eye altering alters all" in "The Mental Traveller." The poem is a rhapsodic, Blakean, Whitmanesque illumination of the realm of the actual, the material world. If we accept and observe attentively, if we see, Ginsberg tells us, then all is reconciled and all is recognized for what it in essence truly is: holy, divine.

The eye can become discerning in the deepest sense. Perceiving the inscape of each object, each event and life, we can perceive the divine presence. We can see the angel in every human form; we can see "eternity in time"; we can even see "the Angel in Moloch." Perception is a reciprocal process. You are what you behold; what you behold is what you are. ("Who digs Los Angeles IS Los Angeles"—i.e., we can see either the dirty, lonely city of woe and weakness or the City of the Angels.) The essence of everything, of every being, is holy; only the form may be foul or corrupted; therefore, "holy the visions . . . holy the eyeball." In this way Ginsberg's earlier assertion that "Heaven . . . exists and is everywhere about us" is extended and fulfilled. If we can wake up in Moloch, we can awake out of Moloch.

The acceptance of the body is essential for Ginsberg, for the senses can be a way to illumination. The body is where we must begin. Throughout "**Howl**" sexual repression or disgust with the body or denial of the senses have been seen as forms of Mental Moloch: "Moloch in whom I am a consciousness without a body!"; "where the faculties of the skull no longer admit the worms of the senses." That is why the "**Footnote**" proclaims: "The soul is holy! The skin is holy! The nose is holy! The tongue and cock and hand and asshole holy!" Body and spirit are affirmed and reconciled.

Heracleitus taught that "the way up and the way down are the same way." For Ginsberg, in his night-sea journey, the path of descent described in the first two sections of "**Howl**" has become the path of ascent, of victory and vision, as presented in section three and in "**Footnote to Howl.**" "**Howl**" records a solstice of the soul, a nadir of darkness, and then a growth again towards light. The poem exemplifies Jack Kerouac's understanding that to be Beat was "the root, the soul of Beatific."

For many of the romantic writers the loss of vision and the return to the actual was a permanent defeat: their lives and their art became sorrowful and passive; they languished and mourned; their behavior became self-destructive, even suicidal. Ginsberg transforms his season in hell into new resolve and purpose. Like Coleridge's ancient mariner, he has returned from a journey of splendors and wonders and terrors and intense suffering with a new vision of human community, a new reverence for life. Like Blake's Bard, his is a voice of prophetic anger, compassion, and hope. Implicit in Ginsberg's vision in "**Howl**" of human solidarity and ultimate victory is the Blakean vow as expressed in "A New Jerusalem": "I shall not cease from mental fight . . . till we have built Jerusalem. . . ."

Ginsberg's sense of our common human necessity to redeem light from darkness, to seek vision and to practice virtue, is communicated in verse by the breath-measured, long-line, chant rhythm of "**Howl.**" Andrew Welch observes that:

> "The chant rhythm is a basic use of language that both reflects and directs social action toward community goals, a force that seems never to be far away when this rhythm enters poetry." In the Eskimo dance song, in the Navaho and Australian chants, in the prophecies of the Ghost Dance and of the Maya poet Chilam Balam, and in the poems of Ginsberg and Baraka, there is rhythmically and thematically a strong sense of movement and action, a communal rhythm enforcing communal participation and communal identity.

In this way, "**Howl**" is linked not only to the romantic tradition but also to the preliterary, oral, magic incantations of the universal shamanist tradition. "**Howl**" not only invokes and participates in the tradition of vatic poetry but significantly contributes to and furthers that tradition.

The poem's considerable achievements, by Ginsberg's use of myth, rhythm, and prophetic vision, are the resolution of the problems associated with transcendence and the embodiment in verse of a new syncretic mode of spiritual awareness, a new social consciousness. A quarter of a century later, **"Howl"** is still on point, still vital and still pertinent. Rather than a literary artifact, the poem is likely to become a classic.

"Kaddish"

SCOTT HERRING (ESSAY DATE FALL 2001)

SOURCE: Herring, Scott. "Her Brothers Dead in Riverside or Russia: 'Kaddish' and the Holocaust." *Contemporary Literature* 42, no. 3 (fall 2001): 535-56.

In the following essay, Herring relates "Kaddish" to the Holocaust.

Allen Ginsberg's death, on April 5, 1997, was the end of a full and flamboyant life—so flamboyant, indeed, that, as literature, his poetry is somewhat eclipsed by his good-natured public eccentricity. One can see the process at work in his obituaries, in which his poems were remembered in great part for the riotous living detailed therein; the popular press thus mirrored the popular impression of him, remembering the celebrity more than the poetry.[1] For most of us, Ginsberg remains Ginsberg the performer, the advocate of psychedelic drugs, the spokesman of sexual liberty, the man who attempted to levitate the Pentagon, most of all the king of the Beats. The spectacle that was Ginsberg makes it harder to read his work; now that he is done creating his legend, however, it may be easier to look again at his poetry, understanding that here was a poet who was also a sensitive observer of the history of his brutally eventful times.

The text I wish to reread is Ginsberg's 1961 elegy for his mother, **"Kaddish"**; this essay will examine a presence of brooding importance to the poem, that of Adolf Hitler. Ginsberg was a member of the first generation of young Jewish intellectuals forced to come to grips with the murder of six million Jews. No one of his background, writing an elegy based in part on the Hebrew prayer for the dead, could use the name "Hitler" without evoking evil connotations, evil beyond description. In Ginsberg's case, the evil had a quite personal impact. Naomi Ginsberg, the poet's mother, had come to the United States in 1905 from the western Soviet Union—from the very place, that is, where Heinrich Himmler sent his *Einsatzgruppen*. Naomi's paranoia, in which Hitler plays a prominent role, is not simply a family tragedy. Though tangled with genuinely irrational fears, her dread of the Nazis was, for a Russian Jew, not so irrational at all; Ginsberg recreates her not as a lunatic but as a modern Cassandra. Finally, if we broaden the scope of our reading, we also broaden the scope of Ginsberg's mourning. **"Kaddish"** becomes not just an elegy for a single woman but for all the dead of the Holocaust.

Placing **"Kaddish"** within the context of the Holocaust does not invalidate previous criticism on the text, which has established, I think, a valid groundwork from which to expand. The focus of this criticism, however, has been on the private, emotional impact Naomi Ginsberg's illness visited upon her son.[2] With an important exception, to be examined later in this essay, commentary has been relatively ahistorical; critics have probed Ginsberg's psychology and decoded his metaphysics but have never adequately read the poem as a contingent text, embedded both in the era when Ginsberg composed it and in the era of its remembered history.[3] Yet one aspect of this history, Hitler's Final Solution, is omnipresent within the text; despite few critics having seemed to notice its presence, the Holocaust looms large in **"Kaddish."**[4] First, there is the presence of Adolf Hitler throughout; he is almost a major character, nearly equal to Naomi, Allen, Louis, and Eugene. Just as Hitler was the central force behind the murder of European Jewry, Ginsberg makes him the central force driving Naomi's madness. He first appears early in the "Narrative" section of the poem, the initial portion of which is an account of what Michael Schumacher calls Ginsberg's "most harrowing childhood experience" (17), set in the winter of 1941-42. Naomi convinces her son to take her to a rest home in Lakewood, New Jersey, as a means of escape from her proliferating "enemies." During the trip, as Ginsberg relates it, she details the plot against her. She has seen her mother-in-law

> 'On the fire escape, with poison germs,
> to throw on me—at night—maybe Louis is
> helping her—he's under her power—
> 'I'm your mother, take me to Lakewood'
> (near where Graf Zeppelin had crashed
> before, all Hitler in Explosion) 'where I can
> hide.'
>
> (213)

Ginsberg has Naomi begin her catalog of enemies with her mother-in-law, then move on to her husband Louis; so far, she seems to be suffering the sort of delusions typical of clinical paranoia. Their destination, however, evokes in Ginsberg a peculiar and striking memory: Lakewood, New Jersey, is near Lakehurst, where the airship *Hindenburg* had exploded a few years previously. Ginsberg provides an explanatory sentence in the notes to ***Collected Poems, 1947-1980*** and goes further; quite unnecessarily, he adds the famous photograph of the last moments of the *Hindenburg,* a fireball consuming both the aft section and the fins, which had been decorated with swastikas. On the opposite page (764) is a photograph of an apparently happy Ginsberg family enjoying the New York World's Fair in June 1940. When the volume is open to these pages, the two images confront each other in stark contrast, the smiling family looking out unaware at the terrible, spectacular disaster that Ginsberg has so closely tied to Naomi's next breakdown. And he calls the airship "all Hitler in Explosion." It represents Hitler's regime in the text as it did in fact, a world-traveling embodiment of German technological prowess and advertisement for the New Order. In "**Kaddish**," the *Hindenburg*'s destruction is a small *Götterdämmerung* that foreshadows any number of coming calamities. At the same time, it represents both Naomi's insanity and Nazi Germany; from the start, it is clear that Ginsberg draws his mother and Hitler tightly together.

Having left his mother in a rest home, the young Allen collapses into hopelessness at the probable outcome (and indeed, after he leaves, she will break down completely):

> I left on the next bus to New York—laid
> my head back in the last seat,
> depressed—the worst yet to come?—abandoning
> her, rode in torpor—I was only 12.
> Would she hide in her room and come
> out cheerful for breakfast? Or lock her door
> and stare thru the window for sidestreet
> spies? Listen at keyholes for Hitlerian invisible gas?
>
> (213)

As he remakes the scene, Ginsberg adjusts his age, arriving at one more appropriate for so overwhelming a situation; both Schumacher (17-21) and Barry Miles (30-34) establish that the event took place when he was fifteen, just as the Second World War was beginning for the United States. Here—significantly, as we shall see—he links Hitler with one of Naomi's obsessions, that her enemies are trying to poison her.

Throughout the rest of "**Kaddish**," Ginsberg joins his mother and the Nazi leader more and more closely. He speculates on her thoughts after her release from the hospital in 1943, obviously not much improved:

> May have heard radio gossip thru the
> wires in her head, controlled by 3 big sticks
> left in her back by gangsters in amnesia,
> thru the hospital—caused pain between her
> shoulders—
> Into her head—Roosevelt should know
> her case, she told me—Afraid to kill her,
> now, that the government knew their
> names—traced back to Hitler—
>
> (218)

The *Führer* is now chief of the conspiracy besetting Naomi. Ginsberg also recalls Hitler as the agent behind another of her obsessions, that three "sticks" have been inserted into her back, in order to monitor her thoughts. Hitler has by now thoroughly entered her head. She once "went half mad—Hitler in her room, she saw his mustache in the sink" (220). As she enters her final decline, the plot that Hitler leads against her has so terrorized Naomi that she turns vicious, lashing out against the family itself:

> But started kicking Elanor, and Elanor
> had heart trouble—came upstairs and asked
> her about Spydom for hours,—Elanor
> frazzled. Max away at office, accounting for
> cigar stores till at night.
> 'I am a great woman—am truly a beautiful soul—and because of that they (Hitler,
> Grandma, Hearst, the Capitalists, Franco,
> Daily News, the '20s, Mussolini, the living
> dead) want to shut me up—Buba's the head
> of a spider network—'
>
> (221)

Her madness now reduces itself to its essence, and Hitler entirely takes over her mind: "I banging against her head which saw Radios, Sticks, Hitlers—the gamut of Hallucinations—for real—her own universe—no road that goes elsewhere—to my own—No America, not even a world" (221). Ginsberg here prefigures his farewell in "Hymmnn," in which the *Führer* has become so much a force in Naomi's life that he is like a part of her body:

> farewell
> with your sagging belly
> with your fear of Hitler
> with your mouth of bad short stories
> with your fingers of rotten mandolins
>
> (226)

Her fear is now so strong that it has become a physical, palpable thing, like belly, mouth, and fingers. A kind of *Anschluss* has been launched, successfully; Hitler has taken over Naomi.

Ginsberg suffuses "**Kaddish**" with other evocations of the Holocaust, both direct and oblique;

many others are discussed below. Adolf Hitler, however, is the most important vehicle by which he accomplishes this evocation—the evil Hitler, who oppresses and finally overwhelms his mother. This name functions in the text as a kind of synecdoche: to name Hitler is to name the Holocaust. That his name should have this synecdochic function is inevitable given his historical role as the initiator and driving force behind the Holocaust. More than Pan-Germanism, more than *Lebensraum,* more than the "stab in the back," a homicidal anti-Semitism became the central obsession of Hitler's life from an early date:

> *Today it is not princes and princes' mistresses who haggle and bargain over state borders; it is the inexorable Jew who struggles for his domination over the nations.* No nation can remove this hand from its throat except by the sword. Only the assembled and concentrated might of a national passion rearing up in its strength can defy the international enslavement of peoples. Such a process is and remains a bloody one.
>
> (*Mein Kampf* 651)

At one level, "**Kaddish**" sets up contrasting instances of paranoia, Naomi's and that of her Nazi adversary. Although we should not identify it as a result of mental illness, an identification that might seem to absolve Hitler, his beliefs about Jews had a strongly paranoid cast. He too was beset by a grand conspiracy. In his mind, the Jewish conspirators were capable of the most extraordinary feats of infiltration and sabotage. From their secret meeting places, and with unnatural ingenuity, they reached out to manipulate the whole world, seeking to poison the bloodstream of the German *Volk.* A large part of Naomi's fear actually had its origin in Hitler's fear of her and everyone like her. Given the ultimate outcome of Hitler's paranoia, Naomi's paranoia begins to look less incongruous, and more like a proportional response.

Hitler's name, then, evokes all the actions of the regime of which he was the unquestioned *Führer.* How else does "**Kaddish**" evoke the Holocaust? One way that it does so, paradoxically, is by elegizing a woman whose very existence would have been abhorrent to any right-thinking Nazi—by elegizing, that is, the very sort of person whom the Final Solution was intended to destroy. Ginsberg gives us a Naomi who almost seems to have designed her life to be in every way an affront to the principles of German National Socialism. Before Ginsberg was born, Naomi worked as a school-teacher; as Miles puts it, "her specialty became teaching educationally disadvantaged children, and she was very good at it" (14). This early vocation appears in "**Kaddish**," although Ginsberg describes Naomi's pupils in less decorous language. He imagines her during a period of rebound after an early breakdown; she is relaxing in the country,

> or back teaching school, laughing with idiots, the backward classes—her Russian specialty—morons with dreamy lips, great eyes, thin feet & sicky fingers, swaybacked, rachitic—
>
> great heads pendulous over Alice in Wonderland, a blackboard full of C A T.
>
> Naomi reading patiently, story out of a Communist fairy book—
>
> (214)

The pupils to whom she devotes herself sound, from Ginsberg's description, rather like the extras in any number of Nazi propaganda films warning of the threat such unfortunates posed to the genetic health of the Master Race. One of the first legislative acts Hitler's government passed, on July 14, 1933, was the Law for the Prevention of Genetically Diseased Offspring, which provided for the sterilization of anyone suffering "any of several 'genetic' illnesses, including feeblemindedness, schizophrenia, manicdepressive insanity, genetic epilepsy, Huntington's chorea, genetic blindness or deafness, or severe alcoholism" (Proctor 96). Under the Nazi regime, Naomi's students would first find themselves sterilized and later perhaps subjected to euthanasia. Under an order given by Hitler himself in October 1939, tens of thousands of the mentally retarded and mentally ill were killed in German hospitals, led in groups into what appeared to be showers and dispatched with poison gas. One historian has called this mass euthanasia "the stage rehearsal for the subsequent destruction of Jews, homosexuals, communists, Gypsies, Slavs, and prisoners of war" (Proctor 177), another "a pilot scheme for the [H]olocaust" (Weindling 548). Worse still, Ginsberg has his mother teach her students from a "Communist fairy book." Naomi herself—Jewish, a communist, subject to repeated hospitalization for insanity lasting years at a time—would be a fine candidate for euthanasia.

In Nazi eyes, however, Naomi's greatest capacity to do harm lay in her ability to pass on her dangerous genes; her motherhood is her greatest crime. Indeed, the one figure in the poem who may be more offensive than Naomi, in the Nazi scheme of things, is her son, a leftist, a pacifist, an antiwar activist, an experimenter with numerous alternative lifestyles who celebrates his homosexuality in a very public way. Ginsberg himself is exactly what Hitler was trying to keep from being born. Despite all their myriad problems, Ginsberg praises his mother in terms which suggest that he credits her madness for making him a poet: "O glorious muse that bore me from the womb, gave suck first mystic life & taught me talk and music, from whose pained head I first took Vision" (223). Throughout "**Kaddish**," mother and son together thumb their noses at Nazism.

Given the ubiquitous presence of Adolf Hitler in the text, when Naomi's students appear, the reader may think of a specific act of his regime, the murder of mental patients in the late thirties, which led directly to the first mobile execution vehicles used against Jewish prisoners at Chelmno. In similar ways, this presence summons memories of the Holocaust throughout the text. It has this effect, for instance, when Ginsberg combines it with his mother's fear that her enemies are trying to kill her with poison gas. Ginsberg refers to this fear often, and it often appears to be only the sort of delusion typical of paranoid schizophrenia, merely a symptom of personality breakdown: "and you covered your nose with motheaten fur collar, gas mask against poison sneaked into downtown atmosphere, sprayed by Grandma" (212). Yet when Naomi breaks down at the rest home in Lakewood during the first winter of the war, Ginsberg imagines her listening "at keyholes for Hitlerian invisible gas." One naturally thinks of events then occurring in Europe, where the increasing use of poison gas to kill large numbers of people was a key technical innovation that made the Final Solution possible. Similarly, Ginsberg foregrounds his mother's belief that devices have been inserted in her back during previous stays in the hospital, as she explains to young Allen during the bus ride to Lakewood: "Allen, you don't understand—it's—ever since those 3 big sticks up my back—they did something to me in Hospital, they poisoned me, they want to see me dead—3 big sticks, 3 big sticks" (213). On the surface, her fear again appears to be purely delusional, but in the context, it resonates. Both Ginsberg and his mother believe, rightly, that the treatment to which the hospitals subject her is highly questionable. In an endnote, Ginsberg explains that one of the drugs the doctors gave her—Metrazol, which "had made her fat" (217)—was "[u]sed with insulin for shock treatment in common but now abandoned mental therapy experiments" (766). In the context, we may remember that many thousands of victims of the Holocaust were tortured to death in bogus medical experiments, that German pharmaceutical firms, as Philip Friedman has shown (323-24), used the inmates at Auschwitz as guinea pigs for the testing of new drugs.

But Ginsberg creates his most striking allusion to the Holocaust as he is narrating Naomi's return from the hospital in 1943. The shock treatments have made her more calm; her disease now manifests itself in spells of dreamy abstraction during which she tries to "think beautiful thoughts." Ugly thoughts, however, keep intruding:

> Or a No-shake of her body, disgust—some thought of Buchenwald—some insulin passes thru her head—a grimace nerve shudder at Involuntary (as shudder when I piss)—bad chemical in her cortex—'No don't think of that. He's a rat.'
>
> Naomi: 'And when we die we become an onion, a cabbage, a carrot, or a squash, a vegetable.' I come downtown from Columbia and agree. She reads the Bible, thinks beautiful thoughts all day.
>
> (219)

In a scene set two years before the Allied armies would open the camps, Ginsberg has Naomi perceive that something evil is happening at Buchenwald. The existence of a concentration camp there was no great secret, but the true enormity of its horrors would not be widely known until the war was nearly over. As then-General Eisenhower wrote to George C. Marshall, having visited Buchenwald on April 19, 1945, shortly after his troops liberated it: "We continue to uncover German concentration camps for political prisoners in which conditions of indescribable horror prevail. I have visited one of these myself and I assure you that whatever has been printed on them to date has been understatement" (qtd. in Hackett 11). It also seems significant that Ginsberg follows Naomi's "nerve shudder" with her thoughts on how the dead become vegetables; as she speaks, the ashes of the dead blanket the farmland around the extermination camps in Poland. He continues her odd revelation:

> 'Yesterday I saw God. What did he look like? Well, in the afternoon I climbed up a ladder—he has a cheap cabin in the country, like Monroe, N.Y. the chicken farms in the wood. He was a lonely old man with a white beard.
>
> 'I cooked supper for him. I made him a nice supper—lentil soup, vegetables, bread & butter—miltz—he sat down at the table and ate, he was sad.
>
> 'I told him, Look at all those fightings and killings down there, What's the matter? Why don't you put a stop to it?

ON THE SUBJECT OF...

EDWARD MARSHALL

Edward Marshall's fame stems in large from the poem "Leave the Word Alone," written in 1955 and first published in the *Black Mountain Review.* Ginsberg cited the poem as a source of inspiration for **"Kaddish,"** stating in his introduction to the 1979 Pequod Press printing "I copied [Marshall's] freedom of form, and wildness of line, and homeliness of personal reference." The poem is focused on Marshall's mother—who was committed to an insane asylum when he was still a newborn—and on the madness that he felt in himself. A man of religious passions, Marshall infuses "Leave the Word Alone," with a theological fervor. Despite the recognition it brought him, Marshall did not include "Leave the Word Alone" in either of his first two collections. His first book, *Hellan, Hellan,* a collection of nine poems, was published in 1960; *Transit Gloria* was published in 1967. It was not until 1979 that Marshall's most famous poem appeared in the collection bearing its name.

> 'I try, he said—That's all he could do, he looked tired. He's a bachelor so long, and he likes lentil soup.'
>
> (219)

Ginsberg alludes to the Holocaust itself; he also alludes to the literature in which the Holocaust is represented, as he does here. It is a regular (and inevitable) feature of such literature that God is depicted as dead, wounded, or missing, in some way profoundly defective, or simply inadequate. As George Steiner puts it, writing of Exodus 33.22-23, "God can turn His back." God must do so because he has bungled the Creation: "Perhaps because through some minute, hideous error of design the universe is too large for His surveillance, because somewhere there is a millionth of an inch, it need be no more, out of His line of sight. So He must turn to look there also. When God's back parts are toward man, history is Belsen" ("Survivor" 142). Or God may be a sadist, as the young Elie Wiesel (to whom Steiner's essay is dedicated) decides in Auschwitz: "Why, but why should I bless Him? In every fiber I rebelled. Because He had had thousands of children burned in His pits? Because He kept six crematories working night and day, on Sundays and feast days? Because in His great might He had created Auschwitz, Birkenau, Buna, and so many factories of death?" (*Night* 64). A fellow inmate of Auschwitz, Primo Levi, agrees that God is to be scorned: "Today I think that if for no other reason than that an Auschwitz existed, no one in our age should speak of Providence" (157-58). Ginsberg participates in this developing literary tradition and adds a new element to it: in his mother's recreated vision, God becomes a comical—if sad—nebbish.

Ginsberg has Naomi reveal her eccentric visions—of the dead become produce, of God as an elderly pensioner—immediately after she shudders at "some thought of Buchenwald." He plainly links her visions with the concentration camp; foremost among the "killings" that Naomi wishes God would stop, one feels, are those happening in Buchenwald and all the other camps that Buchenwald represents. Again, as Ginsberg re-creates the scene, the killing is happening as she speaks; the collapse of Germany is still far in the future, yet she knows the truth—and, with the compelling obscurity of a Greek oracle or biblical prophet (note that she "reads the Bible" as she "thinks beautiful thoughts"), she speaks it. Hitler, as Ginsberg has her insisting all along, is an apocalyptic threat. She is labeled a madwoman in large part because, with her three big sticks and poison "sprayed by Grandma," she is genuinely delusional, but she does share the label with the prophets throughout human history whose visions were more than normal, workaday people could stand, although the visions were true.

Ginsberg has constructed his poem in a way that permits us to explain her vision, the awareness of events in Buchenwald he grants her, in either rational or occult terms. The choice is left to the reader. If one prefers the rational, one need only note that the Nazis did not entirely succeed in keeping the Final Solution a secret; Fortress Europe was not leakproof. The facts were available in the United States, although as Deborah E. Lipstadt demonstrates in her study of contemporary press reactions to the Holocaust, they were widely disregarded as exaggerations or propaganda lies: "Over the course of the years to 1945 the details would multiply, but the doubts would never be completely erased." In June 1942, for instance—a year before Naomi and Allen have the conversation about God in his loft—the Polish government-in-exile in London released an accurate report of what was happening to Jews on its soil; newspapers printed accounts, but only short ones buried far from page 1. The incredulity was durable:

> By early in the Nazis' rule a pattern had emerged which would characterize the reaction of the press as well as the public to the entire Nazi persecution. Americans did not doubt that things were difficult for the Jews but seemed reluctant to believe that they were as bad as reporters on the scene claimed. Whether the story was of Jewish judges being dragged from their courtrooms or Jews being rounded up and shot en masse, the news was greeted with both horror and disbelief, condemnation and skepticism.
>
> (38-39)

Paul Fussell, among others, blames this skepticism on the widespread mistrust of the press that the propaganda of the First World War had created: "No one can calculate the number of Jews who died in the Second War because of the ridicule during the twenties and thirties of Allied propaganda about Belgian nuns violated and children sadistically used. In a climate of widespread skepticism about any further atrocity stories, most people refused fully to credit reports of the concentration camps until ocular evidence compelled belief and it was too late" (316). Only a few took the reports as seriously as they deserved to be taken. To tell the truth about what was happening to the Jews of Europe was to risk being thought gullible, alarmist, or perhaps insane.

The awareness of the Holocaust Ginsberg accords his mother has a rational explanation, yet he does appear to add an element of occult knowledge; he frames her understanding so that it seems preternatural. At some level, her madness, and its brutal "treatment," makes her sensitive to the truth. Her "thought of Buchenwald" may also be a "bad chemical in her cortex" or a moment when "some insulin passes thru her head." The relationship between madness and insight is also clear when Hitler makes one of his last appearances in the text:

> only to have known the weird ideas of Hitler at
> the door, the wires in her head, the three
> big sticks
> rammed down her back, the voices in the ceiling
> shrieking out her ugly early lays for 30
> years,
> only to have seen the time-jumps, memory
> lapse, the crash of wars, the roar and silence
> of a vast electric shock . . .
>
> (225)

In Ginsberg's construction, the "vast electric shock" has somehow made Naomi exceptionally sensitive to Hitler and "the crash of wars," and it has made her capable of "time-jumps." It has enabled her to transcend what George Steiner calls the "time relation" (the term appears in the same essay that Stingo ponders in *Sophie's Choice* as he recalls the life he led—safely ensconced at Duke—at the same time that Sophie was enduring Auschwitz [Styron 216]). "One of the things I cannot grasp," Steiner admits, "though I have often written about them, trying to get them into some kind of bearable perspective, is the time relation." While the death camps were running,

> the overwhelming plurality of human beings, two miles away on the Polish farms, five thousand miles away in New York, were sleeping or eating or going to a film or making love or worrying about the dentist. This is where my imagination balks. The two orders of simultaneous experience are so different, so irreconcilable to any common norm of human values, their coexistence is so hideous a paradox—Treblinka *is* both because some men have built it and almost all other men let it be—that I puzzle over time.
>
> ("Postscript" 156)

The reason few in the Allied countries believed contemporary reports of the Holocaust, Steiner continues, may have been

> the sheer incapacity of the "normal" mind to imagine and hence give active belief to the enormities of the circumstance and the need. Even those—and they may have been few—who came to believe that the news out of eastern Europe was authentic, that millions of human beings were being methodically tortured and gassed in the middle of the twentieth century, did so at some abstract remove, as we might believe a piece of theological doctrine or an historical occurrence far in the past. The belief did not relate.
>
> (158)

Not so for the Naomi of "**Kaddish**"; her insanity breaks down barriers of time and space. It seems to enable her to see what is happening in Europe. Perhaps, then, Ginsberg makes the result also a cause, and the vision her insanity gives her also makes her more insane. Perhaps he constructs her insanity as a sympathetic response to the plight of the Jews of Europe, caught in the teeth of an insane ideology—an ideology that, to note only one aspect of its lunacy, saw the same Jewish conspiracy behind both international finance capitalism and Soviet communism.

"**Kaddish**," then, represents more than a family tragedy; Naomi is not just a victim of mental disease but is a Cassandra figure, an unheeded prophet. By making her a seer ("from whose pained head I first took Vision"), the poem again participates in the evolving tradition of literature about the Holocaust, in which the unheeded warning has become a kind of topos. It appears in Thomas Keneally's *Schindler's List* in the figure of Bachner the pharmacist, who is deported with a group of Cracow Jews to a camp, escapes, and returns to tell those still in the ghetto that the deportees have all been gassed: "All the way down Lwówska and into the streets behind Plac Zgody he carried his story. He had seen the final horror, he said. He was mad-eyed, and in his brief absence his hair had silvered" (135). He is greeted with skepticism. An unheeded warning figures in Art Spiegelman's *Maus,* when the family watches Anja's grandparents taken away to, they think, Theresienstadt; the grandparents will actually go immediately to the gas chambers at Auschwitz. The family has been warned. "When did you first hear about Auschwitz?" Art asks. "Right away we heard," Vladek replies; "even from there—from that other world—people came back and told us. But we didn't believe" (88).

In Aharon Appelfeld's *Badenheim 1939,* disbelief is the major response to the opening moves of the Final Solution. Insanity is another. Most of the temporary residents of Badenheim, faced with deportation to Poland (and ultimately to the death camps, though they do not know this), try to look on the bright side. Salo the salesman tells himself and others that "a man should broaden his horizons. Ever since he was a boy he had loved traveling" (97). Some characters, though, respond by losing their sanity, like the "half-Jewish waitress" who mutilates herself (48-50), or Trude, "haunted by a hidden fear, not her own," or her husband Martin, "infected by her hallucinations" (10-11). While the rest of the town consumes the drugs looted from his pharmacy, "Martin's sorrow knew no bounds"; however, "his was a voice calling in the wilderness" (108). Unheeded warnings, taken as evidence of insanity, appear recurrently in Elie Wiesel's *Night.* One is delivered by a woman on the train to Auschwitz. She begins to scream, "Look! Look at it! Fire! A terrible fire!" The others attempt to ignore her: "Powerless to still our own anguish, we tried to console ourselves: 'She's mad, poor soul'" (22-23). Another is delivered by Moshe the Beadle, who, like Bachner, has escaped certain death at the hands of the Nazis:

> Through long days and nights, he went from one Jewish house to another, telling the story of Malka, the young girl who had taken three days to die, and of Tobias, the tailor, who had begged to be killed before his sons. . . .
>
> Moshe had changed. There was no longer any joy in his eyes. He no longer sang. He no longer talked to me of God or of the cabbala, but only of what he had seen. People refused not only to believe his stories, but even to listen to them.
>
> "He's just trying to make us pity him. What an imagination he has!" they said. Or even: "Poor fellow. He's gone mad."
>
> (4-5)

So, too, is Naomi considered mad. In Wiesel's view, however, the truly devastating insanity of the Holocaust emerged not in its victims. In "A Plea for the Dead," Wiesel discerns it in those outside Hitler's empire (he names Roosevelt, Churchill, Eisenhower, and the Pope) who learned of the killing and did nothing to stop it: "I take my head in my hands and I think: it is insanity, that is the explanation, the only conceivable one. When so great a number of men carry their indifference to such an extreme, it becomes sickness, it resembles madness" (191). Naomi's insanity, as Ginsberg constructs it, may be a sympathetic response; it may suggest powers of prophecy. Wiesel's comment suggests still another possibility: that in the historical situation in which the poet and his mother find themselves, the conventional definitions of "sane" and "insane" may no longer apply. The entire world, it seems, is no longer sane—and sanity, as Ginsberg suggests, can be "a trick of agreement" (212). It may not be necessary to choose among the above options to account, within the context of the poem, for Naomi's madness; all operate at one point or another in **"Kaddish."** Nor do I mean to suggest that her insanity is in any way beneficial or is anything but a disaster for the Ginsberg family. Still, she is more than merely insane; Ginsberg too carefully fuses the family's disaster to a global one.

At this point, a qualification is necessary. It will, however, lead to my final, and perhaps most important, point: that the poem may be seen as a Kaddish for all the dead of the Holocaust, all the victims of insanity. One might object that to focus closely on Naomi's temporal perspective, as the poem constructs it, is to miss the point; the crucial temporality of **"Kaddish"** is not that of Naomi looking forward, into a catastrophe that will not be fully revealed for some time, but of her son looking back. Summoning the Holocaust from the vantage of the late 1950s, that is, Ginsberg looks back on events that have been investigated and widely publicized. The presence of Adolf Hitler in his poem says less about Naomi than about the poet and his own cultural and emotional position as—to use George Steiner's phrase—a kind of survivor.

Understanding the temporality of **"Kaddish,"** however, is not a matter of choosing one or the other, the mother's notional view of the future or the son's poetic view of the past. The two work together, both the poet and his subject cooperating in the task of grieving. An analogy that could clarify how these two temporal viewpoints work together to mourn both Naomi and the victims of the Holocaust may be found in Leon Wieseltier's recent *Kaddish,* his record of his year of ritual mourning for his father. Immersing himself in centuries of rabbinic commentary on the Mourner's Kaddish, Wieseltier finds a thread that appeals to him, that "the dead are in need of spiritual rescue; and that the agent of spiritual rescue is the son; and that the instrument of spiritual rescue is prayer, notably the kaddish" (127). Like Ginsberg, he has his doubts. "I do not believe that I can save you," he tells his dead father; still, "I am your son and I will persevere" (280). His year of ritual grief is a culmination of the regular reversal that takes place in the life of a family, "when the parent becomes the child and the child becomes the parent. . . . I think that kaddish is the perfect symbol of such a reversal. Suddenly the chain of transmission turns around. *He* needs *me*" (174). Wieseltier draws a similar but broader analogy between the Mourner's Kaddish and the keeping of tradition and history: "The son's redemption of the dead father, the dead father's protection by the son: is this not an allegory for the power of the present over the past? For the past is at the mercy of the present. The present can condemn the past to oblivion or obscurity" (144). It seems apt that Wieseltier should thus broaden his analogy, since his family has not lost only one member. His thoughts turn often to his close relatives on both sides of the family who were murdered by the Nazis, who did not have, as his mother puts it, "a proper end" (150). His mourning expands to include them; their names will be engraved on his father's and, eventually, his mother's tombstones.

Ginsberg, too, makes himself custodian of the past, in two senses: Naomi lives on in his poem, and so do Naomi's memories. In spite of his disbelief in the consolations of formal religion, he takes on the traditional work of chanting the departed soul out of Gehenna, in Naomi's case the Gehenna of insanity. If only in the context of the poem, he at least temporarily succeeds: "Now wear your nakedness forever, white flowers in your hair, your marriage sealed behind the sky" (223). The reversal that Wieseltier embraces takes place very early in "**Kaddish**"; when Ginsberg is still an adolescent, his mother is already dependent on him. By the end of her life, she is helpless, and Ginsberg has largely taken over the role of guardian (a role abandoned by her husband, Louis). He is even, in places, a parent, scolding her, consoling her, trying to make her behave. Yet his ascendancy is not complete; as noted, he thanks her for making him a poet. In important ways, their relationship is not a matter of dependence or guardianship. They form, rather, an alliance. He remembers his mother placing an extraordinary trust in him, greater than the trust one would normally expect a mother to have in her son—greater because her mind is not normal. Ginsberg seems the only member of the family whom Naomi trusts not to belong to the grand conspiracy that besets her; indeed, she relies on his protection against the conspiracy. We have seen what similar personalities they exhibit in "**Kaddish**," their lives structured to enact ideologies that are the direct opposites of Nazism. The alliance continues after her death. By foregrounding her dread of Hitler—her vision of what Hitler will do—he joins her sadness to his own.

At least one critic has read "**Kaddish**" as an expression of a wider grief, and at this point his analysis is pertinent; in an essay written when the poem first appeared, Allen Grossman sees, in Ginsberg's lament for his mother, an inclusive sense of loss. Grossman further locates the origin of this loss in the Holocaust, if briefly. "In America, which did not experience the Second World War on its own soil," he argues, "the Jew may indeed be the proper interpreter of horror." For Ginsberg, "the extreme situation, the American analogy of the bombed city and the concentration camp, is mental illness and the horrors of private life" (157-58). Grossman reads the work of Ginsberg and others of his generation as arising directly from recent catastrophes:

> The characteristic literary posture of the postwar poet in America is that of the survivor—a man who is not quite certain that he is not in fact dead. It is here that the Jew as a symbolic figure takes on his true centrality. The position can be stated hypothetically from the point of view of a European survivor who has made the Stygian crossing to America: "Since so many like me died, and since my survival is an unaccountable accident, how can I be certain that I did not myself die and that America is not in fact Hell, as indeed all of the social critics say it is?" Ginsberg's poetry is the poetry of *a terminal cultural situation.* It is a Jewish poetry because the Jew is a symbolic representative of man overthrown by history.
>
> (153)

In Grossman's reading, Ginsberg represents the arrival of this "terminal cultural situation" in Naomi's utter ruin and death. She is not simply the poet's mother; she is a highly inclusive symbol. Naomi "is Ginsberg's version of the Jewish mother and, simultaneously, of the Shechinah, the wandering soul of Israel herself. Ginsberg is the last dutiful son of Israel reciting Kaddish at the grave of his mother and of the symbolic image of his people" (154). Indeed, as Norman Finkelstein argues, Grossman considers Ginsberg "a kinsman," at least "in terms of cultural situation." In part, Finkelstein contends, Grossman is motivated by his conviction that "poetry is one of the few resources left that may help us understand the Shoah, along with the other catastrophes of the twentieth century." Further, at the time that he reviewed **"Kaddish,"** Grossman felt himself "a young poet called into utterance after the devastation of World War II and the Shoah, who must somehow speak for the dead."[5]

Ginsberg, too, speaks for the dead, for the six million as well as for his mother. Further, as the custodian of Naomi's memories, Ginsberg evokes both the Holocaust and the world that it destroyed, the world of her childhood. He alludes often to Russia, and near the end of the poem he recalls her "lone in Long Island" at the close of her life, "her brothers dead in Riverside or Russia" (225). In the context, we can read "brothers" in the more general sense of "brethren" or "comrades." Our perception of Ginsberg and Naomi as together mourning the dead of the Holocaust gains strength if we look closely at what happened to the childhood world she had left in 1905. In closing, it is worthwhile to pause and remember that this world—the place where the sequence of memory in **"Kaddish"** has its temporal starting point—was systematically destroyed, and with unerring brutality. Reading and rereading **"Kaddish,"** we need to keep in mind (as her son certainly does) who Naomi Ginsberg was: a Jewish communist born and partly raised in the western Soviet Union, where the behavior of the Nazis reached its most feral depths.

Naomi was from the small town of Nevel; her family left first for Vitebsk, then for the New World, to escape—as seems appropriate—a pogrom. The German *Wehrmacht* occupied the region in early summer 1941; close behind the army followed *Einsatzgruppe* B. It seems unlikely that Ginsberg knew the precise details of what followed, but the fate of Nevel was repeated hundreds of times across the Soviet Union. In the extant communications from the *Einsatzgruppen* to headquarters in Berlin (preserved in the Bundesarchiv in Germany), Nevel first appears in a report dated September 4, 1941:

> Sonderkommando 7a carried out another action in Nevel against the Jews, in which 74 persons were shot. . . .
>
> The action was carried out as a punitive measure for arson committed by Jews in Nevel. According to the voluntary confession of many Jews, many members of that race participated in these arsons which destroyed the center of the town which was only slightly damaged during the fighting.
>
> (Arad et al. 122)

One wonders what actually happened; who, for instance, set the fires, and what was involved in extracting the "voluntary confession." Unfortunately, the Nazis are nearly our only source of information, an exception being some otherwise nameless "Russian witnesses of mass shootings in Nevel," located by Daniel Romanovsky, who "recall with respect how Jewish men met death from Nazi executioners without a single sound or plea for mercy, standing straight and looking their murderers in the eye" (247). Nevel did not survive the month of September. One study of the *Einsatzgruppen* reports to headquarters uses Nevel as an example of the "more heinous crimes mentioned throughout the reports. These were the occasions when the entire Jewish and/or non-Jewish population of a village was killed and/or the whole village was then burned down" (Headland 61). The actual report—dated September 23, 1941, a few months before Naomi's catastrophic breakdown in Lakewood—is terse:

> In the Nevel ghetto which was set up approximately 3 km outside the city and which comprised several wooden houses, scabies broke out according to the diagnosis of a German doctor. In order to prevent further contagion, 640 Jews were liquidated and the houses burned down.
>
> (Arad et al. 152)

Nevel was, in short, a Soviet Lidice—with some important differences. Unlike Lidice, the destruction of Nevel went unnoticed; no songs were composed, no streets renamed, no propaganda issued in its memory. No one mourned. From Nevel, no one was deported to a camp, as the women were from Lidice, and the children, of course, were not sent to the Reich to be raised as Aryans. Every Jew died. There were no known survivors—unless one counts the farsighted Livergant family, whose second-born was Naomi. She and her son had ample reason to mourn together.

Notes

I wish to thank Michael Hoffman for his generosity in reading earlier versions of this essay and providing valuable insights.

1. *Time* described Ginsberg as the "quintessential beatnik poet" who "first raged into public view in 1956 with *Howl,* a profane tirade that railed against a conformist society and dealt, rather graphically, with his homosexuality" ("Milestones" 31). *Newsweek* recalled *Howl* as the poem that "made him notorious," one that seemed, when it first appeared, "to be a Dantesque tour of the Eisenhower era's scary, repressed subconscious: buggery, blasphemy, benzedrine, be-bop and the bomb" (Gates 60). While the two newsweeklies were fairly neutral toward Ginsberg's work, *Rolling Stone* was wholly laudatory, devoting most of an issue to elegy. Yet here, too, much of the strength of the poetry lies in his genius for unabashed revelation: "More than anything . . . Ginsberg was someone who summoned the bravery to speak hidden truths about unspeakable things" (Gilmore 36).

2. Critical attention has had this focus from the start. In an essay published on the first appearance of "Kaddish," for instance, Paul Carroll helped set the tone that continues to prevail: "Allen Ginsberg's real accomplishments as a poet do not come from his public image or his political and social poems. The great Ginsberg poems are private" (94).

3. For instance, James Breslin psychoanalyzes Ginsberg. He sees great value in *Howl* and "Kaddish" in part because "these poems derive from deep, long-standing private conflicts in Ginsberg—conflicts that ultimately stem from his ambivalent attachment to his mother" (67). Other critics may begin by interrogating Ginsberg's inner states and expand to more cosmic issues. Thomas F. Merrill reads "Kaddish" as both an act of mourning and a vehicle for fierce eschatological speculation: "because of the inevitable interplay between the confident assurance of the 'Mourner's Kaddish' of Reform Judaism and Ginsberg's reworking of the litany, there is great opportunity for irony of the most relevant sort: the irony of the certainty of the official prayer placed against the anguished uncertainty of humanity thrown, in the twentieth century, into a secularized world" (71).

4. Not that critics have totally ignored the historicity of "Kaddish"; one scarcely could, given its elaborate network of allusions to the public events of Naomi's lifetime. The central fact around which Ginsberg weaves this network is Naomi's communism. The allusions play a role in M. L. Rosenthal's reading of "Kaddish": "Clearly, Naomi's unstable personality found the pressures of the 1930s unbearable"; the "Hitler terror" and the "hysterical obsessions with 'Trotskyism'" had an impact on her mental health "that should not be discounted" (103). Rosenthal is surely correct that Naomi's politics exacerbated her paranoia; a communist in the age of Stalin lived in a very frightening world. Naomi's political fears are sometimes joined with what is more clearly clinical insanity: "The enemies approach—what poisons? Tape recorders? FBI? Zhdanov hiding behind the counter? Trotsky mixing rat bacteria in the back of the store?" (216). There are various shades of paranoia in "Kaddish," levels of fear in Naomi that range from the wildly irrational to the rather sensible. Ginsberg calls attention to the difficulty of defining whether fear is irrational or not for one of Naomi's political persuasion when he lists the "accumulations of life" that have worn her out. He includes "your Communism—'Paranoia' into hospitals" (211), the quotation marks seeming to ask whether she had been entirely paranoid. Although she shared the fear with millions, it was not rational for her to fear an international conspiracy of left-deviationist Trotskyite saboteurs, wreckers, and counterrevolutionaries, to adopt the febrile language of the time. Yet among Naomi's enemies listed above, Trotsky and Zhdanov are joined with the FBI; for an immigrant communist to fear federal law enforcement, especially J. Edgar Hoover's FBI, may often have been simply prudent. And for a Jewish communist to fear Hitler, even though he was never closer than an ocean away, exhibits a soundness of judgment that sadly was not as common as it might have been.

5. Norman Finkelstein, *Not One of Them in Place: Modern Poetry and Jewish-American Identity.* I am grateful to the author for letting me see this work in manuscript form.

Works Cited

Appelfeld, Aharon. *Badenheim 1939.* Trans. Dalya Bilu. Boston: Godine, 1980.

Arad, Yitzhak, Shmuel Krakowski, and Shmuel Spector, eds. *The Einsatzgruppen Reports: Selections from the Dispatches of the Nazi Death Squads' Campaign Against the Jews, July 1941-January 1943.* New York: Holocaust Library, 1989.

Breslin, James. "Allen Ginsberg: The Origins of *Howl* and *Kaddish.*" 1977. *The Beats: Essays in Criticism.* Ed. Lee Bartlett. Jefferson, N.C.: McFarland, 1981. 66-89.

Carroll, Paul. "The Pentecostal Poems of *Kaddish.*" *On the Poetry of Allen Ginsberg.* Ed. Lewis Hyde. Ann Arbor: U of Michigan P, 1984. 94-95.

Finkelstein, Norman. *Not One of Them in Place: Modern Poetry and Jewish-American Identity.* Albany: State U of New York P, 2001.

Friedman, Philip. "Crimes in the Name of 'Science.'" *Roads to Extinction: Essays on the Holocaust.* Ed. Ada June Friedman. New York: Jewish Publication Society of America, 1980. 322-32.

Fussell, Paul. *The Great War and Modern Memory.* New York: Oxford UP, 1975.

Gates, David. "'Holy the Bop Apocalypse!': Allen Ginsberg, American Poet, 1926-1997." *Newsweek* 14 Apr. 1997: 60.

Gilmore, Mikal. "Allen Ginsberg, 1926-1997." *Rolling Stone* 29 May 1997: 34+.

Ginsberg, Allen. "Kaddish." 1961. *Collected Poems, 1947-1980.* New York: Harper, 1984. 209-27.

Grossman, Allen. "The Jew as an American Poet: The Instance of Ginsberg." 1962. *The Long Schoolroom: Lessons in the Bitter Logic of the Poetic Principle.* Ann Arbor: U of Michigan P, 1997. 150-58.

Hackett, David A., ed. *The Buchenwald Report.* Boulder, CO: Westview, 1995.

Headland, Ronald. *Messages of Murder: A Study of the Reports of the Einsatzgruppen of the Security Police and the Security Service, 1941-43.* Cranbury, N.J.: Associated University Presses, 1992.

Hitler, Adolf. *Mein Kampf.* 1925. Trans. Ralph Manheim. Boston: Houghton, 1943.

Keneally, Thomas. *Schindler's List.* 1982. New York: Simon, 1993.

Levi, Primo. *Survival in Auschwitz: The Nazi Assault on Humanity.* 1958. Trans. Stuart Woolf. New York: Simon, 1996.

Lipstadt, Deborah E. *Beyond Belief: The American Press and the Coming of the Holocaust, 1933-1945.* New York: Free, 1986.

Merrill, Thomas F. *Allen Ginsberg.* Rev. ed. Twayne's United States Authors Ser. 161. Boston: Twayne, 1988.

Miles, Barry. *Ginsberg: A Biography.* London: Viking, 1990.

"Milestones." *Time* 14 Apr. 1997: 31.

Proctor, Robert N. *Racial Hygiene: Medicine under the Nazis.* Cambridge, MA: Harvard UP, 1988.

Romanovsky, Daniel. "Soviet Jews under Nazi Occupation in Northeastern Belarus and Western Russia." *Bitter Legacy: Confronting the Holocaust in the USSR.* Ed. Zvi Gitelman. Bloomington: Indiana UP, 1997. 230-52.

Rosenthal, M. L., ed. *The New Poets: American and British Poetry since World War II.* New York: Oxford UP, 1967.

Schumacher, Michael. *Dharma Lion: A Critical Biography of Allen Ginsberg.* New York: St. Martin's, 1992.

Spiegelman, Art. *Maus: A Survivor's Tale. My Father Bleeds History.* New York: Pantheon, 1986.

Steiner, George. "A Kind of Survivor." *Language and Silence: Essays on Language, Literature, and the Inhuman.* New York: Atheneum, 1967. 140-54.

———. "Postscript." *Language and Silence* 155-68.

Styron, William. *Sophie's Choice.* New York: Random, 1979.

Weindling, Paul. *Health, Race and German Politics between National Unification and Nazism, 1870-1945.* Cambridge: Cambridge UP, 1989.

Wiesel, Elie. *Night.* 1958. Trans. Stella Rodway. New York: Bantam, 1982.

———. "A Plea for the Dead." *Legends of Our Time.* New York: Holt, 1968. 174-97.

Wieseltier, Leon. *Kaddish.* New York: Knopf, 1998.

Reality Sandwiches: 1953-1960

THOMAS S. MERRILL (ESSAY DATE 1981)

SOURCE: Merrill, Thomas S. "Allen Ginsberg's *Reality Sandwiches.*" In *The Beats: Essays in Criticism,* edited by Lee Bartlett, pp. 90-106. Jefferson, N.C.: McFarland, 1981.

In the following essay, Merrill analyzes the poems collected in Reality Sandwiches.

I The Menu

Ginsberg's poem **"On Burroughs' Work"** concludes with the stanza:

> A naked lunch is natural to us.
> we eat reality sandwiches.
> But allegories are so much lettuce.
> Don't hide the madness
>
> [***Reality Sandwiches*** 40].

The title of this fourth volume of collected poems thus pays homage to two of his most influential friends: Jack Kerouac, who suggested "Naked Lunch" as an appropriate title for Burroughs' novel, and, of course, Burroughs himself. Burroughs contends that "[*Naked Lunch*] means exactly what the words say: NAKED Lunch—a frozen moment when everyone sees what is on the end of every fork."[1] ***Reality Sandwiches*** presumes to exhibit twenty-nine such "frozen moments" that span a full seven years of Ginsberg's development (1953-60).

Both Ginsberg's and Burroughs' titles promise the reader a taste of pure reality and demand that he savor its sweetness and bitterness with a vital palate. Both writers presume to serve an Existential feast devoid of hypocritical condiments which might disguise "the madness." In either case, the program is ambitious and suggests the radical, synesthetic entreaty that Ginsberg once made to Peter Orlovsky when he dedicated ***Kaddish and Other Poems*** to him: "Taste my mouth in your ear."

The reader gets a good taste of Ginsberg's mouth in his ear in this collection, which, as usual, is uninhibitedly and often flamboyantly honest. As a poetic method, unadulterated honesty is hardly a new departure for Ginsberg. The limits to which honesty have led him are marked by jail sentences, obscenity trials, and a "second-rate creep image that was interpreted to the public via mass media."[2] Honesty has also led him to the lonely regions of isolation where death and self struggle to negotiate a viable program of being. There is much discussion in these poems of what Heidegger would have called the "authentic" versus the "inauthentic" life as well as some further jousting with the problem of Death. The menu is varied and the service is erratic; but, true to his word, Ginsberg is sparing with the lettuce in his sandwiches and the taste of madness is strong.

II Illuminations

The initial poem, **"My Alba"** (7), is an experiment within traditional forms which bears, as do so many of Ginsberg's early verses, a strong affinity to the style of William Carlos Williams. The subject is wasted time, and the method is the catalogue. Williams' poem, *"Le Médecin malgré Lui,"* might easily stand as the model; but Ginsberg thrusts beyond the structural ennui of *"Le*

Médecin" to arrive at a description of a human being poised for a spring into authentic existence. It is a morning song that anticipates an awakening. The poet seems to be undergoing the shock of discovering that his life has been non-being; his metaphor is the paraphernalia of the business office. His life is not measured in coffee spoons, but worse: "Sliderule and number / machine on a desk / autographed triplicate / synopsis and taxes. . . ." This catalogue documents a wasted "five years in Manhattan / life decaying / talent a blank."

One successful technique is the sense of boredom that has been created by the incessant run-on lines and by the complete avoidance of punctuation of any kind. The result of the lack of punctuation is an abundance of suggestive liaisons which occur between thought patterns: ". . . Manhattan / life decaying . . . blank / talking disconnected / patient . . . mental / sliderule. . . ." The feeling that Ginsberg creates and sustains by the use and the structure of language in the body of the poem is decisive in making possible the structural tension that the title lends to the entire poem. The juxtaposition of the awakening, implicit in the title "**My Alba**," with the ostentatiously banal poem which follows is an example of Ginsberg's borrowing of Williams' typical method of creating significance from structure.

As reinforcement to the structural significance of the poem, Ginsberg also adds a final note of Existential urgency: "I am damned to Hell what / alarmclock is ringing." By this time, the reader realizes that the preceding stanzas have attempted to chart the precincts of Hell and that the ringing of the alarm clock is the sudden awareness of a crisis. The "autographed triplicate / synopsis" is a carbon-copy existence; it is inauthentic, and it is time to awaken to a naked breakfast.

The penultimate stage of illumination that this poem suggests reminds the reader of traditional experiences of religious regeneration in which one is "reborn" to a new understanding of existence. The second selection in this volume, a Zen poem called "**Sakyamuni Coming Out from the Mountain**," deals with the difficulty of being twice-born: "how painful to be born again / wearing a fine beard, / reentering the world" (10).

The form of this poem seems to be once again derivative from the experiments of William Carlos Williams with the three-step, variable foot line in *Paterson, The Desert Music and Other Poems,* and *Journey to Love.* A single specimen from *Paterson II* suffices to illustrate the similarity:

> The descent beckons
> as the ascent beckoned
> Memory is a kind
> of accomplishment
> a sort of renewal
> even
> an initiation . . .[3]

The obvious characteristics of this style are that each of the three steps is intended to be equal and that, after each step down, there is a caesural pause. The effect is rather like syncopation; the lines come, as John Ciardi has suggested, just "off the beat" of iambic pentameter, and they follow the general rhythmic patterns of modern jazz.[4] For Williams, the method was "a way of escaping the formlessness of free verse,"[5] and the intention was also presumably Ginsberg's. At the same time, however, the Oriental flavor of the poem was an additional concern for Ginsberg, and one could easily make a case for the form's congeniality with *haiku.*

Liang-k'ai was a painter of the Sung dynasty (959-1279), and his work represents a relationship between man and nature which ignores priorities. In other words, his landscapes depict "a world to which man belongs but which he does not dominate."[6] This attitude does much to explain the final declaration of Ginsberg's poem: "humility is beatness / before the absolute World," which in turn provides a nexus to Heidegger's thesis that the predicament of man is that he has been "thrown" into a world with which he must come to terms. Hence, the poem is rich in philosophical possibilities which emerge from a matrix of Taoism, Zen, Beatness, and Existentialism.

The theme of the aimless life, so characteristic of Zen thought, is presented in the opening description of Arhat who "drags his bare feet / out of a cave . . . wearing a fine beard, / unhappy hands / clasped to his naked breast . . . faltering / into the bushes by a stream" (9). The issue of priority between man and nature is then introduced: "all things inanimate / but his intelligence." The function of the intelligence within the context of the Zen attitude is not to separate man from nature but to perform as a receptor of momentary glimpses—glimpses, perhaps, into authentic Being which testify to man's oneness with the world. Humility (Beatness) begins to emerge in the reader's mind as a state whereby a man realizes that he is nothing special in the face of "the absolute World." This recognition seems to be the denouement that the narrative poem offers.

Arhat has been seeking Heaven "under a mountain of stone," and in typical Zen fashion he has "sat thinking" (not imposing his thoughts upon nature, but passively awaiting an understanding) until an awakening occurs. He realizes that "the land of blessedness exists / in the imagination." This realization is analogous to the ringing of an alarm clock, and Arhat is reborn; his "inauthentic" existence is authenticized and he is made humble:

> he knows nothing
>   like a god:
>   shaken
> meek wretch—
>
> [10]

In essence, Ginsberg's poem supplies an answer to one of the fundamental questions that Existentialism poses:

> . . . are we disclosed to ourselves as existents who are always already in a world—a world with which we are concerned and involved in all kinds of ways—so that it is out of this total situation that we must seek after whatever understanding of Being may be possible for us; or are we, as the traditional Western philosophy has been inclined to regard us, primarily thinking subjects, before whom there is spread out for our inspection a world, and this world is to be understood in a genuine way only along the lines of detached theoretical inquiry?[7]

Clearly, "beatness" or "humility" understands only the first option.

"Over Kansas" (42) is another poem which describes a similar illumination, but a contemporary American backdrop replaces the misty forests and lonely rocks of the Sung landscape painters. The situation of the poem is an airplane journey across the United States, one that becomes, in the poet's consciousness, a subjective journey that takes him from ego-less non-being, through a vision of Kansas at night, to a form of self-realization. Two implicit themes seem to embrace in the consummation of this poem: death and nakedness. Death haunts the stanzas in the several references to "death insurance by machine" and the hypothetical poet below in Kansas who is "Someone who should collect / my insurance!" More profoundly, however, death enters the meditations of the traveler as he ponders the fact that he is "Travelling thru the dark void / over Kansas yet moving nowhere / in the dark void of the soul." Death is also present in his mind when he muses that "Not even the human / imagination satisfied / the endless emptiness of the soul."

Clearly, this latter appreciation of death is more than biological: it is a death bred of a man's forgetfulness of what it means to be. Hence, the poem takes an Existential turn which recognizes that anxiety over death brings a new seriousness to life which awakens one to an authentic life. The poet moves from the airport waiting room crowded with businessmen to the dark, isolated sky above "imaginary plains / I never made afoot." He finds himself in "the dark void" above the ground where men actually live, breathe, make love, and "collect the streets and mountain tops / for storage in . . . [their] memory." The illumination comes "in a sudden glimpse" by the poet of his own non-being in the airplane ("me being no one in the air / nothing but clouds in the moonlight . . ."), while underneath him living creatures copulate.

The solution to the dilemma of being versus non-being is summed up in Ginsberg's ubiquitous metaphor: nakedness. All of his poetry is about nakedness, he is always ready to assert; but precisely what "nakedness" means is rarely explained. In this poem, for example, he says, "Nakedness must come again—not sex, / but some naked isolation." This statement seems to suggest an unqualified openness to being, but the sexual suggestiveness of the term is certainly overt in such expressions as "that football boy / in sunny yellow lovesuit. . . ." The reader is also told that "the starry world below [Hollywood]" also expresses nakedness:

> that craving, that glory
> that applause—leisure, mind,
> appetite for dreams, bodies,
> travels: appetite for the real,
> created by the mind
> and kissed in coitus—
> that craving, that melting!

But this is merely an expression of nakedness, imaginary because it is "created by the mind." It is only an appetite for nakedness rather than the real thing, and the reader is immediately informed that "Not even the imagination satisfies / the endless emptiness of the soul."

Then comes the official illumination over Hutchinson, Kansas, where the poet peers beyond his own reflection in the window ("bald businessman with hornrims") and sees a "spectral skeleton of electricity"

> illuminated nervous system
> floating on the void out
> of central brainplant powerhouse
> running into heavens' starlight
> overhead.

The vision is an emblem, presumably. The lights of Hutchinson emanating out of a "central brainplant powerhouse" (the human mind) "floating on the void." Because this "illuminated nervous system" is seen by the poet to be "running into heavens' starlight / overhead," it seems apparent that "the vision" reveals the potentiality of the human imagination to connect the heavens and this world—in a word, mysticism.

What the reader is up against, then, is the familiar credo of the Angel "hipster." "It'd be a lot easier if you just were crazy," Ginsberg has said, ". . . but on the other hand what if it's all true and you're *born* into this great cosmic universe in which you're a spirit angel. . . . ?"[8] After the illumination, the poet is in Chicago between flights and decides that this city is "another project for the heart,"

six months for here someday
to make Chicago natural,
pick up a few strange images.

This spirit angel is on the lookout for missionary work, and it begins to come clear that "nakedness" is merely the unaccommodated man finding in his misery that all are brothers under the skin, that all are angels. In Ginsberg's world, unauthenticated angels rarely fly; their feet trod the dusty earth where life takes place:

Better I make
a thornful pilgrimage on theory
feet to suffer the total
isolation of the bum,
than this hipster
business family journey
—crossing U.S. at night—

There are so many complex constituents to Ginsberg's illuminations that it is often difficult to analyze or even comprehend precisely the response that is expected. The fact that Ginsberg himself often confesses that he is usually not aware of exactly what he means at the time of writing lends little comfort.[9] Nevertheless, even when exegesis fails, communication of a sort often breaks through. Graffiti collectors are reported to have uncovered this interesting specimen in a men's lavatory: "Ginsberg revises!" If the legend were true, perhaps the task of the explicator would be simplified. For good or for bad, Ginsberg does not write for expositors but for angels; and one must be alert to Wordsworth's counsel that "We murder to dissect."

"Sather Gate Illumination" (54-58) may not present as many problems as **"Over Kansas,"** but the honest lyricism of its celebration of a moment in space and in time manages to avoid the straining for effect that many of the poems in ***Reality Sandwiches*** exhibit. The poem is Whitman inspired through and through from the gracious "Dear Walter, thanks-for-the-message" tribute in the beginning to the illumination proper at the end: "Seeing in people the visible evidence of inner self thought by their treatment of me: who loves himself loves me who love myself." Almost any line picked at random from "Song of Myself" serves to explicate the general theme of Ginsberg's piece:

I CELEBRATE myself, and sing myself,
And what I assume you shall assume,
For every atom belonging to me as good belongs
to you.

or

There was never any more inception than there
is now,
Nor any more youth or age than there is now,
And will never be any more perfection than
there is now,
Nor any more heaven or hell than there is now.

Even more informative are the lines: "Clear and sweet is my soul, and clear and sweet is all that is not my soul / Lack one lacks both, and the unseen is proved by the seen, / Till that becomes unseen and receives proof in its turn."[10]

"Dear Walter's" message is no stopgap communiqué for Ginsberg, but a program of positive perception as well as a healthy dose of self-vindication. It reaffirms the brotherhood of angels: "Why do I deny manna to another? / Because I deny it to myself" (54). The key to the illumination is the acceptance of self which the poem affirms from the start: "Now I believe you are lovely, my soul, soul of Allen, Allen—/ and you so beloved, so sweetened, so recalled to your true loveliness, / your original nude breathing Allen / will you ever deny another again?"

There is precious little that is new so far as content is concerned in this poem, and its effect probably rests on the fact that the poet's mind has been liberated for mere observation. There is a dazzling array of commonplace scenes and incidents raised to significance by the slender support of Whitman's insight and buttressed by poetic sensitivity. There is also moral tension structurally built into the poem by the leitmotif of the "Roar again of airplanes in the sky" whose pilots "are sweating and nervous at the controls in the hot cabins" (54). These bombers with their "loveless bombs" perform as a mobile umbrella shadowing both the giggling girls, "all pretty / everywhichway," and the crippled lady, who "explains French grammar with a loud sweet voice: / Regarder is to look."

Looking is the genius of this poem, and it is not only the "scatological insight"[11] that Ginsberg's eye exploits as he observes the "pelvic energy" of the crippled girl's bouncing body, but it is the deeper vision of the "unseen" being "proved by the seen." Professor Hart, "enlightened by the years," walks "through the doorway and arcade he built (in his mind) / and knows—he too saw the ruins of Yucatan once—" (56). The unseen which the poet reveals through his perception surely is the sense of community that binds all mankind together: ". . . we all look up," Ginsberg observes, "silence moves, huge changes upon the ground, and in the air thoughts fly all over filling space" (58).

The salutary moment is both spiritual and poetic. "My grief at Peter's not loving me was grief at not loving myself," the poet concludes. Minds that are broken in "beautiful bodies [are] unable to receive love because not knowing the self as lovely." The illumination is no less poignant because it derives from Whitman. Indeed, from Whitman the poetic impulse behind the creation becomes much clearer; for, in the words of the "True American," Walt Whitman, Ginsberg's literary foundation can be seen: "I know I am solid and sound / To me the converging objects of the universe perpetually flow, / All are written to me, and I must get what the writing means."[12]

III Love and Nakedness

The doctrine of "nakedness" that Ginsberg continually preaches is implicit in **"Sather Gate Illumination"**; and it, too, owes much to Whitman. "Undrape! you are not guilty to me, nor stale nor discard," one reads in "Song of Myself": "I see through the broadcloth and gingham whether or no, / And am around, tenacious, acquisitive, tireless, and cannot / be shaken away."[13] Clothes are not only a hindrance to lovemaking; they are the garments of illusion with which men shamefully hide their humanity. Mind, too often, is the grim tailor, which appears to be one of the underlying themes of **"Love Poem on Theme by Whitman"** (41). In this poem, the poet shares the nuptial bed of "the bridegroom and the bride" of humanity whose "bodies fallen from heaven stretched out waiting naked and restless" are open to his physical visitation. As he buries his face "in their shoulders and breasts, breathing their skin . . . bodies locked shuddering naked, hot lips and buttocks screwed into each other," he hears the "bride cry for forgiveness" and the groom "covered with tears of passion and compassion." What is described so sensually is an orgasm of community—a nude coming together of primal human hearts from which the poet rises "up from the bed replenished with last intimate gestures and kisses of farewell."

The graphic extremity to which the erotic description takes one is an all-out blitzkrieg against shame. The bed is a possible world of contracted time and space—the identical bed threatened by the "busy old fool, unruly Sunne" that John Donne so beautifully has celebrated.[14] In Ginsberg's poem, however, it is not the "Sunne" which is the intruding landlady of this secret tryst but the mind. Once again, the "cold touch of philosophy" withers primordial love. The conclusion of Ginsberg's poem drops an ironic veil between love and life as it is lived. Shameless physical love occurs

> all before the mind awakes, behind shades and
> closed
> doors in a darkened house where inhabitants
> roam
> unsatisfied in the night, nude ghosts seeking
> each
> other out in the silence.

Some of the pathos of Ginsberg's personal attempts to revive "nude ghosts" can be appreciated in his mock-heroic epic, **"The Green Automobile"** (11-16), a visionary, yet autobiographical excursion with Neal Cassady to Denver, where the two latter-day cavaliers seek to

> . . . be the angels of the world's desire
> and take the world to bed with us before
> we die.
> Sleeping alone, or with companion,
> girl or fairy sheep or dream,
> I'll fail of lacklove, you, satiety:
> all men fall, our fathers fell before . . .
> [15].

Love is the prize, the holy grail, of these deprived wanderers, and the urgent necessity of drinking from this universal cup erases hetero- and homosexual boundaries. **"Malest Cornifici Tuo Catullo"** (47) is just one of Ginsberg's several poetic, homosexual confessions; and few can deny the poignancy of its brief, candid apology:

> Ah don't think I'm sickening.
> You're angry at me. For all of my lovers?
> It's hard to eat shit, without having visions;
> when they have eyes for it's like Heaven.

IV The Ubi Sunt

One of the universals of poetic expression is the mood which remembrance of things past evokes. The modern *"Ubi sunt"* sometimes arouses a poignancy that rivals even the most powerful of the Old English lyrics. The subject is the same: alienation; the mood, however, is more personal because the bygone times are less distant and the feelings are closer to man's sense of how rapidly the ravages of time close in upon him. "The Wanderer" and "The Seafarer" give a taste of the loneliness of the unaccommodated *scop,* bereft of his mead hall and the comfort of his protecting thane. Modern mead halls lack the magnificence of Heorot; "matter is water" (72) the twentieth-century singer must confess. And so the heavy nostalgia of an Anglo-Saxon heritage must be translated into faster tempos and tawdrier, less localized scenes. The universal feeling has not changed, but the props are demythologized. The result is a poem such as **"Back on Times Square Dreaming of Times Square"** (70-71).

The conflict of this poem is measured by the collision of actuality with memory. The medium is place—Times Square—and the kinetic throwoff of the poem is the sad contrast of what *is* with what *was.* Times Square, a "memorial of ten years," is now emotionally neutralized by the imposing facticity of "the green & grooking McGraw/Hill offices" (70). A "sad trumpeter" is petitioned to "stand on the empty streets at dawn / and blow a silver chorus to the buildings of Times Square"; but obviously the time for silver choruses is long past—ten years past—and what music now exists belongs to a solitary cop walking by who is "invisible with his music."

Surprisingly, the contrast is not traditional; that is, present loneliness versus past joy. The contrast is between two distinct types of loneliness which superimpose one quality of alienation with a deeper tint of the same. The polar symbols are the McGraw-Hill offices of the present moment and the "Globe Hotel" of memory. Both poles share a grimness which the fine discrimination of the poet separates with the subtle reminiscence. "I was lonely," he confesses, just as he implicitly avows his present loneliness. The modern mead hall ("The Globe Hotel") boasted little of the comfort and solace of its historical antecedents, for it was a place where "Garver lay in

> grey beds there and hunched his
> back and cleaned his needles—
> where I lay many nights on the nod
> from his leftover bloody cottons
> and dreamed of Blake's voice talking . . .
>
> [70].

Returning to this place is acknowledging the quickened pace of mutability: "Garver's dead in Mexico two years, hotel's vanished into a parking lot / And I'm back here—sitting on the streets / again" (70).

The *"Ubi Sunt"* lament which speaks through this poem is the forlorn query: Where are the not-so-good old days before mass media raped man's special mission? It is a lament to the stolen Beat Generation—an attitude that was popularized to extinction:

> The movies took our language, the
> great red signs
> A DOUBLE BILL OF GASSERS
> Teen Age Nightmare
> Hooligans of the Moon
>
> [70].

Underlying the lament is the apologetic protest of misrepresentation:

> But we were never nightmare
> hooligans but seekers of
> the blond nose for Truth
>
> [71].

The theme, then, of this poem is missionary martyrdom. From the ashes of an apparently defeated memory arises the poet's conviction about the prophetic validity of what had once occurred. "We are legend," he concedes, "invisible but legendary, as prophecied" (71).

The next poem, **"My Sad Self"** (72), is less protestant, less prophetic. It is difficult to defend much of this poem from the charge of "crude sentimentality" which the *Times Literary Supplement* insists "is of a piece with the equally crude rhetoric, the hamfisted philosophizing, and the wholesale misuse of imagist and neosurrealist techniques" which pervade ***Reality Sandwiches.***[15] This poem is a sentimental one, but it is somewhat superior to **"Tears"** (63) which is indeed an example of Ginsberg's apparent "belief that an emotion stated is an emotion conveyed."[16] **"My Sad Self"** baldly states an emotion: sadness; and this emotion is presented more or less as a premise as the poet gazes at New York from the top of the RCA Building. From this vantage point he catalogues various places, each with its attendant nostalgia ("my history summed up, my absences / and ecstasies in Harlem"). The universalizing lever in this poem—the device that lifts it from pure nostalgic sentimentality—is the concept of transiency that is suggested in the final lines of the first stanza:

> —sun shining down on all I own
> in one eyeblink to the horizon
> in my last eternity—
> matter is water.

Ginsberg owns all he sees because of his subjective relation to it ("Who digs Los Angeles Is Los Angeles!" [*H*, 21]). The natural corollary to this stance is the intransigence of things: "matter is water" (72).

The remainder of **"My Sad Self"** is a meandering journey through New York with the usual Ginsbergian reactions to the things he sees about him. For example, he stares "into all man's / plateglass, faces, / questioning after who loves . . ." (72); and, near the end of the poem, he unleashes his prophetic voice and painfully observes that "this graveyard . . . once seen / never regained or desired / in the mind to come . . . must disappear" (74).

V Spontaneity and Meditation

Norman MacCaig, who has admitted that "there's a great head of pressure built up in all that Allen Ginsberg writes," remarks that "the trouble is that often the fabric of the poem can't contain it—it explodes messily in your face, spattering you with gobbets and fragments of what may have been a fine body of experience."[17] This description seems an accurate one of

FFFFF U U NN N
F U U N N N
FFFFF U U N N N
F U U N N N NY DEATH
F U U N N
F UU N N

"I Beg You Come Back & Be Cheerful," "Aether," and several others. In these poems, "syntax is shot at sight, things are described in a catalogue of gasps, the light is lurid, distances enormous [and] . . . the wind blows from hysteria."[18] **"Aether,"** perhaps, contains the justification for these excursions:

Yet the experiments must continue!
Every possible combination of Being—all
the old ones! all the old Hindu
Sabahadabadie-pluralic universes
ringing in Grandiloquent
Bearded Juxtaposition. . . .

[84]

Many of these experiments were accomplished under the influence of various stimulants and drugs, but the literary significance is clear: the method is spontaneous dictation of experience without benefit of after-thought. Perhaps the typical reaction is, again, MacCaig's, whose summary is: "Terribly Romantic, in a diabolical sort of way. And tediously self-regarding. . . . It's the continuous pumping-up that I distrust."[19]

"Siesta in Xbalba," the best poem of ***Reality Sandwiches,*** is not "pumped up" at all; but, as James Scully feels, it "recalls . . . the quieter vision of Henry Vaughan."[20] What is reminiscent of Vaughan is control more than anything else. The reader is not asked to fill his mind with abstract eternities or chaotic meanderings of a turgid mind; instead, he finally has something tangible to deal with. Ginsberg presents in this poem a real, vibrant world to consider; and, at the same time, it is a world pregnant with intimations of immortality.

Like Vaughan's "The World" ("I saw Eternity last night . . ."), **"Siesta in Xbalba"** makes the effort for revelation:

Late sun opening the book,
blank page like light,
invisible words unscrawled,
impossible syntax
of apocalypse—

[21]

The poem even programs a method: "let the mind fall down" (21). From the very beginning of the poem, therefore, there is a yearning for an apocalyptic vision—a setting almost assured of producing the proper mystic mood—and, finally, a yielding up of the rational discipline so that the poet becomes almost pure receptor. What occurs in the poem from this point on is what George Poulet might describe as the "infinite receptivity" which is the genius of Walt Whitman's thought. Ginsberg obviously enjoys the stance. He is in a hammock, suspended, so to speak, above the world and yet still of it, while white doves copulate underneath him (21) and monkeys bark. The reader is told that the poet has "succumbed to this temptation" of "doing nothing but lying in a hammock" (21); and he is prepared for observation and apocalyptic musing.

The musing initially takes place in the form of a dream flashback—"an eternal kodachrome" (22), Ginsberg calls it—where his friends at a party are frozen in his mind. Clearly, the idea is to present an *inauthentic* contrast to the *authentic* situation the poet is in at Xbalba because the people are described as "posed together," with "stylized gestures" and "familiar visages." They are all, he concludes, "posturing in one frame, / superficially gay / or tragic as may be, / illumed with the fatal / character and intelligent / actions of their lives" (23).

Immediately following this dream flashback is a description of the poet's own pretentiously stark surroundings: "And I in a concrete room / above the abandoned / labyrinth of Palenque / measuring my fate, / wandering solitary in the wild /—blinking singleminded / at a bleak idea—" (23). Clearly, there is a note of superiority here. Friends are trivial, but "I" am serious is the note Ginsberg seems to strike; there is, of course, the usual cosmic trump card to be played: the oncoming mystic vision. Fatigued from gazing at the bleak idea, the poet awaits the moment when

> my soul might shatter
> at one primal moment's
> sensation of the vast
> movement of divinity.
>
> [23]

There is obviously an inchoate quest operating in the debris of the mind that has fallen down, and it seems to be directed toward the usual eternity which so often is the misty goal of Ginsberg's poems. The reason is probably the same as Whitman's: "Eternity gives similitude to all periods and locations and processes, and animate and inanimate forms, and . . . is the bond of time." Such a valuable commodity as this bond is certainly worthy of the highest poetry, and it helps once again to explain Ginsberg's views concerning drugs. If eternity is the "bond of time"—the thing which glues everything together into community and permits everyone to be an angel—then it is reasonable that any access to this state would be well worth the price. Even without drugs the search for Eternity can be salutary:

> As I leaned against a tree
> inside the forest
> expiring of self-begotten love,
> I looked up at the stars absently,
> as if looking for
> something else in the blue night
> through the boughs,
> and for a moment saw myself
> leaning against a tree. . . .
>
> [23]

Time and eternity, as the glue that binds all things together, is developed as a concept later in the poem when Ginsberg meditates upon a death's-head. Part of his fascination with the death's-head is its relevance to the principle of prophecy. He is impressed by the fact that it "thinks its way / through centuries the thought of the same night in which I sit / in skully meditation" (26). Here is an instance of eternity indeed obliterating time but in the fashion of biblical prophecy. The anterior artisan, the maker of the death's-head, sculpted his artifact until it fully represented his idea; but now, Ginsberg muses, the death's head communicates that idea across time:

> but now his fine thought's vaguer
> than my dream of him:
> and only the crude skull figurement's
> gaunt insensible glare is left. . . .
>
> (26)

The philosophical substratum of this small passage of the poem would seem to be the idea that truth (even history) is entirely subjective. Works of art, be they poems or death's-heads, have the capability of triggering or exciting thoughts in future individuals. The sense of oneness that eternity brings with it acts as a sort of guarantee of this phenomenon and presents the possibility of bridges across time. Real history, then, does not operate chronologically, logically, or rationally. History is apocalypse, so that Ginsberg can say:

> I alone know the great crystal door
> to the House of Night,
> a legend of centuries
> —I and a few indians.
>
> [29]

Any other access to history—any other solution to the "impossible syntax" of the hieroglyphics—cannot possibly yield what the death's-head potentially can surrender subjectively to the eternalized viewer. Unless the mind is allowed to "fall down," the rational apparatus will filter out the past:

> Time's slow wall overtopping
> all that firmament of mind,
> as if a shining waterfall of leaves and rain
> were built down solid from the endless sky
> through which no thought can pass.
>
> [28]

The first part of the poem ends with a rejection and a tentative affirmation: "There is a god / dying in America" (33) which is the institutionalized religious impulse. At the same time, there is also "an inner / anterior image / of divinity / beckoning me out / to pilgrimage" (33).

Part Two of this poem, **"Return to the United States"** (33), possesses a stark, generally crisp descriptive style and only one real intrusion of Ginsbergian metaphysics. The reader is told, finally, that "The problem is isolation" (36), a statement later followed by the lament: "What solitude I've finally inherited" (37). What these lines appear to mean is that Ginsberg has failed in a way. If what he hoped to retain from his night in Xbalba was a vision of Whitman's "vast similitude [which] interlocks all, / All spheres grown, ungrown, small, large, suns, moons, planets, / All distances of place however wide, / All distances of time . . . ,"[23] what he actually returned with was less ambitious: a few Traditions, / metrical, mystical, manly / . . . and certain characteristic flaws" (38). The isolation, it would seem, is not entirely his own; it's the isolation of the whole universe. The temptation for social criticism becomes too strong in the final lines, and the *real* loneliness and the *real* isolation are finally diagnosed as natural consequences of "The nation over the border [America]" which "grinds its arms and dreams of war" (39).

Intellectual sentimentality appears to be Ginsberg's Achilles' heel, and one reason for the success of **"Siesta in Xbalba"** is the fact that the thundering onslaughts upon God, upon eternity, upon the cosmos, and so on, are kept unusually under control. There is more attention to things in this poem than in most of the others, which anchors it to a refreshing empirical plane too often missing in the later work. An Oriental clarity in some places in the poem even brings metaphysics nearer to the reader's grasp, much in the way suggested in **"Cézanne's Ports,"** for example. One such instance is the simple description of the night in the midst of the rain forest:

> I can see the moon
> moving over the edge of the night forest
> and follow its destination
> through the clear dimensions of the sky
> from end to end of the dark
> circular horizon.
>
> [25]

If nothing else, the idea in this short excerpt is *rendered* rather than garrulously bellowed. It is structural, not strident; and the quiet control of **"Siesta in Xbalba"** is a welcome reminder that the best poems are most often made rather than notated.

VI Assessment

It is very difficult to assess ***Reality Sandwiches*** as a whole because the book, which spans seven years of poetic development, modestly claims to be merely "scribbled secret notebooks, and wild typewritten pages, for yr [*sic*] own joy." It would be silly to pretend that many of the poems are not simply amateurish, pretentious, clumsy, and, at times, even downright dull. One bittersweet reviewer of the *Times Literary Supplement* has conceded that "in among this amateurish material . . . there are moments of real excitement, and poems which are firmly restrained and delicately balanced. There are not many, but there are enough to give one hope for Mr. Ginsberg's future development."[24] The assessment is probably true, but what the reviewer hopefully regards as signs of "future development" are perhaps more accurately carry-overs from Ginsberg's less flamboyant earlier versifying. Ginsberg is not working *toward* what would be considered traditional control; he is fleeing from it as rapidly as possible.

One is left, then, with the kind of response to which James Scully invariably resorts when he reviews Ginsberg's work: Scully finds Ginsberg's worth in his "sense of humanity." The phrase is ambiguous and slippery, and even Scully's attempt to clarify does no more than suggest the type of power that he finds in the poems. Nevertheless, according to Scully this sense of humanity is Ginsberg's attempt "to uncover a community";[25] and such attempts have perfectly respectable credentials. Walt Whitman, for example, was doing the very same thing when he wrote:

> Divine am I inside and out, and I make holy
> whatever I touch
> or am touched from,
> The scent of these arm-pits aroma finer than
> prayer,
> This head more than churches, bibles, and all
> creeds.[26]

In a way, Whitman's liturgy of the divine, human self appears to be the one constant, yet elusive, goal toward which Ginsberg has been striving throughout most of his career.

Notes

1. William Burroughs, *Evergreen Review,* IV (January, 1960), 15.
2. Letter from Allen Ginsberg to this author, November 22, 1966.
3. William Carlos Williams, *Paterson II* (New York, 1948).
4. John Ciardi, "How Free Is Verse?" *Saturday Review* (October 11, 1958), 38.
5. William Carlos Williams, *I Wanted to Write a Poem,* ed. Edith Heal (Boston, 1958), p. 92.
6. Alan W. Watts, *The Way of Zen* (New York, 1959), p. 173.
7. John MacQuarrie, *Studies in Christian Existentialism* (Philadelphia, c. 1965), pp. 48-49.
8. "The Art of Poetry VIII," *Paris Review,* XXXVII (Spring, 1966), 40.
9. See *Ibid.,* 22.
10. *Song of Myself,* XX, 403-405.
11. James Scully [review of *Reality Sandwiches*], *Nation,* CXCVII (November 16, 1963), 330.
12. Walt Whitman, *Song of Myself,* XX, 403-405.
13. *Ibid.,* VII, 145-47.
14. "The Sunne Rising."
15. *Times Literary Supplement,* CCXII (September 20, 1963), 706.

16. *Ibid.*

17. Norman MacCaig, "Poemburgers" [review of *Reality Sandwiches*], *New Statesman,* LXVI (July 5, 1963), 20.

18. *Ibid.*

19. *Ibid.*

20. James Scully [review of *Reality Sandwiches*], *op. cit.,* 330.

21. George Poulet, *Studies in Human Time* (New York, 1959), p. 342.

22. Walt Whitman, *The Complete Poetry and Prose,* ed. M. Cowley (New York, 1948), II, 92.

23. *Ibid.,* I, 249.

24. *Times Literary Supplement* [review of *Reality Sandwiches*], *op. cit.,* 706.

25. Scully [review of *Reality Sandwiches*] *Nation,* CXCVII (November 16, 1963), 330.

26. *Song of Myself,* XXIV, 524-26.

"Wichita Vortex Sutra"

PAUL CARROLL (ESSAY DATE 1968)

SOURCE: Carroll, Paul. "I Lift My Voice Aloud, / Make Mantra of American Language Now . . . / I Here Declare the End of the War!" In *The Poem in Its Skin,* pp. 81-101. Chicago: Follett Publishing Company, 1968.

In the following essay, Carroll examines Ginsberg's long poem "Wichita Vortex Sutra."

Is **"Wichita Vortex Sutra"** a major American poem? The great act of imagination at the core of this long work seems to demand that the reader consider the poem either as a notable and even monumental achievement or as a roaring and pretentious failure. Either this poem is incandescent in that Allen Ginsberg succeeds in assuming the role of poet as priestly legislator and as Baptist of a mantra whose dispensation brings peace and love or it is opaque in that he fails to become little more than mock creator of a harangue whose dispensation brings bad rhetoric and banality.

This is of course relentlessly univocal. Yet the poem demands such univocal judgement due to the sheer heroism and daring of its declared intention. With admirable sincerity and making no bones about it, Ginsberg attempts to assume the role called for by Shelley in the celebrated if somewhat petulant assertion that poets are "the unacknowledged legislators of the world."[1] Ginsberg assumes this role when he attempts to legislate by declaring the end of hostilities in Viet Nam in these astonishing lines which occur about two-thirds of the way through the poem:

> I lift my voice aloud,
> make Mantra of American language now,
> pronounce the words beginning in my own
> Millennium—
> I here declare the end of the war!—
> Ancient Days' illusion!
> Let the States tremble,
> let the nation weep,
> let Congress legislate its own delight
> let the President execute his
> own desire—
> this Act done by my own voice,
> nameless Mystery—

What makes this assertion so original is the means by which Ginsberg strives to give validity and authority to his act of legislation: he declares the end of the war by making a mantra. More specifically, it is a mantra of the American language. The central implication seems clear. If the mantra of the American language "works," then it should be able in some vigorous, magical or religious way to end the slaughter in Viet Nam. But first, what exactly is a mantra?

The dictionary explains that mantra comes from the Sanskrit term for sacred formula or counsel and defines it as "a mystical formula or invocation or incantation in Hinduism or Mahayana Buddhism"; but since I am ignorant about Eastern religions, I asked Ginsberg if he would explain his understanding of mantra, as well as to indentify some of the important but obscure allusions to Hindu or Buddhist mysticism—for example, the litany of gurus, swamis, yogis, saints and demigods whom he invokes in the section beginning: "I call all Powers of imagination / to my side in this auto to make Prophecy . . ." In August 1966, the poet generously replied in the form of a letter and notes written in the margins of a xerox copy of the poem.[2] Here is Ginsberg's definition of mantra: "a short magic formula usually invoking an aspect of the Divine, usually given as meditation exercise by guru to student, sometimes sung in community or 'kirtan'—the formula is considered to be identical with the god named, and have inevitable power attached to its pronunciation. Oft used in chanting or invocation."

The mantra made in **"Wichita Vortex Sutra,"** then, seems to consist of three parts. First, there is the litany beginning "I call all Powers of imagination," invoking the holy men, demigods and gods from whom the poet asks assistance in the making of his mantra. Then there is the creation of the mantra itself: "I lift my voice aloud, / make mantra of American language now . . ." Finally, the mantra is put to work as the poet announces his act of declaring the end of the war and then pronounces benediction on the United States, Congress and President Johnson; and then as part of the mantra he ritualistically enumerates the five "leaps" or "skandas"—the areas of apportionment of consciousness mentioned in the Buddhist Sutras: the liberation of his own form, sensations, thought, imagination, and "all realms within my consciousness."

The intention of the mantra is heroic and ambitious. If it works, it functions as a magic formula whose power can end the war and also as the formula which invokes that which is eternal and divine and free in the poet himself, as well as that which is holy and free in the members of Congress and in the President. Clearly here is one of the supreme moments of imagination in American poetry. There has been nothing to equal its grandeur, it seems to me, since Whitman's "Passage to India."

What is impressive about this mantra is that it isn't merely a Hindu or Buddhist prayer for peace and for the liberation of the holy in the poet and in his fellow Americans. Instead, Ginsberg attempts to make a mantra out of the American language itself. What exactly could this mean? The poet explains in his reply to my original letter in which I mentioned that I'd been thinking of his poem as fulfilling Shelley's assertion that poets are the unacknowledged legislators of the world: "Not *only* a question of legislator as Shelley's formula. Merely that the war has been created by language . . . & Poet can dismantle the language consciousness conditioned to war reflexes by setting up (mantra) absolute contrary field of will as expressed in language. By expressing, manifesting, his DESIRE (BHAKTI in yoga terminology—'adoration')."

Here, then, is the dramatic and crucial tension created by the making of the mantra: the poet expresses his desire for peace and the liberation of the divine and free in himself and his countrymen by creating a mantra made with American words; but the mantra will succeed in bringing peace and liberating the holy and free in Americans only if its language can oppose and finally dismantle the corrupt and evil language which has conditioned the American people to "war reflexes"—the corrupt and evil language which (according to the poet) created and sustains the current Viet Nam war. In brief, the mantra is one of true or beatific language; its job is to dissipate and annihilate the slaughter and moral barbarism created by false or evil language. In this sense, **"Wichita Vortex Sutra"** is primarily a poem embodying an experience of contemporary American language and what that language can or cannot accomplish.

When read in the light of this tension between false and true language, the poem divides into three parts. The first section is the longest, containing five stanzas of some 365 lines, all of which document in one way or another aspects of the false and evil language which created and sustains the Viet Nam war. The second section, beginning with the stanza "I call all Powers of imagination / to my side in this auto to make Prophecy . . ." depicts in some 50 lines the creation of the mantra. The final section opens in "the chill earthly mist" 60 miles from Wichita and contains some 130 lines in two stanzas in which the mantra of true language is put to work in opposing the false words of the first section.

Let us look at some of the outstanding examples of the false and evil use of the American language in the first section and attempt to see how such perverted uses drive the poet to declare: "The war is language, / language abused / for Advertisement, / language used / like magic for power on the planet / Black Magic language, / formulas for reality . . ."

At the very beginning of the poem, the poet encounters an example of black magic language as he hears the voice of Senator Aiken [Republican, Vermont] on the interview program "Face the Nation" coming over the radio in his Volkswagen driving on a Sunday morning in February 1966 past Hickman, Nebraska, along Route 77, bound south for Wichita. The Senator claims that Secretary of Defense McNamara made "no more than a Bad Guess" when he predicted in 1962 that only "8000 American Troops [could] handle the / Situation." Here are at least two examples of misused or twisted "formulas for reality." By calling McNamara's miscalculation only a bad guess, the Senator distorts what that miscalculation in all events actually was: namely, a calculated sop thrown to pacify the American people and soften or quiet whatever moral opposition they may have felt against our involvement in Viet Nam, as well as a sop to mollify whatever objection they might feel in the near future to the increasing escalation of aggression by American pilots against Viet Cong troops and civilian villages. What makes the Senator's description false is that the Secretary of Defense might possibly have known in 1962 that America would increase its "commitment" and aggression on the large scale that it actually did.

A minor but equally false perversion of language occurs when Senator Aiken describes the war as "the Situation." To call napalm bombing, machine-gunning and destruction of helpless villages by United States pilots—not to speak of the massacre of our own soldiers by the Viet Cong—a "situation" is precisely that kind of official gobbledygook which refuses to call an event by its correct name (however ugly that name is) and by so refusing only helps to blunt moral perceptions of what that reality might be.[3] Bombing with intent to destroy and kill, intricate tactical strategies, abortive attempts to negotiate peace, and swelling rosters of dead or wounded on both sides: this is not a "situation:" this is war.

Other examples of perverted use of words bombard the poet as he reads newspaper headlines. "Rusk Says Toughness Essential for Peace" declares the *Omaha World Herald*. Toughness? What's accomplished by the use of this virile noun? Such a word only flatters a nation's image of itself and helps to dissipate whatever reservations Americans may have about the morality of our slaughtering in Viet Nam by conjuring the image of the American as Wild West hero who refuses to let anybody push him around or make a sissy out of him. What the use of the word tends to ignore or varnish over is the moral reality: What right do Americans have to act "tough" with Oriental peasants who are fighting for what is, after all, their own country? Thirty years ago, a German newspaper could have said: "Hitler Says Toughness Essential for Final Solution"—meaning the extermination of countless Jews who were in no rational or legal sense enemies of the Third Reich. Then there's the headline: "Vietnam War Brings Prosperity." Here the perversion exists in the word "prosperity." By claiming that the war brings prosperity, the headline implies that the aggression is not only reasonable and valuable but condoned by the god of capitalism. No sensible man denies that prosperity is a good thing; but the use of the word here blunts the vital issue: Prosperity at what moral cost? Antebellum slavery brought prosperity to Southern planters and to the entire economy of the South. Barbaric working conditions and immoral wages brought prosperity to owners of Chicago meat packing houses and New England textile mills in the late 19th century. And so on.

Examples of perverted black magic language heard over the radio or read in the newspapers continue to assault the poet throughout the long first section of the poem as he comes to know how persuasive and corrupting the perversion has become. One example is the old misuse of the word "Communism" to encourage a growing "war reflex" both in American statesmen and military men and in the citizens as a body. While eating ham steak in the warm cafe, the poet broods how "Communism is a 9 letter word / used by inferior magicians" and funky warlocks which resulted in the "Communion of bum magicians / congress of failures from Kansas & Missouri / working with the wrong equations / Sorcerer's Apprentice who lost control / of the simplest broomstick in the world: / Language . . ." whose perversion may erupt in the "deluge of radiation" flooding the living rooms of America.

Nor is the black magic language limited only to the present. In one of the most memorable passages in the poem, Ginsberg recalls an episode of the perversion of the Word which occurred in 1956 when President Eisenhower "knelt to take / the magic wafer in his mouth / from Dulles' hand / inside the church in Washington . . ." Here the "magic" communion wafer given by Dulles (acting as lay presbyter) seems to symbolize all of the abuses and perversions of the American language: it is the Word abused. Presumably the wafer represents the false advice given by the then Secretary of State that America should continue its involvement in the Viet Nam civil war, although on strictly moral grounds this country had no justification whatsoever for its increasingly active participation in that Asian conflict.

Misuses of language also occur in the examples from mass communication (symbolized by the almost comic monster NBCBSUPAPINSLIFE) and from the advertising industry. Not only does "Time Mutual" present the "World's Largest Camp Comedy" by turning the Viet Nam reality inside out but the poet also notices the pathetic but droll misuse of words by advertising companies. One billboard informs him that his generation is not the Lost Generation or the Generation of 1776 or the one of Manifest Destiny: it is "the Pepsi Generation"; another billboard tells him how Marines are "in love" with a local bread made by a Pop Art icon called Aunt Betty.

On a more profound level, one also notices how the poet himself suffers from the abuses done to the American language by fork-tongued politicians, hysterical columnists, mass media and by those Barnums of exaggerated and phony language—the gentlemen of advertising. What could be more trite, flat and prosaic, for example, than his own description of the Nebraska landscape: "icy winter / grey sky bare trees lining the road / South to Wichita"? Here is an ultimate indignity created by false language: it leaves a contemporary American poet with only shabby equipment with which to try to do his job. Even his grasping at those masters of the spoken American idiom—Walt Whitman and Ezra Pound—as possible antibiotics to counteract the infections in our language turns into a buffoon episode in which the only words Ginsberg has are: "Ham steak waitress please."

What do all of these examples of perverted black magic language add up to? The poet tells us clearly in the desperate passage quoted a moment ago, beginning: "The war is language . . ." All of the perversions of black magic language in the opening section, the passage implies, not only helped to encourage and condone the original involvement of America in the internal affairs of Viet Nam but the false, evil idiom helps to perpetuate that involvement by distorting the bald reality that United States troops are engaged in a murderous aggression waged against Oriental peasants who have never threatened or harmed America in any way whatsoever.

Then what must the mantra accomplish? It must oppose and dismantle the "war reflexes" conditioned by the false, evil misuses of the American tongue. How? Through language. Fire must fight fire.

For one thing, the true and beatific language must call events and moral realities by their correct names. And it must accomplish this tough task by embodying a vocabulary which is not only accurate but powerful and *magical* in the profound and mysterious sense of that word. Indeed, this true language must be something like the idiom used by the mystical alchemists of the Middle Ages—those extraordinary men who (as Jung documents in his important study *Psychology and Alchemy* (1953)) were hardly concerned with such trivial, childish goals as discovering how to transform cheap iron or matter into gold; rather, they were striving to create out of gross matter nothing else than the God Incarnate.

The true and beatific language, in short, must be brilliant and memorable enough to create and sustain the "absolute contrary field of will" which alone can cure the moral disease resulting from the false and evil idiom and, by so doing, end the war in Viet Nam. The language of the last 180 lines must be the language of great poetry.

Is it?

The language of the creation of the mantra certainly is if not great, then memorable poetry. In strong, vivid and lucid words Ginsberg not only creates the possibility of an original supernatural reality for the American consciousness but he calls for the liberation of the holy and free in himself and in his fellow countrymen.[4]

But what about the language in the stanzas following the making of the mantra? Does it have the ring of great or memorable poetry?

No.

On the contrary, the shocking thing seems to be that the language of the final section of **"Wichita Vortex Sutra"** sounds much the same if not even worse than the black magic vocabulary of the first section. One hears the same flat, boring descriptions of the landscape, the same type of newspaper headlines, the same Rand-McNally catalogue of Kansas towns and cities, ending with a doggedly accurate map of Wichita streets and the names of office buildings, gas stations, the McConnell Air Force Base and the Lutheran Church of the Redeemer past which the poet's Volkswagen drives, heading for the Hotel Eaton on Douglas Street.

Not only is the language undistinguished and prosy but in several crucial instances the diction disintegrates into bad or flashy rhetoric. Take the section in which Bob Dylan is invoked as an Angel of Glad Tidings. As the Volkswagen speeds past the "endless brown meadows" and the small Kansas town of Burns, the folk-rock singer's voice floats over the radio, singing "Won't You Come See Me, Queen Jane?" Here is the entire Dylan section:

> Oh at last again the radio opens
> blue Invitations!
> Angelic Dylan singing across the nation
> "When all your children start to resent you
> Won't you come see me, Queen Jane?"
> His youthful voice making glad
> the brown endless meadows
> His tenderness penetrating aether,
> soft prayer on the airwaves,
> Language language, and sweet music too
> even unto thee,
> hairy flatness!
> even unto thee
> despairing Burns!

In what sense is Dylan "angelic"? And why does his voice gladden the brown, endless meadows? Why should the town of Burns be in despair?

And even if its citizens are suffering from despair, why should Dylan's "soft prayer" and "sweet music" alleviate their unhappy condition? Answers to such questions remain in my mind a total blank: the poem does nothing to clarify them. Instead, it seems to fall back on an adolescent rhetoric in which the mere mention of Dylan and the epithet "angelic" are supposed to persuade the reader that here is an angel of language who embodies the true and beatific American idiom which puts to rout the effects of the earlier language of black magic. Even worse: Burns is in despair presumably because its small-town natives are writhing in unhappiness (the reader is encouraged to imply) because they don't hear Dylan often enough. Unfortunately, the melancholy effect of such rhetoric is to make the reader suspect that such writing is no better in kind than the rhetoric of Senator Aiken and the copy writer who describes the "love" of Marines for Aunt Betty's loaves of bread.

An even more glaring example of bad rhetoric occurs in the (by now) celebrated final lines:

> The war is over now—
> Except for the souls
> held prisoner in Niggertown
> still pining for love of your tender white bodies
> O
> children of Wichita!

Even if one understands children here in the metaphorical sense which translates into "white citizens," one doubts if it is their bodies for which the ghetto Negro pines: it is more likely their necks. In a less melodramatic sense, it's neither white bodies (the hoary Caucasian fantasy that black men possess magical sexuality which if not castrated will lure white females away forever) nor white necks for which most Negroes "pine": rather, it's the more mundane opportunity to obtain and earn the jobs, prestige and buying power taken for granted by the majority of whites. Here I'm not interested in the compassion of Allen Ginsberg (he clearly is the speaker in the poem) for the American Negro; I am concerned with why the concluding lines disintegrate into piously liberal but sentimental rhetoric. Nothing in the body of the poem justifies the switch from Viet Nam to the Negro Revolution. Even less organic is the creation of the figure of the Loving Negro.[5]

Notice that until these lines the poem hasn't once mentioned civil rights or the Negro Revolution. Then why does the speaker switch horses, as it were, in midstream? To argue that, after all, both the Viet Nam conflict and the Black Revolution are both "wars" and that the victims of both are victims of White American aggression and that the poet here attempts to end all types of war and aggression: this is pious liberal sentiment which has nothing to do with this poem as a poem. What the sudden and unprepared introduction of the loving Negroes of Wichita accomplishes, on the other hand, is to create the nagging suspicion that the speaker himself feels his mantra has failed, despite his assertion that "The war is over now," and that he tries to gloss over or even to ignore the suspicion of failure by turning to that last resort of the rhetorician: the instant cliché or self-righteous sentimentality. The conjuring of the loving Negroes is part of the same kind of rhetoric one hears from a rhetorician of the John Birch Society who invokes the cartoon of the Pilgrim Father with the White Face or the Henry Ford of Free Enterprise in an argument attempting to annihilate all that is not white or capitalistic or Protestant Christian.

Still a third example of bad rhetoric occurs in the Carry Nation section. The reader is asked to believe that the crusader for temperance—who in the 1890s marched into saloons throughout Kansas to hurl vituperations at the drinkers and smash furniture and fixtures with her hatchet ("hatchetation" of "joints," as she put it)—is responsible for beginning the "vortex of hatred" evident in Wichita today. Moreover, this vortex now defoliates the Mekong Delta and also murdered the poet's mother by driving her insane "one decade long ago." One accepts the existence of the vortex discovered by the poet in the same sense that one accepts the wasteland discovered by Eliot. No reasons exists within **"Wichita Vortex Sutra,"** however, to clarify how Miss Nation created the vortex or why the vortex is responsible either for the war in the Mekong Delta or for the insanity of Mrs. Naomi Ginsberg. (I trust this doesn't sound flippant: I don't intend it to be.) Obviously his mother's insanity is a moving memory for Ginsberg—as the reader may recall from that great elegy **"Kaddish"**—but he still fails to perform the ancient task of the poet: to render why or how any connection whatsoever exists between her insanity and Carry Nation or between the two women and the current aggression of the United States against the Viet Cong. To feel that the connection should be obvious merely because of the poet's wounded feelings is not enough, in my opinion. Such a reading, in fact, only responds to the sentimental rhetoric of the lines and not to the lack of genuine poetry in them.

And this brings us to a final and perhaps profound issue: Why does the language fail to be great poetry? One approach to a possible answer would be to explore still another question: Does the mantra "work"?[6]

As far as additional news of war is concerned, the mantra seems to be working: we hear only of conflicts which happened a few days or even few hours ago as the poet reads an edition of the *Wichita Eagle-Beacon* of the 100 Viet Cong deaths near Bong Son and how soldiers "charged so desperately they were struck with six or seven bullets / before they fell." And he tells us clearly that he feels the mantra is working because:

> The War is gone,
> Language emerging on the motel news stand,
> the right magic
> Formula, the language that was known
> in the back of the mind before, now in the black print
> of daily consciousness

Even though we hear no more of present conflict, however, there seem to be several more subtle ways in which the poem itself suggests doubts that the mantra is "working" not only in the sense of the cessation of war but also in the sense of releasing the holy and free in both the speaker and in his countrymen. The most obvious of these doubts occurs when we hear what does come over the radio now that there's no more news of war. What the poet hears are the voices of angels.

We've seen how the voice of the first angel—Bob Dylan as the Angel of Glad Tidings—fails in an important way to embody the incandescent language promised by the making of the mantra: his "blue invitation" disintegrates into sentimental rhetoric. Then the poet hears the voices of the Angels of Apocalypse—"Now radio voices cry population hunger world / & unhappy people"—who also prophesy the nativity of the new American Adam who presumably will overcome the Whore of Babylon of Famine and who also seems to fulfill the prophecy made in the first section of the poem: "I claim my birthright! / reborn forever as long as Man / in Kansas or other universe—Joy / reborn after the vast sadness of War Gods!" But the new Adam is parodied and rendered merely comic by the voice of the mock Angel of Advertising which suddenly floats over the air waves with a fragment from a soap commercial: "you certainly smell good / the radio says . . ." False or evil language, in short, infects what at first appear to be the healthy voices of the new dispensation made possible by the creation of the mantra.

On still another level, the poem corrodes one's hope that the mantra is working in the sense that it has released the divine and free in the speaker and, by extension, in his countrymen. And that is: it ends in a loneliness or lack of love more exacerbating than the loneliness and hatred which pervades the opening section and which the poet discovers in himself and in his fellows and which he cries out against in the moving stanza beginning: "I'm an old man now, and a lonesome man in Kansas / but not afraid / to speak my lonesomeness in a car, / because not only my lonesomeness / it's Ours, all over America, / O tender fellows . . ."

Loneliness pervades all of the stanzas leading up to the creation of the mantra. One notices how desolate the loneliness feels in that the Nebraska landscape through which the speaker drives is without people. All one hears are faceless voices. In fact, the only faces seen are in the grotesque photo in *Life* depicting adolescent Marines "blowing the air thru their cheeks with fear." And it is this loneliness which compels the speaker to feel:

> All we do is for this frightened thing
> we call Love, want and lack—
> fear that we aren't the one whose body could be
> beloved of all the brides of Kansas City,
> kissed all over by every boy of Wichita—
> O but how many in their solitude weep aloud like
> me . . .

But is this acute American loneliness and lack of love alleviated by either the making of the mantra or the realities experienced once the mantra begins its dispensation?

At first, it appears that both loneliness and lack of love are dispelled—particularly in the intimacy between poet and the Indian holy men summoned in the litany at the beginning of the creation of the mantra. Notice the vividness of detail in the summoning of the ten saints: "Shambu Bharti Baba naked covered with ash / Khaki Baba fat bellied mad with the dogs / Dehorahava Baba who moans Oh how wounded, / how wounded"—and so on. This is the kind of specific, intimate knowledge of another person that only a close friend or lover has. But the reader may also begin to notice a paradox: once the speaker begins to summon the supernatural beings whom the saints worship, the sense of intimacy evaporates. The poet calls on them in increasingly formal and depersonalized epithets: "Allah the Compassionate / Jaweh Righteous One"—and so on. Here the irony is that the speaker seems to end lonelier than he began.

And the loneliness only becomes more exacerbated as he continues driving toward Wichita. Even voices disappear as he enters Wichita itself and sees only a gas station, factory, supermarket, "crowds of autos moving with their light shine," an insurance company and the De Voors Gurad's funeral home. At the end his only companions are ghosts and faceless abstractions—the ghosts of Carry Nation and his mad mother, and the anonymous souls of Negroes and the bodies of the "children" of Wichita. The poem ends, in truth, in a nightmare vortex of loneliness.

Still a third way in which the poem suggests that the mantra hasn't worked its "right magic / Formula" is in the spiritual vacuum which pervades the final section. As we've seen, the mantra promises a release of the divine in both speaker and fellow countrymen. Instead of continued communion with the gods or an awareness of divinity in Americans, however, the poet sees statues commemorating the only god this country knows: the god of the pragmatic, concrete, materialistic present. It is as if Wichita itself becomes a cathedral filled with "statues" of signs advertising hamburgers and Skelley gas, the Kansas Electric Substation, Texaco, the Lutheran Church, the (felicitously named) Titsworth Insurance Company, the funeral parlor—and so on. And instead of the release of divine energy in Americans, the poet experiences only the re-release of hatred (in the figure of Carry Nation), paranoia (his mother), and racial violence (the Negroes of the ghetto). In short, the concluding stanzas depict a spiritually empty whirlpool, irresistible and catastrophic in power, in which the poet suffers the desolation of existence in a nation without gods or spiritual realities.

All of these doubts of the mantra's efficiency raised by the poem contribute to suggest that **"Wichita Vortex Sutra"** fails to achieve the intention stated by the poet: namely, to dismantle "the language consciousness conditioned to war reflexes by setting up (mantra) of absolute contrary field of will as expressed by language."

But does the poem itself fail? The answer might seem obvious. If the mantra fails and the language continues to be diseased by false or evil idioms, then Ginsberg's act of legislation fails too and obviously the poem itself is a failure.

But such a verdict depends of course on discursive analysis. Such analysis can help to reach an intelligent grasp of some aspects of a poem but it is almost useless if not a hindrance once the reader moves (as he should move) beyond what the poem *appears* to be saying and begins an adventure into the deeper and more obscure areas of the complex of experience which the poem may *in reality* embody.

In short, it should prove valuable to explore: *Why* does the mantra fail?

How could it have succeeded? When we examine the irony created by the meeting of the two equal but separate powers in the final section—the poet as holy man and America as secular nation—it should become clear how and why the mantra must fail.

On the one hand, there's the religious act of the poet as holy man. As priestly legislator, he invokes saints and deities to help in the creation of the mantra; and then as Baptist, he announces the dispensation of the mantra by calling on "Proud Wichita! vain Wichita" to repent of its sin in having sustained the vortex of hatred, and he announces in the composite figure of the Loving Negro and the white "children" of Wichita the advent of the Lamb of peace, love and brotherhood. The Lamb is of course the new American Adam proclaimed earlier by the Angel of Apocalypse. The Baptist arrives in Wichita, in short, to make the prophecy announced in several passages throughout the poem.

But to whom? The America to whom the Baptist speaks is, on the other hand, clearly alien if not hostile ground for such a dispensation and Messiah.

How is America depicted in the poem? As we've seen, it seems a wilderness containing expanses of fields and meadows vacant of people but infested by the voices of "angels" of evil or false language, and containing small towns and the secular cathedral called Wichita—both of which are also empty of people (with the exception of the faceless crowd in Beatrice, Nebraska). In addition, Wichita contains statues commemorating the gods of commerce and technology, as well as a vortex of hatred filled with war reflexes, paranoia and ghettoes.

To think of this America as merely the wilderness surrounding the Jordan, however, would be an understandable but serious error. Notice how the poet himself responds to the alien reality, strength and beauty contained not only in the farmlands of Nebraska and Kansas but also in some of the small towns and in Wichita itself. Rural elegance is acknowledged in lines such as: "A black horse bends its head to the stubble / beside the silver stream winding thru the woods / by an antique red barn on the outskirts of

Beatrice—/ Quietness, quietness / over this countryside"; and in the view glimpsed through the chill earthly mist of "houseless brown farmland plains rolling heavenward / in every direction." And the excitement of a happening is contained in the haiku of the burning garage in Beatrice: "Water hoses frozen on the street, / Crowd gathered to see a strange happening in the garage—/ How red the flames on Sunday morning / in a quiet town!" Wichita too contains elegance and a kind of muscular or existential beauty: the poet responds to its "mysterious families of winking towers" grouped around the quonset hut on the hill, the aluminum robot of the Kansas Electric Substation signalling through thin antennae towers to the solitary derrick that "pumps oil from the unconscious / working day and night," the "green jewelled" traffic lights, the Texaco sign "starred / over streetlamp vertebrae"—and so on.

In short, the America here is the everyday middle class America which in its natural resources, standard of living, and commercial and technological genius is the most prosperous nation men have ever known. The "alien gods" of this country are of course the gods of the practical, existential present. And the implication seems clear, in my opinion, that such gods condone this nation's continued commitment to the South Vietnamese in their civil war with the North for the most obvious reason: it might be most practical to protect this American middle class life by helping to defeat Communism in Viet Nam and truncate its potential growth.

The irony, in brief, is this: the Baptist announces the coming of the Lamb in a country which neither desires nor recognizes the authority of such a Messiah.

And the irony cuts of course both ways. As we've seen, the Baptist is himself a distinguished victim of the black magic language which created the vortex of war and hatred he would oppose with the Lamb of peace and brotherhood: the Baptist speaks in the idiom of the New Testament Pharisee and not in the tongue of the Old Testament prophet. And the irony at the expense of middle class America cuts as deep. The greatest nation in the sense of material prosperity and power the world has known is capable of producing a language which is perhaps among the most barbaric the world has ever heard. Contemporary American language not only conditions "war reflexes" which result in a harvest of slaughter among Oriental peasants but in its banality, its glut of clichés and adolescent vocabulary with which to express complex adult feelings and ideas, this language affords no decent words with which a powerful American poet might express desire for peace and love and brotherhood.

The mantra fails, then, because it couldn't possibly have succeeded. If the mantra had "worked," the poem would have been false. How could the religious act of the poet, which is doomed to expression in language which embodies worship of alien gods, affect that language and what it has created and sustained?

One problem still remains: Does the failure of the mantra contain all of the complex of experience within this poem? What prompts me to raise the question is the heroic quality in the final image of the poet as Baptist.

Although the concluding lines with the image of the Loving Negro and the white children contain an ironic example of that false rhetoric which the mantra attempts to oppose, the lines when read from another view also contain genuine poetry. What makes the final lines moving, it seems to me, is the fact that they are spoken at all. Everything opposes this last and almost desperate attempt to make the mantra effective: the poet stands as Baptist crying in a false language in a secular wilderness; yet he refuses to stop his attempt to dismantle the vortex of hatred and death which seems about to envelop him.

In this sense, "**Wichita Vortex Sutra**" can be read as a poem of noble desire. The desire it embodies is the ancient one: that the Lamb of God come among this people, bringing peace, love and salvation. This desire not only seems to inspire the creation of the mantra in the first place but also encourages the poet to continue trying to build a Jerusalem of peace and brotherhood in the teeth of such a hostile or indifferent environment. In a striking sense, this is the same desire which we have heard in Blake's famous lines from "Milton":

> And did those feet in ancient time
> Walk upon England's mountains green?
> And was the holy Lamb of God
> On England's pleasant pastures seen?
>
> And did the Countenance Divine
> Shine forth upon our clouded hills?
> And was Jerusalem builded here
> Among these dark Satanic Mills?
>
> Bring me my bow of burning gold!
> Bring me my arrows of desire!
> Bring me my spear! O clouds, unfold!
> Bring me my chariot of fire!
>
> I will not cease from mental fight,
> Nor shall my sword sleep in my hand,

Till we have built Jerusalem
In England's green and pleasant land.

Finally, the nobility of the desire of the poet who refuses to cease from mental fight accounts, it seems to me, for some of the memorable passages throughout the poem which in their intensity and magnanimity seem unequalled by any American poet since Whitman.

Reread that passage on United States Foreign Policy, for instance, which occurs a little over half way through the first section as the Volkswagen nears Marysville, Kansas, beginning: "Is this the land that started war on China?" and ending with the indictment of the Dulles law firm for the alleged greed which prompted its support of the overthrow in 1954 of the Guzmán regime in Guatemala which had favored agrarian reform and encouraged Communists to hold key posts in government. Then there's the section depicting the Human Mystical Body which begins as the station wagon passes through Waterville, Kansas and which ends: "When a woman's heart bursts in Waterville / a woman screams equal in Hanoi." Or take the Loneliness of Americans section (which some might censure for its sentimentality but which I find genuine poetry because of the incandescence of the desire) which opens with the confession: "I'm an old man now, and a lonesome man in Kansas" and continues with the meditation on God the Creator and concludes with the poet searching for the language "that is also yours."

In the light of such passages embodying Ginsberg's desire for peace and brotherhood, we should reread the Indictment of Wichita section, beginning with the entrance of the Volkswagen into the "Centertown ganglion" and ending with the final exhortation to the children of Wichita. When seen in the broader context of the poem as statement of desire, this section no longer seems, in my opinion, as rhetorical or sentimental as it once did. Now it blazes with compassion.

When the entire poem is seen as being a statement of desire, it seems irrelevant to circumscribe our critical appreciation by such questions as: Does the mantra fail? or Is this an anti-Viet Nam poem? What matters is that the poem embodies and sustains throughout the statement of Ginsberg's complex desire to assume the function of poet as priestly legislator and as Baptist announcing the dispensation of peace, compassion and brotherhood for all Americans. In this sense, then, "**Wichita Vortex Sutra**" is a major work.

Notes

1. W. B. Yeats offers more practical advice to poets who want to think of themselves as legislators. Shortly before retiring from political life—he served as Senator in the Irish Senate from 1922 to 1928—Yeats admonished his old friend Ezra Pound: "Do not be elected to the Senate of your country. Neither you, nor I, nor any other of our excitable profession can match those lawyers, old bankers, old business men, who, because all habit and memory, have begun to govern the world." Poets would be as much out of place in a Senate and in political life in general, Yeats continued, as would "the first composers of Sea-chanties in an age of Steam."
2. The text of the letter and notes appears in Appendix One. At first, I thought that the proem to "Wichita Vortex Sutra" mentioned by the poet in his letter should be included in an essay exploring the poem; but when I learned that both the proem and poem were portions of an extremely long poem-in-progress tentatively called "These States," I decided to limit my remarks to a discussion of the poem which has impressed me as a complete and self-contained work of art since it first appeared in *The Village Voice* (April 28, 1966). The reader might be interested to know that the entire text of "These States" comes from an almost literal transcription of the tape recording made by the poet as he wandered around America as a Guggenheim Fellow in Poetry during the fall of 1965 and winter of 1966.
3. A copy of the first draft of the essay on his (or her) poem was sent to each poet in the hope that comments and/or variant readings would help to clarify awkward or wrong interpretations. In a letter dated November 22, 1967, Ginsberg offers variant readings of several crucial passages in "Wichita Vortex Sutra." Although his comments proved helpful and stimulating when I rewrote the essay, I decided to keep my original reading of most of the passages in question. But in case the reader might want to compare the two readings, I have included the poet's comments in Appendix Two. The first comment concerns the lines about Senator Aiken's statement to the reporters about Mr. McNamara's "bad guess."
4. I will never forget the feeling that swept over me as I heard the poet recite the lines of the creation of the mantra at The University of Chicago one evening in February 1967. Here was an American poet calling—for the first time in our literature perhaps and certainly for the first time since Whitman—for the possibility of the existence of the ancient verities in the life of these States. Ginsberg was calling for communion with the gods and for release of love and peace in the souls of Americans. He was calling, in truth, for the realization by himself and by all of us that the Kingdom of God is within everybody. And as I remember the figure of the poet chanting his prayer on the stage of Mandel Hall, I hope that never again will I have to hear or read the wide-spread but boring criticism of Ginsberg which scolds or condemns him because he is supposed to be the Rasputin of American Poetry: the degenerate who is out to subvert or tarnish the Stars and Stripes, Mom, Home, and the Boys of the 4-H Club, as well as *The Oxford Book of American Verse*. The man on stage that evening was a holy man.
5. Nor can the final lines be understood (as far as I can see) as an example of the "impure" discussed in the concluding essay and in the essay on Frank O'Hara's

"The Day Lady Died." The concept of the impure doesn't apply here because the final lines clearly are intended by the poet to be the conclusion of what is an extremely well-structured and organic poem.

6. I am dismissing without discussion another possible answer as to why the language fails. This is that answer which those readers and fellow poets who dislike (or envy) Ginsberg and his poems might be tempted to argue: namely, that the language fails because Ginsberg is a bad poet. I dismiss this view with the most basic observation. Any poet whose imagination could have created the mantra in the first place is one I will bear with and follow to the end, assured that he will take the poem into areas in which few American poets have dared to explore.

Planet News

THOMAS PARKINSON (REVIEW DATE SPRING 1969)

SOURCE: Parkinson, Thomas. "Reflections on Allen Ginsberg as Poet." *Concerning Poetry* 2, no. 1 (spring 1969): 21-4.

In the following review, Parkinson discusses Planet News *and addresses critics of the time who questioned whether or not Ginsberg's work is poetry in the traditional sense.*

Allen Ginsberg is a notoriety, a celebrity; to many readers and non-readers of poetry he has the capacity for releasing odd energetic responses of hatred and love or amused affection or indignant moralizing. There are even people who are roused to very flat indifference by the friendly nearsighted shambling bearded figure who has some of the qualities of such comic stars as Buster Keaton or Charlie Chaplin. And some of their seriousness.

His latest book ***Planet News*** grants another revelation of his sensibility. The usual characteristics of his work are there, the rhapsodic lines, the odd collocations of images and thoughts and processes, the occasional rant, the extraordinary tenderness. His poetry resembles the Picasso sculpture melted together of children toys, or the sculpture of drift-wood and old tires and metal barrels and tin cans shaped by enterprising imaginative young people along the polluted shores of San Francisco Bay. You can make credible Viking warriors from such materials. Ginsberg's poetry works in parallel processes; it is junk poetry, not in the drug sense of junk but in its building blocks. It joins together the waste and loss that have come to characterize the current world, Cuba, Czechoslovakia, the Orient, the United States, Peru. Out of such debris as is offered he makes what poetry he can.

He doesn't bring news of the earth but of the planet. Earth drives us down, confines, mires, isolates, and besides there is less and less earth available to perception and more and more artifice. The late C. S. Lewis might not have enjoyed having his name brought into this discussion, but his great trilogy that begins with *Out of the Silent Planet* and ends with *That Hideous Strength* demonstrates the same concern with the planet as Ginsberg's new book. Both of them see Earth as a planet, part of a solar system, part of a galaxy, part of a universe, cosmic. But where Lewis wrote out of hatred, indignation, and despair at the destruction of tradition by mindless technology, Ginsberg writes from sad lost affection. I think Ginsberg is our only truly sad writer, sad with a heavy, heavy world, and somehow always courageous and content to remain in the human continuum with all his knowledge of human ill and malice clear. He persists.

But is it poetry? This question is so often asked that it does require answering not only within the confines of Ginsberg's work but generally. I am not entirely sure what the question means, since it could legitimately be asked of Whitman or Hart Crane, has been asked of them. What Ginsberg's work represents is an enormous purging and exorcising operation; it is in the area of religious and spiritual exploration rather than that of aesthetic accomplishment. In the dispute between Whistler and Ruskin over the concept of artistic "finish," Ginsberg's poetry would stand with Whistler's painting. He tends to use the term "poet" not as "maker" but revealer at best; at worst he accepts the notion that makes "poets" out of all confused serious persons who are genuinely unquiet about their souls and the condition of the planet. This is a widely embracing category. What troubles many readers of Ginsberg's work, if they are frank about it, is the continuous and consequently tedious reference to semen, excrement, masturbation, buggery, fornication, and the limited series of variations on such substances and processes. Who needs all the soiled bed-sheets? The only proper answer is that Ginsberg does—or did. They were reminders of the shame, guilt, and disorder that apparently afflicted his sexual life and obsessions; they needed to be purged and declared innocent, and the poems attend seriously to that very problem. To some readers they are frank, courageous, out-spoken; others find them violations of the artistic principle of reticence. Both arguments seem to me trivial, having to do with civil rights or social formalities. What occurred in Ginsberg's work seems to me at once more rational and more historically determined than many readers seem willing to admit.

If Ginsberg is nothing else, he is a large contributor to the *Zeitgeist.* Legally and linguistically, he not merely reflected the drift of his time but diverted and channelled it, not out of any sensational interest in so acting but out of the necessities that his being exacted from history. The co-incidence of his particular hang-ups—and there is no other way to describe them—with the tabus of the society generated a freely inevitable kind of writing. For in addition to the concern for his own troubled being, he was involved in liberating his body and liberating his mind so that both could function properly: spontaneous me, I sing the body electric. In their most considerable work, both Whitman and Ginsberg are intent on destroying those cerebral bonds that impair their sympathy with their bodies and with others. For others appear only in the body. The irony in both writers is that their most rationally ordered poems are those that argue against the rational faculties. In fact, their real quarrel is with the misuse of cerebral power; they share this sense of imbalance with Blake and Lawrence. And there must be moments when Ginsberg would ruefully agree with Lawrence who answered a correspondent who questioned his intellectual fulminating against the intellect by saying, in effect, that yes, he reminded himself of Carlyle who once said that he had written fifty books on the virtue of silence.

When such paragraphs as the preceding one place Ginsberg in the realm of Whitman, Blake, Lawrence, and Carlyle, a certain uneasiness might justly prevail. I think that this is more a matter of habit than of perception. When the Epstein statue of Blake was placed in Westminster Abbey, I felt slightly miserable—it seemed that the British talent for retrospectively accepting the eccentric had over-reached itself. I don't want to see Ginsberg canonized because it would take the edge off his work. With contemporary poets, all question of relative evaluation with the mighty dead is impertinent. Some years back an acquaintance of mine was bad-mouthing Robert Frost and ended with what he took to be an unanswerable question, "Will he last?" and I tried to bring him back to biological reality by murmuring, "None of us will." What we can ask from our writers is a willingness to face up to the troubled planet.

Returning again to the sexuality of Ginsberg's work, I find that in this book, arranged chronologically, there seems to be a steady diminution of concern with the vocabulary and processes that bother many otherwise sympathetic readers. Several of the poems are among his very best work: **"Kral Majales"**; **"Who Be Kind To"**; **"Wichita Vortex Sutra"**; **"Wales Visitation."** I can't imagine Ginsberg ever solving to his satisfaction the problems that have troubled his being for so many years; but he does seem to have undergone some profound religious experiences during the past five years that give his work a new density and fullness. He is one of the most important men alive on the planet. We should all be grateful for his presence.

But is he a poet? Again I find the question meaningless. He has written over a dozen first-rate poems; he has brought back to life, through his studies in French and Spanish verse, the Whitman tradition and informed it with a new pulse; he has served as a large part of the prophetic conscience of this country during its darkest period; he has been brave and productive. He has gone off on side-tracks; he has indulged himself publicly in some poems that seem better confined to note-books. But when a man liberates the sense of prosodic possibility and embodies in his work a profoundly meaningful spiritual quest that is compelling and clarifying to any reasonably sympathetic reader, well, yes, he is a poet. Only envy and spite could deny the title.

ON THE SUBJECT OF...

JOANNE KYGER ON MEETING THE DALAI LAMA WITH GINSBERG

And then Allen Ginsberg says to him how many hours do you meditate a day, and he says me? Why I never meditate, I don't have to. The Ginsberg is very happy because he wants to get instantly enlightened and can't stand sitting down or discipline of the body. He always gobbles down his food before anyone else has started. He came to India to find a spiritual teacher. But I think he actually believes he knows it all, but just wishes he *Felt* better about it.

Kyger, Joanne. Excerpt from "Letter to Nemi April 10 1962" in *Strange Big Moon: The Japan and India Journals: 1960-1964.* Berkeley, Cal.: North Atlantic Books, 2000, 281 p.

PAUL ZWEIG (REVIEW DATE 1969)

SOURCE: Zweig, Paul. "A Music of Angels." In *On the Poetry of Allen Ginsberg,* edited by Lewis Hyde, pp. 195-9. Ann Arbor: University of Michigan Press, 1984.

In the following review, which originally appeared in the Nation *in 1969, Zweig analyzes the poems collected in* Planet News.

Communicating vases: so the French Surrealists described them. Between the inner and the outer vase, a boil of suffering; memories churning over the psychic obstacles, on their way to be captured in the nets of grammar and consecutive statement. If there is one man who has helped us to believe in and to practice the mystery of these communicating vases, it is Allen Ginsberg, whose new book, ***Planet News,*** contains some of his finest poems. Between the planet earth and the planet Ginsberg, a banter of loves and disasters has been carried on; between this aging space of ecstasies, who insists aloud:

> I am that I am I am the
> man & the Adam of hair in
> my loins This is my spirit and
> physical shape I inhabit
> this Universe

and that other jet-diminished globe, riddled with places: Warsaw, New York, Calcutta, Wales . . . titles of so many personal, gritty moments from which poems arise.

What Ginsberg forced us to understand in **"Howl,"** twelve years ago, was that nothing is safe from poetry. His argument was not for new poetic subjects, for speech rhythms, for more emotions, or for mysticism. Argument in fact, is not the word for the unsettling spell Ginsberg-as-shaman chanted, suffered and danced in **"Howl."** In life, as in poetry, the shaman does not argue. He climbs the psychic hill, beyond the last familiar stone, and then disappears. Later the wind will blow disquieting noises back to us. Morality has pursued him like a clean razor and dismembered his body; his spirit has been assaulted by righteous chancres; rumors abound that he has been nailed to a tree, where the animals will play upon his bones forever, like a harp. But then the poet-shaman reappears, carrying the sick soul he had gone to save: anyone and everyone's soul, his own too, for the shaman must have suffered from all the ills he can cure. He comes back, but he is changed, for he has seen, played before him, all the fantasies of the hidden psyche, and all the possibilities of the will. He has learned the demanding truth that Montaigne discovered in his tower: "I am a man, and nothing human is foreign to me." Here, I think, lies the generous fantasy of ***Planet News.*** Ginsberg has brought back the sick soul—his own, mine, yours. In payment, he has received the gift of love. Now nothing human is foreign to him.

We know how much what we are is bound up in what, and how, we remember. Our character, and therefore what we do, depends upon—and is—the style of our remembering. I insist upon the word "style," for quantity, the sheer bulk of what we have been, has nothing to do with it. It is like stringing beads out of a huge box of beads. I work in reds, you in shades of green, and you in sharp edges. The "I" is selective, distrustful. And when, beguiled by travel, drugs or women, I recklessly string a rainbow stone, or a piece of turd, that too is part of the pattern. I have learned to be selectively reckless. On principle I open a certain third eye, let if flicker on the marvel of endless possibility, and then hurry it shut, afraid I will be convicted of "too much."

Ginsberg has made "too much" the affair of his life. Like Whitman, Blake, Traherne, Rabelais, he has enacted what it means to say: "I am the greatest lover in the universe." It is the mystery of seeing, and not judging, of understanding, and not discriminating. If such a life can have a program, then Whitman formulated it:

> This is the meal equally set,
> this the meat for natural hunger,
> It is for the wicked just the same as for the
> righteous,
> I make appointments with all,
> I will not have a single person slighted or left
> away,
> The kept-woman, sponger, thief, are hereby
> invited,
> The heavy-lipp'd slave is invited, the venerealee
> is invited;
> There shall be no difference between them and
> the rest.

In ***Planet News,*** the quintessential poem of "too much," is **"Television Was a Baby Crawling Toward That Death-chamber."** It is a poem which, like electricity, is sustained by its own movement. And the movement arises from Ginsberg's magical ability to know all the beads, and yet select none, for he selects all. Here as elsewhere, Ginsberg opens a hot line to every recess of his roomy, endless body. Like the infinite interconnection of all phenomena in the physical world (when I spit into the ocean, it rises; when I blow, the wind changes direction), the tangled relationships of everything with everything speak in Ginsberg's poem. He has faith that this is so; that all fishing in the dark water is successful. When Ginsberg is at his best, his mad leaps of association are perfect; they imitate the ideal knowledge of a Monad linked, lovingly, to the whole planet: even to cat vomit, Peruvian skulls, disappointed old body, or LSD pastoral worships:

> That's what I came here to compose, what I knocked off my life to
> Inscribe on my grey metal typewriter,
> borrowed from somebody's lover's mother got it from Welfare, all
> interconnected and gracious a bunch of Murderers
> as possible in this Kalpa of Hungry blood-drunkard Ghosts—

The shape of "**Television . . .**" is the shape of "too much," which is to say that it works against the very idea of poetic form. And yet, by creating the experience (or enchantment) of "too much," it claims for itself all the privileges of form, i.e., the privilege of being this irreplaceable, absolutely achieved word-vision. Ginsberg, like Whitman, does not forget the place he occupies in the spectrum of cultural forms. He has the pleasure of knowing, from some shy Victorian refuge in his own psyche, that he is being a bit ridiculous. And so he acts out for us our temptation to judge his "too-muchness," and to contain it. What I mean is that Ginsberg, like his spiritual godfather, Walt Whitman, has a sense of comedy. He is an American humorist:

> Dusty moonlight, Starbeam riding its own flute, soul
> revealed in the scribble, an ounce of looks, an Invisible
> Seeing, Hope, The Vanisher betokening Eternity
> one finger raised warning above his gold eyeglasses—
> and Mozart playing giddy-note an hour on the Marxist gramophone—
>
> . . . . .
>
> The Bardo Thodol extends in the millions of black jello
> for every dying Mechanic—We will make Colossal
> movies—
> We will be a great Tantric Mogul & starify a new Hollywood with our unimaginable Flow—Great Paranoia!

The humor is part of the generosity of ***Planet News.*** Ginsberg, in his expansive way, is trying to convince us to wade out from the moralizing beaches where we have learned too well to string our beads. The water is fine, he says. If only we could stop judging and disdaining, we would realize how simple it is to paddle around in the world (and in ourselves).

Often ***Planet News*** modulates from the glutted, sexual fantasy of "too-muchness," to a quieter, more intimate vision. When the Kalpas of extended space collapse momentarily, Ginsberg remembers himself: the citizen of an aging body, uprooted, humanly unhappy, and yet far from lament, for—and this is the peculiar strength of these moments—he has learned to love even his own aging despair:

> Allen Ginsberg says this: I am a mass of sores and worms
> & baldness & belly & smell I am false Name the prey
> of Yamantaka Devourer of Strange Dreams . . .
>
> . . . . .
>
> and I lay back on my pallet contemplating $50 phone bill,
> broke, drowsy, anxious, my heart fearful of the
> fingers dialing, the deaths, the singing of telephone
> bells

Ginsberg in ***Planet News,*** has given us a music of angels. Not Christian holy angels, but the angels of which Rilke spoke: "those almost deadly birds of the soul." They are almost deadly, because they ask what is most difficult to do: to love even what is not lovable, to serve up the meal for everyone, to love fate while seeing with intelligent, discriminating eyes what fate is.

I have insisted on evoking the ancestry of Ginsberg's vision because there is in this poetry of "too-muchness" a tradition and a genre which deserve to be noticed. In "**Journal Night Thoughts,**" for example, Ginsberg echoes a conventional form and uses it, with humor, to express his continuous fantasy. It is a poem of night images, traveling a path of the mind's peregrinations in New York. One thinks, inevitably, of Young's "Night Thoughts," of Whitman's lovely poem, "The Sleepers." Ginsberg has confidence that form, once rhetorical shapes have been discarded, can arise from life itself, referring backward and forward, in the fashion of a psychic genre, to a larger shape of human experience. Here Ginsberg writes the "night-ode" or whatever name we give it: a form more ample for our total needs than sonnet, epic, or other hanger for old clothes.

FURTHER READING

Biographies

Fredman, Stephen. "Allen Ginsberg and Lionel Trilling: The Hasid and the Mitnaged." *Religion and Literature* 30, no. 3 (autumn 1998): 67-75.

Details Ginsberg's relationship with Lionel Trilling.

Kramer, Jane. *Paterfamilias: Allen Ginsberg in America.* New York: Random House, 1969, 202 p.

Account of Ginsberg's life during the 1950s and 1960s.

Miles, Barry. *Ginsberg: A Biography.* New York: Simon & Schuster, 1989, 588 p.

Comprehensive portrayal of Ginsberg's life and career by a personal friend and associate.

Criticism

Breslin, James. "Allen Ginsberg: The Origins of *Howl* and *Kaddish.* In *The Beats: Essays in Criticism,* edited by Lee Bartlett, pp. 66-89. Jefferson, N.C. and London: McFarland, 1981.

Explores the background of two of Ginsberg's most famous poems.

Breslin, James E. B. "Allen Ginsberg's *Howl.*" In *From Modern to Contemporary: American Poetry, 1945-1965,* pp. 77-109. Chicago: The University of Chicago Press, 1983.

Regards "Howl" as a series of poetic experiments combining the idealism of nineteenth-century verse with contemporary urban realities.

Burns, Glen. *Great Poets Howl: A Study of Allen Ginsberg's Poetry, 1943-1955.* Frankfurt am Main: Verlag Peter Lang, 1983, 540 p.

Formalist study of Ginsberg's poetry.

Clark, Thomas. "The Art of Poetry VIII: Allen Ginsberg, an Interview." *The Paris Review,* no. 37 (spring 1966): 13-55.

Transcribes a detailed interview that covered a wide range of subjects, including censorship, art, Ginsberg's relationship with fellow Beat writers, and his celebrated visions of William Blake.

Cox, Harvey. "An Open Letter to Allen Ginsberg." *Commonweal* (April 1967): 147-49.

Compares hippies and the Beat movement to Christianity.

Davie, Donald. "On Sincerity: From Wordsworth to Ginsberg." *Encounter* 31, no. 4 (October 1968): 61-6.

Discusses Ginsberg's work as part of a tradition of confessional poetry.

Diggory, Terence. "Allen Ginsberg's Urban Pastoral." *College Literature* 27, no 1. (winter 2000): 103-18.

Explores Ginsberg's desire for a simple life of writing poetry and meditation.

Fiedler, Leslie. "Into the Cafés: A Kind of Solution." In *Waiting for the End,* pp. 233-49. New York: Stein and Day, 1964.

Asserts that Ginsberg stands apart from other poets of the Beat movement and explores the influence of Walt Whitman on his works.

Foster, Edward Halsey. "Ginsberg." In *Understanding the Beats,* pp. 84-127. Columbia: University of South Carolina Press, 1992.

Focuses on the political aspects of Ginsberg's poetry.

Grossman, Allen. "The Jew as an American Poet: The Instance of Ginsberg." *Judaism: A Quarterly Journal of Jewish Life and Thought* 2, no. 4 (fall 1962): 303-08.

Explores the role of Jewish culture in Ginsberg's poetic identity.

Pinckney, Darryl. "The May King." *Parnassus* 10, no. 1 (spring-summer 1982): 99-109.

In the following essay, Pinckney traces Ginsberg's development as a poet.

Podhoretz, Norman. "My War with Allen Ginsberg." *Commentary* 104, no. 2 (August 1997): 27-40.

Podhoretz recalls his history of disputes with Ginsberg and provides a critical assessment of his work and contribution to American poetry.

Portugés, Paul. *The Visionary Poetics of Allen Ginsberg.* Santa Barbara, Calif.: Ross-Erikson, 1978, 181 p.

Discusses Ginsberg's work as visionary in the tradition of William Blake.

Rosenthal, M. L. *The New Poets: American and British Poetry Since World War II,* pp. 89-113. New York: Oxford University Press, 1967.

Examines the political and aesthetic properties of "Howl" and "Kaddish."

Shechner, Mark. "Allen Ginsberg: The Poetics of Power." In *After the Revolution: Studies in the Contemporary Jewish American Imagination,* pp. 180-95. Bloomington: Indiana University Press, 1987.

Investigates the capability of Ginsberg's poetry to crossover to popular culture and affect social history.

Van der Bent, Jaap. "'O fellow travelers I write you a poem in Amsterdam': Vinkenoog, and the Dutch Beat Connection." *College Literature* 27, no 1. (winter 2000): 199-212.

Traces Ginsberg's influence on Dutch Beat poetry.

Widmer, Kingsley. "The Beat in the Rise of the Populist Culture." In *The Fifties: Fiction, Poetry, Drama,* edited by Warren French, pp. 155-73. Orlando: Everett/Edwards, Inc., 1970.

Charts the role of "Howl" and other poems in the escalating popularity of the Beat movement in the 1950s and 1960s.

Woods, Gregory. "Allen Ginsberg." In *Articulate Flesh: Male Homo-Eroticism and Modern Poetry,* pp. 195-211. New Haven: Yale University Press, 1987.

Analyzes Ginsberg's use of homoeroticism in his poetry.

OTHER SOURCES FROM GALE:

Additional coverage of Ginsberg's life and career is contained in the following sources published by the Gale Group: *American Writers Supplement,* Vol. 2; *Authors and Artists for Young Adults,* Vol. 33; *Authors in the News,* Vol. 1; *Concise Dictionary of American Literary Biography, 1941-1968*; *Contemporary Authors,* Vols. 1-4R; *Contemporary Authors New Revision Series,* Vols. 2, 41, 63, 95; *Contemporary Literary Criticism,* Vols. 1, 2, 3, 4, 6, 13, 36, 69, 109; *Contemporary Poets,* Ed. 7; *Dictionary of Literary Biography,* Vols. 5, 16, 169, 237; *DISCovering Authors*; *DISCovering Authors 3.0*; *DISCovering Authors: British Edition*; *DISCovering Authors: Canadian Edition*; *DISCovering Authors Modules: Most-studied Authors,* and *Poets*; *Gay & Lesbian Literature*; *Major 20th-Century Writers,* Eds. 1, 2; *Poets: American and British*; *Poetry for Students,* Vol. 5; *Reference Guide to American Literature,* Ed. 4; *Twentieth-Century Literary Criticism,* Vol. 120; *World Literature Criticism*; and *World Poets.*

BARBARA GUEST

(1920 -)

American poet, novelist, playwright, essayist, biographer, editor, and art critic.

Like—but not with—the Beat writers, Guest performed her works at the Living Theater and other Greenwich Village locales during the 1950s. One of the five founding members of the New York School of Poets and its only founding female, Guest has enjoyed an expansive career as a Modernist poet and author. While critical attention has often passed her by in favor of cofounders Frank O'Hara and John Ashbery, Guest nevertheless has earned a distinctive reputation as an experimental and innovative poet. Interested in the language of poetry rather than the narrative or ideas, she also avoids political and social commentary in favor of developing the visual potential of the poetic medium. Her many volumes and collaborations are rich testaments to her unique vision and the influence of abstract imagery and surrealism on poetics, and viewing her development as an innovative poet who developed separately from—but during the same era as—her contemporaries in the Beat Generation, provides a unique perspective on the literary and social culture of the time.

BIOGRAPHICAL INFORMATION

Biographers know that Guest was born on September 6, 1920, in Wilmington, North Carolina, to James Harvey and Ann (Hetzel) Pinson, but little has been written about Guest's childhood. In 1943 she obtained a B.A. from the University of California, Los Angeles, and in 1949 she married Lord Stephen Haden Guest, with whom she has one child. The couple divorced in 1954, the same year she married her second husband, Trumbull Higgins, a professor of military history, with whom she has a second child.

In the early 1950s Guest relocated from the West Coast to New York, where she worked for *Art News* magazine and drew upon an extensive background and interest in the visual arts. The influence of modernism, surrealism, cubism, and abstract expressionism on her growing interest in literature led Guest to form a friendship with four other aspiring writers and artists—O'Hara, Ashbery, James Schulyer, and Kenneth Koch—who shared her creative interests. Their collective artistic philosophy united the informal group of authors, who came to be known as the New York School of Poets. Their poetry is recognized for its celebration of New York, a passion for abstract expressionist painting, their experimental surrealist style of writing, and their rejection of traditional narrative and linguistic methods. Of the New York School of Poets, Ashbery and O'Hara rose to the greatest critical prominence, while Guest has remained relatively unknown.

She published her first volume of poetry, *The Location of Things,* in 1960 and subsequently published over fourteen works of poetry, biography, drama, and fiction, while regularly contributing essays on literary and art criticism to periodicals. Her work has been inconsistently anthologized over the years, which has led in part to some critical ambivalence toward her work. Most widely read for her poetry in the 1950s and 1960s, Guest continued to write and experiment with language, poetics, and art throughout the next three decades. In 1999 Guest was awarded the Poetry Society of America's Robert Frost Medal for Lifetime Achievement, which Robert Kaufman claims "officially places her in the select company of such previous Frost-Medal recipients as Wallace Stevens, Marianne Moore, and John Ashbery." In the late twentieth and early twenty-first centuries, there has been an increasing momentum in Guest scholarship as her significance to the New York School of Poets and her innovative style and perspective captured the imaginations of new generations of experimental poets and critics.

MAJOR WORKS

With a wide body of poetry, including *Poems: The Location of Things, Archaics, The Open Skies* (1962), *Moscow Mansions: Poems* (1973), *Fair Realism* (1989), and her collection *Selected Poems* (1995), Guest's oeuvre can be characterized as being significantly influenced by her background in the visual arts and painting. Disinterested in traditional narrative styles or in political statements, Guest's poetry is often motivated by the language itself rather than the ideas it conveys. Painting with her pen, Guest employs abstract and surrealist perspectives as she writes to and about other painters, works of art, and music. Her work is refined rather than emotional, and this has often left readers feeling unsure of their relationship to her work and its author. Guest's prose further explores her interest in imagism and abstraction. Her novel *Seeking Air* (1978) employs stream-of-consciousness as it follows Morgan Flew and his attempt to gain control over his life and the world around him. The experimental novel uses the small moments of everyday life and the spaces between events to examine daily experiences in New York and Paris and to explore issues of memory, coincidence, time, and disorder. Guest's interest in imagism led her to write a biography of the original Imagist poet H. D. (Hilda Doolittle). *Herself Defined: The Poet H. D. and Her World* (1984) examines the life and experiences of H. D., who wrote free-verse poetry and employed vivid imagery as she moved in literary circles that included D. H. Lawrence and Ezra Pound. This biography met with significant attention for its careful consideration of H. D. and its examination of an important literary period.

CRITICAL RECEPTION

While there have been no full-length biographies of Guest, and criticism of her early work is limited, the late twentieth century saw a significant increase in Guest scholarship. In 2001 *Women's Studies: An Interdisciplinary Journal* devoted an entire volume to Guest with prominent Guest scholar Sara Lundquist considering the writer's placement in the New York School of Poets. Likewise, Arielle Greenberg examines the poet's use of humor and levity in her work. In that same year, the National Poetry Foundation published a collected work of criticism on the New York School of Poets, in which Lynn Keller considers Guest's work in the context of the burgeoning feminist movement and Betty Friedan's seminal work *The Feminine Mystique*. Other critics have found rich material for exploration in Guest's writing for and about painting and artists, as well as in the musicality of her language. The apolitical nature of her work has led some critics to consider her significance as a woman poet in a largely male subgenre of Modernist poetry. While Guest is now a respected and honored American poet, many critics feel the true critical appreciation of this experimental, innovative writer is yet to come, and many reviewers have expressed hopes for increasing appreciation of her contributions.

PRINCIPAL WORKS

The Ladies' Choice [produced in New York, Artists Theatre] (play) 1953

The Location of Things (poetry) 1960

The Office [produced in New York, Café Chino] (play) 1961

Poems: The Location of Things, Archaics, The Open Skies (poetry) 1962

Robert Goodnough, Painter [with Bernard Harper Friedman] (poetry) 1962

Port [produced in New York, American Theatre for Poets] (play) 1965

The Blue Stairs: Poems (poetry) 1968

I Ching: Poems and Lithographs [with Shelia Isham] (poetry and art) 1969

"Jeanne Reynal"; published in journal *Craft Horizons* (essay) 1971

Moscow Mansions: Poems (poetry) 1973

"Helen Frankenthaler: The Moment and The Distance"; published in journal *Arts Magazine* (essay) 1975

The Countess from Minneapolis (poetry) 1976

Seeking Air: A Novel (novel) 1978

The Türler Losses (poetry) 1979

Biography (poetry) 1980

Quilts (poetry) 1980

Herself Defined: The Poet H. D. and Her World (biography) 1984

"A Reason for Poetics"; published in journal *Ironwood* (essay) 1984

"June Felter at 871 Fine Arts"; published in journal *Arts in America* (essay) 1985

"Leatrice Rose"; published in journal *Arts Magazine* (essay) 1985

"Mysteriously Defining the Mysterious: Byzantine Proposals of Poetry"; published in journal *How (ever)* (essay) 1986

Musicality [illustrations by June Felter] (poetry) 1988

Fair Realism (poetry) 1989

"The Vuillard of Us"; published in journal *Denver Quarterly* (essay) 1990

The Altos [illustrations by Richard Tuttle] (poetry) 1991

"Shifting Persona"; published in journal *Poetics Journal* (essay) 1991

Defensive Rapture (poetry) 1993

Selected Poems (poetry) 1995

Stripped Tales [with Anne Dunn] (poetry) 1995

Quill, Solitary Apparition (poetry) 1996

The Confetti Trees: Motion Picture Stories (poetry) 1998

If True, Tell Me: Short Poems (poetry) 1999

Rocks on a Platter: Notes on Literature (criticism) 2000

Symbiosis [art by Laurie Reid] (poetry and art) 2000

Miniatures and Other Poems (poetry) 2002

GENERAL COMMENTARY

SARA LUNDQUIST (ESSAY DATE SUMMER 1997)

SOURCE: Lundquist, Sara. "Reverence and Resistance: Barbara Guest, Ekphrasis, and the Female Gaze." *Contemporary Literature* 38, no. 2 (summer 1997): 260-86.

In the following essay, Lundquist considers the critical perception that Guest's work is refined rather than passionate and that Guest favors language and texture to narrative. Lundquist attempts to refute this perception by exploring Guest's poetry to, for, and about paintings for the ways it reveals the inner life of the poet.

Composer John Gruen, in his reminiscence of the New York arts scene during the 1950s and 1960s, employs both photographs and text to show how ardent artistic endeavor merged in those days with fervent socializing. He chronicles the doings of a group of people whose admiration of each other's as-yet-unrecognized work coincided with delight in each other's conversation and company. Studio photographs of artists at work are mixed with photographs of parties in bars and on beaches; pictures of elegant gallery openings are mixed with comical posings and blurred informal snapshots of leisure and levity. A typical photograph full of people is accompanied by a half-page list of names—of poets, painters, sculptors, scriptwriters, musicians, everyone who was anyone or hoped to be. One photograph, tagged "Another patio group shot—another party" (from 1961), particularly compels interest because of the elusive presence there, among the crowd, of "poet Barbara Guest" (154). Barbara Guest sits far to the left in the photograph, on its very margin, her face turned from the camera and hidden by her hair, one of the few people who does not look aggressively or self-consciously out of the photograph toward its contemporary and future viewers. Her attention is entirely inward toward the company, and she thus deflects the attention of the viewer; she is *difficult to see,* mysteriously not there at the same time that she is ostensibly there.

Trying to see Barbara Guest in this photograph is similar to trying to "see" Barbara Guest in any of the many venues in which contemporary poets come to the attention of readers. She is provocatively *there,* by name in literary histories, by reputation in the written reminiscences of others, and as a primary source for writers of literary biographies. She was present as an influential art critic who wrote essays for *Partisan Review* and helped edit *Art News* during the 1950s. Her biography of H. D. is generally acknowledged to be an important contribution to the reappraisal of the poet, "whose work, especially the long myth-laden poems of her later years, offers a uniquely female twist on modernism," in the words of one reviewer of Guest's book (Pollitt 7). But as a poet, Guest has remained strangely elusive, her volumes of poetry often difficult to obtain, reviews of her work infrequent, and academic critical studies sparse. Her name, in literary histories and anthologies, is almost invariably linked with those of Frank O'Hara, John Ashbery, Kenneth Koch, and James Schuyler as a member of the New York school of poets. Yet her poetry has not yet garnered the attention paid to the other four, certainly not the intense interest directed toward Ashbery and O'Hara from academic critics.

This disregard registers as particularly curious since Guest seems to fit so securely among these poets, engaged like them in beginnings, celebrations, *le merveilleux,* like them "saturate[d] . . . in language, the spoken, ordinary language, partly colloquial, partly slangy . . . wish[ing] to heighten the surface of a poem by intense, sophisticated interest in individual words" (Myers 24). And, like theirs, her poetry derives significant inspiration from painting. In books from ***The Location of Things*** in 1960 to ***Defensive Rapture*** in 1993, Guest has written poems about, for, and to paintings by artists as varied as Pinturicchio, Delacroix, Miró, Gris, Matisse, Kandinsky, Giacomo Balla, Robert Motherwell, Warren Brandt, Grace Hartigan, Mary Abbott, and Helen Frankenthaler. These poems can match Ashbery's and O'Hara's famous ekphrastic poems for sophistication, power, and subtlety.[1] But as Ashbery and O'Hara (and to a lesser extent Schuyler and Koch) have, over the years, entered the literary mainstream—favored by anthologists, reviewed in the literary and general presses, studied by literary scholars, critics, and theorists, and, as Geoff Ward puts it, "airlifted to the slippery slopes of the university syllabus" (9)—Guest's work remains marginal, or perhaps "out front." She is still likely to publish single poems in avant-garde publications like *Sulfur, Blue Mesa, Hambone, O.blek,* and *Temblor.* Her poem **"On the Verge of the Path"** must surely comment ruefully on the way her playful companions "Frank" and "John" of the 1950s have become "the shelves of O'Hara and Ashbery" (***Moscow Mansions*** 68), strangely transformed, from her point of view, into "name" poets.

Of the two anthologies that responded to the new popularity of avant-garde poetry in New York—Ron Padgett and David Shapiro's *An Anthology of New York Poets* (1970) and John Myers's *The Poets of the New York School* (1969)—one (Myers's) includes more than twenty pages of Guest's poetry, beginning with a large, startlingly vivid photograph of the poet and interspersing reproductions of paintings by Robert Goodnough. The other (Padgett and Shapiro's), although it includes three times as many poets (twenty-seven as opposed to Myers's nine), leaves out Barbara Guest.[2] Again a curious impression of absence/presence is created by considering the anthologies together: in one, Guest is securely in place and valued, and from the other she is carelessly or carefully excluded. Investigation into her reception and reputation yields a double sense of her both being there and not being there, creating a suspicion that, as Rachel Blau DuPlessis has suggested, "gender marginalization and invisibility have been an issue," and that Guest's career has suffered from the "strained and unexamined relationship to their female participants" often characteristic of groups dedicated to innovative poetries, which manifests itself in a "cavalier attitude toward women" ("Flavor" 23).

When Guest's poetry does come under critical discussion, it is likely to be described in such a way as to reinforce three persistent, true, but ultimately simplistic assumptions about her work: first, that it is difficult to the point of obduracy; second, that it is refined and cool, rather than passionate, personal, or emotionally urgent; and third, that it invariably avoids the political in favor of the aesthetic, preferring the sensualities of surface, texture, and wordplay over narrative, social commentary, and political naming.[3] "She seems serenely confident in her calling," writes Anthony Manousos, unbeset by "the political ardors of Denise Levertov and Adrienne Rich or with the confessional intensity of Sylvia Plath and Anne Sexton" (299, 296). While admiring her "assurance, taste, and intelligence" (Manousos 299), critics have noted the poetry's stylistic inaccessibility and have characterized her subject matter and tone as elite, perhaps elitist, working to refine rather than popularize American poetry. "She is . . . the most elegant of the New York poets," writes Robert F. Kiernan. "There is an inveterate chill to her poetry—a cosmopolitan refinement that supersedes anything truly personal" (144). Reviewing ***Moscow Mansions*** (1973), Alicia Ostriker claims: "the values are essentially and purely esthetic—line, texture, color, tone—rather than, say, moral, intellectual, or emotional"; "[The poems] are a little like conversations in refined places among refined persons. They are, like Alice's biscuits, very dry" (qtd. in Manousos 298,

296).[4] In an era when the poetry of women and feminist poetic theories richly sustain each other, Guest appears less than ardently feminist, difficult to place on a literary map whose coordinates are gender-based. This perhaps accounts for her exclusion from both editions of Florence Howe's influential anthology of twentieth-century poetry by women, *No More Masks!,* and for the troubling omission of any discussion of Guest's work from *Stealing the Language,* Ostriker's panoramic examination of American women's poetry. Unlike other women poets slighted by the literary mainstream, Guest has not yet, with the notable exception of DuPlessis, been embraced or promoted by feminist readers.[5]

The issues of difficulty and the personal urgency and feminist vision of Guest's poems can be reevaluated by looking at her numerous ekphrastic poems, that is, her poems about paintings. In this kind of second-order discourse one finds the inner life, the erotic life, the conflicts and confusions, and the intellectual exigencies of Guest's poetic personality lying half-concealed and half-revealed. There one is also disabused of the notion that her poetry engages only in the driest and coolest of refined, cultural "high talk." Her stylistic choices also come to seem less dauntingly difficult if they are read as precise and passionate expressions of feeling, thought, vision, and commitment experienced in the presence of a particularly compelling painting. Guest herself becomes more visible when one acknowledges that the act of seeing is crucial to her art, and much can be learned by assessing the nature and quality of her gaze.

Ekphrasis is the literary term for poetry that is "verbal representation of visual representation," in James A. W. Heffernan's succinct definition (3). Inquiry into the complex relations between word and image has been pursued most recently by W. J. T. Mitchell in *Picture Theory* (1994), by Heffernan in his book on the history and poetics of ekphrasis, *Museum of Words* (1993), by Murray Krieger in *Ekphrasis* (1992), and by Wendy Steiner in *Pictures of Romance* (1988). Thanks to this work on ekphrasis, it is possible to recognize and analyze the lively and conflicted emotional, intellectual, and linguistic activity that lies subsumed under the words "inspired by." A vocabulary now exists to investigate the arena of conflict or seduction that a poet enters when she or he re-presents in words what has already been presented in images.

Guest's ekphrastic poems perform and illumine questions central to the genre of ekphrasis, which are usefully phrased by Mitchell this way: "what motivates the desire to construct an entire text as an evocation, incorporation, or substitute for a visual object or experience? Why do texts seem compelled to reach out to their semiotic 'others,' the objects of visual representation?" (109). The poetry also invites its readers to speculate on the fact of choice: why this painting, and why now? What does it reveal about the poet's temperament, her character, her situation in time and place? What does it reveal about her sense of self as artist, her aesthetic, political, and moral position vis-à-vis her chosen painter? Because Guest's work offers the rare perspective of a woman in the position of viewer, respondent, "envoicer," and maker of the poetic meaning, it offers to complicate and inform theories of gendered art criticism which analyze the male gaze. To look at a painting via a poem by Barbara Guest is to enter the arena of the "female gaze" and also compels us to consider in what respects Guest is indeed a feminist.

In Guest's work we encounter an embarrassment of riches in the ekphrastic genre.[6] Her work charts an entire lifetime of engagement with painting and sculpture, resulting in some of our century's most complex and beautiful ekphrastic poems, poems that help define what viewing art means in our time. The poems explore how (indeed *if*) aesthetic perception of the visual can be translated into the signification of words, and what is problematic or enabling about the attempt to do so. Guest's imagination engages both representational and abstract art, evoking the postmodern situation of having the entire history of art to "walk through" and choose form. A comprehensive list of her ekphrastic poems would require much space, but notable examples include **"Piazzas"** (for Mary Abbott Clyde), **"Heroic Stages"** (for Grace Hartigan), **"All Elegies Are Black and White"** (to Robert Motherwell), **"Roses"** (about Gertrude Stein and Juan Gris), **"The Rose Marble Table"** (about Matisse), **"The View from Kandinsky's Window," "Dora Maar," "Wild Gardens Overlooked by Night Lights," "The Screen of Distance," "The Nude,"** and **"The Surface as Object."** "Painting is the poems' cosmology," Barbara Einzig writes, "and the world is read as a painting" (9).

Two particular poems about paintings, because they are distinctly different, can serve as examples and illustrations and give a sense of the range of Guest's capabilities. The first is titled **"The Poetess,"** from the collection ***Moscow Mansions*** (1973). The poem, short, compressed, and pointed, describes a lyrical, abstract gouache and oil painting of shifting shapes and colors by the Spanish modernist painter Joan Miró titled *La Poétesse*. The second poem, **"The Farewell Stairway,"** from ***Fair Realism*** (1989), is long, repetitious, and meandering, lavishly spread over six pages of ***Selected Poems***. It responds to a rigorously realist painting of three women descending a staircase, completed in 1909 by the Italian futurist Giacomo Balla. Both poems invite analysis of their gender configurations and contexts, since both are about paintings of women and present a female poet in colloquy, as it were, with a male painter. The paintings enhance access to the poems and vice versa, and both are revealing of the poetic personality of Guest herself. Similarly, the poems, though resplendently aesthetic, are not merely so; when contextualized, they reveal Guest's strong, judicious, clear understanding of cultural and social issues central to women.

"The Poetess," with its epigraph "after Miró," claims outright its ekphrastic nature, its entanglement with an Other. The painting *La Poétesse* is one in a series of twenty-three collectively titled *Constellations,* completed by Miró during World War II, smuggled out of occupied France, and first displayed at the Pierre Matisse Gallery in New York in 1945.[7] When, in April 1994, Brown University held a conference to celebrate Guest's work, the announcement of the event reprinted **"The Poetess"** alongside a reproduction of *La Poétesse*. Such a singling out of this poem enhances its status as a "signature" poem, which bears distinctive marks of identity, individuality, personality. It can, in fact, be read as a subtle and powerful autobiographical poem, as if the reader were looking over the shoulder of Guest as she looked in a mirror, seeing her see herself. When an interviewer asked Guest, "Did you go in for confessional poetry?" she answered simply, "I think all poetry is confessional" ("Barbara Guest" 23). This response expresses, I believe, Guest's awareness that all artistic representation functions as autobiographical projection, necessarily telling a story of self. In ekphrastic poetry (by definition a representation of a representation), the central story of self becomes complicated and enriched by the simultaneous centrality of an Other. Two visions consort and conflict with each other, seduce and serve, bewilder and explain each other. In poems such as these, Guest is creating a risky, open-ended portrait of self-as-artist, a portrait that is always strangely and necessarily relational.

The title, **"The Poetess,"** invites reading of the poem for understanding of how Guest defines herself as a poet, and specifically as a woman poet. The title also begs the question of why a woman poet would so closely align herself with the troublesomely gendered word "poetess." The tradition of American women's poetry has been haunted by the specter of the poetess; most women poets took pains to dissociate themselves from her devalued status. In a refrainlike phrase, DuPlessis repeatedly expresses the fears and longing of H. D. about her career amid male modernist poets: "It was the struggle not to be reduced, not to become 'poetess.'" Women poets live and work, she writes, with inscribed "drives to self-abnegation . . . [that] could easily help to create poetesses from the raw material that would have made poets" (***Pink Guitar*** 27, 28). Just a decade before Guest's poem was published, Robert Lowell, intending to extend high praise to Sylvia Plath's achievement in *Ariel,* declared her "certainly not another 'poetess'" (vii), while a generation earlier, a male critic, seeking to undermine the powerful poet and critic Amy Lowell, employed the humorous but immensely hurtful epithet "Hippo-poetess" (Gould 231-33).

It is strange and significant that a "signature" poem should also be an ekphrastic poem, one that owes its existence to another, one generated and interpolated by another. The poem has its eye trained not inward but outward, at a painter's brush marks, and yet those marks look to Guest like a mirror. The poet, it seems, has adopted Miró's *La Poétesse* as an amenable portrait of a woman poet, and an altogether truer and more satisfactory representation of her own self-as-poet than the stereotype of the "wailing" or "scribbling" poetess that has haunted literary criticism and the popular imagination. As the only woman poet of the first-generation New York poets, Guest may have seen in Miró's painting a visual validation of the inventive, humorous, fluid, elusive, urbane, whimsical, postsurrealist work she and they were doing and rejoiced to find it labeled feminine.

Neither painting nor poem, of course, is in any way a conventional portrait. The painting is essentially abstract: against a luminous brown-grey background geometrical and calligraphic shapes splay out over the painting's surface. Although J. H. Matthews complained that "however much good will we muster, we cannot be sure we discern a poet of either sex" (95), and although distinction between the figure and her surroundings is purposely minimized, a humanoid shape can be discerned and once seen is difficult to unsee. The poetess's body, with upraised "arms" reaching into the top corners, is drawn with a single continuous line, a section of which runs roughly parallel to the bottom margin of the painting. The contours of the body suggest a flowing and capacious robe as the poetess's apparel. Her head, in profile looking right just above the center, is marvelously odd but entirely Miróesque. Her eye, with its dilated pupil, startling white section, and eyelashes, is shaped like a stylized baby bird. Her nose or forehead is greatly elongated, even phallic shaped, and sports two extra sets of breasts. Her mouth is opened to reveal three sharp teeth. What is "inside" the poetess is very similar to what is "outside" her defining line: the same intense black, white, brown, and green, with primary yellow, red, and blue, the same linear tracery, curlicues, arabesques, asterisks, hourglass shapes, crescents, circles, barbells, triangles. Whenever line cuts through shape, it causes a color change. Inside the poetess's body, triangular shapes seem to represent breasts, and she displays the "awesome red and black vagina" that William Rubin has pointed out in another of the *Constellations* paintings (82). There are two of Miró's ubiquitous, mysterious "escape ladders." There are other "personages" and scattered minor characters in the form of childlike stick figures, biomorphic shapes, and floating eyes. The whole gives an impression of rhythm, humor, and delirious play among elements that are nonetheless delicately related and balanced.

La Poétesse, like the other *Constellations,* is imbued with spatial mystery and with sexuality that is "warm, abandoned, clean-cut, beautiful, and above all intense," in Robert Motherwell's description (117). About the period in which the paintings were made, Miró wrote:

> We had to leave Varengeville in haste. In this region which had remained calm the Germans opened up pitiless bombardments. With the Allied armies completely defeated and continuous bombardments we took the train from Paris. Pilar [Miró's wife, Pilar Juncosa de Miró] took Dolores, who was then a little girl, by the hand and I carried with me under my arm the portfolio containing those *Constellations* that were finished and the remainder of the sheets which were to serve for the completed series. . . .
>
> At this time . . . I was very depressed. I believed in an inevitable victory for Nazism, and that all that we love and that gives us our reason for living was sunk forever in the abyss. I believed that in this defeat there was no further hope for us, and had the idea of expressing this mood and this anguish by drawing signs and forms . . . which would go up and caress the stars, fleeing from the stink and decay of a world built by Hitler and his friends.
>
> (qtd. in Penrose 100-102)

Given the bleak and brutal context of world war in which these paintings were made, they seem to reflect Miró's wishful and stubborn need to assert human loveliness, sensuality, tenderness, humor, and benevolence in the order of things: in short, they posit what might be called a "feminized" cosmology. Miró, by titling *La Poétesse* as he did, made this painting stand out among the others and no doubt contributed to Guest's attraction to it.[8] The title suggests that the "mute ekphrastic object awaiting the . . . poetic voice already has a voice of its own" (as Mitchell puts it in another context [173]); indeed that it, *she,* "speaks" for the whole of the endangered world. In the cosmos of *Constellations,* the poet figure is a *poetess,* a circumstance in which Guest positively revels. She wrote in a letter about the poem: "Miró, being ignorant of the pejorative attitude toward the word Poetess, I believe, in his genuine educative ignorance chose the word as the correct word for a woman who was a poet. I took him at his word, and fearlessly had my own hyjinks with the painting." In other words, the poem does not partake of a recurrent motif among ekphrastic poems, what Mitchell calls "ekphrastic anxiety"—fear that the powerful image will silence and paralyze the poet who would approach it (170-76). To Guest, writing forty years after the fact, *La Poétesse* seems to have conferred instead a sense of entitlement and permission, an access to speech.

Here then is Guest's **"The Poetess"** (after Miró):

> A dollop is dolloping
> her a scoop is pursuing
> flee vain ignots   Ho
> coriander darks   thimble blues
> red okays adorn her
> buzz green circles in flight
> or submergence?   Giddy
> mishaps of blackness make
> stinging clouds what!
> a fraught climate
> what natural c/o abnormal
> loquaciousness   the
> Poetess riddled
> her asterisk
> genial!   as space
>
> (***Selected Poems*** 78)

Compact and concrete, elegant and capricious, joyously "frontal" in its persistent present tense, this poem exuberantly describes Miró's painting. Guest emulates the painting's sensual surface, its oscillating rhythms. She sees both the poetess and her consequence, the difference she makes in occupying her field, the ripples she sends out, the stir and sensation she causes.

The poem leaps from the page like what Charles Olson would call a "high energy construct," in which words and phrases are shifting and indeterminate—in their parts of speech, in their syntactical relationships, in their symbolic depth and import. This effect is heightened by a lack of punctuation to order the affiliation of word with word, phrase with phrase. What punctuation there is—one question mark and two exclamation points—contributes to an aura of suggestion rather than assertion, possibility rather than certainty, excited discovery rather than orderliness or deliberation. Radical enjambment agitates both line and sentence. The "dollop" and the "scoop" probably refer to the two creatures in Miró's painting that flank the poetess's head. The dollop (to the left) is a pear-shaped, heavily jowled and mustached fellow, with staring red eyes; the scoop (on the right) is white and snakelike, with a black snout and ears and a blue pointed tail. In the first lines of the poem, the inert dollop undergoes a swift transformation from noun to verb and then, due to a deft enjambment, from intransitive verb to transitive. Even so lumpish a character in such a lively setting cannot merely be but must do, and do to. As the dollop dollops the poetess, the scoop courts her, chases her, attempts to capture her, perhaps in the recess of his scooplike body. Yet these minor characters are collectively referred to by a neologism of charming and dismissive brevity—"ignots," which connotes, along with the adjective "vain," their ignorance, perhaps their ignominy, and their diminutive size in a field so clearly commanded by the poetess herself.

There are words of percussive interjection: "Ho" expresses surprise and joy and discovery. The word "dark" becomes plural, and "darks" are curiously characterized as "coriander"—to suggest, perhaps, the freshness, greenness, flavor of darkness in the painting. "Thimble," usually a noun, serves as an adjective describing blue, or perhaps blue is a verb, something the thimble does. "Okays" take on the concreteness of red-colored adornments. Are the buzzing "green circles in flight / or submergence"? Is "what!" meant to express strong excitement and elicit agreement? Or is it a breathless inability to say what "mishaps of blackness" do to "stinging clouds" in this "fraught climate"? Is "as space," the final phrase of the poem, part of a metaphor that describes how genial the poetess's asterisk is, or does it begin a new, unseen sentence drifting off onto the white page, into space itself?

"Riddle" is what this poetess does, the compact poetic mode of surprise and enigma that, like Emily Dickinson, she has chosen. But she is also "riddled," shot through with the whole objective world, her boundaries, as in the painting, astonishingly permeable. One riddling phrase—"natural c/o abnormal"—forms a verbal labyrinth in its own right, a conundrum of skewed paradox describing the "loquaciousness" of the poetess. DuPlessis hears in this short phrase an entire mocking debate on the issue of women's speech ("Flavor" 23). By jamming two words into an adjectival phrase describing loquacity, Guest seems to question how fluency and readiness of speech in women can be "natural" and "abnormal" at the same time. On the other hand, the admiring tone of the phrase in which these words appear seems to strip both words of their pejorative sting. "Natural" speech, if by this we understand speech that is spontaneous and free from artificiality, affectation, or inhibition, is carried into poetry in the care of ("c/o") "abnormal / loquaciousness." Here we can read "abnormal" as the necessary deviation of poetic language from standard language, a deviation that revitalizes perception, emotion, thought, and standard language itself.

Pervasive variability is described in the poem as "a fraught climate." This "fraughtness" is a quality of both poem and painting, in the sense that they are both highly charged, full to their own edges, volatile, mercurial, sexual. The poetess lives and breathes this climate; she also creates it as an emanation of her natural, abnormal will toward speech. Poem and painting deny the notion of static essence in a celebration of motion, change, multiplicity, all that is dynamic; both imply a denial of the passivity, weakness, piety, sentimentality, and humorlessness traditionally understood to be inherent in the term "poetess." "Poetess," argues Svetlana Boym, will come to serve as a useful critical term only if it can be "rewritten and reinvented to resist all cultural insults and condescendingly precautionary quotation marks" (240). Guest recognized that Miró's abstract rendering of a woman poet is presented as just the kind of (very rare) poetess "without quotation marks" that Boym would like to see—a poet whose feminine suffix does not read as "a sign of cultural inferiority" (192). Miró's poetess generates and inhabits fraught space that is, by consequence, also "genial" space, conducive to life, growth, and comfort, and even (reviving an obsolete meaning of the word) "relating to or marked by genius." Like Miró, working inside and against the stresses of his wartime context, Guest can and does transform the critical context represented by the word "poetess" by an act of lyric and ekphrastic translation.

The second poem, **"The Farewell Stairway,"** also declares epigraphically its ekphrastic status: "After Balla." The poem responds to the futurist Giacomo Balla's painting of 1909 that is titled *Salutando* (*Saying Goodbye*) or *Gli Addii Scala* (*The Stairway of Farewells*). The painting depicts, from an uncustomary angle of vision, three women descending a staircase. So precisely and geometrically rendered are Balla's lines and angles, so naturalistic are his scaling and foreshortening that his painting, when reduced in size and reproduced in black and white, is often mistaken for a photograph. Guest's poem about this painting is divided into eleven sections, as if it contrived to be eleven successive looks at the painting, each with its own shape, its own lyric agenda, its own management of the page's white space. Guest presumes to name the figures in the painting, and to attribute to them emotions and thoughts not explicit there. Also, she "adds" to the painting what cannot be seen in it—usually fragments of outdoor imagery, strangely portentous and evasively allusive, but also bits of autobiographical reference. All of this creates a degree of dissonance between painter and poet that is absent from **"The Poetess."** Here there is a sense that Guest wishes to enter into an imaginative dialectic with Balla, rather than posit him as precursor to be admired and emulated. The poem evinces an intriguing mixture of reverence and resistance, displaying admiration for the painting but pointedly foregrounding and emphasizing all the ways in which *Salutando* does not correspond to the futurists' political and artistic agenda.

Here, the fact of choice is of immense significance, since Guest has chosen to respond to a painting executed by an ardent proponent of futurism *before he became a futurist,* before his period of greatest notoriety. She chose a painting from 1909, rather than one of those paintings from the next decade which, by and large, erase the human figure in favor of abstract depictions of light, movement, color. This puts Guest in the position of examining a "lost" moment in the history of modern art. She claims in the poem "I saw it futurally" and that the women in the painting are "futurally extended." I want to make much of the substitution of the word "futural" (coined as far as I can determine by Guest herself) for "futurist" or "futurism." The poem seems to wonder about and mourn the loss of female figures and female sensibility from Balla's artistic world, and the transformation of an artist capable of thinking and creating futurally into one who began to think and create and act futuristically instead. The suffix *-al* is amenable in its neutrality to Guest's appreciation of *Salutando:* it makes a noun adjectival in order to convey the unvexed meaning "of, related to, or characterized by." The suffix *-ist* (especially in the case of "futurist") denotes advocacy of a specified doctrine, theory, or system of principles. Guest's admiration of and identification with *this* painting (expressed in a future beyond futurism) suggests a subtle reproof of futurist thought and propaganda.

The Italian futurists were "a tightly knit, ardently committed amalgam" (C. Taylor 1) whose aim was to express the energetic, dynamic, and violent quality of contemporary life, which they accomplished partly through a series of revolutionary manifestoes written between 1909 and 1933. They intended to blast through what they saw as current complaisance and compromise with a combination of "arrogance, bombast, and buffoonery" (C. Taylor 3). Futurism began with what Marjorie Perloff calls a period of "utopian buoyancy . . . a short-lived but remarkable rapproachement between avant-garde aesthetic, radical politics, and popular culture" (*Futurist Moment* xvii), but it later became known for its innate machismo, its glorification of war, its virulent disparagement of the female temperament, and after 1917 its much contested relationship with Fascism in Italy. Guest's poem responds most appreciatively to the features of Balla's painting that owe nothing to these negative components of futurist ideology.

First, Guest sees Balla celebrating an ordinary moment in present time, which is serene and domestic rather than aggressive or feverish, a moment remarkable for its nonrevolutionary aspect.[9] This choice would seem to contravene the intent of the futurists to "create[] eternal, omnipresent speed" and to "exalt aggressive action, a feverish insomnia, the racer's stride, the mortal leap, the punch and the slap" (Marinetti 22, 21). Secondly, she points at the subject of his painting, three women carefully and respectfully depicted, which does not seem to evince the "scorn for woman" (whom futurists considered to be fatally passive,

Barbara Guest reads poetry at the Living Theatre in 1959.

weak, and incapable of the hygienic violence of war) so pointedly called for in the manifestoes of futurism (Marinetti 22). And thirdly, she shows how the painting can be convincingly and successfully read in terms of mythology, despite the futurists' rejection of the "smelly gangrene" of mythological and historical subjects, their determination to "[s]weep the whole field of art clean of all themes and subjects which have been used in the past" (Boccioni et al. 26), and their declaration that "Mythology and the Mystic Ideal are defeated at last" (Marinetti 20). What Balla the modernist had to disparage and throw away, Guest the postmodernist can resuscitate and interpolate into Balla's painting itself.[10]

A description of the painting: the viewer's perspective is that of one who stands on the top landing of a spiral staircase, looking downward. Five turnings of the staircase are visible, each concentrically smaller, receding deep into the picture's space, each becoming less defined than the one before, until the limit of the visible is reached. The steps and the balusters fan out, precisely spaced, outlined by the curved brown line of the railing. The light is from above, suggesting a skylight. Color darkens from whites and grays to browns and purples as the stairway descends. The sensation is of a vortex, a drawing of the eye downward, inward, toward that blank, unseeable center of the staircase, which in the painting is off-center to the right and bisected by the bottom frame. The upper, outward region of the painting, where the staircase is wide and white, suggests openness, airiness, release; the inner, downward region suggests tightening, darkening, inexorable pull.

On the first turning of the staircase, three women are caught in the act of descending, their feet directed forward and downward, but all three have turned their heads and upper bodies backward and upward in gestures of farewell. They form a triangle. One wears a long purplish dress and a white hat; her right hand is on the inner railing. She seems to smile. Beside her stands a woman dressed all in black, her left hand resting on the outer rail, her right hand lifted in a wave. Of the three, she is the least distinct, her facial features most blurred, her figure most in shadow. The third woman, two steps above the other two, also raises her right (gloved?) hand. She wears pink; her dress floats. She wears a white hat; one has the impression that she is the youngest of the group. The three women express in their bodies' language a fleeting moment in going of staying. It is this looking backward, and Balla's care in depicting it, that feels unlike a futurist's stance. Also, the scene is domestic, social, even bourgeois: three well-dressed ladies, having made a visit, now descend the stairway to depart into the city and into the rest of the day. The techniques of photography rather than those of futurism provide visual drama here—not futurist whorls, force lines, vibrating intervals, and chaotic excitement, but photography's flattening of the image, the aerial view, the cropping rather than centering of the subject, the snapshot's ability to catch its subject in a normally unobserved daily activity.

Yet for all its ordinariness, its technical precision and photographic realism, the painting resonates with something mysterious and enigmatic, prompting, I think, Guest's impulse toward remythologizing it. When she speaks of, to, and for this painting, Guest names the women as Greek goddesses, as if stylish Roman matrons in the midst of their daily activities were unconsciously enacting ritual—their movements, when stilled, speak ancestrally, mythically, iconically. No commentary on this painting that I have seen makes this startling, inspired connection. To come "after Balla" is to re-mythologize, personally and vitally, what Balla has carefully, pointedly stripped of mythologies grown, for him and his generation of young men, conventional and stale. (Or perhaps she catches him in a moment of inadvertent, soon-to-be-disparaged mythologizing.) Guest "voices" Balla's silent painting in terms of the mythical tale of Demeter, Persephone, and Hecate, revealing in the process her full-blown, personal involvement with the classic myth of periodic descent, female sexuality, relationships among women, and the position of human beings in relation to time and the future.

Guest's poem, however, evinces none of the feverish rush toward the future that characterizes futurism. Perhaps in admiring imitation Guest has built a poem that declines poetry's and mythology's access to the available "future" of its protagonists. Instead, the poem holds its futural promise firmly in check, obsessively retelling, rephrasing, and correcting its opening line—"The women without hesitancy began to descend" (***Fair Realism*** 48)—in each of the ten other sections of the poem. Never do the women finish their descent, or even progress beyond the point of beginning it. A single moment in time, a single setting in space (the time and space that Balla captures with his snapshot-like picture) are revisited and retold in suggestive fragmentary descriptions and floating metaphors rather than in passages of forward-moving event. This lack of plot-driven narrative has, in fact, been Guest's practice in making use of mythological stories since she published the poems called "**Archaics**" in 1962. There likewise she does not attempt to narrate entire myths but instead captures Greek and Roman mythological personages in resonant moments of present time, as if the outcomes of their famous stories were yet unknown. Atalanta, famed for her swiftness in running, is pictured pacing in strenuous restlessness, heedless of the future, while the reader knows she will eventually be overtaken in a race by her future husband. The separate arbitrary and lazy doings of Hero and Leander are recounted in the hours before their fateful meeting. The poems set up a dialectic between the reader's prior knowledge of the stories' outcome and the richness of the present moments they portray.[11] In the present lyric moment of "**The Farewell Stairway**," the reader must acknowledge the characters' situatedness in time, their wonderful ignorance of the future, and also must experience intimations that their story might have proceeded and ended otherwise. In this way the poem profoundly comments on and even "performs" the meaning of futurity, since it remains stuck in a perpetual present.

Because Guest, following Balla, refuses to "see" the future of the myth she has introduced, stops frames her retelling of the Persephone myth at the moment of descent, depicts the women descending together, declares that they descend "without hesitancy," and declines to characterize the dark center ("Hades at the bottom" [48]), she seems to prefer one version of this famous myth to the other.

One account of the story is that Persephone and her mother, Demeter (Guest calls her by her Roman name, Ceres), were picking flowers together in a valley when Persephone was abducted by Hades, who forced her to descend into the underworld and become his wife. Hecate heard Persephone cry out, but did not (or could not) prevent the abduction. Demeter grieved so at the loss of her daughter that she neglected her duties as goddess of the earth, causing the earth's vegetation to shrivel and die. Persephone was later allowed to return to her mother for two-thirds of the year. Hecate, after assisting in the search for Persephone, lighted her way back to earth.

The story has been important to feminist readers, who focus on Hades' abduction and rape of Persephone, interpreting it as "an encoding of patriarchal violence" (in Elizabeth T. Hayes's words), a representation of traumatic loss and grief, a resonant story of forced separation from matriarchal sources of identity and love, a paradigm of marriage as primitive abduction severely limiting the freedom of women, and an allegory of feminine power usurped by a dominant male, then partially restored, but in a derivative and damaged form (Hayes 9).

In another (older) version of the myth (which has also been important to feminists), there is no abduction; instead Persephone goes seriously but willingly to a Hades portrayed not as a man, or a male god, but as unpredictable mystery, the unknown, the dark, the future. She descends in fear and attraction to Hades, which is both vibrant with sexuality and redolent of death. In this version, the journey that Persephone takes through shadowy realms of uncertainty is read as a journey into the future and into maturity, leading ultimately to gains in wisdom and selfhood, rather than to irrevocable damage and loss of integrity.

"**The Farewell Stairway**" reveals Guest as more attracted to this second reading of the Persephone myth than to the first, as her opening line declares: "The women without hesitancy began to descend." The agency in this movement downward belongs entirely to the women; all suggestion of outside coercion is erased. At this determining moment all three women are together, serving as guides, companions, and models for each other. Guest renders the women in Balla's painting with deft and simple phrases of ekphrastic description in which they reveal their ancient personalities. Ceres/Demeter, of the three the one understood as representing the aspect of woman in full maturity, the goddess of agriculture, appears "harried" and "bragg[ing] of cultivated grain" (48). She has pressing responsibilities; she is possessed of important accomplishments appropriate to middle age. She appears in the Balla painting as the woman dressed in purple. Hecate appears there as the woman dressed in black, the most indistinct of the three, the most shadowy, and in Guest as "the gray-wrapped woman. / in lumpy dark," who "managed me" (48, 51). Hecate's role is that of the dread and wise crone; she stands for the old age aspect of woman, "funerary priestess and death mother . . . owner of the sacred lore," as Barbara Walker describes her, claiming her "our best guide in this long, dark, labyrinthine spiritual journey" (14). She haunts the fringes, as the goddess of the threshold and the crossroad; she "represents the seriousness and precariousness of all transitions" (Downing 234). That leaves the pink dress woman as Persephone; of the maiden-mother-crone triad, she alone remains unnamed in the poem, but significantly, it is she who merges from time to time with the narrative "I."[12] The "I" seems to be by turns the poet who looks at the picture and a character in the picture, both viewer and viewed.

In the poem, the women seem to oscillate back and forth between their mythological, portentous aspect and their contemporary ordinariness. The second line—"leaving flowers"—on the one hand evokes an image of the modern Roman women, having brought flowers and left them as a gift. On the other hand, read into the myth, it recalls the valley of flowers that Persephone "left" to begin her descent into Hades. Throughout the poem, mythological imagery and everyday imagery (borrowed from Balla, or making reference to the poet's own life) hold each other in balance, almost in an embrace. Sections referring to "tiny Arachne" and "gnarled Charon" (the boatman who carries the souls of the dead to Hades), "birds dropping south out of the wind," and the Greek town of Nauplia alternate with "common" scenes more linkable to the painting, where the women's clothes are described as "modish," the "*scala,*" or stairway, is described as being "polished" and situated in the neighborhood of the "*stazione.*" But either way, the poem holds the future in abeyance, refusing to foreknow it, refusing to fill in the darkness at the bottom of Balla's stairway, and, most significantly, refusing to name abduction, rape, violation of will, and severing of ties between women as the inevitable nature of "Hades." Instead, Guest sees Persephone, the "I" of the poem, in one section laughing and in another tearful, but always poised at a moment of choice, "pull," and desire as she steps into the future. This is accomplished daily, moment by moment, in the most unremarkable ways, Guest implies, trusting Balla the painter more than Balla of the manifestoes. Yet, she suggests, such moments are also crossed with immense significance, which can and should be understood in mythological terms. Suddenly speaking intimately to the reader who is outside both poem and painting, Guest invites her to imagine the future as vortex, inexorably "pulling" and yet, paradoxically, somehow also allowing "free movement":

> you who are outside. over there.
> can't feel the pull. it makes you wonder—
>
> the oscillation. the whirling. urgent.
> indicating air revolving in a circuit.—
>
> without interruption. free movement
> in *cielo puro*—
>
> (52)

Much art criticism and most discussions of ekphrastic poetry have assumed that the viewer of the art will be male, engendering an entire literature describing the desires and the appropriations of the "male gaze." Some theorists have even characterized the act of looking as itself characteristically male, intent on penetration and control, and granting authority to the viewer. Mitchell, among others, has discussed the tendency of poems in the ekphrastic tradition to treat the image as a "female other." The genre, he writes, "tends to describe an object of visual pleasure and fascination from a masculine perspective, often to an audience understood to be masculine as well" (168). Surely Linda Nochlin, in this passage, assumes that both the makers and the consumers of art have been and will be masculine:

> representations of women in art are founded upon and serve to reproduce indisputably accepted assumptions held by society in general, artists in particular, and some artists more than others, about men's power over, superiority to, difference from, and necessary control of women, assumptions which are manifested in the visual structures as well as the thematic choices of the pictures in question.
>
> (13)

Besides working to understand the pervasive and powerful "male gaze," feminist critics document those many painful moments in art and literature when the female viewer or reader fails to find her image, or finds it distorted, disturbed and disturbing. Mary Ann Caws, for instance, has analyzed the difficulties that female viewers encounter when viewing fragmented, entrapped, doll-like, dominated, or violated images of women in surrealistic art; she would caution viewers always to ask, "Whose is the pleasure, where is it taken, and from whom?" (117).[13]

But Caws begins to move in another direction when she encourages female viewers, critics, and writers to find and chronicle their responses to positive images of women as well: "Instead of yielding our minds up with our modeled and remodeled bodies, we must give our . . . opinions as to which [images] deserve anger and which celebration" (133). To do so "turns us from consumer and consumed to creator and life-giver" (134). One area in which it is possible to find abundant, complex, surprising, and often beautiful and challenging chronicles of women's responses to art is in contemporary women's ekphrastic poetry, of which Guest has been a consistently vital and thoughtful practitioner.

Indeed, examination of the ways women poets go about seeing and responding to gender content in painting complicates and enriches ekphrastic theory itself, particularly the assertion that the relationship of poetry to painting is always of necessity intensely *paragonal* (to employ the word that James Heffernan likes to use), the assertion that ekphrasis invariably enacts a "struggle for mastery between word and image" (6). Cynthia Messenger, for instance, comes to another conclusion about Elizabeth Bishop's ekphrastic poems: that Bishop's ekphrasis is *not* the kind described by Grant F. Scott as a "cunning attempt to transform and master the image by inscribing it" (302). Instead, she writes, Bishop's poetry is "rather an admission of the impossibility of achieving the same" (109). Perhaps to do this, Bishop must, like Guest, seek out paintings that enable rather than paralyze their (often female) subjects, and therefore enable and give pleasure to their female viewers.

Guest's poems also seem singularly free of that fear of being silenced which provokes verbal acts that strive to dominate or erase the initiating image. Guest does not seem to posit the relationship of poem to painting as one of conflict and competition, but as one of division of labor and dialogue, one of both reverence and resistance, in which she, as viewer and maker of meaning, is equal to the painter as maker of meaning. To the claim of theorists that ekphrastic poetry speaks about, to, and for paintings, Guest's poems add an alternative: they speak *with* the paintings and, through them, *with* the painters; they speak relationally rather than paragonally. This ongoing poetic and critical project, never less than difficult, is always, intensely, both personal and political. Guest, responding to a friend's paintings, wrote in sympathetic infinitives that might also describe her own ekphrastic desires and accomplishments: "To find the picture, the animus, both physical and metaphysical; to be directed and to direct; to clarify and intensify; to be absorbed and to be free; to allow thought to enter passion as silence interrupts movement, these are the urgencies of a Goodnough painting" ("Robert Goodnough" 23). These are also the subtle and powerful urgencies of a Barbara Guest poem about painting.

Notes

1. James A. W. Heffernan calls Ashbery's "Self-Portrait in a Convex Mirror" "the most resoundingly ekphrastic poem ever written and certainly one of the longest" (170-71). For discussions of Ashbery and O'Hara in this regard, see also Altieri; Diggory; Miller; Moramarco; Perloff, *O'Hara;* and Wolf.
2. Twenty-two years later, David Shapiro wrote apologetically about this lapse: "It was a youthful indiscretion that Ron Padgett and I were not able to include her in our motley [anthology]: a misjudgment we have apologized for over the years, and an indication of the lopsided dogmatism of youth" (39).
3. It is true that, from her earliest collection of poems in 1960, Guest has exploited, for her own ends, much of the poetic experimentation that has contributed to difficult poetry of our century: the spareness and juxtapositional ambiguity of imagism, the allusive freedom of verbal collage, the arbitrary fictiveness and metonymic oddity of dada and surrealism, the broken "cubist" writing reminiscent of Gertrude Stein. Early and late, she has been a practitioner of "disjunctive" poetics, which has often manifested itself in severe paratactical fragmentation. In this, and because of the associative and improvisatory quality of her work, she has been admired and imitated recently by the language poets.
4. By no means have all Guest's readers been puzzled or faint in their praise. Some substantial appreciative reviews of her more recent poetry have provided useful avenues of approach. See DuPlessis, "Flavor"; Einzig; Shapiro; and Welish. See also Guest's 1992 interview with Mark Hillringhouse.
5. DuPlessis's "'All My Vast / Journeying Sensibility': Barbara Guest's Recent Work" discusses two important poems about paintings in which gender content is paramount: "Dora Maar" and "The Nude" (*Fair Realism* 22-25 and 57-64). At the National Poetry Foundation's 1996 conference on American poetry in the 1950s, the session on Guest featured a paper by Linda Kinnahan about women and experimental poetics, one by Lynn Keller titled "Barbara Guest's Feminine Mystique," and my "'The Imagination's at Its Turning': Barbara Guest's Ekphrastic Poems from the 1950s."

6. In addition to writing ekphrastic poetry, Guest has produced collaborative works with visual artists June Felter, Sheila Isham, Richard Tuttle, Warren Brandt, and Anne Dunn.

7. Guest's poem is not the first ekphrastic response to *La Poétesse.* André Breton's *Constellations,* published in 1959, is a series of surrealist prose poems inspired by Miró's *Constellations.* Part of the poem Breton wrote for *La Poétesse* reads (in translation from the French): "The games of love are going on under the peristyle with detonations of firearms. From the coppices where the bewitching song is brewing, the belladonna's nipple is breaking through in lightning flashes and undulating" (qtd. in Matthews 96).

8. Guest described Miró's act of titling this painting in "The Cradle of Culture": "He took a piece of crayon from his pocket / he began to draw stars, starfish, pebbles / a woman: 'The Poetess' you saw him write / above the triangles, circles, jingles of color" (*Fair Realism* 76).

9. Susan Barnes Robinson argues that ordinariness may have been precisely the point—that "ever-objective Balla" intended to counter "symbolist excesses," particularly in the form of Edward Burne-Jones's painting of 1880 *The Golden Stairs.* "Three ordinary Roman matrons descending the staircase of a Roman palazzo" represent, Robinson suggests, a realist alternative to Burne-Jones's "improbable architecture and visionary subject matter" (70).

10. The more usual reading of this painting is that it "anticipates some important desiderata of Futurism," explores "the dynamic potential of lines and shapes," and "is an imaginative analogue to the abstract oscillation patterns which Etienne-Jules Marey derived from his chronophotographic images of moving objects" (Guggenheim Museum 48).

11. Barbara Einzig describes Guest's method of handling mythology this way: "personages that are ancient and classical . . . cross over into the text, but they usually swim back, shy of a classical story, appearing instead as shards of their original narratives, clues, fragments of the mythologies of another time" (7).

12. In not naming Persephone, Guest follows precedent. C. Kereńyi reports that during the ancient Elysian mystery rites dedicated to these goddesses, Persephone was never named but referred to as the "ineffable maiden," too sacred to be spoken of among the initiated (26).

13. See Mulvey and Rose as well as Caws and Nochlin for discussions of women as subjects and viewers of painting, photography, and film.

Works Cited

Altieri, Charles. "John Ashbery and the Challenge of Postmodernism in the Visual Arts." *Critical Inquiry* 14 (1988): 805-30.

Boccioni, Umberto, et al. "Manifesto of the Futurist Painters, 1910." Trans. Robert Brain. *Futurist Manifestos.* Ed. Umbro Apollonio. New York: Viking, 1973. 24-27.

Boym, Svetlana. *Death in Quotation Marks: Cultural Myths of the Modern Poet.* Cambridge, MA: Harvard UP, 1991.

Caws, Mary Ann. *The Art of Interference: Stressed Readings in Verbal and Visual Texts.* Princeton, NJ: Princeton UP, 1989.

Diggory, Terence. "Questions of Identity in *Oranges* by Frank O'Hara and Grace Hartigan." *Art Journal* 52 (1993): 41-50.

Downing, Christine. "Hekate, Rhea, and Baubo: Perspectives on Menopause." *The Long Journey Home: Re-Visioning the Myth of Demeter and Persephone for Our Time.* Ed. Christine Downing. Boston: Shambhala, 1994. 233-42.

DuPlessis, Rachel Blau. "'All My Vast / Journeying Sensibility': Barbara Guest's Recent Work." *Sulfur* 39 (1996): 39-48.

———. "The Flavor of Eyes: *Selected Poems* by Barbara Guest." *Women's Review of Books* 13 (1995): 23-24.

———. *The Pink Guitar: Writing as Feminist Practice.* New York: Routledge, 1990.

Einzig, Barbara. "The Surface as Object: Barbara Guest's *Selected Poems.*" *American Poetry Review* Jan.-Feb. 1996: 7-10.

Gould, Jean. *Amy: The World of Amy Lowell and the Imagist Movement.* New York: Dodd, 1975.

Gruen, John. *The Party's Over Now: Reminiscences of the Fifties.* New York: Viking, 1967.

Guest, Barbara. "Barbara Guest: An Interview by Mark Hillringhouse." *American Poetry Review* July-Aug. 1992: 23-30.

———. *Defensive Rapture.* Los Angeles: Sun & Moon, 1993.

———. *Fair Realism.* Los Angeles: Sun & Moon, 1989.

———. Letter to the author. 30 May 1996.

———. *Moscow Mansions.* New York: Viking, 1973.

———. *Poems: The Location of Things, Archaics, The Open Skies.* New York: Doubleday, 1962.

———. "Robert Goodnough." *School of New York: Some Younger Artists.* New York: Grove, 1959. 18-23.

———. *Selected Poems.* Los Angeles: Sun & Moon, 1995.

Guggenheim Museum. *Futurism: A Modern Focus.* Preface by Thomas A. Messer. New York: Guggenheim Foundation, 1973.

Hayes, Elizabeth T. *Images of Persephone: Feminist Readings in Western Literature.* Gainesville: UP of Florida, 1994.

Heffernan, James A. W. *Museum of Words: The Poetics of Ekphrasis from Homer to Ashbery.* Chicago: U of Chicago P, 1993.

Kerényi, C. *Eleusis: Archetypal Image of Mother and Daughter.* Trans. Ralph Manheim. New York: Schocken, 1977.

Kiernan, Robert F. *American Writing since 1945: A Critical Survey.* New York: Ungar, 1983.

Krieger, Murray. *Ekphrasis: The Illusion of the Natural Sign.* Baltimore, MD: Johns Hopkins UP, 1992.

Lanchner, Carolyn. *Joan Miró.* New York: Museum of Modern Art, 1993.

Lowell, Robert. Foreword. *Ariel.* By Sylvia Plath. New York: Harper, 1965. vii-ix.

Manousos, Anthony. "Barbara Guest." *Dictionary of Literary Biography: American Poets since World War II.* Ed. Donald J. Greiner. Vol. 5. Detroit, MI: Gale, 1980. 295-300.

Marinetti, F. T. "The Founding and Manifesto of Futurism 1909." Trans. R. W. Flint. *Futurist Manifestos.* Ed. Umbro Apollonio. New York: Viking, 1973. 19-24.

Matthews, J. H. "André Breton and Joan Miró: *Constellations.*" *Languages of Surrealism.* Columbia: U of Missouri P, 1986. 79-101.

Messenger, Cynthia. "'But How Do You Write a Chagall?': Ekphrasis and the Brazilian Poetry of P. K. Page and Elizabeth Bishop." *Canadian Literature* 142-43 (1994): 102-17.

Miller, Stephen Paul. "'Self-Portrait in a Convex Mirror,' the Watergate Affair, and Johns's Crosshatch Paintings: Surveillance and Reality-Testing in the Mid-Seventies." *Boundary 2* 20.2 (1993): 84-115.

Mitchell, W. J. T. *Picture Theory: Essays on Verbal and Visual Representation.* Chicago: U of Chicago P, 1994.

Moramarco, Fred. "John Ashbery and Frank O'Hara: The Painterly Poets." *Journal of Modern Literature* 5 (1976): 436-62.

Motherwell, Robert. "The Significance of Miró." *The Collected Writings of Robert Motherwell.* Ed. Stephanie Terenzio. New York: Oxford UP, 1992. 114-21.

Mulvey, Laura. *Visual and Other Pleasures.* Bloomington: Indiana UP, 1989.

Myers, John Bernard. Introduction. *The Poets of the New York School.* Philadelphia: Pennsylvania UP, 1969. 7-29.

Nochlin, Linda. "Women, Art, and Power." *Visual Theory: Painting and Interpretation.* Ed. Norman Bryson, Michael Ann Holly, and Keith Moxey. New York: Harper, 1991. 12-46.

Padgett, Ron, and David Shapiro, eds. *An Anthology of New York Poets.* New York: Random, 1970.

Penrose, Roland. *Miró.* New York: Abrams, 1969.

Perloff, Marjorie. *Frank O'Hara: Poet among Painters.* New York: Braziller, 1977.

———. *The Futurist Moment: Avant-Garde, Avant Guerre, and the Language of Rupture.* Chicago: U of Chicago P, 1986.

Pollitt, Katha. "She Was Neither Dryad nor Victim." Rev. of *Herself Defined: The Poet H. D. and Her World,* by Barbara Guest. *New York Times Book Review* 11 Mar. 1984: 7-8.

Robinson, Susan Barnes. *Giacomo Balla: Divisionism and Futurism 1871-1912.* Ann Arbor, MI: UMI Research, 1981.

Rose, Jacqueline. *Sexuality in the Field of Vision.* London: Verso, 1986.

Rubin, William. *Miró in the Collection of the Museum of Modern Art.* New York: Museum of Modern Art, 1973.

Scott, Grant F. "The Rhetoric of Dilation: Ekphrasis and Ideology." *Word & Image* 7 (1991): 301-10.

Shapiro, David. "A Salon of 1990: Maximalist Manifesto." Rev. of *Fair Realism,* by Barbara Guest. *American Poetry Review* Jan.-Feb. 1991: 37-47.

Steiner, Wendy. *Pictures of Romance: Form against Context in Painting and Literature.* Chicago: U of Chicago P, 1988.

FROM THE AUTHOR

EXCERPT FROM GUEST'S POEM "PARACHUTES, MY LOVE, COULD CARRY US HIGHER"

This wide net, I am treading water
Near it, bubbles are rising and salt
Drying on my lashes, yet I am no nearer
Air than water. I am closer to you
Than land and I am in a stranger ocean
Than I wished.

Guest, Barbara. Excerpt from "Parachutes, my love, could carry us higher." In her *The Location of Things.* New York: Tibor de Nagy Editions, 1960, 67 p.

Taylor, Christiana J. *Futurism: Politics, Painting, and Performance.* Ann Arbor, MI: UMI Research, 1979.

Taylor, Joshua C. *Futurism.* New York: Museum of Modern Art, 1961.

Walker, Barbara G. *The Crone: Woman of Age, Wisdom, and Power.* San Francisco: Harper, 1985.

Ward, Geoff. *Statutes of Liberty: The New York School of Poets.* New York: St. Martin's, 1993.

Welish, Marjorie. Rev. of *Fair Realism,* by Barbara Guest. *Sulfur* 26 (1990): 213-15.

Wolf, Leslie. "The Brushstroke's Integrity: The Poetry of John Ashbery and the Art of Painting." *Beyond Amazement: New Essays on John Ashbery.* Ed. David Lehman. Ithaca, NY: Cornell UP, 1980. 224-54.

ARIELLE GREENBERG (ESSAY DATE 2001)

SOURCE: Greenberg, Arielle. "A Sublime Sort of Exercise: Levity and the Poetry of Barbara Guest." *Women's Studies* 30 (2001): 111-21.

In the following essay, Greenberg looks at Guest's poetry in Poems *(1962),* The Blue Stairs *(1968),* The Countess from Minneapolis *(1976), and* The Türler Losses *(1962) to uncover the ways her levity reveals her feminism and at the same time anchors her otherwise often difficult work.*

Much of the recent critical work on Barbara Guest has focused on the importance of *painterly* light in her poems. I would like to discuss the importance of a *different* kind of light—light in the sense of levity, humor. I would ask that we read Guest as a poet possessed of great wit, and as a poet employing feminist strategies. I argue that these two characteristics can be seen as intrinsically linked.

This essay charts a trajectory in Guest's work from 1960 through 1980—from ***Poems*** (1962), ***The Blue Stairs*** (1968), ***The Countess from Minneapolis*** (1976), to ***The Türler Losses*** (1979)—and argues that her use of wit over those two decades parallels a change in her aesthetic: from work influenced by poetic tradition to a more liberated voice. I also argue that the use of levity is a feminist strategy; it serves as an undoing of the dominant order in both poetics and the culture at large. I argue that, ironically, levity *grounds* Guest's reader in poems which are often fragmented and spare, and that while a sense of humor is certainly present in the work of the New York School poets, Guest's work resonates more with that of contemporary avant-garde women writers who use the subversive power of wit to locate themselves within a female community.

As evidenced by this issue of *Women's Studies: An Interdisciplinary Journal* and other attentions paid to her in recent years, Guest has finally begun, in her fifth decade of publishing poetry, to receive real critical attention. But the ways in which she is read still encompass a very limited set of frameworks. As Sara Lundquist notes, discussion of Guest's poetry centers around

> three persistent, *true,* but ultimately simplistic assumptions about her work: first, that it is difficult to the point of obduracy; second, that it is refined and cool, rather than passionate, personal or emotionally urgent; and third, that it [. . .] avoids the political in favor of the aesthetic, preferring the sensualites of surface, texture and wordplay over narrative, social commentary, and political naming.
>
> (263)

I want to argue that Guest actually has that most forgiving and welcoming kind of warmth, the kind manifested in a sense of humor, and that this carries a political power. How can wit in women's writing be considered political or feminist? First, we can understand the very nature of women writing as feminist. From an ideological standpoint, the act of a woman writing is itself a subversive and resistant act, because language is power, and power is male-dominated. If women claim and use that power, we are working in opposition to structural oppressions.

Second, humor disrupts the order of things, celebrating chaos and confusion; it relies on otherness to exist. This is compounded when instigated by a woman. As Regina Barreca notes, "the woman writer's use of comedy is dislocating, anarchic and [. . .] unconventional," because language itself is imagined to be equivalent to the authority of the masculine perspective (*New Perspectives* 6). Barreca states, "Women's humor is about our reclamation of certain forms of control over our own lives. Humor allows us to gain perspective by ridiculing the implicit insanities of a patriarchial culture" (*Untamed* 12). A woman with a sense of humor is proving her intelligence, indicating her confidence, taking action.

By characterizing Guest's humor as *levity* I mean to indicate a breezy use of irony that doesn't betray femininity. The lack of closure often noted in Guest's work is an extension of this breeziness. As Guest uses it, levity allows a person to make light of herself while still retaining her dignity. It also signifies a certain confidence; to quote Lundquist again, "Guest's poems seem singularly free of that fear of being silenced" (283). As I will show, Guest's use of levity is tied to her sense of womanhood, and its development can be tracked along a path from control—of self, of line, of syntax—to liberation—of objects, of identity, and of language.

Guest's first major book, ***Poems,*** finds the poet drawing from a number of poetic movements. There is a lyrical, Romantic aesthetic at work, with metaphoric references to personified seasons, and an epigraph from Verlaine. There is also the influence of the narrative confessional present, with a strong use of the first-person voice. I see little in this book which is deeply resonant with the poems of O'Hara or Koch: the voice rarely gets chatty or witty, and feels rather restrained. The connection with the New York School, if one needs to be made, would probably hinge on Ashbery's more elusive and elegant writing.

What is evident here is a sense of being controlled and a desire for freedom, and many of the poems in this first collection refer to specifically gendered issues. **"All Grey-haired My Sisters"** is a case in point. The poem is addressed from a devoted speaker to a group of mythic women using classical Western roles—sisters, relatives, adventuresses, darlings, ancestresses, mermaids, girls; each term cements the speaker's community with these figures. The women are in concert with nature ("guided by the form and scent / of tree and flower blossoming") and have endured hardships throughout history (*"you walked into the wars"*) (15). These hardships may have also included marriage, as indicated in the lines *"as daises drop at your wrists/which flight are you making? / down the lime aisles"* (16).

This poem also contains lines which I would like to posit as one of Guest's first gendered jokes. In this section, an unidentified second-person emerges—"From your journals"—and then a moment of dialogue is quoted from an unknown "he" and "she" (16):

He said: "In nymphic barque"
She replied: "A porcupine".
And later,
"Reason selects our otherness."

(16)

As I read this, a man is describing a woman in terms of nature and of a feminized creature of sweetness and innocence, the nymph. The response from a woman is a pointed, sharp animal.

A plea for liberty is present in the poem **"The First of May,"** in which the speaker begins: "My eye cannot turn toward you / Night / because it has Day watching" (73). Throughout the poem, the speaker yearns for autonomy and freedom:

I would like to go for a walk
in the dark
without moonbeams

down that path of mushrooms
in my nightdress
without shoes.

(73)

Her desire is manifested in a desire for sexual pleasure and rebellion: "I would like to steal . . . ," "I would like to go to a hotel / with you" (73). Day, the controller, blinds the speaker, and yet the speaker is reluctant to leave Day's power, because if she does disobey and "give you up Day forever," she will be forced to join "the guerrillas" who will "roast my bird / and eat it" (74). Thus freedom is seen as bringing treacherous consequences.

Published six years after ***Poems, The Blue Stairs*** opens with a daring declaration: "There is no fear / in taking the first step" (3). These first lines anticipate the liberation of language, line and spirit, the "quiet authority of [. . .] one," in Wendy Mulford's words, that runs throughout Guest's second collection. ***The Blue Stairs*** establishes the aesthetic now typically associated with Guest. Fragmentation occurs more often and in greater extremes: the average line in the book is five words long. The lines begin to move away from the left margin, with indentations bringing lines halfway across the page. The page looks airy; each idea is given its own room to breathe.

And although the first-person speaker does make appearances here, the first poem in the book, significantly, has hardly any "I" voice at all. In its place is a voice of declarative authority which seems to be calling for courage, ambition and dignity—a climb up a flight of metaphorical stairs: "In fact the top / can be reached / without disaster" (3). In my reading, this is a gendered quest. The speaker knows her own mind and her goal: "Its purpose / is to take you upward" (5). Once she has finished her journey to the pinnacle, she does not want to relinquish her position: "And having reached the summit / would like to stay there / even if the stairs are withdrawn" (6).

In other poems in ***The Blue Stairs,*** we can see a chatty, light-hearted humor which seems more related to the New York School mode than any of the poems in the previous collection. In **"Turkey Villas"** the voice becomes whimsical and intimate:

Or
to make a shorter story
and relate in truth
to my life
as if it were San Francisco
1937

(7)

The speaker later takes on a self-effacing tone, laughing at herself for being so personal. "Now to be a proper historian / of my dreams," she describes

. . . a ship seen from
A Hotel Hilton balcony
Think of that
Balcon Hilton!

(8)

And then, as if sensing her own foray into O'Hara-ish exuberance, she pulls back the reigns: "Enough of this dizziness / let us apply the oars." (8)

But the speaker cannot help herself:

I am spinning with ideas
to the top of the Mosque
I am an ice cream cone
Muezzin

(8)

A critique of gender roles is here, too; in the midst of a list of wishful thinking—"I shall go on collecting pottery / yet it shall be blue"—the speaker laughs "I shall be medieval and slim / at once!," a reference to her own body, and a joke on what is expected of it (9). Revealing this insecurity only adds to the humanity of this poem, and towards its end, the speaker is once again self-effacing: "My dreams / are stupidly turbulent," she claims, and yet as readers, we do not quite believe her (10). Her dreams have proven to be delightful in their wildness.

In the poem **"The Return of the Muses"** the speaker refers specifically to the problems and particulars of the female body. When the Muses leave the speaker, she is forced to alter herself:

> And I went on a diet
> I stopped eating regularly,
> I changed my ways several times
>
> "strict discipline, continuous devotion,
> receptiveness"
>
> were mine.
>
> (19)

In these lines, the speaker refers to dieting as a kind of religious ritual which she happily abandons when the Muses return: "Here you are back again. Welcome. / Farewell, 'strict, continuous, repetitive—'" (19).

The Blue Stairs concludes with one of Guest's most noted poems, **"A Handbook of Surfing."** The tone here is more serious than in previous poems—in an interview, Guest stated, "That poem is really an anti-Vietnam poem"—but the use of language is lively, and foreshadows the kind of fragmentation used in her more recent work (Hillringhouse 26). Lines are often broken in unexpected places; there is a lack of punctuation which makes phrases feel rushed together. This kind of bold usage and heightened language are interspersed with a pseudo-handbook tone, which is then deconstructed by the speaker so that a passage which reads "we would / like to tell here about paddling, standing and turning" receives the response (39),

> Everyone knows how to turn or turn about
> or make a reverse these are daily decisions both
> politic and poetic and they have historic
> sequences
> in the surf they are known as Changing Directions
>
> (39-40)

The Blue Stairs marks a rather dramatic change in direction for Guest, one that is followed through in the book-length poem, ***The Countess from Minneapolis.*** In it, a woman of European royalty is displaced in the American Midwest, where she observes the culture through the "unreasonable lenses" of an outsider (12). The book alternates between lyric, fragmented poems and prose pieces that tend to be more down-to-earth—and humorous.

These prose pieces employ playful strategies: syntactic misuse, lists, parodies of formality, and surrealist juxtapositions. There is something subversive about the voice in these poems, in part because they are prose poems: they do not follow the "rules" of poetic form.

Laughing at the pretensions of European and aristocratic culture is a refrain throughout the prose poems in ***Countess.*** Minneapolis itself is not ridiculed for its perceived shortcomings; the contempt of The Countess is reserved for the cosmopolitan pretension she herself uses to describe her surroundings. Poem fourteen begins in the voice of Signor Reboneri, a visiting lecturer: "The refinement of what's special takes place between the meat and the bun. N'est-ce-pas?" (14). The professor proceeds to compare the Midwestern locals in a bar to Viking "'sauvages,'" but he "like[s] what he saw," a room full of "hefty maidens" and "god-like men" (14). In the end, the joke is on the Signor, who falls into a beer-induced reverie about the "hairy arms" of "these tribes" (14).

Surrealism is found in this text through the juxtaposition of everyday objects out of place. This is the case in poem twenty-five, which begins by pointing out "The further exoticism of reading a British novel while visiting Duluth," and in poem eleven (25):

> There was such an anachronism lurking
> in the snakelike room that Pedersen frequently
> mistook
> the potatoes in his soup for boulders and
> searched
> beneath them for hidden reptiles.
>
> (11)

Most strikingly surrealist (and lovely, and funny) is the list of "ACTIVITIES" which make up poem thirty-seven:

> Grain Belt Beer, He Who Gets Slapped, Vikings
> vs Dolphins,
> ice skating, fishing, Japanese food, meat, square
> dancing, collage, Rimbaud, New York Painting,
> Showboats,
> Baskin-Robbins ice cream, La Strada, Basement
> Studios
>
> (37)

This list points to the strangeness of cultural landscape; it mixes high and low culture in a manner reminiscent of the New York School (which itself is referenced here). In fact, despite the Countess's ancestry, her tone is often extremely casual and New Yorky, as in the letter she composes when an unnamed friend suggests, "'What you need is a sophisticated cat'" (24). The Countess writes a "note to self": "Contact nearest available feline breeding—kennel—was it kennel—was it shed? Whatever. The sooner the better" (24).

Elsewhere Guest delights in the surfaces of language in a light-hearted way, as in the list of names the Countess reels off in poem fifteen, "AT THE GUTHRIE THEATER": ". . . Helm Wulfings and his assistants: Hnaef Hocings, Wald Woings, Wod Thurings, Seaferth Seggs . . ." and so on (15). These lists mock the social order and meaning, which can be read as a feminist strategy, a disruption (by the Countess) of the power structure.

In the last book Guest published in the '70s, a slim volume entitled ***The Türler Losses,*** the speaker, who one is safe to assume is Barbara Guest, has lost several expensive Türler watches, and the poems recount the losses. The *poems* feel likewise scattered. While they are too abstract and complex to utilize the kind of levity present in ***Countess,*** some places find Guest offering a warm welcome to the reader inside a difficult text, as in this section:

> I like innocuous rhythms, don't you?
> Loss isn't so important.
> When nothing lies there wearing its ring.
>
> (3)

In this way, Guest takes herself lightly, and urges us to do the same, joking even about the importance of her watches and her carelessness in losing the costly objects: "After the second Türler loss / a lessening perhaps of fastidiousness / the Timex phase" (6).

I'd argue that by focusing on such a personal theme—the loss of a piece of jewelry—for a sustained experimental work, Guest is again using a feminist strategy: elevating the "woman's sphere" to the place of high art. Of course, the book is also about metaphoric losses, about space and time, but it often reads, between sections of dense imagery and assonant sound-play, more like an ethereal diary than anything else:

> Whisked to hotel. Sleepy hotel morning. Enjoyment of eiderdown. Waiter wheels in lunch. Step outside onto balcony. Clouds. Descend to gardens. Pool where there is wave-making machine, much discomfiture.
>
> (11)

Certainly, this kind of reportage voice seems to be making fun of the very nature of such a personal book: a female voice masquerading as male news anchor. The use of the diary form feels womanly, as she herself remarks in a later section: "Safely home she duly recorded this event in her DIARY, JOURNAL, LETTERS, and the Sunday shopping lists later discovered nestling in the shrubbery outside her workroom" (14). When Guest uses the academic, scientific—i.e., masculine—mode of the footnote with no corresponding notation in the text, she is clearly making fun of it:

> SEE: INDEX, CROSS-FILING, UNIVERSITY, CORRESPONDENCE, ac-Va Yu, post, previous, subsequent, intervening, chronological, summary, additional material, endeavors, travel, quarrels, divorces, demises. N.B. All private papers withheld.
>
> (14)

In ***The Türler Losses,*** the voice is uniquely Guest's, representative of her commitment to the blend of the everyday and the spiritual, the philosophical and the capricious, a commitment which is evident in the poetry which has come since.

I want to close by quoting Guest herself, who once remarked "poetry should have more tension [. . .] I think it is coming into contemporary poetry more and I admire that" (qtd. in Hillringhouse 28). It is out of admiration for Guest that I put forward the reading I've outlined here, which I'm hoping will serve to complicate notions of her aesthetic—to heighten the tension, even. But I'm not asking that we read Guest only in this light. Rather, I see this essay as part of an exciting new effort—evidenced by this issue of *Women's Studies,* the recent panel on her work at the National Poetry Conference on North American poetry in the 1960s, and other events and publications—to place Guest in a new context, one which appreciates the fresh air she has breathed into language.

Works Cited

Barreca, Regina, ed. *New Perspectives on Women and Comedy.* Philadelphia: Gordon and Breach, 1992.

Barreca, Regina, ed. *Untamed and Unabashed.* Detroit, Wayne State UP, 1994.

Guest, Barbara. *The Blue Stairs.* New York: Corinth Books, 1968.

Guest, Barbara. *The Countess from Minneapolis.* Providence: Burning Deck, 1976.

Guest, Barbara. *Poems The Location of Things, Archaics, The Open Skies.* New York: Doubleday & Company, Inc., 1962.

Guest, Barbara. *The Türler Losses.* Montréal: Mansfield Book Mart Ltd., 1979.

Hillringhouse, Mark. "Barbara Guest: An Interview by Mark Hillringhouse." *The American Poetry Review* July/August 1992: 23-30.

Lundquist, Sara. "The Midwestern New York Poet: Barbara Guest's 'The Countess From Minneapolis.'" *Jacket* #10: online, October 1999. Available: www.jacket.zip.com.au/jacket10/mulford-on-guest.html.

Lundquist, Sara. "Reverence and Resistance: Barbara Guest, Ekphrasis, and the Female Gaze." *Contemporary Literature* 38.2 (1997): 260-286.

Mulford, Wendy. "The Architecture of Dream: Barbara Guest's 'The Blue Stairs,' Corinth, 1968." *Jacket* #10: online, October 1999. Available: www.jacket.zip.com.au/jacket10/mulford-on-guest.html.

FURTHER READING

Bibliography

Lundquist, Sara. "Bibliography." *Women's Studies* 30 (2001): 135-41.

Bibliography of works by and about Guest.

Criticism

Atlas, James. "A Chronicle of Younger Poets." *Poetry* 113, no. 6 (March 1969): 428-33.

A brief review of four new publications, including Guest's The Blue Stairs.

Bennett, Robert. "'Literature as Destruction of Space': The Precarious Architecture of Barbara Guest's Spatial Imagination." *Women's Studies* 30 (2001): 43-55.

Considers Guest's unconventional spatial imagery as an offshoot of Modernist art and examines its relationship to her poetry.

Bernstein, Charles. "Introducing Barbara Guest." *Jacket* 10 (2000): 1-4.

A brief overview of Guest's life and career.

Caples, Garrett. "The Barbara Guest Experience." *Women's Studies* 30 (2001): 123-29.

Considers Guest's poetry as primarily linguistic and examines the form of her work, noting elements of surrealist imagery.

Dickey, William. "Responsibilities." *Kenyon Review* 24, no. 4 (autumn 1962): 756-64.

A review of six new publications, including Guest's Poems: The Location of Things, Archaics, The Open Skies.

Diggory, Terence. "Barbara Guest and the Mother of Beauty." *Women's Studies* 30 (2001): 75-94.

Explores Guest's aesthetic ideal as a commitment to beauty.

Einzig, Barbara. "The Surface as Object: Barbara Guest's *Selected Poems*." *American Poetry Review* 25, no. 1 (January-February 1996): 7-10.

Examines Guest's Selected Poems *as modern compositions filled with tension. Includes text of several poems, including "Roses."*

Fraser, Kathleen. "One Hundred and Three Chapters of Little Times: Collapsed and Transfigured Moments in the Fiction of Barbara Guest." In *Breaking the Sequence: Women's Experimental Fiction,* edited by Ellen G. Friedman and Miriam Fuchs, pp. 240-49. Princeton, N.J.: Princeton University Press, 1989.

Considers Guest's experimental novel Seeking Air *in terms of its poetic compression and Cubist style to discover the ways it challenges presentations of narrative truth.*

Hillringhouse, Mark. "Barbara Guest: An Interview by Mark Hillringhouse." *American Poetry Review* 21, no. 4 (July-August 1992): 23-30.

An interview with Guest exploring her influences, her thoughts on poetry, and her motivation as an artist.

Kasper, Catherine. "Introduction." *Women's Studies* 30 (2001): 1-6.

Introduction to a special issue devoted to Guest with an overview of her works and career.

Kaufman, Robert. "A Future for Modernism: Barbara Guest's Recent Poetry." *American Poetry Review* 29, no. 4 (July-August 2000): 11-16.

Examines Guest's poetry as Modernist works, questions the future of Modernist poetry, and argues that her experimental poetry may eventually play a role in reviving the genre.

Keller, Lynn. "Becoming 'A Compleat Travel Agency': Barbara Guest's Negotiations with the Fifties Feminine Mystique." In *The Scene of My Selves: New Work on New York School Poets,* edited by Terence Diggory and Stephen Paul Miller, pp. 215-27. Orono, Maine: The National Poetry Foundation, 2001.

Considers ways in which Guest's works of the 1950s and early 1960s reflect social disaffection stemming from cultural expectations of gender and represent an attempt at social rebellion.

Lundquist, Sara. "The Fifth Point of a Star: Barbara Guest and the New York 'School' of Poets." *Women's Studies* 30 (2001): 11-41.

Examines the New York School of Poets and Guest's role as one of its five originators, paying particular attention to the effect her gender had on critical acceptance—or dismissal—of this role.

Rabinowitz, Anna. "Barbara Guest: Notes toward Painterly Osmosis." *Women's Studies* 30 (2001): 95-109.

Considers Guest's work of the 1990s in terms of its increasing abstraction and strong connection to the visual art of painting.

Sadoff, Ira. "Inside/Out." *American Poetry Review* 29, no. 2 (March-April 2000): 9-12.

Examines Guest's poetry alongside works by Alice Notley and Jean Day, discussing the ways Guest's verse moves between the traditional and unconventional to create surprise and tension.

OTHER SOURCES FROM GALE:

Additional coverage of Guest's life and career is contained in the following sources published by the Gale Group: *Contemporary Authors,* Vols. 25-28R; *Contemporary Authors New Revision Series,* Vols. 11, 44, 84; *Contemporary Literary Criticism,* Vol. 34; *Contemporary Poets,* Ed. 7; *Contemporary Women Poets; Dictionary of Literary Biography,* Vols. 5, 193; and *Literature Resource Center.*

JOHN CLELLON HOLMES

(1926 - 1988)

American novelist, essayist, travel essayist, poet, and biographer.

Holmes is best known as a chronicler of the Beat Generation, a term he introduced to the world in 1952. His novel *Go* (1952) is acknowledged as one of the first fictional accounts of the Greenwich Village bohemian scene that revolved around such writers as Jack Kerouac, Allen Ginsberg, William Burroughs, and Neal Cassady. Holmes's novels are marked by vivid characterizations and a meticulous, poetic prose style, and his essays on the Beat Generation are respected for their objectivity and lucidity in explaining the ethos of the movement.

BIOGRAPHICAL INFORMATION

Holmes was born on March 12, 1926, in Holyoke, Massachusetts, the son of John McClellan Holmes, a sales representative, and Elizabeth (Emmons) Holmes. His father's job required constant relocation, and Holmes grew up in various New England states and in California. Partly because of the frequent moves and school changes, Holmes quit high school, but enrolled in summer courses at Columbia University in 1943. In 1944 he was drafted and entered the Navy. After completing boot camp he married Marian Miliambro. He was discharged from the Navy for medical reasons in 1945 and returned to Columbia University. In 1949 Holmes attended the New School for Social Research in New York City with Jack Kerouac—whom he met at a party the previous summer—and William Styron. He spent the next two years writing his first novel, *Go*. This period was emotionally turbulent for Holmes and his wife, and they divorced shortly before publication of the novel. In 1953 he married Shirley Anise Allen and moved to Old Saybrook, Connecticut. He published two more novels, numerous poems, and essays. His essays "This Is the Beat Generation" and "The Philosophy of the Beat Generation" helped define the Beat movement and are partially responsible for making the term "Beat Generation" part of the vernacular. After Kerouac's death in 1969, Holmes became a biographer, not only of Kerouac, but of the entire Beat movement. He also began to revise and publish much of his early poetry. Holmes spent the latter part of his career teaching at various universities, including the University of Iowa, Yale University, Brown University, Bowling Green State University, and the University of Arkansas. Holmes died of cancer on March 30, 1988, in a hospital near his Old Saybrook home.

MAJOR WORKS

Holmes's novels depict artists, hipsters, and outcasts whose dissatisfaction with traditional institutions such as family, church, and government cause them to embrace extreme lifestyles and unconventional social views. *Go* portrays the New York City underground scene of the late 1940s and is based on actual events; the characters in the novel are drawn from several prominent members of what would later be called the Beat Generation. *Go* depicts young bohemians searching for identity and commitment in a time of stifling conformity. Paul Hobbes, the protagonist in *Go,* is a young writer torn between living a conventional married life and joining his hipster friends in their wild nocturnal exploits. While sympathizing with the Beats, Hobbes nevertheless remains wary of their self-destructive behavior.

Holmes's second novel, *The Horn* (1958), details the tragic decline of Edgar Pool, a black jazz saxophonist whose characterization is partially based on the lives of jazz musicians Charlie Parker and Lester Young. The novel examines rivalries among musicians and demonstrates the ways many American artists were forced to debase their work ethic in order to survive due to financial need. In *The Horn* Holmes uses metaphors and allegory to equate creating jazz music with a spiritual journey toward the divine.

Get Home Free (1964), Holmes's last novel, concerns a failing love affair between Verger and May, two characters who appeared in *Go*. The couple is disenchanted with their lives and each other, and lack spark in their relationship. When they decide to part, they leave New York City for their respective hometowns in hopes of learning more about their pasts and gaining a better understanding of themselves. While separated, they each meet a person who instills in them the will to survive. Upon returning to New York, they are again drawn together by their mutual newfound zest for life and enjoy a spiritual rejuvenation through an intense physical relationship. After *Get Home Free,* Holmes published a collection of essays titled *Nothing More to Declare* (1967), an acclaimed volume that includes the seminal pieces "This Is the Beat Generation" and "The Philosophy of the Beat Generation," as well as profiles of Kerouac and Ginsberg. *Visitor: Jack Kerouac in Old Saybrook* (1980) and *Gone in October: Last Reflections on Jack Kerouac* (1985) offer reminiscences of the celebrated Beat author and analyses of his works.

Many of Holmes's earlier writings were poems; there were periods when he allegedly wrote a poem a day. These writings were occasionally published in periodicals, but he was unhappy with many of these poems due to his inability to relax his form, and he resolved to cease writing poetry. Later in his career when he was able to revise his style, he began writing poetry again. *The Bowling Green Poems* (1977) is an example of his looser approach. Holmes also completed numerous revisions to his earlier poems, and in combination with newer pieces, these were published in *Death Drag: Selected Poems* (1979), *Dire Coasts* (1988), and *Night Music* (1989).

Before his death Holmes also selected and revised many of his essays. These were published as *Displaced Person: The Travel Essays of John Clellon Holmes* (1987), comprised of pieces he wrote while living in self-imposed exile in Europe during the Vietnam War. *Representative Men: The Biographical Essays of John Clellon Holmes* (1988) includes portraits of Kerouac, Burroughs, Ginsberg, and other members of the Beat movement; and *Passionate Opinions: The Cultural Essays* (1988) features essays on social changes, the sexual revolution, politics, pop culture, and reflections on the Beat era.

CRITICAL RECEPTION

Critical response to Holmes's works has varied and evolved over the years. As with other Beat writers, his writing was initially perceived as extremely unconventional and garnered a mixed reception. Earlier reviewers of his novels were divided between two camps: those who failed to empathize with the disaffected youth of the late 1940s and had no desire to develop an understanding of the group, and those who recognized a new literary voice and embraced the revolutionary writing style. Upon its publication, *Go* was dismissed by many critics as the ramblings of pseudo-intellectuals with little moral character. However, after the Beat Generation began to gain recognition, *Go* steadily gained praise as an objective chronicle of the Beats and their lifestyles. In general, Holmes's later novels were subsequently regarded as enlightening and innovative. Several of Holmes's novels have been lauded for their poetic prose, but his earlier poetry has been faulted as immature and overly dependent on form. Many commentators, including Holmes himself, have found the early poetry stiff and more comparable to a Shakespearean sonnet than the freethinking, looser form for which Holmes was striving. Critics have noted that the later poetry is more personal and introspective in tone and have praised it for a natural rhythm and unforced style. Commentators have also asserted that Holmes's essays on the Beat movement and his reminiscences of his relationships with central Beat figures are passionate in belief and feeling, and have noted their objective point of view. Holmes's essays have been widely considered an invaluable resource for understanding the counterculture of the 1940s and 1950s and those who embraced the Beat lifestyle.

PRINCIPAL WORKS

Go (novel) 1952

The Horn (novel) 1958

Get Home Free (novel) 1964

Nothing More to Declare (essays) 1967

The Bowling Green Poems (poetry) 1977

Death Drag: Selected Poems (poetry) 1979

Visitor: Jack Kerouac in Old Saybrook (reminiscences) 1980

Gone in October: Last Reflections on Jack Kerouac (reminiscences) 1985

Displaced Person: The Travel Essays of John Clellon Holmes (travel essays) 1987

Dire Coasts (poetry) 1988

Passionate Opinions: The Cultural Essays (essays) 1988

Representative Men: The Biographical Essays of John Clellon Holmes (biographies) 1988

Night Music: Selected Poems (poetry) 1989

PRIMARY SOURCES

JOHN CLELLON HOLMES (JOURNAL DATE 1948)

SOURCE: Holmes, John Clellon. "Crazy Days and Numinous Nights, 1948-1950." In *The Beat Vision: A Primary Sourcebook,* edited by Arthur Knight, pp. 73-88. New York: Paragon House, 1987.

In the following journal excerpts written in 1948 and republished in The Beat Vision *in 1987, Holmes reflects on his literary peers and his generation.*

September 8, 1948

The whole world is going berserk and I'm going too, just for laughs . . . I think myself into straitjackets. I wake up yowling out of my dreams. I stay up until two every night and scrape myself out of bed at seven in the morning. It's the binge of the New Age, our Brave New World . . . I don't listen to quite so many news broadcasts anymore, and I've cut myself down to two papers. It was the least I could do to save my stomach . . . I've been listening to bebop. It's the new insane music of this world. It's like the configurations of a wild mind. It pounds on and on, mechanical, disharmonic, the abstraction of an abstraction . . . Look at the young men go off to war! Singing their songs, making their obscene jokes, laughing and uneasy in their hearts . . . Now they go off, without memories, without regrets, the boys who always turned to the sports sections of the daily papers, who went to the shows, who fucked their girls in back alleys or under the stairs in the tenements. They learned to smoke at seven, had their first woman at the whorehouse on 161st street when they were fifteen. They wandered around this city, beating up old men for a lark, writing dirty words in the subway, posting no bills. Now they are finished. Where in hell's name does it lead? . . . There are those of us who don't give a good goddamn anymore. We're sick and tired of caring about the whole rotten swill of life. The boiling cities of the earth swallow us all and masticate us with their cement jaws and spit us out when they can't digest or destroy us. . . . Why shouldn't we take what we can get, possess it absolutely?

December 10, 1948

Kerouac speaks to Harrington (in a letter written and mailed from here) about "the beat generation," the "generation of furtives" . . . They are breaking the laws of this country, almost every one of them. They are drug addicts, or they are drug peddlers. Many of them are thieves, some are murderers . . . But it is interesting to note that Huncke, a street-arab as a child, a junkie, a thief, a second-story man, a miserable derelict, listens to Ginsberg, with interest, and comprehends him in a way. Their experience is the same, they recognize the same mental reality, they have been thru it. They comprehend subtleties that are Dostoyevskian, but only because they are "underground" and know what "the man" is talking about . . . I am called out into the street to try to understand the above-mentioned things, to fit them into my patterns, to change my patterns where that is necessary.

JOHN CLELLON HOLMES (LETTER DATE 4 AUGUST 1972)

SOURCE: Holmes, John Clellon. Letter to Jim White (4 August 1972). American Center for Artists (online) http://www.americanartists.org/Articles/Holmes/on_writing_a_novel.htm> (1999).

In the following letter, written to Jim White while Holmes was a graduate student at Brown University, Holmes relates his work methods and creative process.

Dear Jim:

Sorry it's taken me so long to get back to you. Immediately after closing up shop in Providence, I went to Maine for a while to work on our little clammer's shack up there, and get a rest. When I got back, I had a long (and long overdue) magazine piece to finish, and now we're off again to Maine for the rest of August.

You ask about the novel I'm working on; how do I approach it? Well, the kernal of the idea came to me a long time ago. It came first as a one-act play, which never got beyond the most desultory note-taking. A few years later, I realized that it was a novel—that is, that I was as much interested in the three main characters as I was in the "plot"-idea. It expanded itself naturally, still keeping the severe time-limit-actions of the play-idea, but fleshed out with backgrounds, a stronger, denser sense of milieu, flashbacks, and other subsidiary characters. It germinated for a long time while I was engaged in doing another book. In 1969, I started to get down to work on it, filling a large loose-leaf workbook with notes, sections of prose, and references to journal-entries that were germane to the project. I started serious prosing in early 1970 after a trip to Los Angeles (which is the setting of the book), but immediately had problems of "entry": I had thought to begin the book a year after the major action, and then drop back. This proved unweildy (sic) and cumbersome. I spent a month trying to solve that difficulty and realized that I had conceived the book in the wrong point of view. I made a shift from third to first person, and started the book directly in the middle of the penultimate action (the last day of a complicated, three-way relationship), and it went along fine. I wrote the first three chapters (of a possible eight or ten) in a couple of months. Much of this time was spent getting into the specifics of my character's tone—a complicated tone in that he is a wry, somewhat involuted type, who is addressing the reader, and slips back and forth from the first to the third person. That is, he sometimes speaks of himself as if he was speaking of someone else. The viewpoint, as well, is complicated (perhaps the major theme of the book has to do with identity-sense, and so there's a lot of role-playing, masquerade, and mirroring), and this took time to get accustomed to. By the third chapter, something of a digression, the thing was starting to open up. A minor character, and her involvements, abruptly became more important; I saw reflections of the basic situation in this character—reflections which, towards the end of the book, will become more important, and will serve to build the thing more forcefully towards its end. Then in the fourth chapter, I struck my first serious snag. It was a flashback (which I usually like doing), and I hadn't thought very much about it in advance, but when I got going on it the prose turned bad, my selectivity-gieger-counter went dead, I wrote reams and reams of stuff that I knew I didn't need. This went on for months until I realized that I had placed this particular flashback in the wrong spot. I moved along better for a time, though I still had an uneasy feeling. Then I ran entirely out of money, and had to stop and do magazine-articles, go back to Los Angeles to do a long piece on that city for *Playboy,* an then the job at Brown came along, which put the book off until now.

How do I work? I work in the morning usually, and usually for no more than four-five hours. If I'm hot, I continue, but more than five hours is about as long as anyone can take. I tend to write slowly, and re-write as I go along. I like to have fairly finished product behind me. if I write five hundred words a day it's a good day. In recent years, I've been writing a little faster than that, and usually at the end of a scene it goes rapidly—up to a thousand sometimes in a few hours. I try to work every day, but there are times when you realize you haven't solved the problems, and until you do there's no point in going forward. I guess the way I conceive a novel these days might be described as a process of ACCRETION. If I have the strong central situation, and the characters, I find that other, necessary things and people and reactions attach themselves naturally, or emerge worrying it too much, and then later I go back and see what's out of proportion, what needs to be built up, etc. I go a lot by *feel,* how it feels, how it sort of *hefts* in the mental—hand. I think a lot of structural-sense comes from this sense of feel. It has to do with a feeling for proportion, nuance, balance—it's very architectural, and I'm not sure one can "learn" it, except by reading and becoming more sensitive to balance, etc. The only unities (in the Aristotelian sense) that apply to the novel are, I suppose, a feeling for limiting, or compressing, your material so that maximum aesthetic-tensions build-up, a sense of how a story can be made to move forward by grounding it in time (which is the heart of the novel), and the crucial importance of a strong sense of milieu that will make the characters vivid because of the sense of "world" that the reader gets. I used to be far more hungup on prose than I am now I strove for "fine" writing, every sentence a jewel. This slowed things up for me, and I think did the same thing for the reader. Now I'm more interested in getting *flow,* in breaking up the rhythms, and picking up the pace. I've found that *story* is far more important than I used to believe. By that I think I mean, *movements,* pivots, hinges. The difference between a novel and a short story lies in this matter of movements: a story has only one or at most two. A novel never has less than three. These *changes* (in character, in situation, etc.) are what relate the novel to time, to a feeling of the passage of time. Any great novel can be reduced to these bare bones. Reducing it does it damage in the reader's mind (even if the reader is a writer), but the process makes it clearer to the writer how structure functions in producing the "feeling" of a given book. Hemingway, for instance, was basically a short-story writer. When he comes to the novel, he is often on unsure ground, and that's why you get those magnificent set-pieces in all his novels (the Retreat from Caporetto, El Sordo on the mountain, the last section of *Islands in the Stream*), set-pieces that often seem far more assured and memorable than the novels in which they occur, set-pieces that, on investigation, we see to be marginal to the basic action of the books. They are, in effect, short stories.

Tolstoi, who does great battle scenes too, perhaps the best of all, never uses them as digressions (sic), separate narratives, but always as climaxes for some far more important interior event in his characters lives. Dostoyevski, on the other hand, rarely writes set-pieces. His novels move gigantically along by a process of ever-intensifying acceleration—the method of the thriller until his great climaxes (the trial in Karamazov, Raskolikov's confession, the various murders in *The Possessed*) cap everything off. his method is dramatic: huge, intense scenes placed cheek by jowl with one another like massive building blocks, with very little narrative connective. This is perhaps why so many attempts have been made to transform his novels to the stage or the screen—most of them dismal failures—and failures because his scenes are bigger than life, they explode time. Faulkner works with a kind of mythic flow, he's very Greek in some ways, his people are all doomed, driven by forces they barely comprehend, tiny figures in a vast, exotic landscape of fates. But he, too, is always moving forward, and he keeps the reader's attention by a series of hints-at-future-action, by deliberately withheld information, by a process (influenced by Conrad) of continual circling-back. One could go on. there are limitless possibilities in structuring one's material, but they all involve a *feel* of proportion, attention-riveting, and moving the ball forward. Modern material, modern experience, has demanded all kinds of new techniques, but they are all attempts to solve the same old problems, the major one of which is simply to keep the reader reading ahead. I have found that a strong grip on *theme* is often a help in these matters, because it gives the writer a yardstick by which to measure what is needed, what isn't; what to cut, what to expand. The writer must continually ask himself: what is this book *about*? Because of the length of time that it takes to write a novel this question must be repeated over and over again.

For myself, I find that I can't hurry a novel. that is, I'm constantly learning more about it, cautiously digging its shape out of nothingness, and often I don't know precisely how it's going to turn out until I'm well along in it. Not one novel of mind, except the very first, has come out the way I thought it would when I conceived it, and even the death which ends ***Go*** didn't occur until I'd written almost half the book. ***The Horn*** changed drastically as it went along, and deepened too as I saw more possibilities. ***Get Home Free*** was literally conceived backwards, and the hardest parts to write were the three New York sections. The book suffers a sort of structural schizophrenia as a result. The current novel is strong and simple structurally, and yet I have to beware of becoming too rigid, too imprisoned by the movement of my own events. The danger here is that I'll scant all the "little lower layers", without which it won't work at all. Yet if I succumb to the delight of my leading character's tone, comments, etc. the book will be self-indulgent and outre. Again, a question of finding, and striking, a balance.

Novel-writing is the hardest work I know. At times one can suffer what feels like an actual mental unbalance from trying to get into a character's head. It's very unnatural. Yet, for me, the creation of believable characters is the ball game, people that live, whom we understand below the level of mere intelligence, about whom we intensely care. For me, character is still the core of the novel, but I mean this in Fitzgerald's sense that "action is character". What a character *does* defines him. A writer knows that he's getting it when a character starts acting more or less on his own, when the action emerges out of the character without the author's intervention. The best characters I ever wrote ended up writing themselves. They took on a life that seemed utterly independent of me and my initial conceptions of them. The ones that worked best for me were Stofsky in ***Go,*** Edgar in ***The Horn,*** and May in ***Get Home Free.*** But perhaps this has to do with the amount of difficulty I had in getting them to walk and talk on their own . . .

These are a few very unsystematic reflections, just what comes to mind this morning. Of course you can continue to write to me, and I'll answer any questions that you have. If my replies are tardy sometimes, I know you'll understand it's because I've got my head down in the well.

In any case, I hope you have a great year at Brown, and I'm glad you're getting out of New York. Also, that your health improves. I can't write a coherent sentence when I have as much as a head cold.

All the best,

John

GENERAL COMMENTARY

JOHN CLELLON HOLMES AND TIM HUNT (INTERVIEW DATE 1977)

SOURCE: Holmes, John Clellon, and Tim Hunt. "An Interview with John Clellon Holmes." the unspeakable visions of the individual, *Volume 8: The Beat Journey,* pp. 147-66. California, Pa.: A. and K. Knight, 1978.

In the following interview, conducted on June 10, 1977, Holmes discusses his works, elaborates on his experiences and opinions regarding the Beats and the Beat era, and explains the difficulties he has encountered while writing.

[*Hunt*]: *Reading the introduction to the new edition of* **Go**, *one thing that caught my eye was your feeling that Stofsky had been the most satisfying thing to come out of the novel.*

[Holmes]: Well, I had to work harder on Stofsky as a character. The Jack [Kerouac] character and so many of the others are minor characters. They're just on the margins. Stofsky, more happens to him. He's the conscience of the book in a curious sense, and I think he became so important to me because he was the first character I ever created that came to live on his own for me. By the end of the book I wasn't thinking of Ginsberg anymore, and I didn't have to invent things for the character to do. I didn't have to manipulate him or play a puppeteer with him. He was vivid enough to me in my own imagination by then that it was impossible for me to write him wrong. He just came out right. And also, he is the character in the book who is the matrix of the conflicts, the conflicts of morality and new experiences and so forth. He acts out more of it than anybody else. Hobbes and his wife are rather passive. They're drawn into it. They feel the centrifugal force of this kind of experience, but it's Stofsky who tries to do things—what I call his "earnest interferences" in other peoples' lives.

I have the feeling that Stofsky and Agatson are complimentary figures. If the novel plays off order, conservatism, a sense of holding to past mores over and against something else, both Stofsky and Agatson link up with that something else; but they link up with very different notions of what that something else might be. As much as choosing between order and disorder, or the old and the new, it comes out to be a choice between following Stofsky or following Agatson.

It was intended to be that way. Agatson, of course, was based on a real person, Bill Cannastra, and one thing that I was trying to reflect in the book was the whole series of levels of things: how this new thing that was involving drugs and Beat experience was angled toward spirituality, toward some kind of semi-religious conception of the nature of man as against the simple dissipates which we have always had with us (almost a hangover from the Twenties). Agatson was meant to represent that—a drunkard rather than a drug addict, a nihilist really. This is something Jack disagreed with me about. I did want to show the destructiveness in this kind of experience, not just in the kinds of experience that are reflected in Agatson but also the destructiveness that is implicit to me in Hart Kennedy and some of the Beat stuff too. And of course, Jack at that point and most of the people I knew who were involved in that really thought it was all upbeat and ongoing and celebratory, while I felt that there was also a note of destructiveness and wastage in it.

I think that's best noticed in that scene between Stofsky and Ancke. That's probably the place where the positive-negative side of that comes across most clearly. The place where Stofsky tries to get Hart and Dinah to confront their little games is another. But there, Stofsky seems rather unwitting, and it's only in retrospect that he recognizes what he has done. In the conversation with Ancke, it's right there as a dramatic encounter.

It was one of my intentions with the character when I did the second draft to slowly unpeel these things—that he [Stofsky] was unwitting in the beginning and it was only gradually as things kept developing that he saw what his somewhat awkward attempts to interfere in peoples' lives for good reasons had really resulted in. This is another aspect of the book that many of my friends didn't like. For instance, Allen [Ginsberg] was going to do an introduction for this new edition, and he found he couldn't read it. He wrote me a very interesting and revealing letter about it simply saying, "I can't imagine that I was ever this way." In a sense, he was saying that it brought it all back to him in a way that was both uncomfortable and unpleasant. He didn't say he didn't like the book. He said, "I can't read it." He's a tremendously busy and mercurial kind of person. So, for instance, when he wrote the introduction to *Visions of Cody* he called it "The Great Rememberer", and I said, "Allen you've stolen that. I stole it from Jack, and you stole it from me." And he said, oh yes he hadn't read ***Nothing More to Declare*** in years. He picked the same line out of the book to describe Jack as I did, but I did it first. [laughs] All of us had this problem from the beginning because at one period in our lives we were all dealing with the same material, the same people, so that constantly our stuff kept overlapping. Jack and I used to have fights about this.

I get the feeling that in some ways at this point the visibility of Kerouac and Ginsberg makes it difficult to read the novel as a novel.

I wouldn't be surprised, but when the book came out neither Allen or Jack were known to anybody. Jack had published one novel, but Ginsberg hadn't published anything. People still had difficulty reading the novel. Perhaps the difficulty lies in the fact that it is a *roman a clef.* I had to go back and read the book again for the first time in twenty years to write the introduction, and the first half I found very difficult to read, partially because I think it is badly written in many instances. But beyond that, I think that because I was dealing with real people rather than creatures of the imagination, I relied too much on catching for myself the way they talked and the things that they did instead of getting inside them as fictional characters which is really what you've got to do. The second half of the book I find more successful simply because by then the characters had become themselves and were not just transcriptions of real people. So that if people have difficulty in reading the book, which I am certain they do, I think it's a literary failure on my part more than just an association with people who have since become famous or notorious.

How much of a sense did you have when you shifted from **Go** *to* **The Horn** *of trying to leave behind people that you knew?*

Well, it was a completely different kind of experience. I was aided in a curious way in ***The Horn*** because I didn't know any of the people involved. I didn't know any of these jazz musicians. I had known some jazz musicians, but the people I created in the book were my own imagination of the way they were. And of course the form of the book is completely different. It is not a *roman a clef.* It is not reportorial in any way. Everything in the book was based on things that I had either heard about or imagined. So that it is not the life of Charlie Parker. It is not the life of Lester Young. It's a complete creation. I use, as I say, "rumor and legend" to develop some of the episodes. It was much more a conscious creative effort than ***Go*** was.

To what extent did you have particular musicians in mind for particular characters?

Actually, the way I worked it was this: I wanted to write a book about the artist as American, or the American as an artist, and rather than write about writers—which has never worked and no writer could ever do, I don't think—I picked out to me the most indigenous American artist, which is a jazz musician. a) It is a completely American art, and b) almost all the problems and traumas that the American artist goes through happen most dramatically and most immediately in the life of a jazz musician, that is, all the most commercial problems, the struggle to discover what you mean in your own voice and all that.

I was working on three levels at the same time. I wanted each of these characters to represent an American writer, which is the only reason why I put those little epigraphs in front of every chapter. But I also wanted him to represent a particular kind of jazz musician, and then I had to create a fictional character doing these things, so that Edgar Poole, for instance, is Edgar Allan Poe. It's always seemed to me, as it seemed to Whitman, that the problem of the artist in America is almost best represented by Poe being voted through the streets of Baltimore drunk. So that's who that is, but it's also Lester Young and then it becomes Charlie Parker—I mean the things surrounding Parker's death are the things I use for the death of Edgar Poole, although I had begun the book and written the first chapter some years before Parker died. Geordie is both Billie Holiday and Emily Dickinson. Junius is Thelonious Monk and Nathaniel Hawthorne, and Metro is just any great big yawping tenor sax player, but he's also Walt Whitman. Now I did it this way not because I thought I could say anything profound about all this, but it gave me a control mechanism and a way to think about it and a way to create a character out of whole cloth which is really what I was doing. Curny Finnly is both Dizzy Gillespie and Mark Twain—you know, wordy, funny, weird, also tremendously interested in commercial success as Dizzy is and Twain was but always failing at it as both Dizzy and Twain did. Wing is Charlie Parker and Herman Melville. That one had also been written before Parker died. That was written way back in '52, that chapter. I had already begun the book by then, and I found that I couldn't make the analogy too exact because it wouldn't work. Melville's too big, and he threatened to take over the whole book. And Parker's too big too for that matter. So I had to limit it. But I did have him have his little "Typee experience" with the girl down in New Orleans and stuff like that.

What's your sense of **The Horn** *looking back on it?*

Well, I haven't read it in years. I'm somewhat embarrassed by the lyricism in it. The last time I looked into it, I actually read one chapter at a reading. I read the "Metro" chapter because it's more or less self-contained and not too long. What troubled me most about it were, of course, the technical errors which are rife, but also the rhythm in the book is much too, it's almost iambic pentameter—it isn't broken enough. I couldn't write well enough then to find a prose style that was right for the subject. It wasn't syncopated enough in other words. But, of course, I was writing a mythic kind of book, and I was writing from an omniscient third person. I was tremendously influenced by Melville in those days, and Melville, of course, was working with a Shakespearean rhythm. Jack, you see, solved these problems tremendously successfully, most successfully in *Visions of Cody* where its very rhythmic writing, very tidal writing, and yet it doesn't resemble Melville and it doesn't resemble Shakespeare, who were the two prose people or two stylistic influences on all of us in those years. I think they wrote the best English, the most flowing English that's ever been written. So I don't know what I think of ***The Horn.*** I know it was earnest. I know I was reaching for something. Whether I got it is somebody else's decision to make. I'm not ashamed of it at all. I think there are things in it about jazz and about the problems of being an artist that I would stand on, and the end of it—the end of Edgar, the last twenty-five or thirty pages—I remember writing it and being pleased with it. I was pushing it and handling it right for me, and I was quite moved by it. Shirley is one of my toughest critics, and she's also very candid and very bright. I remember giving her those last two chapters that are both about Edgar and she cried. And I thought WHOOPEEEEE! All writers are ham bones in a way, and you want to make people laugh and cry. I mean at least if you can do that, then you feel, well, you've got to them. If you can change their lives, too, that's marvelous, but that's beyond most of our reach.

As long as we're moving along this track, perhaps we ought to take the next step and look at **Get Home Free.**

Well, ***Get Home Free*** was therapy for me. I had been through a very bad two years in which I couldn't work. I had also started a novel after ***The Horn*** that proved to be beyond my grasp. It was a big thing, and it had a very complicated moral problem in it. It was about non-violence, and this was the fifties. It was about a kind of Beat Ghandi. I struggled with it and struggled with it and wrote about forty thousand words of it. Those forty thousand words were okay, but I was just really getting to the tough part, and it tripped me up, and it froze me. It was the first time I ever really had a block. And then certain things in my personal life went wrong. My father died, and Shirley and I had some trouble. For about eighteen months I couldn't do anything. I mean I wrote all the time, but it was bad. It's something I describe in ***Nothing More to Declare.*** And then finally I was in really bad shape in my head, and I decided that I was going to write or die. So I started one morning. I'd had the idea for **"Old Man Molineaux"** from a few years before. I had met a guy like that up here. So I had the material, and it was such a complete change from the stuff I'd been doing that I thought maybe it would free me, which it did. So I started writing that, and I just wrote every single day and finished it in a couple of months. And then rather than stop, I had this other idea from going South with Shirley; so I started that. I literally finished **"Old Man Molineaux"** one day and started right on to the next one and finished that up in about two or three months. So I had two novellas in effect. Then I had the idea of making a double decker sandwich out of it. And those three sections that are interlarded between the two novellas were the hardest part to write and took me almost a year to get right. So I dedicated the book to December 15, 1960 or whatever it was because that's the day I started and that got me out of my block. So, I ended up slightly more than a year later with a book. It was never really satisfactory. The form was always wrong. It was really meant to be two novellas, but of course you can't publish novellas. They were too long for magazines and too short to be published as a book. So that's why I put those three sections in. But it was good for me—two things: 1) I got back to writing again; 2) I worked harder on the prose to get some of the soft quality that I think is in ***The Horn*** out, to get the prose tougher and harder and more exact.

It's been a while since I looked at **Get Home Free**, *but the structural problems do seem to me to be there. But it's also in* **Get Home Free** *where the prose really takes on its own character.*

One of my problems always is that I set myself dilemmas that are terribly hard to solve. There was no particular—well there was actually—a reason why I had to write the two novellas in the first person, one from a man's point of view and one from a woman's point of view. I'm aware of how difficult it is for a man to write convincingly as if he was a woman. One is in the past tense. The **"Old Man Molineaux"** section is Verger recalling this from years later. The other is much more immediate, and of course the three interlarded sections are all from the third person and working sort of backwards. The book would have been more successful if I could have solved from the very beginning the problem of the voice and the problem of the tense.

Where do you see yourself going with the novel you're working on now? Can you talk about that at all?

Well yes, I can talk a little bit about it. I won't characterize it except that it is a very complicated book, not in the structural sense, but it covers a vast period of time, that of sixty years. It is making demands on my imagination that are going to make its composition slow. That is one reason why I took the steady job because it completely alleviates the economic problem so that I can concentrate what time I have left from teaching completely on this book without having the pressure of having to get it done quickly to get some remuneration from it. I see the book as taking me at least two more years. It's going to be long for one thing, and as I say it's very complicated. It has four major characters whose experiences are not directly related to each other, that is, they are four sisters and it takes them from about 1900 to 1960 or 65. Also, the book is perhaps, in the way its going, more social than anything I've done before. It's going to reflect changing mores. But it also has money problems in it, marriages and all sorts of things. So that's my long term thing. Last year, or eighteen months ago, before I began this book, I wrote a bunch of short stories and found myself for the first time really interested in the short story as a form, as a form into which I could put my own material. I've written short stories for years, but not many of them. I always found problems in getting the kind of things that I am interested in in fiction into the short story form. It seemed much too constrained. But as I say, eighteen months ago I had a kind of breakthrough. I found out how I could do it. I'd love to do more short stories. I've taken up poetry again. I hadn't written any poetry for years when I wrote all the novels, but I've taken it up again and am publishing it here and there. Primarily, I don't feel any longer the sense of pressure and push and hurry I used to feel. Part of that, half of that, is age, just getting older. You can't live under that sense of tremendous competition and pressure, both intellectual and financial, when you're fifty years old. At least I can't. I've lived much too hard, and I'm tired, frankly. But I mean I'll go on writing. I've written, since the last book came out, a whole other book which hasn't been published yet, that travel book, which is a complete long book. Almost everything in it has been published in magazines but the thing itself has not been published yet. And then I've rewritten another book, and I'm working on getting the collection together that we talked about. But primarily, my effort has gone into this novel, but I'm not going to rush it.

What's the other book you've rewritten? Is it a novel?

Yes. Right after ***Go*** and before ***The Horn*** I wrote another novel which was, as I mentioned in the introduction to ***Go,*** meant to be the first book in a trilogy. I wrote the second book. It was longer than ***Go*** and much more complicated in terms of its problem. It had the same characters as its stepfather. It was never published when I submitted it. It had a serious structural defect which I couldn't seem to solve. So I abandoned it. I was so tired from writing it that I just wanted to get away from it. So what I did was get into the third novel, which is the one I couldn't do because it was even more complicated. So a couple of years ago I went back to the second book, which is called *Perfect Fools*. Actually, I had looked at it a couple of times in the intervening years, and I still couldn't figure out how to solve the problem. But a couple of years ago, it all became clear to me—that it was much too long and that the major character was not very likeable. So what I did was go back and rewrite it, mainly a cutting job. I cut 150 pages out of it and rewrote the bad prose and finished it to my satisfaction. So far, nobody likes it. [laughs] It's about the fifties. It was ahead of its time when I first wrote it, and now it's behind its time. It's not a nostalgic view shall we say. I don't know what will happen to it. I'm going to start going to small presses and see what they say. My agent has just been trying the big New York houses, and they don't like it. It's gotten good rejection slips, but with that and twenty-five cents you can get downtown. So in other words, I've got those two books floating around. I don't worry about them. They may never be published, but that's what I've been doing since ***Nothing More to Declare*** came out. I mean I haven't been just fooling around.

In **Nothing More to Declare** *you talk about the way you and your friends as young writers felt forced to go against the prevailing literary, academic models—that one had to strike out on his own at tremendous risk. Isn't that also different for your students?*

It's different right now than it was even five or ten years ago. The sixties produced no literature to speak of. With the exception of Pynchon and a few people like that, nobody under thirty-five has written anything of interest. There was some poetry but not even much of that. Most of the literary effort went into song lyrics. The best poet of the sixties is Bob Dylan and people like that. Now that the ferment of the sixties and its political involvements, its drug involvements, and its music involvement has quieted down, I find that students I've been teaching in the last year or two are much more serious about writing than they used to be. They don't write in hip slang anymore. They don't write the anti-father story, the anti-establishment story, the Haight Ashbury story, the commune story, all of which during the sixties if one was teaching literature one got just dozens of those stories. They're not doing that now. They rewrite a lot more. They're more aware of style. They're dealing with subtler problems. I don't see them as writing against the grain. I don't see them as trying to challenge their elders as much—I don't mean personally, but I mean in writing. It is not a radical generation in other words. I also don't see any particularly new perception that distinguishes them from their older brothers and sisters. Whereas my group at least did have a perception about something, or we fancied we did, about the world but also about literature itself, its uses, its possibilities. I don't see them doing that. They're writing the traditional stories pretty much. They're writing about their own experiences and their own lives, which are different from ours, but mostly they are writing about personal problems. They don't see themselves as a distinct generational group with shared experience which is different from the experience of older people. They're sick of the sixties and the attitudes of the sixties. They all grew up in the sixties; they know about that. Some of them were even involved in that as teenagers, but I see them as being much more introspective, much more venturesome in terms of literary styles and attitudes and structures and so forth. I think of it as a transition period.

It seems almost as if it helps to have somebody to knock down.

But they are not knocking anybody down.

Isn't that partly because there's no monolith to beat against?

Could be. They don't have any particular political attitude. The war, after all, was a tremendous catalyst for the generation of the sixties. It gave them a cause; it anguished them. It made many things seem less important than they had before. And this bunch of people, people in their early twenties, don't have that. They yawn at it. It is not a factor. There is not the draft hovering over their lives or the possibility of having to go into exile or do something that they don't want to do. Things have quieted down. I think that there are an awful lot of good young writers coming along because they are working harder at it. They are not spending as much time doing other things. Whereas my crowd, whether by accident or some perception, felt that we could yoke an attitude towards the world and towards life, a conception of the nature of man in other words, could yoke that with what were primarily literary interests. We didn't get out in the streets. We were home writing all the time.

What are some of the ways in which your generation influenced things?

Whether we directly influenced anything at all, I don't know. We certainly didn't affect the country in any way. I think that ironically and to some degree gratuitously, we saw something underneath the rather calm and cautious veneer of American life that finally surfaced, and by the time it surfaced in the sixties, we had written about it. So that when young people came along who were dissatisfied with the life into which they'd come, who were interested in consciousness, who started to flirt with drugs, who were the heirs of a time of sexual freedom, if they looked to see if this had been reflected anywhere they came to Kerouac, Ginsberg, and me and Burroughs and all the others simply because we had written about all that. So maybe we gave them a way to think about what they were feeling anyway, but that, in so far as I can see, is the only real influence we had. We gave them a way to think about what they were feeling anyway. Our music was jazz; theirs was rock. Our drugs were primarily pot; they got into acid and stuff like that. They were interested in madness; we had already written about it. We had written about unconventional sexual behavior, and they were into that too. And then of course there is the figure of Allen Ginsberg. I think he really had an influence, a direct personal influence on thousands of young people in the sixties. He was out there reading to them and talking to them too and living. He was a role model to some degree because that's the way he chose to live. And also because he has a messianic streak in him, he's a born teacher. So I think that he perhaps actually had some direct influence on people. That is, I keep meeting people saying, "God when I was eighteen I saw Allen Ginsberg read, and afterwards I talked to him and he was perfectly available and accessible." In those days, Kerouac was no influence at all, while now I increasingly get letters from people about Jack. Now that all the uproar is over that something sweet and tender and caring that is in Jack's work is speaking to people again. But that's the only influence; those items are the only things that I could say had any direct influence on anybody. I don't think literature does influence anybody. It makes nothing happen, unfortunately. I believe that a lot of stuff that we created is going to last because it wasn't just *Been Down So Long It Looks Like Up To Me*. The attitudes (and I like that book rather), the attitudes in that book have passed, while the attitudes in Jack's books haven't and never will. There will be times when they will be seen in different ways, but they're rich enough to be seen in many ways and will last even as things change.

One shift you can look back and see coming from Kerouac's fiction, Ginsberg's poetry, and your nonfiction is a seriousness about the popular arts and pop culture and not putting up that tremendous barrier between pop culture and serious culture.

Well that seemed natural to us. I guess it was because we were the first generation in America to be totally involved in popular culture as kids, going to the movies, the comics, the popular musics. These were the things we grew up with, and even when our interests deepened, if you will, or when we wanted to be serious writers and so forth, this was the stuff of our imagination. It seemed absolutely natural to us to use it, and we didn't make a distinction between high culture and low culture. It all seemed like culture. If you'd gone to W. C. Fields movies or the Marx Brothers movies, you didn't feel embarrassed by saying these are great men; these are great artists. Long before we read Shakespeare, we had seen Chaplin, and as I say in ***Nothing More to Declare,*** it wasn't a college professor who sent me to Tolstoy, it was Greta Garbo. I mean I saw *Anna Karenina* and only then read the book. This happened time after time. I saw *David Copperfield* long before I read the book, and it got me to read the book. Of course, I liked the book much better than I liked the film, but the two are connected in my head. Whenever I read about Mr. Micawber, it is W. C. Fields; it's got to be. In terms of the music, most of us grew up at end of the swing era, which was the popular music more widely accepted among young people than any music until rock. And from swing, we got into jazz. Now that was not widespread, but jazz is an art music basically, anyway, in which, particularly in modern jazz, it is the moment of individual creativity which is stressed. So when we confronted literary problems, which are art problems, the example of the jazz musician was never very far from our idea about how these things might be solved. This is why Jack continually compared his writing to the problem of spontaneous creation, which is what jazz musicians do. It did not seem a cheap analogy; it seemed a most apt analogy. Also in that period right after the war, popular culture was taken quite seriously for the first time by certain people. [Jay] Landesman and [Gershon] Legman were both primarily interested in popular culture. They were critical of it in many cases, but they took it very seriously. For one thing, popular culture was so widespread then that we were among the first people to see what an enormous influence it had on people—sometimes for good, sometimes for bad. But it wasn't just something that happened over there. It seemed more serious than so called high culture. I mean more people read *Superman* than *The Partisan Review,* and even the people who read *The Partisan Review* were also reading *Superman.* They just wouldn't admit it. Let me put it this way; this is more apt. All the editors of *The Partisan Review* were going to movies two or three times a week, but they wouldn't let that into the pages of their magazine. That seemed to us tremendously hypocritical.

Part of what you say when you say that pop culture seemed even more serious seems to reflect an almost inevitable attitude for an American artist raised with figures like Melville, Hawthorne, and Whitman, particularly Whitman—you know, that American art to be significant has to reach many people; simultaneously one has to be an individual, not one of the crowd, while also in some way being a member of the crowd by reaching it in large numbers.

Whitman and Melville, Whitman particularly, were writing about the life of the streets, the life of the country, the real experiences. This seemed more relevant to us than W. H. Auden or T. S. Eliot. It just seemed more relevant to us. It spoke to us more loudly and more succinctly in a curious way than the literary idols we were supposed to worship. Pound and Williams were the only two big poet figures that escaped our neglect. I mean we all talked about Eliot, but none of us liked him. None of us felt much relevance in his poetry to what we were doing. Auden, of course, was the big figure in New York then. And we all liked Auden, and we all tried to write like Auden. Ginsberg tried to write like Auden and did. It's all been published now, but I'll never forget the discontent that we felt that this wasn't our way and wasn't our voice and didn't reflect what was really happening to us. So that Allen quit writing poetry and went off to Yucatan, which is where he broke out of that murderously compacted style that he was getting into, that metaphysical style. I quit writing poetry completely because I couldn't get out of it.

Isn't there a problem for anyone who wants to be an "American writer" caused by our sense that one must be individual, even idiosyncratic, and yet be popular, even though, as Whitman found, the two things very seldom come together?

I think it's always been true in America. I see no immediate solution to it. We're not a country that values our culture at all, I'm afraid. We only value it when it is out of date. Kerouac ends up on lists in fiction classes, but in his own lifetime he was not appreciated. He made a few bucks, and he was notorious, but his work was not taken seriously. This is because, I suppose, we have an encapsulated culture. Books are not very popular, when you figure that if you sell 10,000 copies you're doing very well—of anything! Any book that sells a million copies is an overnight smash, and this is a country of over 200 million people. So your audience—you can't have a wide audience. You want a really wide audience, you have to become a rock star. How this is ever going to be solved, I don't know. The reasons for it would be a whole course in American studies. Like you figure something like this, the Rolling Stones in one night—one night!—make more than Charlie Parker in his whole life. I'm not asking the Stones to be as good as Parker. You can't ask anybody to be that good. But Parker was a genius, and as such he was doomed. He pulled the roof in over his head, sure. If he'd been able to live like a decent man and live like a serious man instead of having to live like a clown, who knows what he might have done. But this has always been true. Look at Melville. Melville died in obscurity. Our greatest writer, one of the greatest writers who ever lived, potentially, and yet half his career was truncated. After *Pierre* the rest of it is fragments. And yet in *Moby Dick* he wrote a world book, one of the great books ever written. And yet it was misunderstood, it didn't sell, and he became disgruntled. Look at Jack. I'm not saying that Jack wouldn't have died as a drunk anyway, but he wrote that astonishing series of books in a short period of time in total obscurity. Fame came, and he was supposed to go on talk shows where he was treated like Marlon Brando. He was treated as a curiosity, not as a serious man, and this inevitably does something to an artist. The greatest artists can withstand it, perhaps, but most of them haven't. Picasso did, but Picasso got fame *and* money pretty early on. He kept going his own way, and he was big enough; Stravinsky the same way. But Fitzgerald is another example—not taken seriously, books out of print, given everything at once, then having it all taken away, having to hustle his ass in Hollywood, treated like a fool out there, as if he wasn't a serious man. The only people who are taken seriously in this country are people who have money, artists that have money. Now Saul Bellow is a good, good writer, and he's fought it all the way through and become a popular writer in so far as a serious writer *can* be popular. Now with the Nobel Prize, it's perfectly acceptable for people to say, "Oh yes Bellow must be a great writer. He's got to be a great writer." His books weren't taken very seriously either.

There's one good thing about this. American artists who are serious can never get complacent, and that's why the best poetry in the English language in this century has been written by Americans. All the really important steps, with certain few exceptions, in the novel have been taken by Americans. In this country, it's not like Italy. When you are in Italy, they call you *professori.* When inn keepers in Italy discovered I was a writer, they called me *scritori* or *professori.* Half of these people couldn't even read, but you see it's very respectable to be a writer. They didn't ask you how much you made. They didn't ask you how the reviews of the last book were. But what that can do, I've seen it in England, what that can do to an artist is make him complacent. The writer is taken very seriously in England. It's a perfectly respectable thing to be, which is one reason why I think English literature in this century has not been very good, with some exceptions of course. Whereas here, this is a jungle, and if you don't keep rolling, you're going to get gobbled up. This is why Mailer's analogy of fighters and boxers to writers, although I find it personally shallow—personally to me it's shallow; I don't mean it's shallow on Norman's part—is an apt analogy because you've got to keep yourself like a street fighter.

GREGORY STEPHENSON (ESSAY DATE 1990)

SOURCE: Stephenson, Gregory. "Homeward from Nowhere: Notes on the Novels of John Clellon Holmes." In *The Daybreak Boys: Essays on the Literature of the Beat Generation,* pp. 90-104. Carbondale: Southern Illinois University Press, 1990.

*In the following essay, Stephenson analyzes a trio of Holmes's novels—*Go, The Horn, *and* Get Home Free*—and explores the themes, metaphors, characters, and situations that recur throughout these novels.*

The body is hip. It is only the mind that knows Nowhere.
John Clellon Holmes, ***Nothing More To Declare***

Night and homelessness are central motifs in the fiction of John Clellon Holmes, metaphors for the state of the human psyche in our century. The convulsive violence and vicious destructiveness of our age are seen by him as expressions of a spiritual void, a vacuum at the heart of humanity. For Holmes, the psychic climate of the postwar world is one approaching an absolute zero of the spirit; we are at Nowhere: benighted, dispossessed, in exile, and overcome by darkness. The motive of his work is to discover an end to the night, to find a way home.

Go, the author's first novel, opens with an image of spiritual nostalgia, as Paul Hobbes, the central figure of the story, yearns for a return to innocence, longing for humankind to live "naked on a plain" (3). In stark contrast, though, to this Edenic ideal, Holmes portrays a world where (in Matthew Arnold's phrase in "The Buried Life") men and women "live and move trick'd in disguises," sharing only mutual fear and shame, a desperate ennui, and the secret craving for love. Such is the state of the soul not only of the mass of men but also of the group of alienated young writers and bohemians on which the novel is centered. They are significant, however, for their attempt to transcend their condition, for their having undertaken a quest for a more authentic life, and for their search for some measure of meaning and peace.

The poles of ***Go*** are nihilism and vision, embodied respectively by the characters Bill Agatson and David Stofsky. The other characters of the novel, including the protagonist, occupy points along a continuum between these two extremities—between denial and affirmation, between fear and love, between zero and infinity. And the poles themselves sometimes meet, coexisting in the same person and ultimately in all humankind.

Agatson, the negative pole, the "black prophet" of the novel, is a demonic, destructive, drunken monster of a man (195). His outrageous and often cruel antics derive from "a fatal vision of the world" and from his "inability to really believe in anything" (19). His death, near the end of the novel, is as absurd and meaningless, as squalid and wasteful, as was his life. Shortly before Agatson's death, Hobbes observes an unguarded expression on his face that seems to epitomize his dark, anarchic life: "He looked like a man who is witnessing the vision of his whole unredeemable existence, seeing it as a savage mockery; but more, perceiving that *all* of life is a blasphemous, mortal joke at everyone's expense, a monstrous joke in which everything is ignoble, ludicrous and without value or meaning" (273).

And yet, Agatson, the monster, the nihilist, is ultimately seen to be an inverted idealist, a sort of saint turned inside out, an unconscious martyr to an unbelieving age. Precisely because he cares so deeply, he wills not to care at all. His essential sensitivity and vulnerability are glimpsed only when he involuntarily relaxes his will, as when he falls asleep once after a marathon binge revealing in sleep "a curious private softness" (74), a "boyishness," and an "innocence" (75). Only one other time does he let his mask slip for an instant in public, when he realizes that he has gone too far in baiting and mocking Verger, and he becomes suddenly contrite and gentle. Otherwise Agatson is determined to play the monster. But as Stofsky perceives, the monster in each of us is in reality no more than "a runny-nosed little boy"—pitiful, miserable, and strangely vulnerable (109).

Stofsky is the counterpart to Agatson. If Agatson may be seen to embody the psychic malady of our age, then Stofsky embodies the cure. Poet and mystic, Stofsky is an earnest quester who experiences a visionary breakthrough, a revelation of the essential duality of being: the material and the spiritual. He sees that the level of ordinary consciousness is characterized by "a chemical piercing fright," but at a deeper level, beneath the dread, there is "an impersonal, yet somehow natural love, cementing the very atoms" (83). This love is the Divine Presence, the Holy Spirit. As a result of this vision, Stofsky embarks on a life of charity and humility, extending compassion and consideration to all. He sees that the only proper and practical response to the "secret lovelessness" of the world and to the helpless, frightened "creatureliness" of man is love, sympathy, and service to others (179).

A measure of the spiritual strength of Stofsky is the notable lack of success of other characters in the book who strive for vision or enlightenment. They achieve only a partial and, therefore, dangerous degree of success in their spiritual endeavors. Bill Waters, for example, though he attains a vision of eternity, succumbs to madness. Daniel Verger, despite his advanced theological studies, remains spiritually immature, and when he is unable to requite his amorous yearnings for May, becomes self-pitying and self-destructive. Finally, Ancke, who through his sufferings achieves a form of egoless resignation, a degree of detachment that could be turned to good advantage in a spiritual context, cannot summon the necessary discipline nor capacity for exertion and so remains passive, unable to raise himself from a life of criminality and addiction to opiates.

Nor do the paths to meaning and enlightenment followed by other more central figures in ***Go*** seem to lead them beyond their restlessness and confusion. The vitalism of Gene Pasternak, who champions the simple and natural life of the body over what he perceives as the sophistries of abstract thought and intellectualism, provides him with no enduring contentment or fulfillment. His love affair with Christine begins in "innocence" but ends in bitterness and pain (59), while his cross-country journeys only bring him back to where he started. He finds no livable truth. In a similar manner, Hart Kennedy's transcendental hedonism generates ecstasies and insights, but ultimately his Dionysian energies show themselves to be equally capable of veering off into nastiness and violence. Both Pasternak and Kennedy seem to be on the right track in their rejection of the rational mind and in their cultivation of the instincts, but their attempts to live fuller, truer lives are imperfectly realized and must be accounted as failures.

Other than Stofsky, the only character to grow and change in a positive manner in the course of the novel is Paul Hobbes. In the beginning, Hobbes feels "brittle and will-less," aimless, and frustrated (3). His marriage to Kathryn is troubled and precarious, and his relations to others are often uneasy, as his motives and reactions are frequently misunderstood. Reticent and unassertive, he is more of an outsider, an observer, than a participant in "the beat generation" (211). Earnestly searching for a direction, a position, a perspective on life, Hobbes is hindered by his emotionally reserved nature. "In the face of an avid passion, Hobbes snapped shut like an oyster on a grain of sand; but like the oyster, the passion festered inside him" (69). Similarly, he feels a simultaneous attraction to and an alienation from both the "hip" world of mystery and kicks and the "square" world of reasonableness and responsibility.

A series of shocks jolt Hobbes into self-examination and greater awareness. Confrontations with Stofsky and Pasternak and Kathryn, the rejection of his novel on which he had staked so much, and the death of Agatson are catalysts in Hobbes' psyche. He begins to perceive the falseness, the shallowness, and the essential selfishness of his relationships to others.

> How insufferable everyone was. . . . They came to fear emotions, to think of human needs as a sign of weakness, and to view isolation, not as a curse and a blight, but as a protection. For the first time, he saw these attitudes in himself. . . . And suddenly his part in all relationships seemed made up of actions blind and cowardly and base, even though they were unconscious.
>
> (292)

Humbled with this new awareness of himself, Hobbes undertakes a further journey into the dark labyrinth of the self, and there in the maze of motives and emotions, he confronts his personal monster. Hobbes' monster manifests itself in the form of a sudden, sickening realization of the "reality of horror, without meaning, with no certain end" (309). Hobbes' monster is the void itself. In the dim, foul men's room of a waterfront saloon, he regards himself in a shattered mirror, a metaphor for his fragmented self. Reading the obscene inscriptions on the walls, Hobbes is overpowered with a knowledge of "the barrenness of the heart" (310). He understands how tenderness and the longing for love become perverted into cruelty and lewdness. With awful clarity he sees the cause of Agatson's wild despair.

> Certainly, somewhere, some time this fatal perception must have entered him like a germ and corrupted his heart and mind. And Hobbes suddenly knew that someone who believes this vision is outraged, violated, raped in his soul, and suffers the most unbearable of all losses: the death of hope. And when hope dies there is only irony, a vicious senseless irony that turns to the consuming desire to jeer, spit, curse, smash, destroy.
>
> (310)

Terrified and appalled by this infernal epiphany, Hobbes exclaims, "I must get out of here!" (310). He wishes to escape not merely the rank latrine and its scrawled obscenities but metaphorically, the state of his mind and spirit. His exclamation is more than a cry of fear and revulsion; it is a vow to amend his life. He must work to extricate himself from the dark hell of lovelessness and selfishness. The novel concludes with Hobbes' tentative reconciliation with Kathryn and with an image of his continuing search for a spiritual home, recalling his longing at the outset of the story for an Edenic home: "'Where is our home?' he said to himself gravely, for he could not see it yet" (311). In the end, Hobbes, more than any other character in the book, represents the burden of his generation—the terrible urgency of the spirit to "get out of here," to get out of hell, to redeem itself (310); and Hobbes most fully embodies the bewildered bereftness and lostness of the soul in an age of murder and perdition.

Much of the meaning of ***Go*** derives from its nervous, ominous mood, its atmosphere of decay and dissolution: the dreary, phony, sad bars of the city; the hostile streets; the glimpsed vignettes of violence, indifference, and affectation, of pretense and evasion; the endless, desperate, joyless parties; the desolate, crumbling cityscapes; the squalor and the sordidness—all seen in the infernal illumination of neon lights and streetlights in a perpetual night. In this dark and this ruin Holmes' hipsters pursue their spiritual quest: lurking, furtive; "connected by the invisible threads of need, petty crimes of long ago, or a strange recognition of affinity"; conspirators in a "revolution of the soul" (36). They are the "children of the night: everywhere wild, everywhere lost, everywhere loveless, faithless, homeless" (310); yet ever searching for a breakthrough, a vision, a center, an answer, ever seeking for some way homeward from Nowhere.

Since mystical revelation, such as that experienced by Stofsky, is not accessible to most people, other forms of communion and spiritual enlightenment must be sought in the faithless wasteland of the postwar world. For the Beat Generation in ***Go,*** the chief means of transcendence, truth, and grace is jazz. In the fluent, organic rhythms of bop they recognize the lost language of the loins and of the heart; they hear the cry of the human in a dehumanized age.

> In this modern jazz, they heard something rebel and nameless that spoke for them, and their lives knew a gospel for the first time. It was more than a music; it became an attitude toward life, a way of walking, a language and a costume; and these introverted kids (emotional outcasts of a war they had been too young to join, or in which they had lost their innocence), who had never belonged anywhere before, now felt somewhere at last.
>
> (161)

Through this music, at once erotic and ethereal, the music of the body and the spirit, the music of revolt and celebration, ***Go*** leads into and is linked with Holmes' next novel, ***The Horn.***

The Horn is a bildungsroman told in reverse: the life history of jazz saxophonist Edgar Pool, known reverently to his fans and fellow musicians as "the Horn." (Pool is a fictional composite of Lester Young, Charlie Parker, and others but essentially a product of the author's imagination.) The central narrative of the novel moves forward in time from dawn to dark on Pool's final day of life, while a series of tributary narratives move backward in time tracing significant events in his life from the most recent to the earliest. Pool is a living legend in the jazz world, a seminal genius of bop, but he is dissipated, impoverished, broken in health and spirit. His object on his last day is to find a way home, to raise enough money to return to his hometown.

Pool is in many ways an extension of Agatson in ***Go***: embittered, cynical, mocking, ironical, outrageous, and self-destructive. He is described as "the Black Angel," a man who has "fled from the light" and who has turned inward on himself in his fierce pride.[1] Like Agatson, there is a demonic quality to Pool, a desperate, driven quality. With his "cold eyes and destructive lips and closed heart" (38), he is likened to "a ruined prince intent upon doom" (107). Unlike Agatson, though, Pool is a musician, an artist, a creator who can turn even his rage and despair into art; and he is thus, in the end, able to redeem himself in despite of himself.

Redemption for Pool occurs only in the fleeting, final minutes of his life when he experiences a "falling away of all veils" enabling him to see himself and to see others clearly at last, to see the world not through the distortions of his fatal, satanic pride but lucidly with love (207). Only in the last minutes of his life does Pool extend kindness and compassion to others; only then does he regret his hauteur and pretense; and only then does he regain the full, true power of his art and understand it at last. In this sense, Edgar Pool does find his way home.

If Agatson in ***Go*** is seen as a sort of martyr, crippled by his lack of belief and acting out the destructive fantasies of a whole community of unbelievers, then Pool is a martyr of a similar sort but for opposite reasons. His is the martyrdom of a prophet unheeded for so long and forced to endure such neglect and humiliation that at last he loses his faith. Ironically and to his further embitterment, when he has lost his faith, others suddenly embrace his former prophecies and testimonies, leaving him "an atheist old man maddened by the certainties of youth" and feeling himself mocked by images of his earlier self (38).

Three interlocked clusters of images convey the thematic movement of ***The Horn***: religious imagery, musical imagery, and the imagery of birds and of flight.

Religious similes and metaphors occur throughout the story, especially in connection with jazz, which is described in terms of a "testament" (10), a "sacrament" (202), and as "holy" (36) and further characterized as a "mystery" and a "prophecy" (154), and as a "ritual" enacted on an "altar" by ecstatic "suppliants" (155).

Music itself is, in turn, a metaphor for the spiritual search of humankind. It brings light to darkness and is the expression of truth. All music is a part of "the one song" (47), "the one continuing song" (243) that evolves in "apostolic succession, song to song, man to man" (76). The musician is "God's own fool" (25) (in both senses) and his music is ultimately "always deeply on God's side" (231), a celebration of the created world and of the spirit.

Imagery of flight and of birds is also central to ***The Horn.*** Allusions to types of birds (such as the goose, the hummingbird, the albatross, the eagle, etc.), to the anatomy of birds (wing, beak, plumage), and to their songs (their squawks and honks) are frequent in the text. The bird imagery is most often applied to jazz musicians, while imagery of flight is applied to the music itself. Pool's saxophone, for example, is compared to "some metallic albatross caught insecurely in his hands, struggling to resume flight" (8). The bird and flight motif suggests transcendence, the soaring of the spirit beyond the limits of the body and the material world, rising and gliding in perfect joy and freedom. In this way, the motif unites the religious and the musical imageries in mutual reinforcement.

The single image that most concisely encapsulates the theme of the novel is song as a defense against the cold, music as a defense against death by freezing. This image emerges from an early experience in the life of Edgar Pool, recalled many years afterward by his boyhood friend Metro. As boys on the bum, riding in an empty boxcar in the dead of winter, they were caught in an "arctic blizzard" (167). In order to generate heat and to stay alive, they sang—spontaneously and defiantly against the cold and the night and, by this means, surviving and triumphing.

The incident serves as a metaphor for the human situation: we are all alone and far from home, frightened and cold, traveling through a storm, heading, like Pool and Metro, through "the exact magnetic eye of that wild, uncaring night, into an absolute shrieking dark" (167). And, like Pool and Metro, we must also find the creative force, the source of song within ourselves, and we must learn to sing or we shall freeze in "the bitter dark and cold" of this godless age (167).

The knowledge that the state of ultimate human nakedness and vulnerability is coupled with an innate redeeming power informs Pool's art and is its secret motive power despite his attempts to deny it. He acknowledges this redeeming power again only as he is dying on stage, and he tries to communicate it to others with his dying words, his final message: celebrate. Pool's saxophone is the symbol of the continuity and the enduring presence of such power and its celebration. At the beginning of his career as a musician, he redeems his first horn from a pawnshop; and at the end of his career, he returns his last horn to a pawnshop. But his pawned horn will, we are told, be redeemed again by a new celebrant, "dreaming a new dream, hoping a new hope, loving a new love" (242); and this singer will "fashion on it a new song—a further chorus of the one continuing song" (243). In defiance of the inertia, the despair, and the surrender emblematized by the pawnshop, the instruments of renewal and hope, of celebration and truth, are passed from hand to hand, from human to human. Like the boys in the boxcar, we can only freeze if we give up, let go, if we allow ourselves to freeze.

Perhaps by way of emphasizing the essential continuity of ***Go*** and ***The Horn,*** Holmes develops points of intersection in the two novels. Both share, of course, certain locations and a similar milieu—the New York city night world of jazz and in particular the jazz club called the Go Hole. Gene Pasternak and Paul Hobbes from ***Go*** make two brief appearances in ***The Horn.*** They are first glimpsed listening to bop outside a record store (150) and later seen in the audience at the Go Hole on the night of Edgar Pool's final gig (232). In both instances they are appraised by the jazz musicians as true communicants, as exemplars of an understanding and appreciation of jazz that is inspiring to the musicians. Their enthusiasm is seen as a necessary nourishment to the artist who, in turn, gives sustenance to the audience. Thus is "the one continuing song" born out of the hearts of all humankind, not just the musician; it is given and received in equal amount, a mutual human endeavor.

Thematically, too, the two novels intersect, both representing aspects of the postwar search for belief, for a unifying vision. In ***Go*** Holmes describes the goal of the quest as being "some end of the night (the night that was a corridor in which they lurked and groped, believing in a door somewhere, beyond which time and the discord bred of time were barred)" (240). In ***The Horn,*** Walden Blue, the successor to Pool, is described as having "groped blindly" for some form of belief as he plays his horn and as feeling that "down in his heart waited a single note of music that he felt would shatter all discord into harmony" (16). The terms of description and the ends of both quests are significantly similar.

Both novels also affirm that the means to transcend discord and darkness lie not in the rational mind, not in the ego, but in the unconscious, the body. In ***Go*** Stofsky speaks of having rejected Aristotelian logic and of cultivating instead "a breakthrough into the world of feeling" (65). In ***The Horn,*** Metro, the "prophet of joy," achieves his ecstatic affirmations by moving beyond the mind, knowing that "only beyond such breaking loose would all things finally be reconciled" (154). His wild, joyful, celebratory music says "a clear and untranslatable 'Yes!' to everything that was not of the mind" (155). To resist alienation and dehumanization and to achieve a psychic reorientation that will restore integrity and coherence to human life, Holmes proposes the energies of the unconscious, the mysterious life of the body.

Holmes' third and last novel, ***Get Home Free,*** is a sequel to ***Go.*** The book follows the lives of certain characters from ***Go*** in the aftermath of the events of that novel. ***Get Home Free*** also shares motifs and themes with ***The Horn*** and may be seen as extending and resolving the concerns of its two predecessors and thus completing a sequence of interrelated novels.

Get Home Free consists of two central, separate episodes divided by an interlude and framed by a prologue and an epilogue. The structure of the two episodes and of the novel as a whole is informed by the archetypal pattern of the night journey: the movement of the psyche through dissolution to a new wholeness, through darkness to light—a process objectified by the temporal movement from night to dawn and daylight. The novel is also unified by the motif of returning to one's geographical home and of finding a spiritual home.

The prologue, titled **"New York: The End,"** is a sort of epilogue to the events of ***Go.*** The desperate energy of the immediate postwar era is now dissipating; there is an air of exhaustion, of "hopelessness and waste," as the forties end and the fifties begin.[2] And with the new decade there is a widespread feeling of apathy, a sense that the moral and metaphysical issues have somehow been obviated. Correspondingly, there is a reassertion of self-interest, self-gratification, a reentrenchment of convention. Personifying the new zeitgeist, the spirit of the fifties, is the character Tertius Streik: brash, insensitive, venal, hedonistic, cynical, and utterly, ruthlessly, unashamedly materialistic. (His name suggests an allusion to baseball: the third strike, the batter's failure to hit the ball, the end of hope for a home run.) Streik's self-satisfaction and his preoccupation with pleasure, career, position, and money is the antithesis of Agatson's despair and Stofsky's mysticism in ***Go.***

ON THE SUBJECT OF...

THE INFLUENCE OF JAZZ ON THE BEATS

In this modern jazz, they heard something rebel and nameless that spoke for them, and their lives knew a gospel for the first time. It was more than a music; it became an attitude toward life, a way of walking, a language and a costume; and these introverted kids (emotional outcasts of a war they had been too young to join, or in which they had lost their innocence), who had never belonged anywhere before, now felt somewhere at last.

Holmes, John Clellon. Excerpt from *Go.* New York: Scribners, 1952.

The prologue also serves to define the specific problems of the main characters Verger and May. Having come together after Agatson's death, Verger and May are now nearing the end of their love affair. There has been "a failure of intimacy between them," a failure that encompasses both sexuality and true heart-to-heart communication through tenderness and openness (16). They are mutually alienated—alienated from their country (Verger rails and raves against America) and, of course, ultimately alienated from themselves. Their failure to love is linked with the horrors of the recent war and with the tensions of the cold war, with the universal human failure to love. "What's *wrong* with us?" May asks, "What happened to everyone?" (27). Verger replies, "Good Lord, what can I say. It sounds so pompous. . . . But Hiroshima, Belsen, the foolishness at Torgau, all that—it reached here somehow, right here . . ." (27-28). The note of disintegration and disjunction introduced and sustained in the prologue reaches its culmination at the end of the section when Verger and May separate.

In the first of the two episodes that form the core of ***Get Home Free,*** Verger, having left May, leaves New York City too and returns to his hometown in rural New England "to come to terms with a stalled life" (55). There he encounters and becomes acquainted with Old Man Molineaux, a local eccentric and reprobate, the town drunk, and the object of much scandalized gossip. A curious affinity develops between the old man and the younger man, and through his association with Molineaux, Verger gains self-awareness and maturity; he discovers or recovers his own identity.

Old Man Molineaux is the heir to an American tradition that goes back to Washington Irving's Rip Van Winkle and comes down through Henry David Thoreau. Molineaux is a free spirit, fiercely independent, stubborn, defiant, a ne'er-do-well and a social outcast, undomesticated, at home in the forests and the fields, a friend of dogs, and an enemy of the authorities (the constable and the politicians), of propriety (the prim, church-going ladies and the respectable productive citizens), and of all convention and orthodoxy. Molineaux is the embodiment of the wild-outlaw-anarchic spirit that has always been the true informing energy of the American republic.

Significantly, Molineaux is in imminent danger of being involuntarily institutionalized, committed to the state hospital upon the recommendation of the town physician and with the consent of his family. The decision to confine this proud, wild, solitary man is entirely appropriate to an age of conformity and complacency and secret anxiety, an age dazzled by affluence and hypnotized by "the Great Gray Eye" of television (90). With the collusion of Verger, Molineaux evades the forces of normality for a time, and when at last he is cornered and forced to capitulate, he does so on his own terms. Molineaux manages to turn his defeat into a sort of victory, transforming his retreat into a tactical withdrawal. By feigning or, at least, by playing up his physical infirmities, he succeeds in preserving his self-esteem and in gaining the opportunity to spend the winter in the comfort of the hospital rather than in his primitive shack. The Old Man may be caught for the time-being, but he remains unreconstructed, unregenerate, unrepentant, and ultimately irrepressible. With the cunning and craft of an old campaigner he continues "the unequal struggle" against society (134), keenly, intuitively aware that, as Emerson states, "society everywhere is in conspiracy against the manhood of every one of its members" and that "whoso would be man must be a nonconformist."

Molineaux has also gained a disciple and an heir in Verger, who, during the course of their adventures, assumes "a filial protectiveness" for the Old Man, and for whom Molineaux becomes a sort of spiritual father (98). In protecting and defending Old Man Molineaux, Verger learns to accept and to affirm the same wild, anarchic, rebellious spirit in himself. He thus becomes the successor to Molineaux, just as the Old Man is himself successor to "the Old Leather Man" of his youth. After passing through a long, drunken night of wandering and misadventures with Old Man Molineaux, Verger manages in the end to bring him safely home. Through this act, he comes safely home himself, finding his true home and his true family by embracing the tradition of "*wild* America . . . Indians, sailors, bums, crazy damn fools with funny notions in their heads" (101). His night journey over, Verger has succeeded in getting home free.

May, too, makes a night journey, undergoing a process of self-refinement and regeneration. Like Verger, May has reached the dead end of herself in New York City and, in an "exhaustion of spirit," returns to her hometown in rural Louisiana (146). But, as did Verger in New England, May feels herself an outsider, a stranger in her community, stifled by the polite inanity and dismal conventionality of her family and her friends. And finally, like Verger, May, too, discovers "*wild* America" and reaffirms her own sense of individuality and of identity.

Abandoning her stuffy, unadventurous, hometown companions of the evening, May spends a night in the fertile chaos of a dilapidated country house inhabited by a collection of nonconforming, blithe, and unrestrained hipsters and free spirits. The house is a sort of oasis of untamed energy, sensuality, and individuality, a sanctuary of "careless anarchy and underground freedom of whim" (187). In the course of a long night of alcohol, marijuana, music, conversation, dance, arguments, and strange encounters (including three sexual propositions), May reaches "a bottomless weariness, beyond despair" (230). She passes then, at dawn, into an almost transcendent state of heightened receptivity to, awareness and acceptance of the ongoing and ever renewed and renewing miracle and mystery of existence:

> I was translucently open to it—the gnats, like a fine cloud of golden specks, swarming in a ray of early sunshine; the wild asters meek and fragile in the glistening grasses; the cock that crew with lazy conceit over near the bayou; all the verdure, and the growth, and the awakening—tiny hidden worlds from which we are mostly excluded by our formulating intelligence—all there in the dewy sanity of the morning.
>
> (234)

There is in this passage a sense of having at last reached the end of the night, the dark night of the soul, and of having moved out of Nowhere to here, to being on the earth, in the world, to a feeling of community of life, communion with creation. There is a sense of deliverance and repristination, of refreshment and restoration, a quality of having been returned to the senses, to the body. May has come through and has found a fulcrum, a meridian, a beginning.

Another character from ***Go,*** Paul Hobbes, also reappears in ***Get Home Free.*** Hobbes, too, has left New York, and, like Verger and May, he is embarked upon a night journey through his psyche. Hobbes is one of the racially-mixed company staying at the old Louisiana farm house. He is divorced, drifting, having forsaken words and writing for music and abandoned intellectuality for an exploration of the dark mysteries of the body. "We've lost touch with something—," Hobbes tells May, "something wild and natural, call it bliss or reality, a capacity for spontaneous love, whatever—but it's the only thing that can renew the consciousness when it's exhausted by anxiety" (198). Learning music under the tutelage of Little Orkie, sexuality under the tutelage of Orkie's sister Billie, submerging himself in the unconscious and the instincts by means of drugs and alcohol, and trying to learn to read the map of his own nervous system, Hobbes is still in midvoyage, at midpassage. His night journey has not yet been completed.

Music is, once again, an important motif in ***Get Home Free,*** a metaphor again for the spiritual search and aspiration of man and a vehicle of expression for certain elusive truths and for a knowledge beyond language. Embodying the wisdom of music is the blind, black singer, Little Orkie, with his message of joyous affirmation: "It's all all right." Orkie possesses an unfallen, Adamic innocence (appropriately, he works as a gardener), and his music reflects a prelapsarian "nakedness" of spirit and a strange, orphic reconciling power (162):

> The voice itself seeming to make its own peace with life's betrayals, the voice speaking for the body out of which it came, and for its humors and agitations and bafflements, a little mournful with the subsiding sob that lingers for a while in a cheered child's first hesitant laugh; somehow suggestive, too, of the grief that purges as usually only art can purge; a voice without an emotional flaw, with no failure of feeling, and, as a result, almost unearthly to hear, because we are so unused to hearing anything so utterly earthly exposed to the disbelief of strangers.
>
> (163-64)

Though blind, Orkie is intensely aware of, involved in, and responsive to the world around him. He retains, as May observes, a childlike sense of wonder at the world and a relatedness to it:

"He's still part of it" (234). Orkie serves as a sort of spiritual teacher or guide for both Hobbes and May, an exemplar of simple, sincere, and unself-conscious faith and grace. He may be seen as the musician that Edgar Pool might have been without his fatal pride: an enraptured celebrant of life.

The last section of the novel, **"New York: The Beginning,"** brings May and Verger back to the city again (Verger by way of Europe) and, as the title indicates, brings them to a new beginning of their lives. Both have achieved maturity and a new self-reliance and composure, a sense of identity. They recommence their affair but on the basis of immediate desires and spontaneous passion without reference to received patterns or abstractions of love or commitment or a long-term relationship. Free of such formal and impersonal conventions with their often distorting and inhibiting pressures and preconceptions, Verger and May discover a new sexual compatibility and a new intensity of erotic desire, one that flourishes "without a word, without a thought" (246). The sheer heightened physicality of their lovemaking serves to bring them closer together at a psychic level than ever before and constitutes a form of transcendence. "Their two desires fused into that single cleaving need in which the mind is extinguished at last . . . and the astounded moan of pleasure comes abruptly of itself, abolishing something—some illusion of the isolated self" (249). In their new union May and Verger have rediscovered an elemental, sacramental, regenerative energy; they have found a way leading homeward from Nowhere.

The title of the novel, ***Get Home Free,*** suggests the successful resolution of the quests that were begun in ***Go*** and were pursued in ***The Horn.*** Verger and May come home in at least three ways: they come home to themselves, attaining their identity, their individuality, and discovering a tradition, a community in which to participate; they come home to their homeland, reconciling themselves to the "creative turmoil" of America, its violence and anger, its joy and aspiration, its continuing potential for evolution (248); and, finally, they come home to that wholeness, that mysterious unity of being which exists beyond the exile of the isolate ego.

John Clellon Holmes' three novels propose three different but complementary ways of countering human destructiveness and of finding a solution to our common crisis of spirit. These ways or paths out of Nowhere are mysticism, art, and sexuality. Although these may, at first sight, seem to be irreconcilable and incompatible, ultimately they may be seen to share some essential qualities and characteristics. Each involves a surrender of the ego to a greater entity or energy; each in its way represents a form of communion with the numinous; each is rooted in the unconscious; and each draws upon the deepest creative energies of our being. Like Blake and Lawrence, Holmes perceives the subversive, liberating nature of sexuality and art—both expressions of Eros, both reflections and revelations of eternal beauty and bliss—and discerns the deep congruence and affinity of sexuality and spirituality—both expressions of the same urge to transcend the subjective self.

Holmes' novels record and interpret the inner conflicts and problems of the immediate postwar period, a crucial juncture of contemporary history. He focuses upon representative members of the generation that came of age during the Second World War and during the cold war that followed, the Beat Generation, which was the first to register the effects of the collective trauma of the war and to react to it, seeking the cause and the cure of their condition. In the acute response of his fiction to the social, moral, and metaphysical issues of postwar America and in his resolute quest for remedial means and measures, strategies for renewal, for the realization of a new consciousness and for a new human wholeness, Holmes' work is prophetic and possesses an enduring pertinence to our time. A bold explorer of the antipodes and terrae incognitae of the psyche, Holmes has shown us that the night and the void can be traversed and that a homeward passage can be effected.

Notes

1. John Clellon Holmes, *The Horn* (London: Jazz Book Club, 1961), 15, 18, 21. Further parenthetical references are to this edition; when necessary for clarity page references are preceded by *Horn.*

2. John Clellon Holmes, *Get Home Free* (London: Corgi Books, 1966), 13. Further parenthetical references are to this edition; when necessary for clarity page references are preceded by *Home.*

JAAP VAN DER BENT (ESSAY DATE NOVEMBER-DECEMBER 1994)

SOURCE: van der Bent, Jaap. "The Maples Will Enleaf Again, and Consciousness Relent: The Poetry of John Clellon Holmes." *American Poetry Review* 23, no. 6 (November-December 1994): 55-61.

In the following essay, van der Bent examines the stylistic and thematic changes in Holmes's poetry and details the revisions Holmes made to earlier poems.

To most readers, John Clellon Holmes (1926-1988) is probably still mainly known because of his connection with the Beat Generation. Even those not specifically interested in the Beats are now often aware that it was in a conversation with Holmes, in 1948, that Jack Kerouac coined the term "beat generation," and that Holmes's novel ***Go*** (1952) was the first adequate depiction of that generation to appear in print. All too often, however, attention has been paid to Holmes's work primarily because of his association with the Beats, whom he frequently defended against hostile critics. While his efforts in this field helped to pave the way to academic and critical success for several of his Beat colleagues, the merits of Holmes's own work have never been widely recognized. Yet ***The Horn*** (1958) is an engaging novel about the jazz world of the late forties and early fifties. And as is shown convincingly by the three-volume edition of his essays which came out in the late 1980s, Holmes was also one of America's most distinguished postwar essayists, with a good eye for societal changes and what usually remains hidden beneath the surface of everyday reality. However, not only as a novelist and essayist, but also as a poet he deserves a larger audience.

Like many authors, Holmes started to write poems long before he began to attempt to express himself in prose. According to Holmes himself, he wrote his "first poems of any interest at all when [he] was thirteen," even publishing "one or two in local New Jersey newspapers."[1] After he had enrolled at Columbia University in the fall of 1945, he not only began work on a first novel that was never completed, but also continued to write poems, "sometimes at a rate of one per day."[2] These early poems owed a great deal to Auden and Yeats; under the influence of the New Criticism, they were highly formal and allusive, strongly affected by Elizabethan and metaphysical poets. In this respect, although Holmes was more skillful at the use of orthodox metres and rhymes, his early poems are not unlike the poems that Allen Ginsberg wrote before 1950, which have been described as "decorative, overwritten, full of conceits and poetic diction . . . all in the style of the sixteenth and seventeenth century mystics and sonnetteers."[3] However, while around 1950, under the influence of William Carlos Williams's aesthetics, Ginsberg gave up trying to use an Elizabethan voice and was able to relax into a more spontaneous style, the much more cerebral Holmes was unable to do so for some time to come.

A characteristic specimen of Holmes's early poetry is **"Fear in the Afternoon,"** one of his first poems to appear in a well-known literary magazine (it was written in 1947, and published in *Poetry* in July, 1948):

> Watched and sleeping all the sodden afternoon,
> Listened until the creeping song began to moan
> And sleeping stealthy sang along but did not
> mean.
>
> And the slow blinds so drawn against the sun,
> Or the sly yawn that signifies one's really sane,
> And the clouds that fawn on sky and gather
> soon.
>
> All this blots out the ancient ruined wall,
> The twilight flute, the incense, and the Druid
> wail,
> And this is NOW, and all, though final, still is
> well.[4]

This strange poem is rather cryptic but revealing of Holmes at the same time. Its impersonal aspect, partly due to the fact that it is not written in the first or third person, is in line with the poem's content, which concerns the creation of a defense against new, disturbing experiences. The unsettling nature of these experiences is effectively emphasized by the consonance of the end rhyme, and connected with "the ancient ruined wall, / The twilight flute, the incense, and the Druid wail" of the third stanza. However, in the first stanza these elements are already announced by a "creeping song" that begins to "moan." Instead of wholeheartedly responding to this song, the person described in the poem only sings along furtively; he does not "mean," but guards himself by drawn blinds, a sly yawn and, even, gathering clouds. This armature allows him to hold on to the present, and gives him the illusion that everything, although "final," is still all right.

The impersonal character of **"Fear in the Afternoon"** makes it a hazardous undertaking to explain the poem in biographical terms. Still, because it deals with a defense of the self, one can hardly avoid a connection with the character armour that Holmes's persona, Paul Hobbes, in ***Go*** is both battling against and dependent upon, as it shields him from the lifestyle of his Beat friends, which is at the same time threatening and attractive to him. When Holmes wrote **"Fear in the Afternoon,"** he had not yet met either Kerouac or Ginsberg, and both the poem's form and its subject matter show that in 1947 he was not at all prepared for the "Druid wail" that would characterize the later work of such a typical Beat poet as Ginsberg (whose "Howl" was in fact re-titled "Wail" by Kerouac in *The Dharma Bums*).

Between 1948 and 1952 Holmes wrote many more poems that illustrate his skills in versification. At the same time, however, his technical dexterity was a stumbling block that interfered with the expression of his personal voice. It is striking that, unlike Ginsberg and even though the subject matter of his poems sometimes begs for it, at this time Holmes was unable to break into the use of more open forms. While Kerouac and Ginsberg were "really talking about freedom of being, feelings rushing out, candor and honesty,"[5] it was especially the ironic tone of his own work with which Holmes grew increasingly disenchanted:

> That's why I stopped writing poetry. Because I couldn't get out of that tone . . . which was terribly constricting . . . The last poem that I wrote then before I started again was a poem about Christ . . . And I wrote a poem about Jesus Christ . . . in the tone of W. H. Auden—who'd already done it many times. And I decided, "Fuck this shit man. If you can't find a way to talk out, then you'd better shut your fucking mouth."[6]

The poem to which Holmes refers here is entitled **"Good Friday."** It was written in 1952 and, although its remarkable use of consonance attests once more to Holmes's competence, it is in fact one of his most literary and affected poems. **"Good Friday,"** which Holmes himself called "perfect and empty," made him decide not to write another poem until "emotion overcame craft."[7]

Holmes did not write poetry again until the autumn of 1959. In August of that year his father had died of injuries sustained in an automobile accident on the New Jersey turnpike. When, in letters to friends, Holmes found himself unable to describe how he felt about his father's death, it became clear to him that his feelings demanded "a more heightened expression,"[8] and he tried to articulate them in a long poem to and about his father, **"Too-Late Words to My Father (1899-1959)."** Although he had decided to do away with metre and rhyme, Holmes still discovered that he had trouble using freer forms, and he kept on working on the poem, off and on, all through the sixties. During that period he wrote many other poems as well. In these poems, no longer influenced by Auden and Yeats but by Williams, Ezra Pound, Theodore Roethke, Gary Snyder and "particularly the T'ang poets of China, and certain of the Japanese,"[9] he was finally able to use the open forms he was striving for. In the early seventies Holmes reworked most of these poems into the versions in which, from 1974 onward, they started to appear in literary magazines both in America and Great Britain.

Holmes finally completed **"Too-Late Words to My Father"** to his satisfaction in the spring of 1974. By the beginning of February of that year he had started to rework, "between other chores," the version of the poem he had on his hands then:

> It started to shape itself into uneven stanzaic patterns, I chopped away at the rhetoric, trying to build the emotion as deep into the lines as I could. The little tags at the end of each stanza gave me a direction to move towards, and they also reminded me of the gradual shortening of lines toward the bottom of New England headstones.[10]

The extent to which Holmes was able to do away with rhetoric and to write clearly and directly is illustrated by the opening of the poem:

> Camden nights dire with honeysuckle,
> back of hospital streets,
> stoops murmurous with baseball—
> Sucking peppermints in an alien town,
> I carried plastic tubes of sleeping pills,
> aspirin, iodine, and oil of camphor—
> prepared against myself but ill-prepared for vigils
> in South Jersey shipyard Whitman night,
> or the irony of turnpike smashup
> that brought you there,
> my urbane father.[11]

Especially in the second and longest part of **"Too-Late Words to My Father,"** which Holmes called "probably the best poem I've ever written,"[12] it becomes an expression of all the things he never said to his father in life, "the recognition of his inherent value as a man and a father, the too-late tribute of a grieving son."[13] The value Holmes attributes to his father is illustrated by the fact that he feels that it is because of the influence of his father that he became a writer:

> Now you won't read to me again
> though I write stories and this poem
> because you read me Dickens before sleep—[14]

The same stanza, however, also suggests some of the antagonism that, according to the poem and to remarks made by Holmes in interviews, clearly existed between the poet and his father:

> From you I caught a taste for language,
> never to confess it in our wrangles.
> Though proud of me, the use I put it to
> left the Jeffrey Farnol in you
> speechless.

The highly effective phrasing of the first two parts of **"Too-Late Words to My Father"** also characterizes the rest of the poem, in which Holmes describes his recent reconciliation with his father and the latter's funeral, and in which, in the poem's fifth and last part, he returns to a scene at his father's deathbed. The description of that scene reveals that the poem's poignancy is to a large extent due to a mixture of grief and toughness on the part of the poet. This comes out very well when Holmes describes his father's "thin fleet meatless legs learning / something new to do in bed at sixty."[15] These lines, which refer to Holmes's father having to adapt himself to the new situation of being confined to a hospital bed, take on a very moving quality when one realizes that elsewhere in the poem, as well as in at least one interview, Holmes described his father as having always been very much a ladies' man. Moreover, the unsentimental quality of suchlike lines allows Holmes in other places to give free reign to the formulation of his deepest feelings, such as those described in the conclusion of the poem:

> I talked on with awful pointlessness,
> embarrassed by my breaking voice.
> But I spoke out of time and its ego—
> the shame of something-more-to-lose—
>
> And end this now,
> become your son
> at last.[16]

Although **"Too-Late Words to My Father"** is a very fine and successful poem, it is not necessarily Holmes's best. Among the poems that he started to write from 1959 onward there is a considerable number that equal it in quality. Most of these poems deal with the conflict between intellect and emotion, and many of them describe a situation in which the poet moves from a feeling of disharmony to a sense of being, at least temporarily, at one and at ease with the world. This definitely holds for **"North Cove Revenant,"** a poem in four parts that Holmes started to write in November 1959 and which, like **"Too-Late Words to My Father,"** he finally completed in 1974. In the opening of the poem, in fact, Holmes seems to refer to his father's death, with which late in 1959 he was trying to come to terms:

> Create against death
> and its contagion—
> After a death, a poem—
> clove-apple of the mind.[17]

The extent to which the poet feels out of tune at the beginning of the poem is convincingly expressed by the opening part's next, and last, five lines, whose tapering off is reminiscent of **"Too-Late Words to My Father"**:

> But I am nothing again, and nothing comes
> out of the dank well.
> I am nothing, and search reality
> to redeem my nothingness
> in its appearances.

The course of action proposed in these lines is carried out in the second part of **"North Cove Revenant."** Walking about in the watery North Cove area, Holmes is like the swans that cruise the shore, "looking for life to eat." The swans, however, "are arrogant, / knowing their element," and especially in this last respect they are completely unlike the poet at this particular juncture. Holmes is aware that one reason why he has trouble entering reality is the fact that, even though there are "[n]o secrets in reality— / only happenings, / accidents, / fortuitous events / going unrecorded endlessly," he is bothered by a strong urge to "hold," to "arrest," these events. Still, as the following lines indicate, by letting things take their course, the poet is able to at least weaken the hold death had on him in the opening of the poem. What these lines also show, especially the last three, is Holmes's sharp eye for detail and his fine use of metaphor:

> I'm nothing again
> but the smell of death
> is blown away
> by November riverwind.
> Scavenger gulls look down,
> silvered minnows dart
> like filings to a magnet[18]

The thematic aspects that characterize **"North Cove Revenant"** are also found in many of the poems that Holmes wrote since. In several of them, the poet, though painfully longing for a life in tune with himself, is unable to rise above feelings of failure and frustration. This is the case in **"Women in A.M.,"** originally written in 1961. This poem, short enough to quote in full, movingly describes the poet's being separate from the sense of harmony that Holmes, in a somewhat old-fashioned way, ascribes to women:

> Women drowse through mornings, nurturing
> life.
> Some women never rouse except by twilight.
> They save the real expenditures for dark.
> Drowsing in dream-peopled beds,
> no anguish in their mornings,
> only the flesh-warm linen,
> the whish of rain, the soul at sleep.
> They are ingathering, they are in root,
> and I'm unhappy to be up and writing it.[19]

Many of Holmes's later poems went through numerous revisions and sometimes only reached their definite form years after he first conceived them. By 1975, however, Holmes had found his own, characteristic and highly personal poetic voice, which from that time on enabled him to write his poems down in a form that was almost immediately satisfactory to him. Thus, in April and May 1975, he wrote a nine-poem sequence, ***The Bowling Green Poems,*** which has justly been claimed to be "the strongest sequence he has had published."[20] As Holmes explained in a brief introduction to the first publication of the sequence, at the time of writing these poems he was "living in a northwest Ohio college town as a visiting writer, taking stock of his life and work, both temporarily stalled."[21] It was "a dim time" for him, which was not made easier by the fact that he missed dead friends such as Kerouac and Walker Evans, as well as his wife, who could not come with him. However, a trip to Hartford, Connecticut enables him to spend a weekend with her, and after he has returned to Ohio and has a chance street-encounter with one of his students, "the log-jam in his spirit breaks."

The first and shortest of the nine ***Bowling Green Poems,*** which introduces the setting of the sequence, can be read as a plea for inspiration:

> My bachelor house in order,
> tapes and dishes shelved,
> I putter and make a drink
> waiting to be used,
> waiting to expend myself—
> a gypsy scrivener,
> haranguer of fraternities;
> a winter woodchuck in his burrow,
> nostrils quivering for spring.[22]

In the following three poems the poet takes stock of the situation in which he finds himself in Ohio. In the introduction to the sequence Holmes had already admitted that the landscape in that particular state did not "stir" him. In reality, this is still an understatement for his completely negative attitude towards the Ohio countryside, as the opening of the second poem immediately makes clear:

> Light of empty morning,
> pickle factories in an old bog,
> homely Anderson phone-poles.
> Sense of a frozen sea,
> muds coagulant to the eye's lift,
> vital movement contravened.[23]

In the next two poems Holmes keeps referring to the "mud" and "loam" that are for him the most striking characteristics of "these villages" that "break the will-to-form." Ohio is for him a landscape "inhospitable / to visions," and in the beginning of the third poem of the sequence, Holmes describes himself as "a sea-crab / in an inland swamp." The ultimate put-down of Ohio comes, however, in the ending of the fourth poem, where Holmes writes:

> God put this place underwater
> then some boring asshole
> went and drained it
> to build a filling station.[24]

In view of the poet's low opinion of the area in which he temporarily has to live, it is hardly surprising that in the last line of the second poem he even seems to begrudge the wind its "going elsewhere." Stuck between "the night's void" and the "fissureless day ahead," Holmes can only, like the sea-crab he referred to earlier, pace "a half-dark room, / waiting out the TV-news." Still, as the third poem goes on to reveal, Holmes is aware that it may yet be possible to find a way out of the fix in which he has found himself in Ohio. This part of the poem also clearly shows that what holds Holmes's poetry together is not so much a fixed metre, as an unobstrusive use of interior rhyme and a delicate reliance on alliteration, while the phrase "a stay of sentences," in the second to last line, is again characteristically ambiguous:

> God knows
> the maples will enleaf again,
> the sentience of wrens among them,
> and consciousness relent.
> God knows
> time has its lucky accidents
> no more explicable than birds.
> Best into bed at evening
> with someone else's book
> to drowse despite the six-packs
> of the neighbor boys,
> and Walter Cronkite—
> the great world of the ambitions
> promising another morning,
> a stay of sentences,
> birdsong,
> and *no blame.*[25]

After, in the fifth and sixth poem, reminiscing about Walker Evans and Kerouac, in the seventh poem, Holmes can finally describe the change he anticipated in the quotation above. In this seventh poem, which marks a turning point in the sequence, Holmes writes about the time he is able to spend with his wife in Hartford, where he has travelled to deliver a lecture about Kerouac and the Beats. The first lines of the poem immediately reveal a striking contrast in mood and tone to what has gone before:

> And if there can be love again
> between such wearied people
> there can be oysters
> smiling in their shells,
> Franz Kline, cold marts, bouzouki music.[26]

This joyful mood and its concomitant affirmative tone are sustained in the rest of this part of the sequence. Holmes's brief reunion with his wife has brought them a "return of the old sensual fevers / resting the expended parts of us," as a consequence of which "life's got savor now— / there's grace in it." It is especially the revelation that there could be "flesh-love again" between Holmes and his wife, "hand-colloquies in hotel-beds, / words become tongues," which at least for the moment resigns the poet to his fate, and which shows that there may yet be an end to the "soldiering-through" Holmes described earlier. The poet's having become in tune with reality is perhaps most aptly illustrated in the last stanza of the seventh poem, in which Holmes refers to a well-known Zen parable about the nature of enlightenment:

> I kissed you in the marriage-places,
> grounded again.
> There's nothing more to lose.
> The old Zen canniness occurred—
> mountains were mountains once again.[27]

The sure touch that is typical of ***The Bowling Green Poems*** distinguishes many of the poems that Holmes wrote after 1975. In these later poems the most moving evocation of his longing for transformation is to be found in **"Northfork October Return,"** written in October 1982. This poem can be regarded as a companion piece to **"North Cove Revenant,"** with which it shares its theme and a similar kind of setting, while the titles of the two poems also resemble each other. Although, as in the earlier poem, in **"Northfork October Return"** Holmes again tries to "[c]reate against death," the presence of death is much more threatening now, because he wrote **"Northfork October Return"** in an effort to come to terms with the after-effects of his first bout of cancer. The poem describes how, "after the tumor of July, the radiation-August, / the long depression of September,"[28] in the hope of finding new strength, Holmes returns to a place where he used to spend his summers as a boy, one of the Long Island beaches "where the curse / or blessing took place long ago." In *Interior Geographies: An Interview with John Clellon Holmes,* two years before writing **"Northfork October Return,"** Holmes had already reminisced about the summers he spent on Long Island:

> We summered far out on the North Fork of Long Island at Peconic—BLT's on the rocky beach for lunch, waiting the prescribed hour before I could dive off two special rocks, and, when brave, swim down deep and ginger through their barnacled separation, overhearing talk of Hitler from a second cousin, Margie, just back from a year in Germany, reproducing the fanatic rant of his voice in a language I couldn't understand, but understood. Spain, read about in the pages of the *Herald Tribune* (bought at a little grocery in town), and somehow knowing, even at 10, that something dire was loose in the world. My father called me Yo in those days, short for Johann Sebastian Bach; others called me Buddy. Some severance, some wrenching, happened to me there. I was spanked by my mother with a rugbeater I had retrieved from the tide-line, and I became a bore that late August with the litany of "Nobody loves me—."[29]

While in 1980 Holmes's memories of his summer holidays on Long Island were not entirely positive, at the time of writing **"Northfork October Return"** the North Fork area had come to symbolize for him the safety, strength and health that were taken for granted when he was younger, but that now are painfully lacking. Consequently, it is with a poignant sense of regret that Holmes addresses himself to the scenes of his youth:

> *Lost boyhood haven, still salt-worn*
> *as cloudy bits of bottle glass,*
> *was it for this I was preparing?*
> *The dream of harbor swamped so fast*
> *by chance gusts of an easterly?*[30]

Alternating with descriptive fragments, in which Holmes pictures himself as fighting "assaults of panic, curdling to self-pity" when "the cove he'd hoped for prove[s] phantom," **"Northfork October Return"** contains two more passages in italics. In the first of these the poem becomes a highly moving prayer to the sea at North Fork, to help the poet regain some of the safety he has lost:

> *Sea-sleep,* he begged in secret, *come*
> *and ease my heart, kedge-anchored still*
> *off Horton's Point with no way in.*
> *Cold petrel spirit of these tides,*
> *excuse me for a little, I was innocent*
> *believed life's risks without a tab,*
> *who now, an anxious, aging scold,*
> *must make a final fight or bitter-over—*
> *Scud this sprung dory to some berth.*[31]

Identifying with the gulls that "persist into stiffening wind, / coasting its shoals and currents in the sun / to Greenport's fish-rich jetties east," the poet tries, symbolically and in vain, "to find a long down-draft / to take him also out beyond / Peconic's headlands to the empty beach." Then he speaks to the rocks in terms that can be compared to those in which he appealed to the sea:

> *Stay with me till I mend, you rocks,*
> the ragged teeth of that bedraggled
> coast, *bear up a coward's weight*
> *until tomorrow's fresh with resolutions,*
> *cheap tears turned as tough as brine.*

In the end the poet's prayers are answered and, following the same development that is found in many of Holmes's other poems, the last stanza describes how he finds at least temporarily some of the peace he knew at North Fork when he was a boy:

> The second morning there, it came
> while he was blank, distracted—
> a settling below the heart.
> Amid the ebb-drained strew that dawn,
> three fragile scallop shells,
> chaste as their absent Venuses,
> lay in his empty hand and eye.
> He hunkered down, boy-rapt, to ponder
> their fluted edges perfect as the poem
> already forming in the tide's return.[32]

While in its definitive version "**Northfork October Return**" is still one of Holmes's most personal poems, its private character is even more apparent in the first two of the eight drafts that he wrote for it. In these early versions the poem was not only entirely written in the first person, but it also contained traces of a very understandable but still formless despair that, had the poem been printed then, would probably have overstressed its intimate quality. This goes, for instance, for Holmes's Poundian description of himself as "gone in the teeth" and for his plea "*sweet Jesus, let my heart too come home!*"[33] which were later particularized to "irradiated to the last eyetooth" and "*Scud this sprung dory to some berth.*" Apart from the fact that, beginning with the third draft, the descriptive parts of the poem were written in the third person, Holmes further objectified and universalized his personal experiences by employing the ambiguity on which he also relied in some of his earlier verse. Thus the "*berth,*" in the supplication quoted above, can also imply the rebirth that Holmes eagerly awaits in "**Northfork October Return.**" The same ambiguity is found in the "return" of the poem's title, which not only refers to Holmes's having come back to one of the scenes of his youth, but which, as the last line of the poem suggests, also stands for the turning of the tide that brings Holmes some of the peace of mind he had lost, as well as the poem itself.

"**Northfork October Return**" can serve as a final and clear example of Holmes's great abilities as a poet, although he went on to write a substantial number of poems until the very end of his life. Night Music: Selected Poems (1989), in which many of the poems discussed here can be found, ends in fact with a short poem, Samoan Head," which, as a brief note underneath the poem tells us, was Holmes's "last poem / written in the night," three days before his death on March 30, 1988. It is not one of his best poems, but it helps to remind us that Holmes was a writer (and a poet!) to the backbone.

Notes

1. Dana Burns Westburg, "The Curious Case of John Clellon Holmes" (Amherst, Massachusetts: Amherst College, 1976; unpublished B.A. thesis), p. 7.
2. *Ibid,* p. 21.
3. Paul Portugés, *The Visionary Poetics of Allen Ginsberg* (Santa Barbara, California: Ross-Erikson, 1978), pp. 26-27.
4. John Clellon Holmes, *Night Music: Selected Poems* (Fayetteville, Arkansas: University of Arkansas Press, 1989), p. 3.
5. Dana Burns Westburg, "The Curious Case of John Clellon Holmes," p. 57.
6. *Ibid,* p. 32.
7. Arthur and Kit Knight, *Interior Geographies: An Interview with John Clellon Holmes* (Warren, Ohio: The Literary Denim, 1981), p. 5.
8. Richard Ardinger, An Annotated Bibliography of works by John Clellon Holmes (Pocatello, Idaho: Idaho State University Press, 1979), p. 17.
9. *Ibid.*
10. *Ibid.*
11. John Clellon Holmes, *Night Music,* p. 25.
12. Arthur and Kit Knight, *Interior Geographies: An Interview with John Clellon Holmes,* p. 7.
13. *Ibid.*
14. John Clellon Holmes, *Night Music,* p. 27.
15. *Ibid,* p. 30.
16. *Ibid.*
17. John Clellon Holmes, *Death Drag: Selected Poems 1948-1979* (Pocatello, Idaho: Limberlost Press, 1979), p. 5.
18. *Ibid,* p. 6.
19. John Clellon Holmes, *Night Music,* p. 32.
20. Richard Kirk Ardinger, "John Clellon Holmes," in *The Beats: Literary Bohemians in Postwar America,* ed. Ann Charters (Detroit: Gale Research Company, 1983), p. 260.
21. John Clellon Holmes, *The Bowling Green Poems* (California, Pennsylvania: The Unspeakable Visions of the Individual, 1977), p. 4.
22. *Ibid,* p. 7.
23. *Ibid,* pp. 7-8.
24. *Ibid,* p. 12.
25. *Ibid,* p. 10.
26. *Ibid,* p. 15.
27. *Ibid,* p. 16.

28. John Clellon Holmes, *Night Music,* p. 62.

29. Arthur and Kit Knight, *Interior Geographies: An Interview with John Clellon Holmes,* p. 2.

30. John Clellon Holmes, *Night Music,* p. 62.

31. *Ibid,* p. 63.

32. *Ibid,* pp. 63-64.

33. All eight drafts of "Northfork October Return" are in the John Clellon Holmes Collection at Boston University.

TITLE COMMENTARY

Night Music

FRANK MIELE (REVIEW DATE SPRING 1990)

SOURCE: Miele, Frank. "John Clellon Holmes and the Burden of Maturity." *Literary Review* 33, no. 3 (spring 1990): 381-7.

In the following review, Miele offers a mixed assessment of Night Music, *a collection that encompasses Holmes's entire career. Miele contends that Holmes's early poetry is poorly written with stiff form and childish lyrics, but believes that Holmes's later poems possess a maturity of theme and freedom of form that offers a vast improvement over earlier efforts.*

The so-called Beat Generation writers have not aged well, if they have aged at all. Jack Kerouac, the patron saint of the movement and arguably its most original talent, died in 1969 at the age of 47. Allen Ginsberg has not died yet but has garnered all the advantages of death by attaining the status of myth in life. Though his early poems were replete with incendiary confession and searing social criticism, he has spent the past thirty years skating on the thin ice of reputation. Another luminary of the '50s, novelist William Burroughs, has continued to produce work of originality through the years but of such increasing idiosyncrasy that it speaks to no one now but Mr. Burroughs himself and a band of devoted sycophants. A host of other Beat-era stars such as Gregory Corso, Lawrence Ferlinghetti, and Peter Orlovsky are now extraordinarily irrelevant, perhaps also dead.

One other name from the era that might well seem irrelevant is that of John Clellon Holmes, who died in 1988. It was Holmes who had the distinction of announcing to the world the official baptism of the Beat Generation, he having been present when Kerouac pronounced the epithet for the first time. He also might be remembered for having anticipated Kerouac's *On the Road* by a few years (as far as publication is concerned) with his novel, ***Go,*** a jejune but sincere attempt to pin down some of the same themes that Kerouac eventually made his own.

But to Holmes's disappointment, and no doubt to the disappointment also of many critics who would find his establishment approach much less unsettling than Kerouac's mile-a-minute "typing" (to repeat Truman Capote's famous insult), there was surprisingly little to show at the end of Holmes's career of four decades of professional writing. Three novels, three books of poetry, and three books of nonfiction. There were also three books of selected essays and now this book, ***Night Music,*** a collection of selected poems that spans the entire career from 1946 to 1988. What is especially interesting about the book, regarding its relevance to Holmes's generation, is its organization into two sections: early poems from 1946 to 1952 and later poems from 1959 to 1988. We thus see the poet during the years when the Beat Generation was coming into being and during the years when it was coming apart in disarray. Somehow, the years 1953 to 1958—when the movement was at its height—did not elicit any poetry deemed worthy of inclusion in this thin volume. That seems almost a tacit admission that the Beat writings were ephemeral, that the generation itself was more lost than it ever knew. And the writings that are included allow a significant contrast to be drawn between the younger and older Holmes, perhaps helping to shed some light on why the Beat Generation has not aged well and why Holmes never quite lived up to his early potential.

First of all, it must be said that unlike his early prose, the early poems are imitative and traditional. Holmes shows himself to be at heart a formalist and a romantic. The latter puts him squarely into the Beat Generation, but the former drives a wedge between him and the freer spirits of his age. Such a poem as **"Instructions for the World Librarian,"** with its stuffy opening lines, must have embarrassed the more deliberately radical element of the Beat writers:

> When this grave's mould is broken up again—
> whatever reason your new times may find—
> let any ghoul or statistician then
> dismiss the lines of our age that was blind . . .

This imitative formal voice dominates throughout the early work, to such an extent that one can much more easily imagine the young Holmes at his ease in a London tavern with the donnish Auden than on the road with Kerouac.

Search as we may, there's no hint of rebellion or revolution in the writing itself, in the style of the poems (which reveals the nature of the man much more honestly than the few overt, posturing challenges to authority in the message). Most tellingly, in any case, these early poems are too often just badly written. Some of the worst offenses, for instance, are found in the title poem, **"Night Music"**:

> Do not be afraid
> though the light is far
> Dawn has been delayed
> on another star.
> Though it's very far,
> do not be afraid.

How, the reader might well ask, did dawn manage to get onto another star? Not just another planet, which would have been silly enough, but another star. And why should we not be afraid? Dawn delayed for any reason is an utterly terrifying concept, a concept which cannot be glossed over. But here, the phrase has no significance other than as a sophomoric ingredient in what is little more than a youthful recipe for a rhyming poem.

Such fascination with form is endemic among the early poems, and Holmes almost eagerly succumbs to the many traps that formal verse holds for bad writers. Then, in **"The Memoirs of an Imaginary Man,"** an equally bad poem, he indicts himself for his unfulfilling poses.

> I grew to manhood like a paper flower
> that has no roots . . .
>
> I hid behind elaborate attitudes . . .
>
> I tried to press my life in books
> and give to everything a sense of mission . . .
>
> Certainly my heart knew semaphore
> but always sent its messages in prose.
> It was not capable of reaching far
> but grew most urgent in request for praise.

Though Holmes probably did not realize it, this list appropriately describes the shortcomings of his own verse and not just those of the generalized literary man that is the intended target of the 1951 poem. It is just such a sense of manhood without root as he describes that is apparent in these early poems, written when the poet was in his twenties. Here as much as anything the poet is trying to fake roots by imitating the poetry of the universities, and falsely parading his knowledge as something earned rather than something merely borrowed.

The later poems, evincing a much larger self-awareness however, show evidence of the poet finally trying to put down roots the honest way, by exploring the tension between his own romantic ideals and the less than romantic life he led. Perhaps those six years of the 1950s that are not represented here were in fact well spent. The writing shows evidence that Holmes grew in both understanding and talent, dropping almost completely his early efforts at versifying and taking up the challenges of free verse that Robert Lowell notably, among others, was defining for a generation. How far from that misplaced dawn of **"Night Music"** he had come by the early '60s is evident in the finely etched opening of **"Cold Window"**:

> Crow pecking a patch of last ice—
> live beak against the wind's knife.
> Shabby firs,
> grass without nutrients,
> nothing behind the dead sky.
> No God
> or atheist certainty.

Holmes has by this time clearly learned the art of the specific, and knows finally the value of uncertainty in art. The early poems, as so many of the early Beat Generation credos, as ultimately so many of the postulations of youth, were mere posturing. Their certainty was based on inexperience. In an undated prologue poem, Holmes writes: "Strangeness, bentness, interest, / come again with the quirk / of my special mind." It is just those qualities which inform much of the latter half of the book and are absent from the predictable early poems. Interestingly enough, in a 1968 poem, **"Unwanted 1943 Chappaqua Flashback,"** Holmes himself hits on some insights that are useful in understanding his two-pronged career:

> I remember now in the rueful way
> of remembering wonder when one
> has less wonder left,
> knowing it is better to be a foolish, rapt young
> poet,
> "knowing" nothing, than to be
> a serious writing man, recalling it,
> worrying the words,
> trying to be accurate . . .
>
> Having learned to live with death
> as with an old wife,
> the struggle over,
> the bickerings over with at last,
> burdened with maturity,
> able to forbear,
> not proud of compromise but prisoned in it,
> no longer fevering.
> Nevertheless I know the loss of the sap of life

The first of these stanzas tells, perhaps, why Holmes remained a minor poet to the end. His romantic image of the "foolish, rapt young poet" corresponds exactly to what we find of Holmes in the early poems. And by dismissing his later self, "the serious writing man . . . worrying the words, trying to be accurate" (the author of **"Cold Window"** for instance), he devalues the very craft that he had begun to master by the early '60s. The "serious writing man," it turns out, can't take himself seriously because he doesn't measure up to the early romantic image that the "rapt young poet" had conjured up years before. Thus, despite increasing sureness of tone and command of language, Holmes still falls victim to his fanciful notions of the writerly life. "There seemed to be a way to pluck romance from anything," he writes of his younger self, but even if he is "no longer fevering" in 1968 when this poem was written, he continues to long for the fever, to try to recapture its blurry heat in such gauzy lines as ". . . (spring's freshet having / flooded into summer's pond) / now, in sere autumn, the soul fermenting." This obsession, sadly, puts no distance between the writer of the later poems and the self-consumed tyro of earlier years. Even the language harks back to bygone days, and not by accident. Clearly, despite his proud claim, it is not death that Holmes had to learn to live with, but his own youth.

Indeed, as a romantic he was if anything too familiar with death, and if the struggle there was already ended, clearly the struggle with his own juvenile yearnings remained largely unresolved. The poem, notably, is an "unwanted" flashback. He never comes to grips with his beginnings. And in the phrase, "burdened with maturity," he tells us that he never came to grips with his later years either, seeing his own increasingly individual life and voice as burdens. Here finally we may see John Clellon Holmes as an exemplary life of the Beat Generation. Though he chose to see himself as a man who had somehow outlived his time, Holmes clearly carried the traits of his generation with him as he went, and it was rather the generation which had outlived its usefulness. For, in hindsight, it is easy to see that the Beat Generation (like earlier romantic movements) represented little more than a kind of neurotic rebellion against responsibility. By banding together behind a philosophy that codified their rebellion, however informally, the members of this generation were able to avoid the burdens of maturity and live life "on the road."

Holmes seems to have recognized how completely his own life was shaped by that era, that philosophy. In one of the last poems in the book, he calls himself "A rootless, aging man, imagining home" (**"Dire Coasts,"** p. 67). Over and over, in fact, he addresses his lost innocence, and though it often is represented as the era of his childhood, we might well understand the true source of Holmes's nostalgia to be those long-lost days and nights with Kerouac and the boys. Clearly, the Beat ideal pays no respect to age or maturity, but only to image and motion. Holmes had outlived his own image of himself and had settled into rather a humdrum life as *"an anxious, aging scold"* (italics in original, 63) whose pangs are "drowned in bourbon" (59).

Ironically, however, in certain of the later poems there are moments of greatness, moments especially when Holmes addresses that very "burden of maturity" that he bemoaned in 1968. For one of the burdens that time puts on the backs of poets is to be honest to the moment, to live in the now absolutely, and to face the truth about themselves and their world. A mature poet cannot maintain the illusions of romanticism. He cannot live in the past. Holmes, perhaps maturing against his will, moved accordingly from the "big" sententious poems like **"Instructions for the World Librarian"** to smaller personal poems like **"Fayetteville Dawn (I),"** **"Fayetteville Dawn (II)"** and the wholly mature poem **"Vignette,"** written in 1988 and full of both unpredictably and familiarity:

Down some mud alley
  in back of a Kansas town
on a night made memorable by rain,
  garbled curses red threats
    doomed inventions
made the night as extraordinary
  as news in a place where
    nothing happens
only a bitter boy choking on mud
  and the bittersweet dream
    the gunshot soured
and the yapping yellow dog.

Here the language comes alive with real feeling and not just the romantic idea of feeling. This is the burden of maturity for a poet, and Holmes had the talent if not the consistent will to wield it. Perhaps, it was this very distinction of real and imagined feeling that killed off the Beat movement itself as it will kill off all movements of youthful energy that speak from limited experience.

Not surprisingly then, Holmes's true burden turned out to be the burden of discipline. When he kept his focus small, and limited his desire to philosophize and wax poetic, he was capable of writing solid, mature verse. But when he returned to the indiscipline of the rebellious Beat era for his inspiration, he wrote trite meandering poems that were mere self-indulgence. A writer of true genius such as Ginsberg could get away with this, for a few years at least, but a writer of limited means such as Holmes couldn't count on producing any work of significance merely by shouting long and loud. For him the good poems needed to be crafted into shape—by "worrying the words / trying to be accurate," as he put it. Instead, too often, he squandered his talent in the service of a romantic ideal that was long since dead.

And perhaps this too was always the quotient that had set Kerouac apart from his followers and imitators, for Kerouac labored under no romantic illusions. He understood the burden of discipline as much as any writer ever did (not excepting Truman Capote), producing a body of work that will last for years. He was the Prometheus for his generation, doing real hero's work, and cannot be blamed for the arsonists that came after him. As Sal Paradise, the narrator of *On the Road* says, "The only people for me are the mad ones, the ones who are mad to live, mad to talk, mad to be saved, desirous of everything at the same time, the ones who never yawn or say a commonplace thing, but burn, burn, burn, like fabulous yellow roman candles exploding like spiders across the stars." If Kerouac, propounding this philosophy, burned himself out, that is surely no excuse for the rest of his generation to turn icy before mundane experience which is the root of poetry. Yet that seems to be exactly what has happened. John Clellon Holmes's career as a poet is exemplary of this process, seeming in large part frozen around those few years when the Beat culture flourished. And yet it must also be admitted that Holmes, being to the end a devoted student of Kerouac, managed, after an extended career of juvenilia that borrowed its spark from Kerouac and others, to finally produce a handful of mature poems that had the flame of originality, too. It is that keen fire which makes the burden of maturity worth bearing, yet makes it also hard to handle and so easy to cast aside. Holmes, regrettably, makes it clear that at whatever cost to his art he'd much rather reflect on the meager youthful spark he had been handed by Kerouac years ago than take the risk of becoming his own Promethean hero in a quest for the dangerous fire within.

FURTHER READING

Biographies

Gifford, Barry, and Lawrence Lee. In *Jack's Book: An Oral Biography of Jack Kerouac,* pp. 167-74. New York: St. Martin's Press, 1978.

Recounts the birth of the term "Beat Generation" and delves into the personal and literary relationships among Holmes, Jack Kerouac, and Allen Ginsberg.

"Obituary of Mr. John Clellon Holmes: Chronicler of the Beat Generation." *Times* (London), (2 April 1988).

Provides an overview of Holmes's life and literary career.

Criticism

Regier, Gail. "Sudden Wisdom." *American Scholar* 59, no. 4 (fall 1990): 618.

*Examines essays in three collections—*Displaced Person, Representative Men, *and* Passionate Opinions*—and explains how these writings emphasize Holmes's influence on and perspective of the Beat Generation.*

Tytell, John. "An Interview with John Clellon Holmes." In *the unspeakable visions of the individual, Volume 4: The Beat Book* pp. 37-52. California, Pa.: A. and K. Knight, 1974.

Provides Holmes's perspective on the major figures of the Beat Generation and their literary pursuits.

OTHER SOURCES FROM GALE:

Additional coverage of Holmes's life and career is contained in the following sources published by the Gale Group: *Contemporary Authors,* Vols. 9-12R, 125; *Contemporary Authors New Revision Series,* Vol. 4; *Contemporary Literary Criticism,* Vol. 56; *Dictionary of Literary Biography,* Vols. 16, 237; and *Literature Resource Center.*

HERBERT HUNCKE

(1915 - 1996)

(Full name Herbert Edwin Huncke) American short story and memoir writer.

While Huncke has received scant attention as a writer, he has been the subject of considerable commentary on his role as a principal catalyst of the Beat Generation. Jack Kerouac, Allen Ginsberg, and William S. Burroughs were inspired by Huncke's unconventional street life, and this veteran of the urban drug culture served as their guide into a world that had previously been unknown to them. He was first and foremost a hustler, drug addict, and petty criminal, an ethos that Beat writers found irresistibly exotic and, in comparison to middle-class existence during the Eisenhower era, compellingly authentic. Huncke served as the model for characters in several major Beat works, including Kerouac's *On the Road* (1957), Burroughs's *Junky* (1953), and Ginsberg's "Howl" (1956), and it is a commonly-held opinon that Huncke was the originator of the term "Beat." Huncke's published writings are comprised of autobiographical sketches and short stories. His prose style, which is similar to Kerouac's automatic writing method, applies a frequent use of pauses and dashes, mirroring the sense of ephemerality, loss, and weariness that characterized his Bohemian lifestyle. In his later years, Huncke became a frequently consulted source of information on the details of the private lives of Beat Generation notables.

BIOGRAPHICAL INFORMATION

Huncke was the son of Herbert Spencer Huncke, a machine part distributor, and Marguerite Bell Huncke, the daughter of a prominent Wyoming rancher. He was born in Greenfield, Massachusetts, on January 9, 1915, and moved to Detroit and then Chicago in his early childhood. His parents divorced when he was twelve, and he quickly became an chronic runaway. As a seventeen-year-old, he began to hitchhike to New York City. In Chicago, Huncke began using marijuana and heroin and began working as a prostitute and drug dealer shortly thereafter. He met Elsie John, a circus hermaphrodite who was later the subject of one of Huncke's better-known stories, and the two were arrested for selling heroin when Huncke was fifteen. Huncke dropped out of high school during his sophomore year. After working odd jobs in Nashville, Memphis, and New Orleans, Huncke returned to Chicago in 1938. His mother left Chicago for California that same year, and Huncke moved permanently to New York City in 1939. Huncke lived for years as a hustler on Forty-Second Street. His long-time interest in music—he began sneaking and pleading his way into jazz clubs as a youth—led him to meet Charlie Parker, Billie Holiday, and Dexter Gordon. He also briefly served in the merchant marines during World War II before returning to New York.

Huncke first met Burroughs in 1945, when the latter sought a buyer for some stolen goods, including morphine and a tommy gun. Huncke was immediately suspicious of Burroughs's neatly groomed and respectable appearance, and Burroughs was curious about Huncke's lifestyle. The two became friends, and Huncke introduced Burroughs to heroin. Through Burroughs, Huncke met Kerouac and Ginsberg, also becoming their guide to the illicit subculture of New York City. He introduced them to Dr. Alfred Kinsey, of the Kinsey sex reports: Kinsey had paid Huncke to discuss the details of his sex life as a hustler and then paid Huncke for each new interviewee he could find. During this time Huncke, who had written occasionally throughout his life, began writing more often in earnest, quickly turning out the sketches that would later be published as *Huncke's Journal* (1965). Huncke's friends used him to develop their writing, and Huncke benefitted from their offers to provide room and board. Burroughs paid for Huncke to accompany him and his common-law wife, Joan, to their marijuana farm in New Waverly, Texas, where Huncke lived for a few years before returning to New York. In 1949, Huncke broke into a New York doctor's office, was caught, and went to prison for five years. After his release he resumed his lawless life-style and was sent back in prison in 1955.

During his incarceration, the Beat writers who had romanticized Huncke as a criminal-saint failed to correspond with him. Huncke and Kerouac and Ginsberg had gone in very different directions: the latter two authors were published, successful, and famous by the end of Huncke's last prison term. After his release, Huncke sought out Ginsberg, who took it upon himself to look after Huncke, helping him find an apartment and later assisting him in obtaining psychiatric care at Jacoby Hospital. Huncke continued making well-placed friends who were charmed by his open, compassionate nature as well as his gift for storytelling. These friends eventually guided him toward the publication of *Huncke's Journal*. Based on the commercial success of his journal, Huncke was invited to perform readings and an appear on *The David Susskind Show*. During the 1970s Huncke met Louis Cartwright, a photographer who became a benefactor and Huncke's partner until Cartwright's death in 1994. It was also during the 1970s that Huncke met R'lene Dahlberg, who published two of his short stories as *Elsie John and Joey Martinez* (1979). A larger collection of Huncke's stories, *The Evening Sun Turned Crimson,* was published in 1980. He remained friends with Ginsberg, who helped him into a methadone program, and enjoyed the financial support of other admirers; Jerry Garcia, lead singer of the Grateful Dead, was rumored to have paid Huncke's rent at the Chelsea Hotel for several years. In 1990 Huncke published the autobiography *Guilty of Everything* and continued touring and speaking well into his late seventies. Although he remained in a methadone program until his death in 1996, he was never able to abandon drugs completely. At the age of eighty, Huncke tested positive for heroin, cocaine, marijuana, and Valium; he died of congestive heart failure on August 8, 1996, at the age of eighty-one.

MAJOR WORKS

Huncke's Journal and Huncke's short stories—some of them retitled sections from the *Journal*—are both highly autobiographical and generally fragmented in form. He wrote in a series of sentence fragments connected by dashes, which has been viewed as an effective means of conveying the weariness of Huncke's existence and experiences on Forty-Second Street. Many of his sketches and stories, including "Spencer's Pad," "Russian Blackie," "Detroit Redhead 1943-1967," and "Whitey" give Huncke's impressions of men he met while hustling on Forty-Second Street; "Elsie John" recalls this early figure in Huncke's criminal life in Chicago. Though many of Huncke's characterizations focus on societal misfits and criminals, his writings about them reveal a compassion and egalitarianism that has been judged as exceeding the efforts toward inclusiveness of the more successful Beat writers. Huncke's autobiography, as Burroughs described it, combines his misadventures as a drug addict and thief with the author's unique perspective on an unusual time and place in history. *The Herbert Huncke Reader* was published in 1997, and includes previously unpublished letters from Huncke to his Beat friends.

CRITICAL RECEPTION

Assessments of Huncke's work range from praise for the author's personal, honest, and empathic approach to dismissal for exploitative sensationalism and cheapness. By the time he was a published author, Huncke's literary status was widely considered to be limited to his coining the term "Beat" and introducing Burroughs to heroin. Later critics have maintained that Huncke was not the first Beat author merely because of his criminal activities, drug use, and lack of literary ambition. These commentators explain that from a very early age Huncke wrote in the jagged, brutally honest style that the more successful Beat writers would later adopt, and that while his friends strived to write important works, Huncke's goal was to capture his own experiences as honestly as possible and was not interested in gaining notoriety. Ginsberg in particular recognized Huncke's talent and urged him to publish; other literary figures of the 1960s and 1970s, including Irving Rosenthal, Eila Kokkinen, and Diane di Prima, also attempted to promote Huncke's writing, though the grim stories and transparently honest tone were not highly marketable at that time. Huncke's earlier works have generally fared better with critics; the energy and feeling of the stories have been lauded as evocative and emotionally poignant, and valuable for their portrayal of a generally unknown segment of American society. As a romanticized criminal, Huncke has earned comparisons to thief-writers Francois Vilon and Jean Genet. Clive Bush observes that while Huncke lacked the artistic aspirations of Genet, he achieved the similar aura of "sainthood" with his peculiar brand of integrity and amorality. Huncke's autobiography, *Guilty of Everything,* was less successful with critics. Some reviewers assessed it as a lifeless narration of the sordid life of a junkie, indicating that it lacked the energy and atmosphere of the times that his earlier works had conveyed.

PRINCIPAL WORKS

Huncke's Journal (sketches and memoirs) 1965

Elsie John and Joey Martinez (short stories) 1979

The Evening Sun Turned Crimson (short stories) 1980

Guilty of Everything: The Autobiography of Herbert Huncke (autobiography) 1990

The Herbert Huncke Reader (memoirs, sketches, short stories, and letters) 1997

PRIMARY SOURCES

HERBERT HUNCKE (SHORT STORY DATE 1979)

SOURCE: Huncke, Herbert. "Elsie John." In *Elsie John and Joey Martinez: Two Stories by Herbert Huncke,* pp. 1-4. New York: Pequod Press, 1979.

The following short story by Huncke, "Elsie John," is considered emblematic of the author's writing style: direct, personal, and detailed. Huncke's familiarity with both hipster jargon and a variety of narcotics is evident as is his fascination with the underbelly of American society.

Sometimes I remember Chicago and my experiences while growing up. I remember in particular the people I knew and, as frequently happens, I associate whole periods of time as indicative of certain changes within myself. But mostly I think about the people, and I recall one person rather vividly, not only because he was obviously out of the ordinary, but also because I now recognize what a truly beautiful creature he was.

He was a giant, well over six and one-half feet tall with a large egg-shaped head. His eyes were enormous and of a very deep sea blue with a hidden expression of sadness as though contemplating the tragedy of his life. Also there were times when they appeared gay and sparkling and full of great understanding. They were alive eyes always and had seen much and were ever questing. His hair was an exquisite shade of henna red, which he wore quite long like a woman's. He gave it special care. I can see it reflecting the light from an overhead bulb which hung shadeless in the center of his room while he sat cross-legged in the middle of a big brass bed fondling his three toy Pekes whom he loved, and who were his constant companions. His body was huge with long arms which ended with thin hands and long, tapering fingers whose nails were sometimes silver or green or scarlet. His mouth was large and held at all times a slightly idiot smile and was always painted bright red. He shaded his eyelids green or blue and beaded the lashes with mascara until they were often a good three quarters of an inch long. He exhibited himself among freaks in sideshows as the only true hermaphrodite, and he called himself Elsie-John. When I met him, he was in his early thirties.

He came originally from somewhere in Germany and, before coming to this country, had traveled—or travailed if you prefer—over much of Europe and could talk for hours of strange experiences he'd had. He was a user of drugs and, although he liked cocaine best, he would shoot-up huge amounts of heroin, afterward sitting still like a big, brooding idol.

When I first knew him, he was living in a little theatrical hotel on North State Street. It was an old hotel and in all probability is no longer in existence. Apparently at one time it had been a sort of hangout for vaudeville actors. It was shabby and run-down, and the rooms were small and in need of fresh paint. He lived in one of these rooms with his three dogs and a big wardrobe trunk. One of the things I remember distinctly was his standing in front of a long, thin mirror which hung on the wall opposite his bed applying make-up, carefully working in the powder bases and various cosmetics creating the mask which he was seldom without.

When I met him, I was coming out of a Lesbian joint with a couple of friends and, upon seeing him for the first time, was struck dumb. He was so big and strange. It happened that one of the girls knew him, and he invited us all up to his room to smoke pot—tea it was called in those days. His voice was rather low and pleasant with a slight accent which gave everything he said a meaning of its own. When we were leaving, he suggested I come back; it was not too long until I became a constant visitor and something of a friend.

He liked being called Elsie, and later when I introduced him, it was always as Elsie.

We began using junk together, and sometimes I would lie around his place for two or three days at a time. A friend of mine named Johnie joined us, and we became a sort of three-some. Johnie was later shot to death by narcotic bulls in a hotel while making a junk delivery; they grabbed him as he was handing the stuff over, and he broke free and ran down the hall, and they shot him. But as I say, at this time we were all together.

Elsie was working an arcade show on West Madison Street and, though junk was much cheaper then than now, he wasn't really making enough to support his habit as he wanted to. He decided to begin pushing. As a pusher he wasn't much of a success. Everybody soon got wise; he wouldn't let you go sick, and as a result, much more was going out than coming in. Eventually one of the cats he'd befriended got caught shooting up and, when asked where he scored, turned in Elsie's name. I will never forget the shock and the terror of the moment when the door was thrust open and the big red-faced cop, shouting "Police," shoved into the room followed by two more. Upon seeing Elsie he turned to one of the others saying, "Get a load of this degenerate bastard. We sure hit the jackpot this time. This is a queer sonofabitch if I ever saw one. And what the hell are these?" The dogs had gathered around Elsie and were barking and yipping. "God-damned lap dogs. What do they lap on you?" he said, as he thrust himself toward Elsie.

Elsie had drawn himself up to his full height. "I'm a hermaphrodite, and I've papers to prove it." He tried to shove a couple of pamphlets which he used in his sideshow act toward the cop. Meanwhile, one of the others had found our works and the stash of junk, about half an ounce, and was busy tearing apart Elsie's trunk, pulling out the drawers and dumping their contents in the center of the bed. It was when one of the cops stepped on a dog that Elsie began to cry.

They took us all down to the city jail on South Street, and since Johnie and I were minors, they let us go the next morning.

The last time I saw Elsie was in the bullpen. He was cowering in the corner surrounded by a group of young Westside hoods who had been picked up the same night we were. They were exposing themselves to him and yelling all sorts of obscenities.

ROBERT MCG. THOMAS JR. (OBITUARY DATE 9 AUGUST 1996)

SOURCE: McG. Thomas, Robert, Jr. "Herbert Huncke, the Hipster Who Defined 'Beat,' Dies at 81." *New York Times* (9 August 1996): B7.

In the following obituary for Huncke, Thomas provides a brief overview of Huncke's life and recounts the author's significance to the Beat Generation.

Herbert Huncke, the charismatic street hustler, petty thief and perennial drug addict who enthralled and inspired a galaxy of acclaimed writers and gave the Beat Generation its name, died yesterday at Beth Israel Hospital. He was 81.

The cause was congestive heart failure, said Jerry Poynton, his friend and literary executor.

Mr. Huncke had lived long enough to become a hero to a new generation of adoring artists and writers, not to mention a reproach to a right-thinking, clean-living establishment that had long predicted his imminent demise.

In an age when it was hip to be hip Mr. Huncke (whose name rhymes with junkie) was the prototypical hipster, the man who gave William S. Burroughs his first fix, who introduced Jack Kerouac to the term beat and who guided them, as well as Allen Ginsberg and John Clellon Holmes, through the netherworld of Times Square in the 1940's.

They honored him in turn by making him an icon of his times. He became the title character (Herbert) in Mr. Burroughs's first book, *Junkie* (1962). He was Ancke in Mr. Holmes's 1952 novel, *Go.* He appears under his own name in innumerable Ginsberg poems, including "Howl" (1956) with its haunting reference to "Huncke's bloody feet."

And if it was the fast-talking, fast-driving Neal Cassady who became Mr. Kerouac's chief literary obsession, as the irrepressible Dean Moriarty in Mr. Kerouac's 1957 breakthrough classic, *On the Road,* Mr. Huncke (who was Elmo Hassel in *On the Road*) was there first.

As Junkey, he was the dominant character in the urban half of Mr. Kerouac's first book, *The Town and the City,* and made later appearances as Huck in *Visions of Cody* and *Books of Dreams.*

All this for a teen-age runaway who said he was using drugs as early as 12, selling sex by the time he was 16, stealing virtually anything he could get his hands throughout his life and never once apologizing for a moment of it.

"I always followed the road of least resistance," he said in a 1992 interview. "I just continued to do what I wanted. I didn't weigh or balance things. I started out this way and I never really changed."

Actually, he didn't quite start out that way. Born into a middle-class family in Greenfield, Mass., on Dec. 9, 1915, he moved with his family to Detroit when he was 4 and two years later to Chicago, where his father ran his own machine-parts distributing company.

By his own accounts he seems to have had an uneventful early childhood, but his parents divorced, and by the time he was in his early teens he was on the street, acquiring a lifelong passion for drugs and discovering the joys—and lucrative possibilities—of sex with men. He was also beginning a life of crime, first as a runner for the Capone gang and later as a burglar and thief.

Hitting the road early, he served for a time with the Depression-era Civilian Conservation Corps. He traveled around the country until 1939, when he arrived in New York and found a psychic home in Times Square.

Making his base of operations the Angler bar at 42d Street and Eighth Avenue, he sold drugs at times and himself at others, not always with notable success. Mr. Huncke once confided to a friend that he had not been a successful hustler: "I was always falling in love," he said.

It was in 1945 that an elegantly dressed man in a Chesterfield coat knocked on the door of an apartment where Mr. Huncke was living. The visitor, who was in search of Mr. Huncke's roommate in the hope of selling him a sawed-off shot gun, was William S. Burroughs. Mr. Huncke would recount that he took one look and told his roommate to get rid of him. "He's the F.B.I.," he said.

Mr. Burroughs proved anything but, and within days Mr. Huncke had introduced him to heroin and sealed a lifelong friendship that included a 1947 visit to a marijuana farm Mr. Burroughs had started in Texas.

It was through Mr. Burroughs that Mr. Huncke soon met Mr. Ginsberg, then a Columbia undergraduate, and Mr. Kerouac, a recent Columbia dropout who became so enchanted with Mr. Huncke's repeated use of the carny term "beat," meaning tired and beaten down, that he later used it as his famous label for the Beat Generation. (Mr. Kerouac later clouded things by suggesting it was derived from "beatific.")

An aspiring, Columbia-centered literary crowd was soon learning at Mr. Huncke's feet. Among other things, he introduced them to Alfred Kinsey, who after meeting Mr. Huncke at the Angler had interviewed him about his colorful sex life and hired him to recruit other subjects.

Though it seemed strange to some people that such a wide array of literary figures found Mr. Huncke so enchanting, he was always more than he seemed. For all his disreputable pursuits, he had elegant, refined manners and a searing honesty. He was also uncommonly well read for someone who had never been to high school, and such a natural and affecting storyteller that he could keep a table of admirers enthralled until the wee hours.

He also had a code of honor. Yes, he might steal from his friends if he needed a fix, but did not inform on them, something he proved on a number of occasions when the police sought his help in developing charges against his celebrity friends.

Mr. Huncke, who spent a total of 11 years in prison, including almost all of the 1950's, was unrepentant, a man whose acceptance of crime as his fate bolstered his friends' views that he was a victim of a rigid, unfeeling society.

If his friends saw him as fodder for their literary work, Mr. Huncke as he later claimed, saw them as marks. There is, perhaps, a certain paradox in Mr. Huncke's use of his literary friends as literary fodder. Mr. Huncke himself began writing in the 1940's, locking himself in a stall in the men's room in the subway. He described it as the only place he could work in peace, scribbling away in his notebooks.

Taking the Kerouac idea of writing nearly automatic prose even further than Mr. Kerouac did, Mr. Huncke turned out a series of memoirs that have been praised for their unaffected style. Those who heard him regale listeners say his books read as if he were telling a spontaneous anecdote around a table at the Angler.

Huncke's Journal, (1965) was followed by ***Elsie John and Joey Martinez*** (1979), and ***The Evening Sun Turned Crimson,*** (1980) and ***Guilty of Everything,*** published by Hanuman Books in 1990.

The books and Mr. Huncke's role in a brash new literary movement made him famous to a younger generation, and he had several successful lecture tours in recent years.

His books did not make much money, but they didn't need to. Friends contributed willingly to the upkeep of Mr. Huncke, who seemed proud that he had no talent for regular work.

It was a reflection of his continued standing among self-styled counterculturists that one of his most generous benefactors was a man who had never met him: Jerry Garcia of the Grateful Dead, who is said to have helped with his rent at the Chelsea Hotel.

Mr. Huncke, whose longtime companion, Louis Cartwright, was killed in 1994, is survived by his half-brother, Dr. Brian Huncke of Chicago.

GENERAL COMMENTARY

CLIVE BUSH (ESSAY DATE 1996)

SOURCE: Bush, Clive. "'Why Do We Always Say Angel?': Herbert Huncke and Neal Cassady." In *The Beat Generation Writers,* edited by A. Robert Lee, pp. 128-57. London: Pluto Press, 1996.

In the following essay, Bush considers Huncke's role as a model for the Beat writers and how they viewed his criminality as a sign of sainthood. Bush interprets Huncke's writing by comparing him to Jean Genet, whose work Huncke had read, and as with Genet ascribes Huncke's "angel" status to his confident amorality.

> 'It seems anyway that I am wrong in everything I think so I might as well believe everybody and be a saint and make money in television.'
>
> Allen Ginsberg to Neal Cassady[1]

> 'The innaresting thing about Cocteau is his ability to bring the myth alive in modern terms.'
>
> "Ain't it the truth?" said Allerton.
>
> William Burroughs, *Interzone*[2]

> Assuredly we bring not innocence into the world, we bring impurity much rather: that which purifies us is triall, and triall is by what is contrary. That vertue therefore which is but a youngling in the contemplation of evill, and knows not the utmost that vice promises to her followers, and rejects it, is but a blank vertue, not a pure; her whitenesse is but an excrementall whitenesse.
>
> John Milton, *Areopagitica*[3]

In the America of the 1950s the literary tradition appeared to many to have run out of steam, and a dullness policed by the New York literary set ensured that approved literature was as polite as it was dead, as academic and class-bound as it was minimally inventive in form.

There were parallels in political life because the American society in which the Beat writers came to public attention was the society of 'hidden persuaders', the 'power elite', the 'organisation man', the 'mechanical bride' and 'the feminist mystique', to choose among many of the decade's descriptive epithets. These suggestions of largely hegemonic controls were matched by, and based upon, the actual politics of the era of unchallenged American mid-century power which produced McCarthyite witchtrials, the Korean War, the Dulles-Eisenhower manipulation of foreign governments, not to mention the virtually feudal oppression and ghettoisation of black people. America's once magnificent Enlightenment conceptions of freedom were being co-opted to promote a market-driven, ever-increasing productivity which promised to destroy nature itself: a veritable logic of historical reason which out-Hegeled Hegel.

At the personal level, the ambition of the Beat writers was to recover a sense of self which married a visionary tradition to a recovery of individual worth which challenged the historic, normative values of postwar America. At the artistic level, the ambition was to create new American forms of prose and poetry out of a deep and wide-ranging reading (from the Vedic texts to Dostoevsky), and to free them from academic categories and the abstract banalities of most then-current academic criticism. At the political level (and the practice, as will be shown, varied widely from 'social' challenge to actual 'political' practice), the aim was to subvert the apparent consensus of the suburban American dream.

Yet there was another peculiarly American strain, the need for a religious metaphysic to underwrite personal authenticity. Whitman had reinforced the romantic and visionary tradition from the texts of Indian religions. In early American literature, religious Eastern texts were classically given romantic attention by Emerson and Thoreau in their different ways. The Beats, too, would variously embrace Buddhism, Catholicism, forms of Zen and Taoism, and, in the case of the Cassadys, for example, religious cranks like Edgar Cayce and his followers. At best the resources of non-Western religions (meditation techniques especially, certain drug experiences) enabled the writers to steady themselves for creative work at the heart of the frantic chaos of urban America. At worst, the Beats were in danger of sometimes forgetting Camus' warning: 'There is no compromising between the literature of apologetics and the literature of rivalry.'[4] William Burroughs was one of the few in the circle to be intensely sceptical about the sacred. When his Tibetan Holiness, Chögyam Trungpa Rinpoche, got so drunk that he fell down the stairs and suffered concussion, and then claimed it was his karma, Burroughs inwardly exclaimed with one of his mocking parodies, 'O excellent foppery of the world! As if we were fools and drunkards by heavenly compulsion.'[5]

How did Neal Cassady and Herbert Huncke fit into this? What models on every level did they provide for the great writers of the Beat generation: for Ginsberg and Kerouac? Their actual written works are, after all, minimal. The first and most obvious fact is that their lives, on and off the record, posed a challenge to the specifically personal and social values of Cold War America. In 1961 (oddly enough, when the initial radicalising sexual and drug-related iconoclasms of the movement were being safely commercialised), J. Edgar Hoover stated publicly that the beatniks were one of the three greatest threats to America.

On the positive side, Huncke and Cassady were more than survivors. At best they lived with wit, grace and flair; at worst they succumbed to that careless, driven egotism of the human being trapped in situations where society left few choices but psychopathic revenge. Cassady's excessive jail sentence for 'possession' compounded by a vicious judge's definition of his 'attitude' only serves as an exemplary instance.[6] They served the writers they befriended, not always willingly, with models of how to survive without material goods, and they confirmed continuously, in Olson's words, that 'man is larger than / his social reformation'.[7] Huncke and Cassady could provide living instances of 'rebels without a cause' (a phrase reeking with a massive evasion of political and social definition) and of the 'white negro', Mailer's attempt to theorise a post-existentialist model of behaviour to counter emotional plague.[8]

Yet the very term 'psychopathic' poses problems. In essence, it transfers legal and political and social definitions to a medicalised discourse, with all the dangers that implies. By the end of the 1950s in America, it had been replaced by the term 'delinquent'. The word 'psychopath' was just too convenient for the kinds of replacement of legal by the professionally expert judgement outside the courtroom and of which Thomas Szasz gave so brilliant an account throughout the 1950s. Mailer's effort to reclaim the term for his 'white negro', as a means for the subject to get to a position where choice and a capacity for risk and courage in a deadened society might again become possible joins the radical psychologists' attempt of the same period to reclaim desire as an ally rather than as an enemy of freedom.

Yet another term must be added. Cassady and Huncke provided American instances of what Kerouac called the 'fellaheen': a word borrowed from Spengler (massively influential in the ideology of the Beat movement) and applied by them, in the first instance, to the inhabitants of a Utopianised Mexico experienced as pure Other. Carolyn Cassady saw the 'construction' of this particular 'subject' as legitimation for a type of irresponsible male behaviour.[9] But for Kerouac it was at least as much a construction which helped him to articulate a sense of cross-cultural global solidarity with oppressed and deprived peoples who could be romanticised as being without nationality, as primitive, instinctual, cunning and in tune with the 'cosmos'.[10] Ginsberg saw it as a biblical perception, the Bible being the only text educating the American perception of 'the primaeval earth-conscious non-machine populace that inhabits 80 per cent of the world'.[11] Ruling out descriptive accuracy, the 'primitivism' proposed countered heuristically the logics of the bureaucrat; the connection with the cosmos challenged, by pure dissent, the belief in legitimations of pure racial difference and the secret metaphysics of those who thought they had none; and, finally, the pan-nationalism of the image helped to confirm

Zukofsky's observation that 'If there must be nations, why not / Make it clear they're for business?'[12]

Via Rilke and Lorca, the angel-headed hipster of the poetic imagination defeated the categorisations of liberal sociologist, academic criminologist, worn-out teacher, parent, indeed any authority figure, whether despairing wives, mothers, fathers, or powerful old men. How to account for the beauty of the young men who come into being programmed into poverty, urban blight, conscription and death, labour that would insult an animal, and into hunger and unemployment? Within a largely homophilic perspective, the celebration of a brief angelic flowering already corrupted within a fateful universal wastage was not the least of the Beat writers' achievements. 'Allen accepted Jack's notion that there were "fallen angels" full of secret love, who loved even if they didn't show it.' And yet the dreamers of angels were challenged by the angels themselves: 'Why', wrote Cassady to Ginsberg, repeating Kerouac's question, 'do we always say angel?'[13]

Why indeed? Part of the answer can be suggested in Sartre's great work on Genet. The aura of the sacred haunts Huncke and Cassady, whose roles as life-models, friends, lovers, destroyed writers, thieves, wastrels, jailbirds and drug suppliers were both succoured and sucked dry by the writers who had not lived very similar lives.

Citing Eliade, Sartre states: 'Genet has no profane history. He has only a sacred history, or, if one prefers, like so-called "archaic" societies, he is continually transforming history into mythical categories.'[14] Modern commentators only tend to emphasise the dangers, but the transformations of mythic thinking may not be simply posed as pure opposition to reality: 'In the light of mythological, events and persons can seem true or false to the true story of who I am.'[15] Thus Cassady's joyriding 2000 cars in two years turns him into a hero, but the precise lineaments of the intelligibility of the fact have all the complexity that mythic thinking requires. Was it a case of the 'true pleasure of the thief [being] the fictive pleasure of the fake owner'?[16]

Huncke will embrace the designation of thief to a far greater extent, but without Cassady's intellectual sensibilities. Cassady will choose among his contrary actions. He will stop stealing cars, but not fucking, and he will choose a religion to support the distinction.[17] His sexual conquests are of a kind: a number of his partners have declared the encounters as machine-like, demonstrating a violent one-sided pleasure, ending in exhaustion. Like his society, Cassady wills his own nothingness: the final dereliction of himself as a sanctification of instinct. The society whose psychological goal is homogeneous repetition, within the desire that nothing will happen, needs a perverse fiction of itself as super-active outside the law of its own reality. *Exhaustion* is the goal of both states. Huncke and Cassady, but more especially Cassady, are mythic heroes of exhaustion. Thus, their beauty is as real and compelling as any sacrificed hero; the transactions become: my fiction for your fiction, my sex for your bed and board, my drug for your money, your witness to my destruction to preserve your tranquillity, my satisfaction (as victim) of your need for power to preserve the fiction of the freedom of my fateful luck. Yes indeed they are 'angels'—human beings with wings, with all the freedom of air: 'the phenomenon of saintliness appears chiefly in societies of consumers'.[18]

The saint and hero merit social approval by practising on themselves the 'magnificent destruction which represents the ideal of their society'.[19] The aim is pure activity without reflection, what Paul Goodman called 'an action, not a reflection or comment'.[20] The pragmatic tradition of America favours action before reflection, or attempts, as Goodman does, to equate it with a religious (here Taoist) legitimation of 'living with independent integrity'. How you know integrity without reflection he doesn't say. The practical and the mystical tended to remain only absolute options. Plummer comments that embracing the doctrines of Cayce led Carolyn Cassady to 'positive thinking', while it led Neal to 'Gurdieff and P.D. Ouspensky'.[21]

Other Beat figures were more actively and politically engaged. Carl Solomon at Columbia was a member of the American Youth for Democracy (known as the Tom Paine Club at CCNY), which later became the Communist Political Association. Solomon argued with Ginsberg over the legacy (political versus sexual) of Whitman.[22] Ginsberg himself, as Carolyn Cassady noted, somewhat astonished his friends by telegraphing Eisenhower over the Rosenbergs' execution in 1953.[23] Presumably they had forgotten, or did not know of, Ginsberg's youthful dream of being a labour leader as well as a poet. As a reporter on the *Labor Herald,* the official journal of the New Jersey AFL, he had gotten to know Paterson better than ever, as he reported to William Carlos Williams.[24] Eric Mottram noted that his picketing in the San Francisco anti-Madame Nhu demonstration of 1963 had Ginsberg stating that this was the first time 'I've taken a political stand', and commented that Ginsberg, to a certain extent, wards off that easy co-option by the state of a familiar American anarchism by 'the intelligence of his body's convictions for freedom'.[25] Mottram's criticisms necessarily harden later, while praising Ginsberg as a witness to his times.[26]

In the later 1960s, many Beat writers were active in the anti-Vietnam war movement. For Gary Snyder, the attitudes of some of the Beat writers changed when Castro took over Cuba, and when Martin Luther King's movement got off the ground.[27] To a degree these facts challenge Goodman's comment: 'Considered directly their politics are unimpressive.'[28]

But it was the literature that challenged the more social and personal preconceptions and prejudices of a generation. The Beat writers ransacked many literary traditions in truly American style and created a staggeringly impressive new art, which struck at the heart of American consensual deadness. The younger writers were fortunate in their mentors. Justin Brierly, Denver lawyer and high school counsellor, encouraged Neal Cassady to report to him on his reading of Kant, Schopenhauer, Nietzsche, Santayana, Shakespeare, Dostoevsky and Proust.[29] Burroughs was mentor to Kerouac and Ginsberg, introducing them to Céline, Genet, Kafka, Wilhelm Reich, Cocteau, Spengler, Korzybski, as well as Herbert Huncke, his morphine connection.[30] A few academics also assisted the reading list. John Clellon Holmes and Kerouac sat in on Alfred Kazin's classes on *Moby Dick* at the New School for Social Research. Raymond Weaver, Mark Van Doren's office colleague and the discoverer of the manuscript of Melville's *Billy Budd,* read sympathetically Kerouac's Wolfean outpourings, *The Sea is my Brother,* suggesting readings also in Gnostic literature, Chinese and Japanese Zen and the American transcendentalist tradition.[31] The reading list included Melville's *Pierre* and *The Egyptian Book of the Dead.*[32]

In their different ways, the Beat writers would draw strength from the most challenging European literature from the Romantics onwards, freely intermingled with Gnostic texts and Eastern religious texts in a project familiar to America writers since the transcendentalists. With the exception of Burroughs and Huncke, there is always a visionary strain mingling the sacred and the profane, employing anything that came to hand—including radio shows, popular fiction and comics.

For Cassady, as for the others, Proust was key. The long sentences provided the vehicle for a recall of detailed memory and, structured within an American-Denver working-class speech, resulted in a prose which had profound effects on Cassady, Ginsberg and Kerouac.[33] Spengler was of equal importance. His *Decline of the West* was in the mode of the grand epic narrative of civilisation which has always appealed to Americans. Cycle, fatality, destiny and heroic, historical pessimism made Spengler as American as a John Ford Western; here could be enacted a drama promoting an aesthetics of the will to power, without alibis of historical, scientific or religious salvation in which civilisation itself performed the last act of manifest destiny. Céline, Genet, Kafka and Cocteau could be seen in their various ways to write footnotes to the results of the unholy bargains of Faustian man. In Spengler's words, science had failed, it was the 'soul of the culture that [had] had enough'.[34]

Spengler led back to Nietzsche, to the recovery of myth to be hurled against the *Irony* of the historical and scientific consciousness alike. Hayden White long ago pointed out that the Nietzschean concepts of memory, time and history were more complex than their interpreters in the twentieth century had reckoned with. Crippled by 'the ironical self-consciousness' of conventional historical scholarship, art and religion offer themselves as a means to forget and to turn away from the consciousness of becoming: 'The unhistorical and the superhistorical are the natural antidotes against the overpowering of life by history; they are the cures of the historical disease.'[35] It is in this sense that Dean Moriarty (Neal Cassady) is the pupil of Chad (Brierly), the 'Nietzschean anthropologist' and that 'western kinsman of the sun', whose character is 'Western, the west wind, an ode from the Plains, something new, long prophesied, long a-coming (he only stole cars for joy-rides)'.[36]

In Nietzsche's *Genealogy of Morals,* the conditions for the self are laid down: 'To be oneself is to deny the obligations which both past and future lay upon one, except for those obligations that one chooses for oneself and honors simply because one finds them "good".'[37] Activity is more important than adaptation. White points to the anti-communal nihilism of Nietzsche's thought; it is not surprising that a postwar generation of American writers would have been attracted to him, given the profound disquiet of the years following 1945. Indeed, they were in a sense returning to the writers of sixty years before, for whom Dostoevsky and Nietzsche had been the heroes of historical pessimism and that new world of the 'id', with its theory of natural drives, rationalisations, sexual masochism and sublimation, of guilt as a product of cultural thwarting—so close, as Hughes points out, to Freud's own work.[38]

The Beats' 'holy fools' are to be less self-reflexive and, to a degree, less socially engaged than Dostoevsky's. With Dostoevsky's Prince there is always that enormous chasm of doubt as to the sincerity and precise motives of the teller of the tale: 'But what sort of an idiot am I now when I know myself that people take me for an idiot?'[39]

Dostoevsky makes his Idiot appear withdrawn, yet deeply social. He catches his holy fool in a network of sexual, class and ethical fictions which structure the responses of those who encounter him. No less than with Nietzsche, traditional ethics (and their accompanying moral fables and melodramas) become chips in a game of aesthetically passionate manipulation. This less-than-holy innocent ends up in a Swiss clinic, delivering himself of a few happy and intelligent truisms; a fate which, while it avoids the malign erotics of crucifixion and transfiguration, scarcely holds out hope for a life in which ecstatic and imaginative intuition is a primary moral requirement.

The hope of the Beats to the contrary was that through breakdown was the hope of breakthrough.[40] Ginsberg survived his clinic, and, with varying degrees of skill, both resisted and transformed his role, but as a poet of an American tradition of visionary experience, not as a psychologist or philosopher.

Yet the dangers were that the holy fool could not but feed on the thing he opposed: that suicidal arsenal of his own anxieties. The contortions of difficulty (of one holy fool to another) are most complexly recorded, though not resolved, in a letter from Neal Cassady to Ginsberg of 3 August 1948 and in Ginsberg's reply, later that same month:

> I've long ago escaped admiration—as such—however, you stimulate whatever degree of hero-worship I've left. But beyond all this, you stand head and shoulders above any one man I've ever known—that, in itself, is love—calls for love. Again, look at yourself as Prince Mischkine—the idiot—you manifest more of the mystic, the Dostoievskian religious, the loving Christ, than does anyone else. Or, even as young Faust, you show more of these supposedly virile, masculine . . . However, off the intellectual now, you are not an abstract symbol to me; nor quite a personal love which I must combat, fear—or flee. Rather, (at last I reach the point) I have a new vision to add to our collection—you are my father . . . The above paragraph is a beginning of sincerity, and the vision of the father—a good *partial* one—. . .[41]

The subtext is that Ginsberg found himself more in love with Neal than the reverse. But it would be cheap to simplify the complex issues in such a way. Cassady is painfully ransacking his reading as a means of articulating his own difficulties and confusions. Thus, the Nietzschean hero is democratically refused though his temptations remain. The ambivalent erotic feelings are sentimentalised into a simplistic reading of Mischkine. Unable to find a middle way of characterising his relation with Ginsberg between a less than whole personal love and the abstract symbol of the master, 'father' becomes a tropological term for creating an emotional distance under pressure. It is less the psychological father, for the relation is unsubtly equalised with 'wife' (Carolyn) and 'brother' (Jack Kerouac). Ginsberg naturally was stung enough to reject the equalisation. The lover does not want to be admitted into the family on equal terms.

Ginsberg's own reply is a narrative which combines confession and the conversion experience, with its transcendental personal moment, directed both to fend off his feelings for Cassady and promote a practical poetics. Here is one moment in this important letter:

> I am glad you at last recognise in me the elements of Myschkin; it has taken me this long to recognise them and to be able to affirm them myself, at least the true elements. My intuition before led me into a presumption of love, where there was no true love (of world) but nonetheless, these phantasies were shadows of the truth that is within me and which will one day emerge in all its power and intensity. I cannot be your father: you putting yourself in a false situation, perhaps, apropos; Jack & Caroline: but that is none of my affair except as your fellow human & your lover. As to young Faust and the 'enigma problems' that you speak of, that is perhaps also true, that I contain or show, rather more than they . . . However, I cannot speak of their souls, nor yours, for I do not know them as well as I do my own. How I am learning to know my soul in relation to itself, not to others; and to know it in relation to 'god'.[42]

Ginsberg deliberately plays on the traditional and special sense of 'father' used here and, with Whitman-like blitheness, insists on the equation of 'fellow human' and 'lover'. There is a retreat here and it is a religious one with its Thoreauvian echoes of the greater importance and conviction of self-knowledge in contradistinction to the knowledge of others. Myschkin is then to be declared true and false—not because of *his* complex relation with others—but because of the partiality of his truth along some ineffable transcendental way. Ginsberg's unhappinesses are patent: 'I long more to go to God than to you, and perhaps you are a temptation rather than an angel', and the final PS outlines a reading list of the visionary texts of Blake, Yeats, Eliot and St John of the Cross.

The postscript is important, for what Ginsberg is doing here under intense emotional pressure is attempting to articulate intimations of his precise poetic role and strength. The homiletic and imaginatively moral aspects of the Prince (the story of Marie, the brilliant inveighing against the death penalty) will also provide part of a poetic persona in a tradition which stretches back to Whitman. He will 'contain or show' *more* than they.

Cassady's treatment of the 'soul', however, is to a degree less transcendental than Ginsberg's and, in the following passage, he takes up the Emersonian themes of language, nature and poetry. He speaks here of the 'physicist of the inner world':

> But the very words that he selects, to notify to others the results of his intellectual labors, betray him. The word as utterance, as poetic element, may establish a link, but the word as notion, as element of scientific prose, never. Easier to break up a theme of Beethoven with a knife than break up the soul by methods of abstract thought. Images—likenesses, are the only way for spiritual intercourse yet discovered.[43]

In a tradition going back via the symbolists (Rimbaud especially) to Emerson and beyond, Cassady creates a prose in which the juxtaposing of abstract and concrete terms turns philosophy into an aesthetics of creativity, the image into a rival (at the semantic level) of syntax, science into a handmaiden of theory, whose validations are predicated on a metaphysical psychology.

Relying on a theory of Emersonian correspondences, the word is declared both divine and available, inseparable from utterance and obliterating the distinction between the world of science and the world of art. In so doing, it appeals to what Barthes called the 'something beyond language', which for Americans is less 'the threat of a secret' than a *confidence* in an intuited set of correspondences.[44] For the Beats it became intimately connected with Eros itself. Benjamin's comments on Kraus' language are of assistance here in looking at this cluster of problems in another way. He said of Kraus' language, 'It has done away with all hieratic moments. It is the theatre of a sanctification of the name', and cites Kraus' words which are close in spirit to the dialogue between Cassady and Ginsberg: 'The more closely you look at a word the more distantly it looks back.'[45]

The transcendentalist disposition toward aphorism is also evident: 'Easier to break up a theme of Beethoven with a knife than break up the soul by methods of abstract thought'; its imperfect dualism combines the New Testament homiletic prophetic style ('It is easier for a camel etc. . . .') with Old Testament psalmic poetic parallelism. The Platonism of the argument is obvious, but the association of 'image', 'likeness' and that 'gesture' of 'imperceptible movement' have their roots deep in an American Puritan visionary tradition.

In February 1952, Ginsberg was supplying Cassady with further huge book lists. He had been reading Balzac, Hesse, Kafka, Faulkner, William Carlos Williams, Robert Lowell, Goethe, Lawrence, Hardy, Gogol, Stendhal, Anson on Auden, and Genet. He was reading and translating Genet's 'Un condamné a mort'. For Ginsberg, the 'golden-obscene poetry' of Genet turns the Dostoevskian terror of those who *know* they are already dead into an erotics of a love forbidden by those who clamour for state murder. Like Genet, Ginsberg will speak *as* the homosexual lover not *on his behalf*. Unlike Genet, however, neither Ginsberg nor Cassady claim evil as their good, not because they do not know that evil will escape their embrace of it, but because they have the ultimately liberal hope that they can transcend or escape it. They lack ultimately the radicalism of de Sade, even though they too 'made the brutal discovery that there was no conciliation possible between social existence and private pleasure'.[46] Protesting, yet somehow less conscious of evil, they never quite transform transgression into glory.[47] A certain depth of mockery is absent from Cassady and Ginsberg, though perhaps for slightly different reasons.

For Ginsberg, Cassady had the simplicity of a Blakean angel, the redeemed man of the visionary experience with its simple poetic truth that it is possible to imagine things other than they seem to be:

> I sometimes see you afresh, a great erotic and spiritual existence, after all the dross of history is washed down the drain and you emerge pristine as I first knew you shining and triumphant like an angel rejoicing in the strength of your own imagination, your own self-creation fostered in the sweetness of naked idealism.[48]

The relation of 'the dross of history' and that 'great erotic and spiritual existence' was managed poetically, not ideologically. The debate, however, between the two possibilities was intense. While Raymond Weaver, for example, instructed Kerouac in Melville's *Pierre,* Plotinus, Zen and the Gnostics, Alfred Kazin at the New School for Social Research brought a greater sense of socialist analysis to the courses he taught. When, however, Kerouac bombarded Kazin with pages of *Dr Sax* the latter thought him crazy.[49]

The great twentieth-century classic which deals with the claims of the sacred against the political logic of the powerful is unquestionably Genet's *The Thief's Journal* (1949), and it is a work of especial interest for this essay because it was read intensively by the Beat writers in the 1950s. Its greatness lies less in the abstracted content of what it reveals—the banality of petty betrayal, sexual manipulation and violence among men who never had a chance—than in its capacity through tone and structural/aesthetic consideration to mock the moralising legitimations of law, police, petty officialdom and bureaucracy. The mockery is all the more powerful because Genet insists, radically, that it is a condition to which both sides have given their consent. The world Genet depicts is without compassion and invokes the absolute pride of solitude.

The work provides a benchmark for looking at Huncke and Cassady. Not only is it the work of the genre most self-conscious of its procedures, but it will here also provide a crucial sense of difference between the European and American texts. The immediate difference is in the question of *glory.* The European angel-headed hipster glories to a greater extent in punishment, cruelty, and self-abnegation as the part of the necessary confirmation and support of 'our world'.

The difference is one of culture. America had no formally adopted Church. The Italy, France, Germany and Spain of Genet's wanderings are dominated by an unbroken tradition of Catholic tradition and morality. The choice of religious explanatory discourse is a preoccupation of the Beats; in Genet's work, it could be assumed as given.

> I knew the formula, as I had already begged for others and myself: it mixes Christian religion with charity; it merges the poor person with God; it is so humble an emanation from the heart that I think it scents with violet the straight and light breath of the beggar who utters it.[50]

In parallel with the holy fool in Russia, the beggar, covered with lice, filthy and degraded can be inscribed paradoxically within a narrative of extreme self-control, and victory: 'Poverty made us erect. All across Spain we carried a secret, veiled magnificence unmixed with arrogance' (p.20). Loss, defeat, victimisation, poverty, degradation, suffering have high visibility within the traditional culture of Catholic Europe. Not so in America.

For Genet, the difference is that religious discourse is too inscribed in the given meanings to give any hope of transcendence, or of breaking the vicious circle. In Cassady and Ginsberg, the hope has not been given up. One cannot imagine any of the Beats adopting a stance of 'being good' as a lucky charm to commit a crime, (p.24) nor seeking love in order [to] gain the power to destroy it (p.36).

Except, perhaps, for Burroughs. Like Burroughs' fictions, Genet's are essentially those of melodrama: the genres and topics of rightwing newspapers. They are narratives of spies, outlaws, diamonds, drugs, smugglers, police, murderers, crooks, Legionnaires, prostitutes, cross-dressing homosexuals. The narratives act out their crypto-realities on national borders, in ports, in slums, in jails. Sardonically and actually, Genet insists on the perfect order his fictions represent for they reach deep into a betrayed romantic psychology of individual freedom. In this world the palace *is* the prison, mirroring it in its rituals and in the sumptuous destitution of its solid ruins. The alliance of aristocrat and sentimentalised criminal is directed against the actual power of the moralistic bourgeoisie.

Further, necessity, like the power of money, does not differentiate between its objects: objects themselves become a nexus of human relations under a condition of hierarchies of power to which the vengeful discipline of self-abnegation gives its consent. Genet combines the insights of Nietzsche and Marx as he moves through a world of nightmare in which he claims an ever more innocent expertise: 'Yet I was not going through Europe but through the world of objects and circumstances, and with an ever fresher ingeniousness' (p.94). In writing this world, legibility and legend converge to provide a new emotion: that of poetry itself (p.98). Here the very agency of perception itself is claimed by the power of objects. The panic of theft (the inverse of the pleasure of buying, as adultery is to marriage) creates an hallucinatory consciousness by breaking the taboo of ownership in which reified nature again asserts its own power: 'The trees were surprised to see me. My fear bore the name of panic. It liberated the spirit of every object, which awaited only my trembling to be stirred' (p.105).

Thus the saint, the creator and criminal are of a piece in Genet's work: individuality, renunciation, destruction, loss of self, 'forcing the Devil to be God', underwrite what these roles have in common (p.170). Genet differs from the Beats in that he struggles to be what the crime has made him, and caught, 'I shall perform with slow, scrupulous patience the painful gestures of the punished' (p.214).

The aloneness of the European hoodlums and pimps is in their beauty. Yet, as Sartre points out, this beauty has its own categorical imperative: 'the aesthete's will must be not only a will to Beauty but a beautiful will; needs, life, death itself must be consumed in beautiful, blazing gestures which all at once transform their authors into actors, the spectators into extras and the place into a stage set'.[51] Thus, the aesthetic, which detaches itself from the world of the purposeful, and the legitimations of the political order combine to re-enter it as a validating tone of the ritual. It is more than tone, however; it is foundation of the symbolic eroticism of sovereignty itself: that absolute desire for a once for all sovereignty in Genet that Bataille correctly criticised Sartre for not emphasising enough.[52] Norman O. Brown once commented: 'The drama enacted in the sex act is the ritual drama of divine kingship. Sex is *le theatre des pauvres* [Talleyrand]; every man a king; King Oedipus . . . The phallic personality and the receptive audience are in coitus; they do it together, when it comes off.'[53]

If I can't be king, I'll be a magnificent beggar is the tragic cry of those who realise they will not make it in the ludicrously banal world of capitalist imperatives for 'work'. 'Poverty', said Genet, 'makes us erect' (p.20). The conjunction of punishment, sovereignty and sexual display is inscribed in the elaborately fetishistic and grubby apparel of every unemployed and briefly defiant streetkid in Europe. In London, postcards displaying their faces are sold alongside portraits of diamond-bestrewn Queen Mothers and Princesses by newsagents in the neighbourhoods of tourist hotels. Together they constitute the interlocked sovereign icons of the nation.

In an early published journal of 1965, Huncke's **'Song of Self'** immediately shows the more detached nature of the American criminal. Uttering his own name 'creates an almost weary and loathsome feeling in me'.[54] The emphasis is on impending insanity, accompanied by thoughts of suicide. Unlike Genet, Huncke does not adopt his loathsomeness, he passively regrets it. Seduced when fifteen years old by a Russian Jew in his late twenties, he also seduces the Russian's lover in order to celebrate his power over his seducer. Immediately he regrets this action: 'I was filled with a sudden sense of loneliness—which I have never lost.'[55]

When Huncke, and he has clearly been reading Genet, declares himself a thief, the differences become even more apparent:

> As I became a thief and less concerned with surface evaluations—the opinions of the majority—recognizing only a few friends—and not always sure of them—learning at the same time of the world of the spirit—linking me—all of us—together—it not mattering our outer husk—only in this world—this life—beginning to secure the oneness of the inner force—observing the drive and what became to me the direction of the individual entity toward the 'is' of life—feeling instinctively—and with assurance—all becomes the one God—the one indestructible force—power—energy—drive—call it what you choose—or by any word—I became more fully aware of a sense of peace.[56]

In Genet, surface and depth are not separate but locked in a static mirror reflection of each other. The world of thieves endlessly betrays, there is no transcendental 'is' transforming the existential moment, and, while there is a similar sense of a vitalistic force, there is no notion of 'peace'. God appears to Genet in the monstrousness of his lovers; God for Huncke is a hopeful transcendental nothingness. Genet earns his solitude; Huncke fears it. Genet sees his guilt as simplifying the path to sainthood; Huncke just suffers.

Nostalgia is the first and last mood of Huncke's autobiography ***Guilty of Everything,*** published only recently, in 1990. Today's, as opposed to yesterday's drug scene, the milieu of the saint, is cold-blooded and rapid, mirroring the impersonal world of the corporation and take-over wars, and the contingent interchanges of the city. There is a sense that the book's groundbass theme is a 1930s, or even 1920s sense of the glamour of the carnivalesque (Harlem Renaissance) alternative scene, associated with drugs and linked to the demimonde through fashion and dealing. It involved manfacturing a style (Huncke is as obsessed with clothes as Dreiser) to hurl at the centrist compromises of the bourgeoisie:

> In the old days, believe it or not, a junkie used to be a role model of a sort. He'd be on the corner draped down with his Italian silk suit, his hand-made shoes, his Stetson or his specially-made hat that had to be handled just so and tilted just right;

> and with his new car, and his old lady by his side wearing just this side of Bergdorf Goodman.[57]

Though Huncke lacked Kerouac's literary skills and his guilt-strewn Catholicism, he could cope with his drug habit better, and was mercifully unencumbered by the damage of Oedipal relations. ***Guilty of Everything*** is a combination of confession, personal narrative, and cautionary tale. It feeds into and plays with major American anxieties. For example, an early incident involves being shaken down by 'the biggest, blackest man you ever saw in your life with the longest blade you've ever seen' (p.2) and stripped naked. The difference between 1980s New York, say, and prewar Amsterdam, is the impersonality of that threat. Genet, who dreamed of being fucked by a black man, would have had in an actual encounter other multiple links with his would-be attacker in a sociality of underclass liaisons. He might also have imagined his delicious crucifixion at such a person's hands.

Huncke's take on the situation has all the humour of the mumbling, grumbling *practical* victim, built over the absence of any moralistic, guilty, or even panicking response. The humour is the distance between the high drama of the death threat and the inability to summon up anything but a low key (not even deadpan) response. Consequently there is neither guilt nor panic in his response. There's a practical 'sauve qui peut' which constitutes part of the humour, but nothing else:

> They took the coat. I happened to have good clothes. (I always tried to keep myself fairly well groomed.) Here was a good winter coat that I'd just bought—gone. Then my gloves went, my suit—the suit didn't fit either one of them but they figured they might be able to get in hock. In those days you could hock clothes in hock shops for money.
>
> (p.3)

The humour of the response mixes the sentimental with the Gothic. Huncke is a pundit in the grand American tradition, his tone edges into the archness of a Huckleberry Finn.

For the upper-middle-class school boy (no less than for Burroughs), there was nonetheless a searching curiosity about the urban underworld, then a string of jobs to support developing habits with varieties of drugs. For six years from roughly 1934-40 he 'didn't do anything but float around the country' (p.37), presumably with a lot of other unemployed men, though no sense of the world of the Depression comes through at all, just as any wider sense of political life is absent in Genet. Here, the details are tantalisingly brief (as throughout the book), but what comes across is a life of adventures initially prompted by fury at the betrayals of the bourgeois world and its limitations.

Huncke is a radical Utopian anarchist: one extreme of that complex individualism. He is unremittingly curious about his fellow human beings, but placed under the necessity of cheating them in order to survive. The absence of moral judgement parallels that of Genet, and enables him to survive by cruising, busting cars, dealing, shipping out (one time getting over to Wales in war time and slipping the ship's sugar and bananas to the people of the Rhondda valley), doing time: 'It turned out to be my first prison experience and although in many respects unpleasant, at the same time very interesting' (p.46). The difference between Huncke here and the later Timothy Leary is crucial. Huncke has an absorbing curiosity about the world *outside himself.* He earns through deviance and courage the absolute right to his own quiet self-confidence.

Huncke's sense of reality was born of necessity. One major difference between a Huncke and a Burroughs was that he always risked, in a tight fix, *not* having family or friends to bale him out. The winter of 1948 is an exemplary moment for the kind of isolation and class discrimination Huncke could face on his way to ending up in Sing-Sing. Busted for robbery with Allen Ginsberg (who had been naïvely receiving and hoarding stolen goods), Jack Melody, and Vickie Russell, their immediate respective fates expose the legal and punishment system in the US in very clear ways. Ginsberg had at this point to his credit literally pulled Huncke out [of] the gutter and had been naïve and generous to the point of confusion in his dealings with the three petty thieves as the episode is told in Miles' biography of Ginsberg.[58] Told from Huncke's side, however, it's clear he took the rap: 'I ended up doing a bit. Somebody had to do it' (p.108).

The hierarchy of punishments had everything to do with personal relations with the 'straight' world. Ginsberg had a lawyer brother who pulled him clear. His distinguished poet and labour-leader father and Lionel Trilling got him to the Psychiatric Institute rather than to Sing-Sing. He had the support of famous men like Van Doren of Columbia who, however, told him that if he thought Huncke an 'illuminated saint' he should go to jail for his beliefs. Meyer Schapiro was more sympathetic for he had once been 'arrested and put in jail for being a "stateless bum" in Europe as a young traveler'.[59] Jack Melody got off with psychiatric treatment for a year. He was the son of the Secretary Treasurer of the eastern seaboard Mafia, and his wife, Jackie's mother, 'looked like someone out of a wild gypsy story—an old crone with henna-red hair that stood out like a halo round her face' (p.103). Mama Melody 'knew everybody . . . Jackie was her baby and she wasn't going to stand for him being put in jail' (p.104). Vickie Russell's father was a magistrate judge from a respectable family in Grosse Point, Michigan. In Huncke's words, 'he flew to New York and got his darling daughter' (p.108).

A more delightful display of the discreet charm of the bourgeoisie would be hard to imagine: The University, The Law, and The Mafia in cahoots, clucking over their children. Huncke at least had the dignity—and the misfortune—not to have institutional deals legitimated by the natural morality of the family, done over his head in defiance of equality before the law. Naturally, though, they tried. The parole board summoned his parents against Huncke's express wish—he was 33 years old—thus depriving him of his rights as a citizen. His father (whose truth is legitimated *a priori*) incriminated his son by speaking of the defiance of parental love (a lie). So armed, family and parole board prejudged him together. The one bright spot in the entire shoddy episode is that the actual judge (acting strictly on legal considerations and on a plea from the prisoner) gave him only half the maximum sentence.

Huncke quickly learnt the ritualistic moves of his oppressors, making distinctions between police and detectives, manipulating the hierarchies of power within the system, and getting wise to the psycho-theatre of arrest, charge and prison. Once inside the prison, Huncke is both wise to and naïve about the way the prison functions as a inner microscopic space of the world outside. There is no glory in Huncke's mood in the prison world, just a slightly world-weary and fatalistic acceptance of the way things are. The prison moment, however, created feelings of abandonment. Little given to self-pity Huncke remarks: 'I was cut off completely from the outside world I knew. It was a funny feeling not hearing from anyone. I admit I felt very bitter when I came out, I really did' (p.117).

He refused, however, the 'help' of offical state psychiatric hospitals, and that moment produces one of the few declarations of his own values and standards in the book:

> If I had to die a lingering death I did not want it to include personality and behavior adjustments at the hands of bureaucratic psychologists and their cohorts—the do-good social service types, conscientious and specialized in psychiatry. I believed myself far too old and settled in my ways for rehabilitation and had no desire to join the so-called society of present standards, nor to concede for one moment that it is other than maladjusted . . . If I take drugs it is most certainly my business, and if it is against the law and I am caught that becomes my loss and I must pay in their coin. But they have no right to force me into a position where I must submit to mental probing and investigation under the guise of what is supposedly best or right for me.
>
> (p.181)

The strength of Huncke's book is his commitment to disengagement and dissent. Death by expert judgement as Szasz writes is a function of 'the increasing complexity of our artifical environment', a situation in which 'democracy may easily become technocracy'.[60] Huncke does not glory in his punishment, but he wants to take it on terms which preserve and acknowledge his transgression, to preserve the dignity of his antagonism to the state. Therapeutic intervention, declares Szasz, has two functions: 'one is to heal the sick, the other is to control the wicked'.[61] Huncke refused to see the two as synonymous.

Nonetheless Huncke lives, given his habit, from an early age that alternating ecstasy and despair of the absolute consumer. In that sense, his life is central to the contemporary world. But the saint, ever in need and without possessions, is caught in a permanent state of flux, which is only a delirium of freedom. Huncke wishes to escape the material world, but is caught again nonetheless when the drug itself becomes the universal equivalent of value. The moment of possession vicariously transcends the need and reproduces it. The roles are reversed. The body becomes parasite to the host of the drug itself. Whoever I give love to, I steal from. Losing and finding, the guest and the enemy, sacrifice and salvation become exact equivalents, as in the Christian injunction.

Huncke finds his 'home' in the tawdry, commercial brilliance of Times Square, at the heart of the intersections of the twenty-four hour city, where the square and hip world meet, where everyone is on display, where products become pure electronic signs and the tourist-freak couple perform their arhythmic dances of self-congratulation. The noisiest, the loudest, the most spectacular win a fleeting attention. Yet his role is paradoxically modest, even self-effacing, curiously detached in his manner with a touch of the nostalgia for the good old values, where carnival was something *worth* watching, and to be a junkie made you different, exotic, someone who took their freedom on their own terms and lived by it, who preferred personal individualised danger to mass murder, lived by their own code rather than participating as a 'normal' human being in the mass-madness that will destroy the planet. In that sense he is paradoxically close in character to Chandler's detective, Philip Marlowe.

The photographs tell a great deal. The clean, pressed white shirt, the transparent delicacy of the post-addiction facial skin against the irreducible context of a New York that still appears to have its soul in the movies of the 1930s. His is the ravaged city face that sometimes seems bemused at the attention of the famous and, at other times, half drawn in and out of memories, animated in the company of the young, but always in place with a sense of attention.

If Huncke was the passive angel, Cassady was the reluctant angel. There are at least two possible approaches to Cassady: as envisioned by others, and envisioned by himself in the vision of his own more crafted work.

As envisioned by others, he is variously: 'the American person that Whitman sought to adore';[62] Mailer's White Negro raised exponentially';[63] 'cocksman and Adonis of Denver';[64] 'a natural Buddhist';[65] 'a provincial Mouth shooting naif';[66] and 'a Billy Budd'.[67]

The mythic figure as such was calculated to offend positivist (rightwing) criminologist and old-fashioned liberal equally. The actual ritual breakout of young men usually ends by their early twenties and is ritualistic to the extent of engaging in a pattern of denunciation and retribution by society. However the 'Delinquent is casually, intermittently, and transiently immersed in a pattern of illegal action.'[68] Prolonged into adulthood, beyond the socio-biological cycle, this activity creates a new meaning rather than predictable behaviour. In Goodman's words, referring to Dostoevsky's characters, they were 'adult delinquents' and he added, 'In our time Genet has made of the doomed delinquent culture a powerful thought and poetry.'[69]

In real life, in the 'dominant culture of modern America—ranging in its portrayal from ascetic puritanism to the oath of boy scouts . . . delinquency is mandatory'.[70] As such, it threatens no one, except the poor. Breakout, containment and punishment follow in a dreary cycle. Cassady will not fit Goodman's category of 'old fashioned poor',[71] except in his capacity to survive.

The greatest mythicisation of Cassady was of course Kerouac's. What is at issue here is not the 'truth' of the real life/myth opposition, but the construction of the myth within differing discourses.

Kerouac's mythicising was of a different order, and the figure that emerged was not homogeneous or simple. Gerald Nicosia is perhaps right to say that: 'Jack promoted Neal as a myth figure, just as Allen had done for Jack; in effect, Jack and Neal's relationship became a mirror image of the intense, almost priestly bond between Jack and Allen.'[72]

In *On The Road,* as well as holy fool and angel, Dean Moriarty (Cassady) is perhaps most of all the scapegoat. As well as being an embodiment of social and individual energy in Dionysian form, close to the ecstasy of the jazz rhythms, articulating the sacredness of sexual exchange, the eternal hope of renewal after divorce, and the hope of the eternal return itself, he is also the sacrificial victim. Here the sainthood of the beautiful man confronts the sainthood of the mother. Destiny is confirmed in the rejection of the one by the other. Pietà: the dead Christ in the arms of the holy mother: the nihilistic centre of the sacred.

The reverse and complementary figure of the sacrificial victim is the betrayer: two modes of the pseudo-passivity of evil. Genet embraces the role of betrayer consciously; Dean Moriarty, in his dual role as scapegoat and betrayer, unconsciously and furtively, protests his innocence. In that sense, Dean Moriarty is less evil than Genet for he lacks shrewdness. In the same way the women who represent the 'social good' indicate no more than a crude economic utilitarianism accompanied by piety: the Carolyn Cassady who in real life did not like the naughty words in McClure's 'Fuck Ode'.

In *Visions of Cody,* Cassady, as Holmes once observed, is a more monumental than a dramatic figure.[73] Here, the ambiguity of the presentation in *On The Road* moves into obsessive contradiction. Cassady is at once devil and angel. The street speech and style that works its way from Cassady's into Kerouac's prose is clearly an occasion of guilt. The debt is reversed in the quasi-paranoid perception. 'Cody' is a 'devil, an old witch, even an old bitch from the start . . . he can read my thoughts, and interpret them on purpose so I'll look on the world as he does'.[74] As *The Vision of Cody* progresses, so the dream vision of Cassady as Cody himself filters in. Here is one moment:

> It is a face that's so suspicious, so energetically upward-looking like people in passport or police line up photos, so rigidly itself, looking like it's

about to do anything unspeakably enthusiastic, in fact so much the opposite of the rosy coke-drinking boy in the Scandinavian ski sweater ad, that in front of a brick wall where it says *Post no Bills* and it's too dirty for a rosy boy ad you can imagine Cody standing there in the raw gray flesh manacled between sheriffs and Assistant D.A.s and you wouldn't have to ask yourself which is the culprit and which is the law. He looked like that, and God bless him he looked like the Hollywood stunt man who is fist-fighting in place of the hero and has such a remote, furious, anonymous viciousness (one of the loveliest things in the world to see and we've all seen it a thousand times in a thousand B-movies) that everybody begins to be suspicious because they know the hero wouldn't act like that in a real unreality. If you've been a boy and played on dumps you've seen Cody, all crazy, excited and full of glee and power, giggling with the pimply girls in back of fenders and weeds till some vocational school swallows his ragged blisses and that strange American iron which later is used to mold the suffering man-face is now employed to straighten and quell the long wavering spermy disorderliness of the boy. Nevertheless the face of a great hero—a face to remind you that the great Assyrian bush of a man, not from an eye, an ear or a forehead—the face of a Simon Bolivar, Robert E. Lee, young Whitman, young Melville, a statue in the park, rough and free.[75]

This passage is in a tradition of the portrait of the American hero as composite myth. Melville had done the same for Billy Budd in his posthumously published story, particularly in the opening sequences. Read carefully, this passage shows Kerouac, too, building a pattern of conflicting characterisations from innocent hoodlum to the petrified hero of history. In terms of the American fictional hero, he is Leslie Fiedler's good bad boy, opposed for ever to the blond, good boy. He is also the Whitmanian average man transposed, via the movies, to the twentieth century. There is a grand binary allegory of order and disorder here which is the passage's strength and weakness. Its strength is its clear will to be on the side of the too-soon-crushed discarded young. The weakness is in the very need to create that Manichean world between 'nature' and 'iron' which recalls the psychological naturalism of the early part of the century, and between the oppositional types which merely play the system as carnival.

Turning now to Cassady's own account of himself, several things becomes clear at once. The first is that it is Cassady's the language whose diction and rhythms Ginsberg and Kerouac worked into their own different synthetic styles to an astonishing extent. Robert Stone, a friend of Kesey's described it as 1940s stuff: 'old time jail and musician and street patter . . . American-Denver talk, what Kerouac liked to think of as Okie drawl, but with free-lancing Proustian detail'.[76] Yet the inventiveness goes beyond street talk with its buzz words, repetitions and proverbial variations. The language of the earlier part of the Prologue is quite different in its brilliant crispness and artful simplicity from the longer more 'Proustian' sentences it develops into later. There is, in fact, more than a touch of West, imitating Voltaire, in the piling up of incidents of woe in the earlier pages. It is Defoe with a hint of mockery in the narrative voice at its own omnipotence. Here, Neal describes his father with affectionate humour and with the authority of absolute historical statement:

> Anyway, he enlarged his social life immeasurably, and if one can point to a period in Neal's lifetime that was most balanced and contentedly full, it must be in the year or eighteen months following the mutilation of his nose. He was literally at his peak and the happiest he ever was to be.[77]

In short, there is artfulness in the style which gives the lie to Ferlinghetti's 'homespun, primitive prose', and a different slant to Carolyn Cassady's remark that 'he knew he was neither trained nor equipped to think of writing in terms of literary merit'. Kerouac, of course, admired his prose intensely, and neither he nor Ginsberg spared their efforts to encourage him.[78] That his radical nervousness and lack of intellectual self-discipline (almost an impossibility in any case, given the extraordinary disorder of his early life) frustrated his clear promise does not alter the case.

There is an epic quality of entry into the story, the journey to settlement of the days of the pioneers. It signals that sense of movement, once a historic fact, now a psychological restlessness, which will structure the movement throughout the work's compellingly irreducible and discrete details. But the epic requires that those details become enlarged into representative moments of archetypal conflict. The fight of the good and evil brothers, with the acquittal by jury of the good killer (the grandfather), who is victor points to a major American obsession with personal justice and law. Neal (the father), himself sixth and last child, is bullied by his brothers and partially protected by his sister. In a recurring pattern of small-town violence, and persecuted and humiliated by his sadistic school-teaching brother, Neal Sr makes the first of his attempts to flee from home.

In this initial section, the language has a decorum which fits the subject matter precisely. The stubborn and empirical detail is often placed alongside a qualified abstraction, which might be taken as an inexperienced writer's search after authoritative literariness, but in fact, given the way Cassady handles it, manages to sidestep the danger to create a strangely haunting cadence, which mingles a tone of nervousness with elusive authority, and makes narrative itself the servant of mood: nostalgia, fear, and the shocks of accident.

Neal Jr, whose affection for his father seems to have been the one steadfast love of his life, went, as he lugubriously puts it, at six years old with 'his wino father into the lowest slums of Denver' to become the 'natural son of a few score beaten men' (pp.46-7). The resultant 'freedom' is a freedom from that experience of the internalised emotional and physical violence of the American family under economic pressure, and rightwing imperatives to consider the family a holy site of biosociality. The father provided a role model of the life of absolute failure which, given the American context in which economic failure is sign of a moral and spiritual degeneracy, has a particular poignancy. The father is the unconscious, will-less, speechless version of Genet's articulate saint:

> In his weakness, Father accepted complete subjugation to the power of his vice and, thus gripped by its onslaught, his unrebelling slavery to drink produced the sustaining force for a saint-like gentleness always displayed when he was sober. Deeply penetrated by the destroying excess of an uncontrolled flaw, his soul assumed the guilt which made unquestionable the right of his suffering, and without evident bitterness he would innocently accept the torment administered, as though unaware that he could protest. In him this Christian virtue of 'turning the cheek' was no pretension . . .
>
> (p.77)

Cassady reacted to the helpless and beloved father with the only response he could draw on: *speed*—of both mind and body. It was the *slowness* of the father, his endless still passion which formed such a powerful antithesis to the American Way. For Cassady needed movement and noise against the immobility and dumbness of the father. But he also internalised that furious speed that America's own commitment to its futuristic destiny, its competitive restlessness, seemed to require. Virilio speaking of the futurists once declared: 'In fact the human body huddling in the "steel alcove" is not that of the bellicose dandy seeking the rare sensations of war, but of the doubly-unable body of the proletarian soldier.'[79]

In her magnificent essay, 'Must we Burn Sade?', Simone de Beauvoir declared herself tempted to make 'a very cautious comparison between this conception of perpetual motion [the exhaustion of Sade's repetitive excursions into dissolution exhaustion and annihilation] and the Hindu doctrine of *samsara*':

> Nature's aspiration to escape from herself in order to recover an unconditioned state would seem to be a dream much like that proposed by the notion of Nirvana—at least to the extent that a Western man has a capacity for such dreams. Sade, rather than setting off on the path which Schopenhauer searched for, thrashes out the one Nietzsche was to follow: the acceptance of *samsara*, the *eternal return of the same thing.*[80]

Certainly that erotic movement and the spiritual existence have their repetitive convergences in their search for innocence.

The young Cassady's movement has not yet obtained the yo-yo-like self-hypnosis of petrochemical-injected movements across the continent. The journeyings are journeyings of marvellously told, youthful nostalgias on foot, where the poor could still *walk* through the city in the sun without harassment on quiet Sundays, through the deserted business warehouses whose Christian owners resisted capitalism's final speeding up of commercial life into twenty-four-hour business, seven days a week. Without the family, notoriously quarrelsome because taken off the labour fix for a day, Neal Sr and Neal Jr could make something of the 'sabbath-deserted street'. No less than for Melville's Ishmael, the Sabbath streets lead to water, to where 'the South Platte River passes beneath the 15th Street bridge of angle-iron and wood that squeaked aloud in protest as autos pass over its rapidly deteriorating surface . . .' (p.82). The Platte provided the 'flexuous corridor for my travels', a difference in tone and emphasis from Kerouac's description of Riverside Street in *Dr Sax,* which leads to a more transcendent Merrimac and to a more cosmic sea.[81] Though geographically far away, technologically the world is that of Williams' *Paterson:* an industrial world of iron, mill, brick, steam, country viaducts which provided superb climbing frames for boys. The still places are the factories and schools which crush the spirit. They exist at the nexus of intersecting points of movement.

With its echoes of Proust the walk to school is one of the virtuoso passages in the book. There is a visionary quality to these pages where mastery over self-initiated movement is developed in the long run to the schoolhouse: dribbling the tennis balls, avoiding pavement cracks, creating a zig-zag route to save time, skirting banks whose 'enormous bronze doors of scrolled bas-relief (featuring charioteered archers, mostly) were never opened'.

Each detail has the quality of a sign which moves beyond its immediate meaning, like the fleeting glimpses of a city which become dream icons of consciousness in a French *nouvelle vague* movie.[82] Or, perhaps, details are closer to images—the same quality to be found in Ginsberg's poetry which he took in turn from Whitman's 'haiku' style.[83]

The zig-zag route is the enforced penitents' journey through the maze—here recaptured for the authority of the self. The cracks in the pavement are ancient signs of taboo and superstition. In the words of the Opies, when the child walks to school, the 'day ahead looms large and endless in front of him, and his eyes are wide open for the prognostics which will tell him his fortune'.[84] The same authors also report that, in the United States, 'pavement lore' is more uniform than in Britain. In Illinois, Iowa, New Jersey, Louisiana, New York State, Ohio, and Texas, the child says 'Step on a crack' and continues 'You'll break your mother's back' or 'You'll break your grandmother's back' or 'Break the devil's back'.[85]

'The block of Arapahoe Street whorehouses' speaks of more adult matters, and of more than one social rape. The 'mighty colonnaded Post Office' hanging over the cheap stores of Curtis street is a rival for that scrolled bas-relief of the bank's doors. Its neo-classical style, in the tradition of American architecture and once signifying the democracy of Athens, is now a sign of power whose presence intimidates the shopkeepers and bums of the poor city streets. There's humour here, too, as he hears in his swift journey 'from the depths of musty second hand clothing stores, screech sounds of serious adolescent violin lessons'. Again, tone and meaning hesitate between endorsement and rejection.

Indeed, many of the fleeting images point to a sense of potential entrapment which the boy's run circumvents by skill and speed. The image of the public fountain flowing through winter and sometimes choked by ice, the movement of the young boy on to it to drink before getting his feet wet, and the sententious motto inscribed on its base, 'Desire rest but desire not too much', all indicate the potential for being trapped between the stern authoritarian and therefore contradictory commands of simultaneous movement and stasis. The 'weaving run' moves between the colonnaded Stout street, along the tightrope of the 'angled top of a half-foot high sidewalk border' of the Federal Building. But all the self-testing is on his own terms. Crossing spaces without taking breath in long takes is a favourite activity, and is linked with his later car escapades. First and foremost, said Huizinga, 'play is a voluntary activity'.[86]

Here, that voluntary activity is set within the shadow of its opposite: the unfulfilling labour America offers to the young and poor. Unlike Huizinga's 1940s anthropological and structuralist self-balancing universe of adaptive play, there is a strange sense of menace in Cassady's run to school. The boy's feat of leaping from the top of a swing's arch onto the iron pipe guardrail of the playground, not only suggests obvious lurking danger but a kind of Gothic potential of escape from the prison by exceptional feats of daring. The Denver business school nestles between a Catholic church with 'matching slender spires of rough stone' and the Denver Bible Insitute, 'whose odd belfry was a squat clapboard affair of afterthought'. It's business as usual between the Catholic senses and the Protestant spirit.

The threat to the body and soul is about equal. This Wordsworthian education by beauty and fear is even captured in the deliberately archaic phrase—'often the chase led upwards' (on the homeward run)—but it ends on arrival at school with the shades of the prison house: 'Around the entire block-square schoolyard ran a seven foot woven wire fence that enclosed all and was made by a U.S. Steel subsidiary, as a metal tag attached every few yards testified.' The sign attached to fences seems magically to invest the very patrolling of borders with the public product's privatised name. It is indeed a man's retrospective dream of a boy's freedom in a world of slavery but it is placed within a prosody which indicates full consciousness of the fact in every image.

It is speed which holds the whole thing together. And finally it is not enough. It moves toward the vertiginous melancholy of its own solipsistic centre. As early as 1948, Cassady was writing to Ginsberg about his 'periods of semi-consciousness', where he speaks of the conjuncture of marijuana and psychology as seeming to open possibilities of both freedom and imprisonment. The passage in this letter of 1948 describes a condition which seems to lead to that more productive, more potentially creative foreground, which Bachelard would call *reverie*—'not dreams, nor guilt nightmares, but, are great impressions of things'.[87]

It is clear that Cassady has great difficulty in distinguishing the poetics of reverie from the troubling nightmares of guilt, frustration and wish-fulfilment, and it is also clear, particularly in the letter, that Bachelard's words, 'Writing a book is always a hard job. One is always tempted to limit himself to dreaming it', are all too appropriate.[88] In *The First Third,* however, Cassady's speculations on consciousness are more complexly thematised. His perpetual fear of suffocation, though he gives the actual origins of the fear, has the quality of psychological exemplar and, as written, joins an American theme which goes back to Poe, and to the intense examination of dream, drug, and religious vision in William James.[89] Characteristically, in the following example, he speaks of the sensation of speed, of spinning sensations, the acceleration of time:

> But the prime requisite—to hold still as death and listen intently for the inner ear to speed up its buzz until, with regular leverlike flips, my mind's gears were shifted by unknown mechanism to an increase of time's torrent that received in kaleidoscopic change searing images, clear as the hurry of thought could make them, rushing so quickly by that all I could do was barely catch the imagery of one before another crowded . . . I failed to match these mental eruptions firmly enough to any reasonable explanations in reality, so that the cause, cure or real workings of these singularly fresh and concise visions were forever beyond my diagnosis, in fact beyond my remembering, except as residue, almost every flashing scene once it had spun by.
>
> (p.113)

The passage can be read in many different ways, as a 'romantic' attempt, neo-Platonically, to describe the threshold and absence of original vision; as a reworking of the thematics of the book in relation to memory, speed, and failure; and as a description of the drug experience. In fact, however, the general argument is sadly predicated not on the poet's confidence in reverie, but on the failure of the ordinary world to validate the experience, thus producing a general sense of impotence. Time is drugged, not suspended in the magic of the imagination's ability to close down the world of anxiety. It perhaps sums up Cassady's relation to the more disciplined writers of the circle. He internalises their more articulate, diagnostic and memory-rich sense of himself, he becomes the object of their dreams and is robbed of that *reverie œuvrant,* the reverie that prepares books—except, paradoxically, in this one instant, where he records the failure of speed to produce that tranquillity which would make him the author of his own solitude.[90] For, finally, it is just in that record of failure that the stories of Huncke and Cassady are most moving. They turn failure into celebration in the face of a society which denies that very possibility.

Notes

The question [in the title] is Kerouac's. Ginsberg to Cassady, quoting Kerouac, 4 September 1953 in *As Ever: The Collected Correspondence of Allen Ginsberg & Neal Cassady,* Foreword by Carolyn Cassady, Afterword by Allen Ginsberg, ed. and introd. Barry Gifford (Berkeley, California: Creative Arts Book Company, 1977), p. 153. This work will be referred to hereafter as *The Collected Correspondence.*

1. Ginsberg to Cassady, [n.d., Sept] 1948 in *The Collected Correspondence,* p. 51.
2. William Burroughs, *Queer* (London: Pan Books, 1986), p. 49.
3. John Milton, *Areopagitica; a Speech of Mr John Milton For the Liberty of Unlicenc'd Printing* (London, 1644) p. 12.
4. Philip Thody, ed. and trans., *Albert Camus: Selected Essays and Notebooks* (Harmondsworth: Penguin Books, 1970) p. 271.
5. Ted Morgan, *Literary Outlaw, the Life and Times of William S. Burroughs* (New York: Henry Holt and Company, 1988) p. 487.
6. Carolyn Cassady, *Off the Road: Twenty Years with Cassady, Kerouac and Ginsberg* (1990; rpt London: Flamingo, 1991) p. 313.
7. George Butterick (ed.), *Charles Olson & Robert Creeley: The Complete Correspondence,* Vol. 1 (Santa Barbara: Black Sparrow Press, 1980) p. 47.
8. Norman Mailer, 'The White Negro: Superficial Reflections on the Hipster', *Dissent* (Summer, 1957) pp. 276-93, rpt in *Advertisements for Myself* (New York: Putnam, 1957).
9. Carolyn Cassady, *Off the Road: Twenty Years with Cassady, Kerouac and Ginsberg* (London: Flamingo, 1991) p. 166.
10. Tom Clark, *Jack Kerouac: A Biography* (1984; rpt New York: Paragon House, 1990) p. 5.
11. Jack Kerouac, *Visions of Cody,* introd. Allen Ginsberg (London: André Deutsch, 1973) p. xi.
12. Louis Zukofsky, 'A' 4 in *'A'* (Berkeley, Los Angeles and London: University of California Press, 1928) p. 32.
13. Cassady to Ginsberg, 4 September 1953 in *The Collected Correspondence,* p. 153.
14. Jean-Paul Sartre, *Saint Genet, actor and martyr,* trans. Bernard Frechtman (New York: Pantheon Books, 1963), p. 5.
15. Robert Duncan, *The Truth and Life of Myth: An Essay in Essential Autobiography* (Fremont, Michigan: The Sumac Press, 1968) p. 8.
16. Ibid., p. 14.
17. William Plummer, *The Holy Goof: A Biography of Neal Cassady* (New York: Paragon House, 1990) p. 98.
18. Sartre, *Saint Genet,* p. 195.
19. Ibid., p. 200.

20. Paul Goodman, *Growing Up Absurd: Problems of Youth in the Organized Society* (New York: Vintage Books, 1960) p. 189.

21. William Plummer, *Holy Goof,* p. 101.

22. 'John Tytell Talks with Carl Solomon', in Arthur and Kit Knight (eds), *The Beat Vision: A Primary Sourcebook* (New York: Paragon House, 1987) p. 242. Hereafter referred to as *The Beat Vision.*

23. Carolyn Cassady, *Off the Road,* p. 222.

24. Barry Miles, *Ginsberg: A Biography* (London: Viking, 1990), p. 127.

25. Eric Mottram, *Allen Ginsberg in the Sixties* (Brighton: Unicorn, 1972) p. 15.

26. See Eric Mottram, 'The Wild Good and the Heart Ultimately: Ginsberg's Art of Persuasion', *Spanner,* Vol. II, No. 5 (July 1978).

27. Interview with Gary Snyder by James McKenzie in *The Beat Vision,* p.10.

28. Goodman, *Growing Up Absurd,* p. 187.

29. Gerald Nicosia, *Memory Babe: A Critical Biography of Jack Kerouac* (Harmondsworth: Penguin Books, 1986) p. 146.

30. Plummer, *Holy Goof,* p. 35.

31. Allen Ginsberg and Allan Temko respectively in Barry Gifford and Lawrence Lee, *Jack's Book: An Oral Biography of Jack Kerouac,* pp. 42-3, 66.

32. Nicosia, *Memory Base,* p. 139.

33. James McKenzie, 'An Interview with Allen Ginsberg', in Arthur and Kit Knight, *Kerouac and the Beats: A Primary Sourcebook,* Foreword by John Tytell (New York: Paragon House, 1987) p. 254.

34. Quoted by Wolf Lepenies, *Between Literature and Science: the Rise of Sociology,* trans. R. J. Hollingdale (Cambridge: Cambridge University Press, 1988) p. 255.

35. Hayden White citing 'The Use and Abuse of History' in *Metahistory: The Historical Imagination in Nineteenth-Century Europe* (Baltimore and London: The Johns Hopkins University Press, 1973) p. 355.

36. Jack Kerouac, *On the Road* (London: Pan Books, 1961) p. 12.

37. White, *Metahistory,* p. 361.

38. Stuart H. Hughes, *Consciousness and Society: The Reorientation of European Social Thought 1890-1930* (New York: Vintage Books, 1977) p. 105.

39. Fyodor Dostoevsky, *The Idiot,* trans. and introd. David Margashack (Harmondsworth: Penguin Books, 1955) p. 97.

40. Mottram, 'The Wild Good', p. 71.

41. Neal Cassady to Allen Ginsberg, 3 August 1948 in *The Collected Correspondence,* p. 38. Cassady remarks in the next paragraph: 'of course we've all been long familiar with Dost.'s work The Idiot. Personally, I first read it in 1943 in a reform school on the pacific coast . . .'.

42. Neal Cassady to Allen Ginsberg, [August 1948] in *The Collected Correspondence,* p. 43.

43. Neal Cassady to Allen Ginsberg, 25 November 1950 in *The Collected Correspondence,* p. 86.

44. Roland Barthes, *Writing Degree Zero,* trans. Annette Lavers and Colin Smith (New York: Hill and Wang, 1967) p. 20.

45. Walter Benjamin, 'Karl Kraus' in *One Way Street and Other Writings,* trans. Edmund Jephcott and Kingsley Shorter (London: New Left Books, 1979) pp. 282-4.

46. Simone de Beauvoir, 'Must we burn Sade?', introd. to The Marquis de Sade, *The 120 Days of Sodom and Other Writings,* compiled and translated by Austryn Wainhouse and Richard Seaver (New York: Grove Press, 1966) p. 7.

47. Beauvoir, 'Must we Burn Sade?', p. 29.

48. Allen Ginsberg to Neal Cassady, 14 May 1953, *The Collected Correspondence,* p. 144.

49. Nicosia, *Memory Babe,* p. 253.

50. Jean Genet, *The Thief's Journal,* trans. Bernard Frechtman (Harmondsworth: Penguin Books, 1967) p.13. Further references follow in the text.

51. Sartre, *Saint Genet: actor and martyr,* trans. Bernard Frechtman (New York: Pantheon Books, 1963) pp. 379-80.

52. Georges Bataille, 'Genet and Sartre's Study' in *Literature and Evil,* trans. Alastair Hamilton (London, New York: Marion Boyars, 1985) pp. 173-208.

53. Norman O. Brown, *Love's Body* (New York: Vintage Books, 1968) p. 132.

54. Herbert Huncke, *Huncke's Journal, Drawings by Erin Matson* (New York City: The Poet's Press, 1965) p. 1.

55. Ibid., pp. 9-10.

56. Ibid., p. 27.

57. Herbert Huncke, *Guilty of Everything, the Autobiography of Herbert Huncke,* Foreword by William S. Burroughs (New York: Paragon House, 1990) p. 207. Further references to this work follow in the text.

58. Miles, *Ginsberg,* pp. 105-16.

59. Ibid., p. 119.

60. Thomas S. Szasz, *Psychiatric Justice* (New York: The Macmillan Company, 1965) p. 11.

61. Thomas S. Szasz, *The Myth of Mental Illness,* rev. edn (New York: Harper and Row, 1974) p. 69.

62. Jack Kerouac, *Visions of Cody,* p.xi. Allen Ginsberg commented on Neal's relation with Jack Kerouac: 'Whitman's adhesiveness! Sociability without genital sexuality between them.' See Allen Ginsberg: *The Visions of the Great Rememberer: with Letters by Neal Cassady and Drawings by Basil King* (Amherst, Mass.: Mulch Press, 1974) p. 27.

63. Plummer, *Holy Goof,* p. 9.

64. Allen Ginsberg, 'Howl' in *Collected Poems, 1947-1980,* p. 128.

65. Jim Holms in *Jack's Book,* p. 94.

66. Nicosia, *Memory Babe,* p. 175. This was a general reaction of Ginsberg's group when Cassady first appeared in New York.

67. Pierre Delattre in *The Beat Vision,* p. 59.

68. David Matza, *Delinquency and Drift* (New York, London and Sydney: John Wiley, 1964) p. 28. Matza distinguishes the culture of delinquency sharply from 'the radical or bohemian tradition', p. 37. I am most grateful to Dr S. Groarke for drawing my attention both to this and to other works of criminology on delinquency.

69. Goodman, *Growing Up Absurd,* p. 197.

70. Matza, *Becoming Deviant* (Englewood Cliffs: Prentice Hall, 1969) p. 19.

71. Goodman, *Growing Up Absurd,* pp. 64, 168, 185.

72. Nicosia, *Memory Babe,* p. 250.

73. Knight, *Kerouac and the Beats,* p. 154.

74. Kerouac, *Visions of Cody,* p. 298.

75. Ibid., p. 48.

76. Cited in Plummer, *Holy Goof,* p. 129.

77. Neal Cassady, *The First Third, & Other Writings,* rev. and expanded edn, with a new Prologue (San Francisco: City Lights, 1981) p. 26.

78. Lawrence Ferlinghetti, editor's note to *The First Third,* and Carolyn Cassady, *The First Third,* p. 140. Further references to this work follow in the text.

79. Paul Virilio, *Speed and Politics,* trans. Mark Polizzotti (New York: Semiotext, 1986) p. 62.

80. Simone de Beauvoir, 'Must we Burn Sade?', p. 79.

81. Jack Kerouac, *Dr Sax* (1959; rpt New York: Grove Weidenfeld, 1987) pp. 7-9.

82. I am especially thinking of Agnes Varda's *Cleo from 5 to 7* (1961).

83. Ginsberg in conversation with author, at Warwick University, 1983, spoke of the phrasal image in Whitman's poetry as 'haiku'.

84. Iona and Peter Opie, *The Lore and Language of School Children* (London: Paladin, 1977) p. 233.

85. Ibid., p. 242.

86. Johan Huizinga, *Homo Ludens: A Study of the Play-Element in Culture,* author's translation (Boston: The Beacon Press, 1955) p. 7.

87. Neal Cassady to Allen Ginsberg, 4 August 1948, in *The Collected Correspondence,* p. 41.

88. Gaston Bachelard, *The Poetics of Reverie: Childhood, Language and the Cosmos,* trans. Daniel Russell (Boston: Beacon Press, 1969) p. 66.

89. See the author's study of James' hypnogogic vision in *Halfway to Revolution: Investigation and Crisis in the Work of Henry Adams, William James and Gertrude Stein* (New Haven and London: Yale University Press, 1991) pp. 249-58.

90. The phrases used here are Bachelard's. See *The Poetics of Reverie,* pp. 173, 182.

RAYMOND FOYE (ESSAY DATE 1997)

SOURCE: Foye, Raymond. Introduction to *The Herbert Huncke Reader,* by Herbert Huncke, edited by Benjamin G. Schafer, pp. xv-xviii. New York: William Morrow, 1997.

In the following essay, Foye combines personal remembrances of Huncke with a positive assessment of Huncke's clear and simple prose. Foye suggests that Huncke captured what Kerouac and Ginsberg were seeking: a form of writing that approximated life experience and actual speech.

There remains an indelible image of Herbert Huncke the writer, forever frozen in time: homeless and alone, crouched in a Times Square pay toilet with notebook on his knees, furtively composing his latest tale from the underground. It was before he had met Kerouac, Burroughs, and Ginsberg, long before any notion of literary recognition. Toiling in obscurity, he transcribed his travels and adventures as a hobo, drug user, and petty criminal, since leaving his upper-middle-class Chicago home in the late 1920s. "To live outside the law you must be honest," sang Bob Dylan, and Huncke's code of honor speaks to this higher order. It also speaks of a lost America, of boxcars and all-night cafeterias, pool halls and rooming houses, and always the open road.

The discovery of Herbert Huncke by the Beats in the late 1940s was something akin to novice explorers' stumbling upon a great archaeological find. He was the *Ur*-Beat: Kerouac's lonesome traveler, Burroughs's junky, Ginsberg's angel-headed hipster. Primitive and incipient, Huncke's life and writings became the Rosetta Stone of Beat sensibility, not only for the experience imparted therein but for the prose itself. Spontaneous prose and cutups were mature elaborations in Beat literature. The earliest writings of Kerouac and Burroughs were marvels of clarity. This clarity is best embodied and preserved in Huncke's deceptively simple and plainspoken style. To write as one speaks is one ideal of literature, and Huncke's prose accomplishes just that, to such a degree that the experience of reading him is akin to sitting across from him in one of those famous all-night sessions, where tales were unraveled and the human condition examined into the early hours of the morn.

I first met Herbert Huncke in 1978 in a bar on New York's Upper West Side, at a book party for his old friend William Burroughs. I was standing at the bar with a friend when Herbert passed by, and we called to him. He was elegantly dressed (as always) in suit and tie, olive-green in color, set off by a russet wool knit sweater. He drank brandy from a snifter, and smoked Players cigarettes, likewise William's current brand. Of course I knew who he was. If ever someone's reputation preceded him, it was Herbert Huncke. Yet I was unprepared for the refined gracefulness of his speech and deportment. He was loquacious, but his choice of words was exacting. His manner was elevated and noble. He was aware of his charm, and wielded it deftly. All in all, he bore the air of one from another era, which indeed he was. Whatever one might say of him, he was unmistakably a *writer.*

And yet there was another level operative in this encounter, and I would call it aversion. There was a sense of danger to this character. A confidence game was being played. I sensed that not only would he cheat, con, or deceive, but moreover he would probably do so on general principles. Little did I realize how true that would be. Over the next eighteen years I, like all those who knew Herbert, was given my share of instruction from the master: engage me at your own risk, accept me for who I am, and complain not of the consequences. To befriend Herbert was to enter into a consensual agreement in which nearly all rules of conduct were challenged, save those of acceptance and style. He was the Duke of Deception and bore the office with the haughty air of ruined nobility. He was one of nature's aristocrats, and more often than not what he rankled in me was my own hypocrisy or pride. In the end I came to feel that Herbert embodied a higher morality than the common one he so cavalierly betrayed. Call it Huncke's Paradox. If there was one notion that Herbert returned to in his conversation, time and again, it was the relativeness of all experience: everything is determined by its relation to something else. "It's all in the way you see it," Herbert would often reiterate. "I see it one way, you see it another. Both are valid." Or, in an even more familiar and succinct phrase of his: "So be it."

There is no shortage of war stories on the part of anyone who knew Herbert. Trading these stories was (and still is) a common activity of his friends. Why then, one might ask, did one continue to associate with the man? The reasons for this are less remarked upon. To engage Herbert Huncke was to enter into a world in which life was examined with a broad, knowing eye. Herbert was a philosopher of the streets. Human nature was his subject, and he approached it with sympathy and penetration. In this regard his range was truly Shakespearean: life as the Human Comedy. Not that all of it is funny, but that it is all so various and improbable. And what he loved most was to sit late into the night, in a bar, a cafeteria, or later in his Chelsea Hotel room, and discuss the peculiarities of human behavior that so delighted him. He was a student of the human condition and he sketched his ideas and observations with a writer's eye. To be in his presence was to participate in this great act of creation: the bringing into existence of a world so vivid that one felt more alive and connected to the very cosmos than one did at any other point in one's life. It was also to experience the lost art of conversation, for he listened as carefully as he spoke.

Until Herbert entered his eighties, he was remarkably fit and healthy, maintaining a busy daily routine that began with a visit to his methadone clinic, usually followed by lunch with friends, visits to local booksellers, and various small errands around town. On occasion he would give readings or attend book signings. I recall an appearance before an eager freshman English class at New York University, where his honesty and charm won him a crowd of new admirers. Although his range of friends was all-inclusive, he valued the company of young people above all. Often he would impart sage advice, not without an ironic chuckle, that he should be counseling others on how to live. He loved to wander the

FROM THE AUTHOR

HUNCKE ON THE 1950S NEW YORK CITY DRUG SCENE

The funny thing was that the drug scene was no longer confined to just any one neighborhood. It started to happen in all neighborhoods, much more so than previously when you'd cop, say, in Harlem. More and more people, different types, began to use—not only heroin and morphine but amphetamine too. When I came back to the scene after my second bit, in '59, it was even more obvious. It was the younger generation becoming more involved, a batch of new junkies were making their move, and the old-timers—guys that dated back to the days of Welfare Island—were leaving.

Huncke, Herbert. Excerpt from *The Herbert Huncke Reader.* New York: Morrow, 1997, p. 268.

streets of Manhattan, and to accompany him on such walks was to see the city as an open book. Every block held stories of crash pads, speakeasies, all-night jam sessions with Charlie Parker or Dexter Gordon.

In his eightieth year his health began to fail. His small furnished room, number 828 in the Chelsea Hotel, now became the center of his activities. The Grateful Dead, in a fitting homage, paid his rent in the final years. Here he continued to write and to receive friends. Photographers, rock journalists, and literary historians increasingly sought him out, and he was unfailingly generous with his time. "Talk is my stock in trade," he told one visitor.

Almost daily medical attention, and frequent hospitalizations, became the norm in his final year. Dr. Gabe Zatlin and his colleagues at Beth Israel Hospital attended to him with great professionalism and kindness, often making house calls in the summer heat. Without a penny to his name, recompense was out of the question. But like everyone who knew him, they were repaid with an uncommon mixture of old-world wisdom and charm. I can still see Herbert in those final weeks, sitting on the edge of his bed, wrapped in a favorite Guatemalan shawl, taking in the marvelous view of lower Manhattan and the Hudson. "I wish I could say I'd hit upon the answers to the great mysteries of life," he mused, as if to sum up his life. "But it doesn't make any more sense to me than it did on day one."

JAMES CAMPBELL (ESSAY DATE 1999)

SOURCE: Campbell, James. "The Muses: Huncke-Junkie and Neo-Cassady." In *This is the Beat Generation: New York-San Francisco-Paris,* pp. 39-64. London: Secker and Warburg, 1999.

In the following excerpt, Campbell focuses on Huncke's connection to William Burroughs, using Huncke's writings to illuminate his role as inspirer, storyteller, and criminal influence within the original Beat circle.

Burroughs first heard the word 'beat' used as a desirable piece of argot in the same year as *Really the Blues* was published; but in his case, it came with criminal, rather than musical, overtones. Burroughs had no friends in the jazz world, and no ear for the music, but he was developing a taste for the rascally and picaresque, with the end in view of finding a resting place for his misfit soul, and he liked the sound of 'beat' and the concept of 'underside', 'at odds', that it contained.

It wasn't the first time that he had felt the gravitational pull of low life. It had been tugging since his boyhood. The tone of the 'beat' world, as Burroughs first perceived it, chimed with the world of Jack Black, a hobo-crook whose memoir of larceny and fugitiveness, *You Can't Win* (1926), had encouraged young, wolfish Burroughs in his search for a replacement for the imperturbable gentility of his family in St Louis. The society of burglars, jewel-thieves, travellin'-men, dope-users, safe-crackers, D and D men (who beg under the pretence of being deaf and dumb), brothel-keepers and the rest suggested a rosy alternative to a hearth and home constructed on the profits of a machine used for doing sums.

Recuperating at home, following his brush with the law in the Carr-Kammerer affair, Burroughs might have had time to take down his copy of *You Can't Win* and read again about the sub-crust where all the bums carried razors, 'for shaving, fighting, or cutting through a sleeper's clothing to get into his pocket'; where 'if he is feeling bad, a fiend takes a jolt so he will feel good. If he is feeling good, he takes one to make him feel better'; where strangers asked: 'How long you been on the road?', and where jewel-thieves such as the Sanctimonious Kid would coo over the spoils of a heist with a quotation from Shakespeare: 'There's a stone, kid, that "A Jew would kiss and an Infidel adore."'

It was this world, the 'carny' world, the beat, off-beat world, that Burroughs began to seek out when he returned from St Louis to New York City in 1945. And he found it in the Lower East Side apartment of Herbert Huncke, which appeared to Burroughs as an updating of the Jack Black realm to which his boy's imagination had sneaked off to escape the dreariness of social clubs and pruned gardens and conversations about flower-arranging (on which Mrs Burroughs was an expert). It was from the mouth of Huncke that Burroughs first heard 'beat' and other bits of jive talk close up. Huncke was well beat, a committed reject, a hustler *engagé.*

He was a small, faintly Arabic-looking man, with heavily lidded eyes and a countenance which Kerouac was later to characterize as 'sincerely miserable'. Not yet thirty when Burroughs encountered him, Huncke had seen the insides of half-a-dozen prisons, and was familiar with outlaws of every type, including sexual outlaws. One of his friends from a spell in Chicago before he came to New York was Elsie-John:

> His mouth was large and held at all times a slight idiot smile and was always painted bright red. He shaded his eyelids green or blue and beaded the lashes with mascara until they were a good three-

quarters of an inch long. He exhibited himself among freaks in sideshows as the only true hermaphrodite.

When Huncke was not in prison, or doing something which was likely to lead to prison, he was on the road, 'beating it'—travelling in freight trains—criss-crossing America with other hoboes, black and white and red, just as Jack Black was doing half a century before. Here is Huncke:

> Through the whole period of the 30s and after '34 for six years I didn't do anything but float around the country. If I've hit New Orleans once, I've hit it four or five times. Same with California. A favourite of mine was Route 66, because I could make it straight across the country.

Here is Jack Black:

> It was springtime. Sundown found me miles away on a country road, walking westward. Darkness was coming on, but it did not strike me as unusual that I had no supper or room for the night.
>
> I came to a bridge and stopped when I heard voices below . . .
>
> 'Where you from, kid?'
>
> 'The city,' I answered.
>
> 'Where you goin'?'
>
> 'Oh, just west, anywhere, everywhere.'

Drifting to New York, Huncke began to haunt Times Square and 42nd Street, the basin of cheap urban outlawry. There were to be found the single-room hotels and shabby cafeterias which housed a population of prostitutes, sailors and slummers, and the thieves, such as Huncke, who were at once their companions and who preyed on them. When he couldn't afford a room, Huncke stayed in one of the all-night movie theatres, or packed himself into a toilet cubicle in Penn Station.

Huncke is pronounced to rhyme with 'junkie', which was his principal occupation. Jack Black could write of the Western boom towns that 'morphine and opium were almost as cheap as tobacco', but in mid-century New York a drug habit was expensive and, therefore, time-consuming. Huncke would get double satisfaction when he succeeded in locating a croaker—a crooked doctor—who was willing to write out prescriptions for morphine. From the supply, he could keep himself straight, and sell the remainder to prostitutes crawling around Times Square in search of a 'john' who would pay them enough for a 'jolt'. If the croaker was willing to write out the prescriptions liberally, then the junkie could restrict himself—much as the prostitute might hope to do—to a few regular customers.

Huncke was also known in his circle as a good story-teller, and occasionally, while shifting from 'doorway to doorway, to restaurant and subway entrances, and along the side of graystone buildings seeking shelter from the cold', or in the scented privacy of his toilet cell, he would write one of his stories down. He carried his worldly goods with him in a cigar box, a beat Dick Whittington. They amounted to little more than a toothbrush, a shaving razor, a handkerchief, and maybe a syringe. Without self-consciousness, he was an archetype in letters: the queer, drug-addicted poet-thief. A muse for the behatted, begloved, besuited William S. Burroughs II.

At the turn of the year, in obedience to his natural downward urge, Burroughs came into possession of a strange cargo. It consisted of a Thompson submachine-gun—a tommy gun—the cartridge-clip for an automatic pistol, and several boxes of the disposable, ready-to-fix capsule called the 'morphine syrette', a small tube, like a toothpaste tube, with a needle sticking out the end. Like the weaponry, the syrettes had been stolen from a Navy store by a casual acquaintance. He had asked Burroughs if he knew of anyone who would like to buy them, and, just to see what it felt like to buy narcotics, which he had never used, to snap the firing-pin on a real tommy gun, to place himself definitively among the shady and the shifty, Burroughs offered to find someone.

An acquaintance called Bob Brandenburg, who worked in a drugstore in the vicinity of Columbus Circle, said he might have a buyer. He led Burroughs downtown to an apartment on Henry Street, overlooking the Brooklyn Bridge, and here Burroughs found what he had been looking for: Jack Black's *You Can't Win* come to life.

Herbert Huncke was among the occupants. But he thought Burroughs was a policeman, or, as he said (in another bit of jive talk), 'heat': the hat, the coat, one hand in glove, the other glove in hand, the altogether grey look. Then, on second thoughts, maybe not; heat would have taken trouble to disguise the grey look. No heat looked this much like heat. Also in the apartment were Phil White, a professional pickpocket and 'lush worker' (specializing in mugging drunks on the subway), who had once killed a man in the course of a robbery; Little Jack Melody, a safecracker, and Little Jack's lover, Vicki Russell, the daughter of a Philadelphia judge. She was described as amazonian; she was a full foot taller than Little Jack, and kept herself in drugs—and sometimes the others, too—by working in a related industry, as a middle-rank, non-street-walking, prostitute.

The walls of the living-room were black, with yellow panels, and matching black-and-yellow drapes kept out natural light at all times. The ceiling was painted red, and, to give an oriental effect, the medallion in the centre of it had been coloured plum, green, orange and yellow. A china Buddha with a votive candle placed before it was conspicuous among the exotic bric-à-brac. Every day, they got high in front of the Buddha and gossiped about crime and other criminals.

Huncke wanted nothing to do with Burroughs, even after he was persuaded that the stranger with the guns and drugs was not from the FBI. 'He obviously didn't know any of the underground language', Huncke recollected. 'He appeared like a fish out of water to me.' But Phil White bought the stuff, and Burroughs returned to Henry Street a second and then a third time. While Kerouac worked at a soda fountain next door to his mother's house in Queens, and Ginsberg continued to go to classes at Columbia, Burroughs was with Vicki Russell as she shared her trade secrets—how to keep a john happy: 'Build him up. If he has any sort of body at all, say "Oh please don't hurt me"'—and with Phil White talking about dead drunks coming alive on subway trains while he was rummaging through their pockets.

Eventually Huncke became less wary, and on one of his visits Burroughs asked to be included when the others started preparing their injections. Huncke advised him what to expect:

> Morphine can be pretty frightening the first time you shoot it up mainline, because it gives a terrific pins and needles sensation. You can literally feel the drug travelling through the system, and it usually hits the back of the neck. You get this flush feeling, a sort of heatwave, and if you're not prepared for it, it's pretty frightening.

After Huncke and Phil White had had their regular shot, Huncke indicated to Burroughs that there was enough left over for him.

> So Bill said, 'Well, what do you think? How should I go about this? . . .
>
> We tied him with a very effective tourniquet. He rubbed a little alcohol on, then turned his head the other way. I got the needle in and drew up a little blood. I said, 'Loosen the tourniquet.' He loosened it, peering down at his arm, and began to feel the sensation as I shot the morphine into him. All of a sudden, he said, 'Well—that's quite a sensation . . . that's very interesting.' He gave the impression of being scientific-minded about everything. He hadn't given me any indication of where his intentions lay, but he was so methodical about everything that I felt his approach came from a purely scientific standpoint. As I discovered later, it was. He became a drug addict principally as a result of research.

By this time, the circle that had broken up in the autumn of 1944 had reformed. Joan Vollmer had found another large apartment, a few blocks down from the last one, at 419 115th Street, at the back of Barnard College. Edie Parker Kerouac came and went from Grosse Pointe, Céline began to hang around, and one by one the members of the boy-gang drifted back.

Kerouac had asked Edie for a divorce less than six months after they had pledged themselves to one another eternally under the watchful eye of Detective Shea, but he still wrote to friends and family about how wonderful she was, even though his sexual instinct was sniffing around elsewhere (around Céline, for example). The real problem for any wife or girlfriend was the other woman, the one Jack could never leave: Gabrielle Kerouac—known as Mémère—nursing her concern in Ozone Park, forever in the act of preparing the bedroom-study for her son's next visit. When Leo Kerouac died in 1946, their need for one another grew stronger than ever.

By this time, too, Ginsberg had had his first face-to-face meeting with a psychiatrist—a meeting to talk about him, that is, and not his mother. Still only nineteen in 1945, Ginsberg was sometimes patronized by Kerouac. Everything about Ginsberg was 'little' or dumb: he was 'little Allen' and 'little friend' and 'jeune singe' (young monkey). 'I shall answer all your questions, as there is nothing else to do', Kerouac might write; or 'Your little letter moved me'. Should Ginsberg have been wondering why that might be so, Kerouac provided the answer: 'because you'd been and still are sick'.

That was the way others saw him, too, including the Associate Dean of Columbia, N. M. McKnight. In March, Dean McKnight had written to Louis Ginsberg:

> I regret exceedingly to be obliged to send you a copy of a letter which I have just written to your son . . . The two principal elements are obscene writings on his window, and giving over-night housing to a person who is not a member of the College and whose presence on the Campus is unwelcome.

The unwelcome guest was Kerouac, who had been declared persona non grata on campus following the Carr affair and his part in it. Attention was drawn to his presence in Ginsberg's dormitory in Livingston Hall by the cleaner one early morning (they had slept in the same bed, without sexual contact). Having Kerouac in bed was bad enough (though it was a common enough thing for two men to sleep in one bed, and homosexual love was probably far from the thoughts of the Dean), but the primary objection concerned the 'obscene writings' Ginsberg had fingered in the grime which coated the window. The intention was to shame the cleaner into washing it. Ginsberg took the extreme route. 'Butler has no balls', he wrote—referring to Nicholas Murray Butler, President of Columbia—and 'Fuck the Jews'. Underneath, he made a crude drawing of a prick, and another of a skull and crossbones.

The result was suspension from the College. Ginsberg was told that he would not be permitted to re-enroll until he had seen a psychiatrist. Even that might not be enough, as Dean McKnight told Louis in a further letter; he wished to correct Louis's misunderstanding 'that Allen's opportunity to resume his work in Columbia College will rest upon the presentation of a letter from a psychiatrist stating that he is well enough to do so'. Medical opinion would have a bearing on the question, but the final decision rested with the College. McKnight suggested that Ginsberg work at a job for a year. What he needed was 'a dose of reality'.

A diversionary expedition into Ginsberg's sexuality of the time takes the traveller through 'Mountains of homosexuality, Matterhorns of cock, Grand Canyons of asshole'. It was not a land of content. The Matterhorns and Grand Canyons, Ginsberg told Burroughs, who was participating with him in an ad hoc form of psychoanalysis, posed 'a great weight on my melancholy head'. He was not ready to admit his homosexuality fully—if he should burst out with his desires to a friend, such as Burroughs or Kerouac, it had the immediate kickback of a depression and inward withdrawal—and for many years to come he would keep on hoping that a woman, or a psychoanalyst, would cure it.

In the meantime, cast out from college, he enrolled in the Maritime Service Training Centre, to become a merchant seaman. (The sea, as much as literature, gave the boy-gang cohesion; Huncke had just returned from the Caribbean and Pacific islands when Burroughs first met him, and Burroughs himself would make several unsuccessful efforts to gain seaman's papers. On the final occasion, in August 1945, it was the dropping of the atom bomb on Hiroshima—expertly developed at his old school—that kept the Los Alamos old boy out; VJ Day was declared, and the training centre where Burroughs had intended to join Ginsberg was closed down.) Sailors, the traditional partners for secretive homosexuals, provided Ginsberg with momentary respite, but the aftershock from those encounters would push him down into the depressing valleys between the mountains and Matterhorns. 'I feel more guilty and inferior for reasons of faggishness than intellectualization will admit is proper', he wrote to Burroughs.

It was Kerouac, the seaman-poet, who particularly inflamed him. One night, while they were walking in Greenwich Village, Ginsberg made a pass, and to his surprise Kerouac responded sympathetically. Standing between two trucks where the elevated West Side highway passes over Christopher Street—'Oh, just west, anywhere, everywhere'—Ginsberg masturbated his friend. (It was doubtless an act of kindness more than desire on Kerouac's part, but he had had sex with men before—rudimentary, sometimes oral, usually out of doors or aboard ship; when he mentioned a 'sexual problem' to friends from Lowell, as he had done, they probably didn't imagine that he meant this, rather than paralysing stage fright or the imagined smallness of his penis. From first to last, when drunk and belligerent in a bar, Kerouac was apt to throw out the invitation: 'Come on, I'll fuck you.')

Jewishness was another area of self-consciousness for Ginsberg, and he was, of course, continually worried about his mother's madness and its effects—long-term, short-term, psychic, domestic—on the rest of the family. And while he was not happy about the teaching he received at Columbia, he had been unable to bring himself to quit. So his scrawled collection of messages on the dormitory window at Livingston Hall seems to have drawn all the strands of his unhappy mind together in a convocation to demand a solution.

Evicted from Livingston Hall, he went in search of his dose of reality at 115th Street.

Where there was now a new member of the fraternity.

Joan had let out one of the spare rooms to a Columbia student from Denver, Hal Chase, 'a hero of the snowy West', as Ginsberg saw him. Like the incarcerated Lucien, he was intellectual and impetuous; like Lucien, he was blond and good-looking; like Lucien, he was attracted to Céline, who became his lover. (She recognized in him 'that feeling of futility . . . that reminds me of Lucien'.)

Hal Chase made two contributions to boy-gang life, a minor intellectual one and a major social one. First, he came up with the concept of 'Wolfeans' and 'non-Wolfeans'—that is, those who were in the rugged American tradition, expansive, encompassing, healthily panting for the future; and those who were rooted in European sensibility and tended towards the degenerate and the effete—and, by implication, faggishness.

The distinction was based on two types of contemporary American writer. Thomas Wolfe was one sort, an all-embracing melting pot of a writer, a 'putter-inner', as Kerouac said. The other kind was personified by F. Scott Fitzgerald, refined, old-world, a 'leaver-outer'. Hal Chase made a division among the 115th Street boys: he and Kerouac were the life-loving Wolfeans, he declared, while Burroughs and Ginsberg were non-Wolfeans. (Ginsberg took it as yet another rejection.) The girls, not being writers, did not qualify for a reckoning.

Out West, Chase had done some work with Native American artefacts in the Denver Museum; he had served in the ski troops, training in the Rockies; and he was influenced, in his conception of the essential American spirit as an open-hearted, on-the-move, creaturely thing, by one of his Denver acquaintances, Neal Cassady. He told the others about Cassady. Neal was a 'cocksman', so keep an eye on your women; he had made a living before the war as a poolhall shark and done a little time inside; and he had read his way through the Denver Public Library, from A to Z. There was no one like Neal. They would see for themselves: he was coming to town.

The 'prize room' in Joan's apartment—according to Huncke, who had begun to visit—was reserved for Burroughs: 'a beautiful room, in which he kept his books and a desk and a bed for himself'. His other bed was in Joan's room. They had become lovers. Although Burroughs was primarily attracted to men, homosexuality was not a fixed state, and he was not without experience of women; on the whole, Burroughs appreciated feminine smoothness in young men, while responding to strong intelligence in women. In Joan, slightly older than the others, Burroughs found the maturity that had been lacking in his friendships since the death of Kammerer. Like him, she was interested in ideas, and could answer his talk of Freud and Korzybski, his theories of hypnotism and mind-control, of multiple personalities concealed in the unconscious, with ideas of her own. Burroughs enjoyed her sharp city wit.

The other flourishing aspect of their lives was the use of drugs. As Burroughs continued his narcotics research, Joan stepped up her doses of Benzedrine. It was a punishing habit, and had completely overcome the 'soft and dewy' side of Joan that Edie had liked so much. In addition to causing body sores, the amphetamine addiction brought difficulties of blood circulation, so that by the age of twenty-five Joan was walking with a limp, occasionally assisting herself with a cane. As well as having to put up with Burroughs's strange routines, she had her baby daughter to care for. Once Kerouac—who made raids on 115th Street from his mother's hearth when in need of his own dose of reality—caught sight of her in Times Square on her way to buy in a stock of inhalers, hobbling along with little Julie in tow, one arm swinging loosely at her side.

Some time around the end of 1945, she began telling Ginsberg and the others that she was able to hear the voices of the people in the apartment below. Allen replied that he couldn't hear a thing, but Joan explained this by saying that the drugs she was taking had heightened her auditory faculty. She would elaborate: they were an elderly couple; they had fights; they said vile things about her and her friends. They also knew that everyone upstairs was a dope fiend (as they would say, not yet having the hip word, 'junkie'), and they wanted to call the police. Joan listened to everything they said with great attention, sometimes conveying it on down the line as it was happening. No one else could hear a thing.

One night, she announced that the couple were having a dreadful brawl. The old man was threatening his wife. He had a kitchen knife. Now he was chasing her round the apartment with it. Kerouac and Ginsberg rushed downstairs and banged on the door, but there was no answer. No one lived there.

Paul Adams, Joan's lawful husband, returned from military service to find that the pretty Barnard student he had left behind to look after their baby daughter had become the leading lady in an avant-garde expressionist drama, which, to him, was incomprehensible. He went away and didn't come back. Gradually, unceremoniously, Joan Vollmer, Joan Adams, began to call herself Joan Burroughs. She told her new man that he made love like a pimp. In the theatre of 115th Street, it was considered a compliment.

Under the tutelage of Phil White, who had probably pimped in his time, Burroughs learned a new trade, a Jack Black trade: he became a lush-worker. His monthly $200 allowance from his parents was not enough to feed a growing drug habit. Phil White showed him how to rob drunks in the subway, and how to talk the lingo at the same time: rolling lushes like this was 'working the hole'.

The natural, Huncke, watched as Burroughs studied the ways of the street. By now, he had overcome his suspicions that Burroughs might be a lawman, but with the true deadbeat's respect for proper learning, he could not help but be sceptical about Burroughs's latest enterprise:

> They informed me they were making the hole together as partners with Burroughs learning to act as a shill and cover-up man for Phil—helping to pick pockets by standing near, holding a newspaper open, spread wide—Phil reaching behind Bill, fingers feeling the inside breast pocket of the mark's suit jacket or perhaps the overcoat pockets searching for the wallet—or poke, as Phil referred to it. Somehow there was something ludicrous about a man of Bill's obvious educational background becoming a business partner with knock-around, knock-down, hard hustling Phil.

Burroughs's anthropological studies—which would later be ploughed into his first book, an autobiography thinly disguised as fiction, a lost chapter from *You Can't Win*—were terminated in April 1946.

It began with Huncke, who was fingered by a boy who had agreed to cooperate with the police in exchange for lenient treatment. By this time, Burroughs had rented a place on Henry Street next to the apartment where he had taken his original morphine shot, and Huncke was living there and using it as a storehouse for stolen goods. Following a trail, the police began to pick up Huncke's associates one by one, eventually arriving at 115th Street to arrest Burroughs on a charge of forging a doctor's signature on stolen blank prescriptions. They took him to the Tombs.

His new life had got him into trouble, but his old life could be relied on to get him out of it. Long-suffering Mortimer Burroughs made the journey to New York again to bail his son out of prison for the second time in eighteen months. In June, the case came before the courts, and Burroughs, technically a first offender (and a Harvard graduate), was sternly ordered by the judge to spend the summer at his parents' home in St Louis. Huncke, a graduate of the school of vagabondage, got four months in prison. When he was released, he found a room at 115th Street.

Joan liked Huncke, but did not welcome the criminal flotsam and jetsam that drifted in his wake. Whoever took pity on Huncke found themselves in trouble sooner or later. One story in his later recollections involves a Polish guy, a black queen, a stolen car, and a missing valise; then the police at Joan's apartment, with 'this black queen looking very righteous' and accusing Huncke of taking the valise:

> They knocked on the door and just came in. Joan was absolutely horrified. This was the first experience with the law she'd ever had. Of course, they couldn't touch her. They were primarily interested in me . . . The queen pointed out the car downstairs in front of the house. She was really very spiteful. Sure enough, all three of us ended up in the Bronx jail with this case on our hands. Well, I beat it . . . they couldn't do anything to me.

For Joan, it was a further twist in the downward spiral. Her beauty had gone, and her mind was following. She cleaned the apartment obsessively. She was apt to strip naked in front of visitors. In the several accounts of her state at this time, her Benzedrine habit is mentioned frequently, her daughter Julie scarcely ever.

At the beginning of October, John Kingsland, the teenage student who for a term had been her lover but who had since been reclaimed for respectability by his parents, paid a call at 115th Street. When he left the apartment, he wrote a letter to Ginsberg: 'I saw Joan last weekend. She seems to be losing her mind.' Two weeks later, she was picked up off the street and taken to the Bellevue psychiatric ward. 'It's a shame, don't you think?' asked Kingsland.

As Joan entered her brief confinement, Lucien Carr emerged from his. The conditions of his parole made it unwise for him to socialize too often with his old libertine friends, especially as he could not help but notice the addition of hard criminality to what had been (until his own notorious deed, as it happened) a prankish bohemianism.

Ginsberg met him and confessed, for the first time, his desire for men (including Carr). Carr seemed shocked. The words 'homosexual', 'queer', 'fairy', 'faggot', conjured up a dingy picture of stinking toilets and restless shame. Carr had gone to prison for killing a homosexual, in what many onlookers at the trial had regarded as an honour slaying. He told Ginsberg that it was a 'sorry life'. Ginsberg, suitably sorry, replied that he was planning to see a psychiatrist and seek a cure.

Kerouac, who had been so deeply involved in the events of August-September 1944, saw little of Carr. He was too wary, and too deeply involved in his writing. He came and went at 115th Street, but his year had been taken up with a novel, *The*

Town and the City ('The Sea Is My Brother' had been abandoned). It told the story of a family growing up in a mill town on a river, very much like Lowell. It was very Wolfean and very long, and Kerouac discovered in writing it the deep capacity of his memory, its fine net for detail, and its ability to fetch up a great amount of story in the course of a single day. Kerouac was memory's servant. Sometimes he would write up to 4,500 words in a night. By the end of 1946, the manuscript of *The Town and the City* was approaching 1,000 pages.

While storms blew about him—as Burroughs willingly went down to a life of drugs and crime, as Ginsberg got lost in Grand Canyons of asshole, as Carr knifed his pursuer and Joan went mad—Kerouac was gifted with the ability to take one step back, to take the passenger seat, to take notes, and to think of shaping them into a book. By Christmas, there was a new chapter.

A brief tour of Huncke's New York.

Start at Bryant Park, behind the New York Public Library at 42nd Street, originally a potter's field, or pauper's graveyard, latterly the resting place (in life) of every sort of human detritus New York's famous tide of energy throws up. In the 1940s, Bryant Park was hustler Huncke's base of operations. On one occasion, he used a 'Keep Off the Grass' sign to smash a car window, intending to steal the contents and sell them for drug money. He was caught, and spent six months in Rikers Island, his first visit to that prison.

Walk west along 42nd Street, towards Eighth Avenue. At no. 210 42nd Street was Chase's Cafeteria, a notoriously lowdown place, which Kerouac fictionalized as Ritzy's Bar: 'You don't see a single girl', he wrote.

Next door to Chase's stood Grant's Cafeteria, housed in the Chandler building (named after the Coca-Cola magnate).

Across the street, at no. 225, was Bickford's, an all-night place where Huncke was often in residence, when not in a movie theatre or a station toilet. He could spend up to eighteen hours a day in Bickford's, reliably stationed at the window in view of pushers, ponces, and friends such as amazonian Vicki and Little Jack Melody. The place had the novelty of a jukebox. The light was described by Ginsberg as 'submarine'. The food was said to be good and cheap.

Cross the street again, and stop at no. 250. Here stood the Horn and Hardart Automat. Automats were an experiment in food dispensing, in which diners used a nickel to open a little window on to their choice of dish. Macaroni and cheese was a favourite. The absence of disapproving waiters was a welcome feature to idlers, such as Huncke, and to other thieves who used the automats as 'meets' where they could discuss the sale of overcoats and what-not, and the corresponding purchase of drugs. The automats were also open all night, making them a top attraction to the submarine community.

Turn right into Eighth Avenue, and walk one block north. On the corner of 43rd Street stood the Angler Bar (also known in books as the Angle Bar), a favourite of Burroughs and an overcoat thief he had befriended called Bill Garver. Burroughs recalled Huncke at the Angler, 'always high on something—weed, benzedrine, or knocked out of his mind on "goof balls" . . . his head kept falling down onto the bar'. Burroughs also provided a snapshot of the typical clientele:

> Roy and I were standing at the end of the Angle Bar. Subway Mike was there, and Frankie Dolan. Dolan was an Irish boy with a cast in one eye. He specialized in crummy scores, beating up defenceless drunks, and holding out on his confederates. 'I got no honor', he would say. 'I'm a rat.'

It was at the Angler that Huncke met Alfred Kinsey, and related details of his sex life for honest cash, details later integrated into Kinsey's *Sexual Behaviour in the Human Male.* 'The one thing I could not supply him with was the size to my penis', Huncke wrote later. 'He finally gave me a card and asked me to fill it out and send it to him . . . I never did.'

Walk east to Broadway, then turn north in the direction of 44th Street. At 1506 Broadway, between 43rd and 44th, was Hector's, one of a chain of Jewish cafeterias in New York. Kerouac loved its 'glittering counter', its 'decorative walls', and above all its 'noble old ceiling . . . almost baroque, plaster now browned a smoky rich tanned color'. Hector's was the first stop in New York City for Neal Cassady and his child bride LuAnne, after they stepped down at the Greyhound Terminal on 50th Street, in December 1946. They ate, according to Kerouac's memory, glazed cakes and creampuffs.

FURTHER READING

Biographies

Burroughs, William S. Foreword to *The Herbert Huncke Reader,* by Herbert Huncke, edited by Benjamin G. Shafer, p. ix. New York: William Morrow, 1997.

Recalls briefly William Burroughs's impressions of Huncke, including their first meeting.

Ginsberg, Allen. "The Hipster's Hipster." *New York Times Magazine,* (29 December 1996): 39.

Details aspects of Allen Ginsberg's relationship with Huncke, including Huncke's appearance in "Howl."

Tytell, John. "An Interview with Herbert Huncke." *Unspeakable Visions of the Individual* 3, no. 1-2 (1973): 3-15.

Recalls the Beat era from the perspective of a more settled lifestyle.

Watson, Steven. "Insert Name of Chapter Here." *The Birth of the Beat Generation,* pp. 72-6. New York: Pantheon Books, 1995.

Discusses Huncke's childhood, as well as the Times Square haunts of the Beats.

Criticism

Ansen, Alan. Review of *Guilty of Everything,* by Herbert Huncke. *Review of Contemporary Fiction* 10, no. 3 (fall 1990): 227-8.

Suggests that Huncke's importance stems primarily from his literary connections.

Bronski, Michael. "Dark Angels." *Advocate,* (11 September 1990): 71-2.

Reviews Huncke's Guilty of Everything, *finding it less energetic than his earlier writings.*

Douglas, Ann. "Beat Angel." *Village Voice,* (16 December 1997): 97.

Reviews The Herbert Huncke Reader *and observes that loneliness and inclusiveness are major motifs in Huncke's writing.*

Herman, Jan. "The Beatnik's Beatnik." *New York Times Book Review,* (10 June 1990): 22.

Describes Huncke's autobiography as an oral history of his life on the street, plain-spoken but still vague, and honest.

OTHER SOURCES FROM GALE:

Additional coverage of Huncke's life and career is contained in the following sources published by the Gale Group: *Contemporary Authors,* Vols. 130, 153; *Contemporary Authors New Revision Series,* Vol. 61; *Dictionary of Literary Biography,* Vol. 16; and *Literature Resource Center.*

INDEXES

The main reference

Kerouac, Jack 1922-1969 **1:** 2, 14-18, 20, 21-25, 34, 37-41, 43, 49-52, 106-9, 118-21, 133-34, 141-42, 157-59, 161, 163, 164, 169-71, 179-80, 196, 213-14, 240-46, 305-6, 357-58, 363-68, 398-411; **2:** 113, 123-24, 127-30, 141-50, 318, 379-80, 490; **3:** 4-7, 9-11, 63, **63-142,** 207-8, 272, 471

lists the featured author's entry in either volume 2 or 3 of The Beat Generation; *it also lists commentary on the featured author in other author entries and in volume 1, which includes topics associated with the Beat Generation. Page references to substantial discussions of the author appear in boldface.*

The cross-references

See also AAYA 25; AITN 1; AMWS 3; BPFB 2; CA 5-8R; CANR 26, 54, 95; CDALB 1941-1968; CLC 1, 2, 3, 5, 14, 29, 61; CPW; DA; DAB; DAC; DAM MST, NOV, POET, POP; DLB 2, 16, 237; DLBD 3; DLBY 1995; GLL 1; MTCW 1, 2; NFS 8; RGAL 4; TCLC 117; WLC; WP

list entries on the author in the following Gale biographical and literary sources:

AAL: Asian American Literature
AAYA: Authors & Artists for Young Adults
AFAW: African American Writers
AFW: African Writers
AITN: Authors in the News
AMW: American Writers
AMWR: American Writers Retrospective Supplement
AMWS: American Writers Supplement
ANW: American Nature Writers
AW: Ancient Writers
BEST: Bestsellers (quarterly, citations appear as Year: Issue number)
BLC: Black Literature Criticism
BLCS: Black Literature Criticism Supplement
BPFB: Beacham's Encyclopedia of Popular Fiction: Biography and Resources
BRW: British Writers
BRWS: British Writers Supplement
BW: Black Writers
BYA: Beacham's Guide to Literature for Young Adults
CA: Contemporary Authors
CAAS: Contemporary Authors Autobiography Series
CABS: Contemporary Authors Bibliographical Series
CAD: Contemporary American Dramatists
CANR: Contemporary Authors New Revision Series
CAP: Contemporary Authors Permanent Series
CBD: Contemporary British Dramatists
CCA: Contemporary Canadian Authors
CD: Contemporary Dramatists
CDALB: Concise Dictionary of American Literary Biography
CDALBS: Concise Dictionary of American Literary Biography Supplement
CDBLB: Concise Dictionary of British Literary Biography
CLC: Contemporary Literary Criticism
CLR: Children's Literature Review
CMLC: Classical and Medieval Literature Criticism
CMW: St. James Guide to Crime & Mystery Writers
CN: Contemporary Novelists
CP: Contemporary Poets
CPW: Contemporary Popular Writers
CSW: Contemporary Southern Writers
CWD: Contemporary Women Dramatists
CWP: Contemporary Women Poets
CWRI: St. James Guide to Children's Writers
CWW: Contemporary World Writers
DA: DISCovering Authors
DA3: DISCovering Authors 3.0
DAB: DISCovering Authors: British Edition
DAC: DISCovering Authors: Canadian Edition
DAM: DISCovering Authors: Modules
- *DRAM:* Dramatists Module; *MST:* Most-Studied Authors Module;
- *MULT:* Multicultural Authors Module; *NOV:* Novelists Module;
- *POET:* Poets Module; *POP:* Popular Fiction and Genre Authors Module

DC: Drama Criticism
DFS: Drama for Students
DLB: Dictionary of Literary Biography
DLBD: Dictionary of Literary Biography Documentary Series
DLBY: Dictionary of Literary Biography Yearbook
DNFS: Literature of Developing Nations for Students
EFS: Epics for Students
EXPN: Exploring Novels
EXPP: Exploring Poetry

EXPS: Exploring Short Stories
EW: European Writers
FANT: St. James Guide to Fantasy Writers
FW: Feminist Writers
GFL: Guide to French Literature, Beginnings to 1789, 1798 to the Present
GLL: Gay and Lesbian Literature
HGG: St. James Guide to Horror, Ghost & Gothic Writers
HLC: Hispanic Literature Criticism
HLCS: Hispanic Literature Criticism Supplement
HW: Hispanic Writers
IDFW: International Dictionary of Films and Filmmakers: Writers and Production Artists
IDTP: International Dictionary of Theatre: Playwrights
LAIT: Literature and Its Times
LAW: Latin American Writers
JRDA: Junior DISCovering Authors
LC: Literature Criticism from 1400 to 1800
MAICYA: Major Authors and Illustrators for Children and Young Adults
MAICYA: Major Authors and Illustrators for Children and Young Adults Supplement
MAWW: Modern American Women Writers
MJW: Modern Japanese Writers
MTCW: Major 20th-Century Writers
NCFS: Nonfiction Classics for Students
NCLC: Nineteenth-Century Literature Criticism
NFS: Novels for Students
NNAL: Native North American Literature
PAB: Poets: American and British
PC: Poetry Criticism
PFS: Poetry for Students
RGAL: Reference Guide to American Literature
RGEL: Reference Guide to English Literature
RGSF: Reference Guide to Short Fiction
RGWL: Reference Guide to World Literature
RHW: Twentieth-Century Romance and Historical Writers
SAAS: Something about the Author Autobiography Series
SATA: Something about the Author
SFW: St. James Guide to Science Fiction Writers
SSC: Short Story Criticism
SSFS: Short Stories for Students
TCLC: Twentieth-Century Literary Criticism
TCWW: Twentieth-Century Western Writers
WCH: Writers for Children
WLC: World Literature Criticism, 1500 to the Present
WLCS: World Literature Criticism Supplement
WLIT: World Literature and Its Times
WP: World Poets
YABC: Yesterday's Authors of Books for Children
YAW: St. James Guide to Young Adult Writers

AUTHOR INDEX

The Author Index lists all of the authors featured in The Beat Generation *set. It includes references to the main author entries in volumes 2 and 3; it also lists commentary on the featured author in other author entries and in volume 1, which includes topics associated with the* Beat Generation. *Page references to author entries appear in boldface. The Author Index also includes birth and death dates, cross references between pseudonyms or name variants and actual names, and cross references to other Gale series in which the authors have appeared. A complete list of these sources is found facing the first page of the Author Index.*

A

B

C

D

E

F

TITLE INDEX

The Title Index alphabetically lists the titles of works written by the authors featured in volumes 2 and 3 of The Beat Generation *and provides page numbers or page ranges where commentary on these titles can be found. English translations of foreign titles and variations of titles are cross referenced to the title under which a work was originally published. Titles of novels, dramas, nonfiction books, and poetry, short story, or essay collections are printed in italics; individual poems, short stories, and essays are printed in body type within quotation marks.*

A

B

C

D

E

F

G

H

I

J

K

L

TITLE INDEX

M

N

O

P

R

S

T

SUBJECT INDEX

The Subject Index includes the authors and titles that appear in the Author Index and the Title Index as well as the names of other authors and figures that are discussed in the Beat Generation *set. The Subject Index also lists titles and authors of the critical essays that appear in the set, as well as literary terms and topics covered in the criticism. The index provides page numbers or page ranges where subjects are discussed and is fully cross referenced. Page references to significant discussions of authors, titles, or subjects appear in boldface; page references to illustrations appear in italic.*

A

SUBJECT INDEX

C

D

E

F

SUBJECT INDEX

G

H

K

L

M

SUBJECT INDEX

SUBJECT INDEX

S

T

U

V